Warman's®
Americana & Collectibles
10TH EDITION

EDITED BY ELLEN T. SCHROY

Published by

**krause
publications**

700 E. State Street • Iola, WI 54990-0001
Telephone: 715/445-2214

Please, call or write us for our free catalog of antiques and collectibles publications.
To place an order or receive our free catalog, call 800-258-0929.
For editorial comment and further information,
use our regular business telephone at (715) 445-2214.

Library of Congress Catalog Number: 84-643834
ISBN: 0-87341-976-6

Printed in the United States of America

Table of Contents

Part 1

Acknowledgments 4
Introduction 5
Board of Advisors 10
Auction Houses 12
Abbreviations. 17

Part 2

Categories 18

Part 3

Index 392

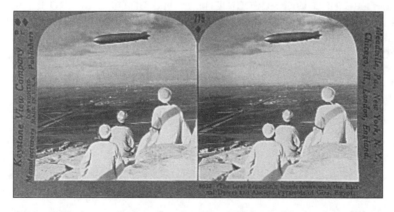

One of the new categories in this year's guide is zeppelins.

Acknowledgments

Since it's creation in 1984, *Warman's Americana & Collectibles* has grown and changed with the shifts of the antiques and collectibles marketplace. New categories are included that show what folks are collecting as we embrace a new century. New collectibles are drawing folks to antique shows, shops, flea markets, and browsing the Internet. Perhaps it's living in a country and society where you are free to decide what to collect, how to spend your money, or perhaps my aging Baby-Boomer philosophy, but I believe every dedicated collector brings their own unique dedication and enthusiasm to the hobby. Thankfully there are collectors for almost every type of object, keeping the hobby lively.

No edition of *Warman's* would ever be complete without a special thanks to the members of the Board of Advisors, a wonderful, dedicated group. Some new names have been added, helping to give this edition a very up-to-date and wide-geographical flavor, while providing some solid information about some hot topics. Through the mail, telephone, and e-mail, I've been in contact with each and every one, heard about what's important to their collecting interests, as well as what's new in their lives. Through these conversations and their warm wishes of support, we've created an even better *Warman's Americana & Collectibles.*

The fine staff of Krause Publications continues its nurturing support of *Warman's.* Perhaps you have noticed some of the additional books that now include "Warman's" in their titles, like *Warman's Advertising, Warman's Country, Warman's Sports,* and *Warman's Depression Glass.* Collectors should be assured that every title that contains that familiar Warman's name is full of good information, as well as solid, up-to-date pricing. So with a special thanks to Kris Manty and her talented co-workers in production, layout, and photography, we'll now offer you a new edition of *Warman's Americana & Collectibles.*

Here's hoping you enjoy it as much as we enjoy creating it for collectors and dealers like you.

Ellen Tischbein Schroy
June 5, 2001

INTRODUCTION

Welcome to *Warman's Americana & Collectibles*, the cornerstone of the Warman's Encyclopedia of Antiques and Collectibles. In 1984, the first edition of *Warman's Americana & Collectibles* introduced the collecting community to category introductions featuring collecting hints, history, references, periodicals, and reproduction and copycat information complemented by detailed, accurate listings and values. As a result of the enthusiastic acceptance of this format, it was extended to *Warman's Antiques and Collectibles Price Guide* and ultimately to volumes in the Warman's Encyclopedia of Antiques and Collectibles.

Warman's Americana & Collectibles was a pioneering work, the first general price guide to mass-produced 20th-century objects. It helped define and solidify the modern collectibles market. As the collectibles market has matured, so has *Warman's Americana & Collectibles*. If you have a copy of the first edition, compare the categories listed in it to those found in this 10th edition. Times *have* changed. Perhaps this is why so many individuals find the collectibles market so exciting.

Collectibles are the things with which your parents, you, and your children have played and lived. The things that belonged to your grandparents are now *antiques.* The evolution of an object from new to desirable to collectible to antique within one's lifetime, i.e., an approximately 50-year span, is difficult for some to accept. However, it is reality.

Warman's Americana & Collectibles takes you on a nostalgic trip down memory lane. Sometimes it's sad to think back about things that have been passed on to others, perhaps have been broken or discarded. However, it's better to be thrilled by the value of the things that were saved. Do not hesitate to buy back the things from your childhood that evoke pleasant memories. As you do, you will find that the real value of objects is not monetary, but the joy that comes from collecting, owning, and, most importantly, playing and living with them once again.

As we embrace a new century, it's our philosophy that collectors should enjoy what they treasure so passionately and take the time to learn more about their specialties. *Warman's Americana & Collectibles* is based on the premise that it is acceptable to collect anything you wish. Remember one simple fact: All of today's antiques were collectibles in the past.

What is a collectible?

The definition of an antique remains clear, while what constitutes a collectible has become more confusing.

For the purpose of this book, an antique is anything made before 1945. A great many individuals in the antiques and collectibles field disagree with this definition, but with each passing year, it becomes harder and harder to deny this premise. The key is the war years of 1942-1945. During this period, production switched from domestic to wartime products. When the war ended, things were different. American life and expectations were very different in 1948 than in 1938. New war technology modified for productive civilian use was partially responsible. However, the most-telling fact of all is that well over half the population living in America today was born after 1945 and approximately two-thirds grew up in the post-1945 era.

Keeping this in mind and seeking technical definitions, a collectible then becomes an object made between 1945 and 1965, and a "desirable" an object made after 1965. The difference between a collectible and a desirable is that a collectible has a clearly established secondary market, while a desirable exists in a market rampant with speculation.

Actually, the post-1945 era is broken down into three distinct collecting periods: 1945-1965, 1965-1980, and post-1980. Goods from the 1965-1980 period are moving out of their speculative mode into one of price stability.

Within the Warman's Encyclopedia of Antiques and Collectibles, *Warman's Americana & Collectibles* is the volume designed to deal with objects from the 20th century. Three criteria are applied when preparing the book: Was the object mass produced? Was it made in the 20th century, preferably after 1945? Do the majority of the items in the category sell for less than $200? The ideal collectible fits all three qualifications.

Since collecting antiques became fashionable in the early 20th century, there have been attempts to define certain groups of objects as the "true" antiques, worthy of sophisticated collectors, and to ignore the remaining items. Most museums clearly demonstrate this attitude. Where do early 20th-century tin toys, toy soldiers, or dolls fit? Those made before 1915 are antique. No one argues this any longer. Those made between 1920 and 1940 are in transition. We designate them "prestige" collectibles, objects changing in people's minds from collectible to antique.

In some collecting areas, such as advertising, dolls, and toys, *Warman's Americana & Collectibles* offers readers descriptions and values for 20th century items that might not be covered in *Warman's Antiques & Collectibles*. Other topics covered in *Warman's Americana & Collectibles* expand on the information found in that companion book. Areas like costume jewelry and Star Wars can better be addressed in *Warman's Americana & Collectibles*. When *Warman's Americana & Collectibles* was initially launched, it was hoped that this book could capture that segment of the market place that was missing from other price guides. Today, that fine tradition continues as *Warman's Americana & Collectibles* evolves again to respond to the collectibles marketplace.

To clarify the distinction between antique and collectible, consider Webster's definition of collectible: "an object that is collected by fanciers, especially one other than such traditionally collectible items as art, stamps, coins, and antiques."

International Market

Collectibles began to draw worldwide interest at the end of the 1980s. All of a sudden, American buyers found themselves competing with buyers from Europe and Japan on their home turf. In head-to-head competition, the American buyers frequently lost. How can this be explained?

The largest portion of the 2000's collectibles market is made up of post-World War II material. During this period, the youth of the world fell under three dominant American influences: movies, music, and television. As the generations of the 1950s, 1960s, and even 1970s reached adulthood and started buying back their childhood, many of the things they remember and want have American associations.

America is the great mother lode of post-war collectibles. At the moment, it is packages and boxes of American collectibles that are being sent abroad. It will not be too much longer before the volume reaches container loads.

American collectors also are expanding their horizons. They recognize that many objects within their favorite collectible category were licensed abroad. They view their collections as incomplete without such examples. Objects are obtained by either traveling abroad or by purchasing from foreign sources through mail or auction.

The addition of the Internet and its auctions, dealer Web sites, and collector club Web sites has created additional buying opportunities. Collectors no longer have to set aside time to travel to their favorite haunts and search for hours for something to add to their collection. Sometimes it's as easy as sitting down at their computer and reading what's posted for sale. Some collecting areas are also benefiting from chat rooms dedicated to their specialties, allowing collectors to explore and learn from each other in ways and with speed only now available. This new openness is creating more savvy collectors and allowing information to flow globally.

Price Notes

Prices in the collectibles field are not as firmly established as in the antiques area. Nevertheless, we do not use ranges unless we feel they are absolutely necessary.

Our pricing is based on an object being in very good condition. If otherwise, we note this in our description. It would be ideal to suggest that mint, or unused, examples of all items do exist. In reality, objects from the past were used, whether they be glass, china, dolls, or toys. Because of this, some normal wear must be expected.

The biggest problem in the collectibles field is that an object may have more than one price. A George Eastman bubble gum card may be worth $1 to a bubble gum card collector, but $35 to a collector of photographic memorabilia. I saw the same card marked both ways. In preparing prices for this guide, we have considered the object in terms of the category in which it is included. Hence, a girlie matchcover may be valued at 25¢ to 50¢ in the matchcover category and $2 to $5 in pinup art. However, for purposes of making a sale, if all you can find are matchcover collectors, take the quarter and move on.

Organization of the Book

Listings: We have attempted to make the listings descriptive enough so the specific object can be identified. Most guides limit their descriptions to one line, but not *Warman's*. We have placed emphasis on those items which are actively being sold in the marketplace. Nevertheless, some harder-to-find objects are included in order to demonstrate the market spread. A few categories in this book also appear in *Warman's Antiques and Collectibles Price Guide*. The individual listings, however, seldom overlap except for a few minor instances. We've tried to include enough objects to give readers a good base for comparison. After all, that is what much of the collectibles marketplace uses to establish prices: comparables. To properly accomplish this task, some overlapping between books is unavoidable. It is our intention to show objects in the low- to middle-price range of a category in *Warman's Americana & Collectibles* and the middle to upper range in our main antiques guide, *Warman's Antiques and Collectibles Price Guide*, thus creating two true companion lists for the general dealer or collector.

Collecting Hints: This section calls attention to specific hints as they relate to the category. We note where cross-category collecting and nostalgia are critical in pricing. Clues are given for spotting reproductions. In most cases, we just scratch the surface. We encourage collectors to consult specialized publications.

History: Here we discuss the category, describe how the object was made, who are or were the leading manufacturers, and the variations of form and style. In many instances, a chronology for the object is established. Finally, we place the object in a social context—how it was used, for what purpose, etc.

References: Many general references are listed to encourage collectors to learn more about their objects. Included are author, title, most recent edition, publisher, and a date of publication. If published by a small firm or individual, we have included the address when known.

Finding many of these books may present a problem. The antiques and collectibles field is blessed with a dedicated core of book dealers who stock these specialized publications. You may find them at flea markets, antiques shows, or through their advertisements in leading publications in the field. Many dealers publish annual or semi-annual catalogs. Ask to be put on their mailing lists. Books go out-of-print quickly, yet many books printed more than 25 years ago remain the standard work in a field. Also, haunt used-book dealers for collectible reference material.

The reference lists in *Warman's Americana & Collectibles* should be a good starting point, but don't assume we've listed every reference book pertaining to a particular topic. That would be a wonderful feature to offer, but would leave little room for price listings. We try to list the most current books to assist you in your search for information.

Collectors' Clubs: The large number of collectors' clubs adds vitality to the collectibles field. Their publications and conventions produce knowledge which often cannot be found anywhere else. Many of these clubs are short-lived; others are so strong that they have regional and local chapters. Many collector clubs are now going on-line, offering chat rooms and other benefits to their members.

Periodicals: In respect to the collectibles field, there are certain general monthly periodicals to which the general collector should subscribe:

Antiques & Collecting Hobbies, 1006 South Michigan Ave., Chicago, IL 60605.

Antique Trader Weekly, P.O. Box 1050, Dubuque, IA 52001; http://www.csmonline.com.

AntiqueWeek, P.O. Box 90, Knightstown, IN 46148; http://www.antiqueweek.com.

Maine Antique Digest, P.O. Box 358, Waldoboro, ME 04572; http://www.maineantiquedigest.com.

Several excellent periodicals relating to the collectibles marketplace are published by Krause Publications, 700 East State Street, Iola, WI 54990-0001; http://www.krause.com. Check out these interesting publications:

> *Coin Prices*
> *Coins*
> *Goldmine*
> *Numismatic News*
> *Sports Cards*
> *Sports Collectors Digest*
> *Toy Shop*

Many of the categories included in *Warman's Americana & Collectibles* have listings of specialized periodicals and newsletters. Please refer to your specific collecting interest for these additional references.

Museums: The best way to study any field is to see as many documented examples as possible. For this reason, we have listed museums where significant collections are on display. Special attention must be directed to the Margaret Woodbury Strong Museum in Rochester, New York, and the Smithsonian Institution's Museum of American History in Washington, D.C.

Reproduction Alert: Reproductions are a major concern, especially with any item related to advertising. Most reproductions are unmarked; the newness of their appearance is often the best clue to uncovering them. Where the words "Reproduction Alert" alone appear, a watchful eye should be kept on all objects in the category.

Reproductions are only one aspect of the problem; outright fakes are another. Unscrupulous manufacturers make fantasy items which never existed, e.g., a depression glass Sharon butter dish reproduced in Mayfair blue.

Research

Collectors of objects in the categories found in this book deserve credit for their attention to scholarship and the skill with which they have assembled their collections. This book attests to how strong and encompassing the collectibles market has become through their efforts.

We obtain our prices from many key sources—dealers, publications, auctions, collectors, the Internet, and field work. The generosity with which dealers have given advice is a credit to the field. Everyone recognizes the need for a guide that is specific and has accurate prices. We study newspapers, magazines, newsletters, and other publications in the collectibles and antiques fields, as well as spending more and more time on-line. All of them are critical to understanding what is available in the market. Special recognition must be given to those collectors' club newsletters and magazines which discuss prices.

Our staff is constantly monitoring the field, paying attention to all parts of the country. We accomplish this by reading trade publications and using the Internet and its vast resources to reach many places. Frequent visits to several different Web sites yield valuable information as to what is being offered for sale and what people are looking for, as well as insights into collecting clubs and new collecting interests. Our Board of Advisors provides regional, as well as specialized information. More than 100 specialized auctions are held annually, and their results provided to our office. Finally, private collectors have worked closely with us, sharing their knowledge of price trends and developments unique to their specialties.

Buyer's Guide, Not Seller's Guide

Warman's Americana and Collectibles is designed to be a buyer's guide, a guide to what you would have to pay to purchase an object on the open market from a dealer or collector. **It is not a seller's guide to prices.** People frequently make this mistake and are deceiving themselves by doing so.

If you have an object mentioned in this book and wish to sell it, you should expect to receive approximately 35 to 40 percent of the value listed. If the object cannot be resold quickly, expect to receive even less. The truth is simple: Knowing whom to sell an object is worth 50 percent or more of its value. Buyers are very specialized; dealers work for years to assemble a list of collectors who will pay top dollar for an item.

Examine your piece as objectively as possible. If it is something from your childhood, try to step back from the personal memories in evaluating its condition. As an antiques appraiser, I spend a great deal of my time telling people their treasures are not "gold," but items readily available in the marketplace.

In respect to buying and selling, a simple philosophy is that a good purchase occurs when both the buyer and seller are happy with the price. Don't look back. Hindsight has little value in the collectibles field. Given time, things tend to balance out.

Where to Buy Collectibles

The collectible has become standard auction house fare in the new millenium. Christie's East, Sotheby's Arcade, and Skinner's conduct collectibles sales several times each year. Specialized auction firms, e.g., James Julia, Inc. and Bill Bertoia Auctions in advertising, toys, and a host of other categories, have proven the viability of the collectible as a focal point.

The major collectibles marketing thrust has changed from the mail auction to Internet auctions. Hake's Americana & Collectibles is the leader in mail auctions. More and more collectible mail auctions are sprouting up all across the country. Add to this the excitement of buying online and even participating in online auctions, and you can see why so many expand their collections using these venues.

It is becoming easier and easier to buy and sell collectibles on-line. There are numerous auction sites, including ebay.com, Collectoronline.com, etc. The same excitement of buying collectibles at a real auction can be achieved. However, this arena is growing quickly and is not yet regulated. Buyers need to be cautious, know what they are buying and learn to set limits on what to spend. Buyers should feel comfortable with the venue before jumping in on the bidding and should feel free to ask questions of the seller, just as they would in a more traditional-selling setting. With on-line services and live auctioneers merging and forming new alliances, it is now possible to live bid on objects being auctioned off at a major auction house. This is a brand new area to explore and hopefully it will bring excitement and energy to the antiques and collectibles market as we begin the new millennium.

Direct-sale catalogs abound. Most major categories have one or more. These dealers and many more advertise in periodicals and collectors' clubs' newsletters. Most require payment of an annual fee before sending their catalogs.

Of course, there are an unlimited number of flea markets, estate and country auctions, church bazaars, and garage sales. However, if you are a specialized collector, you may spend days looking for something to add to your collection. If you add in your time, the real cost of an object will be much higher than the purchase price alone.

All of which brings us to the final source—the specialized dealer. The collectibles field is so broad that dealers do specialize. Find the dealers who handle your material and work with them to build your collection.

Board of Advisors

Our Board of Advisors is made up of dealers, authors, collectors, and leaders of collectors' clubs throughout the United States. All are dedicated to accuracy in description and pricing. If you wish to buy or sell an object in their field of expertise, drop them a note. Please include a stamped, self-addressed envelope with all correspondence. If time permits, they will respond.

We list the names of our advisors at the end of their respective categories. Included in the list at the front of this book are mailing address for each advisor and, when available, phone number and/or e-mail address.

Comments Invited

Warman's Americana & Collectibles is a major effort dealing with a complex field. Our readers are encouraged to send their comments and suggestions to P.O. Box 392, Quakertown, PA 18951-0392; or via e-mail to schroy@voicenet.com.

Editorial Staff

Ellen T. Schroy
Editor

Board of Advisors

Bob Levy
The Unique One
2802 Centre Street
Pennsauken, NJ 08109
(856) 663-2554
e-mail:theuniqueone@world-net.att.net
Slot Machines; Pinball Machines; Vending Machines

Patricia McDaniel
Old Storefront Antiques
411 W. 28th St.
Connersville, IN 47331
(765) 825-6295
Drugstore

Nancy McMichael
P.O. Box 53132
Washington, DC 20009
Snowdomes

**Gary L. Miller &
K. M. Scotty Mitchel**
Millchell
2112 Lipscomb
Fort Worth, TX 76110
(817) 923-3274
Electrical Appliances

Joan Collett Oates
685 South Washington
Constantine, MI 49042
(616) 435-8353
Phoenix Bird China

Clark Phelps
Amusement Sales
7610 South Main Street
Midvale, UT 84047
(801) 255-4731
Web site: http://www.Punch-boards.com
Punchboards

Evalene Pulati
P.O. Box 1404
Santa Ana, CA 92702
Valentines

Arthur Rein
Lottery Collector's Society
642 Locust Street, Apt 2J
Mt. Vernon NY 10552-2620
(914) 237-7417
e-mail: Lotteryfan@aol.com.
Lottery Tickets

Julie P. Robinson
P.O. Box 117
Upper Jay, NY 12987
e-mail: Celuloid@frontier.net
Plastics

Jim & Nancy Schaut
7147 W. Angela Drive
Glendale, AZ 85308-8507
(602) 878-4293
e-mail: Jnschaut@aol.com
Horse Collectibles, Western Collectibles

Kenneth E. Schneringer
271 Sabrina Court
Woodstock, GA 30188
(707) 926-9383
Web site: old-paper.com
e-mail: trademan68@aol.com
Catalogs

Richard Shields
The Carolina Trader
P.O. Box 769
Monroe, NC 28112
(704) 289-1604
e-mail: Carotrader@trellis.net
Scouting

Judy Smith
1702 Lamont Street NW
Washington, DC 20010-2602
(202) 332-3020
e-mail: Reamers@quiltart.com
Reamers

**Lissa Bryan-Smith
and Richard Smith**
7 Baldtop Heights
Danville, PA 17821-0768
(717) 275-7796
e-mail: Lissabryan@aol.com
Christmas Items; Holiday Collectibles; Santa Claus

Connie Swaim
c/o Antique Week
P.O. Box 90, 27 North Jefferson
Knightstown, IN 46148
(800) 876-5133
e-mail: TheLorax50@aol.com
Dr. Seuss Collectibles

Dixie Trainer
P.O. Box 70
Nellysford, VA 22958
(804) 361-1739
e-mail: SouvenirBu@aol.com
Souvenir Buildings

Lewis S. Walters
143 Lincoln Lane
Berlin, NJ 08009
(609) 589-3202
e-mail: lew69@erols.com
Radios

AUCTION HOUSES

The following auction houses cooperate with Warman's by providing catalogs of their auctions and price lists. This information is used to prepare *Warman's Antiques and Collectibles Price Guide*, volumes in the Warman's Encyclopedia of Antiques and Collectibles. This support is truly appreciated.

Albrecht & Cooper Auction Services
3884 Saginaw Rd
Vassar, MI 48768
(517) 823-8835

Sanford Alderfer Auction Company
501 Fairgrounds Rd
Hatfield, PA 19440
(215) 393-3000
Web site: http://www.alderfer-company.com

American Social History and Social Movements
4025 Saline Street
Pittsburgh, PA 15217
(412) 421-5230

Andre Ammelounx
The Stein Auction Company
P.O. Box 136
Palantine, IL 60078
(847) 991-5927

Antique Bottle Connection
147 Reserve Rd
Libby, MT 59923
(406) 293-8442

Apple Tree Auction Center
1616 W. Church St.
Newark, OH 43055
(614) 344-4282

Arthur Auctioneering
RD 2, P.O. Box 155
Hughesville, PA 17737
(717) 584-3697

Auction Team Köln
Jane Herz
6731 Ashley Court
Sarasota, FL 34241
(941) 925-0385

Auction Team Köln
Postfach 501168 D 5000
Köln 50, W. Germany

Noel Barrett Antiques & Auctions, Ltd.
P.O. Box 1001
Carversville, PA 18913
(610) 297-5109

Robert F. Batchelder
1 W Butler Ave.
Ambler, PA 19002
(610) 643-1430

Bear Pen Antiques
2318 Bear Pen Hollow Road
Lock Haven, PA 17745
(717) 769-6655

Beverly Hills Auctioneers
9454 Wilshire Blvd., Suite 202
Beverly Hills, CA 90212
(310) 278-8115

Bill Bertoia Auctions
1881 Spring Rd
Vineland, NJ 08360
(609) 692-1881

Biders Antiques Inc.
241 S. Union St.
Lawrence, MA 01843
(508) 688-4347

Brown Auction & Real Estate
900 East Kansas
Greensburg, KS 67054
(316) 723-2111

Buffalo Bay Auction Co.
5244 Quam Circle
Rogers, MN 55374
(612) 428-8440
Web site:
www.buffalobayauction.com

Butterfield, Butterfield & Dunning
755 Church Rd
Elgin, IL 60123
(847) 741-3483
Web site: http://www:butterfields.com

Butterfield, Butterfield & Dunning
7601 Sunset Blvd.
Los Angeles, CA 90046
(213) 850-7500
Web site: http://www:butterfields.com

Butterfield, Butterfield & Dunning
220 San Bruno Ave.
San Francisco, CA 94103
(415) 861-7500
Web site: http://www:butterfields.com

C. C. Auction Gallery
416 Court
Clay Center, KS 67432
(913) 632-6021

Cerebro
P.O. Box 327
East Prospect, PA 17317
(717) 252-3685

W. E. Channing & Co., Inc.
53 Old Santa Fe Trail
Santa Fe, NM 87501
(505) 988-1078

Chicago Art Galleries
5039 Oakton St.
Skokie, IL 60077
(847) 677-6080

Childers & Smith
1415 Horseshoe Pike
Glenmoore, PA 19343
(610) 269-1036
e-mail:
    harold@smithautionco.com

Christie's
502 Park Ave.
New York, NY 10022
(212) 546-1000
Web Site: http://
    www.christies.com

Christie's East
219 E. 67th St.
New York, NY 10021
(212) 606-0400
Web Site: http://
    www.christies.com

Cincinnati Art Galleries
635 Main St.
Cincinnati, OH 45202
(513) 381-2128

Mike Clum, Inc.
P.O. Box 2
Rushville, OH 43150
(614) 536-9220

Cobb's Doll Auctions
1909 Harrison Road
Johnstown OH 43031-9539
(740) 964-0444

Cohasco Inc.
Postal 821
Yonkers, NY 10702
(914) 476-8500

**Collection Liquidators
Auction Service**
341 Lafayette St.
New York, NY 10012
(212) 505-2455
Web site: http://
    www.rtam.com/coliq/bid.html
e-mail:

**Collectors Auction
Services**
RR 2, Box 431 Oakwood Rd
Oil City, PA 16301
(814) 677-6070
Web site: http://
    www.caswel.com

**Collector's Sales and
Service**
P.O. Box 4037
Middletown RI02842
(401) 849-5012
Web site: http://
    www.antiquechina.com

**Coole Park Books
and Autographs**
P.O. Box 199049
Indianapolis, IN 46219
(317) 351-8495
e-mail: cooleprk@indy.net

Copeke Auction
226 Route 7A
Cokepe, NY 12516
(518) 329-1142

Samuel J. Cottonne
15 Genesee St.
Mt. Morris, NY 14510
(716) 583-3119

Craftsman Auctions
1485 W. Housatoric
Pittsfield MA 01202
(413) 442-7003
Web site: http://
    www.artsncrafts.com

Dargate Auction Galleries
5607 Baum Blvd.
Pittsburgh, PA 15206
(412) 362-3558
Web site: http://
    www.dargate.com

Dawson's
128 American Road
Morris Plains, NJ 07950
(973) 984-6900
Web site: http://
    www.idt.net/-dawson1

DeWolfe & Wood
P.O. Box 425
Alfred, ME 04002
(207) 490-5572

Marlin G. Denlinger
RR3, Box 3775
Morrisville, VT 05661
(802) 888-2775

Dixie Sporting Collectibles
1206 Rama Rd.
Charlotte, NC 28211
(704) 364-2900
Web site: http://
    www.sportauction.com

Dorothy Dous, Inc.
1261 University Drive
Yardley, PA 19067-2857
(888) 548-6635

**William Doyle
Galleries, Inc.**
175 E. 87th St.
New York, NY 10128
(212) 427-2730
Web site: http://
    www.doylegalleries.com

Dunbar Gallery
76 Haven St.
Milford, MA 01757
(508) 634-8697

Early Auction Co.
123 Main St.
Milford, OH 45150
(513) 831-4833

Fain & Co.
P.O. Box 1330
Grants Pass, OR 97526
(888) 324-6726

**Ken Farmer Realty &
Auction Co.**
105A Harrison St.
Radford, VA 24141
(703) 639-0939
Web site: http://kenfarmer.com

Fine Tool Journal
27 Fickett Rd
Pownal, ME 04069
(207) 688-4962
Web site: http://
    www.wowpages.com/FTJ/

Steve Finer Rare Books
P.O. Box 758
Greenfield, MA 01302
(413) 773-5811

Fink's Off the Wall Auctions
108 E. 7th St.
Lansdale, PA 19446
(215) 855-9732
Web site:
   www.finksauctions.com

Flomaton Antique Auction
P.O. Box 1017
320 Palafox Street
Flomaton, AL 36441
(334) 296-3059

Fontaine's Auction Gallery
1485 W. Housatonic St.
Pittsfield, MA 01201
(413) 488-8922

William A. Fox Auctions Inc.
676 Morris Ave.
Springfield, NJ 07081
(201) 467-2366

Freeman\Fine Arts Co. of Philadelphia, Inc.
1808 Chestnut St.
Philadelphia, PA 19103
(215) 563-9275

Garth's Auction, Inc.
2690 Stratford Rd
P.O. Box 369
Delaware, OH 43015
(740) 362-4771

Greenberg Auctions
7566 Main St.
Skysville, MD 21784
(410) 795-7447

Green Valley Auction Inc.
Route 2, Box 434
Mt. Crawford, VA 22841
(540) 434-4260

Guerney's
136 E. 73rd St.
New York, NY 10021
(212) 794-2280

Hake's Americana & Collectibles
P.O. Box 1444
York, PA 17405
(717) 848-1333

Gene Harris Antique Auction Center, Inc.
203 South 18th Ave.
P.O. Box 476
Marshalltown, IA 50158
(515) 752-0600
Web site:
   www.harrisantiqueauction.com

Norman C. Heckler & Company
Bradford Corner Rd
Woodstock Valley, CT 06282
(203) 974-1634

High Noon
9929 Venice Blvd.
Los Angeles CA 90034
(310) 202-9010
Web site: www.High Noon.com

Randy Inman Auctions, Inc.
P.O. Box 726
Waterville, ME 04903
(207) 872-6900
Web site:
   www.inmanauctions.com

Michael Ivankovich Auction Co.
P.O. Box 2458
Doylestown, PA 18901
(215) 345-6094
Web site: http://
   www.nutting.com

Jackson's Auctioneers & Appraisers
2229 Lincoln St.
Cedar Falls, IA 50613
(319) 277-2256
Web site: http://
   www.jacksonauction.com

James D. Julia Inc.
Rt. 201 Skowhegan Rd
P.O. Box 830
Fairfield, ME 04937
(207) 453-7125
Web site:
   www.juliaauctions.com

J. W. Auction Co.
54 Rochester Hill Rd
Rochester, NH 03867
(603) 332-0192

Lang's Sporting Collectables, Inc.
31 R. Turthle Cove
Raymond, ME 04071
(207) 655-4265

La Rue Auction Service
201 S. Miller St.,
Sweet Springs, MO 65351
(816) 335-4538

Leonard's Auction Company
1631 State Rd
Duncannon, PA 17020
(717) 957-3324

Howard Lowery
3818 W. Magnolia Blvd.
Burbank, CA 91505
(818) 972-9080

Joy Luke
The Gallery
300 E. Grove St.
Bloomington, IL 61701
(309) 828-5533

Mapes Auctioneers & Appraisers
1729 Vestal Pkwy
Vestal, NY 13850
(607) 754-9193

Martin Auctioneers Inc.
P.O. Box 477
Intercourse, PA 17534
(717) 768-8108

McMasters Doll Auctions
P.O. Box 1755
Cambridge, OH 43725
(614) 432-4419

McMurray Antiques & Auctions
P.O. Box 393
Kirkwood, NY 13795
(607) 775-2321

Metropolitian Book Auction
123 W. 18th St., 4th Floor
New York, NY 10011
(212) 929-7099

Gary Metz's Muddy River Trading Company
P.O. Box 1430
Salem, VA 24135
(540) 387-5070

Wm. Frost Mobley
P.O. Box 10
Schoharie, NY 12157
(518) 295-7978

Wm. Morford
RD #2
Cazenovia, NY 13035
(315) 662-7625

Neal Auction Company
4038 Magazine Street
New Orleans, LA 70115
(504) 899-5329
Web site: http://
    www.nealauction.com

New England Auction Gallery
P.O. Box 2273
W. Peabody, MA 01960
(508) 535-3140

New Orleans Auction St. Charles Auction Gallery, Inc.
1330 St. Charles Avenue
New Orleans, LA 70130
(504) 586-8733
Web site: http://
    www.neworleansauction.com

New Hampshire Book Auctions
P.O. Box 460
92 Woodbury Rd
Weare, NH 03281
(603) 529-7432

Norton Auctioneers of Michigan Inc.
50 West Pearl at Monroe
Coldwater MI 49036
(517) 279-9063

Nostalgia Publications, Inc.
21 S. Lake Dr.
Hackensack, NJ 07601
(201) 488-4536
Web site:
    www.nostalgiapubls.com

Old Barn Auction
10040 St. Rt. 224 West
Findlay, OH 45840
(419) 422-8531
Web site: http://
    www.oldbarn.com

Ohio Cola Traders
4411 Bazetta Rd
Cortland, OH 44410
(330) 637-0357

Richard Opfer Auctioneering Inc.
1919 Greenspring Dr.
Timonium, MD 21093
(410) 252-5035
Web site:
    www.opferauction.com

Pacific Book Auction Galleries
133 Kerney St., 4th Floor
San Francisco, CA 94108
(415) 989-2665
Web site:

Past Tyme Pleasures
PMB #204, 2491 San Ramon
    Valley Blvd., #1
San Ramon, CA 94583
(925) 484-6442
Fax: (925) 484-2551
Web site:
e-mail: Pasttyme@excite.com

Phillips Ltd.
406 E. 79th St.
New York, NY 10021
(212) 570-4830
Web site: http://
    www.phillips-auction.com

Postcards International
2321 Whitney Ave., Suite 102
P.O. Box 5398
Hamden, CT 06518
(203) 248-6621
Web site: http://
    www.csmonline.com/post-
    cardsint/

Poster Auctions International
601 W. 26th Street
New York, NY 10001
(212) 787-4000
Web site:
    www.posterauction.com

Profitt Auction Company
P.O. Box 796
Columbia, VA 23038
(804) 747-6353

Provenance
P.O. Box 3487
Wallington, NJ 07057
(201) 779-8725

David Rago Auctions, Inc.
333 S. Main St.
Lambertville, NJ 08530
(609) 397-9374
Web site: http://
    www.ragoarts.com

Lloyd Ralston Toys
173 Post Rd
Fairfield, CT 06432
(203) 255-1233

James J. Reeves
P.O. Box 219
Huntingdon, PA 16652-0219
(814) 643-5497
Web site:
    www.JamesJReeves.com

Mickey Reichel Auctioneer
1440 Ashley Rd
Boonville MO 65233
(816) 882-5292

Sandy Rosnick Auctions
15 Front Street
Salem MA 01970
(508) 741-1130

Thomas Schmidt
7099 McKean Rd
Ypsilanti, MI 48197
(313) 485-8606

Seeck Auctions
P.O. Box 377
Mason City, IA 50402
(515) 424-1116
Web site:
    www.willowtree.com/~seeck-
    auctions

L. H. Selman Ltd.
761 Chestnut St.
Santa Cruz, CA 95060
(408) 427-1177
Web site: http://
    www.selman.com

Sentry Auction
113 School St.
Apollo, PA 15613
(412) 478-1989

Skinner Inc.
Bolton Gallery
357 Main St.
Bolton, MA 01740
(978) 779-6241
Web site: http://
www.skinnerinc.com

Skinner, Inc.
The Heritage on the Garden
63 Park Plaza
Boston MA 02116
(978) 350-5429
Web site: http://
www.skinnerinc.com

C. G. Sloan & Company Inc.
4920 Wyaconda Rd
North Bethesda, MD 20852
(301) 468-4911
Web site: http://
www.cgsloan.com

Smith & Jones, Inc., Auctions
12 Clark Lane
Sudbury MA 01776
(508) 443-5517

Smith House Toy Sales
26 Adlington Rd
Eliot, ME 03903
(207) 439-4614

R. M. Smythe & Co.
26 Broadway
New York, NY 10004-1710
(212) 943-1880
Web site: http://
www.rm-smythe.com

Sotheby's
1334 York Ave.
New York, NY 10021
(212) 606-7000
Web site: http://
www.sothebys.com

Southern Folk Pottery Collectors Society
220 Washington Street
Bennett, NC 27208
(336) 581-4246

Stanton's Auctioneers
P.O. Box 146
144 South Main St.
Vermontville, MI 49096
(517) 726-0181

Stout Auctions
11 W. Third St.
Williamsport, IN 47993-1119
(765) 764-6901

Michael Strawser
200 N. Main St., P.O. Box 332
Wolcottville, IN 46795
(219) 854-2859
Web site:
www.majolicaauctions.com

Swann Galleries Inc.
104 E. 25th St.
New York, NY 10010
(212) 254-4710
Web site:
www.swanngalleries.com

Swartz Auction Services
2404 N. Mattis Ave.
Champaign, IL 61826-7166
(217) 357-0197
Web site: http://
www/SwartzAuction.com

The House In The Woods
S91 W37851 Antique Lane
Eagle River, WI 53119
(414) 594-2334

Theriault's
P.O. Box 151
Annapolis, MD 21401
(301) 224-3655
Web site: http://
www.theriaults.com

Toy Scouts
137 Casterton Ave.
Akron, OH 44303
(216) 836-0668
e-mail:
toyscout@salamander.net

Treadway Gallery, Inc.
2029 Madison Rd
Cincinnati, OH 45208
(513) 321-6742
Web site: http://
www.a3c2net.com/tread-
waygallery

Unique Antiques & Auction Gallery
449 Highway 72 West
Collierville, TN 38017
(901) 854-1141

Venable Estate Auction
423 West Fayette St.
Pittsfield, IL 62363
(217) 285-2560
e-mail: sandiv@msn.com

Victorian Images
P.O. Box 284
Marlton, NJ 08053
(609) 985-7711
Web site:
www.tradecards.com/vi

Victorian Lady
P.O. Box 424
Waxhaw, NC 28173
(704) 843-4467

Vintage Cover Story
P.O. Box 975
Burlington, NC 27215
(919) 584-6900

Bruce and Vicki Waasdorp
P.O. Box 434
10931 Main St.
Clarence, NY 14031
(716) 759-2361

Web Wilson Antiques
P.O. Box 506
Portsmouth, RI 02871
1-800-508-0022

Winter Associates
21 Cooke St. Box 823
Plainville, CT 06062
(203) 793-0288

Wolf's Auctioneers
1239 W. 6th St.
Cleveland, OH 44113
(614) 362-4711

Woody Auction
Douglass, KS 67039
(316) 746-2694

York Town Auction, Inc.
1625 Haviland Rd
York, PA 17404
(717) 751-0211
e-mail:
yorktownauction@cybe-
ria.com

ABBREVIATIONS

The following are standard abbreviations which we have used throughout this edition of Warman's.

3D = three dimensional
ADS = Autograph Document Signed
adv = advertising
ALS = Autograph Letter Signed
approx = approximately
AQS = Autograph Quotation Signed
b&w = black and white
C = century
c = circa
cov = cover
CS = Card Signed
d = diameter or depth
dec = decorated
dj = dust jacket
DS = Document Signed
ed = edition, editor
emb = embossed
ext. = exterior
ftd = footed
gal = gallon
ground = background
h = height
horiz = horizontal
hp = hand painted
illus = illustrated, illustration, illustrator
imp = impressed
int. = interior
irid = iridescent
j = jewels
K = karat
l = length
lb = pound
litho = lithograph
LS = Letter Signed

MBP = mint in bubble pack
mfg = manufactured
MIB = mint in box
MIP = mint in package
MISB = mint in sealed box
mkd = marked
MOC = mint on card
MOP = mother of pearl
n.d. = no date
No. = number
NRFB = never removed from box
opal = opalescent
orig = original
oz = ounce
pat = patent
pc = piece
pcs = pieces
pg = page
pgs = pages
pr = pair
PS = Photograph Signed
pt = pint
qt = quart
rect = rectangular
Soc = Society
sgd = signed
SP = silver plated
SS = sterling silver
sq = square
TLS = Typed Letter Signed
vol = volume
w = width
yg = yellow gold
# = numbered

A

Abingdon Pottery

Collecting Hints: Like wares from many contemporary potteries, Abingdon Pottery pieces are readily available in the market. The company produced more than 1,000 shapes and used more than 150 colors to decorate its wares. Because of this tremendous variety, it is advisable to collect Abingdon Pottery with particular forms and/or colors in mind.

Abingdon art pottery, with its vitreous body and semi-gloss and high-gloss glazes, is found at all levels of the market, from garage sales to antiques shows. For this reason, price fluctuations for identical pieces are quite common.

Black (gunmetal), a semi-gloss dark blue, a metallic copper brown, and several shades of red are the favored colors. Decorated pieces command a premium of 15-20 percent.

History: The Abingdon Sanitary Manufacturing Company, Abingdon, Illinois, was founded in 1908 for the purpose of manufacturing plumbing fixtures. Sometime between 1933 and 1934, Abingdon introduced a line of art pottery. In 1945, the company changed its name to Abingdon Potteries, Inc. Production of the art pottery line continued until 1950 when fire destroyed the art pottery kiln.

After the fire, the company once again placed its emphasis on plumbing fixtures. Eventually, Abingdon Potteries became Briggs Manufacturing Company, a firm noted for its sanitary fixtures.

Reference: Joe Paradis, *Abingdon Pottery Artware 1934-1950, Stepchild of the Great Depression*, Schiffer Publishing, 2000.

Collectors' Club: Abingdon Pottery Collectors' Club, 210 Knox Hwy S, Abingdon, IL 61410.

Ashtray, #456 ....36.00
Bookend
    Goose, #98, single 42.00
    Horse Heads, black, #441 ....75.00
    Seagull, single, #305 ....70.00
Candleholders, pr
    Double scroll, blue, gold trim, wear to gold 35.00
    Shell, peach 20.00

Compote, white, #568, mkd "Abingdon USA #568," 5" h, 2" sq base 25.00
Console Bowl
    #377, yellow, handle continues into bowl, #377, stamped "Abingdon, U.S.A.," 14" w, 3-3/4" h 50.00
    #532, leaf, green, 10" l 27.50
    #532, scroll, blue, mkd "Scroll/MD/14.5Sl/1941," 14-1/2" l, 3-3/4" h, age crazing 25.00
    #532, shell, peach/beige, floral decals, gold trim, stamped with name and number, 1940s, 14" l 45.00
Cookie Jar
    Daisy 45.00
    Little Miss Muffet, #622 .... 220.00
    Money Bag, #588 ....80.00
    Pineapple, lid repaired 75.00
    Sunflower 45.00
    Windmill, #678 .... 250.00
Cornucopia, pink 20.00
Figure
    Goose, blue, #571 ....45.00
    Peacock, pink 40.00
Planter
    Fan shape, light blue, ink mark "Abingdon U.S.A.," imp number, 4-1/2" h, 8" l 35.00
    Mexican and cactus, #616D 70.00
    Sailing Ship, rope handles, sea green glaze 40.00
Salt and Pepper Shakers, pr, Little Bo Peep 45.00
String Holder, mouse 90.00
Tray, green, 10-3/4" x 8" 22.50
Vase
    Alpha, antique white, handles, #105, 8" h 35.00
    Art Deco style, dusty rose, #114 .37.50
    Baluster, dusty blue, two handles, #117, 9-3/4" h 45.00
    Box, white, 5-1/2" h 70.00
    Boyne, pale peach, mold defect at one handle, 9" h 35.00
    Cameo, pink, sgd, dated "4-16-52," mkd "Special Star Flower," 6-1/4" h, 6-1/4" d 125.00
    Double Cornucopia, white, 11" l ..35.00
    Fan, salmon, mkd "Abingdon USA 513," 9" h 25.00
    Ship, peach, hairline at top, 7" h, 6-1/2" w 12.00
Wall Pocket
    Book 50.00
    Calla Lilly 60.00
Window Box, #476 ....20.00

Action Figures

Collecting Hints: This is one of the hot, trendy collecting categories. While there is no question that action figure material is selling—and selling well—much of the pricing is highly speculative. Trends change from month to month as one figure or group of figures becomes hot and another cools off.

The safest approach is to buy only objects in fine or better condition and, if possible, with or in their original packaging. Any figure that has been played with to any extent will never have long-term value. This is a category with off-the-rack expectations.

Be extremely cautious about paying premium prices for figures less than ten years old. During the past decade, dealers have made a regular practice of buying newly released action figures in quantity, warehousing them, and releasing their stash slowly into the market once production ceases.

Also examine packaging very closely. A premium is placed on a figure in its original packaging, i.e., the packaging which was used when the figure was introduced into the market. Later packaging means a lower price.

History: An action figure is a die-cast metal or plastic poseable model with flexible joints that portrays a real or fictional character. In addition to the figures themselves, clothing, personal equipment, vehicles, and other types of accessories are also collectible.

Collectors need to be aware of the following attempts to manipulate the market: 1) limited production—a deliberate act on the part of manufacturers to hold back on production of one or more figures in a series; 2) variations—minor changes in figures made by manufacturers to increase sales (previously believed to be mistakes, but now viewed as deliberate sales gimmicks); and 3) prototypes—artists' models used during the planning process. Any prototype should be investigated thoroughly—there are many fakes.

The earliest action figures were the hard-plastic Hartland figures of popular television Western heroes of the 1950s. Louis Marx also included action figures in a number of playsets during the late 1950s. Although Barbie, who made her appearance in 1959, is poseable, she is not considered an action figure by collectors.

G.I. Joe, introduced by Hassenfield Bros. in 1964, triggered the modern action-figure craze. In 1965, Gilbert introduced action figures for James Bond 007, The Man from U.N.C.L.E., and Honey West. Bonanza figures arrived in 1966, along with Ideal Toy Corporation's

Captain Action. Ideal altered the figures by simply changing heads and costumes. Captain Action and his accessories were the hot collectible of the late 1980s.

In 1972, Mego introduced the first six super heroes in what would become a series of 34 different characters. Mego also established the link between action figures and the movies when the company issued series for "Planet of the Apes" and "Star Trek: The Motion Picture." Mego's television series figures included "CHiPs," "Dukes of Hazzard," and "Star Trek." When Mego filed for bankruptcy protection in 1982, the days of eight- and twelve-inch fabric-clothed action figures ended.

The introduction of Kenner's "Star Wars" figure set in 1977 opened a floodgate. Action figures enjoyed enormous popularity, and manufacturers rushed into the market, with Mattel quickly following on Kenner's heels. Before long, the market was flooded, not only with a large selection, but also with production runs in the hundreds of thousands.

Not all series were successful—just ask companies such as Colorform, Matchbox, and TYCO. Some sets were not further produced when initial sales did not justify the costs of manufacture. These sets have limited collector value. Scarcity does not necessarily equate with high value in the action-figure market.

References: Tom Heaton, *The Encyclopedia of Marx Action Figures,* Krause Publications, 1999; Sharon Korbeck, *Toys & Prices, 1999,* 6th edition, Krause Publications, 1998; Paris & Susan Manos, *Collectible Action Figures,* 2nd ed., Collector Books, 1996; John Marshall, *Action Figures of the 1980s,* Schiffer Publishing, 1998; Stuart W. Wells, III, *Science Fiction Collectibles: Identification & Price Guide,* Krause Publications, 1999.

Periodicals: *Action Figure News & Review,* 556 Monroe Tpk, Monroe, CT 06468; *Tomart's Action Figure Digest,* Tomart Publications, 3300 Encrete Lane, Dayton, OH 45439.

Collectors' Clubs: Captain Action Collectors Club, P.O. Box 2095, Halesite, NY 11743; Captain Action Society of Pittsburgh, 516 Cubbage St., Carnegie, PA 15106.

Additional Listings: G.I. Joe Collectibles, Super Heroes, Star Wars, Star Trek.

Star Trek, Capt. James T. Kirk, space suit, 1994, Playmates, MOC, $20.

Alien, Slasher, Spider-Man, loose.......7.50
Angela, Spawn, MacFarlane Toys,
    MOC 20.00
April O'Neil, Playmates, MIB.............15.00
AT-AT Commander 40.00
Austin Powers, MacFarlane Toys, 6" h,
    MOC 15.00
Baltar, Battlestar Galactica, loose 35.00
Banzai...10.00
Bedrock, Spawn, loose.....................15.00
Belly Bustin, Mask, Kenner, MOC 18.00
Bespin Guard Black, 3" h 12.00
Best of West Sam Cobra, 1974, many
    accessories 68.00
Betty Mustin, Mask, Kenner, MOC ...20.00
Boba Fett, Star Wars, two circles,
    MIP 25.00
Brett Hull, Starting Lineup, 1994 ......10.00
Bryant, Starting Lineup, extended, 1996,
    MBP 80.00
Captain Jean-Luc Picard, Star Trek,
    movie edition, MIB 15.00
Carcass 25.00
Charo, Clash of the Titans, Mattel, 1980,
    3-3/4" h, MOC..............................35.00
Chompin' Milo, Mask, Kenner,
    MOC 18.00
Clear Iceman, X-Men.......................25.00
Clemens, Starting Lineup, 1999,
    MBP 10.00
Cornelius, Planet of the Apes,
    Kenner..30.00
Deadproof, #1, X-Men 25.00
Death Star Commander, Star Wars ..10.00
Die Hard, MacFarlane Toys, MIB 15.00
Dorian, Mask, Kenner, MOC.............20.00
Dream Team, Starting Lineup, 1996 Basketball, set 1 of 2.............................30.00

Dr. Alex Durant, Black Hole, 12-1/2" h,
    Mego, © 1979, WDP, MIB...........50.00
Dr. Evil, MacFarlane Toys, MOC 15.00
Dr. Zaius, Planet of the Apes,
    Kenner...25.00
Duncan, Starting Lineup, 1997,
    MMP...50.00
Emplate, Marvel, Toy Biz, MIB 15.00
Elvira, DC Direct, 7-1/2" h, regular (serpent and chainsaw) or witch variant,
    each...15.00
Eric Lindros, Starting Lineup, 1996,
    MOC 24.00
Flash Gordon, Defenders of the Earth,
    Galoob, 1985, MOC....................35.00
Fonzie, Happy Days, Mego, loose ..35.00
Garax Swordship, Defenders of the Earth,
    Galoob, 1985, MIB 45.00
Hannibal, A-Team, Galoob, MOC....20.00
Heads Up Dorian, Mask, Kenner,
    MOC 20.00
Human Torch, Fantastic Four 7.50
Indiana Jones, Raiders of the Lost Ark,
    Kenner, MOC..............................325.00
James Bond, 007, adjustable ring, set of
    nine: Scuba Bond, Tux Bond, Dr. No.
    Bond, Moneypenny, Domino, Dr. NLE,
    M, Goldfinger, Odd Job, loose ...40.00
Jim Carey, Starting Lineup, 1996.....15.00
Joker, Legends of Batman...............15.00
Laserscope Fighter, Battlestar Galactica,
    Italy, loose 195.00
Leia Organa, Star Wars, ...20.00
Lone Ranger, GI Joe, 1989, 3-3/4" h,
    loose 14.00
Lothar, Defenders of the Earth, Galoob,
    1985, MOC 35.00
Lt Commander Data, Star Trek, movie edition, 1994......................................15.00
Lt Commander Geordi LaForge, Star
    Trek, MIB.....................................15.00
Luke Skywalker, Star Wars, 1st issue,
    12" h, MIP 38.00
Luke, X-Wing, 3" 12.00
McGwire, Starting Lineup, 1999,
    MBP 15.00
Mercy, Hobby Exclusive, gold edition,
    7" h 17.50
Mystique, Marvel, 10" h, loose.........15.00
Nightcrawler, Uncanny X-Men, Marvel,
    Toy Biz, MIB 18.00
Pandora, Bolt, MOC 15.00
Peter Palmer, Spider-Man, loose 10.00
Phalanx, Generation X, Marvel, Toy Biz,
    MIB..15.00
Phantasm, Batman, animated, foreign
    card..24.00
Phantom, Defenders of the Earth, Galoob,
    1985, MOC 35.00
Picard, Star Trek, loose 10.00
Power Droid, 3" h, loose....................8.00
Quick Draw, Mask, Kenner, MOC....20.00
Ralph, Happy Days, Mego, MOC ...65.00
Ritchie, Happy Days, Mego, MOC ..65.00

Rodman, Starting Lineup, red, 1994, MBP..............................50.00
Rogue, Marvel, 10" h, loose 12.00
Sabretooth #1, X-Men.......................10.00
Shaggy, Scooby-Doo, 8" h, MIB.....15.00
Sinthia, Princess of Hell, Skybolt Toys, Lightning Comics, MOC..............17.00
Spawn, poseable bendy cape, gun, knife, arm pad straps, McFarlane Toys, MIP 35.00
Spider-Man, super poseable, 10" h .10.00
Splinter, Playmate, MIB...................15.00
Steve Bono, Starting Lineup, MOC..12.00
Tornado, Mask, Kenner, MOC.........20.00
Tremor, Spawn, loose 12.00
Troll, Spawn..15.00
Usage Yojimbo, Antartic Press, 5" h 12.00
Vampire, Spawn, loose....................17.50
Velma, Scooby-Doo, MIB 15.00
Venom, Marvel, Supersize, ToyBiz, 1991, MIB..30.00
Werewolf, Spawn, loose 20.00
Wetworks Mother-One, Spawn, MacFarlane Toys, MOC 20.00
Widow Variant, MOC 15.00
Wild Wolf, Mask, Kenner, MOC........18.00
Willie Mays, Starting Lineup.............20.00
Wolfman, 3-1/2" h, vinyl clothes, 1960s...90.00
Wolverine, X-Man, mask and sword, fully poseable, ToyBiz, 1991, MIB 35.00
World War I Aviator Ace, GI Joe mail-in...60.00
Xena, DC Direct, Series II, Harem, 6-1/2" h..9.00

Advertising

Collecting Hints: Many factors affect the price of an advertising collectible: the product and its manufacturer, the objects or people used in the advertisement, the period and aesthetics of design, the designer and illustrator of the piece, and the form the advertisement takes. In addition, advertising material was frequently used to decorate bars, restaurants, and other public places. Interior decorators do not purchase objects at the same price level as collectors.

In truth, almost every advertising item is sought by a specialized collector in one or more collectible areas. The result is diverse pricing, with the price quoted to an advertising collector usually lower than that quoted to a specialized collector.

Most collectors seem to concentrate on the period prior to 1940, with special emphasis on the decades from 1880 to 1910. New collectors should examine the advertising material from the post-1940 period. Much of this material is still very inexpensive and likely to rise in value as the decorator trends associated with the 1950s through the 1970s gain importance.

History: The earliest advertising in America is found in colonial newspapers and printed broadsides. By the mid-19th century, manufacturers began to examine how a product was packaged. The box could convey a message and help identify and sell more of the product. The advent of the high-speed, lithograph printing press led to regional and national magazines, resulting in new advertising markets. The lithograph press also introduced vivid colors into advertising.

Simultaneously, the general store branched out into specialized departments or individual specialty shops. By 1880, advertising premiums such as mirrors, paperweights, and trade cards arrived on the scene. Through the early 1960s, premiums remained popular, especially with children.

The advertising character developed in the early 1900s. By the 1950s, endorsements by the popular stars of the day became a firmly established advertising method. Advertising became a lucrative business as firms, many headquartered in New York City, developed specialties to meet manufacturers' needs. Advertising continues to respond to changing opportunities and times.

References: Pamela E. Apkarian-Russell, *Washday Collectibles,* Schiffer Publishing, 2000; Donna S. Baker, *Chocolate Memorabilia,* Schiffer Publishing, 2000; Donald A. Bull, *Beer Advertising,* Schiffer Publishing, 2000; Fred Dodge, *Antique Tins,* Collector Books, (Book I, 1997 values, Book II, 1998, Book III, 1999); Robert Forbes and Terrence Mitchell, *American Tobacco Cards: Price Guide and Checklist,* Tuff Stuff Books, 1999; Sharon and Bob Huxford, *Huxford's Collectible Advertising,* 4th ed., Collector Books, 1999; Don and Elizabeth Johnson, *Warman's Advertising,* Krause Publications, 2000; Ray Klug, *Antique Advertising Encyclopedia,* Vol. 1 (1978, 1993 value update), Vol. 2 (1985, 1990 value update), L-W Book Sales; Linda McPherson, *Modern Collectible Tins,* Collector Books, 2001; Curtis Merritt, *Advertising Thermometers,* Collector Books, 2001; Rex Miller, *The Investor's Guide to Vintage Character Collectibles,* Krause Publications, 1999; David Zimmerman, *Encyclopedia of Advertising Tins,* Vol. II, Collector Books, 1999.

Periodicals: *Advertising Collectors Express,* P.O. Box 221, Mayview, MO 64071; *Let's Talk Tin,* 1 S Beaver Lane, Greenville, SC 29605; *National Association of Paper and Advertising Collectors (P.A.C.),* P.O. Box 500, Mt. Joy, PA 17552; *Paper Collectors' Marketplace (PCM),* P.O. Box 128, Scandinavia, WI 54977; *Tin Fax Newsletter,* 205 Brolley Woods Drive, Woodstock, GA 30188; *Tin Type Newsletter,* P.O. Box 440101, Aurora, CO 80044; *Trade Card Journal,* 143 Main St., Brattleboro, VT 05301.

Collectors' Clubs: Advertising Cup and Mug Collectors of America, P.O. Box 680, Solon, IL 52333; Antique Advertising Association of America, P.O. Box 1121, Morton Grove, IL 60053, Ephemera Society of America, P.O. Box 95, Cazenovia, NY 13035, www.ephemerasociety.org; Inner Seal Collectors Club, 4585 Saron Drive, Lexington, KY 40515; National Association of Paper and Advertising Collectibles, P.O. Box 500, Mount Joy, PA 17552; Porcelain Advertising Collectors Club, P.O. Box 381, Marshfield Hills, MA 02051; Tin Container Collectors Association, P.O. Box 440101, Aurora, CO 80044; Trade Card Collector's Association, 3706 S. Acoma St., Englewood, CO 80110.

Reproduction Alert.

Grading Condition. The following numbers represent the standard grading system used by dealers, collectors, and auctioneers:

10	=	Mint
9	=	Near Mint
8.5	=	Outstanding
8	=	Excellent
7.5	=	Fine+
7	=	Fine
6.5	=	Fine – (good)
6	=	Poor

Bank, Boscul Coffee, W. S. Scull Co., 2-1/2" d, 2-1/4" h, $17.50.

Ashtray

Coors Beer, 6" d, ceramic 4.00
Hodges Candy Company, Liberal, Kansas, clear glass, blue pryoglaze, 4-1/2" sq, 3/4" h 7.50
Nevada Club, Lake Tahoe, glass, 1967 calendar, illus of club, 6-3/4" x 5-3/4" 10.00
TP & W Coal Co., painted plaster, figural, stacked coal lumps, diamond logo at front for Toledo, Peoria & Western Co., seated Indian figure holding peace pipe in one hand, unmarked loose glass insert tray, maker "Plastco/Chicago," c1950 .... 140.00
Windsor Lock Company, CT, 4" sq, clear glass, multicolored adv, wear 5.00

Bill Clip, 1-3/4" celluloid on metal disk, attached to steel spring gripper club Boulevard Velvet, red and white logo, blue lettered in white, sponsored by "A Wimpheimer & Bros., New York City," early 1900s 25.00
Edison Portland Cement Company, Philadelphia, PA, location, yellow and black design, tiny inscription for "Thomas A. Edison Trademark," early 1900s, some wear 25.00
Hoyt's Flintstone Belting, New York City sponsor, global logo, blue, and yellow design, white ground, black lettering, early 1900s 25.00

Bill Hook, Breakfast Cheer Coffee, Campbell & Woods, Pittsburgh, celluloid mounted to wire hanger loop, 4" stiff wire barbed hook, shows red package, early 1900s, 2" x 2-3/4" 40.00

Book

B. F. Goodrich, *Wonderful Book of Rubber,* 36 pgs, 1947, 7" x 10", some wear 20.00
Metropolitan, *Metropolitan Life Insurance Company,* 9-1/4" x 12-1/2", 242 pgs, 1914 .... 10.00

Nestle's Mother Book, *About the Care & Feeding of Babies,* 72 pgs, 1923, 4-3/4" x 6-1/2" 17.50
Bookcover, Kress, Scholastic School Supplies, 1958-59, emblem, school year calendar, place for name, subject, etc., folded flat 10.00
Bookmark, Lebanon, PA, piano and organ dealer, little Victorian girl, pink dress, bouquet of pink roses, 2" w, 6" l, some roughness, tear 15.00

Box, Fairy Soap, Gold Dust Corp., 2-3/8" x 3-7/8", $24.

Box

Andy Gump Sunshine Biscuits, cardboard, 5" x 3" x 2" 425.00
Baker's Chocolate, 12 lb size, wood 25.00
Bob Cat Candy Bar, It's A Wow, black, white, and orange, c1940, 9" x 12" x 2" 10.00
Fairies Bath Perfume, unopened, 1920s 12.00
Ferry Standard Seed, dovetailed wooden display box with dividers, c1895 .... 235.00
Love Lass, red, white, and blue, Luscious Banner Candy Co., young couple in heart shaped medallion, c1930, flattened, 3" x 10" 3.00
My Baby Lamp Safety Pins, brass, colorful graphics 65.00
National Lead Co., paint chip samples 25.00
Regal Underwear, cardboard 20.00
Whitman's Pleasure Island Chocolates, cardboard, pirate scenes on five sides, map on bottom, 1924 .... 28.00

Bridge Tallies, Angelus-Campfire Stretchum, 7" x 9-1/4" punch-out sheet holding parts for 3-D dog, boy, girl, and monkey scoring cards, c1930s, unused 45.00

Brochure

Arm & Hammer, Cleansing Help for the Housewife, 1922 .... 4.50

Electrol Automatic Oil Heating, 1937 .... 5.00
Larkin Soap, 1885 .... 17.50
Magic Yeast 7.50
Philco Radio, fold-out, 1936 .... 9.00
Seymour-Smity & Son, Pruning, 1935 .... 7.50
Westinghouse, Today's Ben Franklin, 1943 .... 5.00

Brush, American Clay Machinery Co., Bucyrus, OH, World's Best Clay Working Machinery, 1909, 4" d 15.00
Paristian Novelty Co., factory scene in center, round, some wear to black paint 50.00

Calculator

Funk's G' High Profit Trio Corn Calculator, for grain, how much to plant per acre, fertilizer per acre, etc. 9.50
Perfection B.T. U. Calculator, Perfection Stove Company, Cleveland, Ohio, 1948, measures BTU's in cubic feet 10.00

Calendar

C. I. Myers Truck Lines, Knox City, MO, 1952, cowgirl and horse, No. 1443, Western Girl, U.I. Co., Made in USA, 12" w, 20-3/4" l, unused 24.00
Compliments of Oriental Tea Co., E. J. Helmer, Prop, Dubuque, Iowa, diecut of Victorian children, top only 22.00
Cudahy's Puritan Meat Products, celluloid, full color illus from "Priscilla and John Alden" series, 1926 calendar, 2-1/4" x 3-3/4" 18.00
Dundee Savings Bank of Dundee, Iowa, 11" w, 9" h, framed 35.00
Singer Sewing Machine, 1905, four prints, 7" x 10" 85.00
Smith Drug Store, Lincoln, Nebraska, wind chart back 3.00
Walter A. Baker, Lincoln, Nebraska, Alka-Seltzer ad, wind chart back 3.00

Candy Tin

Hershey's, A Kiss for You 55.00
Sovereign Toffees, litho tin, hinged, full color American Indian scene, c1950, 3" x 3-1/2" x 5-3/4" 38.00
Whitman's Salmagundi, 4-1/4" x 7-1/2" x 2", litho tin, hinged, Art Nouveau design of young lady, copyright S. F. W. & S. Inc., 1920s, scattered nicks and scratches 20.00

Canister, Woodfield's Fresh Oysters, Galesville, MD, tin litho, c1930, 6-1/2" d, 7-1/2" h 18.00

Charm, Bull Durham, 3-D, brass bull, left side with product name, early 1900s 12.00

Clip

Bengal Ranges, 1-1/2" l, multicolored celluloid, spring clip mkd "Ever Handy Letter Clip No. 2," made by C. H. Hunt Pen Co., 1920s 40.00
Dold Food Products, oval celluloid log, blue, yellow, and red, 1920s 25.00
Golden Blend Coffee, black, white, and red waiter bringing coffee cup, "Here You Are Sir!" 48.00

Rochester Automatic Oiler, black, white, and red celluloid, red lettering 45.00

Clock, Winston Cigarette, electric, neon, 20" h, 16-1/2" w, 4" d 95.00

Coffee Tin

Capitol Mills, 5-1/2" h, 5" d, Lincoln, Seyms & Co., small top, canister 60.00

Comrade, 3-1/2" h, 5" d, J. A. Folger & Co., 1 lb, keywind 170.00

Copley Coffee, First National Stores, Somerville, MA, 1 lb 15.00

Dining Car, 4" h, 5" d, scene of passengers eating in train's dining car, 1 lb, keywind 95.00

Forbes Coffee, Jas. H. Forbes Tea & Coffee Co., St. Louis, Mo, 1 lb., pry top lid, grade 9+ 95.00

Golden Wedding, 3-3/4" h, 5-1/4" d, old couple at breakfast table, The Ennis-Hanly-Blackburn Coffee Co., 1 lb, snap top 60.00

Lindley's Motor, 3-1/2" h, 5" d, images of electric motor on both sides, 1 lb, keywind 50.00

Old Berma Coffee, Grand Union Co., 1 lb, 6-1/4" h, minor blemishes 50.00

Old Judge, 5-3/4" h, 4-1/4" d, titled "Settles the Question," David O. Evans Coffee Co., 1 lb, slip lid 70.00

Seal of Minnesota, 6-1/4" h, 4" d, Philip B. Hunt & Co., Illinois Can Co., farmer working land, Indian warrior on horseback in background, 1 lb, missing slip lid 85.00

Universal, 6-1/2" h, 4" d, E. B. Miller & Co., Uncle Sam image, knob top, 1 lb, even wear 50.00

Wedding Breakfast, 4" h, 5" w, 1 lb, keywind 50.00

Comic Book, giveaway type

Porky Pig, Lobel's Shoe Store imprint on back cover, #71, 1951 copyright, 7-1/8" x 10-1/4" 24.00

Red Ball, tennis shoes, 32 pgs, 1947, 7-1/2" x 10-1/4" 3.00

Collapsible Cup, Knox, 2" d silvered metal canister, removable lid emb "Knox" logo, 1897 patent date 18.00

Compass, Bryant Devices, celluloid disk, insert compass paper and genetic needle under glass, celluloid inscribed in black and red lettering on white for "Superior Wiring Devices," plain silvered insert 15.00

Counter Sign, Hershey's Chocolate Soldier, cardboard, 1936, 6" h 75.00

Creamer and Sugar, Handy Flame, National Gas Industries, painted and glazed, blue, black eyes, red tongue, 1940s, copyright, one mkd "Indianapolis," each 6" h, professional repair to creamer 18.00

Display

Crescent Tool, figural carpenter in overalls and cap, mkd "Stand Pat Easel Co., Detroit, Mich, Pat Oct 25, 04," 4-1/2" w, 5-1/2" h, some discoloration on front 27.50

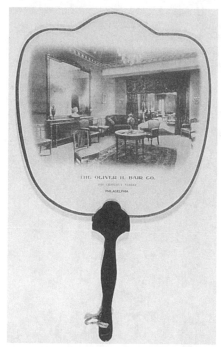

Fan, The Oliver H. Bair Co., Chestnut Street, Philadelphia, interior scene showcasing furniture, black lacquer handle, $20.

Yeast Foam, yellow and red litho tin, 27-1/4" h, 2-3/4" w 140.00

Display Cabinet, counter top

Van Haagen's Fine Toilet Soaps, German silver, curved corners, front glass etched with name, some denting to moldings 525.00

Zeno Gum, wood, emb Zeno marquee with fancy filigree, 18" h, 10-1/2" w, 8" d 575.00

Display Rack, Redi Ade Home Drinks, 19" h, three tiers, some paint loss 115.00

Doll

Aunt Sarah's Pancake House, Aunt Sarah, 15" h stuffed cloth, blue, black, and white, yellow accents, c1970, minor wear, stitched repair 20.00

Hostess Munchies, 14" h stuffed cloth, bright orange plush, orange flannel chest, mkd "Best-Made Toys Ltd. of Toronto," 1980s 18.00

Jack Frost, 19" h stuffed cloth, printed fleshtone face, yellow hat, matching outfit, early 1970s 20.00

Jewel Skippy, 6" h soft white vinyl, squeeze type, blue paint on nautical hat, collar, and trousers, black facial features and chest buttons, unpainted reverse, name on rear of jacket, c1970 .... 58.00

Quaker Crackels, boy, 15" h stuffed cloth, green vest, red pants, brown shoes, box of Quaker Crackels in back pocket, 1924-30, some soiling and fabric settling 45.00

Fan

Alva Hotel, Philadelphia, diecut cardboard, 5-1/2" l wood handle, full color

of nude toddler holding thermometer in process of shattering from heat while talking on candlestick telephone, sweating puppy looks on, early 1900s, 9-1/2" h, 8" w 60.00

Tip-Top Bread, diecut cardboard, full color stars artwork, reverse with six red, white, and blue illus of suggested snacks using bread, c1930, 7-1/4" x 9-1/4" 25.00

Wallace's Farmer and Iowa Homestead Newspaper, little girl standing in front of school, holding book and blue metal lunch box, 1955, 10" w, 10-1/2" h 35.00

Figure

Big Tex, 13" h hollow hard vinyl, cowboy, copyright 1961 for Ottis Stahl, Dallas, TX 60.00

Free-Speech Mike, KMPC, 5-3/4" h painted plaster figure, upper torso image of radio microphone, patriotic finish to hat crown, call letters for Los Angeles radio station, late 1960s 170.00

Jockey, 14" h, man in jockey suit, wooden base, mkd "Jockey Mensware" 110.00

Michelin Man, 3-1/4" h hollow soft rubber white figure of Mr. Bib, suspended on thin elastic stretch cord loop, c1950 .... 60.00

Nabisco, 9-1/2" h, plaster, youngster in rain slicker, carrying product package, engraved brass inscription plate "Kroger Sav-On/1982 1 Million Dollars/Nabisco Brands" 135.00

Obocell Medicine, 4-1/2" h, 1950 .... 75.00

Scribbles, 4-3/4" h painted plaster, blond boy, country outfit, broad brimmed hat, bib overalls, title on base front, copyright Hall Brothers (predecessor of Hallmark Cards) on back, c1940 .... 50.00

Tagamet Rx, orig wrapper 50.00

Flip Pin, diecut, thin celluloid hanger, short stickpin fastener, early 1900-20s

Ali Ghan Temple, nude youngster drying by white towel with brown stripes, 2" l 45.00

Armour's Verbest Brisket Beef, multicolored, young girl in chef hat, frilled dress, dark blue ground, inscription on reverse 42.00

Beechnut Sliced Bacon, multicolored jar, back inscribed "Send 10 Cents for Sample," 1905 patent date 12.00

Have Some Junket, multicolored, young waitress serving desserts on two plates, ad text on back 20.00

Roesch's Standard Meats, ham in white wrapper, blue and white diagonal label, inscribed "Dellicious-Mild-Pure-Hams-Tongue-Bacon," blank reverse, 1905 patent date 8.00

Folder, Mail Pouch Chewing Tobacco, black and white, diecut of baby laying on blanket next to Mail Pouch tobacco package, copyright 1938 .... 15.00

Handwriting Analysis Guide, Compliments of Folger's, by Lorne A. Milne, c1935, top turns to different types of writing, shows appropriate personality characteristics, worn 30.00

Ink Blotter
Ace Rubber-Elastic Bandage, 1954 calendar, set of four 12.00
Cornell Company, Bethesda, MD, Lawson Wood monkey cartoon, 1950 monthly calendar 5.00
Eagle White Lead, York Hardware, 3" x 6" 7.50
H. J. Cutshall, Lincoln, NE, 1949, Lawson Wood cartoon of monkey being stung by bees, "A bad case of hives," adv for Hi-Temp Lubricants, Penn-Central Oil Co., calendar for July, 1949 .... 2.75
Lakeside Dye Works, full color illus of Jane House in swimsuit, 1940s monthly calendars 7.50
Levi's, full color art, black and white imprint of local dealer store, unused, 1960s, 2-3/4" x 6-1/4" 20.00
Libby's Food Products, three cardboard ink blotters under celluloid cover, steer head plus six food packages, Libby, McNeill & Libby, Chicago, capped river with black and white portrait of gentleman, printed by F. F. Pulver Co., Rochester, early 1900s, 3" x 5-1/2" 45.00
Marble Granite Works, Westport, CT, "A Happy Future," fortune telling Mammy, Harry Roseland print, 1906, 6-1/2" x 3-1/2" 40.00
Morton's Salt, 3-1/2" x 6-1/8" 7.00
Optimist Week, Nov. 1955, yellow, 4" x 8" 5.00
Shores Company, Cedar Rapids, IA, Lawson Wood monkey cartoon, 1943 monthly calendar 5.00
Watermans Fountain Pen, H. G. Govers Store, Central Michigan Normal School Supplies, Mt. Pleasant, MI, 1922 calendar 10.00

Key Holder, celluloid disk, metal ring Lion Milk, product illus on one side, other with holly sprig and "Compliments of Lion Brand Condensed Milk" 25.00
New York Edison Co., silvered metal circular clip, black, white, red, and gold celluloid disk on both sides 20.00

Letter Opener, Coshocton Glove Co., celluloid, work glove shape, some red accent striping at wrist, early 1900s, 8-1/2" l, 2" w at wrist 48.00

Lunch Box
Central Union Cut Plug, The United States Tobacco Co., Richmond, VA, 4-1/4" x 7" x 4-5/8", grade 9 .... 210.00
Cut Plug Tobacco, R. J. Reynolds, George Washington litho, 4-1/4" x 7-1/2" x 4-3/4" h, some wear 195.00
Fashion Cut Tobacco, 4-1/4" x 7-3/4" x 5", some wear and nicks, grade 8-8.5 .... 250.00

Mayo's Cut Plug, collapsible tin, 5-7/8" x 7-7/8" x 4-7/8", grade 9 .... 550.00
Round Trip Tobacco, 6-1/2" h, 5" l, 3-1/2" d 100.00

Magazine Ad
Camel Cigarettes, from Popular Science Magazine, May, 1942, Joe DiMaggio's mighty swing, framed, 9" x 11" 15.00
Catalina Swim Suits, 1952 .... 5.00
Ivory Soap, from Century Magazine, March, 1892, "Use Ivory Soap-It Floats!" old 7" x 9" frame 17.50
Wrigley's Gum, 1931, "Chewing Wrigley's Gum Keeps Your Lips Looking Young!" framed, 9-3/4" x 13-3/4" 15.00

Match Safe
International Tailoring Co., silvered brass, hinged case, "King of Tailors" logo, standing Indian warrior and symbolic commerce lady, 1904 patent year, insert and text paper 35.00
Schlitz Brewing Co., combination match safe and stamp holder, wear, 3-1/2" x 1-1/2" x 1/4" 95.00

Memo Book
Agrico Fertlizer, 1947 calendar 4.00
Bond Clothes, Cleveland, OH, 1934 calendar, 2-3/4" w, 3-7/8" h 8.00
Compliments of W. M. Lazzari, Plaza Terrace, St. Petersburg, FL, 1959/60 calendar, some pages used, 4-1/4" x 3" 2.00
Dwinell-Wright Co., Coffees, Teas, Spices, Shopping Memorandum, White House Coffee adv on reverse, aluminum cover, two blank cardboard pages, black and white ad, c1910, some scratches 15.00
Libby's Food Products, Libby, McNeill & Libby, celluloid cover, full color view of Chicago factory, six examples of packaged products, 14 pages, printed by Whitehead & Hoag Co., 2-1/2" x 4-1/2" 55.00
Mother's Oats & Expo, diecut celluloid covered tablet, grommet fastener, 1-1/2" x 2-1/4" 75.00
Reese's Corn Remover, 1936-37 calendar 4.50
Sunbeam, celluloid cover with young lady, swirling hair, sheer fabric, pale yellow sun rays, published by Bastian Bros. Co., 2-1/2" x 4-3/4" 40.00

Mirror, Pocket
Angelus Marshmallows, multicolored winged cherub holding trumpet, announcing "A Message of Purity," sponsor Rueckheim Bros. & Eckstein, Chicago 90.00
Brunswick Phonograph Record, black and white, figural record shape, Brunswick-Balke-Collender Co. label, 1920s 40.00
Buster Brown Shoes, multicolored portrait of Buster and Tige, lighted aged collet, traces of scratching 175.00

Mirror, Dingman Soap, red ground, white letters, printed, emb, 1-7/8" d, $25.

Fargo School Shoes, C. H. Fargo & Co., Chicago, silvered tin rim 40.00
Horlick's Malted Milk, multicolored milkmaid and cow in wooded setting, gold rim 55.00
Jansen Bros. Dancing and Bowling, multicolored profile portrait of brunette young lady, wearing sheer pale green top, Covington, KY address 80.00
Kansas Expansion Flour Mills Co., Wichita, Kansas, 2" d 75.00
Lyon & Healy, Chicago, IL, Everything Known in Music, 1901-05 calendar, celluloid 55.00
Pennisular Stove Co., blue and white, ornate home heating stove 60.00
Victrola Phonograph Record, black and white, figural record shape, red label for Victor Talking Machine Co., tiny Nipper and phonograph symbol, record titled "Her Bright Smile Haunts Me Still," by Edward Johnson, 1930s 55.00

Paperweight
American Oil Products, Somerville, Mass, "We Want To Do Business With The Man On The Other Side," domed glass with silvered reverse, red on white design of elephant within circular title, 1920s, 3" d 55.00
A. P. Smith Mfg. Co, East Orange, NJ, silvered white metal, figural 2-3/4" h fire hydrant, finely detailed raised aerial view of factory building, maker Van Gytenbeek Inc., New York City, inscribed on base, 1920s, 6" w, 3-1/2" h 60.00

Pencil Clip
Driekorn's Bread, cello on silvered tin, orange, blue, white, and yellow wrapped loaf of bread, white ground, c1930 .... 12.00
Dunbak Sportsman's Clothing, gold luster metal, red, white, and blue enamel accents, center image of spoked wheel, 1930s 20.00
Use Victor Flower, red and yellow on white design 15.00

Worcester Iodized Salt, cello on silvered tin, inscription in white letters outlined in black, orange ground..8.00

Pendant, Armour's Shield Lard, chocolate brown, emb brass loop, product name on one side, image of product canister, inscribed "Pure Leaf Lard," 1930s 10.00

Pinback button, Favorite Stoves and Ranges, $20.

Pinback Button
Bantam Anti-Friction Co., black and white, Bantam rooster poised within cutaway view of roller bearing 10.00
Big Chef White Bread, black, white, and red, white lettering, 1930s ...12.00
Buster Brown Bread, multicolored, red rim lettering, Buster as sign painter, "Resolved that the Best ..Bre(a)d People eat Buster Brown Bread" 24.00
Chocolate Mason Mints, blue on silver, slogan "Soothing Cooling Flavor," 1940s 8.00
Cinderella Rubberetts, red, white, and blue litho, "Replacable At Knees/No Sewing," c1930s............................8.00
Cinderella Stoves and Ranges, multicolored, red, white, blue, and gold accents 15.00
Dakota Gold Turkey, blue and yellow design, red lettering, 1940s 12.00
Dry Yeast Baking Powder, yellow, brown, and white canister, white background, black letters, c1898 ....15.00
Dunning Boiler, black and white, cast iron heating boiler.........................12.00
Farm Boy Bread, blue and white farm youth, chicken, cow, and milk can, white ground, red lettering, "Hankey's My-T-Fine Bread," c1920.............20.00
Favorite Stoves and Ranges, multicolored, yellow and red rising sun rays... 15.00
Ferguson's Honey Bread, multicolored toasted brown plump loaves, yellow background, red and black lettering 12.00
Freeman's Milk, blue bottle on white and light blue ground, c1920......15.00
Golden Sheaf Bread Bungalow, multicolored scene of ranch style contest prize house, "Located in Rock Ridge Park," black lettering, c1920.......75.00

Good Humor Know America Club, red, white, and blue, 1930s.........45.00
Heusner's Bread, two browned plump bread loaves, red ground, white letters 15.00
It's Levi's Week, 2-1/4" d, metal covered by blue denim fabric, white slogan, red and white Levi's logo, 1980s..15.00
Machinists Supplies, red and white, center image of hammer and anvil, Chandler & Farquhar, Boston......10.00
Maxwell House Coffee, blue and white, slogan "The People Choice," 1850s..8.00
Old Master Coffee Elf, multicolored pixie character, red cap, green ground 20.00
Sunshine 'Takhome' Biscuits, red, white, and blue packaged product..20.00
Sunny Jim Bran-Dandes, multicolored trademark character running in haste, "Be a Regular Fellow," early 1900s...35.00
Van Camp's Pork and Beans, 7/8" d, multicolored product canister, white ground 20.00
Vote for Betty Crocker, red, white, and blue litho, 1970s...........................8.00
White House Coffee, multicolored, black and white image of White House, slogan "Thrice A Day Every Day/White House Coffee is the Mainstay of the Inner Man"..................40.00
Widow Jones Suits Me, multicolored, attractive auburn-haired young lady in stylish gray suit, pale blue ground, dark blue lettering, New England clothier..18.00
Wool Soap, multicolored, youngsters comparing length of nightshirts, one says "My Mamma Used Wool Soap," one in shorter shirt regrets, "I Wish Mine Had" 15.00
Yale Bread Wins, blue and white image of pennant, yellow ground, blue lettering, solid tin reverse.............18.00

Pin Holder
Buckwalter Stoves, diecut thin celluloid covers over insert of cotton wafer, full color illus of bronze/silver "Real Apollo" cooking stove, black, white, and red logo on other side, early 1900s...12.00
Hotel Broadway-Central, Oklahoma, diecut, heart-shape aluminum panels, red fabric wafer to hold pins, 1890s...12.00
Prudential Insurance, paper covering, felt insert, white battleships passing Prudential rock of Gibraltar, "The Fleet Protects the Nation, Prudential Life Insurance Protects The Home," underside paper text with sponsor info 12.00

Plate, Havana Post Tobacco, Morn English, La-Tarde-Castello, tin, women holding jug, patent date Feb 21, 1905...150.00

Post Card
Dutch Boy Painter, National Lead Co., 1906, divided back, unused 20.00
Haines the Shoe Wizard Show House, black and white aerial scene, 3-1/2" x 5-1/2", late 1930s 8.00

Heinz Peanut Butter Girl, Mama's Favorites, adv on back, used 20.00
Sharples Tubular Separator, Farm Pleasures, adv for H. O. Blodgett Exhibit at Chautauqua County Fair, Aug, 1907, divided back, unused..20.00

Record, Get More From Your Kenmore, 33-1/3 rpm, 6" sq red cardboard sleeve, multicolored label of Jean Shaw/Director Home Economics Laboratory, 1950s..........................18.00

Salesman's Sample, bathtub, American Standard, porcelain, plastic base, mkd "Contour Bath by American Standard"......................................90.00

Sharpening Stone, Pike Mfg. Co., Pike, NH, gold luster finish metal case, pike fish passing through letter "P," rect whetstone, some wear to stone and luster 45.00

Shoe Horn
Brown's 5-Star Shoes, St. Louis, litho metal, red and yellow dec, made by Chas W. Shonk Co., Chicago, 1920s, 4-1/2" l 45.00
T. G. Plant Co., Boston, Queen Quality Shoes, ivory white celluloid, full color portrait of young regal lady, curled top, regional info on reverse, 1920s, 6" l 50.00

Sign
Croft's Swiss Milk Cocoa, litho wood, cocoa beans, product bottle, 1901 copyright, Croft & Allen Co., Philadelphia, 9-3/4" x 11-3/4" 75.00
Dupont Defender Photographic Products, 15" x 18" matched buff gray wooden frames holding black and white semi-gloss photo enlargements on cardboard, scenic mountain view and three posed young ladies, "Defender" centered on frame, applied yellow and blue paper sticker with Dupont slogan "Better Things For Better Living Through Chemistry," orig hanger wire, 1940s, price for pr...60.00
Eddie's Everlasting Black Dye, 6-1/2" x 8-1/2", hanging diecut, lightly emb litho tin, E-Jay-R Mfg. Co., Baltimore, boxed and bottled product, plus 25 illus for use, 1920s 70.00
Edgeworth Tobacco, metal over cardboard, 9-1/4" x 13-1/4".............475.00
Fall Sale, orange, blue, and black, flying geese, 1930s, three fold lines, 50" x 12-3/4"...............................45.00
Hatchet Brand Spices, reverse paint on glass, framed, 22-1/2" x 16-1/2"......................................895.00
Italian Swiss Colony Tavern, 5" x 9", painted plaster, 6" h to top of gentleman's hat, Asti, California, wine sponsor, Plasto Mfg. Co., Chicago, c1950...85.00
King's Quality Shoes for Men, 9-1/2" x 12", diecut litho tin shield, emb crown, made by Mayer & Laverson Co., NY, some wear, c1920......................60.00
Kinney Tobacco Co., Manufacturers of Special High Class Cigarettes, framed litho of pretty woman, 14-1/4" x 8-1/2"...350.00

Model Smoking Tobacco, tin, 5-3/4" x 15" 235.00

Par-T-Pak, metal, 1930s, 54-1/2" l, 18-1/2" h 125.00

Principe Alfonso Clear Havana, S. Ottenberg and Bros., NY, tin, wood frame, 15" x 12" 875.00

Rawlings Track Equipment, heavy cardboard, easel back, 1940s, 17-3/4" x 13-3/4" 80.00

Republic Tires, tin, wood frame, c1935, 26-1/2" x 72" 325.00

Trade at Grand Union, Cattle Crossing, porcelain, blue letters on white ground, 21" sq 300.00

Spinner Top, Sun-Proof Paint, cello inserted at center of wooden spinner dowel, orange smiling sun, white ground, made by C. A. Loew, Milwaukee 50.00

Spoon Rest, Fuller Brush Co., pear shape, red plastic 5.00

Stud

Garland Stoves and Ranges, cello on metal, colorful logo, white ground, blue lettering "World's Best," c1896 ....12.00

New Home Sewing Machine, black, white, and red celluloid on metal, faded red lettering reads "Better Than Silver or Gold," black and white image of sewing machine, c1896 ....15.00

Quaker Oaks, dark charcoal luster finish, raised relief image of smiling young boy's head, rim inscription "The Smile That Won't Come Off, Make Somebody Smile Today" 12.00

P & F Brand Syrups, 3/4" d, red, white, and blue enamel, gold luster metal 10.00

Smoke Blackwell's Genuine Durham, cello on metal, center red drawing of livestock bull on white, black letters, early 1900s 15.00

Tile

Haines Tile and Mantel Company, Wichita, KS, Batchelder Tile Co. 235.00

Hermosa Line, Gladding McBean, 6-1/8" w 70.00

Tin

Amsterdam Brand Pure Linseed Oil, Kelloggs & Miller Inc., Amsterdam, NY, five gallon, 9-1/4" w, 9-1/4" d, 13-1/2" h, lid cover missing 48.00

A & P Peanuts, 7 ozs, red, white, and yellow label, "Made for the Great Atlantic & Pacific Tea Company, New York, NY," orig price tag, can mkd "CANCO," 3-1/2" d, 3" h, grade 8+ 38.00

Handy Hatter, The Perfect Powder, Triple Acting Cleaner for Fine Felt Hats, Hawley & Jones, Phila, paper label, 1-3/4" d, 3" h 18.00

Laiglon, French dry cleaning, Windsor-Lloyd products, 1933, 9-1/2" x 3" x 10" 90.00

Union Carbide Highest Gas Yield, World's Best Quality Trade Mark, Manufactured by Union Carbide for Carbide Gas Lamps and Lanterns, blue and gray, some denting and rusting, 3-1/2" d, 5-1/4" h 18.00

Tip Tray

B.P.O.E., Philadelphia, 21st Annual Reunion, July, 1907, rect, 4-7/8" x 3-1/4" 135.00

Bull Brand Feeds, Maritime Milling Co., Buffalo, NY, rect 185.00

C. D. Kenney, Thanksgiving theme 90.00

Cleveland and Buffalo Line, 4-1/8" d 400.00

Fraternal Life & Accident Insurance, rect, 4-7/8" x 4-1/4" 135.00

Fred Halsteads Suburban Hotel, Baltimore, MD, 4-1/4" h 225.00

Frost Wire Fence Co., Cleveland, OH, 4-1/4" h 245.00

Helvetia Milk Condensing Co., 3-1/2"d, very light crazing 145.00

Jap Rose Soap, James S. Kirk & Co., Chicago, adv on back, 4-1/4" d 250.00

La Tisona 5 cent Segar, Wm Tigner's Son Co. Makers, Lima, Ohio, 4-1/2" d, some wear 300.00

Mokane is the Best of all Liquers, 4-5/8" x 3" rect, edge wear 225.00

National Cigar Stands Company, beautiful lady in center, 6" d 195.00

Puritan Hams, Cudahy Packing Co., 4-1/4" d 310.00

Quick Meal Ranges, 4-1/2" x 3-3/8" oval, edge wear 225.00

Treasure Line Stoves & Ranges, D. Moore Co., Ltd. Hamilton, Ontario, 7-1/2" x 4-1/8", some oxidation to gold background 290.00

Yuengling's Bottled Beer, 4-1/8" d 270.00

World's Best Table Water, White Rock, scantily clad female kneeling, looking into water, rect, 6-1/8" x 4-1/8", some scratches, grade 8 ....100.00

Tobacco Jar (Humidor), Imperial Cube Tobacco, white ground, bright graphics, wear to gold trim, 6" d, 7" h 295.00

Tobacco Tin

Bagley's Old Colony Mixture, John J. Bagley & Co., Detroit, MI, 3-1/8" x 4-1/2", minor scuffs, grade 8.5 ....325.00

Black and White, vertical, 4-3/8" x 3" x 7/8", very minor scratches on lid, grade 8.5 ....625.00

Buckingham Smoking Tobacco, sample, full, 2-1/8" w, 2-7/8" h 275.00

Bull Dog, vertical, paper on cardboard, orig tax stamp 875.00

Caromel Twist, R. J. Reynolds Tobacco Co., round cardboard container, full, unbroken tax stamp, 4-3/8" d, 7" h 400.00

Chicago Cubs Chewing Tobacco, Rock City Tobacco Co., Ltd., Quebec, 1936, 6" d, 3-1/4" h 255.00

Culture Tobacco, vertical, 3" x 4-1/2" 175.00

Edgeworth Free Tobacco Sample, cardboard, full, 3-1/8" x 2" 285.00

Forest and Stream, vertical, 4-1/4" x 3" x 7/8", grade 9 ....725.00

Granulated Sliced Plug 54, vertical, free sample, 2-1/4" x 3", grade 8.5 ....350.00

Half and Half, 1 lb, paper stamp, small amount of rust on bottom 42.00

Hand Made Flake Cut, vertical, some roughness 365.00

Liggett & Myers Tobacco Co., early horse drawn fire engine, cardboard, metal ends, 5-1/4" d, 6" h 275.00

Mayo's Cut Plug, handle, some rust, small dents, 7-3/4" w, 3-1/4" d, 4-3/4" h 55.00

Niggerhair Tobacco, B. Leidersdorf, Milwaukee, WI, bail handle, 5-3/8" d, 6-5/8" h, grade 8.5.......................525.00

North Pole Cut Plug Tobacco, United States Tobacco Co., Richmond, VA, oval slip top, 5-1/4" x 6-1/8" x 4-1/8", grade 8.5+ 1,100.00

Pat Hand, Globe Tobacco Co., Detroit, MI, yellow hand, 2-1/2" x 2-7/8", wear on edges, grade 8 ....295.00

Philip Morris, 2-1/4" w, 1" d, 3" h . 45.00

Q-Bold Cube Cut, vertical, 3-3/8" x 4", grade 9.5 ....345.00

Toy

A. C. Spark Plug, pull toy, 4-1/2" diecast metal horse, mkd "A. C. the quality Spark Plug" 250.00

Laszios Car Wash, Flushing, Bay Shore, Copiague, NY, friction car 50.00

Michelin, walker, 3" h orange plastic Mr. Bibb with black tire, inscription, "We Walk By Ourselves," in five languages, 4-1/2" sq orig card, 1960s, MOC 95.00

Raid Bug, wind-up walker, green blended to yellow, hard plastic bug, green vinyl antennae, sponsor S. C. Johnson & Son, 3" x 3" x 3-1/2" mailing carton, 1980s 60.00

Trade card, Marshall & Ball Clothiers, advertising on back, 4-3/8" l, 3-1/8" h, $9.

Trade Card

Agate Iron Ware, duck in teapot, sailor in cup, 3-7/8" x 2-3/4" 45.00

Arm & Hammer Co., set of nine cards from Fish and Game series, mounted on brown paper, 1900-04 ....55.00

Boraxine Oat Meal Soap, Niagara Falls scene 18.00

Chocolat du Planteur, woman in red coat and muff 20.00

Demorest Emporium of Fashions for Girls, little girl with feather 8.00

Domestic Sewing Machine Co., Chicago, 1883, adv on back 6.50

Empire Mower, Gies & Co., Buffalo, NY, rabbit family 6.00

Enamieline Stove Polish, paper doll type, rose, distributed by J. L. Prescott & Co., 11 Jay St, 1900s, 5" h 30.00

Hoyt's German Cologne, E. W. Hoyt & Col, Lowell, MA, 1890 calendar on back, wear on one corner 14.00
Jas. S. Kirk & Co. Soap Makers, full color
  Calendar 5.00
  Columbia 5.00
  Queen of the Laundry 5.00
  Savon Imperial 5.00
  White Ceylon 5.00
McLaughlin's XXXX Coffee, girls having tea party, 1887 calendar on back 12.00
Tyrrell Trips Seeing Portland, automobiles... 15.00
Scotch Oats Essence, full color art of young lady stirring contents of barrel, assisted by nude cherubs, adv on back, 4" x 6" 12.00
8th Wonder or Engle Clock, Capt J. Reid and his wife standing next to giant mechanical clock, Hazelton, PA, c1890 .... 8.00
Tip Tray, Bakers Cocoa, Walter Baker Company, Dorchester, Mass, 6" d 295.00
Tray
 Bartlett Spring Mineral Water, doe and fawn drinking from pure mountain spring, oversized bottle of mineral water in background, Kaufmann & Strauss Co. litho, 13" d 150.00
Beamer Shoes, Victorian woman, c1900 .... 75.00
Enterprise Brewing Co. Old Tap Ape, toothless happy old man, minor wear to rim, some staining to background 175.00
Golden West Brewing Co., factory scene, early trolleys and horse drawn carts, American Art Works, some chipping and soiling 300.00
Heck's Capudine Medicine 215.00
Kaiser Willhelm Bitters Co., oversized bottle with trademark label, "For Appetite and Digestion" 70.00
National Brewery Co. White Seal Beer, factory scene, horse drawn wagon, early blob top bottle, Griesedieck Bros., proprietors, chipping and scratching 185.00
Olympia Brewing Co., trademark Turnwater "It's the Water," Savage Manufacturing Co., 12" d, overall scratching, soiling, and light surface rust 90.00
Pacific Brewing & Malting Co., Mt. Tacoma illus, orig 1912 work order from Chas. W. Shonk Co. on back 50.00
Park Brewing Co., factory scene, early railroad, horse drawn carts, and automobilia, Chas. W. Shonk Co. litho, some in painting, 12" d 60.00
Ruhstaller Brewery, elderly man in Turkish outfit enjoying his pipe and stein of beer, H. D. Beach Co. litho, 16-1/2" l, 13-1/2" w, some rubbing and chipping to rim 300.00
Stahley's Flour, horse and girl, 1905 .... 50.00
Wolverine Toy Co., c1920, 4" x 6" 95.00

Tumbler, Miss Dairylea, clear glass, maroon-red images of Miss Dairylea and "Drive Slow," c1950, 3-1/2" d, 3-1/8" h 15.00

Whistle, Baby Ruth, Curtis Candy Co., red ground, white text, $15.

Whistle
  Buster Brown Shoes, litho tin, full color image of Buster and Tige on top, slogan "Tread Straight Feature That Helps to Walk Toes Straight Ahead to Health" 20.00
  Butter-Krust Bread, red and white celluloid, tin backing panel, 1930s 20.00
  Endicott Johnson Shoes, litho tin, black on yellow, made by Kirchof Co., Newark, NJ 15.00
  Golden Royal Milk, yellow and black 7.50
  Hurd Shoes, litho tin, red inscriptions, ivory ground 15.00
  Old Reliable Coffee 10.00
  Oscar Meyer Weiner, painted 15.00
  Poll Parrot Shoes, litho tin, full color parrot, yellow ground 15.00
  Red Goose Shoes, litho tin, trademark red goose, yellow ground 25.00

Advertising Characters

Collecting Hints: Concentrate on one advertising character. Three-dimensional objects are more eagerly sought than two-dimensional ones. Some local dairies, restaurants, and other businesses developed advertising characters. This potential collecting area has received little attention.

History: Americans learned to recognize specific products by their particular advertising characters. In the early 1900s, many immigrants could not read but could identify the colorful characters. Thus, the advertising character helped to sell the product.

Some manufacturers developed similar names for inferior-quality products, like Fairee Soap versus the popular Fairy Soap. Trade laws eventually helped protect companies by allowing advertising characters to be registered as part of a trademark.

Trademarks and advertising characters are found on product labels, in magazines, as premiums, and on other types of advertising. Popular cartoon characters also were used to advertise products.

Some advertising characters, such as Mr. Peanut and the Campbell Kids, were designed to promote a specific product. The popular Campbell Kids first appeared on streetcar advertising in 1906. The illustrations of Grace G. Drayton were originally aimed at housewives, but the characters were gradually dropped from Campbell's advertising until the television industry expanded the advertising market. In 1951, Campbell redesigned the kids and successfully reissued them. The kids were redesigned again in 1966. Other advertising characters (e.g, Aunt Jemima) also have enjoyed a long life; some, like Kayo and the Yellow Kid, are no longer used in contemporary advertising.

References: Warren Dotz, *Advertising Character Collectibles,* Collector Books, 1993; ——, *What a Character,* Chronicle Books, 1996; David Longest, *Character Toys and Collectibles,* 1st Series (1984, 1992 value update), 2nd Series (1987, 1990 value update), Collector Books; Rex Miller, *The Investor's Guide to Vintage Character Collectibles,* Krause Publications, 1999; Robert Reed, *Bears and Dolls in Advertising,* Antique Trader Books, 1998; David and Micki Young, *Campbell's Soup Collectibles from A to Z,* Krause Publications, 1998.

Collectors' Clubs: Campbell Kids Collectors, 649 Bayview Dr., Akron, OH 44319; Campbell's Soup Collector Club, 414 Country Ln Ct, Wauconda, IL 60084; Peanut Pals, 804 Hickory Grade Rd, Bridgeville, PA 15017; R. F. Outcault Society, 103 Doubloon Dr., Slidell, LA 70461.

Reproduction Alert.

Additional Listings: Advertising, Advertising Logo Watches, Black Memorabilia, Cartoon Characters, Fast Food, Planter's Peanuts.

AC Spark Plug, diecast, diecast horse in bathtub...250.00
Alka Seltzer, Speedy
   Figure, 5-1/2" h, plastic, 1960s....20.00
   Paper Cup, 1977 ....12.00
   Sign, 10" w 65.00
Aunt Jemima
   Button, "Aunt Jemima Breakfast Club," tin litho, 4" d, color image of smiling Jemima, red background, black text, "Eat a Better Breakfast," Green Duck Co., Chicago, c1960 ....35.00
   Cookbook, Aunt Jemima's Album of Secret Recipes, 1935, 33 pgs, soft cover, booklet form......................32.00
   Hat, Aunt Jemima's Breakfast Club, paper, fold-out style.....................20.00
   Magazine Tear Sheet, Aunt Jemima Pancakes, 1949, 13" x 5".............15.00
   Place Mat, paper, full color, Story of Aunt Jemima, "Story of Aunt Jemima and her Pancake Days…has devoted her time to working with service clubs…on her community Pancake Day Festivals…," unused, 1950s, 10-1/2" x 13-1/2"..........................45.00
   Restaurant Table Card, diecut face, full color, "Folks…It's a treat to eat out often…Bring the whole family…time for Aunt Jemima Pancakes," 1953, 4-3/4" x 3" 55.00

Buster Brown, plate, multicolored transfer, gold rim, 5-1/4" d, $45.

Buster Brown
   Book, *Buster Brown's Drawing Book,* 1906, 12 pgs, 3-1/2" x 5", full color cover, premium from Emerson Piano Co..350.00
   Box, Buster Brown Stockings, c1905, 11" x 4" x 3"................................150.00
   Game
      Buster Brown Game and Play Box, Andy Devine photo, unused..................................80.00

   Pin-The-Tail, c1910, 24" x 30" color litho poster 110.00
Pattern, stuffed doll, uncut, full color, makes 17" Buster Brown doll and 11" Tige, 42" x 18" sheet, 1924 .... 275.00
Pinback Button
   Buster Brown Hose Supporter, multicolored, 1920s 25.00
   Buster Brown Shoes, sepia letters, brown rim 20.00
Playing cards, copyright 1906, each card 1-3/4" x 2-1/4".................... 180.00
Postcard, sgd by Outcault, dated 1903..20.00
Ring, sq flicker ring, 1950s..........50.00
Transfer Kit, Buster Brown Rub-A-Doodles Time Machine, 6-1/4" x 7-3/8", 8 page stiff paper folder, full color art images, c1969 ....12.00
California Raisins
   Bank, hard vinyl, dark purple body, black arms and legs, white hands, orange and white sneakers and sunglasses, copyright 1987 CALRAB, orig box, 3" x 6" x 6-1/2" 18.00
   Doll, 14" d, 18" h, stuffed plush and fabric, copyright 1988 CALRAB, and "Acme" inscription for Applause...38.00
   Figure, 5-1/2" h, flexible polyvinyl, male with microphone, black arms and legs, white gloves and spats, 1987 CALRAB copyright 24.00
   Toy, wind-up, hard plastic, built-in key, dark purple body, movable black arms, hard plastic hands, Applause, copyright 1988 CALRAP, 3" x 5" x 3-1/4" 20.00
Campbell Kids
   Bank, ceramic, 1970s..................70.00
   Christmas Ornament 25.00
   Doll, boy and girl, vinyl, orig clothes, pr 145.00
   Radio, MIB 45.00
   Sign, 16-1/2" x 22-1/4", paper, full color, Campbell Kids, tomato soup can, school chalkboard design, c1950 ....48.00
   Soup Bowl, Campbell Girl on inside, alphabet and "Christine" on bottom, c1940 ....30.00
   Truck, semi, chunky soup adv 65.00
Charlie the Tuna, Sunkist
   Bracelet, 1-1/4" disk centered by high relief figure, c1970 ....12.00
   Necklace, 1-1/4" h pendant with relief image of Charlie on anchor, c1970 ....15.00
   Pin, 1" h raised figural Charlie, two tiny blue rhinestones in eyeglasses, 10 tiny white rhinestones on chest, c1970 ....18.00
Dutch Boy Paint, Dutch Boy
   Desk Set, 3-1/2" x 9-1/2" marble base, 4-1/2" h painted cast metal Dutch Boy figure, brass perpetual calendar with paper reel, plastic pen holder and ballpoint pen, 1950s, some wear... 135.00
   Hand Puppet, 12" h, fabric body, painted soft vinyl head, c1960 ....35.00
   Marker, diecut thin cardboard inserted into slotted wooden base, front side with Dutch Boy Painter, reverse with

black and white image of paint can, inscribed, "Paint with Dutch Boy White Lead," c1930..............................20.00
Paint Booklet, *The Adventures of the Dutch Boy and the Color Sprites,* published by Jon T. Lewis & Bros., Philadelphia, 1914, 20 pgs, 5" x 8", some pages neatly painted 12.00
Pinback Button, multicolored......15.00
Sign, 49" h, 26-1/2" w, linen cloth, "Now for another good paint job!" painter getting into overalls next to Dutch Boy holding bucket of Dutch Boy White Lead, Sweeney Litho Co., artist Rundle, c1932 ....125.00
Statue, composition figure, holding full pail of paint, 36" h, some denting to base...400.00
Elsie the Cow, Borden
   Cartoon Book, 3-1/4" x 4", 16 pgs, "Compliments of Elsie," c1940 ... 32.00
   Christmas Card, 4-3/4" x 6-1/2", glossy stiff paper, color pop-up of family retrieving Christmas dec from attic, printed greeting, "From Elsie, Elmer, Beulah, Beauregard and all of us at Borden's," copyright 1940 .... 45.00
   Drinking Glass, 3" h, Aunt Elsie, Little Lola, and Baby Beulah, blue illus, red trim stripe, short verse on back, late 1940s/early 1950s, set of three... 40.00
   Drinking Glass, 5" h, Beauregard, Elsie, and Elmer, Spirit of '76 costumes, drums and fife, c1976..... 18.00
   Folder, 6-1/4" x 12", New York World's Fair, Elsie, Trylon and Perisphere, promotes Borden's Chateau cheese, 1939, folded 18.00
   Gift Box, 9-1/2" x 12" x 3-1/2", vinyl over cardboard, dark olive green, gold lightly emb Elsie head, inscribed "Borden's Van Wert, Ohio, The World's Largest Cheese Factory," orig hinge replaced, 1950s 45.00
   Paper Napkin, 6-1/2" x 6-3/4", white, colorful graphics of Elsie in sunburst design, floral pattern, copyright Borden Co., 1960s............................. 8.00
   Pencil Case, 4" x 7-1/2", blue vinyl, metal zipper top edge, Elsie image on one side, two plastic insert eyeballs, c1970, unused 88.00
   Plush Toy, Elsie and Beauregard, vinyl faces, orig Borden signature ribbon on Elsie, orig tags "My Toy Creations," 1950s, pr.................................... 85.00
   Push Puppet, 2-1/2" x 2-1/2" x 5-1/2", jointed wood, brown, pink, and white, knotted string tail, green base with "Elsie" on yellow decal, Mespo Products Co., late 1940s 75.00
   Sign, 11-1/2" x 18", Borden's Fine Cheeses, rigid cardboard, copyright 1944, disk wheels to determine "Real Money" product price in any combination of numerals up to 99¢, orig cardboard easel and cord hanger... 195.00

Train, Food Line, 4 sheets of cardboard with litho punch-outs to create train, unpunched 350.00

Entenmann's
Cookie Jar, 11" h, heavy ceramic jar, baker hat lid, inscribed "Fine Baked Goods, Quality Since 1898," mkd "Exclusively for Entenmann's 1st Collectors Series/JCK 1992," made in Brazil 90.00
Piggy Bank, 8-1/2" h ceramic piggy baker, 7" d hat, glossy white, blue hat dec, neckerchief, accents, black eyes and shoes, rubber trap, inscribed "Created Exclusively for Entenmann's," foil Made in China sticker, 9" x 9" x 10-1/2" orig carton, early 1990s 30.00

Esquire, Esky, figure, 5-1/2" h, jigsawed wood, painted features 70.00

Exxon Tiger
Bank, tiger, figural, plastic...........35.00
Beverage Set, 3-1/2" h white glass mugs, 13" d litho tin serving tray, light wear 35.00
Drinking Glass, Esso Tiger, "Put a Tiger in Your Tank," slogan printed on back in eight different languages, 5" h 18.00
Mug, 3-1/2" h, white glass, full color tiger portrait, 1970s 8.00

Florida Orange Bird, Tropicana
Bank, 4-3/4" h orange vinyl, yellow accent, green leaf petal hair and wings, Hong Kong, c1960 ....35.00
Bell, 5-1/2" h, white china, small bisque clapper, Walt Disney Productions design copyright, 1970s.....12.00
Nodder...150.00
Radio...30.00
Squeeze Toy, figural, MIB............95.00

Green Giant
Dancing Doll, cloth, mail-away premium, 40" h 125.00
Figure, Sprout, vinyl......................20.00
Telephone, Little Sprout, 14" h.....65.00

Hawaiian Punch, Punchy, figure, hard plastic, blue or orange 12.00

Heinz 57, Aristocrat Tomato, figure, 2-1/2" x 2-1/2" x 5-3/4" h, painted hard rubber, c1940 ....185.00

Hush Puppies, basset hound figure, 8" h, hard vinyl, 4-1/2" d base, c1970 ....18.00

Keebler, Elf
Bank, figural, ceramic 65.00
Cookie Jar, cookie tree, raised figures 95.00
Doll, Ernie, plush, talking mechanism not working 15.00
Mug, 3" h hard plastic, raised letters, fleshtone, white hair, red outfit trim, orig plain brown shipping box, label with maker "F & F Mold & Dye Works, Inc.," copyright 1972...................25.00
Telephone, advertising Pecan Sandies, 1985............................125.00

Kellogg's, Tony The Tiger
Bank, figural vinyl 40.00
Doll, Tony the Tiger, cloth 25.00
Radio...30.00
Spoon, SP, emb "Kellogg's" 10.00

Kool Cigarettes

Figure, Dr. Kool, 4-1/2" h, black and white, painted plaster, full figure walking along carrying satchel with name on side, wearing stethoscope, late 1930s, professional repair to base chip... 136.00
Pinback Button, Willie between donkey and elephant, 1930s 25.00
Salt and Pepper Shakers, pr, Willie and Millie, figural, 3-1/2" h, black and white plastic, yellow accent beaks, red accent necklace and dark red hair bow on Millie, c1950 ....35.00

Mennon, Hard Hat, figural bottle, clear glass, smiling man in jacket, bright orange replica hard hat, white plastic cap, 1950s, 3" w, 9" h...................15.00

Mr. Bubble
Figure, plastic...............................25.00
Wash Mitt, printed blue image on peach colored sponge, 1970s, unused, 6" x 6-1/2" 18.00

Nestle's Quik
Figure, 6" h, bendable, "Q" chocolate bunny, brown, cream, dark blue "Q" on chest, 1980s 8.00
Mug, 4" h, fully dimensional hard plastic, Quik rabbit, brown, tan face, black eyes, red nose, two handles form ears, c1970 ....10.00
Spy-Scope, 4" x 20" cardboard periscope, brown, red, white, and yellow, unassembled, c1960..................12.00

Purple Cow, Pick-Ohio Hotel, Youngstown, OH, mustard jar, Shenango China, $10.

Philip Morris, Johnny
Pinback Button, black, white, red, and fleshtone, 1930s..........................35.00
Place Card, figural 17.50
Sign, emb tin, well worn, 12" x 14"...95.00

Pillsbury Co., Dough Boy
Action Cut-outs, Play Bakery, c1936, unpunched, orig mailing envelope.......................................75.00
Cookie Jar, heavy ceramic, 5" x 5-1/2" x 10-1/2" h, glossy white, blue markings, c1970..................................28.00
Doll, 7-1/4" h, vinyl, smiling full figure boy, blue accent eyes, button on cap, copyright 1971 Pillsbury Co. Minneapolis 18.00

Mug, Choo Choo Cherry , 3" h, red hard plastic, black and white hat and face, copyright 1969 ....18.00
Mug, Goofy Grape, 3" h, purple hard plastic, green hat, black and white eyes and teeth, copyright 1969 ....18.00
Salt and Pepper Shakers, Poppin Fresh and Poppie, hard white plastic shakers, blue eye dot dec 25.00

RCA Victor, Nipper
Coffee Mug, plastic 8.00
Hanger Pin, His Master's Voice, diecut thin celluloid, black, white, and red, figural Nipper, inscribed, "Owens Music Store Spencer, Ind." 40.00
Pinback Button, 1-1/4" d, diecut celluloid, red, white, and blue, dealer's name on back 40.00
Snowdome 40.00

Red Goose Shoes
Bank......................................150.00
Egg Layer, 27" h, 22" w, plastic red goose sitting atop cardboard box, slight paint loss.........................200.00
Figure, 2" w, 2" h diecut cardboard, slotted wooden base, 1930s 28.00
Punch-Out Book, *Red Goose Shoes Chimpanzee Show in 3-D,* 9-3/4" x 10-1/2", punch-outs feature St. Louis Zoo Chimpanzee Show, Ken Giles Tuk-A-Tab Play Kit, 1950s 50.00
Ring, secret compartment, glow, photo..150.00
Spinner Top, Red Goose Shoes, cello disk inserted at center of wooden spinner dowel, red goose, yellow ground, 1930s, made by Parisienne Novelties.......................................50.00

Reddy Kilowatt
Banner, fabric, 39" x 53", individual letters stitched to pale yellow fabric, figure of Reddy with hand painted accents, wooden hanger rod missing knob cap, c1960, made by retiree of Rural Electric Assn, Mansfield, PA..48.00
Beanie Baby, 8" h 20.00
Bib, 8" x 10", textured white fabric, tie strings, black, white, red, blue, and yellow image, red lettering, "I Am Your Pal, Bo-Peep, Boy Blue, Ready To Help With Whatever You Do," unused..38.00
Brochure and Pin, Northern States Power, 1" l, gold and red, "I'm a Busy Little Atom Providing Heat, Light & Power" 35.00
Dexterity Slide Puzzle, 3-1/2" x 3", red and white 15.00
Employee Pin, 2-1/8" d, yellowish-white background, red Reddy, "Reddy Kilowatt Your Electric Servant"......5.00
Figure, 5" h, stuffed felt, unmarked, c1950..120.00
Hot Pads, 6" x 6" octagon, heat-resistant material, red artwork on black background, c1950.....................24.00
Memo Case, 4" x 6-1/2", dark brown hard plastic, holds 3" x 5" paper, made by Autopoint, Chicago, Reddy copyright on underside, c1950...........60.00
Neon Sign, diecut, 36" h, white enamel, red diecut vinyl outline 6,500.00

Nodder, 7" h, MIB 20.00
Pinback Button, 1-1/4" d, "Please Don't
Litter" 20.00
Pinback Button, 3-1/4" d, Ohio Edison
Company, celluloid, red image, Pari-
sian Novelty Co., Chicago,
1940s 95.00
Place Mat, 10" x 14", printed in red and
pink on white, Reddy flanked by elec-
tric service questions and answers,
Massachusetts Electric Co. of New
England System, diecut scalloped
edges, unused, 1960s 12.00
Playing Cards, 1" x 3-3/4" x 5" slipcase
box, two complete 52 card decks,
unused, c1960............................38.00
Stove Pad, 7" x 7" litho tin, "Table of
Weights and Measures," Pro-Tex textile pad insert, black, white, and red
image of Reddy a chef,c1950 ....32.00
Trophy, 6" h, brass and pewter, wood
base, issued by Northern States
Power 200.00

Sinclair Oil
Booklet, 1960s 20.00
Toy, dinosaur, 3" x 6" white, red, green,
and pink paper backing, plastic bag
containing four small hard plastic
dinosaurs, text, c1960 ....30.00

Tony the Tiger
Growler Attachment, 3" d, 4" l, hard
plastic noisemaker, underside bracket
and bolts to attach to bicycle,
Kellogg's premium, c1970 ....60.00
Pencil Sharpener, 2-1/2" x 3-1/2" x 4",
soft vinyl, orange replica head,
threaded black plastic base, Kellogg's
premium, c1960 ....80.00
Toy, 3-1/2" x 4-1/2" x 5-1/2" plastic display case, diecast metal and plastic
vehicle in image of Kellogg's Frosted
Flakes box, oversized dune buggy
wheels, Tony as driver, Buddy L,
unopened, 1980s 45.00

Willie Wiredhand, restaurant china coffee cup, eggshell, black rim trim, 1" h
Willie logo, mkd "Buntingware"...45.00

Advertising-Logo Watches

Collecting Hints: Advertising-logo watches are an increasingly popular collectible. They reflect popular culture, are interesting technically and artistically, and are possible to find. Numerous themes, subjects, and types create a high degree of cross-collectibility. Watches are often tie-ins to a trend, movie, or TV program.

Age and demand affect value; demand can change with an increase or decrease in popularity. Look for clean, complete, watches in excellent condition. The newer the piece, the better the condition must be. Original mint packaging can double or triple value. Information regard-

ing the source and the associated printed matter (original offers, boxes, enclosures, outer wrap/mailer etc.) are also important.

The earlier and scarcer pieces for popular companies and characters can have good value, but even a brand new ad-logo watch can be highly collectible if available for only a short time.

Copyright dates can lead to confusion about the year of issue and age of a watch. The date generally refers to when the character or logo was first "published" and cannot be relied upon to date a watch.

Finding new product watches involves first finding the watch offer. Offers can appear on "SMPs" (specially marked packages). A combination of Proofs of Purchase and cash will be required. Newspaper Sunday Supplements and store order forms on tear-off pads are also a source for new offers. Companies sometimes issue "catalogs" of logo merchandise. Logo merchandise now commonly appears on corporate Web sites. The Premium Watch Watch Newsletter lists details of known offers.

Look for older watches in collecting publications, house and garage sales, rummage sales, flea markets, and antiques and collectibles shows. Knowledgeable collector friends/dealers might be the most reliable way to acquire both watches and information.

Internet auctions are currently the primary source for collectible ad watches. www.ebay.com is the largest and has the most watch listings. Purchases can be safely made with caution. Both buyers and sellers should use the feedback feature to check on the other person. Ask questions of sellers about the watch. Don't rely on fuzzy pictures or fuzzy descriptions. Check the details of postage.

Collectible ad watches include: giveaways and premiums; retail, catalog, Web site "store" ad watches; mechanical wind-up and battery operated pocket and wrist watches; digital and analog (with hands) watches, plastic and metal; dress and sport watches; company logo and characters; licensed characters and events; in-house awards, events, and commemoratives.

Collectibility is increased by appealing, colorful graphics. Popular trademarks, such as: Company character—Charlie the Tuna, Ronald McDonald; company product name—SPAM, Coca-Cola; company logo—Oscar Meyer Weinermobile; contract licensed character—Where's Waldo by Life Cereal; or contract licensed event—1996 Super Bowl XXX by Kraft, all add to the collectibility of advertising logo watches.

History: The earliest ad-logo timepieces are pocket watches. Advertising on the pocket watch face first appeared around the turn of the 20th Century. Earlier, 19th Century pocket watches might feature a company name engraved on the case, but advertising watch fobs attached to the watch chain were more popular.

The internal movements and cases of the pocket watches were cheaply made; few early ones survive. The cases are usually chrome plate and the "crystals," often made from an early plastic, are yellowed with age. Only a company name is likely to appear on the face. Pocket watches were worn by men, and the ads have masculine orientation.

Wrist watches came into popular use in the 1920-30s, but pocket watches remained common through the 1950s and experienced a resurgence in the 1990s.

The first documented trademark character wrist watch, featuring Twinkie the Brown Shoe Elf, was issued by the Hamilton Brown Company in the mid-1920s. A Twinkie pocket watch was released as well. Chevrolet issued a salesman's award wrist watch around the same time; it has a clever radiator shaped case.

A smattering of ad watches from the 1940-60s are known, but it wasn't until the 1970s that the constant visibility of wrist watches was recognized, and more and more were produced.

Watch Features By Decade:

1970s: Mechanical wind-ups with heavy metal cases, generally marked "Swiss Made." Wide leather or plastic straps with snaps. Earliest revolving disks and mechanical digitals. The value is from $75-$300.

1980s: Battery operated, both digital and analog. Slim, plastic cases common. New features include electronic hands only visible when the battery is good, clam shell case digitals, pop-up digitals, and printed plastic straps. Hanger cards and other elaborate packaging common. The value is from $10-$75 in mint condition.

1990s: New features include holograms, revolving sub-dials, "talking" features, water filled cases and straps, game watches, stopwatches and timers, Giga Pet watches, and clip-on "clocks," clear printed resin straps and laser cut straps. Special boxes and printed tins important. Value is rarely above $25, and the plastic watches range $10-$15.

References: Hy Brown, *Comic Character Timepieces,* Schiffer Publishing, 1992; Shugart and Gilbert, *The Complete Guide to Watches,* published annually by Cooksey Shugart Publications.

Periodical: *The Premium Watch Watch,* 24 San Rafael Drive, Rochester, NY 14618. E-mail: watcher1@rochester.rr.com

Advisor: Sharon Iranpour.

Reproduction Alert: Watch faces can be color copied and old ones replicated or the copy can be put in the wrong cases. Fantasy watches are offered for sale that combine modern artwork and older pocket watch cases.

Ball Park Franks, 1989, black plastic case with red upper strap and yellow lower strap, big hot dog in center of face with words, "They plump when you cook 'em," mint 15.00
Burger King, 1970s, silvertone case with blue suede strap, face has blue background with old style Burger King raising his arms, good 50.00
Campbell Soup Co., 1982, "Original Edition," set of four. All are mechanical windups, made by Criterion, each marked on back, clear plastic box has holder for watch and slip cover printed with the Kids pictures:
  Boy Kid, 1" goldtone case, black plastic strap, face shows boy in green shorts carrying lunch box, MIB 40.00
  Boy Kid, 1-1/8" goldtone case, black plastic strap, face shows the boy in orange jacket, blue jeans, MIB ... 40.00
  Girl Kid, 1" goldtone case, red plastic strap, face shows girl in red jacket carrying school bag, MIB 40.00
  Girl Kid, 1-1/8" goldtone case, black

plastic strap, face shows girl in green dress with mirror in hand, MIB 40.00
Captain Midnight, Ovaltine, 1988, digital watch, yellow plastic case, blue plastic strap, face shows rocket taking off and the words, "S.Q. Secret Squadron Member," orig letter from Ovaltine included, mint 40.00
Charlie the Tuna, Star-Kist, dated on face
  1971, heavy goldtone 1-3/8" case, blue leather double strap, pink plastic box has "Charlie the Tuna" printed on lid, MIB 75.00
  1971, lightweight goldtone 1-1/8" case, blue leather double strap, Mint with offer insert 50.00
  1973, 1-1/4" silvertone case, date window on face, blue plastic strap with four double sets of holes on each side, mint 40.00
  1977, 1-1/4" silvertone case, blue plastic strap with four double sets of holes on each side, no date window, mint 40.00
  1986, 1-1/4" silvertone case, black leather strap, "25th Anniversary 1961-1986" on face, brown box, MIB 30.00
  1990, 15/16" goldtone case, black leather strap, white box, MIB.......25.00
  1992, 1-1/8" black metal case, black leather strap, white box with red "Star-Kist," MIB......................................25.00
  1998 1-1/4" blue plastic case, plastic strap has yellow upper and red lower, silver box, MIB 15.00
Coppertone 40th Birthday, 1980s, both men's and women's goldtone styles have brown leather straps, face has classic girl and dog with balloons and "Happy 40th Birthday!" each, mint 25.00
Energizer Bunny, 1992, black plastic case, black leather strap, face shows pink bunny with drum on revolving disk, mint 20.00
Icee Bear, Hassis Watches, 1971, stainless steel case, white strap with snaps, face has silvertone background with red and blue Icee Bear, holding a drink in each hand, mint 125.00
Keebler Elf
  1970s, Swiss windup, silvertone case, blue denim-look wide plastic strap with snaps, porcelain face, Ernie stands with arms held to his side, mint 75.00
  1980s, silvertone case, black leather strap. Ernie's arms are the watch hands, MIB 25.00
  1990s, silvertone case, black leather strap, similar to the 1980s watch, but Ernie is printed and stationary, MIB 20.00
Little Hans, Nestle, 1971, made by Piet, Israel, silvertone case, Little Hans in center of face, eyes move side to side, VG 50.00
Major Moon, Moonstone Cereal, 1970, silvertone case, wide plastic blue denim-look strap with snaps, face shows character holding the yellow words "Moonstone," VG 75.00

Max Headroom, 1987, black plastic case, red strap, face has red and yellow stripes, Max wears sunglasses, can of Coke is at the bottom, man's or woman's styles, each, mint 15.00
M&Ms, Mars Candy, most with plastic cases and straps, dated front or back
  1980s, rectangular 3/4" x 1-1/4" goldtone metal case, black leather strap, yellow face with brown M&Ms looks like candy box, MIB 75.00
  1987, yellow case with red and green strap, face has yellow, green, orange, and red M&Ms, mint................... 20.00
  1990, 50th Birthday Watch was included in Birthday Club Package which contained many additional paper items, watch has yellow case, red and green strap, party hat on face, complete in 9" x 12" printed Tyvik envelope, mint 40.00
  1993, red case with yellow and green strap, face has orange, red, green and yellow M&Ms, mint 15.00
  1994, Cool Moves Watch, red case and brown printed strap, face has red M&M with skateboard, on revolving disk, MIB...................................... 20.00
  1996, New Blue Watch, black case and strap, Mr. Blue plays saxophone, M&Ms on revolving disk, MIB 20.00
  1997, Fun Watch, black case with M&M characters on black laser cut strap, face has white M on red circle, MIB.. 20.00
  1997, Minis Watch, painted yellow metal case with M&M figures on purple laser cut strap, Minis on revolving disk, MIB...................................... 15.00
  1998, Canadian Minis Sports Watch, blue and yellow sports style, black plastic strap, mint 25.00
  1998, Crew Pocket Watch, brasstone case with "Official Factory Crew" on face, black velveteen bag, mint in bag.. 60.00
  1998, International M&Ms Watch, clear yellow case, yellow back printed resin strap, packaged in yellow box with two packs of candy, complete, MIB.. 30.00
  1998, Millennium Watch, silvertone case, embossed black leather strap. "The Official Candy of the Millennium" on crystal, face has red M&M, mint 15.00
  1999, Crispy Watch, silvertone case, blue and black woven strap, speeding Crispies appear on sub-dial, MIB.. 25.00
  1999, Minis Watch, blue plastic case with back printed XO graph resin strap. Minis on face, MIB 20.00
  1999, Racing Team Watch, silvertone case, black leather strap, red and yellow pit crew on face, mint 15.00
Peter Pan Peanut Butter, S&M Inc., 1980s, small 7/8" red plastic case and strap, face shows dancing peanut butter jar with feet, his hands are watch hands, MIB.. 20.00
Punchy, Hawaiian Punch
  1970s, Swiss digital wind-up, heavy

rect goldtone case, wide red leather strap with snaps, face shows Punchy at one side, hours and minutes display in separate windows, VG 100.00
1971, Swiss wind-up, goldtone case, shiny red strap with snaps, face has Punchy with his arms as the watch hands, mint 50.00
1980s, blue plastic case, face has Punchy next to volcano, his feet and skateboard printed on white plastic strap, mint 20.00
1980s, red plastic case, blue plastic strap, face has blue outer ring with red numbers, electronic hands which don't show when the battery dies, mint 20.00
Raid Bug Spray, Swiss wind-up, 1970s, goldtone case, Raid can on face, bug on revolving disk 175.00
Reddy Kilowatt Pocket Watch, 1930s, silvertone case, "Compliments of Philadelphia Light & Electric" on face, several case styles, VG 200.00
Ritz Cracker
1971, made by the Continental Watch Co, silvertone case, black vinyl strap with snaps, face has red and blue crackers at hour marks, with yellow printed "Ritz," box has white top and black bottom, red velvet insert, MIB 200.00
1999, red plastic case and strap, face with blue background, yellow printed "It's Ritz Time," MIB 20.00
Scrubbing Bubbles, Dow, Marcel, 1970s, goldtone case, wide blue plastic strap with snaps, face has center character and "Scrubbing Bubbles" printed, VG 50.00
Shell Golden Oil Pocket Watch, Girard Perregaux, 1940s, case has a crystal on both front and back, works visible, Roman numerals, "Shell" on watch movement, VG 250.00
Snickers Anniversary, Mars, Advance Watch Co, 1990, goldtone case, brown leather strap, goldtone face with embossed stars, revolving subdial features Snickers wrappers as they changed over time, mint 35.00
Stanley Powerlock, Stanley Tools, 1980, black plastic case, yellow strap printed to look like tape measure, yellow face with black "Stanley Powerlock," MIB 25.00
Swiss Miss, Elam Watch Co., Swiss wind-up, 1981, goldtone case, brown leather strap, Swiss Miss in a blue dress on face, printed "Swiss Miss," MIB 25.00
Tony the Tiger, Kellogg's Frosted Flakes, Swiss wind-up, 1976, silvertone case, black vinyl strap with snaps, face pictures striding Tony, box has a shiny orange top and black bottom, MIB 200.00
Toppie the Elephant, Tip Top Bread, Ingraham, 1951, small 7/8" chrome case, gray leather strap, face has pink polka dotted elephant wearing cape with "Toppie," good 100.00

Westinghouse Refrigerator Pocket Watch, New Haven Clock Co., 1940s, silvertone case, red face with a yellow wedge between the 10-12 hour marks, "Westinghouse kitchen-proved refrigerator, 10 out of 12 hours uses no current at all," green box with yellow top, MIB 100.00

Akro Agate Glass

Collecting Hints: The Akro Agate mark—"Made in USA"—often includes a mold number. Some pieces also have a small crow in the mark.

Akro Agate glass is thick, and somewhat susceptible to chips. Therefore, collectors should buy only mint pieces. The marbleized types of Akro Agate were made in many color combinations. The serious collector should look for unusual combinations.

History: The Akro Agate Co. was formed in 1911, primarily to produce marbles. In 1914, the owners moved from near Akron, Ohio, to Clarksburg, West Virginia, where they opened a large factory. They continued to profitably produce marbles until after the Depression. In 1930, the competition in the marble business became too intense, and Akro Agate Co. decided to diversify.

Two of its most successful products were the floral ware lines and children's dishes, first made in 1935. The children's dishes were very popular until after World War II when metal dishes captured the market.

The Akro Agate Co. also made special containers for cosmetics firms, such the Jean Vivaudou Co. and Pick Wick bath salts (packaged in the Mexicali cigarette jar). Operations continued successfully until 1948. The factory, a victim of imports and the increased use of metal and plastic, was sold to the Clarksburg Glass Co. in 1951.

References: Gene Florence, *Collectors Encyclopedia of Akro Agate Glassware,* revised ed., Collector Books, 1975, 1992 value update; Roger and Claudia Hardy, *Complete Line of the Akro Agate,* published by author, 1992.

Collectors' Clubs: Akro Agate Art Association, P.O. Box 758, Salem, NH 03079; Akro Agate Collector's Club, 10 Bailey Street, Clarksburg, WV 26301.

Reproduction Alert: Pieces currently reproduced are not marked "Made In USA" and are missing the mold number and crow.

Children's Dishes, small unless otherwise noted
Cereal Bowl
Concentric Ring, blue, large 27.50
Interior Panel, green, transparent, large 25.00
Stacked Disk and Interior Panel, blue, transparent, large 35.00
Creamer
Chiquita, cobalt blue, baked-on 10.00
Interior Panel, topaz transparent 20.00
Octagonal, sky blue, open handle, large 25.00
Stacked Disk, green 10.00
Stacked Disk, pink 25.00
Stippled Band, green, large 30.00
Cup
Chiquita, opaque green 8.50
Chiquita, transparent cobalt blue 14.00
Concentric Rib, green, opaque 6.00
Interior Panel, green transparent, large 15.00
J. Pressman, lavender 32.00
Octagonal, closed handle, dark green, large 8.00
Stacked Disk, aqua blue 5.00
Stacked Disk, green opaque 6.00
Stacked Disk, green transparent 12.00
Stacked Disk Interior Panel, pumpkin 38.00
Stippled Band, green, large 20.00
Cup and Saucer
Chiquita, green opaque 8.00
Interior Panel, green and white marble 37.50
Stippled Band, cobalt blue, large 35.00
Stippled Band, green, large 30.00
Stippled Band, green, small 30.00
Demitasse Cup and Saucer, J. Pressman, green 22.00
Pitcher
Interior Panel, blue transparent 35.00
Stacked Disk, blue opaque 15.00
Stacked Disk and Panel, green transparent 45.00
Stippled band, green transparent 18.00
Plate
Chiquita, opaque green 8.00
Concentric Rib, opaque green 3.00
Concentric Ring, dark blue, 3-1/4" d 10.00
Interior Panel, blue opaque, medium 15.00
Interior Panel, green opaque, large 15.00
Interior Panel, topaz transparent 10.00
J. Pressman, green, baked-on, 3-3/4" d 5.00
Octagonal, green, large 12.00
Octagonal, white, small 8.00

Stacked Disk, green 10.00
Stacked Disk, medium blue 6.00
Stacked Disk and Panel, transparent
cobalt blue, large 22.00
Stippled Band, green, small 15.00
Stippled Band, topaz, large 10.00
Saucer
Chiquita, opaque yellow 12.00
Concentric Rib, white 3.00
Concentric Ring, ivory 4.50
Interior Panel, medium blue, opaque,
large 9.00
Octagonal, dark pink 8.00
Octagonal, white, large 12.00
Stacked Disk, green 7.00
Stacked Disk and Panel, transparent
green, small 12.00
Set
Chiquita, tea set, 16 pcs 150.00
Concentric Ring, green plates, green
cups, white saucers, blue creamer
and sugar, blue teapot with white lid,
16 pcs, orig box 200.00
Interior Panel, green cups and sau-
cers, green creamer, pink sugar, pink
teapot, white lid, small size 290.00
Interior Panel, topaz transparent, service for four, cups, saucers, plates,
creamer and sugar, teapot with
lid 215.00
Octagonal, large, orig box,
21 pcs 350.00
Stippled Band, amber, two cups and
saucers, two dinner plates, covered
teapot 60.00
Sugar, cov
Chiquita, green opaque 8.00
Chiquita, transparent cobalt
blue 8.00
Stacked Disk, green 10.00
Stacked Disc, pink 50.00
Teapot, cov
Chiquita, green opaque 18.00
Chiquita, transparent cobalt
blue 35.00
Interior Panel, green, white lid,
large 45.00
Interior Panel, green, white lid,
small 25.00
Interior Panel, medium blue opaque,
lid missing, large 36.00
Stacked Disk, azure blue, white
lid 10.00
Stippled Band, green, small 35.00
Stippled Band, green, large 115.00
Tumbler
Interior Panel, green transparent,
2" h 12.00
Octagonal 20.00
Stippled Band, transparent
green 11.00
Stacked Disk and Interior Panel, trans-
parent green, 2" h 12.00
Stacked Disk, white or pink 18.50
Water Set
Octagonal, open handle, blue pitcher,
two dark and two light green
tumblers 70.00
Stacked Disk and Interior Panel, trans-
parent green, seven pcs 70.00
Stacked Disk, green pitcher, white
tumblers, orig box 145.00

Stippled Band, green, pitcher, six tum-
blers 110.00

Sugar bowl, Concentric Ring, closed handles, yellow, small, $6.50.

Household Items
Ashtray
2-7/8" sq, blue and red marble 8.50
4-1/2" w, hexagon, blue and
white 35.00
Basket, two handles, orange and
white 35.00
Chinese Checkers Marbles, boxed set of
60, complete, orig paper dividers, box
mkd "Chinese Akro-Agate Checkers
Manufactured by the Akro Agate Co.,
Clarksburg, W. Va, U.S.A." 90.00
Cornucopia, 2" w, 3" h, orange and white,
mkd #765 .... 12.00
Electric Fan, 13" h, oxblood base, metal
fan and fittings 200.00
Flowerpot
2-1/4" h, Ribbed, green and
white 10.00
2-1/2" h, Stacked Disk, green and
white 12.00
4" h, Stacked Disk, blue and
white 25.00
5-1/2" h, Scalloped Top, blue 32.00
Jardiniere, Darts, pumpkin 65.00
Lamp
5-1/2" d, ribbed base 115.00
12" h, brown and blue marble, 4" d
black octagonal top, Globe
Spec Co. 75.00
Mexicalli Jar, cov, cactus and guitar
player
Green and white 30.00
Orange and white 40.00
Tan and white, mkd "Mexicali, Pick-
wick Cosmetic Corp., Fifth Ave., New
York," 3" h, 2-3/4" d, lid missing 9.00
Mortar and Pestle, black, mkd
"JV Co." 25.00
Pen Holder, black golfer, light green and
rust base 165.00
Planter
Flowers, orange and white, 5-1/2"
x 3" 9.00
Graduated Dart, 8-1/2" l, oval, scal-
loped, dark blue 30.00
Lily, green and white, crow flying
through "A" mark, 5-1/2" l,
2-1/4" h 17.00
Powder Jar, Colonial Lady, yellow 65.00
Vase
3-3/4" h, green, marble 15.00
4-1/4" h, lily, marble 17.50

4-5/8" h, 4-1/4" w, flared, green and
white marble, rust streaks, raised
flower on each side, mkd "Made in
USA" with backwards S, crow over let-
ter A 28.00
8" h, 4-1/4" d top, ribbed, pumpkin,
slight roughness 90.00

Aluminum, Hand Wrought

Collecting Hints: Some manufacturers' marks are synonymous with quality, e.g., "Continental Hand Wrought
Silverlook." However, some quality
pieces are not marked and should
not be overlooked.

Check carefully for pitting, deep
scratches, and missing glassware.

History: During the late 1920s, aluminum was used to make many decorative household accessories.
Although manufactured by a variety
of methods, the hammered aluminum
with repoussé patterns appears to
have been the most popular.

At one time, many companies
were competing for the aluminum
giftware market. In order to be more
competitive, numerous silver manufacturers added aluminum articles to
their product lines during the Depression. Some of these aluminum
objects were produced strictly as
promotional items; others were
offered as more affordable options to
similar silver objects. Many well-
known and highly esteemed metal-
smiths contributed their skills to the
production of hammered aluminum.
With the advent of mass-production
and the accompanying wider distribution of aluminum giftware, the
demand began to decline, leaving
only a few producers who have continued to turn out quality work using
the age-old and time-tested methods
of metal crafting.

References: Marilyn E. Dragowick
(ed.), *Metalwares Price Guide,*
Antique Trader Books, 1996; Everett
Grist, *Collectible Aluminum,* Collector Books, 2000; Dannie A. Woodard,
*Hammered Aluminum Hand Wrought
Collectibles, Book Two,* Aluminum
Collectors' Books, 1993; ——, *Revised
1990 Price List for Hammered Aluminum,* Aluminum Collectors' Books,
1990; Dannie Woodard and Billie
Wood, *Hammered Aluminum,* published by authors, 1983.

Periodical: Aluminist, P.O. Box 1346,
Weatherford, TX 76086.

Silent butler, Chrysanthemum, Continental Silverlook, 7-1/2" d, 12" l, $45.

Ashtray
    3-1/4" d, Stanhome, Stanley Home Product, center relief dec of house 5.00
    4-3/4" d, Whirlpool, Open House, Oct 1965, Marion Division 8.00
Basket
    9" l, rose finial on handle, mkd "Continental Trade Mark Hand Wrought Silverlook 654" 25.00
    14" l, 10-1/2" w, 10" h, fire-side shape, rose dec, piecrust edge, mkd "The Beauty Line, Designed Aluminum," with a rose....................................20.00
Bowl
    7-1/2" d, DePonceau, apple blossom dec, mkd..20.00
    8" d, Wendell August Forge, Pine Cone pattern..................................45.00
    11-3/4" d, Continental Silverlook, Chrysanthemum pattern, applied leaves, #715 ....20.00
Bread Tray, 13-1/4" l, 7-3/4" w, Continental, chrysanthemum decoration, #572 ....25.00
Butter Dish, Buenilum, round, domed cover, double-loop finish, glass insert 35.00
Candleholder, 6" h, Buenilum, beaded edge base, aluminum stem with wood ball..10.00
Candy Tray, 8" d, chrysanthemum dec, unmarked....................................10.00
Casserole, 9-7/8" d, 6-1/2" h, Buenilum, mkd "B (castle) W" 24.00
Chafing Dish, cov, 11" h, dish, stand, candle holder warmer, 1-1/2 qt glass insert, mkd "Buenilum"................30.00
Coaster Set, Everlast Forged Aluminum Co., Bamboo pattern, set of eight in matching aluminum holder 25.00
Compote, 5" h, Continental Hand Wrought Silverlook, wild rose dec, #1083 ....18.00
Creamer and Sugar, Continental Hand Wrought Silverlook, Chrysanthemum pattern, grooved handles, applied leaves, matching tray................30.00
Crumb Catcher Set, unmarked........10.00
Desk Set, Everlast Forge, Bali Bamboo pattern, price for 3 pc set............45.00

Dish, 6" l, 4" w, pear shaped, background etching, mkd "Neocraft," Everlast Metal Products 25.00
Ice Bucket
    8" d, rosette finial, minor wear 20.00
    8-3/4" d, 12" h, aqua porcelain liner, 1950s.. 100.00
Lazy Susan
    15-1/2" w, Art Deco leaping stags dec, mkd "Everlast Forged Aluminum" 30.00
    15-1/2" w, 4-1/2" h, Everlast Forged Aluminum Co., pears, berries, and leaves, 8-1/2" d removable glass insert..25.00
Lemon Squeezer, hammered aluminum handles, five drainage holes, small penguin mark 30.00
Nottingham Jar Base, Kensington, #7472 ....30.00
Nut Bowl, 9" d, 4" h, floral design inside bowl, center nut pick holder........20.00
Plate, flying ducks and cattails, 5" d...6.00
Silent Butler, 6" d, Canterbury Arts, Celtic knot pattern 30.00
Tidbit Tray, 10" h, 13" d, 3 tiers, Dogwood pattern, mkd "Wilson Specialties Co., Inc., Brooklyn, NY" 30.00
Tray
    9-3/8" x 5-1/8", floral and ivy design, mkd "Everlast Metal #569"..........20.00
    10-1/2" x 15", floral dec, high raised handles.......................................18.00
    14" x 9", Wendell August Forge, #606, Barley pattern...............................35.00
    18" x 11", Arthur Armour Deco, gold world map 80.00
    18-1/2" x 11-1/2", fruit and floral dec, crimped piecrust edge, curved handles, mkd "Hand Finished Aluminum"....................................30.00
    19" x 11", Canterbury Arts, Art Deco geometric pattern, handles 18.50
    20" d, round, heavily emb paisley design, Keystone, few scratches.....................................25.00
Water Pitcher, 8-1/2" h, 5-1/2" w, handle knotted and riveted to body, mkd "World (globe) Hand Forged" 35.00

American Bisque

Collecting Hint: When searching for American Bisque products, look for a mark consisting of three stacked baby blocks with the letters "A," "B," and "C." This common mark is readily found.

History: The American Bisque Company was founded in Williamstown, West Virginia, in 1919. Although the pottery's original product was china-head dolls, it quickly expanded its inventory to include serving dishes, cookie jars, ashtrays, and various other decorative ceramic pieces. B. E. Allen, founder of the Sterling China

Company, invested heavily in the company and eventually purchased the remaining stock. In 1982, the plant was sold and operated briefly under the name American China Company. The plant closed in 1983.

Sequoia Ware and Berkeley are two trademarks used by American Bisque, the former used on items sold in gift shops, and the latter found on products sold through chain stores. Cookie jars produced by this company are marked "ABC" inside blocks.

References: Susan and Al Bagdade, *Warman's American Pottery and Porcelain,* 2nd ed., Krause Publications, 2000; Mary Jane Giacomini, *American Bisque,* Schiffer Publishing 1994.

Bank
    Dancing Pig, 4-3/4" h 35.00
    Elephant, 6" h 85.00
    Piggy.. 70.00
Basket, get well type, wire handle.. 45.00
Cookie Jar
    African Violet, 11-1/2" h, oval on front with flower, mkd "American Bisque USA" on back............................. 65.00
    After School Cookies, schoolhouse with bell in lid, inside rim chip..... 55.00
    Bear, lacy blue rompers, holding pink daisy cookie, 11-1/4" h.............. 105.00
    Beehive, 11-3/4" h 165.00
    Candy Baby, 11" h.................... 130.00
    Cat, gray, pink, and yellow........ 235.00
    Chalkboard Clown, paint loss, faint hairline crack 375.00
    Cheerleaders, two cheerleaders with flashing eyes, megaphone mkd "Cookie Time," mkd "USA #802," 11" h.. 475.00
    Chef, yellow 95.00
    Clown, round body, 12" h, 10" w, wear to paint.. 85.00
    Coffee Pot, yellow coffee cup and cookies on front, 7-1/2" d, 9-1/2" h... 75.00
    Cookie Churn, yellow, 10" h 30.00
    Cookie Truck, mkd "USA 744," 11" h.. 195.00
    Davy Crockett, 11-1/2" h 750.00
    Dutch Boy, blond hair, blue eyes, 13" h, some paint crazing 175.00
    Fred and Dino, 14-1/2" h, minor glaze crazing, neck repair 550.00
    French Poodle, 10-3/4" h, slight glaze imperfection on top 135.00
    Granny, yellow and pink, brown hair.. 200.00
    Jack in the Box, smiling figural lid, blue and yellow base with blue "Cookies," 12" h.. 185.00
    Kitten with Yarn, black and white kitten, lime green ball, brown and white kitten on lid, 9-1/2" h.............. 115.00
    Majorette, 11" h....................... 385.00
    Milk Wagon, mkd "USA 740" 165.00
    Pig, multicolored....................... 225.00

Popeye, 10-1/2" h 1,000.00
Rubbles House, 10" h, 9" w 950.00
Saddle, 12" h 350.00
Sitting Horse, 11" h, 7" w 1,100.00
Spaceship, 12-1/2" h, 8" w 385.00
Swirl, blue ground, white lid,
  1940s 25.00
Tea Kettle 50.00
Toy Soldier, mkd "USA 743,"
  11-1/4" h 225.00
Yogi Bear, sgd "Hanna
  Barbera" 450.00
Door Stop, 8" h, Keystone Cop, blue hat
  and pants, white jacket 115.00
Flower Frog, swan 45.00
Flower Pot, two handles, peach
  colored 38.00
Lamp, television type, black panther,
  maroon base back, 1950s 70.00
Planter
  Bear sitting on log, 5-1/2" l, 6" h .. 18.00
  Couple in front of TV set 45.00
  Dutch Boy, pink, 9" h 35.00
  Gazelle, 6-1/2" l, 5" h 20.00
  Kitten playing with yarn, 5-1/2" w,
  3-7/8" h 20.00
Salt and Pepper Shakers, pr, egg
  shape, white ground, multicolored
  polka dots, c1940 .... 45.00

Animation Art

Collecting Hints: A very specific vocabulary is used when discussing animation cels. The differences between a Courvoisier, Disneyland, master, key production, printed, production, and studio background can mean thousands of dollars in value. Auction houses selling animation art do not agree on terminology. Carefully read the glossary section of any catalog.

A second of film requires more than 20 animation cels. The approximate number of cels used to make that cartoon can be determined by multiplying the length of a cartoon in minutes times 60 times 24. The question that no one seems to be asking as prices reach the ten- and hundred-thousand dollar level is, "What happened to all the other animation cels?" Vast quantities of cels are in storage.

There is no doubt that Walt Disney animation cels are king. Nostalgia, legend, and hype drive pricing more than historical importance or workmanship. The real bargains in the field lie outside the Disney material.

Although animation art has a clearly established track record, it also is an area that has been subject to manipulation, representational abuse, and shifting nostalgia trends.

It is not the place for the casual collector.

Avoid limited edition serigraphs—color prints made by silk screening. Although they may appear to be animation cels, they are not.

History: According to film historians, the first animated cartoon was Winsor McCay's 1909 "Gertie the Dinosaur." Early animated films were largely the work of comic strip artists. The invention of the celluloid process (a "cel" is an animation drawing on celluloid) is attributed to Earl Hurd. Although the technique reached perfection under animation giants such as Walt Disney and Max Fleischer, individuals such as Walter Lantz and Paul Terry—along with studios such as Columbia, Charles Mints and Screen Gems, MGM, Paramount/Famous Studios, UPA, and Warner Brothers—did pioneering work.

Leonard Maltin's *Of Mice and Magic: A History of American Animated Cartoons* (A Plume Book/New American Library, revised and updated edition, 1987) is an excellent source for historic information.

References: Jeffrey M. Ellingport, *Collecting Original Comic Strip Art,* Antique Trader Books, 1999; Jerry Weist, *Original Comic Art,* Avon Books, 1992.

Periodicals: *Animation Film Art,* P.O. Box 25547, Los Angeles, CA 90025; *Animation Magazine,* 4676 Admiralty Way, Ste 210, Marina Del Ray, CA 90292; *Animato!,* P.O. Box 1240, Cambridge, MA 02238; *In Toon!,* P.O. Box 217, Gracie Station, New York, NY, 10028; *Storyboard/The Art of Laughter,* 80 Main St., Nashua, NH 03060.

Collectors' Club: Greater Washington Animation Collectors Club, 12423 Hedges Run Dr. #184, Lake Ridge, VA 22192.

Museums: Baltimore Museum of Art, Baltimore, MD; International Museum of Cartoon Art, Boca Raton, FL; Museum of Cartoon Art, Rye Brook, NY; Museum of Modern Art, New York, NY; Walt Disney Archives, Burbank, CA.

Donald Duck, orig layout drawing, Donald swinging ring on his finger, wearing straw hat 650.00
Fat Albert and the Cosby Kids, Filmation Studios, 1970s, tempera background sheet, framed 950.00

Fred and Wilma Flintstone, Barney and Betty Rubble, orig production cel, multi-cel set mounted on full celluloid, framed, glazed, 16" x 19" 450.00
Hercules, Walt Disney Productions, running, wearing sandals, 12-1/2" x 17" sheet size, 1997, certificate of authenticity, matted 500.00
Jungle Book, Walt Disney, 1967, Baloo, 6-1/2" x 4", gouache on celluloid, cel trimmed, unframed 900.00
Ludwig Von Drake, Walt Disney Studios, artist's field paper, 2-3/4" x 1-1/2" image size, matted 75.00
101 Dalmatians, The Colonel, c1958, 8" x 6-3/4" cel, 13" x 13-1/2" frame ... 425.00
Peanuts, Charles Schulz, blue and colored graphite drawings on artist's field paper, 1980s
  Sally, 2-3/4" x 1-1/2" image size, matted 75.00
  Snoopy, 3-1/2" x 2" image size, matted 45.00
Pink Panther, Depatie-Frelang Studio, gouache, 10-1/2" x 12-1/2", c1960 .... 125.00
Pooh and Tigger, Walt Disney Productions, seri-cel, 5-1/2" x 7-1/2", Walt Disney silver seal 145.00
Robin Hood, Walt Disney Productions, Sir Hiss, 10" x 13" sheet size, orig Walt Disney sticker, matted 480.00
Sleeping Beauty, Walt Disney Productions, King Hubert, 7-1/2" x 4-1/2" image size, matted 75.00
Smurf, numbered, matted, 11" x 14" 95.00
Simpsons, Bart, dopey expression, black and orange pencil drawing, 4-1/2" x 1-1/2" image size, matted 25.00
Sword in the Stone, Walt Disney Productions, production cel, #55 in sequence, Sir Ector drinking wine, 7" x 6-1/2" image size, certificate of authenticity, matted 65.00
Sylvester, orig production cel, gouache on full celluloid, accompanied by orig layout drawing, c1960, 17" x 32", mounted, framed 450.00
Teenage Mutant Ninja Turtle, certificate of authenticity, copyright dates 1985 to 1991, matted, 11" x 14" 85.00
Tom and Jerry Golfing, Turner Home Entertainment seal, 11" x 14" sheet size, matted 115.00
Yogi Bear, Hanna Barbera, 5-1/2" h image of Yogi, colorful 13" x 11" laser background, late 1970s or early 1980s 85.00

Autographs

Collecting Hints: The condition and content of letters and documents significantly influences value. Signatures should be crisp, clear, and located so that they do not detract from the rest of the item. Whenever possible, obtain a notarized statement of authenticity, especially for pieces worth more than $100.

Forgeries abound; copying machines compound the problem. Furthermore, many signatures of political figures (especially presidents), movie stars, and sports heroes were signed by machine or by a secretary rather than by the individuals themselves. Photographically reproduced signatures resemble originals. Use a good magnifying glass or microscope to check all signatures.

Presentation material, something marked "To_____," has less value than a non-presentation item. The presentation personalizes the piece and often restricts interest to someone with the same name.

There are autograph mills throughout the country run by people who write to noteworthy individuals requesting their signatures on large groups of material. They in turn sell this material on the autograph market. Buy an autograph of a living person only after the most careful consideration and examination.

History: Autograph collecting is an old established tradition. Early letters were few, hence, treasured in private archives. Municipalities, churches, and other institutions maintained extensive archives to document past actions.

Autograph collecting became fashionable during the 19th century. However, early collectors focused on the signatures alone, clipping off the signed portion of a letter or document. Eventually collectors realized that the entire document was valuable.

The popularity of movie stars and sports, rock 'n' roll, and television personalities brought about changes in the way autographs were collected. Fans pursued these individuals with autograph books, programs, and photographs. Collectors requested that autographs be signed on everything imaginable. Realizing the value of their signatures and the speculation that occurs, modern stars and heroes are often unwilling to sign material under certain circumstances.

References: Mark Allen Baker, *All Sport Autograph Guide,* Krause Pub-

lications, 1995; ——, *Advanced Autograph Collecting,* Krause Publications, 2000; ——, *Collector's Guide to Celebrity Autographs,* 2nd ed., Krause Publications, 2000; *Standard Guide to Collecting Autographs,* Krause Publications, 1999; Kevin Keating and Michael Kolleth, *The Negro Leagues Autograph Guide,* Tuff Stuff Books, 1999; Kevin Martin, *Signatures of the Stars,* Antique Trader Books, 1998; Tom Mortenson, *Standard Catalog of Sports Autographs,* Krause Publications, 2000; Kenneth W. Rendell, *Forging History: The Detection of Fake Letters and Documents,* University of Oklahoma Press, 1994; ——, *History Comes to Life,* University of Oklahoma Press, 1996; George Sanders, Helen Sanders, and Ralph Roberts, *Sanders Price Guide to Autographs,* 5th ed., Alexander Books, 2000.

Periodicals: *Autograph Collector,* 510-A S Corona Mall, Corona, CA 91720-1420, http://www.autographcollector.com/acm.htm; *Autograph Review,* 305 Carlton Rd, Syracuse, NY 13207; *Autograph Times,* 1125 W. Baseline Rd., #2-153-M, Mesa, AZ 85210-9501, http://celebrityconnection.com/at.htm; *Autographs & Memorabilia,* P.O. Box 224, Coffeyville, KS 67337; *The Collector,* P.O. Box 255, Hunter, NY 12442; *Celebrity Access,* 20 Sunnyside Ave., Suite A241, Mill Valley, CA 94941-1928; V.I.P. *Autogramm-Magazine,* 3000 W. Olympic Blvd., Blvd. 3, Suite 2415, Santa Monica, CA 90404, http://www.vip-entertainment.com.

Collectors' Clubs: International Autograph Collectors Club & Dealers Alliance, 4575 Sheriden St., Suite 111, Hollywood, FL 33021-3575, http://www.iacc-da.com; Manuscript Society, 350 N Niagara Street, Burbank, CA 95105-3648, http://www.manuscript.org; Universal Autograph Collectors Club, P.O. Box 6181, Washington, DC 20044; Washington Historical Autograph & Certificate Organization, P.O. Box 2428, Springfield, VA 22152-2428, http://www.whaco.com.

Libraries: New York Public Library, New York, NY; Pairpoint Morgan Library, New York, NY.

Abbreviations: The following are used to describe autograph material and size.

ADS   Autograph Document Signed

ALS   Autograph Letter Signed

AQS   Autograph Quotation Signed

CS   Card Signed

DS   Document Signed

FDC   First Day Cover

LS   Letter Signed

PS   Photograph Signed

TLS   Typed Letter Signed

Sheet music, Suzanne Joret Gill, "Will You Tell Me Fair Young Lady," words and music by Gill, $50.

Autograph Letters Signed (ALS)

Ford, Edsel B., fund-raising letter, typed, 8" x 10" 85.00
Heath, Vernon L., L. S. Heath & Sons, maker of "America's Finest Candy Bar," 7-1/4" x 10-1/4" buff colored stationery, 1957 typewritten letter inviting guest to luncheon at headquarters in Robinson, IL, sgd in blue ink 15.00
Hepburn, Katharine, one page 8" x 10", Oct 18, 1973, typed, thank you note, orig envelope 185.00
Kraft, James L., Chairman of Board, Kraft Foods Co., May 19, 1947, typewritten on 7-1/4" x 10-1/2" Kraft letterhead, sgd in black ink, accompanied by mailing envelope and leaflet 15.00
Leigh, Vivien, personal stationery, 1959 .... 650.00
Sellers, Peter, personal stationery, 1959 .... 125.00

Book Signed

Ellison, Ralph, *The Invisible Man,* 1952, leather binding 750.00
Garcia, Ted, *The Irreverent Angel,* William Reed, Frontier Heritage Press, 1971 .... 35.00
Geisel, Theodore Seuss, *The Grinch Who Stole Christmas,* long whimsical inscription 750.00
Scott, Commander, *Romance of the Highways of California,* Griffin-Patterson Co., 1947 .... 10.00

Stewart, Michael, *Monkey Shines,* 1983, first edition, orig dj 15.00
Whitehouse, Eula, *Texas Flowers in Natural Colors,* first edition, 1936 .... 48.00

Cards Signed (CS)

Adargo, Everett, Deep Sea Diver, Catalina Island, CA, real photo post card 5.00
Billingsley, Barbara, 3" x 5" black and white card, sgd "Love, Barbara Billingsley" 8.00
Bogart, Humphrey, framed with Warner Bros. promotional photo 820.00
Bridges, Lloyd, 3" x 5" white card, inscribed, "Best Wishes David, Lloyd Bridges" 35.00
Bush, Barbara, First Lady, Blair House stationery, 3" x 2" 60.00
Cravath, Gavvy, 3" x 5" card, sgd in fountain pen 250.00
DeHaven, Gloria, 3" x 5" black and white card, sgd "Best of luck always, Gloria DeHaven" 20.00
DiMaggio, Joe, post card, 9/42, sgd in fountain pen 350.00
Garner, James, black and white post card 24.00
Hickman, Dwayne, 3" x 5", sgd, "To David, Best wishes, Dwayne Hickman 'Dobie'," 5.00
Kipling, Rudyard, 2-1/2" x 4" lined card, sgd in fountain pen 150.00
McCarthy, Joe, Hall of Fame back and white post card, inscribed and dated Feb, 1965, accompanied by 1939 8" x 10" photo of McCarthy in Yankee uniform from the inside cover of *Baseball Magazine* 85.00
Oritz, Roberto, 3" x 5" card, inscribed in Spanish, 1968 .... 125.00
Schirra, Wally, 3" x 5" white card 25.00
Takei, George, Star Trek, 3" x 2" white card, dark blue Star Trek imprinted at top, blue Enterprise image 75.00

Document Signed (DS)

Andrews, Julie, two sgd checks 82.00
Eisenhower, Dwight David, poster, military attire, card stock 475.00
Fleitas, Angel, players contract with Washington Senators, 1944, also sgd by William Harridge, and Clark Griffith, four pgs 350.00
Fox, Nellie, check, 4/66, neatly laminated 425.00
Grant, Maxwell, The Shadow, check for cash, filled out and signed in ink, c1950, 2-3/4" x 6-1/2" 35.00
Hughes, Langston, sheet music, lyrics by him 395.00
Murphy, Dale, print, Atlanta Braves, 16" x 20" 30.00
Niven, David, two sgd checks 164.00
Robinson, Jackie, check, dated 10/73, accompanied by letter of authenticity from Rachel Robinson 550.00
Ryan, Nolan, *Legends Magazine* cover 150.00

Serling, Rod, writer and producer, bank check, June, 1968 .... 295.00
Wakely, Jimmy, *Western Song Parade,* 1947, magazine cover 75.00
West, Mae, theater playbill, 6" x 9" program for stage production of Kenley Players production of "Come On Up, Ring Twice," July 7, 1952, 12 pgs 75.00
Yastremzski, Carl, post card, postmarked Aug, 1961 .... 275.00

Equipment

Baseball
Koufax, Sandy 185.00
Musial, Stan, sgd in blue pen, sgd, "Stan 'The Man' Musial HOF 69" 60.00
Rose, Pete, sgd in blue pen 50.00
Williams, Ted, ball holder 175.00
Basketball Jersey
Helton, Todd, Rockies 295.00
Leonard, Buck, Homestead Grays 350.00
Batting Helmet, game used
Guillen, Ozzie, White Sox 225.00
Winfield, Dave, Twins 750.00
Boxing Gloves, Joe Frazier 90.00
Cap, autographed on visor
Mantle, Mickey 225.00
Molitor, Paul, Blue Jays 50.00
Nicklaus, Jack, Las Vegas golf cap 75.00
Schmidt, Mike, Phillies 90.00
Football Helmet
Steel, Curtain, Steelers helmet 400.00
Marino, Dan, NFL licensed mini helmet 125.00
Tripp, Charlie, St. Louis Cardinals helmet 295.00
Team Ball, Official National League ball
Boston Braves, 1945, 20+ signatures 395.00
Brooklyn Dodgers, 24 signatures 550.00
Cardinals and Giants, sgd by Mel Ott, Bill Terry, Johnny Mize, Luke Hamlin, Van Mungo, Curt Davis, Joe Medwick, few other illegible signatures 275.00
Philadelphia Phillies, 1966, 24 signatures 225.00
Pittsburgh Pirates, 1945, 20+ signatures 595.00

First Day Covers (FDC)

Astaire, Fred and Ginger Rogers, honoring the 50th Anniversary of Talking Pictures, canceled Hollywood, 1977 .... 195.00
Paige, Janis, Palmomar Mt. Observatory, postmarked 1948 .... 10.00
Prince Rainer, honoring Great American Presidents, Washington, Lincoln, FDR, and Eisenhower, canceled 1966, blue ink signature 50.00
Yeager, Chuck and Scott Crossfield, honoring Glenn Curtiss, canceled NY, 1980 .... 50.00

Photograph Signed (PS)

Aguilera, Christina, 8" x 10" black and white, early career pose 125.00
Allen, Marty and Steve Rossi, 8-1/8" x 9-1/8" black and white, sgd by both 15.00

Anderson, Pamela, 8" x 10" color, Bay Watch set, red bathing suit, with certificate of authenticity 125.00
Bloch, Robert, 8" x 10" black and white, smiling Bloch at left, artwork of demon scowling in background, c1970 .... 30.00
Curly Joe, 8" x 10" black and white photo of Three Stooges, facsimile signatures of all three, plus bold ink Curly Joe signature, late 1950s 48.00
Davis, Betty, 8" x 10" black and white, orig envelope 35.00
Davis, Marian, 9" x 12", black and white, matte finish 18.00
Hayward, Susan, Johnny Downs, and Gregory Ratoff, 8" x 10" black and white group shot at party 375.00
Kostelanetz, Andre, 8" x 10" black and white, personally inscribed 15.00
MacDonald, Jeannette, 5" x 6", black and white, orig envelope 30.00
Mackaill, Dorothy, 8" x 10" black and white 400.00
Madonna, 8" x 10" color, Sweet Rapunzel 15.00
Milland, Ray, 8" x 10" black and white 15.00
Mitchum, Robert, 5" x 7" black and white 15.00
Rush, Barbara, 8" x 10-1/8" black and white, personally inscribed 12.00
Spears, Britney, 8" x 10" color, field of flowers, with certificate of authenticity 125.00
Young, Gig, 8" x 10" black and white, personally inscribed 25.00
Wayne, John, 8" x 10" color, cowboy hat 590.00
Winters, Jonathon, 8-3/16" x 10" black and white, photo of Winters holding up two masks of his face 15.00

Aviation Collectibles

Collecting Hints: This field developed in the 1980s and is now firmly established. The majority of collectors focus on personalities, especially Charles Lindbergh and Amelia Earhart. New collectors are urged to look at the products of airlines, especially those items related to the pre-jet era.

History: Most of the income for the first airlines in the United States came from government mail-carrying subsidies. The first non–Post Office Department flight to carry mail was in 1926 between Detroit and Chicago. By 1930, there were 38 domestic and five international airlines operating in the United States. A typical passenger load was ten. After World War II, four-engine planes with a capacity of 100 or more passengers were introduced.

The jet age was launched in the 1950s. In 1955, Capitol Airlines used British-made turboprop airliners for domestic service. In 1958, National Airlines began domestic jet passenger service. The giant Boeing 747 went into operation in 1970 as part of the Pan American fleet. The Civil Aeronautics Board, which regulates the airline industry, ended control of routes in 1982 and fares in 1983.

Major American airlines include American, Delta, Northwest, Pan Am, TWA, United, and USAir. There are many regional lines as well. As a result of deregulation, new airlines are forming; some lasting longer than others.

References: *Air Transport Label Catalog,* Aeronautica & Air Label Collectors Club of Aerophilatelic Federation of America, n.d.; Stan Baumwald, *Junior Crew Member Wings,* published by author, n.d.; Jon A. Maguire and John P. Conway, *American Flight Jackets: A History of U. S. Flyers' Jackets from World War I to Desert Storm,* Schiffer Publishing, 2000.

Periodical: Airliners, P.O. Box 52-1238, Miami, FL 33152.

Collectors' Clubs: Aeronautica & Air Label Collectors Club, P.O. Box 1239, Elgin, IL 60121; C.A.L./N-X-211 Collectors Society, 226 Tioga Ave., Bensenville, IL 60106; Gay Airline Club, P.O. Box 69A04, West Hollywood, CA 90069; World Airline Historical Society, 3381 Apple Tree Lane, Erlanger, KY 41018.

Commercial

Almanac, 7" x 4-1/4", PLUNA, Uruguayan airline, desk type, plastic, 1950s 55.00

Ashtray, 4-3/8" sq, 1-3/4" h, Lufthansa, deep blue, logo on four sides, mkd "Made in Austria" 20.00

Bowl, Delta Airlines, VIP International Flights, mkd "Delta Airlines, Mayer China" 20.00

Cup, china
TWA, mkd "ABCO Japan" 25.00
TWA, mkd "Michaud Japan" 25.00

Drinking Glass
2-1/2" h, 2-1/2" w, United Airlines, white logo 15.00
4-1/2" h, Eastern Airlines, "New Type Constellation, Compliments of Eastern Airlines," applied signature of "Eddie V. Rickenbacker" 36.00

First Day Cover, Pennsylvania Airlines 5th Anniversary, 1932, black stamped cancel 18.00

Lunch Box, National Airlines on front and back, Ohio Art, 1960s 40.00

Magazine Ad, United Stewardesses, 1966, color, 10" x 13" 40.00

Menu Card, United Airlines
Flight from Denver, CO, prepared by Conrad Kung, Chef, issued about the Mainliner 20.00
Flight from Los Angeles, CA, prepared by Max Burkhardt, Chef, shows United Nations Building, NY, back with emblem for 50th Anniversary of Powered Flight 15.00
Flight from San Francisco, CA, prepared by Frank Hurliman, Chef, shows Mt. Hood, adv "United Mainliners offer direct service to 14 Pacific Northwest cities" 15.00

Model Airplane, Matchbox, diecast, Sky Busters series, MIBP
Aero Mexico DC10, 4-3/4" l, 3-1/2" wingspan 35.00
Air France Airbus, 4-1/8" l, 3-1/2" wingspan 35.00
Air France Concord, 5-1/2" l, 2-1/2" wingspan 35.00
KLM 747, 4-3/8" l, 3-3/4" wingspan 35.00
Pan Am 747, 4-3/8" l, 3-1/2" wingspan 35.00

Plane, 21" l, 28" wingspan, American Airlines, pressed steel, 1940s, some scratches 325.00

Candy container, figural, glass, Army bomber, $35.

Post Card
Disneyland TWA Airlines, unused, copyright Disneyland, Inc., 1955 .... 22.00
TWA's Jetstream, Zamparelli's Interpretation of Paris, info on back about mural, unused 15.00

Silverware Set, Pan Am, fork, spoon, and knife, engraved logo on handles, International Silver Co. 24.00

Swizzle Stick, TWA, set of 2, green from Hong Kong, red from Africa 12.00

Toy
Jeep, Lufthansa German Airlines Airport Service, tin litho, friction, mkd "T. T. Japan," c1960, 2" x 4" x 2-1/2" h 18.00
Truck, Trans World Air Lines, metal and plastic, Japan, 1980s, 3-1/2" l 25.00

Whiskey Bottle, United Airlines Menehune, foil sticker for Jim Beam Distilling Co., inscription for 10th anniversary of Hawaiian Open, 1975, 12-1/2" h 28.00

General

Ashtray, Naval Aviation Museum, Pensacola, FL, figural airplane, souvenir decal, gold lettering, incised "Japan," 7" l 28.00

Badge and Ring, American Aviator, 4-1/2" x 5-1/4" red, white, and blue stiff paper card, text for American Boy Outfit, 3" brass accent badge with propeller, wing design, small brass accent child's ring with relief image of military eagle symbol, M.P. & Co., USA, 1940s 24.00

Book, *Concorde, The Story of the World's Most Advanced Passenger Aircraft,* F. G. Clark and Arthur Gibson, Crescent Books, 1975 .... 9.00

Card Game, Soco/Transatlantic Flight, bufftone stiff paper, red and green printing, copyright C. Carey Cloud, Chicago, 1946, 2-1/4" x 3-1/4" 20.00

Chart, Join the Maltex Good Health Squadron, 8-1/4" x 10-1/2", full color sheet, four sets of airplanes flying in formation, numbered weeks next to each group, instructs user to color plane day that 100% breakfast is eaten, Maltex Co., VT, early 1940s 24.00

Cigarette Lighter, chrome plated, desk type, propeller, lighter compartment in wing, c1937 .... 95.00

Magazine Tear Sheet, Bendix Aviation Corp., 1947, *Saturday Evening Post* 4.00

Medallion, National Air Races, Meritorious Participation Award, 1932, inscription, "Happy Landings-Presented by Miss Fidelty-Home Port Wheeling West Virginia,"" pewter-like silver finish .. 150.00

Membership Card, Flying Aces Club, 2-1/2" x 4", orange, black text, wings logo mounted, premium from Flying Aces Magazine, 1932 .... 24.00

Membership Kit, Kool-Air Junior Aviation Corps, Perkins Products Co., copyright 1938, hat, membership card, letter, and News-O-Gram, certificate filled out in ink, two facsimile signatures of TWA pilot and hostess ... 60.00

Model Plans, Tailspin Tommy Flying Club, Douglas DC-3 model, specifications, illus chart, orig envelope, c1936 .... 35.00

Pinback Button, 5/8" d, High Flyers, three primitive bi-planes in flight, back paper for David Cook Publishing Co., c1920 .... 8.00

Plate, 10-1/2" d, Martin Aviation, Vernon Kilns, brown illus of 5 aircraft, titles, c1940 .... 55.00

Post Card, Quakertown Airport, Quakertown, PA, black and white, shows six small planes, unused 7.50

Premium Model, Deny Starling Plane, balsa wood, instruction sheet, orig 15" l mailing tube, return address from Bireley's, CA, c1930, wear 30.00

Stickpin, Nestle's Sky Club, silvered metal wings, center shield emblem, blue enamel accents, 1960s 15.00
Store Sign, Sky Blazers, 30" x 37-1/2", thick cardboard, thin wax coating, 1930s, adv CBS radio show and sponsor Wonder Bread, minor wear, some age discoloration 45.00

Personalities

Book
  Alone, account of Richard Byrd in Antarctica, 1934, autographed 125.00
  That's My Story, Douglas Corrigan, published by E P Dutton & Co, 1938, 5-1/2 x 8-1/4", hard cover, 221 pgs, 56 sepia photos 20.00
Christmas Light Bulb, 3" h, Charles Lindbergh wearing aviation uniform ..65.00
Film, *Lindbergh's Paris Flight,* Pathex Motion Pictures 50.00
Game, Howard Hughes Game, 11 x 17 x 3", Family Games, Inc., thick brown plastic box designed as attaché case, orig cardboard label and shrink wrap, copyright 1972..........................100.00
Money Clip, Spirit of St Louis, silvered brass, spring clip, finely detailed illus of Lindbergh aircraft, Anson Co...125.00
Pinback Button
  7/8" d, Corinth Airport Dedication, photo of Col. Roscoe Turner, 1930s 12.00
  7/8" d, Welcome Lindbergh, blue and white...75.00
  1" d, Plucky Lindy/Flexible Flyer, black and white center Lindbergh portrait, yellow sled with red runners, inscription, "Two Great Flyers," late 1920s 20.00
  1-1/4" d, Atlantic, Newfoundland to Wales, Amelia Earhart and passengers Lou Gordon and William Stultz, 1928 ....325.00
  1-1/4" d, General Balbo portrait, sepia, leader of Italian air fleet visitation to Chicago World's Fair, 1933 ....50.00
  1-1/4" d, Welcome Wiley Post, black and white, aviator with patch over blinded eye, 1930s.....................150.00
  1-3/8" d, red, white, and blue litho, photo of Lindbergh, eagle, Spirit of St. Louis, Statue of Liberty, and Eiffel Tower, American flags 120.00
  2" d, Orville Wright, black, white, and buff litho, "Orville Wright-American/ First Man To Fly," 1930s...............20.00
Photograph, 31" x 41", Wright Bros. first flight, 1903, framed 165.00
Plate, 8-1/2" sq, Lindbergh commemorative, yellow ground, multicolored transfer center, marked "Limoges China, Sterling, Golden Glow"................35.00
Pocket Mirror, 2-1/4 x 3-1/2", celluloid, Lindbergh and plane in flight, maroon and white 125.00
Post Card, 3-3/4 x 5-1/2", air mail, black and white, issued to welcome Lindbergh, Milwaukee, Aug, 1927, back text endorses air mail 30.00
Sheet Music, 9-1/4 x 12-1/4", *Lindy, Lindy,* Wolfe Gilbert and Abel Baer, 1927 copyright, black, white, and orange cov...25.00

Tapestry, Charles Lindbergh, large center portrait, Spirit of St. Louis on left flying over New York skyscrapers, Statue of Liberty, right with Spirit of St. Louis flying over Paris, Eiffel Tower, 50" x 20", made in France.........................400.00

Avon Collectibles

Collecting Hints: Avon collectibles encompass a wide range of objects, including California Perfume Company bottles, decanters, soaps, children's items, jewelry, plates, and catalogs. Another phase of collecting focuses on Avon Representatives' and Managers' awards.

Avon products are well marked with one of four main marks. There is a huge quantity of collectibles from this company; collectors should limit their interests. Although they may be harder to find, do include some foreign Avon collectibles. New items take longer to increase in value than older items. Do not change the object in any way, as this destroys the value.

History: David H. McConnell founded the California Perfume Co. in 1886. He hired saleswomen, a radical concept for that time. They used a door-to-door technique to sell their first product, "Little Dot," a set of five perfumes; thus was born the "Avon Lady," although by 1979 they numbered more than one million.

In 1929, California Perfume Co. became the Avon Company. The tiny perfume company grew into a giant corporation. Avon bottles began attracting collector interest in the 1960s.

References: Bud Hastin, *Hastin's Avon Collector's Encyclopedia,* 16th ed., Collector Books, 2000.

Periodical: *Avon Times,* P.O. Box 9868, Kansas City, MO 64134.

Collectors' Clubs: National Association of Avon Collectors, Inc., P.O. Box 7006, Kansas City, MO 64113; Shawnee Avon Bottle Collectors Club, 1418 32nd NE, Canton, OH 44714; Sooner Avon Bottle Collectors Club, 6119 S. Hudson, Tulsa, OK 74136; Western World Avon Collectors Club, P.O. Box 23785, Pleasant Hills, CA 94523.

Museums: Hagley Museum and Library, Wilmington, DE; Nicholas Avon Museum, Clifton, VA.

Reproduction Alert.

Hand lotion, coffee pot, 10 oz, full, $4.

Beauty Products

Bottle

After Shave
  Automobile, Electric Charger, two-seater, black, red decal trim, Wild Country 35.00
  Bear, Wild Country, little orig contents.....................................22.00
  Big Mack Truck, Windjammer, orig contents, inner packaging, labels, and box..95.00
  Bull dog pipe, 6" h.......................25.00
  Champion Spark Plugs, Wild Country, pair of bottles, orig contents, inner packaging, labels, and box.........75.00
  Chess Set Rook, empty, 5-1/2" h...................................20.00
  Chevy, 1955 style, Wild Country, orig contents, inner packaging, labels, and box..90.00
  First Volunteer, fire truck, Tail Winds, orig contents, inner packaging, labels, and box......................................90.00
  German Shepard, Wild Country, little orig contents, 6-1/2" h 22.00
  Goodyear Blimp, Everest, some contents leaked, orig box stained 10.00
  Haynes-Apperson, 1902 firetruck, orig contents, inner packaging, labels, and box..85.00
  Irish Setter Dog, 7" l.....................10.00
  Magic Lamp, green, 7-1/2" l 12.00
  Mustang, Avon Spicy After Shave, orig contents, orig labels....................55.00
  Solid Gold Cadillac, Leather, orig contents, inner packaging, labels, and box, 7-1/4" l.............................125.00
  Statue of Liberty, 7-1/2" h............10.00
  Studebaker, Wild Country, orig contents, inner packaging, labels, and box..75.00
  The Capitol, Wild Country, empty...10.00
  Thunderbird, 1965 style, deep blue, 5" l, empty..................................30.00
  Touring Model T, Excalibur, orig contents, inner packaging, labels, and box..75.00

Bubble Bath
 Christmas Tree, gold, 1968-70......6.00
 Schroeder, Snoopy character,
  1970 ....9.50
Cologne
 American Schooner, orig contents and
  box, 7" l, 5" h 25.00
 Bell, milk glass, hobnail, empty ..10.00
 Birds, set of four, Bird of Paradise,
  American Belle, Moonwind, and Dutch
  Maid 60.00
 Bride and Groom, Delicate Daisies,
  1978-99, 5" h.............................. 10.00
 Bust of Abraham Lincoln, orig con-
  tents and box, 7" h 22.50
 Bust of George Washington, orig con-
  tents and box, 6-1/2" h 22.50
 Cruet, red glass, strawberry shaped
  stopper, 5-1/2" h..........................10.00
 Depot Wagon, orig contents and box,
  5" l, 4-1/2" h 25.00
 Dusenberry Automobile, orig contents
  and box, 8" l, 2" h 27.00
 Globular, clear, pressed glass, silver
  colored top, Mist, 4" h 10.00
 Globular, white milk glass, gold cat
  cap, Rapture, 4 oz, 1971..............6.00
 Gone Fishing, fisherman in fishing
  boat, orig contents and box, 8" l, 4" h,
  wear to box top............................20.00
 Maxwell Automobile, Golden Rocket,
  orig contents and box, 7" l, 6" h ..25.00
 Mini-bike, orig contents and box, 6" l,
  5" h 22.50
 Moose, orig contents and box, 5" l,
  9" h, minor scrapes on box 25.00
 Old Time Soda Glass, metal holder,
  Pretty Peach Cologne, some rust,
  straws missing 25.00
 Pistol, 10" l, filled, orig box 22.50
 Race Horse, orig contents and box,
  5-1/2" l, 6" h 25.00
 Stein, Antique Cars, 1979, 8" h ...25.00
 Stein, English Setter on one side, rain-
  bow trout on reverse, 8-1/4" h 18.00
 Stein, Tall Ships, rope shaped handle,
  orig Clint Cologne bottle, orig box,
  1977, 9-1/4" h..............................32.00
 Stein, Train, 1982, 8" h 25.00
 Stein, Western, 1980, 8" h 25.00
 The Atlantic, 4-4-3 locomotive, orig
  contents and box, 8" l, 3-1/2" h ...25.00
 The General, 4-4-0 locomotive, orig
  contents and box, 7" l, 4" h..........25.00
 Thermos, plaid, Sweet Honesty, worn
  orig box..12.00
 Wedding Flower Maiden 5.00
Set
 Gay Look, compact and lipstick, black
  faille cover, red lining, Spark of Fire
  shade, orig box..........................100.00
 Lavender Ensemble, 4 oz bottle of
  Lavender Toilet Water, bar of Lavender
  soap, small foil wrapped packet of
  bath salts, orig box slightly soiled,
  5-3/4" x 7-1/2" x 1-1/2" h 27.50
 Quaintance Bath Bouquet, two bottles
  of Quaintance cream lotion, cologne,
  blue bar of soap, orig white box with
  red rose on lid, orig protector sleeve,
  1955, 7-3/4" w, 2" h 25.00
Tin, talc
 Cotillion, Good Housekeeping guarantee on back, orig plastic lid cracked,
  1940s 8.00

 Lady Skater, Ariane, full, orig plastic
  lid 7.50
Glassware
Cape Cod pattern, red
 Beverage Set, ftd, MIB 17.00
 Bread and Butter Set, orig box....25.00
 Candlesticks, pr............................22.00
 Candy Jar, cov, 6" w, 3" h............18.00
 Champagne Glass.........................20.00
 Creamer and Sugar.......................25.00
 Dessert Plate, 7-3/8" d, set of
  four...35.00
 Dinner Bell, 10-1/2" d 25.00
 Hurricane Lamp, 2-1/2" h, 3" w at
  top...18.00
 Napkin Rings, 1-3/4" d, 1-1/2" h, set of
  four...45.00
 Salad Plate, 7-1/2" d 12.00
 Serving Bowl, #98-363-364, MIB, price
  for pr...22.00
 Tumbler, 5-1/2" h 20.00
 Vase, 8" h.......................................35.00
 Water Pitcher, 48 oz, 7-1/2" h.......40.00
 Wine Goblet, 4-1/2" h....................45.00
Coin pattern, candy jar, cov, Fostoria,
  amber 65.00
Mount Vernon pattern, cobalt blue,
 Fostoria
 Creamer, Mt. Vernon 12.00
 Dresser Tray, wrapped soaps, orig
  box...15.00
 Goblet, George Washington 5.00
 Goblet, Martha Washington...........7.50

Jewelry
Bracelet, bangle, goldtone, ivory colored
  flowers..20.00
Brooch, acorn, gold wash, set with
  pearls..20.00
Choker, small green butterfly on side,
  goldtone, 15" l, sgd......................15.00
Necklace
 Cameo pendant, 1-1/4" pink cameo,
  fine 31" goldtone chain, sgd......20.00
 Chain, goldtone, five graduated sized
  gold balls......................................22.00
 Cross, goldtone, 3" l filigree cross with
  ruby red center stone, sgd..........35.00
 Cross, silvertone, 24" l, 2-3/4" x 2" filigree cross with ruby red center stone,
  four multicolored stones, sgd......30.00
 Flower pendant, 1-1/4" l rect white with
  yellow flower and leaves pendant, 18" l
  fine goldtone twisted chain, sgd .20.00
 Flower tassel, fine silvertone chain,
  sgd 20.00
 Heart, silvertone, three goldtone
  puffed hearts in center, sgd 20.00
 Pendant, 3" l brown plastic and goldtone pendant, 23" l goldtone chain,
  sgd...20.00
 Pendant, 3-1/2" l black pendant, 24"
  silvertone chain, sgd 30.00
 Perfume Pendant, swirl dec, 26" l thick
  goldtone chain, perfume intact, sgd,
  orig box..35.00
 Row of three goldtone chains, sgd
  "Barrera for Avon".........................45.00
Necklace and Matching Earrings
 Beads, black and white flat beads with
  gold spacers, clip-on earrings,
  sgd...25.00
 Beads, coral beads, 22" l, matching
  pierced earrings, sgd 25.00
 Beads, turquoise beads with goldtone
  balls, 22" l, matching pierced earrings,
  sgd...25.00

 Choker, fine chain with goldtone knots,
  matching pierced earrings 25.00
 Open link goldtone chain with pearls
  and gold balls in between links,
  pierced pearl and goldtone earrings,
  sgd 25.00
 Rope chain, fine goldtone, 22" l, oval
  1-3/8" x 1-1/8" flower pendant, pierced
  earrings 22.00
Perfume Brooch
 Cameo, orig box............................35.00
 Goldtone leaf, orig perfume
  insert 27.50
 Owl, orig box 35.00
Pin
 Avon's 50th Anniversary.............40.00
 Cat, goldtone, full bodied cat prowling
  on fish tank, trying to catch dangling
  fish, sgd 15.00
Pin and Earrings, goldtone flower blos-
  som, 2-1/4" w pin with large pearl cen-
  ter, matching pierced earrings, sgd,
  orig box..30.00
Ring
 Goldtone band, green marbleized oval
  stone, filigree around stone and black
  antiquing on ring, perfume
  insert 18.00
 Sterling silver, small synthetic
  stone 30.00

Miscellaneous Collectibles
Barbie
 Spring Blossom Barbie, first edition,
  MIB 40.00
 Strawberry Sorbet Barbie, 1998, shoe
  replaced, orig stand and box 30.00
Candleholder
 Chicken, 5-1/2" h, 4-1/2" w.......... 12.00
 Triangular, plastic liner, initial "P" on
  front as oval sticker, 4-7/8" x
  3-7/8"...10.00
Canister Set, set of four ceramic house
  containers, roofs as lids 55.00
Collector's Plate
 Fifth Anniversary, Giant Oak theme,
  8" d 75.00
 1974, Freedom 35.00
 1976, blue and white, Enoch Wood,
  pr...35.00
Dinner Bell, silverplate, scalloped
  edge 20.00
Egg, crystal, 4-1/2" x 3" 20.00
Figure, Avon Images of Hollywood, Dorothy and Toto, Wizard of Oz........25.00
Soap Dish
 Chicken, 5-1/2" l, 4-1/2" w,
  4-1/2" h...12.00
 Snoopy, 7" l, some wear..............10.00
Statue, A Mother's Love, 1982,
  6" h 15.00

Sales Awards and Ephemera
Albee Award Figurine, Staff President's,
  1989, 9-1/2" h 60.00
Brooch, sterling silver, designed by
  Angela Cummings, stamped "Tiffany
  & Co.," orig box and felt pouch, early
  1980s 100.00
Catalog, salesman's, 169 pgs, spiral
  bound, 1950s, 10-1/2" x 7"..........30.00
Clock, President's Club, hand painted,
  mkd "Designed and hand painted
  exclusively for Avon Rose Circle," orig
  box...85.00

B

Banks, Still

Collecting Hints: The rarity of a still bank has much to do with determining its value. Common banks, such as tin advertising banks, have limited value. The Statue of Liberty cast-iron bank by A. C. Williams sells in the hundreds of dollars. See Long and Pitman's book for a rarity scale for banks.

Banks are collected by maker, material, or subject. Subject is the most prominent, focusing on categories such as animals, food, mailboxes, safes, transportation, and world's fairs. There is a heavy crossover of buyers from other collectible fields.

Banks are graded by condition. Few banks are truly rare. Therefore, only purchase examples in very good to mint condition—those which retain all original paint and decorations.

History: Banks with no mechanical action are known as still banks. The first still banks were made of wood or pottery or from gourds. Redware and stoneware banks, made by America's early potters, are prized possessions of today's collectors.

Still banks reached their golden age with the arrival of the cast-iron bank. Leading manufacturing companies include Arcade Mfg. Co., J. Chein & Co., Hubley, J. & E. Stevens, and A. C. Williams. The banks often were ornately painted to enhance their appeal. During the cast-iron era, banks and other businesses used the still bank as a form of advertising.

The tin lithograph bank, again frequently a tool for advertising, was at its zenith between 1930 to 1955. The tin bank was an important premium, whether a Pabst Blue Ribbon beer can bank or a Gerber's Orange Juice bank. Most tin advertising banks resembled the packaging of the product.

Almost every substance has been used to make a still bank—die-cast white metal, aluminum, brass, plastic, glass, etc. Many of the early glass candy containers also converted to a bank after the candy was eaten. Thousands of varieties of still banks were made, and hundreds of new varieties appear on the market each year.

Reference: Don Cranmer, *Collectors Encyclopedia: Toys-Banks,* L-W Book Sales, 1986, 1994–95 value update; Beverly and Jim Mangus, *Collector's Guide to Banks,* Collector Books, 1998; Earnest and Ida Long and Jane Pitman, *Dictionary of Still Banks,* Long's Americana, 1980; Andy and Susan Moore, *Penny Bank Book,* 3rd ed., Schiffer Publishing, 2000; Charles V. Reymolds, *Collector's Guide to Glass Banks,* Collector Books, 2001; Vickie Stulb, *Modern Banks,* L-W Book Sales, 1997.

Periodicals: *Glass Bank Collector,* P.O. Box 155, Poland, NY 13431; *Heuser's Quarterly Collectible Bank Newsletter,* 508 Clapson Rd, P.O. Box 300, West Winfield, NY 13491.

Collectors' Club: Still Bank Collectors Club of America, 1456 Carson Ct, Homewood, IL 60430.

Museum: Margaret Woodbury Strong Museum, Rochester, NY.

Reproduction Alert.

Advertising

Boston Baking Company, 27 State St., Boston and 44 Front St., Worcester, heavy metal, 3-1/2" d round 50.00
Eagle Pencil Co., tin canister, insert celluloid on top with black, white, and gold eagle symbol, designed to hold $2.50 in dimes, silver flashing finish worn 40.00
Electrolux Refrigerator, cast iron, 4" h, 2" w, 1-1/2" d 50.00
Mister Thrifty, tin litho, mailbox shape, comical face with coin eyes, red, white, and yellow plaid, Ohio Art, 1960s..15.00
Poll Parrot Shoes, cardboard sides, tin top and bottom, 1-3/4" x 1-1/4" x 2" 45.00
Saltines, Indian Warrior................35.00
Tetley Tea, Gaffer, Wade, 6" h 42.00
Western Savings Fund, tin canister, capped by celluloid panels with color design of pale blue and dark blue, Philadelphia sponsor address 65.00

Ceramic

Barnaby Bee 50.00
Eagle, Emigrant Industrial Savings Bank 18.00
Entenmann's Baker, unused........40.00
Garfield, 6" h, 1981 ....50.00
Pig, white body, pink rosebuds, green trim..25.00
Snoopy, with Woodstock, 40th Anniversary, orig hang-tag, unused ...30.00
TP Thompson Products, Indian and Teepee, company logo on teepee, c1950, 5" x 6-1/4" x 6-3/4" 140.00

Metal

Atlas Storage, litho tin 24.00
Atomic, diecut litho tin, Hobbyville Toy Co., 1950s, 10" h...................... 110.00

Bank Building, litho tin, cupola, blue, red roof, c1870 ....70.00
Barrel, litho tin, Happy Days, Chein 30.00
Black Face, cast iron, googlie eyes, 4-1/2" w, 4" h 55.00
Cable Car, Citizens Federal Savings, orig key 27.50
Cat, cast iron, with ball............. 175.00
Clock, cast iron, emb "A Money Saver," Arcade, c1910 ....65.00
Elephant, diecast, ivory enamel finish, 5-1/2" h, 6" l 235.00
Furnace, cast iron, mkd "Fobrux," tin accents, 5-1/2" h 200.00
Lion, cast iron, copper colored paint..55.00
Mercury Eight 1940 Car, greenish-gray, white wood wheels, c1940, 1-3/4" x 5" x 1-3/4"......................65.00
Mr. Zip, litho tin, Ohio Art, mail box shape 70.00
Sheep, 3" h, 5" l 36.00
Slot Machine, diecast, mkd "Madley Mfg. Co." 225.00
Uncle Sam's Cash Register 60.00

Plastic and Vinyl

Barney Rubble, with bowling ball 45.00
Bionic Man................................40.00
Bionic Woman 42.00
Bozo the Clown, figural, 6" h 35.00
Bullwinkle, 1973 ....75.00
Bus, Greyhound Amercruiser, Jimson, Hong Kong, 10" l, MIB................60.00
Esso Tiger....................................35.00
Garfield, Feed the Kitty, Enesco, MIB..45.00
Hitachi Panda............................35.00
Hobo Joe, Dakin..........................45.00
Hockhua Bank............................35.00
Icee Bear 25.00
Ice Fire Jean Boy 35.00
Mr. Brasso 200.00
Nestle Chamyto..........................35.00
Political Senator, smiling reindeer, Taiwan..50.00
Rountrees, adv 30.00
Shmoo, figural, 1948, orig card, cello wrapper 95.00
Snoopy, orange airplane, Flying Ace decals, Determined, ©1977 ....45.00
Speedy Alka Seltzer..................150.00
Street Fighter, Capcom 25.00
Wonder Bread Fresh Guy, orig paper label and closure......................125.00

Penny banks, porcelain bug, ceramic purse, glass globe, and glass Liberty Bell, sold as one lot for $150. Photo courtesy of Joy Luke Fine Art Brokers and Auctioneers.

Porcelain

Hubert the Lion, Lefton, red and gold foil label, mkd "H13384," 7-1/2" h..58.00

Humpty Dumpty 70.00
Pig, 6" h, mkd "Hull Pottery,
#196"... 125.00
Pig, 6" l, 3-3/4" h, hp, pink cheeks,
ears, nose, blue bow around neck,
blue blushed highlights, pink rosebuds and green leaves outlined in
brown, wreath of yellow and pink flowers with green leaves around one ear,
dark red rose mouth, black eyebrows
and lashes, stopper missing....... 35.00
Pink Poodle, Kreiss, gold glitter
dec 55.00

Barbershop and Beauty Collectibles

Collecting Hints: Many barbershop collectibles have a porcelain finish. If chipped or cracked, the porcelain is difficult, if not impossible, to repair.

Buy barber poles and chairs in very good condition or better. A good appearance is a key consideration.

Many old barbershops are still in business. Their back rooms often contain excellent display pieces.

Collectors are also starting to appreciate the products used in early beauty parlors. Some collectors now include home beauty products in their collections. Watch for attractive packaging and endorsements by famous people.

History: The neighborhood barbershop was an important social and cultural institution during the 19th Century and first half of the 20th Century. Men and boys gathered to gossip, exchange business news, and check current fashions. "Girlie" magazines and comic books, usually forbidden at home, were available for browsing, as were adventure magazines and police gazettes.

In the 1960s, the number of barbershops dropped by half in the United States. Unisex shops broke the traditional men-only barrier. In the 1980s, several chains began running barber and hairdressing shops on a regional and national basis.

References: *Barbershop Collectibles*, L-W Book Sales, 1996; Lester Dequanine, *Razor Blade Banks: An Illustrated History and Price Guide*, published by author (39 W. Main St., Box 14, Meriden, CT 06451-4110); John Odell, *Digger Odell's Official Antique Bottle and Glass Collector Magazine Price Guide Series*, Vol. 1, published by author (1910 Shawhan Rd, Morrow, OH 45152), 1995.

Collectors' Clubs: National Shaving Mug Collectors' Association, 320 S. Glenwood St., Allentown, PA 18104;

Safety Razor Collectors' Guild, P.O. Box 885, Crescent City, CA 95531.

Museum: National Saving and Barbershop Museum, Meriden, CT.

Advertising Trade Card, S. Kain for the Best Harrow, "Strict Attention to business" as he cuts ear off patron, adv on back, 2-3/4" x 4-1/2"....................... 30.00
Antiseptic Container, 8" h, plated brass.. 48.00
Barber Bottle
  Amethyst Glass, enameled dec, 7-1/2" h 140.00
  Crackle Glass, hand blown, hobnail dec, pontil scar 50.00
  Green Glass, enameled white flowers with orange centers, 9" l 250.00
  Milk Glass, decorated, stopper repaired 80.00
  Overshot, orig screw on top, polished pontil, 7-1/4" h 150.00
Barber Pole, 22" d, 35" h, wood, red, white and blue worn paint.................. 145.00
Barber Chair, green porcelain, all orig condition, pump lift does not work 2,500.00
Blade Bank, figural
  Shaving Brush, ceramic, 6" h 25.00
  Treasure Chest, Ever Ready adv, litho tin 25.00

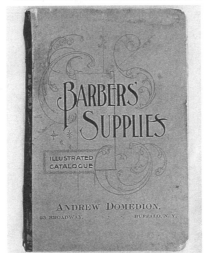

Catalog, Andrew Domedion, Buffalo, NY, illus, 140 pgs, $60.

Catalog
Crown Hair Goods Co., New York, NY, 1920s, 48 pgs, 8" x 10-3/4", hair pieces, wigs, beauty parlor furniture 82.00
Theo. A. Kochs, Co., Chicago, IL, 1932, 16 pgs of professional chairs for beauty parlors, 8-1/2" x 11".......... 65.00
Clippers, Andis, c1940 .... 25.00
Comb Holder, Barbacide................. 30.00
Counter Mat, 9" x 8", Wardonia Razor Blades, rubber............................... 20.00
Display Case, West Hair Nets, 15" h, 6" w, 5" d, tiered display case, tin litho picture of flapper lady in touring car inside lid 60.00
Facial Kit, Revlon, Moondrops at Home, orig packaging............................ 45.00

Flicker Pin, Clairol Hair Coloring, image changes between fleshtone face and hair image with slogan, "Will She Or Won't She," to full-color image of blond, inscribed, "Clairol Says She Will," early 1960s 40.00
License, framed, c1960 .... 10.00
  Liquor Bottle, Gay Fad Rye, milk glass, painted singing barbershop quartet dec, sgd "Gay Fad," clear glass stopper 24.00
Magazine Tear Sheet, Joe DiMaggio homers for Blue Brylcreem, from Men's Hairstylist and Barber's Journal, 1968.. 4.00
Mirror, 16" h, 6" d beveled round mirror, silver plated, brush holder and wooden handle "Rubberset" brush, c1890, floral and geometric engraving on mirror, mkd "Wallace Bros. Silver Co.," some wear to plating . 125.00
Neck Duster, cherry handle 30.00
Photo, 5" x 7" sepia toned photo of shop interior, two customers, two male barbers, female attendant, young Black man, c1920................................. 18.00
Razor, Burham Razor, 1-1/2" w, 3-3/4" l, 3/4" h, tin litho safety razor tin, orig razor, three blades in orig envelope, complete, unused, red ground, black lettering 160.00
Razor Tin
  Gem Cutlery Co., 5-3/8" h, 1-3/8" d, image of gentleman shaving on front, adv on back................................ 300.00
  Yankee Blades, 1-1/4" w, 2-1/4" l, tin litho, eagles and center image of man shaving, red ground................. 200.00
Shaving Brush, Every Ready, blue box, black celluloid handle, dark bristles, MIB.. 15.00
Shaving Mug
  Occupational, butcher, steer head, cleaver, saw, sharpener, and knife, name on other side, gold trim, mkd "K. T. K.," 3-3/4" h 250.00
  Tavern scene lithophane scene in bottom, bird and butterfly transfer dec, gold accents, 3-5/8" h, 3-1/2" d 125.00
Shaving Mug Rack, 38" h, pine, holds 24 mugs.. 200.00
Sign
  Barber, Bastian Bros., NY Allied Printing, Rochester, 15" x 6" 155.00
  Klondike Head Rub, 11" x 8-3/8", emb, blue letters, cardboard................ 22.00
Strop, 9" x 2-1/2" x 2", leather, two-sided, mkd "Horse Hair Burl Finish" 20.00
Tin
  Sweet Georgia Brown Hair Dressing Pomade, Valmore Products Co., 1-1/8" d, black, white, and red, stylish male and female young blacks, instructions for use on back, c1930 .... 35.00
  Watkins Medical Co., Winona, MN, Watkins Tooth Powder, 5-1/2" h x 2-1/2" w, tin litho, cameo of woman on both sides 120.00
Vending Machine, Gillette Razor Blades, 17" h.. 125.00

Barbie

Collecting Hints: Never forget that a large quantity of Barbie dolls and related material has been manufactured. Because of this easy availability, only objects in excellent to mint condition with original packaging (also in very good or better condition) have significant value. If items show signs of heavy use, their value is probably minimal.

Collectors prefer items from the first decade of production. Learn how to distinguish a Barbie #1 doll from its successors. The Barbie market is one of subtleties.

Recently collectors have shifted their focus from the dolls themselves to the accessories. There have been rapid price increases in early clothing and accessories, with some of the prices bordering on speculation.

History: In 1945, Harold Matson (MATT) and Ruth and Elliott (EL) Handler founded Mattel. Initially, the company made picture frames but became involved in the toy market when Elliott Handler began to make doll furniture from scrap material. When Harold Matson left the firm, Elliott Handler became chief designer and Ruth Handler principal marketer. In 1955, Mattel advertised its products on "The Mickey Mouse Club," and the company prospered.

In 1958, Mattel patented a fashion doll. The doll was named "Barbie" and reached the toy shelves in 1959. By 1960, Barbie's popularity was assured.

Development of a boyfriend for Barbie, named Ken after the Handlers' son, began in 1960. Over the years, many other dolls were added. Clothing, vehicles, room settings, and other accessories became an integral part of the line.

From September 1961 through July 1972, Mattel published a Barbie magazine. At its peak, the Barbie Fan Club was second only to the Girl Scouts as the largest girls' organization in the United States.

Barbie is now a billion-dollar baby, the first toy in history to reach this prestigious mark—that's a billion dollars per year, just in case you're wondering.

References: J. Michael Augustyniak, *Collector's Encyclopedia of Barbie Doll Exclusives and More,* 2nd ed., Collector Books, 2000; Stefanie Deutsch, *Barbie, the First 30 Years,* Collector Books, 2001; Sibyl DeWein and Joan Ashabraner, *Collector's Encyclopedia of Barbie Dolls and Collectibles,* Collector Books, 2000 values updated; Connie Craig Kaplan, *Collector's Guide to Barbie Doll Vinyl Cases,* Collector Books, 1999; Patricia Long, *Barbie's Closet, Price Guide for Barbie & Friends Fashions and Accessories,* 1959-1973, Krause Publications, 1999; Lorraine

Mieszala, *Collector's Guide to Barbie Doll Paper Dolls,* Collector Books, 2000; Kitturah B. Westenhouser, *The Story of Barbie,* 2nd ed., Collector Books, 2000.

Periodicals: *Barbie Bazaar,* 5617 6th Ave., Kenosha, WI 53140; *Barbie Fashions,* 387 Park Ave. So, New York, NY 10016; *Barbie Talks Some More,* 19 Jamestown Dr., Cincinnati, OH 45241; *Collector's Corner,* 519 Fitzooth Dr., Miamisburg, OH 45342; *Miller's Price Guide & Collectors' Almanac,* West One Summer #1, Spokane, WA 99204.

Accessories

Clothing Case, Ken, Rally Day, vinyl case, by Ponytail, 1962 Mattel copyright, mustard yellow, blue, black, and yellow, wear 10.00
Country Kitchen, #7404, 1974, NRFB 105.00
Display Background, for Gone with the Wind Barbie, sold through Spiegel, 1994, folds 35.00
Dog N' Duds outfit, #1613, red velvet dog coat, gold braid trim, 1964 .. 10.00
Flasher Disk, "I Love Barbie," full-color portrait, blue ground, slogan in yellow, c1970, 2" d 3.00
Ring, brass base, thin expansion band, top with diecut design with clear acrylic cover over colorful insert, one butterfly, one bouquet of flowers, one pink heart with center full color Barbie portrait, F.A.O. Schwarz, 1997, price for set of three 12.00
Swimming Pool and Deck, inflatable pool, decking, ladder, slide, etc .. 20.00
Thermos Bottle, 7" h, black, tan cup, wear 15.00
Wardrobe Booklet, Barbie, Ken, and Midge, blue cover, 32 pgs, Mattel catalog #0850-1170, 1962, 3" x 4" 10.00
Wristwatch, Fossil, 35th Anniversary, light pink wristband, Ponytail head, powder puff, pompon shoe, and sunglasses on dial, light pink cardboard decoupage hatbox with purple cord fastener, matching decoupage head scarf, certificate of authenticity, MIB 50.00

Clothing

After Five, #934, black dress with shawl collar, white hat with black velvet ribbon band, one black open toe shoe, played-with condition 45.00
Ballerina, #989, paper tiara missing, 1961-65 .... 150.00
Belle Dress, 1962-63, pink 80.00
Dreamy Pink, #1857, 1968, slippers missing 40.00
Dress Coat, #1906, Skipper, red velvet jacket, button accents, matching hat, purse, one white glove, white flat shoes, Skipper booklet 20.00
Fancy Dress, #1858, knit dress with hot pink top, lace trim, green skirt, matching green jacket with hot pink trim, flower print sheer stockings, pink molded box shoes 100.00
Faux Fur, skirt and jacket 80.00
Floating Gardens, #16 .... 350.00
Floral Petticoat, #921, 1959-63, bra, comb, and brush missing 50.00

Friday Night Date, #979, 1960-63, orig package, some edge damage 125.00
Garden Party, #931 .... 155.00
Icebreaker, #942, 1962-64 .... 140.00
Let's Dance, #978, 1960-62, pearl on chain missing 120.00
Orange Blossom, bride's maid dress, #987, 1961-64 .... 135.00
Pajama Fun 8.00
Raincoat, #949, 1963 .... 155.00
Singing the Shower, #988, 1961-62 .... 135.00
Skirt, sheath, orange cotton, telephone, 1962, telephone cord missing 20.00
Sleep-Ins, #1463, pink nylon nightgown, matching pink robe with floral pattern, fuzzy pink slippers, tag slightly frayed 20.00
Sorority Meeting, #937, brown sheath dress, brown felt hat with braid trim, brown open toed shoes, played-with condition 10.00
Sweater Girl, #976, 1959-62 ..... 140.00
Sweet Dreams, #973, yellow, 1959-63, shoes, apple, clock, and diary missing 50.00
Tennis Anyone, #941, white tennis dress, white sweater with red trim, white cotton socks, white tennis shoes, two white tennis balls, plastic tennis racquet, blue glasses, clothing slightly aged colored, one side of tennis racquet melted 35.00
Tuxedo, Ken, jacket and solid black trousers, 1974 .... 8.00
Winter Holiday, 1959-63, black tights pants, red plastic gloves, multicolored zipper hooded sweater top, red and white lined plastic jacket, orig tags inside 40.00

Barbie, bubblecut, brunette, red nylon swimsuit, black wire stand, white cover Barbie, Ken, Midge booklet, red open toe shoes in cellophane bag, original box, $215. Photo courtesy of McMasters Doll Auctions.

Doll, Barbie

American Girl Barbie, ash brown hair, repainted lips, orig one-pc swimsuit, gold wire stand, Exclusive Fashion by Mattel Book, aqua open toe shoes in cellophane bag, slightly age discolored, wear to orig box 975.00

Ballroom Beauties, Midnight Waltz, 2nd in series, black and white gown, 1996, NRFB 95.00

Bloomingdales, Calvin Klein Jeans Barbie, 1996 .... 60.00

Bob Mackie Design, MIB, doll has been removed from orig packaging, some slight damage to box

Empress Bride Barbie, #4247, 1992 .... 350.00

Goddess of the Sun, #14105, 1996 .... 125.00

Masquerade Ball Barbie, #10803, 1993 .... 200.00

Neptune Fantasy Barbie, #4247, 1992 .... 350.00

Platinum Barbie, #2703, 1991 .... 250.00

Queen of Hearts, #12046, 1994 .... 155.00

Starlight Splendor, #2704, 1991 .... 325.00

Bubblecut Barbie

Brunette, red nylon swimsuit, black wire stand, cardboard box insert, white cover Barbie, Ken, Midge booklet, red open toe shoes in cellophane bag, age discolored box worn around edges 215.00

Brunette, #1683 Sunflower dress, played-with condition 140.00

White ginger hair, black and white striped knit swimsuit, black wire stand, face slightly darker than body, wear to orig box 375.00

Coca-Cola Series

After the Walk Barbie, second in series, 1997, NRFB, box slightly scuffed 50.00

Soda Fountain Sweetheart Barbie, # 15762 .... 250.00

Color Magic Barbie, yellow hair in orig set, blue barrette and nylon head band, one-piece swimsuit with ribbon belt, wrist tag, Color Magic Changer packets A and B, blue tulle, brush with sponge, three metal hair barrettes, four hair ribbons, gold metal stand, orig box age discolored, box liner creased and torn where stand prongs insert, accessories loose in package 1,625.00

Couture Collection Edition, Portrait in Taffeta, 1996, NRFB, orig cardboard shipping box 55.00

FAO Schwarz Special Limited Edition, NRFB

Circus Star, # 13257 .... 140.00

Jeweled Splendor, 1995, NRFB, orig cardboard shipping box 100.00

Night Sensation, # 2921 .... 195.00

Rockettes, # 2017 .... 375.00

Silver Screen, # 11652 .... 265.00

Statue of Liberty, American Beauties series, 1995, NRFB, small crease on box flap 45.00

Great Eras Collection, NRFB

Egyptian Queen, #11397 .... 160.00

Elizabethian Queen, #12792, 1994 .... 130.00

Flapper Barbie, #4063 .... 240.00

Medieval Lady, #12791, 1994 .... 120.00

Southern Belle, #11478, 1993 .... 95.00

Happy Holidays

1988, red net dress with velvet bodice, shoes and earrings missing 350.00

1989, dusty box 150.00

1990, white, fuchsia gown, NRFB 225.00

1991, white, green velvet dress, NRFB 200.00

1992, white, silver gown, NRFB 150.00

1993, white, red and gold gown, NRFB 125.00

1994, European, red and gold gown, orig box 120.00

1994, white, gold gown, NRFB 125.00

1997, MIB 45.00

Harley

Barbie #1, #2, two different Buddy L Harley trucks, orig package 800.00

Barbie #3, 1999, NRFB 95.00

International Series, NRFB, slight age discoloration to box

Eskimo Barbie, 1981 .... 50.00

Icelandic, 1986 .... 65.00

India Barbie, 1981 .... 55.00

Korean Barbie, 1987 .... 50.00

Royal Barbie, 1979 .... 125.00

Russian Barbie, 1988 .... 40.00

Scottish Barbie, 1980 .... 75.00

Swedish Barbie 55.00

Swiss Barbie 50.00

Limited Edition Porcelain Collection, orig certificate, stand, accessories, NRFB, cardboard shipping box

Benefit Performance, #5475, 1987 .... 120.00

Enchanted Evening, #5415, 1986 .... 105.00

Gay Parisienne, #9973, 1991 .... 135.00

Golden Anniversary, #14479, 1995 .... 100.00

Holiday Jewel, #14311, 1995 .... 65.00

Solo in the Spotlight, #7615, 1989 .... 75.00

Macys, Nicole Miller, limited edition, 1996, NRFB 95.00

Philippine Centennial, pin, NRFB

#9980, green and white heart dress, side ponytail 25.00

#9982, green floral dress, long braid 25.00

Ponytail Barbie

#4, brunette hair, orig top knot, gold hoop earrings, Solo in Spotlight black sequin dress with tulle and flower accents, black nylon gloves,

#1 light navy blue open toe shoes with holes, four strand bead choker, pink scarf, microphone on stand, pink cover Barbie booklet in cellophane bag, black pedestal stand mkd "T.M.," doll near mint, some flaws, wear to orig box 4,100.00

#5, blond hair, orig ponytail, black and white striped swimsuit, pearl earrings in box, black wire stand, white rimmed glasses with blue lenses, black open toe shoes, NMIB 450.00

#5, titian hair in orig set, black and white striped swimsuit, some loose hair strands, faded green discoloration at ears, minor skin blemishes, no box 165.00

#6, brunette hair in orig set, red nylon swimsuit, pearl earrings, green discoloration on both ears, faded dark dot on left leg, no box 105.00

#6, brunette hair, orig topknot, red nylon swimsuit, pearl earrings, gold wire stand, Exclusive Fashions Book 2, near mint, name written on lower front of orig box 370.00

Service Merchandise, Definitely Diamonds, first in scries, 1998, NRFB, box slightly scuffed 40.00

Spiegel Limited Edition, Winner's Circle Barbie, 1996, NRFB 35.00

Swirled Ponytail Barbie, brunette hair in orig set with yellow ribbons, red nylon swimsuit, wrist tag, cardboard box inserts, gold wire stand, Exclusive Fashions Book 1, face and arms slightly darker than rest of body, name written on box flap 410.00

35th Anniversary, # 11591, 1994 reproduction of orig 1959 Barbie 285.00

Talking Busy Barbie, blond, red shirt, matching headband, blue satin jumper, green belt and knee-hi boots, wrist tag, clear plastic stand, accessories, NRFB, non-working 325.00

Toyland Barbie, Canadian, hula hoop, teddy bear, shopping bag, clothes, 1997, NRFB 50.00

Toys R Us, 1995, Sapphire Dream, NRFB 125.00

Twist 'n' Turn Barbie, ash blond, ribbon tied, two piece swimsuit with net cover-up, wrist tag, clear plastic stand, booklet, MIB, box age discolored, paper label on front of box discolored 550.00

Wear and Share, Rapunzel, pink and gold outfit, 36" h, played with 150.00

Winter Fantasy, # 5946, NRFB .. 240.00

Winter Princess, Evergreen, 1994, NRFB 100.00

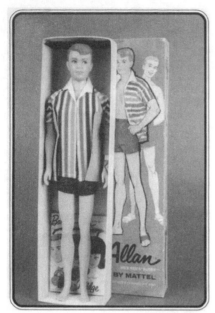

Allan, painted red hair, orig jacket, blue swim trunks, wrist tag, white cover booklet, cork sandals in cellophane bag, original box, $95. Photo courtesy of McMasters Doll Auctions.

Doll, Barbie's Friends and Family

Allan, painted red hair, orig jacket, blue swim trunks, wrist tag, white cover booklet, cork sandals in cellophane bag, black wire stand, cardboard box insert, orig box discolored, age discoloration to clothes........95.00

Carla, black hair, bendable legs and arms, orange dress with white trim, foreign issue, NMIB 70.00

Hair Happenin's Francie, blond, wearing T'n'T Francie swimsuit, no box 100.00

Ken, red swim trunks, cork sandals
  Brunette flocked hair, black wire stand, NMIB.................................70.00
  Painted blond hair, several dark spots of paint along hairline, small paint rubs, played-with condition30.00

Live Action Ken, painted brown hair, print shirt, brown suede vest, gold satin pants, brown shoes, no box 80.00

Living Fluff, blond hair, bendable arms and legs, dress with striped knit top and orange vinyl skirt, yellow skateboard, stand, end of wrist tag creased, box damaged and age discolored 95.00

Living Skipper, Trade-In, blond hair in orig set, bendable arms and legs, green, blue, and hot pink nylon swimsuit, orig box with Living Barbie and Living Skipper booklets in cellophane bag, NMIB 50.00

Malibu Christie, Sun Set, black hair, red nylon swimsuit, white terry cloth towel, NRFB 190.00

Malibu Skipper, Sun Set, blond hair, two pc orange nylon swimsuit, NRFB...85.00

Midge, titian hair, striped knit one piece swimsuit, gold wire stand, Exclusive Fashions booklet, aqua open-toe shoes in cellophane bag, original box, $375. Photo courtesy of McMasters Doll Auctions.

Midge
Blond, #1694 Pink Moonbeams outfit, no box, small rubs on doll 85.00

Titian hair, striped knit one pc swimsuit, gold wire stand, Exclusive Fashions booklet, aqua open toe shoes in cellophane bag, orig box, one arm slightly darker than body, ends of box lining creased and torn at one side where stand protrudes 375.00

Nan 'n' Frank, Pretty Pairs, black doll with black hair, bendable arms and legs, flannel floral print pajamas, matching pink flannel cap, slippers, wrist tag, holding black doll with black hair, pink flannel body, lace and ribbon accents, plastic hands, MOC.. 195.00

Pose n' Play Skipper, blond hair in orig set, bendable arms and legs, one pc blue/white outfit, NM, no box 55.00

Quick Curl Miss America, blond, silver and white gown, attached white Miss America ribbon, red cape with fur trim, plastic scepter, near mint, no box 75.00

Ricky, painted red hair, blue swim trunks, black wire stand, no box, age discoloration to clothes................45.00

Skooter, brunette, replaced red velvet ribbon, orig two pc red and white swimsuit, orig box, wear to doll and box...90.00

Todd, brown hair, bendable arms and legs, red shirt, blue shorts, foreign issue, NMIB..................................40.00

Tutti, blond hair, pink ribbons, yellow dress with white lace trim, orig box slightly discolored 50.00

Twiggy, blond, blue, green, and yellow knit striped dress, yellow boots, arms lightly colored with faint stains.... 95.00

Twist 'n' Turn Julia, dark hair, nurse's outfit, NRFB, box discolored..... 150.00

Twist 'n' Turn Stacey, light blond hair, pink and blue floral nylon swimsuit, clear plastic stand, played-with condition 110.00

Ornament, Hallmark
  1st in series, 1993, box ripped ... 60.00
  2nd in series, gold and white gown, white faux fur, MIB 45.00
  3rd in series, Yuletide Romance, green velvet and satin gown, 1996....... 50.00

Trading Card, deluxe first edition set, never removed from orig box, 300 cards plus 20 fashion portfolio, 1990... 40.00

Baseball Cards

Collecting Hints: Condition is a key factor—collectors should strive to obtain only cards in excellent to mint condition.

Concentrate on the superstars; these cards are most likely to increase in value. Buy full sets of modern cards. In this way, you have the superstars of tomorrow on hand. When a player becomes a member of the Baseball Hall of Fame, the value of his cards and other memorabilia will increase significantly.

The price of cards fluctuates rapidly, often changing on a weekly basis. Spend time studying the market before investing heavily.

Reproduced cards and sets have become a fact of life. Novice collectors should not buy cards until they can tell the difference between the originals and reproductions.

The latest, highly speculative trend is collecting rookie cards, i.e., those from a player's first year.

History: Baseball cards were first printed in the late 19th century. By 1900, the most common cards, known as "T" cards, were those made by tobacco companies such as American Tobacco Co. The majority of the tobacco-related cards were produced between 1909 and 1915. During the 1920s American Caramel, National Caramel, and York Caramel candy companies issued cards identified in lists as "E" cards.

During the 1930s, Goudey Gum Co. of Boston (from 1933 to 1941) and Gum Inc. (in 1939) were prime producers of baseball cards. Following World War II, Bowman Gum of Philadelphia (B.G.H.L.I.), the successor to Gum, Inc., lead the way. Topps, Inc., (T.C.G.) of Brooklyn, New York, followed. Topps bought Bowman in 1956 and enjoyed almost a monopoly in card production until 1981 when Fleer of Philadelphia and Donruss of Memphis became competitive. All three companies now produce annual sets numbering 600 cards or more.

References: Robert Forbes and Terence Mitchell, *American Tobacco Cards*, Krause Publications, 2000; Jeff Kurowski and Tony Prudom, *Sports Collectors Digest Pre-War Baseball Card Price Guide*, Krause Publications, 1993; Mark Larson (ed.), *Baseball Cards Questions & Answers*, Krause Publications, 1992; ——, *Sports Collectors Digest Minor League Baseball Card Price Guide*, Krause Publications, 1993; ——, *Sports Collectors Digest: The Sports Card Explosion*, Krause Publications, 1993; Bob Lemke (ed.), *Sportscard Counterfeit Detector*, 3rd ed., Krause Publications, 1994; ——, *2001 Standard Catalog of Baseball Cards*, 10th ed., Krause Publications, 2001; *101 Sports Card Investments*, Krause Publications, 1993; ——, *Premium Insert Sports Cards*, Krause Publications, 1995; ——, *2001 Standard Catalog of Baseball Cards*, 10th ed., Krause Publications, 2000; Alan Rosen *True Mint*, Krause Publications, 1994; *Standard Catalog of Baseball Cards*, 6th ed., Krause Publications, 1996; Sports Collectors Digest *Baseball's Top 500 Card Checklist & Price Guide*, Sports Collectors Digest, Krause Publications, 1999; ——, *2000 Sports Collectors Almanac*, Krause Publications, 2000; ——, *2001 Baseball Card Price Guide*, 18th ed., Krause Publications, 2001.

Periodicals: The following appear on a monthly or semi-monthly basis: *Baseball Update,* 220 Sunrise Hwy, Ste 284, Rockville Centre, NY 11570; *Beckett Baseball Card Monthly*, 4887 Alpha Rd, Ste 200, Dallas, TX 75244; *Beckett Focus on Future Stars*, 4887 Alpha Rd, Ste 200, Dallas, TX 75244; *Card Trade*, 700 E. State St., Iola, WI 54990; *Diamond Angle*, P.O. Box 409, Kaunakakai, HI 96748; *Old Judge*, P.O. Box 137, Centerbeach, NY 11720; *Sports Cards*, 700 E. State St., Iola, WI 54990; *Sports Collectors Digest*, 700 E. State St., Iola, WI 54990; *Your Season Ticket*, 106 Liberty Rd, Woodsburg, MD 21790.

Collectors' Clubs: There are many local card collecting clubs throughout the United States. However, there is no national organization at the present time.

Reproduction Alert: The 1952 Topps set, except for five cards, was reproduced in 1983 and clearly marked by Topps. In addition, a number of cards have been illegally reprinted including the following Topps cards:

1963 Peter Rose, rookie card, #537
1971 Pete Rose, #100

1971 Steve Garvey, #341
1972 Pete Rose, #559
1972 Steve Garvey, #686
1972 Rod Carew, #695
1973 Willie Mays, #100
1973 Hank Aaron, #305
1973 Mike Schmidt, rookie card, #615
Notes: The prices below are for cards in excellent condition. The number of cards in each set is indicated in parentheses.

Bowman Era

1948 Bowman, black and white
Complete Set (48) 1,500.00
Common Player (1-36) 10.00
Common Player (37-48) 12.50
6 Y Berra 165.00
36 S Musial 340.00
1949 Bowman
Complete Set (240) 7,000.00
Common Player (1-36) 7.50
Common Player (37-73) 8.50
Common Player (74-144) 6.50
Common Player (145-240) 35.00
85 J Mize 125.00
100 Gil Hodges 30.00
157 Walt Masterson 22.00
1950 Bowman
Complete Set (252) 2,850.00
Common Player (1-72) 12.00
Common Player (72-252) 8.00
18 E Robinson 10.00
178 Fitzgerald 125.00
219 Bauer 275.00
248 Sam Jethroe 6.50
1951 Bowman, color
Complete Set (324) 8,350.00
Common Player (1-252) 9.50
Common Player (253-324) 6.50
32 Elliott 60.00
134 W Spahn 80.00
143 T Kluszewski 36.00
305 W Mays 1,250.00
1952 Bowman, color
Complete Set (252) 900.00
Common Player (1-216) 2.50
Common Player (217-252) 4.00
4 R Roberts 24.00
8 Pee Wee Reese 80.00
14 C Chambers............................5.00
22 W Ramsdell.............................8.00
44 R Campanella 55.00
53 R Ashburn 36.00
100 S Sisty 8.00
158 B Harris 175.00
159 D Leonard 12.00
200 K Silvestri 12.00
1953 Bowman, color
Complete Set (160) 4,500.00
Common Player (1-96) 15.50
Common Player (97-112) 16.50
Common Player (113-128) 26.00
Common Player (129-160) 18.00
40 L Doby...................................24.00
57 L Boudreau 24.00
63 McDougald 395.00
125 F Hatfield...........................35.00
153 W Ford............................... 185.00
1954 Bowman
Complete Set (224) 850.00
Common Player (1-128) 4.00
Common Player (129-224) 4.50

1 P Rizzuto 60.00
50 G Kell 16.00
73 Mueller 25.00
74 J Gilliam 20.00
135 Pesky 55.00
1955 Bowman, color
Complete Set (320) 2,900.00
Common Player (1-96) 6.50
Common Player (97-224) 7.50
Common Player (225-320) 14.00
10 Rizzuto 13.00
29 Schoendienst 18.00
102 Thomson 65.00
156 Hughes 6.00
201 Reynolds 7.50
252 Smalley 50.00
1991 Bowman, factory set 65.00
1992 Bowman, complete set.........320.00
1993 Bowman, complete set.........65.00
1994 Bowman, complete set 100.00
1995 Bowman, complete set.........300.00
1996 Bowman, complete set.........120.00
1997 Bowman, complete I set.........75.00
1997 Bowman, complete II set........60.00
1998 Bowman, complete I and II set,
    BB 115.00

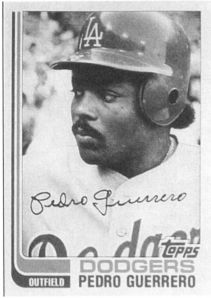

Topps, Pedro Guerrero, #247, 1982, $.25.

Topps Era

1951 Topps, blue backs
Complete Set (52) 725.00
Common Player (1-52) 12.00
3 R Ashburn 22.00
37 B Doerr 20.00
50 J Mize 25.00
1951 Topps, red backs
Complete Set (52) 350.00
Common Player (1-52) 3.10
1 Y Berra................................... 27.50
31 G Hodges 10.00
38 D Snider................................ 20.00
1952 Topps
Complete Set (407) 4,850.00
Common Player (1-80) 14.00
Common Player (81-252)............. 6.50
Common Player (253-310) 12.00

Common Player (311-407)..........25.00
33 W Spahn 20.00
48 J Page, error 45.00
88 B Feller.................................20.00
400 B Dickey 225.00
1953 Topps
Archives Set..............................60.00
Complete Set (280) 5,000.00
Common Player (1-165)............11.50
Common Player (166-220)..........7.50
Common Player (221-280).........42.50
1 J Robinson...........................175.00
10 S Burgess 16.00
62 M Irvin 8.00
100 B Miller...............................20.00
149 D DiMaggio 31.00
1954 Topps
Archives Set..............................85.00
Complete Set (250) 7,900.00
Common Player (1-50)................7.00
Common Player (51-75)..............8.00
Common Player (76-250).............5.00
3 Irvin......................................10.00
30 Matthews..............................30.00
32 Snider.................................925.00
63 Pesky..................................10.00
66 Lepcio.................................37.50
94 Banks.................................175.00
177 Milliken................................4.00
222 Wilson................................17.00
248 Smith.................................10.00
1955 Topps
Complete Set (210) 7,300.00
Common Player (1-160)..............6.00
Common Player (161-210)...........7.50
6 Hack.......................................6.50
31 Spahn..................................30.00
90 Spooner 7.50
120 Kluszewski..........................20.00
177 Robertson-High 145.00
182 H Robinson.........................22.00
1956 Topps
Complete Set (340) 3,000.00
Common Player (1-180)..............2.50
Common Player (181-260)...........3.50
20 Kaline.................................875.00
33 R Clemente.........................265.00
180 R Roberts...........................15.00
181 Martin...............................695.00
226 Giants Team........................11.00
1957 Topps
Complete Set (407) 3,500.00
Common Player (1-88)................3.50
Common Player (89-176).............3.00
Common Player (177-264)...........6.00
Common Player (265-352)...........8.50
Common Player (353-407)...........2.50
18 D Drysdale..........................110.00
20 H Aaron................................85.00
25 Ford...................................275.00
59 D Williams............................75.00
120 B Lemon.............................10.00
154 R Schoendienst.....................3.00
366 Lehman...............................50.00
1958 Topps
Complete Set (495) 2,600.00
Common Player (1-110)..............3.50
Common Player (111-440)...........3.00
Common Player (441-495)...........2.00
52 Clemente............................165.00
58 Groat...................................40.00
70 Kaline..................................50.00
310 Banks.................................50.00

440 Matthews............................10.00
485 Williams..............................50.00
1959 Topps
Complete Set (572) 4,150.00
Common Player (1-10) 3.50
Common Player (11-198) 2.75
Common Player (199-506)...........2.50
Common Player (507-572)...........7.50
8 Phillies Team............................8.00
102 F Alou, RC..........................11.00
315 Adcock...............................55.00
317 Ashburn/Mays......................24.00
462 Colavito's Catch...................75.00
467 H Aaron HR...........................7.00
478 Clemente...........................365.00
480 Schoendienst.......................45.00
543 Corsair Trio, Clemente, SGC 92-
8.5 ....595.00
1960 Topps
Complete Set (572)............... 3,350.00
Common Player (1-506) 2.50
Common Player (507-572)...........2.00
73 Gibson.................................17.00
132 F Howard.............................70.00
136 Kaat...................................20.00
302 Phillies Team.........................4.00
464 Braves Coaches.....................6.00
584 Mincher 8.00
1961 Topps
Complete Set (589) 4,650.00
Common Player (1-522) 1.00
Common Player (523-589)...........7.00
2 R Maris..................................25.00
35 R Santo RC...........................16.00
42 AL Batting Leaders.................50.00
47 NL Pitching Leaders...............50.00
98 Checklist................................7.50
360 Minoso...............................55.00
388 Clemente...........................225.00
405 Gehrig Benched.................100.00
570 Fox...................................125.00
1962 Topps
Complete Set (598)............... 4,600.00
Common Player (1-370) 3.50
Common Player (371-446)...........5.00
Common Player (447-522)...........7.50
Common Player (553-598).........20.00
5 S Koufax..............................105.00
50 Musial, SGC 88-8................195.00
73 N Fox....................................3.50
384 KS Team.............................30.00
470 Kaline.................................75.00
490 C Boyer..............................40.00
530 B Gibson.............................85.00
548 Del Greco...........................45.00
1963 Topps
Complete Set (576)............... 4,200.00
Common Player (1-196) 2.50
Common Player (197-446)...........2.00
Common Player (447-506)...........2.00
Common Player (507-576)...........1.50
10 Leaders.................................4.00
79 Checklist................................4.00
128 Alou....................................6.00
138 Pride of NL..........................35.00
439 Zimmer...............................19.00
492 Wickersham.........................85.00
542 St Louis Team.....................135.00
553 Stargell, SGC 88-8.............205.00
1964 Topps
Complete Set (587)............... 2,550.00
Common Player (1-370) 50
Common Player (371-522) 75

Common Player (523-587)...........1.25
5 Koufax/Drysdale.......................5.00
125 P Rose................................55.00
243 H Aaron 35.00
423 Aaron/Mays, SGC
92-8.5...................................595.00
573 Duffalo, SGC 92-8.5 ....35.00
579 Red Sox Team, SGC
96-9....................................195.00
580 Podres SGD 92-8.5.............55.00
1965 Topps
Complete Set (598) 3,350.00
Common Player (1-506) 1.00
Common Player (507-598)...........1.50
10 NL Pitching Leaders 28.00
27 Mets Team.............................7.00
30 Bouton.................................50.00
87 Cardinals Team.......................8.00
232 Lopez..................................5.00
159 Duffalo...............................24.00
1966 Topps
Complete Set (598)...............3,500.00
Common Player (1-506)..............1.00
Common Player (507-598)...........3.50
70 Yastrzemski..........................20.00
194 Senators Team......................6.00
221 Leaders...............................5.00
420 Marichal..............................11.00
428 Alomar................................65.00
551 Purkey................................30.00
590 Skowron..............................95.00
1967 Topps
Complete Set (609) 4,450.00
Common Player (1-533)..................75
Common Player (534-609).......... 2.00
103 Mantle Checklist #2, SGS
96-9....................................295.00
215 Banks, SGC 92-8.5 ....205.00
325 Cardenas SGC 92-8.5 ....27.50
480 W McCovey..........................20.00
609 T John................................25.00
1968 Topps
Complete Set (598) 2,750.00
Common Player (1-457)..................75
Common Player (458-598)..............50
30 Torre.....................................9.00
45 Seaver, SGC 92-8.5..............250.00
144 Morgan 5.00
145 Drysdale.............................80.00
158 WS Winners Celebrate, SBC
96-9.....................................50.00
408 Carlton, SGC 96-9...............195.00
460 Lonborg, SGC 88-8 ....25.00
497 Cardinals Team 7.00
571 La Russa............................12.00
1969 Topps
Complete Set (664) 2,200.00
Common Player (1-218)..................50
Common Player (219-327).............30
Common Player (328-512).............25
Common Player (513-664).............30
7 Leaders 6.00
35 Morgan.................................11.00
75 Aparicio................................90.00
95 Bench, SGC 92-8.5..............325.00
107 Checklist............................10.50
379 K Boyer...............................20.00
564 Hodges...............................45.00
659 Podres................................35.00
1970 Topps
Complete Set (720) 1,150.00
Common Player (1-132).................20
Common Player (133-459).............20

Common Player (460-546) 25
Common Player (547-633) 35
Common Player (634-720) 60
140 R Jackson 15.00
210 Juan Marichal 2.50
537 J Morgan 2.25
700 F Robinson, SGC
92-8.5 .... 175.00
1971 Topps
Complete Set (752) 2,000.00
Common Player (1-523) 25
Common Player (524-643) 35
Common Player (644-752 75
180 A Kaline 10.00
709 D Baylor 50.00
1972 Topps
Complete Set (787) 1,500.00
Common Player (1-394) 20
Common Player (395-525) 20
Common Player (526-656) 25
Common Player (657-787) 65
26 B Blyleven 5.00
79 Fisk, SGC 92-8.5 .... 150.00
595 N Ryan 75.00
588 Cardinals Team 3.50
761 Oglive/Cey, SGC 92-8.5 ...... 60.00
777 Wilhelm SGC 92-8.5 .... 45.00
1973 Topps
Complete Set (660) 700.00
Common Player (1-396) 20
Common Player (397-528) 40
Common Player (529-660) 45
31 B Bell 1.75
193 C Fisk 1.75
245 C Yastrzemski 5.00
615 M Schmidt RC 235.00
1974 Topps
Complete Set (660) 500.00
Common Player (1-660) 15
Team Checklist Set 60.00
Traded Set 40.00
50 R Carew 2.75
283 M Schmidt 25.00
456 D Winfield 30.00
1975 Topps
Complete Set (660) 750.00
Common Player (1-660) 50
61 D Winfield 25.00
70 M Schmidt 25.00
223 R Young Mini RC 65.00
370 T Seaver 7.00
1976 Topps
Complete Set (660) 300.00
Common Player (1-660) 10
Traded Set 40.00
19 G Brett 6.00
340 J Rice 6.00
480 M Schmidt 6.25
1977 Topps
Complete Set (660) 250.00
Common Player (1-660) 10
110 S Carlton 2.25
400 S Garvey 1.75
473 Rookies Outfielders 9.00
1978 Topps
Complete Set (726) 235.00
Common Player (1-726) 10
36 E Murray 18.00
72 A Dawson 2.00
360 M Schmidt 2.50
1979 Topps
Complete Set (726) 180.00
Common Player (1-726) 10

39 D Murphy 4.00
469 L Parish 1.75
650 P Rose 2.50
1980 Topps
Complete Set (726) 165.00
Common Player (1-726) 06
70 Gary Carter 1.25
77 D Stieb 1.00
482 R Henderson 15.00
1981 Topps
Complete Set (726) 145.00
Common Player (1-726) 06
315 K Gibson 2.50
479 Expos Future Stars 7.00
700 G Brett 1.75
1982 Topps
Complete Set (792) 100.00
Common Player (1-792) 05
70 T Raines 1.25
254 J Bell 9.00
668 D Murphy 1.50
1983 Topps
Complete Set (792) 115.00
Common Player (1-792) 05
Traded Set 35.00
49 W McGee 2.00
163 C Ripken 4.50
251 A Wiggins 50
1984 Topps
Complete Set 40.00
Traded Set 40.00
1985 Topps
Complete Set 200.00
Traded Set 12.00
1986 Topps
Complete Set 30.00
Traded Set 18.00
1987 Topps
Complete Set 18.00
Factory Set 25.00
Traded Set 10.00
1988 Topps
Complete Set 18.00
Factory Set 20.00
Traded Set 12.00
1989 Topps
Complete Set 18.00
Factory Set 20.00
Traded Set 30.00
1990 Topps
Factory Set 25.00
Traded Set 5.00
1991 Topps
Factory Set 25.00
Traded Set 12.00
1992 Topps
Gold Factory Set 120.00
Gold Traded Set 290.00
Traded Set 120.00
1993 Topps
Factory Set 50.00
Traded Set 50.00
1994 Topps
Factory Set 60.00
Traded Set 80.00
1995 Topps
Factory Set 90.00
Traded Set 65.00
1996 Topps
Factory Set 60.00
Upper Deck
1989, Factory Set, BB 280.00

1993, Complete Set, SP BB 160.00
1996, Complete Set, BB 80.00
1997, Complete Set, BB (550) .. 200.00
2000, Victory, Factory set 25.00

Baseball Collectibles

Collecting Hints: Baseball memorabilia spans a wide range of items that have been produced since baseball became the national pastime more than 100 years ago. This variety has made it more difficult to establish reliable values, leaving it to the individual to identify and determine what price to pay for any particular item. This "value in the eye of the beholder" approach works well for the experienced collector. Novices should solicit the advice of a reliable dealer or an advanced collector before investing heavily. Fluctuating market trends are compounded by the emerging interest in—and inordinately high prices paid for—unique pieces, especially items associated with superstars such as Cobb, Ruth, and Mantle.

Because of the unlimited variety of items available, it is virtually impossible to collect everything. Develop a collecting strategy, concentrating on particular player(s), team(s), or type of collectible(s), such as Hartland Statues or Perez-Steele autographed postcards. A special emphasis allows the collector to become more familiar with the key elements effecting pricing within that area of interest, such as condition and availability, and permits building a collection within a prescribed budget.

History: Baseball had its beginnings in the mid-19th Century and by 1900 had become the national pastime. Whether sandlot or big league, baseball was part of most every male's life until the 1950s, when leisure activities expanded in a myriad of directions.

The superstar has always been the key element in the game. Baseball greats were popular visitors at banquets, parades, and, more recently, at baseball autograph shows. They were subjects of extensive newspaper coverage and, with heightened radio and TV exposure, achieved true celebrity status. The impact of baseball on American life has been enormous.

References: David Bushing and Joe Phillips, *Vintage Baseball Bat 1994 Pocket Price Guide*, published by authors (217 Homewood, Libertyville, IL 60048), 1994; ——, *Vintage Baseball Glove Pocket Price Guide*, No. 4, published by authors (217 Homewood, Libertyville, IL 60048),

1996; Larry Canale, *Mickey Mantle: The Yankee Years*, The *Classic Photography of Ozzie Sweet*, Tuff Stuff Books, 1998; Kevin Keating and Michael Kolleth, *The Negro Leagues Autograph Guide*, Tuff Stuff Books, 1999; Mark I. Larson, *Complete Guide to Baseball Memorabilia*, 3rd ed., Krause Publications, 2000; Tom Mortenson (ed.,) *2000 Standard Catalog of Sports Memorabilia*, Krause Publications, 2000.

Periodicals: *Baseball Hobby News*, 4540 Kearney Villa Rd, San Diego, CA 92123; *John L. Raybin's Baseball Autograph News*, 527 Third Ave., #294-A, New York, NY 10016; *Sports Collectors Digest*, 700 E. State St., Iola, WI 54990; *Tuff Stuff*, P.O. Box 1637, Glen Allen, VA 23060.

Collectors' Clubs: Glove Collector, 14057 Rolling Hills Lane, Dallas, TX 75210; Society for American Baseball Research, P.O. Box 93183, Cleveland, OH 44101, members receive *Baseball Research Journal The SABR Bulletin and National Pastime*.

Museum: National Baseball Hall of Fame and Museum, Cooperstown, NY.

Reproduction Alert: Autographs and equipment.

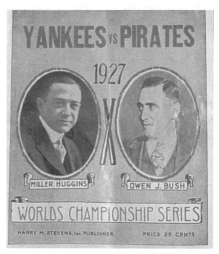

Program, Yankees vs. Pirates, 1927, $125.

Autograph
   Barrett, Bill, 2-1/2" x 4-1/2" card, baseball design, "Hall of Fame Baseball" imprinted on top, center space for signature, bold fountain pen signature 150.00
   Cabrera, Lorenzo "Chiquitin," 8-1/2" x 12" page from payroll ledger book for Mariano Cuban baseball team ...65.00
   Dean, James H. "Dizzy," 3" x 5" card...75.00
   Doyle, Carl, cut from album page, attached to 3" x 5" card 45.00

   Duryea, James "Jesse," 4" x 6" autograph album page, sgd in pencil...225.00
   Larsen, Don, 8" x 10" color photo taken by fan from center field seats during 1956 World Series game, sgd and inscribed, "WS Perfect Game 10-8-56"...............................35.00
   Sewell, Joe, Baseball Hall of Fame plaque post card 8.00
Autographed Ball
   McGwuire, Mark, official American League Baseball, sgd 1988.....995.00
   Home Run Hitters, signatures of 11 players, Mickey Mantle, Ted Williams, Frank Robinson, William Mays, Harmon Killebrew, Reggie Jackson, Hank Aaron, Mike Schmidt, Ernie Banks, Eddie Matthews, and Willie McCovey 495.00
   Joe DiMaggio, certificate of authenticity, Sept. 4, 1999....................... 250.00
Autographed Glove
   DiMaggio, Joe, 1950s Hollander, documentation 950.00
   Kluszewski, Ted, 1950s MacGregor...............................75.00
   Lynn, Fred, 1970s Rawlings, very minor bleeding............................55.00
   Pinson, Vada, 1950s Reach 225.00
Autographed Mini Helmet, serialized Certificate of Authenticity, security decal
   Agbayani, Benny, Mets...............45.00
   Carlton, Steve, Phillie 45.00
   Doby, Larry, Indians.....................50.00
   Gooden, Dwight, Mets.................50.00
   Killebrew, Harmon, Twins 60.00
   Larson, Don, Yankees..................35.00
   Murphy, Dale, Braves 80.00
   Ripken, Cal, Orioles 110.00
   Rose, Pete, Reds.........................70.00
Autographed Payroll Check, NY Yankees
   George Pipgras, May 1924...... 175.00
   Monte Pearson, June 1939 ...... 125.00
Autographed Shoes, Spotbilt cleats 125.00
Book
   Our Base Ball Club and How It Won The Championship, Noah Brooks, Button, 1884, intro by A. G. Spaulding.................................. 350.00
   Pitchin' Man, by Leroy (Satchel) Paige as told to Hal Lebovitz, 1948, softcover, 96 pgs, cover detached.....................................10.00
   30 Years of Baseball's Greatest Moments, Joseph Reichler, Ruthledge Books, 1973 ....9.75
Button Stud, Mickey Mantle Westerns, from jean plant in Commerce, OH, silver, red baseball-like stitching.....10.00
Character Jug, The Baseball Player, Royal Doulton, #D6878, Brittiana Ltd. Backstamp............................... 150.00
Game Bat, used
   Brett, George, Louisville 950.00
   Carter, Gary, Adirondack, hairline crack.. 275.00
   Clark, Will, Adirondack 225.00
   Mantle, Mickey, 1972 Old Timer's Game, Philadelphia 2,915.00
Glove, catcher's mitt, child's, Ben Warren, Rawlings 210 Professional Model, single tunnel web, hinge is stamped in the leather 55.00

Glove, fielder's, Ed Brandt, Wilson, split finger, leather soft and supple, some cracking inside............................ 90.00
Glove, first base mitt, Wilson, right handed, early 1940s, stamped patent number 55.00
Jersey, Roger Clemens, Yankees, pinstripe 300.00
Hartland Figurine
   Bat Boy, 25th Anniversary, MIB... 100.00
   Berra, 1 .... 350.00
   Drysdale, 2 .... 450.00
   Fox, 2 .... 200.00
   Killebrew, 25th Anniversary, MIB... 50.00
   Mantle, 4 .... 150.00
   Minor Leaguer, black base 250.00
   Minor Leaguer, white............... 150.00
   Maris, 1 .... 600.00
   Matthews, 2 .... 150.00
   Musial, 1 .... 350.00
   Ruth, 2 .... 150.00
Limited Edition Collector's Plate, Best of Baseball Series, Sports Impressions, "Legendary Johnny Bench," 6-1/2" d, MIB.. 40.00
Magazine
   Life, April 13, 1962, Burton and Taylor cover, Mantle and Maris baseball cards 145.00
   Sports Illustrated, Aug 16, 1954, first issue, night baseball cover, card pages intact.............................. 225.00
Miniature Bat, Louisville Slugger, endorsed by Jackie Robinson.... 95.00
Ornament, Baseball Heroes series, Babe Ruth, first edition, 1994 .... 45.00
Paperweight, 2-3/4" x 4-1/4", glass
   Mickey Mantle holding baseball bat, accompanied by donor card with info about Mantle............................... 20.00
   Ted Williams holding bat.............. 20.00
Player's Contract, NY Yankees, 4 pgs, 8-1/2" x 11", Allen "Dusty" Cooke, also sgd by E. S. Barnard, Jacob Ruppert.. 250.00
   Art Fletcher, coach's contract, also sgd by E. S. Barnard, Ed Barrow 250.00
   Joe Glenn, 1936, also sgd by William Harridge...................................... 125.00
   Jack Saltzgaver, 1934, also sgd by William Harridge, Ed Barrow..... 125.00
Photograph, Roger Clemens, Triple Exposure, 16" x 20"............................ 175.00
Plate, Philadelphia As, 1911 .... 855.00
Pocket Knife, Babe Ruth, bat shape.. 90.00
Post Card, "The National Game, Making a Homer," emb cupid wearing hat playing baseball, unused 20.00
Poster
   Pittsburgh BBC, 1894, lithography, some professional restoration............................... 3,550.00
   U. S. Coast Guard, 1930s...... 1,050.00
   Press Pen and Original Artwork, used by Balfour Co., 1953 New York Yankees World Series 995.00
Print, limited edition, Lance Richbourg artist, shows McGraw watching Travis Jackson, sgd and numbered in pencil 90.00

Punchboard, one cent board, shows
   player sliding into home, catcher and
   umpire waiting, unpunched,
   1920s 100.00
Salt and Pepper Shakers, pr, 5" l baseball
   bat salt shaker, 2" h baseball
   pepper 12.00
Sign, pub type, New York Yankees, illus of
   batter 50.00
Ticket Stub, used
   AAA Red Birds vs. Nashville Sounds,
   7-30-99, autographed by Adam
   Kennedy.......................................25.00
   Mets, 8-22-99, Mark McGwire's 49th &
   50th home runs............................15.00
   Yankees, 5-30-46..........................65.00
   Yankees, 9-11-49..........................30.00
Trophy, Spaulding, fielder's, orig
   condition 3,550.00
Wrist Watch, Montreal Expos, Bulova,
   Sportstime, quartz, 1980s,
   MIB...100.00

Basketball Collectibles

Collecting Hints: The NBA is trying
hard to make collectors out of all their
fans. Enjoy the hoopla as more and more
collectibles are being generated. Save
those programs, promotional pieces, and
giveaways. Collectors should pay careful
attention to the growing interest in
women's collegiate basketball and the
enthusiasm it's creating.

History: The game of basketball originated in Springfield, Massachusetts, in
1891, under the direction of Dr. James
Naismith of the YMCA. Schools and colleges soon adopted the game, and it
began to spread worldwide.

Basketball was added to the Olympic
games in 1936. The National Basketball
Association was founded in 1949 after
professional teams became popular.
Today the NBA consists of 27 teams in
two conferences, each having two divi-
sions.

Basketball is generally considered to
be an indoor game, but almost every
town in America has some place where
locals gather to shoot a few hoops. Regu-
lation games have two teams with five
players each. Courts are 92 feet long and
50 feet wide and have a hoop attached to
a backboard at each end.

References: *2001 Standard Catalog of
Basketball Cards*, 4th ed., Krause Publications, 2000; Sports Collectors Digest
ed., *Football, Basketball & Hockey Price
Guide,* 2nd ed., Krause Publications,
2000.

Periodical: *Sports Collectors Digest*,
700 E. State St., Iola, WI 54990.

Museum: Naismith Memorial Basketball Hall of Fame, Springfield, MA.

**Playmate Toys Inc. talking Michael
Jordan figure, from the movie
"Space Jam," $45.**

Advertising
   Dream Team, display, orig Dream
   Team 10 members, USA uniforms, orig
   shipping box 350.00
   Keds, letter regarding star athlete, orig
   envelope, sgd by Pete Maravich 85.00
Badge, 3-1/2" d, Harlem Globetrotters,
   celluloid, full color team photo, white
   ground, blue letters, small gold stars,
   c1970 ....24.00
Basketball, autographed
   Red Auerbach, official Spaulding NBA
   leather ball................................. 150.00
   Larry Bird, sgd and numbered limited
   edition, Spaulding leather all-star
   game ball 400.00
   Larry Bird and Red Auerbach, official
   Spaulding NBA leather ball...... 300.00
   Boston Celtics, 20 team autographs,
   official Spaulding NBA leather ball,
   numbered............................... 2,500.00
   Julius Erving and Connie Hawkins,
   ABA 30th Year Reunion ball 400.00
   Grant Hill, Christian Laettner, Bobby
   Hurley, Duke University, Final four
   ball.. 275.00
   Magic Johnson, Kareem, Baylor, and
   West, special inscription by all 4 to
   Wilt, numbered out of #250 ...... 550.00
   Scottie Pippen, Spaulding leather all-
   star game ball, 1994................. 375.00
   Rick Pitting, official Spaulding indoor/
   outdoor NBA ball 85.00
Jersey, double tags
   Larry Bird, Celtics, green.......... 275.00
   Kobe Bryant, LA Lakers, Champion
   Pro, rookie year 250.00
   John Havlicek, Boston Celtics,
   NBA 250.00
   Magic Johnson, Lakers, gold... 275.00
   Keith Michale, Upper Deck authenti-
   cated 300.00
   Robert Parish, Upper Deck authenti-
   cated 200.00
   Dennis Rodman, Lakers,
   Nike 325.00
Keychain, Chicago Bulls, #2203........8.50
Lithograph
   Los Angeles Lakers, five greatest
   players, artist Ann Neilsen, hand
   signed by Wilt Chamberlain, Jerry
   West, Magic Johnson, Elgin Baylor,

and Kareem Abdul-Jabbar, limited to
   1992 pcs, 22" x 39" unframed... 695.00
   UCLA Legends, Coach John Wooden,
   Jabbar, Goodrich, Warren, Johnson,
   Walton, Erickson, action photos and
   portraits, sgd in blue underneath each
   player, 22" x 40" unframed 150.00
Magazine
   Basketball Digest, November 1980,
   Larry Bird cover........................... 15.00
   Maravich, tribute for Pete Maravich,
   Pistol Pete action cover, 9" x 12", black
   and white, color cover,
   uncirculated............................... 125.00
   Sports Illustrated, November 1977,
   Larry Bird and Cheerleaders
   cover... 45.00
Notebook, Spaulding Official NBA,
   unused... 20.00
Photograph, autographed
   Kenny Anderson, 8" x 10" 20.00
   Vic Baker, 8" x 10"...................... 15.00
   Kenny Carr, 8" x 10".................... 15.00
   Wilt Chamberlain, 100 point game,
   8" x 10" 125.00
   Julius Erving, Dr. J., 16" x 20", sgd and
   numbered 165.00
   C. Fitzsimmons, 8" x 10".............. 15.00
   George Gervin, 8" x 10"............... 35.00
   Brian Grant, 8" x 10" 20.00
   H. Grant, 8" x 10" 20.00
   Grant Hill, 8" x 10"....................... 45.00
   Juwan Howard, Univ of Michigan,
   8" x 10"... 7.50
   Magic Johnson and Larry Bird, 1997
   NCAA Finals, 15" x 19", signed only by
   Bird... 165.00
   Magic Johnson and Larry Bird, Upper
   Deck, authenticated, 16" x 20", signed
   by both.. 350.00
   K. C. Jones, 8" x 10" 8.00
   Bob Knight and Steve Fisher, 11" x 14",
   signed by both 75.00
   J. Lucas, 8" x 10" 25.00
   Moses Malone, 8" x 10".............. 15.00
   Meadowlark Lemon, 8" x 10" 25.00
   Theo Ratliff, Wyoming, 8" x 10" 5.00
   Dennis Rodman, 8" x 10"
   Lakers 60.00
   N. Thurmond, 8" x 10" 25.00
   Robert Traylor, Univ of Michigan, 8" x
   10" 12.00
   C. Webber, 8" x 10"...................... 25.00
   Jerry West and Magic Johnson, 16" x
   20", from Magic's retirement
   night 285.00
Photograph, vintage, shows team, Grove
   City, OH, 5" x 7", 1930s 32.00
Poster, Michael Jordan
   Caricature, uncirculated,
   40" x 60" 150.00
   Space Jam, unreleased, Nike, Looney
   tunes, 1992................................. 55.00
Program
   1982 NCAA Final Four 125.00
   Retirement, Kevin McHale, Jan 1994,
   McHale vs. Lakers cover, full ticket,
   mini replica banner 50.00
   St. Louis Hawks and Boston Celtics,
   1982, autographed by Bill Russell,
   Bob Cousy, Sam Jones, Jim Loscutoff,
   Tom Sanders 275.00
   Seal and Diecut, Dennison, orig cello-
   phane envelope, 4" h 5.00

Shoes, game used, dual autograph
   Patrick Ewing 425.00
   Larry Johnson, Converse 200.00
   Alonzo Mournng, Nike Air
      Force 325.00
   Steve Smith, Reebok 150.00
Soap, Shaq Shower Suds, 8 oz tube, orig
   contents 8.00
Tie-tac, chain, figural basketball
   player 12.00
Trading Card
   Finest 1, 1998/99, MIB 90.00
   Fleer, uncut sheet, 1990/91.........18.00
   Fleer II Metal, 1996/97, MIB 35.00
   Icee Bear, 1972, Jabbar, SGC
      92-8.5 ....95.00
   NBA Hoops, Michael Jordan, #5,
      1990-91, Most Valuable Player, good
      condition 3.00
   NBA Hoops, Michael Jordan,#298,
      1992-93, All Star Weekend 2.00
   NBA Hoops, Michael Jordan,#30l
      1991-92, Most Valuable Player, good
      condition 3.00
   NBA Hoops, Michael Jordan,#358,
      illus by Ken Goldammer, 1990......2.00
   NBA Hoops, Michael Jordan,#536,
      1991-92, All-Time Active Leader Scor-
      ing 2.00
   Pacific Prism Draft, 1996/97,
      MIB...40.00
   SkyBox, 1990/91, hand
      collated 20.00
   Stadium Premium I, 1998/99,
      MIB..60.00
   Topps, 1957/58, #7, Sears SGC
      88-8 ....275.00
   Topps, 1970/71, #50, Chamberlain,
      SGC 88-8 ....150.00
   Topps, 1980/81, wax pack..........55.00
   Upper Deck, 1991/92, factory
      sealed 20.00
   Upper Deck, 1992/93, Italian series,
      foil, wax, MIB..............................25.00
Uniform, autographed, Wilt Chamberlain,
   LA Lakers, double tagged,
   home 450.00
Wire Service Photo
   Los Angeles Lakers Earvin Johnson
      and Miami Heat Sylvester Gray,
      1989 ....3.50
   Los Angeles Lakers, Earvin Johnson,
      Supersonics Reynolds, 1989 ....3.50
   Los Angeles Lakers, Magic Johnson,
      1989 ....3.50
   Los Angeles Lakers, Magic Johnson
      and Seattle's Jerry Reynolds,
      1989 ....3.50
   Los Angeles Lakers, Kareem Abdul
      Jabbar, A.C. Green, and Magic
      Johnson, 1989 ....3.50
   Los Angeles Lakers, Magic Johnson
      and Phoenix Suns Tyrone Corbin,
      1989 ....3.60
Yearbook
   Boston Celtics, 1974/75, Silas and
      Chaney on cover, Dick Raphael pho-
      tos...40.00
   Chicago Bulls, 1984/85, Orlando
      Woolridge and Michael Jordan on
      cover 125.00

Captain Blushwell, litho tin and cloth, Japan, original box, 11" h, $85.

Battery-Operated Automata

Collecting Hints: Prices fluctuate greatly, but operating condition is a key factor. Many pieces were originally made with accessory parts; these must be present for full value to be realized. The original box, especially if it has a label, adds 10 to 20 percent to the price. Also, the more elaborate the action, the higher the value.

History: Battery-operated automata began as inexpensive Japanese imports in the 1950s. They were meant for amusement only, many ending up on the shelves of bars in the recreation rooms of private homes. They were marketed through 5 and 10¢ stores and outlets.

The subjects were animals—bears being favored—and humans. Quality of pieces varies greatly, with Linemar items being among the best made.

Bear Drummer, bright orange plush-
   covered bear, tan drum, 1970s, orig
   box, 5-1/2" x 7-1/2" x 11", played with
   condition.......................................20.00
BMW 3.5 CSL turbo car, Dunlop and
   Bosch Electric advertising, tin,
   MIB 120.00
Brainstorm Beany, blue felt beanie,
   yellow lettering and trim, orig 6" x 6" x
   4" deep box, light bulb attached to top
   center of hat, back cord connects to
   cardboard and tin cylinder for battery,
   Electric Game Co., Inc.,
   c1950 ....45.00
Brave Eagle, beating drum, raising
   war hoop, MIB.......................... 145.00
Bubble Blowing Monkey, plush-cov-
   ered monkey, soft vinyl face, black,
   white, red, and yellow plaid shirt, small
   bowl missing, orig box, 4-1/2" x 5-1/2"
   x 10-1/2" h....................................70.00
Carnival Choo Choo, plastic, Hong
   Kong, 1970s, MIB 55.00

Comical Clara, MIB 495.00
Covered Wagon, soft plastic, dark
   brown wagon, yellow cover, 3-D cowboy, pair of brown horses, orig box,
   1970s, 4" x 11" x 4-1/2" h............45.00
Flip Over Car, hard plastic, silver, large
   black wheels, blue transparent dome
   with 3-D astronaut, red, white, and
   blue NASA decal, mkd "Made in Hong
   Kong," 1970s, orig box with some
   damage, 4-1/2" x 7" x 4", does not
   work properly...............................30.00
Ford Mustang GT, 6" x 16" x 4" plastic
   car, black, white, blue, and orange
   box designed as garage, orig decals
   have been applied to one side, including "Kendall GT 1/Cobra Driver Troy,"
   racing stripes, orig "Motorized Mustang Operator's License," AMF Wen
   Mac Division, c1967...................95.00
Happy Miner, MIB 1,075.00
Knock-Out Boxers, orig box 295.00
Love-Love Volkswagen Beetle, blinking light in back window, tin, orange,
   Mobil, Champion, Goodyear sayings,
   VW on hubcaps, MIB 145.00
McGregor, Scotsman smoking cigar,
   raises up and down from pirates
   chest, MIB 195.00
My Fair Dancer, litho tin, dancer in
   naval outfit, seahorse graphics on
   base, 11" h, MIB 225.00
Picnic Bear, NM toy, box fair..... 125.00
Police Autocycle, 3" x 10" x 8" h, hard
   plastic cycle with police officer, orig
   red, white, blue, and black box with
   display window, Bandai,
   1970s.. 18.00
Poodle, walking, 4" x 11" x 10" h, white
   plush poodle, bright red, gray, yellow
   plaid fabric body, pink neck bow and
   top of head, c1950, some
   fading..20.00
Princess French Poodle, 4" x 8" x 8" h
   fabric and gray/black plush, black,
   blue, and red plaid jacket and hat,
   remote control battery box, Alps,
   Japan..20.00
Rex, copyright 1987 Jamina World
   Corp., 5" x 9" x 12" h...................35.00
Roller Coaster, plastic, Hong Kong,
   1970s, MIB 55.00
Rosko, bartender, shakes mixer,
   pours, and drink, smoke rises from
   ears, MIB 75.00
Santa Claus, C-10 toy, C-8 orig
   box..225.00
School Bus, tin litho, switch to open
   front and back doors, headlights light
   up.. 175.00
Slurpy Pup, litho tin doghouse, green
   plastic base, plush covered dog's
   head, red plastic bowl, T. N. Japan,
   1960s, 4" x 6" x 4" h 30.00
Smoking Grandpa, Japan, smokes,
   but pipe doesn't light 85.00
Sniffy Dog with Bee, Modern Toys,
   Japan, 1970s, MIB 55.00
Space Explorer, Gakken, Japan, turn-
   over action, MIB 100.00
Sparky, litho tin doghouse, 3" long
   wood dog, copyright M. P. 1949 (Multi
   Products), orig box with some
   defects...20.00
Surrey Rider, hard plastic brown, red,
   and black surrey, attached brown
   horse, man in blue suit holding whip,

woman in ink dress, 4" x 10" x 45-1/2" h......................................40.00
Traffic Policeman, MIB..............490.00
Train, 55 Special Express, tin litho, gray, red, white, and yellow, mkd "Made in Japan, T. N.," c1980, 3" x 14" x 4" h................................28.00
Trans Am, '83, hard plastic, bright yellow, copyright 1983 Royal Condor, orig box with display window, 2-1/4" x 6" x 1-3/4" h................................18.00
Tumbles the Bear, Yanoman, 1970s, MIB..85.00
Universe Boat, red, white, and blue tin litho, yellow accents, white plastic dome on front, red plastic rockets on back, detachable tin antenna, name on side, mkd "Gyro Action" on back, mkd "Made in China," c1970s, 5" x 9" x 6" h...38.00
US Army Helicopter, C-7.............90.00
Walking Gorilla, MIB...............1,275.00
Waltzing Matilda, MIB................875.00

Bauer Pottery

Collecting Hints: Bauer pieces range in style from Art Deco to Streamlined Modern. Focus on highly stylistic, designer forms; interest in utilitarian redware and stoneware pieces is minimal.

Remember that jiggered and cast production pieces were made in large quantities. Unfortunately, hand-thrown pieces by Matt Carlton and Fred Johnson, which were made in limited numbers, are not marked. Learn to identify them by studying photographs of known examples. Among the more desirable shapes are oil jars—the taller the jar, the higher the price.

Some colors of dinnerware are more highly prized than others. Premium prices are paid for burgundy, orange-red, and white pieces in all patterns.

History: In 1885, John Bauer founded the Paducah Pottery in Paducah, Kentucky, to manufacture stoneware and earthenware utilitarian pieces such as crocks and jugs. Bauer died in 1898, and John Andrew Bauer continued the business in Paducah until 1909, at which time the plant was moved to Los Angeles, California.

Bauer's initial California production consisted of redware flowerpots. Stoneware production did not resume immediately after the move to California because of the difficulty of locating suitable stoneware clay. Utilitarian ware such as bean pots and mixing bowls remained a company staple.

In 1913, Matt Carlton, an Arkansas potter, and Louis Ipsen, a Danish designer, developed an artware line of glazed bowls, jardinieres, and vases. The company won a bronze medal at the Panama-California Exposition of 1915-16, but within a short time period, the firm's art-ware was replaced by a line of molded stoneware vases.

In 1922, John Andrew Bauer died. Just prior to his death, he established a partnership with Watson E. Brockmon, his son-in-law. The firm prospered under Brockmon's leadership.

In the early 1930s, the company introduced a line of popular dinnerware designed by Ipsen and covered with glazes developed by Victor Houser, a ceramic engineer. In 1931, "ring" ware was introduced to contrast with the plain ware of the previous year. Eventually, more than a hundred different shapes and sizes were manufactured in table and kitchenwares. Brusche Contempo (1948-61), La Linda (1939-59), Monterey (1936-45), and Monterey Moderne (1948-1961) were some of the more successful tableware lines. Ipsen's Aladdin teapot design was part of the Glass Pastel Kitchenware series.

The company continued operations during World War II, reformulating the glazes to correspond to wartime restrictions. Wheel-thrown artware featuring the designs of Carlton and Fred Johnson was made, and cast forms were kept in production. Tracy Irwin, a designer, developed a modern line of floral containers.

Following the war, the company faced stiff competition in the national as well as in the California market. A bitter strike in 1961 signaled the end, and in 1962, W. E. Brockmon's widow closed the plant.

References: Susan and Al Bagdade, *Warman's American Pottery and Porcelain*, 2nd ed., Krause Publications, 2000; Jack Chipman, *Collector's Encyclopedia of Bauer Pottery*, Collector Books, 1998; Lois Lehner, *Lehner's Encyclopedia of U.S. Marks on Pottery*, Porcelain & Clay, Collector Books, 1988.

Atlanta
 Mixing Bowl, cobalt blue, No. 24................................65.00
 Pot, 4" d, white 40.00
Kitchenware, Gloss Pastel
 Bowl, 11 1-1/2" l, 2 2-3/4" h, light green 25.00
 Casserole, cov, 1 qt.....................48.00
La Linda
 Ashtray, 4" sq, cobalt blue...........25.00
 Tumbler, chartreuse, price for set of six 95.00
Miscellaneous
 Carafe, jade, Plainware 75.00
 Coffee Cup, green-gray, 4" d.......14.00
 Console Bowl, cream colored 20.00
 Corsage Vase, Russel Wright, white 350.00
 Dog Dish, large, cobalt............ 150.00
 Flowerpot, large, peach colored 65.00
 Planter, swan, large, yellow and white 170.00
 Salt Box, Grape & Cherries, wood lid 145.00
 Serving Dish, gray, 9" l.................25.00

Monterey
 Butter Dish, cov, red....................85.00
 Teapot, cov, yellow 145.00
Ring-Ware
 Batter Bowl, yellow 35.00
 Bowl, 10" d, green 50.00
 Butter Dish, cov, green or Delph, light blue 135.00
 Candleholder, yellow....................20.00
 Canister, wooden lid, oval, orange, "Coffee" 80.00
 Casserole, cov, individual size
  Green....................................55.00
  Red, wooden frame 60.00
 Chop Plate
  12" d, orange.........................80.00
  14" d, green............................75.00
  14" d, orange.......................140.00
 Coffee Server, red, copper handle 65.00
 Cookie Jar, cov, red...................695.00
 Creamer
  Delph, light blue 35.00
  Ivory......................................125.00
  Red..35.00
 Gravy Boat, bright yellow, imp "Bauer USA Los Angeles," 10" w, 4" h....30.00
 Jardiniere, white, 4" d, rim chip 100.00
 Juice Tumbler, black, some flea bites to glaze 60.00
 Mixing Bowl
  5-3/4" d, No. 36, orange.........40.00
  7" d, No. 24, blue....................24.00
  8" d, No. 12, turquoise 42.00
  10" d, No. 9, black...............250.00
 Mug, barrel
  Jade.......................................300.00
  Yellow....................................300.00
 Plate
  7-1/2" d, salad, mixed colors, set of six 100.00
  9" d
   Red.................................20.00
   Yellow.............................15.00
  10-1/2" d, dinner
   Black or ivory...................75.00
   Red.................................50.00
 Salt and Pepper Shakers, pr, black, short 95.00
 Sherbet, ftd, yellow......................35.00
 Spice Jar, red, 3 quart...............595.00
 Sugar, cov, Ivory 125.00
 Sugar Shaker, jade.....................350.00
 Teapot, cov
  Cobalt blue, six cup.............350.00
  Red.......................................150.00
  Rust, Hi-Fire line 60.00
 Tumbler, black, 6 oz, wooden handle..60.00
 Water Set, carafe and six tumblers, wooden handles, red and yellow tumblers, price for set 250.00
Strawberries
 Cookie Jar, snack bar dec........225.00
 Muffineer, "For Cinnamon Toast," some crazing 95.00
 Salt Shaker, oval canister, no lid 35.00

Beanie Babies®

Collecting Hints: Here's a collecting category where much of the present-day value depends on the toy being in mint condition with the original tag. The collecting frenzy created by this toy has excited the collectibles marketplace and still continues.

A whole new set of abbreviations, such as MWWT, MWM3T, etc. have evolved, along with terms such as "tush tag" and "string tag." This kind of enthusiasm and creativity in ways to communicate about the collectibility of Beanie Babies will help foster continued interest, as will the Internet, where Web sites and cha rooms about Beanie Babies are numerous.

History: When H. Ty Warner founded Ty, Inc., in 1986, he hoped to make an impact on the toy market with his stuffed toys. By using good quality fabrics and interesting designs, plus stuffing them with beans and making them affordable to children, he was well on his way. The original set of nine Beanie Babies was released in late 1993. That set included: Chocolate the Moose, Cubbie the Brown Frog, Flash the Dolphin, Legs the Frog, Patti the Platypus, Pincher the Lobster, Splash the Whale, Spot the Dog, and Squealer the Pig. Several of these original nine have been retired and have since increased significantly in value from their original issue price of $5.

By the spring of 1994, a second generation of string tags was developed (today there are five generations) and also the second generation of tush tags (today there are seven different types). Retiring animals, mistakes, changes in tag design, and other variations fueled speculation in the market place. By November of 1997, there were 78 releases of different animals and variations.

References: *Shawn Brecka, The Bean Family Pocket Guide 1999 Values & Trends*, Antique Trader Books, 1998; Sharon Korbeck, ed., *Toys & Prices*, 1999, 6th edition, Krause Publications, 1998.

Periodicals: *Beanie Collector*, Mary Beth's Beanie World; *Mo's Beanie Baby News Magazine; Toy Shop; White's Guide to Collecting Beanie Babies*, plus more. Visit a local newsstand or book store for the latest publications.

Abbreviations: Here's a list of some of the new language which has evolved because of Beanie Babies and their dedicated collectors:

MWMT – mint with mint tag
MWM3T – mint with mint three tags (including Canadian tag)
MWCT – mint with creased tag
MWBT – mint with bent tag or mint with both tags

Note: Prices below are for toys in mint condition, with original tags.

Bessie the Cow, $60.

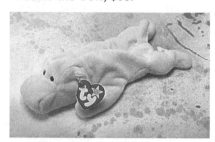

Happy the Hippo, $20.

Pouch the Kangaroo, $8.

Advertising

A & W Rootbeer Bear 18.00
Caesar's Pizza, Christmas, 1997 .... 15.00
Coca-Cola, set of six 50.00
Dairy Queen Cone 15.00
Energizer Bunny 15.00
Ernie the Keebler Elf 15.00
Harley Davidson, series II 50.00
Hawaiian Punch 15.00
M & M's, four-pc set 45.00
McDonald's, Teeney Beanies 1998, set of six, Pinchers, Happy, Bongo, Mel, Inch, Twiggs 50.00
1999, set of four, Glory Bear, Britannia Bear, Maple Bear, Erin Bear 65.00
Mr. Peanut, Planters 10.00
NBC Studios, peacock 25.00
Pillsbury Doughboy 15.00
Travel Lodge Sleep Bear 15.00

Retired

Ally the alligator 48.00
Ants the anteater 6.00
Baldy the eagle 10.00
Bernie the St. Bernard 6.00
Bessie the cow 60.00
Blizzard the white tiger 6.00
Bruno the terrier 6.00
Bubbles the fish 145.00
Cassie the collie 7.50
Cubbie the bear 18.00
Daisy the cow 6.00
Ears the bunny 12.00
Fetch the golden retriever 6.00
Flash the dolphin 95.00
Flip the cat 24.00
Glory 7.50
Goldie the goldfish 55.00
Gracie the swan 7.00
Grunt the razorback 160.00
Holiday Teddy Bear, acid-free bag tag protector 42.00
Hoot the owl 40.00
Humphrey the Camel 185.00
Inch the worm 16.00
Issy 20.00
Jester the clown fish 6.00
Kuku the cockatoo 8.00
Libearty 58.00
Lizzy the lizard 20.00
Manny the manatee 150.00
Patti the platypus 15.00
Princess Bear, orig TY tag, 1997 55.00
Quackers the duck 8.00
Radar the bat 160.00
Rover the dog 16.00
Seamore the seal 135.00
Sly the fox 6.00
Smooch 20.00
Sneaky the leopard 5.00
Snort the bull 6.00
Speckles 10.00
Splash the whale 95.00
Sting the ray 150.00
Tank the armadillo 70.00
Waddie the penguin 17.00
Weenie the dog 18.00
Ziggy the zebra 10.00
Zip the cat 20.00

Beatles

Collecting Hints: Beatles collectibles date from 1964 to the present. The majority of memorabilia items were produced from 1964 to 1968. The most valuable items are marked "NEMS." Most collectors are interested in mint or near-mint items only, although some items in very good condition, especially if scarce, have considerable value.

Each year major auction houses hold auctions which include Beatles memorabilia, primarily one-of-a-kind items such as guitars and stage costumes. The average collector can participate in these sales now in person or on-line.

History: The fascination with the Beatles began in 1964. Soon the whole country was caught up in Beatlemania. The members of the group included John Lennon, Paul McCartney, George Harrison, and Ringo Starr. The group broke up in 1970, after which the members pursued individual musical careers. Beatlemania took on new life after the death of John Lennon in 1980.

References: Jeff Augsburger, Marty Eck, and Rick Rann, *Beatles Memorabilia Price Guide*, 3rd ed., Antique Trader Books, 1997; Barbara Crawford, Hollis Lamon and Michael Stern, *The Beatles: A Reference & Value Guide*, 2nd Edition, Collector Books, 1998; Editors of *Goldmine Magazine*, *The Beatles Digest*, Krause Publications, 2000.

Periodicals: *Beatlefan*, P.O. Box 33515, Decatur, GA 30033; *Instant Karma*, P.O. Box 256, Sault Ste Marie, MI 49783.

Collectors' Clubs: Beatles Connection, P.O. Box 1066, Pinellas Park, FL 34665; Beatles Fan Club, 397 Edgewood Ave., New Haven, CT 06511; Beatles Fan Club of Great Britain, Superstore Productions, 123 Marina, St. Leonards on Sea, East Sussex, England TN38 OBN; Working Class Hero Club, 3311 Niagara St., Pittsburgh, PA 15213.

Reproduction Alert: Records, picture sleeves, and album jackets have been counterfeited. Sound quality may be poorer on the records, and printing on labels and picture jackets usually is inferior to the original. Many pieces of memorabilia have been reproduced, often with some change in size, color, or design.

Apron, paper, white, black pictures, name, and song titles 75.00
Bag, 9-1/2" x 10", textured vinyl, red, portraits, black inscription and signatures, cord carrying strap, 1964 .... 165.00
Bank, 7-1/2" h, plastic, Yellow Submarine, bust figures of each Beatle, 1960s, price for set of four, minor damage.................................... 1,400.00
Banner, printed nylon, black images of four Beatles, blue printed "The Beatles," Memphis, 1966 .... 1,150.00
Beach Towel, 34" x 57", terry cloth, Beatles in bathing suits, c1960 .... 115.00
Billfold, red, four white signatures on one side, picture on other 90.00
Blanket, 62" x 80", wool, tan, printed black and red bust figures and instruments, "The Beatles" center, mfg by Whitney 165.00
Bobbing Head, Ringo, 8" h, 1964 .... 90.00
Book, *Yellow Submarine*, Signet Book, Oct, 1968, paperback, 128 pgs . 20.00
Bubble Gum Cards, Topps, black and white, 1964.................................... 2.00
Calendar, 12", spiral bound, 1969, Golden Press, orig brown paper envelope 65.00

Cake Decorating Kit, figurals, playing instruments, set of four, MIB 195.00
Coat Hangers, Yellow Submarine, set 295.00
Coaster, 4" sq, Yellow Submarine, cardboard, set of 12 .... 65.00
Coloring Book, 8-1/4" x 11", Saalfield, 1964 NEMS copyright, includes eight black and white photos, unused 65.00
Doll, 5" h, Paul McCartney, Remco, 1962 .... 85.00
Drum, 14" d, red sparkle finish, "The Beatles Drum" on skin, metal stand, mfg by Mastro 325.00
Figure, 6-1/2" h, painted and glazed plaster, set of four, 1960s 150.00
Fun Kit, 1964, orig sealed plastic 70.00
Handkerchief, 8-1/2" sq 20.00
Hummer, 10-1/2" l cardboard tube, full color paper label of Beatles portraits against blue background, black text "Hum Along With Your Official Beatle Hummer," Merrimaker, ©1964 NEMS Enterprises Ltd., yellow plastic cap, funnel end missing 20.00
Limited Edition Collector Plate, Delphi
    Sgt. Pepper, 25th Anniversary, 1992, orig box 75.00
    The Beatles Live in Concert, first edition, 1991, orig box 65.00
    The Beatles Rubber Soul, 1992, orig box 65.00
Lunch Box
    Blue, rim wear 285.00
    Yellow Submarine, some edge wear 125.00
Magazine Cover and Story
    Life, Nov. 7, 1969, Paul McCartney and family 15.00
    Life, Aug. 6, 1981, Yoko story 15.00
    Pop Pics Super, 1964 .... 12.00
    Sixteen, August 1966 .... 15.00
    Teen World, July 1965 .... 15.00
    Time, Dec. 22, 1980, John Lennon 10.00
Mug, 4" h, 3" d, ceramic, bust photos of group wearing blue jackets, England, c1964 .... 85.00
Notebook, three ring binder, red vinyl cov, Standard Plastic Products 135.00
Paddle Ball Game 100.00
Pencil Case, 8" x 3-1/2", vinyl, blue, group picture and facsimile autographs, zipper top, Standard Plastic Products 35.00
Pencil Tablet, 7-3/4" x 10", full color photo cover, facsimile signatures, Lewis F. Dow Co., ©NEMS Ltd. London, dated 1967.. 35.00
Pennant, 23" l, felt, white, red, and black, printed illus and facsimile signatures, red trim and streamers, "Official Licensee"" copyright, c1964 .... 80.00
Photograph, official, 8" x 10", printed in USA, set of four 45.00
Pin, enamel, Yellow Submarine, 1-1/4" h, set of four 60.00

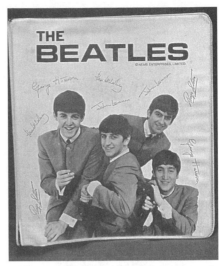

Notebook, white, black letters, sepia toned figures, NEMS Enterprises, $40.

Pinback Button, 3-1/2" d, set of four buttons for Yellow Submarine, 1968 .... 30.00
Program, tour, Beatles pictured in playing cards, 1964 British tour, minor folds 230.00
Puzzle, Yellow Submarine, MIB 55.00
Records
    All Things Must Pass, George Harrison, three-record set, Apple 25.00
    Hard Days Night, soundtrack 40.00
    Help, soundtrack, Apple 18.00
    Sgt. Peppers Lonely Hearts Band, Capitol Records, orig cellophane wrapper, c1967 .... 30.00
    The Beatles Rock N Roll Music, Volumes I and II, 1980 .... 25.00
Ring, flasher type, 1960s, set of four 25.00
School Bag, 12" x 9"x 3-1/2", tan, "The Beatles" printed on flap, handle, and shoulder strap 215.00
Scrapbook, NEMS, 1964 .... 50.00
Soap Container, 10" h, plastic, Ringo, removable head, Colgate-Palmolive Co., 1965 NEMS copyright 85.00
T-shirt, Beatles '65, size large 17.00
Tile, 6" sq, ceramic, group picture, "The Beatles," mfg by Carter Tiles 85.00
Wallet, 3-1/2" x 4-1/2" tan vinyl, browntone photo, black facsimile signatures, Standard Plastics Products, © Ramat & Co., Ltd., 1964 .... 85.00

Beer Bottles

Collecting Hints: Beer bottles often are found by digging in old dumps or wells. Although these bottles may be discolored and flaked, the key is whether or not they are broken. Damage to the bottle is of greater concern in pricing than the discoloration.

Concentrate on the bottles from one brewery or area. When an example is sold in the area in which it originated, it is likely to command more money than when sold outside that local region

Over the years, breweries usually changed bottle styles several times. This also is true for the paper labels found on later bottles.

Early bottles had special closures, and a bottle is worth more if the closure is intact. Presence of the metal caps is not critical to the value of later bottles. However, collecting metal caps is a growing field.

History: Breweries began in America shortly after the arrival of the first settlers. By the mid-19th century, most farmsteads had a small brewery on them. Local breweries dominated the market until the arrival of Prohibition. The majority of breweries closed although a few larger ones survived.

When Prohibition ended, a much smaller number of local breweries renewed production. The advertising, distribution, and production costs of the 1950s and 1960s led to the closing of most local breweries and the merger of many other breweries into a few national companies.

In the 1960s, imported beers from Europe entered the American market. Some companies signed licensing agreements to produce these foreign labels in the United States. In more recent years, beers brewed in Canada and Mexico have been gaining popularity.

References: *Donna S. Baker, Vintage Anheuser-Busch, An Unofficial Collector's Guide*, Schiffer, 1999; Donald A. Bull, *Beer Advertising*, Schiffer Publishing, 2000; Don and Elizabeth Johnson, *Warman's Advertising*, Krause Publications, 2000; Ralph and Terry Kovel, *Kovels' Bottles Price List*, 11th ed., Crown Publishers, 1999; Michael Polak, *Bottles*, 3rd ed., Quill, 2000.

Collectors' Club: American Breweriana Association, Inc., P.O. Box 11157, Pueblo, CO 81001.

Embossed

Hand Brew Co., Pawtucket, RI, aqua 15.00
Iroquois, Buffalo, Indian head, amber 12.00
Monongahela Valley Brewing Co., Clinton, PA, brown, 12 oz, buck head raised on front 10.00
North Eastern Breweries Lt., Blackhill Middlesboro Sunderland, trademark of motorized brewers dray cart, green, 10" h 45.00
Pabst Milwaukee, raised label, clear glass, 12 oz, bottom reads "WF & Sons" 6.00
Piel Bros., East New York Brewery, fancy logo, aqua 19.00
Pittsburgh Brewing Co., brown glass, raised words 6.00
Schlitz, emb "Royal Ruby Anchor Glass," Anchor Hocking, elongated neck, 1950s, 8" h 45.00

Painted Label

Augusta Brewing Co., Augusta, CA, 7" h, aqua 15.00
Rolling Rock Extra Pale, blue and white label, green label, unopened 20.00
Schlitz Brewing Co., 9-1/2" h, amber 10.00

Paper Label

Central Brand Extra Lager Beer, 9-1/4" h, aqua 8.00
Cooks 500 Ale, 9-1/2" h, aqua 5.00
Diamond Jim's Beer, 9-1/4" h, aqua 6.50
Jordan Beer, Mankato Brewing, Mankato, MN, orig paper label 15.00
Pabst Extract, amber, two labels 12.00
Rolling Rock Beer, Mountain Springs, Latrobe, PA, unopened 30.00
Southern Brewing Co., machine made, 9-1/2" h, green 4.00

Stoneware

Bowack Brothers Edinburgh, Genuine Brewed Ginger Beer, two tone stoneware with swing stopper, horseshoe trade mark, 9" h 24.00
R. Douglas Kircaldy and Ladybank, Stone Ginger Beer, champagne shape, two tone stoneware, orig hard rubber stopper with 1923 date, imp mark "Buchan Portobello Edinburgh," 8" h 18.00
W. B. Reid Newcastle-Upon-Tyne, Brewed Ginger Beer, two-tone stoneware, internal screw closure, imp mark "Buchan Portobello Edinburgh," 9" h 18.00

Beer Cans

Collecting Hints: Rusted and dented cans have little value unless they are rare examples in some respect. Most collectors remove the beer from the cans. Cans should be opened from the bottom to preserve the unopened top.

As beer can collecting became popular, companies issued special collectors' cans which never contained beer. Many were bought on speculation; value has been shaky.

History: Before Prohibition, beer was stored and shipped in kegs and dispensed in returnable bottles. When the Prohibition Act was repealed in 1933, only 700 of 1,700 breweries resumed operation. Expanding distribution created the need for an inexpensive container that would permit beer to be stored longer and shipped safely. Cans were the answer.

The first patent for a lined can was issued to the American Can Co. on Sept. 25, 1934, for its Keglined process. Gotfried Kruger Brewing Co., Newark, New Jersey, was the first brewery to use the can. Pabst was the first major company to join the canned-beer movement.

Continental Can Co. introduced the cone-top beer can in 1935, and Schlitz was the first brewery to use this type of can. The next major change in beer can design was the aluminum pop-top in 1962.

Reference: Thomas Toepfer, *Beer Cans*, L-W Book Sales, 1976, 1995 value update.

Collectors' Clubs: Beer Can Collectors of America, 747 Merus Ct, Fenton, MO 63026; Capitol City Chapter of the Beer Can Collectors of America, P.O. Box 287, Brandywine, MD 20613; Gambrinus Chapter of the Beer Can Collectors of America, 985 Maebelle Way, Westerville, OH 43081.

Museum: The Museum of Beverage Containers and Advertising, Goddlettsville, TN.

Abbreviations: The following abbreviations are used in the listings:

CR - Crowntainer-type cone top
CT - cone type
FT - flat top
ML - malt liquor
PT - pull top.

Left: Old Topper Snappy Ale, CT, 1940, $55; right: Hanley's Ale, CT, c1940, $25.

ABC Ale, Wagner, Columbus, OH, PT, 12 oz 4.00
Ace Hi M.L., Ace, Chicago, IL, FT, 7 oz 115.00
Aero Club Pale Select, East Idaho, Pocatello, ID, CT, 12 oz 125.00
Atles, National, Detroit, MI, FT, 12 oz 40.00
Ballantine, P Ballantine, Newark, NJ, PT, 12 oz 5.00
Bantam, Goebel, Detroit, MI, FT, 8 oz 27.50
Berghoff, Ft Wayne, IN, FT, 12 oz 75.00
Breuing's, Rice Lake, Rice Lake, WI, FT, 12 oz 7.50
Budweiser, Anheuser-Busch, PT, 10 oz 5.00
Butte Special, Butte, MT, FT, 12 oz 25.00
Chief Oshkosh, Oshkosh, WI, FT, 12 oz 15.00

Colt 45 M.L., National, PT, 8 oz 2.00
Dutch Treat, Phoenix, AZ, PT,
12 oz 2.50
Eastside Old Tap, Pabst, Los Angeles,
CA, FT, 12 oz 15.00
Fabacher Brau, Jackson, New
Orleans, LA, PT, 10 oz.................12.00
Falstaff Premium Quality Beer, Falstaff
Brewing Co., St. Louis, MO, opened at
bottom, grade 8 ....35.00
Fisher Light, General, PT, 12 oz 2.00
Fitzgerald's Pale Ale, CT, some
rusting 85.00
Gablinger's, Forrest, New Bedford,
MA, PT, 12 oz..............................6.50
Goebel Ale, Goebel, Detroit, MI, FT,
8 oz...35.00
Hamm's, Hamm, St Paul, MN, PT,
12 oz 4.00
Heidelbrau, Heileman, LaCrosse WI,
PT, 12 oz.....................................2.50
Horlacher Pilsner, Horlacher, Allen-
town, PA, FT, 12 oz 10.00
Iron City Pittsburgh Pirate Beer, 1979
World Series, opened from
bottom 12.50
Kentucky M.L., Fehr, Louisville, KY, FT,
12 oz 45.00
Lucky Lager, San Francisco, CA, FT,
7 oz..12.00
Manheim, Reading, PA, FT,
12 oz 12.00
Milwaukee's Best, Miller, Milwaukee,
WI, PT, 12 oz 7.50
National Bohemian, National, Detroit,
MI, FT, 12 oz 15.00
North Star, Associated, PT, 12 oz..4.00
Old Crown Ale, Ft Wayne, IN, FT,
12 oz 50.00
Old Topper Snappy Ale, CT, rust spot,
some corrosion, 5-1/2" h 55.00
Olympia Light, Olympia, Olympia, WA,
PT, 7 oz.......................................8.50
Pearl Draft, Pearl, PT, 12 oz...........1.00
Piels Real Draft Premium Beer, Piels
Bros., Allentown, PA 7.00
Pike's Peak M.L., Walter, Pueblo, COP,
FT, 8 oz.......................................45.00
Prager Bohemian Light Lager, 12 fluid
oz, tap top, empty, but never
opened...9.00
Premium Richbrau Beer, Home Brew-
ing Co., Richmond, VA, CT, orig cap,
some rusting 35.00
Queens Brau, Queen City, Cumber-
land, MD, FT, 12 oz......................55.00
Rahr's Green Bay, Green Bay, WI, CT,
12 oz 55.00
Red Top, Drewrys, South Bend, IN, PT,
12 oz 10.00
Rolling Rock, Labrobe, Latrobe, PA,
PT, 7 oz..4.50
Schaefer, PT, 10 oz 3.50
Schlitz Light, Schlitz, 6 cities, PT,
12 oz 1.00
Senate Beer, Washington, DC,
FT 50.00
Stag Premium Dry, Griesedieck-West-
ern, 2 cities, CT, 12 oz 35.00
Stein Haus, Schell, New Ulm, MN, PT,
12 oz 4.00
Tavern Pale, Atlantic, Chicago, IL, FT,
12 oz 30.00

Tech Premium, Pittsburgh, PA, FT,
8 oz..60.00
Topper, Eastern, Hammonton, NJ, PT,
12 oz 4.00
Utica Club Pale Ale, West End, Utica,
NY, FT, 12 oz 50.00
Valley Forge, Valley Forge, Norristown,
PA, FT, 12 oz...............................20.00
Walter's Light, Walter, Pueblo, CO, PT,
12 oz 4.00
West Virginia Pilsner, Little Switzerland,
Huntington, WV, PT, 12 oz............5.00
Yuengling, Yuengling, Pottsville, PA,
PT, 12 oz.....................................6.00
Ye Tavern, Lafayette, IN, CT,
12 oz 95.00

Beswick

Collecting Hints: Collectors have shortened the name of these interesting ceramics from House of Beswick to simply Beswick. There are five common marks that consist of "Beswick, England." Some include shape numbers and other information.

History: Beswick characters are well known to collectors and include figures from children's literature, as well as animals and other subjects. The firm was created by James Wright Beswick and his sons, John and Gilbert Beswick in 1894. Initial production was plain and decorated wares. By 1900, they were producing jugs, tea ware, dinner ware, flower pots, pedestals, figurines, vases, bread trays, and other household items. The factory was a family-run organization for decades. Gilbert Beswick is credited with creating the company's shape numbering system and shape book in 1934 while he was sales manager and his nephew, John Ewart Beswick, was chairman and managing director.

The first full-time modeler, Arther Gredington, was hired in 1939. Many of the designs he created are still in production. James Hayward was an outstanding decorator and created many new patterns and shapes. He also is credited with experimenting and perfecting glazes used on Beswick wares.

By 1969, the family members were nearing their retirement years and had no successors, so the company was sold to Royal Doulton Tableware, Ltd. Many of the Beswick animals are still being continued by Royal Doulton, but several have been discontinued. In August of 1989, the animal line was renamed as "Doulton Animals" and numbering system instituted that includes DA numbers rather than the Beswick backstamp.

References: Diana Callow et al., *The Charlton Standard Catalogue of Beswick Animals*, 3rd ed., Charlton Press, 1998;

Diana and John Callow, *The Charlton Standard Catalogue of Beswick Pottery*, Charlton Press, 1997; Jean Dale, *The Charlton Catalogue of Royal Doulton Beswick Figurines*, 6th ed., Charlton Press, 1998; Harvey May, *The Beswick Price Guide*, 3rd ed., Francis Joseph Publications, 1995, distributed by Krause Publications.

Bookends, Spaniel Dog, 5" h, drizzled
glaze, mkd "England" 145.00
Character Mug
Falstaff, inscribed "Pistol with Wit or
Steel, Merry Wives of Windsor," imp
"Beswick, England, #1127," 1948-73,
4" h 90.00
Hamlet, inscribed "To Be or Not To
Be," imp "Beswick, England, #1147,"
1949-73, 4-1/4" h 90.00
Mr. Bumble, mkd "Beswick #2032,
Parish Beadle," 4-3/4" h 65.00
Mr. Micawber, #310, 1970-73,
8-1/2" h.....................................125.00
Sairey Gump, #371, 1936-73,
6-1/2" h 125.00
Child's Feeding Dish, Mickey and Donald
on bicycle 140.00
Decanter, Loch Ness Monster, Beneagles
Scotch Whiskey, modeled by A. Hal-
lam, 1969 ....75.00
Figure
Amiable Guinea Pig, mkd "Beswick,
England, #37, F. Warne & Co., Ltd.,
Copyright 1967," slight dent in hat,
attributed as factory flaw,
3-1/2" h......................................240.00
Barnaby Rudge 60.00
Benjamin Ate A Lettuce Leaf, mkd
"Beswick, Made in England, Beatrix
Potter, F. Warne & Co., 1992 Royal
Doulton," 4-3/4" h 40.00
Benjamin Bunny, Royal Albert, mkd
"Beswick, Made in England, Beatrix
Potter, F. Warne & Co., 1948, 1989
Royal Doulton"............................36.00
Buffalo, 5-1/4" h 150.00
Bulldog, white and tan,
2-1/4" h 45.00
Bunnykin, bride 165.00
Bunnykin, groom 165.00
Bunnkyin, minstrel 130.00
Cardinal, #927, 6-1/4" h 150.00
Charalais Cow and Calf, 4-1/4" h x
7-1/2" h cow, pr.........................235.00
Chippy Hackee, Beatrix Potter, copy-
right 1979, 3-3/4" h 55.00
Foxy Whiskered Gentleman, mkd
"Beswick, Made in England, Beatrix
Potter, F. Warne & Co., 1954, 1989
Royal Doulton," 4-3/4" h 36.00
Girl, holding doll behind her back,
designed by Joan Walsh Angland,
4-3/4" h 175.00
Hereford Bull, 4-3/4" h,
7-1/2" l 185.00
Hereford Bull, 6" h, 9" h 225.00
Hereford Cow, 4-1/2" h,
6-3/4" l 165.00
Miss Moppet, 1954-78, BP-2 back
stamp, 3" h.................................225.00
Mr. Alderman Ptolemy, BP38 ....150.00

Old Mr. Brown, Beatrix Potter character, 1955-72, 3-1/4" h 125.00
Owl, Winnie the Pooh, 1968-90, 3" h 125.00
Palomino Horse, #1261, 6-3/4" h 165.00
Peter Rabbit, mkd in gold "Beswick Ware, Made In England, 1997, Royal Doulton" 65.00
Puddleduck, Beatrix Potter, F. Warne & Co., 1997 Royal Doulton, "#33, #15, #29," MIB 55.00
Samuel Whiskers, BP2 .... 250.00
Scottie, white, ladybug on nose, #HN804, 1940-69 .... 225.00
Siamese Cat Standing, #1896, 1963-80, oval mark, 6-1/2" h 100.00
Swish Tail Horse #1182, orig Beswick sticker, 8-1/2" h, 10" l 225.00
Tommy Brock, 1955-74, BP-2 backstamp, 3-1/2" h 600.00
Top Cat and Choo Choo, Hanna-Barbera, 1996, designed by Andy Moss, 4-1/2" h 160.00
Walking Horse and Jockey, #1037, mkd "Beswick England," #55, 8-1/2" h, 10-1/2" l 475.00
Plate, 7" d, Disney characters 95.00
Pitcher, Palm Tree pattern, mold number 1073, beige 175.00
Teapot, Sairey Gamp, #691, 5-1/2" h 300.00
Vase, 11-1/2" h, 9-1/4" w, #432, double handles, mkd "Beswick, Made in England, #432" 95.00

Bicycle Collectibles

Collecting Hints: Collectors divide bicycles into two groups—antique and classic. The antique category includes early high wheelers through safety bikes made into the 1920s and 1930s. Highly stylized bicycles from the 1930s and 1940s represent the transitional step to the classic period, beginning in the late 1940s and running through the end of the balloon-tire era.

Restoration is an accepted practice, but never pay a high price for a bicycle that is rusted, incomplete, or repaired with non-original parts. Replacement of leather seats or rubber handle bars does not effect value since these have a short life.

Make certain to store an old bicycle high (hung by its frame to protect the tires) and dry (humidity should be no higher than 50 percent).

Do not forget all the secondary material that features bicycles, e.g., advertising premiums, brochures, catalogs, and posters. This material provides important historical data for research, especially for restoration.

History: In 1818, Baron Karl von Drais, a German, invented the Draisienne, a push scooter, that is viewed as the "first" bicycle. In 1839, Patrick MacMillan, a Scot, added a treadle system; a few years later, Pierre Michaux, a Frenchman, revolutionized the design by adding a pedal system. The bicycle was introduced in America at the 1876 Centennial.

Early bicycles were high wheelers with a heavy iron frame and two disproportionately sized wheels with wooden rims and tires. The exaggerated front wheel was for speed, the small rear wheel for balance.

James Starley, an Englishman, is responsible for developing a bicycle with two wheels of equal size. Pedals drove the rear wheels by means of a chain and sprocket. By 1892, wooden rim wheels were replaced by pneumatic air-filled tires, and these were followed by standard rubber tires with inner tubes.

The coaster brake was developed in 1898. This important milestone made cycling a true family sport. Bicycling became a cult among the urban middle class—as the new century dawned, more than four million Americans owned bicycles.

The automobile challenged the popularity of bicycling in the 1920s. Since that time, interest in bicycling has been cyclical although technical advances continued. The 1970s was the decade of the ten speed.

The success of American Olympiads in cycling and the excitement of cycle racing, especially the Tour d'France, have kept the public's attention focused on the bicycle. However, the tremendous resurgence enjoyed by bicycling in the 1970s appears to have ended. The next craze is probably some distance in the future.

References: Jim Hurd, *Bicycle Blue Book*, Memory Lane Classics, 1997; Jay Pridmore and Jim Hurd, *The American Bicycle*, Motorbooks International, 1996; Neil S. Wood, *Evolution of the Bicycle*, Vol. 1 (1991, 1994 value update), Vol. 2 (1994), L-W Book Sales.

Periodicals: *Antique/Classic Bicycle News*, P.O. Box 1049, Ann Arbor, MI 48106; *Bicycle Trader*, P.O. Box 3324, Ashland, OR 97520; *Classic & Antique Bicycle Exchange*, 325 W. Hornbeam Drive, Longwood, FL 32779; *Classic Bike News*, 5046 E. Wilson Rd., Clio, MI, 48420; *National Antique & Classic Bicycle*, P.O. Box 5600, Pittsburgh, PA 15207.

Collectors' Clubs: Cascade Classic Cycle Club, 7935 SE Market St, Portland, OR 97215; Classic Bicycle and Whizzer Club, 35769 Simon, Clinton Twp, MI 48035; International Veteran Cycle Association, 248 Highland Dr., Findlay, OH 45840; National Pedal Vehicle Association, 1720 Rupert, NE, Grand Rapids, MI 49505; The Wheelmen, 55 Bucknell Ave., Trenton, NJ 08619.

Museum: Schwinn History Center, Chicago.

Advertising Mirror, Bakersfield Cyclery and Novelty Works 20.00
Air Speed Indicator, 2-1/2" d x 1" h deep white metal, clasp ring, black and white celluloid window, aluminum marker for indicating miles per hour, D. A. Comstock & Co., Post Cereals premium, c1940 .... 15.00
Badge
  L.A.W. 18th Annual Meet/Philadelphia/ Aug. 4-7, 1897, diecut brass link, "Souvenir," pendant in shape of victory wreath around star symbol centered by logo of League of American Wheelman 65.00
  YMCA Bicycle Club/New Brunswick, NJ, 1896, gold luster metal link, inscribed "Mileage" hanger bar, pendant with victory wreath motif and YMCA inscription around triangle logo, back professionally engraved "Century-1896 YMCA Bicycle Club/New Brunswick, NJ" 75.00
Bicycle
  Ace Cycle and Motor Works, metal label reading "George Tenby-Cycling champion of Wales- retired, 1879-1889," as-found orig condition . 150.00
  Ames and Frost Co., Model #36 Imperial 500.00
  AMF Roadmaster 500.00
  Bronco, boy's 5,500.00
  Chilion, wood frame, 1898 ..... 1,100.00
  Cleveland, lady's drive shaft model, 20" frame 290.00
  Columbia
    Expert, 1887, 54" wheel, orig condition 2,500.00
    Fire Arrow 300.00
  5 Star Superb, 75th Anniversary edition 375.00
    Standard, 1883, 48" front wheel, restored condition 2,700.00
    Twinbar 3,200.00
  Dayton Champion 4,620.00
  Elgin
    Black Hawk, 1934 .... 2,200.00
    Miss America, 1939, balloon tires 1,320.00
  Elliot, hickory safety, wooden spokes and fellows, c1898, as-found condition, needs retiring 470.00
  Excelsior, man's motor, orig olive drab, no tires 1,050.00
  High Wheeler, Scottish, 42" h front wheel, primitive, excellent condition 3,100.00
  Huffy, Radiobike 2,000.00
  Lady's, hard tired safety type, 1891, good unrestored condition 3,600.00
  Monarch, Silver King, hex tube 825.00
  Montgomery Ward, Hawthorne, girl's, mid-1950s, orig paint, 26" 125.00
  Overman Wheel Co., Victor Light, safety, man's, 25" frame, butterfly handlebars, c1894 .... 395.00
  Pope Mfg Co., Columbia Model #50, drive-shaft, orig condition 400.00
  Roadmaster, Luxury Liner 600.00

Rollfast, Custom Built, Model
V200 ....2,750.00

Schwinn Black Phantom, repainted blue, orig chain guard, S2 rims, handle bars, spring fork, and drum brake, repro tank, seat, fenders, luggage rack, head and tail lights, tires, $1,400. Photo courtesy of Clark Phelps.

Schwinn
  Aerocycle Model 34 ....8,500.00
  Autocycle, B-107 ....1,750.00
  Corvette 300.00
  Hornet 400.00
  Mark II Jaguar 750.00
  Panther, Model D-77, girl's ...900.00
  Phantom, Model D0-27 ....900.00
  Starlet, Model D0-67 ....500.00
  Seaman, wood frame 3,630.00
Sears, Elgin
  Bluebird 7,000.00
  Robin.................................3,500.00
  Skylark 2,000.00
  Twin 30...............................700.00
Shelby, Donald Duck 2,000.00
Springfield Roadster, c1888, 50" to 100" ratchet drive, orig condition 5,100.00
Sterling, tandem, lady's front three gear, c1897, orig condition 1,200.00
TRB Alenax, ratchet drive, nice condition.....................................110.00
Unknown Maker, hard-tired safety type 700.00
Western Wheel Works, Chicago, IL, Otto, boy's, c1900, late high wheel, wooden spokes 1,350.00
Whizzer, Model H, 1948 ....2,310.00
Bike Horn, Hopalong Cassidy, orig handlebar clamp 150.00
Book
  Around the World on a Bicycle, Fred A. Birchmore, autographed 30.00
  Patterson, 150 line drawings.......70.00
  Bicycling World, four-volume set.......................................1,265.00
  Riding High, A. Judson Palmer, autographed 82.50
  The Wheel and Cycle Trade Reviews, 25 volume set 4,100.00
Brochure, Schwinn-Built Bicycles, 3-1/4 x 6", illus of nine bicycles, c1948...55.00
Cabinet Card, man with high wheeler.......................................120.00
Catalog
  Eclipse, Elmira, NY 46.00
  Flying Merkel, 1916 ....250.00
  G. W. Stevens Bike Suits, orig fabric swatches 100.00
  Imperial 25.00

Indian Bicycle 90.00
Iver Johnson, 1914 ....120.00
Mead Cycle Co., Chicago, IL, c1923 ....14.00
NSU Motorcycle........................110.00
Rollfast...70.00
Springfield Roadster 110.00
Victor Bicycle, 1898 ....200.00
White Flyer, 1890.......................880.00
Dance Card, 3-1/4" x 5-1/2", Nashua Cycle Club, 1888, cardboard folder 25.00
Display, Dunlop Cycle, repair display and repair outfit 70.00
Lamp
  Argonaut....................................45.00
  Evel Knievel Tail Light, Mego, 1974, MOC...35.00
  Lucas, Silver King, petroleum 95.00
  Majestic Lamp 25.00
  P & H Ltd., The Winner 15.00
  Solar Model S.............................55.00
Lapel Stud, 7/8" d, celluloid on metal, c1896 America, red letter on white "Buy The America and You Can't Go Wrong"......................................20.00
  Bicycle Saddles, red, and white, winged gargoyle trademark, Muller Mfg Co., NY..................................25.00
  Colonial Bicycles, red, white, and blue, patriot shield symbol 20.00
  Columbia Bicycles, black and white, nameplate inscribed "You See Them Everywhere"................................20.00
  Conroy Bicycle, Willard & Conroy, CO, NY, black, white, and red.............15.00
  Crescent Bicycles, red lunar crescent, white ground, black letters 20.00
  Dey's Bike, red, white, and blue figural wheel......................................20.00
  Falcon, olive green and pink logo, tiny falcon image 20.00
  Frontenac Bicycles, brown and white 15.00
  Northampton Bicycles, olive green, black, and white............................15.00
  Oquaga, white letters, rose pink ground..15.00
  Phoenix Bike, black, white, and red, trademark Phoenix bird rising from ashes, slogan "It Stands The Racket"...................................20.00
  Richmond Bicycle Company, black and white.....................................15.00
  Spaulding, black, white, and red 10.00
  Sylph Cycles Run Easy, black and white 15.00
  The Fowler Bicycles, white letters, plum ground................................20.00
  The Liberty, black letters, peach ground, tiny slogan "American's Representative Bicycle" 25.00
  The Winton, white letters, deep purple ground..15.00
  Yellow Fellow, black letters, orange ground, "Trans-Continental Relay Souvenir," sponsored by NY Journal Examiner 30.00
Lap Robe, cycling motif.................. 320.00
Magazine Tear Sheet
  Murray Bicycles, Eliminator, Murray Lightweights, and Murray Wildcats, *Boys' Life, 1967*.............................3.00

Raleigh, Chopper, *Boys' Life,* 1970..3.00
Roadmaster, half sheet, *Saturday Evening Post,* 1951 ....2.00
Schwinn Christmas, Krates, Orange Krate, Lemon Peeler, Apple Krate, and Pea Picker 3.00
Membership Cards, L.A.W., 1886 to 1907..130.00
Model, Enterprise, Cycle Miniatures series, c1950, 4" x 6" x 1" orig box Old High Wheeler......................9.00
  Tandem, Bicycle Built for Two.......7.50
Nameplate, early 1900s
  2-1/2" h, aluminum, Bloomingdale's Lexington, New York 18.00
  2-1/2" h, silvered sheet metal, Ward's Hawthorne 15.00
  3" h, curled brass, Roamer 20.00
Photo Album, two cabinet cards, ten tintypes of bicyclists........................700.00
Photograph, William Witaschek, The Great Calvert, 1937, 30th year on road...60.00
Pinback Button, 7/8" d, celluloid, c1896
  Bells Bicycles, multicolored 25.00
  Ellsmore Bicycles, multicolored, red and black lettering 30.00
  Mak-Nu, Expressly For Bicycle Use..15.00
  Member Bicycle Riders Thrift League 23.00
  Ride a Pope Bicycle, black, white, and blue, green Tribune model..........25.00
  Stewart's Cycle Brake, blue image, red letters, white ground....................15.00
  Superb Ajax Cycles, white letters, blue ground 15.00
Playing Cards, Monark, King Cooper, 1895 ....300.00
Quadracycle, leather seat and fenders, tiller steering, handles for pumping 1,000.00
Ribbon, Clerk of the Course, 1896...45.00
Seat
  DeLuxe Messenger, leather, balloon tire type bicycle 20.00
  Monarch, twin..............................30.00
Sheet Music, *Velocipedia*.............. 110.00
Spoke Reflectors
  7/8" x 3", flat plastic, relief image of Garfield on top, copyright United Features Syndicate, 1978, blue with serious expression, yellow with smiling expression 8.00
  2-1/2" x 3-1/2", molded flat plastic, warrior shape, two yellow with yellow reflector, one red with red reflector, Kellogg's cereal premium, copyright 1985, set of three........................8.00
Stickpin, 7/8" d celluloid, Lovell Diamond Cycles, black and white, diamond logo, c1896............................30.00
Tandem, Victor............................ 1,760.00
Tire Setter, Improved Peerless 150.00
Toy, tricycle, 2-1/2" x 4-1/2" x 6", wind-up, built-in key, boy riding red, white, and blue tricycle, plastic balloon attached to handlebars mkd "Happy Days," mkd "MTU/Made in Korea," 1970s, orig colorful box 24.00
Trade Card, Clark Bicycle Co., Christmas, Santa on high wheeler, 1880s...25.00

Tricycle
    Boy's, butterfly handlebar, leather padded seat......................................190.00
    Gendron, c1900, tiller steering, 20" wheel, restored..........................370.00
    Girl's, tiller steering, 28" rear wheels, front treadle drive.......................270.00
    Homer Benedict, invalid type....325.00
    Hopalong Cassidy......................660.00
    Victor, 25" wheels, c1890.......1,000.00

Big Little Books

Collecting Hints: Ongoing research on Big Little Books is a factor in shifting values. Condition always has been a key. Few examples are in mint condition since the books were used heavily by the children who owned them. Each collector strives to obtain copies free from as many defects (bent edges on cover, missing spine, torn pages, mutilation with crayon or pencil, missing pages, etc.) as possible.

The main character in a book will also determine price since collectors from other fields vie with Big Little Book collectors for the same work. Cowboy heroes, Dick Tracy, Disney characters, Buck Rogers, Flash Gordon, Charlie Chan, and The Green Hornet are a few examples of this crossover influence.

Until recently, little attention was given to the artists who produced the books. Now, however, books by Alex Raymond and Henry Vallely command top dollar. Other desirable artists are Al Capp, Allen Dean, Alfred Andriola, and Will Gould. Personal taste still is a critical factor.

Little is known about production runs for each book title. Scarcity charts have been prepared but constantly are being revised. Books tend to hit the market in hoards, with prices fluctuating accordingly. However, the last decade has witnessed price stabilization.

The introduction to Larry Lowery's book includes an excellent section on the care and storage of Big Little Books. He also deserves credit for the detailed research evident in each listing.

History: Big Little Books, although a trademark of the Whitman Publishing Co., is a term used to describe a wealth of children's books published from the 1930s to the present day. Whitman and Saalfied Publishing Company dominated the field. However, other publishers did enter the market. Among them were Engel-Van Wiseman, Lynn Publishing Co., Goldsmith Publishing Co., and Dell Publishing Co.

The origins of Big Little Books can be traced to several series published by Whitman in the 1920s. These included *Fairy Tales*, *Forest Friends*, and *Boy Adventure*. The first actual Big Little Book appeared in 1933. Ten different page lengths and eight different sizes were tried by Whitman prior to the 1940s.

Whitman also deserves attention for the various remarketing efforts it undertook with many of its titles. It contracted to provide Big Little Book premiums for Cocomalt, Kool Aid, Pan-Am Gas, Macy's, Lily-Tulip's Tarzan Ice Cream, and others. Among its series are *Wee Little Books*, *Big Big Books*, *Nickel Books*, *Penny Books*, and *Famous Comics*.

In the 1950s, television characters were introduced into Big Little Book format. Whitman Publishing became part of Western Publishing, owned by Mattel. Waldman and Son Publishing Co. under its subsidiary, Moby Books, issued its first book in the Big-Little-Book style in 1977.

References: Bill Borden, *The Big Book of Big Little Books*, Chronicle Books, 1997; Glen Erardi, *Collecting Edgar Rice Burroughs*, Schiffer Publishing, 2000; Larry Jacobs, *Big Little Books: A Collector's Reference & Value Guide*, Collector Books, 1996; Lawrence Lowery, *Lowery's Collector's Guide to Big Little Books and Similar Books*, privately printed, 1981; *Price Guide to Big Little Books & Better Little, Jumbo, Tiny Tales, A Fast-Action Story, etc.*, L-W Book Sales, 1995.

Collectors' Club: Big Little Book Collector Club of America, P.O. Box 1242, Danville, CA 94526.

Additional Listings: Cartoon Characters, Cowboy Heroes, Disneyana, Space Adventurers.

Barney Baxter in the Air with the Eagle Squadron, Whitman #1459, copyright 1938, small loss to cover.............18.00
Buffalo Bill Plays a Long Hand, 1939, spine missing...............................15.00
Daktari, Night of Terror, cover bent..16.00
David Copperfield, Whitman #1148, 1934, movie edition, W. C. Fields, Freddy Bartholomew................100.00
Don Winslow USN, Whitman #1107, 1935...50.00
Ella Cinders and the Mysterious House, Whitman #1106, 1934..................55.00
Flash Gordon and the Witch Queen of Mongo, Alex Raymond................75.00
Foreign Spies, Doctor Doom and the Ghost Submarine, 1939, tear at top of spine...15.00
Inspector Wade of Scotland Yard, Saalfield Publishing, 1940...........20.00
Just Kids and the Mysterious Stranger, Saalfield Publishing, 1935, spine missing, first 10 pages loose..............12.00
Kazan in the Revenge of the North..25.00
Lassie, Adventure in Alaska, 1967...12.00
Lil Abner, Among the Millionaires, 1939, front and spine missing..............10.00
Little Red School House, Dickie Moore, several front pages missing........20.00
Lone Ranger and the Black Shirt Highwayman, 1939..........................20.00

Lone Ranger and the Menace of Murder Valley, 1938, spine broken away from cover..20.00
Major Matt Mason Movie Mission, 1968...20.00
Mickey Mouse and Pluto the Racer, 1936, some cover wear and soiling, pages yellowed...35.00
Mickey Mouse, Mystery at Dead Mans Cove, copyright 1980 Walt Disney Productions.....................................30.00
Pluto the Pup, Whitman #1467, 1938...65.00
Radio Patrol, Outwitting the Gang Chief, 1939, spine broken away from front cover..15.00
Rex Beach's Jaragu of the Jungle, Whitman #1424, title page and first eight pages missing, other wear...........2.00
Snow White and the Seven Dwarfs, Walt Disney Enterprises, 1938, C-7....45.00
Stan Kent, Freshman Fullback, Saalfield Publishing, 1936..........................15.00
State Trooper and the Kidnapped Governor, Jim Craig, 1938...................42.50
Sybil Jason in Little Big Shot, Whitman, #1149, title page and copyright page missing, pencil markings..............8.00
Terry & War in the Jungle, 1936, worn cover, name written inside, 4-1/2" x 3-1/2"...25.00
The Man from U.N.C.L.E., the Calcutta Affair, 1967................................15.00
The Story of Jackie Cooper, 1933, spine missing..20.00
Tom and Jerry Meet Mr. Fingers......20.00
Tom Beatty, wear to cover...............25.00

Better Little Book, *Red Ryder, Acting Sheriff*, #702-10, Fred Harman, artist and author, 1948, $28.

Better Little Book

Brer Rabbit From Song of the South, Whitman #1426, 1947 copyright......................................75.00
Bugs Bunny and the Pirate Loot, Whitman #1403, 1947 copyright........40.00
Disney's Cinderella and the Magic Wand, #711-10............................40.00
Disney's Donald Duck, Ghost Morgan's Treasure, #1411................50.00

Disney's Donald Duck, Up in the Air,
1945, wear on cover and spine, light
soiling..25.00
*Disney's Mickey Mouse on Haunted
Island,* #708-10.............................50.00
*Disney's Silly Symphony Presents
Donald Duck,* #1169....................25.00
Disney's Thumper and the 7 Dwarfs,
#1409..40.00
Ghost Avenger, Whitman #1462, 1943
copyright...30.00
G-Men Breaking the Gambling Ring,
Whitman #1493, 1938
copyright...40.00
Inspector Charlie Chan, Whitman
#1424, 1942 copyright.................60.00
Mickey Mouse in the Treasure Hunt,
1941, wear and soiling................45.00
Mr. District Attorney, Whitman #1408,
1941 copyright..............................50.00
Tailspin Tommy All-Pictures Comics,
Whitman #1410, 1941
copyright...25.00

Black Memorabilia

Collecting Hints: Black memorabilia
was produced in vast quantities and variations. As a result, collectors have a large
field from which to choose and should
concentrate on one type of item or a limited combination of types.

Outstanding examples or extremely
derogatory designs command higher
prices. Certain categories, e.g., cookie
jars, draw more collectors, resulting in
higher prices. Regional pricing also is a
factor.

New collectors frequently overpay for
common items because they mistakenly
assume all Black collectibles are rare or
of great value. As in any other collecting
field, misinformation and a lack of knowledge leads to these exaggerated values.
The Black memorabilia collector is particularly vulnerable to this practice since so
little documentation exists.

New collectors should familiarize
themselves with the field by first studying
the market, price trends, and existing reference material. Seeking out other collectors is especially valuable for the novice.

Black memorabilia has developed into
an established collecting field and continues to experience increasing public
attention and interest.

History: The term "Black memorabilia"
refers to a broad range of collectibles that
often overlap other collecting fields, e.g.,
toys and postcards. It also encompasses
African artifacts, items created by slaves
or related to the slavery era, modern
Black cultural contributions to literature,
art, etc., and material associated with the
Civil Rights Movement and the Black
experience throughout history.

The earliest known examples of Black
memorabilia include primitive African
designs and tribal artifacts. Black Americana dates back to the arrival of African
natives upon American shores.

The advent of the 1900s saw an
incredible amount and variety of material
depicting Blacks, most often in a derogatory and dehumanizing manner that
clearly reflected the stereotypical attitude
held toward the Black race during this
period. The popularity of Black portrayals
in this unflattering fashion flourished as
the century wore on.

As the growth of the Civil Rights Movement escalated and aroused public
awareness of the Black plight, attitudes
changed. Public outrage and pressure
during the early 1950s eventually put a
halt to these offensive stereotypes.

Black representations are still being
produced in many forms, but no longer in
the demoralizing designs of the past.
These modern objects, while not as historically significant as earlier examples,
will become the Black memorabilia of
tomorrow.

References: Douglas Congdon-Martin,
*Images in Black: 150 Years of Black Col-
lectibles,* 2nd ed., Schiffer, 1999; Kyle
Husfloen (ed.), *Black Americana Price
Guide,* Antique Trader Books, 1997;
Kevin Keating and Michael Kolleth, *The
Negro Leagues Autograph Guide,* Tuff
Stuff Books, 1999; Jan Lindenberger,
*Black Memorabilia for the Kitchen: A
Handbook and Price Guide,* 2nd ed.,
Schiffer, 1999; —, *More Black Memora-
bilia,* 2nd ed., Schiffer Publishing, 1999; J.
L. Mashburn, *Black Postcard Price Guide*
2nd ed., Colonial House, 1999; Dawn
Reno, *Encyclopedia of Black Collectibles,*
Wallace-Homestead/Krause, 1996; J. P.
Thompson, *Collecting Black Memorabilia,*
L-W Book Sales, 1996; Jean Williams
Turner, *Collectible Aunt Jemima,* Schiffer
Publishing, 1994.

Periodical: *Blackin,* 559 22nd Ave.,
Rock Island, IL 61201; *Doll-E-Gram,* P.O.
Box 1212, Bellevue, WA 98009-1212;
Lookin Back at Black, 6087 Glen Harbor
Dr., San Jose CA 95123.

Collectors' Club: Black Memorabilia
Collector's Association International Golli-
wogg Collectors Club, P.O. Box 612,
Woodstock, NY 12498, http://www.teddy-
bears.com/golliwog; 2482 Devoe Ter,
Bronx, NY 10468.

Museums: Black American West
Museum, Denver, CO; Black Archives
Research Center and Museum, Florida
A&M University, Tallahassee, FL; Center
for African Art, New York, NY; Great Plains
Black Museum, Omaha, NE; Jazz Hall of
Fame, New York, NY; John Brown Wax
Museum, Harper's Ferry, WV; Museum of
African American History, Detroit, MI;
Museum of African Art, Smithsonian Insti-
tution, Washington, DC; National Baseball
Hall of Fame, Cooperstown, NY; Robeson
Archives, Howard University, Washington,
DC; Schomburg Center for Research in
Black Culture, New York, NY; Studio
Museum, Harlem, NY.

Reproduction Alert: The number of
Black memorabilia reproductions has
increased during the 1980s. Many are
made of easily reproducible materials
and generally appear new. Collectors
should beware of any item offered in large
or unlimited quantities.

Note: The following price listing is based
on items in excellent to mint condition.
Major paint loss, chips, cracks, fading,
tears, or other extreme signs of deterioration warrant a considerable reduction in
value, except for very rare or limited production items. Collectors should expect a
certain amount of wear on susceptible
surfaces.

Ashtray, 4-1/2" w, ceramic, black boy with
head in alligator's mouth, Florida sou-
venir...75.00
Baby Rattle, 8" l, celluloid, figural, stand-
ing black man, top hat and tails, holding bouquet of flowers, white, red, and
black, mkd "Made in
Japan"..45.00
Badge, 4" d, Aunt Jemima Breakfast
Club, litho tin, sepia face, pink lips,
yellow and red checkered bandanna,
red ground, white lettering "Eat A Bet-
ter Breakfast," bar pin fastener,
c1960..65.00
Bank, still, cast iron
Darky Sharecropper, 5-1/4" h, A. C.
Williams, painted, c1901...........165.00
Mammy, 5-1/2" h........................125.00
Save and Smile, 4-1/4" x 4",
England......................................425.00
Birthday Card Golliwogg, 1950s.....24.00
Black boy blowing out candles on
cake, © Hall Brothers, 1940s, 4" x
5"...25.00
"Happy Birthday Wishes – Guaran-
teed Not to Fade, Hoping that your
happiness is the kind that's sure to last
– may all your birthday joys be Bright
and true, and Color-Fast!," little black
girl in wooden tub on front, sgd, dated
1942...30.00
Book
*America Dilemma, The Negro Problem
& Modern Democracy,* Gunnar
Myrdal, Harper Bros., 1944, 1,483
pgs, some underlining, fading,
wear...16.00
Army Life in A Black Regiment, Went-
worth, 1870, 296 pgs.................45.00
*Black Troops in the Union Army, 1861-
1865, The Sable Arm,* Dudley Cornish,
1956...42.00
*Human Cargo: The Story of the Atlan-
tic Slave Trade,* White, c1972, illus,
engravings, drawings.................35.00

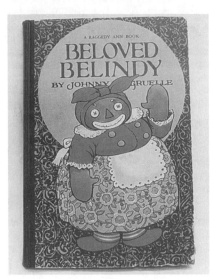

Children's book, *Beloved Belindy*, Johnny Gruelle, 1926, $25.

The Negro in the Civil War, Quarles, 1953 .... 35.00
The People Could Fly, American Black Folktales, Virginia Hamilton, Knopf, 1985, 178 pgs, inscribed 10.00
The White Man's Burden: Historical Origins Of Racism in the US, Winthrop D. Jordan, Oxford Press, 1974, ex. Library copy 15.00

Booklet
  4" x 5-1/2", "Vote Against Jim Crow," Socialist Workers Party, 1940, worn 45.00
  4-1/2" x 8", "Equality, Land and Freedom-a Program for Negro Liberation," Communist Party publication, League of Struggle for Negro Rights, New York, 1933, 48 pgs 75.00
  5-1/2" x 8-3/4", "Songs, Sketch of the Life, Blind Tom, the Negro Boy Pianist," biography, reviews, and sample songs, c1888, soil, wear 125.00

Bottle Opener, 7" h, figural, minstrel, painted wood 42.00

Box, Mason's Challenge Blacking, 11-1/2" w wood box, paper label 85.00

Children's Book, *Suremma,* Whitcombe, c1940 .... 30.00

Cigar Box Label, 6-1/4" x 10", glossy paper label, Booker T. Perfecto Cigars, c1930, unused 18.00

Creamer and Sugar, stacking type, black clown 85.00

Dish Towel, embroidered Mammy 35.00

Doll, Cream of Wheat Chef, stuffed cloth, 1960s 80.00

Feather Duster Holder/Bank, 3" x 4-1/2" x 8" h, painted plaster, black boy, blue pants, one gold colored metal loop earring, standing next to oversized orange, yellow, and green pineapple, hold in top to hold wood handle feather duster, coin slot in back, mkd "Japan," 1960s 40.00

Figure
  1-1/4" x 2-1/2" h, kneeling celluloid boy, red shorts, surprised expression at dice roll, reglued to base, thumb missing, small tourist decal worn away, Japan, c1930 .... 25.00
  2-1/4" w, 2-1/2" h, little black boy peeking in outhouse door at another black boy, titled "One moment please," mkd "Made in Japan" 20.00
  4-1/2" h, bisque, woman, native clothing, mkd "Occupied Japan" 24.00

Game
  Chocolate Splash, Willis G. Young Mfg., Chicago, 7" x 10" x 1-1/2" cardboard box, paper label, target game, 1916 .... 175.00
  Sambo, Wyandotte Toys, 14" x 23" dart board, litho tin, grinning black boy, some wear and scratches 100.00
  The Game of Hitch Hiker, Whitman, 13" x 13" x 1-1/2" box, 1937 .... 95.00

Incense Burner, 5" h, cast iron, standing Mammy, green dress, yellow shawl, balancing wide shallow yellow basket on head, chips to paint 95.00

Lobby Card, Come Back Charleston Blue, 1972, 8" x 10" 8.00

Magazine, *Labor Defender,* June 1931, cover of young Black man with head in noose, cover story "Dreiser on Scottsboro," minor wear 150.00

Magic Lantern Slide, man playing banjo 24.00

Match Holder/Ashtray, little girl eating watermelon, chalkware 38.00

Mirror, pocket, 1-3/4" x 3-3/4", oval celluloid, photo of W. T. Brown Jr., Black Chicago funeral home director, 1920s 125.00

Needle Book, Luzianne Coffee adv 22.50

Nodder, 4-1/4" h, painted metal, boy in yellow hat, smoking cigar, mkd "Occupied Japan" 55.00

Notepad and Pencil Holder, 6" x 10-1/2", painted hard plastic, wall hanger, 3-D Mammy image, insert pencil as broomstick in one hand, orig paper tablet, yellow and black accents, 1950s 165.00

Palm Puzzle, tin rim holding glass over emb glossy paper image, caricature black face, blue shirt, green ground, dark red mouth slot, five tiny balls serve as teeth, German, c1920 165.00

Pennant, 25" l, New York Black Yankees, felt 200.00

Photograph, ambrotype, 2" x 2-1/2", cased, half length portrait, seated Black woman, wearing print dress, white collar, brooch, wide-brimmed hat, mid-19th C, separation at hinge of leather case 200.00

Pinback Button
  Don't You Love Me No Mo? Black girl in pigtails, wearing skimmer hat, daisy flower 25.00
  I Raise You, black man in uniform holding cable with word "elevator" next to him, art by Goldberg 35.00
  Ten Days-Smoke Up, caricature of black man standing before judge, art by Tep, c1912, 7/8" d 35.00

Pin Cushion, sitting black baby, movable arms and legs, tape measure 90.00

Perfume bottle, Golliwogg figural bottle, orig box and contents, 3-7/8" h, $90.

Post Card, 3-1/2" x 5-1/2"
  Card #53, caricature of youngster being booted out of doorway, designed by F. G. Long, published by Kaufmann & Strauss Co., copyright 1904, inked personal message, slight use 38.00
  Card #57, caricature of youngsters playing dice, inked personal message on front, designed by F. G. Long, published by Kaufmann & Strauss Co., 1906 .... 24.00

Program, Penn Wheelman Frolic, 1927, Minstrels, Orpheum Theater, 64 pgs 42.00

Recipe Booklet
  Aunt Jemima, Quaker Oats, 15 pgs, c1932 .... 45.00
  Aunt Jemima's Magical Recipes, 25 pgs, 1952 .... 16.50

Salt and Pepper Shakers, pr, figural
  Butler and Mammy, flowers on dress 135.00
  Jonah and Whale 90.00
  Kids in Basket 85.00
  Native and Hut 70.00
  Native on Hippo 215.00
  Salty and Peppy, Pearl China ... 245.00

Sheet Music
  Cotton Fluff, Clayton F. Summy Co., tape reinforcing on sides 25.00
  It Takes A Long Tall Brown-Skin Gal To Make A Preacher Lay His Bible Down, red, brown, and white cover art, 10-1/2" x 13-1/2" h, 1917 copyright 25.00
  Sam the Accordion Man 20.00

Sign, "Out to Lunch, Sappy's Barbershop, Colored Only," Pittsburgh, 1929, cardboard 25.00

Song Book, *Favorite Negro Spirituals,* Shawnee Press, 30 songs, 1938 .... 25.00

Spice Shaker, Aunt Jemima, plastic, mkd "F & F Mold & Die Works," paprika, 1950s 55.00

Stove Pipe Vent Cover, 9-1/2" d, multicolored, black youngster with straw hat, holding banjo, looking at car made out of ear of corn, watermelon wheels,

passenger with pink plumed hat, brass frame, hanging chain, asbestos backing, c1900............................145.00
String Holder, figural
Boy, bending beside watermelon 65.00
Mammy 45.00
Tip Tray, 4" d, Cottolene Shortening, litho tin..85.00
Toy
Trapeze Artist, squeeze type, painted wood 45.00
Wakouwa Boxing Champs, 5" h, painted wood 90.00
Tray, 12" d, Green River Whiskey, black man and horse, litho tin..100.00
Wall Pocket, Blackamoor, mkd "Royal Copley" 70.00

Tobacco jar, bisque, seated Black woman holding pug dog, 8" h, $550. Photo courtesy of Joy Luke Fine Art Brokers and Auctioneers.

Blue Ridge Pottery

Collecting Hints: Blue Ridge patterns are among the most established of the collectible American dinnerwares. Collectors pay a premium for artist-signed pieces. The Talisman Wallpaper dinnerware pattern, because of its original failure to attract buyers, is the most difficult dinnerware pattern to find. Among the harder-to-find shapes are the China demipot and the character jugs.

Patterns and forms made in the 1940s are the most popular. As in most dinnerware patterns, hollowware pieces command higher prices than flat pieces. Demi-sets that include the matching tray are considered a real find. Blue Ridge collectors must compete with children's dish collectors for miniature pieces.

Because the wares were hand decorated, identical pieces often contain minor variations. Develop a practiced eye to identify those that are most aesthetically pleasing. Minor color variations can change a pleasing pattern into one that is ordinary.

History: In 1917, the Carolina Clinchfield and Ohio Railroad, in an effort to promote industry along its line, purchased land along its right-of-way and established a pottery in Erwin, Tennessee. Erwin was an ideal location because of the availability of local white kaolin and feldspar, two of the chief ingredients in pottery. Workers for the new plant were recruited from East Liverpool and Sebring, Ohio, and Chester, Virginia.

In 1920, J. E. Owens purchased the pottery and received a charter for Southern Potteries, Incorporated. Within a few years, the pottery was sold to Charles W. Foreman. Foreman introduced hand painting under glaze and trained girls and women from the nearby hills to do the painting. By 1938, Southern Potteries, Incorporated, was producing Blue Ridge "Hand Painted under the Glaze" dinnerware. The principal sales thrust contrasted the Blue Ridge hand-painted ware with the decal ware produced by most other manufacturers.

Blue Ridge maintained a large national sales organization with eleven showrooms scattered nationwide. Few catalogs were issued and trade advertising was limited. As a result, researching Blue Ridge is difficult.

Most of the patterns used on Blue Ridge originated at the plant. Lena Watts, an Erwin native, was chief designer. Eventually, Watts left Blue Ridge and went to Stetson China Company.

Blue Ridge also made limited-production patterns for a number of leading department stores.

As the 1930s came to a close, Southern Potteries was experiencing strong competition from inexpensive Far Eastern imports, but World War II intervened and changed the company's fortune. Southern Potteries' work force increased tenfold, production averaged more than 300,000 pieces per week, and the company experienced a period of prosperity that lasted from the mid-1940s into the early 1950s.

By the mid-1950s, however, imports and the arrival of plastic dinnerware once again threatened Southern Potteries' market position. The company tried half-time production, but the end came on January 31, 1957, when the stockholders voted to close the plant.

References: Betty and Bill Newbound, *Collector's Encyclopedia of Blue Ridge Dinnerware*, Collector Books, 1994, 1999 value update; —, *Southern Potteries, Inc.*, 3rd ed., Collector Books, 1989, 1999 value update; Frances and John Ruffin, *Blue Ridge China Today*, Schiffer Publishing, 1997.

Periodicals: *Blue Ridge Beacon Magazine*, P.O. Box 629, Mountain City, GA 30562; *National Blue Ridge Newsletter*, 144 Highland Drive, Blountville, TN 37617.

Collectors' Club: Blue Ridge Collectors Club, 208 Harris St., Erwin, TN 37650.

Museum: Unicoi Heritage Museum, Erwin, TN.

Annette's Wild Rose, milk pitcher, 4-1/2" h................................115.00
Applejack, skyline shape
Coffeepot, Ovide......................245.00
Dinner Plate, 9" d.........................20.00
Platter...30.00
Vegetable Bowl, divided 40.00
Becky
Dinner Plate, 10" d 15.00
Eggcup..30.00
Luncheon Plate, 8" d 10.00
Big Blossom, pitcher, Grace shape, 5-3/4" h..95.00
Bluebell Bouquet
Bowl, 9" d, some crazing 20.00
Dinner Plate, 9" d.........................8.50
Gravy Boat....................................25.00
Calico
Candy Box.....................................185.00
Teapot, cov, colonial shape 170.00
Carnival, creamer and sugar............30.00
Cash Family, pitcher, mkd "Made by the Cash Family handpainted" 65.00
Chick, creamer, floral, 5-1/2" h.......110.00
Chintz
Cake Plate, maple leaf shape, loop handle, 10" l................................60.00
Candy Dish....................................90.00
Chocolate Pot.............................325.00
Christmas Tree, plate 65.00
Cock of the Walk, dinner plate, 10" d..75.00

Vegetable dish, Dogwood, yellow and brown floral decoration, 9-1/2" x 7", $24.

Cocky Locky, platter......................140.00
Colonial Rose, dinnerware set, 61 pcs..495.00
Daffodil
Cereal Bowl, 6" d.........................12.00
Creamer..12.00
Cup and Saucer..........................12.50
Dinnerware Set, piecrust shape, 45 pcs.......................................575.00
Dinner Plate, 10-1/2" d 15.00
Dahlia, creamer 15.00

Delicious, dinnerware set, Candlewick
edge, 45 pcs 425.00
Dogtooth Violet, candy dish, cov,
round 265.00
Dorothy, bon bon 55.00
Dutch Bouquet, colonial shape
Bread and Butter Plate, 6" d........10.00
Cereal Bowl, 6" d 12.00
Cup and Saucer 15.00
Dinner Plate, 9-34" d.....................17.50
Easter Parade
Bon Bon, flat 150.00
Cake Plate..................................125.00
Celery Dish, leaf 75.00
Chocolate Pot..............................195.00
Creamer, pedestal 75.00
Relish, round 75.00
Sugar...75.00
Elegance, sugar, pedestal, 6" w,
3-1/2" h......................................50.00
Faimede Fruit, pitcher, Alice shape,
6-1/4" h......................................90.00
French Peasant
Bon Bon 170.00
Butter Pat 75.00
Candy Box, cov 165.00
Chocolate Pot, cov 500.00
Demitasse Cup and Saucer........75.00
Dinner Plate, 9" d 100.00
Server, center handle 95.00
Soup Plate, two handles.............135.00
Fruit Basket, relish, narrow leaf 75.00
Fruits, bon bon, shell, flat,
9-1/2" w 110.00
Gloriosa, dinnerware set, skyline shape,
20 pcs 250.00
Grapes, salad set, bowl, four
plates 145.00
Gypsy Dancer, teapot, cov, colonial
shape 135.00
Hampton, vase, hibiscus shape,
5-1/2" h......................................80.00
Harvest Time, dinnerware set, modern
shape, 50 pcs............................475.00
Helen, milk pitcher, 4-1/2" h.............95.00
Hilda, dinnerware set, 55 pcs 450.00
Jigsaw, child's feeding dish 90.00
Lyonnaise
Demittasse Cup...........................75.00
Sandwich Tray, 11-1/2" w 110.00
Mardi Gras
Creamer 12.00
Dinner Plate, 9" d, Colonial
shape 10.00
Pie Plate, used, age spots 20.00
Teapot, cov 185.00
Martha, pitcher, earthenware, 7" w,
6-1/2" h......................................75.00
Milady, water pitcher, ftd,
7-3/4" h.....................................250.00
Mirror Image, dinnerware set,
43 pcs 500.00
Nocturne
Cup and Saucer, colonial shape, red
edge..15.00
Dinner Plate, sq 15.00
Nova Rose
Dish, shell shape 90.00
Salt and Pepper Shakers, pr,
5-1/2" h.......................................82.00
Palisades, pitcher, mid-1950s...........90.00
Petite Point, child's tea set, four cups and
saucers, four plates, creamer, sugar,
teapot...850.00

Poinsettia, colonial shape
Bread and Butter Plate, 6" d..........3.50
Creamer 8.00
Cup and Saucer............................12.00
Dinner Plate...................................6.50
Fruit Bowl, 5" d..............................6.50
Luncheon Plate 5.50
Queen's Lace, plate, 10-1/2" d,
used...10.00
Red Letter Day, teapot, cov, colonial
shape, 10" w, 8" h......................120.00
Rock Rose, batter set tray, 8-1/2" x
13-1/2" 120.00
Rooster, cigarette box, cov, sq,
4-1/4" w 125.00
Rosebuds, Candlewick shape
Salad Bowl, 11" w 55.00
Salt and Pepper Shakers, pr,
6" h..75.00
Rose Hill, teapot, cov, fine panel
shape 130.00
Rose of Sharon, creamer,
pedestal 90.00
Rustic Plaid, snack set, plate and
cup...7.50
Sculptured Fruit
Pie Server 35.00
Pitcher, 6-1/2" h 135.00
Pitcher, 7-1/4" h 125.00
Skeeter, demitasse cup and saucer, "PV"
in circle mark, 4-3/4" w.................48.00
Stanhose Ivy, skyline shape, dinnerware
set, 45 pcs.................................425.00
Summertime, celery tray, leaf,
10-3/4" l......................................85.00
Sunshine, demitasse tray, 9-1/2" l, small
chip..85.00
Sweet Clover, dinner plate.................8.00
Trailee Rose, water pitcher,
spiral..135.00
Tuffie Muffie, celery tray, leaf
shape 50.00
Tuna Salad, party plate with cup,
10-1/2" d plate..............................46.00
Velvet Petals, celery tray, leaf,
10-3/4" l......................................85.00
Verna, maple leaf shape
Cake Plate..................................125.00
Dish, 10" w...................................90.00
Weathervane
Bread and Butter Plate, 6" sq,
cock..60.00
Dinner Plate, 10-1/2" d.................45.00
Fruit Bowl......................................18.50
Saucer 15.00
Wild Strawberry, sugar....................135.00
Winnie, skyline shape, dinnerware set,
31 pcs 325.00
Yellow Nocturne, salad bowl,
11" l..70.00

Bookends

Collecting Hints: Since bookends
were originally designed to be used in
pairs, make sure you've got the proper
set. Check for matching or sequential
numbers as well as damage or loss of
decoration. Single bookends are sometimes marketed as doorstops or shelf sitters, and a careful eye is needed to find
one-of-a-kind items.

History: No formal history of bookends
is available, but it is not too difficult to
imagine those eager for knowledge that
began to accumulate books searching for
something to hold them in an orderly
fashion. Soon decorators and manufacturers saw the need and began production of bookends. Today bookends can
be found in almost every type of material,
especially metal and heavy ceramics,
which lend their physical density to keep
those books standing straight.

Bookends range from artistic copies of
famous statuary to simple wooden
blocks, offering collectors an endless
adventure.

References: Louis Kuritzky, *Collector's
Guide to Bookends*, Collector Books,
1998; Robert Seecof, Donna Seecof, and
Louis Kuritzky, *Bookend Revue*, Schiffer
Publishing, 1996.

**Squirrels, metal, mkd Bronzart, $90.
Photo courtesy of Joy Luke Fine Art
brokers and Auctioneers.**

American Eagle, cast iron with copper
finish, holding ribbon in mouth with "E.
Pluribus Unum," holds arrows in one
claw..125.00
Arts & Crafts, Roycroft, copper, emb
teardrop shapes, orig felt, 4" w,
5" h...175.00
Bear, New Martinsville, clear glass,
4-1/2" h.......................................110.00
Book, alabaster, 3" w, 5-1/2" h 85.00
Bowl of Flowers, bronze, mkd "Armour
Bronze, Inc.," c1923, 7" h 235.00
Boy, little nude boy sitting on stump,
hands up to mouth, dog with head on
boy's leg, mkd "J. L. Drucklieb," 6-1/4"
h, worn down to pot metal 80.00
Bust
Abraham Lincoln, cast iron, gold
finish, copyright 1928 with triangle in
circle mark, 5-1/4" h, some rust ..50.00
Civil War Generals, Grant and Lee,
pot metal, 6" h.............................30.00
Oliver Wendell Holmes, cast iron,
bronze finish 135.00
Cathedral Window, attributed to Brad-
ley & Hubbard, cast iron, 6" w,
6-1/4" h......................................165.00
Cheshire Cat, brass, c1930......145.00

Clematis, white flowers, blue ground, Roseville Pottery 300.00
Clipper Ships, cast iron with copper finish..25.00
Cocker Spaniel, Frankart, white metal, c1934, 7-1/2" h............................165.00
Conestoga Wagons.....................80.00
Cottage, composition, 6-1/2" h....30.00
Cowboy on bucking horse, arm in air, hat flying, fence in background, gold painted cast iron, 5-3/4" h, some wear to paint 50.00
Dice, white, black and red, sq marble base 40.00
Dog, Goebel, crown mark.........135.00
Eagle
    Cast bronze with hand finishing, brass column, marble bases 350.00
    Copper, taking flight 95.00
Elephants
    Cast Iron, Connecticut Foundry shopmark, c1930, 5-3/4" h..........85.00
    Glass, New Martinsville, clear 170.00
Farmer and Wife, giving thanks in field, male resting against a tree, woman with lunch basket, bicycle, bronzed metal, 4-3/4" h 50.00
Fisherman in rowboat, gold painted cat iron, 3-1/2" h, some wear to paint 48.00
Flowers in Basket, multicolored painted flowers, blue basket, cast iron 65.00
Flying Mallards, Shawnee Pottery, sgd "Shawnee USA 4000," 6" h 115.00
Ford, 1901 model, ceramic.........50.00
Galley Slaves, slaves pulling a rope, cast iron, coppery brown paint, c1930, no felt.......................................220.00
Garfield and Odie, orig Enesco paper label, glazed ink stamp mark, 1983, 5" h, 2" w..235.00
Gazelles
    Frankart, 7-1/4" l, 6-1/4" h.....225.00
    Mahogany, carved, 5" w, 7-1/2" h...................................90.00
Gladiator, man fighting beast, bronzed cast iron, name incised on reverse, 5-1/4" h 50.00
Good Luck Owls, gray, white, and yellow owl perched on 2" sq block, marble, 4" h 15.00
Graceland Gates, Clay Art..........90.00
Greyhounds, Art Deco style, bronze 250.00
Horseheads, glass, clear, Fostoria, 4-3/4" w, 3-1/4" d, 5-3/4" h 35.00
Horse Grazing, bronze finished metal, 3-3/4" h 45.00
Horse Tamer, Littco Mfg. Co., iron, copper-clad finish, inscribed "Horse Tamer," orig felt, 6-1/2" w, 4-3/4" h 110.00
Hunting Dogs, Hubley, bronze, orig paint dec, c1925 ....185.00
Indian
    Brave, wearing headdress, cast iron, mustard-colored paint, book rack, expands to 23-1/2" l, 6" h .220.00
    Head, brass, detailed...........125.00

Profile, pot metal, orig paint, mkd "K Co.," c1935 ....150.00
Riding horse, with spear, bronze, 6" h...185.00
Kissing Fish, Littco Mfg. Co., cast iron, coppery brown paint, c1925, 6-1/8" h, one with orig felt, wear to paint...250.00
Lions
    Book rack, emb lions on each side, expands to 22" l, 5" h 185.00
    Cast iron with black finish, catwalk pose, Bradley and Hubbard 165.00
    Glass, Cambridge, amber, made for National Cambridge Collectors, 1978..155.00
Lost Hope, K & O Mfg Co., gray metal with polychrome finish, 1920-40s 125.00
Oriental Boy and Girl, Burmese, black glaze, Roseville Pottery, c1950 ....400.00
Peony, Roseville, yellow floral dec 145.00
Poodle, white bisque, gray tints, white book base, gold trim, red Lefton paper label, 5" x 3" base, 6" h 50.00
Praying Hands, brass, 6-1/2" h ...75.00
Puppies, set of three puppies resting heads together, bronzed pot metal, felt base...70.00
Race Horse and Jockey, bronzed white metal, Art Deco 95.00
Sailing Ships, cast iron, mkd "Verona," 5-1/4" h 45.00
Scotties
    Ceramic, light blue bows, orange base, mkd "Made in Japan"........85.00
    Glass, clear, Cambridge, 6-1/2" h 175.00
    Pot metal, painted ivory, orig felt, 7" h, wear to paint 65.00
Septarian Nodules, mined in Utah, 5-3/4" h 60.00
Setters, ceramic, mkd "Made in Japan" 45.00
Signing of Declaration of Independence, four men seated at table, including George Washington and Thomas Jefferson, Liberty Bell, and flags, bronzed cast iron, mkd "copyright," CP logo, 5-1/8" h 50.00
Snow White, Schmid, Walt Disney Productions copyright.......................55.00
Spinning Scene, woman seated at spinning wheel, brass covered cast iron, c1930, 3-7/8" h, wear to paint..60.00
Stage Coach, pulled by 2 teams of horses, sunset in background, bronze finished metal, mkd "Old Coaching Days," 4-1/4" h 45.00
Terriers
    Cast iron, Judd Mfg. Co., brown paint, orig felt, Judd logo, inscribed number, c1930, 3-1/4" w, 4-1/2" h 165.00
    Pot metal, 5-1/2" h, worn, tarnished 75.00

The Thinker, gold painted cast iron, 5-3/8" h 65.00
U.S. Olympic Yachting Trials, San Francisco, CA, 1956, wooden with round medallions........................85.00
Wagon Train, American Hardware Co., cast iron, dated 1931, minor paint loss 90.00
Ye Olde Inn Stagecoach, three men, partial Syroco label, 1940 ....55.00

Bookmarks

Collecting Hints: The best place to search for bookmarks is specialized paper or advertising shows. Be sure to check all related categories. Most dealers do not keep bookmarks together but rather file them under subject headings, e.g., Insurance, Ocean Liners, World's Fairs, etc.

History: Bookmark collecting dates back to the early 19th century. Bookmarks—any object used to mark a reader's place in a book—have been made in a wide variety of material including celluloid, cloth, cross-stitched needlepoint in punched paper, paper, sterling silver, wood, and woven silk. Heavily embossed leather markers were popular between 1800 and 1860. Advertising markers appeared after 1860.

Woven silk markers are a favorite among collectors. T. Stevens of Coventry, England, manufacturer of Stevengraphs, is among the most famous makers. Paterson, New Jersey, was the silk weaving center in the United States. John Best & Co., Phoenix Silk Manufacturing Company, and Warner Manufacturing Co. produced bookmarks. Other important United States companies that made woven silk bookmarks were J. J. Mannion of Chicago and Tilt & Son of Providence, Rhode Island.

Collectors also search for colorful folk art quality of cross-stitched bookmarks created between 1840 and 1920. These were a popular handicraft made by young women who followed the design imprinted on pre-punched paper strips. Plain strips were available for those wishing to design their own bookmark. Most have a religious theme, but examples have been found commemorating birthdays or Christmas, or depicting temperance (anti-drink) or other themes. Most were attached to colorful silk ribbons.

Periodical: *Bookmark Collector*, 1002 West 25th St., Erie, PA 16502.

Collectors' Club: Antique Bookmark Collector's Association, 2224 Cherokee St., St. Louis, MO 63118.

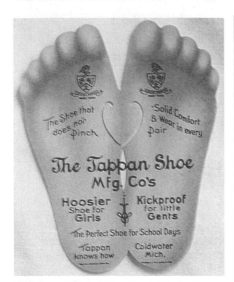

Tappan Shoe Mfg Co., flesh tone, black letters, $20.

Advertising

Cameron Steam Pump, celluloid, multicolored, Scottish bagpiper, product text, New York City, blank reverse 70.00
Eberhart & Miller, Shoes & Rubbers, Warren, PA, aluminum, emb floral design, attached silk cord.............7.50
Maltine, diecut thin celluloid, multicolored image, brown and white owl, lengthy text on reverse.................45.00
Morrell's Meats, heart-shaped diecut celluloid, slogan "Iowa's Pride Meats," black and white text on reverse 42.00
Palmer Violets Bloom Perfume, gold trim 15.00
Printzless, celluloid, multicolored image of lady in stylish white plumed hat, matching gown, brown fur accessories, black and white text.........75.00
Snickers, 3" w, 4-1/4" h, 1987........2.50
Standard Publishing Co., Cincinnati, multicolored image of female cardinal, "Search The Scriptures".......25.00
Theo F. Siefert Furs, Philadelphia, celluloid, multicolored image of delivery truck 40.00
United States Fidelity & Guarantee Co., brass, etched logo and "Home Office Baltimore USF & G" 5.00

Figural

Carriage, brass.............................25.00
Cross, diecut, translucent plastic, Lord's Prayer written on front, 1-1/2" x 4-3/4" 6.00
Heart, sterling silver, 1-3/4" h.......20.00
Hoof, clamped, sterling silver mkd "W & S Sorenson, Denmark, Sterling"...45.00
Horse, brass, running with weathervane directions N and S, 4-1/2" h, 1-3/4" w 35.00
Letter "A," Apollo Silver Co., sterling silver, c1899-4905 ....35.00
Teardrop shape, sterling silver, mkd "S. Kirk & Son," 1" x 2-1/2"...........35.00

Woven

Cloth, oval silhouette of Lincoln at top, quote from Gettysburg address, black on cream, orig card, c1935.........20.00
Silk, cream, oval vignette of George Washington, Chinook jargon saying on one side, English translation on other, 1-7/8" w, 6-1/2" h, lightly soiled 30.00
Silk, T. Stevens, Coventry, England, Home Sweet Home, black bungalow center, floral pattern, 1-1/2" x 6-3/4", c1890 ....38.00

Books

Collecting Hints: Many types of books relating to people's lives, such as biographies and autobiographies, can be found in the antiques and collectibles marketplace. Watch for well-illustrated, complete, and clean copies. Condition is always a key to prices. Keep an eye open for autographed copies, as well as first editions.

Today's book collectors now have a wealth of Web sites, which cater to locating vintage titles. Just as in the real world, it pays to shop around in this new cyber market.

History: This edition of *Warman's Americana & Collectibles* is going to concentrate on biographies and autobiographies, books about interesting people. Some were written during the person's lifetime, others are compilations of information obtained from their diaries, letters, historical accounts, etc. Many readers found them interesting when they were first published and today collectors actively seek them out.

References: Allen Ahearn, *Book Collecting: A Comprehensive Guide*, G. P. Putnam and Sons, 1995; Allen and Patricia Ahearn, *Collected Books: The Guide to Values*, G. P. Putnam and Sons, 1997; *American Book Prices Current*, Bancroft Parkman, published annually; Sharon and Bob Huxford, *Huxford's Old Book Value Guide*, 13th ed., Collector Books, 2001; Norma Levarie, *Art & History of Books*, available from Spoon River Press, 1995; Caroline Seebohm, Estelle Ellis, and Christopher Simon Sykes, *At Home with Books: How Book Lovers Live with and Care for Their Libraries*, available from Spoon River Press, 1996.

Periodicals: *AB Bookman's Weekly*, P.O. Box AB, Clifton, NJ 07015; *Biblio Magazine*, 845 Wilamette St., P.O. Box 10603, Eugene, OR 97401; *Book Source Monthly*, 2007 Syosett Dr., P.O. Box 567, Cazenovia, NY 13035; *Firsts, The Book Collector's Magazine*, P.O. Box 65166, Tucson, AZ 85728, http://www.firsts.com; *Rare Book Bulletin*, P.O. Box 201, Peoria, IL 61650.

Collectors' Club: Antiquarian Booksellers Association of America, 20 West 44th St., 4th Floor, New York, NY 10036.

Gone with the Wind, large-print edition, two volumes, hardcover, with dust jacket, $25.

The Life and Adventures of Santa Claus, by L. Frank Baum, $45.

A Streak of Luck: The Life & Legend of Thomas Alva Edison, Robert Conot, 1979, Book of the Month Club, 565 pgs..8.00
Autobiography of an English Soldier in the United States Army (Mexican/American War 1846), Lakeside Classic, 1986 ....35.00
Dr. Seuss and Mr. Geisel, A Biography, Judith and Neil Morgan, Random House, 1995, dj.........................20.00
DuPont, The Autobiography of an American Enterprise, 1952, 138 ps, illus 9.00
Dwight D. Eisenhower, a Gauge of Greatness, Reiman Morin, 1969, 251 pgs..8.00
Everybody Who Was Anybody, Janet Hobhouse, Putnams, 1974, 1st ed. 8.50
F. Lee Bailey w/Harvey Aronson, The Defense Never Rests, Stein & Day, 1971, 262 pgs, dj 8.50
Frederick Catherwood, Architect, Victor Wolfgang von Hagen, Oxford, 1950..30.00
Life of John Wesley Hardin (Gunfighter) as Written by Himself, 1896, 150 pgs.......................................45.00
John G. Johnson, Barnie F. Winkleman, 1942, 315 pgs.....................9.00

Fannie Kemble, A Passionate Victorian, Margaret Armstrong, Macmillan, 1938, 382 pgs..................................9.00
George Washington, A Biography, Douglas Southull Freeman, 1948-57, seven volumes, slight wear.........45.00
George Washington Himself-Written from His Manuscripts, J. C. Fitzpatrick, 1933, sgd by Henry Steel Commager, ex-library copy............................16.00
Granville: Tales and Tail Spins from A Flyer, Diary, Abingdon Press, 1919......................................75.00
Hirohito, Emperor of Japan, Leonard Mosley, 1966, 371 pgs..................9.50
Jack London and His Times, An Unconventional Biography, Joan London, Book Leaque, 1st ed., dj.....15.00
John Marsh Palmer Pioneer, The Life Story of a Trail Blazer of Six Frontiers, George D. Lyman, Scribners, NY, 1934, 394 pgs..............................12.50
Kit Carson's Autobiography, Milo Quaife, ed., Lakeside Press, 1935.......................................65.00
Life of Abraham Lincoln, Joseph H. Barrett, 1865.........................57.50
Life of Clara Barton-Angel of the (Civil War) Battlefields, Ross, 1956......35.00
Lindberg, The Lone Eagle, George B. Fife, A. L. Burt, 1930, ex-library copy, cracked hinge, worn spine.........19.00
Lone Cowboy, My Life Story by Will James, Scribner, 1930, 1st ed., illus by author...37.50
Maxfield Parish, Coy Ludwig Watson, 1973, 3rd printing.........................58.00
Memoirs of General William T. Sherman, 1957 reprint of 1875 edition, two volumes in one.............................15.00
Memoirs of My Own Times, Gen. James Wilkinson, four volumes, including atlas, 1973 reprint of 1815 edition..65.00
My Forty Years with Ford, Chas. E. Sorensen, 1956, 345 pgs...........19.00
My Lord, What a Morning, An Autobiography Marian Anderson, Viking, 1956, 4th printing, worn dj..........10.00
Of Flight and Lives, Charles A. Lindbergh, Putman, Charles Schribner, 1927, 1st ed., dj.............................40.00
On Board with the Duke, John Wayne and the Wild Goose, Capt. Bert Minshall, Seven Locks Press, 1992, dj 12.00
Pat Nixon, The Untold Story, Julie Nixon Eisenhower, Simon & Schuster, 1986, 461 pgs, dj 7.50
Picasso-Creator and Destroyer, Arianna Stassinopoulos Huffington, Simon & Schuster, 1988, 1st ed. 12.00
Plain Speaking, An Oral Biography of Harry S. Truman, 1974, 448 pgs, dj 12.00
Remembered Laughter, The Life of Noel Coward, Cole Lesley, Knopf, 1977, 481 pgs, dj 8.50
Rufus Jones, Master Quaker, David Henshaw, 1951, 306 pgs, dj.......12.00
Simon Kenton, His Life and Period, 1755-1836, Edna Kenton, 1930, illus, ex-library 20.00

Stanley Vestal-Champion of the Old West, Tassin, Arthur H. Clark, 1973, 300 pgs, photos...........................65.00
Thayendanegea Joseph Brant-Life of the Mohawk Indian War Chief, H. Thomas, 1988, 200 pgs, dj................65.00
The Autobiography of Betrand Russell, Betrand Russell, volumes 1 and 2, wear.......................................18.00
The Brass Ring, A Memoir, Bill Bauldon, W. W. Norton, 1971, 1st ed., 275 pgs, illus and cartoons, wear to dj..16.00
The Fabulous Showman, The Life and Times of P. T. Barnum, Irving Wallace, Knopf, 1959, dj.............................8.00
The Gershwins, Robert Kimball and Alfred Simon, Altheneum, 1973, 1st ed..17.50
The Life of George Washington, John Marshall, 1836, Philadelphia, two volumes, full leather, 460 and 448 pgs 85.00
The Life of Lady Randolph Churchill, Ralph G. Martin, Prentice Hall, 1969, 9th printing, 395 pgs.....................8.50
The Life of William Penn: With Selections of His Correspondence and Autobiography, S. Janney, 1852, 1st ed., scuffed leather covers..........65.00
The Logbook of the Captain's Clerk-Adventures of the China Seas, Sewall, 300 pgs 35.00
The Lonely Lady of San Clements, The Story of Pat Nixon, Lester David Crowell, 1978, 224 pgs, dj 7.50
The Secret Life of Henry Ford, John C. Dahlinger, told by Frances Leighton, 1978, 1st ed., wear to dj...............9.50
Thirteen Days, Robert Kennedy, W W Norton & Co., 1969, 1st ed., BOMC, 29 pgs of photos, dj....................12.00
Thomas Pownall, Gov. of Mass. Bay, Author, Letters of Junius, CA Pownell, 1907, 526 pgs, foxed throughout, minor faults..................................15.00
War Within and Without, Diaries & Letters of Anne Morrow Lindbergh, Harcourt Brace Jovanovich, 1980, dj, 452 pgs 8.50
Will Rogers, Ambassador of Good Will, Prince of Wit and Wisdom, P. J. O'Brien, Navy Aviation Service, WW, appreciation by Lowell Thomas, Winston, Co., 1935, 288 pgs 12.00
Will Rogers, His Life and Times, Richard M. Ketchum, 1973, 415 pgs, dj..13.50
Winston Churchill, Rene Karus, Lippencott, 2nd edition, 1941, dj 10.00

Bottle Openers, Figural

Collecting Hints: Condition is most important. Worn or missing paint, repainted surfaces, damage, or rust result in lower value.

Figural bottle openers are one type of bottle openers that collectors have been attracted to for generations. Another growing area of bottle openers is advertising-related openers. Look for examples with crisp lettering and detailed information about the product or bottle opener manufacturer.

History: Figural bottle openers were produced expressly to remove a bottle cap from a bottle. They were made in a variety of metals, including cast iron, brass, bronze, and white metal. Cast iron, brass, and bronze openers are generally solid castings; white metal openers are usually cast in hollow blown molds.

The vast majority of figural bottle openers date from the 1950s and 1960s. Paint variations on any particular figure are very common.

References: Donald Bull, *Price Guide to Beer Advertising, Openers and Corkscrews*, published by author, 1981; *Figural Bottle Openers*, Figural Bottle Opener Collectors Club, 1992.

Collectors' Clubs: Figural Bottle Opener Collectors Club, 3 Ave. A, Latrobe, PA 15650; Just For Openers, 3712 Sunningdale Way, Durham, NC 27707.

Reproduction Alert.

Advertising

Anchor Beer, 3-1/2" h, some rust 3.00
Arrow Beer, It Hits the Spot, flat handle, loop type................................ 6.00
Atlas Prager Beer............................ 6.50
Bell Telephone, hard hat shape, cast iron, white, blue and yellow stripes, Bell logo on each side, made by Scott Products, Inc., Newark, NJ, orig box.. 50.00
Blatz Milwaukee Beer, iron loop type, name emb on both sides of handle, slight rust 8.00
Canadian Ace Beer....................... 5.00
Canadian Act Brand Beer & Ale, church key type, slight rust........... 6.00
Dixie Beer Co., iron loop type, name emb on both sides of handle...... 20.00
Drink Kamm's Quality Beer, loop opener 7.00
Drink National Beer 6.00
Edelweiss Beer, reads "Eidelweiss Beer A Case of Good Judgement" on one side, "Sehaehofen Edelweiss Co., Chicago, Illinois" on other side, silver color, 4-3/4" h................................. 4.00
Esslinger's Premium Beer 6.00
Floral handle, sterling silver, 6" l 35.00
Fort Pitt Beer, red, yellow, and green plastic handle 9.00
Fox Deluxe Beer............................. 5.50
Foxhead 400 Beer........................... 7.00
Genesee Beer-Ale.......................... 6.00
Goebel Beer 5.50

Drunk leaning on palm tree, painted white metal, 4" h, $35.

Graupner's Beer, loop opener 6.00
Gunthers Beer 5.00
Hamm's Beer from the Land of Sky Blue Waters 4.50
Hamm's Beer, sketch of bear 7.40
Horlocher Pilsner Beer, church key type, slight rust 6.00
Hyde Park Beer 5.00
Jackson Brewing Co., New Orleans, LA, wall type, "JAX" on upper section, base with full name, patent number, Brown Co., N. News, VA 20.00
King Edward, brass, coronation souvenir 8.50
Kirin Beer, iron loop type, name emb on both sides of handle 10.00
Krueger's Finest Beer, Lord Essex Stout, Old Surrey Porter, Boar's Head Ale, Kent Ale on one side, G. Krueger Brewing Co., Newark, NJ, on other side, loop handle, slight rust 7.50
Leinenkugel's Beer, iron loop type, name emb on both sides of handle 8.00
Make Friends with Valley Forge Beer on one side of loop, Rams Head Ale, the Aristocrat of Ales on other side 6.00
Neuweiler Beer & Ale, flat type 7.00
Old Reading Beer and Ale, loop opener 6.00
Old Regal Beer, bottom engraved "H R Ransom & Co.," 5" l 10.00
Ortleib's Beer, loop opener 5.50
Pabst Blue Ribbon Beer, loop top, bottle design on handle 5.00
Pale Ginger Ale, 2-3/4" l, broken rim, some rust 1.00
Piel's Beer Les N.F.S., beer can and bottle opener combination 5.00
Prior Beer, iron loop type, name emb on both sides of handle 8.00
Rainier Beer-Ale, iron loop type, name emb on both sides of handle 6.50
Royal 58 Beer 6.00
Schaefer Fine Beer, beer bottle shape 5.00
Stoney's Pilsner Beer, Esquire Premium Beer 5.50
Sunshine Premium Beer, church key type, slight rust 6.00

Tennis Rackets and ball, brass, 4-1/2" x 2-1/2" 10.00
Tru-Blu Beer and Ale, curved flat metal 5.00
West Bend Lithia Beer 6.00
Wiedemann's Fine Beer 5.00
Yusay Pilsner Beer 5.00

Figural

Cathy Coed, cast iron, preppy girl holding stack of books, green base, white front, sgd "L & L Favors," 4-1/8" h 375.00
Cockatoo, cast iron, orange and yellow, 3-1/4" h 150.00
Donkey, white metal, painted, 3-5/8" h 30.00
Elephant, sitting, trunk in circle, gray, pink and white highlights, Wilton Products, 3-1/16" h 50.00
Pelican, cast iron, head up, cream, orange beak and feet, green base, John Wright Co. 190.00
Sailor, hitchhiking pose, white uniform, blue tie and shoes, white sign with black trim, John Wright Co., 3-3/4" h 60.00
Sea Horse, brass, green, white highlights, green base with blue and black highlights, 4-1/4" h 85.00
Skunk, cast iron, black and white 150.00

Boxing Collectibles

Collecting Hints: Collectors of boxing memorabilia might wish to limit their collections to specific fighters. Today's fighters often retire and re-enter the ring, and new collectibles are being generated at a rapid rate.

History: Boxing, also known as prize fighting, is an old sport. The Romans enjoyed boxing competitions, and the sport was revived in the early part of the 18th century in England. The marquess of Queensberry introduced rules for the sport in 1865 and required the use of boxing gloves. Boxing became an Olympic sport in 1904.

Boxing was illegal in America until 1896, when New York became the first state to legalize it. Every state has a boxing commission or athletic organization to regulate the sport. Competition, limited to timed three-minute "rounds," takes place in a ring, which is usually 20 feet square. Professional boxers are divided into eight weight classes, ranging from flyweight to heavyweight.

References: David Bushing, *Sports Equipment Price Guide*, Krause Publications, 1995; Michael McKeever, *Collecting Sports Memorabilia*, Alliance Publishing, 1966.

Periodicals: *Boxing Collectors Newsletter*, 59 Bosson St., Revere, MA 02151; *Sports Collectors Digest*, 700 E. State St., Iola, WI 54990.

Collectors' Clubs Boxiana & Pugilistica Collectors International, P.O. Box 83135, Portland, OR 97203.

Museum: International Boxing Hall of Fame, Canastota, NY.

Autographed Glove, Muhammad Ali, red Everlast glove sgd "Muhammad Ali aka Cassius Clay" 150.00
Autographed Inaugural Induction Covers, 6-10-99
   Foster, Bob 20.00
   Griffith, Emile 25.00
   Saddler, Sandy 20.00
Autographed Photo
   Ali, Muhammad, 16" x 20" photo of Olympic torch lighting ceremony 500.00
   Ali, Muhammad, 16" x 20" photo of Sonny Liston, black and white 475.00
   Marciano, Rocky, 4 x 6", black and white, bold blue ink signature, matted and framed 995.00
Badge, 3" d black and white cello, "Tommie Smith-Ali Charity Fight," picturing Mayor Smith of Jersey City, NJ, as "The Urban Fighter" in preparation for exhibition charity bout with Muhammad Ali, also pictured, June 29, 1979 .... 55.00
Book
   Boxing Record Reference, 5" x 7-1/4", paperback published by Everlast Sports Publishing Co., 1929, 392 pgs, fighter profiles and portraits, green, black, and white cov 35.00
   Jack Dempsey/The Idol of Histiana, 1936 revised edition, Nat Fleischer, 158 pgs, inked autograph 35.00
   Ruby Roberts Alias Bob Fitzsimmons, Robert Davis, George H. Doran Company publishers, 1926, hard cover, orig dust jacket, several Fitzsimmons photos 100.00
   Muhammad Ali, belt buckle 20.00
Bottle Cap, Joe Louis Punch, red and white tin cap, c1940 .... 30.00
Boxing Gloves, Rocky Graziano, orig box 145.00
Bust, John Sullivan, Red Top Beer 250.00
Charm, Jack Dempsey, bright gold luster plastic, boxing glove, inscribed name on top, early 1950s 35.00
Game, Muhammad Ali's Boxing Ring, mechanical, Mego Corp., 1976 copyright, Herbert Muhammad Enterprise Inc., orig box 65.00
Magazine, *Sports Illustrated*, June 18, 1973, George Foreman on cov 20.00
Photograph
   Ali-Ellis, 8" x 10" glossy black and white, ten different Muhammad Ali facial expressions and contortions explained by photo release caption "Actor, Fighter, Or Both-A Study in

Many Faces of Muhammad Ali," lists live closed circuit telecast, July 26, 1971, Houston Astrodome 40.00
Dempsey-Loughran, 7" x 9" glossy black and white, press release caption by Associated Press attached to rear, March 23, 1938 release date, Jack Dempsey in left, Tommy Loughran at right, attending Philadelphia dinner honoring State Boxing Commissioner Julies Aronson pictured in center 25.00
Dempsey, US Army Signal Corps, 8-1/4" x 10" glossy black and white, Dempsey in military dress uniform, other military personnel and civilians, Signal Corps stamp dated Jan. 19, 1944 on back 30.00
Pinback Button
Cerdan, Marcel, black and white photo, European middleweight who held U.S. championship, c1948 .... 35.00
Frazier-Ali, black and white, March 8, 1971, Madison Square Garden 35.00
LaMotta, Jake, black and white photo, c1949 .... 30.00
Moore, Archie, gray and black photo, c1956 .... 15.00
Poster, Koncert King Promotions presents Farewell to a Legend Muhammad Ali in His Last Ring Appearance, March 12, Providence Civic Center, Providence, RI, also features bout with Marvelous Marvin Hagler in 10-bout round 180.00
Press Badge, diecut octagon cardboard, inked authorization for "H & E Photog" for "Loughran vs. Walker" bout March 29, 1929, Chicago Stadium, pink silhouettes of boxers under inked name, printed "24" serial number, grommet for hanging 85.00
Record Book, Blue Book, 1922 .... 60.00

Boyd Crystal Art Glass

Collecting Hints: Boyd Crystal Art Glass objects are usually made in a specific run of colors. The mark used has changed over the years. The first mark was a "B" in a diamond. Starting in 1983, an embossed line was added, and an additional line was added every five years thereafter. Counting the lines around the diamond will give the collector a clue as to the year of production. The latest mark includes an embossed "R," meaning the mold has been retired. Check out the Web site to get a good idea of the variety of colors this company has perfected over the years.

History: The Boyd Crystal Art Glass Company was founded in Cambridge, Ohio, on October 10, 1978, by father and son Bernard C. Boyd and Bernard F. Boyd. Today, Bernard F.'s son, John Ber-

nard, has joined the firm and it continues to produce glass collectibles, using 300 uniquely colored formulas.

In 1964, Elizabeth Degenhart asked glassmaker Zachery Boyd to assume the management of her company, Degenhart Glass. Upon Zachery's death in 1968, his brother Bernard C. Boyd assumed the leadership of the Degenhart Glass. Bernard C. and his son, Bernard F., purchased the Degenhart Company in 1978 and changed the name to Boyd Crystal Art Glass. Their initial production used the fifty Degenhart molds. They started issuing new colors in these molds. Over the years, additional molds were added, now numbering more than 200. Some were purchased from other glass companies, such as Imperial, creating some items in colored Candlewick.

Web site: http://www.boydglass.com.

Periodical: *Jody & Darrell's Glass Collectibles Newsletter*, P.O. Box 180833, Arlington, TX 76096, e-mail: scribeink@aol.com.

Angel, introduced 1995
Fantasia 19.00
Millennium Surprise, blue slag 19.00
Rosie Pink 18.00
Bernie the Eagle, introduced 1992
Alexandrite 9.00
Alpine Blue 9.00
Banana Cream 9.00
Capri Blue 9.00
Cardinal Red Carnival 10.00
Cobalt 9.00
Cobalt Carnival 10.00
Columbus White 9.00
Lemon Custard 9.00
Mint Julep 9.00
Nile Green 10.00
Rosie Brown 9.00
Waterloo 9.00
Bow Slipper, 5-3/4" l, 2-1/2" h, Harvest Gold Slag, "B" in diamond with lines mark 12.00
Brian the Bunny, introduced 1986, retired 1988
Alpine Blue 8.00
Cobalt Carnival 9.00
Nutmeg Carnival 9.00
Toffee Slag 9.00
Bulldog Head, 3" w, 3-1/2" h, "B" in diamond with lines mark
Jade Green 15.00
Purple Fizz 17.00
Purple Fizz Satin 18.50
Toffee Slag 17.00
Candlewick Box, cov, 5" l, 4" w, 2-1/2" h, vaseline, "B" in diamond with lines mark 25.00
Capri Box, cov, ftd, 5" l, 4" w, 2-3/4" h, "B" in diamond with lines mark
Aruba Slag 28.00
Jade Slag 28.00
Vaseline 25.00
Cat Slipper, 5-3/4" l, 3" h, "B" in diamond with lines mark
Alpine Blue 12.00

Millennium Surprise (blue swirl) .. 12.00
Millennium White 12.00
Moss Green 11.00
Nutmeg 11.00
Peacock Blue Swirl 12.00
Rosie Pink 12.50
Doberman Head, 3-1/2" w, 3-1/2" h, Purple Fizz, sgd by Bernard Boyd in gold, "B" in diamond with lines mark 17.00
Elizabeth Doll, introduced 1990, retired 1995
Alpine Blue 8.00
Crown Tuscan 9.00
Lemon Custard 9.00
Lemon Splash 8.00
Spring Beauty 9.00
Vaseline Carnival 10.00
Fuzzy Bear, 3" h, retired 1989, "B" in diamond mark
Alpine Blue 15.00
Amber and Red Swirl 12.00
Caramel Slag 17.00
Plum 15.00
Ritz Blue 15.00
Rosie Pink 15.00
Sunflower Yellow 15.00
Hen on Nest, Mirage (pale orchid), 4-1/4" w, 5-1/2" l, 5-3/4" h 20.00
High Boot, 4-3/4" l, 4" h, Daisy and Button pattern, "B" in diamond with lines mark
Peacock Blue 11.50
Tangy Lime 11.50
Jennifer Doll, introduced 1996
Alpine Blue 9.00
Cobalt 9.00
Harvest Gold 9.00
Marshmallow Crème 10.00
Milk Chocolate 9.00
Moss Green 10.00
Purple Fizz Carnival 10.00
Spring Surprise 10.00
Pie Vent, duck, yellow or blue 35.00
Pin Dish, cov, 2-3/4" w, 3-1/4" h, vaseline, "B" in diamond with lines mark 12.00
Puff Box, cov, 4" w, 2-1/4" h, vaseline, "B" in diamond with lines mark 16.00
Sports Car, 1-1/2" w, 4-3/4" l, 1" h, "B" in diamond with lines mark
Harvest Gold 15.00
Millennium White 15.00
Moss Green Slag 15.00
Nutmeg Carnival 18.00
Peacock Blue Slag 15.00
Tomahawk, 7-1/2" l, 4" w, emb Indian head, leaves and berries down handle, vaseline, "B" in diamond mark 15.00
Toothpick Holder, 3-1/2" h, scalloped top, chocolate slag, "B" in diamond with lines mark 30.00
Tractor, 2-3/4" l, set of five, blue irid, carnival irid, red carnival, orange and red slag, blue slag, each mkd "Boyd" on front, mkd "Boyd" without diamond 125.00
Tucker Car, 1-1/2" w, 3-3/4" l, 1" h, "B" in diamond with lines mark
Alpine Blue Carnival, includes emb "R" mark 16.00
Cashmere Pink, includes emb "R" mark 15.00

Dijon, includes emb "R" mark..... 15.00
Indian Orange Slag 15.00
Lime Green, includes emb "R"
mark 15.00
Mirage (pale orchid)................... 16.50
Patriot White, includes emb "R"
mark 15.00
Virgil the Clown, Mirage (pale orchid),
2-1/4" w, 4-1/2" h 12.00

Sascha Brastoff

Collecting Hints: When collecting items made by Brastoff, take special note of the signature. Pieces made exclusively by Brastoff are marked with his full name. A "Sascha B" signature indicates he only supervised the production.

History: Internationally known designer, artist, sculptor, and ceramist Sascha Brastoff began producing ceramic art-ware in 1953. His hand-painted china originally commanded prices ranging from $25 to thousands of dollars for a single item. He also designed a full line of dinnerware.

References: Jack Chipman, *Collector's Encyclopedia of California Pottery*, Collector Books, 1992, values updated 1998; Lois Lehner, *Lehner's Encyclopedia of U.S. Marks on Pottery, Porcelain & Clay*, Collector Books, 1988.

Ashtray
    Alaska, hooded, 5" w, 5" h, Eskimo
    face design, sgd "Sascha B ®,"
    H-3..65.00
    Alaska, hooded, 6-1/2" w, 8-1/2" h, sgd
    "Sascha B ®," #H-3......................75.00
    Freeform, gold ground, orange, green,
    and gold design, sgd "Sascha
    B"..60.00
    Iris OBA, gold signature, some wear to
    gold 20.00
    Jeweled Peacock, slant, gold signa-
    ture, standard mark 25.00
    Turquoise, 6" w..............................40.00
Ashtray and Cigarette Set, 13-1/2" x 5"
    ashtray, 3-3/4" h lighter, 2-5/8" cigarette
    container, Rooftops pattern, c1958,
    lighter not working 150.00
Box, cov
    Alaska, 5" l, 3-1/2" w, 2" h, sgd
    "Sascha B"...................................85.00
    Fruit and leaf design, brown, high
    glaze, sgd "Sascha B" on top of lid,
    slight crazing on base.................60.00
    Minos, 9" l, small int. chip 95.00
    Mosaic, dog finial, rooster
    mark 165.00
    Rooftops pattern, logo and style num-
    ber under roof, 5" x 7-1/2", white back-
    ground.......................................145.00
    Rooftops pattern, logo and style num-
    ber under roof, 6" x 7", pink, black
    background 145.00
Bowl
    9" l, 6" w, Aztec or Mayan, freeform,
    gold floral pattern, sgd "Sascha B ®"
    on front, rooster mark on back....95.00

9-3/4" l, 8-1/2" w, 2-1/2" h, Star Steed,
    three-ftd, starfish shape, gold accents,
    sgd "Sascha B ®" on front, rooster
    mark, #C-14 .... 110.00
14-1/2" l, 12" w, 4-1/4" h, Mosaic, three-
    ftd, sgd "Sascha B" inside bowl,
    rooster mark, minor paint chips around
    rim... 145.00
Cache Pot
    6" d, 4-1/2" h, scalloped top, sgd
    "Sascha B," slight factory flaw 70.00
    6-1/4" d, 4-1/2" h, ruffled top, light and
    dark green, pinks, mauves, white, and
    black trim, sgd "Sascha B" 65.00
Cigarette Holder, 5-1/2" h, pipe shape,
    Jewel Bird....................................50.00
Dish
    7-1/2" d, Aztec or Mayan, gold bird
    design, sgd "Sascha B" on front,
    rooster mark 50.00
    7-1/2" sq, Star Steed, sgd
    "Sascha B" 65.00
    9-1/2" l, 5-1/2" w, Vanity Fair, black
    ground, pink, blue, and burnt orange
    flowers, green grass 125.00
    10" d, Jewel Bird, freeform, sgd
    "Sascha B" on front, rooster mark,
    #F42..85.00
    11-1/2" l, Alaska, shell, gold trim, sgd
    "Sascha B ®" on front, rooster mark,
    #S52 ....95.00
    13" l, 6" w, 2-3/4" h, Rooftops, freeform,
    matte finish, sgd "Sascha B" on front,
    rooster mark 95.00
Figure
    Elephant, upturned trunk, gold glaze,
    8" h.. 400.00
    Horse, prancing, 6" l, Italian marble
    base, brass signature plate "Sascha
    Brastoff" 550.00
    Polar Bear, produced by American
    Bisque from estate.................... 195.00
    Rooster, 17" h 400.00
    Seal, light blue 425.00
    Seal, orange, resin, sgd
    "Sascha B" 295.00
Lamp, light blue base, orig shade,
    sgd 700.00
Plate, 8-1/2" d, ChiChi Bird, back
    sgd 195.00
Platter, 13-3/4" x 8-1/4", Alaska, Matt
    Adams, gray and taupe seal, blue sky,
    c1962-73, sgd "Sascha B" 130.00
Teapot, Surf Ballet, pink and gold,
    large 75.00
Tobacco Jar, 6-1/2" h, Abstract, stainless
    steel lid, F-20, some int. rust
    stains 65.00
Vase
    5-1/2" h, ChiChi Bird, sgd "Sascha B"
    on front, rooster mark...................95.00
    5-1/2" h, 5-1/2" w, Mosaic, sgd, two
    paint flakes and repaired chip 55.00
    5-1/2" h, 8" w, Alaska, Great Eskimo
    face, sgd "Sascha B ®" on front,
    #066.. 110.00
    5-1/2" h, 8-1/2" w, Aztec or Mayan,
    gold horse design, sgd "Sascha B ®"
    on front, rooster mark................ 125.00
    6-1/2" h, 3" w, Alaska, sgd
    "Sascha B ®," #V-4......................60.00
    7" h, gray, white and pink horse on
    hind quarters, 1951 ....95.00

8" h, Elk design, sgd "Sascha B ®,"
    #082...75.00
8" h, Eskimo Totem Pole, sgd "Sascha
    B ®," #082 ....75.00
8" h, Walrus, aqua, sgd "Sascha B ®,"
    #082...75.00
8" h, Walrus, brown and gray, sgd
    "Sascha B ®," #082 ....75.00
8" h, whimsical, flaring top, sgd
    "Sascha B ®" on front, #082.......85.00
8-1/2" h, Rooftops, matte finish, sgd
    "Sascha B" on front, rooster mark,
    #047..115.00
9-1/4" h, white and speckled yellow
    ground, gold leaves, rooster mark,
    sgd "Sascha B," price for pr..... 265.00
10" h, Vanity Fair, rooster mark,
    #F24.. 155.00
12" h, gold and white rings around
    base, white drip design, sgd "Sascha
    B, ®. V-3" 125.00
12" h, orange and gold, sgd "Sascha
    B ®," #V-3................................... 155.00
14" h, fruit design, sgd "Sascha B" on
    front base................................... 145.00
Wall Pocket, Provincial Rooster, 5" w, 4" h,
    sgd "Sascha B" on front, rooster mark,
    #P-1...95.00

Brayton Laguna Pottery

Collecting Hints: Brayton Laguna Pot-tery used three marks. The first mark reads "Brayton Laguna" and was regis-tered in February of 1935. The second one was an arched semi-circle with the letters "Weston-Ware" above a five-leaf decoration and was used about 1945. The third mark was "Brayton Laguna Pot-tery" in a hand-printed type script.

History: Durlin E. Brayton, a graduate of the Chicago Art Institute, began making pottery in his home in South Laguna Beach, California, in 1928. Brayton's bright hand-crafted matte glazed dinner-ware was an instant hit and the business began to flourish. The line was expanded to include cookie jars, lamps, figures, and other decorative objects. Durlin's wife, Webb, joined the firm and continued until her death in 1948. After Durlin died in 1951, employees operated the business. By 1967, competition proved to be too strong and the company ceased opera-tion.

Candleholders, pr, black youth,
    4-3/4" h 125.00
Cookie Jar
    Mammy, copyright 1943 .... 1,100.00
    Partridges, teal background, golden
    brown partridges, black branches, #V-
    11, incised mark 290.00
Creamer and Sugar, Calico Cat and
    Gingham Dog..............................95.00
Figure
    Car, wood tone, 17" l 145.00
    Chicken, blue 145.00

Figaro, crouching, 3-1/2" l 75.00
Fighting Pirates 450.00
Gay Ninety Bar, three men posing at
bar, 7-1/2" w, 8-1/2" h 115.00
Lady with Russian wolfhounds, light
blue dress, c1943, 11" h 115.00
Matilda, holding two planter baskets
across her shoulder, 7-3/8" h 90.00
Miranda 90.00
Owl 75.00
Panther, black 215.00
Pelican 45.00
Purple Cow, 9" l, 5-1/2" h 195.00
Sally, freckled face, 8" h 40.00
Sambo, small repaired chip on back of
hat 140.00
Zizi and Fifi, cats, maroon and green,
two paint flakes, pr 500.00
Flower Ring 45.00
Planter, kneeling black moor 125.00
Salt and Pepper Shakers, pr
Mammy and Chef 195.00
Provincial Man and Lady, 5-1/4" and
5-1/2" h 90.00

Breweriana

Collecting Hints: Many collectors concentrate on items from one specific brewery or region. An item will bring slightly more when it is sold in its original locality. Regional collectors' clubs and shows abound.

History: Collecting material associated with the brewing industry developed in the 1960s when many local breweries ceased production. Three areas occupy the collectors' interest—pre-Prohibition material, advertising items for use in taverns, and premiums designed for an individual's use.

References: Herb and Helen Haydock, *World of Beer Memorabilia*, Collector Books, 1997; Jack McDougall and Steve Pawlowski, *United States Micro/Brew Pub Coaster Guide*, published by authors, 1995; Steve Pawlowski and Jack McDougall, *New Jersey Brewery Coasters*, published by authors, 1995; Dale P. Van Wieren (ed.), *American Breweries II*, East Coast Breweriana Association, 1995.

Periodicals: *All About Beer*, 1627 Marion Ave., Durham, NC 27705; *Barley Corn News*, P.O. Box 2328, Falls Church, VA 22042; *Suds 'n' Stuff*, 4765 Galacia Way, Oceanside, CA 92056.

Collectors' Clubs: American Breweriana Association Inc., P.O. Box 11157, Pueblo, CO 81001; East Coast Breweriana Association, P.O. Box 64, Chapel Hill, NC 27514; National Association of Breweriana Advertising, 2343 Met-To-Wee Ln, Wauwatosa, WI 53226.

Museum: The Museum of Beverage Containers & Advertising, Goodlettsville, TN.

Reproduction Alert: Advertising trays.

Ale Mug
Finn Maccoul Beer, porcelain, Wade,
green, gray, and blue 25.00
Schlitz, brewery emblem on both
sides, scene of barrels brought by
boat being loaded on horse-drawn
cart, 7" h 6.00
Smith's Musty Ale, base mkd "WM
Brunt Pottery Co., E. Liverpool" ... 26.00
Staffordshire, 5-1/4" d, 5-1/4" h, frog in
bottom, c1930 .... 425.00
Ale Muller, copper, George III, English,
c1800, 9-1/4" l, 10-1/2" h 185.00
Ashtray
Coors Beer, white ceramic, red lettering, 6" d 4.00
Gregg & Helen's Standard Tap, pin-up
girl illus, metal, 3-3/4" x 4-1/2" 80.00
Molson's Ale, Porter, mkd "Estd 1786,"
6" d 80.00
Ballot Box, tin, round, maroon and gold
design on pale yellow ground, "Milderized Tavern Pale Beer, Atlantic Brewing Co., Chicago," slit on lid for ballots,
"Ballot Box. Place your vote here for
Miss Tavern Pale Contest, Watch the
Contest on Tavern Pale's Television
Show, WGN TV every Thursday night,"
7-1/2" w, 11-1/4" h 200.00
Banner, Bud Light Beer, Welcome to the
Kemper Open, red and gold, plastic,
rope ties, 112" x 36" 35.00
Bar Light, Schlitz, logo on front and back,
gold-colored plastic, plaster goddess,
glass globe, 1976, 45" h 140.00
Beer Cooler, Hamm's Beer, folding handle, 19" l, 9-1/2" w, 12" h 135.00
Beer Glass, pilsner-type
adv, Holland Brand Beer,
7-3/4" h 8.00
Buick Model "C" dec, red rim, green
leave, red car, yellow tulips, policeman
standing by light post, 1905, set of six,
8-1/2" h 40.00
Valley Forge Beer, red logo, glass handles, set of four 20.00
Beer Stein, Anheuser-Busch
After the Hunt, 9-3/4" h 100.00
American Homestead, retired 1996,
Ceramarte, 7" h 85.00
Babe Ruth, first in Legends series,
8-1/2" h 85.00
Decade of the '50s, 9" h 170.00
Early Delivery Days, 1998,
Ceramarte 100.00
Lighting the Way, 1995, 7" h 100.00
Beer Stein, Budweiser
Clydesdales, 1988, 6" h 25.00
Nina, part of Explorer series 90.00
Olympiad, LA, 1964 .... 100.00
Season's Best, 1991 .... 80.00
Western Boot, brown glazed ceramic,
1994 .... 35.00
Beer Stein, Winchester, 7-3/4" h
Calf Roping, first in series 180.00
Saddle Bronc Riding, third in
series 180.00
Beer Tap, Schlitz, wood and ceramic,
worn 25.00
Book, *Bluegrass, Belles and Bourbon-A
Pictorial History of Whiskey in Kentucky,* Harry Harrison Kroll, AS Barnes,
1967, 224 pgs, photos 42.00
Bottle Opener
Budweiser, pocket-type, 2-1/2" l, mkd
"Made in W. Germany" 12.00

Drink Ale & Beer, Ballantine & Sons,
Newark, NJ, Purity, Body, Flavor,
4-1/4" l, 1-1/2" w 5.00
Harpoon Beer 1.25
Box
Old German Beer, Renner Co., Youngstown, OH, made by River Raixin
Paper Co., Monure, MI, 1954, 16-1/2" x
11" 72.00
Old Oxford Ale, cardboard, made by
Inland Container Co., Indianapolis, IN,
17" x 10-1/2" 72.00
Cap, paper, "Drink Old Stock, Finest Beer
in Town" on one side, "Drink Old
Stock, Philadelphia Brewing Company" on other side, red and white
printing 20.00
Champagne Horn, Dry Monopole,
3" x 3-1/2" x 13" h, formed cardboard,
Heidsleck & Co. stickers,
c1930s 12.00
Clock, Moosehead Canadian Lager Beer,
bottle cap shape, golden moose logo
in center, gold, red, and white, green
ground, composition, battery operated, 9-1/2" d, some paint chips. 50.00

**Coasters, Chesterfield and Lark,
3-1/2" d, each $4.50.**

Coaster
Ballantine, 1967, set of eight,
3-1/2" d 10.00
Dubois Beer, 4-1/8" d 190.00
Fitzgerald's Beer, Troy, NY,
octagonal 2.50
Counter Display
Blatz Beer, metal, baseball scene,
beer bottle as catcher, keg as umpire,
beer can sliding into home base,
20" h 125.00
Gibbons Beer, Gibbons Brewery,
Wilkes-Barre, PA, cardboard, bottle
shape, 1937, 20-1/4" h 50.00
Hamm's Beer, black Santa bear, Wade
Ceramics, 1995 .... 35.00
Hans Shoolerbosch, Inc., New York,
four Clydesdales pulling wagon with
wooden beer barrels, 54" l 550.00
Old Shay Beer & Ale, Fort Pitt Brewing
Co., Pittsburgh, PA, couple riding in
cart, rubber horse, tin wheels, plaster
adv base, 13-1/4" l, 11-1/2" h, some
wear 100.00
Decanter
12" h, Kessler Whiskey, football player,
1950s, small chip 85.00
13" h, 4-1/2" d, Maloney Kentucky
Bourbon, flower child, 1968, blue and
white striped dress, brown boots, mkd
"Royal Enfield Porcelain Liquor Bottle
#185" 45.00
Dexterity Puzzle, 5" h, full sized can of
Miller High Light Beer, orig plastic
wrapper 20.00

Fan, Honest Scotch Snuff, diecut cardboard, full color illus of hunters and product in moonlight wooded setting, black and white product ad and monthly calendars for 1936-37 on back, 3-1/2" l bamboo loop handle, 7-1/2" x 9" 20.00

Foam Scrapper Holder, Ruppert Beer-Ale, bakclitc and catalin, notched cobalt blue glass, 9" h 300.00

Gift Set, Piels Beer, ten Piels coasters, bottle open, seven-page flyer promoting Piels Beer, 10" l illus box, unused 30.00

Lamp and Clock, Coors Beers, red digital numbers, 1970s............................50.00

Lighter, miniature Miller Beer can shape, out of butane, 1" w, 2-3/4" h 10.00

Mug, Schmidt, decal on white ground, 6-1/4" h, $18.

Match Safe and Stamp Container, Schlitz Brewing Co., 3" x 1-1/2", some wear 95.00

Pitcher, 6-1/4" h, ceramic, Bass & Co. Pale Ale, made to commemorate 250th anniversary in 1977, Wade 50.00

Plaque, 8" x 11-1/2" thick wood board, large gold plastic horseshoe, red and white Budweiser logo, color decal of horses, "Horseshoe Worn by Champion Clydesdale Eight-Horse Hitch," 1970s...20.00

Salt and Pepper Shakers, pr
Blatz Old Heidelberg Beer, bottle shape, amber colored glass, metal caps, red and white printing on blue label, 3" h..30.00

Blatz Pilsner Beer, Milwaukee's most exclusive beer, bottle shape, amber colored glass, metal caps, red and gold printing on off-white label, 3" h...28.00

Dooley and Shultz, Utica Beer, 4-1/2" h 125.00

Falstaff Beer, bottle shape, light brown colored glass, metal caps, orig labels, 4" h...10.00

Sign
Ballentines Ale, stand-up type, cardboard, 1951, 12" x 14".................95.00

Bavarian Beer, red, white, and gold, tin over cardboard, 1950s, 6" x 10"..35.00

Carling's Ale, Nine Pints of the Law, tin over cardboard, 1920s............. 140.00

Carling's Black Label, tankard, lighted, plastic..40.00

Fishers Beer, oval wooden back with real taxidermy fish.................... 350.00

Griesendieck Beer, tin, 60" x 36", 1930s... 250.00

Gus Topper Beer, yellow and blue, 1940s, 18" x 24"......................... 175.00

Hanley's Peerless Ale, "The Connoisseur," tin, 11" d 330.00

O'Keefe Canadian Ale, hard plastic, 1980s, 16" x 11"........................... 15.00

Schmidt's Beer, diecut, standing type, three sections, Rip Van Winkle theme, 27" x 18" 125.00

Tiger Ale, winking eye.............. 115.00

Toy, truck, Coors Beer, Winross, semi-tractor trailer 20.00

Tray
Christian Feigenspan Beer, 13-3/8" d 175.00

Falcon International Beer, Falcon logo, red, white, black, and gold, scratches.................................... 18.00

Fitzgerald's Ale, Fitzgerald Bros. Brewing Co., Troy, T. Burgomaster Beer, 13" d, 1-1/4" h 80.00

Hudepohl Cincinnati Fine Beer, 13" d..85.00

Narrangansett Banquet Ale, seal, gold, red, and black, few minor chips 125.00

Rochester Brewing Co., Old Topper, minor rust...................................30.00

Scheidts Valley Forge Beer, Rams Head Ale, Norristown, PA 40.00

Schlitz, Milwaukee, 1962 .... 50.00

We Serve Kaier's Star of Excellence Beer, Kaier Brewing Co., Mahanoy City, PA, red, white, and blue logo in center, 12" d............................... 25.00

White Cap Ale, Special Lager Beer, red, white, and blue, 13" d, chip 275.00

Wall Display, Schlitz Beer, bottle-shaped lamp, electric, 8" w, 9" d, 15" h.. 90.00

Window Sign, Genesee Beer, double-sided, round, late 1950s, 11" d... 18.00

C

Calculators

Collecting Hints: Mechanical calculators found at flea markets are often in very poor condition. Look for models in working order with no missing parts. Crank- or lever-operated machines are desirable, but 110-volt electro-mechanical machines have not attracted collector interest, perhaps because they are still so common.

Slide rules made of wood or metal are widely collected, but plastic models are not. Most slide rules are six to twelve inches in length. Longer rules and circular models are less common and more valuable.

Electronic calculators have no moving parts. Battery-operated or pocket models are desirable, while desktop printing machines generally are not. Like early transistor radios (1955-1965), the first pocket calculators (1970-1980) have become an exciting collectible. But unlike transistor radios, early pocket calculators are still easy to find at thrift stores and flea markets. Best of all, thrift stores often sell 1970s models for less than $5. Models with display numbers that light up (LED type) were made only during the 1970s and are thus obsolete and collectible. Almost all pocket calculators made since 1980 have liquid crystal (black) display numbers. With the exception of novelty types, these newer models are not currently collectible. A very easy way to identify the early (1970s) models is to look for a socket (hole) for an adapter plug. Almost all early pocket calculators have an adapter socket while newer pocket models do not. Collectors generally don't care if the adapter and cord are missing as long as the calculator has a socket. Fortunately for the collector, almost every pocket calculator has both the manufacturer's name and the model number printed clearly on the front or back of the case.

Although most collectors are only interested in small pocket calculators, some large desktop models are now being purchased by collectors. The collectable types do not print on paper tape but have Nixie Tube or CRT (TV screen) displays. Companies that made these desktop calculators include Anita, Canon, Casio, Commodore, Friden, IME, SCM, Sharp, Singer, Sony, Victor, Wang, and Wyle.

History: Although the abacus has been used for more than a thousand years, the first mechanical calculating devices were not invented until the 1600s. Few of these early machines survived, and those that did are now in museum collections. A very early handmade brass calculating device recently sold for several million dollars.

Calculators were not manufactured on a commercial scale until the early to mid-1800s. By the late 1800s, mechanical calculators were being produced by many companies, and some models, such as Felt's comptometer, are still found in flea markets today. Electric motors were added at the turn of this century, and these "electromechanical" calculators were still in common use in the 1960s. During the 1960s, transistorized desktop calculators began to appear but initially cost thousands of dollars.

In the early 1970s, thanks to the invention of the integrated circuit, which packed thousands of transistors onto a microchip, the first affordable electronic calculators began to appear. Pocket-sized electronic calculators came onto the market in 1971-1972 for $200 to $400. This was the end of the line for mechanical calculator and slide rule companies. Competition to produce cheaper electronic calculators soon reached a frenzy, and dozens of companies either went bankrupt or were quickly forced out of the calculator business—bad news for calculator manufacturers, but good news for collectors! By 1973, the price of a basic pocket calculator had fallen to the incredibly "low" price of $100 (about $300 in terms of today's adjusted currency). Today a similar four-function calculator sells for about $5. Note that some manufacturers, like Texas Instruments and Unisonic, made dozens of different models. The first models made by a given company are generally the most sought after. Only two American companies—Texas Instruments and Hewlett-Packard—still produce pocket calculators.

References: William Aspray, *Computing Before Computers*, Iowa State University Press, 1990; Bruce Flamm and Guy Ball, *Collector's Guide to Pocket Calculators*, Wilson/Barnett Publishing (14561 Livingston St., Tustin, CA 92680), 1997; Thomas Russo, *Office Collectibles: 100 Years of Business Technology*, Schiffer Publishing, 2000.

Collectors' Clubs: International Association of Calculator Collectors (IACC), 10455 Victoria Ave., Riverside, CA 92503; The Oughtred Society (slide rules), 2160 Middlefield Rd, Palo Alto, CA 94301.

Museums: Cambridge University Science Museum, Cambridge, England; National Museum of American History, Smithsonian Institution, Washington, DC.

Addometer	25.00
APF Mark 21	25.00
Bohn Instant	30.00
Bonsei 3000	10.00
Bomar 901B	65.00
Busicom Handy LE	250.00
Calcupen	150.00
Canon Pocketronic	150.00
Commodore	
887D	30.00
MM1	70.00
MM2	45.00
MM3	25.00
Corvus 411	30.00
Craig	
4501	50.00
4502	55.00
4509	35.00
Crown CL 130	150.00
Facit 1140	45.00
Heathkit IC2006	50.00
Hewlett Packard	
12C Financial	15.00
35	100.00
55	80.00
HP-01 Calculator	
wristwatch	750.00
Keystone, 390	50.00
Kings Point	
8412	40.00
SC20	35.00
Litronix 2220	25.00
Lloyds 303	20.00
National	20.00
Semiconductor 600	15.00
Omron 606	35.00
Radio Shack EC 425	45.00
Rapid Data 800	35.00
Remington, R-540, German	20.00
Rockwell 76	35.00
Royal Digital 3	100.00
Sanyo ICC 804D	100.00
Sharp	
EL 8	75.00
Elsmite 507	12.50
Sinclair Sovereign	110.00
Summit K09V	45.00

Texas Instruments
TI-83 ....36.00
TI-85 ....45.00
TI-86, sealed 70.00
TI-89 ....95.00
TI-92 ....100.00
TI-1000 ....5.00
Tamaya NC-2,
Astro-Navigation 55.00

Calendars

Collecting Hints: Value increases if all monthly pages are attached. Most calendars are bought by collectors who are interested in the subject illustrated on the calendar rather than the calendar per se.

History: Calendars were a popular advertising giveaway in the late 19th century and during the first five decades of the 20th. Recently, a calendar craze has swept bookstores throughout America. These topic-oriented calendars contain little or no advertising.

Reference: Rick and Charlotte Martin, *Vintage Illustration: Discovering America's Calendar Artists*, Collectors Press (P.O. Box 230986, Portland, OR 97281).

Collectors' Club: Calendar Collector Society, 18222 Flower Hill Way #299, Gaithersburg, MD 20879.

Additional Listings: Pinup Art.

Reproduction Alert.

1890, Hoyt's German Cologne, E. W. Hoyt & Col, Lowell, MA, advertising trade card with calendar on back, wear on one corner 14.00

1892, C. I. Hood Co., Lowell, MA, titled, "The Sewing Circle," complete pad and cover sheet, orig envelope, 8" d 95.00

1894, C. I. Hood Co., Lowell, MA, titled, "Sweet Sixteen," orig pad and cover sheet 140.00

1896, set of twelve actors and actresses 125.00

1899, C. I. Hood Co., Lowell, MA, titled, "The American Girl," orig pad and cover sheet 100.00

1903, Youth Companion, Boston, MA, diecut, some tape off back, 23" x 26" 175.00

1905, Grand Union, little girls on front, listing of Grand Union stores on back, 9-3/4" w, 10" l 295.00

1907, Metropolitan Life Insurance Co., yard-long, four generations of ladies, 8" w, 29-1/2" l 165.00

1908, Antimamnia Tablets, 7-3/4" w, 10" h 150.00

1909, American Clay Machinery Co., pocket size, bound in leather-type material, world maps, populations of US states, 2-1/2" w, 4-1/2" h 12.00

1913, sheep in snow scene, complete pad, 11" w, 7" h 80.00

1918, Swifts Premium, Haskell Coffin art, titled "The Girl I Leave Behind Me," soldier saying goodbye to lady, bottom pieces missing, 8-1/2" w, 15" h 100.00

1929, Kimble Music Store, Greeley, CO, full pad 25.00

1935, Harmon Coal Co., Columbus, OH, weekly memo type 20.00

1936, Seasons Greetings, Moss Grocery Store, Montpelier, MO, 8" w, 16" h, creases to cardboard 7.00

1937, Dr. Miles Products, Alka-Seltzer ad, 6 pages, 10" w, 12-3/4" h 48.00

1938, Mt. Airy Milling, Gold Medal Flour 25.00

1941, Peoples Drug Company, Tulsa, OK, two cute twins eating ice cream cones..75.00

1942, Buick dealership, Three Rivers, MI, green background, picture of cottage house, church, shepherd, flock of sheep, 6-3/4" w, 9-1/4" h 20.00

1946, Esso, Russell Sambrook prints, 8-1/2" w, 15" l 25.00

1946, St. Bernard with young girl, Mrs. Hurd's Bakery, Denver, CO, 8" w, 11-1/4" h 45.00

1947, Chesapeake and Ohio Railway, Charles E. Brucker artist, 15" w, 24" h, $28.

1947, Illinois Bell Telephone, wallet size, adv on front, calendar on back..10.00

1947, Petty, pin-up, minor soiling on January page, 9" x 12" 155.00

1948, appointment, Mother letting little one talk on phone, Wheaten Tavern-Ferd Fetsch, Proprietor, St. Louis County, MO, several months missing, 9-1/2" w, 15-1/2" h 35.00

1948, Four Seasons, Norman Rockwell, cover page quoting Rockwell describing how each painting was created, "Norman A. Smith Co., Limited, Toronto, Canada," address and telephone number on bottom of each page 95.00

1951, Coronet Kiddies, Butler's Sunoco adv...10.00

1951, Four Seasons, Norman Rockwell, cover page quoting Rockwell discussing the sporting spirit of Canadian children, "Norman A. Smith Co., Limited, Toronto, Canada," address and telephone number on bottom of each page 95.00

1952, Kinghon dog, titled "Puzzled Pups," 10" w, 17" h 60.00

1952, Will Rogers, 5" w, 6" l 15.00

1954, collie and pretty girl, titled, "High on a Hilltop," "Strong, Carlisle & Hammond Co., Your Electronic Parts Headquarters, Cleveland and Akron, Authorized Member of Philco Factory, Supervised Service," 10" w, 17" h... 15.00

1954, Esquire Girl, pinup, orig envelope with few tears around edge, 9" x 12" 145.00

1954, Jayne Mansfield, pinup pose, 10-1/2" w, 12" h 85.00

1956, Travelers, Hartford, CT, Currier & Ives prints, double-sided 75.00

1958, Esso Family, Dec 1957 to Dec 1958..10.00

1959, Ramco Piston Rings, tin, stand-up type..12.00

1959, Santa with bag of toys, "Merry Christmas and Happy New Year," St. Joseph's Aspirin, Blue Mound Pharmacy, weather chart and almanac, 8" w, 15" l 32.00

1961, International Edition, *Best* magazine, in English, French, and Spanish.......................................30.00

1963, Brownies, Ramon's Pills, Wiest & Boyd, General Merchandise, Gerrardstown, WV, black and red... 15.00

1968, Grove Funeral Home, Christian Home illus...................................8.00

1969, Kennedy Brothers United, Alton S. Tobey, some personal notations on pages, right corner damaged, thumbtack holes, 12" w, 14" h ... 20.00

1970, Hummel figures, Goebel 8.00

1974, Marilyn Monroe, orig envelope.......................................30.00

1975, Avoyelles Trust and Savings Bank, Louisiana, note pockets for each month, sealed in orig plastic, 10" w, 14" h.. 7.00

1977, hunting scene, Weaver & Son Food Market, Merriam, KS 12.00

1978, Arizona Highways...................7.00
1984, dollhouse illus, 9" x 12".........10.00
1992, Pop Tarts, Dweezil Twins, from October 1991 to Dec 1992........10.00

Cameras and Accessories

Collecting Hints: Because of the sheer numbers of antique and classic cameras available, collectors often concentrate on specific eras, types, models, manufacturers, or country of origin.

Leica has been the top name in 35mm photography since the German company of Ernst Leitz introduced its landmark camera in 1925. Although prices are relatively stable, Leica cameras are generally expensive. Demand for them exists worldwide.

Kodak has been American's favorite camera since the introduction of the low-cost Brownie in 1900. As a result of the company's mass production and marketing, there is a surplus of many common models, both antique and modern.

The commercial success of Polaroid's instant-picture cameras has resulted in a surplus in the marketplace. Introduced in 1948, Polaroid cameras are not widely collected, and prices for most models remain low. The few exceptions are Polaroid cameras outfitted with superior optics.

Condition is of utmost importance unless the camera in question is particularly scarce. Shutters should function properly. Minimal wear is generally acceptable. Avoid cameras that have missing parts, damaged bellows, or major cosmetic problems.

In addition to precision instruments, camera collectors look for the odd and unusual models. Examples run the gamut from an inexpensive plastic camera that looks like a can of soda to a rare antique camera disguised to look like three books held together by a leather strap.

History: Of all the antique and classic cameras available, the most prized are those that took the earliest photographs known as daguerreotypes. The process was successfully developed by Louis-Jacques-Mandé Daguerre of Paris in 1839. These photographic images, made of thinly coated silver on copper plate, have a legion of collectors all their own. However, few of the cameras that photographed daguerreotypes have survived.

Edward Anthony became America's first maker of cameras and photographic equipment by founding E. Anthony in 1842. The company later became Ansco. Stereoscope photos were shown at London's Great Exhibition in 1851 and soon became the rage in Britain and Europe. Stereo cameras are recognized by their horizontally mounted twin lenses. Tintype photographs were introduced in 1856.

George Eastman's introduction of the Kodak camera in 1888 made photography accessible to the general public. Made by Frank Brownell for the Eastman Dry Plate & Film Co., it was the first commercially marketed roll-film camera. The original Kodak camera was factory loaded with 100 exposures. The finished pictures were round and 2-1/2 inches in diameter. Eastman Kodak's No. 2 Brownie, a box camera made of cardboard, became a best-seller shortly after it was introduced in 1902.

After manufacturing microscopes and optical equipment for 75 years, Ernst Leitz of Wetzlar, Germany, introduced the first Leica 35mm camera in 1925. Japanese companies entered the photography market with Minolta (Nifca) cameras circa 1928, Canon (Kwanon) in 1933, and Nippon Nogaku's Nikon range-finder cameras in 1948.

References: Rudolpf Hillebrand and Gunther Kadlubek, *Photographica: The Fascination with Classic Cameras*, Schiffer Publishing, 2000; Michael McBroom, *McBroom's Camera Blue Book 1993-1994*, Amherst Media, 1993; Jim and Joan McKeown (eds.), *Price Guide to Antique and Classic Cameras 1997-1998*, Centennial Photo Service, 1996; Douglas St. Denny, *Hove International Blue Book Guide Prices for Classic and Collectable Cameras*, Hove Foto Books, 1992.

Periodicals: *Camera Shopper Magazine*, P.O. Box 1086, New Canaan, CT 06840; *Classic Camera*, P.O. Box 1270, New York, NY 10157; *Shutterbug*, 5211 S. Washington Ave., Titusville, FL 32780.

Collectors' Clubs: American Society of Camera Collectors, 4918 Alcove Ave., North Hollywood, CA 91607; International Kodak Historical Society, P.O. Box 21, Flourtown, PA 19301; Leica Historical Society of America, 7611 Dornoch Lane, Dallas, TX 75248; National Stereoscopic Association, P.O. Box 14801, Columbus, OH 43214; Nikon Historical Society, P.O. Box 3213, Munster, IN 46321; Photographic Historical Society, P.O. Box 39563, Rochester, NY 14604; The Movie Machine Society, 50 Old Country Rd, Hudson, MA 01749; Zeiss Historical Society, 300 Waxwing Drive, Cranbury, NJ 08512.

Museum: International Museum of Photography at George Eastman House, Rochester, NY.

Advisor: Tom Hoepf.

Ansco, Binghamton, NY

3A Folding Ansco, 1920s folding camera for postcard-size prints, chrome-plated fittings 25.00
Memo, c1927, half-frame 35mm camera, wooden vertical box body, black leather, knob on back advances film 75.00
Pioneer, c1950, plastic eye-level camera, 2 1/4 x 3 1/4 exposures on PB20 film 5.00
Standard Speedex, c1950, horizontal folding camera, f6.3 Anastigmatic lens 25.00
Vest-Pocket No. 2, c1917, strut-type folding camera, 120 roll film, f7.5 Modico Anastigmatic or f6.3 Ansco Anastigmatic lens, Bionic shutter, hinged lens cover.....................30.00

Argus, Ann Arbor, MI

Argoflex Seventy-Five, inexpensive twin lens reflex camera with flash unit, leather case...........................12.00
C3, 35mm range finder, c1939-66, nicknamed "brick" for its size and heft, with case 25.00

Beacon Two-Twenty-Five, Whitehouse Products, Brooklyn, NY, inexpensive plastic 620 roll-film camera with flash unit
Black models...........................10.00
Color models 50.00

Ciro Cameras, Delaware, OH

Ciro 35, 35mm range finder, f3.5 50mm Wollensak lens, chrome body 30.00
Ciroflex, common 1940s twin lens reflex camera............................40.00
Detrola Corp., Detroit, MI, Detrola G, basic 1940s miniature camera, Ilex or Detrola Anastigmatic f4.5 lens .. 34.00
Diana, inexpensive plastic 120 roll-film camera, eye-level viewer, popular for distorted effects produced by its cheap lens 40.00

Eastman Kodak, No. 2, Bull's Eye, 1896-1913, leather covered wood box, top load, $24.

Eastman Kodak, Rochester, NY
  Kodak disc 8000 camera, c1983, top-of-the-line model, 8 x 10.5mm image on disc film, motorized film advance, built-in electronic flash, alarm clock, original price: $119.95, discounted to $89.96, in original plastic display case 20.00
  Kodak Petite, c1930 folding Vest Pocket Model B in colors blue, gray, green, lavender, rose, with matching case 100.00
  Kodak Stereo, 1950s 35mm camera with f3.5 35 mm Anaston lenses 120.00
  Vanity Kodak, c 1930 folding vest pocket camera in colors blue, brown, gray, green, red, in matching satin-lined box 250.00

Perfex Fifty-five, Camera Corp. of America, Chicago, IL, 1940s mini-camera, f3.5 Wollensak lens, focal plane shutter 40.00

Realist Stereo, David White Co., Milwaukee, WI, 1950s 35mm stereo camera, Model 1041, f3.5 lenses 150.00

Red Baron Premium Photo Ace, Red Baron Pizza giveaway (recyclable) camera, 1996, plastic body with illustrated cardboard covering, 12 exposures 15.00

Spartus Corp., Chicago, IL
  Spartus folding cameras, 1940s, various models 20.00
  Spartus Press Flash, 1940s, Bakelite box camera with built-in flash unit 10.00

Camera Related
  Jack-in-the-Camera, Commonwealth Plastics Corp., Leominster, MA, 1940s minicam novelty toy; press the shutter release and a little smiley face springs through the lens opening, orig box 25.00
  Kodak kerosene lantern darkroom safelight, tin with red glass lens... 30.00
  No. 1 Kodak Trimming Board, paper cutter, 5 x 6 wooden base 20.00

Candlewick Pattern

Collecting Hints: Select pieces without chips, cracks, or scratches. Learn the characteristics, shapes, and types of pieces Imperial made. Many items that are similar to Candlewick have been made by other companies and are often mixed with or labeled "Candlewick" at shops and shows. Learn to identify look-alikes and reproductions

History: Candlewick, Imperial Glass Corporation's No. 400 pattern, introduced in 1936, was made continuously until October 1982 when Imperial declared bankruptcy. In 1984, Imperial was sold to Lancaster-Colony Corporation and Consolidated Stores International, Inc. Imperial's assets, including inventory, molds, buildings, and equipment, were liquidated in 1985. Imperial's Candlewick molds were bought by various groups, companies, and individuals.

At the liquidation sale, the buildings and site were purchased by Anna Maroon of Maroon Enterprises, Bridgeport, Ohio, with the intent of developing the site into a tourist attraction, Imperial Plaza. The Imperial glass outlet, The Hay Shed, the Bellaire Museum, and a few small businesses moved into the building, but the project failed, and the Imperial building deteriorated and was demolished in July 1995.

The Hay Shed outlet relocated to a building near the Imperial site and operates as a consignment shop for Imperial and other glass. At its 1996 convention, the National Imperial Glass Collector's Society started a drive to establish an Imperial museum and preserve the heritage of glassmaking that took place at Imperial for more than 80 years.

Candlewick is characterized by the crystal-drop beading used around the edges of many pieces; around the bases of tumblers, shakers, and other items; in the stems of glasses, compotes, and cake and cheese stands; on the handles of cups, pitchers, bowls, and serving pieces; on stoppers and finials; and on the handles of ladles, forks, and spoons. The beading is small on some pieces, larger and heavier on others.

A large variety of pieces were produced in the Candlewick pattern.

More than 650 items and sets are known. Shapes include round, oval, oblong, heart, and square. Imperial added or discontinued items as popularity and demand warranted. The largest assortment of pieces and sets were made during the late 1940s and early 1950s.

Candlewick was produced mostly in crystal. Viennese Blue (pale blue, 1937-1938), Ritz Blue (cobalt, 1938-1941), and Ruby Red (red, 1937-1941) were made. Amber, black, emerald green, lavender, pink, and light yellow pieces also have been found. From 1977 to 1980, four items of 3400 Candlewick stemware were made in solid-color Ultra Blue, Nut Brown, Verde Green, and Sunshine Yellow. Solid-black stemware was made on an experimental basis at the same time.

Other decorations on Candlewick include silver overlay, gold encrustations, cuttings, etchings, and hand-painted designs. Pieces have been found with fired-on gold, red, blue, and green beading. Blanks, i.e., plain pieces, were sold to many companies which decorated them with cuttings, hand paintings, and silver overlay, or fitted them with silver, chrome, or brass bases, pedestals, or lids. Shakers sold to DeVilbiss were made into atomizers. Irving W. Rice & Co. purchased Candlewick tray handles and trays and assembled boudoir sets consisting of a puff jar, two perfume bottles and a Candlewick tray. They also sold hand mirrors with large bead handles and Candlewick clocks made from ashtrays. Imperial made and sold Candlewick lamp parts, globes, and shades to several companies, including Lightolier Co., Midwest Chandelier Co., and H. A. Framburg & Co. Ceiling and wall fixtures, table and floor lamps have been found with Candlewick parts.

References: Myrna and Bob Garrision, *Imperial's Boudoir*, Etcetera, 1996; National Imperial Glass Collector's Society, *Imperial Glass Encyclopedia, Vol. I: A-Cane*, The Glass Press, 1995; Virginia R. Scott, *Collector's Guide to Imperial Candlewick*, 1997 edition, available from author (275 Milledge Terrance, Athens, GA 30606); Mary M. Wetzel-Tomalka, *Candlewick: The Jewel of Imperial*, Books I and II, available from author (P.O. Box 594, Notre Dame, IN 46556-0594); —, *Candlewick, The Jewel of Imperial, Personal Inventory & Record Book*, available from author, 1998; —, *Candlewick, The Jewel of Imperial, Price Guide '99 and More*, available from author, 1998.

Periodicals: *Glasszette*, National Imperial Glass Collector's Society, P.O. Box 534, Bellaire, OH 43528; *Spyglass Newsletter*, Michiana Association of Candlewick Collectors, 17370 Battles Rd, South Bend, IN 46614; *The Candlewick Collector Newsletter*, National Candlewick Collector's Club, 6534 South Ave., Holland, OH 43528; *TRIGC Quarterly Newsletter*, Texas Regional Imperial Glass Collectors, 2113 F. M. 367 East, Iowa Park, TX 76367.

Collectors' Clubs: Candlewick Crystals of Arizona, 1122 W. Palo Verde Drive, Phoenix, AZ 85013; Fox Valley Northern Illinois Imperial Enthusiasts, 38 W 406 Gingerwood, Elgin, IL 60123; Maryland Imperial Candlewick Club, 23 Ashcroft Court, Arnold, MD 21012; Michiana Association of Candlewick Collectors, 17370 Battles Rd, South Bend, IN 46614; National Candlewick Collector's Club, 6534 South Avenue, Holland, OH 43528; National Imperial Glass Collector's Society, P.O. Box 534, Bellaire, OH 43528; Ohio Candlewick Collector's Club, 613 S Patterson, Gibsonburg, OH 43431; Texas Regional Imperial Glass Collectors, 2113 F. M. 367 East, Iowa Park, TX 76367.

Museum: Bellaire Museum, Bellaire, OH 43906.

Reproduction Alert: When Imperial Glass Corp. was liquidated in 1985, all the molds were sold but no accurate records were kept of all the buyers. It is known that Mirror Images, Lansing, Michigan, purchased over 200 of the molds, and Boyd Crystal Art Glass, Cambridge, Ohio, purchased 18 small ones. Other molds went to private individuals and groups.

Since the late 1980s, Boyd Crystal Art Glass has used Candlewick molds to make items in various slag and clear colors. Boyd has marked their reproductions with their trademark, a "B" inside a diamond, which is pressed on the bottom of each article.

In 1985, Mirror Images had Viking Glass Co., New Martinsville, West Virginia, make the six-inch Candlewick basket, 400/40/0, in Alexandrite, and a four-piece child's set (consisting of a demitasse cup and saucer, six-inch plate, and five-inch nappy) in pink. In 1987, Viking produced clear plates, bowls, saucers, flat-based sugars and creamers (400/30 and 400/122), and the 400/29 tray for Mirror Images in crystal. These pieces have ground bottoms, are somewhat heavier than original Candlewick pieces, and are not marked. Shapes of items may differ from original Candlewick.

In late 1990, Dalzell-Viking Corporation, successor to Viking, began making Candlewick in Mirror Image's molds. It made five-piece place settings in crystal, black, cobalt, evergreen, and red. Most of these are marked, either "DALZELL" for the first-quality pieces, or "DX" for seconds. In January 1991, Dalzell added handled plates, bowls, and a five-section 400/112 center-well relish in crystal. A new pastel shade, Cranberry Mist, was added in 1992.

Since late 1995, Dalzell-Viking has offered Candlewick Gold, clear with gold beads; Candlewick Pastels, also called Satins, in azure, crystal, green, yellow, and cranberry; eight-, ten-, and twelve-inch plates, cups, and saucers, and 6-inch bowls were made, all marked only with a paper label.

In 1996, Dalzell added a punch bowl set with gold beads and also began to make Candlewick with silver beads. The Pastel Satin production has been extended to include the following: 400/231 three-piece square bowl set; 400/161 butter dish; 400/154 deviled-egg tray; 400/68D pastry tray with a heart center handle; 400/87C and /87F vases; a six-inch bowl on an eight-inch oval tray; and a four-ounce sherbet, similar to 400/63B compote. Dalzell also added Candlewick Frosts, dark amber, plum, blue, and sage green with frosted finish. All of the above are marked only with a Dalzell-Viking paper label. Dalzell Viking Corp. went out of business in May, 1998. All glass on hand, including Candlewick, was sold. Dalzell Candlewick is now being sold by many dealers, often mixed with Imperial Candlewick, sometimes marked "Rare Candlewick." Great care must be taken by collectors to learn the characteristics, many colors and decorations of the glass made by Dalzell-Viking. The future use of Candlewick molds has not been announced by the owner, Mirror Images.

Glass with beaded edges closely resembling Candlewick is being made and imported to the United States by companies in Germany and Taiwan. The look-alikes are being sold by many stores and through mail-order catalogs. Clear bowls, plates, and cake stands, some with gold beads, have been widely offered in catalogs and stores. Frosted candle tumblers and small plates with gold beads and a "Taiwan" label also are being sold in stores and by catalogs.

Ashtray
    400/60, match holder
      center 150.00
    400/118............................... 12.00
    400/150, 6" d, round, large beads
      Caramel slag 120.00
      Cobalt blue 50.00
      Crystal 8.00
      Pink 15.00
    400/176, 3-1/4" square, large
      beads 12.00
    400/450, nested set, 4", 5", and 6"
      Colored, 4" blue, 5" yellow, 6"
      pink 50.00
      Crystal 25.00
    400/450, nested set, 4", 5", and 6",
    patriotic dec
      Colored, blue, yellow,
      pink 75.00
      Red, white, and blue 175.00
    400/650, nested set, orig Imperial
      sticker 135.00
Atomizer
    400/96 shaker, atomizer top, made by
      DeVilbiss 125.00
    400/167 shaker, atomizer top, amethyst 175.00
    400/167 shaker, atomizer top,
      aqua 175.00
    400/247 shaker, atomizer top, amethyst 150.00
    400/247 shaker, atomizer top,
      aqua 150.00
Baked Apple Dish, 400/53X,
    6-1/2" 25.00
Banana Stand, 400/103E, 11" d, two turned-up sides, four-bead stem, crystal 1,500.00
Basket, crystal
    400/37/0, 11", applied handle. 150.00
    400/40/0, 6-1/2", turned-up sides, applied handle 50.00
    400/273, 5", beaded top, beads on top of handle 225.00
Bell, 400/108, 4", 4-bead handle ... 60.00
Bonbon, 400/51T, 6", heart shape, curved-over center handle, beaded edge
    Crystal 30.00
    Light Blue 90.00
    Ruby red, crystal handle 250.00
Bowl
    400/3F, 6", nappy, crystal 12.00
    400/52, 6" d, divided, crystal 20.00
    400/49H, 5" d, heart shaped 175.00
    400/73H, 9" d, heart shape 55.00
    400/74SC, 9" d, four ball toes, crimped

Black, painted flowers..........250.00
Crystal....................................60.00
Light blue.............................100.00
Ruby red...............................275.00
400/75B, 10-1/2" d, crystal........40.00
400/84, 6-1/2" d, divided...........20.00
400/92B, 11" d, float bowl, cupped
edge, crystal, fuchsia
cutting......................................75.00
400/103C, 10" d, fruit, ftd.........185.00
400/104B, 14" d, belled, large beads
on sides...................................75.00
400/427B, 4-3/4" d, 6" d, 7" d and
8-1/2" d, crystal, price for nested
set...75.00

Bud Vase, crystal
400/25, 3-3/4" h, beaded foot, ball
shape, crimped top...................35.00
400/28C, 8-1/2", trumpet shaped top,
crimped, beaded ball bottom....75.00
400/107, 5-1/4" h, beaded foot, large
beads, crimped top...................45.00
400/227, 8-1/2" h, beaded ball bottom, narrowed top slants, applied
handle......................................95.00

Buffet Set, 400/9266, 14" d 400/92D
plate, 5-1/2" d 400/66E cheese compote, plain stem, two pcs..........70.00

Butter, cov, crystal
400/161, quarter pound, graduated
beads on cov............................25.00
400/276, 6-3/4" x 4", California
Beaded top, c1960..............100.00
Plain top, c1951..................125.00
Cake Stand, crystal
400/67D, 10" d, wedge marks on
plate, one-bead stem
Dome foot, c1939..................85.00
Flat foot, c1943.....................70.00
400/103D, 11" h, tall, three-bead
stem..95.00
400/160, 14" d, 72 candle
holes.......................................400.00

Candleholder, crystal
400/40CV, 5" h, round bowl, beaded
or fluted vase insert...................75.00
400/79R, 3-1/2" h, rolled saucer, small
beads.......................................15.00
400/81, 3-1/2" h, dome ftd, small
beads, round handle, pr..........115.00
400/86, mushroom shape, pr....85.00
400/115, 9" h, oval, beaded base,
three candle cups...................125.00
400/115/2, 9" h, two eagle
adapters.................................350.00
400/175, 6-1/2" h, three-bead
stem..95.00
400/207, 4-1/2" h, pr................250.00
400/224, 5-1/2" h, ftd, three sections
of arched beads on stem........175.00
400/1752, 9" h, three-bead stem,
adapter, prisms......................250.00

Candy Dish, cov, crystal
400/59, 5-1/2" d, two-bead
finial...40.00
400/110, 7" d, three-part, two-bead
finial.......................................175.00
400/140, 8" d, one-bead stem
Domed beaded foot,
c1942...................................500.00
Flat plain foot, c1944..........275.00
400/245, 6-1/2" d, round bowl, sq cov,
two-bead finial.......................300.00

400/259, 6-3/4" w, beaded rim, two-
bead finial on cov....................110.00
Celery Tray, crystal
400/46, 11" l, oval, scalloped
edge...75.00
400/105, 13" l, oval, two curved
beaded handles.......................35.00
Champagne, 3400, flared belled top, 5
oz, four graduated beads in stem,
crystal.......................................15.00
Cheese and Cracker Set, 400/88,
5-1/2" ftd 400/88 cheese compote,
10-1/2" d 400/72D handled plate,
crystal.......................................65.00
Cheese, Toast or Butter Dish, 400/123,
7-3/4" d plate with cupped edge,
domed cov with bubble knob,
crystal.....................................275.00
Cigarette Set, 400/29/64/44 or 400/29/6,
dome ftd 3" 400/44 cigarette holder,
small beads, four nested 400/64 2-3/
4" d ashtrays, 400/29 kidney-shaped
tray...95.00
Clock, 4", large beads, New Haven
works, crystal...........................400.00
Cocktail, 4000/190, bell-shaped bowl,
beads around foot, 4 oz, 3 bead
stem, crystal.............................18.00
Cocktail Pitcher, 400/19, 40 oz,
8-1/2" h..................................250.00
Cocktail Set, crystal, 400/97, 6" d 400/39
plate with 2-1/2" off-center indent,
#111 1-bead cocktail glass.......35.00
Compote, crystal
400/48F, 8" d, beaded edge, 4-bead
stem..75.00
400/48F, 8" d, beaded edge,
5-bead....................................200.00
400/67B, 9" d, flat, large bead stem,
c1943.....................................100.00
400/67B, 9" d, ribbed bowl, dome ftd,
large bead stem, c1937..........150.00
400/103F, 10" d, crimped, 3-bead
stem, hp pink roses, blue
ribbons...................................350.00
400/220, 5" d, 3-part, beaded edge,
arched....................................145.00
Console Set, crystal, bowl, pr candleholders
400/100, 12" 400/92F flat bowl,
cupped edge, pr 400/100 2-lite candleholders, center circle of large
beads.......................................90.00
400/8063B, bowl and
candleholders...........................95.00
400/8692L, 13" 400/92L mushroom
bowl on 400/127B 7-1/2" d base, pr
400/86 mushroom
candleholders.........................125.00
Condiment Set, crystal
400/1589, jam set, two cov 400/89
marmalade jars, three-bead ladles,
oval 400/159 tray......................95.00
400/1769, 6 oz 400/119 cruet, pr 400/
96 salt and pepper shakers, 8" 400/
171 tray...................................100.00
400/2946, oil and vinegar, pr 400/164
and 400/166 beaded foot cruets, kidney-shaped 400/29
tray...90.00

Cordial, 3400, flared belled top, four
graduated beads in stem,
crystal.......................................48.00
Cordial Bottle, 15 oz, beaded foot, three-
bead stopper, handle
400/82, crystal, handle,
c1938.....................................225.00
400/82, crystal, handle, red stopper
and base, c1938....................275.00
400/82/2, crystal, no handle,
c1941.....................................200.00

**Creamer and sugar, 400/31, plain foot,
question mark handles, c1941, $25.**

Creamer and Sugar Set
400/18, domed foot, large beads,
creamer with plain handle attached at
bottom, no handle on sugar,
1954-55...................................125.00
400/29/30, flat base, beaded ques-
tion mark handles, 400/30, 7" l 400/29
tray, crystal...............................30.00
400/31, beaded foot, plain handles,
c1937
Crystal...................................40.00
Blue.......................................60.00
400/31, plain foot, question mark handles, c1941, crystal..................25.00
400/122, individual, pr...............22.00
Cruet, 400/119, orig stopper..........25.00
Cup and Saucer, beaded question mark
handles
400/35, tea, round 400/35 cup,
400/35 saucer...........................12.00
400/35/252, no beads on cup handle
Crystal...................................25.00
Light blue...............................40.00
400/37, coffee, slender 40/37 cup,
400/35 saucer...........................15.00
400/77, after dinner, small, slender
5-1/2 d beaded saucer.............20.00
Decanter, 400/163, beaded foot, round
stopper
Crystal...................................195.00
Crystal with red foot and stopper,
c1938.....................................250.00
Dessert Tumbler, crystal
400/18, domed beaded foot, rounded
top, 6 oz...................................40.00
400/19, beaded base, straight sides,
5 oz...14.00
Deviled Egg Tray, 400/154, 11-1/2" d,
twelve indents for eggs, heart-
shaped center handle,
crystal.....................................110.00
Dresser Set, I. Rice Co., 400/151 round
mirrored tray; powder jar, beaded
base, three-bead cover; two round
perfume bottles, beaded base, four-
bead stoppers, 1942,
four-pc set..............................250.00

Epergne Set, 400/196, 9" ftd 400/196FC flower candle holder, one-bead stem, 7-3/4" h two-bead peg vase, beaded top, peg to fit into candle cut, crystal......................................175.00

Goblet, water, crystal
400/190 Line, bell shaped bowl, hollow trumpet shaped stem with beads around foot, 10 oz......................24.50
3400 Line, flared bell bowl, 4 graduated beads in stem, 9 oz Crystal...15.00
Solid Colors, Verde Green, Ultra Blue, Sunshine Yellow, Nut Brown, c1977-80 ....40.00

Iced Tea Tumbler, crystal, 12 oz, ftd
400/18, domed beaded foot, rounded top..50.00
400/19, beaded base, straight sides..15.00
3400 Line, solid Colors, Verde Green, Ultra Blue, Sunshine Yellow, Nut Brown, c1977-80.........................40.00

Jelly Server, crystal
400/52, 6" d, divided dish, beaded edge, handles...........................20.00
400/157, 4-3/4" d, ftd, one-bead stem, no cover 35.00
400/157, 4-3/4" d, ftd, one-bead stem, two-bead cov 65.00

Juice Tumbler, 400/18, domed beaded foot, straight sides, 5 oz.............12.00

Lamp, Hurricane
400/79R, 3-1/2" saucer candleholder, 9" chimney, two-pc set
Bohemian, cranberry flashed chimney, gold bird and leaves dec..125.00
Crystal...................................100.00
400/152R, candleholder, chimney, and 100/152 adapter, crystal, three pc 200.00

Lemon Tray, 400/221, 5-1/2" l, arched handle, crystal 35.00

Marmalade Jar
400/130, round 400/89 base, beaded cover with notch, two-bead finial, 400/130 three-bead ladle 35.00
400/8918, 400/18 old fashion tumbler, beaded notched cover with two-bead finial, 400/130 three-bead ladle.75.00

Mayonnaise Set, bowl, plate with indent, and ladle, crystal
400/23, 5-1/4" d 400/32D bowl, 7-1/2" d 400/23B plate, 400/135 three-bead ladle 35.00
400/52/3, 400/23D 7-1/2" d handled plate with indent, 400/52B 5-1/2" d handled bowl, 400/135 ladle 40.00
400/84, 6-1/4" divided bowl with silver overlay, 8-1/4" underplate..........85.00

Mint Dish, 400/51F, 5" d, round, applied handle 20.00

Mirror, domed beaded base, crystal, brass holder and frame, two-sided mirror flips on hinges, made for I. Rice Co., 1940s 250.00

Mustard Jar, 400/156, beaded foot, notched beaded cov with two-bead finial, 3-1/2" glass spoon, fleur-de-lis handle, crystal...........................40.00

Old Fashion Tumbler, 400/19, beaded base, straight sides, 7 oz...........20.00

Parfait, crystal, 3400, flared bell top, one-bead stem, 6 oz..................50.00

Pastry Tray
Crystal, 400/68D, 11-1/2" d beaded plate, center heart-shaped handle 35.00
Red, center handle 12" d.........600.00

Pitcher, crystal
400/16, 16 oz, beaded question mark handle, plain base 175.00
400/18, 16 oz, plain handle, beaded base 225.00
400/18, 80 oz, plain handle, beaded base 200.00
400/24, 80 oz, beaded question mark handle, plain base 165.00

Plate, crystal
400/1D, 6" d, bread and butter 8.00
400/3D, 7" d, salad...................7.00
400/5D, 8-1/2" d, salad/dessert 10.00
400/7D, 9" d, luncheon 15.00
400/10D, 10-1/4" d, dinner.........35.00
400/72C, 10" d, w handles, crimped..................................25.00
400/145D, 12" d, two open handles.....................................30.00

Punch Bowl Set, crystal
400/20, 13" d six quart 400/20 bowl, 17" d 400/20V plate, twelve 400/37 punch cups, 400/91 ladle, 15-pc set..265.00
400/128, 13" d 400/20 bowl, 10" 400/128 belled base, twelve 400/37 punch cups, 400/91 ladle........300.00
400/210, 14-1/2" d ten quart 400/210 bowl, 9" bolled 400/210 base, twelve 400/211 punch cups with round beaded handles, 400/91 ladle, 15-pc set..800.00

Relish, beaded edge, crystal
400/54, two-part, 6-1/2" l, two tab handles...................................15.00
400/57, 8-1/2" l, oval, pickle/celery...30.00
400/112, 10-1/2" d, three-part, well for mayonnaise jar..........................75.00
400/208, 10" l, three part, three toes.......................................145.00
400/213, three-part, 10" l, handle 75.00
400/214, 10" l, oblong, cover with beaded top handle...................250.00
400/215, three-part on one side, one section on other, 5-1/2" l, two tab handles...................................50.00
400/234, two-part, 7" sq...........140.00
400/256, two-part, 10-1/2" l, oval, two tab handles 25.00
400/262, three-part, 10-1/2" l, two tab handles...................................100.00

Relish and Dressing Set, crystal
400/1112, 10-1/2" five-part 400/112 relish, 400/89 jar fits center well; long ladle, c1941 ....95.00

400/1112, 10-1/2" five-part 400/112 relish, 400/289 jar fits center well; three-bead ladle, c1945............ 70.00

Salad Set, crystal
400/17, 14" 400/92D plate, 10-1/2" 400/17F bowl, old style ribbed fork and spoon 85.00
400/735, 9" d handled heart-shaped 400/73H bowl, 700/75 fork and spoon set................................... 150.00
400/75B, 10-1/2" d beaded 400/75B bowl, 13" d cupped 400/75V plate, five-bead handles 400/75 fork and spoon set................................... 110.00
400/106B/75, 12" d bell 400/106B bowl, graduated beads on both sides, fork and spoon 80.00

Salt and Pepper Shakers, pr, beaded foot, crystal
400/96, bulbous, eight beads, chrome tops 20.00
400/96, nine beads, flat bottom, plastic tops, c1941........................... 30.00
400/109, individual chrome tops 12.00
400/116, one-bead stem, no beads on foot, plastic or metal tops..... 75.00
400/190, trumpet foot, chrome tops... 65.00

Salt Dip, 400/61, 2"....................... 12.00

Sauce Boat Set, 400/169, oval gravy boat with handle, 9" oval plate with indent.................................... 125.00

Seafood Icer, 400/190, one-pc coupette 90.00

Sherbet, 3400 line, flared bell top
Low, 5 oz 12.00
Tall, 5 oz..................................... 15.00

Tidbit Server, 400/2701, two tiers, 7-1/2" d and 10-1/2" d plates joined by metal rod, round handle at top
Crystal 60.00
Emerald green......................... 750.00

Tidbit Set, 400/750, three-pc nested hearts, 4-1/2", 5-1/2", 6-1/2", beaded edges
Crystal 40.00
Milk glass, 1950 .... 50.00

Torte Plate
400/20D, 17" d, flat, crystal 40.00
400/20V, 17" d, cupped, crystal 60.00

Tray, 400/159, 9" oval, concentric circles in bottom, rect Farberware chrome holder with cut-out lacy pattern on each corner 75.00

Tumbler, water, ftd, crystal
400/18, domed beaded foot, rounded top, 9 oz................................... 45.00
400/19, beaded base, straight sides, 10 oz, 4-3/4" h 18.00

Vase, crystal
400/87C, 8" h, crimped beaded top 35.00
400/87F, 8" h, fan shaped 30.00
400/87R, 7" h, rolled over beaded top 40.00

Wine
400/190 Line, belled bowl, hollow trumpet stem with beads, 5 oz, crystal... 25.00

3400 Line, flared belled bowl, four graduated stems in base, 9 oz
Crystal....................................25.00
Ruby red bowl.....................125.00
Solid Colors, Verde Green, Ultra Blue, Sunshine Yellow, Nut Brown, c1977-80...............................40.00

Candy Containers

Collecting Hints: Candy containers with original paint, candy, and closures command a high premium, but beware of reproduced parts and repainting. The closure is a critical part of each container; its absence detracts significantly from the value.

Small figural perfumes and other miniatures often are sold as candy containers. Study all reference books available and talk with other collectors before entering the market. Watch out for reproductions.

History: One of the first candy containers was manufactured in 1876 by Croft, Wilbur and Co., confectioneries. They filled a small glass Liberty Bell with candy and sold it at the 1876 Centennial Exposition in Philadelphia.

Jeannette, Pennsylvania, was a center for the packaging of candy in containers. Principal firms included Victory Glass, J. H. Millstein, T. H. Stough, and J. C. Crosetti. Earlier manufacturers were West Bros. (Grapeville, Pennsylvania), L. E. Smith (Mt. Pleasant, Pennsylvania), and Cambridge Glass (Cambridge, Ohio).

Candy containers, which usually sold for 10 cents, were produced in shapes that would appeal to children. The containers remained popular until the 1960s, when they became too expensive to mass produce.

References: Jack Brush and William Miller, *Modern Candy Containers & Novelties*, Collector Books, 2000; *Candy Containers*, L-W Book Sales, 1996; Douglas M. Dezso, J. Leon Poirer, and Rose D. Poirer, *Collector's Guide to Candy Containers*, Collector Books, 1998, 2001 values; George Eikelberner and Serge Agadjanian, *American Glass Candy Containers*, revised and published by Adele L. Bowden, 1986; Jennie Long, *Album of Candy Containers*, published by author, 1978; Robert Matthews, *Antiquers of Glass Candy Containers*, published by author, 1970.

Collectors' Club: Candy Container Collectors of America, P.O. Box 8707, Canton, OH 44711.

Museums: Cambridge Glass Museum, Cambridge, OH; L. E. Smith Glass, Mt. Pleasant, PA.

Reproduction Alert.

Left: train engine; right: fire truck with metal wheels, sold as pair, $200. Photo courtesy of Joy Luke Fine Art Brokers and Auctioneers.

Cardboard

Round, Christmas, mkd "Made in Western Germany," 3-1/4" d
Santa Claus following little girl carrying Christmas tree...............30.00
Santa Claus leading child riding donkey, another walking with lantern.....................................30.00
Train, Candyland Express, Loft's Candy, NY, pressed litho cardboard diecut, wooden rear wheels and cart, orig string and wooden bead, some wear....................60.00

Glass

Airplane, 4-1/4" l, 4-1/4" w..........75.00
Ambulance, Red Cross, paper label printed with Red Cross symbol, gold screw cap, printed "T. H. Stough".....................................115.00
Bath Tub, emb "Dolly's Bath Tub," open top, painted white...........315.00
Battleship Maine, 5-1/2" l...........35.00
Bear..45.00
Bulldog, sitting, orig paint..........90.00
Boat, 5-1/4" l.............................35.00
Boot, 3-1/8" h............................30.00
Carpet Sweeper, all orig..........215.00
Duck on Nest, milk glass...........65.00
Fire Engine, Little Boiler No. 1...70.00
Girl, two geese, orig closure......55.00
Hanging Basket, attached chain, emb grape and vine dec, gold paint.....................................35.00
Hat, milk glass, screw-on tin brim, 2-7/8" w at brim, 2-1/8" h, some loss of paint.....................................35.00
Horn...25.00
Hunchback, orig tin cap, painted, Mu-Mu, Argentina, 6-1/4" h........90.00
Jeep, mkd "Jeanette Glass Co. & J. H. Millstein Co.," 4-1/2" l, chip...25.00
Lantern, beveled panel squares, orig closure.....................................75.00
Locomotive, #888, 4" l.................35.00
Mantel Clock, orig dial, back mkd "Contents 3 oz AV"...................245.00
Pistol, Annette, PA, orig closure, 3-3/4" l.....................................35.00
Rabbit, J. H. Millstein Co., 4" x 1-3/4" x 6-1/2" h.........................35.00

Racer, #4, orig closure.............95.00
Railroad Lantern, red metal top, 1-3/4" d, 3-1/2" h......................70.00
Santa, J. H. Millstein, Jeanette, PA, black boots and belt, some white, red sleeves, plastic screw-on cap, 5" h...95.00
Scottie.......................................35.00
Telephone...................................50.00
Willys Jeep, J. H. Millstein, 1-1/2" x 4-1/4" x 2", 1950s.....................38.00

Metal

Cup, Zig Zag/Clark's Teabury Chewing Gum, D. L. Clark Co., Pittsburgh, PA, 1-3/4" d, 1-1/8" h, some paint flaking..75.00
Truck, Cherrydale Farms, movable wheels, labeled "Nobel Hall Made in China," 7" l, 3-1/2" w, 4" h...........5.00

Papier-Mâché

Black Cat, sitting on pumpkin, mkd "Germany"................................80.00
Boot, red and white....................25.00
Christmas Book, 7" l, 4" d at top, 8" h...90.00
Irishman, top hat and pipe........12.00
Rabbit with basket on back, 5" d, 6" h...45.00
Singing Apple..........................200.00

Plastic

Black Cat with Pumpkin, 3" h...35.00
Fire Hydrant, Fleer Co., Philadelphia, 3" h...5.00
Rabbit, yellow and green..........18.00
Reindeer and Sled, 8-1/2" l.......................................24.00
Rockette, Disney, full, late 1980s, MIB...8.00
Santa, standing, opening for candy in back, Rosbro Plastics, 5" h.......30.00
Santa, waving, yellow sled, 4" h...45.00

Candy Molds

Collecting Hints: Insist on molds in very good or mint condition. The candy shop had to carefully clean molds to ensure good impressions each time. Molds with rust or signs of wear rapidly lose value.

History: The chocolate or candy shops of Europe and America used molds to make elaborate chocolate candy items for holidays and other festive occasions. The heyday for these items was 1880 to 1940. Mass production, competition, and the high cost of labor and supplies brought an end to local candy shops.

Chocolate mold makers are often difficult to determine. Unlike pewter ice cream molds, makers' marks were not always on the mold or were covered by frames. Eppelsheimer & Co. of New York marked many of its molds, either with its name or a design resembling a child's toy shop and "Trade Mark" and "NY."

Many chocolate molds were imported from Germany and Holland and are marked with the country of origin and, in some cases, the mold-maker's name.

References: Ray Broekel, *Chocolate Chronicles*, Wallace-Homestead, out of print; Eleanore Bunn, *Metal Molds*, Collector Books, out of print; Judene Divone, *Anton Reiche Chocolate Mould Reprint Catalog*, Oakton Hills Publications, 1983.

Museum: Wilbur's Americana Candy Museum, Lititz, PA.

Reproduction Alert.

Pewter, dancer, mkd #1574/#2/ Anton/Reichet/Dresden, $70.

Chocolate Mold

Clamp type, no hinge, two pieces, copper, Indian, 7-1/2" h, marked "Germany" 45.00
Clamp type, no hinge, two pieces, pewter, dancer, 6-3/4" h, marked "Anton/Reichet/Dresden"...........35.00
Clamp type, no hinge, two pieces, tin
    Basket, 1-1/2" x 4"..................40.00
    Bulldog, seated, 3" h..............45.00
    Chick on Egg, 4" w, 6" h, sgd "Anton Reichet A. G. Dresden Agents Bramigk & Co., London," also numbered 50.00
    Easter Egg, 3-1/2" d, mkd "England"..............................25.00
    Log, 9" l.................................45.00
    Rabbit, 6-1/4" h, standing, marked "Made in Germany"...............25.00
    Rooster, 6-1/4" h 45.00
    Santa, #427, 4-1/2" h, two small holes in body 125.00
    Teddy Bear, 11" h, marked "2644" 165.00
    Witch.......................................40.00
Frame or Block Type, hinged, tin
    Chicks, 5" h, wearing bonnets, two cavities, marked "Made in Germany".................................40.00

Cowboy, holding lasso 45.00
Heart, emb cupid, double hinges................................65.00
Jenny Lind, three parts...........95.00
Lamb, small 50.00
Lion...50.00
Rabbit, eyeglasses, paint brushes, and pail, three part 115.00
Rooster, 10" h 100.00
Tray Type
    Car, four-door sedan, 3" x 5"..................................15.00
    Cherries, three rows with six indentations, 7-7/8" x 4-1/8" 24.00
    Disney, Sweet Treats Candy Mold, SunHill, two plastic double molds of Mickey and Donald, single sheet of 12 bite-size heads of Disney characters, some orig paper fluted display cups, orig recipe book, dated 1982, orig display box, some use..40.00
    Egg, nine cavities, 15" l 20.00
    Lamb, set of three interconnected figures 65.00
    Leaf, thirty rect bars, 2-1/2" x 10-1/2" 45.00
    Millennium, wafer type, plastic square with nine oval molds, eight are 2" long, one is 5-3/4" l, all have "2000" in bottom of mold..........5.00
    Santa, four cavities, 4-1/2" h, 9-1/4" l, marked "Dresden/US Distributor/T.C. Weyland, NY"......95.00

Hard Candy

Chicken on Nest, clamp type, two pcs, pewter 65.00
Rose Lollipops, six cavities, clamp type, tin.....................................55.00
Maple Sugar
    Dog's head, tin, clamp type, two pcs 65.00
    Elephant, clamp type, two pcs 45.00
    Fish, 8-1/2" l, 3-3/8" w, hand carved wood.......................................55.00
    Girl and dog, buff clay, 4-1/4" w, 4-1/2" h 35.00
    Rabbit, wood, 1-3/4" w, 2" h, marked "Germany"................40.00

Cap Guns

Collecting Hints: Condition is crucial to pricing. A broken spring that can be replaced is far less critical than a crack that cannot be repaired. Many older cast-iron cap pistols rusted and suffered other ravages of time. While restoration is acceptable, an unrestored gun in fine condition is more valuable than a restored example.

Beware of restrikes, reproductions, and new issues. Recasts often have a sandy or pebbled finish and lack the details found on the original pieces. Several of the molds for cast-iron cap pistols have survived. Owners have authorized restrikes as a

means of raising money. New issues are frequently made with the intention of deceiving, and the restrikes are sold to the unknowing as period examples. Two prime examples are the Liberty Bell cap bomb and the Deadshot powder keg cap bomb.

It is important to know the full history of any post–World War II cap pistol, especially if it is one of a pair. Toy guns associated with a character or personality sell better than their generic counterparts. Some of the price differences are negated for products from leading manufacturers, e.g., Hubley. The presence of the original box, holster, and/or other accessories can add as much as 100 percent to the value of the gun.

History: Although the first toy gun patents date from the 1850s, toy guns did not play an important part in the American toy market until after the Civil War. In the 1870s, the toy cap gun was introduced.

Cast-iron cap pistols reached their pinnacle between 1870 and 1900, with J. & E. Stevens and Ives among the leading manufacturers. Realism took second place to artistic imagination. Designs ranged from leaf and scroll to animal and human heads. The use of cast iron persisted until the advent of World War II, although guns made of glass, lead, paper, rubber, steel, tin, wood, and zinc are known from the 1920 to 1940 period.

In the 1950s, die-cast metal and plastic became the principal material from which cap guns were manufactured. Leading manufacturers of die-cast guns were Hubley, Kilgore, Mattel, and Nichols. Many of the guns were associated with television cowboys and detective heroes. Often the guns were part of larger sets that consisted of a holster and numerous other accessories.

Collecting cap and other toy guns began in the 1930s with the principal emphasis on cast-iron examples made between 1875 to 1915. In the mid-1980s, the collecting emphasis shifted to the cap pistols of the post–World War II period.

References: Rudy D'Angelo, *Cowboy Hero Cap Pistols*, Antique Trader Books, 1997; James L. Dundas, *Cap Guns with Values*, Schiffer Publishing, 1996; Jerrell Little, *Price Guide to Cowboy Cap Guns and Guitars*, L-W Book Sales, 1996; Jim Schlever, *Backyard Buckaroos: Collecting Western Toy Guns*, Books Americana/Krause Publications, 1996.

Periodical: *Toy Gun Collectors of America Newsletter*, 312 Sterling Way, Anaheim, CA 92807.

Collectors' Club: Toy Gun Collectors of America, 3009 Oleander Ave., San Marcos, CA 92069.

Dynamite, MIB 85.00
Hamilton, Cheyenne Shooter..........70.00
Hubley
 Cowboy, gold plated, black
  grips...200.00
 Disintigrator, diecast, space
  gun...600.00
 Early American Flintlock Jr.,
  MIB...95.00
 Flintlock Jr. 35.00
 Rodeo Patrol, cowboy on bucking
  horse, red, white, and blue, orig
  box 150.00
 Texan, revolving cylinder, lever on
  side 165.00
 Western Cap Pistol, white grips, black
  steer 50.00
Kilgore
 Border Patrol, cast iron 70.00
 Buck, No. 407, red, navy, and white,
  black grips, orig box................125.00
 Deputy, single holster, 2-1/4", fancy
  belt 200.00
 Derringer, sealed, MOC.............70.00
 Eagle...40.00
 Mountie, orig box.......................45.00
 Roy Rogers, illus 185.00
Leslie-Henry
 Gene Autry, gold tone, MIB 550.00
 Wild Bill Hickok, gold tone.......250.00
Lone Ranger, cast iron, unfired 750.00
Lone Star/Wicke
 Dueling Pistol, 1970s, all metal,
  8" l..35.00
 Golden Eye 007 PPR, silencer,
  MOC...65.00
 Tomorrow Never Dies 700 Glock,
  silencer, MOC 55.00
Mattel
 Fanner, 50, orig holster 75.00
 Shootin' Shell, double,
  holster.......................................250.00
 Red Ranger, cavalry style belt
  holder..175.00
 Winchester Saddle Gun, orig
  box 500.00
Nichols
 Derringer....................................48.00
 Spit Fire Rifle, 8-1/2" l................75.00
 Stallion .45 Mark II, black grips,
  unfired 225.00
Pony Boy, celluloid handle, 10" x
  4-1/2"...50.00
Roy Rogers
 Classy Guns & Holster, set 900.00
 Double holster and gun set, Roy's
  image on belt buckle, jeweled
  holster 1,250.00
 Mini-cap gun, holster, belt 175.00
Schmidt
 Buck n' Bronc Deputy, unfired.225.00
 Roy Rogers, guns in holster .1,250.00

Stevens, J & E
 Buffalo Bill, repeating, 1920s, orig
  box 320.00
 Lint Tom, cast iron, pistol 400.00
Unidentified Maker
 Big Scout, cast iron, white
  grips...100.00
 Captain Cutlass Pirate, diecast metal,
  1970s, 10" l...............................75.00
 Hero, cast iron, cowboy on
  grips...45.00
 Western 50.00
 Wyandotte, Red Ranger, dragoon
  style...175.00
 XTLD, pressed steel, colt .45,
  1940s..35.00

Cartoon Characters

Collecting Hints: Many collectible categories include objects related to cartoon characters. Cartoon characters appeared in advertising, books, comics, movies, television, and as a theme in thousands of products designed for children.

Concentrate on one character or the characters from a single comic or cartoon. Most collectors tend to focus on a character that was part of their childhood. Another collector concentrates on the work of a single artist. Several artists produced more than one cartoon character.

The most popular cartoon characters of the early period are Barney Google, Betty Boop, Dick Tracy, Gasoline Alley, Li'l Abner, Little Orphan Annie, and Popeye. The movie cartoons produced Bugs Bunny, Felix the Cat, Mighty Mouse, Porky Pig, and a wealth of Disney characters. The popular modern cartoon characters include Garfield, Peanuts, and Snoopy.

History: The first daily comic strip was Bud Fisher's Mutt and Jeff, which appeared in 1907. By the 1920s, the Sunday comics became an American institution. One of the leading syndicators was Captain Joseph Patterson of the News-Tribune. Patterson, who partially conceived and named Moon Mullins and Little Orphan Annie, worked with Chester Gould to develop Dick Tracy in the early 1930s.

Walt Disney and others pioneered the movie cartoon, both as shorts and full-length versions. Disney and Warner Brothers characters dominated the years from 1940 to 1960. With the advent of television, the cartoon characters of Hanna-Barbera, e.g., the Flintstones, added a third major force. Independent studios produced cartoon characters for television, and characters multiplied rapidly. By the 1970s, the trend was to produce strips with human characters, rather than the animated animals of the earlier period.

Successful cartoon characters create many spin-offs, including comic books, paperback books, Big Little Books, games, dolls, room furnishings, and other materials which appeal to children. The secondary market products may produce more income for the cartoonist than the drawings themselves.

References: Bill Blackbeard (ed.), *R. F. Outcault's Yellow Kid*, Kitchen Sink Press, 1995; ——, *Comic Strip Century*, Kitchen Sink Press, 1995; Jeffrey M. Ellinport, *Collecting Original Comic Strip Art*, Antique Trader Books, 1999; Ted Hake, *Hake's Price Guide To Character Toys*, 3rd ed., Collector Books, 2000; Robert Gipson, *The Unauthorized Collector's Guide to Garfield and the Gang*, Schiffer Publishing, 2000; Maurice Horn and Richard Marshall (eds.), *World Encyclopedia of Comics*, Chelsea House Publications, out of print; David Longest, *Character Toys and Collectibles*, 1st Series (1984, 1992 value update), 2nd Series (1987, 1990 value update), Collector Books; ——, *Cartoon Toys & Collectibles*, Collector Books, 1998; Rex Miller, *The Investor's Guide to Vintage Character Collectibles*, Krause Publications, 1999; Andrea Podley with Derrick Bang, *Peanuts Collectibles, Identification and Value Guide*, Collector Books, 1999.

Periodical: *Frostbite Falls Far-Flung Flier (Rocky & Bullwinkle)*, P.O. Box 39, Macedonia, OH 44056.

Collectors' Clubs: Betty Boop Fan Club, 6025 Fullerton Ave., Apt 2, Buena Park, CA 90621; Peanuts Collector Club, 539 Sudden Valley, Bellingham, WA 98226; Pogo Fan Club, 6908 Wentworth Ave. S, Richfield, MN 55423; Popeye Fan Club, Ste. 151, 5995 Stage Rd, Barlette, TN 38184; R. F. Outcault Society, 103 Doubloon Drive, Slidell, LA 70461.

Museum: The Museum of Cartoon Art, Port Chester, NY.

Additional Listings: Disneyana; also see the index for specific characters.

Andy Panda, Walter Lantz Cartoon
 Apple Andy, #493, Castle Films, 8mm,
  headline edition, orig
  box... 10.00

Comic Book, *Andy Panda*, Dell, #240, 1949 .... 5.00

Figure, 4-3/4" h, Miranda Panda, Don Roberto, Los Angeles, mkd "Lantz Productions," orig foil label 95.00

View-Master Reel, Andy Panda in Mystery Tracks, Sawyer, #822 .... 4.00

Archie
Character Drinking Glass, Welch's, 1971, Hot Dog Goes to School 5.00

Comic Book, Vol. 1, #97, December, 1958 .... 27.50

Doll, Archie, Jughead, Betty, and Veronica, 1975, Marx, NRFB, price for set .. 200.00

Paper Dolls, orig box, played with condition 45.00

Barney Google
Comic Book, Barney Google & Snuffy Smith, four color 120.00

Pep Pin, Kellogg's, Barney, 1946 .... 18.00

Betty Boop
Alarm Clock, metal, 8" w 38.00

Bathroom Set, toothbrush holder, soap dish, and mug, purple, black, and silver, three-pc set 55.00

Character Drinking Glass, 6" h, frosted
Betty Boop on Motorcycle 20.00
Cute & Curvy 17.00
I'm Just Your Average Super Star 18.00

Doll, 14" h, all cloth, orig tag "Play by Play Toys & Novelties" 15.00

Perfume Bottle, figural, glass bottle, wooden head, painted features, stamped "P.E.F.5" 30.00

String Holder, chalk, face and shoulder post, 7-1/2" h 650.00

Bringing Up Father
Doll, Schoenhut, carved jointed wood, orig paper label with 1924 copyright, price for pr 600.00

Movie Poster, "Jiggs and Maggie in Society," Monogram Pictures, 1948, 22" w, 27-1/2" h 60.00

Bugs Bunny
Advertising Counter Display, Sunoco promotion, six different 3-4" rubber Looney Tunes figures, 1989, 17" x 15" 60.00

Bank, 50th Birthday Commemorative, Applause Co., c1900, MIB 50.00

Character Drinking Glass
Happy 50th Birthday Bugs, copyright 1990 .... 4.00
Pepsi, Warner Brothers Looney Tunes, copyright 1966 .... 8.00

Comic Book, Bugs Bunny, Dell
No. 59, Feb-March, 1958 .... 20.00
No. 69, Oct-November, 1959 ...... 18.00
No. 72, April-May, 1960 .... 18.00

Cookie Jar 40.00

Hand Puppet, plush, tag "Bugs Bunny 50th Birthday Celebration," 1990, 14" h 12.00

Limited Edition Collector's Plate, Mother's Day, 1977, Dave Grossman design, licensed Warner Brothers Products, copyright 1977, orig box, 7-1/2" d 16.00

Little Golden Book, *Bugs Bunny At The Easter Party*, Warner Bros. Cartoons, Inc., 1953, 28 pgs 12.00

Lunch Box, tin, 6" x 5-1/2" x 2" 18.00

Planter, Evan K. Shaw, 1940s, 4" w, 5" h 90.00

Rub-Off-Pictures, fourteen wipe-off cards, 1955, used 25.00

Toy, jack-in-the-box, Matty Mattel Presents, Mattel Toymakers, 1951-53, does not play 65.00

Casper and Friends, Harvey Comics
Premium Ring, thin copper luster metal band joined to circular copper luster frame which holds convex metal insert with color image of character against white background, mkd "copyright 1979 ...... Harvey Comics," seven of Casper, two of Wendy, one horse Nightmare, set of ten, some wear 65.00

Push Puppet, Casper 100.00

Radio, figural, MIB 130.00

Daffy Duck, character drinking glass, Pepsi, Warner Brothers Looney Tunes, copyright 1980 .... 8.00

Deputy Dawg, premium ring, thin copper luster metal band joined to circular copper luster frame which holds convex metal insert with color image of character against white background, mkd "Copyright Terrytoons," c1977, set of two 15.00

Dick Tracy, Chester Gould
Play Set, Ideal, orig box 150.00

Pop-On Ring, dark green plastic base, stamped in letters on top, 3-D pale blue full figure of Tracy pointing gun 40.00

Soap, Sparkle Plenty, figural, c1950, diecut dec box 95.00

Felix the Cat, King Features
Cookie Jar 50.00

Figure, cast lead, c1920 .... 385.00

Record, Peter Pan, 45 rpm, ©1959 King Features Syndicate, Inc. 30.00

Fred Flintstone, bank, molded plastic, marked "BDS" on back, Homecraft Products, Vinyl Prod. Corp., 1971, 12-3/4" h, $50.

Flintstones, Hanna-Barbera
Ashtray, Barney, 5-1/4" x 8", pottery, emb image of Barney bowling, mkd "Art

Houseware Products, Chicago" 90.00

Character Drinking Tumbler, plastic
Arthur Treacher's Fish & Chips, Betty, 1974, yellow 6.00
Don Penotti, Fred, Betty, and Wilma on beach, orig lid 9.00

Coloring Book, Flintstones Color by Number, Whitman 24.00

Cookie Jar 50.00

Mug, 5-1/2" h, glass, Bedrock U, Grand Canyon, Arizona 12.00

Playset, #4672, copyright 1961, 15" x 24" x 4" orig box, played-with condition 165.00

Plush Toy, Barney Rubble, 14" h, felt hat, shirt, and pants, tag "NANCO/Country of Origin: Thailand, copyright 1989 Hanna-Barbera Productions, Inc." 22.00

Pop-On Ring, Bamm Bamm, black plastic base, lime green character, c1966 .... 24.00

Pop-On Ring, Fred, black plastic base, red character, c1966 .... 24.00

Premium Ring, Betty Rubble, off-white plastic, expansion band, diecut portrait, c1960 .... 25.00

Heckle and Jeckle
Children's Book, Whitman, wear 5.00

Premium Ring, thin copper luster metal band joined to circular copper luster frame which holds convex metal insert with color image of black crow against white background, mkd "Copyright Terrytoons," c1977, set of three 18.00

Huckleberry Hound, Hanna Barbera, lamp, 20" h, plastic 30.00

Jetsons, Hanna-Barbera
Character Drinking Glass, 1990, Kraft
George 42.00
Jane 42.00

Word Search puzzle book, 64 pgs, 1978, unused, 5-1/8" w, 7-1/2" h 10.00

Li'l Abner, Al Capp
Bank, Smoo, blue plastic 50.00

Big Little Book, Li'l Abner, Among the Millionaires, Whitman Publishing, 1939, spine missing, cover detached 10.00

Flicker Ring, 1" h, blue square 10.00

Hand Puppet, Baby Barry, 1957, played with condition 65.00

Magazine Ad, Cream of Wheat Breakfast Food, Rastus on front of Cream of Wheat box, 5" x 11" 20.00

Pin, Shmoo, 1-1/2" h, brass tone 15.00

Toy, Dog Patch Band, litho tin wind-up, two arms missing 415.00

Maggie and Jiggs, figures, 9" h Maggie, 8-1/2" h Jiggs, composition faces, wood hands and feet, original costumes, $850.

Moon Mullins, Frank Willard
Salt and Pepper Shakes, pr, figural, glass, black hard plastic hats, red painted ties and shoes, mkd "Made in Japan"..95.00
Toothbrush Holder, bisque, incised "Moon Mullins & Kayo, copyright F.A.S."................................... 135.00

Mutt and Jeff, Bud Fisher
Comic Book, Mutt & Jeff, #44 .... 8.00
Doll, jointed, felt clothing, cotton shirts, Buchere, Switzerland, price for pr...500.00
Sheet Music
Moonlight, 1911, caricature cover, pages separated.....................12.00
Mutt and Jeff in Panama, mkd "Gus Hill presents Bud Fisher's original creation and latest success, Mutt and Jeff in Panama," shows Hill with Mutt and Jeff, wearing long fake noses and crazy clothes, cover sheet only...5.00

Peanuts, Charles Schulz
Address Book, Peanuts, United Feature Syndicate, Inc., 3-3/4" x 2-1/2".....6.00
Character Drinking Glass, Snoopy's Kitchen.................................5.00
Children's Dishes, different characters on three plates and three saucers, whole gang on tray, mkd "United Features-Peanuts caricature by Schulz," played-with condition, some rust and scratches...................................7.50
Coin, "The Great Pumpkin," 30th anniversary, silver, limited edition of 1,996 pcs, black case, certificate of authenticity..80.00
Cookbook, Peanuts Cook Book, Scholastic Book Services, January, 1970, 1st printing 25.00
Figure, Charlie Brown and Peggy Jean, sitting on grass, orig box with graphics of whole Peanuts gang, 4" l.........18.00
Lunch Box and Thermos, plastic, red ground, some loss to graphics, 1965 ....65.00
Soakee, Camping Snoopy, 9-3/4" h 12.00

Pogo, Walt Kelly
Children's Book
Pogo Peek-A-Book, Walt Kelly, Simon & Schuster, 1955, 6-5/8" x 9-3/4" 40.00
The Pogo Papers, Walt Kelly, Simon & Schuster, 1951, 5-1/4" x 8", 192 pgs..................................38.00
Poster, 17" x 11", "The World of Pogo, Walt Kelly's menagerie of characters from Okefenokee Swamp," made for exhibit held at the Museum of Fine Arts, Springfield, MA, 1971........55.00

Popeye, E. C. Segar
Child's Record and Coloring Book, Popeye & Becky in Wimpy's Sunken Treasure, 45 rpm record, 17 pg coloring book, 1980, unused 15.00
Doll, 10-1/2" h, rubber head, cloth stuffed body, played-with condition..................................135.00
Flicker Ring, Popeye and Sweet Pea, plastic, 1960s.............................15.00
Game
Board, 1983, unused...................45.00
Ring Toss, Popeye Pipe Toss, 1939, thick cardboard and wood, copyright King Features Syndicate, Inc. and Rosebud Art Company, NY, Sole Licensee 110.00
Mug, 4-1/2" d, 3" h, Popeye eating spinach, copyright King Features, slight wear..98.00
Pencil Sharpener, figural, Bakelite, copyright 1929 King Features Syndicate, 1-3/4" h 75.00
Soap, figural, 1930s, 4" h 30.00
Stereoview Film Card, Tru-Vue Stereo Film Card, Popeye in Spinach Bait, #T-28, King Features Syndicate, Inc., 1959, MIP.....................................10.00
Tin, Popeye Yellow Popcorn, packed by Pure Mills, Inc., Dixon, Ill, pry-top lid, litho "Just a Better POP," image of Popeye on both sides, King Features Syndicate, copyright 1943, 3-1/4" w, 4-3/4" h 200.00
Toy, Popeye with punching bag, Chein, litho tin wind-up, blue, red, and white, green painted base, 1830, 8" h 700.00

Porky Pig, Leon Schlesinger, Warner Bros.
Big Little Book, Porky Pig and His Gang, Whitman #1404 ....50.00
Character Drinking Glass, Pepsi, Warner Brothers Looney Tunes, copyright 1966 ....8.00
Soakie, 9-1/2" h, molded vinyl, plastic body, hard plastic removable head, 1960s...28.00

Quick Draw McGraw, Hanna-Barbera, lamp, 22" h, plastic, c1950, shade mkd "Hanna-Barbera," repaired......................................20.00

Rocky and Bullwinkle, Jay Ward
Bendie, MOC 20.00
Character Drinking Glass, Pepsi logo, Bullwinkle, circus, balloons, Ward Brocking, 1970s.........................16.00
Character Drinking Mug, 3" h, milk glass, yellow panel with brown dec 18.00
Charm, figural 15.00

Musical Instruments, set of three plastic toy instruments, 1969, MOC 50.00

Sylvester, Warner Bros.
Character Drinking Glass, Sylvester, Pepsi, Warner Brothers Looney Tunes, copyright 1966................. 5.00
Character Drinking Glass, Tweety Bird, Pepsi, Warner Brothers Looney Tunes, copyright 1973................. 5.00
Cookie Jar, Sylvester and Tweety, Applause 55.00
Hot Water Bottle, Sylvester holding Tweety, Warner Brothers, Inc., Duarry, Spain, 12-1/4" h 75.00
Spinning Ring, silvered metal frame, thin expansion band, clear acrylic cover over shaded color portrait, 1990s 10.00

Tom and Jerry, Hanna-Barbera
Character Drinking Glass, Pepsi, Jerry, name in black letters, 1975, some small scrapes to decals 8.00
Comic Book, #240, Gold Key 2.00
Mug, scenes of Tom and Jerry, Staffordshire, 1970, mkd "MGM," 3-1/4" h 36.00
Pinback Button, Sunbeam Bead, 1-1/4" d 10.00
Puzzle, child's, copyright 1954, 5" x 15", one small pc missing 8.00
Stereo-View Film Card, The Two Mouseketeers, #T-32, 1956, Lowe's Inc., Tru-Vue Co., Beavertown, OR 10.00

Underdog
Premium Ring, Charlton Comics, silvered plastic base, black image on day-glo red sticker 30.00
Premium Ring, Simon Bar Sinister, white plastic, expansion bands, circular top disk, wear to gold accents, c1975... 65.00

Woody Woodpecker, Walter Lantz
Bank, 7" h, ceramic, figural, red, yellow, blue, white, black, and brown, plastic stopper 40.00
Children's Book, Woody Woodpecker Pogo Stick Adventures, Tell-A-Tale, 1954... 10.00
Cookie Jar, 9" h, Woody mixing up batch of cookies, c1950, mkd "A3391/ww" 325.00
Doll, 13" h, plush, stain on front... 12.00
Game, Travel with Woody Woodpecker, Walter Lantz, Cadaco, lids detached from two containers, all pieces present, played-with condition.................................... 115.00
Harmonica, 5-1/2" h, nodding head, red plastic, Lantz copyright on chest, some decal missing from eyes 25.00
Little Golden Book, Woody Woodpecker, Walter Lantz, copyright 1952 .... 12.50
Ring, thin brass adjustable band, diecut brass Woody facing right, black, white, red, and yellow enamels, mkd "Walter Lantz Productions 1977" 20.00

Salt and Pepper Shakers, pr, Woody and Winnie, paper label "W. Lantz, 1990"...50.00

Spoon, child's, mkd "W.L.P.," stamped "IS," c1950, silverplating worn 6.00

Stereo-View Film Card, Pony Express, #T-23, Walter Lantz, 1951, Tru-Vue Co., Beavertown, OR.................10.00

Toothbrush Holder, 3-3/4" h, 1940s, unmarked.....................................125.00

Yellow Kid, pinback button, policeman's uniform, High Admiral Cigarettes, copyright 1898, $45.

Yellow Kid, R. F. Outcault

Cigar Box, 5-1/2" x 9" x 4", wood, hinged lid with lightly engraved portrait of Kid, other images, orig red label "Smoke Yellow Kid Cigars, Manuf'd by DR Fleming, Curwensville, PA," early 1900s 345.00

Ice Cream Mold, 4-3/4" h, hinged, full figure...215.00

Pinback Button, High Admiral Cigarettes
No. 3, Kid standing in barrel, Mrs. Murphy mends clothes.................35.00
No. 14, Kid with large white collar, dressed to go to ball 45.00

Yogi Bear, Hanna-Barbera

Lamp, 20" h, mkd "Hanna Barbera Productions"......................................30.00

Premium Ring, non-adjustable plastic base with gold luster, black plastic top, portrait and character name along studio initials "H-B"

Dixie, wear to gold luster 45.00
Huck...48.00
Mr. Jinks, some scratches 45.00
Yogi Bear...48.00

Yosemite Sam, Warner Bros., ring, wide brass expansion band, diecut figure with multicolored enamel, foil tag "J.R.S./Warner Bros./1970/Hand-Painted".......................................20.00

Catalina Pottery

Collecting Hints: Many dinnerware patterns, in addition to a wide variety of decorative pieces, were produced

under the Catalina name. From 1937 to 1947, many of the artware lines were made by Gladding, McBean and Company. Although the island plant was closed, many pieces made during this period were still marked "Catalina Island." In order to distinguish between pieces made before and after the Gladding, McBean takeover, collectors must learn the subtle differences in the various marks used.

History: The Catalina Pottery began producing clay building products in 1927 at its original location on Santa Catalina Island. In 1930, the pottery expanded its inventory to include decorative and utilitarian pieces. Dinnerware was added in 1931. Gladding, McBean and Company bought the firm in 1937 and closed the island plant, limiting production to the mainland. Ownership of the trademark reverted to the Catalina Island Company in 1947.

References: Susan and Al Bagdade, *Warman's American Pottery and Porcelain*, 2nd ed., Krause Publications, 2000; Jack Chipman, *Collector's Encyclopedia of California Pottery*, Collector Books, 1992, values updated 1998; Steve and Aisha Hoefs, *Catalina Island Pottery*, published by authors, 1993.

Ashtray
Fish, small, blue 60.00
Sleeping Mexican, matte green, cold paint 285.00

Bowl
7" sq, Matrix, blue 60.00
8" l, oval, Matrix, yellow and maroon 40.00
10" l, 6" w, undulating rim, light orange ext., turquoise int., c1950 ....28.00
12" d, round, low, Matrix, blue 45.00
15" d, Angeleno........................90.00
17" d, oval, fluted, Matrix, yellow and green 90.00

Bud Vase, Angeleno, C105 ....45.00

Candlesticks, pr, Matrix, blue 40.00

Centerpiece Bowl and Underplate, 12" d x 4-3/8" h bowl, 14" d underplate, lobed form, scalloped edge, imp "Catalina Island" in block letters...350.00

Charger, 17" d, red, few slight kiln misses, knife marks, unmarked.....................................350.00

Cigarette Box, cov, horse's head, ivory...475.00

Console Set, Art Deco style, light butterscotch, 4" x 9" pr three-lite candleholders, 13" x 13-1/4" bowl with raised dec base, 3-1/2" x 9" three-tier flower frog, brown ink mark "Catalina Made in USA".......................................400.00

Dinner Plate
10-1/4" d, reddish-orange, some dark marks on back from firing 80.00
10-5/16" d, green, stamped "Catalina Island 4," slight glaze defect 80.00

Dish, 6-1/2" l, 4-1/2" w, rect, white ext., blue int., blue ink mark "Catalina Pottery, Made in USA" 25.00

Egg Plate, 10" d, Matrix, blue.........24.00

Flower Bowl, low, flat, Capistrano
C406, buff, satin green..............40.00
C412, rect..................................35.00
C419, oval 48.00

Jardiniere, 4-5/8" d, 3-5/8" h, floral design...145.00

Pipe Rest, Ivory Siesta, repaired.. 250.00

Tray, Catalina Blue, 13-1/2" d 150.00

Vase
5" h, white ext. and ext., mkd "Catalina Pottery" 35.00
6-1/2" h, C335, white ext., blue int., leaf shape, mkd "Catalina Pottery, C335, Made in USA" 60.00
7" h, C333, blue ext. and int., mkd "Catalina Pottery, C333, Made in USA"...45.00
8" h, 7-1/4" w, white ext., blue int., relief branch of flowers, pleated sides, brown ink mark "Catalina, Made in U.S.A." 125.00
9" h, 7" w at top, 4" w at base, tan ext., green int. 125.00
10" h, 4" d, fluted top, white, blue ink mark, "Catalina Pottery, Made in USA"...225.00

Catalogs

Collecting Hints: The price of an old catalog is affected by the condition, date, type of material advertised, and location of advertiser.

History: Catalogs are excellent research sources. The complete manufacturing line of a given item is often described, along with prices, styles, colors, etc. Old catalogs provide a good way to date objects.

Sometimes old catalogs are reprinted so that collectors can identify the companies' specialties. Such is the case with Imperial and The Cambridge Glass Co.

References: Ron Barlow and Ray Reynolds, *Insider's Guide to Old Books, Magazines, Newspapers, and Trade Catalogs*, Windmill Publishing (2147 Windmill View Rd, El Cajon, CA 92020), 1996.

Advisor: Kenneth Schneringer.

W. F. Dougherty & Sons, Philadelphia, PA, 1921, 212 pgs, 8-1/2" x 11", $78. Photo courtesy of Kenneth Schneringer.

American Hoffman Corp., New York, NY, no date, six pgs, 10-1/4" x 11-1/2", 11-1/2" x 31" sheet folded in as issued, Hoffman Blue Ribbon Motorcycles for the Discriminating Rider..65.00

Big Gem Art Advertising Calendars, US, 1936, 10" x 16-1/2", salesman's demo kit, 10" x 16-1/2" folder with two 14" x 8-1/2" calendars laid down, green folder wraps, gold lettering........30.00

Byrnes & Kiefer, Pittsburgh, PA, c1933, 27 pgs, 3-1/2" x 7-1/2", Manufacturers of Specialties to the Food Industry Presents Recipes Guaranteed to Work with the Products They Manufacture 8.00

Chrysler Sales Division, Detroit, MI, 1950, 18 pgs, 8" x 10", 24" x 30" sheet folded as issued, color, shows 19 models 24.00

Columbia Shade Cloth Co., New York, NY, c1910, 24 pgs, 6-1/2" x 9", drapery hardware and shade sundries 36.00

Cresson-Morris Co., Philadelphia, PA, c1928, 8 pgs, 8-1/2" x 11", 20th Century Woodworker, overhead saw 14.00

Dougherty, W. F., & Sons, Philadelphia, PA, 1932, 212 pgs, 8-1/2" x 11", food service equipment 80.00

8 in 1 Pet Products, Inc., New York, NY, 1955, 24 pgs, 4-1/4" x 7-1/4", canary and parakeet supplies, breeding and mating tips 10.00

Eugene Dietzgen Co., Anabasis, NY, c1939, 56 pgs, 5-3/4" x 8-3/4", Catalog No. 39A, Essential Drawing Instruments and Materials 22.00

Fisher Body Corp., Detroit, MI, 1933, 4 pgs, 10-1/4" x 13-1/2", folded to 5" x 7-1/2" as issued, "A New Motoring Thrill, Cooling Breezes in the Hottest Weather," ventilation system for car comfort and safety, 7 illus 10.00

Frank & Son, Inc., New York, NY, c1912, 8 pgs, 3" x 6", The "Frankson" all-purpose household stool................10.00

Gifford-Wood Co., Hudson, NY, 1922, 84 pgs, 6" x 9", Ice Tool Catalog No. 50, cuts of elevator planners, ice tools..85.00

Gray Brothers, Cleveland, OH, 1924, 176 pgs, 7-1/2" x 10-1/2", Net Price Catalog, carriage, auto supplies, and tools..50.00

Heckerman, H. C., Bedford, PA, 1908, 32 pgs, 7" x 8-1/2", Catalog of Presents for Return Happy Bill Certificates..24.00

Holtzman-Cabot Electric, Boston, MA, 1905, 4 pgs, 6-3/4" x 9-1/2", Bulletin No. 310, Magneto Power Generators 15.00

Jenkinson, G. H., Co., Sioux City, IA, c1906, 42 pgs, 10-1/4" x 14", Catalog No. 22, stapled two-pg colored sheet of printed linoleum, billiard and pool tables, supplies........................365.00

Jorden, Albert, Co., New York, NY, c1925, 32 pgs, 8-1/4" x 11", Dick & Wusthof Cutlery Catalog, cuts of round and oval knife sharpeners 28.00

Kochs, Theo. A., Chicago, IL, 1915, 180 pgs, 9" x 12", Catalog No. 31, picturesque wraps, 19 colored sheets with barber equipment, 1918 price list laid-in, damped along upper edge 475.00

Lazerus Bros., New York, NY, c1930, 30 pgs, 6" x 9", Clothing Bargains, Take A Shot At These Values!, mail-out catalog for men and boys clothing.12.00

Maher & Gross, Toledo, OH, no date, early, 96 pgs, 7" x 10", Catalog No. 46, How to Use A Razor, quality goods, shears, razors, shaving materials, pocket knives, vertical fold in center 42.00

Meneely Bell Co., Troy, NY, 1912, 46 pgs, 6-1/4" x 9-1/2", $75. Photo courtesy of Kenneth Schneringer.

Meneely Bell Co., Troy, NY, 1912, 46 pgs, 6-1/4" x 9-1/2", manufacturers of bells for church, chime, academy, towers, court house, fire alarm, etc. 75.00

Merrell, J. S., Drug Co., St. Louis, MO, 1919, 103 pgs, 9-1/2" x 12-1/4", drug store fixtures, fountain supplies, pencil marks on front wrap............ 150.00

Munves, Mike, Corp., New York, NY, 1955, 28 pgs, 8-3/4" x 11-3/4", illus of arcade games, juke boxes, baseball, football, hockey, bowling, and skeet ball machines, etc. 138.00

National Lumber Mfgrs, Washington, DC, 1929, 30 pgs, 8-1/4" x 11", Lumber & Its Utilization, house framing details, illus how to assemble structural parts of frame buildings.... 20.00

Paine Lumber Co., Ltd., Oshkosh, WI, 1924, 54 pgs, 8-1/2" x 11", Paine Miracle Doors, illus, descriptions, specifications, water damage throughout 24.00

Patch, F. R., Mfg. Co., Rutland, VT, c1930, 16 pgs, 8-1/2" x 11", Catalog of Patch Planers, Belt and Motor Driven, cuts of 48" x 48" open side planer 20.00

Ridabock & Co., New York, NY, 1880s, 48 pgs, 6-3/4" x 8", Successors to J.H. McKenney & Co., military goods 70.00

Russell Uniform Co., New York, NY, 1929, 64 pgs, 5-1/2" x 8-1/2", Catalog No. 35 of Uniforms, semi-military and naval designs, trimmed collars and cuffs, embroidered sleeves and collar devices, doormen, ushers, liveries, uniforms and coats 98.00

Safe Cabinet Co., Chicago, IL, c1931, 40 pgs, 6" x 9", 4 pgs laid-in, Oxo Gas Heating Appliances 15.00

Schenfeld & Sons, New York, NY, no date, 1970s, 24 pgs, 6-3/4" x 9-1/2", House of Schenfield Bridal & Formal Fabrics, 58 material swatches tipped in 24.00

Standard Mail Order Co., New York, NY, c1925, 64 pgs, 6" x 9", Clothing Catalog, men's and women's............ 15.00

Todhunter, New York, NY, 1929, 16 pgs, 8-1/2" x 11", price list laid-in, authentic reproductions of hand wrought lanterns... 45.00

United States Rubber Co., New Orleans, LA, c1940, 12 pgs, 9" x 12", Ked Catalog of Footwear...................... 32.00

Wanamaker, John, New York, NY, 1920s, 8 pgs, 4-3/4" x 6", March is the Month of China, offering china and glassware 36.00

Ward's Natural Science, Rochester, NY, c1910, 8 pgs, 6" x 9-1/4", The Frank A. Ward Foundation of Natural Science of the University of Rochester, South African shells for sale...... 10.00

Warsaw-Wilkinson Co., Warsaw, NY, 1925, 16 pgs, 6" x 9", four pages directions and price list laid in, Climax Pneumatic Feed & Ensilage Cutters, dusted 28.00

Wrinch & Sons, London, Great Britain, 1910, 52 pgs, 6-1/4" x 10", Designs of Folding Chairs, Tables, Garden and Seaside Tents, etc. 65.00

Yawman & Erbe Mfg Co., Rochester, NY, c1929, 17 pgs, 8" x 10-3/4", Y & E Efficiency Desks, tinted color cuts of executive and departmental desks, chairs 60.00

Zeiss, Carl, New York, NY, c1930, 58 pgs, 6" x 8-1/4", Zeiss Field Glasses 50.00

Cat Collectibles

Collecting Hints: Cat-related material can be found in almost all collecting categories—advertising items, dolls, figurines, folk art, fine art, jewelry, needlework, linens, plates, postcards, and stamps, to name just a few. Antique cats are scarce, but modern objects d'feline are plentiful. The better ones, the limited editions and pieces created by established artists, are future collectibles.

The cat collector competes with collectors from other areas. Chessie, the C & O Railroad cat, is collected by railroad and advertising buffs; Felix, Garfield, and other cartoon characters, plus cat-shaped toys and cat-related games, are loved by toy collectors. And cat postcards are collected by postcard collectors in general.

Because cat collectors are attracted to all cat items, all breeds, and realistic or abstract depictions, they tend to buy many items. It is best to specialize. Popular categories are fine art, antique porcelain cats, stamps, advertising, postcards and unique or unusual pieces. Up-and-coming collecting categories include first-day covers, phone cards, and dolls. Kliban's cats, especially the ceramic examples, art by Louis Wain, good Victorian paintings, and cartoon cats are best-sellers in the secondary market.

History: The popular view of cats has been a roller coaster of opinion, from peaks of favoritism to valleys of superstition. Cats were deified in ancient Egypt and feared by Europeans in the Middle Ages. Customs and rituals resulted in brutal treatment of felines. Cats became associated with witchcraft, resulting in tales and superstitions which linger to the present. This lack of popularity adds to the scarcity of antique cat items.

References: Pauline Flick, *Cat Collectibles*, Wallace-Homestead, 1992; Marbena Jean Fyke, *Collectible Cats*, Collector Books, 1993.

Collectors' Club: Cat Collectors, P.O. Box 150784, Nashville, TN 37215, Web site: www.catcollectors.com

Museums: British Museum, London, England; The Cat Museum, Basel, Switzerland; Metropolitan Museum of Art, New York, NY.

Advisor: Karen Shanks.

Reproduction Alert.

Advertising trade cards, A. B. Sealey, 1861, set of six, $120.

Book, *Old Possum's Book of Practical Cats*, T. S. Eliot, Faber & Faber, Ltd., London, 1957 ....42.00

Bookends, pr, ceramic, one with black and white cat stretching his paw through to other bookend, second bookend has gray mouse with mallet, ready to strike extended cat's paw, incised "©1983" and ceramist's initials 35.00

Chalkware Figure, 7-1/2" h, Persian Cat, sitting up, pale yellow head, darkens to black chin and tail 55.00

Child's Play Dishes, cup and saucer, cat on twig of pussy willows, mkd "Made in Japan" 15.00

Clock, 9" h, Sessions Clock Co., white ceramic cat holding clock, plastic cat as second hand, 1950s 50.00

Comic Book, *Felix The Cat*, All Pictures Comics, 1945 ....50.00

Figural
4" h, pottery, pair, white with yellow and black spots, blue bases, stamped in blue "Staffordshire, England".................................35.00
4" h, 2-3/4" l, three pink kittens, attached and seated on blue Victorian-style sofa with gold trim, stamped "©1959 Bradley Onimco" 25.00

Figure, gray striped cat, boot, 4-3/4"h, Staffordsire, $70. Photo courtesy of Joy Luke Fine Art Brokers and Auctioneers.

8" h, Siamese, ceramic, model #4693, paper label "Lefton Japan" 28.00
8-1/4" h, porcelain, repro of Dresden cat, long haired, white, marked in blue "Museo First Edition," Mann Japan paper label, c1975 ....145.00
10-1/2" h, Egyptian cat, museum repro, incised mark "© Austin production 1965" 75.00

Handkerchief, embroidered 5.00

Letter Opener, 9" l, solid brass, arched back cat atop, incised "England" 55.00

Mug, 3-1/4" h, ceramic, cat face, white, dark blue floral collar and handle, incised "Avon" 18.00

Nodder, 4-1/4" h, yellow, black stripes, fuzzy, blue rhinestone eyes, paper label "Made in Hong Kong" 8.50

Pitcher, 8-1/4" h, glass, cat shape, tail forms handle, incised "WMF Germany" 25.00

Planter
6" l, composition, laying down cat holds balls of yard from sewing basket, incised "Pompadour 1984" .. 6.50
6" l, 5" h, pottery, stylized laughing cat, aqua, script "Weller Pottery" mark..75.00

Plaque, bisque, applied full figure cat dancers, c1850-60 ....75.00

Plate
6" d, china, cream colored, gold pattern around border, long-haired golden tabby cat transfer, Mount Clemens Pottery hallmark, c1935 .. 25.00
8" d, 1985 series, titled "Minou-ettes" by Vista Allegra, C. Pradalie, series includes various breeds, all with lacy curtain backgrounds 20.00

Postcards, full color, Clivette, white long-hair cats, neck ribbons of various colors, short verse of inspiration or sentimental nature, used, c1906, set of six, 3-1/2" x 5-1/2" 30.00

Puzzle, 10-1/2" x 14", cardboard, yellow cat in blue pants and white sailor hat, playing concertino 10.00

Salt and Pepper Shaker Sets, ceramic Cat shaped, Holt Howard, ©1958, meowers not working.................20.00
Garfield with Fishburger sandwich....................................60.00
Hello Kitty, three-pc set..............60.00
Mr. and Mrs. Black Cats, stamped "Japan" 15.00
Sylvester and Tweety Bird with mallet...60.00

Scrapbook, greeting and note cards, some with envelopes, approx 125 cards, c1940 to present...........200.00

Serving Tray, 15" x 21", metal, painted gold, aqua border, two Siamese cats in center, sgd "Alexander".........65.00

String Holder, 6-1/2" h, cat face shape, black and cream, blue ball of string, stamped with partial name of company, "James___ Chicago, Il"..65.00

Tape Measure, celluloid case, pictures of playing cats, tape mkd "Made in U.S.A."..35.00

Toby Mug, 9" h, porcelain, Puss n' Boots, Kevin Francis, modeled by Andrew Moss, limited edition.................295.00

Toy, 6" l, tin yellow and red cat, red ball and wheels, leather ears, push tail down and cat moves forward, mkd "MAR Toys Made in USA"..........95.00

TV Lamp, ceramic, shape of two Siamese cats, incised "© 1958 Lane & Co., Van Nys, CA, U.S.A."......85.00

Wall Plaque, 6-1/2" h, chalkware, Tabby cat face, red ears and big bow, green eyes..45.00

Ceramic Arts Studio

Collecting Hints: Collectors should seek pieces which are free of damage and defects. Since this collecting area is relatively new, it behooves collectors to buy the best quality they can while prices are low. A careful eye should be used to find those unique pieces by designers such as Harrington.

A single firing process was used to make Ceramic Arts Studio wares. The pieces were fired after decorations were applied to the soft greenware. The firm's specially developed glazes have remained stable with little discoloration or crazing.

History: The Ceramic Arts Studio, Madison, Wisconsin, was originally formed by Lawrence Rabbit in 1940, while he was a student at the University of Wisconsin. He researched Wisconsin clay for a class project, and later produced hand-thrown pottery. By January of 1941, he went into partnership with fellow University of Wisconsin Student Reuben Sand. Sand became responsible for the administration, distribution, marketing, and management of the studio.

Betty Harrington, who began her career in 1942, designed more than 600 figures and other items for the studio through her 14-year career. She was influence by Martha Graham's modern dancers. In addition to her theater series, she created storybook character and nursery rhyme series. These series included figures, head vases, salt and pepper shaker sets, shelf sitters, and wall plaques. Harrington trained other designers, but was responsible for most of the designs until the studio closed in 1956.

During peak production years in the late 1940s, more than 100 people produced 500,000 pieces a year. The molds were sent to Japan after the studio closed. Japanese pieces are sometimes found in the marketplace, but the depth of the color and clarity does not equal that of the originals.

Ceramic Arts Studio wares were inexpensive—in the $2 to $3 range—and were marketed through department stores and by catalog sellers such as Montgomery Ward.

Collectors' Club: Ceramic Arts Studio Collectors Association, P.O. Box 46, Madison, WI 53701.

Bell, Summer, 5-1/4" h, clapper missing.......................................80.00
Figure
   Black boy on crocodile, 4-5/8" l, 2-1/2" h.....................................220.00
   Black boy on elephant, 1952, 7-3/4" h..200.00
   Dance Modern Man, 9-1/2" h....................................115.00
   Gay Nineties Couple, 6-1/2" Harry, 6-3/8" h Lillibeth, c1954.................90.00
   Mr. And Mrs. Skunk, 2-7/8" h....................................100.00
   Pan American Couple, 4-1/2" h Pepita, 4-1/4" h Pancho, 1954 ....90.00
   Polish Couple, 6-1/2" h..............98.00
   Russian Couple, 5-3/8" h Petrov, 5-1/4" h Petrushka.....................85.00
   Sultan on pillow, 4-3/4" h............80.00
Head Vase
   Becky 80.00
   Mei-Ling 85.00
Pitcher, Adam and Eve 65.00
Razor Bank.....................................80.00
Salt and Pepper Shakers, pr
   Bears, mother and cub, brown, snugglers...85.00
   Boy and Chair, blond boy looking over back of 2" h stuffed chair 60.00
   Clown and Dog 175.00

Cows, 5-1/4" h mother, 2-1/4" h calf, snugglers.................................... 190.00
Elephants, 3-3/4" h male, 3-1/4" h female... 70.00
Fighting Chickens 50.00
Gingham Cat and Calico Dog, 2-7/8" h cat, 2-3/4" h dog........... 95.00
Gorilla and baby, snugglers.... 100.00
Monkeys, 4" h mother, 2-1/2" h baby, snugglers.................................. 80.00
Polar Bears, 4-1/2" h mother, 2-1/4" h baby, white, snugglers 70.00
Scottie Dogs........................... 75.00
Thai and Thai-Thai.................... 72.00
Wee Eskimos........................... 80.00
Shelf Sitter
   Banjo Girl........................... 65.00
   Collie, large 80.00
Nip and Tuck, 1954, 4-1/4" h..... 65.00
Vase, 6" h, Wing-Tang, playing mandolin, bamboo vase, 1947 copyright.. 70.00
Wall Plaque, Cockatoo................. 50.00
Wash Basin and Pitcher, 15" d bowl, 7" w x 11" h pitcher, floral dec........... 85.00

Cereal Boxes

Collecting Hints: There are two keys to collecting cereal boxes. The first is graphics, i.e., the box features the picture of a major character or personality or a design that is extremely characteristic of its period. The second hinges on the premium advertised on the box.

Cereal boxes are divided into vintage boxes (those dating before 1970s) and modern boxes. Hoarding of modern cereal boxes began in the mid-1980s. Beware of paying premium prices for any boxes made after this date.

More desirable than cereal boxes themselves are large countertop and other cereal box display pieces. Cereal box collectors actively compete against advertising collectors for these items, thus driving up prices.

Many cereal box themes also cross over into other collecting categories. In many cases, these secondary collectors are responsible for maintaining high prices for some boxes. Once the outside demand is met, prices drop. Carefully study which market component is the principal price determinant.

History: Oatmeal and wheat cereals achieved popularity in the 19th century. They could be purchased in bulk from any general store. The first packaged, ready-to-eat breakfast cereals appeared around 1900. Initially, the packaging pitch contained an appeal directed to mothers.

Everything changed in the late 1930s and early 1940s. Companies such as General Mills, Quaker, Post, and Ralston redirected the packaging appeal to children, using as a hook the lure of premiums sent in exchange for one or more box lids or coupons. Many of these promotions were geared to the popular radio shows of the period. However, television advertising was most responsible for establishing a firm link between cereal manufacturers and children.

In the 1940s, General Mills successfully used the premium approach to introduce Cheerios and Kix. In the 1950s, sugar-coated cereals were the rage. By the 1960s and 1970s, cereal manufacturers linked the sale of their brands to licensed characters. As the popularity of characters faded, boxes—but not the cereal contents—were changed. Today an endless variety of cereal brands parades across supermarket shelves, some brands lasting less than a year.

References: Scott Bruce, *Cereal Box Bonanza*, Collector Books, 1995; —, *Cereal Boxes & Prizes: 1960s*, Flake World Publishing, 1998; Scott Bruce and Bill Crawford, *Cerealizing America*, Faber and Faber, 1995; Jim Harmon, *Radio & TV Premiums*, Krause Publications, 1997.

Periodical: *Flake*, P.O. Box 481, Cambridge, MA 02140.

Collectors' Club: Sugar-Charged Cereal Collectors, 92B N. Bedford St., Arlington, VA 22201.

Cereal Box

Cheerio's, 7-1/2" x 10" x 2", front panel offer of reproduction Confederate money, slight dusting, c1954.....35.00
Kellogg's Corn Flakes
  6-1/2" x 2-1/2" x 8-1/2" h, white cardboard, red and green printing, back adv baseball related premiums, expiration date of Dec 31, 1942......................................140.00
  7" x 10" x 2", side panel ad for punch-out cardboard walkie-talkie, c1940 18.00
  8-1/2" x 12-1/2" x 3", full color cut-out Tomahawk mask on back panel, c1955......................................28.00
  10" x 15" flattened color box, copyright 1956, flying platform ad 40.00
King Brand Rolled Oats...................45.00
Kix
  6-5/8" x 8-1/4" x 2-1/2", Astral Ace model airplane cut-outs, copyright 1947, #4 in series of eight......38.00
  6-5/8" x 8-3/8" x 2-1/2", Cosmic Cruiser model airplane cut-outs, copyright 1947, #6 in series of eight......38.00

  6-5/8" x 8-1/2" x 2-3/8", Radar Raycraft model airplane cut-outs, copyright 1947, #7 in series of eight 38.00
Nabisco Rice Honey's, 8-1/4" x 10-1/4", tiger shark premium offer, mid 1950s..45.00
Wheaties, Cal Ripken, plain black jersey, unopened...................................75.00

Cereal Box Back

Cheerios
  American Airlines Travel Game, back and side panel, 8" x 9", uncut, 1950s....................................12.00
  Hall of Fun, 3-D picture of Groucho, 8-1/2" x 9", uncut, 1942...........18.00
Kix, Country Fair, #5, ferris wheel, back and side panel, 8" x 9", uncut, 1950s......................................3.00
Quaker Puffed Rice Model Farm, set of five uncut 8" x 9" backs, c1950..30.00
Wheaties
  Elinor Smith, aviatrix, orange, blue, white, and black, 6" x 6", 1930s, one corner missing...................8.00
  Marie McMillin, U.S. Record-Breaking Woman Parachutist, black, white, and orange, facsimile signature, c1930, 6" x 6-5/8"...................15.00
  Orange, white, two shades of blue, and yellow, Ray "Crash" Corrigan in scene from Republic film "Roarin' Lead," 6" x 8", uncut 10.00

Cereal Box Cutout

Quaker Puffed Wheat, Sgt. Preston
  Action Picture, neatly watercolored, 5-12" x 5-3/4" 15.00
  The Great Yukon River Canoe Race board game, 8" x 9" 15.00
Wheaties, Adventures on Wheels, 9" x 12", 1950s, uncut
  Circus wagon.................................3.00
  Covered wagon 4.00
  Gypsy wagon.................................3.00
  Roman chariot...............................3.50
  Stagecoach...................................4.00

Cereal Premiums

Collecting Hints: The rising collectibility of cereal premiums reflects the shift of emphasis from collectibles of the 1920-1940 period to those of the post-1945 era. The radio premium generation is getting older. They have watched the price of scarcer examples of their childhood treasures rise beyond the point of affordability. Further, these collectors are reaching an age when selling, rather than buying, dominates their mind-set. It is time for a new generation to enter the picture—herald the arrival of the cereal premium.

At the moment, collectors do not differentiate between premiums that were found in the box and those that were obtained by sending in the req-

uisite number of box tops. As collectors become more sophisticated, look for this distinction to occur.

The cereal premiums of most interest in the current market are those associated with a fictional advertising, cartoon, or television character. As a result, much of the pricing in this category is being driven by the non-cereal premium collector. This does not appear likely to change in the decade ahead.

Collectors of cereal premiums narrow their collecting by focusing on the premiums found in a single brand or those of one particular manufacturer—variables dependent on whether the concentration is on the 1945-1962 or post-1962 period. The lack of a comprehensive list of manufacturers, brands, and premiums often makes attribution a problem. When buying a cereal premium with which you are unfamiliar, insist that the seller indicate the manufacturer, brand name, and date on the sales receipt.

The importance of original packaging—much of which was nondescript—is unclear at the moment. Current collectors tend to leave sealed any unopened packages. Most examples on the market have not retained their original packaging.

At the moment, there is little enthusiasm for generic pieces. However, anyone who compares the history of Cracker Jack premium collecting with that of cereal premiums will quickly see the long-term potential for generic material.

History: Cereal premiums were introduced in the 1930s when manufacturers such as General Mills, Post, Quaker, and Ralston offered premiums to individuals who sent in the requisite number of box tops or coupons. Many of these premiums had a radio show tie-in.

Although the use of in-the-box premiums and on-pack promotions dates from the 1930s, this approach achieved its greatest popularity in the post-1945 period. Buildings, dolls, games, masks, and puzzles were just a few of the many items that a child could cut out by carefully following the directions on the back of a cereal box. Many in-box and on-pack promotional premiums related to a popular television program or movie.

When sugar-coated brands were introduced in the mid-1950s, advertising characters were developed to assist in the merchandising effort.

Characters such as Captain Crunch, Sugar Bear, Tony the Tiger, and Toucan Sam achieved widespread recognition. Often in-box and on-pack promotions tied in directly with these characters.

In the 1970s, tie-ins were often more short-lived. Cereal manufacturers responded almost immediately to the latest movie or television craze, and local and regional promotions became prominent. One result of this trend is the shift in emphasis from the premium to the box itself as the important collectible unit. Cereal box collecting is now a separate category. The value of most boxes now exceeds any value for the premium associated with it.

References: Scott Bruce, *Cereal Box Bonanza*, Collector Books, 1995; —, *Cereal Boxes & Prizes: 1960s*, Flake World Publishing, 1998; Scott Bruce and Bill Crawford, *Cerealizing America*, Faber and Faber, 1995; Jim Harmon, *Radio & TV Premiums*, Krause Publications, 1997.

Periodical: *Flake*, P.O. Box 481, Cambridge, MA 02140.

Airplane, Kellogg's, balsa wood, 1930s Vultee V1A Richman and Merrills' Lady Piece, model by Mego, orig mailing box 45.00

Animated Specs, Coco-Wheat, stiff cardboard, brown, each temple with Coco-Wheats name, attached flap on back with diecut eyeballs that move as glasses are worn, noticeable browning on back 12.00

Bird House Kit, Post Cereal, wooden parts, Gallow Mfg. Co., Wisconsin, 3-3/4" x 6-1/2" x 1-3/4" tan box ... 15.00

Booklet, *Peeks Behind The Scenes of Tom Breneman's Breakfast in Hollywood*, 5-1/2" x 8-1/2" black and white booklet, 24 pgs, red accents, 5-3/4" x 8-3/4" black and white envelope with Kellogg's imprint, slight soiling .. 15.00

Bowl, 6" x 6" x 1-1/2" deep white china, blue accent rim, 2" h full color image of soldier lad in center, military parade outfit, Vita B on hat, 1930s, some wear 20.00

Charm-Glow Sheet, 6" x 8-3/4", Coco-Wheats, eight cartoon illus of animals and birds, 1944 copyright, orig envelope, unused 10.00

Coin Folder, Wheaties, International, European and Midwest, blue, white, and orange, 4" x 6", c1950, 4 of 15 coins missing 10.00

Deed, Sgt. Preston Kondike Big Inch Land Co., 5" x 8" paper certificate, Quaker Oats, c1955, orig owner's name entered 18.00

Doll, 3" h, Snap, Crackle, Pop, soft vinyl squeeze type, each with individual name and Kellogg's copyright, c1975, set of three 90.00

Explorer's Kit, Quake, Quaker, 8" x 11" black and white sheet listing parts, four fold-out maps, 4-1/2" l geologist's hammer with Geiger counter, four different ore/rock specimens, magnifying glass, tweezers, stand unit, goggles, small pair of mirrors, complete, unused 120.00

Figure, dinosaur, Kellogg's, glow-in-the-dark, soft plastic diecut, flat backs, raised features, early 1970, set of three 12.00

Flashlight, 4-1/2" l, 1-1/2" d, Jack Armstrong, torpedo shape, cardboard tube with metal caps, Wheaties premium from Louis F. Dow Co., St. Louis, 1939 .... 20.00

Flying Saucer, Cap'n Crunch, yellow plastic, raised design, black rubber launcher, c1981-82 .... 10.00

Game
  Cap'n Crunch, finger tennis game, blue plastic, shows Cap'n and LaFoote, c1981-82, unused 15.00
  The Big Ten Football Game, Jack Armstrong Wheaties Premium, 1936, 8-1/2" x 11" diecut green, red, white stiff paper stadium with diecut slide rule openings, 11" x 17" orange and yellow stiff paper football game chart with black and white text, small bag with numbered wooden blocks and diecut field markers, orig 9" x 12" manila envelope with some wear, tears 40.00

Handbook, *Kellogg's Cadet Aviation Corps*, 6" x 9", 32 pgs, copyright 1938, some wear and minor splits 18.00

Mask, Wheaties, clipped back and side panels, c1950, 8" x 9"
  Cannibal character, black and orange, tinted blue accents, name partially clipped off, wear 5.00
  Cartoon Dog, uncut eyes 2.50
  Elf, cut eyes 2.00
  Fierce tiger, uncut eyes 2.50
  Oriental, uncut eyes 2.50
  Robot, black, white, and orange, name clipped off 5.00

Model
  Cap'n Crunch Sea Cycle, unused parts for model, figures of Crunch and Seadog, c1970, 5" x 7" x 2" shipping box 20.00
  Kellogg's Pep, 2-1/2" x 6-1/2" balsa sheet printed with Curtis Helldriver Dive-Bomber airplane, orig paper envelope with printed instructions, small cut-out insignias, c1945 ... 30.00

Mug, Kellogg's Apple Jacks, 3" d, 3" h, red, two eyes, inset mouth, copyright 1960 .... 15.00

Patch, 3-1/4" x 4-1/4" fabric, Future Champions of America, Wheaties, red, white, and blue, c1943 .... 30.00

Manual, *Straight Arrow Injun-nity Manual*, Book 3, Nabisco Shredded Wheat, National Biscuit Co., green lettering, 1949, 3-7/8" w, 7-3/8" h, $15.

Pedometer, 2-1/2" d, Quaker, Sgt. Preston, tin litho insert of Preston and King, belt clip, 1952 .... 35.00

Picture Booklet, Kellogg's Rice Krispies, 3-1/2" x 5-1/2", color illus by Vernon Grant, Snap, Crackle, Pop, copyright 1934, changeable picture segments 15.00

Premium Ad Proofs, Kellogg's Corn Flakes, 8-1/2" x 15", newsprint, full color, one for Whizooka, other for Snozaloony, price for pr 15.00

Premium Comic Page Offer, 15-1/2" x 21-1/2", full color Sunday comics page
  Kellogg's Pep Turbo-Jet Plane premium offer, March, 1949 .... 5.00
  Quaker Puffed Wheat/Puffed Rice Sparkies, Movie Star Buttons premium offer, June 1948 .... 5.00

Premium Order Form
  6-7/8" x 7" black and white, art and text showing Sgt. Preston and Yukon King, coupon for pedometer, Quaker Puffed Wheat or Rice box top offer 30.00
  8-1/2" x 8-3/4" dark green and white, two sided, Canadian, four illus coupon sections for Kellogg's F-87 Jet Plane, Chiquita Banana Doll, Play Baseball Game Ring, English and French text, c1948 .... 15.00

Premium Ring Paper, 2" x 4" folded instruction sheet opens to 4" x 17", illus instructions for using Post Grape-Nuts Flakes Fireball Twigg Explorer's Ring, c1948................................12.00

Premium Set, Cape Cheerios Rocket Base, orig 5" x 8" x 4" deep cardboard mailing box, 8" h white hard plastic rocket launching unit, eight blue soft plastic rocket men, full color illus sheet, instructions to cut other buildings from back of Cheerios boxes, Marx, c1960..............................48.00

Puzzle Card, Kellogg's, Milton The Toaster, 3-1/8" x 4-1/2", full color, Milton driving car, copyright 1973....8.00

Racer, Pink Panther, RPX race car, 3" l pink hard plastic car, 1973, assembly instructions, 3" x 5" cellophane pack..48.00

Ring, Quaker, Devil Dog's, adjustable brass ring, wing designs on side, fierce bulldog top, c1935..........65.00

Rocket, Post Krinkloc, Viking Rockets, hard plastic orange and glow-in-the-dark white spring loaded rocket launcher, three 2-1/2" l Viking rockets, instructions, c1952, 3" x 4" x 1" orig mailing box..............................145.00

Sign, Kellogg's Pep Whole Wheat Flakes, 19-1/2" x 26", paper, cereal box design, black, white, red, gray, and orange, black and white photo of young boy, 1950s.....................22.00

Stamp Album, Cap'n Crunch, Crunch-berry Beast's Farm Animals Stamp Album, eight pgs, full-color animal stamps, c1981-82, 2-1/2" x 5-1/2", unused.......................................15.00

Stencil, Kellogg's Rice Krispies, Snap, Crackle, Pop, vinyl, 3" x 5-1/2" green soft vinyl, diecut images of characters, copyright 1970.....................5.00

Story Display Sign
Kellogg's Pep, 19" x 23" stiff cardboard, designed like box of Kellogg's Pep Whole Wheat Flakes, white, red, and blue lettering and illus, c1940...........................30.00
Pop, 9" x 22" stiff cardboard diecut, color art by Vernon Grant, printed signature lower right, cardboard ease...120.00

Trail Kit, Sgt. Preston, Quaker, 3/4" dia by 6" l red plastic, metal clip, clear plastic top designed a pen, flashlight, whistle, compass, sundial, telescope, magnifying glass, metal fastener clip, Sgt. Preston seal in relief on top, c1958...........................170.00

Toy, Quisp Cycle, 1-1/4" x 2" x 1-1/2" h, blue hard plastic cycle, Quisp figure, attached wheels, 1970s.............40.00

Watch, Trix, secret compartment, attached wrist strap, white, 1970...6.00

Weather House, 2" x 6" x 6", Post, hand-painted wood house, Swiss chalet style, stamped "Italy" under base, man and woman on small platform, swivels to indicate sunny or rainy day, orig instruction sheet, c1959.....15.00

Character and Promotional Glasses

Collecting Hints: Contemporary character and promotional glasses are usually produced in series. It is important to collect the full series, including any color variations. This is not as easy as it sounds. Sports-team glasses are frequently issued regionally, i.e., Philadelphia Eagles glasses may appear just in the Philadelphia market, while San Diego Charger glasses may be available only in the area around San Diego. Before paying a great deal of money for a recent glass, ask yourself if what may be rare in your area is common somewhere else. Any serious collector needs this sense of perspective.

Some early examples were decorated with lead-based paint. They should not be used for drinking purposes.

Collectors place a premium on glasses with out-of-the-box luster. The mere act of washing a glass, in a dishwasher or even by hand, can lessen its value. Avoid examples with any evidence of fading.

Because of their wide availability, character and promotional drinking glasses should be collected only if they are in excellent to mint condition. Pay premium prices only for glasses that pre-date 1980. After that, distributors, dealers, and collectors hoarded glasses in quantity.

History: Character and promotional drinking glasses date to the movie premier of "Snow White and the Seven Dwarfs" in December of 1937. Libbey Glass and Walt Disney designed tumblers with a safety edge and sold them through variety stores and local dairies. The glasses proved extremely popular. Today collector glasses can be found for almost every Disney character, cartoon, and movie theme.

In 1953, Welch's began to package its jelly in decorated tumblers that featured Howdy Doody and his friends. Once again, the public's response was overwhelming. Welch's soon introduced tumblers with other cartoon characters, such as Mr. Magoo.

In the late 1960s, fast food restaurants and gasoline stations started to use drinking glasses as advertising premiums. Soft-drink manufacturers like Coke and Pepsi saw the advertising potential and developed marketing plans focused on licensed characters and movies. Sport's team licensing also entered the picture. By the early 1980s, hundreds of new glasses were being issued each year.

As the 1980s drew to a close, plastic drinking cups replaced glasses, although the use of licensed images continued. While most collectors still prefer to collect glass, a few far-sighted individuals are stashing away pristine plastic examples.

References: Mark Chase and Michael Kelly, *Collectible Drinking Glasses: Identification and Values*, Collector Books, 1996; John Hervey, *Collector's Guide to Cartoon & Promotional Drinking Glasses*, L-W Book Sales, 1990, 1995 value update; Carol and Gene Markowski, *Tomart's Price Guide to Character & Promotional Glasses*, 2nd ed., Tomart Publications, 1993.

Periodical: *Collector Glass News*, P.O. Box 308, Slippery Rock, PA 16057.

Collectors' Club: Promotional Glass Collectors Association, 3001 Bethel Road, New Wilmington, PA 16142.

Animal Crackers, 1978
Dodo...8.50
Lyle..9.00
Annie and Sandy, Swenson's, 1982..7.50
Arby's
BC Ice Age, riding on wheel, 1981...9.00
Bullwinkle, Crossing the Delaware, 11 oz, 1976..........................9.00
Charlie Chaplin, Movie Star series...7.50
Daffy Duck, Head in Star............6.00
Little Rascals..............................8.00
Monopoly, Just Visiting.............18.00
Rocky, In The Dawn's Early Light, 11 oz, 1976.................................9.00
W. C. Fields.................................3.00
Wizard of Id, 1983.....................12.00
Zodiac, Scorpio.........................10.00
Archies, 1971, 8 oz
Archie Takes The Gang For A Ride...4.50
Betty and Veronica Fashion Show..4.00
Hot Dog Goes To School.............4.00
Aquaman, Chipper-Up Soda, Galena, IL..46.00
Battlestar Galactica, 16 oz, Universal Studios, Inc., 1979
Commander Adama..................15.00
Cylon Warriors..........................15.00
Starbuck....................................15.00
Brockway, Al Capp, 1975
Daisy Mae.................................65.00

Lil Abner 55.00
Mammy 55.00
Sadie Hawkins 55.00

Burger Chef
Endangered Species, Bengal Tiger,
1978 .... 6.50
Jefferson, President Series 6.00
Washington, Bicentennial
Series 7.00

Burger King
Burger King, 1989 .... 10.00
Denver Broncos, Riley Odomos .. 5.00
Grand Opening, Londonberry, New
Hampshire, Feb 1984, black,
4-5/8" h 15.00
Have It Your Way, two drummers,
piper, 1976 .... 10.00
Mark Twain Summer Festival, 1985,
set of 4 in orig box 35.00
Shake A Lot, 1979 .... 9.00

Burger King and Coca-Cola, Star Wars
Empire Strikes Back, 16 oz, copyright
Lucasfilm, 1980
Darth Vadar 15.00
Lando Calrissian 18.00
Luke Skywalker 15.00
R2-D2 and C-3PO 15.00
Return of the Jedi, 16 oz, copyright
Lucasfilm, 1983
C-3PO at the Ewok Village 15.00
Jabba, Leia, and the Rebo Band,
slightly faded 12.00
Luke & Han, Fighting on
Tatooine 15.00
Luke Fighting Darth in the Throne
Room 20.00

Coca Cola
Bag of French Fries, 1992, 6" 8.00
Betty, tray girl 12.00
Collegiate Crest, University of Wis-
consin, Milwaukee 18.00
Disney on Parade 5.00
Happy Chef, stained glass
design 5.00
Heritage Collector Series, Washing-
ton, Revere, Jones, and Henry .. 12.00
Holly Hobbie, Simple Pleasures, Fill
Your Day with Happiness 5.00
Kollect-A-Set, Popeye 6.00
Kollect-A-Set, Brutus 5.00
Kollect-A-Set, Swee' Pea 8.00
Kollect-A-Set, Wimpy 6.00
Mothers Pizza, collector series
#2 of 6 .... 8.00
National Flag Foundation,
Alamo 9.00
National Flag Foundation, California
Bear Flag 8.00
National Flag Foundation, Washing-
ton's Cruisers 8.00
Outdoor Scene, buttered corn 5.00
Santa and Elves 7.50
Sign of Good Taste Around the World,
Cairo, Egypt 5.00
Winter Wonderland, Sundblom image
inside wreath, Coke logo on reverse,
5-3/4" h 5.00

DC Comics, Pepsi
Aquaman, 16 oz, 1978 .... 15.00
Batman, 1966 .... 7.50
Green Lantern 8.50
Superman, 1975 .... 7.50

Disney
Double Character, Donald Duck and
Daisy 9.00
Double Character, Pinocchio and
Jiminy Cricket 3.00
Goofy holding up arms, Monkeys of
Melbourne, frosted, 6" h 14.00
Mickey Mouse Club, Donald Duck
building brick wall 3.00
Peter Pan, keyhole with Peter and
Hook on plant 26.00
World on Ice, Snow White Kissing
Dopey's head 14.00

Domino's Pizza, 1988, Avoid the Noids,
complete set of four 25.00

Dr. Pepper
Happy Days, Pizza Hut, The
Fonz 10.00
Hot Air Balloon 9.00
Star Trek, Dr. Spock, 1976 .... 8.00

Garfield
100% Cattitude, frosted, 6" h 8.00
Peek-A-Boo, frosted, 6" h 8.00

Hanna Barbera Productions, Inc.
Hair Bear mug, blue plastic,
1971 .... 10.00
Larosa Pizzaria Parlor, 16 oz, Fred
and Wilma, Yogi and Mr. Ranger,
Scooby, Luigi, 1973 .... 30.00
Square Bear mug, yellow plastic,
1971 .... 10.00

Hardee's, Flintstones, The First 30 Years
- 1964, 16 oz, 1991
Going to the Drive-In 5.00
Little Bamm-Bamm 5.00
The Blessed Event 6.50
The Snorkasaurus Story 6.00

Marvel Comics
Amazing Spider-Man, 1977 .... 5.00
Howard the Duck, 1977 .... 4.00
Hulk, 1978 .... 3.50

McDonalds
All-Time Greatest Steelers, #1,
1982 .... 4.00
Big Mac, McVote, 1986 .... 5.00
Disneyland, Adventureland 3.00
Disney World 25th Anniversary, set of
four 30.00
Garfield, Are We Having Fun Yet,
5-7/8" h 5.00
Mayor McCheese Taking
Pictures 5.00
McDonald Action Series, 16 oz,
1977 .... 5.00
Ronald McDonald Saves The Falling
Star, 1977 .... 6.00
Seattle Seahawks, Beeson Eller/Bea-
mon 10.00

Mobil, football, ten different logos, price
for set 20.00

National Periodical Publications
Batman 15.00
Robin, 6 oz, 1960s 25.00
Superman, Fighting the Dragon,
5-1/4" h, 1965 .... 12.00
Wonder Woman 10.00

Paramount Pictures
Gulliver's Travels, 1939 .... 40.00
Happy Days - Fonze, "Hey!" 16 oz,
1977 .... 15.00

Pepsi
Batman, 16 oz, 1978, minor paint
loss 15.00
Bugs Bunny and Martian, ray gun,
1976 .... 48.00
Bullwinkle 30.00
Chilly Willy, 16 oz 38.00
Cool Cat/Hunter 28.00
Daffy Duck and Tasmanian Devil,
1976 .... 15.00
Dudley Do-Right, black lettering, 16
oz 30.00
Flash, 16 oz, 1976, minor
mispaint 15.00
Foghorn Leghorn, 16 oz, 1973,
slightly faded 10.00
Happy Birthday Mickey, 1978 ..... 4.00
Harvey Cartoons, Wendy, black let-
ters 50.00
Leonardo TTV, Underdog,
16 oz 14.00
Natasha, 12 oz, copyright P.A.T.
Ward, slight fading 35.00
Rescuers, Orville 5.00
Robin, 16 oz, 1978 .... 18.00
Simon Bar Sinister, 12 oz 40.00
Speedy Gonzales, black letters .. 3.00
Springfield Restaurant Group, red
logo, 6" h 11.00
Super Auction Baseball, Count on
Schmidt, 1981 .... 7.00
Superman, 1975, slightly
faded 15.00
Tweety, 16 oz, thin glass, white letter-
ing, 1973 .... 15.00
United Oil Baseball, Babe
Ruth 15.00

Pizza Hut
All-Time Greatest Denver Broncos, #4
of four 11.00
Bullwinkle, blue truck 8.00
Care Bears, Friend Bear 18.00
Denver Broncos, 25th Anniversary, #3
of four 3.00
Dudley Do-right, helicopter 8.00

7-Up, Indiana Jones and the Temple of
Dome, 16 oz, 1984
Down the River Rapids 8.00
High Priest Mola Ram 10.00
Indiana Jones and the Temple of
Doom, Thugee Guards 4.00
The Spiked Boom 10.00

Marvel Comics, Howard the
Duck 17.00

Sunday Funnies
Gasoline Alley, 16 oz, copyright Chi-
cago Tribune, Uncle Walt, Nina, Judy,
Skeezix, 1976, slight paint
loss 15.00
Little Orphan Annie, 16 oz, copyright
New York News, Orphan Annie,
Sandy, Daddy Warbucks, ASP, Pun-
jab, 1976 .... 15.00
Moon Mullins, 16 oz, copyright New
York News, Lord Plushbottom, Kayo,
Willie, Lady Plushbottom, and Moon
Mullins, 1976 .... 18.00
Smilin' Jack, 16 oz, copyright New
York News, Rev Bob, Jack, Sizzle,
Cindy, Sable, The Head, Fat Stuff,
and Jim S 15.00

Taco Bell, Star Trek III, 16 oz, copyright
  Paramount Pictures Corp., 1984
  Lord Kruge 12.00
  The Search for Spock Enterprise
  Destroyed 15.00
Tommy Tucker Kola, Omaha,
  NE 40.00
Walt Disney
  Goofy, 1937 .... 140.00
  Goofy, Goofy and Pluto on back, 16
  oz, Pepsi, copyright Walt Disney Pro-
  ductions, 1978 .... 12.00
  Minnie Mouse 30.00
Warner Bros., Pepsi
  Beaky Buzzard, 16 oz, thin glass,
  1973 .... 15.00
  Cool Cat and Beaky Buzzard, 16 oz,
  1976 .... 15.00
  Daffy Duck, 4 oz, 1976 .... 15.00
  Elmer Fudd, 6 oz, 1976 .... 15.00
  Speedy/Slo Poke, hammer, orig
  Brockway sticker on base,
  1976 .... 175.00
  Taz and Bugs, #4 of 8 .... 10.00
Welch's, 8 oz
  Archies, Betty & Veronica Give a
  Party 5.00
  Archies, Fashion Show 4.00
  Archies, Reggie Makes the
  Scene 4.00
  Archies, Sabrina Calls the
  Play 5.00
  Davy Crockett, Fought the War,
  orange and white 17.50
  Flintstones 6.00
  Kagran, Howdy Doody, Doodyville
  Circus, Clarabell, green 20.00
  Speedy Snaps up the Cheese,
  Sylvester, 1974 .... 4.00
  That's All Folks, Elmer, 1974 .... 6.00
  Yosemite Sam, 1976 .... 7.00

Children's Books

Collecting Hints: Most collectors look for books by a certain author or illustrator. Others are interested in books from a certain time period, such as the 19th century. Accumulating the complete run of a series, such as Tom Swift, Nancy Drew, or the Hardy Boys, is of interest to some collectors. Subject categories are popular, too, and include ethnic books, mechanical books, first editions, award-winning books, certain kinds of animals, rag books, Big Little Books, and those with photographic illustrations.

A good way to learn about children's books is to go to libraries and museums where special children's collections have been developed. Books on various aspects of children's literature are a necessity. You also should read a general reference on book collecting to provide you with background information. Eventu-ally, you will want to own a few reference books most closely associated with your collection.

Although children's books can be found at all the usual places where antiques and collectibles are for sale, also seek out book and paper shows. Get to know dealers who specialize in children's books; ask to receive their lists or catalogs. Some dealers will try to locate books for your collection. Most stores specializing in used and out-of-print books have a section with children's books. Regular bookstores may carry the most recent works of authors or illustrators who are still working.

When purchasing books, consider the following: presence of a dust jacket or box, condition of the book, the edition, quality of illustrations and binding, and prominence of the author or illustrator. Books should be examined very carefully to make sure that all pages and illustrations are present. Missing pages will reduce the value of the book. Significant bits of information, particularly details of the book's edition, can be found on the title page and verso of the title page.

Try to buy books in the best condition you can afford. Even if your budget is limited, you can still find very nice inexpensive children's books if you keep looking.

History: William Caxton, a printer in England, is considered the first publisher of children's books. *Aesop's Fables*, printed in 1484, was one of his early publications. Other very early books include John Cotton's *Spiritual Milk for Boston Babes in 1646, Orbis Pictis* translated from the Latin about 1657, and *New England Primer* in 1691.

Early children's classics were *Robinson Crusoe* (1719), *Gulliver's Travels* (1726), and *Perrault's Tales of Mother Goose* (translated into English in 1729). The well-known "A Visit from St. Nicholas" by Clement C. Moore appeared in 1823. Some of the best-known children's works were published between 1840 and 1900, including *Lear's Book of Nonsense*, Andersen's and Grimm's *Fairy Tales, Alice in Wonderland, Hans Brinker, Little Women, Tom Sawyer, Treasure Island, Heidi, A Child's Garden of Verses*, and *Little Black Sambo*.

During the late 1800s, novelty children's books appeared. Lothar Meggendorfer, Ernest Nister, and Raphael Tuck were the best-known publishers of these fascinating pop-up and mechanical, or movable, books. The popularity of this type of book has continued to the present, and some of the early movable books are being reproduced, especially by Intervisual Communication, Inc., of California.

Series books for boys and girls were introduced around the turn of the century. The Stratemeyer Syndicate, established about 1906, became especially well known for series such as Tom Swift, the Bobbsey Twins, Nancy Drew, and the Hardy Boys.

After the turn of the century, biographies, poetry, and educational books became popular. *Van Loon's Story of Mankind* received the first Newbery Medal in 1922. This award, given for the year's most distinguished literature for children, was established to honor John Newbery, an English publisher of children's books.

Picture books became a major part of the children's book field as photography and new technologies for reproducing illustrations developed. The Caldecott Medal, given for the most distinguished picture book published in the United States, was established in 1938. Dorothy Lathrop's *Animals of the Bible* was the first recipient of this award which honors Randolph Caldecott, an English illustrator from the 1800s.

Books that tie in with children's television programs, e.g., "Sesame Street," and toys, e.g., Cabbage Patch dolls, have become prominent. Modern merchandising methods include multimedia packaging of various combinations of books, toys, puzzles, cassette tapes, videos, etc. There are even books which unfold and become a costume to be worn by children.

References: E. Lee Baumgarten, *Price Guide and Bibliographic Check List for Children's & Illustrated Books 1880-1960*, published by author (Note: all the Baumgarten books are available from 718-1/2 W. John St., Martinsburg, WV 25401), 1996; ——, *Price List for Children's and Illustrated Books for the Years 1880-1940*, Sorted by Artist, published by author, 1993; ——, *Price List for Children's and Illustrated Books for the Years 1880-1940*, Sorted by Author, published by author, 1993; David & Virginia Brown, *Whitman Juvenile Books, Collector Books*, 1996, 1999 values updated; Alan Horne, *Dictionary of 20th Century British Book Illustrators*, available from Spoon River Press, 1994; Simon Houfe, *Dictionary of 19th Century British Book Illustrators*, revised ed., available from Spoon River Press, 1996; E. Christian Mattson and Thomas B. Davis, *A Collector's Guide to Hardcover Boys' Series Books*, published by authors, 1996; Diane McClure Jones and Rosemary Jones, *Collector's Guide to Children's Books, 1850-1950*, Volumes I and II, Collector Books, 1997, values updated 2000, 2001; —, *Collector's Guide to Children's Books*, 1950-1975, Volume Three, Collector Books, 2000; Steve Santi, *Collecting Little Golden Books*, 4th ed., Krause Publications, 2000; Albert Tillman, *Pop-Up! Pop-Up*, Whalesworth Farm Publishing, 1997.

Periodicals: *Book Source Monthly*, 2007 Syosett Drive, P.O. Box 567, Cazenovia, NY 13035; *Firsts, The Book Collector's Magazine*, P.O. Box 65166, Tucson, AZ 85728, http://www.firsts.com; *Martha's KidLit Newsletter*, P.O. Box 1488, Ames, IA 50010, http://www.kidlitonline.com; *Mystery & Adventure Series Review*, P.O. Box 3488, Tucson, AZ 85722; *The Authorized Edition Newsletter*, RR1, Box 73, Machias, ME 04654; *Yellowback Library*, P.O. Box 36172, Des Moines, IA 50315.

Collectors' Clubs: Louisa May Alcott Memorial Association, P.O. Box 343, Concord, MA 01742; Horatio Alger Society, 4907 Allison Drive, Lansing, MI 48910; International Wizard of Oz Club (L. Frank Baum), 220 N. 11th St., Escanaba, MI 49829; Thorton W. Burgess Society, Inc., P.O. Box 45, East Sandwich, MA 02537; Burroughs Bibliophiles (Edgar Rice Burroughs), Burroughs Memorial Collection, University of Louisville Library, Louisville, KY 40292; Randolph Caldecott Society, 112 Crooked Tree Trail, Moultrie Trails, RR #4, Saint Augustine, FL 32086; Lewis Carroll Society of North America, 617 Rockford Rd, Silver Spring, MD 20902; Dickens Society, 100 Institute Rd, Worcester Polytech, Dept. of Humanities, Worcester, MA 01609; Kate Greenaway Society, P.O. Box 8, Norwood, PA 19074; Happyhours Brotherhood, 87 School St., Fall River, MA 02770; Kipling Society (Rudyard Kipling), c/o Dr. E. Karim, Dept. of English, Rockford College, Rockford, IL 61107; New York C. S. Lewis Society, c/o J. L. Daniel, 419 Springfield Ave., Westfield NJ 07092; Melville Society (Herman Melville), c/o D. Yannella, Dept. of English, Glassboro State College, Glassboro, NJ 08028; Mystery and Detective Series Review, P.O. Box 3488, Tucson, AZ 85722; Movable Book Society, P.O. Box 11645, New Brunswick, NJ 08906; Mythopoetic Society, P.O. Box 6707, Altadena, CA 91003; National Fantasy Fan Federation, 1920 Division St., Murphysboro, IL 62966; Series Book Collector Society, c/o J. Brahce, 5270 Moceri Ln, Grand Blanc, MI 48439; Society of Phantom Friends, P.O. Box 1437 North Highlands, CA 95660; Stowe-Day Foundation (Harriet Beecher Stowe), 77 Forest St., Hartford, CT 06105; American Hobbit Association (J. R. R. Tolkien), Rivendell-EA, 730-F Northland Rd, Forest Park, OH 45240; American Tolkien Society, P.O. Box 373, Highland, MI 48031; Tolkien Fellowships, c/o Bill Spicer, 329 N. Ave. 66, Los Angeles, CA 90042; Mark Twain Boyhood Home Association, 208 Hill St, Hannibal, MO 63401; Mark Twain Memorial, 351 Farmington Ave., Hartford, CT 06105; Mark Twain Research Foundation, Perry, MO 63462.

Libraries and Museums: Many of the clubs maintain museums. *Subject Collections* edited by Lee Ash contains a list of public and academic libraries which have children's book collections. Large collections can be found at Florida State University, Tallahassee, FL; Free Library of Philadelphia, Philadelphia, PA; Library of Congress, Washington, DC; Pierpont Morgan Library, New York, NY; Toronto Public Library, Toronto, Ontario, Canada; Uncle Remus Museum (Joel Chandler Harris), Eatonton, GA; University of Minnesota, Walter Library, Minneapolis, MN; University of South Florida, Tampa, FL.

Reprints: A number of replicas are now appearing on the market, most having been published by Evergreen Press and Merrimack. A new Children's Classics series offers reprints of books illustrated by Jessie Willcox Smith, Edmund Dulac, Frederick Richardson, and others.

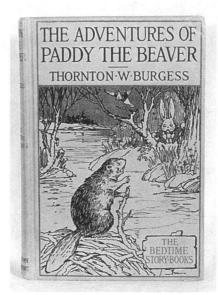

The Adventures of Paddy the Beaver, **Thornton W. Burgess, $20.**

A Child-World, James Whitcomb Riley, Bowen-Merr Publ, 1898, Riding Hood and other stories in dialect 35.00

Adventures of Galloping Gas Stove, Howard Garis, Grossett & Dunlap, 1926, illus by Lang Campbell ... 20.00

Aesop's Fables, illus by Nora Fry, eight color plates, Longmeadow Press, 1988 .... 10.00

Alice's Adventures in Wonderland, MacMillan, 1872, 42 illus by John Tenniel, cover scuffed and soiled 17.50

And To Think I Saw It On Mulberry Street, Dr. Seuss, Vanguard Press, 1937, 3rd printing 35.00

Around the Mulberry Bush, color illus by Fern Bisel Peat, Saalfield, 1933 .... 55.00

A Treasury of Verses, six color plates by Willy Pogany, black and white dwgs, MacMillian, 1900 .... 15.00

Daniel Boone, Wilderness Scout, Stewart Edward White, 1948 .... 8.00

Dolly and Molly At the Seashore, Elizabeth Gordon, color illus by Frances Breen, Rand McNally, 1904 ...... 50.00

Don Sturdy on the Desert of Mystery, Victor Appleton, illus by Walter S. Rogers, Grossett & Dunlap, 1925 ...... 8.00

Favorite Tales of Thornton Burgess, illus by Harrison Cady, 1969 .... 15.00

Five Little Peppers and How They Grew, Margaret Sidney, Lathrop, 1881, very worn green cover 9.00

Good Stories, Easy Growth in Reading, 1st Reader, Level 2, Gertrude Felton, John Winston, 1940 .... 10.00

Heidi, Johanna Spyri, illus Jessie Wilcos Smith, ten color plates, Longmeadow Press, 1986 .... 10.00

Heidi Grows Up, Charles Tritten, Johanna Spyri's translator, illus by Pelagie Doane, Grossett & Dunlap, 1938, black and white illus, one color illus, cover stained, worn 25.00

Hitty, Adventures of a Wooden Doll, Rachel Field, McMillian, 1929, 1st ed. 95.00

Joyful Poems for Children, James W. Riley, 1946, 1st ed. 28.00

Little Women, Louisa May Alcott, John Winston, 1926, embossed picture cover 25.00

Lullaby Land, Eugene Field, Scribner, 1911, illus by Charles Robinson 15.00

More Silver Pennies, Blanche Jennings Thompson, illus by Pelagie Doane, 1945, wear to dj 12.00

Mother Goose in Silhouettes, cut by Katherine Buffum, Hough-Mifflin, 1907, 1st ed. 40.00

Pinocchio, the Adventures of a Mario-nette, C. Collodi, six color plates by Charles Copeland, 1904 .... 45.00

Pinocchio, The Story of a Puppet, C. Collodi, eight color plates by Marie Kirk, 1916 .... 22.50

Pollyanna Grows Up, E. H. Porter, illus by H. W. Taylor, The Page Co., 1915, 1st ed. 22.00

Racketty Packetty House, Frances H. Burnett, Century, 1906, 1st ed., 20 color plates by Harrison Cady ... 85.00

Raggedy Ann and Andy and the Camel With the Wrinkled Knees, Johnny Gruelle, Volland, 1924, 1st ed. .. 85.00

Raggedy Ann Stories, Johnny Gruelle, Volland, 1918, 1st ed., color illus 65.00

Rainbow Valley, L. M. Montgomery, Frederick Stokes, 1919, 1st ed., green cloth cover 95.00

Rick Brant The Lost City, John Blaine, black and white frontis, Grossett & Dunlap, 1947, dj 8.00

Rip Van Winkle, Washington Irving, McKay Publishing, 1921, nine color illus by N. C. Wyatt, black and white drawings 45.00

Son of the Black Stallion, Walter Farley, black and white illus by Milton Manasco, Random House, 21st printing, 1947 .... 12.00

Stocky, Boy of West Texas, Elizabeth W. Baker, illus by Chars. Hargens, John Winson & Co., 3rd printing, 1946 .... 8.00

Stories from Hans Andersen, 15 tipped in color pics by Edmund Dulac, 1st ed. 135.00

The Adventures of Holly Hobbie, Richard Dubelman, Delacourt Press, 1980, 1st ed., wear to dj 15.00

The Adventures of Tom Sawyer, color plates by Tom Hurd, Winston, 1931 .... 22.50

The Big Book of Burgess Nature Stories, T. Burgess, H. Cady, Grossett & Dunlap, 1945 .... 24.00

The Bobbsey Twins and Baby May, Laura Lee Hope, Grossett & Dunlap, 1924, 1st printing, green cover, top and bottom edges rough 12.00

The Bobbsey Twins at the Circus, Laura Lee Hope, Grossett & Dunlap, 1932, 1st printing, 250 pgs, green cover, top and bottom edges rough 12.00

The Bobbsey Twins on a Houseboat, Laura Lee Hope, Grossett & Dunlap, 1915, 244 pgs, green cover, top and bottom edges rough 10.00

The Christopher Robin Reader, Dutton, 1929, dj 75.00

The Christopher Robin Verses, A. A. Milne, Dutton, 1932, 1st printing, 12 color plates 65.00

The Hardy Boys, The Missing Churn, Franklin Dixon, Grossett & Dunlap, 1928, dj taped to cover 12.50

The Hardy Boys, The Secret of the Old Mill, Franklin Dixon, Grossett & Dunlap, 1927, dj taped to cover 12.50

The Mouse and the Motorcycle, Beverly Cleary, illus by Louis Darling, Wm. Morrow, 1963, Weekly Readers Club, wear to cover 6.00

The Outdoor Girls On Cape Cod, Laura Lee Hope, Grossett & Dunlap, 1924, some soiling, wear 17.00

The Secret World of Teddy Bears, A Privileged Glimpse into Their Lives When You're Not There, Pamela Prince, photos by Elaine Faris Kennan, Harmony Books, 1983, 1st ed., dj ... 15.00

The Shore Road Mystery, Hardy Boys, Franklin Dixon, Grossett & Dunlap, 1928, 1st ed., red cover 45.00

The Tale of Little Pig Robinson, story and illus by Beatrix Potter, Frederick Wayne, 1930, 6 color plates, black and white illus 18.00

The Tale of the Good Cat Jupie, Neely McCoy, author and illus, MacMillian, 1926, 1st edition 10.00

The Water Babies, Charles Kinglsey, 12 tipped in color plates by Jessie Wilcox Smith, Dodd-Mead, 1916, 1st ed., 362 pgs 250.00

Wizard of Oz Picture Book, Whitman, #865, 1939 copyright, 8-1/2" x 12" 28.00

The Wonderful Adventures of Paul Bunyan, Louis Untermeyer, color illus by Everett Gee Jackson, Heritage Press, 1940s 15.00

The Yearling, Marjorie Kinnan Rawlings, Scribner's, 1947, school set 12.00

When We Were Very Young, A. A. Milne, Dutton, 1948 .... 8.00

Wild Animal Ways, Ernest Thompson Seton, 200 black and white drawings by author, Doubleday, Page & Co., 1922 .... 25.00

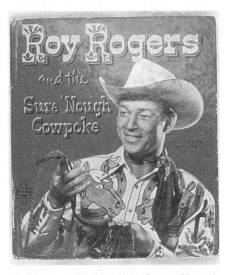

Roy Rogers and the Sure 'Nough Cowpoke, Tell-A-Tale Books, story by Elizabeth Beecher, illustrations by Randy Steffen, copyright 1952, $10.

Children's Dishes

Collecting Hints: Children's dishes were played with, so a bit of wear is to be expected. Avoid rusty metal dishes and broken glass dishes.

History: Dishes for children to play with have been popular from Victorian times to the present and have been made in aluminum, tin, china, and glass.

Many glass companies made small child-size sets in the same patterns as large table sets. This was especially true during the period when Depression glass was popular, and manufacturers made child-size pieces to complement the full-size lines.

References: Maureen Batkin, *Gifts for Good Children, Part II, 1890-1990*, Antique Collectors' Club, 1996; Doris Anderson Lechler, *Children's Glass Dishes, China and Furniture*, Book I (1983, 1991 value update), Book II (1986, 1993 value update), Collector Books; Lorraine Punchard, *Playtime Kitchen Items and Table Accessories*, published by author, 1993; —, *Playtime Pottery & Porcelain from Europe and Asia*, Schiffer Publishing, 1996; —, *Playtime Pottery and Porcelain from the United Kingdom and the United States*, Schiffer Publishing, 1996; Noel Riley, *Gifts for Good Children*, Richard Dennis Publications (available from Antique Collectors' Club), 1991; Margaret and Kenn

Whitmyer, *Collector's Encyclopedia of Children's Dishes*, Collector Books, 1993, 1995 value update.

Collectors' Club: Toy Dish Collectors, Box 159, Bethlehem, CT 06751.

Additional Listings: Akro Agate.

Tea Set, porcelain, white ground, multicolored transfer of woman and children, marked "Germany," $45.

Aluminum
Coffeepot, black wooden handle and knob 25.00
Cook Set, The Griddlette, three pcs, orig red card, 1950s..........................25.00
Measuring Cup, graduated, handle 10.00
Silverware Set, four spoons, two forks, knife, pie server 10.00
Teapot, black wooden knob, swing handle 20.00
Tumbler Set, 2-1/4" h, two green, silver, and gold, Japan, 1950s, set of six...28.00
Utensil Rack, emb flowers and leaves, two spoons, 1920s.....................65.00

Cast Iron, skillet, 5" from handle to edge, mkd "8"............................. 15.00

China
Blue Willow
    Creamer 18.00
    Cup, 1-3/4", Occupied Japan..................................... 15.00
    Cup, 2" 12.00
    Cup, 2-3/4" 10.00
    Cup and Saucer, 2-1/4" cup, 2-3/4" saucer 15.00
    Cup and Saucer, 2-3/4" cup, 3-3/4" saucer 15.00
    Plate, 3-3/4" d 9.00
    Plate, 4-1/2" d...............................8.75
    Platter, 6-1/4" x 3-3/4", oval 25.00
    Saucer, 3-1/4" d, Occupied Japan..8.00
    Set, 26 pc...............................485.00
    Sugar, cov 25.00
    Teapot, cov, 4".............................50.00
Geisha Girl, tea set, four-place setting, creamer, sugar, teapot, chips 125.00
Moss Rose
    Cup and Saucer...........................7.50
    Platter, oval...............................10.00
    Tea Set 125.00

Occupied Japan, teapot, cov..85.00
Depression-Era Glass
Bowl, Little Deb, ribbed 15.00
Creamer
    Cherry Blossom, pink 45.00
    Laurel, jadeite 45.00
Creamer and Sugar, Moderntone, pink.......................................30.00
Cup and Saucer
    Cherry Blossom 45.00
    Diana, pink 45.00
    Doric & Pansy, pink................43.00
    Moderntone, beige 20.00
Cup
    Homespun, crystal 30.00
    Moderntone, blue, pink, or yellow.................................14.50
Mixer, Glassbake, 3 ftd 40.00
Plate
    Cherry Blossom, Delfite Blue 14.75
    Doric & Pansy, pink................15.00
    Homespun, pink 15.00
    Laurel, red trim.......................15.00
    Moderntone, blue, green, pink, or yellow 12.00
Saucer
    Doric & Pansy, teal.................15.00
    Moderntone, blue, green, or pink..10.00
Set
    Cherry Blossom, 14-pc, blue delphite 250.00
    Diana, crystal, gold trim, rack, price for 12-pc set.......................................125.00
Pattern Glass
Berry Bowl, Fine Cut X 20.00
Butter, cov, Doyle's 500, amber.......................................100.00
Creamer
    Fernland 18.00
    Hawaiian Lei 15.00
Cup and Saucer, Lion 45.00
Mug, Fighting Cats.....................35.00
Pitcher, Nursery Rhyme 100.00
Punch Bowl Set, punch bowl and six cups
    Flattened Diamond and Sunburst...............................75.00
    Tulip and Honeycomb 90.00
Spooner, Menagerie Fish, amber.......................................150.00
Sugar, cov
    Hawaiian Lei 35.00
    Nursery Rhyme.......................48.00
Table Set, four pcs
    Arrowhead in Oval 95.00
    Beaded Swirl......................... 125.00
Tumbler
    Nursery Rhyme.......................20.00
    Sandwich Ten Panel, sapphire blue 145.00
Plastic
Chocolate Set, Banner, service for four, napkin holder, silverware ...95.00
Dinnerware Set
    9 pcs, Tinkerbelle, Walt Disney, service for two.............................25.00
    11 pcs, Queen of Hearts with rabbit, two plates, cups, creamer, forks, spoons, wear to decal, Plasco.....................................8.00

17 pcs, Alice in Wonderland, Plasco, service for four, beige.................................... 45.00
17 pcs, Tupperware, service for four, multicolored...................65.00
Silverware Set
    6 pcs, two knives, forks, and spoons, Plasco, pink, orig cardboard 9.00
    8 pcs, serving set, two knives, forks, and spoons, Bestmade, red, orig cardboard 7.50

Christmas Collectibles

Collecting Hints: Beware of reproduction ornaments. They are usually brighter in color and have shinier paint than the originals. Older ornaments should show some signs of handling. It is common to find tops replaced on ornaments.

History: Early Christmas decorations and ornaments were handmade. In 1865, the Pennsylvania Dutch brought the first glass ornaments to America. By 1870, glass ornaments were being sold in major cities. By the turn of the century, the demand created a cottage industry in European countries. Several towns in Germany and Czechoslovakia produced lovely ornaments, which were imported by companies such as F. W. Woolworth and Sears Roebuck and Company, who found a ready market.

References: Robert Brenner, *Christmas Through the Decades*, Schiffer Publishing, 1993; Beth Dees, *Santa's Guide to Contemporary Christmas Collectibles*, Krause Publications, 1997; Constance King, *Christmas Customs, Antiques, Decorations & Traditions*, Antique Collectors' Club, 1999; Clara Johnson Scroggins, *Silver Christmas Ornaments*, Krause Publications, 1997; Leslie Pina and Lurita Winfield, *Nativity Creches of the World*, Schiffer Publishing, 2000; Lissa Bryan-Smith and Richard Smith, *Holiday Collectibles*, Vintage Flea Market Treasures Price Guide, Krause Publications, 1998.

Periodicals: *Golden Glow of Christmas Past*, 6401 Winsdale St., Golden Valley, MN 55427; *I Love Christmas*, P.O. Box 5708, Coralville, IA 52241; *Ornament Collector*, RR #1, Canton, IL 61520.

Collectors' Club: Golden Glow of Christmas Past, 6401 Winsdale St., Golden Valley, MN 55427.

Museums: Many museums prepare special Christmas exhibits.

Reproduction Alert.

Additional Listings: Santa Claus.

Advisor: Lissa Smith.

Soldier, dimestore, Santa on skis, Barkley, $45.

Christmas Village/Garden

Animals
  Camel, 6" h, composition, flocked, wood legs, mkd "Germany" 45.00
  Chicken, 1-1/2" h, composition, metal feet 10.00
  Cow, 3-1/2" h, celluloid 12.00
  Duck, 1-1/2" h, celluloid, metal feet 10.00
  Elephant, 5" h, composition, bone tusks, mkd "Germany"...............75.00
  Goat, 4" h, composition, wool covering, wood legs, metal horns 30.00
  Horse, 5" h, composition, wood legs, mkd "Germany" 35.00
  Lamb, 1-1/2" h, plaster, standing, grassy base, mkd "Germany" 7.50
  Ram, 3-1/2" h, celluloid................8.00
  Reindeer, 3" h, celluloid, brown ...8.00
  Reindeer, 5" h, composition, brown, glass eyes, wood legs, mkd "Germany" 60.00
  Sheep, 5" h, composition, wool covering, wood legs, paper collar with bell, mkd "Germany" 45.00
  Stork, 3" h, celluloid body and legs 12.00
Buildings
  Bank Office, 4" h, plastic, multicolored 15.00
  Barn, 6" h, litho cardboard, "Built-Rite"..30.00
  Church, 4" h, cardboard, white, mica, mkd "Japan" 10.00
  House, 4" h, cardboard, cellophane windows, mkd "Japan" 8.00
Fence
  Plastic, 2" h, white, "Plasticville," six sections.....................................24.00

Wood, 5" h, picket, white, wired for Christmas lights on each post, four sections, 24' l 55.00
People
  Couple, 2" h, sitting on park bench, metal, USA 20.00
  Skater, 2-1/2" h, metal, USA 15.00
  Sled Rider, 2" h, removable figure, mkd "France" 18.00

Non-Tree Related Items
Bank, 5" h, snowman, white, black bowler hat, red scarf, orig box 15.00
Book
  Christmas Carols, Little Golden Book, Simon & Schuster, 1946 ....10.00
  Merry Christmas, Happy New Year, Phyllis McGinley, Viking Press, 1968 ....7.00
  The Night Before Christmas, color painting by Grandma Moses, published by Random House, 1961 ....35.00
Calling Card, 3-1/4" l, Season's Greetings, emb holly...........................5.00
Candleholders, 2-1/2" w, 6" l, 1-1/8" h, brass, poinsettias, price for pr 125.00
Candy Box
  4-1/2" l, cardboard, string handle, Merry Christmas, Happy New Year, carolers in village, 1920s..........8.00
  10-1/2" l, cardboard, paper label, "Charms," red background, coach driving through village scene.....................................18.00
Candy Container, 7-1/2" h, snowman, pressed cardboard, black hat, opening in base, USA...................................40.00
Figure, Choir Boy, 3-1/2" h, hard plastic, red and white 4.50
Nativity
  Boxed set, 14" h, 20" l, cardboard, fold-out, USA, 1950s.................................24.00
  Redware, Foltz, 1977 ....145.00
Pinback Button
  7/8" d, metal, "Health to All," National Tuberculosis Association.............................7.50
  1-1/4" d, celluloid, "Shop in Danville," Santa head............................15.00

Post card, Wishing You Christmas Cheer, $25.

Postcard, 3" x 5"
  "A Hearty Christmas Greeting", sledding Victorian children.......4.00

"Wishing You A Very Happy Christmas", dog with riding crop in mouth, toy horse 5.00
Stocking
  10" d, red cellophane, silver foil trim, electric candle inside..... 18.00
  12" l, red flannel, stenciled Santa and sleigh...............................15.00
Tag, 2-3/4" l, Christmas Greetings, dog in wrapped box, made in USA 2.00
Toy, 16-1/2" l, pull toy, St. Nicholas, cast iron, gilt, blue, and black sleigh, two white horses................... 1,400.00

Tree-Related Items
Beads, 48" l, glass, blue, paper tag, German 20.00
Candy Cane, 6" l, chenille, red and white 4.00
Icicles, 4" h, metal, twisted, color or silver, each 1.00
Light Bulb
  Bubble, Noma......................... 3.50
  Japanese Lantern, 4" h, milk glass 14.00
  Santa head, 2" h, milk glass .. 24.00
  Snowman, 3" h, milk glass 20.00
Ornament, beaded, 3" h, cross, double-sided, Czechoslovakian 24.00
Ornament, chromolithograph, tinsel trim, German
  Angel, 7" h 20.00
  Bell, 4" h, girl's face 17.50
Ornament, glass
  Clown bust, 2" h 35.00
  Grape Bunch, gold, 5-1/2" l, 19th C 210.00
  Heart, 3-1/2" h, red 15.00
  Pinecone, 3-1/2" d, unsilvered, tinsel inside 15.00
  Round, 2-1/2" d, plain, red, pink, green, gold, or silver, each 3.00
  Round, 3" d, striped, unsilvered, paper cap 6.00
  Santa, 3" h 35.00
Reflector, 3" d
  Foil, set of six........................ 6.00
  Metal, pierced tin 5.00
Tinsel, lead strips, orig box... 12.00
Tree
  1-1/2" h, brush, green, red wood base.................................... 4.00
  3" h, brush, green, mica trim, red wood base............................... 5.00
  3" h, feather, green, red wood base................................... 18.00
  5" h, brush, green dec, glass beads, red wood base 12.00
  12" h, feather, white sq red base, mkd "West Germany" 72.00
  36" h, feather, green, candle clips, round wood base, mkd "Germany".......................... 300.00
Tree Stand, tin litho, lighted... 48.00
Tree Topper
  6" h, angel, cardboard and spun glass 25.00
  9" h, silvered glass, multicolored........................... 20.00

Cigar Collectibles

Collecting Hints: Concentrate on one geographical region or company. Cigar box labels usually are found in large concentrations. Check on availability before paying high prices.

History: Tobacco was one of the first export products of the American colonies. By 1750, smoking began to become socially acceptable for males. Cigar smoking was most popular from 1880 to 1930, when it was the custom for men to withdraw from the boardroom or dining table and participate in male-only conversation or activities.

Cigar companies were quick to recognize national, political, sports, and popular heroes. They encouraged them to use cigars and placed their faces on promotional material.

The lithograph printing press brought color and popularity to labels, seals, and bands. Many people have memories of cigar-band rings given by a grandfather or family friend. Cigars took second place to cigarettes in the 1940s. Today, there is less cigar- than cigarette-related material because fewer companies made cigars.

References: Edwin Barnes and Wayne Dunn, *Cigar-Label Art Visual Encyclopedia with Index and Price Guide*, published by authors (P.O. Box 3, Lake Forest, CA 92630), 1995; Don and Elizabeth Johnson, *Warman's Advertising*, Krause Publications, 2000; Gerald S. Petrone, *Tobacco Advertising*, Schiffer Publishing, 1996; —, *Cigar Box Labels: Portraits of Life*, Mirrors of History, Schiffer, 1998.

Periodical: *Tobacco Antiques and Collectibles* Market, Box 11652, Houston, TX 77293.

Collectors' Clubs: Cigar Label Collectors International, P.O. Box 66, Sharon Center, OH 44274; International Lighter Collectors, P.O. Box 536, Quitman, TX 75783; International Seal, Label and Cigar Band Society, 8915 E. Bellevue St., Tucson, AZ 85715; Pocket Lighter Preservation Guild, P.O. Box 1054, Addison, IL 60101.

Museum: Arnet Collection, New York Public Library, New York, NY.

Banner, 12" h, 9-1/2" w, Seminola 5¢ Cigar, painted velvet, Indian princess in center 350.00

Book, *Lorillard and Tobacco 200th Anniversary*, 7-1/2" x 10-1/2", 61 pgs, 1960 ....20.00

Cigar Box
    Chancellor, wood and litho paper, blue and gold labels, c1900-20, 5" x 8"...4.00
    Kenwood Club, wood and litho paper, full color, c1900-20, 5" x 8"...........5.00
    Little Chancellor, wood and litho paper, blue and gold labels, c1900-20, 5" x 8"..................................4.00
    Little Tom, wood and litho paper, inside with full-color graphic of man dressed in turn-of-century frock, wear, 2" x 5" x 8".....................10.00
    Seal of Minneapolis/Lafayette, wood and litho paper, full color, c1900-20, 5" x 8"...5.00

Cigar Box Label, unused
    Blue Ribbon, c1900 ....2.00
    Dan Patch 4.50
    Flor De Bouquet, color litho, pretty woman in center, garden setting, copyright June 12, 1874 ....15.00
    Oceanic Steamer 3.00
    Old Soldier, Union soldier shown, c1920...5.00
    Trump, Sutro & Newmark, 6" x 10", browntone litho, 1876.................20.00

Cigar Cutter, figural
    Boar's tusk................................245.00
    Pelican, cast iron........................75.00

Cigar Holder
    Amber, solid gold band 65.00
    Tortoiseshell 10.00

Cigar Piercer, 3" l, silvered brass, celluloid wrapper band inscribed "Westchester County Bar Association, Annual Dinner, 1995," sharp metal point....................................60.00

Dish, covered with cigar bands, green felt back, 7-1/8" d, $30.

Dish, 7-1/8" d, all over multicolored cigar bands, diecut beautiful woman in center, green felt back 35.00

Humidor, silverplated, bottle shaped, holds matches, cigars, cutter ..400.00

Label
    American Citizen..........................7.00
    Canadian Club 7.00
    Tampa Girl 20.00

Lighter, 4-1/2" h, counter type, cast iron, bulldog-shape 90.00

Matchbook Holder, blued metal, c1920 1-1/8" x 1-5/8", Muriel Cigars, celluloid insert, woman in multicolored portrait, small gold frame, dark red ground 65.00
    1-1/2" x 2-1/4", 1-1/2" oval celluloid, multicolored insert inscribed "For Gentlemen of Good Taste," well dressed gentleman seated in wicker chair, smoking cigar 75.00

Match Safe, Union Made Cigars, bright silvered brass, celluloid cover with light blue Union Cigar label, black inscriptions and artwork, issued by Cigar Makers Union #97, Boston 95.00

Notepad, 2" x 3", Hemmeter Cigar Co., floral and cigar design on cover, calendar, unused 25.00

Pinback Button
    Bachelor Cigars, 100% Havana Filler, green and white, red serial number, c1930 .... 20.00
    Dutch Masters, blue lettering, white ground, "President" in red letters, 1950s...................................... 8.00
    Enjoy A Cigar, brown on yellow, slogan "Join The Cigar Enjoyment Parade," c1930 .... 30.00
    Little Cigar Smokers," short product slogan on back paper, early 1900s...................................... 40.00
    Recruit Little Cigars, 1" d, military cadet, red ground, white letters "Join The Army of Recruit Smoke Pecker Cigars, black lettering, white ground, late 1890s............................... 15.00

Pocket Mirror, 2-1/8" d, Union Made Cigars, celluloid, detailed union label, light blue, black lettering, c1900...................................... 65.00

Sign
    10" h, 13-1/2" w, Imperial Club Cigars, emb self-framed tin, full box of cigars, Sentenne & Green litho 150.00
    1-2/3" h, 17-1/2" l, Charles The Great Cigars, tin, shows full box of cigars, ashtray, fancy match safe, c1910, framed 275.00
    12" h, 10" w, Roi-Tan Cigars, self framed tin over cardboard, oval, raised frame, couple looking at each other as lady lights his fire, c1910..................................... 650.00
    14-1/2" d, Bill Dugan, cardboard, image of Dugan, framed 175.00
    17-1/2" h, 13-1/2" w, three-dimensional emb paper and cardboard, Seminola Cigars, cameo of Indian princess, framed 700.00

Tin
    Lord Tennyson Puritanos, 5" d, 5-1/4" h, grade 8.5, minor wear... 195.00
    Old Abe Cigars, round, paper label... 65.00
    Possum Cigars, full 175.00
    Reichard's Cadet Cigar.............. 85.00

Watch Fob, 1-3/4" d, United Cigar Makers League, black and white, mirror back, metal strap loop, c1900 .. 65.00

Cigarette Items

Collecting Hints: Don't overlook the advertising which appeared in the national magazines from the 1940s to 1960s. Many stars and public heroes endorsed cigarettes. Modern promotional material for brands such as Marlboro and Salem has been issued in large quantities, and collectors have put much aside. Most collectors tend to concentrate on the pre-1950 period.

History: Although the cigarette industry dates back to the late 19th century, it was during the decades of the 1930s and 1940s that cigarettes became the primary tobacco product. The cigarette industry launched massive radio advertising and promotional campaigns. In the 1950s, television became the dominant advertising medium.

The Surgeon General's Report, which warned of the danger of cigarette smoking, led to restrictions on advertising and limited the places where cigarettes could be smoked. The industry reacted with a new advertising approach aimed at 20- to 40-year olds and at females. Recent government regulations and changes in public opinion towards smoking in general have altered the style and quantity of cigarette-related collectibles.

References: Larry Clayton, *The Evans Book: Lighters, Perfumers, and Handbags*, Schiffer Publishing, 1998; Urban K. and Christine Cummings, *The World's Greatest Lighter*, Bird Dog Books (P.O. Box 1482, Palo Alto, CA 94302), 1996; James Flanagan, *Collector's Guide to Cigarette Lighters*, Books 1 and 2, Collector Books, 2000; Robert Forbes and Terrence Mitchell, *American Tobacco Cards: Price Guide and Checklist*, Tuff Stuff Books, 1999; Don and Elizabeth Johnson, *Warman's Advertising*, Krause Publications, 2000; Phillip A. Taggart, *Zippo Advertising Lighters*, Schiffer Publishing, 2000; Nancy Wanvig, *Collector's Guide to Ashtrays*, Collector Books, 1997, 2001 value update; A. M. W. van Weert, *Legend of the Lighter*, Electa, 1995; Neil Wood, *Collecting Cigarette Lighters* (1994), vol. II (1995), L-W Book Sales; ——, *Smoking Collectibles*, L-W Book Sales, 1994.

Periodical: *Tobacco Antiques and Collectibles Market*, Box 11652, Houston, TX 77283.

Collectors' Clubs: Ashtray Collectors Club, P.O. Box 11652, Houston, TX 77293; Cigarette Pack Collectors Association, 61 Searle St., Georgetown, MA 01833; International Lighter Collectors, P.O. Box 536, Quitman, TX 75783; International Seal, Label & Cigar Band Society, 8915 E. Bellevue St., Tucson, AZ 85715; Pocket Lighter Preservation Guild, P.O. Box 1054, Addison, IL 60101.

Cigarette box, hammered brass on cedar, covered emblem with stylized Diana the Huntress and an antelope surrounded by palm trees, four small brads missing, stamped "Haggenauer, Made In Austria," 2-1/4" x 4-1/4" x 3-1/2", $300. Photo courtesy of David Rago Auctions.

Ashtray, unused, orig box
    Chesterfield 20.00
    Lucky Strike 20.00
Banner
    Chesterfield, Jerry Lewis and Dean Martin 195.00
    Old Gold Cigarettes, Not A Cough In The Car Load, 42" x 120" 95.00
Carton, Chesterfield, Christmas 12.00
Cigarette Card, American
    Allen & Ginter, Pirates of the Spanish Main, 1888 .... 15.00
    Kinney Tobacco Co., military and naval uniforms, 1887 .... 5.00
    Wing Cigarettes, first series of fifty 50.00
Cigarette Card Album
    Allen & Ginter, Napoleon 60.00
    W Duck & Sons, Terrors of America 65.00
Cigarette Case
    2-1/2" x 3", tan leather and cardboard, Fatima, veiled lady in gold, "Ninth Annual Convention/A.A.C. of A./Baltimore, June 1913" on reverse 35.00
    3" x 4", enameled, woman's, black, envelope style, red stone dec ... 35.00
Cigarette Holder, 4" l, aluminum top, brown Bakelite mouth piece, stamped "Denicotea Cunni" 55.00
Clock, Vantage Cigarettes, battery operated 10.00
Dexterity Puzzle, Camel Lights, clear styrene plastic keychain case, miniature replica of cigarette pack, small

square opening in top to capture nine miniature filter tip cigarettes in filter ends up, c1980 .... 25.00
Display Sign, 7" x 8", molded hard plastic, Ronson Table Lighters, full color photo of lighter being used over cocktails by young couple, raised image of cigarette, easel back, c1950 .... 18.00
Game, Camels, The Game, MIB, 1992 .... 10.00
Lighter
    ASR, Ascot hidden watch, swivels 82.00
    Beatti Jet, pipe lighter, chrome 35.00
    Beny, England, lift arm, lift top, c1930, worn silver plating over brass ... 65.00
    Canon Camera, Zippo 45.00
    Consolidated Amusement Co. 12.00
    Corona, gun shape, chrome, black 33.00
    Crestline, musical, Colonel Reb & Confederate flag 50.00
    Dunhill, with ruler 70.00
    Dupont, 1950s, silver plated, slight wear 50.00
    Dupont, 1960s, gold plated butane 175.00
    Flaminaire, Limoges, cobalt blue and gold, table model, 3-1/2" h 30.00
    Jet 200, torpedo shape, black plastic and aluminum, MIB 15.00
    MEB, Austrian, pull part, patent April 2, 1912 .... 22.00
    Playboy, brass, engraved bunny, MIB 30.00
    Rexxy, chrome, 1930s, four-hinge mechanism, Swiss 37.00
    Rite Point, pocket clip, pen shape 9.50
    Ronson, Standard, England, hallmarked sterling silver, picture of Queen 85.00
    Stankyo, musical, brass, large .. 45.00
    Zippo, 1959, Boston, ME RR, MIB 42.50
    Zippo, 1966, pin-up girl in collector's tin 30.00
    Zippo, 1968, slim submarine, Tullibee, SSN 35.00
Matchbook Holder, hanging, Kool Cigarettes 10.00
Matches, Jokers for Smokers, Bang Matches, risqué covers, price for set of twelve 20.00
Money Clip, Chesterfield Cigarettes, white enamel and chrome, Liggit & Myers Tobacco Co., made by Robbins Co., c1950s 20.00
Pack, Picayune 6.00
Pinback Button
    High Admiral Cigarettes, red, white, and blue flag, white ground, blue letters "A National Favorite/High Admiral," c1896 .... 35.00
    Perfection Cigarettes, multicolored image of lady, back paper with list of tobacco products 20.00
    Philip Morris Cigarettes, black, white, and fleshtones, c1930 .... 50.00
Playing Cards, Camel Cigarettes 25.00

Poster, Camel Cigarettes, Aerial War Fleet Which Will Play An Important Part in Europe's Terrible War, lists aircraft of Germany, Austria, England, France, and Russia, 1914, 11" x 18" image size, 16" x 23-1/2" frame......................................1,750.00

Radio
Chester Cheetah, MIB................35.00
Marlboro Pack, MIB....................65.00

Server, chrome, smokestack shape, Chase Chrome............................66.00

Silk
1" l, Wm Randolph Hearst for Governor..10.00
3-3/4" l, Wm McKinley................25.00

Sign
12" x 18", high gloss paper, model in negligee, glamour pose, Brown & Williamson Co., c1940s, two archival tape repairs on back.................65.00
19-1/2" h, 11" w, Mecca Cigarettes, paper, Art Deco lady with hat, Earl Christy artist, orig frame stenciled "Mecca Cigarettes"..................275.00
30-1/2" h, 20-1/2" w, Egyptienne Straights, paper, titled "Absolutely Pure," Mormon-type lady in bonnet over full pack, framed..............200.00
38" h, 24-1/2" w, El Principal Cigars, diecut cardboard, two full boxes of cigars, titled "The taste pleases - it really does"................................60.00

Thermometer
Marlboro, Marlboro Man............40.00
Winston Taste Good...Like a Cigarette Should, 9" d, round, metal.........60.00

Tin
Black Cat Cigarettes..................15.00
Cavalier, 100, oval.....................12.00
Lucky Strike 100, round.............20.00
Murad, 5-1/2" x 3" x 1-1/4", Canadian, 1897 stamp.............................40.00
Pall Mall, 7" x 8", Christmas dec..15.00
Phillip Morris, 50, round.............12.00

Circus Items

Collecting Hints: Circus programs are one of the most popular items in this category. Individuals have collected them since the 1920s. Programs prior to the 1930s are hard to find; post-1930 material is readily available.

Model building plays an active part in collecting. Some kits are available; however, most collectors like to build models from scratch. Great attention is placed on accurate details.

There are many books published about the circus. These are sought by collectors for intrinsic, as well as research, value.

History: The 18th-century circus was a small traveling company of acrobats and jugglers, and the first record

of an American troupe is from that time. Washington is known to have attended a circus performance.

By the mid-19th century, the tent circus with accompanying side shows and menagerie became popular throughout America. P. T. Barnum was one of the early circus promoters. His American Museum in New York featured live animal acts in 1841. Other successful Barnum promotions included Jenny Lind in 1850, Tom Thumb from 1843 to 1883, and Jumbo, who was purchased from the London Zoo in 1883.

The Ringlings and Barnum & Bailey brought a magical quality to the circus. The golden age of the tent circus was the 1920s to the 1940s, when a large circus consisted of more than 100 railroad cars.

As television challenged live entertainment, the tent circus fell on hard times. Expenses for travel, food, staff, etc., mounted. A number of mergers took place, and many smaller companies simply went out of business. There are a few tent circuses remaining. However, most modern circuses now perform inside large convention centers.

Periodical: *Circus Report*, 525 Oak St., El Cerrito, CA 94530.

Collectors' Clubs: Circus Fans Association of America, P.O. Box 59710, Potomac, MD 20859; Circus Historical Society, 743 Beverly Park Pl, Jackson, MI 49203; Circus Model Builders International, 347 Lonsdale Ave., Dayton, OH 45419.

Museums: Circus World Museum Library-Research Center, Baraboo, WI; P. T. Barnum Museum, Bridgeport, CT; Ringling Circus Museum, Sarasota, FL.

Baraboo Script, 50th Anniversary 1883-1933, Celebration of the Founding of Ringling Bros. Shows at Baraboo, Wisconsin, pictures and names of different brothers, different script value on each, expiration date of Nov. 1, 1933, 2" x 4", set of three..........12.00

Broadside and Ephemera, 30-1/2" h, 22" w, litho, bright multi color image, various acrobats and jugglers balancing balls, tables, American shield in upper right hand corner surmounted by full spread winged eagle and bust of Edward Earle, sign reads, "Edward Earle the Great American Equilibrist," Halbert Litho, Plymouth, England, sold with seven cabinet photos and other photos of Mr. Earle, three cabinet views of other acrobats, one titled "Fredericks Gloss Lavan, celebrated American trio from Barnums Great American Circus USA," letter on Earle's personal stationery..............................1,200.00

Calendar, Circus World Museum, 1974..5.00

Child's Book
The Jolly Jump-Ups Book, See The Circus, Ringling Bros., The Greatest Show, McLaughlin Bros., 1944, six pop-up scenes........................95.00
Toby Tyler or Ten Weeks With A Circus, James Otis, G & D, 1923, dj, some wear..................................9.00

Christmas Card
Clyde Beatty-Cole Bros., black, white, blue, and yellow, holiday dates on back, 8" x 9-1/2"......................20.00
Seasons Greetings from Ringling Brothers and Barnum & Bailey, cartoon elephant family enjoying Christmas in tropical setting, 1954 pencil date, 6" x 7-1/2" paper folder....20.00

Circus Pass
Circus Hall of Fame, Sarasota, FL..3.50
Covina, California Jr. Chamber of Commerce....................................3.50
Garden Grove Breakfast Lions Club..3.50
King Bros., sponsored by fire company..3.50
United Nations Circus, Bridgeport....................................3.50
Von Bros. Three Ring Circus.......3.50
Wallace & Clark Trained Animal Circus..3.50

Letterhead, Ringling Bros., multicolored, five brothers with crest, 1909....18.00

Magazine, Martin Bros. Circus, 1936, 7" x 10"......................................115.00

Menu, Greatest Show on Earth, Nov. 12, 1898, full color........................100.00

Model, 1" scale
Bareback riders, man and woman, two horses..............................800.00
Clarke Bros Circus, two-wheel hitch...50.00
Hay wagon and harness, blue and red...300.00
Railroad flat car.......................200.00
Side show paraphernalia, fourteen set-ups..................................1,120.00

Newspaper, *The Circus News*, 15" x 23" four-page newspaper, Sixteenth Year, Volume 70, 1970, Carson and Barnes Circus, top half of front features Sky King's appearance at circus, black and white illus and photo of Kirby Grant, orig fold lines..................30.00

Pinback Button
Barnum '76 Festival, red, white, and blue...10.00
Cole Bros, Clyde Beatty, 1930s...25.00
King Reid Shows, black and white clown, red, yellow, and green accents, light blue ground, c1950...30.00
Little Hip And His Owner Prof Andre, trained elephant, c1910............45.00
Setlin & Wilson Shows, 1-3/4" d, black and white clown, red, yellow, and green accents, light blue ground, dark blue rim border, c1940......50.00

Playing Cards, Ringling Bros and Barnum & Bailey Circus, miniature size... 12.00

Poster, Ringling Bros., 20" x 28," $115.

Poster
Arthur Bros.
1940, Big Railroad Show, arrival parade with showgirls on horses and elephants............................90.00
1943, Amusing Wire Display, navy, orange, and red, tightrope walker in top hat.............................170.00
Barnum & Bailey
1894, The Grand Equestrian Tournament, rough riders, inset Civil and Military horsemanship illus, Strobridge litho 725.00
1913, Lion and Tiger, reclining jungle cats, circus logo, Strobridge litho...275.00
Clyde Beatty Circus, holds reign over field of wild jungle cats, date tag "July 4, Glendale Speedway".............50.00
Cole Bros, All the Marvels, animals in cages, Erie Litho......................210.00
Hagenbeck-Wallace, 1925, Capt. Clyde Beatty, World's Most Daring Trainer, posing with lions, tigers, and leopards pyramid.............................270.00
King Bros., 1946, clown face, red and yellow, advertising arrival 210.00
Ringling Bros. and Barnum & Bailey
1935, jolly clown portrait, blue ground, Erie Litho.................270.00
1938, The Greatest Wild Animal Display, presents Terrell Jacobs, World's Foremost Trainer, Strobridge Litho 625.00
1940, The Great Alzanax, high wire act, red ground....................150.00
Program
Barnum & Bailey, 1953 ....10.00
Cole Bros. Clyde Beatty, 1969, 24 pgs, 40 photos..............................5.00
Gentry Bros. & James Patterson, 1924 ....15.00
Hamid-Morgan, 1948....................7.00
New York Hippodrome, Archie Gunn orange and blue cover art, 8" x 12", staples rusty, pages loose 10.00
Ringling Bros. Barnum & Bailey, 1962, 53 pgs, 10 articles, 90 photos.....6.00
Puzzle, Milton Bradley, early 1900s, worn 10" x 11" x 1" box 20.00

Record, Old Time Circus Calliola, Wurlitzer, Calliola, Paul Eakin's Gay 90s Village...5.00
Routebook
Barnum & Bailey, 1906 ....225.00
Cristiani Bros. Circus, 1958 ....25.00
Forepaugh, Adam, shows, 1891 ....225.00
Sign, 43" x 65", Aqua Circus, wood, painted, scallop border, woman in 1890s garb with parachute......140.00
Souvenir Book, Ringling Bros. and Barnum & Bailey Circus, 1939 ....15.00
Ticket Booklet, Von Bros. 3 Ring Circus, 1940s, 2" x 5"................................6.00
Ticket, Ringling Bros., 4-14-56 ....20.00
Tour Route Schedule
Hubert Castle International 3 Ring Circus, 1973, #4, British Columbia......................................5.00
Kelly Miller Circus, 1966, #22, NY, NJ, DE, MD..5.00
King Bros. Circus, 1967, #6, NY, PA, OH 5.00
Polack Bros. Circus, 1969, #1, MI, VA, NC, KY, IN, PA.............................5.00
Polack Bros. Circus, 1969, #4, AZ, CO, MO, UT, NV, CA 5.00
Polack Bros. Circus, 1969, #6, WA, NV, OR...5.00
Polack Bros. Circus, 1969, #8, TN, WV, VA, MD, MI, IL, IN.................5.00
Toy
Paper, Clyde Beatty, Hingee, unpunched, 1945.......................85.00
Playset, Marx, played-with condition, few broken pieces....................475.00
Set, Bergen Toy & Novelty Co., plastic figures, orig box, #250, eight pcs 100.00
Wagon Wheel, wood, metal rim, red, white, and blue painted spokes.....................................250.00

Cleminson Clay

Collecting Hints: Each piece produced by this firm was hand decorated with colored slip, which accounts for the slight variations from piece to piece. The Distlefink dinnerware line is currently finding favor with many collectors.

History: In 1941, Betty Cleminson established Cleminson Clay in the garage of her home in El Monte, California, with her husband, George, handling the business affairs. In 1943, the company expanded to a new plant constructed in El Monte, and its name was changed to The California Cleminsons. In addition to a popular line of tableware called Distlefink, the pottery produced hand-decorated artware and kitchen accessories including pie birds, lazy Susans, spoon holders, and pitchers.

Reference: Jack Chipman, *Collector's Encyclopedia of California Pottery*, Collector Books, 1992, values updated 1998.

Bowl, cov, 2-1/2" h, sides dec with "Gram's" in light blue letters, lavender trim, white ground 30.00
Child's Cup, clown head with comical hat cover, red, green, and blue, some wear...80.00
Clothes Sprinkler, Chinaman, 8" h..90.00
Cookie Jar, cov
Candy House 95.00
Card King, gold trim on hearts......................................400.00
Christmas House................150.00
Creamer, Rooster 45.00
Egg Separator 20.00
Hair Receiver, girl, 2 pcs...............35.00
Lazy Susan, Distlefink 85.00
Pie Bird, rooster, 4-1/2" h
Brown, blue, and lavender........95.00
Pale green, light blue, and brown.......................................98.00
Pink, lavender, and yellow.........95.00
Pitcher, Distlefink 40.00
Plate, hillbilly...............................24.00
Razor Bank, domed top, white and green, sgd "Betty Cleminson 8/12/95"..................................65.00
Ring Holder, bulldog 28.00
Salt and Pepper Shakers, pr, male sailor "Old Salt," and female sailor "Hot Stuff," 5-1/4" h............................75.00
String Holder, "You'll always have a 'pull' with me!," heart shape, 5" h..110.00
Timer, Timothy Timer, orig instructions 45.00
Wall Plaque
Coffeepot.................................30.00
Spray of flowers........................60.00

Clickers

Collecting Hints: Clickers with pictures are more desirable than clickers that display only printed words. Value is reduced by scratches in the paint and rust. Some companies issued several variations of a single design—be alert for them when collecting.

History: Clickers were a popular medium for advertising products, services, and people; and subjects ranged from plumbing supplies, political aspirants, soft drinks, and hotels, to beer and whiskey. The most commonly found clickers are those which were given to children in shoe stores to advertise brands such as Buster Brown, Poll Parrot, and Red Goose. Many shoe-store clickers have advertising-whistle mates.

Clickers were not confined to advertising. They were a popular holiday item, especially at Halloween. Impressed animal forms also provided a style for clickers.

The vast majority of clickers were made of tin. The older and rarer clickers were made of celluloid.

Advertising
    Barton's Store, green on white, "New Hampshire's Biggest Store/Established 1850," tin flange snaps loudly.................................35.00
    Flavor-Kist Saltines, 1-3/4" l.......40.00
    Gunther's Beer, white litho tin, red letters "The Beer That Clicks," Kirchof Co., 1930s..................................25.00
    Hughes Crescent Cottage Paints, multicolored image of can, white background, not working...........30.00
    Lyon & Sons Brewing, Newark, NJ, Lyon's Beer 60.00
    Oshkosh.....................................65.00
    Quaker State, 1-7/8"....................65.00
    Reach for Old Style Beer...........25.00
    Red Goose Shoes, tin, 2" l.........40.00
    Tip Top Bread, Cisco Kid, six shooter gun, cardboard, 9-1/2" x 4-1/4".....................................95.00
    Twinkie Shoes, 1-7/8" l...............80.00
    Weatherbird Shoes, 1-3/4" l.......27.50
    Weston's....................................38.00
Mechanical
    Beetle, diecut metal...................15.00
    Boxer...210.00
    Cricket, yellow and black litho tin, 2" l..10.00
    Cowboy.....................................245.00
    Gun, figural Red, 1950s.............35.00
    Tommy Gun, plastic, yellow and green, 1950s................................8.00
Halloween, cat, plastic, 2-1/4" l......20.00
Ladybug, red and black litho tin, 1946..10.00
Political, "For Governor Lewis Emery Jr.," black, white, and red, silver horseshoe symbol, small green shamrocks, portrait framed by slogan "Let's Polish Off the Gang," Lincoln Party candidate, early 1900s, metal clicker..65.00

Clocks

Collecting Hints: Many clocks of the 20th century were reproductions of earlier styles. Therefore, dates should be verified by checking patent dates on the mechanism, makers' labels, and construction techniques.

The principal buyers for the advertising and figural clocks are not the clock collectors, but the specialists with whose area of interest the clock overlaps. For example, the Pluto alarm clock is of far greater importance to a Disneyana collector than to most clock collectors.

Condition is critical. Rust and non-working parts have a major affect on prices.

History: The clock always has served a dual function: decorative and utilitarian. Beginning in the late 19th century the clock became an important advertising vehicle, a tradition which continues today. As character and personality recognition became part of the American scene, clocks, whether alarm or wall models, were a logical extension. Novelty clocks, especially figural ones, were common from 1930 to the 1960s.

Since digital wristwatches and clocks became popular in the 1970s, clocks have been less commonly used as promotional items.

Reference: Robert and Harriet Swedberg, *Price Guide to Antique Clocks*, Krause Publications, 1998.

Periodical: *Clocks*, 4314 W. 238th St., Torrance, CA 90505; *Watch & Clock Review*, 2403 Champa St., Denver, CO 80205.

Collectors' Club: National Association of Watch and Clock Collectors, Inc., 514 Poplar St., Columbia, PA 17512.

Museums: American Clock & Watch Museum, Bristol, CT; Greensboro Clock Museum, Greensboro, NC; Museum of National Association of Watch and Clock Collectors, Columbia, PA; Old Clock Museum, Pharr, TX; Time Museum, Rockford, IL.

Additional Listings: See *Warman's Antiques and Collectibles Price Guide*.

Advertising
Busch Beer, electrical, horse and rider scene, crossing valley near mountains of Busch 35.00
Cincinnati Reds, logo, wood frame, electric, 1940s..................................60.00
Coca-Cola, "Drink Coca-Cola in Bottles," sq. wood case, electric, Selected Devices Co. NY.......................215.00
Four Roses Whiskey, 14" sq, lights up, orig wiring, metal, glass front, 1950s.......................................250.00
Frostie Root Beer, metal, fluorescent bulb 150.00
General Electric, peach, mirror, electric..55.00
Jefferson "Golden Hour," electric ...85.00
John Deere, 14"d, round, electric ...65.00
Kodak, "Pictures Are Priceless-Use Kodak Film," 15-1/2", sq, lights up 35.00
Lord Calvert, "Custom Distilled for Men of Distinction," black wood case, 11 x 12", 1940s..................................70.00
Piels Beer, 15" x 11" 85.00

Schlitz, lights, 1959 ....60.00
St. Joseph's Aspirin, neon............300.00
Tetley, Tea Time, 13", blue and gray, tin, Art Deco 85.00
Warren Telephone Co., Ashland, MA, oak..80.00
Wise Potato Chip, owl, electric 75.00
Alarm
Bradley, brass, double bells, Germany....................................35.00
Hello Kitty, MIB 65.00
Mickey Mouse, metal, Phinney-Walker, West Germany.......................40.00
Peter's Shoes, New Haven Clock Co., 4" x 4", Art Deco, c1930 ....50.00
Purina Poultry Chows, electric, three dials, red, white, and blue checkerboard bag........................40.00
Tweety, Looney Tunes, talking, Janex, battery operated, 1978 ....65.00
Animated
Fish swimming around dial, Art Deco style, Sessions........................250.00
Haddon, rocking grandmother..........................175.00
Mastercrafter's, fireplace................115.00
United, ballerina, music box 150.00
United, boy, gold fishing, 1950s .. 175.00
Character
Davy Crockett, wall, pendulum.......75.00
Donald Duck, 9" h, wall, glazed china, 2-1/4" d case inscribed "Blessings," blue outfit, green glazed ground, orig gold sticker marked "Waechtersbach," inscribed "Walt Disney Productions, J.A. Sural Hanua/Main-Made in Germany," c1950 ......175.00
Howdy Doody, talking 65.00
Mickey Mouse, Bradley animated hands..45.00
Pluto, 4" x 5" x 9", electric, black, white, and red plastic, bone hands, moving eyes and tongue, c1940 ....100.00
Sesame Street, schoolhouse shape..25.00
Trix The Rabbit, alarm, c1960 ....15.00

Figural, horse, United, Brooklyn, NY, bronze-colored finish, 1950s, $115.

Figural
Artist's Palette, bakelite 35.00
Chef, 10-1/2" h, electric, wall, white, Sessions Clock Co., Forestville.......24.00
Doghouse, 11" h, iron, dog looking out, flowers 80.00
Donut, 8-3/4" h, dark herbal green glaze, Clifton Art Pottery...................85.00
Refrigerator, 8-1/2" h, metal, painted white, GE label, Warren Telechron Co., Ashland, MA 185.00

Spinning Wheel, Lux,
animated 80.00
Wall, Smiley Face, "Have A Happy
Day," 7" d hard plastic, Robertshaw
Controls Co., Lux Time Division, some
wear 25.00

Clothing and Clothing Accessories

Collecting Hints: Vintage clothing should be clean and in good repair. Designer labels and original boxes can add to the value.

History: Clothing is collected and studied as a reference for learning about fashion, construction, and types of materials used. New collectors to this segment of the market are being attracted by designer label accessories, such as compacts and handbags. Other buyers of collectible clothing are looking for costumes for theater or other events, such as re-enactors.

References: LaRee Johnson Bruton, *Ladies' Vintage Accessories*, Collector Books, 2000; Blanche Cirker (ed.), *1920s Fashions From B. Altman & Company*, Dover, 1999; Roseann Ettinger, —, *Handbags*, 3rd ed., Schiffer Publishing, 1999; *20th Century Neckties, Pre-1955*, Schiffer Publishing, 1998; Roselyn Gerson, *Vintage & Vogue Ladies' Compacts*, 2nd ed., Collector Books, 2000; —, *Vintage Vanity Bags and Purses*, Collector Books, 1994; Richard Holiner, *Antique Purses*, Revised 2nd Ed., Collector Books, 1999; Roseanna Mihalick, *Collecting Handkerchiefs*, Schiffer Publishing, 2000; Richard Holiner, *Antique Purses*, Collector Books, 1996 value update; Elizabeth Kurella, *The Complete Guide to Vintage Textiles*, Krause Publications, 1999; Ellie Laubner, *Collectible Fashions of the Turbulent 1930s*, Schiffer Publishing, 2000; Susan Langley, *Vintage Hats and Bonnets*, Collector Books, 1999; Mary Brooks Picken, *A Dictionary of Costume and Fashion: Historic and Modern*, Dover, 1999; Desire Smith, *Fashion Footwear*, 1800-1970, Schiffer Publishing, 2000; Rin Tanaka, *Motorcycle Jackets: A Century of Leather Design*, Schiffer Publishing, 2000; Lorita Winfield, Leslie Pina, and Constance Korosec, *Beads on Bags, 1880s to 2000*, Schiffer Publishing, 2000; Debra Wisniewski, *Antique and Collectible Buttons*, Collector Books, 1997; plus many out of print references.

Periodicals: *Glass Slipper*, 653 S. Orange Ave., Sarasota, FL 34236; *Lady's Gallery*, P.O. Box 1761, Independence, MO 64055; *Lill's Vintage Clothing Newsletter*, 19 Jamestown Drive, Cincinnati, OH 45241; *Vintage Clothing Newsletter*, P.O. Box 1422, Corvallis, OR 97339; *Vintage Gazette*, 194 Amity St., Amherst, MA 01002.

Collectors' Clubs: Compact Collectors Club, P.O. Box 40, Lynbrook, NY 11563; Costume Society of America, 55 Edgewater Drive, P.O. Box 73, Earleville, MD 21919; Federation of Vintage Fashion, P.O. Box 412, Alamo, CA 94507; Living History Association, P.O. Box 578, Wilmington, VT 05363; Textile & Costume Guild, 301 N. Pomona Ave., Fullerton, CA 92632; Vintage Fashion and Costume Jewelry Club, P.O. Box 265, Glen Oaks, NY 11004.

Museums: The Arizona Costume Institute, Phoenix Art Museum, Phoenix, AZ; Boston Museum of Fine Arts, Boston, MA; Chicago Historical Society, Chicago, IL; Detroit Historical Museum, Detroit, MI; Fashion Institute of Technology, New York, NY; Indianapolis Museum of Art, Indianapolis, IN; Los Angeles County Museum of Art, Costume and Textile Dept., Los Angeles, CA; Metropolitan Museum of Art, New York, NY; Missouri Historical Society, Saint Louis, MO; Museum at Stony Brook, Stony Brook, NY; Museum of Art, Rhode Island School of Design, Providence, RI; Museum of Vintage Fashion, Lafayette, CA; National Museum of American History, Washington, DC; Philadelphia College of Textiles & Science, Philadelphia, PA; Philadelphia Museum of Art, Philadelphia, PA; Valentine Museum, Richmond, VA; Wadsworth Atheneum, Hartford, CT; Western Reserve Historical Society, Cleveland, OH.

Apron, white dotted swiss, embroidered red and white hearts 25.00
Baby Bonnet, cotton, tatted, ribbon rosettes......................................15.00
Bed Jacket, satin, pink, lavish ecru lace, labeled "B Altman & Co., NY," 1930s..30.00
Belt, Kenneth Jay Lane, woven goldtone, alternating sizes of coral cabochons, hook clasp, 1" w, 30" l, mkd "KJL" on back 125.00
Bloomers, wool, cream 25.00
Blouse
    Beaded taffeta, black, black glass beads at yoke, hand sewn 85.00
    Chiffon, green, child's, multiple rows of ruffles....................................15.00
    Cotton, white, cutwork, Victorian....................................20.00
    Lace, ecru, evening style, gathered waist, 1950s 18.00
    Poplin, white, middy style, c1910..15.00
    Silk, cream, embroidered, 1900s..65.00
Bonnet
    Beaded, jet beads, 19th C........95.00
    Silk, hand crocheted lace 36.00
    Straw, finely woven, worn silk lining 135.00
Boudoir Cap, crocheted, pink rosettes...................................12.00
Bustle. canvas and woven wire 30.00
Cape
    Girl's, flannel wool, ivory, silk cord embroidery 45.00
    Lady's, mohair, black, ankle length, c1930..75.00
Change Purse, cut steel beads, ecru crochet, push bottom clasp, fringe, leaf dec, 2-1/2" x 3-1/2", inscribed "B Cottle, 1847"............................65.00
Christening Gown, white Cotton, matching bonnet, 47" l 100.00
    Cutwork embroidery bodice, tuck pleats around ruffled skirt 65.00
    Machine sewn, lace, hand embroidery, 42" l.................................50.00
    Net, embroidered, silk slip, 44" l...150.00
Coat
    Baby's, cotton, gathered yoke and capelet, embroidery, flannel lining 25.00
    Boy's, linen, hand stitched, dec cuffs 35.00
    Lady's, evening, black velour, brown highlights, satin lining, large cuffs and stand-up collar, frog closure at neck...275.00
    Lady's, muskrat, bell shaped sleeves, c1940..90.00
    Lady's, velvet, navy blue, beaded dec, black fox collar and cuffs, red satin lining, 1920s 250.00
    Lady's, wool, blue, beaver collar and cuffs, blouson, drop waist style, c1920......................................100.00
Collar
    Beaded, white, 1930s 12.00
    Cotton, white, embroidered, wide, scalloped..................................20.00
Compact
    Avon, oval, lid dec with blue and green checkerboard pattern.....35.00
    Evans, goldtone and mother-of-pearl, compact and lipstick combination............................45.00
    Hudnut, Richard, Deauville, blue, cloisonné tango-chain vanity, metal mirror, compartments for power and rouge, lipstick attached to finger ring chain..200.00
    K & K, brass, colored engine tooled dec basket compact, multicolored silk flowers enclosed in plastic dome lid, emb swinging handle........125.00
    Rowanta, brown enamel, oval petit point compact 65.00

Unknown Maker, enamel, ebony, eight-ball style..........................115.00
Unknown Maker, goldtone, heart shape, brocade lid 50.00
Unknown Maker, Lucite, blue, sterling silver repousse medallion of two doves 135.00
Unknown Maker, plastic, red, white, and blue, Naval Officer's cap shape..85.00
Volupt, USA, Adam and Eve, under apple tree 50.00
Whiting and Davis, Co, Piccadilly, gilded mesh, vanity bag, compact incorporated in front lid, carrying chain 250.00
Woolworth, Karess, polished goldtone, corset shaped, vanity case, powder and rouge compartments............................45.00
Yardley, goldtone, vanity case, red, white, and blue emb design on lid, powder and rouge compartments............................75.00

Cowboy Outfit, child's, Bat Masterson, size 4, unused, MIB.................225.00

Dress, child's
Cotton, day type, gold, net trim, c1900 ....20.00
Georgette, pink, many layers of georgette and chiffon, c1920............75.00
Gingham, blue and white, hand and machine sewn, white embroidery trim, 25" h 50.00
Knit, 2 pc, 1930...........................25.00
Lawn, white, lace, drop waist, c1910 ....60.00
Linen, embroidered wisteria inserts, Irish lace trim............................150.00
Net, silk lining, ruffles at neck, sleeves, pink rosette trim.........120.00
Velvet, red, white nylon, Shirley Temple style, Cinderella tag.............15.00
Wool, pink, lace trim, c1890 ....125.00

Dress, Lady's
Batiste, white, lace, high neck, full skirt, long sleeves, c1900........150.00
Blouson, black, purple, green, and lavender, geometric silk, by Jeanenne Booker, Maggie London, size 10, c1970 ....45.00
Calico, blue, 2 pc, matching bonnet, c1900..165.00
Chiffon, blue, edges trimmed with braided fabric, 1925 ....40.00
Lawn, drop waist........................60.00
Satin, black, 1920s 85.00
Taffeta, blue, embossed dec, 1950s, dinner-type................................10.00

Dressing Gown, satin, ruby red, fagoted ruffled edges, 1930...................28.00

Evening Gown, lady's
Crepe, brown, matching velvet capelet with feather trim, c1930 ....40.00
Net and Taffeta, black, lace flowers, c1940 ....48.00
Organza, white, shirred, rhinestones, c1940 ....45.00

Evening Jacket, crepe, pink, floral patterned sequins, lined, 1940.......58.00

Gloves
Lady's, kid, white, long 20.00

Men's, driving, leather, black, c1910 ....25.00

Handbag, mesh, enamel floral design, white and silver metal frame, chain-link fringe with minor damage, $85.

Handbag
Alligator, suede lining.................18.00
Beaded, abstract design, white and gray, milk glass beads, beaded handle, zipper, 5", marked "Czechoslovakia" 20.00
Florals, pink and blue, shiny beads, gold frame..................................45.00
Lucite, pearlized, round lid, lunch box clasp, twisted handle, seashell dec 17.50
Mesh, enameled, white ground, black leaf spray, Mandalian.................55.00
Patchwork, Seminole, drawstring, grass bottom, blue, c1960.........25.00
Pearl, envelope, Hong Kong label...15.00
Plastic, child's, red, imitation leather, three Scotties dec, silver frame and chain, int. mirror 20.00
Sequins, irid multicolored, silver and seed pearl dec, rhinestone clasp, fancy frame, Belgium.................30.00
Silk, clutch, black, cut steel beads, marked "France," c1930............42.00
Wool, hand-woven, New Mexico, Navajo rug design, white ground, Fred Harvey, c1940....................35.00

Handkerchief, see Handkerchiefs

Hat, lady's
Felt, beanie type, picture of Underdog, Bullwinkle, or Rocky, each 20.00
Felt, cloche, black.....................15.00
Lace and wire, Edwardian, medium brim 130.00
Satin, black, stitched pattern covers upper crown, design of small glass beads and metallic thread on lower crown, rose taffeta lining, label "The Margate Chapeau, Paris, New York," c1916 ....95.00

Satin, pillbox, black, netting...... 18.00
Straw, black, Victorian.............. 95.00
Hat, man's, Stetson, orig box, some wear 150.00
Hat and Purse Set, leopard skin pillbox, matching purse 100.00
Hosiery, color photo of Happy Days, The Fonz, Paramount, 1976 .... 20.00
Muff
Marabou, white....................... 45.00
Rabbit fur, white, child's 25.00
Sable, brown, tails.................. 100.00
Necktie, men's, striped, rayon, 1930s... 3.00
Pajama's, girl's, baby doll style, cotton, pink hearts, 1960s...................... 7.00
Petticoat, cotton, white
Crocheted insert, wide crocheted hem... 45.00
Three rows crochet trim 40.00
Prom Gown
Georgette, yellow, embroidered bodice, strapless, c1960................. 25.00
Net and Taffeta, pink, layered skirt, bow trim, c1950..................... 35.00
Purse, Mexican, tooled leather, brown, white inserts 45.00
Scarf, Maggie Rouff, Paris, black, fuchsia, rose, pink, and off-white, black borders with geometric-style flowers, 1930s, 30" sq........................... 30.00
Shawl
Cotton, mint green, fully embroidered, fringed edges, 1925................. 35.00
Paisley, printed design, 66" x 128", minor wear and stains.............. 60.00
Woven Design, 68" x 69", minor damage 165.00
Shoes, boy's, leather, Oxford style, two-tone brown................................ 35.00
Shoes, children's
Faux crocodile and suede, side buckle, rust, 1930s.................... 36.00
Leather, Mary Jane, two strap style, camel kid, side buttons, Buster Brown brand, 1930s............................ 42.00
Leather, Oxford, black kid, Buster Brown brand, 1930s................. 40.00
Leather, T-strap style, brown leather, black, rust, and tan suede, Red Goose brand, 1930s 40.00
Shoes, lady's
Leather, boots, brown or black, lace up, pointed toes 125.00
Leather, brown, high button top 40.00
Low heels, black kid, black patent toes, Buster Brown brand 145.00
Shoes, men's
Boots, work type, leather, early, 11" h, pr 25.00
Tennis, high top, c1920............. 20.00
Skirt
Linen, gore style, Edwardian type... 40.00
Polished Cotton, floral print, full, c1950.. 24.00
Wool, black, Victorian.............. 40.00

Socks, men's, rayon and silk, cotton toe and heel, black, colored arrow, 1950s 5.00
Suit, boy's, wool
Blazer, short pants, navy, 26" chest, Tom Sawyer brand 42.00
Herringbone, lined, Amish, c1920 ....40.00
Teddy, yellow, pink emb trim on bodice, 1920s 25.00
Travel Kit, gentleman's, alligator, seven accessories, c1940 ....18.00
Wedding Gown, satin, ivory, padded shoulders, sweetheart neckline, waist swag, self train, c1940.............125.00
Wedding Headpiece, pearls and net, 1940s, needs new veiling 95.00
Wedding Veil, mid-length, lace cap, c1920 ....95.00

Coca-Cola Collectibles

Collecting Hints: Most Coca-Cola items were produced in large quantity; the company was a leader in sales and promotional materials. Don't ignore the large amount of Coca-Cola material printed in languages other than English. Remember, Coke has a worldwide market.

History: The originator of Coca-Cola was John Pemberton, a pharmacist from Atlanta, Georgia. In 1886, Dr. Pemberton introduced a patent medicine to relieve headaches, stomach disorders, and other minor maladies. Unfortunately, his failing health and meager finances forced him to sell his interest.

In 1888, Asa G. Candler became the sole owner of Coca-Cola. Candler improved the formula, increased the advertising budget, and widened the distribution. Accidentally, a patient was given a dose of the syrup mixed with carbonated water instead of the usual still water. The result was a tastier, more refreshing drink.

As sales increased in the 1890s, Candler recognized that the product was more suitable for the soft drink market and began advertising it as such. From these beginnings, a myriad of advertising items have been issued to invite all to "Drink Coca-Cola."

Dates of interest: "Coke" was first used in advertising in 1941. The distinctively shaped bottle was registered as a trademark on April 12, 1960.

References: Deborah Goldstein Hill, *Price Guide to Vintage Coca-Cola®*
Collectibles: 1896-1965, Krause Publications, 1999; Don and Elizabeth Johnson, *Warman's Advertising*, Krause Publications, 2000; Allan Petretti, *Petretti's Coca-Cola Collectibles Price Guide*, 11th ed., Krause Publications, 2001; Allan Petretti and Chris Beyer, *Classic Coca-Cola Calendars*, Antique Trader Books, 1999; B. J. Summers, *B. J. Summers' Guide to Coca-Cola*, 2nd ed., Collector Books, 1999; Helen and Al Wilson, *Wilson's Coca-Cola Price Guide*, 3rd ed., Schiffer Publishing, 2000.

Collectors' Clubs: Coca-Cola Collectors Club, 400 Monemar Ave., Baltimore, MD 21228; Coca-Cola Collectors Club International, P.O. Box 49166, Atlanta, GA 30359; Florida West Coast Chapter of the Coca-Cola Collectors Club International, 1007 Emerald Drive, Brandon, FL 33511.

Museums: Coca-Cola Memorabilia Museum of Elizabethtown, Inc., Elizabethtown, KY; The World of Coca-Cola Pavilion, Atlanta, GA.

Reproduction Alert: Coca-Cola trays.

Tie clip, All-Star Dealer Campaign Award, metal and enamel, 1950s, $35.

Ashtray, 4" d, bright red, white logo, 1980s...12.00
Bank
Battery operated, red Coke machine shape 175.00
Coke Year of the Tiger, cute tiger beside large bottle, MIB 40.00
Banner, 11" x 22", printed paper, c1951 ....15.00
Battery Operated, polar bear, reading, head moves back and forth between bottle of Coke and penguin server, Christmas tree in background, 1994, orig instructions and box, 8-1/2" w, 11" h.......................................50.00
Billfold, pigskin, 1950s...................25.00
Binder Cover, 13" x 15-1/2", Advertising Price List, cardboard under textured red oilcloth cover, inner spine four-ring binder, c1950, slight wear..48.00
Blotter, 3-1/2" x 7-1/2"
Full color graphics of smiling Coca-Cola Sprite elf digging bottle of Coke out of snow bank, copyright 1953 Coca-Cola Co. 10.00

Full-color ski scene, copyright 1947, unused......................................18.00
Book, *Portrait of a Business*, 1961, autographed by W. G. Kurtz 75.00
Book Cover, 10" x 14", dark green stiff paper, advertising "Safety A.B.C.'s" motif in brown and red, copyright 1940, unfolded 5.00
Booklet, 2" x 6-1/4", paper fold-out, diecut bottle shape, front and back covers with image, inside 12 pages printed in red and green with information about plant tour, equipment, etc., 1950s......................................24.00
Bottle, commemorative
Cincinnati Reds, World Champs, 1994 ....4.00
Colorado Rockies, 1993 MLB Record Season......................................4.00
Dallas Cowboy Superbowl, commemorative six bottle set 30.00
Denver Broncos 1st Team logo..4.00
Detroit Red Wings, 70th anniversary 4.00
Eskimo Joe's................................3.00
Florida Aquarium......................4.00
Ft. Worth Stock Show 4.00
Graceland, 1995 ....10.00
Houston Rockets, Back to Back Champs, 1995 ....3.00
Kentucky Derby 122 ....4.00
NBA All Star Weekend 1995, desert scene, NBA logo, Feb. date, made and issued in Phoenix, AZ, limited to 300,000, six pack with orig bottles and contents 35.00
Oriole Park at Camden Yards 4.00
Selena, Five Years With You......35.00
Texas Tech Lady Red Raiders 3.00
Bottle Carrier, shopping cart..........50.00
Box, wooden 65.00
Bridge Score Pad..........................12.00
Calendar, 1955..............................52.50
Chalkboard, diner menu 45.00
Check, used
1946, May 3, bottle logo 14.00
1960, July 28, bottle logo, small hole 8.00
1961, April 14, bottle logo........12.00
Cigarette Lighter, miniature............10.00
Clock, 15" sq, electric, metal 115.00
Coaster, Santa Claus, set...............15.00
Cookie Jar, jug shaped, red label with Coca-Cola logo, McCoy............80.00
Cuff Links, pr, bottle shape 45.00
Dart Board, 1950s.........................40.00
Doll, 18" h, porcelain and cloth, boy with scooter, Franklin Mint 55.00
Door Push, 11" x 4", porcelain, 1930s......................................85.00
Folder, 8-1/2" x 11", black, white, and red, four pgs plus overleaf, "More Profit Per Patron," Coca-Cola refreshment counter in movie house lobbies or vending machines, back text describes average weekly gross profits from lobby sales, late 1930s......................................65.00

Game Board
    India Game, Milton Bradley, 9-1/2" x
    18-1/2" hinged cardboard, bottle cap
    kid, early 1950s.............................28.00
    Steps to Health, Coca-Cola of Can-
    ada, 11-1/4" x 13-1/4", folded card-
    board, color playing surface,
    copyright 1938.............................60.00
    Winko Baseball, Milton Bradley,
    9-1/2" x 18-1/2" hinged cardboard,
    instructions on back panel,
    c1945 ....24.00
Glass, set, eight glasses
    10 oz size, sealed in orig carton,
    Libbey, c1960 ....125.00
    16 oz size, Polar Bear, "Always Cool,
    Always Coca-Cola," Indiana Glass,
    1992 ....24.00
Handbill, light pink paper, black print,
    slogan "Coca Cola Delicious,
    Refreshing and Necessary-Why?" 29"
    x 20", some water stains 295.00
Ice Chest, airline cooler...............410.00
Ice Pick, with opener 122.00
Kite, High Flyer, six oz. bottle illus,
    1930s 45.00
Magazine Ad
    Life, March 15, 1963....................7.50
    The Housewife, 1910, matted and
    framed..70.00
Mail Away, model kit, Kit Carson,
    MIB..85.00
Marbles, "Free with every
    carton"..35.00
Menu Board, 1950s 175.00
Movie Lobby Merchandising Folder,
    8-1/2" x 11", black, white, and red,
    four-page folder, "More Profit Per
    Patron," 1930s 24.00
Necktie, c1950................................35.00
Pencil Box, orig contents................35.00
Pencil Sharpener, figural bottle, cast
    metal 45.00
Pinback Button
    Hi Fi Club, red, green, and yellow litho
    tin, brown bottle in center of red 45
    rpm record, 1950s sponsorship of
    teen music TV show....................30.00
    Insignia Series, No. 7, 26th Bombard-
    ment Squadron, orange and gray,
    15-1/6" d, celluloid, Parisian Novelty
    Co, insert back paper with "Drink
    Coca-Cola" trademark along with
    designation of insignia, and series
    number, 1940s 75.00
Playing Cards, "It's The Real Thing,"
    1971 ....8.00
Pocket Knife, black, smooth handle,
    case in shape of Coca-Cola bottle,
    "Coke" engraved on each
    side 200.00
Pocket Mirror, 2-3/4" oval, World War I
    Girl, 1917...................................210.00
Postcard, 5-1/2" x 6-1/2" perforated card-
    board sheets, lower half of back side
    for "Occupant," rest of address
    unused, red and dark green carton
    with white and fleshtone hand, upper
    half of card front with full-color "Take

home a carton" with young lady,
    lower half pictures full-color six-bottle
    carton, coupon for six free bottles
    and deposit of 12 cents, local spon-
    sor Coca-Cola Bottling Works, Fort
    Wayne, IN, late 1930s, price for
    pr 40.00
Poster, girl preparing to ice skate, copy-
    right 1940, well worn................105.00
Pretzel Dish, aluminum, c1938.......45.00
Punchboard, 7" x 8", 1940s,
    unused 8.00
Radio, bottle shape, MIB 45.00
Salt and Pepper Shakers, pr, red, white
    logo, tin can-shape, unpunched
    holes, 1970s, MIB 25.00
Sheet Music, The Coca-Cola Girl,
    1927 ....145.00
Sign
    11-1/2" h, 28" l, porcelain, "Drink
    Coca-Cola Fountain Service," some
    chipping and scratching..........225.00
    12" x 18", porcelain and tin 195.00
    16" x 43", wrap around, fishtail type,
    red and white, 16" x 43", small crease,
    paint chips.................................295.00
Six Pack, full, 1993 Maine Black Bears,
    National Hockey Champs, Ltd., only
    sold in Maine..............................20.00
Thimble, aluminum..........................25.00
Tip Tray, Exposition Girl.................325.00
Toy
    Delivery Truck, Matchbox No. 38,
    1958 ....60.00
    Race Car, Corgi, three diecast cars in
    blister pack, 1979 ....40.00
    Soda fountain dispenser, plastic, four
    miniature glasses 135.00
Tray, metal
    Boy eating sandwich,
    Rockwell.....................................220.00
    Girl preparing to ice skate,
    1940 ....130.00
    Girl with wind in her hair...........120.00
    Hand pouring Coke into glass, "Coke
    Refreshes You Best," 1961 ....10.00
    Menu Girl, 1950...........................55.00
    Picnic basket, c1958 ....80.00
Uniform Patch, "Enjoy Coke"............3.00
Whistle, litho tin, red, yellow, and black,
    "The Pause That Refreshes,"
    1930s...100.00

Cocktail Collectibles

Collecting Hints: One area to concentrate on could be cocktail shakers
that are style statements of their era.
Many have interesting aesthetics,
line, form, and materials that form
principal focus points. A collection
numbering in the hundreds can be
built around examples of the stream-
lined-modern style.

Run your fingers around the edge
of glass shakers to check for chipping. A small chip reduces the price
by a minimum of 30 percent. Shakers
with brilliant sharp colors are more
desirable than those made of clear
glass.

Be on the constant alert for cracks
and fractures. Most individuals want
shakers that are usable and are at
least in fine condition.

Figural shakers are in a class of
their own. Among the more common
forms are bowling pins, dumbbells,
golf bags, and penguins. Shakers
based on the designs of Norman Bel
Geddes often command in excess of
$500.

History: The idea of cocktails traces
its origins as far back as 7000 B.C.
and the South American jar gourd, a
closed container used to mix liquids.
The ancient Egyptians of 3500 B.C.
added spices to fermented grain—
perhaps history's first cocktails. Alcoholic drinks have been a part of
recorded history into the modern era.

By the late 1800s, bartenders
used a shaker as a standard tool.
Passing the liquid back and forth
between two containers created a
much appreciated show.

The modern cocktail shaker
arrived on the scene in the 1920s,
when martinis were in vogue. Shapes
tended to be stylish, and materials
ranged from glass to sterling silver.
Perhaps nothing symbolizes the Jazz
Age more than the flapper dress and
cocktail shaker. When Prohibition
ended in 1933, the cocktail shaker
enjoyed another surge of popularity.

Movies helped popularize cocktails. William Powell showed a bartender how to mix a proper martini in
"The Thin Man," a tradition continued
by James Bond in the 007 movies.
Tom Cruise's portrayal of a bartender
in "Cocktail" helped solidify the collecting interest in cocktail shakers
during the 1980s.

Following World War II, a bar
became a common fixture in many
homes. Every home bar featured one
or more cocktail shakers and/or
cocktail shaker sets. Chrome-plated
stainless-steel shakers replaced the
sterling-silver shakers of the 1920s
and 1930s. Major glass companies,
such as Cambridge, Heisey, and
Imperial, offered cocktail shakers.

Life in the fabulous fifties was filled
with novelties; cocktail shakers were
no exception. Figural and other forms
of novelty shakers appeared.

The electric blender and ready-mix cocktail packets ended the reign of the cocktail shaker, and showmanship was replaced by button pushing.

Reference: Stephen Visakay, *Vintage Bar Ware*, Collector Books, 1997.

Wall-mounted bar, disc, two semi-circular sculpted bronze doors, gold patina, Paul Evans, unmarked, 71" diameter, 18" deep, $2,900. Photo courtesy of David Rago Auctions.

Bottle Stopper, figural
  Kissing Couple 25.00
  Man, tips hat 25.00
  Man, pop-up head 40.00
Cocktail Set
  Art Deco style, glass shaker, six tall glasses, five shorter glasses, stippled frosted surface, gold and colored mid bands, 1950s 65.00
  Farber Brother, two amber, two green, and two smoke cocktail glasses 60.00
Cocktail Shaker
  7-1/2" h, glass base, yellow, orange, and turquoise scenes of Paris, recipes, flat aluminum top and cap 30.00
  8-1/2" h, gold-colored aluminum, mkd "Mirro-The Finest Aluminum, Made in USA," shaker top with insert 18.00
  10" h, glass base, pink elephants and stars dec, aluminum dome top and cap 85.00
  10-1/2" h, glass base, pink, yellow, and green dots and recipes, black glasses, two-part aluminum lidded top with removable cap for pouring 60.00
  10-1/2" h, glass base, red, blue, yellow, and white roosters, all-over white net pattern, aluminum dome top and cap 60.00
  11" h, glass base, black Scotties, red checkerboard pattern around base, aluminum lid, some dents on top cap 85.00
Cordial Set
  Central Glass Co., Balda Orchid pattern, decanter, six matching cordial glasses 375.00

Farber Brothers, chrome plate, seven-pc set 55.00
Cup, Chase Chrome, Blue Moon 99.00
Decanter, orig stopper, glass
  Bohemian, octagonal, clear with greenish tint, engraved forest and deer scene 100.00
  Duncan Miller, First Love, 32 oz 295.00
  Farber Ware, Mandarin gold, 32 oz, 3400/92 .... 60.00
  Fostoria, American pattern, 24 oz, 9-1/2" h 100.00
  Imperial, Cape Cod, etched "Rye" 70.00
Decanter Set, Czechoslovakian, figural owl decanter, four matching cups, blue ground, painted eyes 200.00
Hors d'ouevre Pick
  Fruit, set of twelve 20.00
  Man, top hat 3.50
Ice Bucket
  Aluminum, brown Bakelite handles and knob, mkd "West Bend Penguin Hot and Cold Server," 10" w, 8" h 45.00
  Glass, Cambridge, Apple Blossom, amber 40.00
  Glass, Duncan Miller, Canterbury, clear 45.00
  Glass, Imperial Glass, Cape Cod, clear 125.00
Jewelry, pin and earrings set, large martini glass with olive, silvertone earrings with open-work, 1960s 35.00
Liquor Set
  7" h golf club, shot glass on each end, one holds 1 oz, other 2 oz, golf ball cork screw, 6-1/4" bottle and can opener iron, 9" stirrer iron, orig box with red felt lining, unused 20.00
  14" h, marbleized plastic bowling ball container, chrome dispenser, shot glasses trimmed with red, green, or blue glass rings, gilded metal figural finial 75.00
Martini Pitcher, Duncan Miller, First Love 165.00
Martini Set
  James Bond, 32 oz stainless steel martini shaker, James Bond silhouette logo, two 8 oz martini glasses with satin etched 007 gun logo, United Artists exclusive set, MIB 70.00
  Rooster dec, martini pitcher, four matching tumblers, clear, red and black rooster dec 35.00
  Old Fashioned Tumbler, Fostoria, Coin, crystal 35.00
  Pilsner, Old Sandwich, Heisey, 10 oz, Moongleam green 45.00
  Recipe Card, 4" x 5", full color cardboard envelope, int. card raises by pull tab to show different ingredients and mixing instructions, c1920, wear 18.00
Shot Glass, Russel Wright, Formal Theme 300.00
Stemware, glass
  Champagne, Fostoria, Romance, crystal 22.50

Cocktail, Fostoria, June, rose pink 65.00
Cordial, Cambridge, Caprice, crystal 10.00
Cordial, Heisey, Banded Flute, crystal 100.00
Goblet, Dancing Nymph, French crystal 90.00
Wine, Heisey, Lariat, Moonglow cutting 35.00
Wine, Tiffin, Flanders, mandarian 40.00
Swizzle Stick, glass
  Advertising, colored 3.50
  Amber 1.50
  Black 2.00
  Christmas, set of six 25.00
  Man, top hat 3.50
  Souvenir, Hotel Lexington, amethyst, 1939 World's Fair 20.00
  Spatter knob, clear stirrer 1.00
Toddy Mixer, crystal, green, 12 oz 24.00
Tom and Jerry Set
  Fostoria, American pattern, bowl and eight mugs 340.00
  Hall China, black, ftd bowl, eighteen 5 oz cups 240.00
Traveling Bar, locking case, 12 pc, 12" w, 14-1/2" h 60.00
Tray, 11" d, tin, red, black, and white, martini center, card border 55.00
Tumbler
  Cambridge, Chantilly, crystal 30.00
  Crackle Glass, 5-1/4" h, orange 20.00
  Duncan Miller, Terrace, red 37.50
  Fostoria, June, yellow, ftd 32.50
  Heisey, New Era, ftd, 12 oz 25.00
  Sportsman Series, cobalt blue, white windmill dec, 12 oz 27.50
Whiskey
  Fostoria, June, ftd, yellow 75.00
  Heisey, Yeoman, Sahara yellow 15.00
  Tiffin, Classic, 2 oz 75.00

Comic Books

Collecting Hints: Remember, age does not determine value! Prices fluctuate according to supply and demand. Collectors should always buy comic books in the best possible condition. While archival restoration is available, it's frequently costly and may involve a certain amount of risk.

Comic books should be stored in an upright position away from sunlight, dampness, and insect infestations. Avoid stacking comic books because the weight of the uppermost books may cause acid and oils to migrate. As a result, covers on books near the bottom of the stack may become stained with material that is difficult or impossible to remove.

Golden Age (1939-1950s) Marvel and D.C. first issues and key later issues continue to gain in popularity as do current favorites such as Marvel's *X-Men* and D.C.'s *New Teen Titans*.

History: Who would ever believe that an inexpensive, disposable product sold in the 1890s would be responsible for a current multimillion dollar industry? That 2-cent item—none other than the Sunday newspaper—has its modern counterpart in flashy comic books and related spin-offs.

Improved printing techniques helped 1890s newspaper publishers change from a weekly format to a daily one that included a full page of comics. The rotary printing press allowed the use of color in the "funnies," and comics soon became the newest form of advertising.

It wasn't long before these promotional giveaways were reprinted into books and sold in candy and stationery stores for 10 cents each. They appeared in various formats and sizes, many with odd shapes and cardboard covers. Others were printed on newsprint and resembled the comic books sold today. Comics printed prior to 1938 have value today only as historical artifacts or intellectual curiosities.

From 1939 to 1950, comic book publishers regaled readers with humor, adventure, Western, and mystery tales. Super heroes such as Batman, Superman, and Captain America first appeared in books during this era. This was the "Golden Age" of comics—a time for expansion and growth.

Unfortunately, the bubble burst in the spring of 1954 when Fredric Wertham published his book *Seduction of the Innocent*, which pointed a guilt-laden finger at the comic industry for corrupting youth, causing juvenile delinquency, and undermining American values. This book forced many publishers out of business, while others fought to establish a "comics code" to assure parents that comics complied with morality and decency mores. Thus, the "Silver Age" of comics is marked by a decline in the number of publishers, caused by the public uproar surrounding Wertham's book and the increased production costs of an inflationary economy.

The period starting with 1960 and continuing to the present has been marked by a resurgence of interest in comic books. Starting with Marvel's introduction of "The Fantastic Four" and "The Amazing Spider-Man," the market has grown to the extent that many new publishers are now rubbing elbows with the giants and the competition is keen!

Part of the reason for this upswing must be credited to that same inflationary economy that spelled disaster for publishers in the 1950s. This time, however, people are buying valuable comics as a hedge against inflation. Even young people are aware of the market potential. Today's piggy-bank investors may well be tomorrow's Wall Street tycoons.

References: Mike Benton, *Comic Books in America*, Taylor Publishing, 1993; ——, *Crime Comics*, Taylor Publishing, 1993; ——, *Horror Comics*, Taylor Publishing, 1991; ——, *Science Fiction Comics*, Taylor Publishing, 1992; ——, *Superhero Comics of the Golden Age*, Taylor Publishing, 1992; ——, *Superhero Comics of the Silver Age*, Taylor Publishing, 1992; *Comic Buyer's Guide*, Krause Publications, 1996; Maurice Horn (ed.), *World Encyclopedia of Comics*, Chelsea House, out of print; Dick Lupoff and Don Thompson (eds.), *All in Color for a Dime*, Krause Publications, 1997; Alex G. Malloy, *Comics Values Annual 2001*, Antique Trader Books, 2000; Robert M. Overstreet, *Overstreet Comic Book Price Guide*, 31st ed., Avon Books, 2001; Maggie Thompson and Brent Frankenhoff, *2001 Comic Book Checklist & Price Guide*, 7th ed., Krause Publications, 2000; Stuart W. Wells, III, *Science Fiction Collectibles: Identification & Price Guide*, Krause Publications, 1999; *X-Men—Collector Handbook and Price Guide*, Checkerboard Publishing.

Periodicals: *Comic Book Market Place*, P.O. Box 180900, Coronado, CA 92178; *Comic Buyers Guide*, 700 E. State St., Iola, WI 54990; *Comic Scene*, 475 Park Ave., New York, NY 10016; *Duckburg Times*, 3010 Wilshire Blvd. #362, Los Angeles, CA 90010; *Overstreet Comic Book Marketplace*, 801 20th St. NW, Ste. 3, Cleveland, TN 37311; *Overstreet's Advanced Collector*, 801 20th St. NW, Ste 3, Cleveland, TN 37311; *Western Comics Journal*, 143 Milton St., Brooklyn, NY 11222.

Collectors' Club: Fawcett Collectors of America & Magazine Enterprise, Too!, 301 E. Buena Vista Ave., North Augusta, SC 29841.

Museum: Museum of Cartoon Art, Rye, NY.

Reproduction Alert: Publishers frequently reprint popular stories, even complete books, so the buyer must pay strict attention to the title, not just the portion printed in outsized letters on the front cover. If there's ever any doubt, look inside at the fine print on the bottom of the inside cover or first page. The correct title will be printed there in capital letters.

Buyers also should pay attention to the size of the comic they purchase. The comics offered are exact replicas of Golden Age D.C. titles which normally sell for thousands of dollars. The seller offers the large, 10-by-13-inch copy of Superman #1 in mint condition for $10 to $100. The naive collector jumps at the chance since he knows this book sells for thousands on the open market. When the buyer gets his "find" home and checks further, he discovers that he's paid way too much for the treasury-sized "Famous First Edition" comic printed in the mid-1970s by D.C. These comics originally sold for $1 each and are exact reprints except for the size. Several came with outer covers which announced the fact that they were reprints, but it didn't take long for dishonest dealers to remove these and sell the comic at greatly inflated prices.

Notes: Just like advertising, comic books affect and reflect the culture which nurtures them. Large letters, bright colors, and pulse-pounding action hype this product. Since good almost always triumphs over evil, many would say comics are as American as mom's apple pie. Yet there's truly something for every taste in the vast array of comics available today. There are underground (adult situation) comics, foreign comics, educational comics, and comics intended to promote the sale of products or services.

The following listing concentrates on mainstream American comics published between 1938 and 1985. Prices may vary from region to region due to excessive demand in some areas. Prices given are for comic books in fine condition; that is, comics that are like-new in most respects, but may show a little wear. Comics should be complete; no pages or chunks missing.

Action, #12, Golden Age, first
   Batman 500.00
Adventures Into the Unknown,
   #37 .... 25.00
Adventures Into Weird Worlds,
   #28 .... 175.00
After Dark, #8 .... 30.00

Airboy Comics, Vol. 8, #2 .... 80.00
Alice in Wonderland, #49 .... 95.00
All American Comics, #100, first Johnny Thunder 125.00
All American Men of War, DC, #19 .... 65.00
Amazing Adventures, Ziff-Davis, #4 .... 30.00
Annette's Life Story, Annette Funicello, #1100, Dell, 1960 .... 80.00
Astonishing, #33 .... 25.00
A-Team, Marvel, #2 .... 25.00
Baby Huey, Harvey, #14 .... 8.00
Beetle Bailey, Dell, #552 .... 15.00
Bewitched, #51 .... 18.00
Black Arrow, Classics Illustrated, 1946 .... 28.00
Black Beauty, #60 .... 80.00
Black Cat Mystery, #38 .... 155.00
Black Magic, Vol. 2, #5 .... 160.00
Blue Beetle, #49 .... 75.00
Blue Bolt Weird Tales, #114 .... 70.00
Bold Stories, #1 .... 76.00
Bozo the Clown, Dell, #3, Oct-Dec. 1951, covers lightly rubbed 2.00
Bugs Bunny, Dell
 #3, Christmas Funnies 20.00
 #4, Vacation Funnies, Dell Giant, glossy 40.00
 #59, Shining Knight, Feb-March, 1958 .... 19.00
 #69, Gas Attendant, Oct-Nov. .. 18.00
 #72, Fishing, April-May, 1960
Candy, #60 .... 15.00
Captain America, #30 .... 200.00
Captain Flight, #5 .... 75.00
Casper the Friendly Ghost, Harvey, #30 .... 20.00
Chamber of Chills, #15 .... 135.00
Cheyenne, #734 .... 35.00
Cisco Kid, Dell, #10 .... 8.00
Cow Puncher Comics, Avon, book #1, Jan. 1947 .... 40.00
Crime & Punishment, #89 .... 20.00
Crime Does Not Pay, #102 .... 14.00
Crime Reporter, #2 .... 100.00
Crimes by Women, #54 .... 150.00
Colt 45 .... 20.00
Daffy Duck, Dell
 #14, July-Sept., 1958 .... 19.00
 #15, Oct-Dec., 1958 .... 18.00
 #17, April-June, 1959 .... 18.00
David Copperfield, #48 .... 50.00
Detective Comics, #140 .... 150.00
Dick Tracy, Harvey, #86 .... 18.00
Doctor Solar, Dell, #9 .... 25.00
Donald Duck, Dell, #31 .... 12.00
Eerie, #15 .... 50.00
Elmer Fudd, Dell
 #558 .... 8.00
 #1081, Feb-April, 1960 .... 18.00
Fantastic Fears, #7 .... 370.00
Felix the Cat, #4 .... 18.00
Fighting America, #3, glossy 220.00
Fighting Fronts, Harvey, #5 .... 8.00

Forbidden Worlds, #29 .... 20.00
Gene Autry, Dell, #85 .... 8.00
Goofy, Dell, #562 .... 19.00
Green Lantern, Dell, #32, Oct. 1964 .... 20.00
Green Mansions, #90 .... 20.00
Gypsy Colt, Dell, #568 .... 12.00
Hector Heathcote, #1 .... 25.00
Hopalong Cassidy, DC, #88 .... 30.00
Ivanhoe, Classics Illustrated 20.00
Jace Pearson of the Texas Rangers, Dell, #6 .... 12.00
Jet Fighters, #5 .... 15.00
Jetsons, #1 .... 40.00
Johnny Mack Brown, Dell, #618 .... 35.00
Journey Into Fear, #4 .... 190.00
Jungle, #78 .... 50.00
Konga, #16 .... 30.00
Law Breakers Suspense, #11 .... 100.00
Lawman, #1035 .... 20.00
Little Iodine, Dell, #15 .... 5.00
Little Lulu, French 15.00
Lone Ranger, French 35.00
Lone Ranger's Famous Horse, Hi Yo Silver, Dell, #10 .... 12.00
Looney Tunes/Merry Melodies, Dell
 #139 .... 6.00
 #183, January, 1957 .... 18.00
 #210, Bagpipes, April, 1959 .... 18.00
Love Confessions, #47 .... 10.00
Love Secrets, #48 .... 10.00
Magnus Robot Fighter, Dell, #5 ...... 55.00
Man From U.N.C.L.E., Dell, #9 .... 35.00
Manhunt, #14 .... 100.00
Man in Iron Mask, Classics Illustrated, #54 .... 10.00
Mannix, French 25.00
Marvel Tales, #112 .... 230.00
Maverick, #945 .... 20.00
Mickey Mouse Birthday Party, Dell, #1 .... 25.00
Mighty Samson, Dell, #8 .... 10.00
Moby Dick, Classics Illustrated, #5 .... 45.00
Murder Inc., #1 .... 75.00
Mysteries Weird & Strange, #6 .... 18.00
Mystery Comics, #2G 40.00
Mystery In Space, DC, #3 .... 130.00
Mystic Tales, #7 .... 80.00
Navy Combat, #14 .... 30.00
O. K. Comics, volume 1, #1, 1940, 64 pgs 65.00
Oregon Trail, Classics Illustrated, #72 .... 16.00
Our Army At War, DC, #4 .... 90.00
Perfect Crime, #30 .... 50.00
Peter Panda, DC, #5 .... 25.00
Phantom Lady, #22 .... 125.00
Popeye, Dell, #29 .... 22.00
Porky Pig, Dell, #285 .... 10.00
Prairie, #58 .... 70.00
Punch, #12 .... 100.00

Quest of Zorro, Dell, #617 .... 60.00
Rangers, #14 .... 75.00
Real Heroes, #2 .... 75.00
Rex Allen, Dell, #2 .... 80.00
Rifleman 15.00
Rin Tin Tin, Dell, #12 .... 15.00
Rootie Kazootie, Dell, #4 .... 12.00
Rubber Duck Tales, #1, copyright 1971, 6-5/8" x 9-3/4" 5.00
Rusty Riley, Dell, #554 .... 8.00
Scoop, #2 .... 125.00
Sea Wolf, Classics Illustrated, #85 .... 10.00
Sharp Comics, #2 .... 75.00
Silver Streak, #7 .... 250.00
Smitty, Dell, #5, Feb-April, 1949, spine roll, light wear 2.00
Song of Hiawatha, #57 .... 70.00
Starling, #40 .... 75.00
Strange Adventures, DC, #13 .... 45.00
Strange Fantasy, #11 .... 25.00
Strange Stories of Suspense, #6 .... 135.00
Summer Love, #47 .... 45.00
Superman, #61 .... 125.00
Swiss Family Robinson, #42 .... 10.00
Tarzan, Dell, #113 .... 10.00
Tell It To The Marines, #7 .... 5.00
Terrific, #4 .... 450.00
The Amazing Spider-Man King Size Annual, #2, 72 pgs, copyright 1965 .... 5.00
The Texan, #12 .... 100.00
The Thing, #10 .... 315.00
The Three Stooges, Gold Key, #16, March, 1964 .... 9.00
Thrilling Crime, #49 .... 50.00
Tom & Jerry Summer Fun, Dell, #1 .... 20.00
Tom Brown's School Days, #45 .... 85.00
Tonto, Dell, #15 .... 6.00
Top Cat, #27 .... 20.00
Torchy, #1 .... 150.00
Thunder Agents, Dell, #17 .... 27.00
Uncle Scrooge, Dell, #495 .... 60.00
Underworld Crime, #7 .... 75.00
Wacky Duck, Current Defective Stories, Vol. 1, #1, August, 1948 .... 38.00
Walt Disney Comics and Stories, Dell, #148 .... 10.00
Wanted, #52 .... 50.00
War Birds, #2 .... 16.00
War Front, Harvey, #20 .... 5.00
War Fury, #1 .... 50.00
War Stories, #3 .... 6.00
Western Stories, Classics Illustrated, #62 .... 12.00
Weird Mysteries, #2 .... 75.00
Weird Tales of the Future, #7 .... 125.00
Whack, #3 .... 75.00

Wild West, #2, July, 1948, cover printed slightly off center, light dust soiling 15.00

Wings, #85 ....90.00

Witches Tales, #24 ....15.00

Wizard of Oz, Marvel, large format 35.00

Woody Woodpecker, Dell, #16 ....5.00

Worlds of Fear, #10 ....100.00

Yellow Dog, Volume 2, #2, 1969, newsprint, opens to 11-1/2" x 16" 7.50

Zane Grey's To The Last Man, Dell, #616 ....8.00

Cookbooks

Collecting Hints: Look for books in good, clean condition. Watch for special interesting notes in margins.

History: Among the earliest American cookbooks are *Frugal Housewife or Complete Woman Cook* by Susanna Carter, published in Philadelphia in 1796, and *American Cookery* by Amelia Simmons, published in Hartford, Connecticut, in 1796. Cookbooks of this era were crudely written, for most cooks could not read well and measuring devices were not yet refined.

Collectible cookbooks include those used as premiums or advertisements. This type is much less expensive than the rare 18th-century books.

References: Bob Allen, *Guide to Collecting Cookbooks and Advertising Cookbooks*, Collector Books, 1990, 1998 value update; Linda J. Dickinson, *Price Guide to Cookbooks and Recipe Leaflets*, Collector Books, 1990, 1999 value update.

Periodical: *Cookbook Collectors' Exchange*, P.O. Box 32369, San Jose, CA 95152.

Collectors' Club: Cook Book Collectors Club of America, 231 E. James Blvd., P.O. Box 85, St James, MO 65559.

American Woman's Cook Book, Ella Blackstone, Chicago, 1910, 384 pgs 35.00

Amy Vanderbilt's Complete Cookbook, 1961, 811 pgs 15.00

Anyone Can Bake, Royal Baking Power Co., 1929, hardback, 1st ed. 11.00

A Place Called Sweet Apple-Country Living & Southern Recipes, Clestine Sibley, 1967, dj 10.00

Arm & Hammer Good Things to Eat, Church & Dwight Co., 3" x 5", 1925, 32 pgs 5.00

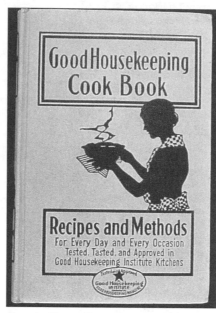

Good Housekeeping Cook Book, white cover, green lettering, 1st edition, 1933, $12.

A World of Vegetable Cookery, Alex D. Hawkes, 1968, 1st printing, 274 pgs 10.00

Betty Crocker's Baking Classics, Best Recipes of 100 Years, Random House, 1979, dj 10.00

Blueberry Hill Menu Cookbook, Elsie Masterson, Crowell, 1966, 1st printing, 373 pgs 7.50

Classic Cooking with Coca-Cola 5.00

Cook's Tour of San Francisco, Doris Muscatine, Scribners, 1963, lower back edge bumped 9.50

Cross Creek Cookery, Marjorie Kinnan Rawlings, Scribners, 1942, 230 pgs 58.00

Dinners Long & Short, A. H. Adair, Knopf, 1929, illus by J. E. Labourer, 257 pgs 32.00

Favorite Foods of Famous Stars, Norge Corp., 8" x 10", 1934 copyright, 32 pgs 10.00

Favorite Recipes From Our Best Cooks Cookbook, Women's Club of Batavia, Ohio, Circulation Service, 1981 ...4.00

Food & Fun for the Invalid, Florence Harris and Dorothy Rider, 1942, 2nd printing, 255 pgs, dj 9.00

Forty Delightful Ways to Serve, Green & Green Co., Dayton, OH, 1928, 16 pgs, 5" x 7" 9.00

From Amish and Mennonite Kitchens, Phyllis Pell and Good & Rachel Pellman, Good Books Publishing, 1984, 420 pgs 10.00

Game Cookery, E. N. & Edith Sturdivant, Outdoor Life, 1967, 166 pgs 6.00

Gebhardt's Mexican Cookery for American Homes, San Antonio, TX, 1932, 35 pgs, 4-5/8" x 7-1/4" 11.00

Heal Thyself Cookbook, A Guide to Natural Living Through Vegetarian Cooking and Holistic Juicing, Diane Ciccone, A&B Books, 1993, 2nd printing 7.00

Helen Corbitt's Cookbook, Houghton Mifflin, 1957, 29th printing, dj 8.00

How To Cook a Wolf, MFK Fisher, Duel Sloane & Pearce, 1942-43, 5th printing 29.00

Jell-O, Rose O'Neill illus, 5-1/4" x 6-7/8" 50.00

Kate Smith's Collection of Famous Dishes from Famous Places/Authentic Recipes from New York's Foremost Eating Places, issued by Diamond Crystal Salt Co., Inc., copyright 1939 ....10.00

Lorain Cooking, American Stove Company, 1930, 180 pgs 9.00

Luchow's German Festival Cookbook, Gene & Fran Schoor, Doubleday, 1976, 1st edition, some edge wear, rubbed, light soil 9.50

Magic in Herbs, Leonie de Sounin, Gramercy, 1941 ....9.50

Martha Washington Log Cabin Cookbook, Philadelphia, 1924, 132 pgs 38.00

Mastering the Art of French Cooking, Julia Child, 1961, 14th printing 15.00

Maxwell House, How to Make Good Coffee, 1931, black and white illus 12.00

Mexico Through My Kitchen Window, Maria A. de Carbia, printed in Mexico, 1937, 215 pgs 22.00

Midwestern Home Cookery, Suggested Recipes by L Szathmary, Promontory Press, 1974 ....11.50

Mrs. Miller's Amish Cook Book, Favorite Recipes From the Family of Miller's Home Cooking, Berlin, OH, Dutch Home Products, 1973, 111 pgs 7.50

Mrs. Rorer's Philadelphia Cook Book, Mrs. S T Rover, Arnold & Co, 1885, 1st edition, 8vo, 581 pgs, 16 pgs of ads 20.00

My Better Homes & Gardens Cook Book, Meredith Publishing, 1935, 10th printing, tabs 7.00

Palatable Dishes, S. Cutter, Peter Paul & Bro, Buffalo, Harness Baking Powder ads, 1891, 920 pgs 110.00

Peanuts Cook Book, Scholastic Books, 1970, cartoon illus by Charles Schulz 5.00

Peanuts Lunch Bag Cook Book, Scholastic Books, 1974, cartoon illus by Charles Schulz 5.00

Secrets of Fat-Free Baking, Sandra Woodruff, Avery Publ, 1994 ....8.00

Southern Food & Plantation Houses, Lee Bailey, 1990, dj 26.00

Southern Sideboards Recipe Book, Junior League of Jackson, MS, 1980, 5th printing, spiral bound, 414 pgs ...9.00

The Art of Cooking with Herbs and Spices...A Handbook of Flavors and Savors, Milo Miloradovich, 1950, 304 pgs 12.50

The Art of Creole Cookery, Wm Kaufman & Sister Mary Ursula Cooper, illus by Margot Tomes, Doubleday, 1962, 1st edition, sgd by Sister Mary........10.00

The Blender Cookbook, Seranne & Gaden, Doubleday, 1961, 288 pgs, dj 5.00

The California Heritage Cookbook, Jr. League of Pasadena, Doubleday, 1976 ....8.50

The Carbondale (PA) Cookbook, Scranton, PA, 1924, 7th ed., 203 pgs 38.00

The Chef's New Secret Cookbook, Louis Szathmary, Hen Regmery, 1975, dj, some wear 9.00

The Cookie Cookbook, Deloris K Clem, Castle Books, 1966, slight edge wear 11.50

The Cookie Jar, Josephine Perry, Gramercy, 1951, some edge wear 9.50

The Home Book of French Cookery, Mme Germaine Carter, Doubleday, 1950, some edge wear.............11.50

The New Butterick Cook Book, Revised and Enlarged, Flora Rose, Butterick Pub Co., NY, 1925, 34d edition 32.75

The New Cookery, Lenna Frances Cooper, Battle Creek, MI, 1916, 5th ed., 472 pgs, illus.............45.00

The Philadelphia Cook Book of Town and Country, Anna Wetherill Reed, Bramhall House, 1963, 346 pgs, dj 15.00

The Poultry Cookbook, Southern Living Cookbook Library, 1977, 192 pgs.............9.50

The Rocky Mountain Cookbook, Menus & Recipes for a Hearty Country Cuisine, Connie Chesnel, Clarkson Potter, 1989, 1st edition, dj 10.00

The Soup and Sandwich Handbook, Campbell Soups, thermal mug on cover, 1971 ....12.00

The Vegetarian Cook Book, E. P. Dutton, Pacific Press, 1914, 271 pgs.....50.00

The Williamsburg Art of Cookery...or...Accomplished Gentlewoman's Companion...5000 Recipes Virginia Cookery, Helen Bullick, Colonial Williamsburg/Holt Rinehart Winston, 1990, 1961, hard back......11.50

365 Ways to Cook Hamburger, Doyne Nickerson, Doubleday, 1960, 189 pgs.............7.00

White Trash Cooking, Ernest Matthew Mickler, The Jargon Society, Berkeley, CA, 1986, 134 pgs, spiral bound.............28.75

Wilken Family Home Cooking Album, Schenely, PA, whiskey distillers, 5" x 9", 1935 ....2.00

Cookie Jars

Collecting Hints: It is not unusual to find two cookie jars made by the same company which have been decorated differently. These variations add some interest to cookie jar collections.

History: The date the first cookie was made is unknown. However, early forms of cookie jars can be found in several mediums, including glass and pottery. Perhaps it was the Depression that caused people to bake more cookies at home, coupled with the pretty Depression-era glass jars that created the first real interest in cookie jars. A canister, complete with matching lid, was made in the popular Kolorkraft line by Brush Pottery Company in Roseville, Ohio, in the 1920s. By embossing the word "Cookies" on it, the piece became one of the first such documented cookie jars. By 1931, McKee Glass Company, Jeannette, Pennsylvania, was advertising a cookie jar that consisted of a 5-1/2 inch jar with a lid, and by 1932 Hocking Glass was advertising a large glass jar with a wide screw-on metal lid. These products were additions to canister sets.

The clever figural jars so often associated with cookie jars were introduced by several companies during the early 1940s. Soon apples, animals, and comic characters were added to more colorful kitchens. Production of American cookie jars flourished until the mid- or late 1970s, when foreign competition became too great for several companies. However, a resurgence in the cookie jar collecting market has helped spur new companies to develop interesting jars, and production is starting to increase. As Americans fall in love with new characters, from "Sesame Street" to "Star Wars," cookie jar manufacturers eagerly fill orders.

References: Fred and Joyce Herndon Roerig, *Collector's Encyclopedia of Cookie Jars*, Book I (1990, 1997 value update), Book II (1994, 1999 value update), Collector Books, Book III (1998, 2001 value update); Mike Schneider, *Complete Cookie Jar Book*, revised and expanded 2nd ed., Schiffer Publishing, 1999; Mark and Ellen Supnick, *Wonderful World of Cookie Jars*, revised ed., L-W Book Sales, 1995; Ermagene Westfall, *Illustrated Value Guide to Cookie Jars* (1983, 1997 value update), Book II (1993, 2000 value update), Collector Books.

Periodicals: *Cookie Jar Express*, P.O. Box 221, Mayview, MO 64071; *Cookie Jarrin'*, RR #2, Box 504, Walterboro, SC 29488; *Crazed Over Cookie Jars*, P.O. Box 254, Savanna, IL 61074.

Collectors' Club: Cookie Jar Collector's Club, 595 Cross River Rd, Katonah, NY 10536.

Reproduction Alert: Reproduction cookie jars are starting to plague the market. Oddly enough, it's not only the old cookie jars being reproduced. The cute blue Cookie Monster made by California Originals in 1970 has been copied. California Originals are clearly marked "© Muppets, Inc. 1970" along the base. Brayton Pottery's Mammy has been reproduced. Unmarked copies have been found in addition to well-made copies with a date on the bottom and new-looking decals on the apron. Other reproductions include American Bisque: Casper; Brush: elephant with an ice cream cone and Peter Pumpkin Eater; California Originals: Count and Cookie Monster; McCoy: Davy Crockett; Regal China: Davy Crockett; Robinson-Ransbottom: World War II soldier and Oscar.

Turkey, brown-glazed ceramic, unmarked, $40. Photo courtesy of Joy Luke Fine Art Brokers and Auctioneers.

Abingdon Pottery
Jack-In-Box, ABC on front, incised mark "611".............125.00
Money Sack.............95.00

Advertising
Blue Bonnet Sue.............40.00
Cookie Bandit, Hallmark 190.00

Keebler Tree House,
Brush-McCoy 100.00
Quaker Oats, 120th
Anniversary 70.00
Regency Insurance, Buick sedan,
royal blue, Glenn Appleman....800.00
Sid's Taxi, Glenn Appleman.....800.00

American Bisque
Cat in a Basket, 12-1/2" h, chips
inside rim....................................40.00
Chef...90.00
Cowboy Boots............................235.00
Churn Boy 225.00
Ernie..95.00
Ice Cream Freezer 460.00
Milk and Cookies 225.00
Mr. Rabbit...................................185.00
Poodle, gold trim........................275.00
Popeye, 10-1/2" h..................1,000.00

Avon
African Village 35.00
Spatter Bear 30.00
Townhouse, small, MIB 15.00

Brush
Bobby Baker 75.00
Clock 185.00
Clown Bust, crazing.................375.00
Elephant, ice cream cone, gray body,
purple jacket..............................610.00
Happy Bunny, heavy crazing ..250.00
Humpty Dumpty, cowboy
hat...350.00
Night Owl 75.00
Panda, black and white...........325.00
Squirrel with top hat, 12" h, mkd "W15
USA"...550.00

California Originals
Koala on Stump 275.00
Seated Turtle...............................45.00
Superman in Phone
Booth..525.00
Tigger...170.00
Winnie-the-Pooh..........................95.00
Woody Woodpecker 1,200.00

Cardinal, French Chef 225.00

Certified International
Barney Rubble.............................65.00
Bugs Bunny 85.00
Christmas Bugs 95.00
Christmas Tweety, in
stocking....................................125.00
Dino and Pebbles 65.00
Fred Flintstone 65.00
Talking Taz...................................95.00

Clay Art
Humpty Dumpty........................125.00
Toaster...60.00
Wizard of Oz 90.00

Cleminsons, Card King, gold trim on
hearts 400.00

Doranne
Coca-Cola Bottle......................150.00
Dragon.......................................275.00
Hound Dog, yellow 30.00
Mailbox..90.00

Enesco
Garfield 90.00
Sugar Town General Store.........60.00

Fitz and Floyd
Autumn Woods Rabbit...............70.00

Busy Bunnies Tree 145.00
Christmas Wreath Santa 150.00
Cotton Tailors Hat Box 95.00
English Garden
Wheelbarrow.............................145.00
Father Christmas......................270.00
Herb Garden Rabbit 95.00
Hydrangea Bears......................150.00
Panda Bear, black and white,
OCI..85.00
Rocking Horse 265.00
Rolls Royce 450.00
Rose Terrace Rabbit 80.00
Santa in airplane 195.00
Santa's Magic Workshop 165.00
Sock Hoppers 290.00
Unicorn..85.00

Goebel, Monk, mkd "Germany,
1957"...800.00

Hall, Gold Lace, Flareware, 9" h, gold
trim, some rim chips...................50.00

McCoy
Clyde Dog 165.00
Coffee Grinder, 10" h, some chips
and age cracks 40.00
Football Boy 225.00
Friendship Space Ship 165.00
Harley-Davidson Hog 650.00
Hamm's Bear 300.00
Keebler Tree House 750.00
Mammy 90.00
Pepper, yellow............................95.00
Raggedy Ann, mkd "USA
741"..150.00
Traffic Light.................................75.00
Woodsy Owl 325.00

Metlox
Apple Barrel 75.00
Ballerina Bear...........................120.00
Chef Pierre 65.00
Cookie Bandit...........................215.00
Fido 245.00
Francine 95.00
Frosty...65.00
Hen 325.00
Hippo, gray 550.00
Mammy, polka dot dress..........450.00
Miss Cutie Pie 250.00
Mona-Monocionius Rose 150.00
Panda Bear 95.00
Puddles, yellow coat...................35.00
Raggedy Andy 165.00
Roller Skating Bear, 13" h..........75.00
Santa, head 600.00
Squirrel, pine cone 95.00
Tulip 425.00
Wally Walrus, 1976, 9-3/4" h 200.00

Pearl China, Mammy, mkd "Pearl China
Hand Decorated, 22 kt gold, USA,"
some wear.................................725.00

Pottery Guild
Elsie the Cow, 12-1/2" h 645.00
Little Red Riding Hood.............225.00
Purinton Pottery, Howdy Doody,
9-3/4" h 900.00

Redwing Pottery
Dutch Girl, two shades of blue,
cracked brown base, faded Redwing
symbol and "Redwing Pottery, Hand
Painted," 10-1/2" h, 6-3/4" w 190.00
Friar Tuck, old nicks 95.00

Regal
Humpty Dumpty 300.00
Quaker Oats 150.00
Jim Beam, cylinder.................. 90.00
Quaker Oats 145.00
RRP CO, Roseville, OH, Peter, Peter
Pumpkin Eater, 9" w, 8" w, small flake
on base in lid opening 230.00

Shawnee
Dutch Girl, mkd "USA," 11-1/2" h,
7-1/2" w................................. 200.00
Jill, 12" h, some age crazing, cracks,
two chips 65.00
King Corn, 10-1/2" h 355.00
Mugsey.................................... 495.00
Puss N Boots........................... 275.00
Sailor Boy, Shawnee Commemora-
tive, limited to 100 jars, designed by
S. A. Corl, produced by Mark Sup-
nick, 1992, black hair............. 495.00
Smiley, blue collar and black
hooves.................................... 270.00
Winnie, combination bank and cookie
jar, 10-1/2" h.......................... 475.00

Treasure Craft
Bart Simpson, holding
cookie...................................... 75.00
Baseball.................................... 75.00
Bird House............................... 45.00
Buzz Lightyear 225.00
Cactus, wearing bandanna and cow-
boy hat.................................... 50.00
Dinosaur, large purple spots, gray
body, blue spines, 11-1/2" h 65.00
Dorothy and Toto, Wizard of Oz,
1994....................................... 350.00
Flop Ear Rabbit 50.00
Mickey Mouse 75.00
Nanna, Mammy-type, USA,
1989....................................... 95.00
Noah's Ark 65.00
Peter Pumpkin Eater 45.00
Pink Panther 175.00
Slot Machine............................ 125.00

Twin Winton
Elf, Collector Series................ 175.00
Friar Tuck................................. 85.00
Gunfighter Rabbit, Collector
Series..................................... 250.00
Magilla Gorilla 275.00
Mother Goose, gray 165.00
Ranger Bear with Badge, mkd "Code
#84".. 60.00
Vandor, Popeye 410.00

Warner Brothers
Bugs Bunny............................. 40.00
Olympics, 1996 .... 75.00
Superman................................. 95.00
Sylvester & Tweety Bird........... 40.00
Tweety on Flour Sack 85.00
Yosemite Sam.......................... 35.00

Cow Collectibles

Collecting Hints: Image is everything. It makes no difference if the
object was made yesterday or 100
years ago, just so long as it pictures
the collector's favorite bovine.

Cow collectors collect in quantity. Advertising and folk art collectors also vie for pieces displaying cow images.

Cow creamers, some dating as early as the 18th century, are a favorite specialized collecting category. Antiques devotees focus on early examples; most cow collectors are perfectly willing to settle for 20th-century examples.

In order for an object to be considered a true cow collectible, it must either be in the shape of a cow or have a picture of a cow on its surface. Milk- and dairy-related items without a cow image are not cow collectibles. T-shirts with cow sayings fall into a gray area.

History: The domesticated cow has been around for more than 8,000 years: cows are part of Greek mythology, the Egyptians worshipped Hathor the cow-goddess, and the Hindus still venerate the cow as a sacred being. Cows have long been a focal point for artists and sculptors.

Some of the more famous nursery rhymes feature a cow, e.g. "Hey, Diddle, Diddle" and "The House That Jack Built." Poetry and literature are rich with cow references.

It is impossible to divorce the cow from the dairy industry. Cow motifs appear throughout a wide range of dairy-product advertising, the three most popular images being the Guernsey, Holstein, and Jersey.

There are a number of famous 20th-century cows: early Disney cartoons featured Clarabelle; the dairy industry created Brooksie, Bossie, and La Vache Qui Ri; and, of course, there is Elsie. When she was at her peak of popularity, only the president of the United States had more public recognition than Elsie the Borden Cow. In the late 1930s, Elsie made her initial appearances in a series of medical journal advertisements for Borden's Eagle Brand condensed milk. Her popularity grew as a result of Borden's 1939-1940 World's Fair exhibition. A 1940 Hollywood appearance further enhanced her national reputation. In 1957, a name-Elsie's-calf contest produced three million entries. Borden briefly retired Elsie in the late 1960s, but the public demanded her return. Today she is once again found on labels, in animated commercials, and at live appearances across the country.

Alas, in this age of equality, the fabled bull receives short shrift. With the exception of Walt Disney's Ferdinand, the male of the species is relegated to a conspicuous second place.

References: Albert and Shelly Coito, *Elsie the Cow and Borden's Collectibles*, Schiffer Publishing, 2000; Emily Margolin Gwathmey, *Wholly Cow!*, Abbeville Press, 1988.

Periodical: *Moosletter*, 240 Wahl Ave., Evans City, PA 16033.

Painting, titled, "Swiss Cattle," scene of two cows in meadow, signed lower left, F. Dearmont, sold in orange gold and black painted frame, 16" x 24", $500. Photo courtesy of Joy Luke Fine Art Brokers and Auctioneers.

Advertising Figure, Milka, hard plastic 10.00

Bank, Nestle Nespray, figural, vinyl 40.00

Blotter, 4" x 9-1/4", Cow Brand Baking Soda, cow illus, c1920 .... 12.00

Booklet, *Milk, An All-Round Food,* Metropolitan Life Insurance, silhouettes on cov, c1930, 8 pgs 3.00

Butter Print, wood, round
  4-1/2" d, standing cow, one piece turned handle, dark finish 350.00
  5-1/4" d, cow with tree and flower, scrubbed white, one piece turned handle 175.00

Charm, 1" d, Swift's Brookfield, brass, emb cow on award base, inscribed "June Dairy Month Award," early 1900s 17.50

Child's Book, *Bossy the Calf Who Lost Her Tinkle Bell*, G. A. Coke, McLoughlin, 1939 .... 20.00

Cookie Jar, cov
  Cow Jumped Over The Moon, Doranne 250.00
  Elsie the Cow, Pottery Guild, late 1940s 250.00
  Purple Cow, Metlox 550.00

Figure, 3" x 5-1/2" x 4", Ferdinand, rubber, Seiberling, Walt Disney Enterprises copyright, c1930 .... 85.00

Membership Pin, Guernsey 4-H Club, full color, plastic, c1940 .... 15.00

Mug, 2-1/2" h, china, white, full color illus of Elsie, blue accent stripe, Juvenile Ware and Borden copyright, c1940 .... 75.00

Pinback Button
  Antarctic Guernsey, multicolored milk cow "Iceberg," identified on back paper as "Born December 19, 1933, on the Byrd Antarctic Expedition II, The Farthest South of Any Dairy Animal" 50.00
  Guernsey-The Only Breed Increasing in Every State, multicolored portrait of cow's head, blue award ribbon, c1930 .... 18.00
  Jerseys For Mine, A.J.C.C., multicolored scene, red rim, white lettering, c1920 .... 55.00
  Livestock Steer, blue and white, blue illus, 1901-12 .... 15.00
  Sharples Cream Separators, multicolored, two young farm girls using product in pasture 50.00
  Whitings Milk, red, white, blue, gold circle accents around logo, 1930s 20.00

Pitcher
  Black, glazed, orig sticker reads "Ellsworth" 35.00
  Stoneware, 8" h 240.00

Poster
  Bull Durham, 19-1/2" x 13-1/2", includes cow figure 375.00
  Evaporated Milk-Pure Cow's Milk, black and white illus of cows, green ground, c1940 .... 25.00
  Swift's Annual Fertilizers, linen, dark blue steer illus and print, 1920s 75.00

Ramp Walker, 3-1/4" l, plastic, brown and white, orig sealed cellophane bag, marked "Made in Hong Kong," 1950s 20.00

Salt and Pepper Shakers, pr, Elsie the Cow, head and shoulders 85.00

Sugar, cov, figural, Elmer, c1940 ... 40.00

Toy, Mozzy Moo-Moo, #190, MIB 270.00

Cowboy Heroes

Collecting Hints: Cowboy hero material was collected and saved in great numbers. Don't get fooled into thinking an object is rare—check carefully. Roy Rogers and Dale Evans material currently is the most desirable, followed closely by Hopalong Cassidy, Tom Mix, and Gene Autry memorabilia. Material associated with the Western stars of the silent era and early talking films still has not achieved its full potential as a collectible.

History: The era when the cowboy and longhorn cattle dominated the Great Western Plains was short, lasting only from the end of the Civil War to the late 1880s. Dime novelists romanticized this period and created a love affair in America's heart for the Golden West.

The cowboy was a prime entertainment subject in motion pictures. William S. Hart developed the character of the cowboy hero—often in love with his horse more than the girl. He was followed by Tom Mix, Ken Maynard, Tim McCoy, and Buck Jones. The "B" movie, the second feature of a double bill, was often of the cowboy genre.

In 1935, William Boyd starred in the first of the Hopalong Cassidy films. Gene Autry, "a singing cowboy," gained popularity over the airwaves, and by the late 1930s, Autry's Melody Ranch was a national institution on the air as well as on the screen. Roy Rogers replaced Autry as the featured cowboy at Republic Pictures in the mid-1940s. Although the Lone Ranger first starred in radio shows in 1933, he did not appear in movies until 1938.

The early years of television enhanced the careers of the big three—Autry, Boyd, and Rogers. The appearance of the Lone Ranger in shows made specifically for television strengthened the popularity of the cowboy hero. "Gunsmoke," "Wagon Train," "Rawhide," "The Rifleman," "Paladin," and "Bonanza" were just a few of the shows that followed.

By the early 1970s, the cowboy hero had fallen from grace, relegated to reruns or specials. In early 1983, the Library of Congress in Washington, D.C., conducted a major show on the cowboy heroes, perhaps a true indication that they are now a part of history.

References: Dana Cain, *Film & TV Animal Star Collectibles*, Antique Trader Books, 1998; Lee Felbinger, *Collector's Reference and Value Guide to the Lone Ranger*, Collector Books, 1998; Michael Friedman, *Cowboy Culture: The Last Frontier of American Antiques*, 2nd ed., Schiffer Publishing, 1999; William Manns and Elizabeth Clair Flood, *Cowboys & The Trappings of the Old West*, Zon International Publishing Co., 1997; Rex Miller, *The Investor's Guide to Vintage Character Collectibles*, Krause Publications, 1999; Jim Schleyer, *Collecting Toy Western Guns*, Krause Publications, 1996; Neil Summers, *Official TV Western Book*, Vol. 1 (1987), Vol. 2 (1989), Vol. 3 (1991), Vol. 4 (1992), The Old West Shop Publishing.

Periodicals: *Collecting Hollywood*, American Collectors Exchange, 2401 Broad St., Chattanooga, TN 37408;

Cowboy Collector Newsletter, P.O. Box 7486, Long Beach, CA 90807; *Favorite Westerns & Serial World*, Rte 1, Box 103, Vernon Center, MN 56090; Westerner, Box 5232-32, Vienna, WV 26105.

Collectors' Club: Friends of Hopalong Cassidy Fan Club, 6310 Friendship Drive, New Concord, OH 43762.

Museums: Gene Autry Western Heritage Museum, Los Angeles, CA; National Cowboy Hall of Fame and Western Heroes, Oklahoma City, OK; Roy Rogers Museum, Victorville, CA.

Additional Listings: Western Americana.

Annie Oakley
Comic Book, #1..........................25.00
Dixie Cup Picture, Barbara Stanwyck....................................50.00
Game, board, Milton Bradley....................................45.00
Record, 45 rpm, mint in sleeve..................................20.00

Bobby Benson
Map, 18-1/2" x 24-1/2", Bobby Benson and the H-O Rangers in Africa, full color, paper, copyright Hecker H-O Co., Inc., 1930s, tack holes on corners, minor damage..................95.00
Record, Bobby Benson's B-Bar-B Riders, 10-1/8" x 10-1/8" illus picture sleeve, 78 rpm record, white and white label, "The Story of the Golden Palomino," Decca #88036, copyright 1950 ....12.00

Bonanza
Charm Bracelet, c1970s, six charms, gold colored metal, MIB 35.00
Coloring Book, unused 30.00
Gun Set, Marx 660.00
Magazine
   Parade....................................25.00
   Police Gazette........................30.00
Playing Cards, shows orig cast, sealed deck of 54 cards, orig plastic box, 1970s 18.00
Poster, Ponderosa, 22-1/2" x 17", c1967, facsimile autographs of cast..18.00
Sheet Music, pictures of 4 stars..................................42.00

Buck Jones
BB Gun, 36", wood stock with printed sundial, metal side with name, metal compass insert, Daisy 90.00
Better Little Book, *Buck Jones and The Two-Gun Kid*, Whitman, #1404, 1937....................................30.00
Big Little Book, *The Fighting Code*, #1104, Columbia Pictures, artists, Pat Patterson, author, 1934, 160 pgs, hard cover, soft spine.................35.00
Book
   Rocky Rhodes, Five Star Library Series, #15, Engel-Van Wiseman, Universal Pictures, artist, adapted by Harry Ormiston, 1935, 160 pgs, hard cover..............................35.00
   Songs of the Western Trails, 60 pgs, words and music, 9" x 12", 1940 copyright........................40.00

Magazine, *Remember When Magazine*, 8-1/2" x 11", Jones on cov, story and black and white photos inside, 1974..7.50
Pinback Button, Bucks Jones Club, enamel on brass, horseshoe, picture in center, 1930s.........................15.00

Buffalo Bill
Cabinet Photo, 4-1/4" x 6-1/2", black and white close-up portrait, c1890..75.00
Figurine, 2-1/8", metal, Blenheim....................................20.00
Show poster 700.00

Cisco Kid
Album, bread label, Freihofer's, 16 labels, 1952............................320.00
Bowl..40.00
Gun, premium, red, white, and blue cardboard, Cisco's picture on handle, clicker mounted inside, advertises TV show and Tip-Top Bread...........45.00
Ring, saddle............................500.00
Snack Set, plate and mug.........50.00

Davy Crockett
Bath Mat, chenille......................50.00
Bib, paper, large......................... 6.00
Doll, 22-1/2" h, plush, vinyl clothing, belt, and tag, "Official Frontierland Doll inspired by Walt Disney's Davy Crockett," c1950, Gund, hat missing 45.00
Frontier Suitcase 60.00
Game, Davy Crockett Rescue Game, compass, 1955.........................45.00
Lamp Shade, orig factory cello wrap..150.00
Potato Chip Bag, Canadian 75.00
Puzzle, frame tray, Fess Parker....................................35.00
Record, Crockett Meets Woody Woodpecker, 78 rpm...............125.00
Ring, brass frame, thin expansion bands, clear sheet of plastic over paper insert with color portrait, c1955..48.00
Ring, plastic, bright copper luster, simulated red plastic stone, raised portrait, c1955 ....18.00
Sheet Music, Fess Parker, for accordion..25.00
Shirt, boy's, unused, orig tags..40.00
Tru-Vue Cards, MIP 60.00
Wrist Watch, arrows as hands, orig band..85.00

Gabby Hayes
Child's Book, *Jack In Box*, hardcover 125.00
Coloring Book, 8" x 10-1/2", *Magic Dial Funny Coloring Book*, diecut television screen opening in front with disk wheel, Samuel Lowe Co, c1950..50.00
Comic Book, Quaker Oats giveaway................................25.00
Dixie Cup Picture, color, Bill Elliott and Gabby..................................50.00
Ring, cannon 185.00
Rocking horse 200.00

Gene Autry
Gun and Holster Set, cast iron..500.00
Lobby Card, Spanish 30.00
Pennant, Gene Autry & Champ, from rodeo show, 1949.....................60.00

Souvenir Program, 20 pgs, c1950, five full page ads for Autry merchandise 25.00
Sweater, child's 65.00
Writing Tablet 55.00

Gunsmoke
Annual, 1975..............................45.00
Board Game, photo cover with James Arness, British............................70.00
Comic Book, #720, 4-color........20.00
Doll, Matt Dillon, limited edition, MIB..................................30.00
Hartland Figure, with horse, no accessories..................................65.00
Little Golden Book, 1958 ....20.00
Magazine, *TV Guide*....................25.00
Notepad, Amanda Blake, unused 45.00
Pencil Box, Hasbro, 1961 ....18.00

Hopalong Cassidy Game, Milton Bradley, copyright William Boyd, 1950, $75.

Hopalong Cassidy
Bag, Jo Mar Ice Cream 50.00
Bedspread, chenille..................100.00
Book
  Hopalong Cassidy Returns, Clarence E. Mulford, Triangle Books, July 1943, 310 pgs, front of dj partially missing...10.00
  Hopalong Cassidy Television Book, 1950, glossy hardcover, mechanical dial moves images around small TV screen on cover, 30-page story, Hoppy and Lucky at Copper Gulch, full color photo on front and back..100.00
  Trail Dust, A. L. Burt edition, dust jacket...75.00
Chow Set, small, dish, plate, and glass..280.00
Comic Book, Bond Bread
  The Mad Barber....................80.00
  The Strange Legacy...............80.00
Drinking Glass, black image, breakfast, lunch, dinner, each...65.00
Ear Muffs, red...........................175.00
Game, board................................75.00
Hair Bow, girl's, hairpin, orig card..100.00
Laundry Bag, plastic, orig container and product card.....................850.00
Little Golden Book, *Hopalong Cassidy & Bar 20*......................25.00
Lobby Card, *Mystery Man*, set of eight, mint in envelope 400.00
Lunch Box, red, cloud decal, no thermos 150.00
Magazine
  Time.....................................120.00
  TV Guide, 1949....................250.00

Manual, Film Exploration............50.00
Neckerchief Slide, steer head, red eyes...55.00
Paperback Book, *Hopalong Cassidy Returns*.....................................30.00
Pencil Box, some orig contents.....................................100.00
Puzzle, frame tray 45.00
Record, double set
  "Hopalong Cassidy and the Singing Bandit" 55.00
  "Hopalong Cassidy and the Square Dance Hold Up" 55.00
Ring, brass, adjustable bands with initials and "XX" brand, loss to black enamel accents.........................50.00
Shooting Gallery, tin litho, 1950s, some wear...............................495.00
Sign, Hopalong Cassidy Rides Again, The Knickerbocker News, cardboard, 11" x 21".................................225.00
Soap, Topper, Castile..............125.00
Spurs, Olympia.........................200.00
Thermos, yellow, no lid 75.00
Wallet, child's, special agent pass...45.00
Wallpaper Section, 3-1/2' x 18'...175.00
Wrist Cuffs, small, black, pr 220.00

John Wayne
Arcade Card, c1950 ....4.00
Clock Plaque, wooden...............45.00
Coin, metal, gold, c1979..............7.50
Coloring Book, 11" x 15", 32 pgs, ten colored pages, Saalfield, #2354-15, 1951 copyright..........................50.00
Doll, Horse Soldier, Effanbee, MIB..185.00
Holster Set, leather belt, two holsters with name on side, orig box, early 1950s...45.00
Knife, memorial, metal and plastic, "The Duke--John Wayne (1907-1979)" 10.00
Movie Still, 8" x 10", black and white 4.00
Paper Dolls, 1980, unused 30.00
Pinback Button, 2-1/2" d, In Memory of a Great American....................5.00
Record Album, Horse Soldiers, soundtrack, 1959 ....50.00
Sheet Music, Put Your Arms Around Me, Honey, 9" x 12", four pgs, black and white photo, of Wayne, Martha Scott and Dale Evans, 1937 copyright 15.00
Standee, cardboard...................35.00

Ken Maynard
Autograph, 8" x 10" black and white glossy photo, black inked signature "Ken Maynard 1941"................125.00
Big Little Book
  Ken Maynard in Western Justice, Whitman, #1430, Irwin Myers, artist, Rex Loomis, author, 1938, standard size, 432 pgs, hard cover.......22.00
  Strawberry Roan, Saalfield, Universal Pictures, artist, Grace Mack, author, 1934, 4-3/4" x 5-1/4", 160 pgs, hard cover 22.00
Premium, photo, 9" x 11", color, black and white "In Old Santa Fe" scenes on back, Dixie 30.00

Kit Carson, gun and holder set...500.00

Lone Ranger First Aid Kit, American White Cross Labs, Inc., New Rochelle, NY, empty, $24.

Lone Ranger
Badge, deputy, secret compartment, secret folder 150.00
Belt, glow-in-the-dark............... 85.00
Caps, repeating roll, 1940s, orig box of 20 rolls, MIB...................... 35.00
Child's Outfit, red shirt, 1940s..................................... 100.00
Flashlight, pistol gun 45.00
Game, horseshoes................... 75.00
Gun, pressed steel................... 60.00
Holster, double, no guns......... 250.00
Insert, Bond Bread, 10¢ insert, uncut sheet, 1938............................... 85.00
Keychain, solid silver bullet 65.00
Membership Kit, letter, certificate, card, orig mailer, Merita Bread, 1939..................................... 125.00
Model, comic scenes, Aurora, MIB
  Lone Ranger.......................... 45.00
  Tonto, orig sealed box 75.00
Ped-O-Meter............................. 30.00
Pencil Sharpener, bullet shape, Merita Bread 40.00
Photo, 8" x 10", color, Lone Ranger and Tonto, facsimile autograph of Clayton Moore 25.00
Ring, gold plastic base, full color portrait against yellow background, sticker mounted on top, clear plastic cover missing, 1950s................. 20.00
Soap, Tonto, figural, Castile, c1940, MIB..................................... 120.00
Star, tin, Merita Bread............... 50.00
Toothbrush Holder, figural, 1930s..................................... 115.00
Toy, litho tin, Marx, Lone Ranger riding Silver, MIB.................... 725.00
Water Pistol, hard plastic, Durham, 1974, figural, MOC.................. 75.00

Maverick
Eras-O Picture Book, 1960, unused, sealed, MIB 100.00
Magazine, *TV Guide*, James Garner cover................................... 30.00

Rawhide, television storybook,
1962 ....60.00

Red Ryder
BB Gun, Daisy, 50th
Anniversary 90.00
Pocket Knife 450.00

Restless Gun
Book, Whitman, 1959 ....15.00
Comic, Dell, #1146 ....20.00
Game, board 60.00

Rin Tin Tin
Big Little Book, *Rin Tin Tin & The Hidden Treasure* 18.00
Comic Book, Dell, #12 ....15.00
Paint By Number, large 60.00
Ring, magic, instructions 450.00
Stuffed Toy, large 45.00
Wonda-Scope 85.00

Roy Rogers
Autograph, 8" x 10" color photo
Roy Rogers 55.00
Roy Rogers and Dale
Evans 65.00
Camera, Herbert George Co., orig
instructions, some damage to orig
box 250.00
Canteen Holder, gold lettering on
suede 95.00
Cereal Bowl, ceramic, 6-1/4" d ..85.00
Child's Book
Roy Rogers and the Desert Treasure, Alice Sankey, color ills by Paul
Souza, Whitman Cozy Corner
Book, 1954 ....20.00
*Roy Rogers and the Outlaws of
Sundown Valley,* Snowden Miller,
Whitman Pub., 1950, 250 pgs 13.50
Trigger to the Rescue 25.00
Dixie Ice Cream Picture
Dale Evans 50.00
Roy Rogers, 1938 ....60.00
Gloves, pr 150.00
Lunch Box, thermos, metal,
used 75.00
Magazine Cover, Roy, Dale and Trigger, *New York News,* 1958 ....48.00
Membership Card, photo, Del Comics, orig mailer 210.00
Mug, Quaker Oats, head
shape 50.00
Pinback Button
Bullet 25.00
Pat Brady 15.00
Roy's Brands 20.00
Roy's Guns 20.00
Sheriff 20.00
Trigger 25.00
Pocket Knife 100.00
Ring
Branding Iron 225.00
Hat, sterling 675.00
Magnifying 120.00
Microscope 125.00
Saddle, silver 450.00
Tie Slide, metal, 2" l, 1950s 30.00

Straight Arrow
Headband, 2" x 10-1/2" thin cardboard, 2 orig red feathers, Nabisco
premium, copyright 1949 ....65.00
Manual, 4" x 7", Straight Arrow Injunuity Manual, 72 pgs, copyright 1951
National Biscuit Co., red, white, and
blue cover, black and white
illus 35.00
Membership Card, 3" x 11-5/8", green
stiff cardboard, black text and artwork of sign language, copyright
1949 National Biscuit Co. 35.00

Patch, shoulder, 3" d, black, red, and
yellow, profile, Nabisco cereal premium, c1950 ....20.00
Premium Card, Straight Arrow Injunuity Index, 4" x 7-1/4" gray stiff paper,
Nabisco Shredded Wheat
Announcement Card, replacement
for card #19, Book #2, Poisonous
Snake Recognition 5.00
Book #1, 29 cards, blue accent art
and text, 1949 copyright, some age
discoloration 35.00
Book #2, missing card #35 of 36,
copyright 1950 ....35.00
Book #4, missing several cards,
copyright 1952 ....30.00
Ring
Arrow 65.00
Face 90.00
Nugget Cave 200.00

The Rifleman
Game, board 85.00
Magazine, *Guns,* Chuck Connors on
cover, article 55.00
Notepad, cover photo of Connors
and Crawford 45.00

Tim McCoy
Autograph, 8" x 10" glossy black and
white photo, purple inked signature
"Best Wishes Tim McCoy,"
c1940 ....75.00
Better Little Book, *Tim McCoy and the
Sandy Gulch Stampede,* Whitman,
#1490, 1939 ....40.00
Big Little Book, *The Prescott Kid,*
Whitman, #1152, Columbia Pictures,
artist, adapted by Eleanor Packer,
1935, 4-5/8" x 5-1/4", 160 pgs, hard
cover, soft spine 25.00
Lobby Poster, 11" x 14", set of eight,
1930s
Fighting Renegade 100.00
Straight Shooter 125.00
Premium, photo, 9" x 11", color,
black and white movie scenes on
back, Dixie 15.00

**Tom Mix, photo card, sepia
tone, 3-1/4" x 5-1/4", $24.**

Tom Mix
Arrowhead, Lucite 85.00
Badge
Straight Shooters, orig
mailer 150.00

Wrangler's 150.00
Decoder Badge, Six Shooter, 1930s
radio show premium 150.00
Fob, gold ore 65.00
Manual, secret writing 100.00
Pocket Knife, Straight Shooters, slight
use 40.00
Ring
Look Around, instructions, orig
mailer 225.00
Magnet, 1930s Ralston Radio show
premium 95.00
Mystery Picture, photo
missing 75.00
Siren, red TV film, instructions, orig
mailer 500.00
Sliding whistle, 1930s Ralston Radio
show premium 135.00
Straight Shooter 100.00
Telescope and Bird Call, Golden Bullet 75.00
Television Set, film, orig
mailer 100.00

Wagon Train
Magazine, *Look,* cast on
cover 20.00
Target Game, English, illus
box 195.00

Wild Bill Hickok
Game, Built-Rite 45.00
Gun and holster, double 500.00

Wyatt Earp
Badge, Marshall's, illus of Hugh
O'Brien on card, 1957 ....40.00
Book, *Wyatt Earp, U.S. Marshall,*
Stewart Holbrook, E. Richardson illus,
Hale Landmark Books, Random
House, 1956, 180 pgs 7.00
Hartland figure, 1958, played with
condition 100.00
Magazine, *TV Guide* 18.00
Paint Box 35.00
Record, "Wyatt Earp Sings," Hugh O'
Brien 35.00
Shirt, child's 40.00

Cracker Jack

Collecting Hints: Most collectors
concentrate on the pre-plastic era.
Toys in the original packaging are
very rare. One possibility for specializing is collecting toys from a given
decade, for example World War II soldiers, tanks, artillery pieces, and
other war-related items.

Many prizes are marked "Cracker
Jack" or carry a picture of the Sailor
Boy and Bingo, his dog. Unmarked
prizes can be confused with gumball
machine novelties or prizes from
Checkers, a rival firm.

History: F. W. Rueckheim, a popcorn
store owner in Chicago, introduced a
mixture of popcorn, peanuts, and
molasses at the World's Columbian
Exposition in 1893. Three years later
the name "Cracker Jack" was
applied to it. It gained popularity
quickly and by 1908 appeared in the

lyrics of "Take Me Out to the Ball Game."

In 1910, Rueckheim included on each box coupons which could be redeemed for prizes. In 1912, prizes were packaged directly in the boxes. The early prizes were made of paper, tin, lead, wood, and porcelain. Plastic prizes were introduced in 1948.

The Borden Company's Cracker Jack prize collection includes more than 10,000 examples; but this is not all of them. More examples are still to be found in drawer bottoms, old jewelry boxes, and attics.

Items currently included in the product boxes are largely paper, the plastic magnifying glass being one exception. The company buys toys in lots of 25 million and keeps hundreds of prizes in circulation at one time. Borden's annual production is about 400 million boxes.

Reference: Alex Jaramillo, *Cracker Jack Prizes*, Abbeville Press, 1989.

Collectors' Club: Cracker Jack Collectors Association, 108 Central St., Rowley, MA 01969.

Museum: Columbus Science Museum, Columbus, OH.

Badge, stud-type, Cracker Jack Junior Detective, dark charcoal luster finished metal, shield shape, c1920-30 .... 90.00
Baseball Score Counter, 3-1/2" 150.00
Bendee Figure, MOC 6.00
Book, *Cracker Jack Painting & Drawing Book*, Saalfield, 1917, 24 pgs ... 40.00
Booklet
    Chicago Expo, 1-1/2" x 2-1/2", 12 pgs, red, white, and blue Cracker Jack box illus, views of 1933 fair 120.00
    Cracker Jack in Switzerland, 4 pgs, 1926 copyright 50.00
    Cracker Jack Riddles, red, white, and blue, cov, 42 pgs, 1920s 60.00
Bookmark, 2-3/4" h, diecut litho tin, printed on one side with brown dog, solid gold flashing on back, 1930s 24.00
Box, 7" h, red, white, and blue cardboard, 1930s 40.00
Cereal Cup, Ralston 5.00
Clicker, aluminum, pear-shaped, 1949 .... 35.00
Coin, 1" d, Mystery Club, emb aluminum, presidential profile, back emb "Join Cracker Jack Mystery Club/Save This Coin," 1930s 20.00
Doll, 12" h, vinyl, Vogue Dolls, orig unopened display card, 1980 copyright 35.00
Fortune Wheel, still paper, two disk wheels joined by center grommet, red, white, and blue art and instruc-

tions, "Jack the Sailor Boy Says To Spell Your Name And Read Your Fortune," 1930s 35.00

Bookmark, tin litho, brown dog, white ground, $20.

Game, Cracker Jack Toy Surprise Game, Milton Bradley, orig box, 1976 .... 35.00
Lapel Stud
    Cracker Jack Air Corps, very dark luster, metal wings, 1930s 45.00
    Cracker Jack Police, dark finish, metal, star badge shape, 1930s 30.00
Lunch Box, metal, Aladdin Industries, c1979 .... 30.00
Pencil, 3-1/2" l, red name 15.00
Pin, Angelus Delivery Wagon, diecut, red, white, and blue litho, horse-drawn wagon, one side with Cracker Jack box, other side with Angelus Marshmallows box, roof inscribed "The More You Eat The More You Want," c1920 .... 95.00
Pinback
    Cracker Jack 5 Cents Candied Popcorn and Roasted Peanuts, multicolored portrait illus of young lady, 1-1/4" d, early 1900s 60.00
    Junior Jackie Club, blue sailor boy, white ground, red lettering, *Chicago Sunday Herald*, 1930s 40.00
    Junior Jackie Club, Little Sisters, blue sailor girl, white ground, red lettering, *Chicago Sunday Herald*, 1930 .. 40.00
    Portrait of Lady, Cracker Jack back paper, multicolored, early 1900s 85.00
Sailor Jack and Bingo, rim inscription for maker Cosmos Mfg Co., Chicago, 1920s 140.00
Pinball Game, MOC 6.00
Post Card, 3" x 5-1/2" d, Cracker Jack Bears #7, bears greeting President Roosevelt, 1907 postmark 25.00
Prize Toy
    Battleship, red enameled white metal, portholes on both sides 17.50

Binoculars, dark finish white metal 12.00
Carnival Barker, black, white, and red litho, stand-up turning chance wheel 50.00
Gun, Smith & Wesson .38 replica, black finish white metal 20.00
Magic Dots, Game No. 2, 1930s, red, white, and blue paper, 1-1/2" x 2-1/2" 15.00
Magnet, silvered wire horseshoe magnet, orig red and white marked "Made in Japan" paper wrapper 15.00
Man's Shoe, dark finish white metal, hobnail sole design 30.00
Model T Touring Car, dark finish white metal 35.00
Owl, red, blue, and yellow emb stiff paper stand-up, marked "Cracker Jack" 40.00
Pocket Watch, dark silver luster white metal, ornate back, 9:27 time ... 30.00
Pocket Watch, dark silver luster white metal, plain back, 4:00 time 35.00
Rocking Chair, yellow enameled litho tin doll furniture chair, curved slat back 20.00
Rocking Horse, dark blue wash tint 20.00
Scottie, bright silver luster white metal 25.00
Spinner Top, red, white, and blue litho, Cracker Jack mystery toy box 35.00
Tank Corps No. 57, diecut, dark olive green, black litho tin tank, c1930-40 .... 40.00
Train Engine, dark white metal, engine and joined coal car 20.00
Train Passenger Car, litho tin, black and yellow, 1930s, some rust ... 25.00
Watch, litho tin, pocket watch, gold flashing, black and white dial, 1930s 50.00
Whistle, green enameled tin, top side inscribed "Close End with Fingers" 35.00

Stand-Up, litho tin
    Lion, green and black, unmarked, 1930s 70.00
    Sailboat Prize, red, white, and blue, mkd "DM 38," and "Dowst Mfg, Chicago, U.S.A.," unmarked, lightly rubbed, 1930s 40.00
Smitty, full color, white background, dark green rim, 1930s 80.00
Tilt Card, sq cardboard, flicker image of sailor passing ball from one hand to the other, back mkd "Tilt Card To And Fro" and Cracker Jack marking, Borden, Inc., Columbus, 1950s 12.00
Watch, litho, 1940s, near mint 75.00

Degenhart Glass

Collecting Hints: Degenhart pressed glass novelties are collected by mold (Forget-Me-Not toothpick holders or all Degenhart toothpick holders), by individual colors (Rubina or Bloody Mary), or by group colors (opaque, iridescent, crystal, or slag).

Correct color identification is a key factor when collecting Degenhart glass. Because of the slight variations in the hundreds of colors produced at the Degenhart Crystal Art Glass factory from 1947 to 1978, it is important for beginning collectors to learn to distinguish Degenhart colors, particularly the green and blue variations. Seek guidance from knowledgeable collectors or dealers. Side-by-side color comparison is extremely helpful.

Later glass produced by the factory can be distinguished by the "D" in a heart trademark or a "D" by itself on molds, where there was insufficient space for the full mark. Use of the "D" mark began around 1972, and by late 1977, most of the molds had been marked. From c1947 to 1972, pieces were not marked except for owls and the occasional piece hand stamped with a block letter "D" as it came out of the mold. This hand stamping was used from 1967 to 1972.

Collecting unmarked Degenhart glass made from 1947 to c1970 poses no problem once a collector becomes familiar with the molds and colors which were used during that period. Some of the most desirable colors, such as Amethyst & White Slag, Amethyst Carnival, and Custard Slag, are unmarked. Keep in mind that some colors, e.g., Custard (opaque yellow), Heliotrope (opaque purple), and Tomato (opaque orange red), were used repeatedly, and both marked and unmarked pieces can be found, depending on production date.

History: John (1884-1964) and Elizabeth (1889-1978) Degenhart operated the Crystal Art Glass factory of Cambridge, Ohio, from 1947 to 1978. The factory specialized in reproduction pressed glass novelties and paperweights. More than 50 molds were worked by this factory including ten toothpick holders, five salts, and six animal-covered dishes of various sizes.

When the factory ceased operation, many of the molds were purchased by Boyd Crystal Art Glass, Cambridge, Ohio. Boyd has issued pieces in many new colors and has marked them all with a "B" in a diamond.

References: Gene Florence, *Degenhart Glass and Paperweights,* Degenhart Paperweight and Glass Museum, 1982.

Collectors' Club: Friends of Degenhart, Degenhart Paperweight and Glass Museum, Inc, 65323 Highland Hills Rd, P.O. Box 186, Cambridge, OH 43725.

Museum: The Degenhart Paperweight and Glass Museum, Inc, Cambridge, OH. The museum displays all types of Ohio valley glass.

Reproduction Alert: Although most of the Degenhart molds were reproductions themselves, there are contemporary pieces that can be confusing, such as Kanawha's bird salt and bow slipper; L. G. Wright's mini-slipper, Daisy & Button salt, and 5-inch robin-covered dish; and many other contemporary American pieces. The 3-inch-bird salt and mini-pitcher also are made by an unknown glassmaker in Taiwan.

Priscilla, Degenhart Green, $60.

Bell, 1976, lavender 12.00
Bernard and Eldena, 7/8" w, 2-3/4" h, price for pr
    Amethyst Carnival 15.00
    Cobalt Carnival 15.00

Cranberry Ice Carnival 18.00
Crystal Carnival 15.00
Green Carnival 15.00
Ice Blue Carnival 15.00
Boot, 2-1/2" h, black slag, "D" in heart mark 25.00
Candy Jar, cov, amberina 24.00
Child's Mug, Stork and Peacock.... 25.00
Coaster, intro 1974, mkd 1975, crystal 9.00
Creamer and Sugar, Daisy and Button, carnival 45.00
Cup Plate
    Heart and Lyre, mulberry 18.00
    Seal of Ohio, sunset 15.00
Hand, mkd, Crown Tuscan 22.00
Hat, Daisy and Button
    Amber.. 12.00
    Amberina 20.00
    Blue 18.00
Hen, covered dish, ebony, 3-1/2"... 24.00
Jewel Box, heart shape, blue 38.00
Owl, 1-3/4" w, 3-1/2" h, introduced 1967, large "D" mark
    Antique Blue.............................. 45.00
    Cobalt Blue Carnival 125.00
    Dark Rose Marie........................ 45.00
    Emerald Green 45.00
    Light Bluefire 45.00
    Midnight Sun 45.00
    Purple Slag............................... 35.00
    Tiger 45.00
Paperweight, early 1950s, John Degenhart
    2-1/2" d, 2-1/2" h, five multicolored flowers, each with controlled bubble center 175.00
    3" d, 3" h, dark blue flower, green ground 250.00
    3-1/4" d, multicolored floral bouquet 250.00
Pooch
    Amethyst.................................... 40.00
    Baby Green 22.00
    Bittersweet................................ 15.50
    Brown 15.00
    Canary 17.50
    Charcoal 20.25
    Cobalt Blue............................... 28.00
    Fawn 17.50
    Henri Blue................................. 15.50
    Heather Bloom 27.50
    Milk Glass, blue........................ 15.50
    Periwinkle 31.00
    Rosemary Pink 18.00
    Royal Violet............................... 24.00
Portrait Dish, portrait of Elizabeth Degenhart, 5-1/2" d, emb name and "First Lady of Glass"
    Amethyst.................................... 50.00
    Clear 30.00
Priscilla, Rose Marie, June, 1976... 65.00

Robin, covered dish, Taffeta, mkd..55.00
Salt and Pepper Shakers, pr, bird, sapphire...............18.00
Tomahawk, 2" w, 3-3/4" l, "D" in heart mark
  Amethyst Carnival.....................18.00
  Chocolate Slag 15.00
  Cobalt Blue 15.00
  Crystal Carnival 15.00
  Pink Carnival 15.00
Toothpick Holder
  Basket, milk glass, white 18.00
  Beaded Heart, lemon custard ...20.00
  Colonial Drape and Heart, custard.......................20.00
  Elephant's Head, jade...............24.00
  Forget-Me-Not, Bloody Mary.....24.00
Wine Glass, Buzz Saw
  Cobalt Blue 20.00
  Milk Glass, blue 22.00
  Vaseline.....................................20.00

Depression Glass

Collecting Hint: Many collectors specialize in one pattern; others collect by a particular color.

History: Depression glass was made from 1920 to 1940. It was an inexpensive machine-made glass and was produced by several companies in various patterns and colors. The number of forms made in different patterns also varied.

The colors varied from company to company. The number of items made in each pattern also varied. Knowing the proper name of a pattern is the key to collecting. Collectors should be prepared to do research.

References: Tom and Neila Bredehoft, *Fifty Years of Collectible Glass, 1920-1970,* Antique Trader Books, Volume I (1997), Volume II (2000); Gene Florence, *Anchor Hocking's Fire-King and More,* 2nd ed., Collector Books, 2000; —, *Collectible Glassware from the 40's, 50's, 60's,* 5th ed., Collector Books, 2000; —, *Collector's Encyclopedia of Depression Glass,* 14th ed., Collector Books, 2000; —, *Elegant Glassware of the Depression Era,* 8th ed., Collector Books, 1999; —, *Florence's Glassware Pattern Identification Guide, Vol. II,* Collector Books, 2000; —, *Glass Candlesticks of the Depression Era,* Collector Books, 1999; —, *Kitchen Glassware of the Depression Era, 6th Edition,* Collector Books, 2000; —, *Pocket Guide to Depression Glass & More, 1920-1960s,* 11th ed., Collector Books, 1999; —, *Stemware Identification Featuring Cordials with Values, 1920s–1960s,* Collector Books, 1997; —, *Very Rare Glassware of the Depression Era,* 1st Series (1988, 1991 value update), 2nd Series (1991), 3rd Series (1993), 4th Series (1996), 5th Series (1996), 6th Series (1999), Collector Books; Phillip Hopper, *Forest Green Glass,* Schiffer Publishing, 2000; Joe Keller and David Ross, *Jadite: An Identification and Price Guide,* 2nd ed., Schiffer Publishing, 2000; Jim and Barbara Mauzy, *Mauzy's Comprehensive Handbook of Depression Glass Prices,* 2nd ed., Schiffer, 2000; James Measell and Berry Wiggins, *Great American Glass of the Roaring 20s & Depression Era,* Book 2, Antique Publications, 2000; Sherry Riggs and Paul Pendergrass, *20th Century Glass Candle Holders: Roaring 20s, Depression Era, and Modern Collectible Candle Holders,* Schiffer Publishing, 1999; Ellen T. Schroy, *Warman's Depression Glass,* 2nd ed., Krause Publications, 2000; Hazel Marie Weatherman, *Colored Glassware of the Depression Era,* Book 2, published by author 1974, available in reprint; —, *1984 Supplement & Price Trends for Colored Glassware of the Depression Era, Book 1,* published by author, 1984; Doris Yeske, *Depression Glass,* 4th ed., Schiffer Publishing, 2000.

Periodicals: *Fire-King News,* P.O. Box 473, Addison, AL 35540; *Kitchen Antiques & Collectible News,* 4645 Laurel Ridge Dr., Harrisburg, PA 17110; *The Daze, Inc.,* P.O. Box 57, Otisville, MI 48463.

Collectors' Clubs: Big "D" Pression Glass Club, 10 Windling Creek Trail, Garland, TX 75043; Buckeye Dee Geer's, 2501 Campbell St., Sandusky, OH 44870; Canadian Depression Glass Club, P.O. Box 104, Mississaugua, Ontario L53 2K1 Canada; Clearwater Depression Glass Club, 10038 62nd Terrace North, St. Petersburg, FL 33708; Crescent City Depression Glass Club, 140 Commerce St., Gretna, LA 70056; Depression Era Glass Society of Wisconsin, 1534 S. Wisconsin Ave., Racine, WI 53403; Depression Glass Club of Greater Rochester, P.O. Box 10362, Rochester, NY 14610; Depression Glass Club of North East Florida, 2604 Jolly Rd, Jacksonville, FL 33207; Fostoria Glass Collectors, Inc., P.O. Box 1625, Orange, CA 92668; Greater Tulsa Depression Era Glass Club, P.O. Box 470763, Tulsa, OK 74147-0763; Heart of America Glass Collectors, 14404 E. 36th Ter., Independence, MO, 64055; Illinois Valley Depression Glass Club, RR 1, Box 52, Rushville, IL 62681; Iowa Depression Glass Assoc., 5871 Vista Dr., Apt. 725, West Des Moines, IA 50266; Land of Sunshine Depression Glass Club, P.O. Box 560275, Orlando, FL 32856-0275; Lincoln Land Depression Glass Club, 1625 Dial Court, Springfield, IL 62704; National Depression Glass Assoc., Inc., P.O. Box 8264, Wichita, KS 67209; Northeast Florida Depression Glass Club, P.O. Box 338, Whitehouse, FL 32220; North Jersey Dee Geer's, 82 High St., Butler, NJ 07405; Peach State Depression Glass Club, 4174 Reef Rd., Marietta, GA 30066; Phoenix and Consolidated Glass Collectors' Club, P.O. Box 182082, Arlington, TX 76096-2082; Southern Illinois Diamond H Seekers, 1203 N. Yale, O'Fallon, IL 62269; 20-30-40 Society, Inc., P.O. Box 856, LaGrange, IL 60525; Western Reserve Depression Glass Club, 8669 Courtland Drive, Strongsville, OH 44136.

Website: *DG Shopper Online,* The WWW Depression Era Glass Magazine, http://www.dgshopper.com; *Mega Show,* http://www.glassshow.com; *Facets Antiques & Collectibles Mall,* http://www.Facets.net

Reproduction Alert: Reproductions of Depression Glass patterns can be a real problem. Some are easy to detect, but others are very good. Now that there are reproductions of the reproductions, the only hope for collectors is to know what they are buying and to buy from reputable dealers and/or other collectors. Most of the current Depression Glass reference books have excellent sections on reproductions. The following items with an † have been reproduced, but beware that they are more reproductions being brought into the marketplace.

Refer to *Antique Trader Guide to Fakes & Reproductions* by Mark Chervenka (Krause Publications, 2000) for good solid information about reproductions.

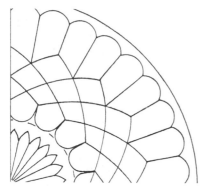

Aunt Polly

Manufactured by U.S. Glass Company, Pittsburgh, PA, in the late 1920s. Made in blue, green, and iridescent.

Item	Blue	Green or Iridescent
Berry Bowl, 4-3/4" d, ind	18.50	9.00
Berry Bowl, 7-1/8" d, master	45.00	22.00
Bowl, 4-3/4" d, 2" h	—	15.00
Bowl, 5-1/2" d, one handle	25.00	15.00
Bowl, 8-3/8" l, oval	100.00	42.00
Butter Dish, cov	215.00	200.00
Candy Jar, cov, 2 handles	42.00	30.00
Candy Jar, ftd, 2 handles	—	27.50
Creamer	48.00	32.00
Pickle, 7-1/4" l, oval, handle	42.00	17.50
Pitcher, 48 oz, 8" h	175.00	—
Plate, 6" d, sherbet	12.00	6.00
Plate, 8" d, luncheon	20.00	—
Salt and Pepper Shakers, pr	220.00	—
Sherbet	15.00	12.00
Sugar	48.00	32.00
Tumbler, 8 oz, 3-5/8" h	30.00	—
Vase, 6-1/2" h, ftd	48.00	30.00

Cherryberry

Manufactured by U. S. Glass Company, Pittsburgh, Pennsylvania, early 1930s. Made in crystal, green, iridescent, and pink.

Item	Crystal or Iridescent	Green or Pink
Berry Bowl, 4" d	7.00	8.75
Berry Bowl, 7-1/2" d, deep	17.50	20.00
Bowl, 6-1/4" d, 2" deep	40.00	55.00
Butter Dish, cov	150.00	175.00

Comport, 5-3/4"	17.50	25.00
Creamer, large, 4-5/8"	40.00	45.00
Creamer, small	15.00	20.00
Olive Dish, 5" l, one handle	10.00	15.00
Pickle Dish, 8-1/4" l, oval	10.00	15.00
Pitcher, 7-3/4" h	165.00	175.00
Plate, 6" d, sherbet	6.50	11.00
Plate, 7-1/2" d, salad	8.50	15.00
Salad Bowl, 6-1/2" d, deep	17.50	22.00
Sherbet	9.00	10.00
Sugar, large, cov	45.00	75.00
Sugar, small, open	15.00	20.00
Tumbler, 9 oz, 3-5/8" h	20.00	35.00

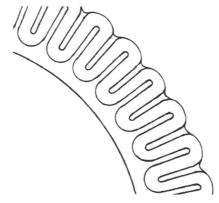

Christmas Candy, No. 624.

Manufactured by Indiana Glass Company, Dunkirk, Indiana, 1950s. Made in crystal and Terrace Green (teal).

Item	Crystal	Terrace Green
Bowl, 5-3/4" d	6.50	—
Creamer	15.00	27.50
Cup	8.00	35.00
Mayonnaise, ladle, liner	24.00	—
Plate, 6" d, bread and butter	6.00	16.00

Plate, 8-1/4" d, luncheon	8.00	28.00
Plate, 9-5/8"d, dinner	12.00	36.00
Sandwich Plate, 11-1/4" d	24.00	65.00
Saucer	5.00	15.00
Soup Bowl, 7-3/8" d.	12.00	75.00
Sugar	15.00	35.00
Tidbit, 2 tier	20.00	—
Vegetable Bowl, 9-1/2" d	—	235.00

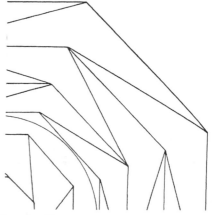

Cracked Ice

Manufactured by Indiana Glass, Dunkirk, Indiana, in the 1930s. Made in pink and green. Often mistaken for Tea Room, look for the additional diagonal line, giving it a more Art Deco style.

Item	Green	Pink
Creamer	30.00	35.00
Plate, 6-1/2" d	15.00	18.00
Sherbet	12.00	15.00
Sugar, cov	30.00	35.00
Tumbler	15.00	18.00

Daisy, No. 620

Manufactured by Indiana Glass Company, Dunkirk, Indiana, from late 1930s to 1980s. Made in amber (1940s), crystal (1933-40), dark green (1960s-80s), fired-on red (late 1930s), and milk glass (1960s-80s).

Item	Amber or Fired-On Red	Crystal, Dark Green or Milk White
Berry Bowl, 4-1/2" d.	9.50	6.00
Berry Bowl, 7-3/8" d deep	17.50	9.50
Berry Bowl, 9-3/8" d, deep	35.00	14.00
Cake Plate, 11-1/2" d	16.50	14.00
Cereal Bowl, 6" d	25.00	10.00
Cream Soup Bowl, 4-1/2" d	13.50	7.50
Creamer, ftd	10.00	8.00
Cup	6.50	6.00
Plate, 6" d, sherbet	3.00	2.50
Plate, 7-3/8" d, salad	7.50	4.50
Plate, 8-3/8" d, luncheon	8.50	6.00
Plate, 9-3/8" d, dinner	10.00	8.00
Plate, 10-3/8" d, grill	15.00	8.00
Plate, 10-3/8" d, grill, indent for soup	15.00	8.00
Platter, 10-3/4" d	15.00	11.00
Relish Dish, 8-3/8" d, 3 part	22.00	12.00
Sandwich Plate, 11-1/2" d	17.50	14.00
Saucer	2.00	2.00
Sherbet, ftd	9.00	5.00
Sugar, ftd	10.00	8.00
Tumbler, 9 oz, ftd	16.00	10.00
Tumbler, 12 oz, ftd	40.00	15.00
Vegetable Bowl, 10" l, oval	18.00	12.00

Doric

Manufactured by Jeannette Glass Company, Jeannette, Pennsylvania, from 1935 to 1938. Made in Delphite, green, pink, and yellow (rare).

Item	Delphite	Green or Pink
Berry Bowl, 4-1/2" d	45.00	12.00
Berry Bowl, 8-1/4" d	135.00	25.00
Bowl, 9" d, two handles		45.00
Butter Dish, cov	—	90.00
Cake Plate, 10" d, 3 legs		30.00
Candy Dish, cov, 8" d	—	42.50
Candy Dish, three part	10.00	9.50
Cereal Bowl, 5-1/2" d	—	65.00
Coaster, 3" d	—	28.00
Cream Soup, 5" d, 2 handles		385.00
Creamer, 4" h	—	17.00
Cup	—	10.00
Plate, 6" d, sherbet	—	7.50
Plate, 7" d, salad	—	20.00
Plate, 9" d, dinner	—	24.00
Plate, 9" d, grill	—	20.00
Platter, 12" l, oval	—	32.00
Relish Tray, 4 x 4"	—	12.00
Relish Tray, 4 x 8"	—	10.00
Salt and Pepper Shakers, pr		40.00
Saucer	—	7.00
Sherbet, footed	10.00	17.50
Sugar, cov		35.00
Tray, 8" x 8", serving	—	30.00
Tray, 10" l, handle	—	25.00
Tumbler, 9 oz, 4-1/2" h, flat		100.00
Tumbler, 10 oz, 4" h, ftd.		90.00
Tumbler, 12 oz, 5" h, ftd.	—	125.00
Vegetable Bowl, 9" l, oval	—	35.00

Early American Prescut

Manufactured by Anchor Hocking Glass Corporation, Lancaster, Ohio, from 1960 to 1999. Made in crystal with some limited production in colors.

Item	Crystal
Ashtray, 4" d	4.00
Ashtray, 5" d	8.00
Ashtray, 7-3/4" d	12.00
Basket, 6" x 4-1/2"	20.00
Bowl, 4-1/4" d, plain rim	20.00
Bowl, 4-1/4" d, scalloped	7.50
Bowl, 5-1/4" d, scalloped	7.50
Bowl, 6-3/4" d, 3 legs	5.00
Bowl, 7-1/4" d, scalloped	18.50
Bowl, 8-3/4" d	9.00
Bowl, 9" d, oval	8.00
Bowl, 11-3/4" d, paneled	200.00
Bud Vase, 5" h, ftd	295.00
Butter, cov, 1/4 lb	7.50
Butter, cov, metal handle, knife	15.00
Cake Plate	25.00
Candlesticks, pr, 2-lite	28.50
Candy, cov, 5-1/4"	12.00
Candy, cov, 7-1/4"	14.50
Chip and Dip, 10-1/4" bowl, metal holder	25.00
Coaster	4.00
Cocktail Shaker, 30 oz	300.00
Console Bowl, 9" d	15.00
Creamer	3.50
Creamer and Sugar Tray	3.00
Cruet, os	9.50
Dessert Bowl, 5-3/8" d	3.00
Deviled Egg Plate, 11-3/4" d	42.00
Gondola Dish, 9-1/2" l	4.50
Hostess Tray, 6-1/2" x 12"	14.00
Iced Tea Tumbler, 15 oz, 6" h	20.00
Juice Tumbler, 5 oz, 4' h	5.00
Lamp, oil	250.00
Lazy Susan, 9 pcs	60.00
Pitcher, 18 oz	12.00
Pitcher, 40 oz, sq	60.00
Pitcher, 60 oz	20.00
Plate, 6-3/4" d, salad	55.00
Plate, 6-3/4" d, snack, ring for cup	40.00
Plate, 10" d, snack	15.00
Plate, 11" d	15.00
Punch Cup	3.00
Punch Set, 15 pcs	35.00
Relish, 2-part, 10" l, tab handle	7.50
Relish, 3-part, 8-1/2" l, oval	6.50
Relish, 5-part, 13-1/2" d	30.00
Salad Bowl, 10-3/4" d	15.00
Salt and Pepper Shakers, pr, ind size	72.00
Salt and Pepper Shakers, pr, metal tops	10.00
Salt and Pepper Shakers, pr, plastic tops	12.00
Serving Plate, 11" d, 4 part	90.00
Serving Plate, 13-1/2" d	15.00
Sherbet, 6 oz	90.00
Snack Cup	3.00
Sugar, cov	4.50
Syrup Pitcher, 12 oz	24.00
Tumbler, 10 oz, 4-1/2" h	6.50
Vase, 8-1/2" h	8.00
Vase, 10" h	15.00

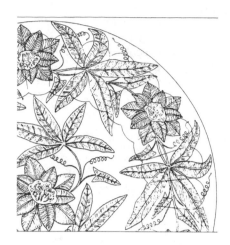

Floral, Poinsettia

Manufactured by Jeannette Glass Company, Jeannette, Pennsylvania, from 1931- to 1935. Made in amber, crystal, Delphite, green, Jadite, pink, red, and yellow. Production in amber, crystal, Jadite, red, and yellow was very limited.

Reproductions: † Reproduction salt and pepper shakers have been made in cobalt blue, dark green, green, pink, and red.

Item	Delphite	Green or Pink
Berry Bowl, 4" d	40.00	25.00
Butter Dish, cov	—	95.00
Candlesticks, pr, 4" h	—	90.00
Candy Jar, cov	80.00	45.00
Canister Set	—	—
Casserole, cov	—	45.00
Coaster, 3-1/4" d	—	15.00
Creamer, flat	—	24.00
Cup	—	15.00
Dresser Tray, 9-1/4" l, oval	—	200.00
Juice Tumbler, ftd	—	24.00
Juice Tumbler, 5 oz, 4" h, flat	—	35.00
Lamp	—	275.00
Lemonade Pitcher, 48 oz, 10-1/4" h	—	265.00
Lemonade Tumbler, 9 oz, 5-1/4" h, ftd	—	60.00
Pitcher, 23 or 24 oz, 5-1/2" h	—	50.00
Pitcher, 32 oz, ftd, cone, 8" h	—	36.00
Plate, 6" d, sherbet	—	8.50
Plate, 8" d, salad	—	15.00
Plate, 9" d, dinner	145.00	30.00
Plate, 9" d, grill	—	185.00
Plate, 10-3/4" l, oval	—	20.00
Platter, 11" l	150.00	25.00
Refrigerator Dish, cov, 5" sq	65.00	65.00
Relish, 2 part oval	165.00	24.00
Rose Bowl, 3 legs	—	500.00
Salad Bowl, 7-1/2" d	—	40.00
Salad Bowl, 7-1/2" d, ruffled	65.00	125.00
Salt and Pepper Shakers, pr, 4" h, ftd †	—	45.00
Saucer	—	12.50
Sherbet	90.00	20.00
Sugar, cov	—	26.00
Sugar, open	75.00	—
Tray, 6" sq, closed handles	—	195.00
Tumbler, 3 oz, 3-1/2" h, ftd	—	18.00
Tumbler, 7 oz, 4-1/2", ftd	175.00	25.00
Tumbler, 5-1/4" h, ftd	—	60.00
Vase, flared, 3 legs	—	485.00
Vase, 6-7/8" h	—	475.00
Vegetable Bowl, 8" d, cov	—	50.00
Vegetable Bowl, 8" d, open	80.00	—
Vegetable Bowl, 9" l, oval	—	35.00

[illustration of Fortune pattern fan motif]

Fortune

Manufactured by Hocking Glass Company, Lancaster, Ohio, from 1937 to 1938. Made in crystal and pink.

Item	Crystal	Pink
Berry Bowl, 4" d	5.00	6.00
Berry Bowl, 7-3/4" d	15.00	15.00
Bowl, 4-1/2" d, handle	4.50	4.50
Bowl, 5-1/4" d, rolled edge	6.00	6.50
Candy Dish, cov, flat	22.50	25.00
Cup	7.50	10.00
Dessert Bowl, 4-1/2" d	5.00	5.00
Juice Tumbler, 5 oz, 3-1/2" h	8.00	10.00
Plate, 6" d, salad	5.00	12.50
Plate, 8" d, luncheon	17.50	17.50
Salad Bowl, 7-3/4" d	15.00	15.00
Saucer	4.00	6.50
Tumbler, 9 oz, 4" h	12.00	12.50

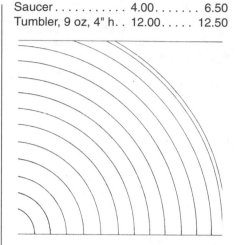

Manhattan, Horizontal Ribbed

Manufactured by Anchor Hocking Glass Company, from 1938 to 1943. Made in crystal, green, iridized, pink, and ruby. Ruby pieces are limited to relish tray inserts, currently valued at $8.00 each. Green and iridized production was limited to ftd tumblers, currently valued at $17.50. Anchor Hocking introduced a similar pattern, Park Avenue, in 1987. Anchor Hocking was very careful to preserve the Manhattan pattern. Collectors should pay careful attention to measurements if they are uncertain of the pattern.

Item	Crystal	Pink
Ashtray, 4" d, round	12.00	10.00
Ashtray, 4-1/2" w, sq	25.00	—
Berry Bowl, 5-3/8" d, handles	20.00	24.00
Berry Bowl, 7-1/2" d	24.00	—
Bowl, 4-1/2" d	9.00	—
Bowl, 8" d, closed handles	28.00	25.00
Bowl, 8" d, metal handle	25.00	—
Bowl, 9-1/2" d, handle	—	45.00
Candlesticks, pr, 4-1/2" h	25.00	—
Candy Dish, 3 legs	—	16.00
Candy Dish, cov	40.00	—
Cereal Bowl, 5-1/4" d, no handles	45.00	—
Coaster, 3-1/2"	19.50	—
Cocktail	15.00	—
Comport, 5-3/4" h	32.00	40.00
Creamer, oval	9.00	17.50
Cup	20.00	160.00
Fruit Bowl, 9-1/2" d, 2 open handles	40.00	35.00
Juice Pitcher, 24 oz	35.00	—
Pitcher, 80 oz, tilted	55.00	85.00
Plate, 6" d, sherbet	7.00	50.00
Plate, 8-1/2" d, salad	24.00	—

Plate, 10-1/4" d, dinner
 . . . . 30.00 . . . . 120.00
Relish Tray Insert . . . 2.50 . . . . 6.00
Relish Tray, 14" d, inserts
 . . . . 40.00 . . . . . 50.00
Relish Tray, 14" d, 4 part
 . . . . 65.00 . . . . —
Salad Bowl, 9" d . . . . 20.00 . . . . —
Salt and Pepper Shakers, pr, 2" h, sq
 . . . . 50.00 . . . . . 48.00
Sandwich Plate, 14" d
 . . . . 22.00 . . . . —
Sauce Bowl, 4-1/2" d, handles
 . . . . 12.00 . . . . —
Saucer . . . . 7.00 . . . . . 50.00
Sherbet . . . . 13.50 . . . . . 15.00
Sugar, oval . . . . 12.00 . . . . 17.50
Tumbler, 10 oz, 5-1/4" h, ftd
 . . . . 16.00 . . . . . 25.00
Vase, 8" h . . . . 20.00 . . . . —
Wine, 3-1/2" h . . . . . 15.00 . . . . —

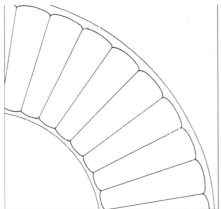

National

Manufactured by Jeannette Glass Company, Jeannette, Pennsylvania, from the late 1940s to the mid 1950s. Made in crystal, pink, and shell pink.

Item	Crystal
Ashtray	4.50
Berry Bowl, 4-1/2" d	4.00
Berry Bowl, 8-1/2" d	8.00
Bowl, 12" d	15.00
Candleholders, pr	30.00
Candy Dish, cov, ftd	20.00
Cigarette Box	15.00
Creamer	6.50
Creamer and Sugar Tray	6.00
Cup	4.00
Jar, cov	15.00
Lazy Susan	40.00
Milk Pitcher, 20 oz	20.00
Plate, 8" d	6.50
Punch Bowl Stand	10.00
Punch Bowl, 12" d	25.00
Punch Cup	3.50
Relish, 3-part	15.00
Salt and Pepper Shakers, pr	10.00

Saucer 1.00
Serving Plate, 15" d 17.50
Tray, 2 handles 17.50
Tumbler, ftd 8.50
Vase, 9" .20.00
Water Pitcher, 64 oz 30.00

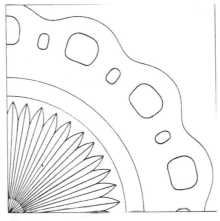

Old Colony, Lace Edge, Open Lace

Manufactured by Hocking Glass Company, Lancaster, Ohio, from 1935 to 1938. Made in crystal and pink.

Item	Pink
Bonbon, cov	.65.00
Bowl, 9-1/2" d, plain	.38.50
Bowl, 9-1/2" d, ribbed	.32.00
Butter Dish, cov	.65.00
Candlesticks, pr	125.00
Candy Jar, cov, ribbed	.65.00
Cereal Bowl, 6-3/8" d	.24.00
Comport, 7" d, cov	.60.00
Comport, 9" d	675.00
Console Bowl, 10-1/2" d, 3 legs	.250.00
Cookie Jar, cov	.75.00
Creamer	.25.00
Cup	.24.00
Flower Bowl, crystal frog	.30.00
Plate, 7-1/4" d, salad	.27.50
Plate, 8-1/4" d, luncheon	.32.00
Plate, 10-1/2" d, dinner	.36.00
Plate, 10-1/2" d, grill	.28.00
Plate, 13" d, 4 part, solid lace . . .	.65.00
Plate, 13" d, solid lace	.65.00
Platter, 12-3/4" l	.42.00
Platter, 12-3/4" l, 5 part	.40.00
Relish Dish, 7-1/2" d, 3 part, deep	60.00
Relish Plate, 10-1/2" d, 3 part . . .	.25.00
Salad Bowl, 7-3/4" d, ribbed	.60.00
Saucer	.15.00
Sherbet, ftd	112.00
Sugar	.25.00
Tumbler, 5 oz, 3-1/2" h, flat	120.00
Tumbler, 9 oz, 4-1/2" h, flat	.22.00
Tumbler, 10-1/2 oz, 5" h, ftd	.95.00

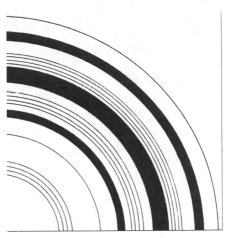

Ring, Banded Rings

Manufactured by Hocking Glass Company, Lancaster, Ohio, from 1927 to 1933. Made in crystal, crystal with rings of black, blue, pink, red, orange, silver, and yellow; green, Mayfair blue, pink, and red. Prices for decorated pieces are quite similar to each other.

Item	Crystal	Decorated or Green
Berry Bowl, 5" d	4.00	. . . . . . 9.00
Berry Bowl, 8" d	7.50	. . . . . 16.00
Bowl, 5-1/4" d, divided	12.50	. . . . . . —
Butter Tub	24.00	. . . . 25.00
Cereal Bowl	—	. . . . . 5.00
Cocktail Shaker	20.00	. . . . . 30.00
Cocktail, 3-1/2 oz, 3-3/4" h	12.00	. . . . 18.00
Creamer, ftd	5.00	. . . . . 10.00
Cup	5.00	. . . . . 3.00
Decanter, stopper . .	25.00	. . . . 35.00
Goblet, 9 oz, 7-1/4" h	7.00	. . . . 14.00
Ice Bucket	20.00	. . . . 33.00
Ice Tub	24.00	. . . . 25.00
Iced Tea Tumbler, 6-1/2" h	8.00	. . . . 15.00
Juice Tumbler, 3-1/2" h, ftd	6.50	. . . . 10.00
Old Fashioned Tumbler, 8 oz, 4" h	15.00	. . . . 17.50
Pitcher, 60 oz, 8" h . .	22.00	. . . . 25.00
Pitcher, 80 oz, 8-1/2" h	25.00	. . . . 30.00
Plate, 6-1/2" d, off-center ring	5.00	. . . . . 8.50
Plate, 6-1/4" d, sherbet	3.00	. . . . 4.50
Plate, 8" d, luncheon	3.00	. . . . . 7.00
Salt and Pepper Shakers, pr, 3" h	20.00	. . . . 40.00
Sandwich Plate, 11-3/4" d	8.00	. . . . 15.00
Sandwich Server, center handle	15.00	. . 27.50

Saucer . . . . 1.50 . . . . . . 2.50

Sherbet, 4-3/4" h . . . 5.00 . . . . . 10.00

Sherbet, flat, 6-1/2" d underplate
. . . . 12.00 . . . . . 18.00

Soup Bowl, 7" d . . . . 10.00 . . . . . 9.00

Sugar, ftd . . . . 5.00 . . . . . 10.00

Tumbler, 4 oz, 3" h . . 4.00 . . . . . . 6.50

Tumbler, 5-1/2" h, ftd
. . . . 6.00 . . . . . 10.00

Tumbler, 5 oz, 3-1/2" h
. . . . 6.50 . . . . . 6.50

Tumbler, 9 oz, 4-1/4" h
. . . . 7.50 . . . . . 7.00

Tumbler, 10 oz, 4-3/4" h
. . . . 8.50 . . . . . —

Tumbler, 12 oz, 5-1/8" h, ftd
. . . . 10.00 . . . . . 12.00

Vase, 8" h. . . . . 20.00 . . . . . 35.00

Whiskey, 1-1/2 oz, 2" h
. . . . 8.50 . . . . . 10.00

Wine, 3-1/2 oz, 4-1/2" h
. . . . 17.50 . . . . . 20.00

Round Robin

Unknown maker, early 1930s. Made in crystal, iridescent, and green. Crystal, produced as the base for iridescent pieces, is found occasionally and is valued slightly less than Iridescent.

Item	Iridescent	Green
Berry Bowl, 4" d 5.00		6.00
Creamer, ftd. 7.50		8.50
Cup 7.50		8.00
Domino Tray . . . . . . —.		40.00
Plate, 6" d, sherbet . 4.00		5.00
Plate, 8" d, luncheon 9.00		12.00
Sandwich Plate, 12" d		
. . . . 15.00		17.50
Saucer 2.50		2.00
Sherbet 8.50		10.00
Sugar 7.50		8.50

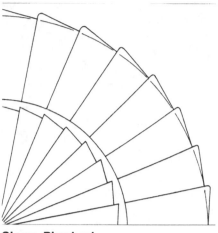

Sierra, Pinwheel

Manufactured by Jeannette Glass Company, Jeannette, Pennsylvania, from 1931 to 1933. Made in green, pink.

Item	Green	Pink
Berry, small 25.00		25.00
Berry Bowl, 8-1/2" d . 40.00		40.00
Butter Dish, cov 75.00		80.00
Cereal Bowl, 5-1/2" d		
. . . . 25.00		20.00
Creamer 25.00		25.00
Cup. 19.50		17.50
Pitcher, 32 oz, 6-1/2" h		
. . . . 160.00		120.00
Plate, 9" d, dinner . . . 30.00		32.00
Platter, 11" l, oval . . . 70.00		65.00
Salt and Pepper Shakers, pr		
. . . . 50.00		50.00
Saucer 10.00		10.00
Serving Tray, 10-1/4" l, 2 handles		
. . . . 25.00		25.00
Sugar, cov. 48.00		48.00
Tumbler, 9 oz, 4-1/2" h, ftd		
. . . . 90.00		80.00
Vegetable Bowl, 9-1/4" l, oval		
. . . . 125.00		80.00

Star

Manufactured by Federal Glass Company, Columbus, Ohio, 1950s. Made in amber, crystal, and crystal with gold trim. Crystal pieces with gold trim would be valued the same as plain crystal.

Item	Amber	Crystal
Bowl, 5-5/8" d . . . . . . —		7.00
Creamer 7.00		9.00
Cup. 10.00		10.00
Dessert Bowl, 4-5/8" d		
. . . . 4.00		5.00
Iced Tea Tumbler, 12 oz, 5-1/8" h		
. . . . 8.00		9.00
Juice Pitcher, 36 oz, 5-3/4" h		
. . . . 10.00		12.00
Juice Tumbler, 4-1/2 oz, 3-3/8" h		
. . . . 4.00		5.00

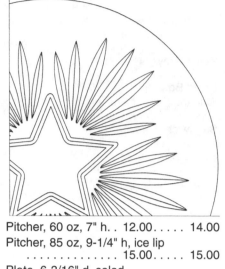

Pitcher, 60 oz, 7" h. . 12.00 . . . . . 14.00

Pitcher, 85 oz, 9-1/4" h, ice lip
. . . . 15.00 . . . . . 15.00

Plate, 6-3/16" d, salad
. . . . 5.00 . . . . . . 6.00

Plate, 9-3/8" d, dinner
. . . . 12.00 . . . . . 14.00

Saucer . . . . 3.00 . . . . . 3.00

Sugar, cov . . . . 15.00 . . . . . 15.00

Tumbler, 9 oz, 3-7/8" h, water
. . . . 7.00 . . . . . . 7.50

Vegetable Bowl, 8-3/8" d
. . . . 10.00 . . . . . 15.00

Whiskey, 1-1/2 oz, 2-1/4" h
. . . . 4.00 . . . . . . 5.00

DISNEYANA

Collecting Hints: The products from the 1930s command the most attention. Disneyana is a popular subject, and items tend to be priced on the high side.

Condition should be a prime consideration before purchasing any item. An incomplete toy or game should sell for 40 to 50 percent less than one in mint condition.

History: Walt Disney and the creations of the famous Disney Studios have a place of fondness and enchantment in the hearts of people throughout the world. The 1928 release of "Steamboat Willie," featuring Mickey Mouse, heralded an entertainment empire.

Walt and his brother, Roy, were shrewd businessmen. From the beginning, they licensed the reproduction of Disney characters on products ranging from wristwatches to clothing.

The market in Disneyana has been established by a few determined dealers and auction houses. Hake's Americana and Collectibles has specialized in Disney material for more than two decades. Sotheby's Collector Carousel auctions and Christie's auctions have continued the trend.

Walt Disney characters are popular throughout the world. Belgium is a leading producer of Disneyana, along with England, France, and Japan. The Disney characters often take on the regional characteristics of the host country; don't be surprised to find a strange-looking Mickey Mouse or Donald Duck. Disney has opened theme parks in Japan and France, Disney retail stores in America, and holds company sponsored collector conventions, all resulting in ever increasing Disney collectibles.

References: Ted Hake, *Hake's Guide to Character Toy Premiums*, Gemstone Publishing (1966 Greenspring, Ste. 405, Timonium, MD 21093), 1996; Robert Heide and John Gilman, *Disneyana: Classic Collectibles* 1928-1958, Hyperion, 1994; Rex Miller, *The Investor's Guide to Vintage Character Collectibles*, Krause Publications, 1999; Maxine A. Pinksy, *Marx Toys: Robots, Space, Comic, Disney & TV Characters*, Schiffer Publishing, 1996; Tom Tumbusch, *Tomart's Illustrated Disneyana Catalog and Price Guide*, Vols. 1, 2, 3, and 4, Tomart Publications, 1985.

Periodicals: *Mouse Rap Monthly*, P.O. Box 1064, Ojai, CA 93024; *Tomart's Disneyana Digest*, 3300 Encrete Ln, Dayton, OH 45439; *Tomart's Disneyana Update*, 3300 Encrete Ln, Dayton, OH 45439.

Collectors' Clubs: Imagination Guild, P.O. Box 907, Boulder Creek, CA 95006; Mouse Club East, P.O. Box 3195, Wakefield, MA 01880; National Fantasy Club for Disneyana Collector & Enthusiasts, P.O. Box 19212, Irvine, CA 92713.

Archives: Walt Disney Archives, Burbank, CA.

Additional Listings: Animation Art.

Advisor: Ted Hake.

Bambi

Bud Vase, 5-1/2" h, Goebel, Bambi figure standing in front of tree stump vase, incised "DJS 428," full bee mark, 1950s 180.00
Comic Book, Walt Disney's Bambi, 7-3/4" x 10-1/4", KK Publications, Inc., 1941 copyright, 32 pgs, glossy cover, large story art and text, used as premium by various stores, room for advertising on back 75.00
Figure, Thumper, 1-1/4" painted and glazed ceramic, tan, brown, and pink, Hagen-Renaker, 1940s 50.00
Poster, 14-1/4" x 20", Prevent Forest Fires, issued by US Dept of Agricultural Forest Service, 1943, reads, "Please Mister, Don't Be Careless. Prevent Forest Fires/Greater Danger Than Ever!" 200.00
Studio Fan Card, 7-1/8" x 9-1/4", stiff tan paper, brown design, facsimile Walt Disney signature, 1942 .... 35.00

Cinderella

Figure, 5-1/4", painted and glazed ceramic, blue and white dress, 1970s 25.00
Magazine, 8-1/4" x 11", Newsweek, Feb. 13, 1950, three-page article, color cover 25.00
Ring, thin sheet of brass forming watch on top, adjustable square-off bands below, small plastic cover over white dial, black lines and numerals, pair of pink blacks hands, underside mkd "Japan," 1950s 35.00
Watch, Bradley, 2-3/4" x 6-1/2" deep blue hard plastic case, hinged lid, 1" dia. goldtone case, white vinyl straps, 1973, full color case insert 45.00

Disneyland

Coloring Book, The Dutch Boy Disneyland Coloring Book, copyright 1957, 8-1/2" x 11", premium from Dutch Boy paints 15.00
Guide Book, 6" x 8-3/4", 20 pgs, stiff glossy covers, artwork, two photos of Walt Disney, c1955 .... 125.00
Magazine, Disneyland Magazine, No. 1, 10-1/4" x 12-1/2", Fawcett Publication, 1972 copyright, 16 pgs, color art 30.00
Pamphlet, Your Guide To Disneyland, 3-1/2" x 8", issued by Bank of America, 1955 copyright, opens to 13-1/2" x 16" with map on one side, other side with text and Bank of America CA locations 30.00
Pinback Button, 4" d, Main Street Commemorative, blue text, 3,000th Performance Sept. 4, 1991, color photo of Main Street Electrical Parade, castle in background 35.00
Plate, 9-1/2" d, white china, gold trim, six large color illus, pierced for hanging, c1950 .... 60.00
Punch-Out Book, Disneyland Punch-Out Book, Gold Press Inc., copyright 1963, 7-1/2" x 13", unpunched 150.00

Donald Duck riding tricycle, bisque, marked "Japan," 3-1/4" h, $35.

Donald Duck

Bank, dime register, 2-1/2" x 2-1/2" x 3/4", tin litho, late 1930s 250.00
Blotter, 4" x 7", Sunoco, color illus of Donald pinning "Quick Starting" medal on gas pump, early 1940s 60.00
Book, *Donald Duck Sees South America*, D. C. Heath & Co., Walt Disney Storybooks, hardcover, 6-1/4" x 5-1/2" 40.00
Comic Book, Donald and Mickey, Firestone Christmas premium, copyright 1947, 7" x 10-1/4", excellent condition 90.00
Figure, bisque
3-1/4" h, Donald with head turned to side, hands straight down at sides, mkd "Japan," 1930s, some paint wear 45.00
4" h, with violin, mkd "Japan," number incised on back 200.00
Matchbox Holder, 1" x 1-1/2' x 1/2", black, hard plastic, high relief images of Donald and nephew, blue and white outfits, pink shirt and hat on nephew, mkd "Potter & Moore/England," c1940 .... 50.00
Nodder, wind-up, 5-1/4" h, celluloid figure attached to domed painted tin base, mkd "TT, Made in Japan," 1930s, fine condition 500.00
Pencil, 5-1/2" l, red, white, and blue, Donald Duck Bread, loaf of bread, imprint of Ungles Baking Co, 1950s 25.00
Pencil Sharpener, 1" d dark green plastic, octagonal, full color decal of Donald waving, c1940 .... 60.00
Ring, silver, adjustable bands, full color raised image on top, int. with WDP copyright and word "Sterling," Ingersoll Watch Co., c1948, wear to orig white glow-in-the-dark material 40.00

Sprinkling Can, 3" h, Ohio Art, tin litho, copyright 1938, Donald walking and tripping over brick, some surface damage......................................145.00

Thermometer, 6" x 6" ceramic Sportsman plaque, Donald as bowler, black text, Kemper-Thomas Co., 1940s 35.00

Viewmaster Set, 4-1/2" x 4-1/2" envelope, color photo, three reels, single inner sleeve, orig story booklet, Donald, Chip n' Dale and Uncle Scrooge, 1960s 25.00

Dumbo

Card Game, 2-1 2" x 3-1/2" x 3/4" deep blue and white box, 45 cards and instructions, English, marked "Pepy Series," c1941 ....125.00

Cookie Jar, 7" x 9" x 13" h, glazed white china, over glaze green, orange, blue, and dark brown paint, turnabout type, Leeds China, late 1940s 100.00

Puzzle, Jaymar, 1950s, orig 7" x 10" box 15.00

Lady and the Tramp

Book, *Lady*, Whitman Tell-a-Tale, 1954 copyright, 5-1/2" x 6-1/2", 28 pgs, color art 20.00

Jock, 2-1/2" x 3-1/2" stiff plastic sheet, punch-out figure of Jock, issued by Scotch Brand tape, c1955 ....25.00

Sheet Music, Hanson Publications, copyright 1955 Walt Disney Music Co., 9" x 12" folio.................................40.00

Lion King

Ring Party Pak, white plastic ring, mkd "Copyright Disney Made in China," each with large flat white plastic top with raised image of character, single metallic color, 1994, unused 10.00

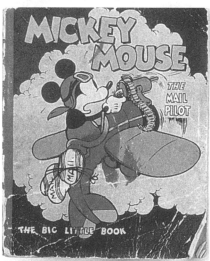

Big Little Book, *Mickey Mouse, The Mail Pilot*, Whitman, 1933, 320 pgs, $35.

Mickey Mouse

Better Little Book, *Mickey Mouse and the Lazy Daisy Mystery*, Whitman, #1433, copyright 1947 ....55.00

Big Little Book, *Mickey Mouse The Mail Pilot*, Whitman, copyright 1933, softcover, 3-1/2" x 4-3/4", some wear...35.00

Book
Mickey Mouse Waddle Book, Blue ribbon Books, copyright 1934, hardcover, 7-3/4" x 10-1/4", 27 pg story, missing waddle figures, fine...85.00

The Adventures of Mickey Mouse Book!, David McKay Co., copyright 1931, hardcover, 5-1/2" x 7-1/2", 32 pgs, shows wear, good condition 55.00

Coloring Book, Another Mickey Mouse Coloring Book, Saalfield Publishing, copyright 1935, 10-3/4" x 15", 28 pgs, used, some signs of aging..........40.00

Doll, 4-1/2" x 7-1/2" x 12" h, Knickerbocker, stuffed cloth and composition, oil-cloth eyes and thick felt ears, 1930s, some fading, played-with condition...................................250.00

Figure
1-1/2" h, bisque, 1930s, red pants, green shoes, one hand raised, Japan 40.00

4" h, glazed bisque, playing violin, mkd "Made in Japan," distributed in Canada...........................150.00

Get Well Card, 4" x 5", diecut, Hallmark, 1930s 35.00

Mug, 2-1/2" h, china, Mickey riding Henry Horse, 1930s, mkd "Made in Japan" 195.00

Pencil Box, 3-1/2" x 5" x 3/4", paper covered cardboard, snap closure, Dixon, 1930s 90.00

Plate, 7" d, Mickey and Pluto, white, orange rim, large color center image, Salem China Co., mkd "Patriot China" and Disney name, 1930s..........150.00

Ring, brass, thin expansion band, diecut brass figure of black, white, and red Mickey in Santa suit, green gloves, copyright "Walt Disney Productions," 1970s...............................12.00

Ring, silver, adjustable bands, full color raised image of Mickey on top, int. with WDP copyright and word "Sterling," Ingersoll Watch Co., c1948, wear to orig white glow-in-the-dark material...40.00

Sand Pail, 8" h, 8-1/4" d, tin litho, Ohio Art Co., copyright 1938, Mickey, Minnie, and Goofy, Donald carrying groceries in wagon pulled by Pluto, very fine condition.............................350.00

Tin, 5-1/2" x 6" x 2", hexagonal, hinged lid, six illus on sides, Australian, 1930s.......................................185.00

Toothbrush Holder, 2" x 2-3/4" x 4" h, china, Disney copyright, Maw & Sons, 1930s.......................................400.00

Watch, Bradley, 2" x 3" x 2" clear and black plastic case, 1" d silvered metal case, 1970s.................................35.00

Wee Little Book, Whitman, copyright 1934, 3" x 3-1/4", from boxed set, very fine condition
Mickey Mouse At The Carnival.................................45.00

Mickey Mouse Wins The Race 45.00

Mickey Mouse Club, news reel with sound outfit, $70.

Mickey Mouse Club

Lunch Box, 7" x 8" x 4", emb metal, Aladdin, c1963............................ 75.00

Membership Certificate, 8-1/2" x 11", tan parchment-like paper, black text, repeated gold Mickey portrait, facsimile Mickey signature and seal design, unused...30.00

Record, Mickey Mouse Club March, 7" x 7" colorful stiff paper sleeve, 45 rpm record, Disneyland label, 1962 copyright...20.00

Stick-Ons Set, 8-1/2" x 13" x 1" deep colorful box, Standard Toykraft, 1961 copyright, colorful fabric pieces, 8" x 9" stiff cardboard section with felt covering...30.00

Thermos, 6-1/2" h, metal, color illus, white cup, Mickey as band leader, other characters playing instruments, Aladdin Industries, 1960s 50.00

Wallet, 3-1/4" x 4", vinyl, snap closure, image of Mickey, flocked ears, 1950s, autographed by Annette Funicello 150.00

Minnie Mouse

Ashtray, green dress, white polka dots, red hat, yellow flower 150.00

Cigarette Holder, 1-1/2" x 3-1/4" x 2-1/2" h, white china, gold trim, Minnie images on both sides, one side brushing hair, other side with finger pointing in the air 225.00

Figure, bisque
3-1/4" h, nurse, yellow dress, dark orange polka dots, gold hat, orange shoes, silver case with orange cross, 1930s 80.00

3-1/2" h, light blue dress, green hat, yellow shoes, holding tan and gold mandolin, 1930s, incised "C69" on back.....................................75.00

Ring, thin brass expansion band, diecut heart on top with black, white, and red image of Mickey and Minnie, white background, int. mkd "Walt Disney Prod.," 1970s......................12.00

Pinocchio

Book, *Pinocchio*, Whitman, copyright 1939, Cocomalt premium, 8-1/2" x 11", excellent condition 35.00
Figure, 3" h, bisque, blue, red, yellow, brown shoes, c1940 ....30.00
Magazine, *The American Girl*, Jan. 1940, 8-1/2" x 11-1/2" l................20.00
Sheet Music, Pinocchio Song Hit Folio, 9" x 12", 16 pgs of words and music, 1940 copyright, Allan & Co, Pty Ltd. Australian issue 20.00
Toy, Pinocchio Pop Pal, 3" h, hard plastic push button, Kohner, c1970, dark brown, tree stump opens to review three-dimensional Pinocchio, squeaks 15.00
Whistle, 1-1/2" h, Jiminy Cricket, aluminum, name, image, and Disney copyright stamped on stem, c1960....10.00

Pluto

Candle, 1-1/2" x 2" x 3-1/2", figural, green base, red and brown dog dish, black and white eye stickers, 1960s, unused 12.00
Card Game, 5" x 6-1/2" box, 35 playing cards, Whitman, 1939 copyright, black, white, and red illus............50.00
Figure, 1-3/4" h, painted and glazed ceramic, brown, black, and white accents, red collar, Shaw sticker missing, 1950s 125.00
Picture, framed, 4-1/4" x 5-3/4", Reliance Art Co., black, and gold wood frame, image printed on back of glass, orig cardboard backing 60.00
Salt and Pepper Shakers, pr, 3-1/4" h, glazed white china, over glaze black and red paint dec, Leeds China, unmarked, 1947 ....30.00
Toy, Marx Wiz Walker, 5" x 9" diecut card, 1-1/2" long hard plastic ramp walker, metal legs, yellow, black, and red, small Disney copyright, c1960 ....25.00

Snow White

Book, *Snow White and the Seven Dwarfs Storybook*, Whitman, copyright 1938, soft cover, 8-1/2" x 11-1/4", very fine..35.00
Cake Decoration Figure, 1-5/8" h, Dopey, bisque, deep pink hat, yellow coat, green pants, tan shoes, c1938 ....35.00
Figure
   3-1/2" h, Happy, hard celluloid head, pipe cleaner beard, arms, and legs, red fabric hat, red felt jacket, black belt, brown pants, green shoes, 1938 ....40.00
   6-1/2" h, Snow White, painted and glazed china, blue and yellow dress, deep pink bow and facial features, black hair, Leeds China, c1949 ....65.00
Mask, diecut stiff paper, premium from Stroehmann's Bread, ad for Snow White Cake, marked "Part-T-Mask/ Eison-Freeman Co, Inc.," poem on back, 1937 copyright

Doc, 9-1/4" x 11" 25.00
Grumpy, 9-1/4" x 13"..............25.00
Snow White, 7-3/4 x 8-1/4" 30.00
Witch, 8" x 10-1/4" 45.00
Paint Book, 10-3/4" x 15", Whitman #696, 1938 copyright, 40 pgs, one pg crayoned, four painted 75.00
Paper Dolls, 10" x 12-3/4", Whitman, 1972 copyright, stiff paper full color covers, six glossy pages of outfits, unused 30.00

Winnie the Pooh

Game, 9" x 17" x 1-1/2" deep colorful box, Parker Brothers, 1964 copyright, 16-1/2" x 16-1/2" board, fabric "grab-bag," plastic disks, four figural playing pieces...30.00
Glass, 4-3/4" h, black design, Canadian, text on back reads "Inspired by Walt Disney's Winnie The Pooh and The Honey Tree," 1965 copyright 40.00
Viewmaster Set, 4-1/2" x 4-1/2" envelope, color photo, three reels, color booklet and catalog, copyright 1964..20.00

Zorro

Book, *Zorro Golden Book*, Golden Press, 1958 copyright, 9-1/4" x 12-1/4", stuff cover, 32 pgs, color and black, white, and red story art, very fine..20.00
Gloves, 4-1/2" x 7-1/2", vinyl cuff section, black fabric fingers, black, white, and red, Zorro image and name, orig staple, red and blue Disneyland Gloves tag, late 1950s, unused ..25.00
Hat, 12" x 12-1/2" x 3", black starched straw, thin felt trim, orig black and white fabric chin strap, black and white patch, c1940 ....60.00
Punch-Out Book, *Giant Funtime Book*, Pocket Books, copyright 1958, 7-1/4" x 13", thin cardboard, four inside pages with punch-outs, unpunched ... 125.00
Viewmaster Set, 4-1/2" x 4-1/2" envelope, color photos, three reels, black and white booklet, copyright 1958...30.00
Wind-Up, 4-1/4" h hard plastic, built-in key, Zorro and horse Toronado, Durham Industries, copyright 1975...40.00

Dog Collectibles

Collecting Hints: A collection of dog-related items may be based on one particular breed or may be composed of items picturing a dog or even dog-shaped objects. With millions of dog owners in the United States, dog collectibles are very popular.

History: Dogs, long recognized as "man's best friend," have been associated with humans since the early cavemen. The first dogs probably were used for hunting and protection against the wilder animals. After man learned that dogs could be taught to provide useful services, many types of dogs were bred and trained for specific purposes. More than 100 breeds of dogs have evolved from the first dog which roamed the earth more than 15 million years ago. Today, dogs are still hunters, protectors, and herders, and are trained to see, hear, and perform routine tasks for handicapped people.

Man has continued to domesticate the dog, developing today's popular breeds. The American Kennel Club has divided the breeds into seven classifications: herding, hounds, sporting, non-sporting, terriers, toy breeds, and working dogs.

The first modern dog show was held in Newcastle, England, in 1859. Its success spawned many other shows. The breeding of prize dogs became popular, and the bloodlines of important dogs were established and recorded. Today, the dogs with the most impressive pedigrees command the highest prices.

As dogs' popularity grew, so did the frequency of their appearance on objects. They became popular in literature, paintings, and other art forms.

References: Elaine Butler, *Poodle Collectibles of the 50s & 60s*, L-W Book Sales, 1996; Dana Cain, *Film & TV Animal Star Collectibles*, Antique Trader Books, 1998; Candace Sten Davis and Patricia Baugh, *A Treasury of Scottie Dog Collectibles*, Collector Books, (Book I, 1998, Book II, 2000); Alice L. Muncaster and Ellen Sawyer, *The Dog Made Me Buy It!*, Crown Publishers, 1990; Patricia Robak, *Dog Antiques and Collectibles*, Schiffer Publishing, 1999.

Collectors' Clubs: Canine Collectibles Club of America, 736 N. Western Ave., Suite 314, Lake Forest, IL 60045; Collieactively Speaking, 428 Philadelphia Rd, Joppa, MD 21085; Wee Scots, Inc., P.O. Box 1512, Columbus, IN 47202.

Museum: The Dog Museum of America, Jarville House, St. Louis, MO.

Print, My Little Playfellow, Currier & Ives, walnut Victorian frame, 16-1/2" x 20-1/2", $125. Photo courtesy of Joy Luke Fine Art Brokers and Auctioneers.

Ashtray, Scottie, Stangl 72.00
Bank
    RCA Nipper, foot reglued 90.00
    Scottie, Hubley 115.00
    St. Bernard, cast iron, painted black and gold 130.00
Book
    Huskies in Action, The Fascination of Sled Dog Racing, Rico Pfirstinger, 1995, color photos 15.00
    Lassie & The Mystery of Blackberry Bog, Dorothea Snow, Whitman, illus by Ken Sawyer, 1946 .... 5.00
    Secrets of Show Dog Handling, M. Miglorina, Arco, 1982, 127 pgs 7.00
    The First Book of Dogs, Gladys Taber, color and black and white illus by Bob Kuhn, Franklin Watts, Inc., 1949, dj 35.00
    The Complete Lab Retriever, It's History, Development & Function As A Sporting Dog, H. Warwick, Howell, 1969, 304 pgs 7.00
    The Dog of the South, Charles Portis, Alfred Knopf, 1979, 1st edition 7.50

Bookends, terriers, chrome plated, marked "434," c1920, 4-1/4" h, $115.

Bookends, pr
    Cocker Spaniel Pups, ceramic, white glossy finish 15.00
    Pekingese, ceramic, glossy finish, mkd "Made in Japan" 45.00
Bowl, 10" d, "DOG" written on side, yellow ware 55.00
Brush, figural, ceramic, Marutomoware, Made in Japan, c1950, 6-3/4" l 22.00
Calendar, Texaco, Scottie and girl on telephone, 1959 .... 20.00
Calendar Plate, 1910, black and white Bulldog, white china, gold trim 45.00
Candy Container, glass, mutt, 3-1/2" h 25.00
Candy Dish, cov, glass, Bulldog 75.00
Child's Book
    Browser the Hound, Thomas Burgess, color illus by Harrison Cady, Little Brown & Co. 50.00
    Mostly About Mutt, Garden City Publishing, 1930s, wear to orig dj 20.00
Cigarette Box, large emb Borzoi heads 35.00
Cigarette Lighter, English Setter, Zippo, painted, 1950 .... 125.00
Cocktail Glasses, Scottie dec, set of six 55.00
Color and Activity Book, 1979, unused 50.00
Cookie Jar, 9" h, mkd "Made in Japan," small nick in lid 25.00
Creamer, large, dog and child, mkd "Teplitz, Stellmacher" 65.00
Dinnerware, Lassie, Melmac, three pc snack set 75.00
Doorstop, painted cast iron
    Setter, on point, side view, black and white, Hubley 300.00
    Terrier 175.00
Dresser Jar, cov, satin glass, dog on top 45.00
Dresser Tray, four French Poodles doing can-can, sgd "Clement" 125.00
Figure
    Basset Hound, Napco 40.00
    Beagle, #1072, Lladro 140.00
    Bloodhound, bronze, David, The Bloodhound of Prince Napoleon, by Jules-Bertrand Gelibert, c1847 .... 7,625.00
    Bonzo Dog, 3" h, bisque, mkd "Germany," c1920 .... 45.00
    Borzoi, Mortens Studios, #749 .... 125.00
    Collie, bisque, black and brown 40.00
    Dachshund, Beswick, #1469 ...... 50.00
    German Shepherd, Royal Dux, porcelain 65.00
    Jack Russell Terrier, bisque, puppy 25.00
    Newfoundland, reclining, bronze, Emanuel Fremiert 1,525.00
    Poodle, sitting, Goebel, matte finish 90.00
    Pug, Mortens Studios, #738 ..... 125.00
    Schnauzer, bronze, dark brown patina, Maximillien-Louis Fiot 2,850.00

Spaniel, 4-1/2" h, china, gold trimmed collar with locket, Staffordshire 135.00
Ink Blotter, The Soap Suds Blues, dog being bathed in tub, Harry N. Johnson, Real Estate & Insurance, Highlands, NJ 10.00
Jewelry, pin
    Bedlingham Terrier 40.00
    Cocker spaniel, sterling silver, emb detail, mkd "Cini" 90.00

Grape label, Spitz Brand, California Fruit Exchange, Selling Agents, c1929, $.50. Label courtesy of Lorie Cairns.

Magazine, *Dog*, 1941 .... 24.00
Model Kit, My Lassie, Gabriel, 1976, MIB 115.00
Nodder
    Dalmatian 80.00
    German Shepherd 75.00
Palm Puzzle, 2" d, aluminum frame, clear glass over cardboard insert, black and white dog, red collar, yellow background, diecut clots for eyebrows and eyes, c1950 .... 15.00
Patch, Rin Tin Tin insignia, set of seven 25.00
Pen Tray, Labrador, bronze 45.00
Pinback Button, Duke the Peters Dog, multicolored, black Labrador clenching Peters shotgun shell carton in mouth, white lettering on black rim 12.00
Pipe Rack, Terrier and Bulldog peeking over fence 35.00
Planter, ceramic
    Cocker Spaniel, white, Royal Copley 40.00
    Spotted Dog, McCoy 145.00
Salt and Pepper Shakers, pr
    Poodle, heads, Rosemeade 165.00
    RCA Nipper, Lenox 75.00
Scarf, cotton, dog print, marked "Occupied Japan" 18.00
String Holder, Scottie, figural 125.00
Stuffed Dog, Lassie, vinyl collar 75.00
Ramp Walker, 3-1/2" l dachshund, brown hard plastic, black and yellow accents, Marx, 1950s 15.00
Toy
    Fisher-Price, #240, boy with dog on tractor, gong bell 70.00
    Snoopy, pull toy, ears move 40.00
    Somersault Dog, 4" x 4" x 5-1/2" h, built-in key, white plush covered body, brown spots, red collar, mkd "Made in Germany," 1960s 18.00
Vase, Poodle, Sascha Brastoff 75.00
Wallet, Lassie, orig mailer 100.00
Wall Plaque, Collie, Mortens Studio 24.00

Dollhouse Furnishings

Collecting Hints: Dollhouse furnishings are children's toys, so some wear is to be expected. It is possible to find entire room sets in original boxes, and these sets command high prices.

History: Dollhouse furnishings are the tiny articles used to furnish and accessorize a dollhouse. Materials and methods of production range from fine handmade wooden pieces to molded plastic items. Several toy manufacturers, such as Tootsietoy, Petite Princess, and Renwal, made dollhouse furnishings.

There is renewed interest in collecting dollhouses and dollhouse furnishings. Many artists and craftsmen devote hours to making furniture and accessories to scale. These types of handmade dollhouse furnishings are not included in this listing. They do, however, affect the market by offering buyers a choice between old pieces and modern handcrafted ones.

References: Charles F. Donovan, Jr., *Renwal-World's Finest Toys, Dollhouse Furniture*, L-W Book Sales, 1999; Flora Gill Jacobs, *Dolls Houses in America*, Charles Scribner's Sons, 1974; Constance Eileen King, *Dolls and Dolls Houses*, Hamlyn, 1989; Jean Mahan, *Doll Furniture, 1950s-1980s, Identification and Price Guide*, Hobby House Press, 1997; Dian Zillner, *Antique Dollhouses and Their Furnishings*, Schiffer Publishing, 1998.

Periodicals: Doll Castle News, P.O. Box 247, Washington, NJ 07882; Miniature Collector, 30595 Eight Mile, Livonia, MI 48152; Nutshell News, P.O. Box 1612, Waukesha, WI 53187.

Collectors' Clubs: Dollhouse & Miniature Collectors, P.O. Box 16, Bellaire, MI 49615; National Association of Miniature Enthusiasts, P.O. Box 69, Carmel, IN 46032.

Museums: Margaret Woodbury Strong Museum, Rochester, NY; Mildred Mahoney Jubilee Doll House Museum, Fort Erie, Canada; Toy and Miniature Museum of Kansas City, Kansas City, MO; Toy Museum of Atlanta, Atlanta, GA; Washington Dolls' House and Toy Museum, Washington, DC.

Little Homemaker Kitchen Furniture, plastic, eight pieces, Plastic Art Toy Corp., Rutherford, NJ, $20.

Baker's Rack, metal, wood cutting board, 3-1/2" w, 6-1/2" h 10.00
Bathroom Set, Tootiestoy, 10 pcs, orig box 80.00
Bath Tub, metal, Tootsietoy 15.00
Bed
    Four poster, patterned cloth spread, matching dust ruffle and canopy 20.00
    Twin, Renwal 10.00
Bedroom Suite, bed, five-drawer highboy, four-drawer dresser, mirror, two side tables, mahogany finish 45.00
Buffet, Petite Princess, MIB 20.00
Canister Set, yellow plastic, four canisters, lids 5.00
Corner Cabinet, oak, 3-1/2" w, 6-1/2" h 20.00
Curio Cabinet, wood 22.00
Dining Room Suite, blond finish, red patterned fabric seats, seven pc 30.00
Dollhouse
    Marx, litho tin, two-story house, detailed living room with fireplace, kitchen cupboard with dishes, toy soldier motif in nursery, 19" l, 8" d, 16" h, front door missing, some rust damage, some play wear 45.00
    Wolverine, litho tin, two-story house, five rooms, bay windows, 10 pcs of period plastic furniture, 22" l, 12" deep, 15" h, chimney missing, some play wear 45.00
Fantasy Room, Ideal, Petite Princess, red, MIB 45.00
Fireplace, Renwal, brown 35.00
Grand Piano and Bench 12.50
Grandfather Clock, door opens to pendulum, 1-1/2" w, 4-1/4" h 10.00
Guest Chair, Ideal, Petite Princess, orig box, some staining 8.00
High Chair, cast iron 25.00

Hostess Chairs, Ideal, Petite Princess, pair of dining room chairs, MIB 20.00
Kitchen Appliances, refrigerator, sink in cabinet, stove, plastic 30.00
Kitchen Suite, plastic, Ideal, c1940, MIB, seven pcs 35.00
Living Room Suite
    Contemporary, floral print, wood and fabric, five pcs 30.00
    Victorian, deep burgundy upholstery, parlor sofa, Queen Anne style side arm and side chairs, coffee table, 1" to 1' scale, four-pc set 40.00
Nightstand, 1" w, 1-1/2" h, price for pr 9.00
Nursery Furniture Set, Marx, crib, high chair, and rocking horse, light blue plastic 15.00
Radio, Renwal 30.00
Rocker and Stool, Bentwood style, red material covering on stool 10.00
Rolltop Desk, wood 10.00
Salon Planter, Ideal, Petite Princess, MIB 25.00
Salon Wing Chair, Ideal, Petite Princess, red brocade fabric, MIB 35.00
Settee, Arcade, cast iron 80.00
Sewing Machine, moveable treadle, wood case, 3-1/8" w, 3" h 5.00
Sofa, Tootsietoy, metal 35.00
Study Suite, mahogany finished wood, red velvet, eight pcs 22.50
Table and Seat, 3-1/4" l table with six legs, four 1" x 1-1/4" matching seats 10.00
Table Set, Ideal, Petite Princess
    Heirloom table with bookends, MIB 40.00
    Palace table set, MIB 20.00
Telephone, Ideal, Petite Princess, MIB 15.00
Treasure Trove Cabinet, Ideal, Petite Princess, MIB 15.00
Wing Chair, matching footstool, floral pattern 12.00

Dolls

Collecting Hints: The most important criteria in buying dolls are sentiment and condition. The value of a particular doll increases if it is a childhood favorite or family heirloom.

When pricing a doll, condition is the most important aspect. Excellent condition means that the doll has all original parts, a wig that is not soiled or restyled, skin surface free of marks and blemishes, the original free-moving sleep eyes, and mechanical parts that are all operational. Original clothing means original dress, underclothes, shoes, and socks—all in excellent and clean condition, and preferably with original tags and labels.

A doll that is mint in the original box is listed as "MIB." Many modern collectible doll prices depend on the inclusion of the original box. Mattel's original Barbie doll, for example, is valued at more than $1,000 MIB. However, without the original box, the doll is worth much less. Another pricing consideration is appeal. How important and valuable a particular doll is depends on the individual's collection.

Modern and 20th-century dolls are highly collectible. They offer many appealing features to collectors, one of which is an affordable price tag. Modern dolls are readily available at flea markets, garage sales, swap meets, etc.

Other determinants for collectors is whether the size of a doll is such that it can be artfully displayed and whether it is made of materials that can be easily cleaned and maintained.

History: The history of modern doll manufacturers is long and varied. Competition between companies often resulted in similar doll-making procedures, molds, and ideas. When Effanbee was successful with the Patsy dolls, Horsman soon followed with a Patsy look-alike named Dorothy. Vogue's Ginny doll was imitated by Cosmopolitan's Ginger. Some manufacturers reused molds and changed sizes and names to produce similar dolls for many years.

Dolls have always been popular with Americans. The early Patsy dolls with their own wardrobes were a success in the 1930s and 1940s. During the 1950s, the popularity of Vogue's Ginny Doll generated the sales of dolls, clothes, and accessories. The next decade of children enjoyed Mattel's Barbie. Doll collecting has become a major hobby, and collectors will determine what the next hot collectible will be.

References: J. Michael Augustyniak, *Collector's Encyclopedia of Barbie Doll Exclusives* and *More*, 2nd ed., Collector Books, 1999; —, *Thirty Years of Mattel Fashion Dolls, 1967 Through 1997: Identification and Value Guide*, Collector Books, 1998; Kim Avery, *The World of Raggedy Ann Collectibles*, Collector Books, 1997, 2000 value update; Carla Marie Cross, *Modern Doll Rarities*, Antique Trader Books, 1997; —, *The Patti Playpal Family*, Schiffer Publishing, 2000; Linda Crowsey, *Madame Alexander Collector's Dolls* Price Guide #25, Collector Books, 2000; —, *Madame Alexander Store Exclusives & Limited Editions*, Collector Books, 2000; Maryanne Dolan, *The World of Dolls, A Collector's Identification and Value Guide*, Krause Publications, 1998; Stephanie Finnegan, *The Robert Tonner Story: Dreams and Dolls*, Portfolio Press, 2000; Jan Foulke, *14th Blue Book Dolls & Values*, Hobby House Press, 2000; Sandra Ann Garrison, *The Raggedy Ann and Andy Family Album*, 2nd ed., Schiffer Publishing, 1999; Beth Gunther, *Crissy Doll and Her Friends: Guide for Collectors*, Antique Trader Books, 1998; Dawn Herlocher, *Antique Trader's Doll Makers & Marks*, Antique Trader Books, 1999; —, *200 Years of Dolls*, Antique Trader Books, 1996; R. Lane Herron, *Warman's Dolls*, Krause Publications, 1998; Judith Izen, *Collector's Guide to Ideal Dolls*, 2nd ed., Collector Books, 1999; Judith Izen and Carol Stover, *Collector's Guide to Vogue Dolls*, Collector Books, 1997, 2000 value update; Polly Judd, *Cloth Dolls of the 1920s and 1930s*, Hobby House Press, 1990; Polly and Pam Judd, *Composition Dolls*, Vol. I (1991), Vol. II (1994), Hobby House Press; —, *European Costumed Dolls*, Hobby House Press, 1994; —, *Glamour Dolls of the 1950s & 1960s*, revised ed., Hobby House Press, 1993; —, *Hard Plastic Dolls*, Book I (3rd ed., 1993), Book II (Revised, 1994), Hobby House Press; Michele Karl, *Baby-Boomer Dolls: Plastic Playthings of the 1950s and 1960s*, Portfolio Press, 2000; Kathy and Don Lewis, *Chatty Cathy Dolls*, Collector Books, 1994, 1998 value update; Michele Karl, *Composition & Wood Dolls and Toys: A Collector's Reference Guide*, Antique Trader Books, 1998; Glenn Mandeville, *Glenn Mandeville's Madame Alexander Dolls*, 3rd Collector's Price Guide, Hobby Hose Press, 2000; Ursula R. Mertz, *Collector's Encyclopedia of American Composition Dolls, 1900 to 1950*, Collector Books, 1999; Patsy Moyer, *Doll Values, Antique to Modern*, 5th ed., Collector Books, 2001; —, *Modern Collectible Dolls*, Vols. I, II, III, IV, V, Collector Books, 1998, 1999, 2000, 2001 values; Doris-anne Osborn, *Sasha Dolls Through The Years*, Gold Horse Publishing, 1999; Robert Reed, *Bears and Dolls in Advertising*, Antique Trader Books, 1998; Cindy Sabulis, *Collector's Guide to Dolls of the 1960s and 1970s*, Collector Books, 2000; Patricia R. Smith, *Collector's Encyclopedia of Madame Alexander Dolls*, Collector Books, 1991, 1999 value update; —, *Effanbee Dolls*, Collector Books, 1998; —, *Modern Collector's Dolls*, Series 1-7 (1973-1995), 1995 value update, Collector Books; —, *Patricia Smith's Doll Values, 11th ed.*, Collector Books, 1995; Evelyn Robson Stahlendorf, *Charlton Standard Catalogue of Canadian Dolls*, 3rd ed., Charlton Press, 1996; Cindy Sabulis, *Collector's Guide to Dolls of the 1960s and 1970s*, Collector Books, 2000; Marci Van Audsdall, *Betsy McCall*, Hobby House Press, 2000.

Periodicals: *Celebrity Doll Journal*, 5 Court Pl, Puyallup, WA 98372; *Cloth Doll Magazine*, P.O. Box 1089, Mt. Shasta, CA 96067; *Costume Quarterly for Doll Collectors*, 118-01 Sutter Ave., Jamaica, NY 11420; *Doll Collector's Price Guide*, 306 E. Parr Rd, Berne IN 46711; *Doll Life*, 243 Newton-Sparta Rd, Newton, NJ 07860; *Doll Reader*, 6405 Flank Dr., Harrisburg, PA 17112; *Doll Times*, 218 West Woodin Blvd., Dallas, TX 75224; *Doll World*, P.O. Box 9001, Big Sandy, TX 75755; *Dolls–The Collector's Magazine*, P.O. Box 1972, Marion, OH 43305; *Rags*, P.O. Box 823, Atlanta, GA 30301.

Collectors' Clubs: Cabbage Patch Kids Collectors Club, P.O. Box 714, Cleveland, GA 30528; Chatty Cathy Collectors Club, 2610 Dover St., Piscataway, NJ 08854; Ginny Doll Club, 9628 Hidden Oaks Circle, Tampa, FL 33612; Ideal Doll Collector's Club, P.O. Box 623, Lexington, MA 02173; Madame Alexander Fan Club, P.O. Box 330, Mundeline, IL 60060; United Federation of Doll Clubs, 8B East St., P.O. Box 14146, Parkville, MO 64152.

Museums: Doll Museum, Newport, RI; Margaret Woodbury Strong Museum, Rochester, NY; Museum of Collectible Dolls, Lakeland, FL; Yesteryears Museum, Sandwich, MA.

Additional Listings: Barbie.

Note: All dolls listed here are in excellent condition and have their original clothes, unless otherwise noted.

American Character. The American Character Doll Company was founded in 1918 and made high-quality dolls. When the company was liquidated in 1968, many molds were purchased by the Ideal Toy Company. American Character Dolls are marked with the full company name, "Amer. Char." or "Amer. Char" in a circle. Early composition dolls were marked "Petite."

Baby, 16" h, composition head, stuffed cloth body and limbs, molded painted brown hair, brown sleep eyes, c1925 ....125.00
Betsy McCall, 8" h, hard plastic, jointed knees, brunette rooted hair, sleep eyes, orig red and white striped skirt, white organdy top, red shoes, c1960 ....45.00
Bottle Tot, 13" h, composition head, body mark, orig tagged clothes.......................................175.00
Carol Ann Beery, 16" h, composition head, 5 pc composition child body, green sleep eyes, closed mouth, orig mohair wig with braid across forehead, orig white pique dress, matching sun suit and bonnet, orig socks and snap shoes, mkd "Petite, Sally" on back of head, "Petite" on body, right foot broken and reglued, tips of right thumb and little finger broken ...440.00
Sweet Sue, 15" h, blond wig, blue sleep eyes, rose dec white taffeta dress, pearl pin, silver dance shoes, all orig...200.00
Tiny Tears, 12" h, hard plastic head, 5 pc rubber body, blue sleep eyes, open nurser mouth, rooted hair, orig pink and white dress, unplayed with condition, orig clothing and accessories appear to never have been removed from box 550.00
Toni, 10" h, collegiate outfit, orig booklet...70.00

Arranbee. This company was founded in 1922. Arranbee's finest dolls were made in hard plastic. Two of Arranbee's most popular dolls were Nancy, and later, Nanette. The company was sold to Vogue Dolls, Inc., in 1959. Marks used by this company include "Arranbee," "R&B," and "Made in USA."
Angel Skin, 13" h, stuffed soft vinyl head, stuffed magic skin body and limbs, molded, painted hair, inset stationary blue eyes, closed mouth, mkd R & B on head, orig tag: The R & B Family/Rock Me/Nanette/Little Angel, Dream Baby/Baby Bunting, Angel Skin/Taffy, c1954, MIB 80.00
Baby Bunting, 15" h, vinylite plastic head, stuffed magic skin body, molded, painted hair, pink fleece bunting, mkd 17BBS/R & B/D6 on head, orig tag reads: Head is of Vinylite Plastic by Bakelite Company 60.00
Dream Baby, 20" h, composition shoulder-head, cloth body, painted hair, redressed, c1925 ....110.00

Little Dear, 8" h, stuffed vinyl body, rooted hair, blue sleep eyes, c1956 ....80.00
Littlest Angel, 11" h, vinyl head, hard plastic body, jointed, rooted dark brown hair, mkd R & B on head, 1959..40.00
Nancy, 21" h, composition, blue glass eyes, orig dress and cut-out shoes 395.00
Nancy Lee, 14" h, composition head, 5 pc composition child body, brown sleep eyes, closed mouth, orig mohair wig in orig set, orig long yellow dress with gold polka dots, matching bonnet, orig yellow taffeta underclothing, socks and shoes, mkd "R & B" faintly on back of head 250.00
Nanette, 15" h, all hard plastic, glued on wig, sleep eyes, walker, cotton pinafore, straw hat, 1952, MIB....... 250.00
Rosie, 19" h, composition, swivel head, cloth body, molded hair, 1935..85.00

Snow White (19" h), and the Seven Dwarfs, (12" h,) $2,200. Photo courtesy of McMasters Doll Auctions.

Character and Personality. Many doll companies made dolls to resemble popular characters found in the funnies, the movies, radio, and later television.

Alf the Alien 30.00
Beany, Mattel................................95.00
Bert, Sesame Street, Knickerbocker, 1981, MIB....................................25.00
Brooke Shields, MIB 30.00
Captain Caveman, stuffed, 30" h 65.00
Carrie, Little House on the Prairie, ©1975, Knickerbocker, MIB 50.00
Charlie Chaplin, 14" h, Louis Amberg & Co., New York, composition head, cloth body jointed at shoulders and hips, composition hands, orig white shirt, red tie, brown plaid jacket with label on sleeve, mauve plaid pants, black felt hat and bamboo cane, orig box... 725.00
Charlie McCarthy, composition, movable mouth, 1930s 185.00
Cher, 12" h, ©1975 Mego, MIB 50.00

Dorothy Lamour, 14" h, cloth, printed blue eyes, open-closed mouth, orig mohair wig with pink flower on side, cloth body jointed at hips, mitten hands, orig pale blue sarong with red and white flowers, plastic flower at waist, orig wrist tag "Autographed Movie Star Dolls, Dorothy Lamour, Popular Paramount Motion Picture Star, Made in California by Film Star Creations, Inc. of Hollywood" ... 150.00
ET, fuzzy, brown, marble eyes 30.00
Farrah Fawcett, 12" h, Mego, MIB... 125.00
General Douglas MacArthur, composition 225.00
Gizmo, squeaker....................... 30.00
Goldilocks, by Diana Effner, Aston Drake, 16" h 130.00
Grinch Who Stole Christmas, Santa hat.. 95.00
Isis, 8" h, Mego, NRFP, orig price sticker 100.00
John Boy Walton, Mego, MIB 75.00
Kristy McNichol, 8" h, MIB 45.00
Little Lulu, MIB 125.00
Mary Ellen Walton, Mego, MIB ... 75.00
Mary Poppin, c1964, MIB 30.00
Portrait of Diana Series, includes Diana, Emissary of Compassion, Diana, Princess of Wales, World's Beloved Rose, Visionary of Style, Aston Drake, all retired, MIB, price for set 700.00
Smokey the Bear, Ideal, talking, MIB... 355.00
Spiderman, 8" h, Mego, NRFP, orig price sticker 85.00
Sunbonnet Baby, Molly, Mandy or May, ©1975, Knickerbocker, MIB, each 25.00
Superman, 8" h, Mego, NRFP, orig price sticker 105.00
Tony Tennille, 12-1/4" h, ©1977 Mego, Moonlight & Magnolias, MIB....... 45.00
Wizard of Oz, Cowardly Lion, ©1974 Mego, MIB 35.00

Cosmopolitan Doll Company. Little recorded history is available about this company. Dolls dating from the late 1940s through the 1960s are found with the mark of CDC. It is believed that the company made many unmarked dolls. One of its most popular dolls was Ginger, made in 1955-1956, which was a take-off of Vogue Doll's Ginny. Many of these Ginger dolls are found with original clothes made by the Terri Lee Doll Company.
Ginger, 7-1/2" h
    Hard plastic, glued on wig, walker, head turns, 1955, ice skating outfit 45.00
    Vinyl head, hard plastic body, arms, and legs, rooted medium blond hair, closed mouth, mkd Ginger on head, 1956 .... 35.00
Little Miss Ginger, 8-1/2" h, vinyl head, hard plastic body, rooted ash blond hair, closed mouth, high heel feet, mkd "Little Miss Ginger," 1956............ 20.00

Merri, 14" h, plastic, rooted blond hair, high heel feet, red gown, white fur trim, mkd AE1406/41, backward AE on lower back, 1960 ....20.00

Deluxe Reading, Deluxe Topper, Topper Corporation, Topper Toy.
Deluxe Reading, Deluxe Topper, Topper Corporation, Topper Toys, and Deluxe Toy Creations are all names used by Deluxe Toys. This company specialized in dolls that can do things. The company went out of business in 1972.

Baby Party, 10" h, vinyl head and arms, hard plastic body and legs, rooted blond hair, painted eyes, blows whistle and balloon, redressed...35.00
Dawn and Friends, 6" h, vinyl, jointed at neck, shoulders, waist, hips, poseable legs, rooted hair, mkd "©1970/Topper Corp/Hong Kong" on lower back, additional mark on head
   Angie, black hair, brown eyes, mkd 51/D10 ....10.00
   Dale, negro, black hair, brown eyes, mkd 4/H86...................12.00
   Dawn, blond hair, blue eyes, mkd 343/S11A........................15.00
Sweet Amy School Girl, 23" h, vinyl head, one pc latex body, mkd "A-!" on head, MIB 50.00

Eegee Doll Mfg. Company.
The owner and founder of this company was E. G. Goldberger. He began his company in 1917, marking his dolls "E.G." Other marks used by the company include "E. Goldberger" and "Eegee." This American doll company is one of the longest lasting doll manufacturers.

Dimples, 11" h, vinyl head, cloth bean bag type body, rooted blond hair, painted eyes, dimples, music box, key wind on back, mkd "148D/Eegee Co." 24.00
Granny, 14" h, vinyl head, plastic body, long white hair in bun, hair grows, mature face, mkd "Eegee/3" 65.00
Karne Ballerina, 21" h, hard plastic and vinyl, rooted hair, sleep eyes, jointed at knees, ankles, neck, shoulders, and hips, ballet shoes, satin and net ballet dress, c1958, MIB 45.00
Layette Baby, 14" h, hard plastic head, latex body, molded, painted hair, glassine sleep eyes, orig layette, c1948, MIB 65.00
My Fair Lady, 19" h, vinyl head and body, blond hair, black net, orig costume, c1958..............................55.00

Effanbee Doll Corp.
The Effanbee Doll Corporation was founded in 1912 by Bernard E. Fleischaker and Hugo Baum. Its most successful line was the Patsy Doll and its many variations. Patsy was such a success that a whole wardrobe was designed and it also sold well. This was the first successful marketing of a doll and her wardrobe. Effanbee experimented with materials as well as molds. Rubber was first used in 1930; the use of

hard plastic began in 1949. Today vinyl has replaced composition. Effanbee is still making dolls and has become one of the major manufacturers of limited edition collector dolls.

Anne Shirley, 15" h, composition head, five-pc composition body, blue sleep eyes, closed mouth, orig mohair wig, orig black velvet dress with gold and red stars, mkd on back, Effanbee Durable dolls on metal heart bracelet 200.00
Baby Dainty, 14" h, composition shoulder head, painted blue eyes, closed mouth, painted teeth, molded and painted hair, cloth body, composition arms and legs, orig blue print dress, matching bonnet and underclothing, orig socks and shoes 150.00
Barbara Lou, 21" h, composition head, 5 pc composition body, brown sleep eyes, open mouth, 4 upper teeth, orig human hair wig, orig blue jumper dress, white blouse, matching romper, white apron, socks, black leatherette flange tie shoes, mkd "Effanbee, Ann-Shirley" on back, clothing pale, lips repainted 350.00
Bobbsey Twins, ©1982 Stratemeyer Syndicates, MIB
   Flossie 45.00
   Freddie 45.00
Dy-Dee Baby, 12" h, hard plastic head, five-pc rubber baby body, blue sleep eyes, open nurser mouth, orig skin wig, orig pink dotted Swiss dress, matching bonnet, orig Effanbee Dy-Dee Baby case with orig clothing, accessories, Mennon products, mkd "Effanbee Dy-Dee Baby (patent numbers)" on back, "Dy-Dee Baby, The Almost Human Doll, An Effanbee Play Product" on inside of case, lightly played with condition................525.00
Honey, orig dress, walking mechanism, hair in orig set, replaced shoes and socks...............................295.00
Madame Butterfly Collection, Madame Butterfly, ©1983, MIB...................45.00
Marilee, 30", composition shoulder head, composition arms and legs, blue tin sleep eyes, open mouth with four upper teeth, orig blond mohair wig, cloth body, orig pale green organdy ruffled dress, matching underclothes and bonnet, mkd "Effanbee, Marilee, Copyr. Doll" on back of shoulder plate, fine crazing......350.00
Patsy-Ann, 19" h, composition head and child body, bent right arm, green sleep eyes, closed rosebud mouth, orig mohair wig over molded hair, orig white dress with green dots and trim, matching romper and hat, orig socks, black straps shoes, mkd "Effanbee, Patsy-Ann," with copyright and patent numbers, some play wear........325.00
Patsy-Joan, 16" h, composition head, 5 pc composition body, bent right arm, green sleep eyes, closed mouth, orig blue and white shorts romper with matching hat, mkd "Effanbee, Patsy-Joan" 300.00
Patsy-Lou, 22" h, composition head, 5 pc composition body, bent right arm, green sleep eyes, closed mouth, molded and painted hair, well-made

copy of Patsy style dress, orig socks and snap shoes, orig blue-green felt coat with gold appliqué and trim, matching tam hat, mkd "Effanbee Patsy-Lou" on back...................375.00
Patsy-Mae, 30" h, composition head, cloth body, composition arms and legs, composition shoulder plate, brown sleep eyes, closed mouth, orig human hair wig, tagged orig white organdy dress with red trim and print, metal heart bracelet, mkd "Effanbee, Patsy-Mae" on back of head, "Effanbee Lovums, ©, Pat. No. 1,383,558" on shoulder plate 800.00
Storybook Doll, Little Bo Peep, MIB..40.00

Hasbro.
Hasbro is primarily a toy manufacturer founded by Henry and Hillel Hassenfeld in Pawtucket, RI, in 1923. One of its most popular dolls was G.I. Joe and his friends. Hasbro is also noted for its advertising and personality dolls.

Amanda, Sweet Dreams, 17" h, stuffed gingham head and body, yarn hair, black felt eyes, button nose, embroidered smile, eyelet lace trimmed night cap, orchid print dress, 1974 ..... 12.00
Charlie's Angels, Kate Jackson, Farrah Fawcett-Majors, and Jacyln Smith, 1977, NRFP, price for set of three 155.00
Choo Choo Charlie, 9" h, soft vinyl head, stuffed cotton bean bag body, rooted hair, painted eyes, mkd "©1973 Quaker City Chocolate & Conf'y Co, Inc."...20.00
Lookin' Smart Maxine, ©1987, MIB...25.00
Maxine's Friend, Ashley, ©1987, MIB...35.00
Maxine's Friend, Kristen, ©1987, MIB...35.00

Horsman Dolls Company, Inc.
The Horsman Dolls Company, Inc. was founded in 1865 by E. I. Horsman, who began importing dolls. Soon after the founding, Horsman produced bisque dolls. It was the first company to produce the Campbell Kids. Horsman invented "Fairy Skin" in 1946, "Miracle Hair" in 1952, and "Super Flex" in 1954. The Horsman process for synthetic rubber and early vinyl has always been of high quality.

Alice in Wonderland, MIB 95.00
Baby Bumps, 12" h, negro, cloth body, arms, legs, painted hair, eyes, large well molded ears, orig romper, c1912..250.00
Baby Dimples, 14" h, composition flange head, child torso, composition arms and lower legs, blue tin sleep eyes, open mouth with two teeth, molded and painted hair, orig tagged dress, leatherette baby shoes, mkd "© E.I.H. Co. Inc.".............................200.00
Babyland Rag, 14" h, cloth, pressed mask face, painted blue eyes, closed mouth, painted wisps of hair around edges of face, cloth body jointed at

shoulders and hips, orig pink pants, jacket, and hood, white oilcloth tie shoes, unplayed-with condition 275.00

Bye-Lo, 14" h, vinyl head, arms, and legs, cloth body, molded straight hair, painted eyes, christening outfit, mkd "Horsman Doll/1972" on head, MIB 50.00

Indian Girl, 13" h, composition flange head, cloth body, composition arms and legs, painted features, molded and painted black hair, orig yellow and red cotton Indian outfit with bead trim, mkd "E. I. H. Co., Inc." on back of head, orig tag on clothing 225.00

Joyce, 18" h, composition shoulder, head, arms, and legs, cloth body, glued on bright red mohair hair ..50.00

Peterkin, 11" h, composition, character face, molded hair, painted side glancing eyes, watermelon smile, c1915 ....215.00

Pram Baby, 19" h, vinyl, jointed head, glass sleep eyes, closed mouth, coos 65.00

Rosebud, 20" h, composition head, arms and legs, cloth body, painted eyes, human hair wig, orig dress 325.00

Ruthie, 12-1/2" h, all vinyl rooted black hair, Oriental hair style, long straight legs, dimpled knees, mkd 12-6aa on upper legs, B-1 on upper arms ..30.00

Toddler, 18" h, composition head, brown tin sleep eyes, open mouth with two upper teeth, molded tongue, orig blond mohair wig, chubby 5-pc composition toddler body, orig dark blue print dress with felt dog, matching bonnet, orig white leatherette shoes, white rayon socks, orig box, mkd "Horsman Doll, Genuine Horsman Art Doll, Made in U.S.A., Horsman Dolls Inc., Trenton, NJ" on box end label...265.00

Ideal, Deanna Durbin, original, 20" h, $1,000. Photo courtesy of McMasters Doll Auctions.

Ideal Toy Corp. The Ideal Toy Company was formed in 1902 by Morris Michtom to produce his teddy bear. By 1915, the company had become a leader in the industry by introducing the first sleep eyes. In 1939, Ideal developed "Magic Skin." It was the first company to use plastic. Some of its most popular lines include Shirley Temple, Betsy Wetsy, and Toni dolls.

Clapping, 15" h, composition flange head, cloth body with clapping mechanism in torso, composition hands, blue sleep eyes, closed mouth, molded and painted blond hair, white baby dress, mkd "Ideal" in diamond, rub on nose, some flaking and soil 115.00

Deanna Durbin, 24" h, composition, pale blue organdy dress with white lace trim.................................... 750.00

Fanny Brice and Mortimer Snerd, 12" h, composition character heads, molded and painted hair, painted blue eyes, open-closed mouth with painted teeth, wooden torso, flexy metal cable arms and legs, composition hands, wooden feet, orig clothing, orig cardboard wrist tag 450.00

Harriet Hubbard, 21" h, vinyl head, blue sleep eyes, closed mouth, saran wig, hard plastic body, vinyl arms, orig flowered pique dress, white organdy pinafore, orig socks and shoes, orig cardboard tag with 3 plastic curlers, orig Stern Brothers price tag, mkd "MK 21, Ideal Doll" on back of head 225.00

Jody the Country Girl, ©1976, MIB 45.00

Miss Ideal, 25" h, Photographer's Model, vinyl head, rigid vinyl body, jointed at shoulders, waist, hips, and ankles, blue sleep eyes, rooted nylon hair, orig clothes, mkd "© Ideal Toy Corp SP-25-S:" on head, "© Ideal Toy Corp P-25" on back orig box with promotional paper, Playwave Kit in orig hatbox, Styling Hints wrist tag, some water stains to orig box 350.00

Revlon, 18" h, vinyl swivel head, blue sleep eyes, closed mouth, pierced ears, rooted nylon hair, vinyl lady body jointed at waist, shoulders, and hips, high heel feet, orig tagged red print dress, blue knit jacket lined with matching fabric, orig tags and wrist booklet, unplayed-with condition, earrings tarnished 310.00

Shirley Temple
15" h, vinyl head, five-pc vinyl body, hazel sleep eyes, open-closed mouth, six upper teeth, dimples, rooted hair in orig set, orig dress with red velvet bodice, white taffeta skirt with nylon overlay, lace trim, orig underclothes, pearl crown, mkd "Ideal Doll ST-15-N" on back of head, c1941 ....325.00
15" h, vinyl head, five-pc vinyl body, hazel sleep eyes, open-closed mouth, six upper teeth,

dimples, rooted hair in orig set, orig blue cotton dress with Spanish-style sleeves, orig box with cellophane window, c1962 ..... 275.00
18" h, composition head, five-pc composition child body, hazel sleep eyes, open mouth with 6 upper teeth, orig mohair wig, orig tagged flower print dress, orig underclothing, socks and shoes, mkd "Shirley Temple" on head and body 600.00

Suntan Dodi and her Suntan Doodles, ©1977, MIB 75.00

Taylor Jones, 12" h fashion doll, hair changes color, ©1976, MIB........ 75.00

Thumbelina, 18", vinyl flange head, cloth body with vinyl arms and legs, painted blue eyes, open-closed mouth, rooted synthetic hair, large wooden knob on back for winding to operate baby wiggling mechanism, orig blue and white knit outfit, mkd "Ideal Toy Corp. 77-16" on back of head, orig box 225.00

Tony, 14" h, hard plastic head, five-pc hard plastic walker body, blue sheep eyes, closed mouth, orig brunette wig, orig blue dress, white organdy bodice, orig underclothes and shoes, mkd "P-90 Ideal Doll" on head and "Ideal Doll 90 W" on back, orig Play Wave set with some orig contents, partial orig box...450.00

Alexander, Flora McFlimsey, 13" h, $800. Photo courtesy of McMasters Doll Auctions.

Madame Alexander. The Madame Alexander Doll Company was started in 1923 by Bertha Alexander. The dolls made by this company are beautifully designed with exquisite costumes. It has made hundreds of dolls, including several series, such as the International Dolls and the

Americana Dolls. Marks used by this company include "Madame Alexander," "Alexander," "Alex," and many are unmarked on the body but can be identified by clothing tags. Today Madame Alexander continues to make dolls which are very collectible. Many dolls are made for a limited time period of one year. Others are offered for several years before being discontinued.

Americana Series, 8" h
    Amish Boy, orig clothes,
      c1965 ....450.00
    Colonial Girl, orig clothes,
      c1962 ....350.00

Alexander, McGuffey Ana, original box, 19" h, $1,100. Photo courtesy of McMasters Doll Auctions.

Binnie, 15" h, hard plastic, blond hair, orig trunk filled with clothes....4,500.00
Bride, 20" h, composition head, blue sleep eyes, closed mouth, orig mohair wig in orig set, five-pc composition body, tagged bride dress, orig underclothes and veil, flowers in hand, factory paint and finish flaws, mkd "Madame Alexander, New York, U.S.A." on dress tag..................525.00
Bridesmaid, 17" h, composition, composition head, brown sleep eyes, closed mouth, orig mohair wig in orig set, five-pc composition body, tagged pink taffeta dress, orig underclothes, flowers in hair, mkd "Mme Alexander" on head "Madame Alexander, New York, U.S.A." on dress tag, unplayed with condition.............................675.00
David Copperfield, 15" h, pressed felt mask face, cloth body, stitch-jointed at shoulders and hips, orig mohair wig, painted brown side-glancing eyes, painted features, closed mouth, orig white shirt, dark blue flannel pants, black flannel jacket, mkd "David Copperfield, Madame Alexander, New York" on clothing tag, "Created by

Madame Alexander, New York, An Alexander Product, Supreme Quality and Design" on paper tag........ 825.00
Emelie, 7" h, composition head, painted brown eyes, closed mouth, molded and painted brown hair, five-pc composition toddler body, orig tagged lavender dress, matching bonnet, socks, center snap leatherette shoes, mkd "Alexander" on back of head, "Dionne Quintuplets, Madame Alexander, New York" on dress tag, name on pin 200.00
Heidi, #1580, orig box, pink tissue paper..85.00
International Series, 8" h
    Germany, ©1975, MIB 50.00
    Greek Boy, jointed knees,
      1968 ....275.00
    Morocco 225.00
    Norway, #584, ©1975,
      MIB 50.00
    Thailand, ©1970 ....135.00
Little Women Series
    #412, Beth, ©1975, MIB 50.00
    #416, Laurie, ©1975, MIB.....50.00
    #1320, Amy, MIB...................65.00
Portrette, 10" h, hard plastic head, hard plastic body jointed at shoulder, hips, and knees, high heel feet, orig wig, clothing, and box
    Melinda, orig teal blue taffeta dress with white lace trim, white straw bonnet, black shoes..275.00
    Renoir, orig navy blue taffeta dress with pleated ruffle at hem, red taffeta hat, black shoes...........215.00
Princess Elizabeth, 17" h, composition head, hazel sleep eyes, open mouth with two upper teeth, human hair wig, five-pc composition child body, orig pink taffeta dress, pink flowers in hair... 245.00
Scarlett, 17" h, composition head, green sleep eyes, closed mouth, orig black human hair wig in orig set, five-pc composition body, orig tagged blue, orange, and green flowered dress, orig underclothes, green velvet coat, matching bonnet, mkd "Mme Alexander" on back of head, "Scarlett O'Hara, Madame Alexander, N.Y. U.S.A. All Rights Reserved" on dress tag, near mint 1,450.00
Sonja Henie, 20" h, composition head, brown sleep eyes, open mouth with six teeth, orig blond human hair wig in orig set, five-pc composition body, orig pink taffeta skating dress, pink marabou trim, gold skates........ 950.00
Wendy-Ann, 9" h, composition, jointed at neck, shoulders, and hips, human hair, wig, painted eyes, orig clothes, mkd "Wendy-Ann Mme Alexander" 265.00

Mary Hoyer. The Mary Hoyer Doll Manufacturing Company was named for its founder, in 1925. Mary Hoyer operated a yarn shop and soon began designing doll clothes. She then wanted a perfect doll and approached well-known sculptor Bernard Lipfert, who designed the popu-

lar doll. The Fiberoid Doll Company, New York, produced composition Mary Hoyer dolls until 1946, when hard plastic production began. Mary Hoyer continued until the 1970s, when all production of these popular dolls ceased. Mary Hoyer's family has recently released a vinyl version of the vintage Mary Hoyer doll.

Cowgirl, 14" h, hard plastic, five-pc hard plastic body, blue sleep eyes, orig set brunette wig, cowgirl outfit, one orig felt boot, mark: Original Mary Hoyer Doll.................................360.00
Girl, 14" h, composition head, five-pc composition body, blue sleep eyes, closed mouth, mohair wig, three-pc navy blue knit outfit, orig socks and black center snap leatherette shoes, mkd "The Mary Hoyer Doll" on back.......................................325.00
Walker, 14" h, hard plastic, five-pc hard plastic body, blue sleep eyes, closed mouth, orig saran wig in braids, peach knit two pc outfit, matching cap and panties, gold sandals, trunk with five complete Mary Hoyer outfits, mkd "Made in U.S.A., Mary Hoyer" in black ink on back, circular mark.................................240.00

Mattel, Inc. Mattel, Inc. was started in 1945. First production of this toy company was in the doll house furniture line. The toy line was expanded to include music boxes, guns, and several character-type dolls. The most celebrated doll they make is Barbie, which was designed by one of the company's founders, Ruth Handler, in 1958.

Bozo The Clown, 16" h, vinyl head, cloth body, pull talk string, c1962...65.00
Cheerful Tearful, 12" h, vinyl head and body, orig clothes, 1966 .... 35.00
Charmin Cathy, 25" h, vinyl head and arms, plastic body and legs, rooted blond hair, blue side glancing sleep eyes, closed mouth, original clothes and metal trunk, 1961 .... 100.00
Chatty Cathy, 20" h, soft vinyl head, hard plastic body, rooted blond dynel hair, blue sleep eyes, open mouth, two teeth, voice box, MIB with orig storybook, dress pattern, clothing, c1965..425.00
Chicken of the Sea Mermaid, 14" h, long blond yarn hair, diamond patterned green body, yellow tail fin with green polka dots, orig box, 1974...45.00
Christie, Twist 'n' Turn, 1970, MIB...275.00
Doctor Dolittle, Polynesia the Parrot, 1968, NRFB 30.00
Francie, no bangs, MIB 1,700.00
Ricky, MIB...................................95.00
Truly Scrumptious, Chitty Chitty Bang Bang, 11-1/2" h, vinyl, straight legs, blond hair, pink and white gown, matching hat, mkd Mattel, #1108, c1969..90.00

Sun Rubber Co. The Sun Rubber Company produced all rubber or lasloid vinyl dolls. Many have molded features and clothes.

Betty Bows, 11" h, rubber, fully jointed, molded hair, blue sleep eyes, drinks and wets, mkd Betty Bows/copyright The Sun Rubber Co/Barberton, OH USA/34A, c1953 .... 35.00
Gerber Baby, 11" h, all rubber, molded, painted hair, open nurser mouth, dimples, crossed baby legs, mkd Gerber Baby/Gerber Products Co on head 45.00
Happy Kappy, 7" h, one piece rubber body, molded painted hair, painted blue eyes, open/closed mouth, yellow hat, mkd The Sun Rubber Co/Barberton, OH/Made in USA/Ruth E. Newton/New York/NY 25.00
Tod-L-Dee, 10-1/2" h, one piece rubber body, molded painted hair, open nurser mouth, molded diaper, shoes, and socks 25.00

Terri Lee Dolls. The founder and designer of the Terri Lee family was Mrs. Violet Lee Gradwohl of Lincoln, Nebraska. She made the first Terri Lee doll in 1948. Jerri Lee, a brother, was trademarked in 1948. Connie Lee joined the family in 1955. Mrs. Gradwohl issued lifetime guarantees for each doll, which were honored until the demise of the company in 1958.

Baby Linda, 9" h, all vinyl, molded painted hair, black eyes, c1951 .. 95.00
Jerri Lee Cowboy, 16" h 600.00
Patty Jo, 17" h, hard plastic, swivel head, jointed hard plastic body, black styled wig, painted brown eyes, closed mouth, orig dress, c1946 .... 450.00
Terri Lee, 10" h, hard plastic head, five-pc hard plastic body, walking mechanism, brown inset eyes, closed mouth, tagged long blue taffeta dress, mkd "©" on head and back, "Terri Lee" on dress, "Tiny Terri Lee, Manufactured by Terri Lee, ® Apple Valley, Calif" on red box 225.00
Tiny Jerri Lee, 10" h, hard plastic, fully jointed, blond curly wig, brown sleep eyes, closed mouth 175.00

Vogue. Vogue Dolls, Inc. was founded by Mrs. Jennie H. Graves. She began a small doll shop which specialized in well-made costumes. The original business of doll clothing lead to a cottage industry which employed more than 500 home sewers in 1950. This branch of the industry peaked in the late 1950s with more than 800 home workers plus several hundred more at the factory. During World War II, the shortages created a market for an American doll source. Mrs. Graves created the Ginny doll and promoted her heavily. The Ginny Doll was the first doll created with a separate wardrobe and accessories. For many years Vogue issued one hundred new outfits for Ginny alone. They continued to produce their own dolls and clothing for other doll manufacturers. Ginny Dolls reached their heyday in the 1950s and are still being made today.

Alpine Lady, 13" h, blond, ethnic costume, 1930s, mkd 200.00
Baby Dear, 12" h, all composition, bent baby limbs, 1961 .... 40.00
Betty Jane, 12" h, all composition, bent right arm, braided pigtails, red plaid woven cotton dress, white eyelet trim; orig tag Vogue Dolls Inc., 1947 ... 85.00
Crib Crow Baby, 7-1/2" h, all hard plastic, curved baby legs, painted eyes, blond synthetic ringlets wig, orig tagged dress, rubber pants, c1949 .... 425.00
Ginny, 7-1/2" h, Dutch Boy and Girl, hard plastic heads, five-pc strung hard plastic bodies, boy with brown sleep eyes, girl with blue sleep eyes, closed mouths, orig wigs, orig blue and white Dutch outfits, wooden shoes, boy has gold felt scarf and buttons, girl has gold cotton apron and hat, orig boxes 625.00
Ginny, 8" h, all hard plastic, painted eyes, molded hair, mohair wig, mkd "Vogue" on head, "Vogue Doll" on back, Springtime, c1948 .... 115.00
Hug a Bye Baby, 22" h, pink pajamas, MIB 40.00
Toodles, Bride, 8" h, composition head, five-pc composition child body, painted blue eyes to side, closed mouth, orig blond mohair wig, orig organdy bride dress with flocked design, orig underclothes, lace trimmed veil, orig white flowers, mkd "Vogue" on back of head, "Doll Co." on back 185.00
Toodles, John Alden, 8" h, composition head, five-pc composition toddler body, painted blue side-glancing eyes, closed mouth, orig mohair wig, orig Pilgrim-type off-white outfit, faint mark on torso, slight aging 175.00
Toodles, Julie, #8-10B, 8" h, composition head, five-pc composition body, painted blue eyes to side, closed mouth, orig mohair wig, orig tagged dark green knit bib pants, red felt squirrel trim, multicolored striped knit shirt and matching hat, orig socks and leatherette shoes, silver hoe with wooden handle, mkd "Vogue" on back, "Vogue Dolls, Inc., Medford, Mass" on pants tag 155.00
Walking Ginny, 8" h, ballerina, poodle cut wig, 1954, walking mechanism, mkd "Ginny Vogue Dolls, Inc., Pat. Pend., Made in USA" 110.00

Drugstore Collectibles

Collecting Hints: There are several considerations when starting a drugstore collection: 1) Buy the best that you can afford. (It is wise to pay a bit more for mint/near-mint items if available.) 2) Look for excellent graphics on the packaging of items. 3) Do not buy anything that is rusty or damp. 4) Before purchasing an item, ask the dealer to remove price tags or prices written on the piece. (If this isn't possible, determine how badly you want the item.) 5) Buy a variety of items. (Consider placing several similar items together on a shelf for increased visual effect.) 6) Purchase examples from a variety of time periods.

History: The increasing diversity of health-related occupations has also encouraged an awareness of pharmaceutical materials, items that appeared in drugstores from the turn of the century through the 1950s. Products manufactured before the Pure Food and Drug Act of 1906 are eagerly sought by collectors. Patent medicines, medicinal tins, items from a specific pharmaceutical company, dental items, and shaving supplies are a key collecting specialties.

The copyright date on a package, graphics, style of lettering, or the popularity of a specific item at a particular period in history are clues to dating a product. Pharmacists who have been in the business for a number of years are good sources for information, as are old manufacturing directories which are available at regional libraries.

References: Al Bergevin, *Drugstore Tins & Their Prices*, Wallace-Homestead, 1990; A. Walker Bingham, *Snake-Oil Syndrome*, Christopher Publishing House, 1994; Douglas Congdon-Martin, *Drugstore & Soda Fountain Antiques*, Schiffer Publishing, 1991; Martin R Lipp, *Medical Museums USA*, McGraw Hill Publishing, 1991; Patricia McDaniel, *Drugstore Collectibles*, Wallace-Homestead, 1994.

Periodical: *Siren Soundings*, 1439 Main St., Brewster, MA 02631.

Museums: National Museum of Health & Medicine, Walter Reed Medical Center, Washington, DC; New England Fire & History Museum, Brewster, MA.

Advisor: Patricia McDaniel.

Beauty Products

Alco-Mist Body Spray, Rexall Drug Company, Los Angeles, St. Louis, Boston, and Toronto, "contains skin softener to prevent dryness, plus hexachlorophene alcohol," 7 oz, 6-1/2" x 4 1/8" round metal can, white with blue stripes in front, broken lid, full..8.00

Breck Hair Spray, John Breck, Inc., Springfield, MA, "Super Hold, Beautiful Hair," 3/4 oz, 4" x 7/8" round, light blue metal bottle with black printing, full..3.00

Matey Easy-Rinse Shampoo, J. Nelson Prewitt, Inc., Rochester, NY, "kind to eyes," 7 fl oz, 7-1/4" x 2-1/4" round green bottle with white label, drawing of children dressed as pirates on boat on the ocean, full 7.50

Nivea Skin Oil, Duke Laboratories, Inc., USA, "Liquid Cream for Dry Skin for Chapping for The Bath," 1 pint, 7" x 2-3/4" x 2-3/4" clear bottle with white and blue label, 1/4 full 12.00

Cold and Cough

Bronchola Special, Bronchola Company, Peoria, IL, "for coughs due to colds," 4 fl oz, 4-1/2" x 1-3/4" round clear bottle, white printing, full bottle 8.00

Coldene, Pharma-Craft Cl., Batavia, IL, "for symptomatic relief of colds, headache, neuralgia and other muscular pains and aches," 20 tabs, 2-1/2" x 1-1/2" x 1-1/2" red box with white lettering, full bottle inside 8.50

Dr. Jayne's Expectorant, Dr. D. Jayne & Son, Inc., Philadelphia, PA, "for coughs due to colds, soothes quickly without opium," 2 fl oz, 5-1/2" x 1-3/4" x 1" brown bottle, white label with red and black printing, picture of frontier man with bulls and covered wagon, full bottle.......................................15.00

Grove's Cold Tablets, Grove Laboratories Incorporated, St. Louis, MO, analgesic, antipyretic, laxative, 20 tabs, 1/2" x 2" x 1-1/2" white box, red and black lettering, enclosed in cellophane 3.75

Mycinaire Antibacterial Nasal Spray, The Pfeiffer Co., St. Louis, MO, decongestant, antihistaminic, "relieves stuffy nose accompanying colds hay fever sinus congestion," 20 cc., 3-3/4" x 2" x 1" white box with burgundy printing, full bottle inside..............................9.00

Dental

Chloresium Dental Ointment, Rystan Company, Inc., Mount Vernon, NY, "A therapeutic chlorophyll preparation," 1/2 oz, white metal tube with dark green, 4 1/8" x 7/8" x-3/4" light green box with white stripes and dark green printing, full tube............................5.00

Dr. West's Insta-Clean Denture Cleanser, Weco Products Co., Chi-cago, IL, "Cleanses 2-5 minutes, dentures, bridges," 4 fl oz, 4-1/4" x 1-7/8" round, clear bottle with white printing, full of red liquid..............................8.00

Kirkman Cleanser, Colgate Palmolive, Peet & Co., 3" d, 4-3/4" h 22.00

Rexall Denturex, Rexall Drug Company, Los Angeles, St. Louis, and Toronto, false teeth cleaner, "No brushing, cleans all by itself," 7-1/2 oz, 6" x 3" x 1 3/8" oval tin, white, red, and light blue, full...8.00

Super-White Kolyno's Toothpaste, Whitehall Laboratories, Inc., New York, NY, "All-new Super-White Kolyno's combines three modern cleansing ingredients in a delightfully refreshing toothpaste. Super-White Kolyno's helps restore natural brightness of teeth, destroy mouth odors and sweeten breath. Brushing teeth after meals with Super-White Kolyno's is as effective in preventing decay as is the use of any dentifrice." 2.8 oz, 6" x 1" x 1" white metal tube with red writing, full 4.00

First Aid

Bell's Camphor Ice, Bell Chemical Cl., Chicago, IL, "for chapped skin, burns, sunburn," 1 oz,-3/4" x 3" x 1-3/4" yellow and brown tin, full.........................12.00

Itch-Me-Not, Sorbol Company, Mechanicsburg, OH, "A palliative aid in relieving the itching and burning of eczema, non-poisonous insect bites, athlete's foot, ivy poisoning and other externally caused skin irritations," 4 fl oz, 4-1/2" x 2" round brown bottle, white, yellow, green and red label, full 12.00

Medi-Quik Medicated Cream, Lehn & Fink Products Corporation, Bloomfield, NJ, "for chapped, cracked skin, detergent hands, minor burns, simple diaper rash," 1-1/2 oz,. 5-3/4" x 1-1/2" x 1-1/4" white box with red and turquoise, full tube inside...................8.25

Red Cross Adhesive Tape, Johnson & Johnson, New Brunswick, NJ, Chicago, IL, adhesive tape, waterproof, 1 inch, 10 yards, 1-1/2" x 3" round tin, white with red and blue printing, unopened.......................................9.00

Sanifit Vaccination Shield, Eagle Druggists Supply Co., Inc., New York, NY, "Celluloid Protector (ventilated) 'curved to fit'," 3-1/4" x 2-1/2" x 5/8" white box with red printing, name in red cross 6.00

Infants and Children

Baby Care Shampoo, Rexall Drug Company, Los Angeles and Toronto, "As gentle as a shampoo can be," 5 fl oz, clear bottle with yellow printing, 6-1/2" x 2-1/2" x 1-1/2" yellow box with white and blue, full bottle.............15.00

Deca-Vi-Sol Chewable Vitamins with Iron, Mead Johnson Laboratories, Evansville, IN, 50 tabs, 3" x 1-3/8" x 1-3/8" brown bottle with white and pink label, boy and girl silhouettes, full bottle 7.00

Feostat Hematinic, Westerfield Laboratories Inc., Cincinnati, OH, "For prevention and treatment of iron deficiency anemia," 6" x 2-1/4" x 1-1/2" brown bottle, white label with red and black printing, large lid with measures marked around outside...............18.00

Playtex Baby Powder, International Latex Corporation, Playtex Park, Dover, DE, "Soothes new born skin (from head to toe). Antiseptic, contains a scientific antiseptic that checks many skin germs," 6 oz, 5-3/8" x 2-1/8" round shaker, shiny pink with flat pink and blue printing, 3/4 full 10.00

Garfield's Seidlitz Powders, laxative, antacid, $12.

Miscellaneous

Cellasin, The Cellasin Co., Buffalo, NY, "Cellasin is derived from fungi, and acts in an alkaline medium and at body temperature. Indestructible, in the system, by acids or by other ferments," 200 tabs, 4-1/2" x 2" x 1-1/2" brown bottle with white label, black writing, edged in red, half full 18.00

Chap-ans Medicated Hand Cream, Miller-Morton Company, Richmond, Virginia, 4 oz, 2-1/2" x 2-1/2" round white jar with red and blue writing, blue picture of hand, full 8.50

Mead's No. 1 Sample Dextri Maltose, 2-1/2" x 2"....................................22.00

Midol, emb with orig instructions, photo of nurse, 24 tablets, 3-1/4" l, 1-1/4" w, " d................................24.00

Pinback Button

Dr. Cole's Tonic, red and white elephant inscribed "Why Suffer, Dr. Cole's Catarrh Cure Cures," early 1900s 10.00

Schering Nurse's Aide, red, white ground, genie lamp, 1960s 3.00

Smith-Junior's Certified Liquid Color Red Shade, Smith-Junior Co., Rochester, NY, 1 pint, 7-1/2" x 3" round clear bottle, white, orange, and black label, 1/3 full of red liquid............15.00

E

Electrical Appliances

Collecting Hints: Small electric appliances are still readily available and can be found at estate and garage sales, flea markets, auctions, antiques malls, and best of all, in the back of your mom's upper cabinets or even in Grandma's attic! Most can still be found at antique malls, etc. for a reasonable price. However, in recent years, due to collectors, decorators, and the foreign market, some appliances, mostly toasters that are "high-style" art deco have been commanding an almost unbelievable and dramatic rise in value. Porcelain and porcelain insert appliances have risen sharply, as well as some electric irons.

Most old toasters, waffle irons, and other appliances still work. When buying an old appliance, ask if it works and ask the *seller* to plug it in to see if it heats. **Note:** use extreme caution, there could be a short due to many factors (dirt, bare wires, etc.). On "flip-flop" type toasters (the most numerous kind) check to see if the elements are intact around the mica and not broken.

Most appliances used a standard-size cord which are still available at hardware stores. Some of the early companies had appliances that would only accept cords peculiar to that company. In such an instance, buy the appliance only if the cord accompanies it.

Unless you plan to use an appliance for display only or for parts, don't buy it if it doesn't work or is in rusted or poor condition.

Dirt does not count! With a little care, time, and diligence, most old appliances will clean up to a sparkling appearance. Aluminum mag-wheel polish, available at auto parts stores, can be used with a soft rag for wonderful results. *No steel wool!* Also, a non-abrasive kitchen cleanser can be a great help.

As with most collectibles, the original box or instructions can add 25 to 50 percent to the value of the piece. Also, beware of brass or copper appliances (usually coffee pots) because these were originally chrome or nickel. Devalue these by 50 percent.

History: The first all electric-kitchen appeared at the 1893 Chicago World's Fair and included a dishwasher that looked like a torture device and a range. Electric appliances for the home began gaining popularity just after 1900 in the major eastern and western cities. Appliances were sold door-to-door by their inventors. Small appliances did not gain favor in the rural areas until the late 1910s and early 1920s. However, most people did not trust electricity.

By the 1920s, competition among electrical companies was keen and there were many innovations. Changes occurred frequently, but the electric servants were here to stay. Most small appliance companies were bought by bigger firms. These, in turn, have been swallowed up by the huge conglomerates of today.

By the 1930s, it was evident that our new electric servants were making life a lot easier and were here to stay. The American housewife, even in rural areas, was beginning to depend on the electric age, enthusiastically accepting each new invention.

Some firsts in electrical appliances are:

1882	Patent for electric iron (H. W. Seeley [Hotpoint])
1903	Detachable cord (G.E. Iron)
1905	G.E. Toaster (Model X-2)
1905	Westinghouse toaster (Toaster Stove)
1909	Travel iron (G.E.)
1911	Electric frying pan (Westinghouse)
1912	Electric waffle iron (Westinghouse)
1917	Table Stove (Armstrong)
1918	Toaster/Percolator (Armstrong "Perc-O-Toaster")
1920	Heat indicator on waffle iron (Armstrong)
1920	Flip-flop toasters (many companies)
1920	Mixer on permanent base (Hobart Kitchen Aid)
1923	Portable mixer (Air-O-Mix "Whip-All")
1924	Automatic iron (Westinghouse)
1924	Home malt mixer (Hamilton Beach #1)
1926	Automatic pop-up toaster (Toastmaster Model 1-A-1)
1926	Steam iron (Eldec)
1937	Home coffee mill (Hobart Kitchen Aid)
1937	Automatic coffee maker (Farberware "Coffee Robot")
1937	Conveyance toaster ("Toast-O-Lator")

References: E. Townsend Artman, *Toasters,* Schiffer Publishing, 1996; Jane H. Clehar, Kitchens and Kitchenware, Wallace-Homestead, 1986; Linda Campbell Franklin, *300 Years of Kitchen Collectibles,* 4th ed., Krause Publications, 1998; Don Fredgant, *Electrical Collectibles, Relics of the Electrical Age,* Padre Publicatios, 1981; Helen Greguire, *Collector's Guide to Toasters & Accessories,* Collector Books, 1997; Earl Lifshey, (ed.), *The Housewares Story,* National Housewares Manufacturers Association, 1973; Gary Miller and K. M. Scotty Mitchell, *Price Guide to Collectible Kitchen Appliances,* Wallace-Homestead, 1991.

Collectors' Club: Electric Breakfast Club, P.O. Box 306, White Mills, PA 18473, The Old Appliance Club P.O. Box 65, Ventura CA 93002.

Advisors: Gary L. Miller and K. M. (Scotty) Mitchell.

Blenders

Berstead Drink Mixer, 1930s, Eskimo Kitchen Mechanic, Berstead Mfg. Co., domed chrome motor, single shaft, lift-off metal base with receptacle for tapered ribbed glass, 12" 60.00

Chronmaster Mixall, 1930s, Chronmaster Electric Corp., NY & Chicago, chrome and black motor, single shaft on hinged black base, orig silver-striped glass 45.00

Dorby Whipper, 1940s, Model E, chrome motor with black Bakelite handle, off/on toggle, clear, measured Vidrio glass 45.00

Electromix Whipper, 1930s, Chicago, ivory colored, offset metal motor housing with push-down break, filler hole in lid, measured glass base, 7-1/2" 40.00

Gilbert Mixer, Polar Cub, 1929, A.C. Gilbert Co., New Haven, CT, 10" h, lift-off gray painted metal, rear switch, blue wood handle, premium for Wesson-Snowdrift, orig box 125.00

Hamilton Beach Malt Machine, forerunner to home malt maker, mid-1920s, Cyclone #1, 19" h, heavy nickel housing, sq stand on marble base, int push-down switch 350.00

Kenmore Hand Mixer, 1940s, Sears, Roebuck & Co., Chicago, small, cream-colored plastic, single 4-1/2" beater, orig box, booklet, warranty and hanger plate 35.00

Kenmore Whipper, 1940s, Sears, Roebuck & Co., Chicago, cream-colored metal domed top, large blue Bakelite knob, clear glass bottom, 8-1/2" h.. 25.00

Knapp Monarch Whipper, mid-1930s, St. Louis, 9-1/2" h, white metal motor, red plastic top handle, round mild glass base with reeded, fin feet, white plastic beater................................65.00

Kwick Way, St. Louis, 7-1/2" h, white metal motor top over angular clear glass base, no switch, decal label..35.00

Made-Rite Drink Mixer, 1930s, Weinig Made Rite Co., Cleveland, light-weight metal, cream and green motor, single shaft, no switch, stamped, permanent support, no glass........................30.00

Silex Blender, 1940s, NY, sq, white cast base, push-button switch, silver foil, Art Deco label, clear glass four-cup top with vertical "Silex" on black stripe, plastic lid.........................35.00

Unmarked Whipper, late 1920s-early 1930s, 7-1/2" h, green metal motor housing, green Depression glass "Vidrio" cup, unusual serpentine shaft...25.00

Chafing dishes

American Beauty, c1910, American Electrical Heater Co., Detroit, MI, three-part, nickel on copper, base serves as hot-water container and has sealed element, separate plugs mkd "fast" and "slow," black painted wood handles and knob........................50.00

Chase Chrome Supper Set, 1930s, 11" x 18" Art Deco chrome body, chamfered corners, four white porcelain inserts with chrome lids, black plastic handles & knobs........................225.00

Manning Bowman, 1930s, Meriden, CT

Chafing Dish, bright chrome Art Deco design, reeded edges, two-part top on hot-plate base, black Bakelite knob and handles 75.00

Supper Set, 19" l oval, chrome, Art Deco body, reeded decoration, two large round Hall Porcelain inserts with chrome lids, black knobs 195.00

Universal, c1910, Landers, Frary & Clark, New Britain, CT, nickel on copper faceted three-part body, sealed element in base hot-water pan, three-prong heat adjuster in base, large black wood handle and knob 50.00

Coffee Makers and Sets

Coleman, percolator, "Electric Brew" model 70, high Art Deco, spherical, glass body, applied glass handle, chrome lid, black knob all mounted on black bakelite base, four vertical, silver fins...95.00

Farberware Coffee Robot, coffee set, 1937, S.W. Farber, Brooklyn, NY, coffee maker #500, set #501, two-part coffee dripolator, creamer, open sugar and tray, nickel chrome, walnut handles, orig booklet, price for set .125.00

Manning Bowman, Meriden, CT

Percolator, 1930s, set #636, tall graceful Art Deco design, bright chrome, reeded decoration around neck and base, 12" h 60.00

Percolator Urn, late 1920s, article #250, three-part aluminum body, unique design prevents re-perking, front spigot, out-turned handles, clear glass insert in domed lid, 12-1/2" h 50.00

Meriden Homelectrics Percolator Set, 1930s, set #636, Manning Bowman Co., Meriden, CT, catalog #32, ser. #4-30, 15" h percolator/urn, creamer, open sugar, nickel chrome vertically faceted bodies, urn on short cabriole legs, up-turned black wood handles, glass knob insert on top, set 95.00

Porcelier, Breakfast Set, 1930s, Greensburg, PA, all-porcelain bodies accented by basketweave design, floral transfers, silver line dec

Coffee Urn............................ 450.00

Cream and Sugar, cov 50.00

Percolator #5007.................. 125.00

Sandwich Grill #5004 .... 195.00

Toaster #5002 .... 850.00

Royal Rochester Percolator, Robeson Rochester Corp., Rochester, NY, percolator

c1912, round chrome body, shaped, clear glass "basket," chrome lid, spigot and attached base, out-turned "feet" 75.00

1930s, #D-30, almost-white porcelain, slight greenish luster around shoulder and spout, spring bouquet floral transfer, chrome lid and base, clear glass insert 125.00

1930s, model D-33, 1930s, high Art Deco design in chrome, cylindrical body with wide black stripe, stepped glass lid with black knob, open, vertical handle, "ding" timer 85.00

Sunbeam Dripolator, 1930s, Model 14, high Art Deco design, cylindrical chrome body with horizontal black stripes, three-part, serving container with hinged lid, large chrome "basket," short hot plate with rotating temperature control, matching creamer and sugar 150.00

Universal

Breakfast Set, 1930s, Landers, Frary & Clark, New Britain, CT, cream-colored porcelain, blue and orange floral transfers, waffle iron on pierced chrome base has porcelain insert, front drop handle

Creamer and sugar, cov.... 45.00

Percolator #E6927 .... 125.00

Syrup, chrome cov 60.00

Waffle Iron E6324 .... 195.00

Coffee Set

c1915, Landers, Frary & Clark, New Britain, CT, coffee urn #E9219, 14" h, squat cabriole legs, large wood ear-shaped handles; nickel bodies, oval tray, price for 4-pc set .. 125.00

1920s, Landers, Frary & Clark, New Britain, CT, urn #E9119-1, 16-1/2" h, chrome, chrome handles, swirl glass insert, octagonal body, handled tray, price for 4-pc set 150.00

Egg cookers

Hankscraft Co., 1920s, Madison, WI, Model #599, yellow china base, large dish on top of domed chrome serves as knob and filler with hole in bottom, instructions on metal plate on bottom...35.00

Rochester Stamping Co., c1910, Rochester, NY, egg-shaped, four-part chrome on small base, interior fitted with skillet with turned black wood handle, six-egg holder with lift-out handle, enclosed heating element...................................... 65.00

Food Cookers

Eureka Portable Oven, 1930s, Eureka Vacuum Cleaner Co., Detroit, MI, 15" x 13" x 19", Art-Deco style, cream-colored painted body, black edges, sides fold down and contain hot plates on chrome surfaces, int fitted with wire racks, controls across bottom front... 200.00

Everhot, 1920s, Swartz Baugh Mfg. Co., Toledo, OH, EC Junior 10, 13" h, large chrome and black cylindrical body, aluminum cov, Art Deco design, "Everhot" embossed on front, int fitted with rack, two open semicircular pans, one round cov pan, three-prong heat control 50.00

Hankscraft, 1920s, Madison, WI, green enamel pan, detachable hinge-pin chrome cov, green ceramic luster-ware knob, chrome base, black wood handles flare from sides of body... 95.00

Nesco Electric Casserole, early 1930s, National Enamel & Stamping Co., Inc., Milwaukee, WI, 9" d, forerunner of crock pot, cream-colored body with green enamel cov, high/low control, three-prong plug 35.00

Quality Brand, 1920s, Great Northern Mfg. Co., Chicago, IL, model #950, 14" h, cylindrical body, insulated sides and cov, fitted int. with cov aluminum pans, brown with red stripe body, lift-out rods.......................................40.00

Westinghouse, roaster oven, 1940s, white metal painted body, aluminum top with window on top, gray plastic handle, includes lift-out gray granite ware pan, three clear glass dishes with lids, matching stand with clock timer and storage door 50.00

Hot plates

Edison-Hotpoint, c1910, Edison Electric, NY, Chicago and Ontario, CA, solid iron surface, clay-filled int., very heavy pierced legs, ceramic feet, copper control with ceramic knob 35.00

El Stovo, c1910, Pacific Electric Heating Co., sometimes mkd "G.E. Hot-

point," solid iron surface, clay-filled int, very heavy pierced legs, pad feet, no control 25.00
Volcano, 1930s, Hilco Engineering Co., Chicago, IL, slightly conical nickel body, black wood handle, slide lever as control on side that lifts grate . 40.00
Westinghouse, 1920s, Mansfield, OH, 7-1/2" d top with green porcelain-metal top surrounding element, hollow legs, no control 25.00

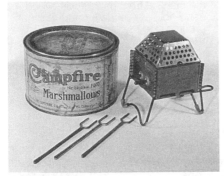

Angelus-Campfire Bar-B-Q Marsh-mallow Toaster, 1920s, $125. Photo courtesy of Gary Miller and Scotty Mitchell.

Miscellaneous

Angelus-Campfire Bar-B-Q Marshmallow Toaster, 1920s, Milwaukee, WI, 3" sq, flat top, pierced pyramid top piece, base on loop, wire legs with rubber-encased feet, flat wire forks, orig box 125.00
Buffet warming oven, Chase Chrome and Brass 130.00
Clock/Timer, late 1930s, made for Montgomery Ward & Co., cream body, silver and red face, curved glass, body swivels on weighted base, clock mechanism winds up manually, cord at back with appliance receptacle 40.00
Coffee Grinder, Kitchen Aid, Hobart, Troy, OH, model #A-9, heavy cream-colored cast base with motor, course/fine adjustment on neck, clear glass jar container with screw-off top serves as storage for beans 75.00
Miracle Flour Sifter, c1934, Chicago, IL, electric, cream body, blue wood hold-down button handle at base, vibrates flour through wire strainer 35.00
Sunkist Juicer, 1930s, 9" h, opaque green Depression glass top, int. metal strainer, chrome body/motor housing with dark green painted center, metal "Sunkist" plate on front 85.00
Universal
  Griddle, late 1930s, large 23" x 15" white porcelain body on short porcelain legs, full aluminum griddle top w/ drain spout, two large red indicator lights, two front round controls with porcelain handles 175.00
  Tea Kettle, c1910, Landers, Frary & Clark, New Britain, CT, model

#E973, bright nickel one-pc squat body and base, long spout, black painted wood high curved handle on pierced vertically curved mounts 45.00
Vita-Juicer, 1930s, Kold King Distributing Corp., Los Angeles, Hoek Rotor Mfg. Co., Reseda, CA, 10" h, heavy, cream-painted cast metal, base motor, container and lid fitted with lock groove and lock-down wire handle, aluminum pusher fits in top holder 35.00
White Cross, oven, 1920s, black steel body, 34" h on short legs, 14" x 12" vertical, small oven and warming compartment, larger top with two hotplates three front, round porcelain and chrome controls 175.00

Handymix mixer, Mary Dunbar, Chicago Electric Mfg. Co., 1930s, 11-1/2" h, $60. Photo courtesy of Gary Miller and Scotty Mitchell.

Mixers

Dominion Modern Mode, 1923-33, Dominion Electrical Mfg. Co., Minneapolis, MN, faceted, angular Art Deco body and base, three-speed rear lever control, runs on A.C. or D.C., two custard glass bowls and juicer, mechanism to control beater height 75.00
General Electric, 1938, G.E. Corp., upright housed motor, no speed control, three synchronized beaters in a row, work light shines in handle, two white glass bowls, black Bakelite handle, ser. #10-A 50.00
Hamilton Beach, 1930s, Racine, WI, model G, cream-colored metal, black Bakelite handle, on/off lever control, "Mix Guide" in window below handle, mixer lifts off base to become portable, two white glass bowls 35.00
Sunbeam Mixmaster
  Attachments, fit most models
    Bean slicer 20.00

Can opener 15.00
Churn 50.00
Coffee grinder 25.00
Drink mixer 15.00
Grater, slicer, shredder, 3 blades 35.00
Grinder/chopper 25.00
Juicer, mayonnaise maker . . 20.00
Knife sharpener 15.00
Pea sheller 10.00
Potato peeler 35.00
Power unit. 10.00
Ricer 20.00
Silver polisher and buffer. . . 10.00
Cabinet, 60-1/2" x 24" 295.00
Mixmaster, early 1930s, Chicago Flexible Shaft Co., model K, cream-colored body, fold-over black wood handle, rear speed control, light green opaque Depression glass bowls, juicer and strainer, orig booklet 65.00

Popcorn Poppers

Berstead, 1930s, model #302, sq, chrome, body with circular int, Fry Glass lid, large black knob on top, rod through lid for stirring 45.00
Excel, 1920s, Excel Electric Co., Muncie, IN, one-pc cylindrical nickel body, metal handles form legs, lock-down levers, hand crank, black wood knob, top vent holes 25.00
Manning Bowman, early 1940s, Meriden, CT, model #500, detachable large aluminum container, fits chrome hot plate, glass lid emb with floral motif, black Bakelite knob, never used 15.00
Rapaport, 1920s, Rapaport Bros., Inc., Chicago, 5-1/2" sq black base, metal legs, round aluminum upper part with attached lid and red knob, chrome handle squeezes through slot in side to agitate corn 25.00
U.S. Mfg. Corp., 1930s, Decatur, IL, #10, body and lid separate from hot plate base, top crank handle...... 15.00
White Cross, c1918, National Stamping & Electrical Co., Chicago, IL, tin can base with heater and cord, wire basket fits onto can, metal top with stirrer mounted through handle, wood handle to side, primitive 30.00

Toasters

Edison Appliance Co., c1918, NY, cat. #214-T-5, open nickel body with free-swinging tab closures at top, single side knob, removable toast warming rack 95.00
General Mills, early 1940s, Minneapolis, MN, cat. #GM5A, two-slice pop-up chrome body, wheat dec on side, black Bakelite base, A.C. or D.C., red knob, light/dark control 45.00
Heat Master, 1923-35, sq chrome body, rounded corners, end opening, two-slice, manual operation, black Bakelite handle and feet 60.00

Kenmore, early 1940s, Sears, Roebuck & Co., Chicago, mechanical, two-slice pop-up, chrome body, rounded edges and sides, black Bakelite handles, mechanical clock mechanism, light/dark control.....30.00

Knapp Monarch Reverso, 1930, cat. #505, light-weight rect nickel body, rounded corners, black painted base, flip-flop doors with tab handles, no mica, wires stretched across 70.00

Montgomery Ward & Co., mid-1930s, Chicago, IL, model #94-KW2298-B, flip-flop type, solid nickel-chrome body, Bakelite handle on end opens both doors simultaneously 50.00

Steel Craft, late 1920s, open, painted green wire construction, flip-flop type, red painted wood knobs and feet 65.00

Sunbeam, early 1920s, Chicago Flexible Shaft Co., model B, 5" x 9", flat, rect dec chrome body, round, reeded legs, hexagonal Bakelite feet, double wire cages flip over horizontally, small drop bail handles for carrying 125.00

Toastmaster, 1927, Waters-Genter Co., Minneapolis, MN, model 1-A-1, recognized as first automatic pop-up, chrome Art Deco body, louvered sides, rounded end, manual clock timer mechanism, light/dark control from A to G, panic button..........250.00

Universal, 1913-15, Landers, Frary & Clark, nickel body, flat base, tab feet, pierced concave spring-loaded doors, permanent warming rack.............60.00

Westinghouse

> Toaster Stove, 1909, Mansfield, OH, flat rect body, four flat strip plates, removable cabriole legs, tray and wire rack, orig box and paper guarantee, never used 175.00
>
> Turnover Toaster, 1920s, Mansfield, OH, cat. #TT3, nickel body, pierced doors and top, flat tab handles, pierced, flat warming rack top 45.00

Waffle Irons and Sandwich Grills

Most popular are porcelain insert waffle irons. These are by most manufacturers in various transfer designs. Any one is worth at least $125.

Armstrong Waffle Iron, 1920, model W, first example with heat read/thermometer light on top, 7" round nickel body, black wood handles, distinctive prongs, with cord..........................45.00

Coleman Waffle Iron, early 1930s, Coleman Lamp & Stove Co., Wichita, KS, high Art Deco style, chrome, low profile, small black and white porcelain top impala insert, black Bakelite handles 85.00

Dominion Electric Co., double waffle iron, 1940s, Mansfield, OH, chrome rect stepped body, two round waffle grills, separate temperature controls, red light heat indicator, walnut handles, top circular dec, special two-headed cord 35.00

Magazine tear sheet showing Westinghouse Products, $20. Photo courtesy of Gary Miller and Scotty Mitchell.

Electrahot Double Waffle Iron, 1940s, Mansfield, OH, two 6" sets of plates mounted on oval base, heat indicators with surrounding dec on top 30.00

Excelsior Waffle Iron, 1930s, Perfection Electric Co., New Washington, OH, 6" round white porcelainized iron body, four little stamped legs, plug in front, turned painted wood handle 25.00

Fitzgerald Star Waffle Iron, 1920s, Torrington, CT, 7", solid flared base, unique handle design locks in position for raising or carrying...................35.00

General Electric Waffle Iron, early 1940s, 8" round chrome body, ivory Bakelite handles and heat control/off front lever, top dec of circle of stars surrounding stripes and leaves...35.00

Hostess Sandwich Grill, 1930s, All Rite Co., Rushville, IN, 5" sq cast-aluminum body, angled at bottom to form feet, screw-off wood handle, orig box and booklet of suggestions 65.00

Hotpoint Waffle Iron, 1920s, Edison, General Electric, Chicago, IL and Ontario, CA, "Automatic" below front handle, rotating cold/hot in small front window, round chrome body, top dec, ivory Bakelite handles, scalloped base dec 35.00

Lady Hibbard Sandwich Grill, 1930s, Hibbard, Spencer, Bartlet & Co., Chicago, IL, nickel rect body, cast cabriole legs, black wood side handles, front handle swivels to form foot for top plate enabling use of both plates as grills, drip spout 25.00

Manning Bowman, Meriden, CT, Twin-O-Matic Waffle Iron, late 1930s, Art Deco design, top heat indicator with rotating knob, chrome body flips over in brown Bakelite stand mounted on chrome base 125.00

Sampson Waffle Iron, 1930s, Sampson United Corp., Rochester, NY, Art

Deco design, chrome boy with wing-like flared Bakelite side handles set asymmetrically, stationary front handle..40.00

Torrid Waffle Iron, 1920s, Beardsley & Wolcott Mfg. Co., Waterbury, CT, flared base, 7-1/2" round plated-chrome body, green up-turned handles and front knob, front window indicates "too cold," "too hot," and "bake"........35.00

Westinghouse Waffle Iron, 1905-21 patent date, rect chrome body, mechanical front handle with wood hand-hold, removable cabriole legs slip into body slots, off/on switch...90.00

Elephant Collectibles

Collecting Hints: There are vast quantities of elephant-shaped and elephant-related items. Concentrate on one type of object (toys, vases, bookends, etc.), one substance (china, wood, paper), one chronological period, or one type of elephant (African or Indian). The elephants of Africa and India do differ, a fact not widely recognized.

Perhaps the most popular elephant collectibles are those related to Jumbo and Dumbo, the Disney character who was a circus outcast and the first flying elephant. GOP material associated with the Republican party is usually left to the political collector.

Because of the large number of items available, stress quality. Study the market carefully before buying. Interest in elephant collecting is subject to phases, and is currently at a modest level.

History: Elephants were unique and fascinating when they first reached America. Early specimens were shown in barns and moved at night to avoid anyone getting a free look. The arrival of Jumbo in England, his subsequent purchase by P. T. Barnum, and his removal to America brought elephant mania to new heights.

Elephants have always been a main attraction at American zoological parks. The popularity of the circus in the early 20th century kept attention focused on elephants.

Hunting elephants was considered "big game" sport, and President Theodore Roosevelt was one well-known participant. The hunt always focused on finding the largest known example. It is not a surprise that an elephant dominates the entrance to the Museum of Natural History of the

Smithsonian Institution in Washington, D.C.

Television, through shows such as "Wild Kingdom," has contributed to knowledge about all wild animals, including the now quite-commonplace elephant.

Periodical: *Jumbo Jargon,* 1002 W. 25th St., Erie, PA 16502.

Figure, elephant with young, bisque, Italian, 21" l, 15-1/2" h, $525. Photo courtesy of Joy Luke Fine Art Brokers and Auctioneers.

Advertising Trade Card, 4-7/8" x 3", Clark's Spool Cotton, Jumbo's Arrival, sepia, white, adv on back 7.50

Ashtray, elephant foot, silver-plate, 3-1/2" d 25.00

Bank
    Cast iron, painted gold, A. Williams, USA, some wear to orig paint ... 110.00
    Chalk, 12" h, orig paint, c1930 . 125.00

Battery Operated, 3-1/4" x 4" x 6", playing cymbal and drum, made by M & M, Japan, c1960 .... 45.00

Book, Edward Allen, *Fun By The Ton* 20.00

Bottle opener, figural, cast iron, sitting, trunk raised
    Brown, pink eyes and tongue, 3-1/2" h 55.00
    Pink, "GOP" on base, 3-1/4" h 55.00

Brooch, 3" w, 3" l, faux jet stones, crystal rhinestones, Butler & Wilson logo on back 135.00

Castor Base, Elephant pattern, pressed glass, wire handle, c1885 .... 180.00

Child's Book, *Kellogg's Funny Jungleland Moving Pictures,* ©1909, published by W. K. Kellogg, patented Jan 15, 1907, fold-out sections 24.00

Christmas Ornament
    3" h, silver emb cardboard, Dresden, Germany 140.00
    3-1/2" l, blown glass, gray body, red blanket 95.00

Cigarette Dispenser, cast iron, orig paint dec 115.00

Clothes Sprinkler Bottle, figural 165.00

Creamer and Sugar, red blankets, Black riding on sugar, Lusterware, mkd "Made in Japan," c1940 .... 190.00

Decanter, 11" l, 9-1/2" h, heavy metal, painted gold, tube to feed liquor through elephant, mkd "Elephant Scotch C.T.S." on both sides 165.00

Figure
    1-1/2" h, 2" l, ceramic, shaded gray glaze 8.00
    3" h, 2-1/2" l, glass, trunk raised .. 12.00
    4-1/4" h, porcelain, acrobat, pastel blue, white, beige, triangular gold "Royal Dux" sticker, oval "Made in Czech Republic" sticker 55.00
    4-1/2" h, maple, child riding on back of elephant with raised trunk, ink stamp "Anri Italy Ferrandiz" 450.00
    23-1/2" h, teak, carved adult and baby, 20th C, one tusk missing 140.00

Lamp, elephant with girl, hand painted, Japan, 14" h 45.00

Letter Opener, 7-1/2" l, celluloid, marked "Depose-Germany," c1900 .... 40.00

Mug, Frankoma, 1970s 20.00

Napkin Ring, Bakelite, navy blue, c1940 .... 65.00

Nodder, 3-1/2" l, 1-3/4" h, celluloid, gray back and head, pink ears, white belly, silver painted tusks 35.00

Pie Bird, mkd "Nutbrown Pie Funnel, Made in England," c1940 .... 185.00

Pin, gold tone, figural 25.00

Pinback Button, Rub-No-More, gray and black image of elephant in household attire, using trunk as shower for baby elephant standing in washing pan 25.00

Pitcher, 6-1/2" h, figural elephant, black man as handle, incised "5020" .175.00

Planter, 8" x 5-1/2", figural, pottery, unmarked 20.00

Post Card, Elephant Hotel, Margate City, NJ, 1953 .... 7.50

Poster, 47" x 58", Lil Nil Cigarette Papers, litho, trumpeting elephant, linen backing 250.00

Salt and Pepper Shakers, pr, figural, mkd "Japan" 24.00

Sign, 15" x 13", Brown's Jumbo Bread, diecut tin, elephant with trunk curled down, blanket on back, c1930 .. 150.00

Tobacco Tag, tin, diecut, Red Elephant Tobacco 7.50

Toy
    3-1/2" h, 4-1/4" l, Jumbo, litho tin wind, mkd "U. S. Zone Germany" 85.00
    5" h, Elmer Elephant, gray, bow tie and hat, rubber, Sieberling 165.00

Vase, figural handle, ivory matte finish 125.00

F

Farm Collectibles

Collecting Hints: The country look makes farm implements and other items very popular with interior decorators. Often items are varnished or refinished to make them more appealing but, in fact, this lowers their value as far as the serious collector is concerned.

Farm items were used heavily; collectors should look for signs of use to add individuality and authenticity to the pieces.

When collecting farm toys, it is best to specialize in a single type, e.g., cast iron, models by one specific company, models of one type of farm machinery, or models in one size (1/16 scale being the most popular). Farm collectibles made after 1940 have not yet achieved great popularity.

History: Initially, farm products were made by local craftsmen—the blacksmith, wheelwright, or the farmer himself. Product designs varied greatly.

The industrial age and the golden age of American agriculture go hand in hand. The farm market was important to manufacturers between 1880 and 1900. Farmers demanded quality products capable of withstanding hard use. In the 1940s, urban growth began to draw attention away from the rural areas, and the consolidation of farms began. Larger machinery was developed.

The vast majority of farm models date between the early 1920s and the present. Manufacturers of farm equipment, such as John Deere, International Harvester, Massey-Ferguson, Ford, and White Motors, issued models to correspond to their full-sized products. These firms contracted with America's leading toy manufacturers, such as Arcade Company, Dent, Ertl, Hubley, Killgore, and Vindex, to make the models.

References: Nick Baldwin and Andrew Morland, *Classic Tractors of the World: A to Z Coverage of the World's Most Fascinating Tractors,* Voyageur Press; C. Lee Criswell and Clarence L. Criswell, Sr., *Criswell's Pedal Tractor Guide,* Criswell Press, 1999; David Erb and Eldon Brumbaugh, *Full Steam Ahead: J. I. Case Tractors & Equipment,* American Society of Agricultural Engineers, 1993; Jim Moffet,

American Corn Huskers, Off Beat Books, 1994; Robert Rauhauser, *Hog Oilers Plus,* published by author (Box 766, RR #2, Thomasville, PA 17364), 1996; C. H. Wendel, *Encyclopedia of American Farm Implements & Antiques,* Krause Publications, 1997; -----, *Unusual Vintage Tractors,* Krause Publications, 1996.

Periodicals: *Antique Power,* P.O. Box 1000, Westerville, OH 43081; *Belt Pulley,* P.O. Box 83, Nokomis, IL 62075; *Country Wagon Journal,* P.O. Box 331, W Milford, NJ 07480; *Farm & Horticultural Equipment Collector,* Kelsey House, 77 High St., Beckenham Kent BR3 1AN England; *Farm Antiques News,* 812 N. Third St., Tarkio, MO 64491; *Farm Collector,* 1503 SW. 42nd St., Topeka, KS 66609, *Iron-Men Album,* P.O. Box 328, Lancaster, PA 17603; *Rusty Iron Monthly,* P.O. Box 342, Sandwich, IL 60548; *Spec-Tuclar News,* P.O. Box 324, Dyersville, IA 52040; *Toy Farmer,* H C 2, Box 5, LaMoure, ND 58458; *Toy Tractor Times,* P.O. Box 156, Osage, IA 50461; *Tractor Classics,* P.O. Box 191, Listowel, Ontario N4H 3HE Canada; *Turtle River Toy News & Oliver Collector's News,* RR1, Box 44, Manvel, ND 58256.

Collectors' Clubs: Antique Engine, Tractor & Toy Club, 5731 Paradise Rd, Slatington, PA 18080; Cast Iron Seat Collectors Association, P.O. Box 14, Ionia, MO 65335; CTM Farm Toy & Collectors Club, P.O. Box 489, Rocanville, Saskatchewan S0A 3L0 Canada; Early American Steam Engine & Old Equipment Society, P.O. Box 652, Red Lion, PA 17356; Ertl Replicas Collectors' Club, Hwys 136 and 20, Dyersville, IA 52040; Farm Toy Collectors Club, P.O. Box 38, Boxholm, IA 50040; International Harvester Collectors, RR2, Box 286, Winamac, IN 46996.

Museums: Billings Farm & Museum, Woodstock, VT; Bucks County Historical Society, Doylestown, PA; Carroll County Farm Museum, Westminster, MD; Living History Farms, Urbandale, IA; Makoti Threshers Museum, Makoti, ND; National Agricultural Center & Hall of Fame, Bonner Springs, KS; Never Rest Museum, Mason, MI; New York State Historical Association and The Farmers' Museum, Cooperstown, NY; Pennsylvania Farm Museum, Landis Valley, PA.

Bank
  Allis-Chalmers, 3" x 5-1/2" x 4" h thin steel, mailbox shape, orange, cream colored flag, black, white, and orange Allis-Chalmers logo sticker, lock and keys, 1970s 15.00
  Iowa Farmers Trust, tin canister, capped top and bottom by celluloid, yellow, black, and white, savings slogans on sides, 1920s, some wear 60.00
Barn Hinge, 27" l, wrought iron, strap type 75.00
Book
  Come Back to the Farm, Jesse Stuart, McGraw Hill, 1971, 1st edition.... 25.00
  Market Milk, Ernest Kelly & Clarence Clement, Wiley & Sons, 1923, 445 pgs. 20.00
  Starting Right with Turkeys, G. T. Klein, MacMillan, 1947, 129 pgs 15.00
Branding Iron, Lazy B, wrought iron 40.00
Card, Olds Patent Wheel Wagon, celluloid, multicolored, white ground, black letters, reverse with detailed aerial factory scene of Fort Wayne, IN 80.00
Catalog
  Adriance Platt & Co., Poughkeepsie, NY, 1905, 48 pgs, 7-1/4" x 9-1/2", farm machinery 48.00
  American Steel & Wire Co., New York, NY, 1913, 22 pgs, 6" x 6-3/4", fencing 17.00
  Buckeye Incubator Co., Springfield, OH, 1900s, 64 pgs, 6" x 9" 24.00
  D. Hill Nursery Co., Dundee, IL, 1930, 40 pgs, 9" x 11-1/2", 75th anniversary evergreen catalog 22.00
  E. A. Strout Farm Agency, New York, NY, 1925, 190 pgs, 7-3/4" x 10-3/4" 36.00
  IHC of America, Inc., Chicago, IL, disk harrow, 1909, 32 pgs, 6-1/2" x 8" 44.00
  Kemp & Burpee Mfg. Co., Syracuse, NY, 1895, eight pgs, 5-3/4" x 8-3/4", four pictures of Kemp Manure Spreader 18.00
  Keystone Farm Machine Co., York, PA, eight pgs, 6" x 9-3/4" 24.00
  Moline Plow Co., Moline, IL, 1908, 32 pgs, 6" x 8-3/4" 32.00
  Pioneer Thresher Co., Shortsville, NY, 1939, 12 pgs, 7-1/2" x 10"........... 28.00
Chick Feeder, tin.................................. 20.00
Clip, Moline Wagon Co., red wagon wheel, orange background, silver lettered inscriptions "Light Running and Durable," insert brass pencil clip 75.00
Corn Dryer, hanging, wrought iron .. 27.50
Egg Candler, 8" h, tin, kerosene burner, mica window 30.00

Egg shipping crate, wood, marked, "Sardiner Egg Carrier, made by New England Box Co., Boston, Mass," 13-3/4" w, 10-1/4" h, $225.

Egg Crate, tin 12.00
Feed Rag, cotton
   Black illus of sheet 12.00
   Floral print, washed 5.00
   Geometric print, yellow and
   green 7.00
Flax Comb, 17-1/2" l, wrought iron, ram's horn finials 135.00
Flicker Tag, Dairylea Milk, cardboard keychain tag, full color image of Miss Dairylea, flicker image "Look Both Ways Before Crossing,"
   c1960 .... 12.00
Flipper Pin, diecut thin celluloid
   Dain Hay Machinery, multicolored image of Great Dane dog, red and white sponsor name on back 50.00
   Globe Scranton Feed, diecut, egg-shaped pin, black and white text, Albert Dickinson Co., early
   1900s 80.00
   Swift's Chicken Feed, black and white farm bird, inscribed, "Swift's Premium Milk Fed Chickens" 25.00
Grain Shovel, wood, carved dec ... 300.00
Hay Rake, 48-1/2" l, varnished 65.00
Implement Seat, Hoover & Co., cast iron 115.00
Magazine Ad, 6" x 10", A. W. Stevens & Son Farm Machinery, little boy and dog, mkd "Gies & Co. Lith, Buffalo, NY," 8-3/4" x 12-3/4" frame 25.00
Memo Booklet, Superior Drill Co., Springfield, OH, celluloid cover, full color illus, tan leather piping, 1907 calendar, four pgs describing farm products, other illus 45.00
Name Tag, Grain Dealers Convention, diecut celluloid, full color illus of train at grain elevator, corn husk background 35.00
Painting
   15-1/2" x 19-5/8", Dorin Cretu, watercolor, titled "In the Fields," workers wearing wooden shoes,
   framed 175.00
   17" x 25", Delores Hackenberger, oil on canvas, old home, gray stone barn,

covered bridge, orig owner's handwriting, name, and town on back, orig frame, 1940s 200.00
Pendant, celluloid, Agriculture Fair, Richfield, NY, 1898, diecut, multicolored horse heads, white ground, black lettering, inserted at top by red, white, and blue striped fabric bow, reverse has celluloid insert centered by multicolored image of various harvest fruit 25.00
Pinback Button
   Boston Hopper, blue and white, red lettering, "Rat-Proof Hopper" 38.00
   Case Farm Machinery Eagle, multicolored, adult eagle, world globe 40.00
   Daybreak Fertilizer, red rooster, white ground, black letters 20.00
   Empire Cream Separator, blue and white image, blue lettering, "I Chirp For The Empire Because It Makes The Most Dollars for Me" 28.00
   Fish Bros. Wagon, Racine, WI, multicolored design, huge river fish being hooked on fishing line 125.00
   Fulton & Walker Co., Best Wagons for Business, Philadelphia, multicolored image of delivery wagon 85.00
   Huber Steam Tractor, multicolored image of "The New Huber," blue rim, white letters 75.00
   Mallard Lake Game Farm, blue and white design, "Turkeys/Quail/Pheasants," c1940 .... 12.00
   New Idea Manure Spreader, multicolored scene of horse-drawn spreader "At Work In The Field" 85.00
   Old Reliable Fertilizers, red star symbol, white lettering, E. Rauh & Sons, Indianapolis 15.00
Page Wire Fence, Adrian, MI, rect aluminum, early 1900s 10.00
   Racine-Sattley Line, red and white logo, black background 10.00
   Russell & Company, The Boss, Massillon, OH, multicolored image of brown bull symbol 60.00
   Sharples Separator, multicolored art scene of mother and young daughter, slogan "Different From The Others" around rim in red letters 25.00
   St. Joseph Pump and Mfg Co., The Only Perfection Water Elevator Purifier, c1896 .... 55.00
   Wright's Stock Food, blue and white, red horseshoe symbol around "Good Luck" inscription 20.00
Pin Holder, Success Spreader, celluloid, two-sided multicolored celluloid centered by thin wafer cardboard insert for holding straight pins, one side figural globe plus iron head logo, ed and black lettering for Kemp & Burpee Mfg. Co., Syracuse, multicolored graphic design of manure spreader on reverse, traces of wear 65.00
Pocket Mirror, Empire Cream Separator, multicolored celluloid, blond milkmaid, ethnic outfit, soft dark green background, slogan "Nothing Else Will Do," early 1900s 150.00

Seed Dryer, chestnut frame, pine spindles, 21" x 43" 85.00
Shove, cast iron, wood handle 30.00
Stickpin
   Anchor Buggy Co., brass, miniature diecu naval anchor symbol 18.00
   Harber Farm Equipment, dark bronze luster finish, ships in harbor trademark, rim design of three spaced sppols of binding twine, inscription, "Harber Bros. Of Bloomington, Ill," back inscription, "If It's From Harber's It's Good Farm Machinery, Binder Twine, Buggies & Wagons" 18.00
   J. I. Case Co., figural, brass logo, eagle poised on world globe, early 1900s 20.00
   Moline Wagon Co., diecut brass, sprinting grayhound dog over spoked wheel, inscribed, "Moline Wagon C., Light, Running, and Durable" 18.00
   Racine-Sattley Line, brass pin, red enameled, early 1900s 25.00
   Sechler Buggy, dark charcoal luster finish diecut, inscribed, "Our Reputation Your Protection, The Sechler Buggy, Cincinnati, O/Sechler & Company" 30.00
Stud
   Detroit Disc, illus of American Harrow Co., Detroit, black in ivory-white celluloid, metal lapel stud fastener 25.00
   IHC, brass, late 1890s 10.00
   Sharples "The Russian," white porcelain, blue and black letters, slogan, "The Bowl Alone Revolves" of cream separator, c1898 .... 60.00
Tape Measure, McCormick Harvesting Machine, celluloid canister, finely detailed black and white aerial illus of Chicago factory, titled "Largest Works in the World," early 1900s harvester machine 80.00
Testimonial Circular, Eureka Mower Co., Towanda, PA, 1883, for new model, testimonials from customers, 44 pgs, 5-3/4" x 8-3/4" 24.00
Toy
   Combine, Case, diecast, 1/16 scale, plastic reel, Ertl, 1974 .... 90.00
   Corn Picker, pressed steel, 1/16 scale, John Deere, Carter, 1952 .... 135.00
   Disc, diecast, 1/16 scale, International Harvester, Ertl, 1965 .... 65.00
   Grain Drill, pressed steel, 1/16 scale, John Deere, Carter, 1965 .... 150.00
   Plow, McCormick-Deering, cast iron, red, yellow wheels, Arcade, 1932 .... 95.00
   Tractor, Ford, Tootsie Toy, rubber wheels 45.00
   Tractor, International Harvester, nickel-plated man, rubber wheels, c1940 .... 325.00
   Tractor, Tru-Scale, Carter, diecast, 1/16 scale, 1975 .... 75.00
Tractor Magneto, K-W Ignition Co., Cleveland, OH, four cylinder brass cover 80.00

Tray, Success Manure Spreader, 3-1/4" x 4-3/4", litho tin, sponsor Kemp & Burpee Mfg Co., Syracuse, early 1900s, light wear 140.00

Wagon Seat, 42" l, wood, wrought iron trim, hinged compartment 250.00

Fast Food Memorabilia

Collecting Hints: Premiums, made primarily of cardboard or plastic and of recent vintage, are the mainstay of today's fast food collector. Other collectible items are advertising signs and posters, character dolls, promotional glasses, and tray liners. In fact, anything associated with a restaurant chain is collectible, although McDo -nald's items are the most popular.

Collectors should concentrate only on items in mint condition. Premiums should be unassembled or sealed in an unopened plastic bag.

Collecting fast food memorabilia has grown rapidly, and, more than ever before, the fast food chains continue to churn out an amazing array of collectibles.

History: During the period just after World War II, the only convenience restaurants were the coffee shops and diners located along America's highways or in the towns and cities. As suburbia grew, young families created a demand for a faster and less-expensive type of food service.

Ray A. Kroc responded by opening his first McDonald's drive-in restaurant in Des Plaines, Illinois, in 1955. By offering a limited menu of hamburgers, french fries, and drinks, Kroc kept his costs and prices down. This successful concept of assembly-line food preparation soon was imitated, but never surpassed, by a myriad of competitors.

By the mid-1960s, the race was on, and franchising was seen as the new economic frontier. As the competition increased, the need to develop advertising promotions became imperative. A plethora of promotional give-aways entered the scene.

References: Gary Henriques and Audre DuVall, *McDonald's Collectibles,* Collector Books, 1997, 1999 value update; Joyce and Terry Losonsky, *McDonald's Happy Meal Toys Around The World, 1875-1995,* 2nd ed., Schiffer Publishing, 2000; —, *The Encyclopedia of Fast Food Toys: Arby's To Ihop,* Schiffer Publishing, 1999; —, *The Encyclopedia of Fast Food Toys: Jack in the Box to White Castle,* Schiffer Publishing, 1999; Robert J. Sodario & Alex G. Malloy, *Kiddie Meal Collectibles,* Krause Publications, 2000; Elizabeth A. Stephan, ed., *Ultimate Price Guide to Fast Food Collectibles,* Krause Publications, 1999.

Periodicals: *Collecting Fast Food & Advertising Premiums,* 9 Ellacombe Rd, Longwell Green, Bristol, BS15 6BQ UK, *Collecting Tips Newsletter,* P.O. Box 633, Joplin, MO 64802; *Fast Food Collectors Express,* P.O. Box 221, Mayview, MO 64071; *World of Fast Food Collectibles Newsletter,* P.O. Box 64, Powder Springs, GA 30073.

Collectors' Clubs: McDonald's Collectors Club, 255 New Lenox Road, Lenox, MA 01240; McD International Pin Club, 3587 Oak Ridge, Slatington, PA 18080; McDonald's Collectors Club, 424 White Rd, Fremont, OH 43420.

A & W

Doll, Root Beer Bear, plush 32.00
Mug, glass 5.00
Pitcher and Glasses, Root Beer Bear and A & W logo, 1970s, seven-pc set 60.00
Puppet, hand, Root Beer Bear, cloth 12.00

Archie's Lobster House

Cup, gold band, mkd "Shenango China, USA, #0-30" 18.00
Egg Cup, 3-3/4" h, 2-3/4" d, gold band, mkd "Jackson China, Falls Creek, PA" 18.00
Salad Plate, 7-1/4" d, mkd "Archie's Lobster House" at top, "Roanoke, VA," at bottom, mkd "Sterling Vertified China, East Liverpool, Ohio, USA" 35.00
Soup Bowl, 6-1/2" d, mustard colored band, mkd "Jackson China, Falls Creek, PA" 18.00

Big Boy

Ashtray, 3-1/2" d, heavy glass, orange image and inscription "Frisch's Big Boy," 1968 .... 12.00
Bank, 8-3/4" h, vinyl, full figure, movable head, red and white checkered outfit, name in black lettering, 1973 copyright under foot, slight scratch, some use 45.00
Menu, punch-out puppet, kiddie menu 45.00
Nodder, papier-mâché head, 5" h 10.00
Patch
1-1/2" x 4" stitched fabric bar, "Frisch's Big Boy," boy below tacked stitching, 1950-60s 40.00
2-3/4" x 4-1/4", stitched fabric, employee type, black and white figure with red stripe accent on trousers and double burger on tan bun, 1950-60s 40.00
Puzzle, 6-1/2" x 9-1/2" orig envelope, 6-1/4" x 9-1/4" frame tray puzzle, printed in color on both sizes, one side with Big Boy image and "Fritsch's," other with double cheeseburger on blue background, "R. C. W." copyright on both envelope and puzzle, c1960 .... 120.00
Pinback Button, Big Boy Club, red, white, blue, and brown hair, c1950 .... 65.00
Salt and Pepper Shakers, pr, china, 1960s 125.00
Tee Shirt, white ground, red, white, and black trademark 10.00

Burger Chef

Character Ring, expandable band, large thin plastic sheet on top, mkd "Made In USA," c1970
Angel, yellow plastic 30.00
Fang, blue plastic 30.00
Jethro, white plastic 30.00
Seymore, orange plastic 30.00

Burger King

Bicycle Clip, colorful wheel spokes, 1981 .... 6.00
Calendar, Olympic games theme, 1980 .... 4.00
Card game, Burger King Rummy, orig box, 1978 .... 12.00
Doll, 16" h, King, cloth, printed red, yellow, flesh, black, and white 7.50
Frisbee, 9-1/2" d, R2-D2, C3PO, and Darth Vader, Empire Strikes Back, 1981 .... 17.50
Glider, King Glider, Styrofoam, 1978 .... 2.50
Lid, 3-1/4" d, red and white, cartoon of Burger King sitting on hamburger, 1970s, unused 8.00
Pinback Button
Happy face, Burger King logo eyes 6.00
Smiley Face, black on yellow litho, two small Burger King symbols, c1970 .... 3.00
Toy
2" x 5", saucer launcher, blue plastic, hand-held launching unit, one saucer, 1979 copyright 10.00
2" x 4" x 1" tall ball launching catapult unit, red plastic, copyright 1980 .... 5.00
3" x 3", Super Pitcher, soft plastic and cardboard, orig cellophane bag, copyright 1978-79 .... 8.00
3" x 4-1/2", King Spinner, soft plastic, orig cellophane bag, copyright 1978-79 .... 7.50
6" l, King's Magic Pipe, hard red plastic pipe, white Styrofoam ball, 1980s 5.00
Trading Cards, The Empire Strikes Back, complete set of 36 .... 37.50
Yo-Yo, Yum Yum, Duncan Yo-Yo, 1979 .... 5.00

Colonel Sanders

Mug, 5-1/2" h, ceramic, high gloss white, crisp black portrait above inscription in red lettering, mkd "Hall, 1272" 18.00

Dairy Queen

Diecut, House of Fun Mirror, 4-1/2" x 6-1/2" stiff paper, diecut image of smiling clown, 3" x 3-1/4" diecut opening holding silver accent aluminum foil, copyright 1960......................................5.00

Meal Box, Hot Doggity, Dennis the Menace 3.50

Salt Shaker, chocolate dip ice cream cone, 4-1/4" h.................................22.00

Spoon, red plastic, long handle, ice cream cone top 1.00

Sundae Dish, 3-1/2" x 8-1/4" x 1-1/4" deep, green molded plastic, designed like boat, curlicue of simulated ice cream scoop for handle, diecut Dairy Queen name, Lynn-Sign Molded Plastic Co., Boston, early 1960s 12.00

Denny's

Menu, plastic coated, c1960 ....2.50

Puppet, hand, Deputy Dan, 1976 ....3.00

Ring, brass, expansion bands, trace of orig yellow paint, center brown "D," 1970s 60.00

Howard Johnson

Ashtray...30.00

Bank...35.00

Drinking Glass, multicolored logo, 4-1/4" h, 2-1/2" d 32.00

Ice Cream Cup, sample size, paper, 1-1/2" h, 1-1/2" d 12.00

Menu, ice cream cover 2.00

Pinback Button, Vote for Howard Johnson's, black lettering on orange, c1950 ....8.00

Post Card, Howard Johnson's Motor Lodge, Middletown, NJ, unused 3.50

Kentucky Fried Chicken

Bank, Colonel Sanders, vinyl, turns, Japan, 1960s 275.00

Box, 1969......................................35.00

Pinback Button, Vote for Col. Sanders, KFC, blue and white, c1972, 1-1/2" d...24.00

Salt and Pepper Shakers, pr, Col. Harland Sanders, figural, 4-1/4" h, smiling full figures, one on white base, one on black base, incised name, Starting Plastics Ltd., London, Canadian premium, c1970 ....34.00

Little Caesar's

Puppet, full body plush figure, copyright 1990.......................................8.00

Ronald McDonald, cloth doll, red, yellow, black, and white, 16-1/2" h, $9.

McDonald's

Action Figure, MOC
Big Mac, blue fabric police uniform, plastic whistle 42.00
Mayor McCheese, fuchsia coat, yellow vest, purple pants........40.00
Ronald McDonald, footed red hair, yellow, red, and white outfit 35.00
Ashtray, 3-1/2" x 6", metal, green, 1970 logo in yellow, street address in silver 18.00
Bank, 6" vinyl figure, made for Canton store opening 20.00
Coloring Book, Ronald McDonald Goes to the Moon, 9" x 12-1/4", 1967, 12 pgs, black and white story, unused 125.00
Cup
Captain Cook, yellow plastic, copyright 1978 ....10.00
Hamburglar, yellow plastic, copyright 1978, some rubs, slight scratch 8.00
Slogan, "McDonald's is your kind of place," red, white, blue, and yellow, 4-3/4" h, 1970s 20.00
Cup Holder, dark blue, orig packaging 3.50
Doll
Hamburglar, played with condition 15.00
Ronald McDonald, stuffed, 1978 ....35.00
Employee Cap, 12-1/2" x 11-1/2", flattened unused service cap, blue cardboard headband with yellow arch symbol on each side, white mesh open crown, mid-1960s...............15.00
Game Sheet, 9" x 12" folded sheet opens to 17-1/2" x 24", full color figures to be cut out, full color photo scene, unused 130.00
Glass Tumbler, 5-3/4" h, set with Ronald, Mayor McCheese, Grimace, Hamburglar, Big Mac, and Captain Cook, bright graphics, 1977 copyright, price for set of six.........................20.00
Happy Meal Box Proof Sheet, 18-1/4" x 23-3/4" white stiff paper printer's proof,

full color image in center, four sided box design
American Tail, Mouse in the Moon puzzle, finger puppets, characters flying away on pigeon Henri, ©1988 McDonald's Corp, unfolded 15.00
Muppet Babies characters, Egyptian theme, ©1986 McDonald's Corp, unfolded 15.00
Happy Meal Display, Marvel Super Heroes 75.00
Happy Meal Prize, Genie and Building 5, from Aladdin and the King of Thieves, MIB.................................4.00
Hat, 8-1/2" x 15", Captain Cook, glossy thin cardboard pirate hat, copyright 1978, unused 18.00
Iron-On
5" x 9-1/2" white tissue sheet with 4-1/2" x 6" black, white, red, and yellow transfer of Ronald and porpoise, early 1970s.................20.00
8" x 9-1/2" white tissue sheet with 6-1/2" x 7" black, white, red, and yellow transfer of Ronald, early 1970s...................................20.00
Lunch Box, orig thermos, 1982...22.00
Map, Ronald McDonald Map of the Moon, 1969................................7.50
Patch, 2-1/2" x 3-1/4", stitched fabric, employee type, yellow arches, red McDonald's name, white ground, blue border, c1960, used 48.00
Photograph, 8-1/2" x 10-1/2", glossy, full color, yellow bands, blue McDonald's ad text, facsimile signatures of Schmid, Franz, Woodrow, Barnaby, Captain Penny, early 1960s 45.00
Plate, Snowman, Melmac, 1977...25.00
Puppet, hand, plastic, Ronald McDonald, c1977........................2.00
Record, Ronald's Christmas, 45 rpm, dark red and silver label, late 1950s, 7" d..24.00
Ring, Polly Pocket Doll, green vinyl base, pink flower petal design top, clear plastic dome with miniature doll in ballerina skirt, mkd "Copyright 1994 Bluebird Toys/China"...................12.00
Ruler, Ronald McDonald, cardboard, early 1970s 12.00
Sandwich Wrapper, 10-1/2" x 14", thin paper, silver foil outer surface, 4-1/2" d center design, gold arch symbol on blue ribbons, "McDonald's Quality" ribbon badge in red and gold, inscribed "New-Juicy" in blue lettering about black "roast beef" title lettering on white, unused, may be test wrapper...45.00
Space Packet, MIP....................16.00
Teenie Beanie Babies, 1997, set of 10, MIP, complete set.........................48.00
Toy Train, wind-up train engine, passenger car, animal cage car, eight sections of railroad track, single golden arch bridge, round café table, happy tree with swing, Ronald, Mayor McCheese and Hamburglar dolls by Remco, some wear and repairs...75.00

Valentines, strip of 6 different valentines, 1978 ....3.00

Pizza Hut

Paper Napkin, logo...........................50
Puppet, hand, Pizza Pete..............2.00

Taco Bell

Banner, full color, Batman & Robin, 1997, full cast, 2' x 25', unused 150.00
Store Display, Godzilla, 18" h, 18" w, holds six premiums, one missing...75.00
Straw, monster eye, MISB, 1997, set of six 20.00
Toy, Godzilla, sealed, 1977, set of seven..20.00

Wendy's

Flying Ring, Fun Flyer, plastic, 3-1/2" d.......................................3.50
Meal Box, The Good Stuff Gang, 1988 ....3.00
Mug, Wendy's Old Fashioned Hamburgers, ceramic, red, white, and black trademark, 1970s 6.50

Fiesta Ware

Collecting Hints: Whenever possible, buy pieces without any cracks, chips, or scratches. Fiesta ware can be identified by bands of concentric circles.

History: The Homer Laughlin China Company introduced Fiesta dinnerware in January 1936 at the Pottery and Glass Show in Pittsburgh, Pennsylvania. Frederick Rhead designed the pattern; Arthur Kraft and Bill Bensford molded it. Dr. A. V. Bleininger and H. W. Thiemecke developed the glazes. A vigorous marketing campaign took place between 1939 and 1943.

The original five colors were red, dark blue, light green (with a trace of blue), brilliant yellow, and ivory. In mid-1937, turquoise was added. Red was removed in 1943 because some of the chemicals used to produce it were essential to the war effort; it did not reappear until 1959. In 1951, light green, dark blue, and ivory were retired and forest green, rose, chartreuse, and gray were added to the line. Other color changes took place in the late 1950s, including the addition of a medium green.

Fiesta ware was redesigned in 1969 and discontinued about 1973. In 1986, Fiesta was reintroduced by Homer Laughlin China Company. The new china body shrinks more than the old semi-vitreous and ironstone pieces, thus making the new pieces slightly smaller than the earlier pieces. The modern colors are also different in tone or hue, e.g., the

cobalt blue is darker than the old blue. Other modern colors are black, white, apricot, orchid, and rose.

References: Susan and Al Bagdade, *Warman's American Pottery and Porcelain,* 2nd ed., Krause Publications, 2000; Mark Gonzalez, *Collecting Fiesta, Lu-Ray & Other Colorware,* L-W Books Sales, 2000; Homer Laughlin Collectors Club, *Fiesta, Harlequin, Kitchen Kraft Tablewares,* Schiffer Publishing, 2000; Sharon and Bob Huxford, *Collectors Encyclopedia of Fiesta with Harlequin and Riviera, 9th ed.,* Collector Books, 2000; Richard Racheter, *Post 86 Fiesta Identification and Value Guide,* Collector Books, 2001; Jeffrey B. Snyder, *Fiesta: Homer Laughlin China Company's Colorful Dinnerware,* 3rd ed., Schiffer Publishing, 2000.

Periodical: *Fiesta Collectors Quarterly,* 19238 Dorchester Circle, Strongsville, OH 44136.

Collectors' Clubs: Fiesta Club of America, P.O. Box 15383, Loves Park, IL 61115; Fiesta Collectors Club, 19238 Dorchester Circle, Strongsville, OH 44136.

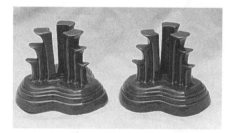

Candleholders, cobalt blue, $115.

Ashtray, 5-1/2" d
   Cobalt blue...................................45.00
   Red 55.00
   Yellow...30.00
Bud Vase, 6-1/2" h
   Ivory, chip...................................60.00
   Red 175.00
Calendar Plate, ivory, 1954, 10" d 55.00
Candleholders, pr, bulb
   Ivory... 115.00
   Light Green 90.00
   Turquoise.................................. 115.00
Candleholders, pr, tripod
   Ivory... 800.00
   Turquoise.................................. 800.00
   Yellow....................................... 700.00
Carafe, cov, light green.................. 185.00
Casserole, cov
   Cobalt Blue 200.00
   Gray 375.00
   Yellow, large 175.00
Chop Plate, 14-1/4" d
   Chartreuse 65.00
   Gray...70.00

   Ivory...60.00
   Yellow...30.00
Coffeepot, cov
   Cobalt Blue............................... 300.00
   Green 225.00
   Ivory... 245.00
   Rose.. 850.00
   Yellow....................................... 135.00
Comport, low
   Turquoise, 12" d....................... 100.00
   Yellow....................................... 125.00
Creamer
   Chartreuse.................................40.00
   Cobalt Blue, stick handle...........50.00
   Medium Green 80.00
   Rose...35.00
   Turquoise, stick handle 115.00
   Yellow, stick handle 50.00
Cream Soup
   Cobalt blue.................................90.00
   Light green 50.00
   Red 50.00
   Rose...95.00
   Turquoise...................................30.00
   Yellow...30.00
Cup and Saucer
   Chartreuse.................................28.00
   Gray 26.00
   Ivory...24.00
   Light Green 20.00
   Medium Green 60.00
   Red 30.00
   Rose...30.00
   Turquoise...................................24.00
   Yellow...24.00
Deep Plate
   Chartreuse.................................50.00
   Gray 50.00
   Ivory...40.00
   Red 50.00
Demitasse Cup and Saucer
   Chartreuse............................... 495.00
   Cobalt blue............................... 100.00
   Ivory...60.00
   Turquoise...................................70.00
   Yellow....................................... 115.00
Dessert Bowl, 6" d
   Gray 40.00
   Medium Green 65.00
   Rose...65.00
   Turquoise...................................30.00
   Yellow...25.00
Egg Cup
   Gray 175.00
   Light Green 65.00
   Yellow...45.00
Fruit Bowl
   4-3/4" d, cobalt blue.................25.00
   4-3/4" d, gray............................25.00
   4-3/4" d, ivory...........................20.00
   4-3/4" d, red..............................30.00
   4-3/4" d, yellow 15.00
   5-1/2" d, ivory...........................20.00
   5-1/2" d, yellow 15.00
Fruit Bowl, 11-3/4" d
   Cobalt Blue............................... 350.00
   Red 420.00
Gravy, turquoise 40.00
Grill Plate, 10-1/2" d
   Cobalt blue................................ 17.50
   Yellow...20.00

Juice Pitcher, disc, 5-1/2" h
  Cobalt blue 135.00
  Yellow 60.00
Juice Tumbler, 4-1/2" h
  Cobalt blue 45.00
  Light green 55.00
  Rose 60.00
  Turquoise 45.00
  Yellow 40.00
Marmalade, red 400.00
Mixing Bowl
  #1, green 200.00
  #1, red 180.00
  #2, cobalt blue 200.00
  #3, ivory 80.00
  #4, ivory 125.00
  #4, light green 85.00
  #5, turquoise 85.00
  #6, light green 110.00
  #7, cobalt blue 200.00
Mixing Bowl Lid, red, medium
  size 750.00
Mug
  Gray 85.00
  Light green 50.00
  Rose 75.00
  Turquoise 50.00
Mustard, cov
  Cobalt blue 245.00
  Turquoise 185.00
  Yellow 175.00
Nappy Bowl, 9-1/2" d
  Cobalt blue 45.00
  Ivory 50.00
  Turquoise 35.00
Onion Soup, cov, ivory 375.00
Plate, 6" d
  Forest green 5.00
  Ivory 7.50
  Medium green 20.00
  Turquoise 5.00
Plate, 7" d
  Green 6.50
  Ivory 8.50
  Turquoise 7.50
Plate, 9" d
  Light green 10.00
  Medium green 40.00
  Turquoise 10.00
  Yellow 10.00
Platter, 12-1/2" l
  Cobalt blue 30.00
  Gray 50.00
  Turquoise 30.00
  Yellow 25.00
Relish
  Cobalt base, red center, light green,
  ivory, yellow, and cobalt blue side
  inserts, slight chips 300.00
  Yellow base, cobalt blue center, four
  yellow inserts, gold trim 135.00
  Yellow base, light green center, red,
  ivory, yellow, and light green side
  inserts 175.00
Salad Bowl, individual size
  Medium green 135.00
  Red 110.00
Salad Bowl, 9-3/8" d, yellow 100.00
Salt and Pepper Shakers, pr
  Cobalt blue 24.00
  Yellow 40.00

Sauce Boat
  Ivory 40.00
  Rose 60.00
  Yellow 45.00
Soup Plate, turquoise 35.00
Sugar Bowl, cov
  Chartreuse 70.00
  Gray 80.00
  Rose 70.00
Sweets Compote
  Light green 75.00
  Yellow 80.00
Syrup, turquoise, green top 150.00
Teapot, cov, medium size
  Red 175.00
  Yellow 140.00
Tray, figure 8, turquoise 300.00
Utility Tray
  Cobalt blue 17.50
  Light green 25.00
  Red 70.00
  Turquoise 20.00
Water Pitcher, disc
  Ivory 140.00
  Light green 165.00
  Turquoise 90.00
Water Set, 5 pc, Sapphire Blue, 7-1/4" h
  pitcher mkd "Still Proudly Made by the
  Homer Laughlin China Co., Genuine
  Fiesta, 60th Anniversary, 1936-1996,"
  four 3-3/4" h tumblers 95.00
Water Tumbler, cobalt blue 80.00

Firehouse Collectibles

Collecting Hints: For a period of time, it was fashionable to put a date on the back of firemen's helmets. This date is usually the date the fire company was organized, not the date the helmet was made.

Firehouse collectibles cover a very broad area. The older, scarcer collectibles, such as helmets and fire marks, command high prices. The newer collectibles, e.g., cards and badges, are more reasonably priced.

History: The volunteer fire company has played a vital role in the protection and social growth of many towns and rural areas. Paid professional firemen are usually found in large metropolitan areas. Each fire company prided itself on its equipment and uniforms. Annual conventions and parades, which gave the individual fire companies a chance to show off their equipment, produced a wealth of firehouse-related collectibles.

References: Andrew G. Gurka, *Hot Stuff! Firefighting Collectibles*, L-W Book Sales, 1994, 1996 value update; Ed Lindley Peterson, *First to the Flames: The History of Fire Chief*

Vehicles, Krause Publications, 1999; Donald F. Wood and Wayne Sorenson, *American Volunteer Fire Trucks,* Krause Publications, 1993; ——, *Big City Fire Trucks, 1900-1950,* Krause Publications, 1996.

Periodical: *Fire Apparatus Journal,* P.O. Box 121205, Staten Island, NY 10314.

Collectors' Clubs: Antique Fire Apparatus Club of America, 5420 S. Kedvale Ave., Chicago, IL 60632; Fire Collectors Club, P.O. Box 992, Milwaukee, WI 53201; Fire Mark Circle of the Americas, 2859 Marlin Dr., Chamblee, GA 30341; Great Lakes International Antique Fire Apparatus Association, 4457 285th St., Toledo, OH 43611; International Fire Buff Associates, Inc., 7509 Chesapeake Ave, Baltimore, MD 21219; International Fire Photographers Association, P.O. Box 8337, Rolling Meadows, IL 60008; Society for the Preservation & Appreciation of Motor Fire Apparatus in America, P.O. Box 2005, Syracuse, NY 13320.

Museums: There are many museums devoted to firehouse collectibles. Large collections are housed at the following: American Museum of Fire Fighting, Corton Falls, NY; Fire Museum of Maryland, Lutherville, MD; Hall of Flame, Scottsdale, AZ; Insurance Company of North America (I.N.A.) Museum, Philadelphia, PA; New England Fire & History Museum, Brewster, MA; New York City Fire Museum, New York, NY; Oklahoma State Fireman's Association Museum, Inc., Oklahoma City, OK; San Francisco Fire Dept. Pioneer Memorial Museum, San Francisco, CA.

Alarm Box, cast iron, pedestal, emb "City of Chicago," restored 285.00
Badge
  1-3/4" x 1-3/4", relief image of fire hydrant on one side, hook and ladder on other, Mineola Fire Dept., c1950 .... 10.00
  2" x 2", relief image of fire hydrant on one side, hook and ladder on other, Mineola Fire Dept., c1950 .... 10.00
Bell, brass, 12" 85.00
Belt, black leather, white lettering 75.00
Booklet, Constitution of the International Brotherhood of Firemen and Oilers, last revision 1971 .... 10.00
Bucket, galvanized tin, red lettering, "Fire Only" 35.00
Commemorative Mug, glass, Roslyn Fire Company, Roslyn, PA, May 21, 1983, Mack Aerialscope Fire Truck 15.00

Daguerreotype, fireman, hat, horn, and uniform, tinted......................500.00

Extinguisher, Harden, hand grenade type, blue glass, patent Aug. 8, 1871..90.00

Fire Engine Name Plate

Ahrens-Fox.....................................15.00

LaFrance.......................................17.50

Mack Trucks, bulldog..................25.00

First Day Cover, 300th Anniversary of Volunteer Firemen's Association, unaddressed...10.00

Hose Nozzle, brass 50.00

Liquor Decanter, Fireman's Thirst Extinguisher 20.00

Little Golden Book, Five Little Firemen, 1949 ....7.50

Magazine

Fire Lines, December 1935.........35.00

NFPA Fireman, 1966.....................7.50

Negative, glass, Chicago Fire Dept. #6 pumper 45.00

Patch, 3-7/8" d, Texas State Fireman's Association 7.50

Photograph

4-3/4" x 6-3/4", silver print of c1900 parade, firemen marching down gaily decorated street 20.00

8" x 11", black and white, aerial truck 10.00

Pinback Button, convention, 1-3/4" d, Pennsylvania State Firemen's Convention

Dark blue cello button, colorful image of Irishman smoking pipe, shaking hands with fireman, light blue ribbon, 1-1/4" green and white "guest" cello button, Harrisburg, PA, October, 1914 ....20.00

White button, colorful image of firehouse and hat, black text around border "Lebanon Co. Firemen's Convention, Myerstown, PA, June 15, 1929," red, white, and blue ribbon..15.00

Plate, Milford Township, Bucks County, commemorative plate, 1974, gold trim 20.00

Post Card, real photo

Firemen searching for victims of 1906 fire, unused 10.00

Main Fire Station, Water Street, Piqua, OH, unused 5.00

Quakertown, PA, firehouse and borough hall, unused...........................8.00

Washington, OH, firehouse, postmarked June 1923 ....12.00

Ribbon

Aug. 18, 1901, Veteran Firemen's Association League Muster, Lawrence, blue ribbon, white celluloid button with fire implements 45.00

1958, Firemen's Celebration, multicolored pinback, some wear to 3-3/4" l ribbon...18.00

Ring, Jr. Fire Marshall, Hartford Insurance, 1950s................................20.00

Salesman Sample, boots, 5" h, rubber, scale model, pull loops, mkd "Candee," c1890 ....70.00

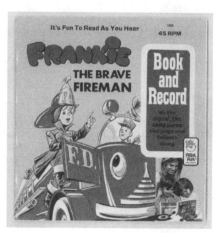

Record, child's, Frankie, The Brave Fireman, book and record, $15.

Tankard, 5-1/2' h, Smokey Bear 40th Anniversary, 1944-1984 New Jersey Forest Fire Service, pottery, mkd "Official Licensee to the NJ State Firemen's Convention," and "Made by Let Us Mug You, Spring Lake, NJ" 60.00

Tie Tac, 1/2" d, "Member, County Firemen's Ass'n," 10K gold mounting, keystone shape, blue and rust colored enamel, center white enamel "6"....................................30.00

Tintype, unidentified fireman wearing dress uniform, holding speaking trumpet...110.00

Toy

Chief Car, litho tin, friction powered, 1960s, 16" l..................................75.00

Marx, tin litho, wind-up car inside firehouse, some play wear, orig box..650.00

Sparkler, 1" x 2-1/2" x 5", tin litho, front showing burning building, pair of thin red transparent plastic windows, illus of person hanging out of window with word "Help" above them, flat tin litho fireman figure pops up to rescue, mkd "Made in Japan," late 1950s.......28.00

Train Accessory, firehouse, MTH, 15" l, 15" h, MIB 175.00

Tumbler, Six County Firemen's 72nd Annual Convention, Kingston, Pa, 1975, firemen's logo.......................5.00

Watch Fob, 1-1/4" d, aluminum, accepted by small red fire helmet, New Kensington, PA, firehouse, inscription "1928 Wet Penna. Volunteer Fireman's Assn," back reads "33rd Annual Convention/The Aluminum City/Aug 1926," black leather strap 15.00

Fire King

Collecting Hints: Anchor Hocking's Fire-King is a contemporary of Pyrex and other "oven-proof" glassware of the 1940s and 1950s. It is only within the past decade that collectors have begun to focus on this material. As a result, prices fluctuate and a stable market is several years in the future.

In 1938, Anchor Hocking introduced a line of children's dishes which became part of the Fire-King line. A popular pattern is Little Bo Peep. Like all children's dishes, these objects command strong prices.

Some Fire-King collectors focus on a single color. Jane Ray, a jadeite-colored pattern, was introduced in 1945. In 1948, the color was first used in a series of restaurant wares and it was discontinued in 1963. This color saw a dramatic increase in prices and collector interest in the last few years.

Fire-King was sold in sets. Add an additional 25 to 35 percent to the price of the individual pieces for an intact set in its original box.

Fire-King pieces are found with two types of marks. The first is a mold mark directly on the piece; the second, an oval foil paper label.

History: Fire-King was a product of the Anchor Hocking Glass Company. In 1905, Isaac J. Collins founded the Hocking Glass Company along the banks of the Hocking River near Lancaster, Ohio. On March 6, 1924, fire completely destroyed the plant, but it was rebuilt in six months. Hocking produced pressed glass dinnerware, many patterns of which are considered Depression glass.

In 1937, Hocking Glass Company merged with the Anchor Cap Company and became Anchor Hocking Glass Corporation. Shortly thereafter, the new company began to manufacture glass ovenware that could withstand high temperatures in a kitchen oven.

Production of oven-proof glass marked "FIRE-KING" began in 1942 and lasted until 1976. Dinnerware patterns include Alice, Charm, Fleurette, Game Bird, Honeysuckle, Jane Ray, Laurel, Primrose, Turquoise Blue, Swirl, and Wheat. Utilitarian kitchen items and ovenware patterns also were produced.

Housewives eagerly purchased Fire-King sets and could also assemble sets of matching dinnerware and ovenware patterns. Advertising encouraged consumers to purchase prepackaged starter, luncheon, baking, and snack sets, as well as casseroles. Oven glassware items included almost everything needed to completely stock the kitchen.

Fire-King patterns are found in azurite, forest green, gray, ivory, jade-ite, peach luster, pink, plain white, ruby red, sapphire blue, opaque turquoise, and white with an assortment of rim colors. To increase sales, decals were applied.

References: Gene Florence, *Anchor Hocking's Fire King & More,* 2nd ed., Collector Books, 2000; ——, *Collectible Glassware from the 40's, 50's, 60's,* 5th ed., Collector Books, 2000; ——, *Kitchen Glassware of the Depression Years,* 5th ed., Collector Books, 1995, 2001 value update; Joe Keller and David Ross, *Jadite: An Identification and Price Guide,* 2nd ed., Schiffer Publishing, 2000; Gary and Dale Kilgo and Jerry and Gail Wilkins, *Collectors Guide to Anchor Hocking's Fire-King Glassware,* K & W Collectibles Publisher, 1991; ——, *Collectors Guide to Anchor Hocking's Fire-King Glassware, Volume II,* K & W Collectibles Publisher, 1998; April M. Tvorak, *Fire-King,* 5th ed., published by author (P.O. Box 126, Canon City, CO 81215), 1997.

Periodicals: *Fire-King Monthly,* P.O. Box 70594, Tuscaloosa, AL 35407; *Fire-King News,* K & W Collectibles, Inc., P.O. Box 374, Addison, AL 35540.

Repro Alert: Reproductions (†) are appearing in jade-ite at an alarming rate.

Dinnerware

Berry Bowl
  Charm, Azurite, 4-3/4" d 5.00
  Jane Ray, ivory 55.00
  Laurel Gray, 4-1/2" d 6.00
  Restaurant Ware, jade-ite, heavy, 4-3/4" d 15.00
Bowl
  Bubble, Peach Luster, 8-3/8" d 9.00
  Turquoise, Splashproof, 3 qt 25.00
Cake Plate, Country Kitchens, 9" d 6.50
Candy Dish, cov, jade-ite, round, 6-3/4" d 140.00
Cereal Bowl
  Charm, Azurite, 6" d 18.00
  Restaurant Ware, jade-ite, heavy, 5" d (†)...35.00
Child's Plate, divided, Turquoise, 7-1/2" d...40.00
Chili Bowl
  Peach Luster, copper tint 7.00
  Restaurant Ware, jade-ite, heavy...15.00
Creamer and Sugar
  Laurel Gray 7.00
  Restaurant Ware, jade-ite, heavy (†) 35.00
  Shell, jade-ite 165.00
Cup and Saucer
  Alice, jade-ite..............................12.00
  Crystal Wheat 8.00
  Honeysuckle 6.00

Jane Ray 15.00
Laurel Gray....................................5.00
Primrose, base reads "Oven Fireking Ware #14 (cup), #35 (saucer), Made in USA".................................9.00
Restaurant Ware, jade-ite, heavy (†) 18.00
St. Denis, jade-ite.........................15.00
Swirl, Azurite..................................8.00
Swirl, Ivory 7.00
Custard Cup, Candleglow 2.50
Demitasse Cup and Saucer
  Fishscale Luster 35.00
  Jane Ray, jade-ite 105.00
  Luster Shell.................................10.00
Dessert Bowl
  Game Bird pattern, Canadian Goose dec 5.00
  Laurel Leaf, peach luster, 4-7/8" d, base reads "Oven Fireking Ware, Made in USA," some scratches from use..2.50
  Royal Ruby 6.50
  Vienna Lace 2.50
Dinner Plate
  Alice, jade-ite 70.00
  Blue Mosaic 8.00
  Game Bird, pheasant dec.............9.00
  Jane Ray, 9" d, ivory 55.00
  Laurel Gray....................................8.00
  Leaf and Blossom, green and pink 8.50
  Restaurant Ware, jade-ite, heavy, 9" d (†) 32.00
  Swirl, Azurite..................................8.50
  Swirl, Ivory, orig label 11.00
  Vienna Lace 3.50
Dinner Set, Jane Ray, six 7 pc place settings, serving pieces, 45 pcs ... 750.00
Grill Plate, Restaurant Ware, jade-ite, heavy..35.00
Luncheon Plate
  Charm, Azurite, 8-3/8" d 5.50
  Restaurant Ware, jade-ite, heavy..85.00
Milk Pitcher, jade-ite, mkd "Fire King," 20 oz..130.00
Mug
  Bubble, Peach Luster 3.50
  Game Bird Pattern, Mallard Duck dec 10.00
  Red Rose 4.00
  Restaurant Ware, jade-ite, heavy (†) 15.00
  Sapphire Blue 25.00
  White, mkd "Anchor Hocking Fireking, Made in USA" 4.00
Pie Pan, Swirl, Ivory, orig label..........15.00
Platter
  Restaurant Ware, jade-ite, heavy, 9-1/4" l (†)..................................60.00
  Shell, jade-ite, oval...................155.00
  Swirl, Azurite, oval.......................20.00
  Wheat, 9" x 12" base reads "Oven Fireking Ware," some scratches from use..12.00
Range Shaker, Swirl, Ivory, orig tulip top...24.00
Relish, Turquoise Blue, 3 part, gold trim...12.00

Salad Plate
  Alice, jade-ite...............................14.00
  Restaurant Ware, jade-ite, heavy (†) 15.00
  Swirl, Azurite 7.00
Serving Plate, Laurel Gray, 11" l....... 40.00
Snack Set
  Colonial Lady, ruby and crystal .. 12.00
  Swirl, Ivory, gold trim 7.50
Soup Bowl
  Jane Ray, 7-5/8" d 30.00
  Meadow Green...............................6.50
  Swirl, Ivory, flat, orig label 12.00
  Wheat, 5-1/2" d, base reads "Oven Fireking Ware, Made in USA, #11".. 5.00
Starter Set
  Swirl, Ivory, orig pictorial box, 4 dinner plates, 4 cups and saucers, set 60.00
  Turquoise, orig box.......................75.00
Tumbler, Game Bird dec, mallard duck, pheasant, or ruffled grouse dec..12.00
Vase, Deco, jade-ite......................18.00
Vegetable Bowl, Luster Shell 6.50

Kitchenware

Batter Bowl, jade-ite (†) 45.00
Bowl, Tulip, 9-1/2" d.........................35.00
Coffee Maker, Silex, 2 cup, 2 pc......25.00
Eggcup, jade-ite...............................40.00
Grease Jar
  Red Dots, white 35.00
  Stripes...35.00
  Tulip, ivory or white......................35.00
Hot Plate, Sapphire Blue 18.00
Lid, Philbe, 5" x 9"............................35.00
Measuring Cup, Sapphire Blue 18.50
Mixing Bowl
  Beaded Rim, white, 4-7/8" d 8.00
  Jade-ite, Colonial rim, 7-1/2" d 118.00
  Jade-ite, splash proof, 9-1/2" d (†) 125.00
Mixing Bowl Set, Swirl, unused (†) 265.00
Nurser, Sapphire Blue, 4 oz 10.00
Refrigerator Jar, Philbe, large, jade-ite, lid missing 40.00
Salt and Pepper Shakers, pr
  Red Dots, white 45.00
  Stripes...37.50
Utility Bowl, Sapphire Blue, 8-1/4" d...20.00

Ovenware

Au Gratin Covered Casserole, Blue Applique, 11" l, mkd "#433 Anchor Hocking Fireking Oven Proof, #9, Made in USA, 1-1/2 Qt, USA" 14.00
Baking Dish
  Blue Applique, 9-1/4" l, deep, quart, mkd "#436 Anchor Hocking Fireking Oven Proof, #18, Made in USA, 1 Qt, USA" 9.00
  Sapphire Blue, individual serving size...4.50

Cake Pan, Wheat, 8" d, bottom stamp reads "#450, Anchor Hocking, Fireking Ovenware, Made in USA, 8," some scratches from use............ 15.00

Casserole, cov
Peach Luster, copper tint, tab lids, orig label.. 7.50
Sapphire Blue, 1 pint.................... 15.00

Custard Cup, crystal, orig label......... 3.00

Loaf Pan
Blue Applique, 10-3/4" l, mkd "Anchor Hocking Fireking Oven Proof, #9, Made in USA," 1 qt, USA 12.00
Sapphire Blue 17.50

Pie Plate
Crystal, 10 oz............................. 4.00
Sapphire Blue, 10-1/4" d 160.00

Roaster, Sapphire Blue,
10-1/2" l 125.00

Utility Bowl, Sapphire Blue, 7" d....... 14.00

Fishing Collectibles

Collecting Hints: The types of fishing items collected are rapidly expanding as the rare specimens become more expensive and harder to locate. New categories include landing nets, minnow traps, bait boxes, advertising signs, catalogs, and fish decoys used in ice spearing.

Items in original containers and in mint condition command top prices. There is little collector value if paint has been spread over the original decoration or if rods have been refinished or are broken.

Early wooden plugs (before 1920), split bamboo fly rods made by the master craftsmen of that era, and reels constructed of German silver with special detail or unique mechanical features are the items most sought by advanced collectors.

The number of serious collectors is steadily increasing as indicated by the membership in the National Fishing Lure Collectors Club which has approximately 2,000 active members.

History: Early man caught fish with crude spears and hooks made of bone, horn, or flint. By the mid-1800s, metal lures with attached hooks were produced in New York State. Later, the metal was curved and glass beads added to make them more attractive. Spinners with painted-wood bodies and glass eyes appeared around 1890. Soon after, wood plugs with glass eyes were being produced by many different makers. Patents, which were issued in large numbers around this time, covered the development of hook hangers, body styles, and devices to add movement to the plug as it was drawn through the water. The wood plug era lasted up to the mid-1930s when plugs constructed of plastic were introduced.

With the development of casting plugs, it became necessary to produce fishing reels capable of accomplishing the task with ease. Reels first appeared as a simple device to hold a fishing line. Improvements included multiplying gears, retrieving line levelers, drags, clicks, and a variety of construction materials. The range of quality in reel manufacture varied considerably. Collectors are mainly interested in reels made with high-quality materials and workmanship, or those exhibiting unusual features.

Early fishing rods, which were made of solid wood, were heavy and prone to breakage. By gluing together tapered strips of split bamboo, a rod was fashioned which was light in weight and had greatly improved strength. The early split-bamboo rods were round and were wrapped with silk to hold them together. As glue improved, fewer wrappings were needed, and rods became slim and lightweight. Rods were built in various lengths and thicknesses, depending upon the type of fishing and bait used. Rodmakers' names and models can usually be found on the metal parts of the handle or on the rod near the handle.

References: Jim Bourdon, *South Bend: Their Artificial Bates and Reels,* John Shoffner (P.O. Box 250, Fife Lake, MI 49633), 1996; Arlan Carter, *19th Century Fishing Lures,* Collector Books, 2000; D. B. Homel, *Antique & Collectible Fishing Rods,* Forrest Park Publishers, 1997; Art, Brad, and Scott Kimball, T*he Fish Decoy,* Vol. II (1987), Vol. III (1993), Aardvark; Monterey Bay Publishing; Dudley Murphy & Rich Edmisten, *Fishing Lure Collectibles,* 2nd ed., Collector Books, 2000; Harold E. Smith, *Collector's Guide to Creek Chub Lures & Collectibles,* Collector Books, 1997, 1999 value update; R. L. Streator with Rick Edmisten and Dudley Murphy, *The Fishing Lure Collector's Bible,* Collector Books, 1999.

Periodicals: *American Fly Fisher,* P.O. Box 42, Manchester, VT 05254; *Antique Angler Newsletter,* P.O. Box K, Stockton, NJ 08559; *Fishing Collectibles,* P.O. Box 2797, Kennebunk-port, ME 04046; *Fishing Collectibles Magazine,* 2005 Tree House Lane, Plano, TX 75023; *The Fisherman's Trader,* P.O. Box 203, Gillette, NJ 07933; *Sporting Classics,* 3031 Scotsman Road, Columbia, SC 29223.

Collectors' Clubs: American Fish Decoy Assoc., P.O. Box 252, Boulder Junction, WI 54512; Carolina Antique Tackle Collectors, 619 Elm Ave., Columbia, SC 29205; Florida Antique Tackle Collectors, P.O. Box 420703, Kissimmee, Fl 34742-00703; National Fishing Lure Collectors Club, P.O. Box 0184, Chicago, IL 60690; Old Reel Collectors Assoc., Inc., 3501 Riverview Dr., P.O. Box 2540, Weirton, WV 26062.

Museums: American Fishing Tackle Mfg. Association Museum, Arlington Heights, IL; American Museum of Fly Fishing, Manchester, VT; Sayner Museum, Sayner, WI; Museum of Fishing, Winter Haven, FL; National Freshwater Hall of Fame, Hayward, WI; National Heddon Museum, Dowagiac, MI.

Reproduction Alert: Lures and fish decoys.

Badge, 1-3/4" d, Fishing, Trapping, Hunting License, NY, 1930 .... 55.00

Bait Trap, Katch-N-Karry, Glassman Mfg. Co., Jackson, TN, patented 1941, wood, 4" dia wire mesh circle, litho of bluegill and roach 375.00

Bank, 3-1/2" x 4" x 7" h, painted composition, bobbing head, round fisherman in hat and sunglasses, mermaid by side, coin slot in back, 1960s, felt covering over base 30.00

Bobber, hand painted
5" l, panfish float, black, red, and white stripes 12.00
12" l, pike float, yellow, green, and red stripes 24.00

Book
Complete Book of Fresh Water Fishing, P. Allen Parsons, 1965, 332 pgs, illus... 11.50
Lures: *The Guide to Sport Fishing,* Keith C. Schuyler, Stackpole Co., 1955, dj................................... 20.00
New Fisherman's Encyclopedia, Ira Gabrielson, Stackpole Co., 2nd ed., 759 pgs.................................... 24.00
Practical Black Bass Fishing, Mark Sosin and Bill Dance, Crown Pub., 1977, illus................................... 10.00
Spinfishing, The System That Does It All, Norman Strung and Milk Rosko, Macmillian, 1973, 1st ed, 339 pgs..................................... 9.75
The New Fisherman's Encyclopedia, Ira Gabriel, ed., Stackpole Books, 1964, 2nd ed., 2nd printing, 759 pgs, worn dj....................................... 12.75

The Origin of Angling and a New Printing of "The Treatise of Fishing With An Angle," John McDonald, paintings by John Langley Howard, Doubleday, 1963, 271 pgs.................................12.50

Cigarette Card, King of England deep sea fishing, New Zealand, 1937 ... 8.00

Clock, mechanical, fish punching hole in side of boat with moving hammer, Hero Clock Co., wind-up, mkd "Made in China"..40.00

Creel
9-1/2" w, 8" d, 8" h, wicker, rear hinged door, repairs...............................110.00
32" w, 6" h, wicker, leather latch with netted fish head, silver tail on other end, late 1940s.........................275.00
35" x 32, wicker, orig 2-1/2" x 1-1/4" paper label "Bestmade, Insist on the Genuine, Occupied Japan, 3616/4 15"..750.00

Dealer Display, Swimmy Bait Co., 12 boxed lures................................155.00

Decoy, trout, Michigan, c1940, 7" l, $70.

Decoy, fish, wood
6-1/2" l, Leroy Howell, gray body, black metal fins...................................115.00
7" l, Ice King, perch, painted, Bear Creek Co. 75.00

Fishing License
Connecticut, 1935, for resident use, yellow, black, and white 65.00
Pennsylvania, 1945, blue and white, black serial number......................18.00

Flask, pewter, emb on both sides, one side with fisherman landing trout, other side with fisherman netting catch, mkd "Alchemy Pewter, Sheffield, England" 175.00

Fly Fishing Display, c1911, painted wood trout replica, fly fishing reel, flies, net, wood case, 39-3/4" l, 3-3/4 " d, 13-1/4" h......................................185.00

License Holder, paper envelope, Florida Game and Fresh Water Commission, stamped with County Judge's name...22.00

Lure
Al Foss Dixie Wiggler, #13, 1928, metal box, extra hook, pocket catalog, 3-1/2" l..................................100.00
Carters Bestever, red and white, pressed eyes, 3" l........................10.00
Creek Chub Giant Pike, 12-1/2" x 2-3/4" orig box.........................195.00
Heddon, Dowagiac Minnow, series 100, wood, red and yellow stripes, olive green strip down back, glass eyes, 2-3/4" l.............................300.00
Meadow Brook, rainbow, 1-1/4" l, orig box, flyrod type.........................120.00
Moonlight Bay #1, c1904, 4" shallow cup...400.00

Musky Minnow 900.00
Paw-Paw, sucker, perch finish, tack eyes.......................................30.00
Pfleuger, Never Fail Minnow, 3 hook, early perch finish, hand painted gill marks, large glass eyes, unmarked props, never-fail take hangers....................................300.00
Sam-Bo, 4" l, bass, pike, pickerel, orig box...215.00
Shakespeare, mouse, white and red, thin body, glass eyes, 3-5/8" l......30.00
South Bend, Panatellia, green crackle-back finish, glass eyes, boxed....50.00
Souvenir, Lucky Lure, Souv of Indian Lake, OH, 3-1/2" l, nude black female, MOC.......................................130.00
Strike-It-Lure, green, yellow, and red spots, glass eyes 40.00

Minnow Bucket, green collapsible canvas, wire bail, orig black painted wooden handle, stamped "No. 08 Mfg for the Planet Co. Patent" 155.00

Patch, 3-3/4" x 5", Atlantic City Surf Fishing Tournament 12.00

Pinback Button, Johnsburg Fish & Game Club, red and white, forest safety theme, 1930s 10.00

Poacher's Gig, hand forged 5 pronged rake-type device, long worn wooden handle, from Eastern Shore, MD or VA, 63" l...145.00

Post Card
Fishing Pier, Asbury Park, NJ, date 1932 in pencil, unused 3.00
Indian fishing scene, white border, used..8.00

Reel
Ambassador 5500C Silver, counter balance, handle, high speed gear rates...120.00
Hardy, Perfect Fly Reel, English, 3-3/8" x 1-1/4".....................................165.00
Hendryx Safety Reel, trout........995.00
Horton #3, suede bag 425.00
Horton #33 Bluegrass Simplex, suede bag...425.00
Julius Vom Hofe, freshwater, casting, Pat. Nov. 17 85, Oct 8, 1887, torn bag...165.00
Meek 33 Bluegrass, suede bag425.00
Penn-Jic Master No. 500, 3" d.....65.00
Pflueger, #1993L, Summit, casting, 1940-50 ....100.00
Pflueger, 1429-3/4 templar, number engraved on side..........................125.00
Pflueger, 1420-1/2 templar, owner's name lightly scratched 175.00
Shakespeare, standard 150.00
Shakespeare, standard professional.................................150.00
Shakespeare, tournament........110.00
South Bend, #1131A, casting, shiny finish, orig box..............................18.00
Union Hardware Co., raised pillar type, nickel and brass 25.00
Unmarked, wood, brass fittings, c1880-1920, 6" d........................85.00
Wilkerson Quadruple, 1900.........95.00
Winchester, Model #1135, fly, black finish 65.00

Rod
Bamboo, fly fishing, orig reel, wear..125.00

Hardy, 7' 2", 1 tip, split bamboo fly, English 200.00
H. L. Leonard, 6-1/2' 1,450.00
Horrocks & Illotson, 9' 3", two tips, split-bamboo fly, maroon wraps...50.00
Kingfisher, brown and red, orig wraps, red agate eyes, paper label 125.00
Montaque, bamboo, two tips, orig case 135.00
Orvis Impregnated Battenkill, 8-1/2', two tips, splint-bamboo fly, cloth bag, aluminum tube..........................250.00
Shakespeare, Premier Model, 9', three pcs, two tips, split-bamboo fly, red silk wrappings, cloth bag, metal tube..75.00
Shakespeare Springbrook, fly fishing, orig bag 100.00
Union Hardware Co., 7-1/2', Kingfisher, saltwater boat rod, split-bamboo fly, dark brown wraps...........35.00

Scale, brass, "Chamllons Improved, New York, Pat. Dec. 10 1967"............30.00

Tackle Box, leather 450.00

Tie Clip, articulated fish, 1-3/4" l 18.00

Tray, aluminum, lady fishing, catches skirt with hook and lifts it up in the back, red and black dec, scalloped edge 165.00

Trout Net, 22-3/4", nice wood, orig net...100.00

Vise, fly tying
7" l, 2-1/2" w, steel and brass, bolts to table...210.00
7-1/2" l, 6" h, cast iron and steel, can be used free standing or bolted down...240.00

Wall Plaque, 13" x 9", large mouth bass...115.00

Flag Collectibles

Collecting Hints: Public Law 829, 77th Congress, approved December 22, 1942, outlines a detailed set of rules for flag etiquette. Collectors should become familiar with this law.

The amount of material on which the American flag is portrayed is limitless. Collectors tend to focus on those items on which the flag enjoys a prominent position.

History: The Continental or Grand Union flag, consisting of 13 alternate red and white stripes with a British Union Jack in the upper left corner, was first used on January 1, 1776, on Prospect Hill near Boston. On June 14, 1777, the Continental Congress adopted a flag design similar to the Continental flag, but with the Union Jack replaced by a blue field with thirteen stars. The stars could be arranged in any fashion. The claim that Betsy Ross made the first Stars and Stripes lacks historical documentation.

On January 13, 1794, Congress voted to add two stars and two stripes to the flag in recognition of Vermont and Kentucky joining the Union. On April 18, 1818, when there were 20 states, Congress adopted a law returning to the original 13 stripes and adding a new star for each state admitted. The stars were to be added on the July 4th following admission. The 49th star, for Alaska, was added July 4, 1959; the 50th star, for Hawaii, was added July 4, 1960.

References: Elizabeth Kurella, *The Complete Guide to Vintage Textiles*, Krause Publications, 1999; Boleslow and Marie-Louis D'Otrange Mastai, *Stars and Stripes*, Alfred Knopf, 1973.

Collectors' Club: North American Vexillological Association, Ste. 225, 1977 N. Olden Ave., Trenton, NJ 08618.

Museums: State capitals in northern states; Hardisty Flag Museum, Hardisty, Alberta, Canada; Prattaugan Museum, Prattville, AL.

Advertising Trade Card
    Major's Cement, 3" x 4-1/4", two American flags decorating display of 125 lb weights holding suspended object, full color, adv "Major's Leather Cement-For-Sale By Druggists and Crockery Dealers" 9.00
    Merrick's Thread, 2-3/4" x 4-1/2", two infant children, one beating Civil War type drum, other waving flag, titled "Young America" 4.00

Armband, World War II, 48 star flag, worn by paratrooper on D-Day invasion, two safety pins 45.00

Badge, with ribbon, gold colored pin "Tower of Jewels, 1915-San Francisco," red white, and blue ribbon, button reads, "Admission day - PPIE Sept 9, 1915, Admit One," US and CA flags and building dec 60.00

Bandanna, 22" x 25", silk, flag inside wreath of 36 stars 140.00

Book, *Proud New Flags*, F. Van Wyck Mason, 1951, orig dj 20.00

Booklet
    Flags and Emblems of Texas, Dept. of Publicity for Texas Centennial Celebration 5.00
    Our Flag, Display and Respect, Marine Corps, 28 pgs, 1942 .... 5.00

Button, 1/2" d, glass dome, flag printed inside, six mounted on card 24.00

Catalog, Chicago Flag & Decorating, Chicago, IL, c1928, 32 pgs, 6" x 9", Catalog No. 30 .... 27.00

Certificate, Betsy Ross Flag Association, 1917, serial #38181, Series N, 12" x 16", C H Weisgerber painting 55.00

Clock, God Bless America, mantel, World War II vintage, small American flag waves back and forth as second hand, Howard Miller Mfg 150.00

Flag
    29 star, 7" x 10", parade flag, coarse cotton material, Great Star pattern, used during Mexican-American War, discolored 145.00
    36 star, 25" x 22", parade flag, printed muslin 115.00
    37 star, 16" x 24", parade flag, 1867-1877, muslin, all printed 50.00
    45 star, 3-1/2" x 2-1/4 ", child's parade type, pattern of 8,7,7,7,7,8 and five point star 35.00
    45 star, 32" x 47", 1896-1908, printed on silk, bright colors, black heading and no grommets 95.00
    46 star, 4" x 5", 1908-1912, stars sewn on, Oklahoma 75.00
    48 star, 5-3/4" x 4-1/2", 1912-1959, printed on heavy canvas-type material, used on D-Day in Infantry invasion, men wore them under the camouflage net on their helmets 95.00

Handkerchief, World War I, flags of US and France, embroidered
    A Kiss from France 15.00
    To My Dear Sweetheart 15.00

Lapel Stud, red, white, and blue enamel flag, white ground, Harrison/Morton 1888, enameled brass 35.00

Letterhead, 11" x 8-1/2", Independence Hall, Liberty Bell, two crossed American flags, Sesquicentennial International Exposition 25.00

Magic Lantern Slide, 42 star flag, c1889, hand tinted, mounted in wood 30.00

Magnifying Glass, pocket, 3/4" x 1-1/4", oval, Voorhees Rubber Mfg Co adv, American flag artwork 37.00

Match Box, 1-1/2" x 2-3/4", Civil War period, emb, picture of Stars and Stripes on one side, Miss Columbia on reverse 65.00

Pinback Button
    Colorado Statehood, For Governor Henry R. Wolcott, black and white photo, red, white, and blue flag, 1898 .... 18.00
    Confederate Flag, white background, 7 white stars, American Pepsin Gum, c1900 .... 30.00
    Welcome to Our President, Roosevelt, cloth flag below, 1-1/2" d pinback with bluetone photo 75.00

Plate
    St. Louis World's Fair, Washington, Jefferson, Lafayette and Napoleon's faces, very colorful, 1904 .... 120.00
    Washington's Headquarters, Newburg, NY, 1783-1883, crossed flags under house, 10" d 95.00

Post Card, printed semblances of Stars and Stripes covering address side, picture of Wm H Taft for president, July 4, 1908, 46 stars, used 18.00

Poster, 14" x 29", lithograph, "History of Old Glory," Babbitt soap giveaway 145.00

Print, 11-1/4" x 15-1/2", Currier and Ives, "The Star Spangled Banner," #481 .... 175.00

Scarf, numerous multicolored flags and expos name and dates in center, sailing ships border, white ground... 95.00

Sheet music, *You're A Grand Old Flag*, words and music by George M. Cohen, copyright 1906, $20.

Sheet Music
    Miss America, two step by J Edmund Barnum, lady with stars, red and white striped dress, large flowing flag . 20.00
    Stars and Stripes Forever March, John Phillip Sousa portrait in upper left hand corner, Old Glory in center, published by John Church Co 20.00

Spoon, 4-1/2" l, Jefferson, eagle, two flags, globe, "1904, St. Louis" on handle, Electric Building in bowl, Louisiana Monument and Cascade Gardens on back, US Silver Co. 55.00

Stevensgraph, post card, "Hands Across the Sea," embroidered English and American flags, hands shaking, mkd "Woven in Silk, R. M. S. Aquitana," used 35.00

Stickpin
    Celluloid, American flag, 48 stars, advertising, S A Cook for US Senator 20.00
    Metal, 1-3/4" h, red, white, and blue painted furling flag at half staff, sign at left "Vietnam 1961-," orig cardboard box with clear plastic window inscribed, "Wear This Pin For Peace," Pace Emblem Company, New York, NY, c1970 .... 35.00

Teapot, 9" h, cream ground, State of Texas, United States, France, Spain, Republic of Texas and Confederacy Mexico flags, titled below, red and blue line on spout cap 475.00

Token, 3-3/4" d, "The Dix Token Coin," Civil War, commemorates the order of General John Adams Dix, Jan. 29, 1861, "If anyone attempts to haul down the American flag, shoot him on the spot," copper-colored coin, picture of "The Flag of Our Union" on one side and quote on the other 10.00

Tray, 13" d, West End Brewing Co., American flag draped over Lady Liberty, standing next to keg of West End Brewing Co. Beer, Kaufmann & Strauss Co. litho........................250.00

Watch Fob, Sesqui-Centennial, Liberty Bell and American flags, dates 1776-1926, crossed rifles at bottom 40.00

Flashlights

Collecting Hints: Flashlight collecting is like many other categories: name brands count, and if the manufacturer is not known, the value is much lower. Check for brand name and/or trademark, patent date, or patent number, and any other information that will help identify the manufacturer and the date the item was made. Also check the overall outside appearance, and look for signs of wear, dents, splits, scratches, discoloration, rust, corrosion, deformities, etc. Carefully look for any cracks in the metal on both ends of tubular flashlights, and determine if both ends can be unscrewed easily. End caps and switches are the most reliable way to identify the date and make since these parts cannot be easily changed. The finish, as well as the design, should be the same on both ends. Check all rivets and make sure they are intact. Brass becomes brittle with age, and it is not uncommon to find splits on both the lens ring and end caps.

The lens cap should be checked for any visible chips and paint chips. The reflector may be silvered and should be checked for tarnish and scratches. A rusty spring or corrosion damage is a clear sign that the batteries have leaked, which may affect the switch mechanism. Make sure the bulb is original, threaded, flanged, or an unusual shape. The entire flashlight should be checked for completeness, making sure the lens caps and rings all match and all switches work.

Flashlight collectors rely on old catalogs and magazine advertisements to help date and identify their flashlights. They are especially drawn to material with detailed illustrations of switches, finishes, and proper end caps.

Many collectors specialize in one type of flashlight, such as pocket watch, vest pocket, pistol, or character flashlights.

History: The flashlight evolved from early bicycle lights. The first bicycle light was invented by Acme Electric Lamp Company of New York City in 1896. A year later, the Ohio Electric Works Company advertised bicycle lights. In 1898, Conrad Hubert, who had been selling electric scarf pins, bought a wood bicycle-light patent and began manufacturing them under the name American Electrical Novelty and Mfg. Co. This company later became the American Eveready Company. Owen T. Bugg patented a tubular bicycle light in 1898. The next year, Conrad Hubert worked with an inventor who patented the first tubular handheld flashlight, which became the basis for the flashlight industry.

Conrad Hubert moved swiftly to take advantage of this unique tubular electrical "novelty." He displayed his products at the first electrical show at Madison Square Garden and again at the Paris Exposition in 1900. He won the only award at the exposition for "Portable Electric Lamps." He had opened offices in London, Berlin, Paris, Chicago, Montreal, and Sydney by 1901.

After the death of Hubert, Joshua Lionel Cowan, founder of Lionel trains, began taking credit for inventing the flashlight. He often gave detailed accounts of his invention, changing specifics from one account to another. However, his timetable, which coincided with that of Conrad Hubert, clouds the facts of flashlight history.

American Eveready has dominated the flashlight and battery industry since the beginning. In 1906, National Carbon bought one-half interest in American Eveready for $200,000. It purchased the remaining interest in 1914 for an additional $2,000,000. Companies such as Rayovac, Yale, Franco, Bond, Beacon, Delta, Uneedit, Saunders, Winchester, Sharpleigh, and Underwood also made many interesting flashlights.

References: *Collector's Digest Flashlights*, L-W Book Sales, 1995; Stuart Schneider, *Collecting Flashlights*, Schiffer Publishing, 1996; Bill Utley, *Early Flashlight Makers & 1st 100 Years of Everready*, printed by author, 2001, (P.O. Box 4095, Tustin, CA 92781).

Collectors' Club: Flashlight Collectors of America, P.O. Box 4095, Tustin, CA 92781.

Character
  CP30, keychain, 1996 .... 4.00
  Elmo, Sesame Street 3.50
  Flintstones, 1975, MOC, 3" h 15.00
  Frankenstein, c1960, 9-1/2" l 48.00
  Hanna Barbera, 3", interchangeable faces, Flintstone, Huckleberry Hound, and Yogi Bear, 1975, MOC 15.00
  Hulk Hogan, WWF, 1991 .... 12.00
  Lion King, Scar, MIP 9.00
  Mickey Mouse, Walt Disney's World on Ice, Happy Lite, Ringling Bros & Barnum Combined Shows, 1991 copyright, blue light swirls on side 10.00
  Mighty Mouse, four color, 1981, MIP 7.50
  Peter Pan, McDonald's 5.00
  Pluto, hard plastic 12.00
  Precious Moments, 4-1/2" h, Heavenly Light, angel, 1980 .... 35.00
  Roy Rogers, orig box 175.00
  Ultimate Warrior, WWF, 1991 .... 11.00
  X-Files 50.00
Diver's, Siebe-Gorman, brass, four brass prongs hold lens, 11" l 300.00
Ever Ready
  Hexagon/dome lens, metal ribbed body, black enamel end cap, on-off thumb switch, 1900s 55.00
  Masterlight, #6662, vest pocket type, nickel plated, ruby push button switch, 1904 .... 30.00
  Octagon, 3 cell, brass 25.00
  #4707, nickel-plated case, large bull's eye lends, 1912 .... 25.00
Irwin, raygun 65.00
Lantern, Delta, Buddy model, 1919 .... 15.00
Lighter, Continental Flashlight, silvered metal, slight wear 20.00
Pistol shape 90.00
Railroad, Jenks, brass, patent July 25, 1911 .... 90.00
Tubular
  Aurora, all nickel case 20.00
  Bond Electric Co., Jersey City, NJ, 1940s, 5-1/4" l 10.00
  Homart, all metal, 1930s, 10-1/2" l 35.00
  Jack Armstrong, 1-1/2" d, 4-1/2" h 85.00
  Loc-Lite, light green Bakelite, 2" x 3" x 1/2" 35.00
  Magnifying Lens, 6-1/2" l metal body, 2-1/2" d glass lens, mkd "Pat. Oct 19 1915," lens scratched, dents to body 20.00
  Pertrix, stamped "Germany," standard white light, side switch for red, blue, or green lens, leather carrying strap, gray painted finish 70.00
  Ray-O-Vac, Billioneer, 7-1/4" l 65.00
  Ray-O-Vac, Space Patrol 40.00
  Rose Brand, MIB 15.00
  Surlite, 1950s 5.00
  Winchester, marble lens, gold-colored body, 1919-26, 5-1/2" l 100.00
  Winchester, Trade Mark Flash Light Made In USA, Pat. Apr. 8, 1919, Dec. 14, 1920 .... 80.00
  Winchester, #1818, 22-K, copper case 35.00

Victorinox, Fieldmaster, combination knife and flashlight......................24.00
Yale, #3302, double ended, flood lens and spot lens..............................30.00
Yale, chrome, heavy glass lens...48.00

Florence Ceramics

Collecting Hints: Pieces of Florence Ceramics are well marked. Most figures have their names marked on the bottom. Six different backstamps were used, all containing a variation of the name of the company, location, and/or ©.

Florence Ceramics is a relatively new collectible. As a result, stable national pricing has not yet been achieved. It pays to shop around.

Several figures have articulated fingers; some figures were issued with both articulated and closed fingers. The former type commands a slight premium.

Look for figures with especially rich colors, elaborate decorations—such as bows, flowers, lace, ringlets, and tresses—and gold trim. Aqua, beige, maroon, and gray, occasionally highlighted with green or maroon, are most commonly found on economy-line figures. Yellow is hard to find.

History: In 1939, following the death of a young son, Florence Ward began working with clay as a way of dealing with her grief. Her first pieces were figures of children, individually shaped, decorated, and fired in a workshop in her Pasadena, California, garage. Untrained at first, she attended a ceramics class in 1942.

She continued to sell her pottery as a means of supplementing her income during World War II. Her business grew, and in 1946 the Florence Ceramics Company moved to a plant located on the east side of Pasadena. Clifford, Ward's husband, and Clifford, Jr., another son, joined the firm.

With the acquisition of increased production facilities, Florence Ceramics began exhibiting its wares at major Los Angeles gift shows. A worldwide business quickly developed. In 1949, a modern factory featuring a continuous tunnel kiln was opened at 74 South San Gabriel Boulevard in Pasadena. More than 100 employees worked at the new plant.

Florence Ceramics produced semi-porcelain figurines that featured historic couples in period costumes and ladies and gentlemen outfitted in costumes copied from late 19th-century Godey fashions. Fictional characters, including movie-related ones such as Rhett and Scarlet from "Gone with the Wind," were made. Inexpensive small figurines of children and figural vases also were manufactured.

Florence Ceramics offered a full line of period decorative accessories that included birds, busts, candleholders, clock frames, smoking sets, wall plaques, and wall pockets. Lamp bases, which were made using some of the figural pieces, were offered for sale with custom shades.

In 1956, the company employed Betty Davenport Ford, a modeler, to develop a line of bisque-finished animal figures. The series included cats, dogs, doves, rabbits, and squirrels. A minimal airbrush decoration was added. Production lasted only two years.

Florence Ceramics was sold to Scripto Corporation following the death of Clifford Ward in 1964. Scripto retained the Florence Ceramics name, but produced primarily advertising specialty wares. The plant closed in 1977.

References: Susan and Al Bagdade, *Warman's American Pottery and Porcelain*, 2nd ed., Krause Publications, 2000; Jack Chipman, *Collector's Encyclopedia of California Pottery*, Collector Books, 1992, 1998 value update.

Periodical: *Florence Collector's Club Newsletter*, P.O. Box 122, Richland, WA 99352.

Bust, white, 9-1/2" h
  Choir Boy...75.00
  Pamela and David 300.00
Cigarette Box, cov
  Lady's head, green, cameo...... 125.00
  Winter 245.00
Dealer Sign....................................350.00
Figure
  Abigail 160.00
  Ava, yellow 300.00
  Bea, teal and rose, 7-1/4" h 150.00
  Blue Boy, 11-3/4" h....................395.00
  Camile 245.00
  Charmaine, green....................460.00
  Chinese Boy and Girl, 8-1/2" h 120.00
  Choir Boy....................................45.00
  Claudia, 8-1/2" h, gray over pink... 200.00
  Della, green and sand, 7-1/4" h 175.00

Douglas 240.00
Edward 430.00
Elaine, white and gold, 6" h 85.00
Elizabeth.....................................600.00
Grace, 7-1/2" h, light green....... 185.00
Irene, beige and green dress, 6" h... 65.00
Irene, gray dress, 6" h 80.00
Irene, pink dress, 6" h 80.00
Jeanette, 7-1/2" h, olive green.. 140.00
Jim, white and gold....................75.00
Lady Diana, 9 1/2" h..................195.00
Matilda, 8" h.............................. 185.00
Melanie, 7-1/2" h, beige with green.. 110.00
Mermaid 125.00
Ming and Toy, 9" h 300.00
Pinkie, 11-1/2" h........................395.00
Priscillia, 7-1/2" h, gray............ 155.00
Rebecca, gray and maroon......250.00
Rhett..350.00
Sarah 125.00
Scarlett..200.00
Sue Ellen, 8", gray with maroon....................................... 150.00
Tess, light green 430.00
Victoria, pink, hat......................530.00
Vivian, pink 360.00
Flower Holder
  Lea, green and rose, 6" h........... 60.00
  Peg, beige and green, 7-1/2" h .. 60.00
Lamp, David and Betsy, price for pr..500.00
Wall Plaque, Cameo, lady in feathered hat... 115.00

Flow Blue China, American

Collecting Hints: As with any Flow Blue china, value for American-made pieces depends upon condition, quality, pattern, and type. Avoid those pieces with flaws which cannot be repaired unless you plan to use them only for decorative purposes.

History: When imported Flow Blue china, i.e., English, German, etc., became popular, American manufacturers soon followed suit. There is great variation in quality. Compared to European makers, the number of U.S. manufacturers is small. The most well-known are the French China Co., Homer Laughlin China Co., Mercer Pottery Co., Sebring Pottery Co., Warwick China, and Wheeling Pottery Co.

References: Mary Frank Gaston, *Collectors Encyclopedia of Flow Blue*, Collector Books, Paducah, KY, 1983; Norma Jean Hoener, *Flow Blue China: Additional Patterns and New Information*, Flow Blue International Collectors Club (11560 W. 95th #297,

Overland Park, KS 66214); Jeffrey B. Snyder, *Historic Flow Blue*, Schiffer Publications, 1994; ——, *Pocket Guide to Flow Blue*, Schiffer Publications, 1995; Petra Williams, *Flow Blue China—An Aid to Identification*, Vols. I, II, and III, Fountain House East (P.O. Box 99298, Jeffersontown, KY 40299), 1971–1991.

Collectors' Club: Flow Blue International Collectors' Club, Inc., P.O. Box 168572, Irving, TX 75016.

Museum: Margaret Woodbury Strong Museum, Rochester, NY.

Additional Listings: See *Warman's Antiques and Collectibles Price Guide.*

Advisor: Ellen G. King

Advertising
  Ashtray, Sebring China, cherub decal in center, 4-1/2" d.........................95.00
  Souvenir, German, shaped like horseshoe, 6" d 80.00
Argyle, J & E Mayer
  Bone Dish 55.00
  Butter Pat 40.00
  Milk Pitcher, 7" h.......................150.00
  Plate, 8" d.................................60.00
Autumn Leaves, Warwick
  Jardiniere, 8" x 71/2" 550.00
  Plate, 10-1/2" d 135.00
  Relish, 8" l...............................110.00
  Syrup Pitcher, squatty, silver plate lid..275.00
Balmoral, Burgess & Campbell, butter pat 45.00
Bathing Beauty, The French China Co., plate, 8" d, colorful decal of woman in bathing suit, c1915......................65.00
Colonial, Homer Laughlin Co.
  Dessert Bowl, 4-3/4" d................40.00
  Plate, 10" d...............................75.00
  Teacup and Saucer.....................95.00
  Vegetable Bowl, round, open, 10-1/4" d.................................125.00
Calico, Warwick
  Creamer.....................................255.00
  Tray, 9" x 6-1/2"..........................130.00
Cracked Ice, International Pottery
  Bowl, round, open, 10" d...........165.00
  Cake Plate, round, open handles, gilting, 10-1/4" d.............................225.00
  Chocolate Pot, lid 450.00
  Demitasse Cup and Saucer........75.00
Delph, Sebring Pottery
  Butter Pat 35.00
  Cake Set, 10" handled round plate, six 6-3/4" d plates, set....................195.00
  Plate, 9" d..................................60.00
  Soup Bowl, 8" d..........................50.00
  Wash Basin, 17" d.....................325.00
Fernery, Knowles, Taylor, Knowles
  Relish, small, oval, 8" l...............65.00
  Soap Dish, cov, no insert 125.00
Hawthorne, Mercer Pottery
  Plate, 8" d..................................60.00

Platter, 13" d 185.00
Vegetable Tureen, cov............. 295.00

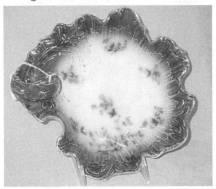

La Belle, bowl with handle, $375. Photo courtesy of Ellen King.

La Belle, plate, 9" d, $60. Photo courtesy of Ellen King.

La Belle/Blue Diamond, Wheeling Pottery
  Biscuit Jar, cov, 8-1/2"............... 495.00
  Bone Dish, individual..................80.00
  Bowl, helmet shape, ftd, 8" d.... 425.00
  Bowl, oval, with handle 375.00
  Bread Tray, 14-1/2" x 6-1/8" 375.00
  Butter Dish, cov, base, insert ... 750.00
  Butter Pat..................................60.00
  Cake Plate, closed handles...... 255.00
  Charger, 11-1/2" d...................... 345.00
  Charger, 14" d.......................... 450.00
  Creamer and Sugar, cov 425.00
  Dessert Bowl, individual, 5-1/2" d 60.00
  Ice Cream Tray, oblong, 13-5/8" l....................................... 375.00
  Jardiniere, octagonal, gilding, 15-3/4" h 2,250.00
  Plate, 7-1/2" d 50.00
  Plate, 9" d..................................60.00
  Plate, 10" d.................................75.00
  Punch Cup, ftd........................... 450.00
  Relish, oval, 8" l......................... 275.00
  Serving Bowl, oval, 10-1/4" x 9"...................................... 275.00
  Serving Bowl, round, 9-1/2" d.... 295.00
  Soup Bowl, 9" d..........................85.00
  Syrup Pitcher, silver plate lid, 4-1/4" 455.00
  Teacup and Saucer 135.00
  Vegetable Tureen, cov............. 350.00

La Francaise, child's cup and saucer, $55. Photo courtesy of Ellen King.

LaFrancaise, The French China Co.
  Butter Dish, cov, insert, worn gold... 125.00
  Butter Pat, plain 30.00
  Butter Pat, gold snowflake 40.00
  Child's Cup and Saucer.............. 55.00
  Creamer, 5" h..............................85.00
  Dessert Bowl, center floral decal, 5" d..30.00
  Plate, center floral decal, 9" d..... 45.00
  Plate, gold tracery, 9" d...............40.00
  Platter, plain, 13-1/2" l................ 75.00
  Salt and Pepper Shakers, pr, round, squatty...................................... 125.00
  Soup Bowl, plain, 8" d 40.00
  Teacup and Saucer, floral decal..80.00
  Vegetable Tureen, cov, ivy pattern 325.00

Luzerne, plate, heavy gilting, 8" d, $65. Photo courtesy of Ellen King.

Luzerne, Mercer Pottery
  Cake Stand, pedestal base, 10" d, 4-3/4" h...................................... 225.00
  Plate, heavy gilding, 8" d 65.00
  Plate, no gold, 10" d................. 100.00
  Platter, 18" l 425.00
  Soup Bowl, 6-1/8" d.................... 55.00
  Soup Bowl, with rim, 8-3/4" d 65.00
  Soup Bowl, with rim, 9-1/2" d 75.00
  Teacup and Saucer................... 125.00
  Teapot, cov 475.00
Paisley, Mercer Pottery
  Butter Pat 55.00
  Creamer, squatty....................... 150.00
  Plate, 8" d...................................65.00
  Plate, 9" d...................................75.00
  Soup Bowl, with rim, 8-7/8" d 75.00

Pansy, Warwick
    Cake Plate, closed handles,
        10" d...225.00
    Charger, 14" d, round 350.00
    Creamer, 6" d 250.00
    Relish, 12-1/2" l 135.00

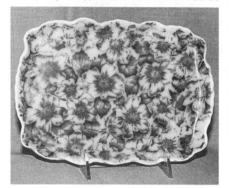

Poppy, tray, 6" x 9", $225. Photo courtesy of Ellen King.

Poppy, Warwick
    Dessert Bowl, individual, 6" d 45.00
    Syrup Pitcher, silver plate lid 375.00
    Tray, 6" x 9"................................225.00
Royal Blue, Burgess & Campbell
    Butter Pat 45.00
    Plate, 9-7/8" d...............................85.00
    Platter, 12-5/8" x 8-1/4"...............325.00
    Soup Bowl, with rim, 9" d.............60.00
Snowflake, Knowles, Taylor, Knowles,
    plate, 9" d.....................................65.00
The Sebring, Sebring Pottery Co.,
    charger, pale green inner rim,
        14" d..350.00
U. S. S. Brooklyn, The French China Co.,
    bowl, round, 10-3/4" d 375.00
U. S. S. Maine, The French China Co.,
    bowl, oval, 9-1/2" x 12-3/4" l 395.00
Wild Rose, Warwick
    Berry Set, 10" d master bowl, six indi-
        vidual bowls..............................375.00
    Chocolate Set, cov chocolate pot, five
        cups and saucers...................1,250.00
Windmill, The French China Co.
    Butter Pat 40.00
    Platter, 13" l................................125.00
    Relish, oval, 10" l..........................55.00
    Soup Bowl, 8" d 45.00
Winona, The French China Co.
    Pitcher, 5" 125.00
    Plate, 6" d.....................................45.00
    Platter, 14" l................................110.00
    Teacup and Saucer 55.00
    Toothbrush Holder, upright........125.00

Football Cards

Collecting Hints: Condition is critical—buy cards that are in very good condition, i.e., free from any creases and damaged corners. When possible, strive to acquire cards in excellent to mint condition. The introduction to *2001 Standard Cata-* *log of Football Cards* (Krause Publications 2001) tells how to determine the condition of a card.

What applies to baseball cards is equally true for football cards. Devise a collecting strategy, such as cards related to one year, one player, Heisman trophy winners, or one team. A large quantity of cards is available; a novice collector can be easily overwhelmed.

History: Football cards have been printed since the 1890s. However, it was not until 1933 that the first bubble gum football card appeared in the Goudey Sport Kings set. In 1935, National Chickle of Cambridge, Massachusetts, produced the first full set of gum cards devoted exclusively to football.

Both Leaf Gum of Chicago and Bowman Gum of Philadelphia produced sets of football cards in 1948. Leaf discontinued production after its 1949 issue; Bowman continued until 1955.

Topps Chewing Gum entered the market in 1950 with its college-stars set. Topps became a fixture in the football card market with its 1955 All-American set. From 1956 thorough 1963, Topps printed card sets of National Football League players, combining them with the American Football League players in 1961.

Topps produced sets with only American Football League players from 1964 to 1967. The Philadelphia Gum Company made National Football League card sets during this period. Beginning in 1968 and continuing to the present, Topps has produced sets of National Football League cards, the name adopted after the merger of the two leagues.

References: *All Sport Alphabetical Price Guide*, Krause Publications, 1995; *Football, Basketball & Hockey Price Guide*, Krause Publications, 1991; *2001 Standard Catalog of Football Cards*, 4th ed., Sports Collectors Digest, Krause Publications, 2000.

Periodicals: *Beckett Football Card Magazine*, 4887 Alpha Rd, Ste 200, Dallas, TX 75244; *Card Trade*, 700 E. State St., Iola, WI 54990; *Sports Cards*, 700 E. State St., Iola, WI 54990; *Sports Collectors Digest*, 700 E. State St., Iola, WI 54990.

Bowman Gum, 1950, top: Y. A. Tittle, Jr., #5, $22; bottom: Glen Davis, #16, $12.

Bowman Card Company
1948
    Complete Set (108)..............6,200.00
    Common Player (1-108)............. 15.00
1951
    Complete Set (144)................ 1,500.00
    Common Player (1-144)............. 18.00
1952, Large
    Complete Set (144)..............12,000.00
    Common Player (1-72)............... 25.00
    Common Player (73-144)............ 35.50
1952, Small
    Complete Set (144)................5,500.00
    Common Player (1-72)............... 18.50
    Common Player (73-144)............ 24.00
1953, #27 Gilmer, SGC 92-8.5....... 250.00
1954
    Complete Set (128)................ 1,600.00
    Common Player (1-64)................. 6.50
    Common Player (65-96)............. 15.00
    Common Player (97-128)............. 5.50
    #102 Tunnel, SGC 92-8.5.......... 105.00
1955, All American
    #18 Heffelfinger, SGC 88-8......... 80.00
    #36 Edwards, SGC 88-8............. 65.00
    #41 Alexander, SGC 88-8........... 65.00
    #42 Tryon, SGC 92-8.5.............. 100.00
    #53 Green, SGC 88-8................. 50.00
    #54 Dooley, SGC 88-8............... 65.00
    #55 Merritt, SGC 88-8............... 65.00
    #57 Hanson, SGC 88-8.............. 65.00
    #64 Friedman, SGC 88-8............ 50.00
    #86 Booth, SGC 88-8................. 65.00
    #87 Schultz, SGC 92-8.5.......... 100.00
1958
    #2 Layne, SGC 88-8................... 85.00

#16 Marchetti, SGC 88-8............45.00
#18 Lary, SGC 92-8.5............55.00
#57 Morrall, SGC 92-8.5............55.00
#90 Jurgensen, SGC 92-8.5.....350.00
#93 Perry, SGC 92-8.5...............75.00
#120 Berry, SGC 92-8.5............150.00

1962
#37 Cleveland Team, SGC
88-8...............................40.00
#79 Matson, SGC 96-9............250.00
#102 Tittle, SGC 92-8.5............150.00

1965
#24 Bass, SGC 92-8.5............50.00
#66 Appleton, SGC 88-8............40.00
#71 Burrell, SGC 88-8............40.00
#109 Robinson, SGC 88-8........40.00

1995
Complete Set (357)......................125.00
Common Player.............................10
Expansion Foil.............................25
Minor Star...................................20
Wax Box.....................................80.00

1998, Chrome
Complete Set (220)....................550.00
Common Player.............................30
Common Rookie.............................3.50
Minor Star...................................80

Fleer
1960
Complete Set (132)....................750.00
Common Player (1-32)..................3.25

1961
Complete Set (220)..................1,625.00
Common Player (1-132).............4.25
Common Player (133-220)...........4.75
Uncut, 132 cards.......................650.00
#187 Otto, SGC 92-8.5............125.00

1963
Complete Set (89)..................1,800.00
Common Player (1-88)................7.50

1990, hand collated set....................10.00

Leaf
1948
Complete Set (98).................6,000.00
Common Player (1-49)...............22.00
Common Player (1-98).............100.00

1949
Complete Set (49)..................2,000.00
Common Player (1-49)...............25.00

1998
Complete Set (300)....................450.00
Common Player.............................15
Common Rookie.............................2.00
Minor Stars...................................30

Philadelphia
1964
Complete Set (198)....................950.00
Common Player (1-198)...............2.00

1966
Complete Set (198)....................950.00
Common Player (1-198)...............2.75

Pro Set
1990
Factory-sealed set..........................5.00
Hand-collated set.........................17.00

Score
1989
Complete Set (330)....................220.00
Common Player (1-330).................10
Minor Star...................................20
Wax Box.....................................500.00

1990, factory sealed set...................10.00

Stadium Club
1991
Complete Set (500)....................90.00
Common Player.............................20
Hand Collated Set.......................90.00
Minor Star...................................40
Wax Box.....................................90.00

1992
Complete Set (700)....................150.00
Common Series 1 (300)..............15.00
Common Series 2 (300)..............15.00
Common Player.............................10

Topps
1956
Complete Set (121)...............1,100.00
Common Player (1-120)..............3.75

1958
Complete Set (132)...............1,350.00
Common Player (1-132)..............3.75

1960
Complete Set (132)...............650.00
Common Player (1-132)..............2.25

1962
Complete Set (176)...............1,825.00
Common Player (1-176)..............3.65

1964
Complete Set (176)...............1,450.00
Common Player (1-176)..............3.50
Common Player SP......................3.00

1966
Complete Set (132)...............1,250.00
Common Player (1-132)..............4.20

1968
Complete Set (219)...............725.00
Common Player (1-131)..............50
Common Player (132-219)...........75

1970
Complete Set (263)...............2,500.00
Common Player (1-132)..............75
Common Player (133-263)............85

1972
Complete Set (351)...............2,300.00
Common Player (1-132)..............50
Common Player (133-263)............75
Common Player (264-351)..........20.00

1975
Complete Set (528)...............355.00
Common Player (1-528)..............25

1977
Complete Set (528)...............225.00
Common Player (1-528)..............15

1979
Complete Set (528)...............125.00
Common Player (1-528)..............15

1981
Complete Set (528)...............250.00
Common Player (1-528)..............20

1983
Complete Set (396)...............50.00
Common Player (1-396)..............10
Common Player DP......................05

1985
Complete Set (396)...............80.00
Common Player (1-396)..............05
Wax Pack, unopened.................90.00

1987
Complete Set (396)...............40.00
Common Player (1-396)..............05

1990
Complete Set (528)...............15.00
Common Player (1-528)..............03

1996, Chrome
Complete Set (165)...............160.00

Common Player.............................25
Common Rookies.........................1.00
Minor Stars...................................50
Wax Box.....................................180.00

1997, Chrome
Complete Set (165)...................180.00
Common Player.............................40
Minor Star...................................75
Wax Box.....................................220.00

Upper Deck
1991
Factory sealed set..................17.00
Hand collated set...................15.00

1996, Game Jersey
Complete Set (10).................4,000.00
Common Player.........................150.00

1997, Game Jersey
Complete Set (10).................3,000.00
Common Player.........................150.00

1998, Super Powers
Complete Set (30).....................45.00
Common Player.............................50
Minor Stars...................................1.00

Football Collectibles

Collecting Hints: Collectors of football items may decide to specialize in one team, one conference, or one type of collectible, i.e., helmets or pennants. Collectors should not overlook the wealth of items generated by colleges, high schools, and even younger participants.

History: The first American college football match was held between Princeton and Rutgers in New Brunswick, New Jersey, in 1869. Harvard documents a more rugby-type game in the 1870s. A professional football association was founded in 1920 and renamed the National Football League (NFL) in 1922. Football really took off after World War II and grew to 28 teams in two conferences by the 1980s. Expansion continued until 30 teams were playing by 1995.

The Super Bowl was created in 1967 and has become the exciting termination of the season for many fans. The Canadian Football League (CFL) was created in 1959 and oversees a professional circuit.

References: Mark Allen Baker, *All Sport Autograph Guide*, Krause Publications, 1994; David Bushing, *Sports Equipment Price Guide*, Krause Publications, 1995; Roderick Malloy, *Malloy's Sports Collectibles Value Guide*, Krause Publications, 2000; Michael McKeever, *Collecting Sports Memorabilia*, Alliance Publishing, 1996; Tom Mortenson, *2000 Standard*

Catalog of Sports Memorabilia, Krause Publications, 2000.

Periodical: *Sports Collectors Digest*, 700 E. State St., Iola, WI 54990.

Autographed NFL Footballs
Allen, Marcus 190.00
Bradshaw, Terry 215.00
Culpepper, Daunte 180.00
Dent, Richard, Super Bowl 20 ... 200.00
Elway, John 250.00
Favre, Brett 200.00
James, Edgerin 180.00
Owens, Terrell 150.00
Marino, Dan 300.00
Montana, Joe 300.00
Rice, Jerry 200.00
Simpson, O. J. 215.00
Smith, Emmitt 210.00
Young, Steve, Super Bowl 29 .... 215.00

Autographed Jersey
Aikman, Troy, pro-cut, Nike 285.00
Csonka, Larry, Dolphins, aqua, Wilson 250.00
Farve, Brett, Packers, green, Nike 300.00
Griese, Bob, Dolphins, Champion 250.00
Marino, Dan, Dolphins, white, Starter 380.00
Montana, Joe, Notre Dame 325.00
Namath, Joe, University of Alabama 300.00
White, Reggie, Packers, green and white, Starter 230.00

Autographed Mini Helmet, accompanied by Certificate of Authenticity and security decal
Alstoff, Mike, Tampa Bay Bucks 80.00
Banks, Carl, New York Giants 50.00
Baugh, Sammy, Washington Redskins 100.00
Bradshaw, Terry, Pittsburgh Steelers 150.00
Brown, Willie, Oakland Raiders ... 80.00
Brunell, Mark, Jacksonville Jaguars 100.00
Buchanan, Ray, Atlanta Falcons 40.00
Campbell, Earl, Houston Oilers .. 80.00
Clayton, Mark, Miami Dolphins ... 50.00
Culpepper, Daunte, Minnesota Vikings 80.00
Curtis, Mike, Indianapolis Colts .. 40.00
Davis, Stephen, Washington Redskins 60.00
Dawson, Len, Kansas City Chiefs 70.00
Dayne, Ron, New York Giants 85.00
Dorsett, Tony, Dallas Cowboys ... 80.00
Dugans, Ron, Cincinnati Bengals 40.00
Elway, John, Denver Broncos ... 200.00
Favre, Brett, Green Bay Packers 150.00
Ferguson, Joe, Buffalo Bills 60.00
Graham, Otto, Cleveland Browns 85.00
Hart, Jim, Arizona Cardinals 45.00
Hornung, Paul, Green Bay Packers 60.00

James, Edgerin, Indianapolis Colts 120.00
Jones, Ed Too Tall, Dallas Cowboys 50.00
Jones, Thomas, Arizona Cardinals 60.00
Kelly, Jim, Miami Hurricanes 90.00
King, Shawn, Tampa Bay Bucks 60.00
Kosar, Bernie, Cleveland Browns 60.00
Lewis, Jamal, Baltimore Ravens 60.00
Marino, Dan, Miami Dolphins ... 170.00
McNabb, Donovan, Philadelphia Eagles 60.00
Moon, Warren, Houston Oilers 80.00
Munoz, Anthony, Cincinnati Bengals 60.00
Namath, Joe, New York Jets 150.00
Pennington, Chad, New York Jets 60.00
Pruitt, Greg, Oakland Raiders 45.00
Reed, Andre, Buffalo Bills 60.00
Sayers, Gale, Chicago Bears 90.00
Sims, Billy, Detroit Lions 50.00
Starr, Bart, Green Bay Packers 150.00
Tarkenton, Fran, Minnesota Vikings 90.00
Taylor, Fred, Jacksonville Jaguars 80.00
Torreta, Gino, Miami Hurricanes 60.00
White, Dez, Chicago Bears 40.00
White, Reggie, Green Bay Packers 100.00
Woodson, Rod, Baltimore Ravens 50.00
Zorn, Jim, Seattle Seahawks 50.00

Autographed Photograph
Blades, B., R. Crockett, K. Scott, and W. White 45.00
Crockett, Ray, Detroit, 8" x 10" 5.00
Eliss, Luther, Detroit, 8" x 10" 5.00
Howard, Desmond, Washington, 8" x 10" 10.00
Mitchell, Pete, Jaguars, 8" x 10" 4.00
Moore, Herman, NFL Official 80.00
Murray, Ed, Detroit, 8" x 10" 5.00
Schembechler, Bo, Univ of Michigan, 8" x 10" 19.00
White, William, Detroit, 8" x 10" 4.00

Autographed Program
Montana, Joe, Super Bowl 24 .... 135.00
Rice, Jerry, Super Bowl 23, sgd "MVP" 140.00

Autographed Ticket, Joe Paterno, Penn State, 9-4-99 .... 38.00

Bobbing Head
Cleveland Browns, sq brown wood base 75.00
Portland Trailblazers, MIB 55.00
Seattle Supersonics, MIB 55.00
St. Louis Cardinal, 6-1/2" h 130.00

Book
Backfield in Motion, A Full-Length Photo-Guide to Playing Quarterback, Running Back and Pass Receiver, Don Smith, Gallahad Books, 1973, 1st ed. 10.00

The Big One, Michigan vs Ohio State, A History of America's Greatest Football Rivalry, Bill Cromartie, Rutledge Press, Nashville, 1988, 399 pgs, dj 10.00
University of Toledo 1970 Football Dope Book, press guide, 64 pgs 17.50

Doll, 7-1/2" h, celluloid head, hands, and feet, straw body, celluloid pinback button with "Yale" with attached ribbon and tin litho football, emb "Japan" on back of head 40.00

Drinking Glass, Seagram V.O. Golden Quarterback Challenge 1990, football player on one side with facsimile signature, VO decal on other, 8 oz, set of eight 24.00

Football, leather, Wilson, NFL 25.00

Game, Tom Hamilton's Pigskin Football Game, 1935 .... 265.00

Hartland Figurine
Arnett 300.00
Browns, orig box 95.00
Giants, orig box 150.00

Jersey, game used
Collins, J, LA Rams, white mesh, 1980s 225.00
Reeves, Eagles, white mesh, 1990s 110.00
Selman, D, Tampa Bay, white mesh, 1970s 325.00
Warren, Univ of Miami, white mesh, Fiesta Bowl, 1990s 245.00
Williams, T, Dallas Cowboys, white mesh, name plate restored, 1980s 145.00

Lunchbox, NFL/AFC, 1978 Broncos Bengals, helmets on side, NFL logo on back, some wear, orig thermos .. 30.00

Magazine Tear Sheet, Wilson football, ball with "grip-ability," Paul Hornung, Boy's Life, 1967 .... 4.00

Patch, Super Bowl V, 1970, Baltimore and Dallas 60.00

Pennant
Chicago Bears, 11-1/2" x 28-1/2" black felt, "Bears" in orange, orange, green, and red football art, orange felt trim strip, late 1940s 25.00
Cincinnati Bengal's Super Bowl 16 AFC Champions, orange 65.00
Denver Broncos World Championship, 1977 .... 45.00
Norte Dame, 1957 Conference Champions, gold filled, football shaped, chain 75.00

Pinback Button, NFL Teams Official Booster Series, mail premium from H. J. Heinz, c1967, 1-5/8" d, litho
Atlanta Falcons, red and black helmet, white ground, black letters 18.00
Baltimore Colts, blue and white, light surface wear 15.00
Detroit Lions, blue and silver, white letters 20.00
New York Giants, black and white helmet, orange ground, white letters 20.00
Philadelphia Eagles, green and silver 18.00

Pinback Button, Super Bowl XV/ABC Sports, 1981, black and white, gray rim, black letters, Superdome, New Orleans, Oakland Raiders and Philadelphia eagles 30.00

Playset, Bob Griese, Gale Sayers, orig box 245.00

Postcard, young boy with football and turkey, postmarked Nov. 23, 1909 ....5.00

Press Badge, U.S.C., blue lettering, taupe gray cello, "Camera" operator at Nov. 1, 1924 game, Los Angeles Coliseum, freshmen teams from Univ of Southern CA and Univ of CA 80.00

Program
New York Giants-Chicago Bears Playoff, 7-3/4 x 10-1/2", Dec. 30, 1956 ....30.00
Notre Dame vs Wisconsin, 1953 ....50.00
Penn State-Navy Homecoming Game, 8" x 10-1/2", Oct.15, 1955, Beaver Field, Penn State Centennial celebration..40.00

Soda Bottle, Dr Pepper, 1972 Commemorative, Miami Dolphins, unopened 95.00

Radio, NFL 50th Anniversary, Chiquita.......................................45.00

Telephone, figural, NFL, NRMIB.......30.00

Ticket Stub
American Football League Championship, 1967, Oakland and Houston.......................................25.00
NFC Division, 1977, Minnesota and LA Rams..12.00
Notre Dame vs Stanford, 1964....15.00
Super Bowl I, 1966, Green Bay and Kansas City...............................125.00

Wire Service Photo, Dallas Cowboys owner Jerry Jones and Jimmy Johnson, 1989 ....3.50

Yearbook, Greenbay Packers, 1974, autographed by coaches and players 35.00

Franciscan Dinnerware

Collecting Hints: The emphasis on Franciscan art pottery and dinnerware has overshadowed the many other collectible lines from Gladding, McBean and Company. Keep your eye open for Tropico Art Ware, made between 1934 and 1937. This company also made some high-style birdbaths, florists' vases, flowerpots, garden urns, and hotel cigarette snuffers. Catalina Art Ware (1937-1941) also is attracting collector attention.

Most buyers of Franciscan's big three patterns (Apple, Desert Rose, and Ivy) are seeking replacement pieces for sets currently in use. As a result, prices tend to be somewhat inflated, especially for hollow pieces. Keep in mind that these patterns were popular throughout the country.

Early Franciscan lines, which are similar to Bauer designs and Homer Laughlin's Fiesta, can be distinguished from their more popular counterparts by differences in shape and color. These pieces are more commonly found on the West Coast than the East.

History: Gladding, McBean and Company, Los Angeles, California, produced the Franciscan dinnerware patterns at its Glendale, California, pottery. The company began in 1875 as a manufacturer of sewer pipe and terra-cotta tile. In 1922, Gladding, McBean and Company acquired Tropico Pottery in Glendale, and in 1933 the West Coast properties of American Encaustic Tile.

In 1934, the company began producing and marketing dinnerware and art pottery under the name Franciscan Ware. Franciscan dinnerware had talc (magnesium silicate) rather than clay as a base. Early lines, which used bright primary colors on plain shapes, include Coronado, El Patio, Metropolitan, Montecito, Padua, and Rancho. As the line developed, more graceful shapes and pastel colors were introduced.

Three patterns are considered Franciscan classics. The Apple pattern with its embossed body, hand decoration, and underglaze staining was introduced in 1940. The Desert Rose pattern (1941) is the most popular dinnerware pattern ever manufactured in the United States. Ivy, the last of the big three, was first made in 1948.

There are three distinct types of Franciscan products: 1) masterpiece china, a high-quality translucent ceramic; 2) earthenware, a cream-colored ware found in a variety of decal- and hand-decorated patterns; and 3) whitestone or white earthenware.

Gladding, McBean and Company became Interpace Corporation in 1963. In 1979, Josiah Wedgwood and Sons, Ltd., acquired the company. In 1986, the Glendale plant was closed, marking the end of American production.

References: Susan and Al Bagdade, *Warman's American Pottery and Porcelain*, 2nd ed., Krause Publications, 2000; Jack Chipman, *Collector's Encyclopedia of California Pottery*, Collector Books, 1992, 1998 value update.

Collectors' Club: Franciscan Collectors Club USA, 8412 5th Ave. NE, Seattle, WA 98115.

Apple, introduced in 1940. Embossed earthenware body, hand decorated and under the glaze stain.
Ashtray.. 25.00
Beer Mug, 17 oz....................... 85.00
Bowl, ftd.................................... 22.00
Bread and Butter Plate............. 14.00
Butter Dish, cov, 8" l................. 95.00
Casserole, cov, individual 55.00
Chop Plate, 14" d 125.00
Coaster 65.00
Cocoa Mug................................ 125.00
Compote, 8" d 175.00
Creamer and Sugar 60.00
Cup and Saucer
Coffee................................... 9.50
Jumbo................................... 70.00
Dinner Plate 20.00
Grill Plate 140.00
Gravy and Underplate 42.00
Jam Jar....................................... 135.00
Juice Tumbler 37.50
Mixing Bowl, 9" d 90.00
Platter, 12-3/4" d 50.00
Salad Plate 18.00
Salt and Pepper Shakers, pr, small.. 36.00
Syrup Pitcher 80.00
Teapot, cov 65.00
Tumbler 20.00
Turkey Platter 320.00
Tureen, ftd.................................. 435.00
Vegetable Bowl, 7-1/2" l 65.00

Arcadia, green, gold trim, gravy boat.. 145.00

Carmel, platinum trim, vegetable, oval 86.00

Coronado, Dinnerware line produced from 1936 until 1956. Made in 15 different colors with both satin and glossy glazes.
Bowl, turquoise, 7-1/2" d 17.50
Bread and Butter Plate, turquoise...................................... 4.25
Butter Dish, cov, turquoise.......... 32.00
Candlesticks, pr, ivory satin 48.00
Chop Plate, 12" d, yellow 20.00
Creamer, yellow.......................... 12.00
Cup and Saucer, coral, matte....... 9.50
Demitasse Cup and Saucer, white.. 37.50
Dinner Plate
Coral, glossy 9.50
Turquoise............................... 12.00
Nut Cup
Maroon 70.00
Turquoise, glossy 70.00
Turquoise, glossy, orig box .. 120.00
Platter, 15" l, oval, yellow 17.50
Sugar, cov, coral, glossy 13.00
Vegetable Bowl, yellow 35.00

Daisy

Milk Pitcher 80.00
Vegetable Bowl 40.00

Del Monte, gravy boat 140.00
Denmark, blue, coffeepot.............110.00
Desert Rose. Introduced in 1941. Embossed earthenware with hand painted under-the-glaze decoration. Known for it's rosebud shaped finials.

After Dinner Cup and Saucer 50.00
Ashtray, individual size...............18.00
Baking Dish
 Oblong.............................275.00
 Square 175.00
Bell, Danbury Mint....................100.00
Bowl, 9" d...............................45.00
Bread and Butter Plate,
6-1/2" d...................................5.00
Butter Dish 30.00
Candlesticks, pr........................75.00
Casserole, 1-1/2 quart.................75.00
Celery Tray, 4-1/2" x 10-1/2" 35.00
Cereal Bowl, 6" d 10.00
Child's Plate 165.00
Chop Plate
 12" d...................................75.00
 14" d...................................95.00
Cigarette Box 140.00
Coffeepot, cov 115.00
Compote 75.00
Creamer and Sugar.....................40.00
Cup and Saucer 15.00
Dessert Plate, coupe...................75.00
Dinner Plate 10-1/2" d.................18.00
Eggcup.................................35.00
Fruit Bowl 6.00
Gravy, underplate 65.00
Grill Plate...............................95.00
Luncheon Plate, 8-1/2" d.............12.00
Milk Pitcher 75.00
Mug, 16 oz 40.00
Party Plate, coupe 200.00
Pickle Dish 45.00
Platter, 19" l...........................225.00
Relish, 3-part..........................90.00
Salad Bowl..............................95.00
Side Salad..............................32.00
Sherbet.................................20.00
Snack Plate...........................195.00
Soup Bowl...............................18.00
Tea Cup and Saucer 10.00
Tea Jar, cov...........................150.00
Tea Tile, square 50.00
Toast Cover............................155.00
Vegetable Bowl, 9" l....................32.00
Water Pitcher, 2-1/2 quart...........95.00

Fremont

Gravy Boat.............................145.00
Platter, large...........................175.00
Vegetable, oval.........................98.00

Fresh Fruit, tile, 6".....................50.00
Granville, gravy boat 120.00
Hacienda, green

Bread and Butter Plate..................8.00
Cup and Saucer 20.00
Dinner Plate 22.00
Platter, 14" l.............................65.00
Salad Plate...............................10.00
Soup Bowl...............................18.00

Indian Summer

Bread and Butter Plate.................4.50
Cereal Bowl, some wear 3.00

Dinner Plate, few knife marks......12.00
Fruit Bowl, some wear 3.00
Salad Plate 7.50
Salt Shaker 5.00
Saucer...................................4.00

Ivy. Introduced in 1948. Embossed earthenware with hand painted under-the-glaze decoration.

Bowl, 7-1/4" d...........................40.00
Bread and Butter Plate,
6-1/2" d..................................12.00
Cereal Bowl..............................22.00
Creamer 30.00
Cup and Saucer..........................20.00
Fruit Bowl, 5-1/4" d....................14.00
Gravy, underplate 80.00
Platter, 12" l............................70.00
Relish, 11" l.............................58.00
Salad Bowl, 11" d, ftd...............150.00
Salt and Pepper Shakers, pr,
small....................................35.00
Sugar, lid................................50.00
Tumbler, 10 oz..........................48.00
Turkey Platter, 19" l..................325.00
Vegetable Bowl, divided..............40.00

Larkspur

Bread and Butter Plate 6.00
Bread Bowl...............................24.00
Dinner Plate..............................14.00
Saucer....................................5.00
Shaker...................................10.00

Magnolia, creamer and sugar 75.00
Mariposa

Salt and Pepper Shakers, pr 98.00
Teapot, cov............................200.00

Meadow Rose

Bowl, 6" d................................9.00
Butter Dish, cov.........................65.00
Cereal Bowl..............................20.00
Goblet..................................175.00
Luncheon Plate, 8" d...................14.00
Side Salad...............................45.00
Snack Plate............................170.00
Teapot.................................200.00

Mesa, gravy boat.......................110.00
Olympic, white violets, gold trim

Platter, medium 128.00
Platter, large 175.00
Sugar Bowl, cov.........................86.00
Vegetable, oval.........................88.00

Palomar, jasper, cov vegetable
bowl 190.00
Poppy

Cup and Saucer..........................32.00
Dinner Plate.............................37.50
Fruit Bowl................................30.00
Gravy, underplate 175.00
Platter, oval............................170.00
Salad Plate, 8" d........................35.00
Salt and Pepper Shakers, pr 60.00
Tumbler.................................148.00
Vegetable Bowl 130.00

Rosemore

Demitasse Cup and Saucer........45.00
Platter, round 110.00

Starburst. Introduced in 1954. Designed by George James, utilizing the eclipse shape.

Ashtray 60.00
Bon Bon Dish 45.00
Butter Dish, cov.........................45.00
Casserole, cov, large 265.00

Chop Plate...............................62.00
Cup and Saucer 25.00
Dinner Plate 18.00
Fruit Bowl 12.00
Jelly Dish 45.00
Nappy...................................35.00
Side Salad Plate, crescent
shape...................................27.50
Soup Bowl...............................20.00
TV Plate.................................75.00

Sundance

Creamer 22.00
Cup and Saucer 15.00
Dinner Plate 16.00
Platter, large............................42.00
Salad Plate 9.00
Soup Bowl 12.00
Sugar Bowl 27.00
Vegetable Bowl 35.00

Westwood, platter, round, light green
band 120.00
Wildflower, plate, 9-1/2" d.............80.00
Willow, chop plate, 14" d.............275.00
Woodside

Gravy Boat.............................140.00
Vegetable, oval.........................92.00

Fruit Jars

Collecting Hints: Old canning jars can be found at flea markets, household sales, and antiques shows. Interest in fruit jars is stable.

Some collectors base their collections on a specific geographical area, others on one manufacturer or one color. Another possible way to collect fruit jars is by patent date. More than 50 different types bear a patent date of 1858. It is important to remember that the patent date does not necessarily indicate the year in which the jar was made.

History: An innovative Philadelphia glassmaker, Thomas W. Dyott, began promoting his glass canning jars in 1829. John Landis Mason patented the screw-type canning jar on November 30, 1858. The progress of the American glass industry and manufacturing processes can be studied through the development of fruit jars. Early handmade jars record bits of local history.

Many devices were developed to close the jars securely. Closures can be as simple as cork or wax seal. Other closures include zinc lids, glass, wire bails, metal screw bands, and today's rubber-sealed metal lids. Lids of fruit jars can be a separate collectible, but most collectors want a complete fruit jar.

References: Douglas M. Leybourne, Jr., *Red Book No. 7*, published by author (P.O. Box 5417, N. Muskegon,

MI 49445), 1993; Dick Roller (comp.), *Indiana Glass Factories Notes*, Acorn Press, 1994; Bill Schroeder, *1000 Fruit Jars*, 5th ed., Collector Books, 1987, 1995 value update.

Periodical: *Fruit Jar Newsletter*, 364 Gregory Ave., West Orange, NJ 07052.

Collectors' Clubs: Ball Collectors Club, 22203 Doncaster, Riverview, MI 48192; Federation of Historical Bottle Collectors, Inc., 88 Sweetbriar Branch, Longwood, FL 32750; Midwest Antique Fruit Jar & Bottle Club, P.O. Box 38, Flat Rock, IN 47234.

Note: Fruit Jars listed below are machine made, unless otherwise noted.

Advance, Pat. App'd For, qt, aqua, ground lip 95.00
Atlas E-Z Seal, qt, dark blue, matching glass lid, wire bial 50.00
Atlas Strongshoulder, qt, light blue 35.00
Atlas Strongshoulder, qt, clear 30.00
Automatic, qt, aqua, #177 .... 225.00
Ball Ideal, pt, aqua, 5-1/2" h 25.00
Ball Perfect Mason, blue, #14 .... 12.00
Beaver, circular, qt, aqua, #424-1 .... 30.00
BBGM Co, qt, aqua, #197 .... 35.00
Brighton, circular, qt, aqua, #512 ..... 85.00
Columbia, qt, pale green, #641 .... 30.00
Crown, qt, apple green, #697 .... 20.00
Crystal Jar, Patd Dec 17, 1878, qt, clear, ground lip 70.00
Dandy, #751, half gallon, aqua 70.00
Everlasting, #952, qt, aqua 35.00
Flaccus, circular, qt, aqua, #1014 .... 75.00
Fruit Keeper, qt, aqua, #1042 .... 65.00
Globe, #1123, qt, aqua 25.00
Griffen's, qt, aqua, #1154 .... 225.00
Helmes, qt, amber, #1235 .... 35.00
High Grade, qt, aqua, ground lip, zinc lid 150.00
Imp, half gallon, aqua 150.00
Independent, qt, light purple, #1308 .... 50.00
Kerr, qt, aqua, #1371 .... 65.00
Mason, #1664-1, qt, aqua 25.00
Mason 1872, #1749, half gallon, aqua 50.00
Mason, square, clear 18.00
P/C, clear, 10" h, wire bail 55.00
Pet, qt, aqua, applied mouth 55.00
Presto Wide Mouth, Owens-Illinois Glass Co., clear, Pat. Re. 1756, metal ring with Good Housekeeping Institute Serial NO. 2285 .... 12.00
Safety, qt, amber, #2534 .... 175.00
Star, qt, aqua, ground lip, zinc insert and screw band 275.00
Sun, qt, aqua, #2761 .... 125.00

The Pearl, qt, aqua, ground lip, screw band 40.00
Whitall Tatum & Co., New York, Philadelphia, blown, clear, open pontil, 8-1/4" h 20.00
Wilcox, qt, aqua, #3000 .... 100.00

Furniture, Modernism Era

Collecting Hints: When buying American 20th century furniture, learn to recognize a particular designer's style. Blending several designers can lead to an interesting look and add texture and color to any decorating scheme.

This sampling of Modernism Era furniture has been taken from prices realized by several major American auction houses. This is an area of furniture collecting that is becoming of interest to collectors. As more examples enter the secondary marketplace, prices may fluctuate, depending on availability and condition.

History: The Modernism Era 20th Century furniture designers were heavily influenced by the International Movement and the events that were changing the attitudes of the world immediately after World War II. This period of furniture starts roughly in the 1940s and extends up to the 1960s when designers of the Pop culture are included. Another influence was the architectural style and type of homes and spaces for which they were designing. Sleek modern homes and office buildings demanded sleek furnishings. Designers were encouraged to incorporate different materials, such as steel, laminates, and chrome. Clean lines were desirable, easily maintained surfaces were demanded by a lifestyle that was changing.

References: Luke Beckerdite (ed.), *American Furniture 1998*, Chipstone Foundation, University Press of New England, 1998; Joseph T. Butler, *Field Guide to American Furniture*, Facts on File Publications, 1985; Anna Tobin D'Ambrosio, (ed.,) *Masterpieces of American Furniture from the Munson-Williams-Proctor Institute*, Syracuse University Press, 1999; Eileen and Richard Dubrow, *American Furniture of the 19th Century: 1840-1880*, 2nd ed., Schiffer Publishing, 2000; —, *Styles of American Furniture, 1860-1960*, Schiffer Publishing, 1997; Oscar P. Fitzgerald, *Four Centuries of American Furniture*, Wallace-Homestead, (Krause Publications,) 1995; Phillipe Garner, *Twentieth-Century Furniture*, Van Nostrand Reinhold, 1980; Cara Greenberg, *Op To Pop: Furniture of the 1960s*, Bulfinch Press, 1999; Myrna Kaye, *There's a Bed in the Piano: The Inside Story of the American Home*, Bullfinch Press, 1998; Leigh and Leslie Keno, *Hidden Treasures: Searching for the Masterpieces of American Furniture*, Warner Books, 2000; Paul McCobb, *Fifties Furniture*, Schiffer Publishing, 2000; Robert F. McGiffin, *Furniture Care and Conservation*, revised 3rd ed., American Association for State and Local History Press, 1992; *Herman Miller 1939 Catalog, Gilbert Rohde Modern Design*, Schiffer Publishing, 1998; John Morley, *The History of Furniture: Twenty-Five Centuries of Style and Design in the Western Tradition*, Bulfinch Press, 1999; Milo M. Naeve, *Identifying American Furniture*, W. W. Norton, 1998; Leslie Piña, *Dunbar: Fine Furniture of the 1950s*, Schiffer Publishing, 2000; —, *Fifties Furniture*, Schiffer Publishing, 1996; Steve and Linda Rouland, *Knoll Furniture, 1938-1960*, Schiffer Publishing, 1999; Steve and Roger W. Rouland, *Heywood-Wakefield Modern Furniture*, 1995, 2001 value update, Collector Books; Ellen T. Schroy, *Warman's American Furniture*, Krause Publications, 2000; Klaus-Jurgen Sembach, *Modern Furniture Designs, 1950-1980s*, Schiffer Publishing, 1997; Robert W. and Harriett Swedberg, *Furniture of the Depression Era*, Collector Books, 1987, 1999 value update; Treadway Gallery, Inc., *The 1950's/Modern Price Guide: Furniture, Volumes 1 and 2*, Treadway Gallery, Inc., 1999.

Bar, Paul Evans, wall mounted, disc, two semi-circular sculpted bronze doors finished with gold patina, unmarked, 71" d, 18" h 3,000.00

Bed

Dunbar, Berne, IN, single size, post war

Head and foot board comprised of bent wood in zig-zag pattern between slender crest rail and two wide cross rails, leather capped feet, light brown finish, metal tag, single size, 41-1/2" w, 37" h 300.00
Walnut, curved rect head and foot board joined by three horizontal

cross stretchers, medium brown finish, metal tag, 42" w, 38" h 200.00

Nakashima, George, c1957, walnut, headboard block, dovetailed, two sliding doors, flush tenons and dowels, orig finish, 74" l, 60" w, 46" h...7,550.00

Nelson, George, Thin Edge, manufactured by Herman Miller, birch frame, orig woven caned headrest, white enameled metal legs, 77" l, 38" w, 34" h 4,750.00

Plymodern Furniture, Plywood Corporation, Lawrence, MA, post World War II, suite of four pieces, double bed, large and small chest of drawers, night stand, curvilinear design, inset drawer pulls, color enhanced reddish brown finish, decal mark, minor wear 825.00

Robsjohn-Gibbings, T. H., manufactured by Widdicomb, headboard only, walnut veneer frame, rattan and brass wrapped edge, 80" w, 36" h 200.00

Rohde, Gilbert, manufactured by Herman Miller, suite, ash veneer, leatherette wrapped pulls, two twin beds, cabinet: 30" w, 18" d, 38" h, vanity: 50" w, 16" d, 27" h, pair night stands: 14" w, 12" d, 24" h, stool: 24" w, 18" d, 17" h 1,400.00

Bookcase, Ettore Sottsass for Memphis, Casablanca, multilevel, 1981, radiating shelves around two door cabinet, three drawers, drop-front compartment, polychrome laminate, metal Memphis tag, 91" x 62-1/2" x 14" 9,000.00

Cabinet, side

Eames, Charles, manufactured by Herman Miller

ESU 200, c1952, rectangular black laminated top with primary colored masonite pulls, zinc angle iron frame, three drawers, perforated metal panel, 47" w, 16" d, 33" h 11,000.00

ESU 400, c1954, primary colored masonite panels in chrome angle iron frame, two drawers, perforated metal panel, X-stretchers, replaced sliding dimple doors, some wear, 47" w, 17" d, 48" h 6,500.00

Knoll, Florence, manufactured by Knoll, credenza

Rectangular white marble top over four drawers, two doors, rosewood veneer, chrome base, roughness to drawers, 75" w, 18" d, 26" h 4,250.00

Walnut veneer, four sliding doors, black leather pulls, interior shelves and drawers, 72" w, 18" d, 28" h 1,325.00

Walnut veneer, two doors, four drawers, chrome metal base, 75" w, 18" d, 26" h 700.00

McCobb, Paul, manufactured by Calvin, from Erwin Collection, bleached mahogany, four drawers, brass base, orig label, refinished, price for pair, 36" w, 19" d, 34" h 1,450.00

Bed, George Nelson for Herman Miller, thin edge bed, caned headboard, 34" x 76" x 35", $1,500. Photo courtesy of David Rago Auctions.

Nelson, George, manufactured by Herman Miller

Birch veneer, four drawers, silverplate pulls, ebonized wood legs, 36" w, 19" d, 30" h 1,750.00

Birch veneer, five drawers, silverplate pulls, ebonized wood legs, 24" w, 19" d, 40" h 1,450.00

Coral lacquer, light walnut case, three drawers, one door, label, scratch to front, 56" w, 19" d, 30" h 1,600.00

Coral lacquer, light walnut case, four drawers, label, light wear, 24" w, 19" d, 30" h...................1,100.00

Orange lacquer, walnut case, three drawers, wooden pulls, label, minor wear to top, 24" w, 19" d, 30" h 1,320.00

Rosewood veneer, three doors, liftup top sections, white coated pulls, cast aluminum legs, interior shelves, 56" w, 20" d, 41" h 7,700.00

Thin Edge, three doors, rosewood veneer, white pulls, cast aluminum legs, label, top refinished, 34" w, 19" d, 31" h........................ 2,860.00

Thin Edge, three doors, four drawers, white pulls, cast aluminum legs, label, worn finish, 80" w, 19" d, 33" h 2,300.00

Thin Edge, four drawers, two drawers, white pulls, cast aluminum legs, worn finish, 67" w, 19" d, 33" h 2,400.00

Walnut veneer, four drawers, one door, orig forest green lacquer, silver-plate pulls, 34" w, 19" d, 30" h 2,100.00

Walnut veneer, two doors, orig forest green lacquer, silver-plate pulls, some wear to top, 34" w, 19" d, 30" h 1,980.00

Woodgrain laminate top, two black sliding doors, tubular legs, repairs to top, 60" w, 18" d, 26" h 950.00

Rhode, Gilbert, manufactured by Herman Miller, pickled veneer, two doors with cutout pulls, tubular metal legs, 36" w, 13" d, 29" h...................1,200.00

Robsjohn-Gibbings, T. H., manufactured by Widdicomb, walnut veneer, rattan wrapped handles, cast brass legs

Four drawers, refinished, 35" w, 21" d, 41" h 850.00

Six drawers, 68" w, 21" d, 32" h......................................750.00

Wegner, Hans, walnut veneer case, roll top front, wear, 28" w, 20" d, 27" h..50.00

Wormley, Edward, manufactured by Dunbar

Dark mahogany, three drawers, three sliding doors, woven fronts, nickel plated base, 62" w, 18" d, 38" h..3,000.00

Pair, seven drawers, curved wooden handles, white lacquer, brass feet, gold tag, 34" w, 21" d, 47" h.................................1,500.00

Cabinet, wall

Evans, Paul, custom design, welded steel door in sunburst motif, enamel and bronze finish, welded signature and date, 20-3/4" x 32-1/2" x 18" 3,000.00

Nakashima, George

Three spindled sliding doors with pandamus panels, free-edge top with extension to one side, 19" x 104" x 19"...........................7,000.00

Two piece, walnut, 1979, free-edge base, dovetailed cases, two matpaneled and spindled sliding doors on top, sliding doors with wooden panels on base, sold with copy of orig invoice, unmarked, 80" x 60" x 21".....................................6,500.00

Chair, arm

Bertoia, Harry, manufactured by Knoll, Diamond Chair, white plastic wire construction, green seat pads, price for pair, 33" w, 25" d, 31" h...250.00

Eames, Charles

Low Wire, manufactured by Herman Miller, black Naugahyde upholstered fiberglass shell, zinc struts, 26" w, 26" d, 24" h......600.00

Soft Pad chair, set of six, manufactured by Herman Miller, channeled red fabric upholstery, cast aluminum frame, tilt and swivel mecha-

nism, casters, wear to arms, 23" w, 23" d, 32" h.........................2,800.00
Frankl, Paul, manufactured by Directional, c1966, sculptural bronze exterior in abstract design, orig gray fabric, price for pair, 28" w, 29" d, 26" h 2,520.00
Nakashima, George, solid walnut, Windsor back, plank seat, price for pair, 25" w, 18" d, 27" h 1,000.00
Nelson, George, manufactured by Herman Miller
  Flexible back in gray fiberglass, rubber and stainless steel fittings, tubular swag leg base, label, 28" w, 20" w, 34" h 1,500.00
  Swagged Leg, molded charcoal fiberglass seat, adjustable back, metal bse, label, 28" w, 26" d, 33" h 2,200.00
  Thin Edge, upholstered in blue fabric, cast aluminum legs, price for pair, 36" w, 32" d, 30" h......2,650.00
Platner, Warren, manufactured by Knoll, 1966, bronze wire construction, orig orange fabric, label, 25" w, 22" d, 30" h 325.00
Rhodes, Gilbert, manufactured by Herman Miller, white leather upholstery, curved wooden legs, 25" w, 25" d, 34" h..750.00
Wormley, Edward, manufactured by Dunbar
  Riemerschmid, set of four, sculptural form, dark mahogany, reupholstered seats, refinished, unmarked, 24" w, 20" d, 31" h...................................2,700.00
  #5705, walnut frame, tufted beige silk upholstery, gold metal tag, minor wear to fabric, c1957, 33" x 27" x 27", price for pr.........1,200.00

Chair, dining

Bertoia, Harry, manufactured by Knoll, set of four, white plastic wire construction, blue seat pads, label, 21" w, 20" d, 30" h................................500.00
Cherner, Norman, manufactured by Plycraft, Lawrence, MA, c1960, set of four, armchair and three side chairs, molded walnut arms, wedge-shaped back, plywood seat, tapered legs, repair to one leg, wear, nicks, price for set of four, 24" w, 22" h, 31" h 920.00
Komal, Ray, manufactured by J. G. Furniture, 1949, Model #939, set of four, one piece molded plywood frame, nickel connector, tubular metal frame, 21" w, 19" d, 28" h........2,200.00
Rhode, Gilbert, manufactured by Herman Miller, set of eight, pickled bentwood frames, reupholstered in black wool, some wear, 18" w, 20" d, 30" h 265.00
Robsjohn-Gibbings, T. H., manufactured by Widdicomb, set of six, two arm and four side chairs, curved slat backs, orig orange upholstery curved legs, 23" w, 20" d, 35" h..........1,650.00
Saarinen, Eero, manufactured by Knoll, c1948, set of six, black fiberglass back, orig tan Naugahyde seat,

satin chrome base, 22" w, 21" d, 22" h...3,750.00
Wormley, Edward, manufactured by Dunbar
  Set of six, two arms and four side chairs, dark mahogany frames, orig Jack Larsen patterned fabric, big "D" label, some fading to fabric, 19" w, 20" d, 39" h....................1,750.00
  Set of six, two arms and four side chairs, dark mahogany frames, rattan backs, 22" w, 18" d, 33" h 1,650.00
  Set of eight, walnut frames, curved tapered legs, rattan backs, black and white vinyl cushions, refinished, 24" w, 21" d, 33" h..1,400.00

Chair, folding, Russel Wright, manufactured by Samson Co., 1940s, molded plywood seat, back, and arms, orig salmon lacquered metal frame, orig labels, set of four, 25" w, 26" d, 31" h..2,875.00

Chair, lounge

Aalto, Alvar, manufactured by ICF, bentwood birch frames, orig black canvas strapping, label, price for pair, 24" w, 27" d, 35" h...................1,850.00
Breuer, Marcel, manufactured by Isokon, c1937-38, chaise lounge, molded plywood seat within bentwood frame, purple fabric upholstered cushion, thru-tenon construction to seat, repairs, 55" w, 24" d, 28" h 5,500.00
Earnes, Charles, manufactured by Herman Miller
  Aluminum Group, channeled charcoal naugahyde upholstery, cast aluminum frame, wear to arm, chair: 26" w, 26" d, 37" h, matching ottoman, 21" w, 22" d, 18" h 550.00
  No. 650 chair and ottoman, black leather upholstery, molded rosewood plywood shells, cast aluminum base, orig label, chair: 33" w, 28" d, 33" h, ottoman: 26" w, 21" d, 16" h 3,500.00
  No. 670 chair and ottoman, molded rosewood plywood shells, tufted black leather upholstery, early down filing, label...............2,900.00
  Soft Pad, green fabric, cast aluminum frame, 24" w, 26" d, 35" h 250.00
Heywood Wakefield, bentwood maple frame, cushions reupholstered in vintage fabric, 30" w, 33" d, 30" h..300.00
Jacobsen, Arne, manufactured by Fritz Hansen
  Egg Chair, sculptural fiberglass shell, reupholstered in purple wool, cast aluminum base, matching ottoman, chair: 32" w, 24" d, 41" h, ottoman: 21" w, 15" d, 17" h 2,925.00
  Swan Chair, c1957, orig purple wool upholstery, cast aluminum base, 30" w, 28" d, 31" h ... 1,430.00
Jeanerette, Pierre, manufactured by Knoll, Scissors Chair, c1947, birch wood frame, chrome plated steel bolts, reupholstered in red fabric, 24" w, 28" d, 32" h......................750.00

Knoll, Florence, manufactured by Knoll, square form, tufted seat and back, orig light tan leather, bronze base, price for pair, 32" w, 32" d, 30" h..2,325.00
Laverne, Erwin and Estelle, manufactured by Laverne International, c1957, Invisible Group, molded Lucite form, circular cushion, 30" d, 23" h................................1,500.00
Mourgue, Olivier, Djinn Chair, manufactured by Airborne International, c1965, sculptural form, orig purple upholstery, price for pair, 28" w, 24" d, 27" h..2,320.00
Nelson, George, manufactured by Herman Miller
  Cantinary, orig channeled wool upholstery, chrome strut base, orig label, price for pair, 30" w, 28" d, 29" h.................................2,400.00
  Coconut Chair, triangular white enameled metal shell, orig blue Naugahyde upholstery, chrome strut frame, 40" w, 32" d, 32" h..............................10,450.00
  Coconut Chair, triangular white enameled metal shell, orig purple woven fabric, unmarked, 40" w, 33-1/2" h.................................3,500.00
  Coconut Chair, triangular white enameled metal shell, reupholstered in blue wool, welded chrome strut frame, some wear to chrome, 40" w, 35" d, 33" h..............2,900.00
Panton, Verner
  Heart Chair, manufactured by Plus-Linje, c1956, metal form, orig blue wool upholstery, chrome base, 40" w, 24" d, 36" h.................13,200.00
  Wire Cone Chair, manufactured by Plus-Linje, c1960, chromed wire construction, circular seat reupholstered in blue wool, 25" d, 30" h.................................1,750.00
Paulin, Pierre, manufactured by Artifort, c1965, Ribbon Chair, sculptural form, white lacquered wood base
  Original blue wool fabric, matching ottoman, orig label, chair: 36" w, 24" d, 28" h, ottoman: 29" w, 19" d, 16" h.................................2,800.00
  Original purple upholstery, 38" w, 24" d, 28" h 2,650.00
Platner, Warren, manufactured by Knoll, 1966, bronze wire construction, orig yellow woven wool fabric, label, chair: 41" w, 35" d, 39" h, matching ottoman: 24" d, 16" h 2,860.00
Risom, Jens, manufactured by Knoll, 1940s
  Brown canvas strapping to molded birch frame, reupholstered, 20" w, 26" d, 29" h 750.00
  Original tan leather strapping to birch frame, orig label, 21" w, 26" d, 29" h.................................1,550.00
Saarin, Eero, manufactured by Knoll
  Grasshopper, upholstered seat, molded birch frame, 26" w, 34" d, 36" h..770.00
  Womb Chair, sculptural fiberglass form, reupholstered in red wool, black metal frame, chair: 29" w, 32"

d, 36" h, matching ottoman: 25" w, 20" d, 15" h..........................2,200.00

Van Der Rohe, Mies, manufactured by Knoll, Barcelona Chair, stainless steel X-frame, tufted black leather seats, label, wear to leather, price for pair, 30" w, 30" d, 29" h.........................2,420.00

Wormley, Edward, manufactured by Dunbar

Chaise Lounge, Listen-To-Me, orig channeled blue-green fabric upholstery, walnut frame, brass and wire stretchers, gold metal tag, 72" w, 26" d, 26" h.....................13,200.00

Curved seat and back, reupholstered in orange velvet, tapered bleached mahogany legs, price for pair, 28" w, 26" d, 32" h......2,325.00

Dark mahogany frames, tilt back, caned sides, upholstered seats in patterned fabric, gold metal tag, price for pair, 26" w, 22" d, 27" h.......................................1,200.00

Rectangular back, reupholstered in blue fabric, bleached mahogany base, marked, 28" w, 28" d, 34" h.......................................200.00

Upholstered seat and back, dark walnut frame, reupholstered in ochre felt, 26" w, 28" d, 30" h.......................................650.00

Woodard, chaise, 1960s, extruded aluminum frame, tufted upholstered, 55" w, 24" d, 28" h, needs reupholstery.............................770.00

Chair, Mandarian, Ettore Sottsass, manufactured by Knoll, c1986, black enameled tubular metal frames, cream leather upholstery, set of six, 26" w, 22" d, 33" h.................................900.00

Chair, side

Cherner, Norman, manufactured by Plycraft, set of four, molded walnut plywood seat and back, bentwood legs, label, 17" w, 19" d, 32" h.............800.00

Eames, Charles, manufactured by Herman Miller

DCM, molded ash plywood back and seat, metal frame, 19" w, 19" d, 29" h.......................................120.00

DCM, molded walnut plywood back and seat, chrome frame, black plastic feet, set of four, 19" w, 18" d, 29" h..............................750.00

DCM, original red aniline dye, patterned upholstered seat and back, orig upholstery label, 19" w, 19" d, 29" h.......................................925.00

Eiffel Tower, c1951, black wire construction, early screw-on footpads, gray fabric bikini pads, set of four, some repairs.....................1,200.00

LCM, molded walnut plywood seat and back, chrome frame, price for pair, 22" w, 24" d, 27" h........750.00

LCW, molded ash plywood seat, back, and frame, 22" w, 23" d, 27" h.......................................1,400.00

LCW, molded birch plywood seat, back, and frame, 22" w, 22" d, 27" h.......................................850.00

Gehry, Frank, Easy Edges, c1972, corrugated cardboard construction, masonite edge, water stain, 16" w, 21" d, 32" h...............................850.00

McCobb, Paul, dowel ladder back, plank seat, wrought iron frame, price for pair, 18" w, 20" d, 34" h........600.00

Nelson, George, manufactured by Herman Miller, caned seat and back, wood frame, white metal base, set of four, c1956, 18" w, 19" d, 33" h.......................................1,700.00

Chair, Toga, Sergi Mazza, manufactured by Martemide, Milan, molded red fiberglass form, impressed marks, price for pair, 28" w, 25" d, 24" h......................................1,320.00

Chest of Drawers

Dunbar, Berne, IN, manufactured by mid-20th C, rectangular top, case with five graduated drawers, recessed handles, platform base, light finish, metal tag, scratches, wear, 28" l, 18" d, 31-1/4" h...............................865.00

Nakashima, George, c1957, walnut, block dovetail top, dowel construction, eight drawers, two walnut slab legs, orig finish, 72" w, 20" d, 32" h...................................6,000.00

Nelson, George, for Herman Miller

Thin Edge, oak, five graduated drawers, white wire pulls, black enameled metal hairpin legs, foil label, minor wear to finish at top, 40-1/2" x 40" x 19-1/2".......4,250.00

Thin Edge, rosewood veneer, eight drawers, conical porcelain knobs, tapering brushed chrome legs, from collection of a George Nelson associate designer, orig foil label, 30-1/2" x 46-1/2" x 18-1/2" 5,500.00

China Cabinet

Frankl, Paul, manufactured by Johnson Furniture Co., mahogany top with three glass shelves, above seven drawers and two doors, mahogany and lacquered cork, 72" w, 21" d, 74" h, some wear 1,000.00

Marx, Samuel, manufactured by Quigley, c1940, eight doors with parchment wrapped front, 62" w, 24" d, 87" h.......................................5,500.00

Parzinger, Tommi, manufactured by Charak, 1940s, contrasting light and dark mahogany, two doors, brass pulls, upper cabinet with lattice glass doors, 36" w, 17" d, 81" h..........950.00

Rhode, Gilbert, manufactured by Herman Miller

Checkerboard walnut veneers, two doors beneath sliding glass top, refinished, 36" w, 14" d, 50" h.......................................750.00

Pickled veneer, sliding glass doors above two doors with cutout pulls, tubular metal legs, 36" w, 13" d, 50" h.......................................775.00

Sottsass, Ettore, overhanging grained wood pediment over two door cabinet, two dark green glass paneled doors, two lower doors, cylindrical legs, entirely covered in mahogany laminate with typographic texture, 84-1/2" x 48-1/2" x 18".........................3,500.00

Daybed

Nelson, George, manufactured by Herman Miller, birch wood frame, dowel legs, orig seat and bolsters, some soiling to fabric, 75" w, 35" d, 25" h.....................................1,500.00

Stein, Richard, manufactured by Knoll, 1940s, biomorphic plywood back, seat, and legs, reupholstered in blue fabric, 76" w, 34" d, 27" h.......2,860.00

Desk

Baughman, Mylo, manufactured by Milo Baughman, 1950s, walnut veneer, two banks of drawers, floating top, dowel legs, wear, 60" w, 28" d, 31" h.................................1,980.00

Dunbar, Berne, IN, rectangular top, cream colored laminated writing surface, curved face front with center drawer flanked by shallow and deep drawers, tapered shaped legs, light finish, metal tag, wear, stains, scratches, 50" w, 21" d, 29-1/4" h...............................4,160.00

Frankl, Paul, manufactured by Johnson Furniture Co.

Cream lacquered cork, seven drawers with wood and brass handles, book shelf, 60" w, 26" d, 29" h.......................................2,400.00

Knee Hole, two-tone, brass pulls, tapered legs, 1940s, 36" w, 24" d, 30" h.......................................950.00

Maloof, Sam, oak, rectangular top over two drawers, dowel detail to top and sides, branded "Design/Made Maloof," 60" w, 25" d, 29" h 5,000.00

Nelson, George, manufactured by Herman Miller

Drop-Leaf, hinged rectangular top, three drawers, brushed chrome base, refinished, 40" w, 24" d, 30" h.......................................825.00

Original black lacquer, red leather writing surface and drawer fronts, lift-up compartment, perforated metal basket, 54" w, 28" d, 41" h.......................................6,500.00

Thin Edge, c1956, rosewood veneer front and sides, white laminate top and writing surface, black metal rolltop, white metal legs, label, 42" w, 25" d, 34" h....6,000.00

Walnut and tan leather writing surface and upper cabinet, satin chrome base, perforated metal file basket, some wear, 54" w, 28" d, 41" h.......................................4,400.00

Robsjohn-Gibbings, T. H., c1940, burled wood, fleur-de-lis inlay, two doors, interior drawers, refinished, 56" w, 22" d, 29" h........................3,850.00

Unknown Designer, 1950s, rectangular formica top above two drawers, ebonized V-base, 40" w, 24" d, 30" h.......................................100.00

Dresser, George Nakashima, cherry, 1968, free-edge top, dovetailed case, twelve drawers with recessed pulls, 30" x 84" x 22-3/4"................14,500.00

Jewelry Chest, George Nelson for Herman Miller, Thin Edge, walnut veneer case, four rosewood drawer fronts, ivory laminate door with conical pulls, orig pedestal and brass legs, Herman Miller label, 10-1/2" x 20-1/4" x 13" 12,000.00

Mirror, Paul Evans, Directional, wall mounted mirror and shelf, gold, copper, and pewter finish, slate top, 30" sq mirror, 70" shelf 650.00

Ottoman

Eames, Charles, manufactured by Herman Miller, black leather, rosewood plywood shell, 26" w, 21" d, 18" h 450.00

Nelson, George, manufactured by Herman Miller, Coconut chair

Original black wool upholstery, chrome metal base, re-foamed, 23" w, 18" d, 10" h 2,200.00

Original blue Naugahyde, chrome base, orig upholstery label, 24" w, 19" d, 16" h..........................5,225.00

Saarinen, Eero, manufactured by Knoll, Grasshopper, upholstered seat, molded birch legs, unmarked, 24" w, 17" d, 16" h..........................750.00

Sideboard/buffet

Evans, Paul, custom designed, wavy front, 1972, slat top, two welded steel doors with enameled and patinated textured ground, high relief biomorphic wave patterns with applied gold leaf, rect black wood base, sgd "Paul Evans," 38" x 76" x 21-1/2" 9,500.00

Unknown Designer, 1940s custom made, orig finish

Chinese red lacquer, two doors, brass trim, Lucite handle, 60" w, 21" d, 37" h..........................2,200.00

White lacquer, two doors, three drawers, brass, and Lucite hardware 1,875.00

Wormley, Edward, manufactured by Dunbar

Light mahogany, central compartment flanked by two doors with ebony and walnut fronts, hinged corner doors, plinth base, brass "D" pulls and keys, orig "D" tag, 80" w, 18" d, 31" h..............1,800.00

Light mahogany, three drawers with four woven front sliding doors, interior drawers and shelf, brass legs, some wear to finish, 82" w, 18" d, 36" h..........................1,800.00

Sofa

Frankl, Paul, manufactured by Directional, c1966, sculptural bronze exterior in abstract design, orig gray fabric, 60" w, 36" d, 24" h...........850.00

Heywood Wakefield, three seat bentwood maple frame, cushions reupholstered in vintage fabric, refinish, 73" w, 33" d, 30" h..........................650.00

Kagan, Vladimir, 1950s, biomorphic cushions, reupholstered in linen fabric, solid walnut base, 96" w, 44" d, 29" h 15,000.00

Nelson, George, Marshmallow

Custom made for the ConEdison Building, New York City, 1958, extended version in orig Alexander Girard multicolored Naugahyde

cushions, brushed steel and black metal frame, one cushion reupholstered, 104" w, 32" d, 29" h, one of two produced, sold by Treadway Gallery, Inc. Dec, 1998... 66,000.00

Manufactured by Herman Miller, 1957, circular cushions in orig Alexander Girard striped red, purple, black, green, and gray fabric, black enameled and brushed steel frame, accompanied by orig sales receipt, some wear, 52" w, 32" d, 30" h 15,400.00

Manufactured by Herman Miller, 1957, circular cushions in orig Alexander Girard, sample version, made to illustrate range of Alexander Girard fabrics available, eighteen cushions each in a different fabric, satin chrome and black enamel frame, 51" w, 32" d, 30" h 15,400.00

Harcourt, Geoffrey, manufactured by Artifort, c1973, Cleopatra, foam and metal frame, orig purple wool upholstery, casters, 74" w, 34" d, 26" d 3,500.00

Matta, manufactured by Knoll, c1968, Malitte seating system, five piece stackable upholstered foam cushions, black and orange, wear to fabric, 62" w, 25" d, 61" h..........................2,000.00

Nelson, George, manufactured by Herman Miller, Steel Frame, reupholstered seat and back, blue fabric, white laminate table, steel frame, 46" w, 30" d, 27" h......................375.00

Saarinen, Eero, manufactured by Knoll, c1948, Womb Settee, organically molded fiberglass shell, reupholstered in blue wool, chrome metal legs, 52" w, 34" d, 36" h..........2,500.00

Unknown Designer, 1940s custom made, rectilinear upholstered form, orig blue lacquered wood base, needs to be reupholstered, 91" w, 32" d, 26" h 900.00

Wormley, Edward, manufactured by Dunbar, V-form, reupholstered in light blue ultra-suede, walnut base, 108" w, 48" d, 32" h 1,750.00

Rocker

Eames, Charles, manufactured by Herman Miller, zinc struts, birch runners

Early gray Zenith shell, rope edge, orig label, some wear to runners, 25" w, 27" d, 26" h..........................1,500.00

Early yellow Zenith shell, rope edge, orig label, 25" w, 27" d, 26" h..1,300.00

Orange fiberglass arm shell, 25" w, 27" d, 27" h..........................1,100.00

White fiberglass arm shell, 25" w, 27" d, 26" h..........................1,100.00

Yellow upholstered fiberglass shell, presentation tag, 25" w, 27" d, 26" h..........................750.00

Gehry, Frank, Easy Edges, c1972, cutout form, corrugated cardboard, masonite edge, 41" w, 23" d, 25" h..........................4,000.00

Takeshi Nii, 1972, Ny X series, high back black canvas seat, wooden armrests, steel tube base, folds flat, 24" w, 28" d, 33" h..........................225.00

Stand, night

Nelson, George, manufactured by Herman Miller, birch veneer, three compartments, pull-out shelves, price for pair, 17" w, 14" d, 40" h...... 1,200.00

Unknown Designer, 1940s, two drawers, side cutouts, orig blue lacquer, silver plate and brass hardware, price for pair, 24" w, 21" d, 26" h.........800.00

Stool, seating

Castiglioni, Achille, manufactured by Zanotta, Mezzadro, metal tractor set, one in black, one in orange, cantilevered chrome and wood base, imp marks, price for pair, 20" w, 22" d, 20" h..........................850.00

Eames, Charles, manufactured by Herman Miller, Time-Life, turned walnut form, concave seat, 13" d, 15" h..........................1,450.00

Saarinen Eero, manufactured by Knoll, circular upholstered seats, white enameled base, orig label, 15" d, 16" h..........................850.00

Wormley, Edward, manufactured by Dunbar, matched set of three, tufted

Sofa and chair, Frank Lloyd Wright for Henderdon, Taliesen design, tufted beige wool design, some wear and pulls to fabric, chair: $475, sofa: $1,100. Photo courtesy of David Rago Auctions.

cushion, bleached mahogany X-base, needs to be reupholstered, 24" sq, 16" h 2,200.00

Table, chess, Isamu Noguchi, manufactured by Herman Miller, c1948, Model IN-61, ebonized plywood with inset plastic markers, fixed top on wooden dowels, two piece base, 22" w, 26" d, 19" h 37,500.00

Table, cocktail, Paul Evans, Directional, cube, copper, bronze, and pewter finish, 3/4" plate glass top, unmarked, 16" x 42" sq 600.00

Table, coffee
Aalto, Alvar, manufactured by ICF, plate glass top, bentwood birch frame, 27" sq, 18" h 100.00
Brown Saltman, 1960s, black and white laminate top, lift-up compartments, walnut frame, minor wear to wood, 41" sq, 16" h 500.00
Butler, Lew, manufactured by Knoll, c1950, black and white laminate top, walnut base, 38" w, 34" d, 16" h 375.00
Eames, Charles, manufactured by Herman Miller
    CTM, circular ash plywood top, four chrome legs with screw-in footpads, 34" d, 16" h 950.00
    Surfboard, elliptical form, black formica, wire strut base, 89" w, 29" d, 10" h 3,550.00
La Verne, Phillip, New York, c1962, "Creation of Man" design in bas-relief on rectangular top, two round fluted bronze legs, signed, some wear and corrosion, 65" l, 23-5/8" d, 17-1/2" h 2,760.00
McCobb, Paul, manufactured by Calvin, circular white glass top, brass base, 42" d, 15" h........................450.00
Mont, James, circular red lacquer top, silver-leaf edge, ebonized base, refinished, 48" d, 14" h........................50.00
Nakashima, George, custom design, 1988, tiger's eye maple burl top, walnut Minguren I base, unmarked, 15" x 59" x 34" 12,000.00
Nelson, George, manufactured by Herman Miller, round walnut veneer top, brushed steel frame, 41" d, 14" h 770.00
Noguchi, Isamu, manufactured by Herman Miller, triangular glass top with early pale green edge, ebonized wood base, 50" w, 36" d, 16" h 1,300.00
Platner, Warren, manufactured by Knoll International, c1966, steel rod hourglass shape, circular glass top, 16" d, 18" h................................550.00
Robsjohn-Gibbings, T. H., manufactured by Widdicomb, plate glass top with polished corners, light walnut and brass base, 45" sq, 12" h 2,100.00
Schultz, Richard, manufactured by Knoll, c1960, Petal, white lacquered segmented top, metal prong base, some wear to top, 42" d, 15" h 550.00
Unknown Designer, 1940s custom made
    Circular white marble top, orig blue lacquered wood base, 40" d, 15" h 100.00

Rectangular glass top, black lacquered base, 58" w, 36" d, 19" h 1,875.00
Unknown Designer, 1950s style, in the manner of Noguchi, triangular plate glass top, ebonized legs, 40" w, 29" d, 14" h... 100.00
Wegner, Hans
    Manufactured by Andr. Tuck, Denmark, rectangular top, chrome base, impressed mark, 47" w, 22" d, 15" h 300.00
    Manufactured by Carl Hansen, Denmark, triangular teak top, tapered teak dowel legs, label, 26" w, 26" d, 17" h 600.00
Wirkkala, Tapio, manufactured by Asko, rectangular top with inset laminate birch designs, tapered laminated dowel legs, marked, very minor wear to top, 39" w, 24" d, 16" h 2,800.00
Wormley, Edward, manufactured by Dunbar
    Black laminate top, light mahogany triangular frame, green tag, 34" sq, 17" h 500.00
    Flip-top, dark mahogany, white laminated shelf, two drawers, 40" w, 17" d, 26" h 850.00
    Glass top, circular, inch thick plate glass top, burlwood pedestal base, paper label, brass "D" tag, 17" x 42"... 650.00
    Long John, bentwood hairpin legs, grooved plank top, Dunbar paper label, 12" x 88-1/2" x 18-1/2" 800.00
    Rectangular dark mahogany top, perforated magazine holders on bentwood legs, green tag, 64" w, 23" d, 20" h 1,300.00
    Rosewood, bronzed sheathed ends, metal "D" tag, orig finish, 16" x 60" x 18"........................... 950.00
    Walnut, sectioned burlwood veneer top, shaped legs, brass capped feet, gold metal tag, 16" w, 58" x 30-1/2"..................................... 1,000.00
    Walnut, six-sided top inset with Tiffany Favrile glass tiles, four legged

base with cross-stretchers, metal Dunbar tag, 17" x 77-1/4" x 19"...............................7,000.00
Sheaf of Wheat, circular terrazzo top, light walnut base, gold metal tag, 38" d, 20" h................................700.00

Table, console
Frankl, Paul, manufactured by Johnson Furniture Co., cream lacquered cork, square cutouts, mahogany shelf with removable magazine tray, 71" w, 21" d, 28" h 3,300.00
Unknown Designer, 1940s, custom made
    Bleached oak, two tiers, tapered legs, brass trim, in the style of Robsjohn-Gibbings, two 57" w, 21" d, 28" h..................................2,200.00
    Lacquered, rectangular top, lattice trestle base, white lacquer, 57" w, 18" d, 36" h 1,875.00

Table, cube, Paul Evans, Directional, copper, bronze, and pewter finish, each with slate top, unmarked, 19" x 13" sq, price for pr....................800.00

Table, dining
Eames, Charles, manufactured by Herman Miller, rectangular walnut plywood top, folding chrome legs, refinished, 54" w, 34" d, 29" h..........950.00
Juhl, Finn, manufactured by Bovirke, 1953, rectangular top, two pop-up leaves, oval teak legs, 59" w, 35" d, 29" h 250.00
Knoll, Florence, manufactured by Knoll
    Elliptical plywood top, chrome pedestal base, 78" w, 49" d, 29" h 1,500.00
    Elliptical oak veneered top, chrome X-base, minor edge damage, 78" w, 48" d, 28" h 1,210.00
Nakashima, George
    Elliptical, cherry, two matched planks joined by four rosewood butterfly joints, trestle base, two 17" leaves for ends, excellent original finish, unmarked, from orig owner, c1950, 29" x 84" x 41-1/2" .7,500.00
    Grass Seat, walnut, unmarked, set of six, 26-3/4" x 23" x 19-1/2"...............................3,500.00

Coffee table, George Nakashima, tiger's eye maple burl top, walnut Minguaren I base, unmarked, 1988, 15" x 59" x 34, $12,000. Photo courtesy of David Rago Auctions.

Nelson, George, manufactured by Herman Miller, Swagged-Leg, circular laminate top with walnut edge, chrome and walnut frame, label, 48" d, 29" h 2,300.00

Noguchi, Isamu, manufactured by Knoll, white laminated top, chrome struts, black enamel base, 48" d, 29" h 2,400.00

Rhode, Gilbert, manufactured by Herman Miller, circular pickled veneer top, tubular metal legs, two leaves, minor wear, 48" d, 28" h 1,540.00

Robsjohn-Gibbings, T. H., manufactured by Widdicomb, radiating walnut veneer top, dowel legs, three leaves, label, 48" d, 29" h 2,310.00

Saarinen, Eero, manufactured by Knoll, circular white laminate top, white cast aluminum pedestal base, 36" d, 29" h 775.00

Woodard, 1960s, circular glass top, extruded aluminum base, 44" d, 29" h 550.00

Wormley, Edward, manufactured by Dunbar

Circular dark mahogany top, tapered legs, three leaves, 50" w, 29" h 1,900.00

Rectangular walnut top, curved sides, tapered slab legs, brass foot, three leaves, refinished, 72" w, 42" d, 29" h 3,750.00

Table, end

Frankl, Paul

Manufactured by Directional, c1966, sculptural bronze exterior, black laminated top, price for set of three, 16" h, 16" h 1,300.00

Manufactured by Johnson Furniture Co., two tiered design, cream lacquered cork top, dark mahogany Greek key frame, price for pair, 36" w, 33" d, 24" h 650.00

.Rhode, Gilbert, manufactured by Herman Miller, pair, two tiers, dark finish, tapered leatherette wrapped tapered legs, single drawer, 29" w, 16" d, 27" h 1,450.00

Table, occasional

Evans, Paul, 1970, circular glass top, sculpted base, sprayed metal exterior, sgd and dated, 42" d, 25" h 260.00

Knoll International, glass and chrome,

rectangular top raised on three tinted glass panels, chromed steel tripartite frame 635.00

Mathsson, Bruno, manufactured by Karl Mathsson, 1940s, rectangular birch top, molded birch legs, label, 29" w, 20"d, 21" h 850.00

Nelson, George, manufactured by Herman Miller, circular white laminate top, white pedestal base, orig label, some wear, 17" d, 22" h 250.00

Platner, Warren, manufactured by Knoll, bronzed finished rod construction, orig glass top, 16" d, 18" h 850.00

Robsjohn-Gibbings, T. H., manufactured by Widdicomb, 1955

Circular walnut veneered top, walnut dowel base, double cross stretchers, orig label, 30" d, 24" h 885.00

Square walnut veneered top, walnut dowel base, double cross stretchers, orig label, 30" sq, 22" h 950.00

Saarinen, Eero, manufactured by Knoll, white circular laminate top, white pedestal base, label, 20" d, 21" h..285.00

Table, side

Eames, Charles, manufactured by Herman Miller, ESU 100, black laminated top, zinc frame, primary blue masonite panel, 24" w, 16" d, 21" h... 2,210.00

Frankl, Paul, manufactured by Johnson Furniture Co., cream lacquered cork top above dark mahogany shelf on triangular legs, some wear, 30" w, 18" d, 21" h............ 350.00

Noguchi, Isamu, manufactured to Knoll, circular white laminate top, wire struts and birch wood base, label, 24" d, 20" h 4,400.00

Wormley, Edward, manufactured by Dunbar

Janus, sculptured dark mahogany frame, Tiffany glass tile top, brass feet, gold metal tag, crack to one tile, 15" sq, 23" h................. 2,900.00

Nesting, bleached mahogany, each with rect top and cloud-lift apron, paper label, orig hangtag, some roughness to orig finish, set of four................................. 1,100.00

Sheaf of Wheat, circular travertine top, ebonized base, metal "D" tags, 20" x 27"......................750.00

Table, suites with chairs

Frankl, Paul, manufactured by Johnson Furniture Co.

Dining Table and Chairs, seven piece set, rectangular cream colored cork top, Y-shaped wooden legs, six V-back armchairs, wear to table top, wear to chair wood frames, table: 96" w, 40" d, 29" h, chair: 25" w, 22" d, 32" h ... 2,750.00

Game Table and Chairs, five piece set, clover shaped cream lacquered cork top, tapered mahogany legs, four arm chairs with striped gold and black fabric, table: 36" sq, 28" h, chairs: 25" w, 24" d, 32" h 385.00

Mendini, Alessandro Mendini and Alessandro Guerriaro, manufactured by Studio Alchimia, 1984, Ollo table and four inset chairs, black and white geometric patterned laminate, orange top, 42" sq, 29" h 5,500.00

Nakashima, George, manufactured by Widdcomb, 1959, seven piece set, rectangular walnut veneer dining table, dovetailed detailed to sides, tapered oval legs, six chairs, two arm and four sides, solid walnut frames, hickory dowel backs and seats, orig label, two leaves for table, table: 72" w, 42" d, 29" h, chair: 25" w, 23" d, 36" h 4,950.00

Robsjohn-Gibbings, T. H., seven pieces, drop-leaf dining table, two arm and four side chairs, all light walnut, table: 40" w, 28" d, 29" h, chairs: 22" w, 20" d, 33" h................................. 775.00

Saarinen, Eliel, manufactured by Johnson Furniture, 1950s, five piece set, rectangular birch veneer top, molded birch legs, four side chairs with curved sets and backs, birch legs, table: 66" w, 40" d, 30" h, chairs: 19" w, 21" d, 33" h..................2,350.00

G

Gambling Collectibles

Collecting Hints: All the equipment used in the various banking games, such as Chuck-A-Luck, Faro, Hazard, Keno, and Roulette, are collected today. Cheating devices used by professional sharpers are highly sought.

Almost all the different types of casino "money" are collected. In the gaming industry, "checks" refers to chips with a stated value; "chips" do not have a stated value. Their value is determined at the time of play.

The methods used by coin collectors are also the best way to store chips, checks, and tokens.

A well-rounded gambling-collectibles display also includes old books, prints, postcards, photographs, and articles relating to the field.

History: History reveals that gambling in America always has been a popular pastime for the general public, as well as a sure way for sharpers to make a "quick buck."

Government agencies and other entities use lotteries to supplement taxes and raise funds for schools, libraries, and other civic projects. Many of the state and city lotteries of the late 18th and early 19th centuries proved to be dishonest, a fact which adds to the collecting appeal. Lottery tickets, broadsides, ads, and brochures are very ornate and make excellent displays when mounted and framed.

Most of the gambling paraphernalia was manufactured by gambling supply houses that were located throughout the country. They sold their equipment through catalogs. As the majority of the equipment offered was "gaffed," the catalogs never were meant to be viewed by the general public. These catalogs, which provide excellent information for collectors, are difficult to find.

References: Art Anderson, *Casinos and Their Ashtrays*, published by author (P.O. Box 1403, Flint, MI 48504), 1994; James Campiglia and Steve Wells, *The Official U. S. Casino Chip Price Guide*, Schiffer Publishing, 2000; Dale Seymour, *Antique Gam*

Good Luck Token, Horseshoe Gold Club, Sparks, NY, 1971, $2.50.

bling Chips, Revised Edition, Past Pleasures, 1998.

Collectors' Club: Casino Chips & Gaming Tokens Collector Club, 5410 Banbury Drive, Worthington, OH 43235.

Advertising Card, Roll-A-Top Bell Twin Jack Pot, Watling Mfg. Co., Chicago, 1941 ....45.00
Ashtray, 5" d, copper-coated metal, Fabulous Las Vegas, emb scenes, glass bottom with working tin red and black roulette wheel, c1950.................30.00
Book
   Blackjack, Winner's Handbook, Patterson 12.00
   Card Tricks, Magic, Gambling Guidebook, 1st ed., ...18.00
   Darwin Ortiz on Casino Gambling 3.50
   The Gambling Man, C. Cookson, 1975, 1st ed. 5.00
   Tricks with Cards, Complete Manual of Card Conjuring, Professor Hoffman, 250 pgs, hardcover, gold lettering, 1st ed., 1889 ....20.00
Bridge Set, Collegiate, 5-12" x 10" x 1" orig box, four score pads, four memotally pads, small pencils, two sets of eight diecut cardboard tallies, one with college boy in long coat, other with college girl in flapper-style outfit, Gibson Co., 1930s, complete, unused 10.00
Card Counter, plated, imitation ivory face, black lettering 20.00
Card Press, 9-1/2" x 4-1/2" x 3", dovetailed, holds 10 decks, handle 140.00
Catalog, H. C. Evans & Co., Secret Blue Book, Gambling Supply, 1936, 72 pgs...55.00
Chuck-A-Luck, red bakelite............75.00
Cigarette Lighter, lucite, dice..........24.00
Cuff Links, dice 17.50

Dice
Bakelite, golf sayings 32.00
   Weighted, black and white, always total 12, set of three..................40.00
Faro Cards, sq corners, Samuel Hart & Co., NY, complete 125.00
Faro Chip Rack, 18" l, 10" w, blue-green billiard cloth lining 80.00
Faro Layout, felt, walnut trim, George Mason & Co., Denver..............575.00
Gambling Sheet, 1935 World Series, unused......................................28.00
Game
   Bing, Beat Dealer's Shake, House Takes All Ties, potable dice game, 1890s, numbered felt board, leather bumper and cup with pair of dice, 23" w, 17-1/2" deep 300.00
   Rollem Dice Games, late 1950s, British Crown Colony Hong Kong, miniature dice roll on spinning table ... 2.00
Keno Cards, 136, wood, paper and material covering, H. C. Evans & Co., Chicago 250.00
Keno Hopper, walnut, blue-green billiard cloth lining bowl, plated metal mouth, acorn finial, three carved feet . 450.00
Label, New Deal, gambling, cards, apple crate size..........................6.50
Matchbook, Golden Nugget, gambling hall on cover.............................1.50
Photo, scene of gambling in old western saloon.......................................37.50
Poker Chip
   Horseshoe Club 14.50
   Mother of Pearl, set of four........24.00
Post Card, black and white, street scene of Palace Club, Reno, Nevada, postmarked 1942 ....17.50
Printer's Proof, 9" x 4-1/2", for playing card wrapper, 1880s 28.00
Roulette Card, 6" x 3-1/2", instructions on hot to play, rates, odds, pay-off at Harold's Club, Reno, 1946, red, black, and white on green ground 22.00
Roulette Chip Rack, walnut, holds 1,500 chips...120.00
Roulette Wheel, 8" d, wood and metal, single and double zero decals, fourprong spinner, cloth layout........45.00
Shot Glass, ribbed dec, porcelain dice in bottom 25.00
Tax Stamp, 4" x 6-1/4", U.S. Internal Revenue Special Stamp, issued to Ramona Club, Tonopah, Nevada, 1945, to operate coin operated amusement devices, some sun streaking discoloration..............16.00
Token
   French, 5 Franc 6.50
   Majestic Casino, $1.....................2.00
   Trump Casino, $1 ....2.25
Watch Fob, Golden Nugget Gambling Hall 12.00
Wheel of Fortune, 20" d, 30 numbers, hand decorated yellow and white, cut-out paneled center, red ground 150.00

Whist Set, Paine's Duplicate Whist 12-Tray Set, orig wooden box, black paper covering, orig cards, instructions, produced by Duplicate Whist Co., Kalamazoo, MI 60.00

Games

Collecting Hints: Make certain a game has all its parts. The box lid or instruction booklet usually contains a list of all pieces. Collectors tend to specialize by theme, e.g., Western, science fiction, Disney, etc. The price of most television games falls into the $10 to $25 range, offering the beginning collector a chance to acquire a large number of games without spending huge sums.

Don't stack game boxes more than five deep or mix sizes. Place a piece of acid-free paper between each game to prevent bleeding from inks and to minimize wear. Keep the games stored in a dry location; but remember, extremes of dryness or moisture are both undesirable.

History: A board game dating from 4000 b.c. was discovered in ruins in upper Egypt. Board games were used throughout recorded history but reached their greatest popularity during the Victorian era. Most board games combine skill (e.g., chess), luck and ability (e.g., cards), and pure chance (dice). By 1900 Milton Bradley, Parker Brothers, C. H. Joslin, and McLoughlin were the leading manufacturers.

Monopoly was invented in 1933 and first issued by Parker Brothers in 1935. Before the advent of television, the board game was a staple of evening entertainment. Many board games from the 1930s and 1940s focused on radio personalities, e.g., Fibber McGee or The Quiz Kids.

In the late 1940s, the game industry responded to the popularity of television, and TV board games were at their zenith from 1955 to 1968. Movies, e.g., James Bond features, also led to the creation of games but never to the extent of television programs.

References: Alex G. Malloy, *American Games, Comprehensive Collector's Guide*, Antique Trader Books, 2000; Rex Miller, *The Investor's Guide to Vintage Character Collectibles*, Krause Publications, 1999; Desi Scarpone, *More Board Games*, Schiffer Publishing, 2000.

Throwing the Bull, $20.

Periodicals: *Toy Shop*, 700 E. State St., Iola, WI 54990; *Toy Trader*, P.O. Box 1050, Dubuque, IA 52004.

Collectors' Clubs: American Game Collectors Association, P.O. Box 44, Dresher, PA 19025; American Play Money Society, 2044 Pine Lake Trail NW, Arab, AL 35016; Gamers Alliance, P.O. Box 197, East Meadow, NY 11554.

Board

Acquire, Avalon 25.00
Action Man, English 45.00
Addams Family Reunion, Pressman, 1991, sealed, MIB 20.00
Alien 25.00
Apple's Way, Milton Bradley, 1974..25.00
Are You Being Served, English.......30.00
Around the World in 80 Days, Transogram, copyright 1957, wear...10.00
Arrest and Trial, Chuck Connors.....35.00
Barney Miller, Parker Bros, 1977 ....24.00
Batman Returns, Parker Bros, 3-D, 1992, MISB....................................25.00
Beat the Clock, Lowell, 1954, 1st ed...65.00
Beat the Drum Game of Skill, Rosebud Art, copyright 1942, 5" x 11" x 1" orig box 40.00
Beetle Bailey 25.00
Ben Hur, C. Heston photo box, British 110.00
Blondie 25.00
Boots and Saddles, Gardner, 1958 ....48.00
Bozo the Clown Circus Game, Transogram 15.00
Branded, Milton Bradley, 1956.......65.00
Camelot Game, Parker Brothers, 1955, 12" x 17-1/2" x 2", light wear.......10.00
Candid Camera 30.00
Candy Land, Milton Bradley, 1949, 1st ed. 45.00
Captain Action, Milton Bradley, 1977 ....30.00

Captain Caveman, sealed 40.00
Captain Gallant Adventure Board Game, Transogram, 1950s 48.00
Captain Video, Milton Bradley, 1950..125.00
Carrier Strike, Milton Bradley, 1977...35.00
Casey Jones...................................30.00
Casper the Ghost...........................75.00
Charge Account, Lowell, 1961 ......12.00
Cheyenne, photo box, British 100.00
Chicago Great Blizzard, C. P. Marino, 1978..85.00
Chutes and Ladders, 1956, 1st ed..20.00
Circus Boy 70.00
Clash of the Titans........................50.00
Clue, Parker Bros., 1949, 1st ed..35.00
Contack, Parker Bros, 1939...........45.00
Dark Towers, Milton Bradley, 1981..150.00
Daytona 500, Milton Bradley, 1990, officially licensed by NASCAR.......35.00
Dick Tracy Crime Stopper, MIB....100.00
Doc Holiday....................................40.00
Doctor Dolittle, 3-D action game, Mattel, sealed......................................125.00
Donn Prairie Race 30.00
Dracula, figural 50.00
Dragnet, Transogram, 1955...........60.00
Dream House 25.00
Dynamite Shack, Milton Bradley, 1968..35.00
Easy Money, Milton Bradley.............7.50
Escape from New York...................40.00
Ewoks 25.00
Family Ties 20.00
Fantastic Voyage...........................25.00
Fess Parker's Trail Blazers Game .. 60.00
Finance, Parker Brothers 45.00
Flintstone Kids, 1967.....................25.00
Fox Hunt, E. S. Lowe Co., 1940s... 20.00
Frankenstein, Jr. 50.00
Fugitive, Ideal, 1964....................280.00
Funky Phantom...............................25.00
Gas Crisis, 1979, factory seal, MIB..12.00
General Hospital, Cardinal, 1982 .. 18.00
Gentle Ben, Mattel, 1968 ....250.00
Get Smart, time bomb, Ideal, 1965...75.00
G-Men, Melvin Purvis, Parker Bros, 1930s......................................200.00
Gilligan's Island 225.00
Goodbye Mr. Chips 35.00
Gray Ghost 95.00
Green Hornet, Milton Bradley, 1966..90.00
Happy Days, Parker Brothers, 1976, sealed......................................45.00
Hardy Boys, 1959...........................35.00

Have Gun Will Travel......................70.00
Howdy Doody, TV show, 1950s....125.00
Huckleberry Hound Bumps, Transogram, 1961...........................50.00
I'm Garry Moore...and I've Got a Secret, Lowell Toy Co., 1956................38.00
I Spy...50.00
It's About Time 200.00
Jackie Gleason, Away We Go, 1956...165.00
King Oil, Milton Bradley, 1974 ....45.00
Knight Rider 25.00
Kooky Chicks Magnetic Game, Milton Bradley, 1964, 11" x 14" x 1" orig box, wear 12.00
Land of the Lost, 1975....................40.00
Lassie, Whiting, 1955 ....25.00
Leave It To Beaver Ambush Game, Hasbro, 1969...................................120.00
Let's Face It, Hassenfield Bros., four plastic Mr. Potato Heads, 15" sq box, 1950s 140.00
Lincoln's Log Cabin Games, W. H. Davidheiser, 1924, 11" x 11" x 1/2" deep colorful tin litho board with illus of young boy reading by fireplace, different bird in each corner, 11-1/2" x 11-1/2" black, white, and red box top 40.00
Little House on the Prairie...............25.00
Little Lulu.....................................180.00
Looney Tunes, 1968.......................45.00
Lost In Space................................135.00
Lucky Town the Build-A-Happy Home Game, Milton Bradley, 1946, wooden playing pcs, 2" x 19" x 1-1/2" box, light wear 24.00
Mad's Spy vs Spy, Milton Bradley, #4600, 1986, slight wear.........................12.00
M*A*S*H, Milton Bradley, 1981.......20.00
Matchbox Traffic Game, 1967 ....50.00
Meet the Presidents Quiz Game, Selchow & Righter, 1950, 10" x 15" x 1-1/4" box, some damage to box 15.00
Midway, Avalon Hill Co., Baltimore, 1965, play wear....................................20.00
Mighty Comics, Super Heroes, Transogram, 1966...........................60.00
Mighty Mouse Rescue, 1950s........45.00
Mod Squad 165.00
Monopoly, Parker Bros., modern......5.00
Mostly Ghostly 30.00
Mr. Ree, Selchow & Righter Co., 1937, 9-3/4" x 19" x 2" blue and yellow box, complete, general scattered wear 30.00
Mr. T, A-Team, Milton Bradley, 1983 ....35.00
My Fair Lady, Standard Toykraft, late 1950s, missing one playing piece 12.00
Mystery Date.................................125.00
Name That Tune, Milton Bradley, 1959 ....20.00

Nancy Drew Mystery Game, Parker Bros., 1959.............................100.00
New Avengers...............................60.00
No Time for Sergeants 25.00
Nurses, Ideal, 1963.......................25.00
Perry Mason, Transogram, 1959 ....45.00
Pinky Lee, Who Am I, 1950s...........60.00
Pit, Parker Bros. 7.50
Pivot Game of Action, Milton Bradley, 1958, 9-1/2" x 14" x 1-1/4" box...10.00
Prisoner of Zenda, Milton Bradley, 1930s..25.00
Quick Draw McGraw Private Eye Game, Milton Bradley, 1960 ....45.00
Raggedy Ann, 1954.......................25.00
Raiders of the Lost Ark, Kenner, 1981 ....48.00
Return A Putt, Bing Crosby, 1950s, MIB...50.00
Road Runner, © Warner Bros., Milton Bradley, 1968 ....70.00
Ruff and Ready, Transogram, 1962 ....35.00
Sea Hunt, Lowell, 1961..................35.00
Sgt Preston, Milton Bradley, 1956...32.00
Shotgun Slade...............................40.00
Sigmund and the Sea Monsters, sealed...40.00
Silly Sidney, Transogram, 1963.......55.00
Six Million Dollar Man, Bionic Crisis, Parker Bros, 1976 ....24.00
Snagglepuss..................................35.00
Social Headaches, Otto Ulbrich, 1930s, four unused question tablets, answer sheet, 6" x 9" x 1/2" h box. MIB ..10.00
Space Angel, Transogram, © 1965 75.00
Spot A Car Bingo 10.00
Spoutsie Hot Potato, Ohio Art, MIB...25.00
Star Trek, Ideal 60.00
Stock Market Deluxe, Whitman, 1963 ....30.00
Sub Search, Milton Bradley, 1973 ..35.00
Superboy, Hasbro, 1950s...............50.00
Surfside Six, Lowell, 1959...............65.00
S.W.A.T. 20.00
Swayze, Milton Bradley, 1954, play wear..40.00
Swoop Space Game, 1969..............30.00
Tank Command, Ideal.....................48.00
Terry Toons, Ideal..........................45.00
The Children's Hour, Parker Bros, 1958, play wear..5.00
The Godfather Game, Family Games, Inc., 1971, 10" x 20" x 1", wear...10.00
The Rebel, Ideal, 1961....................66.00
Three Stooges, Lowell, 1959 ....230.00
Thunderbirds, Parker Bros., 1968 ..55.00
Tic Tac Dough, Transogram, 1957, 1st ed. 25.00
Titanic, Ideal..................................45.00
Tom Hamilton's Pigskin Football Game, Parker Bros., 1946 ....175.00

Treasure Hunt, Milton Bradley..........7.50
Twenty One TV Quiz Game, Lowell Toy Mfg. 50.00
Twiggy 40.00
Twilight Zone 195.00
Uncle Wiggily, 1930s......................45.00
Untouchables, Transogram............55.00
Virginian, Transogram, 1962.........40.00
Watergate Scandal, American Symbolic, 1973...........................18.00
Wolfman, 1960s.............................195.00
Woody Woodpecker 25.00
You're Out, Corey Game Co., 1941...40.00
Zorro, Whitman, 1958.....................30.00

Card

Bewitched 195.00
Carol Burnette 25.00
Dallas..20.00
Dick Tracy......................................45.00
Doctor Dolittle, Whitman 40.00
Dukes of Hazzard..........................15.00
E. T. 25.00
F-Troop 70.00
Howdy Doody..................................48.00
I-Spy 75.00
Llya Kurykakin 35.00
Mork & Mindy 18.00
Munsters..50.00
Panic the Great Wall Street Game, Panic Card Co., copyright 1903, 2-3/4" x 3-1/2" x 1 h" box, slight wear.....18.00
Shazam 15.00
Twelve O'Clock High 40.00

Gardening

Collecting Hints: A collecting category has truly arrived when antique shows of the same name are happening events. The Antique Garden Show in New York is just the place to find vintage garden accessories of all types and price ranges.

History: Gardeners have long enjoyed the beauty of flowers and landscaping. Today, whole outdoor rooms and spaces are being created just as gardeners did decades ago, and antique collectors are fortunate to have a wide range of antiques and collectibles to chose from when creating their unique spaces. Many gardeners also include heirloom plants along with the vintage antiques and find they are perfect companions.

Other collectors are content to decorate with a garden theme, incorporating prints, small garden accessories, such as decorative flower pots and watering cans, into their room-scapes.

References: Barbara Israel, *Antique Garden Ornaments: Two Centuries of American Taste*, Harry N. Abrams, 1999; Alistair Morris, *Antiques from the Garden, Antique Collectors' Club*, 1999; Myra Yellin and Eric B. Outwater, *Garden Ornaments and Antiques*, Schiffer Publishing, 2000.

Bench, wood, mortise and tenon joints through top, weathered green paint, 72" l 90.00

Bird Bath
    19" d, 45" h, cast stone, form of Atlas supporting stylized flower formed basin on his back, socle base 1,760.00
    20-1/2" d, 33" h, cast stone, lotus shape base, circular leaf molded standard, octagonal base 460.00

Book
    An English Country Lady's Book of Dried Flowers, Amanda Docker, Doubleday, 1990 ....12.00
    Crockett's Tool Shed, Gardening Equipment, James Crockett, Little Brown, Boston, photos by Lou Jones, 1989 ....7.00
    Daylilies and How to Grow Them, Ben Arthur Davis, Tupper & Love, 1954, 1st ed, some wear to dj 8.00
    Flower Arrangements to Copy, Tat Shinno, Doubleday, 1966, 246 pgs, author illus, soiled dj 12.00
    How To Tell the Birds From the Flowers and Other Woodcuts, A Revised Manual of Fornithology for Beginners, Robt Williams, Wood, Dood Mead, 1917, 27th ed. 8.00
    No-Work Garden Book, Ruth Stout and Richard Clemence, Rodale Press, 1972, 3rd printing, dj 9.00
    Soiless Growth of Plants-Use of Nutrient Solutions, Water, Sand, Cinder, Etc., Carlton Ellis & Miller W. Swaney, 1938, Reinhold Publishing Co., 155 pgs...7.00
    Successful Gardening with Perennials, Helen Van Pelt Wilson, Doubleday, 1976, 1st edition, worn dj... 12.00
    Taylor's Guide to Gardening, Techniques, Planning, Planting & Caring For Your Garden, Houghton Mifflin Co., 1991, 1st ed. 7.00
    Terrific Tomatoes, How to Grow and Enjoy Them, Catherine O. Foster, Rodale Press, 1975, 1st printing, dj 8.00
    The Complete Book of Dried Arrangements, Raye Miller Underwood, Bonanza Books, 1952, dj.............8.00
    What Kinda Cactus Izzat? Reginald Manning, black and white illus, A Who's Who of Strange Plants of SW America, J. J. Augustin Publ, 1949 ....15.00

Brooch, 1-3/8" h, watering can, goldtone watering can, flowers, faux pearls on handle 22.00

Jardiniere, green, emblem leaf design, 5" d, 4" h, Morton Pottery Works, $45. Photo courtesy of Doris & Burdell Hall.

Child's Watering Can, Mistress Mary, Cohn Toys, Brooklyn, NY, 8" w, 6-1/2" h, wear 115.00

Creche, 16" w, 32" h, weathered wood and slate...............................275.00

Fernery, 32" w, 13" d, 37" h, tôle peinte, molded rect planter inset in arched wirework frame, raised on elaborate cabriole-shaped legs ending in scrolled toes, painted pale yellow with blue accents, French Provincial, fourth quarter 19th C................775.00

Folding Chair, orig green and white cotton striped seat and back, some wear...95.00

Fountain
    23-1/2" d, 45" h, cast iron, putto struggling with large fish, lattice edged basin with reeded body, floral pedestal ending with three applied swans, concave triangular base 750.00
    26" d, 46-3/4" h, cast iron, attributed to J. W. Fiske, NY, 19th C, basin with cast leaf exterior, cranes and cat o'nine tails base, molded circular platform, old white paint, weathered 2,875.00

Fountain Figure
    17" l, 9" h, bronze, alert frog.....360.00
    23-1/2" d, 48-1/2" h, patinated bronze, putto kneeling with one leg on acanthus-like form, holding hand on grapevine, other supporting shell form basin atop his head, circular base molded with clusters of grapes spilling out of barrel 1,320.00
    32" w, 42" h, patinated bronze, kneeling boy playing with frog, naturalistically molded base, applied lotus leaves 1,210.00
    35" h, bronze, naked boy holding goose, socle surrounded by four goslings with open beaks as fonts, greenish gold patina, 20th C....................................6,325.00

Garden Armillary Sphere, Victorian, third quarter 19th C, 38" w, 64" h, later patinated bronze sphere raised on heavily molded cast iron base, fruit, floral and paw designs, plinth base...3,520.00

Garden Bench
    49" l, 14" d, 27" h, cast iron, polychromed, out-scrolling slatted back, conforming seat, rope-twist arms, molded klismos base, price for pr 750.00
    49" l, 41-1/2" d, 29" h, cast iron, slatted construction, naturalistically formed arms, interlocking snake and grapevine legs, leaf shaped feet, price for pr...........................1,650.00
    61-1/2" l, 20" d, 32" h, cast iron, out-scrolling slatted back, conforming seat, scrolled arms, interlocking acanthus legs, plinth feet, price for pr 275.00
    63" l, 22" d, marble, rect seat, backrest carved with Neoclassical scene, satyr and corbel carved supports, Continental 10,925.00

Garden Chair, cast iron, painted and gilded, backrest with drapery and masks above two warriors, openwork frieze, cabriole legs, two painted black, four painted red, gilt highlights, price for assembled set of six 4,350.00

Garden Gate, 42-1/2" w, 70-1/2" h, cast iron, domed form, centered scrolling design, price for four pc set. 3,500.00

Garden Seat, 32-1/2" h, painted arrowback, curving crest above arrowback spindles, shaped arm supports, plank seat, sq splayed legs with stretchers, orig green paint, 19th C, repairs 1,725.00

Garden Suite, cast iron, two 38" h arm chairs, 49" l, 14-1/2" d, 38" h bench, each with arched back, centered armorial within a rosette, surrounded by interlacing branches, topped by trefoils, slatted seat, down-swept scrolling arms and legs, Victorian, price for three-pc set............ 1,760.00

Garden Urn, cast iron
    16" d, 29" h, egg and dart molded lip above neck dec with spray of flowers and wheat over fluted body, circular molded standard, applied scrolling handles, price for pair 750.00
    16" d, 31" h, campana form, egg and dart molded lip, partially reeded body on circular pedestal, pyramidal molded base, price for pr 425.00
    16-1/2" d, 25-1/2" h, campana form, egg and dart molded lip, basketweave molded body, conforming circular base standard, socle, price for pr 825.00
    21-1/2" d, 24" h, campana form, egg and dart molded lip, body dec with scrolling arabesques, circular reeded standard, socle base, applied lion head centered handles, price for pr 500.00
    25" d, 45" h, campana form, everted molded lip, body dec with pr of winged mythical creatures, each centering mosaic with high relief, fluted circular standard, socle base, applied scrolling snake intertwined handles, price for pr............. 1,200.00

25" w, 12" d, 12-1/2" h, rect, rococo manner, serpentine lip above garland and floral motifs dec body, splayed scroll feet, price for pr...350.00

31-1/2" h, three piece construction, scrolled borders with flowers beneath, swallows on wells, scrolled cast detail around base, old worn white repaint, one with welded repair, price for pr 550.00

Garden Urn, cast stone, 18" d, 27" h, everted lip above a partially reeded bulbous body, circular standard, socle base, Italian....................650.00

Garden Urn, terra cotta, 27" d, 52" h, campana form, crested molded lip above body with two Bacchic masks among grapevines, lower fluted part with two rams heads, raised on reeded circular standard, socle base, price for pr 1,100.00

Gate, 29" w, 41" h, cast iron, vine cresting manner "Edward R. Dolan" above willow tree with doves in branches, flanking lambs and flowers below on grassy mound, old black, green, and white paint, America, c1860.1,380.00

Glider, metal, repainted turquoise, working condition 500.00

Hand Tool, normal wear, average price 5.00

Hoe, wooden handle, well used.......7.50

Patio Chair, metal, repainted white, c1950, some wear 125.00

Pendant, celluloid, Agriculture Fair, Pope County, Greenwood, Minn, 1899, diecut, multicolored horse heads, white ground, black lettering, inserted at top by red, white, and blue striped fabric bow, reverse has celluloid insert 25.00

Pinback Button, Nebraska Seed Co., multicolored, "Seeds that Grow" 200.00

Print, Garden of Allah, Maxfield Parrish, House of Art edition, 1918.......500.00

Rack, metal, well used....................10.00

Shears, long wooden handle, wear 25.00

Shovel, wooden handle, well used...8.00

Tumbler, 3-1/4" d, 3-1/2" h, glass, maroon-red image of Miss Dairylea scurrying while holding pail and spade, 1950s............................15.00

Watering Can
Brass, 9-1/2" l, 4-3/8" h, few small dents 8.00
Metal, 12" h, painted black, orig sprinkler attachment 25.00
Porcelain, 8-1/2" h, painted flowers..17.50
Tin, 9" h, sprinkler attachment missing..25.00
Toleware, 9-3/4" d base, 16" h, some rust and surface abrasion........115.00

Wheelbarrow, wooden, removable sides, wear 150.00

Gasoline Collectibles

Collecting Hints: There still is plenty of material stored in old garages; try to find cooperative owners. If your budget is modest, concentrate on paper ephemera, such as maps. Regional items will bring slightly more in their area of origin.

History: The selling of gasoline has come full circle. The general store, livery stable, and blacksmith were the first to sell gasoline. Gas stations, so prevalent from the 1930s to the 1960s, have almost disappeared, partially due to the 1973 gas crises. The loss of independently owned stations is doubly felt because they also were centers for automobile repair. Today, gas sales at mini-markets are common.

The abolition of credit cards by ARCO marked another shift, as did price reduction for cash sales by other brands. The growing numbers of "pay-at-the-pump" stations will also influence the marketplace. Elimination of free maps, promotional trinkets, and other advertising material already is a factor. As more and more stores in shopping centers sell oil, parts, and other related automobile products, it is doubtful if the gasoline station will ever recover its past position.

References: Mark Anderton, *Encyclopedia of Petroliana, Identification and Price Guide,* Krause Publications, 1999; Scott Benjamin and Wayne Henderson, *Gas Pump Globes,* Motorbooks International (P.O. Box 1, Osceola, WI 54020), 1993; Jim and Nancy Schaut, *American Automobilia,* Wallace-Homestead, 1994.

Periodicals: *Hemmings Motor News,* Box 100, Bennington, VT 05201; *Mobilia,* P.O. Box 575, Middlebury, VT 05753; *Petroleum Collectibles Monthly,* 411 Forest St., La Grange, OH 44050.

Collectors' Clubs: American Petroleum Collectors/Iowa Gas, 6555 Colby Ave., Des Moines, IA 50311; International Petroliana Collectors Association, P.O. Box 937, Powell, OH 43065-0937; Spark Plug Collectors of America, 14018 NE. 85th St., Elk River, MN 55330; World Oil Can Collector's Organization, 20 Worley Rd, Marshall, NC 28753.

Reproduction Alert: Small advertising signs and pump globes have been extensively reproduced.

Bank, Wolf's Head, gold and white paper label, tin top and base, 2" d, 4" h, $18.

Banner
8" l, Texaco Havoline, plastic 65.00
36-1/2" h, 60" h, Sunoco Winter Oil and Grease, heavy cloth, Mickey Mouse illus, © Walt Disney 1939.. 650.00

Blotter, Nu-Blue Sunoco Gas, Donald Duck, M. C. Sparks & Son, Ronton, OH, 1948, 4" x 7", slight use...... 24.00

Car Attachment, Shell Oil, 3-3/4" x 5-1/2" metal domed image of Shell symbol, three colorful International Code Flags, late 1930s..................... 190.00

Charm, Mobil Oil Co., Pegasus, red, plastic, 1-1/2" l, 1" h................... 15.00

Child's Hat, Texaco Fire Chief, bull horn speaker system, battery operated.................................. 135.00

Coaster/Ashtray, Mobil Safe Driving Award, 1953, metal, shield logo, 4" dia.. 25.00

Coffee Cup, milk glass
Cities Service, Burl S. Watson... 38.00
Sinclair Oil, Sinclair Dinosaur on each side.. 15.00
Stark Oil, Phillips 66, logo on both sides of cup............................... 12.00

Coloring Book, Esso Happy Motoring, unused...................................... 25.00

Dashboard Memo, Harry's Auto Service, Auto Repairing of All Kinds, Bernard, OH, use to record dates, car servicing info 55.00

Decal Sheet, Esso, 3-1/2" x 3-1/2", white, red letters, beige ground, Palm Brothers, Decalomania Co., NY, c1950.. 3.00

Doll, Texaco Cheerleader, 11-1/2" h, 1960s, MIB 125.00

Employee Badge, Goodyear - Akron, initials, wingfoot logo, silver with blue enamel, 1" x 1/2" 20.00

Fan, 10-1/2" l, 7-5/8" w, Sinclair Opaline Motor Oil, adv on back 75.00

Gas Pump, electric, orig hose, nozzle missing, 16" w, 10" d, 36" h......325.00

Good Luck Penny, 1953, Souvenir of Amoco Dealer Convention, 1953 penny 6.50

Key Chain, flicker
Amoco, As You Travel Ask Us, back side has place for name and address with please return to 12.00
Chevron Supreme, Love That Chevron Supreme, man running towards gas pump, kissing it and throwing his arms around pump, back reads Chevron Supreme Gasoline Now At Calso Stations, Vari-Vue, USA ...24.00

Key Ring
Gulf, Second Triangle Gulf Service Station, Miami, FL, round, orig plastic bag, 1960s...................................5.00
Phillips 66 Philgas, plastic with metal holder 8.00

Kit, Amoco Word Building Contest, 4-1/4" x 8-3/4", black and white envelope, instruction and blank folder, perforated card spelling "American Oil Company," contest dated Jan. 31, 1934, unused 20.00

Lighter, flat style, Atlantic logo one side, Imperial shield reverse, made by Penguin......................................15.00

License Plate Attachment, Sunoco, 1940 ....100.00

Measuring Can, Be-Sure Gasoline, side pouring spout..............................12.00

Measuring Stick, Southern, used to measure in tank, numbered on four sides, 55" l 25.00

Mechanical Pencil, Walter's Service Station, Mobil pegasus logo on top of cream color pencil.....................15.00

Neon Sign, 48-1/2" l, 23" h, Chevrolet Corvette Approved Service ..1,000.00

Oil Can
D-A Speed Sport Oil, yellow full quart with old cars, checkered flags logo, "Racing Division, D-A Lubricant, Indianapolis, Indiana," C9+ 50.00
Farmers Pride Household Oil, Hulman Co., lead spout, 5-3/4" x 2-1/8" x 1-1/4" ova base 365.00

Paper Cup, Gulf Oil, We Enjoy Serving You - Drop In Again.......................4.00

Patch, cloth, Esso, 6" l, 4" w............24.00

Pencil, lead, unused
Gulf Oil 5.00
Marathon Gasoline - Lubricants, Best in the Long Run, Compliments of Your Marathon Dealer 5.00

Globe, Sinclair Gasoline, dinosaur logo, $150.

Pin
Phillips 66, 10-yr pin, 10K gold, screwback, maker's mark..........45.00
Pure Safe Driver Pin, two years, Be Sure with Pure, screw back 35.00
Shell, red cloisonné, gold Shell emblem, marked "NBG, #78, Tuckey S.F." 1920s 95.00
Sun Oil Company Service Pin, 15 years, 14K gold..........................75.00

Pinback Button
Amoco, celluloid, 1" d 15.00
Firestone, celluloid, Ship by Truck, 1920s......................................25.00
Mobil Oil, 1932 ....35.00

Pocket Calendar, 1957, "Esso, You get Something MORE at Your Happy Motoring Store" 5.00

Postcard, Firestone Tire & Rubber Company, 1933, R.R. Donnelly & Sons, Chicago, The Firestone Singing Color Fountain and Multiplane Shadow Sign, A Century of Progress 12.00

Pump Sign, Texaco Sky Chief, 12" x 18", porcelain, dated 3/11/62..........195.00

Puzzle, Sohio Ethyl Gasoline, Mickey Mouse, plastic, 1950s, adv on back 72.00

Salt and Pepper Shakers, pr, Texaco, figural gas pumps, some crazing to decals...50.00

Score Book, Amoco Gin Rummy Score and Bridge Score, 42 sheets, adv, unused 20.00

Shirt, Texaco................................45.00

Sign
Esso Elephant Kerosene, porcelain 875.00
Fisk Tires, porcelain, 1930s...425.00
Good Gulf Gasoline, porcelain, flange 550.00
Goodyear Service Station, Goodyear means Goodwear, porcelain, 1920s......................................895.00
Sinclair Gas, porcelain.............100.00

Tape Measure, Shell Oil, A. C. McLoon & Co., metal 24.00

Thermometer
Shell Anti-Freeze 85.00

Sunoco, 6-3/4" h, 3-3/4" w, tin, raised finish, diecut, emb airplane in flight, adv below, blue and white, black lettering 275.00

Tie Bar, Esso, smiling tiger's head, gold-tone, no makers' marks.............20.00

Token, Shell Safe Driver Award, 1-3/8" dia, brass, 1929, name 50.00

Toy Truck
Hess, 1989, MIB.....................110.00
Texaco #7, 1930 Diamond T Tanker, red and black, MIB..................90.00
Texaco #12, 1910 Mack Texaco Tanker, MIB...............................40.00
Texaco #17, 1919 GMC Tanker Truck 25.00

Tumbler, Sinclair Gasoline, 1916, 5-1/2" h 10.00

Visor Hanger, Sohio-X-70 - Brings Your Car Up To Standard, mileage records, metal, orig envelope...................................38.00

G. I. Joe Collectibles

Collecting Hints: It is extremely important to determine the manufacturing date of any G.I. Joe doll or related figure. The ideal method takes discipline—do a point-by-point comparison with the dolls described and dated in the existing reference books. Be alert to subtle variations; you do not have a match unless all details are exactly the same. It also is helpful to learn the proper period costume for each doll variation.

Accessory pieces can be every bit as valuable as the dolls themselves. Whenever possible, accessory pieces should be accompanied by their original packaging and paper inserts.

G.I. Joe dolls and accessories were produced in the millions. Rarity is not a factor; condition is. When buying dolls or accessories as collectibles, as opposed to acquiring them for play, do not purchase any items in less than fine condition.

History: Hasbro Manufacturing Company produced the first G.I. Joe twelve-inch posable action figures in 1964. The original line consisted of one male action figure for each branch of the military service. Their outfits were styled after uniforms from World War II, the Korean Conflict, and the Vietnam Conflict.

In 1965, the first Black figure was introduced. The year 1967 saw two additions to the line—a female nurse and Talking G.I. Joe. To keep abreast of changing times, Joe received flocked hair and a beard in 1970.

The creation of the G.I. Joe Adventure Team made Joe a prodigious explorer, hunter, deep sea diver, and astronaut, rather than just an American serviceman. Due to the Arab oil embargo in 1976, and its impact on the plastics industry, the figure was renamed Super Joe and reduced in height to eight inches. Production was halted in 1977.

In 1982, G.I. Joe staged his comeback. A few changes were made to the character line and to the way in which the figures were presented. The Great American Hero line now consists of three-and-three-quarter-inch poseable plastic figures with code names that correspond to the various costumes. The new Joes deal with contemporary and science fiction villains and issues.

References: Vincent Santelmo, *Complete Encyclopedia to GI Joe, 2nd ed.,* Krause Publications, 1996; —, *GI Joe Official Identification and Price Guide,* Krause Publications, 1999; —, *Official 30th Anniversary Salute to G.I. Joe,* Krause Publications, 1994.

Periodicals: *GI Joe Patrol,* P.O. Box 2362, Hot Springs, AR 71913. *The Barracks: The GI Joe Collectors Magazine,* 14 Bostwick Pl, New Milford, CT 06776,

Collectors' Club: GI Joe Collectors Club, 12513 Birchfalls Drive, Raleigh, NC 27614; GI Joe: Steel Brigade Club, 8362 Lomay Ave., Westminster, CA 92683.

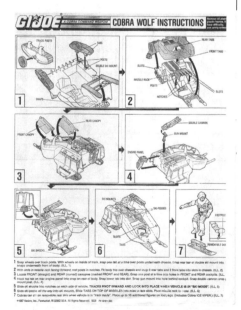

Instruction sheet, for Cobra Wolf, $2.

Accessories Pack, made for sale in Spain, Hasbro, c1975

#1	18.00
#2	19.00
#3	15.00
#4	12.00

Action Figures and Dolls

Action Man Africa Corp., complete	450.00
Action Man Black Soldier, complete	895.00
Action Man Canadian Mountie, complete	495.00
Action Man French Foreign Legion, complete	450.00
Action Man German Tanker, complete	425.00
Action Man Luffwaffe, complete	425.00
Action Man Red Devil, complete	495.00
Action Man SAS Key Figure, complete	395.00
Action Man SAS Parachute Attack, complete	495.00
Action Man SAS Underwater Attack, complete	425.00
Action Man Soldier, 30th Anniversary	150.00
Action Man Underwater Explorer, complete	425.00
Action Marine, 12" h, 1964-1994, NRFB	150.00
Action Marine Medic, equipment	300.00
Action Marine, parade dress uniform	150.00
Action Navy Attack, orange vest	195.00
Action MP, incomplete uniform	195.00
Action Navy, deep sea diver	295.00
Action Navy, shore patrol	295.00
Action Pilot, talking, complete	695.00
Action Sailor, talking, complete	595.00
Action Soldier, combat field jacket and gear	225.00
Action Soldier of the World, British Commando, no medal or clip	400.00
Action Soldier of the World, Japanese Imperial Soldier, no medal, no bayonet	550.00
Action Soldier, orig box, some paperwork	300.00
Action Soldier, talking, red head	175.00
Action Soldier, West Point Cadet	275.00
Adventure Team Commander, 12" h, talking	135.00
Airborne Military Police, Kay-Bee Exclusive	50.00
Air Cadet, complete, painted head	595.00

Arctic Joe Colton, mail order, 12" h	200.00
A.T.A.A. Adventurer, Kung Fu grip, orig box	225.00
Australian Jungle Fighter, complete	495.00
Baroness, 1984, loose	45.00
Capture of the Pygmy Gorilla, complete	395.00
Challenge at Hawk River	15.00
Classic, Historical Commanders Edition, #4, General Colin Powell, MIB	50.00
Cobra Commander, 1992, first issue, Japanese, 3" h, MOC, C-9	40.00
Cobra Officer, 1983, 3" h, carded, C-6	80.00
Cobra, straight arm, 1982, 3" h, carded, C-7.5	140.00
Combat Engineer, complete	995.00
Construction Jack Hammer, complete	895.00
Cover Girl, 1983, loose	17.00
Crash Crew Fire Fighter, complete	475.00
Croc Master, 1987, 3" h, MOC, C-8	30.00
Danger of the Depths, complete	495.00
Deep Freeze, complete, painted head	495.00
Deep Sea Diver, complete, painted head	550.00
Duke, 1983, loose	19.00
Eight Ropes of Danger, complete	495.00
Falcon, 1987, loose	8.00
Fantastic Freefall, complete	495.00
Fighter Pilot, complete, painted head	850.00
French Resistance Fighter	495.00
German Storm Trooper, complete	550.00
G. I. Joe, 50th Anniversary, WWII limited commemorative, Target exclusive, MIB	40.00
Green Beret, all accessories	495.00
Heavy Weapons, complete, painted head	550.00
Hidden Missile Recovery, complete	395.00
Hurricane Spotter, complete	375.00
Iceberg, 1986, loose	6.00
Japanese Imperial Soldier, complete	695.00
Landing Signal Officer, complete	475.00
Marine, Masterpiece Edition, Vol. III, black hair, camouflage fatigues, large cardboard box with illus G. I. Joe book, 1996, NRFB	85.00
Military Police, complete	495.00
Navy Attack, yellow life jacket, complete	795.00
Navy Seal, FAO, 12" h	200.00
Pilot, blond, Masterpiece	100.00

Police State Trooper,
complete 1,495.00

Range Viper, 1990, 3" h, MOC,
C-9 ....20.00

Recsue Diver, complete 850.00

Roadblock, 1984, loose..................15.00

Russian Soldier, complete 550.00

Sailor, black, Masterpiece 75.00

Scarlett, 1992, loose, C-8.5 ....23.00

Scramble Pilot, all accessories, painted
head figure.................................595.00

Set, 1994, pilot, Marine, Navy, Soldier,
3-1/4" h, MIB 100.00

Short Fuse, 1992, loose..................19.00

Smoke Jumper...............................375.00

Sneak Peek, 1987, 3" h, MOC,
C-8 ....18.00

Snow Job, 1983, loose 17.00

Soldier, black, painted black hair, green
fatigues, green plastic cap, black
boots, metal tags, Counter-Intelli-
gence Manual, Hasbro, 1964, slight
age discoloration to box 500.00

Thunder, 1984, loose 9.00

West Point Cadet, complete, painted
head 550.00

White Tiger Hunt, complete 395.00

Coloring Book, 48 pgs, Spanish text,
1989 ....15.00

Foot Locker, 20th
Anniversary 200.00

Gear, Classic Collection

Mission gear, M-60 gunner's pit,
MOC..15.00

U.S. Coast Guard, MIB 30.00

Kite, 42" l, keel-style, plastic, 1980s,
sealed in orig package..............20.00

Outfit

Action Soldier, scuba bottom, orig card,
some tape 175.00

A. T. Dangerous Mission, action outfit,
MOC..50.00

A. T. Jungle Ordeal, MOC...............50.00

Marine Dress Parade Set, #7710,
1964 ....565.00

Pilot Scramble Set, #7807I 1
965 ....450.00

Playset, Atomic Man Secret Outpost,
good box......................................85.00

Ring, 30th Anniversary, reddish-pink
stone 400.00

Set, Home for the Holidays,
Wal-Mart.....................................50.00

Thermos, Aladdin, plastic cup,
1985 ....8.00

Vehicle

Adventure Team Vehicle Set, #7005,
1970, NRFB...............................350.00

Desert Patrol Attack Jeep Set, #8030,
1967 ....3,350.00

Fight for Survival Set, Polar Explorer,
#7982, 1969 ....650.00

Official Sea Sled and Frogman Set,
#8050, 1966 ....600.00

Space Capsule, Convention
Exclusive 200.00

Weapon

Bayonet...15.00

Flare pistol.......................................20.00

M-16 ....30.00

Night stick 20.00

Golf Collectibles

Collecting Hints: Condition is becoming more important as collectors' sophistication and knowledge grow. The newer the item, the better the condition should be.

It is extremely rare to find a club or ball made before 1800; in fact, any equipment made before 1850 is scarce. Few books on the subject were published before 1857.

Most equipment made after 1895 is quite readily available. Common items, such as scorecards, ball markers, golf pencils, and bag tags, have negligible value. Some modern equipment, particularly from the years between 1950 and 1965, is in demand, but primarily to use for actual play rather than to collect or display.

The very old material is generally found in Scotland and England, unless items were brought to America early in this century. Christie's, Sotheby's, and Phillips' each hold several major auctions of golf collectibles every year in London, Edinburgh, and Chester. Golf collectible sales often coincide with the British Open Championship each July. Although the English market is more established, the American market is growing rapidly, and auctions of golf items and memorabilia now are held in the United States, as well as overseas.

The price of golf clubs escalated tremendously in the 1970s, but stabilized in more recent years. For many years, golf book prices remained static, but they rose dramatically in the 1980s. Art prints, drawings, etchings, etc., have not seen dramatic changes in value, but pottery, china, glass, and other secondary items, especially those by Royal Doulton, have attracted premium prices.

History: Golf has been played in Scotland since the 15th century, and existing documents indicate golf was played in America before the Revolu-tion. However, it was played primarily by "gentry" until the less-expensive and more durable "guttie" ball was introduced in 1848. This development led to increased participation and play spread to England and other countries, especially where Scottish immigrants settled. The great popularity of golf began about 1890 in both England and the United States.

References: Sarah Fabian Baddiel, *World of Golf Collectables,* Wellfleet Press, 1992; Chuck Furjanic, *Antique Golf Collectibles, A Price and Reference Guide, 2nd Edition,* Krause Publications, 2000; John F. Hotchkiss, *Collectible Golf Balls,* Antique Trader Books, 1997; Kevin McGimpsey and David Neach, *Golf Memorabilia,* Philip Wilson Publishers, distributed by Antique Collectors' Club, 1999; John M. Olman and Morton W. Olman, *Golf Antiques & Other Treasures of the Game,* expanded ed., Market Street Press, 1993; Beverly Robb, *Collectible Golfing Novelties,* Schiffer Publishing, 1992; Shirley and Jerry Sprung, *Decorative Golf Collectibles: Collector's Information, Current Prices, Glentiques,* 1991; Mark Wilson (ed.), *Golf Club Identification & Price Guide III,* Ralph Maltby Enterprises, 1993.

Periodicals: *Golfiana Magazine,* P.O. Box 688, Edwardsville, IL 62025; *US Golf Classics & Heritage Hickories,* 5407 Pennock Point Rd, Jupiter, FL 33458.

Collectors' Clubs: Golf Club Collectors Association, 640 E. Liberty St., Girard, OH 44420; Golf Collectors' Society, P.O. Box 20546, Dayton, OH 45420; Logo Golf Ball Collector's Association, 4552 Barclay Fairway, Lake Worth, Fl 33467.

Museums: PGA/World Golf Hall of Fame, Pinehurst, NC; Ralph Miller Memorial Library, City of Industry, CA; United States Golf Association, "Golf House," Far Hills, NJ.

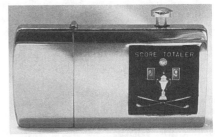

Lighter, score keeper, chrome, marked "Japan," 2-3/4" x 1-1/2", $24.

Ashtray, Senior PGA Golf Tour, ceramic, figural sand trap, green golf flag missing......................................7.00

Ball
Haskell, bramble, patent 1899 ....50.00
Lynx, rubber core.......................18.00
Mitchell, Manchester, gutty.........60.00
Spring Vale Hawk, bramble.......35.00

Book
Arnold Palmer-A Personal Journal, Thos. Hauser, 1994, 1st ed., 192 pgs, photos, dj 18.00
Golf-A New Approach, Lloyd Mangrum, Whittlesey House, 1949, 127 pgs, illus of golf swings 10.00
Golf In The Sun All Year Round, Robert H. K. Browning, 1931 ....38.00
Golf, The History of An Obsession, David Stirk, Price-Stern Sloan, 1987, 1st ed, 190 illus, dj 12.00
How To Play Your Best Golf All The Time, Tommy Armor, Simon & Schuster, 1953, 151 pgs.............10.00
Secrets of Accurate Putting and Chipping, Phil Galvano, c1957 ....4.50
Understanding Golf, John Gordon, 1926 ....40.00

Club
Burke, juvenile, mashie, wood shaft 30.00
C. S. Butchart, scare-head driver, stamped shaft 48.00
Fleetwood, Draper Maynard Co., Plymouth, NH, #4, stainless steel ...25.00
Fleetwood, Draper Maynard Co., Plymouth, NH, #10............................25.00
Hagen, iron-man sand wedge, wood shaft 170.00
Lady Diana, Mashie 5 iron.........50.00
McGregor, Tourney 693W driver, c1953, steel shaft....................150.00
Meadowlark, wood shaft, brass faceplate stamped "Brassie"...................................60.00
Spaulding, Cash-in Putter, steel shaft 65.00
Wilson, wedge, staff model, c1959, steel shaft..................................60.00

Figure, dressed pig finishing stroke, orig 9-1/2" h box...................................36.00

Golf Bag, Osmond Patent Caddy, ashwood, leather handles, straps, canvas club tube, ball pocket 275.00

Medallion, 1" d, inscribed "G. V. C. Golf Chairman 1973," intaglio snowflake design on front, 14K yg 75.00

Mug, hickory shaft, pewter 45.00

Paperweight, US Open, 1980.........32.00

Pen Holder, black golfer, late 19th C outfit, light green Akro Agate with rust marbling..................................165.00

Pin Tray, figural, lady golfer, Schafer & Vater 235.00

Program, Bob Hope Desert Classic, 1967 ....20.00

Graniteware

Collecting Hints: Old graniteware is heavier than new graniteware. Pieces with cast iron handles date from 1870 to 1890; wood handles date from 1900 to 1910. Other dating clues are seams, wood knobs, and tin lids.

History: Graniteware is the name commonly given to enamel-coated iron or steel kitchenware.

The first graniteware was made in Germany in the 1830s. Graniteware was not produced in the United States until the 1860s. At the start of World War I, when European companies turned to manufacturing war weapons, American producers took over the market.

Gray and white were the most common graniteware colors, although each company made their own special shades of blue, green, brown, violet, cream, or red.

References: Helen Greguire, *Collector's Encyclopedia of Graniteware,* Book 1 (1990, 1994 value update), Book 2 (1993, 1997), Collector Books.

Collectors' Club: National Graniteware Society, P.O. Box 10013, Cedar Rapids, IA 52410.

Baking Pan, 9" x 13" x 2-1/2" h, white, black trim, some wear................15.00

Berry Pail, cov, Stransky Steelware, gray and blue 225.00

Bowl
6-1/8" d, blue and white, medium swirl, black trim, c1960 ....35.00
8" w, 3-1/4" h, red and white stripes...................................32.00
8" w, 10-1/2" l, gray, oval 35.00
11-1/2" w, 5-1/2" h, cobalt blue and white, heavy use 25.00

Bread Box, 13" d, 6" h, white, lavender tulip dec, brass handle and latch..95.00

Candleholder, white, round base....65.00

Canister Set, French, some wear
Five cov canisters, orange and cobalt blue, ...425.00
Six cov canisters, cream, red checkered design 585.00

Coffee Boiler, 12-1/2" h, 10" d, gray mottled, side handle, top handle with wood hand-hold, tin lid, some slight discoloration and light rust 135.00

Coffeepot
8-1/4" h, white, red check dec, French, 1920s, chipped on handle and knob 85.00
10" h, stylized floral dec, black pin-stripe, French 325.00
11-1/4" h, 6-1/4" d, cobalt blue, gray graniteware one-pc insert, glass lid mkd "Break-No-More Cardella Mfg. Co., Cleveland, Ohio," some dark spots....................................75.00
11-1/2" h, 10-1/2" w, white, black trim, mkd "Vollrath Co., 7 Cups, Kook King," patent date of 1934, some enamel loss 125.00

12" h, 6-1/2" d, cream and green, green depression-era glass insert, attributed to Lisk Mfg., clear insert.....................................100.00

Corner Strainer, 8-3/4" w, cream and green, use, some light rust 15.00

Cup, cream and green, rolled rim, one ding on edge, wear to edge of handle......................................45.00

Cup and Plate, 4" h x 2-1/4" cup, 9-1/4" d plate, white, black trim, wear, some dings, set of plates..........40.00

Dipper, 14-1/4" l, 5-1/2" x 3" dipper, white, fine speckled black and blue trim, heavy use 30.00

Frying Pan, 7-1/4" w, blue and white speckled, some wear and rust . 45.00

Funnel
4" w, 4" l, white, cobalt blue trim, wear, scuff marks on handle and tip of spout.....................................25.00
6-1/2" w, 6" l, gray, handle 28.00
7-3/4" w, 9" l, gray mottled, some wear..85.00

Grill Plate, 11-1/4" d, green and white, large swirl, black trim, c1960 .... 42.50

Kettle, 14-1/4" d, 8-3/4" h, blue and white, lid missing......................55.00

Ladle, 14" l, white, heavy wear, dings, rust 10.00

Laundry Set, orange and blue, 1920s, three pcs 400.00

Lid, some wear
8-1/2" d, blue and white swirl, wood knob................................10.00
9-1/2" d, brown and white swirl 28.00
10" d, mottled gray 15.00

Lunch Box, cream and white mottled ext., white int...............................70.00

Match Box, hanging, wall type
6-1/4" h, 4-1/4" w, blue and white checkered design, some enamel loss to lower shoulders of backplate.............................195.00
6-1/2" h, blue and white swirl, roughness on lid in striker area 295.00
7" h, 5-1/8" d, white, red check dec, striker on lid 225.00

Mending Kit, Mendets, directions on back, two missing 9.50

Milk Pail
8" h, orange, blue, black, and white Art Deco design, chips around base and lid.......................................70.00
8-1/4" d, brown and white, deco style 75.00
8-1/4" d, red and white plaid, chip on back..95.00

Mixing Bowl
10" d, 4" h, blue and white speckle, darker blue rim trim, some wear, few dings...45.00
11" d, 5-1/4" h, green, black trim, dull int., some wear 30.00
12-1/4" d, 5-1/4" h, green, black trim, flat rim, some wear....................35.00

Mold, 9" d, 3" d, gray, some wear and chipping 35.00

Mug, 4" d, 2-1/4" h, white, black trim, some wear 12.50

Onion Bin 125.00

Oven Thermometer, 3" h, 2-1/2" w, Cooper Cookbook Thermometer, green base, chrome over glass thermometer, graphics of cookbook, dishes with suggested temperatures, thermometer cracked, some rust 50.00

Pan
6" w, 3" h, cobalt blue and white, some wear 30.00
8" w, 4" d, cobalt blue and white, light rust 35.00
12-1/2" x 7", blue and white, 2 handles 75.00

Pan Lid Rack, 7-1/4" w tapers to 2-1/4" w, 24" l, red shades to mustard yellow, 3 hooks 300.00

Pie Plate
9-1/4" d, 1" h, blue swirls 40.00
9-3/4" d, gray mottled, some wear 9.00
10" d, cream and green, some wear 10.00

Pitcher, cov, 6-3/4" h, cobalt swirl, rattan handle, some loosening to handle 425.00

Pitcher
15" h, blue and white, swirl dec, French, 1920s, some damage 225.00
15" h, white and red marble, French, 1920s 235.00

Plate
9" d, cream and green, flat rim, some wear 35.00
9" d, gray and white 20.00
10-1/4" d, orange and white, large swirl, black trim, c1960 .... 35.00

Platter, 14" l, medium blue and white swirl 195.00

Pot, cov
5-1/2" h, 10" d, black and white speckled base and lid, some wear 35.00
6-1/2" h, 7-3/4" d, white, black trim, matching lid, some wear 27.50
6-1/2" h, 11" d, solid black base, bright red lid, int. dull from use 48.00
7-1/2" h, 11" d, white, black trim, some use marks, bottom darkened from use 35.00

Roaster, cov
12-3/4" l, 8" w, 4-1/4" h, cream and green, white int., vents along edge of lid, indented handle, some wear 65.00
17" l, 13" w, 7-1/2" h, gray mottled, metal rack, indented handle, some wear 35.00
17-1/2" l, 11-1/2" w, 8" h, oval, solid cobalt blue, emb "Savory," some wear 60.00
18-1/2" l, 12" w, 9-1/2" h, black base, white lid, some wear 75.00
19" l, 13" w, 8-1/2" h, cream and green, heavy wear 35.00

Salt Box
9-3/4" h, white, red trim, chip around hanging hole, small loss, some int. rusting 175.00
10-3/8" h, white, floral trim 285.00

Sauce Pan, 3-1/2" h, 8-1/4" d, gray mottled 20.00

Soup Plate, 10-1/2" d, dark blue, black trim, some wear, rust, set of 3 .... 35.00

Soup Tureen, gray mottled, mkd "Extra Agate Nickel Steel Ware L & G Mfg. Co.," riveted handles, lid ring, ftd base, chip 395.00

Stew Pot
7-1/2" d, 9-1/2" h, light blue speckled, closed rolled handles, some wear 35.00
8" d, 4" h, white, black trim and lid, dull from use, wear 35.00

Strainer
Blue and white, double handles 50.00
Blue and white, single handle, c1940 .... 30.00
Cobalt blue and white speckled, 10-1/4" d, some wear 35.00
Dark brown and white spatter, 11" d, 3" h, few chips 85.00

Teapot
4-3/4" h, green, orange diamonds dec 165.00
5" h, 9-1/2" w, yellow, red, orange, blue, and green swirls, black handle, spout, and rim, several chips 525.00
10" h, solid blue, chrome lid with clear glass insert knob, slight wear and rust 150.00

Tea Steeper, 4-1/4" h, 4-1/4" d, mottled gray, wear 145.00

Towel Holder, 14-1/2" x 3-1/4", Dutch, Messen, Glazen, Borden, Handen 165.00

Tray, 14-1/2" l, mottled gray, some wear 35.00

Utensil Holder, wall, large, small dippers, skimmer, side dipper, 14-1/2" x 19", deep blue/green 250.00

Utility Pan, 9" l, 2-3/4" h, cream, black trim, some wear 12.00

Wall Pan, 10" w, white, blue trim, spout, mkd "Made in Germany" 35.00

Wash Pan
8" d, 2-1/2" h, gray, some wear .. 15.00
12" d, 3-1/2" h, gray mottled, flat rim with hole for hanging, dull int., some rust 18.00

Griswold

Collecting Hints: Griswold offers varied challenges to all collectors. Griswold made thousands of different products. Griswold made cast aluminum, chrome plated, nickel plated, and porcelain items in addition to cast iron. Griswold items range from a few dollars to several thousand dollars. Griswold also made advertising items, products for companies such as Sears, as well as items only marked with their pattern number. There are still many items made by Griswold that are unknown to the collector community. Condition is very important. Items that are pitted, cracked, warped, rusted or chipped have very little value to collectors.

History: The predecessor company of The Griswold Manufacturing Company, The Selden and Griswold Manufacturing Company, was started as a family enterprise in 1865. In 1884, the Griswolds bought the Seldons' portion of the business and changed the name to The Griswold Manufacturing Company. The business remained in operation in Erie, PA until it was sold to Wagner in 1957. Items with the Griswold and Wagner markings or those with the Griswold logo without Erie, PA were made after 1957 and are not very collectible.

References: Jon B. Haussler, *Griswold Muffin Pans,* Schiffer Publishing, 1997; David G. Smith and Chuck Wafford, *The Book of Griswold & Wagner,* Schiffer Publishing, 1995

Periodical: *Kettles 'n' Cookware,* P.O. Box 247, Perrysburg, NY 14129.

Collectors' Club: Griswold & Cast Iron Cookware Association, (G & CICA), 3007 Plum St., Erie, PA 16508.

Advisor: Jon B. Haussler, 1806 Brownstone Ave., SW, Decatur, AL 35603.

Reproduction Alert: There are reproductions of a few Griswold items. For the most part, the reproductions have a grainy finish and the lettering is uneven and not as sharp as the genuine items. Reproductions do not present a significant problem for the advanced collector. However, new collectors and general line antique dealers are often fooled. The No. 262 small corn stick pan, the No. 0 skillet, and the Santa Claus mold are the most commonly encountered reproduced items. The real Griswold Santa has a tongue and the reproductions do not. There are some fake Griswold items such as a toy Heart and Star waffle iron (Griswold never made one).

Note: Prices are for items that are in excellent as made condition with NO damage.

Abbreviations: EPU is Erie, Pa. USA; HR is Heat Ring.

Skillet

No. 0 Block Logo 85.00
No. 2 Slant Logo 500.00

No. 2 Block Logo Smooth
  Bottom.................................350.00
No. 2 Block Logo HR.................1,000.00
No. 3 Small Logo 20.00
No. 4 Block HR 450.00
No. 4 Block Smooth Bottom 50.00
No. 5 Block HR 450.00
No. 5 Block Smooth Bottom 40.00
No. 5 Victor 500.00
No. 6 Block HR 60.00
No. 6 Victor 150.00
No. 7 Block Smooth Bottom 25.00
No. 7 Victor, fully marked...............40.00
No. 8 Block Smooth Bottom 25.00
No. 8 Erie Outside HR 30.00
No. 8 Erie Spider.......................2,000.00
No. 8 Small Logo 15.00
No. 8 Victor 30.00
No. 9 Small Logo 20.00
No. 10 Block Logo HR...................60.00
No. 11 Block Logo HR.................150.00
No. 12 Block Logo HR...................75.00
No. 12 Erie Outside HR 170.00
No. 12 Small Logo HR...................50.00
No. 13 Block Logo HR.............1,200.00
No. 13 Slant Logo EPU.............1,000.00
No. 14 Block Logo HR.................175.00
No. 15 Oval Fish Skillet................250.00
No. 20 Block Logo EPU...............700.00
Colonial Breakfast Skillet 45.00
5 in 1 Breakfast Skillet.................175.00
Square Egg Skillet 45.00
Square Skillet w/Glass Lid 90.00

Muffin Pan

No. 1 Gem Pan Slant Logo...........250.00
No 2 Gem Pan w/Pattern Number
  (941).....................................400.00

No. 3 Gem Pan Slant Logo EPU...600.00
No. 9 Brownie Cake Pan...............150.00
No. 10 Popover Pan........................35.00
No. 11 French Roll Pan 40.00
No. 12 Gem Pan Slant Logo 500.00
No. 17 French Roll 125.00
No. 18 Popover Pan, fully marked ..60.00
No. 19 Golfball Pan......................450.00
No. 20 Turk Head, mkd
  "Griswold" 550.00
No. 21 Bread Stick Pan................125.00
No. 22 Bread Stick Pan..................35.00
No. 23 Bread Stick Pan................100.00
No. 27 Wheat Stick Pan 225.00
No. 28 Wheat Stick Pan 225.00
No. 32 Danish Cake Pan................35.00
No. 34 Plett Pan, Slant Logo..........60.00
No. 34 Plett Pan, Small Logo 15.00
No. 50 Hearts/Star Pan 2,000.00
No. 100 Hearts/Star Pan 900.00
No. 140 Turk Head Pan................125.00
No. 262 Corn Stick Pan..................60.00
No. 272 Corn or Wheat Stick Pan.125.00
No. 273 Corn Stick Pan..................25.00
No. 283 Corn Stick Pan................100.00

Other

Ashtray with Matchholder
  Round..25.00
  Square.......................................35.00
Double Broiler 250.00
Fluter, Fixed Handle, Erie.............500.00
Griddle, Block Logo, handled
  No. 6..100.00
  No. 7..40.00
  No. 8..30.00
  No. 9..30.00
  No. 10..40.00

Ice Shave
  No. 1 ....100.00
  No. 2 ....150.00
Meat Grinder 22.00
Mold
  Lamb 175.00
  Rabbit.......................................215.00
  Santa 600.00
Patty Mold Set, with box
  No. 1 ....40.00
  No. 2 ....50.00
Pup, marked "Griswold
  Pup 30"..................................275.00
Roaster and Trivet, oval, fully marked
  No. 3 ....600.00
  No. 7 ....500.00
Skillet Lid, Raised Letter
  No. 8 ....40.00
  No. 10 ....125.00
  No. 12 ....250.00
Tite-Top Dutch Oven with Trivet
  No. 6 ....400.00
  No. 7 ....125.00
  No. 8 ....80.00
  No. 9 ....95.00
  No. 10 ....150.00
Tobacco Cutter, Star, No. 3 .... 95.00
Trivet, 7-1/4" d, mkd "The Griswold Mfg.
  Co., Erie, PA, USA, Trivet #7" 45.00
Waffle Iron, American, low base
  No. 6 ....400.00
  No. 7 ....90.00
  No. 8 ....40.00
  No. 9 ....75.00
Waffle Iron, Hearts/Star, No. 18.... 150.00
Wax Ladle, Erie 150.00

H

Haeger Potteries

Collecting Hints: One of the interesting facets of this company's past is that it successfully built and operated a working pottery facility at the Chicago World's Fair in 1933 and 1934. Several different marks were used through the long history of this popular china.

History: Haeger Pottery has an interesting history. Starting as a brick yard in Dundee, IL, in 1871, David H. Haeger formed a company which would develop into an art pottery and commercial pottery. After David was succeeded by son Edmund H. Haeger, in 1900, he began to produce an art pottery line in 1914. Because of their high quality luster glazes and soft pastels, their dinnerware line was a success.

A line named "Royal Haeger" was introduced in 1938, with the Royal Haeger Lamp Company forming in 1939. This expansion was enhanced by the purchase of a pottery building in Macomb, IL, where it soon began to make its florist trade art pottery line.

Today, members of the Haeger family are still involved in the pottery.

Reference: Joe Paradis and Joyce Paradis, *The House of Haeger 1914-1944: The Revitalization of American Art Pottery,* Schiffer, 1999.

Collectors' Club: Haeger Pottery Collectors of America, 5021 Toyon Way, Antioch, CA 94509.

Ashtray, 13-1/2" l, 5-1/4" w, burnt orange, green, blue, and yellow, three small legs, mkd "Royal Haeger SP-12 USA" 25.00
Basket
   8-1/2" h, yellow and green 60.00
   8-1/2" h, 10-1/2" w, stork, pink, glazed over factory flaw 35.00
   13" h, 9" l, pink and white, stamped "Royal Haeger USA" 95.00
Birdhouse, pink, #287, 2 wrens 35.00
Bowl
   7" sq, mauve, low 20.00
   7-1/2" l, 5-1/2" w, white, ribbed, orig foil label, base mkd "Haeger 4020-A U.S.A." 18.00
   8" d, golden brown 18.50
   9" d, 4" h, pale sand-pink, mkd "Royal Haeger USA R G 56" 30.00

10" d, Daisy, light blue, incised "Royal Haeger Roy Hickman USA" 55.00
10" d, burgundy, short pedestal base 40.00
14" l, handle, brown agate blended glaze, ocean motif, #R988 .... 25.00
14" l, 5-1/2" w, orange and green, leaf shape, mkd "Royal Hager 28fS USA" 25.00
18" l, shell shape, mkd "Royal Haeger USA" 18.00
Bowl and Pitcher Set, 6" h pitcher, 7-1/2" d bowl, yellow glaze, raised brown and gold leaves and flowers, incised Haeger #934, pitcher stamped Royal Haeger, number not legible 25.00
Console Bowl, 11" l, 7-1/2" w, yellow, mkd "Haeger USA" 40.00
Console Set, Persian Blue, #316-H, foil label 35.00
Dealer Sign, baby blue glaze 150.00
Figure
   Bird, yellow, mauve, blue, wings spread, mkd R124, 11" h 30.00
   Boxer Dog, 10" l 75.00
   Cat, Mandarian orange, yellow glass eyes, #R616, 15-1/2" h 95.00
   Cocker puppy, lying, 2-3/4" h 25.00
   Fish, salmon-colored, paper label, 10-1/2" w, 17" h 45.00
   Garden Girl, #R995, Royal Haeger stamp mark 35.00
   Gazelle, blue, orig label, 21" h 220.00
   Hound dog, sitting, sad face, dark brown, ink stamp mark, 4" h 40.00
   Nude man and woman, joined at hands and feet, bright shiny black, 14-3/4" w, 14-1/4" h 50.00
   Pheasants, mottled brown, pr, 17" h 225.00
   Ram, maroon, 4" w, 8-1/2" h 130.00
   Swan, yellow, c1938-40, 2" w, 7-1/2" h 75.00
   Swan, uplifted wings, light gray/brown, 9" l 50.00
   Warlord sitting on cushion, pink matte glaze, paper label, 12" w, 12" h 125.00
Flower Bowl and Frog, mermaid, R-224, repaired break on fin 75.00
Jardiniere
   Basketweave, white ground, brown speckles 24.00
   Dripping Color, 10" h, 11" d, used, some glaze chips, etc. 165.00
Pitcher, 60-3/4" w, 6" h, #RG-28, pink, braided handle 55.00
Planter
   Blue, 18" l, 8" w, minor factory flaw 45.00
   Fawn, green, 9" l, 7-3/4" h, mkd "Royal Haeger, R-1913" 25.00
   Green, 11" h, 7-1/2" w, 3-1/2" h 20.00
   Hounddog Shoes, white, mkd "Hounddog Shoes" 55.00
   Koala Bear, Bennington Brown Foam 45.00

Lion, Bennington Brown Foam, slight nick 45.00
Melon ribbed, light green, 9" l, 3-3/4" 18.00
Sunbonnet Girls, 9" w, girls, yellow, c1946, 9" w 130.00
#3264, Madonna and Cherub, blue, orig paper label, 4-1/2" w, 11" h .. 35.00
#3777, light green, 7" d, 6-3/4" h 28.00
Serving Dish, 16", Gold Tweed, mkd "Royal Haeger" 32.00
Store Display, 6-1/2" l, figural green garden house, plaque "Gardenhouse by Haeger," orig label 24.00
Television Lamp
   Leaping deer, Chestnut style, #160, orig tag "Phil-Mar Corp, Cleveland 3, Ohio" 65.00
   Mother and young antelope, brown agate, #160 .... 65.00
   Panther, high gloss chartreuse and yellow, 20" l 20.00
Vase
   7" h, 6 1/2" d, fluted, green 30.00
   7" h, 8" w, Art Deco style, blended light pearl gray to darker pearl gray ... 25.00
   8" h, mottled white and dusty rose pink glaze, 1930s 60.00
   10" h, #R1919, white, concentric black, green, and orchid rings around base, mkd "Royal Haeger USA R1919" 25.00
   10" h, 11" w, Dripping Color, brown, small chip 145.00
   11" h, Madonna with Cherub, #3264, blue, orig sticker 35.00
   12" h, Art Deco-style, pale blue, leaf, mkd "Royal Haeger, made in USA," bruise at left tip 36.00
   12" h, baluster, peacock glaze, #4030 .... 150.00
   12" h, Madonna, #358 .... 36.00
   12-3/4" h, 4" d, deco-style, gray-green textured surface 30.00
   14" h, lily, designed by E. Royal Hickman, blues, greens, and pinks, c1935 .... 100.00
   14-1/2" h, 9" d, ivory, small chip on base 30.00
   15" h, gazelle, #R706 and #R707, one leaping, other standing, hunter green, blue feathering, some scratches on base of one 100.00
   18-1/2" h, pitcher, handle, blended agate glaze, #408 .... 55.00
Wall Pocket, fish, blue 38.00

Hall China

Collecting Hints: Hall China Company identified many of its patterns by name, but some of these are being gradually changed by dealers. A good example is the Silhouette pattern, which is also known as Taverne. Many shapes are also referred to by more than one name, i.e., Radiance is also known as Sunshine, Terrace as Stepdown, and Pert as Sani-Grid.

Because of their high quality, most Hall China pieces are still in wonderful condition. There is no reason to pay full price for imperfect pieces.

History: Hall China Company was formed as a result of the dissolution of the East Liverpool Potteries Company. Robert Hall, a partner in the merger, died within months of establishing the new company. Robert T. Hall, his son, took over.

At first the company produced the same semi-porcelain dinnerware and toiletware that was being made at the other potteries in East Liverpool, Ohio. Robert T. Hall began experiments to duplicate an ancient Chinese one-fire process that would produce a non-crazing vitrified china, with body and glaze fired at the same time. He succeeded in 1911 and Hall products have been made that way ever since.

Hall's basic products—hotel and restaurant institutional ware—are sold to the trade only. However, the firm also has produced many retail and premium lines, e.g. Autumn Leaf for Jewel Tea and Blue Bouquet for the Standard Coffee Co. of New Orleans. A popular line is the gold-decorated teapots that were introduced for retail sale in 1920. In 1931, kitchenware was introduced, soon followed by dinnerware. These lines were made in both solid colors and with decals for retail and premium sales.

Hall is still producing china at its plant in East Liverpool, Ohio.

References: Susan and Al Bagdade, *Warman's American Pottery and Porcelain,* 2nd ed., Krause Publications, 2000; Harvey Duke, *Hall: Price Guide Update,* ELO Books, 1992; C. L. Miller, *Jewel Tea Grocery Products with Values,* Schiffer Publishing, 1996; —, *Jewel Tea: Sales and Housewares Collectibles,* Schiffer Publishing, 1995; Jim and Lynn Salko, *Halls Autumn Leaf China and Jewel Tea Collectibles,* published by authors (143 Topeg Dr., Severna Park, MD 21146), 1996; Margaret and Kenn Whitmyer, *Collector's Encyclopedia of Hall China,* 3rd ed., Collector Books, 2001.

Periodical: *Hall China Encore,* 317 N. Pleasant St., Oberlin, OH 44074.

Collectors' Clubs: Autumn Leaf Reissues Association, 19238 Dorchester Cr, Strongsville, OH 44136; Hall Collector's Club, P.O. Box 360488, Cleveland, OH 44136; National Autumn Leaf Collectors Club, 7346 Shamrock Dr., Indianapolis, IN 46217.

Teapot, Boston shape, Dresden blue, gold dec, 5" h, $24.

Dinnerware Patterns

Autumn Leaf

Premium for the Jewel Tea Company. Produced 1933 until 1978. Other companies made matching fabric, metal, glass, and plastic accessories.

Baker, 2 pint, 6-1/4" d	175.00
Bean Pot, two handles	180.00
Berry Bowl, 5-1/2" d	5.00
Butter Dish, cov, 1 lb	255.00
Coffeepot, cov, rayed, 8 cup, gold double circle mark "Tested and approved by Mary Dunbar, Jewell Homemaker's Institute"	60.00
Cookie Jar, cov	175.00
Creamer and Sugar, cov, ruffled-D	35.00
Cream Soup	35.00
Cup and Saucer, St Denis	50.00
Custard Cup	24.50
Dinner Plate, 9" d	6.50
Gravy Boat	20.00
Hot Pad, tin back, 7-1/4"	35.00
Jug, ball	60.00
Mixing Bowl	
7-1/2" x 4"	35.00
8-3/4" x 4-1/2"	45.00
Platter, 9" x 5-1/2"	25.00
Range Salt and Pepper Shakers, pr	35.00
Salt and Pepper Shakers, pr	15.00
Serving Tray, metal	55.00
Stack Set, three stacking containers, one lid	150.00
Teapot, cov, Aladdin, 6-1/2" h	87.50
Tumbler, glass, frosted	
3-3/4" h	40.00
5-1/2" h	22.00
Vase	210.00
Vegetable Bowl, oval, divided	175.00

Crocus

Dinnerware pattern produced during the 1930s. This decal has multicolored stylized crocuses and green and black leaves. It is also found on a wide array of kitchenware shapes.

Bowl, Radiance	
6-1/8" d, 3" h	45.00
7" d	30.00
9" d	45.00

Bread and Butter Plate, 7-1/4" d	12.00
Butter Dish, cov, 1 lb	555.00
Cake Plate	25.00
Casserole, cov	60.00
Cereal Bowl, 6" d	15.00
Coffeepot, Terrace	110.00
Dinner Plate	38.50
Gravy Boat	32.00
Jug, ball	195.00
Luncheon Plate, 9" d	15.00
Salad Plate, 8-1/4" d	12.00
Platter, 13-1/4" l	35.00
Salt and Pepper Shakers, pr, teardrop shape	45.00
Soup Tureen	395.00
Teapot, banded	175.00
Tidbit, three tier	50.00

Golden Glo

Casserole, 3 qt	30.00
Creamer, 4-7/8" h	30.00
Sugar, 2-1/4" h	30.00

Orange Poppy

Premium for the Great American Tea Company. Introduced in 1933 and discontinued in the 1950s. Dinnerware was made in the C-style shape. Metal accessories are available, though scarce.

Bean Pot	115.00
Cake Plate	20.00
Casserole, 8" l, oval	65.00
Coffee Canister	325.00
Coffeepot	80.00
Custard	6.00
Hot Plate, 9-1/2" d	36.00
Platter, 13" l	18.00
Salad Bowl	12.00
Salt and Pepper Shakers, pr, handled	35.00
Sugar, Great American mark	30.00
Teapot, Boston	350.00
Vegetable Bowl, round	25.00

Pastel Morning Glory

Dinnerware line produced in the late 1930s and readily found in northern Michigan, Wisconsin, and Minnesota. Design consists of large pink morning glories surrounded by green leaves and small blue flowers on white ground. The pattern was also used on kitchenware items.

Bread and Butter Plate, 6" d	6.00
Casserole, cov	48.00
Cereal Bowl, 6" d	20.00
Cup and Saucer	18.50
Custard	15.00
Dinner Plate, 10" d	25.00
Drip Jar, ink	20.00
Fruit Bowl, 5-1/2" d	9.00
Gravy Boat	25.00
Jug, ball, pink	165.00
Luncheon Plate, 9" d	12.00
Pie Baker	30.00
Salad Plate, 8-1/4" d	9.00

Red Dot (a.k.a. Eggshell Polka Dot)

This pattern is found on the Eggshell Buffet Service. Red is the most commonly found Dot color, but the pattern was also produced in blue, green, and orange.

Baker, 13-1/2" l, fish-shape..........45.00
Bean Pot, small, #1.....................95.00
Bowl, 8-1/2" d..........................25.00
Casserole, cov, oval or round.....40.00
Cocette, 4" d, handle..................25.00
Drip Jar, tab handle, #1188.........45.00
Jug, cov, #2 or #4.....................125.00
Mustard, cov, slotted lid..............95.00
Onion Soup, cov........................45.00
Pitcher, Baron 95.00
Range Shakers, salt, pepper, flour,
sugar 150.00
Shirred Egg Dish, 6-1/2" d..........25.00
Tom and Jerry Punch Bowl Set, bowl
and 12 mugs............................250.00

Red Poppy

Premium for Grand Union Tea Company. Produced from mid-1930s until mid-1950s. Complete line of D-style dinnerware and kitchenware in various forms. The design features red poppies and black leaves on a white background. Glass, metal, wood, and cloth accessories were also marketed.
Bowl 10.00
Cereal Bowl, 6" d 18.50
Coffeepot, Daniel, metal
dropper 40.00
Cup and Saucer 15.00
Custard Cup, Radiance 17.50
Dinner Plate, 10" d....................17.50
Drip Jar 30.00
Salt and Pepper Shakers, pr, egg
shape 45.00
Soup Plate, flat.........................20.00
Stack Set..................................75.00

Shaggy Tulip, coffeepot, Kodata drip,
orig strainer 350.00

Taverne

This popular pattern was used as a premium for Hellick's Coffee in Pennsylvania. Other mediums are found with this pattern.
Bowl, Medallion
6" d 20.00
7" d 25.00
Casserole, medallion..................75.00
Coffeepot, 10 cup, metal drip, gold
mark 115.00
Drip Jar, cov.............................40.00
French Baker, 8" d 30.00
Iced Tea Glass...........................50.00
Jug, #3.....................................45.00
Leftover, cov
4" x 8" 70.00
8" x 8" 85.00
Pretzel Jar, cov 165.00
Salad Bowl, 9" d........................25.00
Salt and Pepper Shakers, pr,
5-band....................................75.00
Saucer.....................................10.00
Teapot
Medallion 125.00
Streamline, no lid 100.00

Kitchenware Patterns

Blue Garden/Blue Blossom

This 1939 pattern is a silk-screen decal on a cobalt blue glaze. Hall claims that this was the first time that cobalt blue had been used successfully for vitrified kitchen cooking items.
Batter Jar 250.00
Butter, cov, Radiance.................475.00
Casserole, #4, Sundial...............75.00
Cookie Jar, cov 375.00
Jug, loop handle 245.00
Left Over, loop handle 195.00
Mixing Bowl, 6" d 85.00
Mixing Bowl, 7-1/2" d, thick rim...60.00
Range Shakers, handle...............90.00
Refrigerator Bowl, cov, loop
handle 155.00
Syrup Pitcher, banded 395.00

Chinese Red

This pattern name refers to the bright red color found on various shapes of solid-colored kitchenware. Chinese red is the most commonly found color.
Ashtray, triangular 30.00
Batter Bowl, Five Band 75.00
Bean Pot, #5..............................155.00
Casserole, cov, 8-1/5" d, thick rim,
mkd "Hall's Suporior Quality Kitchenware Made in USA".....................60.00
Creamer and Sugar, cov,
Morning 95.00
Drip Jar, open, #1188 ....35.00
Jug, donut, 1-1/2 quarts, 6-7/8" h, mkd
"Hall's Superior Quality Kitchenware
Made in USA" 185.00
Leftover, Zephyr 165.00
Pretzel Jar, cov 125.00
Ramekin 50.00
Teapot, streamline.....................275.00
Water Bottle, Zephyr 90.00

Rose Parade, mixing bowls, 6",
7-1/2", and 9" d, straight sides, Cadet
blue...110.00

Rose White

Kitchenware pattern with Hi-White body and pink rose decal.
Bean Pot, cov 115.00
Bowl..10.00
Casserole, cov, tab handles........27.50
Jug, 7-1/2" h, Perk......................40.00
Pitcher, small.............................30.00
Salt and Pepper Shakers, pr 35.00

Wild Poppy (a.k.a. Poppy and Wheat)

Kitchenware line introduced in the late 1930s and sold by Macy's.
Bean Pot....................................225.00
Bowl, Radiance, set of four, 6",
7-1/2", 9", and 10".....................140.00
Casserole, cov, round, #76.......110.00
Coffee Canister, cov, 7-7/8" h, mkd
"Hall's Superior Quality Kitchenware
Made in USA" 250.00
Custard, Radiance......................20.00
Flour Canister, cov, 7-7/8" h, mkd
"Hall's Superior Quality Kitchenware
Made in USA" 225.00
Salt Shaker, Radiance, wear to lettering..85.00
Shirred Egg Dish
5-1/4" d 40.00
6" d 40.00
Stack Set, Radiance 175.00
Sugar, handle............................75.00

Tea Canister, cov, 7-7/8" h, mkd "Hall's Superior Quality Kitchenware Made in USA" 250.00
Teapot, cov, 6 cup,
Manhattan................................400.00
Tea Tile, 6" sq 85.00

Water pitcher, covered, General Electric, gray and yellow semi-matte glaze, stamped "GE/Refrigerators/Hall Ovenware China/General Electric," lid rim chipped, 8-1/2" w, 7-1/2" h, $60. Photo courtesy of David Rago Auctions.

Refrigerator Ware and Commercial Ware

Dealer Sign, cobalt blue 35.00
Forman Family Electric Warmer, 3
petite marnites...........................130.00
Game Bird Percolator, gold
trim 120.00
General Electric Adonis, water server
Blue and yellow......................55.00
Gray and yellow 55.00
Hotpoint, leftover, rect 60.00
Interprise Drip-O-Later, 10 cup, orig
instruction book........................175.00
Jolly Green Giant, mug 15.00
Lipton Tea, creamer 135.00
Water Pitcher, cov, Phoenix
Blue..60.00
Westinghouse
Bowl, blue 45.00
Butter Dish, cov, yellow,
Hercules 30.00
Left Over
Delphite 16.00
Yellow, Hercules...............30.00
Pitcher, cobalt blue, Art-Deco
styling, 9" h 125.00
Water Server, delphinium blue,
8-1/4" h...................................85.00

Teapots

Airflow, orange, 6 cup...............100.00
Aladdin, yellow, gold trim,
infusor 45.00
Albany, brown, gold trim 70.00
Baltimore, yellow 50.00
Basket, canary yellow, gold
trim 110.00
Boston, Dresden Blue, gold
mark..95.00
Cube, 1 cup, turquoise 125.00
Doughnut, cobalt blue 165.00

Flareware 60.00
Globe
   Canary Yellow 80.00
   Cobalt Blue, gold trim 225.00
   Emerald Green, gold trim.......95.00
   Light Green, gold trim 80.00
Hollywood, green, gold trim, 4 cup,
wear 70.00
Hook Cover, blue, gold trim, 6 cup,
gold stamp mark 65.00
Manhattan, blue...........................65.00
McCormick, turquoise, 2 cup,
emb..110.00
Melody, maroon and gold,
c1939...550.00
Morning Glory, Aladdin, infuser, mkd
"Hall's Superior Quality Kitchenware,
Tested and Approved by Mary Dun-
bar, Jewel Homemakers
Institute" 160.00
New York, ivory, gold flowers, gold
spout, 6 cup, wear to gold 75.00
Parade, yellow, 6 cup 60.00
Philadelphia, green, gold trim,
c1920 ....75.00
Royal, ivory 150.00
Sundial, yellow, safety handle.....75.00
Teamster, double spout, yellow and
gold...110.00
Twin Spout, emerald green 80.00
Windshield, gold dot dec, gold
label..65.00

Handkerchiefs

Collecting Hints: Collecting handkerchiefs has again become popular with collectors. Perhaps it's the affordability of vintage handkerchiefs, or their cheerful nature. Those shopping for handkerchiefs can still find the best bargains at garage sales, or by patiently rummaging through every basket offered at flea markets and antique malls. For collectors of centuries-old, high-end handkerchiefs, Phillips auction house in London offers three auctions of lace and vintage textiles each year. Shop by catalog or on the Internet at www.phillips-auction.com/uk.

History: The world has not lost its interest in the handkerchief, even after more than a half-century has passed since the invention of the paper tissue. In the first half of the twentieth century, department stores devoted hundreds of square feet of display cases full of handkerchiefs. Today, thousands of those vintage hankies are offered each day on Internet auctions, as well as in basket after basket in flea market and antique malls.

Handkerchiefs were designed for much more than just wiping noses and brows. Decorative lace and embroidered ones were made as wedding keepsakes. Printed ones celebrated everything imaginable: cartoon characters, nursery rhymes, political causes, and souvenirs of every major city or country across the globe.

Handkerchiefs are being bought up for several reasons. Collecting has become easier, with the wide variety offered on the Internet. Those who recognize high-quality workmanship in embroidery and lacemaking are beginning to snap up the truly fine works of art dating from the nineteenth century. Finally, crafty types are recognizing old handkerchiefs to be a wonderful source of fine quality linen and cotton, the raw materials for endless doll dresses, quilts, and other fiber arts.

The handkerchiefs bringing the highest prices at auction are the very old printed ones with stories to tell through great colorfully printed designs. Excellent condition is necessary to draw bidders over the $200 mark.

Designer handkerchiefs of the 1940s to 1960s are gaining notice, and dozens are appearing on the Internet. Only the most innovative designs with the wittiest personalities—dancing zebras, playful animals and figures, great graphic souvenir handkerchiefs of hot tourist scenes like San Francisco, New York and Los Angeles are bringing prices from $20 to $50. Because the handful of collectors are cherry picking the best designs in the best condition, it is too soon to tell if the name of the designer, such as Tammis Keefe or Carl Tait, or the superb graphics are the draw.

Designers like Tammis Keefe, Pat Pritchard, Faith Austin, and Carl Tait were unbelievably prolific. No comprehensive list has surfaced, but a review of handkerchiefs offered on the Internet show Tammis Keefe alone produced more than twenty series: Christmas, Easter, Valentine's Day, souvenir cities, florals, geometrics, witty animal scenes, and exotic harem designs. Perhaps a dozen different designs, each produced in up to a half dozen color combinations, were produced in each series. Although Tammis Keefe designed handkerchiefs for a relatively brief period, from 1944 until her death in 1960, the thousands of Keefe designs should accommodate many more collectors before prices really skyrocket.

Among the lace and embroidered handkerchiefs, the nineteenth and early twentieth century French handkerchiefs are starting to gain a bit of attention. Do your shopping in the United States for these embroidery-encrusted beauties. Handkerchiefs that sell for $100 to $300 in the U.S. bring well over a thousand dollars in France, where their masterful handwork truly is appreciated.

Those offering the best quality early twentieth century Chinese embroidered and drawnwork handkerchiefs on the Internet are wisely sticking to reserve prices well over $100. Although China is again producing brand new white-on-white embroidered and drawnwork handkerchiefs, these do not have the subtle details of scrollwork and shaping on flower petals, the heavy crusting of embroidery, and the elaborate needle lace insertions of the early examples.

Decorative embroidered monograms, especially those with highly decorated white-on-white lettering, are popular as wedding and other presents.

References: Elizabeth Kurella, *The Complete Guide to Vintage Textiles,* Krause, 1999; Roseanna Mihalick, *Collecting Handkerchiefs,* Schiffer, 2000; J. J. Murphy, *Children's Handkerchiefs, A Two Hundred Year History,* Schiffer, 1999; Paolo Peri, *The Handkerchief,* Quite Specific Media Group, 1996.

Advisor: Elizabeth Kurella.

Children's Handkerchiefs

Raggedy Anne and Andy, c1920-30, Anne and Andy and animal characters playing around a maypole........228.00
The Indian Hunter, c1900-10, children dressed as cowboys and cowgirls, shooting at cigar store Indian, 12-1/2" square...66.00

Designer Printed Handkerchiefs (see also souvenir handkerchiefs)

Faith Austin, large old-fashioned keys bordering center of foliage 10.00
Faith Austin, small stylized owls in a tree..3.00
Tammis Keefe, design of whimsical lady scarecrows in a geometric cornfield 15.00
Tammis Keefe, geometric pattern of leaves 5.00
Tammis Keefe, large poodle surrounded by smaller Chihuahua, afghan, and other dogs 12.00
Tammis Keefe, sailors cavorting on the rigging of vintage sailing ship.....18.00
Tammis Keefe, stylized mermaids playing musical instruments 26.00

Carl Tait, "Be My Valentine" motto printed in central field with large heart, cupids arrows and ribbons, surrounded by red and pink hearts 14-1/2" x 14-1/2"............................34.00
Carl Tait, Christmas handkerchief with Santa in the basket of a colorful balloon, in red, purple, green, and other bright colors.................................29.00
Carl Tait, colorful stylized zebras in bright primary colors 59.00

Lace Handkerchiefs

Chinese embroidered handkerchief, late 20th C, floral design outlined in padded satin stitch, some drawnwork, scrolling embroidery..........15.00
Crochet-edged handkerchief, 1" of white crochet lace in unusual scallop design 15.00
Crochet-edged handkerchief, 1/4" of brightly colored crochet lace in simple looping design...............................3.00
French embroidered handkerchief, heavily encrusted with embroidery in floral design, needle lace insertions in flower centers, 18" square.........185.00

Monogram Handkerchiefs

Elaborate scrolling monogram with three scrolling letters intertwined with floral design, white embroidery on white linen 25.00
Simple satin stitch monogram, single letter surrounded with scrollwork and flowers, on white linen 10.00
Simple monogram worked in satin stitch in bright color thread on white linen...5.00

Movie and Cartoon Handkerchiefs

Blondie and Dagwood with sailboat, 8-3/4" square................................48.00
Donald Duck and Alice in Wonderland at a tea party, 8-1/2" square 10.00
Gone with the Wind theme, Scarlet in four different gowns, 13" square .52.00
Minnie Mouse eating a sandwich, 1950s 8.00

Souvenir Printed Handkerchiefs

Chicago theme, Mrs. O'Leary's cow and other city sights, Tammis Keefe...35.00
Dayton, Ohio scenes, central airplane and sq vignettes as border, Carl Tait...38.00
Hollywood Premiere scene, with klieg lights and palm trees, Tammis Keefe..26.00
Niagara Falls, six views of falls, border of red and yellow roses, 10-1/2" square...3.75
San Francisco, colorful "San Francisco" in center surrounded by sq vignettes of local tourist scenes, Carl Tait...52.00

Harker Pottery

Collecting Hints: In 1965, Harker China had the capacity to annually produce 25 million pieces of dinnerware. Hence, there is a great deal of Harker material available at garage sales and flea markets.

Shapes and forms changed through the decades of production. Many patterns were kept in production for decades, and the same pattern was often made using different colors for the background. Patterns designed to have mass appeals include those like Colonial Lady, which was popular at "dish nites" at the movies or other businesses.

Between 1935 and 1955, Columbia Chinaware, which was organized to market Harker products in small towns across the country, promoted enamel ware, glass, and aluminum products. One of Columbia Chinaware's patterns was Autumn Leaf, which is eagerly sought by collectors.

Production of Cameo line at Harker began in 1940. The process was perfected by George Bauer and after the Bauer pottery closed, production began at the Harker Pottery Company. Dinnerware was added in 1941. Bauer continued to own the rights to the process and received a royalty. It was made in blue and pink. Several distinct patterns exist in this line, including Dainty Flower, Shell Ware, Virginia, and Zephyr.

The Harker Company used a large variety of backstamps and names. Hotoven cookware featured a scroll, draped over pots, with a kiln design at top. Columbia Chinaware had a circular stamp showing the Statue of Liberty.

Collectors should consider buying Harker patterns by famous designers. Among these are Russel Wright's White Clover and George Bauer's Cameoware. Or an interesting collection could focus on one object, e.g., a sugar or creamer, collected in a variety of patterns from different historical periods. Watch for unusual pieces. The Countryside pattern features a rolling pin, scoop, and cake server.

History: The Harker Company began in 1840 when Benjamin Harker, an English slater turned farmer in East Liverpool, Ohio, built a kiln and began making yellowware products from clay deposits on his land. The business was managed by members of the Harker family until the Civil War, at which time David Boyce, a brother-in-law, took over the operation. Although a Harker resumed management after the war, members of the Boyce family also assumed key roles within the firm; David G. Boyce, a grandson of David, served as president.

In 1879, the first whiteware products were introduced. The company was able to overcome severe financial problems which were caused by a disastrous flood in 1884. In 1931, the company moved to Chester, West Virginia, to escape repeated flooding. In 1945, Harker introduced Cameoware made by the engobe process in which a layered effect was achieved by placing a copper mask over the bisque and then sand blasting to leave the design imprint. The white rose pattern on blue ground was marketed as White Rose CarvKraft in Montgomery Ward stores.

In the 1960s, Harker made a Rockingham ware line which included the hound-handled pitcher and mugs. The Jeannette Glass Company purchased the Harker Company and the plant was closed in March 1972. Ohio Stoneware, Inc., utilized the plant building until it was destroyed by fire in 1975.

References: Susan and Al Bagdade, *Warman's American Pottery and Porcelain,* 2nd ed., Krause Publications, 2000; Neva W. Colbert, *Collector's Guide to Harker Pottery, U.S.A.,* Collector Books, 1993; Jo Cunningham, *Collector's Encyclopedia of American Dinnerware,* Collector Books, 1982, 1998 value update.

Additional Listings: Russel Wright.

Plate, gray border, 8-1/4" d, $3.

Amy

Rolling Pin, 15" l.........................135.00
Scoop, 6" l...................................65.00

Cameo

Bowl, 8" d, Zephyr, blue 18.00
Casserole, cov, square,
blue 50.00
Cheese Box, cov, Zephyr, blue... 44.00
Creamer, Gem, blue 35.00
Cup and Saucer, Shell Ware,
blue 15.00
Dish, lug handle, Shell Ware,
blue 10.00
Jug, cov, pink, 6-1/2" h 60.00
Mixing Bowl, pink, 9" d, mkd "Cameoware by Harker Pottery Co., Patented USA"..36.00
Pie Baker
Cameoware, Pie Baker, pink, 10" d, mkd "Harker Cameoware By Harker Pottery, Patented USA" 45.00
Plate
7-1/2" d, Shell Ware, blue 10.00
9-3/4" d, Virginia, pink 12.00
Platter, blue, 9" x 11-7/8", mkd "Cameoware by Harker Pottery, Patented USA"..............................38.00
Rolling Pin, 15" l, slight wear 150.00
Salad Bowl, 6-1/2" w, square,
blue 15.00
Sugar, Virginia, blue 20.00
Teapot, cov, 4 cup 65.00
Vegetable Bowl, blue, 9" d, mkd "Cameoware by Harker Pottery Co., Patented USA"..............................30.00

Colonial Lady, platter, 12" sq, mkd "Bakerite Oven Tested Made in USA" 30.00

Deco Dahlia

Jug, cov, 7" h 55.00
Stack Set, two bowls and lid, all with slight crazing 58.00

Ivy

Platter, 12" l...................................35.00
Platter, 16" l...................................55.00
Teapot, cov 135.00

Kelvinator, casserole, cov, Hotoven Ware, black bands, white body, emb, ftd, sq finial, some crazing,
7-1/2" d.. 50.00

Mallow

Fork, patent number on back of handle 35.00
Rolling Pin, 15" l 150.00

Monterey

Jug, cov, 5" h 70.00
Jug, cov, 7" h 95.00
Pie Baker, 10" d, mkd "Hotoven Cookingware Harker The Oldest Pottery In America" 65.00

Petit Point Rose

Batter Bowl..................................60.00
Bowl, 8-1/2" d..............................15.00
Cake Plate....................................20.00
Cake Server 15.00
Casserole, cov, quart, platinum trim, heat stain....................................38.00
Coffeepot 45.00
Cup and Saucer 18.00
Dinner Plate, 8-1/2" d..................12.00

Dinner Set, Royal Gadroon, gold edge trim, five 6" d bread and butter plates, six 10-1/4" dinner plates, eight 8" d flat soups, seven saucers, wear 60.00
Pie Baker 20.00
Spoon 20.00
Sugar, cov 15.00

Red Apple

Decal of large red apple and yellow pear on white background. Red band trim.
Cheese Plate, 10" d 24.00
Custard..8.50
Dinner Plate, 10" d 14.00
Fork..25.00
Mixing Bowl, 9" d 30.00
Pie Baker, 9" d 30.00
Range Set, Apple and Pear, Hotoven, 3 pc set 145.00
Rolling Pin, #2 ....150.00
Salad Bowl, 9" d, swirl.................24.00
Spoon 25.00
Utility Tray, 11" l 22.00
Vegetable Bowl, 9" d...................30.00

Tulip

Pitcher, 9" h 95.00
Rolling Pin, 15" l 150.00

Holiday Collectibles

Collecting Hints: Collectors often start with one holiday and eventually branch out and collect all the holidays. Reasonably priced items can still be found—especially items from the 1950s and 1960s.

History: Holidays are an important part of American life. Many have both secular and religious overtones such as Christmas, St. Patrick's Day, Easter, Valentine's Day, and Halloween. National holidays such as the Fourth of July and Thanksgiving are part of one's yearly planning. Collectors usually consider President's Day, Memorial Day, Flag Day, and the Fourth of July as part of the general category of patriotic collectibles.

Each holiday has its own origins and background and owes its current face to a variety of legends, lore, and customs. Holiday decorations were popularized by German cottage industries at the turn of the century. Germany dominated the holiday market until the 1920s, when Japan began producing holiday items. Both countries lost their place during World War II and U.S. manufacturers filled the American appetite for holiday decorations.

Reference: Lissa Bryan-Smith and Richard Smith, *Holiday Collectibles,*

Vintage Flea Market Treasures Price Guide, Krause Publications, 1998; Charlene Pinkerton, *Holiday Plastic Novelties: The Styrene Toys,* Schiffer Publishing, 1999; Pamela Apkarian-Russell, *Halloween Collectible Decorations and Games,* Schiffer Publishing, 2000.

Periodicals: *BooNews,* P.O. Box 143, Brookfield, IL 60513; *Trick or Treat Trader,* P.O. Box 499, Winchester, NH 03470.

Reproduction Alert.

Additional Listings: Christmas Items, Flag Collectibles, Patriotic Collectibles, Santa Claus, Valentines.

Advisors: Lissa Bryan-Smith and Richard Smith.

Easter

Candle
Easter Bunny holding up top hat, mkd "Gurley Novelty Co.," 3-1/2" h.... 10.00
Easter Lily, green base, white and yellow flower, paper label on base, mkd "Gurley Novelty Co.," 3" 5.00
Rabbit, sitting, off-white, mkd "Tavern Novelty Co.," 5" h, 4" dia 10.00
Candy Container
Birdhouse, cardboard covered with papier-mâché, two cotton batting chicks on top of the house and one in the opening of the birdhouse, cardboard eggs in front of the house, mkd "Nippon," box for candy at the base of the house, 1910-20, 5" h, 4" dia.. 70.00
Chick couple, hard plastic, male chick pink with green tie and top hat, female chick yellow with red hat, opening in their backs for candy, 3-1/2" h.... 12.00
Easter Bunny dressed like cowboy, hard plastic, pulling "wood-look" cart, 1950s, yellow and blue, 13" l...... 22.00
Easter Bunny riding rocket on wheels, hard plastic, pink, blue and yellow, hole in top of rabbit's head for lollipops, 4".. 40.00
Egg and chick, papier-mâché, blue half eggshell with yellow chick coming out of top, 1940s, USA, 5-1/4" h . 55.00
Egg Birdhouse, papier-mâché, yellow egg bird house with orange cardboard roof, mkd "Easter Greetings," script, chicks and flowers all embossed paper attached to birdhouse, mkd "Germany," 7" h, 11" dia............95.00
Rabbit, cotton batting with pink paper ears and pink composition eyes, holding orange cotton batting carrot attached to green reed basket that held candy, mkd "Japan," 4" h ... 35.00
Rabbit, crouching on all fours, papier-mâché, removable head for storage of candy, mkd "Made in Germany, U.S. Zone," 4" x 4" 45.00
Rabbit, molded, crouching with basket on back, papier-mâché, basket colored green, rabbit white with pink highlights, basket is opening for candy, 1940s, USA, 9" l x 5" h..... 65.00

Rabbit, sitting, side view, glass, paper bottom mkd "Peter Rabbit, J.H. Millstein Co.," pressed in glass, mkd "MFG. By J.H. millstein Co., Jeannette, PA – PAT APP FOR," 6-1/4" h 68.00

Rabbit, standing, papier-mâché, white with beading, each ear and head attached with springs, pipe cleaner paws, felt eyes, 1960s, body opens to hold candy, mkd "Made in Western Germany," 11" h..........................38.00

Card Game, Little Grey Rabbit, original box, 44 cards and instruction page, 1940s 22.00

Decoration, cardboard and tissue paper honeycomb, unfolds to set-up, rabbit sitting among lilacs, surrounded by honeycomb eggs and basket, USA, 8-1/2" l 20.00

Egg
Cardboard, violets dec, gold Dresden trim, Germany, 3" l 25.00
Milk Glass, white, gilded lettering "Easter Greetings," painted purple spring flowers, 6" 45.00

Figure
Chick, chenille, paper covered wire feet, paper label attached to foot mkd "Made in Occupied Japan," 1" h ..5.00
Rabbit, chalk, standing, white with pink tipped ears, mkd "Japan," 3-1/2" h..6.00
Rabbit couple, papier-mâché, separate at waist to hold candy, male figure wearing felt jacket and pants, female rabbit wearing felt dress and bandana, 1940s, mkd "Occupied Germany," 7-1/2" h......................450.00

Greeting Card, stand-up
Boy, "All signs point to a Happy Easter," green tissue paper honeycomb base, USA, 7-1/2" h 5.00
Girl, "To Wish you a Happy Easter," yellow tissue paper honeycomb skirt, USA, 7" h.....................................5.00

Handkerchief, child's, yellow cotton with scalloped purple border, decorated with duck family dressed for an Easter Parade, 1950s, 9-1/2" sq 4.00

Postcard
A Peaceful Easter, girl and rabbit looking at Easter eggs, 1911 ....5.00
Easter Greeting, Victorian child cradling rabbit with a nest of colored eggs at her feet, mkd "Series D, No 12," Germany 3.00

Rattle, rabbit, hard plastic, mkd "Irwin"
4" h, pink with blue jacket and holding a blue carrot, dancing 4.00
6" h, pink with blue overalls, standing 8.00

Toy
Musical Easter Basket, cardboard, plastic handle, orig box, mkd "Mattel, 1952," 4" x 6"............................65.00
Rabbit pushing egg buggy with chick, celluloid, VCO trademark .....,......75.00

Halloween, cat lantern, cardboard with paper, minor imperfections, 7" d, $90.

Halloween

Candle
Cat, orange and black, holding pumpkin and tipping hat, mkd on base "Gurley Novelty Co.," 3-1/2" h 5.00
Cat sitting on fence, orange and black, mkd on base "Gurley Novelty Co.," 3-1/2 h 5.00

Candy Box, cov, 5" x 7", yellow and black..8.00

Candy Box Label 3.00

Candy Container
3" h, pressed cardboard black cat head, cutout eyes and mouth, wire handle, Germany 60.00
3" h, 7" l, papier-mâché witch's black shoe, opens on bottom............ 200.00
4" h, painted glass pumpkin, scary face, wire handle, metal screw-on lid 125.00
7" h, papier-mâché pumpkin, cutout eyes and mouth with tissue paper, wire handle, candleholder in base, Germany......................................85.00

Clicker, litho tin, orange and black, frog shape, mkd "T. Cohn, USA" 7.50

Costume, Battling Bunny, child's size, bunny wearing boxing gloves, cloth mask, sateen cloth costume, litho trim, 1940s..20.00

Decoration
Pumpkin man, cardboard, 1960s, jointed arms and legs, jack o'lantern head and body, mkd "Beistle Co.," 29" h..22.00
Set of eight cardboard figures, orig pkg, Beistle Co, mkd "One Assortment of 6 Decorations—Halloween Stand-ups," range in size from 7" to 10-1/2" 40.00

Favor, 4" h, horn, orange celluloid, black stenciled witch, VCO 45.00

Figure
2 3/4" h, cat 15.00
3-1/8" h, cat, hard plastic, jack o'lantern on back...................................22.00
4" h, celluloid witch sitting on moon 345.00
5" h, hard plastic scarecrow with pumpkin head..............................12.00

5-1/4" h, cat, hard plastic, standing with paws on hips, wearing tee shirt, orange, black and green, pouch in back for lollipops..........................50.00
9" h, cardboard black cat, flat, moveable legs and tail, Beistle Co., USA..20.00

Hat, cardboard and crepe paper, Germany
4" h, black and orange...............17.50
10" h, black and orange, gold and black cardboard band................25.00

Horn
8" h, paper, orange and black, wood mouthpiece, Germany 12.00
9" h, cardboard, orange and black, cat, witch, and moon litho figures, USA..15.00

Magazine Cover, *Companion,* October, 1944, black cat standing on pumpkin, 10-3/4" x 13-3/4" 10.00

Mask
Boy, papier-mâché, painted face, cloth ties, stamped "Germany" 35.00
Devil, rubber, red, black, and white, rubber ties 18.00
Duck, buckram, molded bill, cloth ties..30.00

Noisemaker
Pressed cardboard and wood, pickle, mouthpiece, 1920-30s, Germany......................................60.00
Tin, litho, long black handle, round rattle, three litho pumpkin heads, mkd "Made in USA, TC," 9" l..............15.00

Postcard
Girl scared by pumpkin in mirror, Raphael Tuck....................................20.00
The Witch's Dance, postmarked 1909, witch dancing with pumpkin man, mkd Germany......................................15.00
Witch riding broom.......................10.00

Pumpkin, 6" d, metal 35.00

Roly Poly, 3" h, celluloid, black cat, VCO trademark 85.00

Scrap Picture, 6" x 9," cats 35.00

Spoon, child's, bowl depicts witch and cat on broom, handle engraved "Victoria Louise," sterling silver, Mechanics Sterling Co. 200.00

String Holder, winking witch, pumpkin....................................125.00

Tambourine, 6" d, metal 35.00

Toy, 2 3/4" h, witch driving pumpkin vehicle, celluloid, VCO......................90.00

Trick or Treat Bag, brown, litho picture of children trick or treating, 11" x 9" .. 4.00

St. Patrick's Day

Candy Box, 8-1/2" h, green cardboard shamrock....................................18.00

Candy Container
3" h, green and gold cardboard hat, base label "Loft Candy Corp"......25.00
4" l, brown pressed cardboard potato, velvet green and gold shamrock, Germany......................................45.00
4-1/2" h, composition Irish Girl, holding harp, standing on box, Germany....................................75.00

Figure
4" l, green flocked composition pig, Germany....................................50.00

6" h, composition man, green felt coat, spring legs, beer stein.................65.00
7" h, celluloid leprechaun, holding pig, Japan...32.00
Magazine Cover, *Life,* March 15, 1923, cherub wearing Irish hat, playing harp...15.00
Nodder, 3" h, bisque Irish boy, Germany.......................................45.00
Postcard
  Ireland Forever, scenes of Ireland, shamrock, green, and gold...........4.00
  On March 17 May You Be Seen A Wearing Of The Green, Irish man standing on "17," Quality Cards, The A. M. Davis Co., Boston, 1912..4.50
Shamrock, 2-1/2" l, green silk floss-wrapped wire, small bisque hat attached to center.........................5.00

Thanksgiving

Advertisement, Pepsi, 1956, woman and man carving turkey in very 1950s setting, 11" x 14"...............................10.00
Bank, chalkware, turkey, tan, red and yellow, 1950s, USA, 11" h.................85.00
Calendar, framed, November, 1933, from *St. Nicholas Magazine,* 8" x 12" ..25.00
Candle
  Swirl candle, autumn leaves and acorns, mkd "Gurley Novelty Co.," 7" h...5.00
  Turkey, iridescent green and purple, paper label, 4-1/2" h.......................7.00
Candy Container, turkey, wax, white, Fanny Farmer Candy, orig box ...25.00
Decoration, honeycomb tissue paper, table top decoration, two sided lithographed cardboard turkey, mkd USA, 8-1/2" h..15.00
Figure, turkey
  Bisque, green base, mkd Japan, 1" h...7.00
  Chalk, green base, black, white and red, USA, 2-1/4" h........................12.00
  Papier-mâché, cardboard bottom, mkd "Western Germany," 4" h 25.00
Greeting Card, The Mayflower, With Joyful Thanksgiving Wishes....................8.00
Place Card Holder, 2-1/2" h, standing celluloid turkey, holder at base of metal spring legs....................................20.00
Postcard
  A Joyous Thanksgiving, boy carving pumpkin, 1913.................................5.00
  I don't care, that turkey was good while I was eating it, pictures two girls one holding her stomach sitting by empty plate, 1917 postmark, USA...3.00
  Thanksgiving Greetings, boy sitting on fence feeding turkey, 1928 postmark, USA...4.00
Seals, turkeys, orig pkg, Dennison, 12 seals and envelopes.....................3.00

Holt-Howard Collectibles

Collecting Hints: Here is a collecting area that's so hot with collectors, the prices are changing even as the ink is drying on this page. Remember that *Warman's* is a *price guide,* intended to help you determine a fair price. In the instance of Holt-Howard collectibles, we've tried to present accurate prices. So, if you find a great piece at a slightly higher price, that's terrific and if you find one for less than what we've got listed, even better. The whole field of 1950s-'60s ceramics is quite hot right now, with collectors enjoying novelty pieces.

Holt-Howard pieces were marked with an ink-stamp. Many were also copyright dated. Some pieces were marked only with a foil sticker, especially the small pieces, where a stamp mark was too difficult. Four types of foil stickers have been identified.

History: Three young entrepreneurs, Grant Holt and brothers John and Robert Howard, started Holt-Howard from their apartment in Manhattan, in 1949. All three of the partners were great salesman, but product development was handled by Robert, while John managed sales. Grant was in charge of financial affairs and office management. By 1955, operations were large enough to move the company to Connecticut, but they still maintained their New York showroom and later added a showroom in Los Angeles. Production facilities eventually expanded to Holt-Howard Canada; Holt-Howard West, Holt-Howard International.

Their first successful line was Angel-Abra, followed closely by their Christmas line. This early success spurred the partners to expand their wares. Their line of Christmas and kitchen-related giftware was popular with 1950s' consumers. Probably the most famous line was Pixieware, which began production in 1958. Production of these whimsical pieces continued until the 1960s. Other lines, such as Cozy Kittens and Merry Mouse brought even more smiles as they invaded homes in many forms. One thing that remained constant with all Holt-Howard products was a high quality of materials and workmanship, innovation, and good design.

The founders of this unique company sold their interests to General Housewares Corp. in 1968, where it became part of the giftware group. By 1974, the three original partners had left the firm. By 1990, what remained of Holt-Howard was sold to Kay Dee Designs of Rhode Island.

Reference: Walter Dworkin, *Price Guide to Holt-Howard Collectibles and Related Ceramicwares of the '50s and '60s,* Krause Publications, 1998.

Advisor: Walter Dworkin.

Christmas

Air Freshener, Girl Christmas Tree...65.00
Ashtray/Cigarette Holder, Starry-eyed Santa...45.00
Bell, Elf Girl, pr..............................55.00
Candle Climbers, Ole Snowy, snowman, set......................................48.00
Candle Holders
  Camels.......................................38.00
  Christmas Tree, set of six.......38.00
  Elf Girls, NOEL, set of four.....38.00
  Ermine Angels, snowflake rings, set..48.00
  Reindeer, pr...............................38.00
  Santa King.................................85.00
  Totem Pole, Santa....................25.00
  Wee Three Kings, set of 3......60.00
Cookie Jar, pop-up, Santa.........150.00
Cookie Jar/Candy Jar Combination, Santa...155.00
Creamer and Sugar
  Reindeer.....................................48.00
  Winking Santa...........................55.00
Head Vase, My Fair Lady...........75.00
Letter and Pen Holder, Sana...55.00
Napkin Holder, Santa, 4"...........25.00
Pitcher and Mug Set, Winking Santa...70.00
Planter
  Camel...40.00
  Elf Girl in Sleigh.......................58.00
  Ermine Angel.............................38.00
Punch Bowl Set, punch bowl and eight mugs, Santa.............................145.00
Salt and Pepper Shakers, pr
  Cloud Santa...............................38.00
  Holly Girls.................................20.00
  Rock 'N' Roll Santas, on springs.......................................75.00
  Snow Babies..............................35.00
  Winking Santa...........................38.00
Salt and Pepper Shakers, pr, and NOEL candleholder, sterling silver, set..95.00
Server, divided tray, Santa King .55.00
Wall Pocket, Santa ornament......58.00

Cozy Kittens

Bud Vase, pr..............................105.00
Butter Dish, cov.........................105.00
Cookie Jar, pop-up....................250.00
Cottage Cheese Crock..............60.00
Kitty Catch Clip............................38.00
Match Dandy..............................75.00
Memo Minder...............................90.00
Meow Mug....................................35.00
Meow Oil and Vinegar...............175.00
Mustard Condiment Jar............180.00
Powdered Cleanser....................70.00
Salt and Pepper Shakers, pr......20.00
Spice Set..................................110.00
Spoon Rest.................................75.00
String Holder..............................45.00

Sugar Pour 85.00
Totem Pole Stacking Seasons 65.00

Jeeves, butler

Ashtray 70.00
Chip Dish 80.00
Liquor Decanter 165.00
Martini Shaker Set 195.00
Olives Condiment Jar 135.00

Merry Mouse

Cocktail Kibitzers Mice, set of
six 120.00
Corner Coaster Ashtray 55.00
Crock, "Stinky Cheese" 50.00
Desk Pen Pal 85.00
Match Mouse 70.00
Salt and Pepper Shakers, pr 40.00

Miscellaneous

Ashtray
  Golfer Image 110.00
  Li'l Old Lace 50.00
Bank, bobbing
  Coin Closn 135.00
  Dandy Lion 135.00
Bud Vase, Daisy Dorable 70.00
Candelabra, Li'l Old Lace, spiral 50.00
Candle Climbers, Honey Bunnies, with
bases, set 85.00
Candle Rings, Ballerina, set 48.00
Cookie Jar, pop-up, Clown 225.00
Salt and Pepper Shakers with Napkin
Holder, Winking Wabbits 60.00
Salt and Pepper Shakers, pr
  Bell Bottom Gobs (sailors) 50.00
  Bunnies in baskets 32.00
  Chattercoons, Peppy and
  Salty 38.00
  Daisy Doodles, ponytail
  girls 40.00
  Goose' N' Golden Egg 35.00
  Lovebirds, yellow 40.00
  Pink cat, white poodle 35.00
  Rock' N' Doll Kids, on
  springs 75.00

Red Rooster, "Coq Rouge"

Butter Dish, cov 65.00
Candle Holders, pr 30.00
Cereal Bowl 15.00
Coffee Mug 14.00
Coffee Server, 36 oz 65.00
Cookie Jar 100.00
Creamer and Sugar 55.00
Dinner Plate 18.00
Egg Cup 20.00
Electric Coffee Pot, 6 cups 70.00
Mustard Condiment Jar 55.00
Pitcher
  12 oz 45.00
  32 oz 60.00
  48 oz 75.00
Salt and Pepper Shakers, pr,
4-1/2" 25.00
Snack Tray 18.00
Spoon Rest 25.00
Wooden
  Canister Set, 4 pc 85.00
  Cigarette Carton Holder 45.00
  Recipe Box 70.00
  Salt and Pepper Shakers, pr .. 23.00

Homer Laughlin

Collecting Hints: The original 1871 to 1890 trademark used the term "Laughlin Brothers." The next trademark featured the American eagle astride the prostrate British lion. The third mark, which featured the "HLC" monogram, has appeared, with slight variations, on all dinnerware since about 1900. The 1900 version included a number that identified month, year, and plant at which the product was made. Letter codes were used in later periods.

So much attention has been given to Fiesta that other interesting Homer Laughlin patterns have not achieved the popularity which they deserve, and prices for these less-recognized patterns are still moderate. Some of the patterns made during the 1930s and 1940s have highly artistic contemporary designs.

Virginia Rose is not a pattern name but a shape on which several different decals were used. Delicate pink flowers are the most common.

History: Homer Laughlin and his brother, Shakespeare, built two pottery kilns in East Liverpool, Ohio, in 1871. Shakespeare resigned in 1879, leaving Homer to operate the business alone. Laughlin became one of the first firms to produce American-made whiteware. In 1896, William Wills and a Pittsburgh group led by Marcus Aaron bought the Laughlin firm.

Expansion followed. Two new plants were built in Laughlin Station, Ohio. In 1906, the first Newall, West Virginia, plant (#4) was built in. Plant #6, which was built at Newall in 1923, featured a continuous-tunnel kiln. Similar kilns were added at the other plants. Other advances instituted by the company include spray glazing and mechanical jiggering.

Between 1930 and 1960, several new dinnerware lines were added, including the Wells Art Glaze line. Ovenserve and Kitchen Kraft were cookware products. The colored-glaze lines of Fiesta, Harlequin, and Rhythm captured major market shares. In 1959, a translucent table china line was introduced. Today, the annual manufacturing capacity is more than 45 million pieces.

References: Susan and Al Bagdade, *Warman's American Pottery and Porcelain,* 2nd ed., Krause Publications, 2000; Jo Cunningham,

Collector's Encyclopedia of American Dinnerware, Collector Books, 1982, 1998 value update; —, *Homer Laughlin, A Giant Among Dishes, 1973-1939,* Schiffer, 1998; —, *Homer Laughlin China: 1940s & 1950s,* Schiffer Publishing, 2000; Bob and Sharon Huxford, *Collector's Encyclopedia of Fiesta with Harlequin and Riviera,* 9th ed., Collector Books, 2000; Joanne Jasper, *Collector's Encyclopedia of Homer Laughlin China,* Collector Books, 1993, 2000 value update; Richard G. Racheter, *Collector's Guide to Homer Laughlin's Virginia Rose,* Collector Books, 1997.

Periodicals: *Fiesta Collectors Quarterly,* 19238 Dorchester Circle, Strongsville, OH 44136; Laughlin Eagle, 1270 63rd Terrace S., St. Petersburg, FL 33705.

Reproduction Alert: Harlequin and Fiesta lines were reissued in 1978 and marked accordingly.

Additional Listings: Fiesta.

Hen on nest, bisque, 11" l, 7-1/2" h, chip on base, $360. Photo courtesy of Joy Luke Fine Art Brokers and Auctioneers.

American Provincial, Rhythm shape

  Berry Bowl 4.00
  Bread and Butter Plate 5.00
  Cereal Bowl 8.00
  Luncheon Plate, 8" d 8.00
  Platter 16.00

Amsterdam, Nautilus shape, creamer
and sugar 24.00

Best China

  Bread and Butter Plate, 6-1/4" d ... 4.50
  Coffee Mug 5.00
  Cup 3.50
  Dinner Plate, 10-1/2" d 3.25
  Platter, 9" x 11-1/2" 5.00
  Salad Plate, 7-1/4" d 5.00
  Saucer 4.00

Brittany Majestic, Nautilus Eggshell, sugar, cov..............12.00

Calendar Plate, 1953, zodiac symbols..............25.00

Cavalier

Cup and Saucer 10.00
Dinnerware Set, service for 4, plus serving pieces..............80.00
Platter, 13" x 11-1/4"..............6.00

Georgian, eggshell, platter, 10-3/4" x 13-1/2", J40N5, wear..............15.00

Harlequin

Baker, oval, spruce 22.00
Berry Bowl
　Maroon..............6.50
　Spruce 6.00
　Turquoise 6.00
　Yellow 6.50
Candlestick, red 195.00
Creamer, individual size
　Mauve..............23.00
　Orange..............20.00
　Spruce..............25.00
Cream Soup
　Mauve..............22.00
　Orange..............22.00
Cup, rose..............6.50
Cup and Saucer
　Spruce 10.00
　Yellow..............10.00
Deep Plate
　Gray..............45.00
　Mauve..............28.00
　Medium Green..............95.00
　Turquoise 22.00
Dinner Plate, 10" d, mauve..............15.00
Eggcup, double
　Chartreuse..............20.00
　Gray..............24.50
　Maroon..............22.00
　Rose..............24.50
Eggcup, single
　Maroon..............30.00
　Mauve 25.00
　Orange..............25.00
Nappy, 9" d
　Turquoise 18.50
　Yellow..............18.50
Nut Dish
　Mauve 15.00
　Orange..............15.00
　Rose..............20.00
　Spruce 15.00
Platter
　11" l, maroon..............18.00
　13" l, oval, rose 13.00
Relish Insert
　Maroon..............50.00
　Mauve..............75.00
　Red 35.00
　Rose..............90.00
　Yellow..............75.00
Relish Tray, turquoise base, yellow, red, mauve, and turquoise inserts..............495.00
Salad Bowl, individual
　Chartreuse..............45.00
　Light Green..............45.00
　Mauve 45.00

Medium Green..............175.00
Yellow..............25.00
Salt and Pepper Shakers, pr
　Gray..............10.00
　Maroon..............10.00
　Mauve 8.00
　Yellow 12.00
Sauceboat, rose..............15.00

Kitchen Kraft

Cake Server, cobalt blue..............145.00
Casserole, cov, individual
　Cobalt Blue..............200.00
　Light Green..............150.00
　Red..............255.00
　Yellow..............110.00
Casserole, cov, 7 1/2" d, cobalt blue..............70.00
Casserole, cov, 8 1/2" h, yellow...65.00
Cream Soup Bowl, double handle, pink..............6.00
Fork
　Cobalt Blue..............150.00
　Light Green..............85.00
Mixing Bowl, 6" d, red..............110.00
Mixing Bowl, 8" d, green..............120.00
Pie Baker, cobalt blue, 10" d..............32.00
Platter, green..............38.00
Refrigerator Unit, yellow and light green, stacking each..............44.00
Salt and Pepper Shakers, pr, red..............93.50
Spoon, red..............95.00

Magnolia, plate, gold trim, 6-1/4"......6.00

Marigold

Creamer and Sugar 20.00
Cup and Saucer..............11.50
Dinner Plate, 10" d..............18.00
Luncheon Plate, 9-1/4" d..............12.50
Platter, 13-1/2" x 10-7/8"..............30.00
Soup Bowl, 8-1/4" d..............18.00
Vegetable Bowl, 8-1/2" d..............25.00

Mexicana

Baker, oval 25.00
Batter Jug, cov..............80.00
Bowl, 5" d 20.00
Cake Server 30.00
Creamer 20.00
Cup and Saucer..............15.00
Dinner Plate, 9" d 15.00
Fruit Bowl, individual..............18.00
Jar, cov, orig paper label 90.00
Nappy..............25.00
Pie Baker..............35.00
Soup, flat 24.00

Nautilus, plate, 9-1/4" d, eggshell....8.00

Oven Serve, Handy Andy, 8" cream colored bowl, red and platinum lines, chrome holder, black handles........45.00

Priscilla

Cup and Saucer..............8.00
Dinner Plate..............10.00
Gravy Boat 12.00
Mixing Bowl, 8-1/4" d 36.00
Vegetable Bowl, divided..............18.00

Rhythm

Bread and Butter Plate, 6" d, yellow..............6.50

Creamer, gray..............8.50
Gravy Boat, gray..............12.00
Sauce Boat, chartreuse 7.50
Vegetable Bowl, 9" l, chartreuse 8.00

Rhythm Rose

Pie Baker, 9-1/2" d..............28.00
Soup Bowl, 8-1/4" d, coupe shape..............48.00

Riviera

Baker, oval, ivory 15.00
Bowl, 5-1/2" d, ivory..............8.00
Bread and Butter Plate, 6" d
　Ivory..............6.00
　Light green 10.00
　Red 12.00
Butter Dish, cov, 1/4 lb, Century
　Green , ivory or red..............225.00
　Turquoise..............315.00
Casserole, cov
　Green..............125.00
　Ivory..............125.00
　Mauve..............110.00
　Red..............125.00
Creamer, blue or ivory..............9.00
Cup
　Blue..............7.50
　Green..............7.50
　Ivory..............7.50
　Light Green..............12.00
　Red..............8.50
　Yellow..............8.00
Demitasse Cup and Saucer, Century, ivory 95.00
Dinner Plate, 9" d
　Blue..............15.00
　Green..............15.00
　Ivory..............12.00
　Red..............18.00
　Yellow..............18.00
Juice Pitcher, yellow..............185.00
Juice Tumbler
　Green..............85.00
　Ivory..............95.00
　Mauve..............95.00
　Red..............95.00
　Turquoise..............95.00
　Yellow..............85.00
Nappy
　Green..............20.00
　Mauve..............25.00
　Red..............25.00
　Yellow..............20.00
Oatmeal Bowl, Century
　Green..............65.00
　Ivory..............65.00
　Yellow..............65.00
Platter
　Ivory..............12.00
　Yellow..............22.00
Soup Plate, flat, red..............32.00
Saucer
　Green..............3.00
　Ivory..............3.00
　Yellow..............5.00
Sugar, cov
　Green..............10.00
　Ivory..............10.00
　Red..............20.00
Tumbler, handle, Century
　Green..............55.00
　Mauve..............75.00
　Red..............95.00

Silver Patrician, Virginia Rose

    Bowl, 8-1/2" d..............................25.00
    Cup and Saucer..........................10.00
    Dinner Plate, 10" d......................15.00
    Platter, 9-3/4" x 11-3/4"..............25.00
    Platter, 11-1/4" x 13-1/4"...........25.00
    Salad Plate, 8" d.........................18.00
    Saucer...5.00
    Tray, 6" x 9-1/2".........................37.50
    Vegetable Bowl, 7-1/4" x 10".......27.50

Skytone Stardust, coffeepot..........40.00

Song of Spring, bowl, 6-1/2" x 9" oval,
1929 Sears..18.00

Virginia Rose

    Baker, oval, 8" l..........................20.00
    Butter, cov, jade.........................75.00
    Creamer and Sugar, cov.............35.00
    Cup and Saucer............................4.00
    Dinner Plate, 9" d.........................8.50
    Fruit Bowl, 5-1/2" d......................5.00
    Mixing Bowl, large.......................48.00
    Nappy, 10" d...............................20.00
    Pie Baker....................................25.00
    Platter, 13".................................25.00
    Soup Bowl...................................20.00
    Tray, handles...............................25.00
    Vegetable, cov............................45.00

Horse Collectibles

Collecting Hints: The hottest area in equine memorabilia continues to be figures. Early Breyer plastic horse figures are especially sought after. You can tell the early models by their glossy finish, although those with faux wood-grain finish or the unrealistic Wedgewood blue or Florentine gold "decorator" finish are harder to find. Breyers are designed by artists familiar with equine anatomy and are as close as possible as the "real thing." Hartland horses remain popular, especially those representing Western movie and television characters, like Roy Rogers and Trigger or Dale Evans and Buttermilk. Historical characters, especially General Robert E. Lee on his horse, Traveler, are in demand as well. The ears of plastic figures are especially vulnerable, so check the ear tips. Paint rubs greatly reduce the value of plastic model horses.

Ceramic figurines, whether of English origin like Wades and Beswick, German like Goebel, or American manufacture like Hagen-Renaker of California, remain a strong part of the market. Well-detailed ceramic Japanese horse figures made in the 1950s and 1960s have risen in popularity and price. Check ceramic figures carefully for chips, cracks and repairs, especially on legs and tails.

There are few categories of collecting that do not feature some sort of equine image. Advertising featuring the horse has always been popular, especially early memorabilia featuring the famous trotter Dan Patch. Saddle and tack catalogs, Wild West show posters, movie posters, and even Anheuser-Busch advertising featuring its beloved Clydesdale team are all avidly collected by horse lovers.

Kentucky Derby glass prices have leveled off somewhat, except for examples from the 1950s and before. The 1941-44 beetleware (an early plastic) continue to bring thousands of dollars. Carousel horses remain a high-ticket item, but beware of imported hand-carved imitations. These are well done and nice as a decorator item, but don't be fooled into paying the price demanded of a Mueller, Loof or Denzel figure. It is best to find these figures at auctions where you can obtain a written guarantee of their origin.

Horse-drawn toys, whether cast iron or lithographed tin, seem to be a real bargain these days, especially when compared with automobile toys of the same era. Their performance at auctions and sales is just starting to improve, and they still provide a nice, affordable find for the horse enthusiast. The most popular horse-drawn toys remain the circus vehicles, an attraction for circus collectors along with horse lovers. Do be careful buying cast iron, as many of the vehicles have been reproduced. Gaudy paint, ill-fitting parts, and a surface that feels rough to the touch should cause the warning lights to flash. Reproductions are worth maybe $25 as a decorative item, but have no value as a collectible. If you are not sure, it is best to do all your buying from a dealer that you trust.

Collectors are also drawn to equine relatives, especially mules and burros. With the current popularity of Winnie the Pooh memorabilia, everyone from toddlers to grannies want anything featuring Pooh's self-deprecating donkey friend, Eeyore.

History: Horses are not indigenous to the United States, but were brought here by various means. The wild horses of the American Southwest are descended from Spanish Mustangs brought here by the Conquistadors. Later, English stock would arrive with the settlers on the East Coast, where they were used for farming and transportation and even as a food source. In those days, a person's social status was determined by the quantity and quality of the horses he owned. Remember the condescending phrase, "one-horse town?"

Daily life in the early days of the United States would have been much harder on humans were it not for the horse. They were used for transportation of products, pulling plows on farms, rushing a country doctor to his patients and later, for recreational sports like racing and rodeo. Even in the early days of the automobile, horse drawn tankers normally transported gasoline to the local service station from the distributor.

As our means of transportation gradually shifted from the horse to automobiles, trains and airplanes, the horse was no longer a necessity to folks, especially those living in cities and suburbs. Today, horses still earn their keep by rounding up stray cattle, looking for lost people in remote areas, and in competition. For the most part, today's horses are pampered family pets living a sheltered life that the hard-working draft animal of the 1800s could only dream about.

References: Felicia Browell, *Breyer Animal Collector's Guide,* 2nd ed., Collector Books, 2000; Nancy Kelly, *Hagen-Renaker Pottery: Horses and Other Figurines,* Schiffer Publishing, 2000; Gayle Roller, *The Charlton Standard Catalogue of Hagen-Renaker,* Charlton Press, 1999; Jim and Nancy Schaut, *Horsin' Around,* L-W Books, 1990.

Periodicals: *Carousel News and Trader,* 87 Park Avenue W., Suite 206, Mansfield OH 44902; *The Beswick Quarterly,* 7525 W Bernill Rd, Spokane, WA 99208; *The Equine Image,* P.O. Box 916, Ft. Dodge, IA 50501; *The Glass Menagerie,* 5440 El Arbol, Carlsbad CA 92008

Museums: Aiken Thoroughbred Racing Hall of Fame & Museum, Aiken, SC; American Quarter Horse Heritage Center and Museum, Kerrville, TX; American Work Horse Museum, Peaonian Springs, VA; Appaloosa Museum and Heritage Center, Moscow, ID; Gene Autry Western Heritage Museum, Los Angeles, CA; Harness Racing Hall of Fame, Goshen, NY; International Museum of the Horse, Lexington, KY; Kentucky Derby Museum, Louisville KY; Pony Express National Memorial, St. Joseph MO; Roy Rogers Museum, Victorville, CA, Trotting Horse Museum, Goshen, NY.

Advisors: Jim and Nancy Schaut.

Cookie cutter, aluminum, green handle, $4.50.

Horse Equipment and Related Items

Bells
    8" l metal strap, 4 graduated cast bells affixed, attaches to wagon or sleigh shaft..125.00
    84" l leather strap, 40 identical nickel bells, strap shows wear, tug hook 200.00

Bit
    Calvary, Civil War era, "US" spots at cheeks.....................................200.00
    Eagle figure, mkd "G.S. Garcia".......................................950.00
    Silver overlay, floral design, mkd "Crockett"....................................125.00

Blanket
    Canvas with straps, 1930s...........75.00
    Carriage robe, buffalo 875.00
    Saddle, Navajo weaving, early 1900s, some wear 750.00

Bridle
    Calvary, mule bridle, brass "US" spots 225.00
    Horsehair, woven, prison made.......................................2,500.00

Bridle Rosette
    Brass, military, eagle motif 50.00
    Glass with rose motif inside, mkd "Chapman" 40.00

Brush, Calvary, stamped "US," patent date 1850, Herbert Brush Mfg. Co., never used 95.00

Catalog
    Chicago, 1929, polo saddles and equipment....................................75.00
    Kelly Brothers, 1960s, bits, spurs, etc. 60.00

Collar, draft horse, leather-covered wood, brass trim 150.00

Curry Comb, tin back, leather handle, early 1900s 45.00

Harness Decorations (Horse Brasses)
    Lion, rampant in center, England.......................................40.00
    Rearing horse in center, backstamped "England".....................................55.00

Hobbles, chain and leather, sideline type...150.00

Hoof Pick, bone handle, Wastenholm, Germany, patent date 1885 ....55.00

Horse-Drawn Vehicle
    Creators Popcorn Wagon, unrestored 7,500.00
    Stagecoach, Half-scale detailed, excellent condition.................3,500.00
    Watkins Products Delivery Wagon, restored 2,500.00

Horsehide rug, 48" by 72", black & white 250.00

Lasso
    Braided rawhide, Mexican reata...250.00
    Horsehair..................................175.00

Mane and Tail Comb, Oliver Slant Tooth, 1940s..40.00

Newspaper, Horse & Stable Weekly, Boston, Jan. 2, 1891 ....35.00

Saddle, McClelland military type, large fenders, early 1990s 950.00

Spurs, Buermann, star mark and "Hercules Bronze," old leathers.......450.00

Stud Book
    American Quarter Horse Stud Book and Registry, 1959.....................50.00
    Palomino Progress, Stud Book & Registry, 1966 ....75.00

Wagon Seat, springs, padded seat, replaced leather upholstery 250.00

Watering Trough, hollowed-out log, tin liner, 2' by 72" 225.00

Print, color lithograph, two horses, blue ground, orange and yellow details, pencil signed by artist Lebandang, numbered "92/120," 14" x 24" image size, $50. Photo courtesy of David Rago Auctions.

Horse Theme Items

Bank, Ertl, horse and tank wagon, Texaco adv..50.00

Blanket, brown and tan wool, Roy Rogers and Trigger, 1950s, twin size.... 350.00

Book
    American Trotting and Pacing Horses, Henry V. Coats, 1st ed., 1902, 8 volumes 400.00
    Boots and Saddles, or Life in Dakota with General Custer, Elizabeth B. Custer, 1995 ....38.00
    Horse Power-A History of the Horse and Donkey in Human Societies, Brock...38.00
    The Black Stallion, Walter Farley, 1st ed., dust jacket 25.00
    The Horse in Art, John Baskett, NY Graphic Society, Boston, 1980....50.00

Understanding and Training Horses, James Ricci, 1964........................9.50

Calendar, 1907, cardboard, Dousman Milling, cowgirl and horse...........75.00

Carousel Horse, jumper, flag on side, C. W. Parker, American, 1918 ....6,500.00

Catalog, D. F. Mangels Carousel Works, Coney Island, NY, 28 pages, 1918..300.00

Clock, United, brass horse, Western saddle, wood base...........................125.00

Cookie Cutter, prancing horse, bobtail, flat back, 6-1/2" by 7-1/2" 75.00

Cookie Jar, McCoy, Circus Horse....50.00

Decanter, Man O'War, Ezra Brooks .25.00

Decanter, Avon, brown glass thorobred....................................10.00

Doorstop, racehorse, stamped "Virginia Metalcrafters," 1949..................195.00

Fan, Moxie advertising, rocking horse, 1920s...55.00

Figure
    Beswick, reclining foal, 3", brown, white blaze on forehead..............75.00
    Breyer, glossy black rearing horse...125.00
    Hagen-Renaker Pegasus, 1985, mini 35.00
    Hartland, Roy Rogers and Trigger, near mint 225.00
    Heisey Clydesdale, amber glass 95.00
    Rookwood, #6140, 1939...........400.00
    Summit Art Glass, blue, short legs 25.00
    Vernon Kilns, Disney, unicorn, black "Fantasia".................................600.00
    Wade, Tom Smith pony 45.00

Fruit Crate label, Bronco, bucking horse...25.00

Jewelry, pin, figural, celluloid...........35.00

Magazine, *Western Horseman,* Volume 1 #1, 1935.......................................50.00

Mug, Clydesdales, 1st in Series, Certamarte Brazil for Anheuser-Busch...45.00

Nodder
    Donkey in suit, carrying U.S. flag 5.00
    Horse, celluloid, mkd "Occupied Japan" 75.00

Plate, horse leaping white fence, Homer Laughlin....................................55.00

Postcard
    Bucking Bronco, Prescott AZ Rodeo, 1920s..20.00
    Three draft horses, German, pre-1920, used...15.00

Poster
    Berry Exhibitions, Dayton, OH, Saddle Horse Contest, 1913 ....350.00
    Studebaker Wagons, multiple tears and tape, 1909 ....175.00

Program, Kentucky Derby, 1964, signed by artist "Shoofly" 75.00

Rocking Horse, white, black spots, horsehair mane and tail, 75% original paint, handmade, one rocker split......450.00

Salt and Pepper Shakers, pr, figural mules, very detailed..................25.00

Sheet Music, *Dan Patch March,* famous trotter on cover, fair condition......65.00

Sign
Hunter Cigars, tin, 19" by 27", fox hunter with horse 300.00
Mobil Oil, porcelain on steel, 6' long, red pegasus 1,500.00

Snowdome, Budweiser Clydesdales, 1988 limited edition 75.00

Toy
Circus Wagon, 14" long, cast iron, mkd "Kenton".................................1,200.00
Fire pumper, 3 horses, cast iron, Hubley...1,750.00
Hay cart, Gibbs, paper lithographed 495.00

Tray, Genessee Twelve Horse Ale, 12" d...125.00

Valentine, cowboy on horse, 1910, unused..................................30.00

Weather Vane, running horse, with base................................50.00

Windmill Weight, Dempster, bobtail horse, 17" l.................................950.00

Hull Pottery

Collecting Hints: Distinctive markings on the bottom of Hull Pottery vases help the collector to identify them immediately. Early stoneware pottery has an "H." The famous matte pieces, a favorite of most collectors, contain pattern numbers. For example, Camelia pieces are marked with numbers in the 100s, Iris pieces have 400 numbers, and Wildflower a "W" preceding their number. Most of Hull's vases are also marked with their height in inches, making it easy to determine their value. Items made after 1950 are usually glossy and marked "hull" or "Hull" in large script letters.

Hull collectors are beginning to seriously collect the glossy ware and kitchen items.

History: In 1905, Addis E. Hull purchased the Acme Pottery Co. in Crooksville, Ohio. In 1917, A. E. Hull Pottery Co. began to make a line of art pottery for florists and gift shops. The company also made novelties, kitchenware, and stoneware. During the Depression, the company primarily produced tiles. Hull's Little Red Riding Hood kitchenware was manufactured between 1943 and 1957 and is a favorite of collectors, including many who do not collect other Hull items.

In 1950, the factory was destroyed by a flood and fire, but by 1952, it was back in production, operating under the Hull Pottery Company name. At this time, Hull added its newer glossy finish pottery, plus the firm developed pieces sold in flower shops under the Regal and Floraline trade names. Hull's brown House 'n' Garden line of kitchen and dinnerware achieved great popularity and was the main line being produced prior to the plant's closing in 1986.

References: Joan Gray Hull, *Hull: The Heavenly Pottery,* 7th ed., published by author, 2000; ——, *Hull: The Heavenly Pottery Shirt Pocket Price Guide,* published by author, 1999; Barbara Loveless Gick-Burke, *Collector's Guide to Hull Pottery,* Collector Books, 1993; Brenda Roberts, *Roberts Ultimate Encyclopedia of Hull Pottery,* Walsworth Publishing, 1992; ——, *Collectors Encyclopedia of Hull Pottery,* Collector Books, 1980, 1995 value update; ——, *Companion Guide to Roberts' Ultimate Encyclopedia of Hull Pottery,* Walsworth Publishing Co, 1992; Mark E. Supnick, *Collecting Hull Pottery's Little Red Riding Hood,* L-W Book Sales, 1989, 1992 value update.

Periodical: *Hull Pottery News,* 7768 Meadow Drive, Hillsboro, MO 63050.

Advisor: Joan Hull.

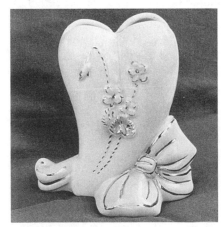

Vase, heart shape, bow base, white ground, blue tone, gold highlights, high gloss, marked "USA," 5-3/4" h, $20.

Pre-1950 Patterns

Bow Knot
B3, 6" vase 250.00
B7, 8-1/2" vase 325.00
B13, double cornucopia...........295.00
B28, 10" d plate.....................1,200.00

Dogwood (Wildflower)
504, 8-1/2" vase 150.00
507, 5-1/2" teapot.....................350.00
514, 4" jardiniere 110.00

Iris
405, 4-3/4" vase 85.00
406, 7" vase...............................155.00

412, 7" hanging planter.............175.00

Jack-In-The-Pulpit/Calla Lily
500/32, 10" bowl.......................185.00
505, 6" vase..............................125.00
550, 7" vase..............................140.00

Magnolia
4, 6-1/4" vase.............................75.00
8, 10-1/2" vase..........................200.00
14, 4-3/4" pitcher........................75.00
22, 12-1/2" vase........................325.00

Magnolia (Pink Gloss)
H5, 6-1/2" vase...........................45.00
H17, 12-1/2" vase......................250.00

Open Rose (Camelia)
105, 7" pitcher 225.00
114, 8-1/2" jardiniere 375.00
120, 6-1/2" vase........................150.00
140, 10-1/2" basket 1,300.00

Orchid
301, 10" vase............................350.00
306, 6-3/4" bud vase 175.00
311, 13" pitcher 700.00

Pinecone, 55, 6" vase..................175.00

Poppy
606, 6-1/2" vase........................200.00
607, 8-1/2" vase........................275.00
609, 9" wall planter 450.00

Rosella
R1, 5" vase.................................35.00
R8, 6-1/2" vase 75.00
R15, 8-1/2" vase 85.00

Stoneware
26H, vase...................................95.00
536H, 9" jardiniere 135.00

Thistle, #53, 6" 175.00

Tulip
101-33, 9" vase.........................245.00
109-33, 8" pitcher 235.00
110-33, 6" vase.........................150.00

Waterlily
L-8, 8-1/4" vase.........................165.00
L-18, 6" teapot 225.00
L-19, 5" creamer 75.00
L-20, 5" sugar 75.00

Wildflower
54, 6-1/2" vase..........................175.00
66, 1001/2" basket.................2,000.00
76, 8-1/2" vase..........................350.00
W-3, 5-1/2" vase 55.00
W-8, 7-1/2" vase 95.00
W-18, 12-1/2" vase 350.00

Woodland (matte)
W1, 5-1/2" vase 95.00
W10, 11" cornucopia................195.00
W25, 12-1/2" vase 425.00

Post-1950 Patterns (Glossy)

Blossom Flite
T8, basket................................125.00
T10, 16-1/2" console bowl.........125.00
T11, candleholders, pr...............75.00

Butterfly
B4, 6" bonbon dish.....................50.00
B13, 8" basket 150.00
B15, 13-1/2" pitcher..................200.00

Ebbtide
E3, 7-1/2" mermaid cornucopia 225.00
E7, 11" fish vase 175.00
E12, 15-3/4" console 200.00

Figural Planters
 27, Madonna, standing 65.00
 82, clown 125.00
 95, twin geese 50.00
Parchment & Pine
 S-5, 10-1/2" scroll planter 95.00
 S-15, 8" coffeepot 175.00
Serenade (Birds)
 S7, 8-1/2" vase 65.00
 S15, 11-1/2" ftd fruit bowl 125.00
Sunglow
 51, 7-1/2" cov casserole 50.00
 80, wall pocket, cup and
 saucer 75.00
 95, 8-1/4" vase 45.00
Tokay (Grapes)
 4, 8-1/4" vase 95.00
 12, 12" vase 125.00
 19, large leaf dish 95.00
Tropicana, T39, 12-1/2" vase 600.00
Woodland
 W-6, 6-1/2" pitcher 65.00
 W-9, 8-3/4" basket 110.00
 W-13, 7-1/2" shell wall
 pocket 95.00

Hummel Items

Collecting Hints: A key to pricing Hummel figures is the mark. All authentic Hummel pieces bear both the signature "M. I. Hummel" and a Goebel trademark. Various trademarks were used to identify the year of production:

 Crown Mark (trademark 1) 1935 through 1949
 Full Bee (trademark 2) 1950-1959
 Stylized Bee (trademark 3) 1957-1972
 Three Line Mark (trademark 4) 1964-1972
 Last Bee Mark (trademark 5) 1972-1979
 Missing Bee Mark (trademark 6) 1979-1990
 Current Mark or New Crown Mark (trademark 7) 1991 to the present.

Collectors are advised to buy pieces with the early marks whenever possible. Since production runs were large, almost all figurines, no matter what the mark, exist in large numbers.

Prices fluctuate a great deal. Antiques newspapers, such as *The Antique Trader,* often carry ads by dealers offering discounts on the modern pieces. The slightest damage to a piece lowers the value significantly.

Before World War II and for a few years after, the Goebel Company made objects, such as vases, for export. These often had the early mark. Prices are modest for these items because few collectors are interested in them; the Hummel books do not even list them. This aspect of Goebel Company production would be an excellent subject for a research project.

History: Hummel items are the original creations of Berta Hummel, who was born in 1909 in Massing, Bavaria, Germany. At age 18, she was enrolled in the Academy of Fine Arts in Munich to further her mastery of drawing and the palette. Berta entered the Convent of Siessen and became Sister Maria Innocentia in 1934. While in this Franciscan cloister, she continued drawing and painting images of her childhood friends.

In 1935, W. Goebel Co. in Rodental, Germany, began producing Sister Maria Innocentia's sketches as three-dimensional bisque figurines. The Schmid Brothers of Randolph, Massachusetts, introduced the figurines to America and became Goebel's U.S. distributor.

In 1967, Goebel began distributing Hummel items in the United States. A controversy developed between the two companies, the Hummel family, and the convent. Law suits and counter-suits ensued. The German courts finally effected a compromise: the convent held legal rights to all works produced by Sister Maria Innocentia from 1934 until her death in 1946 and licensed Goebel to reproduce these works; Schmid was to deal directly with the Hummel family for permission to reproduce any pre-convent art.

References: Carl F. *Luckey, Luckey's Hummel Figurines & Plates,* 11th ed., Krause Publications, 1997; Robert L. Miller, *No. 1 Price Guide to M. I. Hummel: Figurines, Plates, More...,* 8th ed., Portfolio Press, 2000; ---, *Hummels 1978-1998: 20 Years of "Miller on Hummel" Columns,* Collector News, 1998.

Collectors' Clubs: Hummel Collector's Club, 1261 University Dr., Yardley, PA 19067; M. I. Hummel Club, Goebel Plaza, Rte 31, P.O. Box 11, Pennington, NJ 08534.

Museum: Hummel Museum, New Braunfels, TX.

Anniversary Plate
 1975, Stormy Weather, #280,
 FE 165.00
 1979, Singing Lesson 50.00
Ashtray
 Boy With Bird, #166 .... 80.00

 Joyful, #33 .... 75.00
 Let's Sing, #114 .... 75.00
Bank, Little Thrifty, c1972 .... 50.00
Bell
 1975, orig box 65.00
 1980, bas relief, MIB 70.00
Calendar, 1955, 12 illus 15.00
Candlestick, Girl With Fir Tree,
 1956 .... 35.00
Christmas Plate
 1971, Heavenly Angel, #264 .... 725.00
 1972, Hear Ye, Hear Ye, #265 .. 125.00
 1973, Globe Trotter, #266 .... 70.00
 1974, Goose Girl, #267 .... 100.00
 1975, Ride Into Christmas,
 #268 .... 90.00
 1976, Apple Tee Girl, #269 .... 880.00
 1977, Apple Tree Boy, #270 .... 95.00
 1978, Happy Pastime, #271 .... 75.00
 1979, Singing Lesson, #272 .... 85.00
 1980, School Girl, #273 .... 100.00
 1981, Umbrella Boy, #274 .... 100.00
 1983, Postman, #276 .... 110.00
 1984, A Gift From Heaven,
 #277 .... 105.00
 1985, Chick Girl, #278 .... 110.00
 1986, Playmates, #279 .... 135.00
 1987, Feeding Time, #283 .... 135.00
 1988, Little Goat Herder, #284 .. 135.00
 1989, Farm Boy 115.00
Doll
 Carnival, porcelain 190.00
 Chimney Sweep 80.00
 Easter Greetings, porcelain 200.00
 Gretel 60.00
 Hansel 60.00
 Little Knitter 65.00
 Postman, porcelain 200.00
 Rose, pink 50.00

Little girl with doll, #311, three line bee mark, 6-1/2" h, $30.

Figure
 Adoration, #23/111, trademark
 5 .... 375.00
 Artist, #304, trademark 6 .... 90.00
 Barnyard Hero, #195/2/0, trademark
 2 .... 115.00
 Be Patient, trademark 3 .... 145.00

Builder, #305, trademark 4..........82.00
Carnival, #328, trademark 6........80.00
Doll Bath, #319, trademark 5 ......75.00
Doll Mother, stylized bee mark.. 135.00
Duet, #130, trademark 1 ....300.00
Eventide, trademark 3 ....135.00
Farm Boy, #66, trademark 3......350.00
Feather Friends, #344 ....365.00
Friend or Foe, #434 ....285.00
Gay Adventure, #356, trademark
6 ....75.00
Gil with Doll, #239, trademark 6..25.00
Good Hunting, #307, trademark
4 ....130.00
Goose Girl, #47/0, trademark 2 200.00
Happy Birthday, #176/0 ....245.00
Happy Pastime, #69.................190.00
Hear Ye, #15/0, trademark 1 .....300.00
Herald Angels, #37, trademark
2 ....80.00
Just Resting, #112/I, trademark
1 ....300.00
Kiss Me, #311, trademark 4 ......145.00
Little Fiddler, #4, trademark 1 ...250.00
Little Gardener, #72, trademark
2 ....60.00
Little Scholar, #80, Trademark
3 ....55.00
Lot Sheep, #68/0, Trademark 3 ..72.00
Merry Wanderer, #7/II, trademark
1 ....500.00
Out Of Danger, #56B 290.00
Photographer, trademark 2 ....225.00
Retreat to Safety, #201/2/0, trademark
4 ....90.00
School Girl, #81/2/0, Trademark
3 ....60.00
Sensitive Hunter.......................240.00
She Loves Me, She Loves Me
Not 225.00
Sweet Music, #186, trademark
1 ....125.00
Telling Her Secret, #196/0, trademark
2 ....235.00
Tuneful Angel, #359, trademark
6 ....45.00
Village Boy, #51/2/0, trademark
1 ....115.00
Waiter, #154/0, trademark 2 ....1309.00
Wash Day, #321, trademark 4.....80.00
Weary Wanderer, #204, trademark
6 ....80.00
Worship, #84/0, trademark 1.....250.00
Font
Angel Cloud, #206, trademark
4 ....25.00
Angel Sitting, #167, trademark
4 ....40.00
Angel with Birds, #22/0, trademark
6 ....20.00
Angels At Prayer, #91B, trademark
3 ....70.00
Child With Flowers, #36/0, trademark
2 ....48.00
Good Shepherd, #35/0, trademark
6 ....25.00
Madonna and Child, #243, trademark
6 ....25.00
Worship, #164, trademark 2......120.00
Inkwell, With Loving Greetings,
blue 135.00
Lamp
Apple Tree Boy, #M/230, trademark
5 ....165.00

Good Friends, #M/228, trademark
5 ....165.00
Just Resting, #M/225/11, trademark
5 ....175.00
Loves Me, Loves Me Not, #M/227,
trademark 2, c1970 ....190.00
Out of Danger, trademark 2......275.00
Music Box
Chick Girl..................................235.00
Ride Into Christmas 240.00
Nativity Figures
Angel Serenade, #214/D/11........40.00
Donkey, #214/J/11 ....35.00
Infant Jesus, #260.......................80.00
King, kneeling on one knee, #214/M/
11..100.00
Lamb, #214/O/11.........................20.00
Little Tooter, #214/H/11 ....65.00
Madonna, #214/A/M/11 ....110.00
Stable, 3 pc, #214/S11 ....45.00

Hunting Collectibles

Collecting Hints: Sporting-minded collectors can easily find more and more items to add to their collections. Most flea markets yield everything from big-game trophy heads to canoes to hunting licenses.

History: Hunting became a necessity as soon as man discovered it could end hunger pains. Hunting collectibles, also known as sporting collectibles, encompass those items used for hunting, whether fox or big game. Today's hunters often choose to use binoculars and cameras in lieu of rifles, arrows, or caveman's clubs.

Reference: Ralf Coykendall, Jr., *Coykendall's Complete Guide to Sporting Collectibles,* Wallace-Homestead, 1996; Donna Toneilli, *Top of the Line Hunting Collectibles,* Schiffer, 1998.

Periodical: *Sporting Classics,* 3031 Scotsman Road, Columbia, SC 29223; *Sporting Collector's Monthly,* P.O. Box 305, Camden Wyoming, DE 19934; *Sports Collectors Digest,* 700 E. State St., Iola, WI 54990.

Award Badge, NRA
Marksman, dark silver luster, hanger bar, First Class on center bar 12.00
Marksman, First Class, NRA 50 Ft Award, 2" l 18.00
Pro-Marksman, Junior Division, 1-3/4" l 16.00
Sharpshooter, brass link badge on hanger bar, Junior Division 10.00
Book
Hunting, Fishing, and Camping, L. L. Bean, 1942, 103 pgs, illus...........11.50

The Complete Book of Hunting, Clyde Ormond, 1962, 467 pgs, illus 11.50
The Sportsman's Almanac: A Guide to the Recreational Uses of America's Public Lands, with Special Emphasis on Hunting and Fishing, Carley Farquhar, Harper & Row, 1963, 1st ed., 453 pgs, small tear to dj...................... 9.50
Broadside, litho
14-1/2" h, 12" w, DuPont Powders, two anxious duck hunters pecking out of camp, "Just look at 'em," image by Edmund Osthaus, c1910............ 50.00
42" h, 28" w, Western-Winchester, hunter preparing to shoot red squirrel, autumn foliage, Weimer Pursell litho, © 1955.. 70.00
Call
Crow, Charles Perdew, Henry, IL, fair condition 175.00
Duck, Herter's, orig box 35.00
Turkey Hooter Owl, Olt, orig box 35.00
Catalog
Dave Cook Sporting Goods, 48 pgs, 1968... 5.00
Edw Tryon Sporting Goods, 72 pgs, 1923...27.50
Kirtland Bros Sporting Goods, 16 pgs, 1924... 15.00
Winchester Rifle, John Wayne cover, 16 pgs, 1982 .... 8.50
Counter Felt
Dead Shot Powder, ""Kill Your Bird Not Your Shoulder," multicolored on black, trimmed...................................... 90.00
Winchester, "Shoot Where You Aim" 175.00
Decoy Basket, clam-style 200.00
Handbook, Winchester Ammunition, 112 pgs, 1951 .... 13.50
Head, mounted, fine condition
Alaskan Wolf............................. 350.00
Deer 75.00
Elk 400.00
Elk Horns 275.00
Moose 450.00
License
New Jersey, 1928, for resident hunting/fishing, black, white and blue 70.00
New Jersey, 1933, blue and white, black serial number, minor rust on back.. 50.00
New York, 1924, for resident hunting and trapping, buff, black, and white... 85.00
New York, 1932, for resident hunting, trapping, and fishing, peach, black, and white 38.00
North Carolina, 1929-30, pale blue and white, black serial number .. 80.00
Ontario Guide, 1935, black and white, red numerals, worn 20.00
West Virginia, 1934, blue and black, non-resident, black serial number on white band.................................... 80.00
Wisconsin, 1932, black and white, some wear 25.00
Magazine
American Rifleman, August 15, 1924 (cover detached)......................... 12.00

Hunting and Fishing, February, 1938, Myrna Loy and Lucky Strike back cover color ad.............................12.00

Magazine Tear Sheet, half page size, 1949
Western World Champion Ammunition, "Even bull strength is no match for the New Silver Tip"...................3.50
Winchester, "Bag A Buck," model 94, 70, and 12.................................3.50

Pamphlet, Stoeger's Gun Stock, black and white, 16 pgs, 8-1/2" x 11", c1930...8.00

Pinback Button
Ducks Unlimited, multicolored, 1948...95.00
Dupont Smokeless Powder, multicolored, fall hunting scene, pair of black and white pointer dogs, black lettering "Dupont Smokeless-The Champion's Powder"......................................100.00
Nanty Glo Rod & Gun Club, blue lettering on white.............................10.00
Peters Cartridges, multicolored, silver bullet in brass casing, pale green ground, black letters..................45.00
Remington UMC Bears, blue and white cartoon art, red rim, white letters "Shoot Remington UMC Steel Lined Shells,"...140.00

Pinback buttons, upper left: Infallible Smokeless Shotgun, $80; upper right: Winchester Junior Rifle Corps, $45; lower left: Peters, Shoot Peters Shells & Cartridges, $35; lower right: Dupont Powders, the Record Breakers, $55.

Winchester Crosby, multicolored, portrait of W. R. Crosby, The Champion

Shot of the World, and the Shell He Shoots......................................150.00
Winchester Shotgun & Shells, silver and navy blue, red letter "W" outlined in white, rim inscription "Shoot Winchester Shotgun Shells and Shotguns," back paper defaced.......35.00
Winchester Topperweins, husband and wife sharpshooter team, black lettering inscriptions, red circle accent..100.00

Shooter's Box, fired brass shells, 24...280.00

Skiff, gunning, canvas covered, Harve de Grace, MD, tidewaters, c1910 . 500.00

Stickpin, Smith Guns, celluloid, multicolored, oval, brass insert back, inscribed "The Hunter Arms Co, Fulton, NY".......................................120.00

Target Ball, glass
Amber, Bogardus......................255.00
Green, basketweave, shooting figure...185.00

Tintype, 2-3/8" x 3", three young hunters, seated and holding rifles, stack of three more rifles in foreground, late 1800s..18.00

I

Ice Cream Collectibles

Collecting Hints: The ice cream collector has many competitors. Those who do not have a specialty collection are sometimes hampered by the regional collector, i.e., an individual who exclusively collects ice cream memorabilia related to a specific manufacturer or area. Many ice cream collectibles are associated with a specific dairy, thus adding dairy collectors to the equation. Since most ice cream was made of milk, milk and milk-bottle collectors also hover around the edge of the ice-cream collecting scene, and do not forget to factor in the cow collector (ice cream advertising often features cows). Advertising, food mold, kitchen, and premium collectors are secondary considerations. The result is fierce competition for ice cream material, often resulting in higher prices.

When buying an ice-cream tray, the scene is the most important element. Most trays were stock items with the store or firm's name added later. Condition is critical.

Beware of reproductions. They became part of the ice cream collectibles world in the 1980s. Many reproductions are introduced into the market as "warehouse" finds. Although these items look old, many are poor copies or fantasy pieces.

History: During the 1st century A.D. in ancient Rome, nearby mountains provided the Emperor Nero with snow and ice, which he flavored with fruit pulp and honey. This fruit ice was the forerunner of ice cream. The next development occurred in the 13th century. Among the many treasures that Marco Polo brought back from the Orient was a recipe for a frozen milk dessert resembling sherbet.

In the 1530s, Catherine de Medici, bride of King Henry II of France, introduced Italian ices to the French court. By the end of the 16th century, ices had evolved into a product similar to today's modern ice cream. By the middle of the 17th century, ice cream became fashionable at the English court.

Ice cream changed from being a luxury food for kings and their courts to a popular commodity in 1670, when the Cafe Procope (rue de l'Ancienne) in Paris introduced ice cream to the general populace, and by 1700, the first ice cream recipe book appeared. Ice cream was the rage of 18th-century Europe.

Ice cream appeared in America by the early 18th century. In 1777 an advertisement by Philip Lenzi, confectioner, appeared in the New York *Gazette* noting that ice cream was available on a daily basis. George Washington was an ice cream enthusiast, spending over $200 with a New York ice cream merchant in 1790. Thomas Jefferson developed an eighteen-step process to make ice cream and is credited with the invention of baked Alaska.

By the mid-19th century, ice cream "gardens" sprang up in major urban areas, and by the late 1820s, the ice cream street vendor arrived on the scene. However, because ice cream was still difficult to prepare, production remained largely in commercial hands.

In 1846, Nancy Johnson invented the hand-cranked ice cream freezer, allowing ice cream to enter the average American household. As the century progressed, the ice cream parlor arrived on the scene and homemade ice cream competed with commercial products from local, regional, and national dairies.

The arrival of the home refrigerator/freezer and large commercial freezers in grocery stores marked the beginning of the end for the ice cream parlor. A few survived into the post-World War II era. The drugstore soda fountain, which replaced many of them, became, in turn, a thing of the past in the 1970s when drugstore chains arrived on the scene.

America consumes more ice cream than any other nation in the world. But Americans do not hold a monopoly. Ice cream reigns worldwide as one of the most popular foods known. In France, it is called *glace*; in Germany, *eis*; and in Russia, *marozhnye*. No matter what it is called, ice cream is eaten and enjoyed around the globe.

References: Paul Dickson, *Great American Ice Cream Book*, Galahad Books, out of print; Ralph Pomeroy, *Ice Cream Connection*, Paddington Press, out of print; Wayne Smith, *Ice Cream Dippers*, published by author, 1986.

Also check general price guides to advertising and advertising character collectibles for ice cream–related material.

Collector's Club: Ice Screamers, P.O. Box 5387, Lancaster, PA 17601.

Museums: Greenfield Village, Dearborn, MI; Museum of Science and Industry, Finigran's Ice Cream Parlor, Chicago, IL; Smithsonian Institution, Washington, D.C.

Advertising Trade Card, Lightning Blizzard Freezers, diecut, girl giving dish of ice cream out window, mother hand cranking ice cream freezer on reverse 15.00

Book, S*now Ice Cream Makers Guide*, B Heller & Co, 1911 .... 15.00

Carton, Hershey's Ice Cream, one pint, orange and blue 18.00

Catalog, Ice Cream maker's Formulary & Price List, Frank A Beeler, 1910-15 .... 30.00

Christmas Decoration, 6-1/2" x 10" diecut stuff paper string hanger, front illus of Santa making deliveries on foot, holding Christmas wreath under one arm, Merry Christmas placard in other hand, Bartholomay Ice Cream inscription in black on white snow, 1930s 125.00

Clock, Breyer's Ice Cream, wood, sailboat, chrome sails 50.00

Cone Dispenser, glass, copper insert 350.00

Cup, 8-1/2" h, red plastic mug and removable red cap, 4" d brim, Tastee-Free clown, jiggle eyes, c1960 .... 20.00

Doll, Eskimo Pie 12.00

Film, *Ice Cream Face*, Our Gang Comedy, 1930s, 16 mm, 2-1/4" orig sq box 25.00

Freezer Box, Breyers Ice Cream green and red logo, half gallon size, white plastic, clear lid 24.00

Ice Cream Fork, sterling silver, set of 12
  Debussy, Towle 480.00
  Rose Point, Wallace 325.00

Ice Cream Knife, sterling silver, repousse dec, Kirk 85.00

Ice Cream Maker
  Alaska, 4 qt 40.00
  Unknown maker, tin, hand crank, used 80.00
  White Mountain, triple motion 45.00

Ice Cream Mold, pewter
  Cherub 95.00
  Chick, mkd "C & Co." 3-3/8" h, 3-3/4" w 95.00
  Cupid on Heart 40.00
  Ear of Corn, mkd "E & Co. NY" ... 65.00
  Grape Cluster 30.00
  Heart, Eppelsmeier 40.00
  Indian 45.00
  Lady's Shoe 25.00
  Potato 45.00
  Question Mark 50.00

Star in Circle.................................40.00
Turkey...45.00
Ice Cream Scoop Rest, Hendler's Ice Cream, molded brass, inscription, "Friendship of Hendler's The Velvet Kind," 1930-40.............................45.00
Ice Cream Spoon, sterling, set of six
Chantilly pattern, Gorham..........95.00
Etruscan, Gorham.....................365.00
Naturalistic, Gorham.................260.00
Ice Cream Tray, cut glass, American Brilliant Period, hobstars, dandelions, and parallel cuts, sawtooth edge, few chips 150.00
Machine Logo, Kohr's Original Frozen Custard, script, cast brass, chrome plating, 12" l, 6" h 275.00
Mask, 9" x 11", diecut stiff paper, truck driver, white hat, red, white, and blue wings symbol, text on back describing varieties, 1940s, unused 45.00
Menu Clip, Fairmont Ice Cream, 1930-40...18.50
Pennant, Tellings Ice Cream, felt, children making ice cream.........................90.00
Pinback Button
Artic Rainbow Ice Cream Cones, rainbow and ice cream cone image, 7/8" d...75.00
Boston Ice Cream, red lettering on white ground................................15.00
Good Humor Safety Club, blue and white, orange accents, 1930s series 18.00
Melorol Ice Cream, Slim Timblin, blue-tone portrait of caricature Black youngster, portrait flanked by name in blue lettering, red inscription, early 1930s 25.00
Pocket Mirror, Better Made Ice Cream 35.00
Record Brush, Abbotts Ice Cream, celluloid, soft bristles, mkd "Sixth Anniversary," pale red brick left and right, pale blue sky, red lettering, pale blue rim, 3-1/2" d...40.00

Scoop, No-Pak 31, $120.

Scoop
Baskins-Robbins, name emb on front, back emb "Pat. No. 471-449-NSF C2 Buildit Engineering Co., #A-25, Burbank, California, USA"................25.00
Gilchrest #31...............................95.00
Gilchrest #33.............................125.00
No-Pak, #31, hole in scoop........85.00
Williamson, conical, squeeze auction, inside blade mkd "12," chromed steel or brass, black hard plastic handle 175.00
Sign
Borden Dutch Chocolate Ice Cream, Elsie the Cow, paper, 13-1/2" w .50.00

Hancock County Ice Cream, places for seven flavors, 10" w, 20" h, framed 95.00
Jack & Jill Ice Cream Cake Roll, 8-1/2" x 19-1/2", full color, paper, image of housewife holding slice of ice cream cake, © Newly Weds Baking Co., c1940 ....35.00
Song Brochure, Hendler's Ice Cream, 1950s...2.00
Tape Measure, Abbotts Ice Cream, black, white, and red illus......................20.00
Thermometer, Abbottmaid Ice Cream, 2 x 6-1/4", 1920s 45.00
Toy
2" x 4-1/4" x 2", litho tin, Mister Softee Truck, red, white, and blue, silver and black accents, Mister Softee image on three sides, friction, marked "Made in Japan," 1960s............................40.00
2-1/2" l, diecast metal truck, Commer Ice Cream Canteen, Lyons Maid decals in black, white, red, and yellow, white 3-D figure, Matchbox, c1963 ....35.00
4" h, ice cream vendor, litho tin wind-up, Depose France, 1930s....... 795.00
Tray
13" d, Furnas Ice Cream, titled "In Old Kentucky," young girl caressing horse, ©1912, American Art Works litho, some inpainting, bottom rim repainted and relettered............................ 175.00
13" l, 10-1/2" w, Pangburns Pear Food Ice Cream, animated scene of Palmer Cox Brownies and huge dish of ice cream 350.00
Truck Driver's Manual, Jack & Jill, 4-1/2" x 6", black and white, 20 pgs, red accent cover, some scattered spots on cover, late 1930s...........18.00
Whistle, Puritan Dairy Ice Cream, yellow tin litho, black letters, c1930........35.00

Insulators

Collecting Hints: Learn the shapes of the insulators and the abbreviations which appear on them. Some commonly found abbreviations are: "B" (Brookfield), "B & O" (Baltimore and Ohio), "EC&M Co SF" (Electrical Construction and Maintenance Company of San Francisco), "ER" (Erie Railroad), "WGM Co" (Western Glass Manufacturing Company), and "WUT Co" (Western Union Telegraph Company).

The majority of the insulators are priced below $50. However, there are examples of threaded and threadless insulators which have exceeded $2,000.

Fake and altered insulators are a problem to collectors. There is an excellent out-of-print book by Michael G. Guthrie, *Fake, Altered and Repaired Insulators*, (printed by

author in 1988), that is now available on-line. Visit www.insulators.com/books/fake/ to view this important resource.

History: The invention of the telegraph in 1832 created the need for a glass or ceramic insulator. The first patent was given to Ezra Cornell in 1844. The principal manufacturing era lasted from 1850 to the mid-1900s. Leading companies included Armstrong (1938-1969), Brookfield (1865-1922), California (1912-1916), Gayner (1920-1922), Hemingray (1871-1919), Lynchburg (1923-1925), Maydwell (1935-1940), McLaughlin (1923-1925), and Whitall Tatum (1920-1938).

Initially, insulators were threadless. Shortly after the Civil War, L. A. Cauvet received a patent for a threaded insulator. Drip points prevented water from laying on the insulator and causing a short. The double skirt kept moisture from the peg or pin.

There are about 500 different styles of glass insulators, each of which has been given a "CD" (consolidated design) number as found in N. R. Woodward's *Glass Insulator in America* The style of the insulator is the only key to the numbering. Colors and names of the makers and all lettering found on the same style insulator have nothing to do with the CD number.

References: Marilyn Albers and N.R. Woodward, *Glass Insulators from Outside North America*, 2nd Revision, and companion price guide, available from authors (14715 Oak Bend Drive, Houston, TX 77079), 1993; Mike Brunner, *The Definitive Guide to Colorful Insulators*, available from author (6576 Balmoral Terrace, Clarkston, MI 48346), 1999; Michael G. Guthrie, *Fake, Altered and Repaired Insulators*, by Michael G Guthrie, 1988, out-of-print, but available on-line at www.insulators.com/books/fakes; Mark Lauckner, *Canadian Railway Communications Insulators 1880-1920*, available from author (Mayne Island, B.C. Canada V0N-2J0), 1995; *Rarity and Price Guide*, available from author, 1998; John and Carol McDougald, *Insulators*, two volumes, available from authors (P.O. Box 1003, St. Charles, IL 60174) 1990; ——, *1998 Price Guide for Insulators*, available from authors, 1998, ——, *Insulators: A History and Guide to North American Glass Pintype Insulators*, available from authors,

1999; N. R. Woodward, *Glass Insulator in America*, available from author, 1973; Fred Padgett, *Dreams of Glass: The Story of William McLaughlin and His Glass Company*, available from author (P.O. Box 1122, Livermore, CA 94551), 1996; Fred Padgett and Water P. Ruedrick, *Wood Amongst the Wires, The Temporary Solution,* available from author (P.O. Box 1122, Livermore, CA 94551), 2000.

Periodicals: *Crown Jewels of the Wire*, P.O. Box 1003, St. Charles, IL 60174; *Rainbow Riders' Trading Post*, P.O. Box 1423, Port Heuneme, CA 93044.

Collectors' Clubs: Capital District Insulator Club, 41 Crestwood Dr., Schenectady, NY 12306; Central Florida Insulator Collectors Club, 707 NE 113th St., North Miami, FL 33161; Chesapeake Bay Insulator Club, 10 Ridge Rd, Catonsville, MD 21228; Lone Star Insulator Club, P.O. Box 1317, Buna, TX 77612; National Insulator Association, 1315 Old Mill Path, Broadview Heights, OH 44147; Yankee Polecat Insulator Club, 79 New Boltom Rd, Manchester, CT 06040.

Museums: Big Thicket Museum, Saratoga, TX; Edison Plaza Museum, Beaumont, TX.

Website: http://www.insulators.com

Hemingray, #9, aqua, 3-3/4" h, $8.

CD 102, Brookfield, aqua 5.00
CD 102, C. G. I. Co., smoky
  amethyst 10.00
CD 102, Diamond, blue-aqua 3.00
CD 102, S.F., green-aqua, wire groove
  flake... 1.00
CD 102, Star, aqua 7.00

CD 104, New England Tel. & Tel. Co., light
  aqua, wire groove fracture 1.00
CD 106, Denger, aqua, small wire groove
  chip, base flake........................... 10.00
CD 106, Hemingray, light 7-Up
  green 10.00
CD 112, S.B.T. & T. Co., bubbly aqua,
  potstone bruise, stress crack, open
  bubble on base............................ 10.00
CD 115, Maydwell, clear 5.00
CD 115, Mclaughlin, light green......... 6.50
CD 115, Whitall Tatum, No. 3, straw,
  thumbnail ridge chip...................... 1.00
CD 121, Am. Tel. & Tel. Co., emb dome,
  green 20.00
CD 121, California, sage green........ 10.00
CD 121, Lynchburg, aqua................ 15.00
CD 126, Brookfield, Pat. Jan 25, 1870/Pat.
  Feb 22 1870/55 Fulton St., NY, light
  aqua 8.00
CD 128, Hemingray, medium opalescence 95.00
CD 133, Brookfield/45 Cliff St./N.Y./
  (crown) (number) Pat. Jan 25, 1870,
  green, 1" skirt fracture, base
  chipping 15.00
CD 133, H. G. Co., ice aqua 45.00
CD 134, Am. Insulator Co., aqua, underpour at base, two dome pings 25.00
CD 134, C. E. L. Co., jade-ite-type, flat
  base chip, embossing................. 90.00
CD 134, Gaynor, aqua..................... 20.00
CD 134, G. E. Co., aqua.................. 10.00
CD 134, T.H.E. Co., light blue-aqua, base
  flake and bruise 3.00
CD 137, Hemingray, dark aqua........ 10.00
CD 143, Canadian Pacific Railway Co.,
  blue gray 20.00
CD 143, Dwight, light aqua 15.00
CD 143, G.N.R., light aqua, underpour in
  front... 20.00
CD 143, Standard, aqua, two small
  chips 10.00
CD 145, Am. Insulator Co., medium aqua,
  base emb 15.00
CD 145, E. D. R., light blue, bruise,
  chips.. 10.00
CD 145, G.T.P. Tel. Co., GNW blotted out,
  aqua 10.00
CD 145, H.G. Co., petticoat, lime
  green 100.00
CD 145, McLaughlin, light cornflower,
  fracture in front 25.00
CD 145, N.E.G.M. Co., aqua, cing on
  crown... 10.00
CD 145, T.C.R., large Canadian beehive,
  light aqua 15.00
CD 152, Brookfield, aqua 2.00
CD 152, California, light purple, shallow
  base chip 5.00
CD 152, Diamond, blue.................... 10.00
CD 152, Hemingray, green with amber,
  three flakes................................. 20.00
CD 153, Gaynor, blue-aqua, four flaked
  drips.. 4.00
CD 154, Diamond, clear with pink
  tint... 10.00
CD 154, Hemingray, blue 24.00
CD 154, Lynchburg, smoky straw.... 15.00

CD 154, Michigan, light green......... 15.00
CD 155, Armstrong, dark olive 12.00
CD 155, Dominion, ice aqua.............. 5.00
CD 160, California, smoke 15.00
CD 160, Gayner, light blue-aqua 20.00
CD 162, Brookfield, olive green with
  amber swirls, 1" wire ridge chip.. 18.00
CD 162, California, blue-aqua 20.00
CD 162, Hemingray, medium blue 6.00
CD 162, K.C.G.W., dark green, annealing
  fissure in threads 18.00
CD 162, McLaughlin, dark aqua
  sage... 5.00
CD 162, McLaughlin, dark blue
  sage.. 10.00
CD 162, N. E. G. M. Co., green, seed
  bubbles, chip 25.00
CD 164, Brookfield, dark green with
  amber, minor chip flakes............ 15.00
CD 164, Hemingray, ice blue, milk white
  streak 5.00
CD 164, Lynchburg, green 25.00
CD 164, Maydwell, pink 10.00
CD 164, McLaughlin, dark emerald 10.00
CD 164, McLaughlin, light
  yellow-green 10.00
CD 167, Owens Illinois, clear, wire groove
  flake 5.00
CD 168, Hemingray, ice green 10.00
CD 190, Am. Tel. & Tel. Co., blue-aqua,
  short base flakes......................... 15.00
CD 190, Hemingray, blue aqua, chipping
  in pinhole 15.00
CD 190, Hemingray, clear............... 10.00
CD 202, Fred M. Locke Victor NY, dark
  aqua, chip on inner skirt 20.00
CD 216, Whitall Tatum, root beer
  amber 8.00
CD 233, Pyrex, clear 5.00
CD 238, Hemingray, green tint 5.00
CD 239, Kimple-830 Tempered, Made in
  USA, light peach 25.00
CD 251, N.E.G.M. Co., Pat. June 17,
  1890, aqua, chips on inner skirt . 20.00
CD 252, Knowles, blue, amber
  wisps... 20.00
CD 252, Lynchburg, Cable/Made in USA,
  aqua... 12.00
CD 254, Hemingray, dark aqua, light
  amber wisps, one chip 40.00
CD 257, Hemingray, blue-aqua....... 20.00
CD 257, Hemingray, ice green, wide
  groove.. 20.00
CD 259, Cable, aqua, 1" skirt
  chip... 4.00
CD 259, Oakman Mfg. Co., cable, Oakman Mfg. Co./Boston/Pat'd June 17,
  1890, Aug. 19, 1890, light blue, inside
  of outer skirt threaded................. 40.00
CD 263, Hemingray, aqua, ping and drip
  flake 175.00
CD 267, cable, dark aqua 95.00
CD 280, Prism, blue-aqua, chip on innerskirt 30.00
CD 300, Locke, blue-aqua............... 40.00

CD 326, Pyrex, T.M. Reg. U.S. Pat. Off. Made in U.S.A. 453, carnival, 2 crazed spots under saddle top, half dollar crazing on int. of skirt 115.00

Irons

Collecting Hints: Heavy rusting, pitting, and missing parts detract from an iron's value. More advanced collectors may accept some of these defects on a rare or unusual iron. However, the beginning collector is urged to concentrate on irons in very good to excellent condition.

Many unusual types of irons came from Europe and the Orient. These foreign examples are desirable, especially since some models were prototypes for later American-made irons.

Irons made between 1850 to 1910 are plentiful and varied. Many models and novelty irons still have not been documented by collectors.

Electric irons are just beginning to find favor among collectors but are not being added to older collections. Those with special features (temperature indicators, self-contained stands, sets) and those with Deco styling are the most desirable.

History: Ironing devices have been used for many centuries, with the earliest references dating from 1100. Irons from medieval times, the Renaissance, and the early industrial eras can be found in Europe but are rare. Fine engraved brass irons and hand-wrought irons predominated prior to 1860. After 1860, the iron underwent a series of rapid evolutionary changes.

Prior to 1860, irons were heated by three different methods. 1) a hot metal slug was inserted into the body of the iron; 2) a burning solid, e. g. coal, charcoal, or wood, was placed into the body and the heat controlled with dampers, bellows, or other methods to simulate air flow into the burning chamber; and 3) the iron was placed on a hot stove top or over hot coals and by conduction gained heat. After about 1860, liquid and gaseous fuels, such as gasoline, kerosene, alcohol, and natural gas, were introduced into the body and burned.

By the early 1900s, electricity was introduced as a means to heat irons and the evolution changes of different types of irons continued using all the heating techniques for another twenty or thirty years. Finally, only electric irons were being manufactured in the developed countries. In the underdeveloped countries, slug, coal, and conductive heating techniques continue even today.

References: Dave Irons, *Irons by Irons*, published by author, 1994; ——, *Even More Irons by Irons*, published by author, 2001; ——, *More Irons by Irons*, published by author, 1996; ——, *Pressing Iron Patents*, published by author, 1994; Carol and Jimmy Walker, *Year 2000 Pressing Iron Price Guide*, Iron Talk, 1999. Note: The books by Dave Irons are available from the author at 223 Covered Bridge Rd, Northampton, PA 18067.

Collectors' Clubs: Club of the Friends of Ancient Smoothing Irons, P.O. Box 215, Carlsbad, CA 92008; Midwest Sad Iron Collectors Club, 24 Nob Hill Drive, St. Louis, MO 63138.

Museums: Henry Ford Museum, Dearborn, MI; Shelburne Museum, Shelburne, VT; Sturbridge Village, Sturbridge, MA.

Reproduction Alert: The most frequently reproduced irons are the miniatures, especially the swan's neck and flat irons. Reproductions of some large European varieties have been made, but poor construction, use of thin metals, and the unusually fine condition easily identifies them as new. More and more European styles are being reproduced each year. Construction techniques are better than before and aging processes can fool many knowledgeable collectors. Look for heavy pitting on the reproductions and two or more irons that are exactly alike. Few American irons have been reproduced at this time, other than the miniatures.

Advisors: David and Sue Irons.

Charcoal

Box
    Dutch, all brass, cutwork
    sides 300.00
    Eclipse Pat. Aug 25, 1903 .... 150.00
    Ever Ready, Pat. Feb 6, 1917 ... 125.00
    Junior Carbon Iron 300.00
Tall Chimney
    E. Bless, R. Drake, 1852 .... 100.00
    German Dragon, dragon head for
    chimney 800.00
    Tipton, #2, turned chimney 125.00

Children's

Amazoc, Mexican, highly engraved, 3-1/2" 250.00
Block grip, Wapak, #2, 4" 110.00
Brass barrel, goffering iron, "S" standard, 2-1/2" barrel 170.00

Charcoal, tall chimney, 4-1/4" ... 250.00
Enterprise, No. 115, 3-7/8" 100.00
French "PG," low profile, 3-1/2" .. 50.00
Hollow grip, English, handle folded under, 3" 80.00
Ober, double pointed iron, 4" 170.00
Ober, sleeve, 4-1/2" 250.00
Swan, 2-3/4", no paint 120.00
Swan, 2-3/4", yellow with pin-striping 275.00
Two piece lift off top, asbestos sad iron, 4" 45.00
Two piece lift off top, Dover sad iron, 4-1/8" 40.00
Two piece lift off top, Sensible, No. 0, 4" 100.00
Wood grip, Our Pet, 3-1/2" 140.00
Wood grip, star with 12, 4" 150.00

Electric, General Electric, chrome body, late 1930s, $15.

Flat Irons

Asbestos iron, cold handle, two piece 50.00
English, round back, Silvesters Patent 80.00
Enterprise, #70, holes in handle 110.00
French, LeCaiffa, #5 .... 100.00
Griswold, Erie, cold handle 175.00
Hood's, soapstone, cold handle 170.00
Ober, ribbed handle, #6 .... 70.00
Slant handle, two piece, cold handle 160.00
Universal Thermo Cell, cold handle 180.00
Weida's, 1870 Phila, cold handle 250.00
Wrought, from one piece of handle, bell in handle 125.00

Fluters

Combination Type
    Charcoal, Economy, 1906, fluter plate on side 190.00
    Ladies Friend, Racine, Wis, revolves 500.00
    Little Giant, flutes on an angle .. 500.00
Machine Type
    Crown, American Machine Co., orig paint 180.00
    English, box type, fine flutes 300.00
    Original Knox, 1877, orig paint . 300.00
Rocker Type
    Geneva, common 85.00
    Geneva Improved, brass flutes 300.00
    Ladies Friend, two-pc 160.00
    The Best, common 80.00
Roller Type
    American Machine, three pcs .. 125.00

Clarks, 1879, script markings ...300.00
Indicator, temperature needle...450.00

Goffering

Clamp on, European, very pointed 300.00
Double barrel, all brass, Queen Ann tripod base.....................................650.00
Double barrel, cast base, all iron ...500.00
Single "S," wire standard................110.00

Liquid Fuel

Gasoline
    Acorn Brass Mfg. Co., tank in
    handle 400.00
    Coleman Model 4A Red
    Canadian 400.00
    Imperial Self-Heating Flat Iron...100.00
    Improved Easy Iron, Foote
    Mfg. Co. 125.00
Natural Gas
    Acetylene Stone Mfg. Co. 90.00
    Bless & Drake, Newark, NJ.......130.00
    Clarks Fairy Prince, blue
    enamel 200.00
    IWantU Comfort, double
    pointed 110.00

Slug

Box
    Belgium, round base, drop-in-the-
    back 300.00

English, all brass, lift gate......... 100.00
Majestic, A. P. Carver,
    revolving 750.00
Portuguese, dainty brass cut-out
    posts...200.00
Scottish, brass "S" posts 700.00
Figural, swan, 1877, 7-1/2" 5,000.00
Magic, N. R. Streeter, combination
    fluter...500.00
Ox tongue, European.................... 250.00

Miniature, smoothing iron, 3" l, $20.

Special Purpose

Button Hole Iron, removable
    handle.......................................350.00
Crowns, Crown Plaiter...................400.00
Egg, hand held...............................85.00
Flower Iron, 2 pcs, for imprinting
    felt 130.00
Glove Form, all brass, 4 fingers..... 165.00
Hat
    McCoys Patent, raised bottom . 140.00
    Shackle, both sides with movable
    edge for brims 130.00
    Wood Tolliker, curved shape..... 120.00
Hot Water Iron for silk 350.00
Polisher
    Geneva, IL, star on top 120.00
    Gleason, heat shield 130.00
    Hood's, soapstone, 1867.......... 350.00
    Keystone, boat shape............... 110.00
    M. Mahony, leather textured
    bottom.......................................110.00
    Round nose, War Hunt, grid
    button.......................................120.00
    Sweeney Iron, 1894 .... 190.00
Sleeve
    Asbestos Sad Iron......................95.00
    Pluto, electric 200.00

J

Jewelry, Costume

Collecting Hints: Scarcity and demand drive the market for costume jewelry. Demand is greatest for pieces marked with a recognizable and sought-after designer's or manufacturer's name. Name alone, however, does not guarantee high value. Collectors should also consider quality of design and manufacture, size, and color. Condition is of primary importance because costume jewelry is easily damaged and difficult to repair well. Certain types of unsigned pieces, particularly those made of Bakelite and other plastics, generate collector interest. Because costume jewelry is wearable, pieces should be chosen with personal style and wardrobe in mind.

History: The term "costume jewelry" was not used until the 1920s, when Coco Chanel made the wearing of frankly faux jewels an acceptable part of *haute couture*. Prior to the Jazz Age, manufacturers mass-produced imitation jewelry—exact copies of the real thing. Fine jewelry continued to exert its influence on costume jewelry in the 20th-century but, because they were liberated from the costly constraints of valuable gemstones and metals, designers could be more extravagant in producing pieces made of non-precious materials.

By the 1930s, when more cost-effective methods were developed, casting superseded die-stamping in mass-production. The Great Depression instigated the use of the first entirely synthesized plastic, trade named "Bakelite," for colorful and inexpensive jewelry. During World War II, restrictions and shortages forced manufacturers to turn to sterling silver as a replacement for base white metals, and to experiment with new materials such as Lucite (DuPont's trade name for acrylic). Today, Lucite and sterling vermeil (gold-plated) animals and other figurals of the period, known as jelly bellies, are highly collectible. Other World War II novelty items were made of make-do materials such as wood, ceramic, textiles, and natural pods and seeds.

In the prosperous 1950s, high-fashion rhinestone, faux pearl, and colored-glass jewelry signed with the names of well-known couturiers and other designers was sold in elegant department stores. A matching suite—necklace, bracelet, earrings, brooch—was the proper complement to the ensemble of a well-groomed 1950s woman.

References: Joanne Dubbs Ball, *Costume Jewelry: The Golden Age of Design*, Schiffer Publishing, 2000; Jeanenne Bell, *Answers to Questions about Old Jewelry*, 5th Edition, Krause Publications, 1999; Marcia Brown, *Unsigned Beauties of Costume Jewelry*, Collector Books, 2000; Maryanne Dolan, *Collecting Rhinestone & Colored Jewelry*, 4th ed., Krause Publications, 1998; Gabrielle Greindl, *Gems of Costume Jewelry*, Abbeville Press, 1990; Susan Jonas and Marilyn Nissenson, *Cuff Links*, Harry N. Abrams, 1991; Jennifer A. Lindbeck, *Fine Fashion Jewelry From Sarah Coventry*, Schiffer Publishing, 2000; Harrice Simons Miller, *Costume Jewelry*, 2nd Edition, Avon Books, 1994; Karima Parry, *Bakelite Bangles, Price & Identification Guide*, Krause Publications, 1999; ——, *Bakelite Pins*, Schiffer Publishing, 2001; Fred Rezazadeh, *Collectible Silver Jewelry*, Collector Books, 2000; ——, *Costume Jewelry: A Practical Handbook and Value Guide*, Collector Books, 1998, 2000 value update; Christie Romero, *Warman's Jewelry*, 2nd ed., Krause Publications, 1998; Nancy Schiffer, *Fun Jewelry*, revised 3rd ed., Schiffer Publishing, 2001; ——, *Rhinestones*, revised 3rd ed., Schiffer Publishing, 2000; Sheryl Gross Shatz, *What's It Made of?*, 3rd Edition, published by author (10931 Hunting Horn Dr, Santa Ana, CA 92705), 1996; Cherri Simonds, *Collectible Costume Jewelry*, Collector Books, 1997, 2000 value update.

Videotapes: Christie Romero, "Hidden Treasures," Venture Entertainment Group (P.O. Box 55113, Sherman Oaks, CA 91413), 1992, 1995 value update.

Collectors' Clubs: Leaping Frog Antique Jewelry and Collectable Club, 4841 Martin Luther Blvd, Sacramento, CA 95820; National Cuff Link Society, P.O. Box 346, Prospect Heights, IL 60070; Vintage Fashion & Costume Jewelry Club, P.O. Box 265, Glen Oaks, NY 11004.

Reproduction Alert: Recasts and knockoffs are widespread. Copies of high-end signed pieces—e.g., Trifari jelly bellies, Eisenberg Originals, and Boucher—are common. New Bakelite (sometimes called "fakelite") and marriages of old Bakelite parts are also cropping up in many areas.

Bracelet

Ciner, hinged bangle, zebra motif, black and white painted enamel, green cabochon glass eyes, colorless rhinestone accents, sgd, c1960 .... 150.00

Coro, goldtone, pressed glass scarabs, 7" l, 1950s 18.00

Lane, Kenneth Jay, bangle, snake, hinged goldtone, rhinestones, green glass cabochon eyes, sgd "KJL" 155.00

Eisenberg

  Linked clusters of marquise-cut colorless rhinestones, v-spring and box clasp, block letters mark, safety chain, c1950, 7-1/2" l 70.00

  Original, links of large cushion-cut aqua-colored rhinestones alternating with rows of three small circ colorless rhinestones, sgd "Eisenberg Original," c1935-40, 7" l 210.00

Haskell, Miriam, strand of large textured faux pearls flanked by two strands of small textured faux pearls, ornate multi-loop bow motif front clasp of faux seed pearls and colorless rhinestones, sgd on oval plate, c1950, 7-1/2" l 145.00

Hollycraft

  Link, large multi-colored emerald-cut rhinestones flanked by white metal S-scrolls set with multi-colored circ-cut rhinestones, foldover clasp, safety chain, sgd, "Hollycraft COPR 1957," 7" l 82.00

  Sq links set throughout with multi-colored rhinestones, variety of shapes, goldtone metal, foldover clasp, safety chain, sgd "Hollycraft," 7-1/2" l x 1-1/4" w 135.00

Jomaz, hinged bangle, domed oval hinged at the sides, with irregularly-shaped cells of translucent blue and green painted enamel, central crossover design pavé-set with small colorless rhinestones., rhinestone-set thumbpiece on V-spring, c1965, 2-1/4" inside dia 175.00

Lisner, goldtone

  Olive green plastic stones, 7" l, 1" w 10.00

  Pearly pink Lucite beads, faux pearls, pink glass beads 18.00

Renoir, copper cuff, openwork block design, sgd "Renoir," c1950, 2" w 35.00

Tortolani, hinged bangle, goldtone, three-dimensional zodiac figures interspersed with stars, sgd "©Tortolani" in script, snap clasp at center opening, c1960, 2-1/2" w at center, ... 200.00

Unknown Maker, Bakelite

  "Apple juice" colored Bakelite encasing wood Scarab-type ornament 325.00

  Bangle, butterscotch, carved flower design, 2-1/2" d 325.00

  Bangle, pineapple motif, orange and yellow 245.00

Brooch/Pin

Artisan, floral spray with ribbon, nine faux pearl flower buds, three with colorless baguette rhinestone stems, small colorless rhinestones. throughout, all stones replaced, mkd "artisan n.y.," safety catch, c1945, 3-7/8" w x 2-3/4" 100.00

Avon, acorn, gold wash, pearl trim, sgd, 1-1/2" x 1-1/2" 20.00

Boucher
Bunch of three radishes with leaves, red and green enamel, pavé colorless rhinestones around bottom of each, rhodium-plated roots and stems, sgd "MB" with symbol for Marcel Boucher, c1940, 2-1/2" w x 3" 740.50
Flower head, six petals pavé-set with small yellow rhinestones, each bisected by a line of colorless baguette rhinestones, cluster of small blue rhinestones in center, turned edges of petals pavé-set with color-less rhinestones, textured gold-toned finish on rev, mkd "©Boucher" (block letters) # 7713, c1950-60, 2-3/8" 230.00

B.S.K.
Gingo Tree Leaf, gold wash, 2" x 2" 25.00
Floral, goldtone, marquise shapes bezel set, pave rhinestone accents, 2-3/4" x 1-1/2" 18.00
Sunflowers, pale yellow double layer flower petals, amber colored faceted stones in center, green enameled leaf, gold washed metal, 2-1/2" x 2-1/2" 45.00

Caslecliff, goldtone, fish, frosted glass jelly belly, green rhinestone eye, 2-1/4" 60.00

Corocraft
Bow, sterling vermeil, clear rhinestone accents, 3" x 2" 345.00
Leaf, goldtone Florentine finish, center silvertone spray of pave rhinestones, 2-1/4" x 2-1/2" 22.00
Rose, sterling vermeil, rhinestone accents, 2-1/2" x 2" 195.00
Stylized rooster with large faceted rect red glass center, painted enamel tail and features in red, green, black and white, c1940, 2-1/4" w x 2-1/8" ..185.00

DeNiccola, textured goldtone, cupid, clear rhinestones 90.00

Eisenberg
Original, opposed C-scrolls tapering down to point forming fancy shield shape, set throughout with large and med oval, emerald-cut and marquise-shaped pink rhinestones, oulined with small colorless rhinestones, prong-set in gold plated white metal, mkd "Eisenberg Original," c1935-40, 3-1/4" w x 3-1/2".....................................250.00
Overlapping open circles of colorless circ rhinestones and opaque white circ cabochons, outlined with a row of marquise-shaped opaque white cabo-chons along one side, block letters mark, c1950, 2" x 2"...................50.00
Tiger motif, top view, textured gold-tone metal set throughout with small colorless rhinestones, sgd "Eisenberg Ice ©," c1970, 3-1/4" x 1-1/2".......85.00

Emmons, circular motif, faux coral cabo-chons, emerald green and tangerine rhinestones, 2-1/4" d....................35.00

Haskell, Miriam, gold-plated brass wreath of ivy leaves and vines intertwined with opaque green glass seed beads around large central opaque green glass circ cabochon, appl oval plate on rev sgd "Miriam Haskell," c1950, 2" dia.. 105.00

Hollycraft
Floral wreath design, large center circ red rhinestone encircled by goldtone floral and foliate motifs set with small red rhinestones, sgd "Hollycraft, Copr 1954," 1-1/2" w x 3/8" 40.00
Pinwheel design of pale to dark green circ and marquise-shaped rhine-stones, sgd "Hollycraft, Copr 1952," 2" dia... 100.00

Kramer of New York
Rhodium, bar pin with criss-cross clear rhinestone dangles ending in emerald stones, 2-3/4" w, 1" h 95.00
Silvertone, pave set clear rhinestones, circle with floral dec, 1-3/4" d, slight discoloration to one stone 10.00

Lane, Kenneth J.
Butterfly motif, prong set throughout with multicolored marquise-shaped and circ rhinestones, sgd "KJL," c1970, 3" x 3" 57.00
Maltese cross of large green oval cab-ochons and circ green rhinestones around center circ blue rhinestone, outlined in marquise and sq-cut color-less rhinestones, sgd "KJL," c1965, 3" x 3"...35.00

Lisner, jelly fish, pale blue rhinestones, goldtone tentacles, 2-1/2" l, 1-3/4" w, mkd "© Lisner"............................16.00

Mazer
Apple with leaves, sterling vermeil, rhinestone accents, 2-1/2" x 2". 195.00
Bow, sterling, blue glass cabochon and clear rhinestones, 3" x 1-3/4" 185.00

Monet, goldtone, clown, red rhinestone eye for one eye, star on other, open-work collar, 1970s, 1-7/8" x 1-1/4"..12.00

Rader, Pauline, large oval royal blue cen-ter stone surrounded by turquoise and royal blue stones, 2-1/2" h, 2" w.. 165.00

Schreiner
Circ cluster of mottled orange and dark green cabochons interspersed with aurora borealis rhinestones and faux pearls, sgd "Schreiner New York," c1955-60, 2-1/4" dia.................. 100.00
Domed triangular cluster, center circ dark blue rose-cut rhinestone encir-cled by small circ pale blue rhine-stones, three small opaque turquoise cabochons prong-set around circle, large oval and circ light and dark blue rose-cut rhinestones prong-set around outer edges, sgd "Schreiner New York," c1960, 2-1/4" x 2-1/4" 85.00

Trifari
Faux pearl spray, green enamel leaves with colorless rhinestone accents, sgd "Trifari ©," c1950, 2-1/8" w x 1-1/4" 55.00
Flower, retro, enameled and clear rhinestone accents, 1-3/4" x 2-1/2", minor wear 185.00

Unknown Maker, Aurora Borealis, gold wash, Aurora Borealis, champagne, and topaz colored faceted prong set stones, 1-1/2" x 2" 45.00

Unknown Maker, Bakelite
Anchor, red anchor, red, white, and blue dangling plastic anchors, 2-3/4" 295.00
Bar, inlaid orange, red, green, and brown, 3-3/4" l......................525.00
Greyhound, deep blue Bakelite, 4" l 365.00

Unknown Maker, gold, 10 kt, flower spray, prong set blue rhinestones, pink-gold wash flower, yellow-gold wash leaves and stem, sgd "H" with upside down "T" through center

Unknown Maker, goldtone
Basket of Flowers, faceted blue prong set stones, faux pearl centers 35.00
Flower, goldtone wirework flowers, pale green rhinestones, 3" w, 1-3/4" h...................................... 16.00
Flower, prong set blue and green fac-eted rhinestones, 3-D enameled leaves, 3-1/4" l 45.00
Flower, prong set bright pink and green marquis-cut rhinestones, orange center surrounded by white faceted rhinestones, 3-1/4" x 2".. 45.00

Unknown Maker, Rhodium, flower, light blue and milky blue glass cabochons, clear rhinestone accents, worn signa-ture, 1-3/4" x 3", 1940s 210.00

Unknown Maker, sterling vermeil
Flower, retro-style, clear and light blue rhinestones 40.00
Flower, retro-style, clear rhinestones, green glass cabochons, 2" x 2", minor wear 185.00
Pegasus, 3-D wings, 1940s, restored, replated, restoned, 3" x 2-1/2" ..325.00
Rose, 3-D, rhinestone accents, 2-1/2" x 3-1/2" 185.00

Warner, Joseph, circle pin, black japanned metal with prong set scarlet red rhinestones, 1-3/4" d.............32.00

Weiss
Star-shaped cluster of large pear-shaped and smaller marquise-shaped colorless rhinestones prong-set in rhodium-plated wm, sgd "Albert Weiss New York," c1950, 1-1/2" dia 40.00

Chatelaine, Sarah Coventry, gold tone flower with faux pearl center, 3-1/2" x 1-3/4", orig card mkd "Sarah Glo, Chit Chat 6771" 24.00

Choker, Hattie Carnegie, faux emeralds and rhinestones, goldtone mesh chair, 14" l 450.00

Clip

Eisenberg Original
Retro Modern, goldtone floral spray with large emerald-cut green rhine-stone at base, smaller emerald-cut green rhinestone encircled by circ-cut green rhinestones forming flowerhead, marquise-cut green rhinestones in center of second flowerhead, sgd "Eisenberg Original," c1940-45, 3-1/4" w x 2-1/2" 155.00
Sterling, large foliate spray, multiple "branches," each with a line of small

colorless rhinestones terminating in a large oval rhinestone, sgd "Eisenberg Original," mkd "sterling," c1940, 2-1/4" w x 4" 250.00

Staret, openwork shield shape set throughout with large oval and small circ colorless rhinestones (three small stones missing), c1935-40, sgd "Staret," 2-1/8" w x 2-1/2" 115.00

Trifari, painted enamel floral spray, red flowers, colorless rhinestone centers and accents, green leaves, brown stems on rhodium-plated white metal, c1935-40, sgd "Trifari," 1-1/2" w x 2-1/2" 90.00

Cuff Links, pr

Christian Dior, gold filled, textured ovals, orig box, c1960 .... 40.00

Georg Jensen, sterling, rect checkerboard pattern, c1950, sgd "Georg Jensen" in dotted oval, mkd "Sterling Denmark, #113" 170.00

Duette, Coro, sgd
"Jelly belly" fish, sterling vermeil, Lucite centers, colorless rhinestone accents, red glass cab eyes, blue glass cab mouths, c1940, sgd "Coro Duette," mkd "sterling," 1931 pat no., 2-1/2" w x 1-3/4" 300.00
Retro, opposed goldtone swirls set with colorless rhinestones, sgd "Coro Duette," 1931 patent no., 2-1/2" w x 1-1/2" 75.00

Earrings, pr

Alice, gold plated, four leaf clover design, screw backs, 1940s 35.00

Avon, silver double circles set with marquisettes, pierced, c1970 .... 20.00

Chanel, faux pearl "puffy" heart suspended from circ faux pearl surmount, in textured goldtone setting, orig box, c1965-70, sgd "© Chanel," clip backs, 2" l 75.00

Ciner, textured goldtone circ domes, small faux pearls in star-cut settings, c1960, clip backs sgd "Ciner," 1" dia 32.50

Eisenberg, clusters of prong-set cobalt blue marquise and circ rhinestones, small colorless rhinestone accents, c1950, block letter mark, clip backs, 3/4" w x 1-1/4" 55.00

Hollycraft, large multicolored clusters of circ, oval, marquise and baguette rhinestones prong-set in goldtone metal, sgd "Hollycraft Copr 1955," screwbacks, 1-1/2" l 145.00

Matisse, circ domed red-enameled disk with appl copper dome at bottom and appl copper wires at top forming an abstract eye, c1952, one clipback earring mkd "Matisse" in script, 3/4" dia 20.00

Rebajes, copper, oval swirls around central domes, c1950, clip backs sgd "Rebajes," 1" x 1-1/4" 65.00

Robert, flowerhead clusters of green rhinestones, faux pearl centers, c1950, clip backs mkd "Robert," 7/8" dia 34.00

Unknown Maker, antiqued gold finish, foil bead with 4 smaller green glass beads, glove of 10 faceted prong set

white rhinestones, wire strung on antique design clip back, 1-1/2", 1950s 35.00

Weiss, flowerhead clips, large dark blue circ rhinestone encircled by marquise-cut light blue rhinestones, c1950, sgd "Weiss" on clipback, 1" dia 36.50

Necklace

Carnegie, Hattie, goldtone, double strand, peridot green aurora borealis crystals, 20" l 40.00

Caslecliff, three strands, red glass beads, goldtone leaf closure, 22" l 45.00

Coventry, Sarah, goldtone links, 11 faceted aurora borealis crystals, 16" l 18.00

Eisenberg, double row torsade of emerald-cut colorless rhinestones.surmounted by two short rows of circ colorless rhinestones at center, continuing to a small rhinestone-set chain and keyhole clasp mkd "eisenberg," c1950, 1" w (at center), 17-1/4" l 250.00

Florenza, goldtone, Victorian-style, filigree 20.00

Haskell, Miriam, clusters of three molded red glass and brass bead flowerheads with red rhinestone centers, suspended from red molded flowerhead beads, brass and colorless faceted glass rondels, alternating with red faceted glass beads, continuing to a hook clasp, c1960, mkd "miriam haskell" on attached oval hang tag, 20" l 420.00

Trifari
Double strand, goldtone fittings, peridot colored glass beads, 18" l 40.00
Silvertone, Egyptian abstract style, 21" l, 2-1/2" l drop, 1970s 14.00

Unknown Maker, Bakelite, yellow carved cherries 395.00

Vendome, a row of paired circ-cut aurora borealis alternating with single circ-cut amber-colored rhinestones, suspending clusters of small and large circ-cut and emerald-cut green, orange, aurora borealis and amber-colored rhinestones, fancy pronged wm settings, terminating in a rhinestone-set chain and hook clasp mkd "© vendome," appl plaque rev center mkd "Vendôme," c1960, 1-7/8" w x 18" l 125.00

Pearls

Hagler, Stanley, NYC, rhinestone clasp, 29" l 250.00

Haskell, Mariam, pearls with brass drop of pearls surrounded by clear rhinestones, 14" l, 3-1/4" l drop 225.00

Hobe, "potato" pearls, rhinestone and emerald clasp, 25" l, 1965 .... 175.00

Pendant

Eisenberg, owl on a branch in dark, medium, and light green, and black painted enamel, suspended from a gold-plated wm snake chain, pendant rev mkd "eisenberg," c1970, pendant 1-1/4" w x 2-1/2" (with bail), chain 20-1/2 2" l 50.00

Joseff of Hollywood, stamped gold-plated brass in a design of three overlapping circ disks with open scroll and geometric motif, suspending by two outside and two inside crossing chains a large circ disk with geo design, c1950, hook and ring clasp on gold-plated brass foxtail chain, pendant 3" w x 5", chain 16" l 200.00

Unknown Maker
Lucite "ice cube" held by rhodium-plated tongs on matching large curb link chain, pendant 1-3/4" w x 4", chain 30" l 75.00
Red Lucite heart pendant surmounted by appl sterling silver Air Force emblem, suspended from red celluloid chain, c1945, pendant 1-3/4" w x 1-3/4", chain 19" l 165.00

Ring, Vogue, triangular cluster, one large half-round faux pearl, two flowerheads, each center set with five colorless rhinestones encircled by glass cabs, one streaked turquoise colored and other mottled green, c1960, mkd "vogue," adjustable shank, 1-7/8" w x 1-5/8".. 50.00

Sash Ornament, Art Nouveau

Brass, center amethyst stone, 3" x 2" 195.00

Gold Wash, enameled florals, center faux pearl, 4" x 2" 245.00

Stickpin, Anson, owl, sterling, white opal cabochon, 2-1/2" l 25.00

Suite

Boucher, brooch and earrings, rhinestones, 2-1/4" x 2-1/4" pin, 1" x 1-1/2" earrings, 1940s 285.00

Coro, necklace and earrings, necklace of ten linked foliate motifs, each with large central oval blue alternating with green faux moonstone cab framed by smaller circ blue faux moonstones and blue rhinestones set in silvertone metal branches, matching clip earrings, c1950, all pcs mkd "© Coro," necklace with adjustable hook closure, 17-1/2" l, earrings 1/2" w x 3/4" ... 85.00

Eisenberg, brooch and earrings, foliate clusters of circ and marquise large and med rhinestones, shades of green with small colorless accents, c1950, block letter mark, brooch 2-1/4" w x 2-3/4", clip earrings 1" w x 1-1/4" . 225.00

Florenza, necklace and earrings, 2-1/4" l drop with plastic insert with transfer printed flowers, 25" l paperclip chain 18.00

Haskell, Miriam, bracelet, brooch, and earrings, floral clusters of pastel pink and blue glass beads, pale blue seed beads, and pale blue enameled petals on brooch and earrings, bracelet a floral cluster at the top of a double-hinged gold-plated bangle, clipback earrings a single flowerhead, c1960-65, all pieces mkd "miriam haskell" on oval plate, bracelet 1-1/3" w x 2" (at top), 2-1/2" inside dia, brooch 2-3/4" w x 1-1/2", earrings 3/4" dia 335.00

Hobé, necklace and earrings, lariat-style necklace of goldtone metal mesh with circ central ornament and terminals set with marquise-cut citrine- and topaz-colored rhinestones, hook closure, matching clip earrings of clustered marquise rhinestones, , c1950, sgd "Hobé," necklace 26-1/2" l, center 1-3/4" w, earrings 1" w x 1-1/2" .. 108.00

Hollycraft, brooch and earrings, triangular openwork Christmas tree of intersecting ropetwist textured lines forming lozenge pattern, set with red, blue, yellow and green circ rhinestones in centers, surmounted by a rhinestone-set star, matching clipback earrings, c1955-60, mkd "© hollycraft," brooch 1-1/4" w x 2-3/8", earrings 3/4" w x 1-1/8" 150.00

Karu Arke, Inc., brooch and earrings, light yellow, champagne, and aurora borealis prong set rhinestones, orig price tag, 2" x 2" star shaped pin, 1-1/4" l x 1/2" wide clip earrings 24.00

Kramer of New York, collar and bracelet, flexible openwork rows of large and small circ gray and aurora borealis rhinestones, c1950, sgd "Kramer of New York," collar with adjustable hook closure, 16" l, bracelet 7" l, both 1" w 100.00

Mazer Bros., necklace and bracelet, Retro Modern, necklace of open gold-plated links alternating with colorless rhinestone-set links suspending a central gold-plated and rhinestone-set scrolled ribbon bow with two large molded clear glass cherries and three grad clear glass cabs, mkd "Z" on rev, matching bracelet of linked molded glass cherries alternating with clear glass cab and rhinestone-set scrolls, mkd "K" on rev, both pcs mkd "Mazer," c1940, fold-over clasps, necklace 16" l, center 2-1/4" w x 2-1/2", bracelet 1" w x 7-1/2" 175.00

Rebajes, necklace and bracelet, linked pairs of copper leaves, c1950, sgd "Rebajes," 7/8" w, necklace 15" l, bracelet 7-1/2" l, can be joined to form longer necklace 80.00

Regency, bracelet, brooch and earrings, clusters of champagne-colored, aurora borealis and colorless marquise and circ rhinestones, c1955, mkd "Regency," bracelet 7-1/4" l, brooch 2" dia, clip earrings 1-1/2" l 80.00

Trifari
   Bracelet and Earrings, goldtone links, 7" l x 3/4" w bracelet, 1-1/4" l x 3/4" w clip earrings 20.00
   Brooch and earrings, clear and red baguette rhinestones, 2-3/4" x 3" brooch with three swirls, 1" x 2" earrings, 1940s 325.00
   Necklace, bracelet, and earrings, wide links with rhinestone accents, round clip earrings 165.00

Unknown Maker
   Brooch and earrings, royal blue and champagne colored rhinestones, set in gold-washed metal, marquis and round faceted prong set stones, 2-3/4" x 2" pin, 1-1/4" x 3/4" clip earrings, 1950s 75.00

Brooch and earrings, sterling vermeil, clear rhinestone accents, 2" x 2-1/2" apple-shaped pin, 1" x 1-12" clipback earrings, 1940s 245.00
Necklace, bracelet, and earrings, large dark blue rhinestones with surrounding lighter blue rhinestones, chrome setting, 1950s 175.00

Vien, Ann, bracelet and earrings, silver-tone links, purple cabochons and lavender aurora borealis stones, clip earrings with 2" drop, some cloudiness to few stones 40.00

Weiss, necklace, bracelet, and brooch, light blue circ, pear-shaped and marquise glass cabochons and circ rhinestones, necklace of large pear-shaped cab flanked by four smaller pear-shaped cabs alternating with marquise cabs and circ rhinestones, continuing to a chain of circ rhinestones, hook closure, sgd "Weiss," flexible bracelet of alternating circ and marquise cabs between two rows of small circ rhinestones sgd "Weiss," brooch a large star shape of five pear-shaped cabs encircling circ cabs and rhinestones, c1950, necklace 18" l, bracelet 7" l, brooch 2-3/8" dia 75.00

Jukeboxes

Collecting Hints: Jukebox chronology falls into four distinct periods:

In the pre-1938 period, jukeboxes were constructed mainly of wood and resembled a radio or phonograph cabinet. Wurlitzer jukeboxes from this era are the most collectible, but their value usually is under $600.

From 1938 to 1948, the addition of plastics and animation units gave the jukebox a gaudier appearance. These jukeboxes played 78-RPM records. Wurlitzer jukeboxes are king, with Rock-Ola the second most popular. This era contains the most valuable models, e.g., Wurlitzer models 750, 850, 950, 1015, and 1080.

The 1940 to 1960 period is referred to as the Seeburg era. Jukeboxes of this vintage are collected for the "Happy Days" feeling (named for the TV show): drive-in food, long skirts, sweater girls, and good times. The jukeboxes, which play 45-RPM records, rate second in value to those of the 1938-1948 period, with prices usually are under $1,500.

The 1961 and newer jukeboxes often are not considered collectible because the record mechanism is not visible, thus removing an alluring quality.

There are exceptions to these generalizations. Collectors should have a price and identification guide to help make choices. Many original and reproduction parts are available for Seeburg and Wurlitzer jukeboxes. In many cases, incomplete jukeboxes can be restored. Jukeboxes that are in working order and can be maintained in that condition are the best machines to own.

Do not buy any jukebox without taking time to thoroughly educate yourself, making sure you know how collectible the particular machine is and how missing components will affect its value.

History: First came the phonograph. When electrical amplification became possible, the coin-operated phonograph, known as the jukebox, evolved.

The heyday of the jukebox was the 1940s. Between 1946 and 1947, Wurlitzer produced 56,000 model-1015 jukeboxes, the largest production run of all time. The jukebox was the center of every teenage hangout, from drugstores and restaurants to pool halls and dance parlors. They even invaded some private homes. Jukeboxes were cheaper than a live band, and, unlike radio, allowed listeners to hear their favorite songs whenever and as often as wished.

Styles changed in the 1960s. Portable radios coupled with "Top 40" radio stations fulfilled the desire for daily repetition of songs. Television changed evening entertainment patterns, and the jukebox vanished.

References: Michael Adams, Jürgen Lukas, and Thomas Maschke, *Jukeboxes*, Schiffer Publishing, 1995; Jerry Ayliffe, *American Premium Guido to Jukeboxoo and Slot Machines*, 3rd Edition, Books Americana, 1991; Rick Botts, *Complete Identification Guide to the Wurlitzer Jukebox*, published by author, 1984; Stephan K. Loots, *Official Victory Glass Price Guide to Antique Jukeboxes*, published by author, 1997; Vincent Lynch, *American Jukebox*, Chronicle Books, 1990; Scott Wood (ed.), *Blast from the Past, Jukeboxes*, L-W Book Sales, 1992.

Periodicals: *Always Jukin'*, 221 Yesler Way, Seattle, WA 98104; *Antique Amusements, Slot Machine & Jukebox Gazette*, 909 26th St. NW, Washington, DC 20037; *Chicagoland Program*, 414 N. Prospect Manor Ave., Mt. Prospect, IL 60056; *Coin-Op Classics*, 17844 Toiyabe St., Fountain Valley, CA 92708; *Gameroom*, P.O. Box 41, Keyport, NJ 07735; *Jukebox Collector*, 2534 SE 60th Ct #216, Des Moines, IA 50317; *Loose Change*, 1515 South Commerce St., Las Vegas, NV 89102-2703.

Museums: Jukeboxes have not reached the status of museum pieces. The best way to see 100 or more jukeboxes in one place is to visit a coin-op show.

AMI
    Model A..................................1,250.00
    Model B....................................800.00
    Model C 500.00
    Model D 400.00
    Model E....................................500.00

Mills
    Model Empress......................1,500.00
    Throne of Music 850.00
Packard, Manhattan....................2,750.00
Rock-Ola
    Model 1422 ....2,400.00
    Model 1426 ....2,400.00
    Model 1428 ....2,400.00
    Model 1432 ....900.00
    Model 1436 ....900.00
    Model 1438 ....950.00
Seeburg
    Model 147 ....675.00

    Model HF100G.........................950.00
    Model HF100R 950.00
    Model M100B.........................850.00
    Model M100C.........................950.00
    Model V-200 ....1,400.00
Wurlitzer
    Model 412.................................850.00
    Model 600.............................1,200.00
    Model 700.............................3,000.00
    Model 750.............................5,000.00
    Model 800.............................4,500.00

K

Kewpies

Collecting Hints: Study the dolls carefully before purchasing. Remember that composition dolls were made until the 1950s; hence, every example is not an early one.

Many collectors concentrate only on Kewpie items. A specialized collection might include other O'Neill designs, such as Scootles, Ragsy, Kewpie-Gal, Kewpie-Kins, and Ho-Ho.

The vast majority of Kewpie material is sold in the doll market where prices are relatively stable. Pricing at collectibles shows and malls fluctuates because sellers may not be familiar with the overall Kewpie market.

History: Rose Cecil O'Neill (1876-1944) was a famous artist, novelist, illustrator, poet, and sculptor, as well as being the creator of the Kewpie doll. O'Neill's drawing *Temptation* won her a children's art prize at the age of 14 and launched her career as an illustrator.

The Kewpie first appeared in art form in the December 1909 issue of *Ladies Home Journal* in a piece titled, "Kewpies' Christmas Frolic." The first Kewpie doll appeared in 1913. Although Geo. Borgfeldt Co. controlled the production and distribution rights to Kewpie material, Joseph L. Kallus assisted in design and manufacture through his firm, the Cameo Doll Company.

Kewpie dolls and china-decorated items rapidly appeared on the market. Many were manufactured in Germany where 28 different factories made Kewpie-related products during the peak production years.

O'Neill eventually moved to southwest Missouri, settling at Bonniebrook near Bear Creek. She died there in 1944, and in 1947 Bonniebrook burned to the ground.

Production of Kewpie items did not stop at O'Neill's death. Kewpie material still appears as limited edition collectibles.

References: Janet A. Banneck, *Antique Postcards of Rose O'Neill*, Greater Chicago Productions, 1992; *Kewpie Kompanion*, Theriault's, 1994.

Left to right: (49) doll with paper label on chest, 5" h, $150; (39A) doll on sled, 1-3/4" h, $850; (33) doll with paper label on back, 4-1/2" h, $100; (154) pitcher, 6" h, plate, 6-1/4" d, cup (chip) Royal Rudolstadt $275; (9) twin dolls reading book, 3-1/2" h, $450; (39) doll with basket, 2-1/4" h, $800. Photo courtesy of Joy Luke Fine Art Brokers and Auctioneers.

Periodical: *Traveler*, P.O. Box 4032, Portland, OR 97208.

Collectors' Club: International Rose O'Neill Club, P.O. Box 668, Branson, MO 65616.

Museum: Shepherd of the Hills Farm and Memorial Museum, near Branson, MO.

Reproduction Alert.

Bank, 12" h, carnival chalkware, incised "Cast/Craft, Toldeo, O," orig paint and glitter, c1930 .... 155.00
Blanket, 5" x 6", felt fabric, 1914 Rose O'Neill copyright fleshtone images, blue sky, tan buildings, red stitched border 8.00
Candy Container, clear glass, patent date 100.00
Clip, 5/8" l, sterling, imp trademark ..30.00
Cookbook, Jell-O Girl Entertains 25.00
Dealer Sign, "The Rose O'Neill Kewpie Collection by Enesco," sgd "O'Neill," 1991, 3-3/4" h 45.00
Doll
  1-3/4" h, celluloid 40.00
  2-1/2" h, celluloid, some paint missing 20.00
  3" h, cloth, wings, not signed ... 100.00
  8" h, chalk, black skin tone 65.00
  9" h, vinyl, jointed at neck, shoulders, and hips, mkd "Cameo," two small discoloration marks, orig pantaloons 45.00
  10" h, all vinyl, red outfit, Cameo, c1960, slight play wear 75.00
  11" h, all composition, jointed at shoulders, wings on rear, orig heart label on chest, Cameo Co., c1920 .... 495.00
  11" h, all vinyl, black skin tone, orig print floral dress, lace apron, MIB 85.00
  12" h, carnival chalkware, orig paint and glitter 145.00
  13" h, all vinyl, orig clothes, mkd "S4 1965 JLK © Cameo"....................95.00

Figure, Lefton
  Bewildered 12.00
  Content, 5" h 27.50
  Holding foot, 3" h 12.00
  On belly, 3-3/4" l 12.00
  Playing golf, 4" h 35.00
  Puzzled, 5" h 30.00
  Winking, 5" h 32.00
Lamp, 13-1/2" h carnival chalkware jointed arm Kewpie, sticker "Original Sunlite Baby Lamp, Mfg Sunlite Products, Co., Minneapolis, Minn, 2/1926," orig shade and wiring, some paint loss... 185.00
Night Light, figural, orig foil sticker "Lefton Trade Mark Exclusives Japan," #5718 stamped on bottom, 6-1/2" h 75.00
Pendant, small.............................. 10.00
Perfume Bottle, 2-1/2" h, porcelain, painted, glazed, stamped "Germany" in red on base, stopper missing, small chip 135.00
Pin, 2" h, A & M, mkd "Truart Sterling" 40.00
Planter, bisque Kewpie pushing garden cart, mkd "Occupied Japan"...... 25.00
Postcard, "Can't think of an earthly thing to say, Cept I hope you are happy Valentine's Day," Kewpie writing valentines, © Rosie O'Neill, postmarked Feb. 12, 1925, published by Gibson Art Co... 20.00
Tray, Purity Ice Cream, 17-1/2" x 12", large Kewpie holding tray with strawberry sundae on it.............................. 575.00
Vase, 6" h 120.00

Kitchen Collectibles

Collecting Hints: Bargains still can be found, especially at flea markets and garage sales. An appliance's design can help determine its age, e.g., an Art Deco toaster or coffeepot was made around 1910 to 1920.

The country decorating craze has caused most collectors to concentrate on the 1860 to 1900 period. Kitchen products of the 1900 to 1940s, with their enamel glazes and dependability, are popular. Aluminum wares are just coming into vogue as collectors discover their interesting shapes and colors.

History: The kitchen was a focal point in a family's environment until frozen food, TV dinners, and microwaves changed both meal preparation and dining habits.

Many early kitchen utensils were handmade and prized by their owners. Next came a period of utilitarian products made of tin and other metals. When the housewife no longer wished to work in a sterile environment, enamel and plastic products added color, and their unique design served both aesthetic and functional purposes.

The advent of home electricity changed the type and style of kitchen products. Fads affected many items. High technology already has made inroads into the kitchen, and another revolution seems at hand.

References: Ellen Bercovici, Bobbie Zucker Bryson and Deborah Gillham, *Collectibles for the Kitchen, Bath and Beyond,* Antique Trader Books, 1998; Walter Dworkin, *Price Guide to Holt-Howard Collectibles,* Krause Publications, 1998; Linda Fields, *Four & Twenty Blackbirds: A Pictorial Identification and Value Guide for Pie Birds,* published by author, (158 Bagsby Hill Lane, Dover, TN 37058); Linda Campbell Franklin, *300 Years of Housekeeping Collectibles,* Books Americana, 1992; —, *300 Years of Kitchen Collectibles,* 4th ed., Krause Publications, 1997; David T. Pikul and Ellen M. Plante, *Enameled Kitchenware American & European,* Schiffer Publishing, 2000; David G. Smith and Chuck Wafford, *The Book of Wagner & Griswold,* Schiffer Publishing, 2001; Don Thornton, *Beat This: The Eggbeater Chronicles,* Off Beat Books (1345 Poplar Ave., Sunnyvale, CA 94087), 1994; —, *The Eggbeater Chronicles,* 2nd edition, Thorton House, 1999.

Periodicals: *Cast Iron Cookware News,* 28 Angela Ave., San Anselmo, CA 94960; *Cookies,* 9610 Greenview Lane, Manassas, VA 20109; *Griswold Cast Iron Collectors' News & Marketplace,* P.O. Box 521, North East, PA 16428; *Kettles 'n Cookware,* P.O. Box B, Perrysville, NY 14129; *Kitchen*

Antiques & Collectibles News, 4645 Laurel Ridge Dr., Harrisburg, PA 17110; *Piebirds Unlimited,* 14 Harmony School Rd., Flemington, NJ 08822.

Collectors' Clubs: Association of Coffee Mill Enthusiasts, 5941 Wilkerson Rd, Rex, GA 30273; Cookie Cutter Collectors Club, 1167 Teal Rd, SW, Dellroy, OH 44620; Corn Items Collectors Association, Inc., 613 North Long St., Shelbyville, IL 62565; Eggcup Collectors' Corner, 67 Stevens Ave., Old Bridge, NJ 08857; Griswold & Cast Iron Cookware Association, 54 Macon Ave., Asheville, NC 28801; International Society for Apple Parer Enthusiasts, 3911 Morgan Center Rd, Utica, OH 43080; Jelly Jammers Club, 110 White Oak Dr., Butler, PA 16001; Kollectors of Old Kitchen Stuff, 501 Market St., Mifflinburg, PA 17844; National Reamer Collectors Association, 47 Midline Court, Gaithersburg, MD 20878-1996; Pie Bird Collectors Club, 158 Bagsby Hill Lane, Dover, TN 37058.

Museums and Libraries: Culinary Archives and Museum, Johnson & Wales University, Providence, RI; Culinary Institute of America; H. B. Meek Library, Cornell University; Judith Basin Museum, Stanford, MT; Kern County Museum, Bakersfield, CA; Mandeville Library, University of CA, San Diego, CA; Schlesinger Library, Radcliff College; Strong Museum, Rochester, NY; Wilbur Chocolate Co, Lititz, PA.

Additional Listings: Advertising, Cookbooks, Griswold, Kitchen Glassware, Reamers.

Mixing bowls, yellow ware with white slip lines, nested set of five, Morton Pottery Works, $280. Photo courtesy of Doris & Burdell Hall.

Angel Food Cake Pan, 10" d........... 28.00
Angel Food Cake Server, pale green Bakelite with swirls of yellow, metal tines 18.00
Apple Corer, White Mountain, orig box 30.00
Apple Peeler, Turntable No. 98 .... 85.00
Basket, 4-1/2" d, 5-1/2" h, wire, folding, tulip form 45.00
Basting Spoon, granite, cobalt blue handle 15.00
Biscuit Cutter, 1-12" d, tin, bail 10.00
Bowl
    Treasure Craft, green, large, fruit edged handles 10.00
    Walnut, 10" w, 11" l, 3" h 65.00
Bread Board, 12" d, 7-1/2" l, pine handle 90.00
Bread Box, tin, 12" l, white, red top.. 20.00
Breadstick Pan, nickeled cast iron, Wagner Ware 35.00
Bundt Pan, iron, scalloped, 4-1/2" x 10-1/2" 45.00
Butter Churn, Dazy, No. 40, wood paddles 125.00
Butter Fork, 7" x 2-1/2", hand carved maple 25.00
Butter Mold, 1-3/4" x 3-1/2", turned maple, carved floral design 45.00
Butter Paddle, wood, 10" l, 4-1/2" w 48.00
Button Hook, 7/8", Miller's Cocpa, multi-colored celluloid oval, meal hook, c1896 .... 40.00
Cake Carrier, aluminum, copper brushed color 27.50
Cake Mold, 13-3/8" l, 4-3/8" w, 8" h, lamb, cast aluminum 45.00
Cake Pan, tin
    8" d, Swans Down Cake Flour 15.00
    12", black, wire loop handle, Fries 12.00
Candy Scale, Mattocks, 2 lb, orig pan, 7" w, 13" l, 20" h, brass plate on enameled base "Eureka Automatic Scales, No. 35864" 195.00
Can Opener
    Cast Iron, bull's head holds blade, curved tail as handle, 2-1/4" w, 6-1/2" l 55.00
    Cast Iron, fish figure, c1865 ...... 140.00
    Metal, red wood handle 15.00
Canister Set, flour, sugar, coffee, and tea, set of four
    Brushed and polished aluminum, black plastic finials, mkd "AC Heller Hostess Ware, Made in Italy" 40.00
    Copper over aluminum, Lincoln Beauty Works, 1950s 24.00
Catalog
    Calumet Baking Powder Co., Chicago, IL, 1923, 24 pgs, 5" x 8" 12.00
    Revere Copper & Brass Co., Rome, NY, 1936, 8 pgs, 3" x 6", cooking utensils 13.00
    Rochester Stamping Co., Rochester, NY, 64 pgs, 4-1/2" x 7", chafing dishes 26.00
    Standard Electric Stove, Toledo, OH, 1927, 32 pgs, 8-1/2" x 11" 30.00

Cheese Grater, hanging, white china, gold trim, enameled blue forget-me-not dec 70.00

Cheese Slicer, enameled wood handle, marked "Unsco-Germany" 10.00

Cherry Seeder, Dandy 50A, orig damaged box 12.50

Chopping Knife, 6-1/2" l, Henry Disston & Sons, curved steel blade, wood handle 20.00

Cleanser, Guardian Service, unopened, black and silver Art Deco design 35.00

Clothes Sprinkler, ceramic, figural
Chinese Man, Shawnee Pottery 110.00
Elephant 75.00

Coffee Grinder, Olde Thompson, wooden base with dovetailed drawer and sides, iron hopper and handle, wood knob, mkd "Olde Thompson Coffee Mill, The Georges Thompson Corporation, 500 Mission Street, South Pasadena, Calif," 6-3/4" sq base, 8" h 95.00

Colander, aluminum, cone shaped, mkd "Wear-Ever, Made in USA, #4," hand held type 30.00

Cornstick Pan, Junior Krusty Korn Kobs, italic "Wagner Ware" trademark ..85.00

Creamer and Sugar, 3-3/4" w x 4-1/2" h creamer, 3-1/2" w x 2-3/4" h sugar, porcelain, pigs, white body, red-orange mouth, bowties, noses, and ears, black eyes and feet, some wear to glaze, unmarked 35.00

Decorating Tools, cylindrical tube, wooden pusher, changeable disks, mkd "Tala" 75.00

Dish Pan, enamel, gray 15.00

Double Boiler, cov, Porcelier, Sprig, pink, orange, and blue flowers, white ground 40.00

Dough Mixer, Universal, #8 ....125.00

Drink Mixer, Ovaltine, aluminum, 8" h 18.00

Drip-O-Later, Enterprise Aluminum, cream colored, green trim, mkd "Fraunfelter" 30.00

Dust Pan and Broom, Kitchen Prayer Lady 265.00

Egg Beater
9" l, H-L Beater, Tarrytown, NY, No. 0, cast wheel, gears, loop type handle, wood knob, wavy beaters 50.00
9-1/2" l, tin and iron, no markings, wavy beaters 85.00

Eggcup
Baby Bird 45.00
Bonzo, figural, Germany, 1920s 125.00
Charlie McCarthy, lusterware, Canadian, 1930s 60.00
Pluto, 1930s 125.00
Popeye, 1930s, multicolored 110.00

Egg Poacher, red enamel, gray enamel insert, 3-3/4" x 8" 24.00

Egg Separator, aluminum, 9" l 7.00

Egg Timer
Chef 50.00
Girl on phone 50.00

Winking Chef, timer on back 195.00

Egg Whip, spring-type, enameled wood handle 10.00

Figure, Lil Chef, RCA, Whirlpool adv, red plastic, cake decorating tip, 3-1/2" w, 5-1/2" l 10.00

Flour Sifter, Bromweld's, side crank, red wood knob 15.00

Food Chopper
Aluminum shaft and blades, red wooden handle, Hazel Atlas measuring cup base 20.00
Double blades, wood handle, some rust, 5-7/8" blade, 6-1/4" h 185.00
Wrought iron horse shaped shaft, wooden handle, 19th C 250.00

Funnel, Elliptical, gray graniteware ..30.00

Grease Jar, 4-3/8" h, 4-3/8" w, teapot shape, aluminum, strainer fits between lid and pot, mkd "Grease" on front, side mkd "Japan" 30.00

Jelly Mold, 3-1/2" d, 3-1/2" h, tin, Madeline, stamped "Of 539" 25.00

Knife Cleaner, cast iron, painted black, lettering highlighted in white "Spong & Co., Umeek, Patent, Knife Cleaner" 85.00

Lemon Squeezer
6-1/2" l, tin-plated iron 20.00
11" l, hinged maple 65.00

Pot holder, Kriebel's Dairies, Hereford, PA, muslin, 4-1/4" sq, $2.50.

Match Box Holder, ironware, striker bar mkd "C. Parker," also mkd "Pat. Sept. 14, 1869, May 3, 1870," 4-1/4" w, 1-5/8" d, 5-3/4" h 210.00

Mayonnaise Maker, 8-1/4" h, Wesson, glass base, aluminum top and mixer, orig directions 60.00

Meat Grinder, Sargent & Co., Patent March 8, 1892 ....40.00

Meat Tenderizer, 2" x 2-1/2" x 3", rect, iron, heavy handle 40.00

Meat Thermometer, 6" l, hanging, Taylor 10.00

Mixing Spoon, wood handle, slotted bowl, Androck, Made in USA 18.50

Mouli-Julienne, rotary cutter, three interchangeable cutting and shredding discs, orig box, c1950 ....30.00

Oats Crusher, English Pat. No. 448339, white ceramic body, wooden handles, 18" l 125.00

Pea Sheller, 12" h, screw clamp, black wood handle, Vaughans 40.00

Pie Bird
Blue and gray, long neck 90.00
Yellow and brown, long neck 90.00

Pitter, aluminum, hand squeeze type, 1920s 38.00

Potato Masher, 9" h, zig zag wire end, red catalin handle 10.00

Relish Tray, 15" l handle to handle, gold-colored aluminum tray, three-part 8-1/2" l, 7" w glass insert 25.00

Rolling Pin, 10" l, 3-1/2" handles, aluminum 40.00

Rolling Pin, 15" l, Harker China
Floral decal, replaced cork 150.00
Modern Tulip, wear to gold trim ..90.00

Salt Box, 8 x 17-1/2", rect, pine, hinged lid 120.00

Scale, Salter #50, green enameled base, orig 12" d round, 2" deep pan, 8-1/2" w, 14-1/2" h 175.00

Scoop, brass, wood handle, 6-1/2" l 50.00

Sherbet Set, Heller Hostess Ware Colorama, forest green scalloped dishes, anodized gold aluminum bases, set of 12 ....40.00

Shot Glasses, anodized aluminum, set of six tumblers, each a different color, metal stand, orig box 50.00

Sifter, three screens, colorful litho tin 20.00

Skillet, cast iron, Wagner Ware No. 3, italic trademark "Wagner Ware, Sidney-O" 15.00

Spice Set, spun aluminum, copper-colored tops, marked with name of spice, cayenne, allspice, nutmeg, ginger, cinnamon, cloves, mustard, paprika 35.00

Springerie Rolling Pin, 16" l, flag, owl, rabbit, cat, duck, leaf, florals 75.00

Strainer, wire mesh bowl, twisted wire and wood handle 10.00

Strawberry Huller, Nip-It, 1906 ....4.00

Stringholder, 6-1/2" h, table top type, cast aluminum, orig discolored paint, c1900 ....65.00

Sugar Nippers, 9" l, c1800 ....145.00

Tea Caddy, 8-1/2" h, tin, painted, red fruit, yellow leaves, orig cap 265.00

Tea Kettle, copper, gooseneck, dovetailed, sgd "JMWE" and hallmark 175.00

Teapot and Salt and Pepper Shakers, aluminum, four cup teapot, cov with red finial, orig strainer with red handle, orig box, mkd "Highly Polished Aluminum, Made in Japan" 25.00

Tin, rect, Krispy Crackers 35.00

Tom & Jerry Set
9-1/2" d, 4" h white ceramic bowl, eight 3" h x 3" d mugs, gold trim, Homer Laughlin, mkd "USA, E6NS" 75.00
9-1/2" d x 5-3/4" h bowl, eight footed 3-1/2" d cups, white milk glass, green and red dec. unmarked 35.00

11-1/4" d, six 3-1/2" h cups, white milk glass, multicolored scene of young couple in horse drawn sleigh, base mkd "McK," minor wear to decals 75.00

Tomato Slicer, enameled wood handle, orig litho sleeve...........................18.00

Toothpick Holder, Kitchen Prayer Lady, white..15.00

Vegetable Basket, 7" d, 5" h, wire, tapered, bale handle, 1870.........55.00

Vegetable Grater, Schroeter, tin, iron back, wood handle, old blue paint 40.00

Wall Plaque
Fruit, paint scuffed, 1950s.............8.00
Parrot, chalkware, 10" x 6", chips 12.00

Water Pitcher, aluminum
8" h, 6" d, deep red, mkd "Perma-Hues," missing small brad from ice lip..20.00
10" h, cast, black plastic handle. 18.00

Kitchen Glassware

Collecting Hints: Glassware for the kitchen was made in quantity. Although collectors do tolerate signs of use, they will not accept pieces with heavy damage. Many of the products contain applied decals; these should be in good condition. A collection can be built inexpensively by concentrating on one form, such as canister sets, measuring cups, or reamers.

History: The Depression era brought inexpensive kitchen and table products to center stage. The companies in the forefront of production included Hocking, Hazel Atlas, McKee, U.S. Glass, and Westmoreland.

Kitchen glassware complemented Depression glass. Many items were produced in the same color and style. Because the glass was molded, added decorative elements included ribs, fluting, arches and thumbprint patterns. In order to be durable, the glassware had to be thick. This resulted in forms which were difficult to handle at times and often awkward aesthetically. After World War II, aluminum products began to replace kitchen glassware.

References: Gene Florence, *Anchor Hocking's Fire-King & More*, 2nd ed., Collector Books, 2000; ——, *Kitchen Glassware of the Depression Years*, 6th ed., Collector Books, 2001; Joe Keller and David Ross, *Jadite: An Identification and Price Guide*, Schiffer Publishing, 1999; Garry Kilgo and Dale, Jerry, and Gail Wilkins, *Collectors Guide to Anchor Hocking's Fire-King Glassware*, K & W Collectibles Publisher, 1991; ——, *Collectors Guide to Anchor Hocking's Fire-King Glassware, Volume II*, K & W Collectibles Publisher, 1998; Barbara Mauzy, *Depression Era Kitchen Shakers*, Schiffer Publishing, 2001.

Periodical: Kitchen Antiques & Collectibles News, 4645 Laurel Ridge Dr., Harrisburg, PA 17110.

Collectors' Club: Glass Knife Collectors Club, P.O. Box 342, Los Alamitos, CA 90720.

Batter Bowl
Anchor Hocking, set of 7", 8", 9", and 10" d, rimmed, transparent green 95.00
Pyrex, nested set of three, farm motif dec 40.00
Tufglass, two handles, two spouts..45.00

Batter Jug, McKee, red.................175.00

Beer Mug, yellow 40.00

Bowl
5-1/2" d, red, platonite, Criss-Cross.................................12.50
6" d, jade-ite, Jeannette...............16.00
7-1/2" d, cobalt blue, Hazel Atlas..45.00
8" d, green, Hocking.....................15.00
8" d, Orange Dot, custard............32.00
8-1/2" l, oval, Pyrex, beige, two handles, blue dec, 1-1/2 quart..........15.00
10" d, emerald glo...........................50.00

Butter Box, cov, 2 pound size, green 145.00

Butter Dish, cov, 1 pound size
Criss Cross, crystal.....................24.00
Federal, amber, 1 lb.....................35.00
Hocking, crystal 25.00
Jade-ite..95.00

Candle Warmer and Stand, Pyrex, 2-1/2" quart casserole, orig candle warmer and stand with wooden handles, slight use wear....................25.00

Canister
3" h, jade-ite, Jeannette, allspice, ginger, nutmeg, or pepper, each...65.00
5-1/2" h, sq, coffee, jade-ite, Jeannette......................................55.00
6" h, green, screw-on lid, smooth..38.00
16 oz, tea, jade-ite, round.........175.00
20 oz, tea, Delphite, round.......275.00
28 oz, sugar, jade-ite 300.00
40 oz, coffee, Delphite, round..450.00
40 oz, coffee, jade-ite, round....300.00
52 oz, jade-ite, lid........................80.00

Canning Funnel, 4-1/2" d opening at top, 2" d base...................................20.00

Casserole, cov, Pyrex
1 quart, divided, chartreuse, milk glass white cover with green gooseberry dec, MIB...........................25.00

2-1/2 quart, Gold and Black Stripped Ovenware 25.00

Cheese Dish, cov, slicer, opaque white...90.00

Churn, 7" w, 8-1/2" h, Gem Dandy Electric Churn, 4 qt, "Enjoy Delicious Fresh (pointing to milk and butter), Made so easily with Gem Dandy Electric Churn," other side shows churn and cow stating "For use with Gem Dandy Electric Churn, made by Alabama Manufacturing Co., Birmingham, 3, Ala"..45.00

Coffeepot, cov, Pyrex, Model #7759, 9 cup..60.00

Creamer, Criss-Cross, crystal 40.00

Cruet, stopper, Crystolite, amber.....32.00

Curtain Tiebacks, pr
2-1/2" d, knob-type, pink.............38.00
3-1/2" d, flat, floral, green and pink 25.00
4-1/2" d, flat, floral, amber...........28.00

Custard, green, Tufglas 6.50

Double Boiler, Pyrex, orig paper instruction insert 30.00

Drawer Pull, crystal
Double type................................10.00
Knob 3.00

Drippings Jar, cov, jade-ite, Jeannette......................................32.00

Egg Cup, double, black...................12.00

Flour Shaker
Deco, ivory, black lettering 45.00
Roman Arch, ivory.......................45.00

Fork and Spoon, amber handle.......45.00

Fruit Bowl, Sunkist, pink...............335.00

Funnel, green...................................35.00

Furniture Caster, 3" d, transparent green, Hazel-Atlas 40.00

Grease Jar
Red Dots, white...........................30.00
Seville Yellow, black trim.............35.00
Tulips, cov, Hocking.....................15.00

Hand Beater, 32 oz measuring cup base
Green..45.00
Green, stippled texture 45.00

Iced Tea Spoons, colored handles, set of 12 ....60.00

Kitchen Cabinet Coffee Jar, 4" wide, 7" h, clear body, orig tin lid with minor dents, "S" in circle on bottom 48.00

Knife
Block, 8-1/4" l, crystal, orig box 28.00
Flower, pink, 9-1/4" l 50.00
Plain, 9-1/8" l, green....................40.00
Stonex, dark amber, MIB 375.00
Three Leaf, green.........................35.00
Three Star, blue or crystal 38.00

Lemon Reamer
Delphite, Jeannette 80.00
Jade-ite, Jeannette......................35.00
Pink, Hazel-Atlas 35.00

Loaf Pan, cov, 5" x 8", Glassbake, clear, knob finial 35.00

Loaf Pan, open, 9-1/8" l, 5-1/2" w, 2-3/4" deep, Fire King, Sapphire 24.00

Mayonnaise Ladle
Amber, flat 9.75
Pink, transparent 20.00

Measuring Cup
    2 oz, 1/4 cup, jade-ite,
    Jeannette 40.00
    8 oz, Delphite, 1 spout 110.00
    8 oz, Fire-King, 1 spout 18.50
    8 oz, green, transparent.............. 18.00
    16 oz, cobalt blue,
    Hazel-Atlas................................175.00
    16 oz, green, regular
    handle 24.00
    16 oz, green, stick handle, U.S.
    Glass 28.50
    16 oz, white milk glass 24.00
Measuring Pitcher, 7-1/2" h, 4" d, Family
    Measuring Jar, measurements in dry
    pounds and liquid, pouring spout,
    mkd "Family Measuring Jar, Manufac-
    tured by the Rochester Tumbler
    Co." 165.00
Mixing Bowl
    5-3/4" d, Gold and Black Stripped
    Ovenware, Pyrex 25.00
    6-1/2" d, amber, Federal.............. 10.00
    6-1/2" d, green, Restwell 10.00
    7-1/4" d, yellow banded dot,
    Pyrex 10.00
    7-1/2" d, cobalt blue, Hazel-
    Atlas 42.00
    7-1/2" d, Criss-Cross, blue 85.00
    7-1/4" d, 3-3/4" h, green, white ivy
    dec 25.00
    8-1/2" d, cobalt blue, Hazel-
    Atlas 50.00
    8-1/2" d, Criss-Cross, blue 100.00
    9-1/2" d, amber, Federal.............. 18.00
    11" d, Vitrock, white 15.00
Mixing Bowl Set, nested, Pyrex
    Butterprint, 4 pcs 75.00
    Primary colors, 5-3/4" x 3-1/4" blue,
    7-1/4" x 3-3/4" red, 8-5/8" x 4-1/4"
    green, 10-3/8" x 4-1/2" yellow......95.00

Mug, Ranger Joe, Hazel-Atlas, blue or
    red 10.00
Pitcher
    Delphite, 2 cup......................... 150.00
    Jade-ite, sunflower in base 40.00
Range Shaker, sq, flour, jade-ite, Jean-
    nette..30.00
Refrigerator Bowl, cov, Jennyware, pink,
    16 oz, round 48.00
Refrigerator Dish, cov
    4" x 4", Criss-Cross, blue 35.00
    4" x 5", jade-ite............................80.00
    4" x 8", Criss-Cross, blue 100.00
    4" x 8", floral carved, transparent
    green, U.S. Glass.........................30.00
    4-1/2 x 4-1/2" sq, pink,
    Jennyware 35.00
    5" x 8", jade-ite............................80.00
    5" x 10", jade-ite 150.00
    6" x 3", transparent green,
    Tufglass 45.00
    6-1/2" sq, Poppy Cocklebur, transpar-
    ent green, U.S. Glass..................55.00
    8" x 8", sq, amber, Federal..........25.00
    8-1/2" x 4-1/2", jade-ite,
    Jeannette.....................................32.00
Refrigerator Set, Pyrex, Early American
    pattern, some roughness 48.00
Relish, 8-1/2" x 13" oval, delfite, divided,
    Pyrex...20.00
Rolling Pin, clambroth, metal
    handles 125.00
Salad Fork and Spoon, blue.............55.00
Salt and Pepper Shakers, pr
    Cobalt Blue, red lids, Hazel-
    Atlas..30.00
    Jade-ite, ... 150.00
    Jennyware, ftd, pink....................55.00
    Ribbed, jade-ite, Jeannette 22.00
    Roman Arches, black, minor damage
    to lids 45.00

Ships, red trim, red lids 55.00
Salt Box, 4-1/2" x 3-3/4", crystal 25.00
Skillet, jade-ite, 1 spout 150.00
Spice Set, green lids, Scotty Dog dec,
    green tier holder, cinnamon, ginger,
    red, pepper, paprika, mustard, cloves,
    allspice, set................................ 325.00
Spoon, clear, Higbee 25.00
Straw Holder, green transparent.... 500.00
Sugar Jar, slanted, clear glass, base emb
    "Pat. apl. 1.1924," orig lid, small
    chips 35.00
Sugar Shaker, cov
    Criss-Cross design, transparent
    green, Hazel-Atlas....................... 35.00
    Roman Arch, custard, red dot 60.00
Sugar Shaker
    Green... 145.00
    Jade-ite...................................... 175.00
Syrup Pitcher
    Crystal, gold catalin handle 12.00
    Crystal, flower etch..................... 35.00
    Green, Hazel-Atlas 45.00
Syrup Bottle, 6" h, green, Hazel Atlas, orig
    tin lid, handle, pouring spout 60.00
Tom & Jerry Mug, Hazel Atlas, words and
    music to "Auld Lang Syne" on one
    side, 3" h 4.00
Towel Bar, 24" l, crystal, orig
    hardware...................................... 15.00
Tumbler, Hazel Atlas, white
    3-1/2" h, 9 oz............................... 5.00
    4-1/2" h, 16 oz............................. 7.00
Vase, bud, jade-ite, Jeannette 18.00
Water Bottle, clear, glass lid,
    Hocking 27.50

L

Labels

Collecting Hints: Damaged, trimmed, or torn labels are less valuable than labels in mint condition. Collectors prefer labels that can be removed from the product and stored flat in drawers or albums.

History: The first fruit-crate art was created by California fruit growers about 1880. The labels became very colorful and covered many subjects. Most depict the type of fruit held in the box. Cardboard boxes replaced fruit crates in the 1940s, making the labels collectible.

Over the last decade, label collectors have begun to widen their collecting range. Today, can, luggage, and wine labels are sought as well as cigar, fruit crate, and other household-type labels.

References: Joe Davidson, *Fruit Crate Art*, Wellfleet Press, 1990; Gorden T. McClelland and Jay T. Last, *Fruit Box Labels*, Hillcrest Press (3412-G MacArthur Blvd., Santa Ana, CA 92704), 1995; Gerard S. Petrone, *Cigar Box Labels: Portraits of Life, Mirrors of History*, Schiffer, 1998.

Collectors' Clubs: Citrus Label Society, 131 Miramonte Dr., Fullerton, CA 92365; Florida Citrus Labels Collectors Association, P.O. Box 547636, Orlando, FL 32854; International Seal, Label & Cigar Band Society, 8915 E. Bellevue St., Tucson, AZ 85715; Society of Antique Label Collectors, P.O. Box 24811, Tampa FL 33623.

Advisor: Lorie Cairns.

Apple, 10-1/2" x 9"

Apple Kids, two little boys lugging huge apple up a mountain side 4.00
Aurora, three colorful apples on branches, handsome farm scene 2.00
Blewett Pass, 1940s auto on mountain pass road 2.00
Bob White, perky bird, red ground, lug label..50
Carriage Trade, pair of horses pulling carriage with four people, blue ground...2.00
Chief Joseph, Indian Chief, blue ground...4.00
Don't Worry, little boy holding apple with bite taken out of it, black ground ..2.00
Duckwall, pretty wood duck by stone wall, blue ground 1.00

Eatmor, cute boy wearing straw hat and bib overalls, holding apple with bites taken out of it, navy ground...........6.00
Empire Builder, packing house and orchard scene, big red apple 1.00
Falls, huge falls, black ground 2.00
Gilbert Orchards, snowy mountain peaks, two big red apples..........................3.00
Gloriosa, grand orchard vista, snowy mountains.................................5.00
Hesperian, stylized blue Art Deco lady, holding yellow apple, orange ground...3.00
Hy-Land Kids, two red headed boys harvesting big red apple.....................3.00
Independent, blue Liberty Bell, red ground...2.00
Jersey Jerry, cute laughing little boy holding red apple, black ground..........6.00
Kile, two red apples, bold letters, blue ground...2.50
Lake Wenatchee, mountain scene, log cabin by lake, two apples 2.00
Mariposa, colorful butterfly, flowers, navy blue...15.00
Morjon, little boy blowing big horn, two big apples, flowering shrubs.........2.00
My Treat, tri-color apples, blue and black ground...2.00
Nor Cen, big red apple, black ground...2.00
Nuchief, Indian boy holding apple, blue ground...3.00
Oneonta, three bright apples, black ground...4.00
Owl, horned owl looking at three colorful apples...5.00
Pacific, cluster of three colorful apples, inset of battle ships, blue and black ground...2.00
Plen Tee Color, smiling Indian girl, red apple, blue ground 3.00
Red Fox, red fox in field, fence, hills, trees, curved basket label.............6.00
Rose Apples, two big pink roses, blue ground...3.00
Sapphire, big facetted sapphire and gold ring, navy blue ground 2.00
Sky Ranch, apple headed cowboy....2.00
Snomaid, snowgirl admiring big red apple, blue ground 1.00
State Seal, portrait of George Washington, blue ground................................50
Taylor Maid, blond girl, blue ground ..4.00
Teacher's Pet, school scene, little boy offering red apple to smiling teacher 20.00
Top Dog, black poodle seated on apple crate with Top Dog label on it, two apples, red ground, Austrialian...10.00
Washington's Best, three colorful apples, navy blue ground..........................4.00
Wilko, yellow apple, red ground, green border..1.00
Yakima Valley Apples, three colorful apples, Art Nouveau border..........6.00

Baking Powder

Autocrat, heaping plate of biscuits, gilt trim, New Orleans 2.00

Betty Ann, little red haired girl, pink dress, skipping rope, white ground, gilt border, Hastings, NE 3.00
Capitol, capitol dome and building, cream ground, 10 oz, Charleston, WV.. .75
Clabber Girl, little girl carrying plate of biscuits, family scene in blue and white...1.00
Popover, plate of biscuits, white ground 1.00

Blueberry Can

Blueberry Hill, luscious blueberry cluster and blueberry pie, embossed, gilt trim.. 2.50
Forhan's Square, four hands pointing to square, cluster of blueberries embossed, gilt trim......................2.50
Herricks, two images of blueberry clusters on branch 1.50
Raymond, blueberry pie with piece missing, cluster of blueberries, embossed, gilt trim 2.00
Sundrop, cluster of blueberries, 4-1/4" x 7-7/8"..1.00

Grape, 13" x 4"

Arenas, spray of bright red carnations, green leaves, navy blue ground.....50
Baby Marie, cute little girl, yellow and brown ground..................................50

Red Wagon Brand, happy boy pushing red wagon with grapes in it, red-violet background, $.25. Label courtesy of Lorie Cairns.

Rocky Hill America Grapes, Indian Chief on horseback on rocky precipice, blue and black ground, $.75. Label courtesy of Lorie Cairns.

Beaver, big beaver at water's edge, red grapes 75
Big Stump, forest scene with huge redwood tree stump with two people standing on it, light blue ground.....75
Black Bear, comical black bear operating wine press, red ground....................75
Blue Goose, blue goose, orange ground 25
California Beauty, bunch of roses, bunch of grapes 25
Corsage, large white camellia, terra cotta ground 25
Desert Rat, grizzled old prospector and his mule, desert scene................. 1.50
Dewy Fresh, cherub, green leaves, red and white ground 25

Emblem, spray of bright orange California poppies, green leaves, black ground..50

Flying E, yellow, orange, and red shaded "E" with huge wings, black ground. .50

Fremont, silhouette of soldier in orange circle, black ground..........................25

Gold Rush, gold nuggets falling from sky, mountain scene background..........25

Golden West, bay scene, two ships framed by grapes and plums 2.00

Holiday, colorful letters, blue ground 25

Ivanhoe, bright knight Ivanhoe on white horse, red trappings, black ground .25

J.J., two perky bluejays perched on big letter "J"..75

Jo-An, elephant on red sunburst, blue ground..50

La Paloma, gentle dove, bunches of green and red grapes, red and yellow ground...25

Liberty Bell, large bell, blue ground......25

Locomotive Engineer, big "Fruit Special" train speeding through vineyards . 4.00

Mac-D, red to yellow name on Scotch plaid ground 25

Montana, foothill grove scene, snow cap mountains 25

Nile, desert scene, two camels and riders, palms, sphinx, orange sunset...25

Old Mission, Spanish Mission scene with monks, mission bells, green grapes, 1920s 1.00

Out West, cowboy on horseback, lariat encircling words "Out West" 1.00

Pacific Pride, San Francisco Bay scene, bridge, ship, houses, hills, blue ground.. 1.00

Pilgrim, stern faced pilgrim holding bible, green ground 25

Polar Bird, cute penguin standing on iceberg, icicles on maroon ground.......25

Race Track, race track scene, horses on track, cars inside track, bunch tokays within horseshoe in center 75

Rayo Sunshine, orange sunrise, golden rays and skies, lush green vineyards...25

Red Mule, bucking red mule, black ground...75

Royal Choice, jeweled crown on red cushion... 1.00

Sequoia Foothills, farm scene, snowy mountains background 5.00

Setter, Irish Setter, green and blue ground...25

Suncolor, bright red and green grapes, red ground 25

Table Treat, laughing King's face, red ground...25

Top Gun, big revolver, yellow ground... 2.00

Tulare Chief, Indian Chief, black ground... 2.00

Valley Boy, red haired boy wearing beanie, fruit basket...........................75

Western Sky, sunset over San Francisco Bay Bridge, city lights 50

Win, flagman waving checkered flag, bleachers in background 25

Lemon, 12-1/2" x 8-3/4"

Ak-Sar-Ben, Hybrid Lemons, red and black letters, black ground..........50.00

Athlete, three runners reaching finish line in stadium, Claremont.....................5.00

Basket, golden basket holding 5 lemons, blue ground, Lemon Cove 2.00

Bridal Veil, Bridal Veil Falls, Yosemite Park, lemon, Santa Paula 12.00

Channel, seacoast scene, sailing vessels, island, orchards, homes in center, five large flying seagulls, blue ground, Santa Barbara.....................................2.00

Cutter, boat going full speed ahead through choppy seas, orange and gold sky, dated 1937, Oxnard.......3.00

El Merito, lemons, blue, green, yellows, Santa Paula 1.00

Evening Star, star shining over large Spanish mission, palms, groves, mountain city lights in background, San Fernando 2.00

Festival, two bay horses drawing a cart bedecked with pink flowers, two lady passengers, driver, Santa Barbara 2.00

Galleon, sailing high seas, sky background, c1937, Oxnard 6.00

Golden State, four lemons, leaves, map of California, Lemon Cove 2.00

Kaweah Maid, Indian girl wearing turquoise beads, brown ground, Lemon Cove 6.00

Lemonade, three large lemons and leaves, mountain orchards, Ivanhoe..1.00

Lofty, orchard scene, snowy mountain peak, lemons, leaves, glass of lemonade with maraschino cherry and straw, half lemon, pink and maroon ground, Fallbrook.......................................2.00

Meteor, meteor streaking through evening sky, San Fernando 4.00

Morning Smile, lemon on Sunkist wrapper, blue ground, Porterville 1.00

Oxnard, man tilling soil with ox team, mission in background 2.00

Pacific, large center lemon, Hawaiian Islands, maps of Asia, Australia, Pacific coast, trade routes, blue ocean, 1917, Santa Barbara 2.00

Pitcher, lady's face on elegant Victorian silver pitcher, cerise tablecloth, deep blue ground, green border, Santa Paula...4.00

Ramona Memories, romantic Spanish senorita with roses in her hair, San Fernando.................................3.00

Rough Diamond, large "L" in diamond, lime green ground, Santa Paula....1.00

Santa Rosa, man and burro, Spanish style home overlooking lemon orchard, Oxnard...............................2.00

Sea Gull, white flying gulls with black tipped wings, ocean and sky ground, black border, Upland....................8.50

Sespe, mountain scene, river, trees, rocks, black ground, Fillmore........2.00

Shamrock, green shamrock over grove scene, Placentia............................2.00

Silver Moon, large Spanish mission, palms, groves, mountains, lemons, Ivanhoe...2.00

Sunkist Californian Lemons, lemon, yellow letters, black ground, Los Angeles................................... 1.00

Vesper, people going to evening church, maroon ground, Porterville 2.00

Whiz, dynamic lettering on yellow streak, Saticoy...4.00

Orange, 11" x 11"

Airship, old commercial plane, royal blue ground, Fillmore 20.00

Altissimo, pink, aqua, and blue mountains, blue sky background, dated 1918, Placentia..................................2.00

Avenue, palm and eucalyptus tree lined shady avenue, early auto, Riverside... 4.00

Big J, large red and yellow "J" on blue seal, orange leaves, blossom, pale yellow ground, San Francisco 1.00

Brownies, several Brownies preparing orange juice, yellow sun, blue ground, Lemon Cove 8.00

Caledonia, spray of thistles, bright tartan plaid ground, Placentia................. 1.00

Cambria, large brown eagle, two torches, blue ground, brown border, Placentia...................................... 1.00

Corona Lily, white and green speckled lily, black ground, Corona................... 4.00

Dahlia, white daisy, green leaves, black ground, Redlands 3.00

Desert Glow, red shading into yellow letters, blue ground, Highgrove, tangerines, lug size....................................50

Double A, train on trestle supported by two large "A"s as foundations, East Highlands 2.00

Exeter, large Tulare County map, orange, red, and blue ground 2.00

Full O'Juice, partially peeled orange, glass, lavender ground, Redlands 2.00

Gladiola, two large sprays of pink gladiolas on gold-tan ground, Corvina... 3.00

Gold Coast, orange shaped sun over ocean near rocky coast with trees, Fullerton... 7.00

Golden Rod, spray of golden rod, black ground 2.00

Hill Beauty, orchard scene, purple mountains, yellow and blue sky, orange with leaves and blossoms, aqua ground, Porterville...................................... 2.00

Homer, flying homing pigeon, orange, blue, and black ground, Corona .. 2.00

Idyllwild, two oranges, grove, home, scenic, snowy mountains, black ground, Riverside....................................... 2.00

John & Martha, small picture of oranges, white ground, Reedley 1.00

Kaweah River Belle, country scene, Spanish mission, snow capped mountain peaks, bunch of oranges, Lemon Cove 5.00

Legal Tender, $250 bundle of currency, black and blue ground, Fillmore ... 3.00

Lincoln, portrait of Lincoln, orange leaves, Riverside 3.00

Madras, large orange, blossoms, leaves, black ground, Irvine 50

Memory, silhouette of girl in picture frame, glass bud vase, pink roses, Porterville 12.00

National Orange Co., capitol buildings, blue ground, Riverside, strip label 2.00

Orange Circle, large orange circle, two oranges, black and blue ground, Orange Cove 1.00

Orchard King, big orange wearing crown, blue ground, Covina 2.00

Pine Cone, arrowhead on mountain framed inside huge pine cone on bough, orange, Ed. Highlands ... 10.00

Pride of Venice Cove, crowing rooster, two oranges, leaves, blossom, maroon ground, Ivanhoe 3.00

Princess, princess in royal robes, crown jewels, grapefruit, leaves, blue ground, dated 1911, 1939, Corona 2.00

Rebecca, Rebecca by the well, holding water jug, Placentia 7.00

Red Peak, green, brown, and white mountain peak, red sky, Tustin 5.00

Satin, draped pink satin, Sunkist orange, Irvine 1.00

Strathmore, Scottish bagpiper in kilts, thistles, deep blue ground, red plaid border 2.00

Sunflower, huge yellow sunflower, black ground 3.00

Talisman, three roses, leaves, black and blue ground, Redlands 3.00

Treetop, giant twin Sequoia trees, yellow letters, blue ground, Lemon Cove 2.00

Unicorn, galloping pinto unicorn, E. Highlands 25.00

Upland Pride, red rose and bud, navy ground, Porterville 2.00

Victoria, portrait of Queen Victoria, wearing crown, jewels, oranges and leaves nearby, Riverside 2.00

Washington, Washington monument, pool, trees, deep blue round, Exeter 1.00

Woodland Gold, black gnarled tree, lake with gold, purple, and green mountain, Woodlake 2.00

Yokohl, Indian brave fishing by stream, oranges, red ground, Exeter 5.00

Pear, 10-3/4" x 7-14"

A, three pears on branch, aqua ground, gilt border 1.00

All Good, big shaded letters on wood grained ground, green pear 1.50

Blazing Star, big exotic yellow flower on royal blue ground 1.50

Buckingham, cowboy riding bucking pig, blue ground 4.00

Camel, camel and master at sunrise, desert scene 3.00

Silver Tip, Strathmore Grape Growers Assn., brown bear and mountains, black ground, $.50. Label courtesy of Lorie Cairns.

Valley Queen, regal young lady wearing crown, red grapes, vivid colors, 1950s, $.25. Label courtesy of Lorie Cairns.

Cascadian, snowy scene, frozen pond, snow covered trees, pear 1.00

Covered Wagon, pioneers and covered wagon, ox team 4.00

Donner, snowy Lake Tahoe scene, bridge 2.00

Eagle, small eagle in upper left corner, two pears, navy ground 2.00

El Rio Orchards, pair of yellow pears, blue ground 50

Far West, frontiersman gazing at lake 2.00

Golden, yellow train, blue an black ground 4.50

K-O, boxing glove fist delivering punch, yellow border 8.00

Lake Diamond, pear within diamond 50

Life, fisherman catching trout 5.00

Magic Lake, snowy egrets wading in blue lake, mountain background, strip label 1.00

Mr. Pear, cartoon pear with top hat and cane, blue ground 2.00

Oh Yes, We Grow The Best, two big yellow pears, blue ground 50

Piggy Pears, carton character, pink pig wearing clothes and bonnet, carrying green basket of pears, maroon ground 3.00

Poppy, California poppy, two pears, blue ground 1.00

Repetition, three little boys in knitted caps and striped shirts standing behind crates of pears, black ground 2.00

River Made, Dutch girl walking by canal, windmill, lug label 1.00

Sanclar, two big pears on blue Art Deco ground 1.00

Snow Crest, orchard scene, snowy peak, farmhouse framed by forest trees . 1.00

Still Water, serene sylvan scene, big trees, pond, lug label 75

Sun Smile, smiling sun and rays, navy blue ground 2.00

Swan, white swan, black ground 4.00

Tie-It-On, running dog, pear tied to tail, blue ground 2.00

Violet, big punch of purple violets, black ground 4.00

Wagontrain, scene of covered wagons, ox teams, pioneers, buffalos 3.00

Yuba Orchard, two yellow pears, blue ground 50

Tin Can

Arcadia Beauty, bowl cut refugee beans, aqua border, 6-1/2" x 10" 2.50

Bess, two images of tan cow's head 2.00

Cloth of Gold, red bird, bowl of succotash 1.00

Clover Farm, cow and clover blossom, 2-1/4" x 8" 1.50

Ellendale, forest scene, stream, mountains, limas in pods 1.00

Farmers Pride, little girl and elderly man, lima beans 1.00

Isaacs Brand, lake and woods scene, sailboat, tent, peas, and pods 1.50

June Peas, crystal bowl with peas, red roses, and leaves, Baltimore, MD. 2.00

Lark Brand, lark walking in field, trees, house, big tomato, yellow ground 6.00

Mayfield, sunrise country scene, fancy ftd dish of June peas, gilt trim 1.00

Memorial, big white memorial building, red ground, 6-1/2" x 8-1/2" 1.00

Norwich Spinach, two big bunches, light orange and white, gilt ground, 1920s 1.50

Old Black Joe, elderly black man and cabin, black eyed peas 2.00

Page Valley, factory, orchard, red apples, bowl of applesauce 1.00

Preston, lima beans, pods, and leaves, black and red ground 1.00

Red Rose, big red rose and buds, gilt trim, Art Deco design 2.00

Safety, hand pouring evaporated milk into pitcher, red, blue, aqua, and white ground 2.00

Supreme Court, court house, blue shaded Art Deco accents, diced carrots in green bowl 75

Tropic Peas, roaring lion's head, fruits, navy blue on white ground 2.00

Winsom, bowl of diced beets, gilt trim 1.00

Vegetables, 7" x 9"

Beau Geste, Foreign Legion soldier playing bugle in desert 1.00

Big Patch, boy with patched overalls, dog gazing at green farmland 5.00

Bonnie Babe, wide-eyed Scotch lassie holding big head of lettuce, plaid ground 5.00

Challenger, red silhouette of cowboy and bronco in blue circle, blue ground 1.00

Dominator, WWII fighter plane, blue ground 3.00

Flying Colors, three red and white striped flags on blue starred ground 1.00

Gulf, scene with sailboats, beach, palm trees 1.00

Hot Brand, cattle branding scene, cowboys, horse, desert background .. 2.00

Kreme De Koke, blond lady figure skater, navy ground 4.00

Lion, full figure majestic lion, blue and black ground 1.00

Mustang, white horse 1.00

Pinto, vaquero and pinto horse 2.00

Royal Bruce, gold coat of arms, plaid ground 1.00

RRR, rainbow, desert scene 2.00

Tot, baby's face, group of veggies, blue ground 2.00

Up 'N Atom, fighting mad jack rabbit wearing boxing gloves, blue and green ground 2.00

Volume, big blue book titled "Quality Vegetables," red ground 2.00

Yam and Sweet Potato, 9" sq

Bama Yams, yams spilling out of wooden crate with Bama label on it 2.00

Champ, two football players, blue ground 2.00

Deer Mark, stag's head over two sweet potatoes, red ground 1.00

Don't Cry, black youth shooting dice 5.00

Gene-O, man in top hat and tails holding diamond studded cane and big yam .... .75

Honest John, smiling man in bib overalls, straw hat, holding crate of yams ... 6.00

Ken Kat, black cat seated in aqua circle, two yams, navy ground 3.00

LA Grange Sweets, map of LA and state house, three sweet potatoes 1.00

Mary Agnes, little pigtailed blond girl holding big straw hat full of yams . 2.00

Pride of the Farm, farm scene, red roofed homes, barn, yams 1.00

Smoky Jim's, smiling black man with crate of yams 2.00

Sweeties, little girl in green dress holding yam high above her head, rural scene background 1.00

Vitamin, kitchen scene with Mother feeding son vitamins while he's pointing to yams on kitchen table 1.00

Lamps

Collecting Hints: Be aware that every lamp has two values—a collectible value and a decorative value. Often the decorative value exceeds the collectible value, in part because most lamps are purchased as decorative accessories, often as accent pieces in a period room setting.

In the 1990s, the hot lamp collectibles were the odd-shaped examples from the 1950s. Some of these were abstract; some, figural. While 1950s' lamps continue to sell well as part of the 1950s/1960s revival, prices have stabilized primarily because of the market saturation resulting from the large quantity of lamps of this era that survived in attics and basements, due, in large part, to the promotional efforts of J. W. Courter. One man can make a market.

Within the past five years, collector interest is spreading to other manufacturers and into electric lamps, although Aladdin is still one of the most sought after names in lamps.

Just as post-World War II collectors discovered figural transistor and character radios, so also are they discovering motion lamps, many of which are character related. Look for a growing interest in character lamps and a corresponding rise in prices.

History: The kerosene lamp was the predominant lighting device during the 19th century and the first quarter of the 20th century. However, its death knell was sounded in 1879 when Thomas A. Edison developed a viable electric light bulb.

The success of the electric lamp depended on the availability of electricity. However, what we take for granted today did not arrive in many rural areas until the 1930s.

Most electric lamps were designed to serve as silent compliments to period design styles. They were meant to blend, rather than stand out. Pairs were quite common.

Famous industrial designers did lend their talents to lamp design, and their products are eagerly sought by collectors. Bradley and Hubbard and Handel are two companies whose products have attracted strong collector interest.

References: *Better Electric Lamps of the '20s and '30s*, L-W Book Sales, 1997; *Quality Electric Lamps*, L-W Book Sales, 1992, 1996 value update; J. W. Courter, *Aladdin Collectors Manual & Price Guide #18, Kerosene Mantle Lamps*, published by author (note: all the Courter books are available from the author, 3935 Kelley Rd, Kevil, KY 42053), 1998; —, *Aladdin Electric Lamps Price Guide #2*, published by author, 1993; —, *Angle Lamps: Collectors Manual & Price Guide*, published by author, 1992; *Electric Lighting of the '20s & '30s*, Vol. 1 (1988, 1998 value update), Vol. 2 (1994, 1998 value update), L-W Book Sales; Bill and Linda Montgomery, *Animation Motion Lamps*, L-W Book Sales, 1991; Leland and Crystal Payton, *Turned On: Decorative Lamps of the 'Fifties*, Abbeville Press, 1989; Sam and Anna Samuelian, *Collector's Guide to Motion Lamps*, Collector Books, 1998; Tom Santiso, *TV Lamps*, Collector Books, 1999; Calvin Shepherd, *'50s T. V. Lamps*, Schiffer, 1998; Jo Ann Thomas, *Early Twentieth Century Lighting Fixtures*, Collector Books, 2000; —, *Lighting Fixtures of the Depression Era*, Collector Books, 2000.

Periodical: *Light Revival*, 35 W. Elm Ave., Quincy, MA 02170.

Collectors' Clubs: Aladdin Knights of the Mystic Light, 3935 Kelley Rd, Kevil, KY 42053; Coleman Collector Network, 1822 E. Fernwood, Wichita, KS 67216; Historical Lighting Society of Canada, 9013 Oxbox Rd, North East, PA 16428.

Table, figural, mountain goat, brown and green spatter over white, American Art Potteries, 15" h, $45. Photo courtesy of Doris & Burdell Hall.

Akro Agate, lavender and blue marbled shade 350.00

Aladdin, Alacite, electric

  #25 .... 48.00

  #236 .... 55.00

  #266 .... 50.00

  #351, round wall 65.00

  #354, rect wall 65.00

Bedroom

  Art Deco, Chase Chrome, round base, conical shade, c1930 .... 90.00

  Southern Belle, blue, orig shade 80.00

Character

  Fred Flintstone, 13-1/4" h, painted vinyl, black metal base, missing shade 45.00

  Hula Girl, Dodge, Inc., 1938, bronzed metal, shimming grass skirt ... 1,600.00

  Mickey Mouse, 4" d, 6-1/2" h, globular metal base, beige ground, three Mickey decals around sides, Soreng-Manegold Co 85.00

Children's

  ABC Blocks, wood and plastic, linen over cardboard shade 20.00

  Bambi, plastic, 1950s 30.00

  Cookie Monster, figural, Sesame Street characters on shade 45.00

Elephant, figural, ceramic, carousel
beaded shade 195.00
Football Player, 14-1/2" h, hollow plaster, football player standing next to figural football standard, linen over
cardboard shade, WK, Japan, Sears,
Roebuck, 1978 .... 25.00
Dresser
Black Cameo, silhouette of young
woman, surrounded by ribbon, Porce-
lier 48.00
Carved shell, cast brass winged crea-
ture with whole shell body, 1920s wir-
ing, 8" h 385.00
Floor
Brass, swing arm, orig shade ... 275.00
Two green marble sections, orig
matching finial, no shade 330.00
Headboard, pink, chrome 65.00
Lava, Lava Simplex Corp,
c1968 .... 80.00
Motion
Antique Cars, Econolite, 1957,
11" h 120.00
Cheers Bar, sexy girls, MIB 125.00
Fireside Peanut Vendor, dancing devil
graphics, 1930s 400.00
Forest Fire, Econolite, 1955 .... 115.00

Table, Lucite, series of tubular rods arranged in a spiral, circular ftd base, unmarked, 9-1/2" d, 38" h, $20. Photo courtesy of David Rago Auctions.

Fountain of Youth 150.00
Goldfish, green satin glass,
1931 .... 325.00
Niagara Falls, Goodman, extra wide
style 150.00
Snow Scene, bridge,
Econolite 165.00
Organ Grinder, monkey, pink 95.00
Radio, Michael Lumitone 200.00
Stenographer's, Emeralite, clamps onto
desk 395.00
Television
Flamingo, planter base, back incised
"Lane & Co., Van Nuys, Calif, No.
1081," 16" w, 14-1/2" h 495.00

Gondola, ceramic, brown with gold
trim, marked "Copyright Premco Mfg
Co, Chicago, IL, 1954," 16" w,
7" h 45.00
Horse Head, ceramic, 12" x
10-3/4" 25.00
Panther, black, 8-1/2" x 6-1/2" 35.00
Ship, 11" x 10-1/2", gold trim 35.00
Wicker, floor
Eiffel Tower design, shaped shade
with loop designs and latticework panels, base with latticework panels, tight
weaving, scalloped bottom edge,
cane-wrapped legs, brass caps, two
light bulbs, c1920, 26-1/2" d shade,
68-1/2" h 1,450.00
Shaped shade with woven patterns,
scalloped edge, tightly woven base
ending in braiding, three light bulbs,
c1920, 70-1/2" h 1,250.00
Wicker, table
Heywood Wakefield, latticework panels, two light bulbs, c1920, orig label,
26" h 625.00
Latticework panels, round base,
c1920, 24" h 595.00

Limited Edition Collectibles

Collecting Hints: The first item issued in a series usually commands a higher price. When buying a limited edition collectible be aware that the original box and/or certificates increase the value of the piece Be alert to special discounts and sales.

History: Limited edition plate collecting began with the advent of Christmas plates issued by Bing and Grondahl in 1895. Royal Copenhagen soon followed. During the late 1960s and early 1970s, several potteries, glass factories, and mints began to issue plates, bells, eggs, mugs, etc., which commemorated special events, people, places, or holidays. For a period of time, these items increased in popularity and value, but in the late 1970s, the market became flooded with many collectibles and prices declined.

There are many new issues of collector items annually. Some of these collectibles can be found listed under specific headings, such as Hummel, Norman Rockwell, etc.

References: *Collectors' Information Bureau Collectibles Market Guide & Price Index*, 18th ed., Krause Publications, 2000; Pat Owen, *Bing & Grondahl Christmas Plates*, Landfall Press, 1995; Mary Sieber (ed.), *2001 Price Guide to Limited Edition Collectibles,* Krause Publications, 2000.

Periodicals: *Collector Editions*, 170 Fifth Ave., 12th Floor, New York, NY 10010; *Collector's Bulletin*, 22341 E. Wells Rd, Canton IL 61520; *Collectors Mart Magazine*, 700 E. State St., Iola, WI 54990; *Collector News & Antique Reporter*, P.O. Box 156, Grundy Center, IA 50638; *Contemporary Doll Magazine*, 30595 Eight Mile, Livonia, MI 48152; *Hallmarkers Holiday Happening Collectors Club*, 6151 Main St., Springfield, OR 97478; *Insight on Collectibles*, 103 Lakeshore Rd, Ste. 202, St. Catharines, Ontario L2N 2T6 Canada; *International Collectible Showcase*, One Westminster Pl, Lake Forest, IL 60045; *Ornament Trader Magazine*, P.O. Box 7908, Clearwater, FL 34618; *Plate World*, 9200 N. Maryland Ave., Niles, IL 60648.

Collectors' Clubs: Annalee Doll Society, P.O. Box 1137, Meredith, NH 03253; Anri Collector's Society, P.O. Box 380760, Duncanville, TX 75183-0760; Club Anri, 55 Parcella Park Dr., Randolph, MA 02368; Del-Mar-Pa Ornament Kollector's Club, 131 S. Tartan Dr., Elkton, MD 21921; Disney Once Up A Classic Collectors Club, 11443, Dulcet Ave., Northridge, CA 91326; Donald Zolan Collectors Society, 133 E Carillo St., Santa Barbara, CA 93101; Dreamsicles Club, 1120 Califorinia Ave., Corona, CA 91719-3324; Franklin Heirloom Doll Club, U.S. Route 1, Franklin Center, PA 19091; Franklin Mint Collectors Society, U.S. Rte 1, Franklin Center, PA 19091; Gorham Collectors Club, P.O. Box 6472, Providence, RI 02940; Hallmark Keepsake Ornament Collectors' Club, P.O. Box 419034, Kansas City, MO 61441-6034; International Plate Collectors Guild, P.O. Box 487, Artesia, CA 90702; Jan Hagara Collectors' Club, 40114 Industrial Park North, Georgetown, TX 78626; Lladro Collectors Society, 43 W. 57th St., New York, NY 10019; Lowell Davis Farm Club, 55 Pacella Park Dr., Randolph, MA 02368; Modern Doll Club, 9628 Hidden Oaks Cr., Tampa, FL 33612; Precious Moments Collectors' Club, One Enesco Plaza, P.O. Box 1466, Elk Grove Village, IL 60009; Royal Doulton International Collectors' Club, 701 Cottontail Lane, Somerset, NJ 08873; Sarah's Attic Forever Friends Collectors Club, http://www.sarahasttic.com; Wedgwood Society of Boston, 28 Birchwood Drive, Hampstead, NH 03841.

Museum: Bradford Museum, Niles, IL.

Abbreviation: FE = First Edition.

Bells

Anri, J. Ferrandiz, artist, wooden
1976, Christmas, FE 55.00
1977, Christmas 45.00
1978, Christmas 40.00
1979, Christmas 30.00
1980, The Christmas King 15.00
1981, Lighting the Way 15.00
1982, Caring 15.00
1983, Behold 15.00
1985, Nature's Dream 15.00
1987, The Wedding Bell, silver ... 25.00
1988, Bride Belles, Caroline 27.50
1989, Christmas Pow-Pow 25.00
1990, Indian Brave 25.00

Bing & Grondahl, Christmas, annual
1980, Christmas in the Woods 45.00
1981, Christmas Peace 40.00
1982, Christmas Tree 40.00
1983, Christmas in Old Town 40.00
1984, Christmas Letter 40.00
1985, Christmas Eve at the Farm-
house 40.00
1986, Silent Night, Holy Night 40.00
1987, Snowman's Christmas
Eve 40.00
1988, Old Poet's Christmas 40.00
1989, Christmas Anchorage 45.00
1990, Changing of the Guards ... 45.00
1991, Copenhagen Stock
Exchange 50.00
1992, Christmas at the Rectory .. 55.00
1993, Father Christmas in Copen-
hagen 66.00

Danbury Mint, Norman Rockwell artist
1975, Doctor and Doll 50.00
1976, Saying Grace 40.00
1977, Santa's Mail 40.00
1979, Friend in Need 30.00

Enesco Corp., Precious Moments
1981, Jesus Loves Me 40.00
1982, Mother Sew Dear 35.00
1983, Surrounded with Joy 60.00
1984, Wishing You a Merry
Christmas 45.00
1989, Your Love Is Special to
Me 20.00
1990, Here Comes the Bride 25.00
1991, May Your Christmas Be
Merry 30.00
1992, But the Greatest of These Is
Love 25.00

Franklin Mint, 1979, Unicorn,
porcelain 35.00

Gorham, Norman Rockwell, artist
1975, Sweet Song So Young 50.00
1976, Snow Sculpture 45.00
1977, Chilling Chore, Christmas . 35.00
1978, Gay Blades 23.00
1979, Beguiling Buttercup 30.00
1980, Flying High 25.00
1981, Ski Skills, Christmas 27.00
1982, Young Man's Fancy 30.00
1983, Christmas Medley 30.00
1984, Young Love 28.00
1985, Yuletide Reflections 32.50
1986, Home for the Holidays 32.50
1987, Merry Christmas
Grandma 30.00
1988, The Homecoming 37.50

Hummel - see Hummel.
Hutschenreuther, 1978,
Christmas 8.00
Lenox, Songs of Christmas
1991, We Wish You a Merry
Christmas 45.00
1993, Jingle Bells 55.00
1995, Hark the Herald Angels
Sing 60.00
Lladro, Christmas
1987 .... 90.00
1988 .... 80.00
1989 .... 90.00
1990 .... 45.00
1991 .... 40.00
1992 .... 35.00
Pickard
1977, The First Noel, FE 75.00
1978, O Little Town of
Bethlehem 70.00
1979, Silent Night 80.00
1980, Hark! The Herald Angels
Sing 80.00
Reco International
1980, I Love You, FE 20.00
1981, Sea Echoes 20.00
1982, Talk to Me 20.00
1988, Charity 15.00
1989, The Wedding 15.00
Reed and Barton
1980, Noel 65.00
1981, Yuletide Holiday 20.00
1982, Little Shepherd 20.00
1983, Noel 45.00
1984, Noel 45.00
1985, Caroler 25.00
1986, Noel 55.00
1988, Christmas Morning 20.00
1989, Noel 50.00
1990, The Wreath Bearer 15.00
1992, My Special Friend 20.00
1992, Noel 40.00
1995, Christmas Puppy 20.00
River Shore, Rockwell children Series
1977, First Day of School 70.00
1978, Garden Girl 37.00
Schmid
Peanuts
1976, Woodstock 25.00
1977, Woodstock's
Christmas 20.00
1978, Mother's Day 18.00
1979, A Special Letter 25.00
1980, Waiting for Santa 25.00
1981, Mission for Mom 20.00
1982, Perfect Performance 20.00
1983, Peanuts in Concert 15.00
1984, Snoopy and the Beagle
Scouts 15.00
Walt Disney, Christmas
1985, Snow Big 15.00
1986, Tree for Two 15.00
1987, Merry Mouse
Medley 17.50
1988, Warm Winter Ride 18.00
1989, Merry Mickey Claus 24.00
1990, Holly Jolly Christmas 25.00
1991, Mickey & Minnie's Rockin'
Christmas 25.00
Towle Silversmiths, silver plated
1980, ball 19.50
1982, musical 27.50
1984, musical 25.00

1986, ball 30.00
1988, musical 35.00
Wedgwood
1979, Penguins, FE 40.00
1981, Polar Bears 45.00
1982, Moose 40.00
1983, Fur Seals 50.00
1984, Ibex 60.00
1985, Puffin 60.00
1986, Ermine 60.00

Christmas Ornaments

Anri
Disney Four Star Collection, Disney
Studios, 1990, Minnie Mouse 50.00
Ferrandiz Woodcarvings, J. Ferrandiz, artist, 1988, Heavenly
Drummer 250.00
Bing & Grondahl, Santa Claus
1989, Santa's Workshop 55.00
1990, Santa's Sleigh 55.00
1991, The Journey 40.00
1994, Christmas Stories 25.00

Danbury Mint, angel, 4" 45.00

Enesco, Precious Moments, S. Butcher,
artist
1982, Dropping in for Christmas 40.00
1983, O Come All Ye Faithful 55.00
1985, God Sent His Love 35.00
1986, Rocking Horse 25.00
1988, Cheers to the Leader 35.00
1992, I'm Nuts About You 15.00
1994, You Are Always in My
Heart 20.00

Gorham, Annual Snowflake, sterling
silver
1972 .... 110.00
1973 .... 90.00
1976 .... 65.00
1981 .... 300.00
1987 .... 80.00
1990 .... 65.00
1994 .... 55.00

Grossman, Dave, Creations, Rockwell
Collection, annual figurine ornament
1978, Caroler 44.00
1979, Drum for Tommy 28.00
1983, Fiddler 27.00
1987, Skating Lesson 30.00
1992, On the Ice 30.00

Hallmark
1974, Mary Hamilton, orig, Charmer
Design 7.50
1975, Betsy Clark 7.50
1979, Special Teacher, satin 4.50
1980, Baby's First Christmas 15.00
1981, Candyville Express 25.00
1981, Friendly Fiddler 15.00
1981, St. Nicholas, tin 10.00
1982, Cookie Mouse 17.50
1982, Cowboy Snowman 10.00
1982, Jingling Teddy 12.00
1982, Peeking Elf 6.50
1982, Soldier, clothespin,
FE 25.00

Haviland
1972 ....8.00
1973 ....8.00
1974 ....12.00
1975 ....6.00
1976 ....6.00
1977 ....8.00
1978 ....7.50
1979 ....7.50
1980 ....18.00
1981 ....20.00
1982 ....22.00

International Silver, Twelve Days of Christmas, sterling silver, each ...25.00

Lenox, 1982, FE, snowflake emb porcelain, 24K gold finials, date, 6" h...40.00

Lladro, Christmas Ball
1989 ....60.00
1990 ....70.00
1993 ....50.00
1994 ....50.00
1995 ....50.00

Lunt
1974, Trefoil...................................20.00
1980, Medallion 18.00

Reed & Barton
Carousel Horse, silver plated
1988 ....20.00
1990 ....15.00
1994 ....15.00
Christmas Cross, sterling silver
1971 ....355.00
1973 ....90.00
1976 ....80.00
1982 ....140.00
1985 ....80.00
1991 ....75.00
1994 ....55.00
Christmas Cross, 24K gold over sterling silver
1971 ....300.00
1974 ....55.00
1978 ....50.00
1982 ....43.00
1989 ....38.00
1992 ....40.00
1994 ....45.00

Rockwell, by Grossman, 3-1/2"
Bedside Manner, 1999 ....30.00
Homecoming 2000.....................30.00
Triple Self Portrait.......................30.00

Schmid
Paddington Bear, 1982
Ball 5.00
Figural 10.00
Raggedy Ann
1976, FE..6.00
1977 ....3.50
1978 ....3.00
1979 ....3.25
1980 ....3.00
1982, figural................................10.00
Walt Disney
1974, FE......................................15.00
1975 ....5.00
1976 ....10.00
1977 ....5.50
1978 ....5.00
1979 ....6.00
1980 ....4.50
1981 ....4.00
1982, figural................................10.00

Towle
Twelve Days of Christmas medallion, sterling silver
1971, Partridge in a Pear Tree 550.00
1972, Two Turtle Doves 275.00
1973, Three French Hens....100.00
1974, Four Calling Birds.....150.00
1975, Five Golden Rings.....100.00
1976, Six Geese a Laying ...125.00
1977, Seven Swans a Swimming 200.00
1978, Eight Maids a Milking 100.00
1979, Nine Ladies Dancing 100.00
1980, Ten Lords a Leaping . 100.00
1981, Eleven Pipers Piping . 100.00
1982, Twelve Drummers Drumming 100.00
Songs of Christmas Medallions
1978, Silent Night...................70.00
1979, Deck the Halls 70.00
1980, Jingle Bells...................80.00
1981, Hark the Herald Angels Sing 130.00
1983, Silver Bells...................75.00
1984, Let It Snow 75.00
1987, White Christmas 70.00

Wallace Silversmiths
Candy Canes
1981, Peppermint 200.00
1982, Wintergreen 100.00
1983, Cinnamon 60.00
1986, Christmas Candle.........40.00
1991, Christmas Goose.........30.00
1994, Canes...........................20.00
Sleigh Bells, silver plated
1971 ....900.00
1972 ....450.00
1977 ....200.00
1978 ....100.00
1983 ....90.00
1988 ....50.00
1990 ....50.00
1994 ....30.00

Dolls

Annalee Mobilitee Dolls, Inc.
1984, Johnny Appleseed 950.00
1985, Annie Oakley 700.00
1985, Christmas Logo with Cookie 650.00
1988, Sherlock Holmes 450.00
1989, Christmas Morning.........150.00
1991, Christopher Columbus ... 300.00
1992, Back to School..................80.00
1995, Pocahontas.......................80.00

Ashton Drake
Brandon.......................................75.00
Brigitte...95.00
Catherine's Christening 60.00
Glamour of Gibson Girl............ 150.00
Goldilocks 95.00
Hans...85.00
Little Florence.............................85.00
Little Squirt 47.00
Mary...75.00
Michelle 85.00
Miki..85.00
My Secret Pal, Robbie.................85.00
Peek-A-Boo Peter 70.00
Ricky..40.00
Shelley...90.00

Ship & I 80.00
Sweetie 55.00
Victorian Lady.............................95.00
Where's Jamie 65.00
Yummy...47.00

Enesco Imports, Precious Moments
1981, Mikey, 18" h 225.00
1982, Tammy, 18" h 650.00
1983, Katie Lynne, 16" h 185.00
1984, Kristy, 12" h 160.00
1985, Bethany, 12" h 145.00
1986, Bong Bong, 13" h 165.00
1987, Angie, The Angel of Mercy 160.00
1989, Wishing You Cloudless Skies 115.00
1990, The Voice of Spring.........150.00
1991, You Have Touched So Many Hearts 90.00

Franklin Mint
Allison, Ladies Home Journal Centennial, 1920s, MIB...................200.00
Betsy Ross, National Historical Society, MIB 275.00
Deborah, Ladies Home Journal Centennial, 1950s Prom Night, MIB 200.00
Emily, Ladies Home Journal Centennial..200.00

Gorham
1981, Cecile, 16" 750.00
1981, Christopher, 19".............500.00
1982, Allison.........................4,000.00
1982, Baby in apricot dress, 16" 350.00
1982, Baby in blue dress, 12"... 300.00
1983, Ashley.........................1,100.00
1983, Jennifer, bride, 19" 700.00
1984, Holly...............................285.00
1984, Nichole 1,000.00
1985, Alexander, 19" 400.00
1985, Odette, 19" 450.00
1986, Alissa.............................300.00
1986, Colette...........................695.00
1986, Emily, 14" 375.00
1986, Merrie & Mistletoe 300.00
1987, Juliet..............................375.00
1988, Belinda 195.00
1988, Chloe 925.00

Hamilton Collection
1981, Hakata, Peony Maiden.....................................150.00
1985, Heather...........................125.00
1986, Nicole 50.00
1987, Priscilla 50.00
1988, Mr. Spock 75.00
1989, Scotty...............................75.00

Lawton
Crystal Winter 325.00
Emperor's Nightingale..............400.00
Marigold Garden 425.00

Royal Doulton by Nisbet
Little Model 185.00
Pink Sash.................................145.00
Royal Baby...............................350.00
The Muffs 175.00
Winter.......................................180.00

Seymour Mann, Connoisseur Collection
1984, Miss Debutante 180.00
1985, Wendy 150.00
1986, Camelot Fairy 225.00
1987, Dawn 175.00

1988, Jolie..................................150.00
1989, Elizabeth 200.00
1990, Baby Sunshine 90.00
1991, Dephine 125.00

Figurines

Anri, Sarah Kay, artist
1983, Morning Chores, 6",
FE..475.00
1984, Flowers for You, 6"..........400.00
1985, Afternoon Tea, 6"............325.00
1986, Our Puppy, 1-1/2" 90.00
1987, Little Nanny, 4".................180.00
1988, Purrfect Day, 6"................400.00
1989, Garden Party, 4" 195.00
1990, Season's Greetings,
4"..225.00
1991, Season's Joy, 4"..............250.00

Cybis
1963, Magnolia 400.00
1964, Rebecca 345.00
1965, Christmas Rose 750.00
1967, Kitten, blue ribbon............500.00
1968, Narcissus.........................500.00
1969, Clematis with house
wren......................................315.00
1970, Dutch Crocus 750.00
1971, Appaloosa Colt.................285.00
1972, Pansies 350.00
1973, Goldilocks........................325.00
1974, Mary, Mary.......................750.00
1975, George Washington
Bust......................................300.00
1976, Bunny...............................125.00
1977, Tiffin.................................400.00
1978, Edith.................................300.00
1982, Spring Bouquet 750.00
1985, Nativity Lamb...................125.00
1986, Dapple Gray Foal 185.00

Davis, Lowell
Mail Order Bride 95.00
Milk Mouse................................160.00

Department 56, Snowbabies
1986, Hold on Tight 12.00
1987, Down the Hill We Go 20.00
1988, Tiny Trio............................60.00
1989, Icy Igloo 35.00
1990, A Special Delivery............12.00
1991, Just for You 20.00

Enesco Corp., Precious Moments
1979, Jesus Loves Me 30.00
1980, Come Let Us Adore
Him...90.00
1981, But Love Goes on
Forever...................................165.00
1982, I Believe in Miracles 90.00
1983, Sharing Our Season........110.00
1984, Joy to the World................40.00
1985, Baby's First Christmas 35.00
1986, God Bless America...........50.00
1987, This Is the Day the Lord Hath
Made.......................................35.00
1988, Faith Takes the
Plunge....................................30.00
1989, Wishing You Roads of Happi-
ness.......................................50.00
1990, To My Favorite Fan 15.00

Franklin Mint, Princess and the Pea,
bisque, titled "Fairy Tale Surprises,"
1986, Maggie Murphy, hand
painted....................................40.00

Grossman, Dave, Designs, Norman
Rockwell Collection
After the Prom 85.00
American Mother 110.00
At the Doctor 175.00
Back to School...........................50.00
Bride and Groom 50.00
Discovery 160.00
Doctor and the Doll....................35.00
Gramps 75.00
Gramps at the Plate 35.00
Handkerchief..............................95.00
Little Mother...............................55.00
Marble Compass 35.00
Marriage License.......................65.00
New Arrival................................85.00
Puppy Love 35.00
Red Head...................................30.00
Santa at the Globe 35.00
Serenade 30.00
Skaters......................................30.00
Spirit of Education.....................100.00
Stilt Walker 35.00
Sweet Dream.............................75.00
The Pharmist 35.00
The Runaway.............................35.00
Triple Self Portrait 40.00
Young Love 100.00

Hummel - See Hummel.

Lladro
1970, Girl with Guitar 1,800.00
1971, Hamlet............................3,000.00
1971, Oriental Man 1,800.00
1972, Turkey Group 1,500.00
1973, Buck Hunters 2,700.00
1973, Passionate Dance 4250.00
1973, Turtle Doves 2,375.00
1974, Ducks at Pond 5,500.00
1974, Partridge 1,800.00
1978, Car in Trouble....................6,000
1978, Flight of Gazelles 3,000.00
1978, Henry VII 1,100.00
1981, Nest of Eagles, with
base....................................10,000.00
1981, Philippine Folklore 2,000.00
1981, The Rescue..................5,000.00
1983, Bather..................................950
1983, In the Distance 1,100.00
1983, Reclining Nude 650.00
1983, Tranquillity 1,300.00
1983, Youth 1,000.00
1985, Thoroughbred Horse, with
base......................................600.00
1986, Oriental Music, with
base...................................2,400.00
1989, Southern Tea................2,200.00
1991, Champion 1,900.00
1992, Tea in the Garden 9,500.00
1993, Autumn Glow, with
base......................................770.00
1993, Indian Brave.................2,200.00

River Shore
1978, Akiku, Baby Seal, FE 145.00
1979, Rosecoe, red fox kit..........50.00
1980, Lamb................................48.00
1981, Zuela, elephant.................60.00
1982, Kay's Doll 90.00

Royal Doulton
Beatrix Potter
Benjamin Bunny....................70.00
Jemima Puddleduck..............30.00
Lady Mouse...........................30.00
Mrs. Rabbit & Bunnies...........35.00
Old Mr. Brown........................30.00
Peter Rabbit 35.00
Rebecca Puddle-Duck 30.00
Squirrel Nutkin 55.00
Tailor of Gloucester 35.00
Bunnykins
Autumn Days.........................20.00
Ballerina Bunnykins 45.00
Bridesmaid Bunnykins...........45.00
Clean Sweep 15.00
Doctor Bunnykins..................45.00
Easter Greetings 40.00
Family Photograph................24.00
Fortune Teller Bunnykins.......50.00
Friar Tuck 40.00
Grandpa's Story 20.00
Jack and Jill...........................120.00
Little Bo Peep 60.00
Little Jack Horner 50.00
Little John 40.00
Maid Marion 50.00
Mother Bunnykins 40.00
Mystic Bunnykins 60.00
Robin Hood 50.00
Sands of Time 50.00
Sleepy Time...........................18.00
Springtime 20.00
Sundail...................................50.00
Tally Ho 18.00
Royalty
1973, Queen Elizabeth II,
HN2502 ....1,775.00
1981, Duke of Edinburgh,
HN2386 ....440.00
1981, Prince of Wales,
HN2884 ....1,000.00
1982, Princess of Wales,
HN2887 ....1,650.00
1982, Lady Diana Spencer,
HN2885 ....700.00
1986, Duchess of York,
HN3086 ....600.00
1990, Queen Elizabeth, the Queen
Mother, HN3189 ....450.00

Royal Orleans Porcelain, Marilyn Monroe..80.00

Schmid
1979, Country Road 275.00
1980, Two's Company................45.00
1981, Plum Tuckered Out 225.00
1982, Right Church, Wrong
Pew..80.00
1983, Stirring Up Trouble 165.00
1984, Catnapping Too 72.00
1985, Out of Step 45.00Mugs

Royal Copenhagen
1967, large 200.00
1968, large 24.00
1972, large 24.00
1976, large 25.00
1979, small 28.00
1980, small 25.00
1981, large 65.00
1982, small 40.00
1983, small 30.00

Wedgwood
1971, Christmas 35.00
1972, Christmas 30.00
1973, Christmas 40.00
1974, Christmas 30.00
1975, Christmas 30.00
1976, Christmas 30.00
1977, Father's Day....................25.00
1978, Father's Day....................25.00
1979, Christmas 25.00
1980, Christmas 25.00
1981, Christmas 35.00
1982, Christmas 40.00

Music Boxes

Anri
Jemima 100.00
Peter Rabbit...........................100.00
Pigling 100.00

Ferrandiz
Chorale...................................125.00
Drummer.................................185.00
Flower Girl..............................150.00
Going Home 275.00
The Letter...............................150.00
Proud Mother..........................140.00
Spring Arrivals 120.00
Wanderlust..............................110.00

Gorham
Cardinal, double, 6" h, hp, sculptured, porcelain 30.00
Happy Birthday, animals..............35.00
Santa & Sleigh, 6" h 20.00
Sesame Street, Big Bird & Snowman, 7" h 24.00

Schmid
Beatrix Potter
  Jemima Puddleduck 75.00
  Mrs. Tittlemouse 75.00
Peanuts
  30th Anniversary 24.00
  1981, Christmas 30.00
  1981, Mother's Day 20.00
  1982, Christmas 30.00
  1982, Mother's Day 20.00
Raggedy Ann
  1980....................................15.00
  1981 ....15.00
  1982, Flying High 20.00
Walt Disney
  1980, Christmas, FE...............42.00
  1981, Christmas 30.00
  1982, Christmas 25.00

Plates
Anri, Christmas, J. Ferrandiz, 12" d
1972, Christ in the Manger.....................................230.00
1973, Christmas 220.00
1974, Holy Night.........................90.00
1975, Flight into Egypt................80.00
1976, Tree of Life 60.00
1977, Girl with Flowers 175.00
1978, Leading the Way 165.00
1979, The Drummer 170.00
1980, Rejoice............................150.00
1981, Spreading the Word........150.00
1982, The Shepherd Family 150.00
1983, Peace Attend Thee 150.00
Anri, Mother's Day, J. Ferrandiz
1972, Mother Sewing 200.00
1973, Alpine Mother & Child 150.00

1974, Mother Holding Child 150.00
1975, Dove Girl 150.00
1976, Mother Knitting 200.00
1977, Alpine Stroll.................... 125.00
1978, The Beginning 150.00
1979, All Hearts 165.00
1980, Spring Arrivals 160.00
1981, Harmony 150.00
1982, With Love 150.00
Bareuther (Germany), Christmas, Hans Mueller artist, 8" d
1967, Stiftskirche, FE 90.00
1968, Kapplkirche.......................25.00
1969, Christkindlemarkt...............20.00
1970, Chapel in Oberndorf 18.00
1971, Toys for Sale.....................20.00
1972, Christmas in Munich..........35.00
1973, Christmas Sleigh Ride.......20.00
1974, Church in the Black Forest.......................................20.00
1975, Snowman 25.00
1976, Chapel in the Hills.............25.00
1977, Story Time 30.00
1978, Mittenwald.........................30.00
1979, Winter Day 40.00
1980, Miltenberg.........................38.00
1981, Walk in the Forest 40.00
1982, Bad Wimpfen.....................40.00
1983, The Night Before Christmas..................................45.00
1984, Zeil on the River Main........42.50
1985, Winter Wonderland............42.50
1986, Christmas in Forchhe 42.50
1987, Decorating the Tree...........46.50
1988, St. Coloman Church 80.00
1989, Sleigh Ride........................50.00
1990, The Old Forge in Rothenburg 50.00
1991, Christmas Joy....................55.00
1992, Marketplace in Heppenheim 55.00
Berlin (Germany), Christmas, various artists, 7-3/4" d
1970, Christmas in Bernkastel . 130.00
1971, Christmas in Rothenburg on Tauber 30.00
1972, Christmas in Michelstadt...50.00
1973, Christmas in Wendelstein..42.00
1974, Christmas in Bremen 25.00
1975, Christmas in Dortland........60.00
1976, Christmas Eve in Augsburg 30.00
1977, Christmas Eve in Hamburg 32.00
1978, Christmas Market at the Berlin Cathedral..................................55.00
1979, Christmas Eve in Greetsiel 55.00
1980, Christmas Eve in Miltenberg 55.00
1981, Christmas Eve in Hahnenklee................................50.00
1982, Christmas Eve in Wasserburg...............................55.00
1983, Chapel in Oberndorf 55.00
1984, Christmas in Ramsau 50.00
1985, Christmas Eve in Bad Wimpfen 55.00
1986, Christmas Eve in Gelnhaus..................................65.00
1987, Christmas Eve in Goslar 70.00

1988, Christmas Eve in Ruhpolding............................100.00
1989, Christmas Eve in Freidechsdadt.........................100.00
1990, Christmas Eve in Partenkirchen 80.00
1991, Christmas Eve in Allendorf.................................80.00
Bing and Grondahl
Christmas, various artists, 7" d
1895, Behind the Frozen Window...................3,400.00
1896, New Moon Over Snow-Covered Trees.......................1,975.00
1897, Christmas Meal of the Sparrows 725.00
1898, Christmas Roses and Christmas Star 700.00
1899, The Crows Enjoying Christmas 900.00
1900, Church Bells Chiming in Christmas 800.00
1901, The Three Wise Men from the East 450.00
1902, Interior of a Gothic Church 285.00
1903, Happy Expectation of Children 150.00
1904, View of Copenhagen from Frederiksberg Hill................125.00
1905, Anxiety of the Coming Christmas Night 130.00
1906, Sleighing to Church on Christmas Eve 135.00
1907, The Little Match Girl... 175.00
1908, St. Petri Church of Copenhagen 85.00
1909, Happiness Over the Yule Tree....................................100.00
1910, The Old Organist 90.00
1911, First It Was Sung by Angels to Shepherds in the Fields.....80.00
1912, Going to Church on Christmas Eve................................80.00
1913, Bringing Home the Yule Tree......................................90.00
1914, Royal Castle of Amalienborg, Copenhagen 75.00
1915, Chained Dog Getting Double Meal on Christmas Eve........120.00
1916, Christmas Prayer of the Sparrows 85.00
1917, Arrival of the Christmas Boat......................................75.00
1918, Fishing Boat Returning Home for Christmas...............85.00
1919, Outside the Lighted Window................................80.00
1920, Hare in the Snow..........70.00
1921, Pigeons in the Castle Court.....................................55.00
1922, Star of Bethlehem 75.00
1923, Royal Hunting Castle, The Hermitage..............................55.00
1924, Lighthouse in Danish Waters....................................65.00
1925, The Child's Christmas.. 70.00
1926, Churchgoers on Christmas Day 65.00
1927, Skating Couple 80.00
1928, Eskimo Looking at Village Church in Greenland 60.00
1929, Fox Outside Farm 80.00

1930, Yule Tree in Town Hall Square of Copenhagen 85.00
1931, Arrival of the Christmas Train 75.00
1932, Lifeboat at Work 90.00
1933, The Korsor-Nyborg Ferry 70.00
1934, Church Bell in Tower 70.00
1935, Lillebelt Bridge Connecting Funen with Jutland 65.00
1936, Royal Guard 70.00
1937, Arrival of Christmas Guests 75.00
1938, Lighting the Candles 110.00
1939, Ole Lock-Eye, The Sandman 150.00
1940, Delivering Christmas Letters 170.00
1941, Horses Enjoying Christmas Meal in Stable 345.00
1942, Danish Farm on Christmas Night 150.00
1943, The Ribe Cathedral.... 155.00
1944, Sorgenfri Castle.......... 120.00
1945, The Old Water Mill...... 135.00
1946, Commemoration Cross in Honor of Danish Sailors Who Lost Their Lives in World War II 85.00
1947, Dybbol Mill.................... 70.00
1948, Watchman, Sculpture of Town Hall, Copenhagen......... 80.00
1949, Landsoldaten, 19th Century Danish Soldier.................... 70.00
1950, Kronborg Castle at Elsinore 150.00
1951, Jens Bang, New Passenger Boat Running Between Copenhagen and Aalborg 115.00
1952, Old Copenhagen Canals at Wintertime with Thorvaldsen Museum in Background......... 85.00
1953, Royal Boat in Greenland Waters 125.00
1954, Birthplace of Hans Christian Andersen, with Snowman 100.00
1955, Kalundborg Church ... 115.00
1956, Christmas in Copenhagen........................ 140.00
1957, Christmas Candles 155.00
1958, Santa Claus 100.00
1959, Christmas Eve 120.00
1960, Danish Village Church 180.00
1961, Winter Harmony 115.00
1962, Winter Night................. 80.00
1963, The Christmas Elf 120.00
1964, The Fir Tree and Hare 50.00
1965, Bringing Home the Christmas Tree 65.00
1966, Home for Christmas 50.00
1967, Sharing the Joy of Christmas............................. 48.00
1968, Christmas in Church 45.00
1969, Arrival of Christmas Guests.................................. 30.00
1970, Pheasants in the Snow at Christmas............................. 20.00
1971, Christmas at Home 20.00
1972, Christmas in Greenland.......................... 20.00
1973, Country Christmas 25.00

1974, Christmas in the Village.................................. 20.00
1975, The Old Water Mill........ 24.00
1976, Christmas Welcome 25.00
1977, Copenhagen Christmas..................... 25.00
1978, A Christmas Tale.......... 30.00
1979, White Christmas 30.00
1980, Christmas in the Woods.................................. 42.50
1981, Christmas Peace 50.00
1982, The Christmas Tree 55.00
1983, Christmas in Old Town 55.00
1984, Christmas Letter 55.00
1985, Christmas Eve at the Farmhouse................................ 55.00
1986, Silent Night, Holy Night..................................... 55.00
1987, The Snowman's Christmas Eve 60.00
1988, In the Kings Garden 72.00
1989, Christmas Anchorage .. 65.00
1990, Changing of the Guards................................. 60.00
1991, Copenhagen Stock Exchange............................. 70.00
1992, Christmas at the Rectory................................ 65.00
1993, Father Christmas in Copenhagen 65.00
1994, A Day at the Deer Park 80.00
1995, The Towers of Copenhagen....................... 85.00
1996, Winter at the Old Mill 70.00
1997, Country Christmas........ 65.00
1998, Santa the Storyteller 65.00
1999, Dancing on Christmas Eve 65.00
Christmas in America
1986, Williamsburg 150.00
1987, Christmas at the White House...................................... 25.00
1988, Christmas at Rockefeller Center..................................... 45.00
1989, Christmas in New England................................. 45.00
1990, Christmas Eve At The Capitol.................................. 42.00
1991, Christmas at Independence Hall 45.00
1991, Williamsburg, Jubilee ... 45.00
1992, Christmas in San Francisco 45.00
1993, Coming Home for Christmas.............................. 36.00
1994, Christmas Eve in Alaska.................................... 47.00
1995, Christmas Eve at the Mississippi................................... 36.00
Mother's Day, Henry Thelander, artist, 6" d
1969, Dog and Puppies............................... 325.00
1970, Bird and Chicks........... 25.00
1971, Ct and Kitten................ 24.00
1972, Mare and Foal 20.00
1973, Duck and Ducklings..... 20.00
1974, Bear and Cubs 24.00
1975, Doe and Fawns 20.00
1976, Swan Family................ 22.00
1977, Squirrel and Young....... 25.00

1978, Heron...................... 20.00
1979, Fox and Cubs 20.00
1980, Woodpecker and Young...................... 30.00
1981, Hare and Young.......... 30.00
1982, Lioness and Cubs........ 45.00
1983, Raccoon and Young 25.00
1984, Stork and Nestlings 30.00
1985, Bear and Cubs 30.00
1986, Elephant with Calf........ 40.00
1987, Sheep with Lambs....... 50.00
1988, Lapwing Mother with Chicks.................................. 75.00
1989, Cow with Calf 48.00
1990, Hen with Chicks 50.00
1991, The Nanny Goat and Her Two Frisky Kids 75.00
1992, Panda with Cubs 80.00
1993, St. Bernard Dog and Puppies.................................. 55.00
1994, Cat with Kittens 80.00
1995, Hedgehog with Young . 55.00
1996, Koala with Young 60.00

Davis, Lowell
1981, Plum Tuckered Out 65.00
1982, Bustln with Pride 65.00
1987, Country Wedding.............. 65.00
1988, Cutting the Family Christmas Tree, #6 .... 50.00
1991, Christmas at Red Oak II ... 60.00

Franklin Mint
Audubon Society Bird
1972, Goldfinch..................... 115.00
1972, Wood Duck 110.00
1973, Cardinal...................... 110.00
1973, Ruffled Grouse 120.00
Christmas, Norman Rockwell, artist, sterling silver, 8" d
1970, Bringing Home the Tree 275.00
1971, Under the Mistletoe ... 125.00
1972, The Carolers.............. 125.00
1973, Trimming the Tree 100.00
1974, Hanging the Wreath... 100.00
1975, Home for Christmas... 125.00

Haviland & Parlon
Christmas Series, various artists, 10" d
1972, Madonna and Child, Raphael, FE.......................... 80.00
1973, Madonna, Feruzzi........ 95.00
1974, Cowper Madonna and Child, Raphael 40.00
1975, Madonna and Child, Murillo 45.00
1976, Madonna and Child, Botticelli....................................... 50.00
1977, Madonna and Child, Bellini 40.00
1978, Madonna and Child, Fra Filippo, Lippi 65.00
1979, Madonna of the Eucharist, Botticelli 150.00
Lady and the Unicorn Series, artist unknown, 10" d
1977, To My Only Desire, FE.. 60.00
1978, Sight 40.00
1979, Sound 50.00
1980, Touch.......................... 110.00
1981, Scent 60.00
1982, Taste 80.00
Tapestry Series, artists unknown, 10" d
1971, The Unicorn in Captivity.............................. 145.00

1972, Start of the Hunt 70.00
1973, Chase of the Unicorn . 120.00
1974, End of the Hunt 120.00
1975, The Unicorn
Surrounded 75.00
1976, The Unicorn is Brought to the
Castle 55.00

Edwin M. Knowles

American Holidays Series, Don Spaulding, artist, 8-1/2" d
1978, Fourth of July, FE 35.00
1979, Thanksgiving 35.00
1980, Easter 30.00
1981, Valentine's Day 25.00
1982, Father's Day 35.00
1983, Christmas 35.00
1984, Mother's Day 20.00

Gone with the Wind Series, Raymond Kursar, artist, 8-1/2" d
1978, Scarlett, FE 300.00
1979, Ashley 225.00
1980, Melanie 75.00
1981, Rhett 50.00
1982, Mammy Lacing
Scarlett 60.00
1983, Melanie Gives Birth 85.00
1984, Scarlett's Green Dress . 50.00
1985, Rhett and Bonnie 35.00
1985, Scarlett and Rhett:
The Finale 30.00

Wizard of Oz Series, James Auckland, artist, 8-1/2" d
1977, Over the Rainbow,
FE 65.00
1978, If I Only Had a Brain 30.00
1978, If I Only Had a Heart 30.00
1978, If I Were King of the
Forest 30.00
1979, Wicked Witch of the
West 35.00
1979, Follow the Yellow Brick
Road 35.00
1979, Wonderful Wizard of
Oz 50.00
1980, The Grand Finale (We're Off
to See The Wizard) 60.00

Lenox

Boehm Bird Series, Edward Marshall Boehm, artist, 10-1/2" d
1970, Wood Thrush, FE 135.00
1971, Goldfinch 60.00
1972, Mountain Bluebird 40.00
1973, Meadowlark 50.00
1974, Rufous Hummingbird ... 45.00
1975, American Redstart 50.00
1976, Cardinal 58.00
1977, Robins 55.00
1978, Mockingbirds 60.00
1979, Golden-Crowned
Kinglets 65.00

1980, Black-Throated Blue Warblers 75.00
1981, Eastern Phoebes 90.00
Boehm Woodland Wildlife Series, Edward Marshall Boehm, artist, 10-1/2" d
1973, Raccoons, FE 80.00
1974, Red Foxes 50.00
1975, Cottontail Rabbits 60.00
1976, Eastern Chipmunks 60.00
1977, Beaver 60.00
1978, Whitetail Deer 60.00
1979, Squirrels 75.00
1980, Bobcats 90.00
1981, Martens 100.00
1982, River Otters 100.00

Lladro

Christmas, 8" d, undisclosed artists
1971, Caroling 32.00
1972, Carolers 35.00
1973, Boy & Girl 50.00
1974, Carolers 75.00
1975, Cherubs 60.00
1976, Christ Child 50.00
1977, Nativity 70.00
1978, Caroling Child 50.00
1979, Snow Dance 80.00

Mother's Day, undisclosed artists
1971, Kiss of the Child 75.00
1972, Birds & Chicks 30.00
1973, Mother & Children 35.00
1974, Nursing Mother 135.00
1975, Mother & Child 55.00
1976, Virgil 50.00
1977, Mother & Daughter 60.00
1978, New Arrival 55.00
1979, Off to School 90.00

Reco International Corp.

Days Gone By, Sandra Kuck, artist
1983, Sunday Best 55.00
1984, Little Anglers 30.00
1984, Little Tutor 30.00
McClelland's Children's Circus Series, John McClelland, artist, 9"d 1981,
Tommy the Clown, FE 85.00
1982, Katie the Tightrope
Walker 40.00
1983, Johnny the Strongman . 40.00
1984, Maggie the Animal
Trainer 35.00
McClelland's Mother Goose Series, John McClelland, artist, 8-1/2" d
1979, Mary, Mary, FE 250.00
1980, Little Boy Blue 100.00
1981, Little Miss Muffet 30.00
1982, Little Jack Horner 30.00
1983, Little Bo Peep 40.00
1984, Diddle, Diddle
Dumpling 30.00
1985, Mary Had a Little
Lamb 42.00
1986, Jack and Jill 25.00

Reed & Barton, Christmas Series, Damascene silver, 11" d through 1978, 8" d 1979-1981
1970, A Partridge in a Pear Tree,
FE 200.00
1971, We Three Kings of Orient
Are 65.00
1972, Hark! The Herald Angels
Sing 60.00
1973, Adoration of the Kings 75.00

1974, The Adoration of the
Magi 60.00
1975, Adoration of the Kings 65.00
1976, Morning Train 60.00
1977, Decorating the Church 60.00
1978, The General Store at Christmas
Time 67.00
1979, Merry Old Santa Claus 65.00
1980, Gathering Christmas
Greens 75.00
1981, The Shopkeeper at
Christmas 75.00

Rosenthal

Christmas, Bjorn Wiinblad, artist
1971, Maria & Child 700.00
1972, Caspar 550.00
1973, Melchior 375.00
1974, Balthazar 500.00
1975, The Annunciation 190.00
1976, Angel with Trumpet 200.00
1977, Adoration of
Shepherds 225.00
1978, Angel with Harp 275.00
1979, Exodus From Egypt ... 310.00
1980, Angel with a
Glockenspiel 360.00
1981, Christ Child Visits
Temple 365.00
1982, Christening of Christ .. 375.00

Christmas, various artists, 8-1/2" d
1910, Winter Peace 550.00
1911, The Three Wise Men .. 325.00
1912, Shooting Stars 250.00
1913, Christmas Lights 235.00
1914, Christmas Song 350.00
1915, Walking to Church 180.00
1916, Christmas During
War 235.00
1917, Angel of Peace 210.00
1918, Peace on Earth 210.00
1919, St. Christopher with the
Christ Child 225.00
1920, The Manger in
Bethlehem 325.00
1921, Christmas in the
Mountains 200.00
1922, Advent Branch 200.00
1923, Children in the Winter
Wood 200.00
1924, Deer in the Woods 200.00
1925, The Three Wise Men .. 200.00
1926, Christmas in the
Mountains 175.00
1927, Station on the Way 200.00
1928, Chalet Christmas 175.00
1929, Christmas in the Alps . 225.00
1930, Group of Deer Under the
Pines 225.00
1931, Path of the Magi 225.00
1932, Christ Child 195.00
1933, Through the Night to
Light 190.00
1934, Christmas Peace 200.00
1935, Christmas By the
Sea 185.00
1936, Nürnberg Angel 185.00
1937, Berchtesgaden 195.00
1938, Christmas in the Alps . 190.00
1939, Schneekoppe
Mountain 195.00
1940, Marien Church in
Danzig 250.00

1941, Strassburg
Cathedral 250.00
1942, Marianburg Castle 300.00
1943, Winter Idyll..................300.00
1944, Wood Scape..............275.00
1945, Christmas Peace........370.00
1946, Christmas in an Alpine
Valley...................................250.00
1947, The Dillingen
Madonna..............................975.00
1948, Message to the
Shepherds 850.00
1949, The Holy Family..........185.00
1950, Christmas in the
Forest 175.00
1951, Star of Bethlehem.......450.00
1952, Christmas in the
Alps 190.00
1953, The Holy Light 185.00
1954, Christmas Eve 180.00
1955, Christmas in a
Village 190.00
1956, Christmas in the
Alps 185.00
1957, Christmas by the
Sea.......................................195.00
1958, Christmas Eve 185.00
1959, Midnight Mass............195.00
1960, Christmas Eve in a Small Vil-
lage 190.00
1961, Solitary Christmas 225.00
1962, Christmas Eve 185.00
1963, Silent Night 185.00
1964, Christmas Market in Nürn-
berg 225.00
1965, Christmas in Munich ..185.00
1966, Christmas in Ulm........250.00
1967, Christmas in
Regensburg..........................185.00
1968, Christmas in
Bremen 190.00
1969, Christmas in
Rothenburg...........................220.00
1970, Christmas in
Cologne 165.00
1971, Christmas in
Garmisch..............................100.00
1972, Christmas in
Franconia..............................90.00
1973, Christmas in Lubeck-Hol-
stein.....................................110.00
1974, Christmas in
Wurzburg 95.00
Royal Copenhagen, Christmas, various
artists, 6" d 1908, 1909, 1910; 7" d
1911 to present
1909, Danish Landscape..........150.00
1910, The Magi........................120.00
1911, Danish Landscape..........135.00
1912, Elderly Couple by Christmas
Tree..120.00
1913, Spire of Frederik's Church,
Copenhagen...........................125.00
1914, Sparrows in Tree at Church of
the Holy Spirit,
Copenhagen...........................100.00
1915, Danish Landscape..........150.00
1916, Shepherd in the Field on Christmas Night.................................85.00
1917, Tower of Our Savior's Church,
Copenhagen.............................90.00
1918, Sheep and Shepherds......80.00
1919, In the Park......................80.00
1920, Mary with the Child
Jesus......................................75.00

1921, Aabenraa Marketplace 75.00
1922, Three Singing Angels........70.00
1923, Danish Landscape............70.00
1924, Christmas Star Over the Sea
and Sailing Ship 100.00
1925, Street Scene from Christian-
shavn, Copenhagen 85.00
1926, View of Christmas Canal,
Copenhagen..............................75.00
1927, Ship's Boy at the Tiller on Christmas Night 140.00
1928, Vicar's Family on Way to
Church......................................75.00
1929, Grundtvig Church,
Copenhagen 100.00
1930, Fishing Boats on the Way to the
Harbor......................................80.00
1931, Mother and Child..............90.00
1932, Frederiksberg Gardens with
Statue of Frederik VI 90.00
1933, The Great Belt Ferry 110.00
1934, The Hermitage Castle 115.00
1935, Fishing Boat off Kronborg
Castle..................................... 145.00
1936, Roskilde Cathedral 130.00
1937, Christmas Scene in Main Street,
Copenhagen 135.00
1938, Round Church in Osterlars on
Bornholm.................................. 200.00
1939, Expeditionary Ship in Pack-Ice
of Greenland 180.00
1940, The Good Shepherd....... 300.00
1941, Danish Village Church.... 250.00
1942, Bell Tower of Old Church in Jut-
land.. 300.00
1943, Flight of Holy Family to
Egypt 425.00
1944, Typical Danish Winter
Scene 160.00
1945, A Peaceful Motif.............. 325.00
1946, Zealand Village Church.. 150.00
1947, The Good Shepherd....... 210.00
1948, Nodebo Church at Christmas-
time.. 150.00
1949, Our Lady's Cathedral, Copen
hagen 165.00
1950, Boeslunde Church,
Zealand 175.00
1951, Christmas Angel 300.00
1952, Christmas in the
Forest...................................... 120.00
1953, Frederiksborg Castle...... 120.00
1954, Amalienborg Palace, Copen-
hagen 150.00
1955, Fano Girl......................... 185.00
1956, Rosenborg Castle, Copen-
hagen 160.00
1957, The Good Shepherd....... 115.00
1958, Sunshine over
Greenland 140.00
1959, Christmas Night 120.00
1960, The Stag......................... 125.00
1961, Training Ship
Danmark................................... 155.00
1962, The Little Mermaid at
Wintertime 200.00
1963, Hojsager Mill...................80.00
1964, Fetching the Tree.............75.00
1965, Little Skaters 60.00
1966, Blackbird.........................55.00
1967, The Royal Oak 45.00
1968, The Last Umiak...............40.00
1969, The Old Farmyard 35.00

1970, Christmas Rose and
Cat 40.00
1971, Hare in Winter................. 80.00
1972, In the Desert................... 30.00
1973, Train Homeward Bound for
Christmas 22.00
1974, Winter Twilight 30.00
1975, Queen's Palace 20.00
1976, Danish Watermill 35.00
1977, Immervad Bridge 25.00
1978, Greenland Scenery.......... 33.00
1979, Choosing the Christmas
Tree 50.00
1980, Bringing Home the Tree.... 45.00
1981, Admiring the Christmas
Tree 55.00
1982, Waiting for Christmas........ 60.00
1983, Merry Christmas.............. 50.00
1984, Jingle Bells 55.00
1985, Snowman 65.00
1986, Christmas Vacation.......... 55.00
1987, Winter Birds.................... 58.00
1988, Christmas Eve in
Copenhagen 65.00
1989, The Old Skating Pond....... 70.00
1990, Christmas at Tivoli.......... 130.00
1991, The Festival of Santa
Lucia 100.00
1992, The Queen's Carriage....... 85.00
1993, Christmas Guests 95.00
1994, Christmas Shopping........ 75.00
1996, Lighting the Street
Lamp....................................... 70.00
1997, Roskilde Cathedral 80.00
1998, Coming Home for
Christmas 55.00
1999, The Sleigh Ride............... 60.00
Rosenthal
Christmas In Denmark
1991, Bringing Home the
Tree..................................... 48.00
1992, Christmas
Shopping.............................. 45.00
1993, The Skating Party......... 45.00
1994, The Sleigh Ride............ 45.00
1995, Christmas Tales............ 45.00
1996, Christmas Eve............... 45.00
Mother's Day, various artists,
6-1/4" d
1971, American
Mother 125.00
1972, Oriental Mother 60.00
1973, Danish Mother.............. 60.00
1974, Greenland Mother......... 55.00
1975, Bird in Nest.................. 50.00
1976, Mermaids 50.00
1977, The Twins 50.00
1978, Mother and Child 25.00
1979, A Loving Mother 30.00
1980, An Outing with
Mother 35.00
1981, Reunion 40.00
1982, The Children's Hour 45.00
Royal Doulton
Beswick Christmas Series, various artists, earthenware in hand-cast bas-
relief, 8" sq
1972, Christmas in England,
FE... 40.00
1973, Christmas in Mexico 25.00
1974, Christmas in Bulgaria .. 40.00
1975, Christmas in Norway ... 54.00
1976, Christmas in Holland ... 45.00

1977, Christmas in Poland...100.00
1978, Christmas in America...45.00
Mother and Child Series, Edna Hibel, artist, 8" d
1973, Colette and Child, FE......450.00
1974, Sayuri and Child.......150.00
1975, Kristina and Child.......125.00
1976, Marilyn and Child.......100.00
1977, Lucia and Child.........100.00
1978, Kathleen and Child 95.00
Valentine's Day Series, artists unknown, 8-1/4" d
1976, Victorian Boy and Girl......60.00
1977, My Sweetest Friend 40.00
1978, If I Love You.................40.00
1979, My Valentine...............40.00
1980, On a Swing.................40.00
1981, Sweet Music..............35.00
1982, From My Heart 40.00
1983, Cherub's Song.............45.00
1984, Love in Bloom..............40.00
1985, Accept These Flowers .40.00

Schmid
Christmas, J. Malfertheiner, artist
1971, St. Jakob in Groden, FE......125.00
1972, Pipers at Alberobello..120.00
1973, Alpine Horn 375.00
1974, Young Man and Girl ...100.00
1975, Christmas in Ireland 90.00
1976, Alpine Christmas........200.00
1977, Legend of Heligenblut 125.00
1978, Klockler Singers 175.00
1979, Moss Gatherers..........130.00
1980, Wintry Churchgoing ...165.00
1981, Santa Claus in Tyrol....160.00
1982, The Star Singers.........160.00
1983, Unto Us a Child Is Born 150.00
1984, Yuletide in the Valley ..150.00
1985, Good Morning, Good Year............160.00
1986, A Goreden Christmas ..75.00
1987, Down from the Alps ...175.00
Disney Christmas Series, undisclosed artists, 7-1/2" d
1973, Sleigh Ride, FE..........400.00
1974, Decorating the Tree ...175.00
1975, Caroling 20.00
1976, Building a Snowman....35.00
1977, Down the Chimney.......25.00
1978, Night Before Christmas 20.00
1979, Santa's Surprise 20.00
1980, Sleigh Ride 30.00
1981, Happy Holidays 18.00
1982, Winter Games 20.00
1987, Snow White Golden Anniversary 48.00
1988, Mickey Mouse & Minnie Mouse 60th............................50.00
1989, Sleeping Beauty 30th Anniversary 75.00
1990, Fantasia Relief..............25.00
Disney Mother's Day Series
1974, Flowers for Mother, FE......80.00
1975, Snow White and the Seven Dwarfs......................45.00
1976, Minnie Mouse and Friends...............................20.00
1977, Pluto's Pals 25.00
1978, Flowers for Bambi 20.00
1979, Happy Feet...................25.00

1980, Minnie's Surprise 20.00
1981, Playmates 25.00
1982, A Dream Come True.....20.00
Peanuts Christmas Series, Charles Schulz, artist, 7-1/2" d
1972, Snoopy Guides the Sleigh, FE......90.00
1973, Christmas Eve at the Doghouse......120.00
1974, Christmas Eve at the Fireplace 65.00
1975, Woodstock, Santa Claus..................................15.00
1976, Woodstock's Christmas 30.00
1977, Deck the Doghouse 15.00
1978, Filling the Stocking 20.00
1979, Christmas at Hand 20.00
1980, Waiting for Santa 48.00
1981, A Christmas Wish 20.00
1982, Perfect Performance 35.00
Peanuts Mother's Day Series, Charles Schulz, artist, 7-1/2" d
1972, Linus, FE 50.00
1973, Mom? 45.00
1974, Snoopy and Woodstock on Parade..................................40.00
1975, A Kiss for Lucy..............38.00
1976, Linus and Snoopy 35.00
1977, Dear Mom.....................30.00
1978, Thoughts That Count....25.00
1979, A Special Letter 20.00
1980, A Tribute to Mom 20.00
1981, Mission for Mom 20.00
1982, Which Way to Mother? .20.00
Peanuts Valentine's Day Series, Charles Schulz, artist, 7-1/2" d
1977, Home Is Where the Heart Is, FE......25.00
1978, Heavenly Bliss 28.00
1979, Love Match 20.00
1980, From Snoopy, With Love......24.00
1981, Hearts-a-Flutter.............20.00
1982, Love Patch 18.00
Raggedy Ann Annual Series, undisclosed artist, 7-1/2" d
1980, The Sunshine Wagon..................................65.00
1981, The Raggedy Shuffle....25.00
1982, Flying High....................20.00
1983, Winning Streak 20.00
1984, Rocking Rodeo.............22.50

Wedgwood
Calendar Series
1971, Victorian Almanac, FE......20.00
1972, The Carousel 15.00
1973, Bountiful Butterfly 14.00
1974, Camelot.......................65.00
1975, Children's Games.........18.00
1976, Robin...........................25.00
1977, Tonatiuh.......................28.00
1978, Samurai.......................32.00
1979, Sacred Scarab 32.00
1980, Safari...........................40.00
1981, Horses.........................42.50
1982, Wild West.....................50.00
1983, The Age of the Reptiles 50.00
1984, Dogs 55.00
1985, Cats.............................55.00
1986, British Birds.................50.00
1987, Water Birds 50.00
1988, Sea Birds 50.00

Christmas Series, jasper stoneware, 8" d
1969, Windsor Castle, FE 225.00
1970, Christmas in Trafalgar Square 30.00
1971, Piccadilly Circus, London 40.00
1972, St. Paul's Cathedral......40.00
1973, The Tower of London ...45.00
1974, The Houses of Parliament...........................40.00
1975, Tower Bridge...............40.00
1976, Hampton Court 46.00
1977, Westminster Abbey 48.00
1978, The Horse Guards 55.00
1979, Buckingham Palace 55.00
1980, St. James Palace 70.00
1981, Marble Arch 75.00
1982, Lambeth Palace...........80.00
1983, All Souls, Langham Palace..................................80.00
1984, Constitution Hill 80.00
1985, The Tate Gallery 80.00
1986, The Albert Memorial 80.00
1987, Guildhall 80.00
Mothers Series, jasper stoneware, 6-1/2" d
1971, Sportive Love, FE.........25.00
1972, The Sewing Lesson 20.00
1973, The Baptism of Achilles 20.00
1974, Domestic Employment 30.00
1975, Mother and Child 35.00
1976, The Spinner.................35.00
1977, Leisure Time................30.00
1978, Swan and Cygnets 35.00
1979, Deer and Fawn 35.00
1980, Birds 48.00
1981, Mare and Foal..............50.00
1982, Cherubs with Swing.....55.00
1983, Cupid and Butterfly......55.00
1984, Musical Cupids 55.00
1985, Cupids and Doves........55.00
1986, Anemones...................55.00
1987, Tiger Lily......................55.00

Little Golden Books

Collecting Hints: Little Golden Books offer something for everybody. Collectors can pursue titles according to favorite author, illustrator, television show, film, or comic strip character. Disney titles enjoy a special place with nostalgia buffs. An increasingly popular goal is to own one copy of each title and number.

Books published in the forties, fifties, and sixties are in the most demand at this time. Books from this period were assigned individual numbers which are usually found on the front cover of the book, except for the earliest titles for which the title must be checked against the numbered list at the back of the book.

Although the publisher tried to adhere to a policy of one number for each title during the first 30 years, numbers were reassigned to new titles as old titles were eliminated. Also, when an earlier book was re-edited and/or re-illustrated, it was given a new number.

Most of the first 36 books had blue paper spines and a dust jacket. Subsequent books were issued with a golden-brown mottled spine, which was replaced in 1950 by a shiny gold spine.

Early books had 42 pages. In the late 1940s, the format was gradually changed to 28 pages, then to 24 pages in the mid-1950s. Early 42- and 28-page books had no price on the cover. Later, the 25¢ price appeared on the front cover, then 29¢, followed by 39¢. In the early 1950s, books were produced with two lines that formed a bar across the top of the front cover. This bar was eliminated in the early sixties.

Little Golden Books can still be found at yard sales and flea markets. Other sources include friends, relatives, and charity book sales, especially if they have a separate children's table. Also attend doll and book shows—good places to find books with paper dolls, puzzles, or cutouts. Toy dealers are also a good source for Disney, television, and cowboy titles.

Look for books in good or better condition. Covers should be bright, with the spine paper intact. Rubbing, ink and crayon markings, or torn pages lessen the value of the book. Unless extensive, pencil marks are fairly easy to remove by gently stroking in one direction with an art-gum eraser. Do not rub back and forth.

Within the past two years, collecting interest has increased dramatically, thus driving up prices for the most unusual and hard-to-find titles. Prices for the majority of titles are still at a reasonable level.

History: Simon & Schuster published the first Little Golden Books in September 1942. They were conceived and created by the Artists & Writers Guild Inc., which was an arm of the Western Printing and Lithographing Company. More than 1.5 million copies of the initial twelve titles (each 42 pages long and priced at 25¢) were sold within the first five months of publication. By the end of World War II, 39 million Little Golden Books had been sold.

A Disney series was begun in 1944, and Big and Giant Golden Books followed that same year. In 1949, the first Goldencraft editions were introduced. Instead of side-stapled cardboard, these books had cloth covers and were sewn so that they could withstand school and library use. In 1958, Giant Little Golden Books were introduced, most combining three previously published titles into one book. In that same year, Simon & Schuster sold Little Golden Books to Western Printing and Lithographing Company and Pocket Books. The titles then appeared under the Golden Press imprint. Eventually Western, now known as Western Publishing Company, Inc., bought out Pocket Books' interest in Little Golden Books.

In 1986, Western celebrated the one-billionth Little Golden Book by issuing special commemorative editions of some of its most popular titles, such as *Poky Little Puppy* and *Cinderella*.

Notes: Prices are based on a mint condition book from the first printing. The printing edition is determined by looking at the lower right-hand corner of the back page. The letter found there indicates the printing of that particular title and edition. "A" is the first printing, "B" the next, and so forth. Occasionally, the letter is hidden under the spine or was placed in the upper right-hand corner, so look closely. Early titles will have their edition indicated in the front of the book.

Any dust jacket, puzzles, stencils, cutouts, stamps, tissues, tape, or pages should be intact as issued. If not, the book's value suffers a drastic reduction of up to 80 percent off the listed price. Books that are badly worn, incomplete, or badly torn are worth little. Sometimes they are useful as temporary fillers for gaps in a collection.

Reference: Steve Santi, *Collecting Little Golden Books*, 4th, Krause Publications, 2000.

Collectors' Club: Golden Book Club, 19626 Ricardo Ave., Hayward, CA 94541.

Bambi, #B20, 1973	12.00
Bozo the Clown, 2nd ed.	8.00
Bugs Bunny's Birthday, 1st ed., 1950, fair condition	7.00
Captain Kangaroo, #261, 1956, penciled name on front page	5.00
Cars and Trucks, 5th printing, 1971, wear to cover	12.00
Chitty Chitty Bang Bang	20.00
Christmas Carols, 1946, Connie Malvern	10.00
Colors Are Nice, 2nd ed.	5.00
Counting Rhymes, 1946, fair condition	8.00
Daniel Boone, #256, 1956, penciled name on front page	6.00

Walt Disney's Zorro and the Secret Plan, 1958, $12.

Davy Crockett's Keelboat Race, 1955, fair condition	9.00
Dick Tracy, 1962, slight wear to cover	18.00
Ding Dong School, The Magic Wagon, 1st ed., 1955	15.00
Doctor Dan At The Circus, 1st edition, 1960, does not include band-aid, fair condition	40.00
Dumbo's Book of Colors, #1015-23, name written on front page	2.00
Exploring Space, 1958	20.00
Four Little Kittens, #322, 1973, 6th printing, slight wear	4.00
Frosty the Snow Man, 1951	18.00
Gene Autry and Champion, 1956, slight use	25.00
Gordon's Jet Flight, #A48, 1961, activity book, insert missing	65.00
Gunsmoke, 1958	20.00
Hansel and Gretel, 1945	10.00
Home for a Bunny, 1979	4.00
Hop, Little Kangaroo, #558	5.00
Heidi, 1st ed., 1954	6.00
Hopalong Cassidy and the Bar 20 Cowboy, 1952, unused	40.00
Howdy Doody Magic Hats	20.00
Howdy Doody's Circus, 1st ed., 1950	16.00
Lady and the Tramp, #2082	15.00
Little Golden Book of Dinosaurs, #355, penciled name on front page, some rubs	4.00
Little Golden Book of Dogs, #532, some cover damage	4.00
Little Golden Book of Holidays	3.00
Little Golden Book of Wild Animals, #499, 1960, some crayon marks	3.00
Little Golden Dictionary, 18th printing, 1969	4.00
Mickey's Christmas Carol, #459-09, 1983	4.00
My Christmas Treasury, 1979, name written inside	4.00
My First Book, 1942, name written in front	12.00
1-2-3 Juggle with Me, 1st ed.	6.00

Peter Rabbit, #505, 1970, good condition 2.00

Prayers for Children, 1942, 9th printing, some writing on cover, last page missing 10.00

Rudolph the Red Nosed Reindeer, 1958 .... 18.00

Scuffy the Tugboat, #310-41, 1974, some crayon marks 1.00

Seven Dwarfs Found A House, 6-1/2 x 8", Simon & Schuster, 1952 copyright, fourth printing, 1957, 25 pgs, color illus 20.00

Tawny Scrawny Lion, 1991, with orig plush lion 40.00

The Christmas Donkey, 1984 .... 3.00

The Christmas Story, 1952 .... 6.00

The Cold Blooded Penguin, 6-3/4 x 8", Simon & Schuster, 1946 second printing, 24 pgs, full color 60.00

The Emerald City of Oz, L. Frank Baum, adapted by Peter Archer, 1952...25.00

The Friendly Book, 2nd ed. 6.00

The Fuzzy Duckling, 1949 .... 10.00

The Gingerbread Man, 6th ed. 5.00

The Golden Egg, #486, illus by Lillian Obligado 7.50

The Happy Golden ABC's, 1979........ 4.00

The Happy Little Whale, 3rd ed. 5.00

The Little Red Caboose, 13th ed. 5.00

The Monster at the End of this Book, Starring Lovable, Furry Old Grover, Sesame St., 2nd ed. 4.00

The Night Before Christmas, 1946...28.00

The Taxi That Hurried, 1946 .... 17.50

The Tiny Tawny Kitten, 1st ed., 1969 .... 15.00

The Wonderful School, 1st ed.............. 8.00

Things in My House............................. 4.50

Tottle, 1945 .... 12.00

Twelve Days of Christmas, A Christmas Carol, 1983 .... 8.00

Tweety Plays Catch The Puddy Kat, 1975 .... 4.00

Underdog.. 20.00

Walt Disney's Goofy—Movie Star, 1956, red spine 27.50

Walt Disney's Old Yeller, 3rd ed., 1950s 12.00

Walt Disney's Uncle Remus, #D85, 1945 .... 45.00

Walt Disney's Winne-the-Pooh and Tigger, 4th ed. 5.00

Wheels, 1st ed., 1952......................... 8.00

Where is the Bear? 2nd ed................. 6.00

Wizard of Oz, 1st edition 22.00

Woody Woodpecker, 1961................ 24.00

Woodsy Owl, 1974 .... 24.00

Zorro, 1958.. 15.00

Little Red Riding Hood

Collecting Hints: Little Red Riding Hood was a hot collectible in the 1990s. Prices for many pieces are in the hundreds of dollars; those for advertising plaques and baby dishes are in the thousands. As collectors complete their collections, the numbers of active buyers are decreasing.

A great unanswered question at this time is how many Little Red Riding Hood pieces were actually made. Attempts at determining production levels have been unsuccessful. The market could well be eventually flooded with these items, especially the most commonly found pieces. New collectors are advised to proceed with caution.

Undecorated Hull Pottery blanks are commonly found. Their value is between 25 and 50 percent less than decorated examples.

History: The classic story of Little Red Riding Hood has delighted children for decades. Today, collectors have several types of collectibles which reflect their fascination with the tale.

On June 29, 1943, the United States Patent Office issued design patent #135,889 to Louise Elizabeth Bauer, Zanesville, Ohio, assignor to the A. E. Hull Pottery Company, Incorporated, Crooksville, Ohio, for a "Design for a Cookie Jar." Thus was born Hull's Little Red Riding Hood line, produced and distributed between 1943 and 1957.

The traditional story is that A. E. Hull only made the blanks. Decoration of the pieces was done by the Royal China and Novelty Company of Chicago, Illinois. When decoration was complete, the pieces were returned to Hull for distribution. Recent scholarship suggests a somewhat different approach.

Mark Supnick, author of *Hull Pottery's "Little Red Riding Hood": A Pictorial Reference and Price Guide* believes that A. E. Hull only made the blanks for early cookie jars and the dresser jar with a large bow in the front. These can be identified by the creamy off-white color of the pottery. The majority of pieces were made from a very white pottery, a body Supnick attributes to The Royal China and Novelty Company, a division of Regal China. Given the similarity in form to items in Royal China and Novelty Company's Old McDonald's Farm line, Supnick concludes that Hull contracted with Royal China and Novelty for production as well as decoration.

Many hand-painted and decal variations are encountered, e.g., the wolf jar is found with a black, brown, red, or yellow base.

Reference: Mark E. Supnick, *Collecting Hull Pottery's "Little Red Riding Hood,"* L-W Book Sales, 1989, 1992 value update.

Reproduction Alert: Be alert for a Mexican-produced cookie jar that closely resembles Hull's Little Red Riding Hood piece. The Mexican example is slightly shorter than Hull's 13-inch height.

Vase, Little Red Riding Hood, wolf, tree trunk, 15-1/4" h, Staffordshire, $550. Photo courtesy of Joy Luke Fine Art Brokers and Auctioneers.

Children's Book, *Little Red Riding Hood*
  Children's Hour Series, other stories, 80 pgs, hardcover...................... 38.50
  Little Golden Book, #17, 2-3/4" x 2-3/4", 1972 .... 5.00
  Susan Jordan story and illus, 8-1/4" x 7-1/2" 48.00
  Walt Disney Studies, 1934, 33 pgs, soft cover 38.00
Doll
  Avon, porcelain, 1985, 8" h 40.00
  Madame Alexander, #482, 7-1/2" h, bent knees, orig clothes, MIB..... 75.00
  Molley, topsy-turvy, Little Red Riding Hood changes to Wolf, 12" h 300.00
  Nancy Ann Storybook, #116, orig clothes 30.00
  Unknown Maker, papier-mâché body, hand made clothes, c1885, 30" l 815.00
Figure
  Cybis, 1973 .... 325.00
  Pinecone, 4-1/2" h, mkd "Made in West Germany" 45.00
Formula Bottle, 1-3/4" x 2-1/4" x 6-1/2" h, clear glass, red artwork and inscription on front, reverse with emb gauge for measuring formula, threaded glass top, c1940 .... 20.00
Match Holder, Little Red Riding Hood and Wolf, striker, Staffordshire............ 75.00

Hull Pottery Items

Allspice Jar..................................... 375.00
Bank, standing 575.00

Canister	
Cereal	950.00
Coffee	750.00
Flour	450.00
Sugar	650.00
Tea	750.00
Cookie Jar	300.00
Creamer	
Pour through type	300.00
Side pour	150.00
Tab handle	275.00
Lamp	2,000.00
Milk Pitcher	400.00
Mustard, orig spoon	250.00
Range Shakers, pr	150.00
Salt and Pepper Shakers, pr, 3-1/4" h, incised "135889," gold trim	140.00
Sugar Bowl, cov	325.00
Teapot, cov	325.00

Lottery Tickets

Collecting Hints: Most people throw away their losing lottery tickets but there is something else you can do with them. You can collect them and even trade them just like you did with baseball cards when you were younger.

The Global Lottery Collector's Society (GLCS) is an international group of people who collect and trade lottery memorabilia for fun. The roots of the GLCS were formed in 1988 when a group of friends, who lived in different states, decided to collect and trade their state's losing instant scratch-off tickets with each other. These are the tickets that contain latex, which can be rubbed off with the edge of a coin to determine instantly whether they are a winner or loser. Word soon spread about these friends and as more people participated, they decided to form an official club. At that time, they called themselves the Lottery Collectors Society. In 2000, the club merged with another smaller lottery collecting club and now numbers more than 850 members.

The club produces a monthly newsletter that lists the recent instant ticket releases from the 38 U.S. lotteries and the five lotteries from Canada. There are informative articles about many of these tickets, as well as contests and free offers for club members.

Keeping up to date on current tickets is a challenge, but how does one know about the instant ticket releases from a year ago, or two years ago or even 20 years ago? Simple. The GLCS has a ticket catalog that lists every instant ticket ever released. The list is in order by release date and each ticket is given a number.

This acts as a checklist for the tickets from all the U.S. and Canadian lottery jurisdictions, dating back to the very first instant ticket released more than 27 years ago.

The club also holds an annual convention, called the "Lotovention," in which members meet in person to display and trade their lottery memorabilia. Lotoventions have been held every year since 1989 and have been in Atlanta, St. Louis, Chicago, San Diego, Madison, Baltimore, Phoenix, and in British Columbia, Canada.

The goal of the club has always been to promote the hobby of lottery-ticket and lottery-memorabilia collecting. Recently, several club members fought to have two new words introduced into the English language. The first word was "lotology," which is the name they have given their hobby and the second word was, "lotologist," which is what they call themselves. These words will be listed in the next edition of *Miriam Webster's Collegiate Dictionary.*

History: The modern lottery started in New Hampshire in 1964 with the formation of the New Hampshire Sweepstakes Commission, but it was Massachusetts which released the first instant scratch-off ticket in 1974. The game, called, "The Instant Game," was innovative for its time. No longer would people have to wait a few hours or a few days to determine whether they had won. They could now play a game that instantly told them whether they were a winner. In this Massachusetts game, the player could win if any of his four numbers matched "the instant number," a type of game still being played today. That first game cost $1 and while the majority of the games today still cost this amount, tickets have sold for as much as $25 each. In this case, the game was put out by the Connecticut lottery in 1993 and called, "Gift Horse." You still had to match your number to the "gift horse number," but it just cost you more. Because of the cost of this ticket, it was one of the most difficult tickets to find. But it is not the rarest.

The most difficult ticket to find is contained within a set of tickets put out by the Illinois lottery in 1976. The set, called, "Presidents," was a 35-ticket set, with each ticket picturing one of the 35 presidents up until that time. People who purchased those tickets were encouraged to save their losers, since they were told one president would be selected at the end of the contest and then holders of that

particular ticket could send it in as part of a second-chance drawing. The ticket picturing Herbert Hoover was the one selected and is now considered the most difficult ticket to find. Despite these tough tickets, there are thousands of tickets easily available and many are being traded everyday.

Tickets from those early days of the lottery were very small, with some measuring one inch by one inch. Today's tickets come in all sizes. While the majority of them can still fit in the palm of your hand, several have been as large as the Pennsylvania issue, "Super Bingo" from 1996, which measured 8 inches by 6 inches. Some tickets have even taken a less traditional shape than the square or rectangular shapes commonly used. The New Jersey lottery had a ticket in the shape of a Christmas tree for the holiday season. The Oregon lottery had a ticket in the shape of a snowman for a winter theme ticket. The Pennsylvania lottery released a round ticket for a game called "Silver Dollars." Many states have also released a ticket in the shape of a sock during the holiday season called, "Stocking Stuffer." These odd-shaped tickets are called diecuts.

Recently the state lotteries themselves have realized the collecting potential of their tickets by using such popular themes as Star Trek, Harley Davidson, Betty Boop, Nascar, and Wheel of Fortune many times. These tickets are very popular among lotologists. Also, many famous celebrities have appeared on instant scratch-off tickets. Elvis Presley, Marilyn Monroe, Michael J. Fox, John Goodman, Sylvester Stallone, Lucille Ball, the Three Stooges, and Laurel and Hardy are just some of them. Recent tickets have also featured the casts of such television shows as "Baywatch," "Gilligan's Island," and "The Munsters." Even baseball legends, football Hall of Famers and professional wrestlers have been immortalized on instant scratch-off tickets.

Within the past few years, a new type of instant-lottery ticket has been introduced, called "probability games." What makes these games different from the original games is that the player only scratches a small portion of the latex area instead of the entire area. On one particular ticket, a player can only scratch five of the 25 latex spots. The total of the revealed numbers determined whether they were a winner and what the prize would be. Scratching off more than five spots made the ticket void. Because these games are new, they are also being actively sought by lotologists.

There are actually three different types of instant scratch-off tickets collected and traded. The most popular are the tickets that have already been scratched and determined to be losers. These are the most readily available, since the majority of the tickets are losers and can be found thrown in the garbage can of your local retailer. Mint tickets are also collected and traded. These are tickets that have not been scratched, but must be purchased. Then there are the sample-voids, which are promotional tickets given to retailers from the lottery who hide their tickets behind the counter.

While instant scratch-off tickets are the most widely collected, a lotologist can collect just about anything pertaining to the lottery. There are the paper tickets, which are the machine-generated tickets used in either a Powerball game or a daily three-digit number game. Then there are the placards, which are oversized, cardboard reproductions of tickets currently offered for sale. Other items include pull tabs, which is another form of lottery gaming, lapel pins, buttons, magnets, pens, pencils, bet slips, keychains, mugs, bumperstickers and everything else a lottery might use to promote itself. Remember, today's tickets will be sought after by collectors for years.

Periodical: *The Lotologist Monthly*, Stephen Tuday, 608 Victoria Lane, Woodstock, GA 30189-1473.

Collectors' Club: Global Lottery Collectors Society, Arthur Rein, 642 Locust St., Apt 2J, Mt. Vernon, NY 10552-2620; e-mail: Lotteryfan@ aol.com.

Web site: www.Lotterycollectors .com.

Advisor: Arthur Rein.

Australia, group of thirty different Instant Tickets, scratched 16.00
California
    Big Spin, mint, error ticket from 1994, no ticket identification numbers 210.00
    Instant Game, scratched, set of first ten, from 1985 to 1986 .... 14.00
    Winning Spirit, set of five tickets, mint, 1992 .... 35.00
Canada, on-line paper tickets, lot of eleven tickets from 1977 and 1978 .... 25.50
Colorado, Tic Tac Toe, sample void, 1983 .... 15.50
Illinois
    Countdown 2000, sample void, 1999 .... 2.50

Beat the Dealer, Pennsylvania lottery, 1996, trading value only.

Reindeer Games, Pennsylvania lottery, 2000, trading value only.

    Instant Game, "7-11-21," first, scratched, 1975 .... 7.50
Iowa
    Instant Tickets, released only as Sample Voids, Lucky Number and Blackjack, price for pair 32.50
    It's So Easy, sample void picturing Buddy Holly, 1993 .... 6.00
Kentucky, Instant Game, Beginner's Luck, first, scratched, 1989 .... 5.00
Maine, set of four different Lucky Spots probability games, mint, 1999 ..... 62.00
Missouri, five different on-line paper tickets, 2000 .... 4.25
New Hampshire, Double Jackpot, mint, 1981 .... 24.00
New York
    Sample voids, 25 different tickets dating from 1992 to 1997 .... 55.00
    Tax Free Million, mint, error from 1966, background color shifted in printing process 15.75
Oregon, set of 24 Monster Cash tickets, scratched, from 1996 .... 15.50
Pennsylvania, PA Bicentennial, complete set of twenty tickets, scratched, 1976 .... 62.00
Rhode Island, Photo Finish, mint, 1992 .... 11.00
Texas Instant Ticket, Lone Star Millions, first issue, mint, 1992 .... 35.00
Virgin Islands Tickets, sample void, ten different tickets dating from 1994 to 1998 .... 16.00

Lunch Kits

Collecting Hints: The thermos is an integral part of the lunch kit. The two must be present for full value. There has been a tendency in recent years to remove the thermos from the lunch box and price the two separately. The wise collector will resist this trend.

Scratches and rust detract from a metal kit's value and lower it by more than 50 percent.

History: Lunch kits date back to the 19th century when tin boxes were used by factory workers and field hands. The modern children's lunch kit, the form most sought by today's collector, was first sold in the 1930s. Gender, Paeschke & Frey Co. of Milwaukee, Wisconsin, issued a No. 9100 Mickey Mouse lunch kit for the 1935 Christmas trade. An oval lunch kit of a streamlined train, mkd "Decoware," dates from the same period.

Television brought the decorated lunch box into the forefront. The following are some of the leading manufacturers: Aladdin Company; Landers, Frary and Clark; Ohio Art (successor to Hibbard, Spencer, Bartlett & Co.) of Bryan, Ohio; Thermos/ King Seeley; and Universal.

References: Larry Aikins, *Pictorial Price Guide to Metal Lunch Boxes & Thermoses*, L-W Book Sales, 1992, 1996 value update; ——, *Pictorial Price Guide to Vinyl & Plastic Lunch Boxes & Thermoses*, L-W Book Sales, 1992, 1995 value update; Philip R. Norman, *1993 Lunch Box & Thermos Price Guide*, published by author, 1992; Carole Bess White & L. M. White, Collector's Guide to Lunchboxes, Collector Books, 2000; Allen Woodall and Sean Brickell, *Illustrated Encyclopedia of Metal Lunch Boxes*, Schiffer Publishing, 1992.

Periodical: *Paileontologist's Report*, P.O. Box 3255, Burbank, CA 91508.

Collectors' Club: Step into the Ring, 829 Jackson St. Ext, Sandusky, OH 44870.

Archies, 1969 .... 85.00
Astronauts, dome type, 1960 .... 250.00
Battle Kit, 1965 .... 135.00
Bionic Woman, Aladdin, plastic, Canadian flags on lunch box and thermos, 1970s 65.00
Bobby Orr, Aladdin, all plastic, metal snaps, 1970s 125.00
Care Bear Cousins, 1985 .... 18.00
Clash of the Titans, King Seeley, metal, 1980 .... 20.00
Cracker Jack, 1969 .... 75.00
Dark Crystal, orig thermos, 1982, unused 35.00
Dick Tracy, no thermos 150.00
Disney Snow White, orig thermos, 1975 .... 30.00
Donnie & Marie, vinyl, 1977 .... 135.00
Dragon's Lair, orig thermos, 1983 .... 25.00

Dukes of Hazzard, Aladdin, 1980, plastic, orig thermos....................................30.00
Easy Bake, plastic 10.00
E. T., 1982 ....24.00
Fall Guy 35.00
Fat Albert, 1973 ....55.00
Flag, 1970 ....20.00
Flying Nun, Aladdin, 1968, C8 ....150.00
Fritos, generic thermos, 1979 ....90.00
G. I. Joe, orig thermos, 1980............20.00
Green Hornet, 1967 ....525.00
Happy Days, 1977............................65.00
Harlem Globetrotters, 1971..............20.00
Holly Hobbie, vinyl, white, 1972.......30.00
Hot Wheels, red plastic, 1984 ....25.00
Inch High Pirate Eye 40.00
It's About Time, dome top 185.00
Jabberjaw, Hanna Barbera Productions, 1977, orig thermos 60.00
James Bond, metal..........................155.00
Jetsons, dome top 650.00
Jiminey Cricket, two handles, Canadian, 1950s 145.00
Jurassic Park, plastic, no thermos, fair condition 9.00
Kewtie Pie, vinyl 180.00
Knight Rider, 1983 ....22.00
Knitting, Ohio Art, metal, 1960s 30.00

Kung Fu 55.00
Land of the Giants.........................125.00
Legend of the Lone Ranger, Aladdin, 1980, metal, some wear 24.00
Loaf of Bread, metal, dome top..... 175.00
MacDonald's, yellow and white, plastic, 1987...12.50
Masters of the Universe, orig thermos, 1984...20.00
Mickey Mouse Club, red rim, 1977 ..48.00
Miss America, 1972 ....85.00
Mod Tulips, dome top, 1975.......... 450.00
Mork and Mindy, 1979 ....35.00
Muppet Babies, orig thermos, 1985 20.00
New Mickey Mouse Club, orig thermos, 1977...25.00
NFL, 1962..30.00
Paramedics, 1978, no thermos 65.00
Peanuts Gang, playing baseball, orig tags..60.00
Perk's Dragon, thermos, 1978..........30.00
Peter Pan, 1969................................20.00
Pink Panther and Sons, 1984 ....60.00
Plaid, vinyl, steel thermos, 1960s 28.00
Queen Elizabeth, metal, basket style, 1953...40.00
Raggedy Ann & Andy, plastic 75.00
Satellite, used 60.00

Secret of Nimh, orig thermos, 1982, unused...25.00
Smokey the Bear, vinyl, some wear to bottom.. 145.00
Snow White, Ohio Art, 1980............. 22.00
Speed Buggy 35.00
Sports Afield 50.00
Star Trek, plastic, orig thermos, Canadian 100.00
Strawberry Shortcake, vinyl, orig thermos, 1980... 20.00
Supercar, with orig thermos........... 335.00
Tammy and Pepper, vinyl, glossy black, bright color art, Aladdin Industries, 7" x 9" x 3-1/2" 75.00
Teenager Square, used...................... 5.00
U.S. Space Corps, orig thermos, 1984... 420.00
Wags n' Whiskers, 1978.................. 15.00
Western Cowboy, King Seeley Thermos Co., C8,...................................... 130.00
Wild Frontier, magnetic pieces, no thermos 40.00
Young Western, metal, basket style, 1950s... 50.00

M

Magazine Covers and Tear Sheets

Collecting Hints: A good cover should show the artist's signature, have the mailing label nonexistent or in a place that does not detract from the design element, and have edges which are crisp but not trimmed.

When framing vintage paper, use acid-free mat board and tape with a water-soluble glue base, such as brown-paper gum tape or linen tape. The tape should only be affixed to the back side of the illustration. The rule of thumb is do not do anything that cannot be easily undone.

Do not hang framed vintage paper in direct sunlight (causes fading) or in a high-humidity area such as a bathroom or above a kitchen sink (causes wrinkles in both the mat and artwork).

History: Magazine-cover design attracted some of America's leading illustrators. Maxfield Parrish, Erte, Leyendecker, and Norman Rockwell were dominate in the 20th century. In the mid-1930s, photographic covers gradually replaced the illustrated covers. One of the leaders in the industry was *Life*, which emphasized photojournalism.

Magazine covers arc frequently collected according to artist-signed covers, subject matter, or historical events. Artist-signed covers feature a commercially printed artist's signature on the cover, or the artist is identified inside as "Cover by...." The majority of collected covers are in full color and show significant design elements. Black memorabilia is often reflected in magazine covers and tear sheets, and it is frequently collected for the positive affect it has on African-Americans. However, sometimes it is a reflection of the times in which it was printed and may represent subjects in an unfavorable light.

Many of America's leading artists also created the illustrations for magazine advertisements. The ads made characters such as the Campbell Kids, the Dutch Girl, and Snap, Crackle and Pop world famous.

References: Check local libraries for books about specific illustrators such as Parrish, Rockwell, and Jessie Wilcox Smith.

Periodicals: *Illustrator Collector's News*, P.O. Box 1958, Sequim, WA 98392; *Paper Collectors' Marketplace* (PCM), P.O. Box 128, Scandinavia, WI 54977.

Notes: As more and more magazines are destroyed for the tear sheets, complete magazines rise in value proportionate to the decrease in supply. If a magazine is in mint condition, it should be left intact. We do NOT encourage removing illustrations from complete magazines. The complete magazine is the best tool for interpreting a specific historical time period. Editorial and advertising together define the spirit of the era.

The Home, July 1932, Charles Twelvetrees illustration, $20.

Artist Signed
Armstrong, Rolf	35.00
Christy, Howard Chandler	25.00
Drayton, Grace	17.50
Eastman, Ruth	12.00
Fisher, Harrison	35.00
Flagg, James Montgomery	30.00
Gutmann, Bessie Pease	35.00
King, Hamilton	25.00
Leyendecker	30.00
Mucha, Alphonse	50.00
O'Neill, Rose	35.00
Parrish, Maxfield	50.00
Smith, Jessie Wilcox	35.00
Twelvetrees, Charles	30.00

Automobile
Pre-1918, black and white	18.50
Pre-1918, color	20.00
1919-1937, black and white	25.00
1919-1937, color	20.00
1938-1941, black and white	18.00
1938-1941, color	20.00
1942-1955, black and white	15.00
1942-1955, color	20.00

Aviation
Pre-1935, black and white	15.00
Pre-1935, color	17.50
Post-1935, black and white	13.50
Post-1935, color	15.00

Beverage
Beer, identified brand, color	18.00
Coca-Cola, pre-1925, color	20.00
Wines and Liquors	15.00

Black Memorabilia
Cover with personality	20.00
Tear sheet with adv	25.00

Fashion
Pre-1930, color	20.00
Post-1930, color	15.00

Firearms
Christmas Time is Crosman Time, illus of rifles, *Boys' Life*, 1969	15.00
Winchester, *Boys' Life*, 1968, shows models 250, 270, and 290	12.00
Winchester, *Outdoor Life*, 1953, shows model 70, 43, 94, and 12	15.00
Winchester, *Outdoor Life*, 1956	15.00

Food
Campbell Kids, large format	20.00
Clark's Teaberry Gum, 13-1/2" x 5-1/2", 1942, matted and shrink wrapped	25.00
Cream of Wheat, 13-1/2" x 5-1/2", Lil' Abner graphic, matted and shrink wrapped	25.00
Junket Powder, 13-1/2" x 5-1/2", 1943 ad, matted and shrink wrapped	25.00
Kara Syrup, 13-1/2" x 5-1/2", features Dionne Quints, matted and shrink wrapped	25.00

Jewelry, color
	7.50

Miscellaneous
Every Ready Flashlight, 1915, Halloween theme	8.50
Magic Chef, 1946	5.00
HiramWalker with Alfred Glassell, Jr., 1955	8.00
Sunny Brook, 1954	6.00
Watkins Vitamins, 1956	8.00

Tobacco, Philip Morris, 13-1/2" x 5-1/2", matted and shrink wrapped 25.00

Toy
Erector Set	25.00
Trains, Lionel or Ives	18.00
Viewmaster, 13-1/2" x 5-1/2", matted and shrink wrapped	20.00

Magazines

Collecting Hints: A rule of thumb for pricing general magazines with covers designed by popular artists is the more you would enjoy displaying a copy on your coffee table, the more elite the publication, or the more the advertising or editorial content relates to today's collectibles, the higher the price. *Life* magazine went into millions of homes each week, *Harper's Bazaar* and *Vogue* did not. Upper-class families tended to discard last month's publication, while middle-class families found the art on the *Saturday Evening Post* and *Collier's* irresistible and saved them. The greater the supply, the lower the price.

History: In the early 1700s, general magazines were a major source of information for the reader. Literary magazines, such as *Harper's*, became popular in the 19th century. By 1900, the first photo-journal magazines appeared. *Life*, the most famous example, was started by Henry Luce in 1932.

Magazines created for women featured "how-to" articles about cooking, sewing, decorating, and child care. Many of the publications were entirely devoted to fashion and living a fashionable life, such as *Harper's Bazaar* and *Vogue*. Men's magazines were directed at masculine interests of the time, such as hunting, fishing, and woodworking, supplemented with appropriate "girlie" titles.

References: Ron Barlow and Ray Reynolds, *Insider's Guide to Old Books, Magazines, Newspapers, and Trade Catalogs*, Windmill Publishing (2147 Windmill View Rd, El Cajon, CA 92020), 1996; Clark Kidder, *Marilyn Monroe: Cover to Cover*, Krause Publications, 1999; Frank M. Robinson and Lawrence Davidson, *Pulp Culture: The Art of Fiction Magazines*, Collectors Press, Inc., 1998.

Periodicals: *Collecting Cult Magazines*, 449 12th St., #2-R, Brooklyn, NY 11215; *Illustrator Collector's News*, P.O. Box 1958, Sequim, WA 98392; *Paper Collectors' Marketplace (PCM)*, P.O. Box 128, Scandinavia, WI 54977; *Pulp & Paperback Market Newsletter*, 5813 York Ave., Edina, MN 55410.

Notes: General magazine prices listed below are retail prices. They may be considerably higher than what would be offered for an entire collection filling your basement or garage. Bulk prices for common magazines such as *Life, Collier's*, and *Saturday Evening Post* generally range between 50¢ and $1 per issue. Magazine dealers have to sort through many issues to find those which may be saleable, some protect individual issues, covers, or tear sheets with plastic covering, etc. before they can realize a profit for more common magazines.

Airman, Official Air Force Journal, 1961, March 3.00
Alfred Hitchcock Mystery 5.00

Amateur Photographer's Weekly, June 6, 1919 .... 3.00
Amazing Stories, July, 1943, Ziff-Davis Publishing Co., 208 pgs, 7" x 10" .. 5.00
American Childhood, 1941, April 5.00
American Golfer, December 1932 ... 10.00
American Heritage, 1958, October, Pocahontas cover 6.00
American Motorist, 1916 .... 10.00
American Magazine, bound volume of six 1940 issues 35.00
American Rifleman, 1929 .... 15.00
Argosy Weekly, Oct. 19, 1935, 144 pgs, 7" x 10" 2.00
Arizona Highway, 1959, December, Prickly Pear in Bloom 5.00
Atlantic, 1954, July, Churchill cover ... 6.00
Aviation, 1928 .... 15.00
Beckett, Michael Jordon on cover 7.50
Better Homes and Gardens, 1942, December 6.00
Better Photo, 1913 .... 4.00
Billiard's Digest 1.00
Boy's Life
1955, June, Boy Scout Statue cover, Coca-Cola ad 5.00
1970, October, Bill Bradley cover . 6.00
Burr McIntosh Monthly, December 1907, Alphonse Mucha print on cover, poor condition, 12" h, 7" w 40.00
Chatterbox, bound year, 1917, 10" x 7-1/2", 412 pgs 25.00
Child's Life, 1930 .... 4.00
Collier's, Maxfield Parrish cov, rows of soldiers, Nov. 16, 1912 .... 50.00
Confidential, 1966, August, Sammy Davis cover 8.00
Confidential Confessions, 1959, August 3.00
Cosmopolitan, 1910 .... 6.00
Crime Detective, Steve McQueen on cover, 1950s 65.00
Dare-Devil Aces, September, 1937, Fredrick Blakeslee cover, 112 pgs, 7" x 10" 48.00
Delineator, 1904 .... 20.00
Disney, Mickey Mouse is Sixty, animation cel 40.00
Elle, 1997, July, Cindy Crawford 22.00
Ellery Queen Mystery Magazine, 1950s 5.00
Esquire Magazine, July 1935, Ernest Hemingway story 50.00
Etude, 1942, November, West Point choir article 5.00
Everyday Science & Mechanics, August, 1933, world's largest tower on cover 25.00
Family Circle, 1954 .... 5.00
Family Health, September, 1976, John Wayne cover and article 10.00
Famous Fantastic Mysteries, June, 1948, 7" x 9-1/2", lightly worn 5.00
Fantastic Adventures, volume 1, #3, September 1939, graphic cover by H. W. McCauley and Frank R. Paul, splint on front 2.00

Fantastic Adventures, October, 1945, vivid cover art by J. Allen St. John, 178 pgs, 7" x 9-3/4" 10.00
Fantastic Novels, November, 1948, New Publications, Inc., 128 pgs, 7" x 9-1/2" 2.00
Farm & Fireside, 1923, March, boy and dog cover 6.00
Farm Journal
1923, February, boy on cover 9.00
1927, December, Santa and Elves on cover 8.50
1940, March, sheep and lion cover 5.00
Farm Life, 1923, September, cows in pasture cover 6.00
Fate, 1953, Atlantis 7.50
Film Culture, John Ford cover, #25, Summer, 1982 .... 4.00
Flash, volume 1, #1, May, 1941 .... 5.00
Fortune, April, 1941 .... 32.75
Foto, volume 1, #1, June, 1937 .... 5.00
Friends, 1965, May, NY World's Fair cover, Errol Flynn article 9.00
Front Page Detective, 1952, August . 3.00
Gayety Magazine, Alex Schomberg pin-up cover, 1942 .... 45.00
Golden Book Magazine, 1929, six months bound 35.00
Golf Journal Magazine, May, 1967, Jack and Barbara Nicklaus 18.00
Good Housekeeping, 1965 .... 4.00
Hit Parade, 1947, September, Jane Greer cover 7.00
Horticulture, 1959, December, poinsettia cover 3.50
Inside Detective, volume 4, #3, March 1937, 64 pgs, 8-1/2" x 11-1/2" 15.00
Jack & Jill, 1961 .... 10.00
Jewelers' Weekly, 1889, New York, 88 pgs, 7" x 10" 18.00
Jokes Magazine, volume 1, #1, Dell, 32 sepiatone photos, early 1930s, 8-1/2" x 11-1/2" 12.00
Junior Natural History, 1954, April, goat cover 4.00
Junior Scholastic, April 21, 1954, large black and white cover photo of 13 year old student and robot 30.00
Ladies Home Journal, 1960, June..... 5.00
Life
1940, December 30, Britain's Desert Fighters on cover 7.00
1953, July 13, Hillary Climb, Mt Everest, adv with stars 12.00
1961, July 7, Ike Down on the Farm cover 10.00
1962, October 12, Pope John XXIII cover 9.00
1964, March 13, series on World War I 7.00
1968, April 12, Martin Luther King Jr., cover loose 15.00
1970, July 17, Rose Kennedy at 80 cover 11.00
1971, October 15, Disney World Opens cover, Joan Crawford article 9.00
1972, July 7, George McGovern cover, Pandas in DC article 5.00

Literary Digest, 1937, May 1, Princess Elizabeth cover 7.00
Little Folks, April, 1912 .... 5.00
Look
    Davy Crockett, Walt Disney cover 38.00
    Gary Cooper as Lou Gehrig cover 45.00
MAD, #82, October, 1963, Castro smoking cigar 22.00
Mature Outlook Magazine, September/ October, 1987, Charles Schulz and Peanuts cover............................. 12.00
McCall's, 1961, Christmas Make-It Ideas 4.00
Mechanix Illustrated, May, 1954, Creature from the Black Lagoon color cover 65.00
Modern Screen, 1946, August, Gregory Peck cover, Lucy Ball cover photo 15.00
Motion Picture Classic, August, 1927, 9-1/4" x 12" 12.00
Mr. Magazine, volume 1, #1, March, 1950, edge wear.................................... 4.00
National Geographic, 1965, August, tribute to Sir Winston Churchill, 137 pgs 45.00
New England Magazine, 20 issues, 1910-12 .... 22.00
Newsweek, 1974, August 19, Pres Ford cover, special issue 6.00

***Play Mate Magazine*, April 1943, Fern Bisel Peat cover, $12.**

Photo Screen, 1973, July, Waltons cover 8.00
Playthings, 1959 .... 35.00
Popular Aviation, 1933 .... 10.00
Popular Science, Steve McQueen on cover, 1966 .... 40.00
Popular Sports, Fall, 1943 .... 4.00
Quick, 1950, July 24, Princess Elizabeth cover 8.00

Quilter's Newsletter 2.50
Radio and TV Mirror, Lucille Ball, 1950... 50.00
Redbook, June, 1925 .... 5.00
Rexall, 1939, June, Nan Gray cover, Judy Garland article 5.00
Saturday Evening Post
    1955, November 5, Nehru, Rockwell cover 12.00
    1963, January 19, Beverly Hillbillies cover 30.00
    1964, May 2, Fischer Quints cover 12.00
Scouting, 1973, Sept, Soap Box Derby cover 3.00
Scribners Magazine, volume 3 to 59, 1916, bound 11.00
Secrets, 1959, January 3.00
Seventeen Magazine, June, 1970, Susan Dey cover 45.00
Silk, spoof, Monkees 25.00
Silver Screen, 1973, June, Bunkers cover, Brady Bunch article 8.00
Sky Birds, October, 1933, full color art by Tinsley, 7" x 10" 4.00
Song Hits, 1953, March, Janet Leigh cover, Johnnie Ray article 6.00
Sports Illustrated, July 29, 1963, Sonny Liston 15.00
Story Parade, 1952, June 4.00
Successful Farming, 1941, May........ 5.00
Sure-Fire Detective, volume 1, #1, February 1937, 128 pgs, 7" x 10" 40.00
Teen Magazine, Annette kissing Sgt. Garcia (Zorro)................................... 40.00
Ten Dectective Aces, May, 1949, Ace Periodicals, 7" x 10", light wear 6.00
The Crystal Fount, bound issues, Feb thru December, 1847, Baltimore, full calf leather cover, steel engravings ... 45.00
The Granite State (NH) Magazine, volumes 1-6, bound......................... 30.00
The Magazine Antiques, June, 1972... 22.75
The Master Detective, volume 8, #5, July, 1933, 80 pgs, 8-3/4" x 11-1/2", tape repair to cover 10.00
The North American Review, January 1890, includes article about R. E. Lee by Jefferson Davis 15.00
The Spider, November, 1940, Popular Publications, Grant Stockbridge novel, 7" x 10", fading to spine, edge wear... 38.00
Thrilling Wonder Stories, April, 1947, Standard Magazines, 112 pgs, fantasy art cover, 7" x 9-1/2" 2.00
Time
    1933, Dec. 11, 1933, General Chiang.. 75.00
    1942, Nov. 30, Halsey cover 6.00
    1944, June 19, Eisenhower cover. 8.00
    1973, Jan. 29, Nixon caricature cover... 5.00
    1987, Dec. 7, Shirley Maclaine 3.00

***The American Magazine*, December 1923, Earl Christy cover illustration, $10.**

Top Notch Magazine, volume #44, #1, November, 1920, 6-3/4" x 10" 7.50
True Detective, volume 37, #1, October 1941, Bob Hope cover, 120 pgs, 8-1/2" x 11-1/4" 10.00
True Story, January, 1938, 8-1/2" x 11" 2.50
Today's Health, 1960, June, Kate Smith cover 4.00
TV Dial, Roy Rogers, Hopalong Cassidy, Gene Autry on cover 140.00
TV Digest, Lucille Ball and Ricky in motorboat, Philadelphia, 1952 .... 135.00
TV Guide
    Beverly Hillbillies 60.00
    Branded.................................... 25.00
    Lawman..................................... 25.00
    Lil'Abner.................................... 50.00
    Lost in Space.............................. 75.00
    Maverick, James Garner 30.00
    Paladin 25.00
    Rebel 25.00
    That Girl 18.00
    Wild Wild West............................ 30.00
    Zorro, Guy Williams 45.00
TV People, Bonzana cover 40.00
TV Radio Mirror, photo of Honeymooner's Art Carney and others on cover, article on Honeymooners, April, 1960... 20.00
TV Week, Dick Tracy, 1960s............. 35.00
Venture Magazine, April, 1971, 3D picture on cover...................................... 5.00
Vogue, December 1986, Paloma Picasso on cover...................................... 19.00
Wee Wisdom, 1939, July.................. 7.50
Western Horseman, complete run, 1951 through 1963 .... 75.00
Western Story Magazine, Jan. 31, 1925, 144 pgs, 7" x 10" 2.00
Woman's Home Companion, March, 1933, Elizabeth Lansdell Hammell's full color cover artwork of a dish of jonquils, feature by Pearl S. Buck.... 20.00
Woman's World, March, 1936............ 2.00

Wonder Story Annual, volume 1, #1, 1950, 194 black and white pages, 6-1/2" x 9-1/2" 25.00

Workbasket, whole year, 1965 ....5.00

Marbles

Collecting Hints: Handmade glass marbles usually command higher prices than machine-made glass, clay, or mineral marbles. There are a few notable exceptions, e.g., machine-made comic-strip marbles were made for a limited time only and are highly prized by collectors. Care must be taken in purchasing this particular type, since the comic figure was stenciled on the marble. A layer of glass was to be overlaid on the stencil, but sometimes this process was not completed. In such cases, the stencils rub or wear off.

Some of the rarer examples of handmade marbles are Clambroth, Lutz, Indian Swirls, Peppermint Swirls, and Sulphides. Marble values are normally determined by their type, size, and condition. Usually, the larger the marble, the more valuable it is within its category.

A marble in mint condition is unmarred and has the best possible condition with a clear surface. It may have surface abrasions caused by rubbing while in its original package. A marble in good condition may have a few small surface dings, scratches, and slight surface cloudiness. However, the core must be easily seen, and the marble must be free of large chips or fractures.

History: Marbles date back to ancient Greece, Rome, Egypt, and other early civilizations. In England, Good Friday is known as "Marbles Day" because the game was considered a respectable and quiet pastime for the hallowed day.

During the American Civil War, soldiers carried marbles and a small board to play solitaire, a game whose object was to jump the marbles until only one was left in the center of the board.

In the last few generations, school children have identified marbles as "peewees," "shooters," "commies," and "cat's eyes." A National Marbles Tournament has been held each year in June since 1922.

References: Paul Baumann, *Collecting Antique Marbles*, 3rd ed., Krause Publications, 1999; Robert Block, *Marbles Illustrated: Prices at Auc-tion*, Schiffer Publishing, 1999; *Marbles Identification and Price Guide*, 3rd ed., Schiffer Publishing, 1999; Stanley A. Block, *Marble Mania*, Schiffer Publishing, 1998; ——, *Sulphide Marbles*, Schiffer Publishing, 2001; Everett Grist, *Antique and Collectible Marbles*, 3rd ed., Collector Books, 1992, 1998 value update; ——, *Everett Grist's Big Book of Marbles*, 2nd ed., Collector Books, 2000; ——, *Everett Grist's Machine Made and Contemporary Marbles*, 2nd ed., Collector Books, 1995, 1999 value update.

Collectors' Clubs: Buckeye Marble Collectors Club, 437 Meadowbrook Dr., Newark, OH 43055; Marble Collectors Unlimited, P.O. Box 206, Northboro, MA 01532; Marble Collectors Society of America, P.O. Box 222, Trumbull, CT 06611; National Marble Club of America, 440 Eaton Rd, Drexel Hill, PA 19026; Sea-Tac Marble Collectors Club, P.O. Box 793, Monroe, WA 98272; Southern California Marble Club, 18361-1 Strathern St., Reseda, CA 91335.

Museums: Corning Museum of Glass, Corning, NY; Sandwich Glass Museum, Sandwich, MA; Smithsonian Institution, Museum of Natural History, Washington, DC; Wheaton Village Museum, Millville, NJ.

Reproduction Alert: Comic marbles and some machine-made marbles are being reproduced, as are some polyvinyl packages, mesh packages, and original boxes.

Notes: Handmade marbles listed are common examples in mint condition. Unusual examples command prices that are 2 to 20 times higher. Mint condition machine-made marbles priced here have a diameter between 9/16 and 11/16 inch, unless otherwise noted.

Handmade Marbles

End of Day

Onionskin
    Confetti onionskin, 2-3/8" 1,575.00
    Onionskin with mica, 3/4" d 975.00
    Suspended mica 1,200.00

Lutz

    Amber glass ribbon 475.00
    Banded, 1" 265.00
    Black glass............................... 525.00
    Blue and orange ribbon core ... 280.00
    Cranberry ribbon, 1-1/16" d...... 325.00
    Pink onionskin 200.00

Mica

    3/4" d, peppermint 300.00
    1" d 110.00
    1-1/2" 200.00

Other

Clambroth, red on black 250.00
Opaque, red on pink banded........ 250.00
Translucent, Butterfly................... 3,650.00
Sulphide
    Duck, tri-color paint............... 1,100.00
    Girl petting dog 450.00
    Pair of kissing love birds 750.00
    Wild Boar, 2-3/8" d................... 675.00

Swirl, core, yellow and white, multicolored core, 1-5/8" d, $50.

Swirl

Banded, 1" 75.00
Divided Core, 1-3/4" 150.00
End of cane double ribbon 350.00
Indian Swirl, 1-1/6" d, blue bands, translucent 3,550.00
Joseph, multicolored 300.00
Latticino Core
    Bright red swirl 325.00
    Cyan blue 490.00
Green Mist, 1" d, with mica 650.00
Ribbon Core
    3/4" 80.00
    1-1/2" 200.00
Solid Core
    1-7/8", red 2,350.00
    2-5/16", lobed 1,150.00

Machine-Made Marbles

Akro Agate

Boxed Set
    1 red slag, orig box 1,350.00
    100 sparklers......................... 5,300.00
Corkscrew, 1-13/16" d, Royal
    Blue 165.00
Helmet Patch 3.00
Lemonade corkscrew 17.50
Moonstone.. 12.00
Popeye corkscrew, green/yellow 20.00
Swirl oxblood 20.00

Christensen Agate Co.

American Agate 50.00
Cobra/Cyclone 750.00
Electric Swirl 75.00
Flame Swirl, 3 color 300.00
Guinea 350.00
Slag 30.00

Marble King Co.

Color Matrix, multicolor opaque
    Bumblebee................................... 2.00

Girl Scout/John Deere,
　　yellow/green 8.50
Spiderman, blue/red 250.00
Tiger, orange/black 25.00
Wasp, red/black 5.00
Two-Color, white matrix .... .25
White Matrix .... .45

Master Marble Co.

Patch 1.25
Sunburst
　　Clear 22.00
　　Opaque 5.00

M. F. Christensen & Son

Brick, 9/16" to 11/16" 75.00
Opaque, set of 8, orig box 1,600.00
Slag, 1-7/8" d 375.00

Peltier Glass Co.

Boxed Set, five comics 525.00
Christmas Tree, shooter size 220.00
Liberty, 3/4" d 200.00
Moon comic 310.00
Peerless Patch 5.50
Slag 20.00
Sunset, Muddy, Acme Reefer, Tri-Color,
　　7-Up 1.50
Superman, mint, wet 175.00
Two-color Rainbo, old type 20.00

Transitional

Chocolate-brown Navarre transition,
　　resembles a banded agate 1,200.00
Ground pontil oxblood with complete
　　white and yellow design 725.00
Ground pontil hand gathered, green,
　　white, red, and pink 325.00
Horizontal swirl Navarre, 1-1/8" ... 1,350.00

Vitro Agate/Gladding Vitro Co.

All red .... .45
Blackie .... .65
Conqueror 1.20
Hybrid Cat's Eye 2.50
Oxblood Patch 8.50
Patch and Ribbon Transparent .... .45
Victory 3.50

Matchcovers

Collecting Hints: Matchcovers generally had large production runs; very few are considered rare. Most collectors try to obtain unused covers. They remove the matches, flatten the covers, and mount them in albums which are arranged by category.

Trading is the principal means of exchange among collectors, usually on a one-for-one basis. At flea markets and shows, beer or pinup art ("girlie") matchcovers frequently are priced at $1 to $5. Actually those interested in such covers would be best advised to join one of the collector clubs and get involved in swapping.

History: The book match was invented by Joshua Pusey, a Philadelphia lawyer, who also was a chemist in his spare time. In 1892, Pusey put ten cardboard matches into a cover of plain white board and sold 200 of them to the Mendelson Opera Company which, in turn, hand-printed messages on the front.

The first machine-made matchbook was made by the Binghamton Match Company, Binghamton, New York, for the Piso Company of Warren, Pennsylvania.

Few covers survive from the late 1890s to the 1930s. The modern craze for collecting matchcovers was started when a set of ten covers was issued for the Century of Progress exhibit at the 1933 Chicago World's Fair.

The golden age of matchcovers was the mid-1940s through the early 1960s when the covers were a popular advertising medium. Principal manufacturers included Atlas Match, Brown and Bigelow, Crown Match, Diamond Match, Lion Match, Ohio Match, and Universal Match.

The arrival of throwaway lighters, such as BIC, brought an end to the matchcover era. Today, manufacturing costs for a matchbook can range from less than 1¢ to 8¢ for a special die-cut cover. As a result, matchcovers no longer are an attractive free giveaway, and, therefore, many of the older, more desirable covers are experiencing a marked increase in value. Collectors have also turned to the small pocket-type boxes as a way of enhancing and building their collections.

References: Bill Retskin, *Matchcover Collector's Price Guide*, 2nd ed., Antique Trader Books, 1997; H. Thomas Steele, Jim Heimann, Rod Dyer, *Close Cover Before Striking*, Abbeville Press, 1987.

Periodicals: *Match Hunter*, 740 Poplar, Boulder, CO, 80304; *Matchcover Classified*, 16425 Dam Rd #3, Clearlake, CA 95422.

Collectors' Clubs: American Matchcover Collecting Club, P.O. Box 18481, Asheville, NC 28814, http://www.matchcovers.com; Liberty Bell Matchcover Club, 5001 Albridge Way, Mount Laurel, NJ 08054; Long Beach Matchcover Club, 2501 W. Sunflower H-5, Santa Ana, CA 92704; Newmoon Matchbox & Label Club, 425 E. 51st St., New York, NY 10022; Rathkamp Matchcover Society, 2920

E. 77th St., Tulsa, OK 74136; Trans-Canada Matchcover Club, P.O. Box 219, Caledonia, Ontario, Canada NOA-1A0; Windy City Matchcover Club, 3104 Fargo Ave., Chicago, IL 60645; there are also many regional clubs throughout the United States and Canada.

Special Covers

Advertising, Bob's Seasoning Salt, 1" x
　　3-3/4" opened, 1960s, unused 5.00
Apollo Flights, 8-18, Cameo 5.00
Basketball Schedule, U.S.C., 1953-54
　　season 20.00
Chicago Cubs, Diamond Match Co.,
　　complete first set, 1934 .... 175.00

French Casino, Chicago, Lion Match Co., $2.

Dwight D Eisenhower, 5 Star
　　General 17.50
Economy Blue Print, girlies, set of 6,
　　1950s 48.00
Hawaiian Mermaid 2.25
Hillbilly, set of five
　　1950 .... 5.00
　　1953 .... 5.00
　　1954 .... 7.50
　　1556 .... 40.00
Hog's Breath Inn, San Carlos, CA 1.00
KFC, Colonel Sanders, Tampa, FL 2.00
Las Vegas Casino, Jewelite 2.50
Presidential Helicopter, Marine
　　One 12.00
Presidential Yacht, Patricia 12.00
Pull for Wilkie, Pullquick Match 30.00
Stoeckle Select Beer, Giant, Stoeckle
　　Brewery 7.50
Thomas Dewey, For President,
　　1948 .... 1.25

US Royal Tire, Olathe, KS...................2.00
USS Rockbridge Attack Transporter..3.00
Washington Redskins, set of 20.......40.00

Topics

Airlines...45
Americana...15
Atlas, four color 15
Banks 15
Barber Shop..75
Beer and Brewery..................................75
Best Western, stock design 15
Bowling Alleys.......................................15
Cameo's, Universal trademark..............15
Canadian, four color 20
Chinese Restaurants 10
Christmas..25
Classiques 50
Colleges..10
Contours, diecut 20
Conventions..15
Country Clubs..15
Dated...15
Diamond Quality 50
Fairs..25
Features 20
Folities, Universal trademark................10
Foreign 05
Fraternal 15
Full Length 20
Giants..50
Girlies, stock design 50
Group One, non-advertising, old 50
Holiday Inns, stock design...................20
Jewelites 15
Jewels 15
Knot Holes...25
Matchorama's, Universal trademark.....15
Matchtones, Universal trademark.........15
Midgets..25
Navy Ships..35
Odd Strikers..45
Patriotic...25
Pearltone 20
Personalities......................................1.00
Political 1.00
Pull Quick 1.00
Radio and Television 45
Railroads...55
Rainbows, Universal trademark...........25
Restaurants...20
Savings & Loans...................................25
Service, old 25
Ship Lines 25
Signets, Universal trademark...............10
Small towns...20
Soft Drinks...85
Souvenir 25
Sports, old...1.00
Ten Strikes..15
Transportation 25
Truck Lines..20
U. S. Air Force, 1940s.......................1.50
U. S. Army, 1940s 1.00
VA Hospitals..20
Whiskey...35
World War II..1.00

McCoy Pottery

Collecting Hint: Several marks were used by the McCoy Pottery Co. Take the time to learn the marks and the variations. Pieces can often be dated by according to the mark.

Most of the pottery marked "McCoy" was made by the Nelson McCoy Co.

History: The J. W. McCoy Pottery Co. was established in Roseville, Ohio, in September 1899. The early McCoy company produced both stoneware and some art pottery lines, including Rosewood. In October 1911 three potteries merged creating the Brush-McCoy Pottery Co. This firm continued to produce the original McCoy lines and added several new art lines. Much of the early pottery is not marked.

In 1910, Nelson McCoy and his father, J. W. McCoy, founded the Nelson McCoy Sanitary Stoneware Co. In 1925, the McCoy family sold their interest in the Brush-McCoy Pottery Co. and started to expand and improve the Nelson McCoy Co. The new company produced stoneware, earthenware specialties, and artware.

References: Susan and Al Bagdade, *Warman's American Pottery and Porcelain*, 2nd ed., Krause Publications, 2000; Bob Hanson, Craig Nissen and Margaret Hanson, *McCoy Pottery, Volumes I and II*, Collector Books, 1996, 1999 value updates; Sharon and Bob Huxford, *Collector's Encyclopedia of Brush-McCoy Pottery*, Collector Books, 1996, 1999 value update; ——, *Collectors Encyclopedia of McCoy Pottery*, Collector Books, 1980, 1997 value update.

Periodicals: *NMXpress*, 8934 Brecksville Road, Suite 406, Brecksville, OH 44141-2318, http://www.members.aol.com/nmxpress./nmxpress.htm.

Reproduction Alert: Unfortunately, Nelson McCoy never registered his McCoy trademark, a fact discovered by Roger Jensen of Tennessee. As a result, Jensen began using the McCoy mark on a series of ceramic reproductions made in the early 1990s. While the marks on these recently made pieces copy the original, Jensen made objects which were never produced by the Nelson McCoy Co. The best known example is the Red Riding Hood cookie jar, originally designed by Hull and also made by Regal China.

The McCoy fakes are a perfect example of how a mark on a piece can be deceptive. A mark alone is not proof that a piece is period or old. Knowing the proper marks and what was and was not made in respect to forms, shapes, and decorative motifs is critical in authenticating a pattern.

Ashtray, Seagram's VO, Imported Canadian Whiskey, black, gold letters 15.00
Baker, oval, Brown Drip, 9-1/4" l 12.00
Bank, Centennial Bear, sgd, numbered 110.00
Basket, black and white, emb weave ext., double handle 25.00
Bean Pot, brown
  #2 .... 35.00
  #22 .... 60.00
Bird Bath.. 28.00
Bowl, 8-1/2 x 3", green 50.00
Canister, vegetable dec, white ground, mkd "McCoy #216M," 10" h, lid cracked.. 15.00
Casserole, open, Brown Drip............. 4.00
Center Bowl, 5-1/2" h, Classic Line, pedestal, turquoise, brushed gold.... 35.00
Clock, Jug Time, 7" h, c1924, small chip, not running 200.00
Cookie Jar, cov
  Caboose, 7-1/2" h, #182 .... 250.00
  Coffee Grinder............................. 50.00
  Colonial Fireplace 150.00
  Cottage 120.00
  Covered Wagon 155.00
  Elephant, 1943, 11" h............... 175.00
  Engine, 8-1/2" h, mkd "McCoy USA" 295.00
  Kookie Kettle, black 55.00
  Log Cabin.................................. 175.00
  Mammy....................................... 175.00
  Mr. and Mrs. Owl 155.00
  Oaken Bucket.............................. 40.00
  Pontiac Indian........................... 400.00
  Potbelly stove, black 50.00
  Puppy, with sign 135.00
  Rooster 225.00
  Sad Clown 125.00
  Schoolhouse............................... 225.00
  Squirrel....................................... 225.00
  Strawberry, white 35.00
  Tea Kettle, black.......................... 40.00
  Touring Car, 6-1/2" h................. 155.00
  Train, black 150.00
  W C Fields 400.00
  Woodsey Owl 345.00
Cornucopia, yellow............................ 20.00
Creamer
  Brown Drip, 3-1/2" h 6.00
  Elsie the Cow............................... 20.00
Custard Cup, vertical ridges, green .. 5.00
Decanter, Apollo Mission 45.00
Dog Food Dish, emb Scottie.......... 15.00
Figurine, lion, ... 65.00
Flower Bowl, Grecian, 12" d, 3" h, 24k gold marbling 24.00
Hanging Basket, stoneware, marked "Nelson McCoy," 1926............... 20.00

Jar, panda standing on his head, Avon heart-shaped label on one foot. 150.00

Jardiniere, 8" h, Springwood, white, lilac colored flowers, minor hairline 65.00

Lamp, Cowboy Boots, c1956, shade not orig 150.00

Mug
    Surburbia, yellow 10.00
    Willow Ware, brown, c1926 .... 15.00

Oil Jug, 12-1/2" h, 5" d opening, green matte, mkd "NM, USA" 225.00

Pitcher
    Brown, Drip, 5" h, 16 oz 9.00
    Elephant, figural, tan glaze, c1940 .... 32.00
    Water Lily, c1935 .... 20.00

Planter, Uncle Sam, green, 7-1/4" h, $35.

Planter
    Duck and egg, yellow 30.00
    Mums, 8" h, pink flowers, green leaves, mkd "McCoy" 155.00
    Wishing Well 20.00

Salt and Pepper Shakers, pr, figural, cucumber and mango, 1954 ...... 20.00

Spoon Rest
    Butterfly, dark green, 1953 .... 15.00
    Penguin, black, white, and red, 1953 .... 20.00

Strawberry Jar, 12" h, stoneware.... 150.00

Sugar, cov, emb face and scrolls, red glazed cover 10.00

Teapot
    Brown Drip, short spout 20.00
    Grecian, 1958 .... 30.00
    Sunburst Gold, 1957 .... 25.00

Tea Set, Ivy, cov teapot, creamer, open sugar, beige, brown highlights, green flowers and stems, sgd "McCoy USA" 165.00

Vase
    6-1/2" h, cylindrical, applied pink flower 40.00
    7-1/2" h, lily, single flower, three leaves 48.00
    8" h, double handles, green, 1948 .... 60.00
    14-1/2" h, white, purple grapes dec, green leaves 235.00

Wall Pocket
    Basketweave 80.00

Butterfly, white 150.00
Iron Trivet 50.00
Lily 70.00
Wren House 155.00

McKee Glass

Collecting Hint: McKee Glass was mass produced in most colors. Therefore, a collector should avoid chipped or damaged pieces. Collectors should also watch for the distinctive McKee marks.

History: The McKee Glass Company was established in 1843 in Pittsburgh, Pennsylvania, and in 1852, it opened a factory to produce pressed glass. In 1888, the company relocated to Jeannette, Pennsylvania, an area that contained several firms that made Depression-era wares. McKee produced many types of glass, including glass window panes, tumblers, tablewares, Depression glass, milk glass, and bar and utility objects, and continued working at the Jeannette location until 1951, when it was sold to the Thatcher Manufacturing Co.

McKee named its colors Chalaine Blue, Custard, Seville Yellow, and Skokie Green. It preferred Skokie Green to jade-ite, which was popular with other manufacturers at the time. McKee also used these opaque colors as the background for several patterns, including dots of red, green, and black, and red ships. A few items were decorated with decals. Most of the canisters and shakers were lettered in black indicating the purpose for which they were intended.

Reference: Gene Florence, *Kitchen Glassware of the Depression Years*, 6th ed, Collector Books, 1995, 2001 value update.

Batter Bowl, 6-1/2" d, Skokie green, some beater marks 45.00

Bottoms Up Tumbler, orig coaster, Patent #77725, light emerald 175.00

Bowl, 4-1/2" d, Skokie green 12.00

Butter Dish, cov, Seville Yellow, 1 lb, sgd 85.00

Candleholders, pr, double, Rock Crystal, 6-3/4" w, 5-1/4" h 65.00

Canister
    3-1/2" h, 24 oz, open, red ships on white 14.00
    4" h, ivory, round, cov 20.00
    4-1/2" h, red ships on white, open 35.00
    5-1/2" h, 6" w, cov, ivory 40.00
    5-1/2" h, 6" w, cov, Skokie green, coffee 55.00
    6" h, cereal, Seville yellow, open . 47.00

Compote, 8" d, 6" h, amethyst, mkd with shield and "McK," c1935 .... 48.00

Cordial, Rock Crystal 12.00

Creamer, Tappan, 2-1/8" h 20.00

Dinner Plate, Laurel, 9" d 17.50

Dish, cov, 4" x 5", red ships, white ground 20.00

Dresser Tray, milk glass 35.00

Dripping Dish, 4" x 5", cov, Skokie green 30.00

Egg Beater Bowl, ivory, one spout .. 30.00

Egg Cup, custard 8.50

Flour Shaker, Chalaine Blue, square 125.00

Grill Plate, custard, mkd "McK" 25.00

Lemon Reamer, Skokie green 30.00

Measuring Cup
    Red ships, white ground 28.00
    Seville Yellow, four cup, ftd 120.00

Pitcher
    Dark Skokie green, 16 oz 75.00
    Skokie green, 16 oz 37.00
    Wild Rose and Bowknot, frosted, gilt dec 75.00
    Yutec, Eclipse, marked "Prescut" 45.00

Range Shaker
    Lady, salt, pepper, flour, and sugar 135.00
    Roman Arch, custard, blue dots, salt, pepper, flour, and sugar 135.00

Refrigerator Dish
    4" x 5", open, red ships, white ground 7.00
    5" x 4-1/2", cov, ivory 23.00
    8" x 5" x 2-1/2", milk white 95.00

Relish Dish, Rock Crystal, divided, swirl floral design, 11-1/2" d 18.00

Salt and Pepper Shakers, pr
    Amethyst, orig tops, some wear . 24.00
    Custard, Laurel pattern 42.00
    Red ships, white ground 30.00

Sandwich Server, center handle, Rock Crystal, red 165.00

Shaker, Seville Yellow, sq
    Flour 50.00
    Plain 25.00
    Sugar 50.00

Tom and Jerry Mug, white opaque, mkd "McK" in circle 18.00

Toothpick Holder, Tappan, 2-5/8" h, 2-1/8" d 20.00

Tumbler
    4" h, flat, Sextec, crystal 20.00
    4-1/2" h, ftd, ivory 18.00
    4-1/2" h, ftd, Seville Yellow 15.00

Water Cooler Set, vaseline, orig carton 350.00

Metlox Pottery

Collecting Hints: The choices of patterns and backstamps are overwhelming. Collectors should, therefore, concentrate on one specific line and pattern. Among the most popular Poppytrail patterns are California Ivy, Homestead Provincial, and Red Rooster.

The recent cookie-jar craze has attracted a number of collectors to Metlox's cookie-jar line. Most examples sell within a narrow price range. The Little Red Riding Hood jar is an exception, often selling at two to three times the price of other cookie jars.

History: In 1921, T. C. Prouty and Willis, his son, founded Proutyline Products, a company designed to develop Prouty's various inventions. In 1922, Prouty built a tile plant in Hermosa Beach to manufacture decorative and standard wall and floor tiles.

Metlox (a contraction of metallic oxide) was established in 1927. Prouty built a modern all-steel factory in Manhattan Beach to manufacture outdoor ceramic signs, but the Depression impacted strongly on this type of business. When T. C. Prouty died in 1931, Willis reorganized the company and began to produce a line of solid-color dinnerware similar to that produced by Bauer. In 1934, the line was fully developed and sold under the Poppytrail trademark, chosen because the poppy is California's official state flower. Fifteen different colors were produced over an eight-year period.

Other dinnerware lines produced in the 1930s include Mission Bell, sold exclusively by Sears Roebuck and Company, Pintoria, based on an English Staffordshire line, and Yorkshire, patterned after Gladding-McBean's Coronado line. Most of these lines did not survive World War II.

In the late 1930s, Metlox employed the services of Carl Romanelli, a designer of figurines, miniatures, and Zodiac vases. He created a line for Metlox called Modern Masterpieces, which featured bookends, busts, figural vases, figures, and wall pockets.

During World War II, Metlox devoted its manufacturing efforts to the production of machine parts and parts for the B-25 bombers. When the war ended, Metlox returned to dinnerware production.

In 1947, Evan K. Shaw, whose American Pottery in Los Angeles had been destroyed by fire, purchased Metlox. Production of hand-painted dinnerware patterns accelerated: California Ivy was introduced in 1946, California Provincial and Homestead Provincial in 1950, Red Rooster in 1955, California Strawberry in 1961, Sculptured Grape in 1963, and Della Robbia in 1965. In the 1950s, Bob

Allen and Mel Shaw, art directors, introduced a number of new shapes and lines, including Aztec, California Contempora, California Free Form, California Mobile, and Navajo.

When Vernon Kilns ceased operation in 1958, Metlox bought the trade name and select dinnerware molds and established a separate Vernon Ware branch. Under the direction of Doug Bothwell, the line soon rivaled the Poppytrail patterns.

Artware continued to flourish in the 1950s and 1960s. Harrison McIntosh was one of the key designers. Two popular lines were American Royal Horses and Nostalgia, scale-model antique carriages. Between 1946 and 1956, Metlox made a series of ceramic cartoon characters under license from Walt Disney.

A line of planters designed by Helen Slater and Poppets, doll-like stoneware flower holders, were marketed in the 1960s and 1970s. Recent production included novelty cookie jars and Colorstax, a revival solid-color dinnerware.

Management remained in the Shaw family. Evan K. was joined by his two children, Ken and Melinda. Kenneth Avery, Melinda's husband, eventually became plant manager. When Evan K. died in 1980, Kenneth Avery became president. In 1988, Melinda Avery became the guiding force. The company ceased operations in 1989.

References: Susan and Al Bagdade, *Warman's American Pottery and Porcelain*, 2nd ed., Krause Publications, 2000; Jack Chipman, *Collector's Encyclopedia of California Pottery*, 2nd ed., Collector Books, 1998; Carl Gibbs, Jr., *Collector's Encyclopedia of Metlox Potteries*, Collector Books, 1995; Lois Lehner, *Lehner's Encyclopedia of U.S. Marks on Pottery*, Porcelain & Clay, Collector Books, 1988.

Cookie Jar

Clown, 12-1/2" h	200.00
Koala Bear, Poppytrail	225.00
Mammy, yellow polka dot version	550.00
Pancho, bear wearing sombrero, Poppytrail, 13" h	115.00
Wally Walrus, Poppytrail, c1976, 9-3/4" h	200.00
Whale, white, Poppytrail, 9-1/2" h	300.00

Dinnerware

Antique Grape

Casserole	
One quart	55.00
Two quart	75.00
Creamer	18.00

Cup and Saucer	12.00
Gravy, one pint	32.00
Pitcher, water	125.00
Platter	
9" l	32.00
14" l	40.00
Salad Plate, 7" d	10.00
Salt and Pepper Shakers, pr	20.00
Soup Bowl, 7" d	12.00
Sugar, cov	20.00
Teapot, cov	115.00
Vegetable Bowl	
8-1/2" d, divided	35.00
9-1/2" d	
Divided	37.00
Undivided	35.00

Blue Provincial

Bowl, 11" d	44.00
Bread and Butter Plate, 6" d	8.00
Bread Server	65.00
Clock, steeple	145.00
Coffeepot	95.00
Cookie Jar	225.00
Creamer	24.00
Cup and Saucer	14.00
Dinner Plate, 10" d	14.00
Eggcup	50.00
Gravy	36.00
Salad Bowl	175.00
Salad Plate	14.00
Salt and Pepper Shakers, pr	55.00
Soup, lug handle	20.00
Sugar, cov	28.00
Tid-Bit, three tier	185.00

Brown Eyed Susan, teapot, cov, 9" x 7" ... 95.00

California Ivy

Bowl, 9" d	36.00
Bread and Butter Plate, 6" d	2.00
Butter, cov	40.00
Coaster	16.00
Creamer	15.00
Cup	9.00
Dinner Plate, 10-1/4" d	9.00
Gravy Boat, California Ivy	20.00
Hors d'ouevres	25.00
Platter, 13" l, oval	36.00
Saucer	1.00
Sugar, cov	18.00
Tumbler, 16 oz	15.00
Vegetable, 9-3/4" l, oval, divided	32.00

California Provincial

Bread Server	65.00
Chop Plate	75.00
Coaster	20.00
Cocoa Mug	40.00
Coffee Canister	55.00
Coffeepot, cov	85.00
Condiment Set, jam and mustard, lids	65.00
Creamer	22.00
Cup and Saucer	16.00
Dinner Plate, 10" d	17.50
Gravy, handle, 1 pint	40.00

Luncheon Plate, 8" d 32.00
Mug, 8 oz..65.00
Platter, 13-1/2" l 45.00
Salad Plate, 7-1/2" d 10.00
Salt and Pepper Shakers, pr............27.00
Soup Bowl, 5" d, lug handle..............22.00
Sugar Bowl, cov..................................28.00
Sugar Canister.....................................70.00
Tea Canister...70.00
Vegetable
  Covered 85.00
  Open, 8-1/2" d, round, basket
  dec 50.00

California Strawberry

Bowl, 9" d, divided.............................40.00
Bread and Butter Plate, 6" d..............6.00
Butter, cov 45.00
Creamer..20.00
Cup and Saucer 35.00
Dinner Plate, 10" d 15.00
Fruit Bowl, 5-1/2" d.............................10.00
Platter, 13" l, oval 30.00
Salad Bowl...50.00
Salad Plate, 8" d.................................10.00
Soup Bowl, 6-3/4" d 15.00
Sugar, cov 20.00
Vegetable Bowl
  Covered 35.00
  Round...25.00

Camelia California

Bowl, 6-1/2" d.......................................7.00
Bread and Butter Plate 6.00
Dinner Plate...10.00
Salad Plate...8.00
Soup Bowl..15.00
Vegetable Bowl, 10" l, oval 35.00

Colonial Homestead

Coffee Service, cov coffeepot, creamer,
  cov sugar 48.00
Cookie Jar, cov 42.00
Cup and Saucer 6.50
Flour Canister......................................35.00

Contempora, Water Pitcher...........200.00

Della Robia

Bowl, 10-3/4" d....................................32.00
Dinnerware Set, 38 pcs.................200.00
Platter, 14" d..32.00
Vegetable Bowl, cov........................105.00

Homestead Provincial

Bowl, 6" d 10.00
Butter Dish, cov 60.00
Canister Set, 4 pc..............................295.00
Casserole, cov 75.00
Coffeepot, cov, blue 125.00
Cookie Jar, cov 90.00
Creamer and Sugar...........................30.00
Cup and Saucer 12.00
Fruit Bowl, 6" d 12.00
Gravy Boat, one handle 45.00
Matchbox Holder.................................65.00
Platter, 14" l...50.00
Salad Plate, 7" d..................................7.00
Salt and Pepper Shakers, pr............30.00

Tea Kettle, cov...................................115.00

Provincial Rose

Bowl, tab handle 20.00
Butter, cov..55.00
Coffee Server 75.00
Cookies Canister.................................90.00
Creamer..28.00
Cruet Set, 5 pcs 180.00
Gravy, two spouts 28.00
Milk Pitcher..38.00
Mug..35.00
Pitcher, large 68.00
Platter, 9-3/8" l or 14-3/4" l............45.00
Soup, flat 18.00
Vegetable, cov 70.00

Red Rooster

Ashtray, large.....................................30.00
Bowl, 6" d...5.00
Bread Server 50.00
Butter Dish, cov...................................50.00
Canister Set, 8 pcs..........................150.00
Casserole, cov, Kettle 55.00
Cereal Bowl, deep 15.00
Chop Plate..40.00
Coaster...20.00
Coffeepot, cov, 6 cup.........................85.00
Creamer, green 15.00
Cruet Set, 8 pcs 150.00
Cup and Saucer...................................10.00
Dinner Plate, 10" d 7.50
Fruit Bowl...8.00
Gravy, handle 30.00
Luncheon Plate 5.00
Mug..15.00
Mustard Jar, cov..................................45.00
Pitcher, figural, 14" h 695.00
Platter, 13" l...25.00
Salt and Pepper Shakers, pr............15.00
Server, five part, divided 100.00
Soup Bowl, Provincial........................11.00
Teapot, cov, 6 cup...............................80.00
Tumbler, 11 oz.....................................15.00
Turkey Platter 200.00
Vegetable Bowl
  Divided, stick handle 24.00
  Round...28.00

Sculptured Daisy

Apothecary Jar....................................95.00
Bowl, handle
  7" d...28.00
  8" d...35.00
Cereal Bowl, 7" d.................................12.00
Coffeepot...95.00
Creamer..18.00
Cup and Saucer...................................12.00
Dinner Plate, 10" d 15.00
Gravy, handle, 1 pint..........................32.00
Luncheon Plate, 7-1/2" d 8.00
Mug, 7 oz..35.00
Salad Bowl 95.00
Salad Fork and Spoon 125.00
Server, twin, 10" l...............................55.00
Soap Dish...38.00
Sugar, cov 24.00
Tumbler...38.00

Vegetable, cov, 1 quart 45.00

Sculptured Grape

Bowl
  8-1/2" d 27.00
  9-1/2" d 30.00
Canister Set, 4 pc...........................240.00
Cereal Bowl 15.00
Creamer and Sugar....................45.00
Cup and Saucer 16.00
Dinner Plate 17.50
Fruit Bowl 12.00
Platter
  10" l, oval 30.00
  12" l, oval 40.00
Salad Plate, 7-1/2" d 10.00
Vegetable...24.00

Sculptured Zinnia

Bread and Butter Plate, 6" d 7.25
Butter Dish, cov 50.00
Cereal Bowl 14.00
Chop Plate, 12" d 15.00
Creamer..16.00
Cup and Saucer 14.00
Dinner Plate, 10" d 9.50
Fruit Bowl 12.00
Luncheon Plate, 8" d 9.00
Platter, oval
  11" l 28.00
  12" l 38.00
Salad Bowl, 12" d 48.00
Salt and Pepper Shakers, pr............ 16.00
Sugar, cov..17.50
Vegetable Bowl
  8" d...30.00
  8-1/2" d, divided 28.00
  9-1/2" d, divided 32.00

Vernon, Antiqua

Vegetable Bowl, cov
  Fruits dec, cream ground 105.00
  Grape dec 105.00

Model Kits

Collecting Hints: Model kits, assembled or unassembled, are one of the hot collectibles of the 1990s. Even assembled examples, provided they are done well, have value.

In many cases, a kit's value is centered more on the character or object it represents than on the kit itself. The high prices paid for monster-related kits is tied directly to the current monster-collecting craze, which means a portion of the value is speculative.

Box art can influence a kit's value. When individual boxes sell in the $40 to $100 range, it becomes clear that they are treated as *objets d'art*, a dangerous pricing trend. The value of the box is easily understood when you place an assembled model beside the lid. All too often, it is the box that is more exciting.

History: The plastic scale-model kit originated in England in the mid-1930s with the manufacture of 1/72 Frog Penguin kits. The concept caught on during World War II when scale models were used in identification training. After the war, companies such as Empire Plastics, Hawk, Lindberg, Renwal, and Varney introduced plastic model kits to American hobbyists. The 1950s witnessed the arrival of Aurora and Monogram in the United States, Airfix in the United Kingdom, Heller in France, and Hasegawa and Marusan in Japan.

The 1960s was the golden age of the plastic kit model. Kits featured greater detail and accuracy than the early examples, and three scale sizes dominated: 1/48, 1/72, and 1/144. The oil crisis in the 1970s caused a temporary set back to the industry.

A revival of interest in plastic scale-model kits occurred in the late 1980s. At the same time, collector interest began to develop. The initial collecting focus was on automobile model kits from the 1950s and early 1960s. By the end of the 1980s, interest had shifted to character and monster kits.

References: Bill Bruegman, *Aurora*, Cap'n Penny Productions, 1992; Bill Coulter, *Stock Car Model Kit Encyclopedia and Price Guide*, Krause Publications, 1999; Thomas Graham, *Greenberg's Guide to Aurora Model Kits*, Kalbach Books, 1998; Arthur Ward, *Airfix: Celebrating 50 Years of the Greatest Plastic Kits in the World*, Trafalgar Square, 2000.

Periodicals: *Kit Builders and Glue Sniffers*, P.O. Box 201, Sharon Center, OH 44274; *Model and Toy Collector*, P.O. Box 347240, Cleveland, OH 44134.

Videotape: *Aurora Figure Kit*, Time Machine (P.O. Box 1022, Southport, CT 06490-2022).

Collectors' Clubs: International Figure Kit Club, P.O. Box 201, Sharon Center, OH 44274; Kit Collectors International, P.O. Box 38, Stanton, CA 90680; Society for the Preservation and Encouragement of Scale Model Kit Collecting, 3213 Hardy Dr., Edmond, OK 73013.

Jaymar's Wild and Weird Picture Puzzle, left, $20; Lindy Loonys' Road Hog kit, $45.

American Astronaut, Aurora, 1967, MIB 115.00
Apollo Saturn Rocket, Monogram, 1968, MIB 35.00
Anzio Beach, Aurora, built 70.00
Batman, Aurora, MIB 270.00
Bell AH-1G Assault Copter, Aurora, MIB 60.00
Black Night, series 2, Aurora, MIB ... 35.00
Boeing 707 Astrop Jet, Aurora, 1965 .... 55.00
Bonzana, Revell, MIB 150.00
Buck Rogers Marauder, Monogram, sealed, MIB 30.00
Camaro, T-top, AMT 20.00
Cannonball Run Ambulance, MPC, sealed, MIB 30.00
Captain Kidd Bloodthirsty Pirate, Aurora 150.00
Cessna 180, Monogram, some parts assembled, damage to box, 5" x 13" x 1" orig box 5.00
Cherokee Sports roadster, Hawk, 1964, MIB 25.00
Chevy, 51, Fleetline, AMT 45.00
Cobra Tee Way-Out Rod, Pyro, 1/16 scale, MIB 90.00
Corvette, 57, MPC, 1/16 scale, sealed, MIB 65.00
Custom T-Bird, Aurora, 1963 .... 40.00
Dick Tracy Space Coupe, Aurora, sealed 235.00
Don the Snake Prudhomme, 1/24 rear engine dragster, Revell, sealed ... 90.00
Double Whammy, Henri Studebaker, 1953, AMT, sealed 85.00
Dracula
   Aurora 350.00
   Monogram 40.00
Drag Strip, accessory pack, AMT, MIB 40.00
Drop Out Bus, Aurora, box only 20.00
Flying Saucer, Aurora 150.00
Ford, Fairlane, 1956, customizing kit, Revell, 1958, MIB 80.00
Ford, Model T pick-up, Monogram, 1975, MIB 35.00
Forgotten Prisoner 150.00
Frankenstein, glow, Aurora, MIB ... 200.00
George Washington, Aurora, 1965, MIB 125.00

Ghostrider Vette, MPC, sealed, MIB 30.00
Godzilla, glow, Monogram, 1978 ... 250.00
Hunchback of Notre Dame, Aurora, Anthony Quinn box, MIB 275.00
Invaders UFO, Aurora 250.00
Jaguar CC120 Roadster, Aurora, 1961 .... 35.00
Japanese Submarine, Aurora, Young Models Builder's Club box, MIB . 38.00
Knight Rider 25.00
Land of the Giants, snake scene, Aurora, box and instructions only 180.00
Lockhead U-2 Spy Plane, Hawk, sealed, MIB 55.00
Lost In Space Robot, Aurora, MIB . 680.00
Mail Truck, show road, George Barris design, MPC 50.00
Mark II Ford GT, AMT 40.00
Masarati Auto, Aurora, 1966, MIB ... 40.00
MASH Camp Swampy, MIB, sealed 20.00
Mercedes-Benz 300SI Gull-Wing Coupe, AMT, 1960s, motor partially assembled, 5" x 9" x 3-1/2" orig box 24.00
Mister Mulligan Plane, Hawk, BIG ... 15.00
Monogram Relic Kothuga, Revell, sealed, MIB 25.00
Munsters, Koach, AMT, 1964 ...... 1,330.00
Mustang, 1/16 scale, AMT, sealed .. 45.00
Old Ironsides, *USS Constitution*, "S" kit, Revell, 1956, MIB 48.00
Old Timers Stanley Steamer, Aurora, 1961, MIB 100.00
Paul McCartney, Revell, 1964 ...... 300.00
Phantom of the Opera, Aurora, #428, ©1963 Universal Pictures, MIB 300.00
Pilgrim Observer, MPC Space Station, sealed, MIB 25.00
Polaris Nuclear Sub Ethan Allan, Renwal 40.00
Predicta Futuristic Car, Monogram, 1964, MIB 75.00
Prehistoric Scenes, Cro-Magnon Woman, Aurora, sealed, MIB 85.00
Ranch Wagon Western, Revell, horse drawn, 1950s 35.00
Rat Fink, Revell, MIB 115.00
Return of the Saint, Jaguar CJ, Revell, 1/25 scale 25.00
Seaview, Aurora, sealed, MIB 330.00
Scottish Lad, Aurora, MIB 55.00
Scottish Lass, Aurora, MIB 65.00
Sikorsky HH-3 Jolly Green Giant, Aurora, some damage to orig box 40.00
Smokey and the Bandit, Ertl, unbuilt in box 45.00
Sopwith Camel, Aurora, unused 45.00
Spider-Man, Aurora, orig box 200.00
Star Trek, Klingon Battle Cruiser, AMT, MIB 120.00
Street Fever Vette, MPC, 1978, sealed 30.00
Supecharged 56 Chevy, Monogram 40.00
Superman, Aurora, 1963, MIB 375.00

Talos anti-aircraft missile, Revell, 1957,
MIB..45.00
Tarzan, Aurora, 1967, box only........75.00
The Invisible Pigeon, Renwal...........75.00
The Saint's Jaguar XJS, Revell, copyright
1979, 6" x 9-1/4" x 4" deep sealed
box..28.00
The White House, Empire.................75.00
Time Tunnel, Lunar, 1989.............250.00
TransAm, 10th, MPC, MIB...............25.00
US Army MB Munitions Carrier, Aurora,
1/4 scale, plastic, sealed, MIB....75.00
US Navy F4J-4 Corsair Fighter-Bomber,
Monogram, some parts assembled,
orig instructions, most decals
present...5.00
Wacky Back Wacker Machine, Aurora,
1965, MIB....................................350.00
Warlord TransAm, MPC, MIB...........30.00

Monsters

Collecting Hints: This is a category
rampant with speculative fever.
Prices rise and fall rapidly, depending on the momentary popularity of a
figure or family group. Study the market carefully before becoming a participant.

Stress condition and completeness. Do not buy any item in less than
fine condition. Check carefully to
make certain that all parts or elements are present.

Since the material in this category
is of recent origin, no one is certain
how much has survived. Hoards are
not uncommon, and it is possible to
find examples at garage sales. It
pays to shop around before paying a
high price.

While an excellent collection of
two-dimensional material, e.g., comic
books, magazines, and posters, can
be assembled, concentrate on three-
dimensional material. Several other
crazes, e.g., model kit collecting,
cross over into monster collecting,
thus adding to price confusion.

History: The release of Famous Monsters of Filmland in 1958 helped ini-
tiate an avalanche of monster-related
merchandise in the '60s. The popularity of the classic monsters such as
Frankenstein, Dracula, The Mummy,
and the Creature From the Black
Lagoon, plus the additional humorous television spoofs like "The Munsters" and "The Addams Family" set
the foundation for a substantial and
enthusiastic group of collectors in
today's market.

"Star Trek" helped bring about a
shift in the '70s away from monsters
and toward science fiction. There

were still monster toys and games
being made, but they were not nearly
as well received as they had been in
the 1960s. Subsequently, companies
such as AHI, Mego, and Lincoln,
which manufactured monster items
during that period, have become
very popular collecting pieces.

The '80s belonged to a new generation of monsters like Jason,
Freddy Krueger, and Michael Myers.
Even though their movies were amaz-
ingly popular, their ruthless exploits
made it difficult to produce merchandise that could be sold to all ages.
Already a proven success, products
promoting classic monsters were
manufactured and even gained
momentum during that time.

The '90s have seen an explosion
in monster collectibles. Beginning in
1991 with the release of numerous
different monster items by several different companies such as Hasbro,
Exclusive Premier, and Trendmaster,
monster merchandise flooded toy
racks everywhere. The availability
and affordable pricing of these new
items have created an excitement in
monster collecting that will last well
beyond the year 2000.

References: Dana Cain, *Collecting
Japanese Movie Monsters*, Antique
Trader Books, 1998; Ted Hake,
Hake's Guide to TV Collectibles, Wal-
lace-Homestead, 1990; Carol
Markowski and Bill Sikora, *Tomart's
Price Guide to Action Figure Collecti-
bles*, revised ed., Tomart Publica-
tions, 1992; Stuart W. Wells, III,
*Science Fiction Collectibles: Identifi-
cation & Price Guide*, Krause Publi-
cations, 1999.

Periodicals: *Future News*, 5619 Pil-
grim Rd, Baltimore, MD 21214; *G-
Fan*, Box 3468, Steinbach, Manitoba,
Canada R0A 2A0; *Japanese Giants*,
5727 N. Oketo, Chicago, IL 60631;
*Kaiju Review—The Journal of Japa-
nese Monster Culture*, Suite 5F, 301
E. 64th St., New York, NY 10021;
*Monster Attack Team—The Japa-
nese Monster Superhero & Fantasy
Fanzine*, P.O. Box 800875, Houston,
TX 77280; *Questnews*, 12440 Moor-
park St., Suite 150, Studio City, CA
91604.

Collectors' Club: Club 13, P.O. Box
733, Bellefonte, PA 16823.

Advisor: Patrick M. Leer.

Dracula

Beanie, felt, Universal......................16.00
Figure
Imperial, 7-1/2" h, 1986, MOC.....20.00

Limited Edition, Exclusive Premiere
Bela Lugosi Count Dracula.........20.00
Remco, Bela Lugosi...................25.00
Model, Aurora, 1962, in box, excellent
condition...................................275.00
Motionette, Telco Dracula, arms and head
move, eyes flash, laughing sound, 17"
h, MIB...30.00
Photograph, Bela Lugosi as Count Drac-
ula, black and white, 8" x 10"........6.00
Pinback Button, black and white picture,
color background, 1960s...........15.00
Playbill, Ford's Theatre, Nov. 5, 1928,
Raymond Huntley, 4" x 11-1/2"...24.00
Puzzle, Jaymar, 1965, MIB...............65.00

Elvira

Autographed photograph, color 8" x 10",
sexy pose, sgd..........................40.00
Beer Bottle, Night Brew, 1996...........5.00
Poster, Elvira Moonbathing, One Stop
Posters, 1987.............................20.00
Standee, Coors, life-size
Halloween, mint.........................35.00
Inflatable, 1994, mint..................85.00
Video, "Dead of the Night Hosted by
Elvira," VHS Thriller Video..........15.00

Frankenstein

Beanie, felt, Universal.....................16.00
Book, *Frankenstein Or The Modern
Promethus*, Mary W. Shelley, illus by
Nino Carbe, Halycon House, dj
clipped..15.00
Comic Book, *Frankenstein*, Dell Movie
Classic, mint...............................20.00
Figure, Imperial, 7-1/2" h, 1986,
MOC...20.00
Film
"Abbott and Costello Meet Franken-
stein," 8mm, mint.......................20.00
"Frankenstein," Super 8mm film, Cas-
tle, mint.....................................25.00
Magazine, *Life*, Sept. 1964 Boris Karloff
cover, mint..................................10.00
Model, Aurora, assembled, 3" x 7-1/2" x
9-1/4", copyright 1961................30.00
Paddle Ball Game, Frankenstein Classic
Movie Monster Masher...............10.00
Pez, 1960s, mint..........................250.00
Toy, Big Frank, Playskool 1091, 1992,
MIB...50.00

Godzilla

Action Play Set, 4" h Godzilla combat
men and vehicles,
Trendmasters.............................15.00
Figure
Bendable Godzilla, Trendmaster,
1994, 4" h, MOC..........................8.00
Shogun Warrior, Toho, Mattel, 1977,
19" h, with box, mint.................120.00
Game, Godzilla Game, Mattel,
1977...85.00
Inflatable, Giant Godzilla Toho, Imperial,
6', with orig box, mint.................35.00
Poster, Godzilla King of the Monsters, one
sheet, United States Release, 1956,
mint.......................................3,000.00

Hammer

Autographed photograph, color
Christopher Lee, sgd "Dracula"..35.00
Peter Cushing, sgd "Dr.
Frankenstein"...............................45.00
Lobby Card, *Horror of Dracula*, 1958,
mint...100.00
Magazine
Famous Monsters of Filmland, #131
Christopher Lee As Dracula cover,
mint...12.00
Hammer Horror, #1 Christopher Lee as
Frankenstein cover, mint 20.00
Poster, Curse of Frankenstein, theatrical
one sheet, 1957, mint...............225.00
Pressbook, Horror of Dracula, 1958, near
mint...95.00
Trading Card, Hammer Horror, series #1
to 81 cards, each.......................20.00

Game, Barnabas Collins Dark Shadows Game, Milton Bradley, $20.

Miscellaneous

Autograph, Vincent Price, *Crimefantastique*, Jan, 1989.........................100.00
Beanie, felt, Mummy.........................16.00
Game, Monster Madness, Pressman,
MIB..30.00
Magazine, Photon, #22F, The thing from
Another World.............................12.00
Mask, Metaluna Mutant.................150.00
Monster Machine, Gabriel, C-9......125.00
Record, The Thing, soundtrack, John
Carpenter's 15.00
Ring Set, Phantom...........................50.00
Sunken Head Set, Vincent Price,
unused..95.00
Toy
Haunted Tunnel Set, US Zone Germany, two 4" litho cars with horror
scenes and monsters, demons,
ghosts, tin litho track and tunnel,
C-9...235.00
Monster Machine, Gabriel, orig molds,
1970, C-9....................................80.00
Whistlin Spooky Kooky Tree, Marx,
1950s, battery operated, repro
box 1,275.00

Munsters

Coloring Book, The Munsters Coloring
Book, Whitman, 1965, mint.........50.00
Figure
Grandpa, Exclusive Premier Limited
Edition of 12,000, 1998, 9" h,
MIB..30.00
Herman, Presents, 1991, 8-1/2" h,
excellent....................................20.00
Lily, Remco, 1964.....................185.00

Lunch Box and Thermos, King Seely,
1965, near mint.........................275.00
Model Kit, Munster Koach, AMT, 1964,
good condition...........................100.00
Puppet, Herman, Ideal, 1965 Ideal, in
box, excellent...........................350.00
Puzzle, Munster's Puzzle, Dragula, Whitman, 1964 , MIB.........................48.00

The Creature from the Black Lagoon

Film, "The Creature Walks Among Us,"
Castle Films, 8mm 35.00
Game, Creature From The Black Lagoon
Mystery Game, Hasbro, 1963,
MIB..300.00
Model, The Creature, Aurora, assembled
and painted, 6" x 7-1/2" x 8-1/2", copyright 1963 Universal Pictures Co., Inc.,
missing skeleton hand from
base..35.00
Puzzle, Western, 200 pieces, 1990,
MIB..8.00
Robot, litho tin wind-up, 1991,
MIB..135.00
Snow Globe, 4-1/2" h, Hamilton, 1991,
MIB..25.00
Soakie, 10" h, Colgate-Palmolive, 1960s,
mint...140.00
Toy, wind-up, Robot House, 1991,
MIB..155.00
Wax Pack, Creature from the Black
Lagoon, Feature, Topps Gum,
1980..13.00

The Exorcist

Autographed Photograph, Linda Blair, 8"
x 10", Exorcist, Reagan
Possessed..................................40.00
Lobby Card, Reagan Possessed.....12.00
Magazine, *Mad*, #170; October 1974;
Exorcist cover, mint......................5.00

The Nightmare Before Christmas

Book
Box Tree, pop-up, hardcover,
10-1/4" x 10-1/2"..........................35.00
Tim Burton's Nightmare Before Christmas Storybook, illus by Tim Burton,
hardover, 9" x 11-1/4".................30.00
Tim Burton's Nightmare Before Christmas The Film, forward written by Tim
Burton, illus from Burton orig art, complete lyrics from film, Hyperium, 192
pgs, 11" x 8-3/4"..........................70.00
Figure, Hasbro, 1993
Behemoth, MOC 175.00
Evil Scientist, MOC 175.00
Jack as Santa, MOC...................95.00
Jack Skellington, MOC 175.00
Sally, MOC 175.00
The Mayor, MOC 175.00
Werewolf, MOC 175.00
Jack and Sally in Silver Coffins, Junn
Planning Japan, 1993, 12" l,
each...75.00
Mug, Jack's head with box, Applause,
1993...35.00
Neck Tie, Jack in Coffin, Disney,
1993...30.00
Pumpkin, blow-up, Jack and characters,
MIB..35.00

Video, Touchstone, VHS, MIB..........24.00
Walk, Schock and Barrel in Rolling Tub,
Applause, 1993, 4" x 5" 18.00
Watch, Burger King, four different styles,
each...20.00

The Nightmare on Elm Street/Freddy Krueger

Blades, Freddy Krueger Plastic Blades,
Marty Toys, 1984, MOC 25.00
Doll, RIP Horror Collection Series, Limited
Edition, Freddy Krueger, 1998.... 48.00
Figure, Freddy Krueger, LJN, 8-1/2" h,
MOC...20.00
Spitball, Freddy Krueger or victim. LJN,
1989, MOC, each.......................10.00
Toy
Maxx FX, Matchbox, 1989, boxed set,
MIB..40.00
Talking Freddy Krueger, Matchbox, 18"
h, MIB...35.00

Wolfman

Puzzle, Jaymar, 1960s 200.00

Morton Potteries

Collecting Hints: The potteries of
Morton, Illinois, used local clay until
1940. The clay fired out to a golden
ecru color which is quite easy to recognize. After 1940, southern and
eastern clays were shipped to Morton, but these clays fired out white.
Thus, later wares are easily distinguishable from the earlier ones.

Few pieces were marked by the
potteries. Incised and raised marks
for the Morton Pottery Works, the
Cliftwood Art Potteries, Inc., and the
Morton Pottery Company do surface
at times. Occasionally, the Cliftwood,
Midwest, Morton Pottery Company,
and American Art Pottery affixed
paper labels, and some pieces have
survived with these intact.

Glazes from the early period, 1877
to 1920, usually were Rockingham
types, both mottled and solid. Yellowware also was standard during the
early period. Occasionally, a dark
cobalt blue was produced, but this
color is rare. Colorful drip glazes and
solid colors came into use after 1920.

History: Pottery was produced in
Morton, Illinois, for 99 years. In 1877,
six Rapp brothers, who emigrated
from Germany, began the first pottery, Morton Pottery Works. Over the
years, sons, cousins, and nephews
became involved, and the other Morton pottery operations were spin-offs
from this original Rapp brothers' firm.
When it was taken over in 1915 by
second-generation Rapps, Morton
Pottery Works became the Morton

Earthenware Company. Work at that pottery was terminated by World War I.

The Cliftwood Art Potteries, Inc., which operated from 1920 to 1940, was organized by one of the original founders of the Morton Pottery Works and his four sons. It sold out in 1940, and the production of figurines, lamps, novelties, and vases was continued by the Midwest Potteries, Inc., until a disastrous fire in March 1944 brought an end to that operation. By 1947, the brothers who had operated the Cliftwood Art Potteries, Inc., came back into the pottery business. They established the short-lived American Art Potteries. The American Art Potteries made flower bowls, lamps, planters, some unusual flower frogs, and vases. Their wares were marketed by florists and gift shops. Production at American Art Potteries was halted in 1961. Of all the wares of the Morton potteries, the products of the American Art Potteries are the most elusive.

Morton Pottery Company, which had the longest existence of all of the potteries in Morton, was organized in 1922 by the same brothers who had operated the Morton Earthenware Company. The Morton Pottery Company specialized in beer steins, kitchenwares, and novelty items for chain stores and gift shops. It also produced some of the Vincent Price National Treasures reproductions for Sears Roebuck and Company in the mid-1960s. The Morton Pottery closed in 1976, thus ending almost 100 years of pottery production in Morton.

Reference: Doris and Burdell Hall, *Morton's Potteries*, Vol. 2, L-W Book Sales, 1995.

Museums: Illinois State Museum, Springfield, IL; Morton Public Library (permanent exhibit), Morton, IL.

Advisors: Doris and Burdell Hall.

Morton Pottery Works, Morton Earthenware Co., 1877-1917

Bank, acorn, green, Acorn Stove Co. adv, 3-1/2" h 60.00
Butter Churn, brown Rockingham, 4 gallon..250.00
Coffeepot, drip-o-later, 3 pc, 8 cups, brown Rockingham 60.00
Dutch Jug, 3 pint
   Brown Rockingham 60.00
   Cobalt blue 90.00
Jardiniere, leaf dec, 5" d, 4" h
   Brown..20.00
   Cobalt blue 50.00
   Green 45.00

Milk Pitcher, bulbous body, tree bark design, yellow ware, green and brown spatter, 1-3/4 qt 150.00

Morton Pottery Works, bean pot, cov, blue and white sponge ware, $55. Photo courtesy of Doris and Burdell Hall.

Morton Pottery Works, coffeepot, drip-o-later, three pieces, brown Rockingham, $60. Photo courtesy of Doris and Burdell Hall.

Miniature
   Coffeepot, brown Rockingham, 3-1/2" h 75.00
   Jug, 3" h, brown Rockingham 50.00
   Milk pitcher, cobalt blue, 3-3/4" h 60.00
Mixing Bowls, yellow ware, white slip lines, nested set of five 280.00
Mug, one pint, brown Rockingham.................................60.00
Pie Baker, yellow ware, 10" d........ 125.00
Teapot, acorn shape, 3-3/4 cup, brown Rockingham.................................80.00
Urinal, shovel shape
   Brown Rockingham 50.00
   Yellow ware 65.00

Cliftwood Art Potteries, Inc., 1920-1940

Bookends, pr, tree trunk with woodpeckers, chocolate brown drip glaze, 6" x 5" x 3-1/2" 100.00
Compote, four-dolphin base, Old Rose high gloss, 6" h, 8-1/2" d 90.00
Console Bowl, four-dolphin base, matte ivory ext., Old Rose high gloss int., 6" h, 12" l... 100.00
Console Set, bowl and candleholders
   Petal shaped bowl, apple green 75.00

Viking ship bowl, dragon heads at each end, dragon head candleholders, matte ivory/turquoise.......... 225.00
Figure
   Billiken, brown, 11" h 100.00
   Bulldog, Nero, gray grip, 11" h...95.00
   Elephant trumpeting, Blue Mulberry 55.00
   German Shepherd, reclining, brown drip, 11" 150.00
Lamp
   Boudoir, #18, 6-1/2" h, cobalt blue 24.00
   Desk, elephant figure, natural colors, 8" h 80.00
   Donut shape, clock insert, Blue Mulberry, 8-1/2" h 150.00
Mint Compote, ftd, 3-1/2" h, 6-1/2" d, matte blue....................................30.00
Vase, 9" h
   Handled, red and white drip over white..60.00
   Tree trunk, Herbage Green..........70.00
Waffle Set, covered batter pitcher, covered syrup pitcher, on tray, Old Rose drip over white............................ 150.00
Wall Pocket, 8" x 5", handled, cone shape, matte ivory/turquoise 40.00

Midwest Potteries, baseball players, left: catcher, $275; center: umpire, $250; right: batter, $300. Photo courtesy of Doris and Burdell Hall.

Midwest Potteries, duck pitcher, cattail handle, light brown and gray spray glaze, 10" h, $40. Photo courtesy of Doris and Burdell Hall.

Cliftwood Art Pottery, mint compote, 6-1/2" d, 3-1/2" h, matte blue, $30. Photo courtesy of Doris and Burdell Hall.

Midwest Potteries, Inc., 1940-1944

Bookends, Art Deco style base with deer, yellow/gold, 8" h............................25.00

Bud Vase, hand, 6-1/2" h
  Flesh color 18.00
  14K gold 25.00

Figure
  Baseball player, batter, gray uniform, 7-1/4" h...300.00
  Baseball player, catcher, white uniform, 6-3/4" h..............................275.00
  Baseball player, umpire, black suit and cap, 6-1/4" h...............................250.00
  Crane, drip colors, 11" h 35.00
  Deer, stylized, looking back, white, gold dec, 12" h..............................25.00
  Deer, stylized, with antlers, blue-brown spray glaze, 12" h.......................30.00
  Ducks, 3 in a row, 6-1/2" l, 2-1/2" h, white, yellow dec 24.00
  Giraffe, looking over back, yellow/green drip on white, 12" h 35.00
  Heron, blue-yellow spray glaze, gold dec 40.00
  Tiger, natural colors, 7" h, 12" l....40.00

Miniature
  Dog, brown drip, 2" x 2"..............14.00
  Frog, green drip, 1" h...................12.00
  Kissing rabbits, white/gold, 2-1/2" x 3-1/4"......................................30.00
  Lion, brown drip, 2-1/2" x 1-3/4"..14.00
  Rabbit, white and pink, 1-1/2" h..14.00
  Sailboat, blue/tan drip, 2" x 2"....45.00
  Squirrel, brown drip, 2" h.............14.00
  Swan, matte white, 2" h 14.00
  Turtle, green drip, 1" h 12.00

Pitcher, duck, figural, cattail handle, brown/gray spray glaze, 10" h 40.00

Morton Pottery Company, 1922-1976

Bank, hen, hand painted dec, 4" h ..50.00

Bean Pot, cov, blue and white sponge ware, Sears Vincent Price National Treasures, 4 qt 55.00

Cookie Jar
  Basket of fruit, green, naturally colored fruit 50.00
  Hen, chick finial, white, black wash...135.00
  Panda, black and white..............75.00
  Turkey, chick finial, brown 152.00
  Turkey, chick finial, white 225.00

Cliftwood Art Pottery, console set, petal shape bowl, candleholders, apple green, set, $75. Photo courtesy of Doris and Burdell Hall.

Flowerpot Soaker
  Bird, blue and yellow 20.00
  Calla lily, yellow and green 18.00
  Hound dog, brown and white......24.00

Lamp
  Kerosene, brass fixture with glass chimney, cylindrical body with ribbed base, white 50.00
  TV, buffalo figure atop rock base, openings at top of rocks allow animal to be lighted 100.00

Mixing Bowls, Woodland glaze, yellow and green spatter over yellow clay, nested set of four 175.00

Night Light
  Old women in shoe, yellow house, red roof......................................40.00
  Praying child, prayer in wall hanging shadow box..................................40.00
  Teddy bear, brown spray glaze, hand painted dec, heart-shaped nose 50.00

Planter
  Covered wagon, unattached oxen team, price for set.......................55.00
  Davy Crockett as boy, bear beside open stump.................................50.00
  Rabbit, female, with umbrella, beside blue egg 24.00

Salt and Pepper Shakers, chick, white, black wash, 1-3/4" h, each 75.00

Santa Claus head
  Ashtray 15.00
  Mug 18.00
  Nut Cup 14.00
  Plate, 6" d 40.00
  Plate, 12" d 50.00
  Punch Bowl 150.00
  Punch Bowl Set, bowl, 12 mugs, white, rare 360.00

Toothpick Holder, chick, white, black wash, 1-3/4" h...............................75.00

American Art Potteries, 1947-1963

Candleholder, donut shape, three candle cups, green, 6" x 7-1/2"................30.00

Console Set, petal design, 10" l x 6-1/2" h bowl, pr 1-3/4" h candleholders, pink and gray spray glaze ...30.00

Creamer, bird, tail as handle, black and green spray glaze........................18.00

Flower Bowl, Art Deco style, tan with brown spackling, 10" x 4" x 1-1/2".....................................20.00

Lamp, mountain goat figural, brown and green spatter over white, 15" h....45.00

American Art Potteries, candleholder, donut shape, three candle cups, green, $30. Photo courtesy of Doris & Burdell Hall.

American Art Potteries, flower bowl, Art-Deco style, tan with brown spackling, $20. Photo courtesy of Doris & Burdell Hall.

Planter
  Baby buggy, white, hand decorated, 5-1/2" x 7"..................................... 20.00
  Elephant, trumpeting, white, 7-1/2" x 2-1/2".. 30.00
  Lamb, white, pink bow at neck, 8-1/2" x 3"..................................... 25.00
  Pheasant, natural colors, spray glaze, 8-1/2" h, 18" l................................ 40.00
  Swan, orchid/pink, gold dec, 11" x 7".. 25.00

TV Lamp
  Afgan hounds, black, 15" h 75.00
  Conch shell, yellow and green spray glaze, 6" h....................................... 35.00
  Double fish planter, pink-purple spray base, 6" x 9" x 3-1/2" rect base ... 30.00

Vase
  Feather shape, gray and yellow spray glaze, 10-1/2" h.............................35.00
  Ruffled tulip, ivory, pink, and blue spray glaze, 9" h..........................35.00

Wall Pocket
  Apple, red and green, 3 leaves, 5" h...24.00
  Chrysanthemum blossom, mauve and green spray glaze, 7-1/2" h.........28.00

Movie Memorabilia

Collecting Hints: Collectors tend to focus on the blockbuster hits, with "Gone with the Wind" and "Casablanca" among the market leaders. Cartoon images, especially Disney material, are also very popular.

Much of the material is two-dimensional, and collectors have just begun to look for three-dimensional objects, although the majority of these are related to stars and personalities rather than movies.

The market went crazy with speculation in the mid-1970s. Prices fell in the 1980s as a result of self-discipline, compounded by the large number of reproductions, many of European origin, which flooded the market.

History: By the 1930s and into the 1940s, the star system had reached its zenith, and studios spent elaborate sums promoting their major stars. Initially, movie studios and their public relations firms tightly controlled the distribution of material such as press books, scripts, preview flyers, costumes, and props. Copyrights have expired on many of these items, and reproductions abound.

The current interest in Hollywood memorabilia can be traced to the pop-art craze of the 1960s. Film festivals increased the desire for decorative film-related materials, and movie posters became a hot collectible.

Piracy, which has always plagued Hollywood, is responsible for the release of many items into the market. Today the home video presents new challenges to the industry.

References: Mark Allen Baker, *Advanced Autograph Collecting*, Krause Publications, 2000; —, *Collector's Guide to Celebrity Autographs*, 2nd ed., Krause Publications, 2000; Clark Kidder, *Marilyn Monroe: Cover to Cover*, Krause Publications, 1999; Rex Miller, *The Investor's Guide to Vintage Character Collectibles*, Krause Publications, 1999 Marion Short, *Hollywood Movie Songs: Collectible Sheet Music*, Schiffer, 1999; Frank Thompson, *AMC's Great Christmas Movies*, Taylor Publishing, 1998; Stuart W. Wells, III, *Science Fiction Collectibles: Identification & Price Guide*, Krause Publications, 1999.

Periodicals: *Autograph Times*, 2303 N. 44th St., #225, Phoenix, AZ 85008; *Big Reel*, P.O. Box 83, Madison, NC 27025; *Celebrity Collector*, P.O. Box 1115, Boston, MA 02117; *Classic Images*, P.O. Box 809, Muscatine, IA 52761; *Collecting Hollywood*, 2401 Broad St., Chattanooga, TN 37408;

Gone with the Wind Collector's Newsletter, 1347 Greenmoss Dr., Richmond, VA 23225; *Hollywood & Vine*, P.O. Box 717, Madison, NC 27025; *Hollywood Collectibles*, 4099 McEwen Dr., Ste 350, Dallas, TX 75244; *Movie Advertising Collector*, P.O. Box 28587, Philadelphia, PA 19149; *Movie Collectors' World*, P.O. Box 309, Fraser, MI 48026; *Movie Poster Update*, 2401 Broad St., Chattanooga, TN 37408; *Poorman's VHS Movie Collectors Newsletter*, 902 E. Country Cables, Phoenix, AZ 85022; *Silent Film Newsletter*, 140 7th Ave., New York, NY 10011; *Spielberg Film Society Newsletter*, P.O. Box 13712, Tucson, AZ 85732; *Under Western Skies*, Route 3, Box 263H, Waynesville, NC 28786.

Collectors' Clubs: Emerald City Club, 153 E. Main St., New Albany, IN 47150; Hollywood Studio Collectors Club, 3960 Laurel Canyon Blvd., Ste. 450, Studio City, CA 91604; Manuscript Society, 350 N Niagara St, Burbank, CA 91505; Old Time Western Film Club, P.O. Box 142, Silver City, NC 27344; Western Film Appreciation Society, 1914 112 St., Edmonton, Alberta T6J 5P8 Canada; Western Film Preservation Society, Inc., Raleigh Chapter, 1012 Vance St., Raleigh, NC 27608.

Additional Listings: Animation Art, Cartoon Characters, Cowboy Heroes, Disneyana, Movie Personalities.

Advertisement
  Harvey Girls, Judy Garland 15.00
  Heat's On, Mae West 15.00
Almanac, *Motion Picture Magazine*, 1945...42.00
Book
  Flash and Fantasy, The Truth Behind the Fantasy, The Fantasy Behind the Truth in Hollywood, Penny Stallings with Howard Mandelbaum, Bell Publishing, 1981 ....12.75
  Ginger Rogers and the Riddle of the Scarlet Cloak, Lela E. Rogers, Whitman 2378, 1942 ....15.00
  James Bond Show Book, Purnell & Sons, Ltd., London, c1960 ....20.00
  The Road to Oz, Junior Edition, Rand/McNallay & Co., 1939 copyright, 5-1/2" x 6-3/4" 24.00
  The Three Musketeers, Whitman, 1935 copyright, 176 pgs, RKO Radio Picture film, black and white scenes, 5" x 6", covers darkened....................15.00
  Vintage Films-50 Enduring Motion Pictures, Brosley Crowther, Putnam, 1975, worn dj...9.50

Booklet, *Down to the Sea in Ships*, 1920s preview, produced by Elmer Clifton, released by Hodkinson Pictures, 18 pgs...20.00
Card
  Charlie Chaplin, full color, cartoon image, titled "Safety First," 1" x 2"..5.00
  Drums of Fu Mancho, Republic Picture, 1940, 14" x 12" 65.00
  Her Cardboard Lover, Norman Shearer and Robert Taylor, 1942, 14" x 12" 10.00
Catalog, *McGull's Camera & Film Exchange Inc.*, New York, NY, c1942, 84 pgs, 4" x 9", catalog of 16mm silent motion picture film library, Victory edition 25.00
Chair, War of the Worlds, director's chair, Gene Barry 150.00
Christmas Stocking, *ET*, cotton 15.00
Colorforms Kit, Three Stooges, 1959 copyright, 8-14" x 13" box...........28.00
Coloring Book, Jeanette MacDonald, Costume Parade theme, Merrill Publishing, copyright 1941, 68 pgs, some crayoned 18.00
Comic Book, Three Stooges, Gold Key, issue #36, Sept 1967 ....18.00
Cookbook, *Gone With The Wind*, 5-1/2" x 7-1/4", soft cover, 48 pgs, Pebeco Toothpaste premium, c1939...45.00
Dish, 10-1/4" d, white china, blue dec with facsimile signatures of more than 25 movie stars around rim, images of Hollywood Bowl, Ciro's Sunset Strip, Grauman's Chinese Theatre, Earl Carroll's Theatre Restaurant, Brown Derby Restaurant, NBC Studios, mkd "Vernon Kilns," 1940s 120.00
Doll
  Bond, James, 007, Gilbert, 1964, MIB...400.00
  Oddjob, Gilbert, 1965, 11" h, orig first issue box 485.00
Film
  "Have Badge, Will Chase," Abbott and Costello, Castle Films No. 850, 50', 8MM, orig box 22.50
  "Oh Doctor," Three Stooges, 16 mm, 4" sq box 35.00
  "The Fast Getaway," Charlie Chaplin, 16 mm, 2.5" box 25.00
Game, Sons of Hercules, 9-1/2" x 19" box, ©1965 Milton Bradley and ©1968 Embassy Pictures Corp. 65.00
Gasoline Premium, Wings, Herald, sponsored by General Violet Ray Anti-Knock Gasoline, 1927 Paramount Picture, starring Clara Bow, Charles Rogers, Gary Cooper, green tone photos, 4 pgs, 10" x 15-1/2" 40.00
Gum Card Box, Planet of the Apes, Topps, 1967, 24 bubble gum card packs 100.00
Gum Card Set, James Bond, Philadelphia Gum Co, 1965, complete set of 66 photo cards 100.00
Handbill
  Men Are Not Gods, Miriam Hopkins, 6 x 9", 1930s 20.00

Spellbound, Gregory Peck and I Bergmann, 8 x 11", 4 pgs....................25.00

Handkerchief, Gone With The Wind, 13" sq, early 1940s
Bonnie Blue, sheer white fabric, purple, orange, turquoise, and yellow floral design, two corners with image of Rhett and Bonnie Blue, other two corners with Bonnie on horseback ..75.00
Scarlet O'Hara, floral design, yellow, rose, green, black, white, and gold, black diecut foil sticker................60.00

License Plate
Batman, used by Michael Keaton, Gotham City................................165.00
Fargo...15.00

Lobby Card
Chick Carter, Detective, 11" x 14", bluetone photo, Chapter 1, Chick Carter Takes Over, 1948 Columbia Pictures serial 25.00
Gone with the Wind, set of 6, first Italian release, 1948 ....130.00
Lost Horizon, Mexican release, 12-1/2" x 16-1/2"......................35.00
Lovely to Look At, 8" x 10", autographed by Red Skelton, 1952, with certificate of authenticity 40.00
Miss Tatlock's Millions, Robert Stack, Dorothy Wood, 1948, framed......45.00
Pressure Point, set of eight numbered cards for 1962 film, 11" x 14".......15.00
Rawhide Rangers, Johnny Mack Brown, Universal..........................20.00
Target, Tim Holt, RKO, 1952 ....24.00
The Runaway, Paramount, produced by Famous Players-Lasky Corp, starring Clara Bow, Warner Baxter, Georg Bancroft, William Powell, large inscription "A. William de Mile," in pale yellow lettering, gray movie title, 1926, 11" x 14" 40.00
The Sad Sack, Jerry Lewis..........30.00
Who's Minding the Store, Jerry Lewis...30.00

Tin, Gloria Swanson, marked "Beautebox, Canco," 7-1/2" d, $70.

Magazine
The Hollywood Way To A Beautiful Body, 9" x 12", Fawcett, © 1937..20.00
3-D Screen/Hollywood Pin-Ups, 8-1/2" x 11", issue #1, ©1963, 32 pgs, starlet photos.................................55.00

Movie Folder, Son of the Sheik, Valentino......................................25.00

Newspaper Clippings, Gone with the Wind, group of 20, c1948............30.00
Paint Set, Ben Hur, Acorn Industries, 1959, orig box, some contents used..10.00
Pinback Button, Beau James, Bob Hope, 1957, 2-1/2" d.............................38.00
Pistol, used by Bruce Willis for Die Hard...500.00
Playbill, Laffing Room Only, Olsen and Johnson, 1945 ....10.00
Playing Cards, Gone with the Wind, tin container 12.00

Poster
Angel In My Pocket, Andy Griffith, full sheet...100.00
Arson, Inc., three-sheet, 41" x 81", 1949 Lippert Productions, starring Robert Lowery and Anne ..... Gwynne, folded to 10-1/2" x 15"................95.00
Background to Danger, George Raft and Sidney Greenstreet, 1943 movie..85.00
Bomba and the Jungle Girl, six-sheet, 80" x 80", 1953 Monogram Pictures, folded to 11" x 14"......................90.00
Cinderella, full color, 1920s, 20" x 30".. 150.00
Mrs. Bridget O'Brien, John Sheridan, stone litho, 1905, 20" x 30"........ 350.00
Patton, 20th Century Fox, George S. Scott, full color image, folded, 27" x 41"...12.00
Tangier Incident, one sheet, Allied Artists, 1953, George Brent, full color portraits, folded, 27" x 41" 10.00

Press Book
Circus World, John Wayne, 14 pgs 25.00
Girl Happy, Elvis Presley, 1964....25.00
Mary Poppins, Julie Andrews......15.00
The Caine Mutiny, Humphrey Bogart, 18 pcs 35.00

Preview Folder, Manslaughter Herald, Cecil B. DeMille production, Paramount Pictures, 4" x 6" 10.00

Pulp
Doc Savage 35.00
Tell It To The Marines, ©1927, Jacobsen-Hodgkinson Corp, MGM, 128 pgs, 5-1/4" x 8", soft cover...........48.00

Puzzle
Babes in Toyland, Annette and Tommy Sands, WD Jaymar, frame tray, 1961, 9" x 12"..30.00
Little Rascals, Saalfield, frame tray, 1970s, 10" x 14"...........................15.00
No Other Woman, RKO Radio Picture, starring Irene Dunne, Eric Linden, and Charles Bickford, jigsaw, full color, 10" x 15-1/2" orig box..........................40.00

Record, The Wild One, orig motion picture soundtrack, Decca, 1954.. 135.00

Sheet Music, *As Time Goes By, Casablanca,* photographs of Humphrey Bogart, Ingrid Bergmann, and Paul Henreid on cov..........................148.00

Souvenir Album, Ben Hur, copyright 1900, orig ribbon binding............45.00

Souvenir Book
Gone With The Wind, 1939 ...... 115.00
Lawrence of Arabia, Peter O'Toole, colored photos, two fold-out double page maps 18.00

Since You Went Away, Selznick, 1944, 9" x 12", 20 pgs............................25.00
The Song of Bernadette, 9 x 11-1/2", 20 pgs, 1944 religious movie, full color cov Norman Rockwell illus of Jennifer Jones 40.00
White Shadows In The South Seas, MGM, 1928.....................................40.00

Souvenir Program
Citizen Kane, Orson Wells, 1941, 20 pgs, 8" x 12"................................90.00
The Friars, Bob Hope, spiral bound, 144 pgs, 8" x 12" 28.00

Sticker Book, My Fair Lady, 1985, unused, 8" x 11"...........................8.00

Textile, James Bond, pillow case, illus of Bond and other characters......... 70.00

Toy, James Bond Shooting Attached Case, MPC, 1965, orig box ... 1,165.00

Vending Machine Card, Humphry Bogart, The and Now, late 1940s, 3" x 5".. 6.00

Viewer Glasses, 3-D, Bwana Devil, folded 2" x 6" cardboard eyeglasses, Polaroid lenses, 1954 jungle adventure ... 15.00

Window Card
High Noon, Gary Cooper, 14" x 22", 1952...75.00
On The Waterfront, Marlon Brando, 14" x 22", 1954..............................125.00
The Brothers Karamazoo, full color art includes close-up of Yule Brenner, fading, 14" x 22" 8.00

Movie Personalities

Collecting Hints: Focus on one star. Today, the four most popular stars are Humphrey Bogart, Clark Gable, Jean Harlow, and Marilyn Monroe. Many of the stars of the silent era are being overlooked by the modern collector.

Remember that stars have big support staffs. Not all autographed items were or are signed by the star directly. Signatures should be checked carefully against a known original.

Many stars had fan clubs and the fans tended to hold on to the materials they assembled. The collector should be prepared to hunt and do research. A great deal of material rests in private hands.

History: The star system and Hollywood are synonymous. The studios spent elaborate sums of money promoting their stars. Chaplin, Valentino, and Pickford gave way to Garbo and Gable.

The movie magazine was a key vehicle in the promotion. *Motion Picture, Movie Weekly, Motion Picture World,* and *Photoplay* are just a few examples of this genre, although *Photoplay* was the most sensational.

The film star had no private life and cults grew up around many of them. By the 1970s, the star system of the 1930s and 1940s had lost its luster. The popularity of stars is much shorter lived today.

References: Clark Kidder, *Marilyn Monroe: Cover to Cover*, Krause Publications, 1999; Kevin Martin, *Signatures of the Stars*, Antique Trader Books, 1998; Rex Miller, *The Investor's Guide to Vintage Character Collectibles*, Krause Publications, 1999; Stuart W. Wells, III, *Science Fiction Collectibles: Identification & Price Guide*, Krause Publications, 1999.

Periodicals: *Autograph Times*, 2303 N. 44th St., #225, Phoenix, AZ 85008; *Big Reel*, P.O. Box 83, Madison, NC 27025; *Celebrity Collector*, P.O. Box 1115, Boston, MA 02117; *Classic Images*, P.O. Box 809, Muscatine, IA 52761; *Collecting Hollywood*, 2401 Broad St., Chattanooga, TN 37408; *Gone with the Wind Collector's Newsletter*, 1347 Greenmoss Dr., Richmond, VA 23225; *Hollywood & Vine*, P.O. Box 717, Madison, NC 27025; *Hollywood Collectibles*, 4099 McEwen Dr., Ste. 350, Dallas, TX 75244; *Movie Advertising Collector*, P.O. Box 28587, Philadelphia, PA 19149; *Movie Collectors' World*, P.O. Box 309, Fraser, MI 48026; *Movie Poster Update*, 2401 Broad St., Chattanooga, TN 37408; *Silent Film Newsletter*, 140 7th Ave., New York, NY 10011; *Under Western Skies*, Rte 3, Box 263H, Waynesville, NC 28786.

Collectors' Clubs: All About Marilyn, P.O. Box 291176, Los Angeles, CA 90029; Emerald City Club, 153 E. Main St., New Albany, IN 47150; Hollywood Studio Collectors Club, 3960 Laurel Canyon Blvd., Ste. 450, Studio City, CA 91604; Manuscript Society, 350 N. Niagara St., Burbank, CA 91505; Old Time Western Film Club, P.O. Box 142, Silver City, NC 27344; Western Film Appreciation Society, 1914 112 St., Edmonton, Alberta T6J 5P8 Canada; Western Film Preservation Society, Inc., Raleigh Chapter, 1012 Vance St., Raleigh, NC 27608.

Additional Listings: Autographs, Cowboy Heroes, Magazines, Movie Memorabilia.

Abbott & Costello, game, Who's On First, 9-1/2" x 19", Selchow & Righter Co., © ZIV International............................50.00
Allen, Woody, magazine, *Life*, March 21, 1969 ....9.00
Astaire, Fred
  Magazine, *Life*, Dec. 30, 1940 ......7.00

Sheet Music, *My Shining Hour*......7.50
Bacall, Lauren, magazine, *Life*, April 3, 1970...7.00
Bardot, Brigitte
  Book, *Brigitte Bardot*, Francoise Sagan, 1976, 100 pgs, 12-1/2 x 9-1/2"...10.00
  Magazine, *Life*, July 28, 1961......15.00
Bergmann, Ingrid, magazine,
  Life, Oct. 13, 1967 ....8.00
  Look, Nov. 11, 1958 ....12.00
Bow, Clara, arcade card, black and white portrait, tan background...............2.50
Brando, Marlon
  Book, *Brando*, Charles Highman, hard back..10.00
  Magazine, *Life*, Dec. 14, 1962..12.00
Bushman, Francis X., silent star, pennant, Metro 25.00
Cantor, Eddie
  Big Little Book, *Eddie Cantor In An Hour With You*, Whitman, #774, © 1934, 4-3/4" x 5-1/4"....................40.00
  Pin, Eddie Cantor Magic Club, 1-1/2" d, brass, black facial features, red, background, tall hat, Pebeco Toothpaste, 1935 ....50.00
Chaplin, Charlie
  Cartoon Book, *Charlie Chaplin in the Movies*, 1917.................................65.00
  Figure, 2-1/2" x 8", stuffed leather, full length portrait image, inked in black on natural tan leather, black felt back, 1920s..72.00
  Pencil Box, 2" x 8", full figure illus..60.00
  Sheet Music, Charlie Chaplin Walk, © 1915 Rossiter Music Co., Chicago...20.00
Coogan, Jackie
  Arcade Card, black and white portrait, tan background 2.00
  Clicker, metal, adv for peanut butter..24.00
  Pencil Box, red litho tin, black and white portrait on cover, 2-1/4" x 8"..28.00
  Toy, celluloid, soft blue cap, red bib trousers, natural tan face, shirt, and shoes, some wear........................28.00
Cooper, Jackie, big little book, *Jackie Cooper in Peck's Bad Boy*, Saalfield, #1084, © 1934, 4-/4" x 5-1/4", some wear..35.00
Crawford, Joan
  Photograph, black and white, 14" x 17", black and white, facsimile signature..15.00
  Pocket Mirror, black and white photo, mid-1920s, tiny facsimile signature 65.00
Crosby, Bing
  Game, Call Me Lucky, Parker Bros, 1954, black and white portrait on box lid, 19-1/2" sq playing board 30.00
  Magazine, *Look*, June 7, 1960, Bing and family cover 13.00
Davis, Bette
  Coloring Book, 10" x 13", Merrill, 1942..24.00

Movie Poster, Hush Hush Sweet Charlotte, 27" x 41"..............................35.00
Press Book, The Catered Affair, 20 pgs...30.00
Dean, James, scrap book of press cuttings and photographs, anniversary book, and 1955 magazine..........82.00
Etting, Ruth, autographed photo, 8-1/2" x 11-1/2", black and white glossy, soft focus glamour pose 40.00
Farnum, William, silent star, pennant, Fox 25.00
Fields, W. C.
  Lighter, W. C. Fields, figural, painted heavy white metal, 1930s, 4" x 4" x 5-1/4",...70.00
  Record Album, 10-1/2" x 12", Variety Records, United Artist label, © 1946 ....60.00
Funicello, Annette, magazine, *Teen Screen* 22.00
Gable, Clark, photograph, black and white, 14" x 17", black and white, facsimile signature 15.00
Garland, Judy, photograph, black and white, 8" x 10", black and white, checkered Wizard of Oz dress, 1940s... 8.00
Garson, Greer, photograph, black and white, 14" x 17", black and white, facsimile signature 15.00
Grable, Betty, photograph, black and white, 8" x 10" 5.00
Gleason, Jackie, magazine
  Life, Nov. 2, 1959.........................15.00
  Look, Nov. 15, 1966, with Art Carney on cover......................................12.50
Harlow, Jean, post card, 3-1/2" x 45-1/2", glossy, small facsimile signature, fan card, 1930s, unused.....30.00
Hope, Bob, magazine
  Life, Jan. 29, 1971 ....10.00
  Post, Nov. 9, 1963 ....16.00
  Time, Sept. 20, 1943 ....15.00
Kelly, Grace, coloring book, Whitman, 1956, few pages colored 45.00
Lake, Arthur, arcade card, Educational Pictures, black and white, tan background 2.50
Laurel & Hardy
  Arcade Card, Stan Laurel, Paramount Pictures, black and white, tan background 2.25
  Doll, Stan, 9-1/2" h, Bend'em Doll, Knickerbocker Toys, Harry Harmon Pictures Corp., vinyl, flexible legs, orig tags...40.00
  Figure, flat metal, Mignot, Stan wearing gray suit, blue stripes on pants, holds Oliver with one hand, Oliver in dark blue suit, red tie, cane, both hold derby in one hand, 1930s...........48.00
  Movie Poster, *Four Clowns*, 27" x 41"...45.00
  Salt and Pepper Shakers, pr, 1/2" x 2-1/2" x 4" white china tray, 4" h Laurel with black derby, 3" h Hardy with brown derby, Beswick, England, three pcs..115.00
Leigh, Janet, magazine, *Motion Picture*, August 1959 ....10.00

Loren, Sophia, magazine, *Life*, Nov. 14, 1960 .... 15.00

Marx, Zippo, arcade card, black and white portrait, tan background 2.50

Mayo, Virginia, pencil tablet, 12 lined sheets, full color cover, 1950s, unused 3.00

Midler, Bette, magazine, *Time*, March 2, 1987 .... 5.00

Monroe, Marilyn
Cologne Spray, 1983, MIB 45.00
Doll, Tristar, 11-1/2" h 45.00
Newspaper Supplement, New York, Sunday, 1982 .... 20.00

Novak, Kim, fan club kit, wallet, photos, and Christmas card, 1966 .... 25.00

Our Gang
Premium Card, Yuengling's Ice Cream, black and white or color tinted image, set of ten, 1-1/4" x 3", c1930 .... 125.00
Puzzle, 11" x 14" brown envelope, 80 pcs, sponsored by McKesson's Milk of Magnesia, scene of Our Gang characters in a soda fountain 135.00

Pickford, Mary
Magazine, *Photoplay*, September 1914, full color cover, article with photos 45.00
Pennant, Famous Players Film Co. 35.00
Photograph Signed, 1930 .... 55.00

Powell, Eleanor, arcade card, black and white portrait, tan background 2.00

Redford, Robert, magazine, *Argosy*, cover story, August 1974 .... 5.00

Rogers, Ginger
Magazine, *Life*, Nov. 5, 1951 .... 15.00
Photograph Signed, 5" x 7", color, Alhambra Theatre 1940 roster on back 15.00

Rooney, Mickey, photograph, black and white, 14" x 17", black and white, facsimile signature 15.00

Shore, Dinah, Emmy 2,500.00

Sinatra, Frank, magazine
Life, April 23, 1965 .... 15.00
TV Guide, May 14, 1954, New England edition, full color cover photo 45.00

Sparks, Ned, arcade card, black and white portrait, tan background 2.00

Stanwyck, Barbara
Box, Vita-Sert Chocolates 1940s, illus on lid 150.00
Press Book, Gambling lady, 11" x 17", 1934, Warner Bros, some wear ... 30.00

Streisand, Barbara, set of eight lobby cards for "Funny Girl," 27 black and white stills, "Funny Girl" program, two "Funny Girl" records 123.00

Taylor, Elizabeth, photograph, black and white, facsimile signature, 3" x 5" .. 8.00

Taylor, Robert, photograph, black and white, 14" x 17", black and white, facsimile signature 15.00

Temple, Shirley, *see Shirley Temple*

Three Stooges
Fan Photo, 5" x 6", full color, Three Stooges on flying carpet, steering wheel gripped by Larry, facsimile signatures, c1960 .... 20.00
Pinback Button, Carter is Doing the Work of 3 Men, black on yellow, cartoon images, c1980 .... 8.00
Punch-Out Book, 7-1/2 x 13", Golden Press, 1962 .... 75.00

Tucker, Sophie, Christmas card, 5-1/2" x 4-1/4", red, white, and red, folded four-pg postcard, "From My Own Home, Greetings, I'm Singing My Heart Out to Wish You The Merriest Christmas, The Happiest New Year Ever, Sophie Tucker," image of Sophie dressed up as homemaker, apron, large musical note coming from her heart, holding pots and pans in air, R. J. Rincirri, Glen Rock, NJ, c1940 .... 15.00

West, Mae, magazine, *Life*, April 18, 1969 .... 7.00

White, Pearl, silent star, pennant, Pathe 20.00

N

Napkin Rings

Collecting Hints: Concentrate on napkin rings of unusual design or shape. This is one collectible that still can be used on a daily basis. However, determine the proper cleaning and care methods for each type of material. Many celluloid items have been ruined because they were stored in an area that was too dry or were washed in water that was too hot.

Napkin rings with an engraved initial or monogram are worth less than those without personalized markings. Many collectors and dealers have these marks removed professionally, if it will not harm the ring.

History: Napkin rings enjoyed a prominent role on the American dinner table during most of the 19th and early 20th centuries. Figural napkin rings were used in upper-class households. The vast majority of people used a simple napkin ring, although these could be elegant as well. Engraving, relief designs, and carving turned simple rings into works of art. When cast metal and molded plastic became popular, shaped rings, especially for children, were introduced.

The arrival of inexpensive paper products and fast and frozen foods, along with a faster-paced lifestyle, reduced American's concern for elegant daily dining. The napkin ring has almost disappeared from the dining table.

Reference: Lillian Gottschalk and Sandra Whitson, *Figural Napkin Rings,* Collector Books, 1996.

Bone, carved roses, leaves, and stars, 1-1/2" d, $18.

Bakelite, 1940s
    Angelfish, deep blue marbled 70.00
    Elephant, navy blue.....................65.00
    Popeye, orange, some wear to orig decal..140.00

    Rabbit, bright yellow..................75.00
    Rocking Horse, red, orig eye ... 225.00
Brass
    Ring, 1-3/4" d, mkd "Made in India"...2.00
    Two elves, dog, dragon, and leaf dec, emb 20.00
Cloisonné, dragon, white ground...25.00
Glass, twisted hollow tube forms ring, Dorofee Glass, set of 10 ....50.00
Ivory, carved openwork 20.00
Pewter
    Kewpie, 1-3/4" d ring, 2-1/2" h Kewpie 115.00
    Turtle, ring on back, 2-1/2" h........28.00
Porcelain
    Butterfly, porcelain, hand painted, red "Made in Japan" mark, 3" w 6.50
    Girl in Sunbonnet, Erphila Czechoslovakian, 2-1/5" x 4".......................72.00
    Man, Art Deco design, mkd "Noritake" 32.00
    Owl, seated on ring.....................20.00
    Rose, cream ground, gold trim, mkd "Nippon".......................................50.00
Silver, plated
    Bulldog, Dingo Boy.................. 125.00
    Cat, arched back...................... 125.00
    Dog, pulling sled, emb greyhounds on sides, engraved "Sara," Meriden 165.00
    Nude Man, holding torch, sq base.. 150.00
    Parrot, rect base, Rogers Mfg Co. 48.00
    Plain ring with cutout "A," unmarked......................................6.00
Silver, sterling
    Cherubs, pair of seated figures, worn..70.00
    Koala Bear, Australian, 2" x 3" 70.00
    Lily, oval ring, engraved flowers, Rogers and Brothers, c1870, 1-1/2" h 150.00
    Mickey Mouse.............................80.00
    Peacock, standing.......................60.00
    Plain, double border bands.........20.00
    Plain, monogrammed "A.D.A.," worn smooth in places, 1" w, 1-3/4" d ..45.00
    Plain, monogrammed "H. F.," 3-1/4" w, 2-1/4" l...........................35.00
    Swan pulling wheeled napkin ring, Meriden Britannia, c1896, 2-3/4" h 550.00
Wood, child with accordion, painted white ring with red stripes 20.00

New Martinsville-Viking Glass

Collecting Hints: Before 1935, New Martinsville glass was made in a wide variety of colors. Later glass was only made in crystal, blue, ruby, and pink.

Look for cocktail, beverage, liquor, vanity, smoking, and console sets. Amusing figures of barnyard animals, sea creatures, dogs, and bears were produced.

Both Rainbow Art Glass and Viking Glass hand made their products and affixed a paper label. Rainbow Art Glass pieces are beautifully colored, and the animal figures are more abstract in design than those of New Martinsville. Viking makes plain, colored, cut, and etched tableware, novelties, and gift items Viking began making black glass in 1979.

History: The New Martinsville Glass Manufacturing Company, founded in 1901, took its name from its West Virginia location. Early products, made from opal glass, were decorative and utilitarian. Later, pressed crystal tableware with flashed-on ruby or gold decorations was made. In the 1920s, innovative color and designs made vanity, liquor, and smoking sets popular. Dinner sets in patterns such as Radiance, Moondrops, and Dancing Girl, as well as new colors, cuttings, and etchings were produced. In the 1940s, black glass was formed into perfume bottles, bowls with swan handles, and flower bowls. In 1944, the company was sold and reorganized as the Viking Glass Company.

The Rainbow Art Glass Company, Huntington, West Virginia, was established in 1942 by Henry Manus, a Dutch immigrant. This company produced small, hand-fashioned animals and decorative ware of opal, spatter, cased, and crackle glass. Rainbow Art Glass also decorated for other companies. In the early 1970s, Viking acquired Rainbow Art Glass Company and continued the production of the small animals.

The Viking Glass Company was acquired by Kenneth Dalzell in 1986. The company's name was changed to Dalzell-Viking Glass. Production included items made with Viking molds, some animal figures were reintroduced, and other items were made using new colors. In late 1998, Dalzell-Viking closed.

References: Lee Garmon and Dick Spencer, *Glass Animals of the Depression Era,* Collector Books, 1993; James Measell, *New Martinsville Glass,* The Glass Press, 1994; Naomi L. Over, *Ruby Glass of the 20th Century,* The Glass Press, 1990, 1993-94 value update; Hazel Marie Weatherman, *Colored Glassware of the Depression Era,* Book 2, Glassworks, 1982.

Ashtray, fish, 4" d 12.00
Basket, Janice, black, 12" l, 7" w, 9-1/2" h..................................... 190.00
Batter Bowl, 9" w, 5-1/2" h, dark green... 150.00
Beer Mug, pink 25.00

Bowl
5" d, Peach Blow, scalloped rim . 60.00
10" d, Meadow Wreath, crimped 35.00
11" d, 4" h, Teardrop, ftd.............45.00
12" d, Radiance, amber 40.00
Cake Plate, 14" d, Hostmaster,
amber...25.00
Candlestick, clear
Double, etched floral design,
5-1/4" h, 7-1/4" w.....................24.00
Figural, squirrel, 4-3/4" l, 3-1/2" w,
6-3/4" h, pr.................................120.00
Celery Dish, swan, 8" l neck, 6" h.....25.00
Chip and Dip Set, 14" d, orange,
Viking...30.00
Cigarette Holder, cart shaped..........20.00
Compote, fired-on color, handpainted
base trim, wear to gold trim,
4-1/4" h 22.50
Console Set, 11-1/2" w, 9-1/2" h black
swan bowl, pr 5-1/2" w, 5-1/8" h black
swan candleholders 190.00
Cordial, Moondrops, 1 oz, amber, silver
dec 25.00
Creamer and Sugar, individual size,
Moondrops, red 35.00
Cup and Saucer
Fancy Square, jade 15.00
Hostmaster, ruby 10.00
Moondrops, amber.......................15.00
Radiance, red 27.50
Decanter
Nice Kitty, green 55.00
Volkstead Pup, crystal.................75.00
Decanter Set, Moondrops, 12-3/4" h
decanter and six 3-1/4" h tumblers
Cobalt blue 145.00
Ruby...240.00
Figure
Baby Bear, clear, 4-1/4" l 65.00
Bird, clear, 1960s.........................15.00
Chick, baby, clear........................45.00
Dog, 8-1/2" l, orange, Viking,
#1316 ....37.50
Duck, 15" l, orange, Viking 50.00
Eagle, clear...................................60.00
Elephant, clear..............................80.00
Giraffe, 7" h, clear 20.00
Hen, clear 60.00
Horse, head up, clear 90.00
Owl, 8-1/2" h, orange, Viking.....100.00
Polar Bear, clear, 6" l..................95.00
Rooster, large, clear 85.00
Seal, clear 80.00
Squirrel, 5" h, 6" w, clear.............55.00
Goblet
Diamond Thumbprint 12.00
Hostmaster, cobalt blue 24.00
Mt Vernon, cobalt blue 20.00
Guest Set, pink, 6-1/4" h pitcher,
3-1/2" h tumbler, 5-3/4" w, 9-1/4" l tray,
small chips..................................190.00
Handkerchief Bowl, 5" x 5-1/2", crimped,
deep orange, orig red and gold "Hand
Made Viking" sticker....................20.00
Honey Jar, cov, Radiance, ruby.......45.00
Iced Tea Tumbler, ftd, Prelude etching,
crystal...15.00
Lamp Base, 10" h, triangular, black
enamel accents, pink satin
ground...45.00
Marmalade, cov, Janice 25.00
Mug, Georgian, ruby 18.00

Nappy, Prelude, 5" d, heart shaped, han-
dle..20.00
Pitcher, orange, Viking 24.00
Plate
7-1/2" w, Fancy Square, jade.........8.00
8" d, Radiance, red, slight wear ..13.00
8-1/2" d, Moondrops, red.............20.00
11" d, Meadow Wreath, clear 20.00
14" d, Florentine 25.00
Relish Bowl, Radiance, three-part, amber,
9" d..18.00
Relish Set, glass relish dish with three
small feet and orig Viking sticker, Flair
pattern silverplated relish spoon and
pickle fork, mkd "1847 Rogers Broth-
ers," MIB...25.00
Sherbet, #34, jade green..................12.00
Stopper, jade-ite, fan-shaped petals,
2-1/4" w, small crack 6.50
Swan, back forms bowl, 5" x 6" x 5-1/4"
Amber..35.00
Clear 25.00
Tumbler
Georgian, ruby 25.00
Hostmaster, cobalt blue...............10.00
Oscar, red, 4-5/8" h 20.00
Vanity Set, Judy, three pcs, green and
crystal, cologne bottle, stopper,
tray...95.00
Vase
Epic, sapphire blue, Viking,
17-1/2" h 25.00
Shell, leaded crystal, 5" h, pr.....125.00
Whiskey, Moondrops, amethyst 20.00
Wine Set, amethyst, 11-1/2" h decanter,
four 4-5/8" h wine glasses......... 190.00

Newspapers, Headline Editions

Collecting Hints: All newspapers must be complete, with a minimum of chipping and cracking. Post-1880 newsprint is made of wood pulp and deteriorates quickly without proper care. Pre-1880 newsprint was composed of cotton and rag fiber and has survived much better than its wood-pulp counterpart.

Front pages only of 20th-century newspapers command about 60 percent of the value for the entire issue, since the primary use for these papers is display. Pre-20th-century issues are collectible only if complete, as banner headlines were rarely used. These papers tend to run between four and eight pages in length.

Major city issues are preferable, although any newspaper providing a dramatic headline is collectible. Banner headlines, those extending completely across the paper, are most desirable. Those papers from the city in which an event happened command a substantial premium over the prices listed below. A premium is also paid for a complete series, such as all 20th-century election reports.

Twentieth-century newspapers should be stored away from high humidity and out of direct sunlight. Issues should be placed flat in poly-ethylene bags or in acid-free folders that are slightly larger than the paper.

Although not as commonly found, newspapers from the 17th through the 19th centuries are highly collect-ible, particularly those from the Revo-lutionary War, War of 1812, Civil War, and those reporting Indian and des-perado events.

Two of the most commonly reprinted papers are the *Ulster County Gazette,* of Jan. 4, 1800, dealing with Washington's death and the *N.Y. Herald,* of April 15, 1865, concerning Lincoln's death. If you have either of these papers, chances are you have a reprint.

History: America's first successful newspaper was *The Boston Newslet-ter,* founded in 1704. The newspaper industry grew rapidly and reached its pinnacle in the early 20th century. Within the last decade many great evening papers have ceased publi-cation, and many local papers have been purchased by the large chains.

Collecting headline-edition news-papers has become popular during the last 20 years, largely because of the decorative value of the headlines. Also, individuals like to collect news-papers related to the great events which they have witnessed or which have been romanticized through the movies, television, and other media. Historical events, the Old West, and the gangster era are particularly pop-ular subjects.

References: Ron Barlow and Ray Reynolds, *Insider's Guide to Old Books, Magazines, Newspapers, and Trade Catalogs,* Windmill Publishing (2147 Windmill View Rd, El Cajon, CA 92020), 1996; Gene Utz, *Collecting Paper,* Books Americana, 1993.

Periodical: *Paper Collectors' Market-place (PCM),* P.O. Box 128, Scandi-navia, WI 54977.

Advisor: Tim Hughes.

Notes: The following listing includes prices of issues dating more than 200 years old, but concentrates on news-papers of the 20th century. The date given is the date of the event itself; the newspaper coverage usually appeared the following day.

1836, March 6, Battle of the Alamo 375.00
1863, January 1, typical Civil War newspaper 15.00
1863, July 4, the Battle of
Gettysburg.................................300.00

1865, April 14, Lincoln Is Assassinated at Ford's Theater 750.00

1876, June 25, Custer's Massacre, but not reported in newspapers until July 7 and later 260.00

1880, January 1, typical late 19th C newspaper...8.00

1882, April 3, Jesse James is killed 180.00

1886, September 1, final surrender of Geronimo 90.00

1893, June 20, Lizzie Border found not quilty..90.00

War, Japs Bomb US Base, dramatic headline on the attack of Pearl Harbor, $75. Photo courtesy of Tim Hughes.

1901, September 6, President McKinley shot...65.00

1903, December 17, Wright Bros first airplane flight 325.00

1912, February 14, Arizona joins Union..38.00

1912, April 15, *Titantic* hits iceberg and sinks 600.00

1915, May 7, *Lusitania* is sunk 375.00

1917, April 6, war declared, US enters WWI...55.00

1919, June 28, Treat of Versailles signed 27.00

1921, March 4, Harding inaugurated 33.00

1925, July 21, Scopes convicted, Monkey Trial...48.00

1927, May 21, Lindbergh successfully lands in Paris 170.00

1928, November 6, Hoover elected 38.00

1929, February 14, St. Valentine's Day Massacre 170.00

1929, October 28, Stock Market crash (report of Monday's closing) 210.00

1930, October 13, Gangster Legs Diamond is shot 55.00

1932, March 1, Lindbergh baby kidnapped 65.00

1932, May 12, Lindbergh baby found dead 65.00

1932, August 24, Amelia Earhart's record flight across America...................28.00

1933, March 23, Hitler becomes dictator 40.00

1933, April 7, end of Prohibition 60.00

1933, September 6, Dillinger robs Indiana bank...37.00

1933, December 5, Prohibition repealed 68.00

Bonnie & Clyde killed in Louisana, May 23, 1934, $225. Photo courtesy of Tim Hughes.

1934, January 20, Bonnie & Clyde rob Texas bank 40.00

1934, May 23, Bonnie & Clyde killed in Louisana....................................225.00

1934, July 13, Babe Ruth hits his 700th homerun 40.00

1934, October 22, Pretty Boy Floyd killed by FBI in Ohio 65.00

1935, April 14, Bruno Hauptman is sentenced to death............................34.00

1935, September 10, death of Huey Long 40.00

1936, June 19, Max Schmeling vs. Joe Lewis heavyweight fight 26.00

1937, May 6, *Hindenburg* disaster at Lakehurst, NJ 175.00

1937, July 3, Amelia Earhart disappears 85.00

1939, September 1, Germany attacks Poland 43.00

1941, May 25, *Bismark* sunk 39.00

1941, June 2, Lou Gehrig dies.........65.00

1942, June 5, the Battle of Midway ..34.00

1944, June 6, D-Day Invasion of France 60.00

1945, April 12, President Franklin D. Roosevelt dies............................35.00

1945, May 8, Germany surrenders V-E day..60.00

1945, August 9, atomic bomb is dropped on Nagasaki, Japan....................57.00

1945, August 14, Japan quit: V-J Day 65.00

1948, May 14, Israel statehood 58.00

1949, January 20, Truman inauguration 28.00

1950, June 24, North Korea crossed the 38th parallel to invade South Korea...35.00

1951, May 1, Mickey Mantle gets his first home run in his rookie year 39.00

1953, October 5, Yankees win World Series...50.00

1955, September 30, death of James Dean...40.00

1958, July 1, Alaska joins union 25.00

1960, November 8, John F. Kennedy elected 50.00

John F. Kennedy assassinated, Dallas, Nov. 22, 1963, $125. Photo courtesy of Tim Hughes.

1961, October 1, Roger Maris hits his 61st home run, breaking Babe Ruth's record 110.00

1962, February 21, John Glenn orbits the earth...30.00

1962, August 6, Marilyn Monroe dies 120.00

1963, June 12, Medgar Evers is shot in Mississippi....................................39.00

1963, November 22, John F. Kennedy assassinated 35.00

1965, September 9, Sandy Kofax pitches perfect game................................25.00

1968, April 15, Martin Luther King assassinated 48.00

1969, July 21, man walks on moon . 36.00

1969, August 18, beginning of three day concert called Woodstock, near Bethel, NY....................................25.00

Man walks on the moon, July 21, 1969, $36. Photo courtesy of Tim Hughes.

1977, August 17, Elvis Presley dies in Memphis......................................25.00

1989, October 18, stock market crashes 20.00

Niloak Pottery

Collecting Hints: Mission ware pottery is characterized by swirling layers of browns, blues, reds, and cream. Very few pieces are glazed on both the outside and inside; usually only the interior is glazed.

History: Niloak Pottery was made near Benton, Arkansas. Charles Dean Hyten, the founder of this pottery, experimented with the native clay and tried to preserve the natural colors. By 1911, he had perfected a method that produced the desired effect, resulting in the popular Mission ware. The pieces were marked "Niloak," which is Kaolin—the type of fine porcelain clay used—spelled backwards.

After a devastating fire, the pottery was rebuilt and named Eagle Pottery. This factory included enough space to add a novelty pottery line which was introduced in 1929. This line continued until 1934 and usually bears the name "Hywood-Niloak." After 1934, "Hywood" was dropped from the mark. Mr. Hyten left the pottery in 1941, and in 1946 the operation closed.

References: Susan and Al Bagdade, *Warman's American Pottery and Porcelain,* 2nd ed., Krause Publications, 2000.

Collectors' Club: Arkansas Pottery Collectors Society, 12 Normandy Rd, Little Rock, AR 72007.

Ashtray, blue glaze, hat shape......... 12.00
Bud Vase
   7-1/4" h, Ozark Dawn glaze 65.00
   8-1/8" h, Misson Ware................265.00
Cornucopia, 3-3/8" h, teal, price
   for pr..35.00
Creamer, Ozark Dawn glaze.............35.00
Ewer
   7" h, yellow, small brown patch under
   glaze at base of handle...............50.00
   16-1/2" h, Ozark Dawn 150.00
Figure
   Canoe, matte white......................35.00
   Frog, matte green........................30.00
   Polar Bear, matte white................45.00
Flower Pot, hand thrown, ruffled rim,
   matte green glaze, c1920-30....185.00
Planter
   Bear, tan.......................................27.50
   Deer, 4-1/2" h, light matte
   blue 35.00
   Duck, blue and pink 27.50
   Dutch Shoe...................................55.00
   Elephant, 6" h, matte maroon, standing
   on drum with "N" on side 72.00
   Fox, red...27.50
   Frog, 4-1/2" h, chocolate brown..55.00
   Kangaroo, white, brown accents 20.00
   Rabbit, green...............................18.00
   Squirrel...45.00
   Swan, 7-1/2" h, matte blue, detailed
   feathers 65.00

Pot, 5-1/2" d, Mission Ware, blue, dark brown, beige, gray, and terra-cotta swirls, small factory rim flake.... 175.00
Strawberry Vase, pink, gray-green glaze, opening with turkey, tail feathers spread out, orig paper label,
   sgd 65.00
Vase
   3-3/8" w, Ozark Dawn glaze, imp
   mark..38.00
   4" h, Mission Ware, baluster with wide rim, second art mark................. 110.00
   5-1/2" h, Mission Ware, corseted cylinder 175.00
   6" h, hand thrown, hand applied twisted handles, Ozark Dawn glaze, 1930s.. 150.00
   6" h, Mission Ware, inverted bell shape 150.00
   6-1/2" h, double handled, lavender 36.00
   6-1/2" h, Mission Ware, wide shoulders, tapering towards base 195.00
   6-1/2" h, twist, glossy pink glaze...40.00
   7" h, Mission Ware, turkey feather design, blue, orig paper sticker, chip on underside of foot, makers flaw at lip...40.00
   8-3/4" h, hand thrown, gray shading to pink, 1930s............................... 155.00

Nippon China, 1891-1921

History: Nippon, Japanese hand-painted porcelain, was made for export between 1891 and 1921. In 1891, when the McKinley tariff act proclaimed that all items of foreign manufacture be stamped with their country of origin, Japan chose to use "Nippon." In 1921, the United States decided the word "Nippon" no longer was acceptable and required all Japanese wares to be marked "Japan," ending the Nippon era.

Marks: There are more than 220 recorded Nippon backstamps or marks; the three most popular are the wreath, maple leaf, and rising sun. Wares with variations of all three marks are being reproduced today. A knowledgeable collector can easily spot the reproductions by the mark variances.

The majority of the marks are found in three different colors: green, blue, or magenta. Colors indicate the quality of the porcelain used: green for first-grade porcelain, blue for second-grade, and magenta for third-grade. Marks were applied by two methods: decal stickers under glaze and imprinting directly on the porcelain.

References: Joan Van Patten, *Collector's Encyclopedia of Nippon Porcelain,* 1st Series (1979, 2000 value update), 2nd Series (1982, 1997 value update), 3rd Series (1986, 2000 value update), 4th Series, (1997), Collector Books; 5th Series (1998); 6th Series, 2000; Joan F. Van Patten and Linda Lou, *Nippon Dolls & Playthings,* Collector Books, 2000; Kathy Wojciechowski, *Wonderful World of Nippon Porcelain,* Schiffer Publishing, 1992.

Collectors' Clubs: ARK-LA-TEX Nippon Club, 6800 Arapaho Rd, #1057, Dallas, TX 75248; Dixieland Nippon Club, P.O. Box 1712, Centerville, VA 22020; International Nippon Collectors Club, 1417 Steele St., Fort Myers, FL 33901; Lakes & Plains Nippon Collectors Society, P.O. Box 230, Peotone, IL 60468-0230; Long Island Nippon Collectors Club, 145 Andover Place, W. Hempstead, NY 11552; MD-PA Collectors' Club, 1016 Erwin Dr., Joppa, MD 21085; New England Nippon Collectors Club, 64 Burt Rd, Springfield, MA 01118; Sunshine State Nippon Collectors' Club, P.O. Box 425, Frostproof, FL 33843; Upstate New York Nippon Collectors' Club, 122 Laurel Ave., Herkimer, NY 13350.

Reproduction Alert

Distinguishing Old Marks from New:

A common old mark consisted of a central wreath open at the top with the letter M in the center. "Hand Painted" flowed around the top of the wreath; "NIPP. O. Box N" around the bottom. The modern fake mark reverses the wreath (it is open at the bottom) and places an hourglass form not an "M" in its middle.

An old leaf mark, approximately one-quarter inch wide, has "Hand" with "Painted" below to the left of the stem and "NIPP. O. Box N" beneath. The newer mark has the identical lettering but the size is now one-half, rather than one-quarter, inch.

An old mark consisted of "Hand Painted" arched above a solid rising sun logo with "NIPP. O. Box N" in a straight line beneath. The modern fake mark has the same lettering pattern but the central logo looks like a mound with a jagged line enclosing a blank space above it.

Berry Bowl, 8-1/2" d, 3-1/2" h, hand painted raspberries, scalloped edges, blue maple leaf mark 725.00
Berry Set, 9-1/2" d, 2-1/2" h master bowl, six 5" d bowls, open rose dec, green and gold beading 700.00
Biscuit Jar, cov
   8" h, 6" d, hand painted roses, ftd, gold trim, unmarked 495.00
   8-3/4" h, 7" d, teal green ground, deep burgundy, pink, and yellow roses 385.00

Charger, hand painted, bulldog, 12" d, $400. Photo courtesy of Joy Luke Fine Art Brokers and Auctioneers.

Bowl, 9-3/4" d, 3" h, hand painted roses, heavy gold, cobalt blue trim, green ground, ftd 650.00

Butter Dish, cov, florals, mkd "Hand Painted RC Nippon" 40.00

Calling Card Tray, 7-3/4" x 6", Dragonware, blue maple leaf mark 48.00

Charger, 12-1/2" d, grapes, grapevines, two butterflies, gold encrusted border, scalloped rim, blue maple leaf mark, minor paint wear 650.00

Chocolate Set

  Pink roses, hand painted roses, light green leaves, gild and beading, 10" h chocolate pot, cov, five cups and saucers, blue rising sun mark........425.00

  Red roses, hand painted roses, gold beading, 5-1/2" h chocolate pot, five cups and saucers.......................495.00

  White flying bird motif, gold trim, chocolate pot, creamer, sugar, five sets of octagonal cups and saucers, four sets of round cups and saucers, some damage and wear 985.00

Cider Set, 6" h pitcher, six cups, hand painted grapes and leaves pattern, gold trim, blue cherry blossom in circle mark, some wear to gold 375.00

Compote, 8-1/2" d, 4-3/8" h, Wedgwood and rose nosegay dec, wreath mark 200.00

Creamer and Sugar, handpainted florals, gold trim..80.00

Dresser Jar, handpainted floral dec, green wreath mark 100.00

Ferner

  6" w, floral dec, gold beading, four handles, green "M" in wreath mark 125.00

  9-1/2" w, 5-3/4" h, hand painted purple and green florals, Moriage flowers...400.00

Hair Receiver and Powder Dish, pink flowers, light blue center band, gold trim, small brushed gold feet 90.00

Hatpin Holder, 4-3/4" h, florals, wear to gold trim, mkd "Hand Painted Nippon"...95.00

Jam Jar, cov, matching underplate, deep cobalt blue, heavily raised gold cartouches, allover gold dec, pink and pale apricot flowers, two handles, blue leaf mark 145.00

Nut Bowl

  3-5/8" l, 2-3/8" w, handpainted flowers, blue mark "Noritake Nippon" 8.50

5" d, 3 ball feet, bright colors, purple and white grape clusters with leaves, mkd "Hand Painted Nippon" with wreath and "M" in green..............85.00

Open Salt, 3" w, hand painted, mauve flowers, gold trim, pr 30.00

Pitcher, 7" h, slate gray ground, Moriage seal gulls, leaf mark 250.00

Plate

  6-3/8" d, hand painted flowers, "M" in green wreath mark.......................17.50

  6-7/8" d, hand painted floral border, cat face portrait center, set of three, each with different portrait........695.00

Portrait Vase, beautiful lady, floral garland, gold trim, two loop handles, one broken and repaired......................495.00

Serving Tray, 11" d, gold and burgundy medallions inside gold fluted rim, multicolored roses and leaves center, gold open pierced handles, Royal Kinran mark...225.00

Sugar Shaker, white ground, pink and red roses, gold trim, cork bottom, single handle 45.00

Teapot, 6-1/2" h, Dragonware, some wear...32.00

Tea Strainer, pink roses....................50.00

Trivet, 6" d, octagonal, mark #47, pink and blue flowers, brown basket type border, worn gold trim.......................25.00

Tray, 10-1/2" x 11", hand painted roses, double handles, beaded, gold trim... 650.00

Vase

  8" h, handpainted florals, green wreath mark...95.00

  8-1/2" h, two handles, scenic design, blue pagoda mark 165.00

  9-3/4" h, blue floral pattern, green "M" in wreath mark..........................100.00

  11" h, 7-3/8" handle to handle, painted florals 450.00

Noritake Azalea China

Collecting Hints: There are several backstamps on the Azalea pattern of Noritake China. The approximate dates are:

  Prior to 1921: Blue rising sun, printed "Hand painted NIPPON"

  1921-1923: Green wreath with M, printed "Noritake, Hand painted, Made in Japan."

  1923-1930s: Green wreath with M, printed "Noritake, Hand painted, Made in Japan 19322."

  1925-1930s: Red wreath with M, printed "Noritake, Hand painted, Made in Japan 19322."

  1935-1940: Red azalea sprig, printed "Noritake Azalea Patt., Hand painted, Japan No.19322/ 252622."

  Most of the saucers and underplates do not have a backstamp. Those that do are stamped "Azalea 19322/252622."

Most collectors assemble sets and are not concerned with specific marks. Those concentrating on specific marks, particularly the "NIPPON" one, may pay higher prices.

Pieces of Azalea pattern china are available through replacement services.

History: The Azalea pattern of Noritake China was first produced in the early 1900s. Each piece of fine china was hand painted. The individuality of the artists makes it almost impossible to find two pieces with identical painting.

In the early 1900s, the Larkin Company of Buffalo, New York, sold many household items to the American public through its catalog (similar to the Sears Roebuck and Company catalog). In the 1924 Larkin catalog, a basic Azalea pattern serving set was advertised. The set included the larger coffee cups with the blue rising sun backstamp.

Two forces came together in the 1920s to make the Azalea pattern of Noritake China one of the most popular household patterns in this century. First, the Larkin Company initiated its "Larkin Plan," encouraging housewives to sign up to become "Larkin Secretaries." Each Larkin Secretary formed a small neighborhood group of five or more women who would purchase Larkin products. The Larkin Secretary earned premiums based on the volume of orders she obtained and could then exchange these premiums for household items, including Azalea china.

Second, many households in the 1920s could not afford to spend all at one time the amount needed to purchase a complete set of fine china. The Larkin Club Plan enabled them to eventually complete sets of the Azalea pattern by buying items one or a few at a time.

Over the years, and to provide more enticements, additional pieces, such as the nut/fruit shell-shaped bowl, candy jar, and child's tea set were offered. Glassware, originally classified as "crystal," was introduced in the 1930s but was not well received.

It became somewhat of a status symbol to "own a set of Azalea." The Azalea pattern china advertisement in the 1931 Larkin catalog claimed, "Our Most Popular China."

Some Azalea pieces were advertised in the Larkin catalogs for 19 consecutive years, while others were advertised for only four or five years. These latter pieces are scarcer, resulting in a faster appreciation in value.

Most serious collectors would like to own the child's tea set, which we believe was advertised in only two Larkin Fall catalogs, and the so-called salesmen's samples, which were never advertised for sale.

The Larkin Company ceased distribution in 1945.

References: Larkin catalogs from 1916 through 1941.

Notes: The Larkin catalog numbers are given in parentheses behind each listing. If arranged numerically, you will notice gaps. For example, numbers 41 through 53 are missing. Noritake's Scenic pattern, presently called Tree in the Meadow, also was popular during this time period. Many of the missing Azalea numbers were assigned to scenic pieces.

Azalea Pattern, creamer, $40.

Basket (193)	125.00
Bonbon Dish, 6-1/4" d (184)	45.00
Bouillon Cup and Saucer, 5-1/4" (124)	20.00
Bowl, shell shaped	325.00
Bread and Butter Plate	14.00
Butter Pat (312)	65.00
Butter Tub, insert (54)	45.00
Cake Plate, 9-5/8" w, handles (10)	40.00
Casserole, cov (16)	75.00
Celery Dish (444)	250.00
Cereal Bowl	15.00
Cheese Dish, cov (315)	125.00
Coffeepot (182)	500.00
Condiment Set, 4 pc (14)	75.00
Creamer (7)	30.00
Cruet, orig stopper (190)	165.00
Cup and Saucer (2)	25.00
Demitasse Cup and Saucer (183)	125.00
Dessert Bowl	12.00
Dinner Plate (13)	22.00
Egg Cup (120)	55.00
Fruit Bowl	12.00
Grapefruit Bowl (185)	115.00
Gravy Boat (40)	55.00
Jam Jar, cov (125)	110.00
Lemon Tray, handle (121)	30.00
Luncheon Plate (4)	20.00
Mayonnaise Set (3)	50.00
Milk Pitcher, quart (100)	165.00
Pickle Dish	18.00
Platter, medium	75.00
Platter, small	54.00
Relish, four sections (119)	110.00
Relish, undivided, oval	65.00
Salad Bowl, 10" d (12)	35.00
Salad Plate, 7-1/2" d	13.50
Salt and Pepper Shakers, pr	35.00
Soup Bowl, 7-3/8" d	22.00
Spooner (189)	90.00
Sugar Bowl, cov	24.00
Syrup, cov (97)	95.00
Teapot (15)	95.00
Toothpick Holder (192)	95.00
Vegetable Bowl, cov	40.00
Vegetable Bowl, open, oval (101)	45.00
Vegetable Bowl, open, round	30.00

Nutcrackers

Collecting Hints: The most popular modern nutcrackers are the military and civilian figures which are made in East Germany. These are collected primarily for show and not for practicality.

Nutcracker design responded to each decorating phase through the 1950s. The figural nutcrackers of the Art Deco and Art Nouveau periods are much in demand. Concentrating on 19th-century models results in a display of cast-iron ingenuity. These nutcrackers were meant to be used.

Several cast-iron animal models have been reproduced. Signs of heavy use is one indication of age.

History: Nuts keep well for long periods, up to two years, and have served as a dessert or additive to cakes, pies, bread, etc., since the colonial period. Americans' favorite nuts are walnuts, chestnuts, pecans, and almonds.

The first nutcrackers were crude hammers or club devices. The challenge was to find a cracker that would crack the shell, but leave the nut intact. By the mid-19th century, cast-iron nutcrackers in animal shapes appeared. Usually the nut was placed in the jaw section of the animal and the tail pressed as the lever to crack the nut.

The 19th- and early 20th-century patent records abound with nutcracker inventions. In 1916, a lever-operated cracker which could be clamped to the table was patented as the Home Nut Cracker, St. Louis, Missouri. Perhaps one of the most durable designs was patented on Jan. 28, 1889, and sold as the Quakenbush plated model. This hand model is plain at the top where the grip teeth are located and has twist-style handles on the lower half of each arm. The arms end in an acorn finial.

References: Judith A. Rittenhouse, *Ornamental and Figural Nutcrack-*

ers, Collector Books, 1993; James Rollband, *American Nutcrackers,* Off Beat Books (1345 Poplar Ave., Sunnyvale, CA 94087), 1996.

Collectors' Club: Nutcracker Collectors' Club, 12204 Fox Run Drive, Chesterland, OH 44026.

Parrot, cast iron, painted green, red, and gold, 10" l, $295.

Nutcracker	
Cat, brass	50.00
Dog	
6" h, brass	60.00
6" h, 13" l, cast iron, SP	75.00
Elephant, 5" h, 10" l, orig paint, c1920	75.00
Fish, 5" l, brass	30.00
Gendarme, 3" x 6", wood, mkd "Paris"	36.00
Jester, brass, 7" l	195.00
Lady, hip and legs, pewter	30.00
Man's Head, wooden, screw type, whiskered face, brimmed hat, 3" w, 5-1/2" h	40.00
Monkey, head, brass	37.50
Pheasant, bronze	115.00
Pliers Type	
Cast iron	15.00
Steel, adjustable	15.00
Sterling silver	40.00
Punch and Judy, figural, brass	95.00
Rabbit, head, wood, glass eyes, hand carved, German	110.00
Ram, wood, glass eyes	75.00
Rooster, cast iron	35.00
Sailor and Woman, brass	85.00
Screw Clamp type, cast iron, John A. Hurley, Inc., Bridgeport, CT, patent Aug. 19, 1909, 9-1/2" l	100.00
Scottie, cast iron, 6" h	50.00
Set, nutcracker and pick set, red plaid plastic pouch, mkd "HM2"	30.00
Skull and Cross Bones, cast iron	90.00
Squirrel, cast iron	35.00
St. Bernard, adv L. A. Althoff Makers of Headlights, Stoves, and Ranges, Chicago, IL, cast metal, 3" w, 5-3/4" h	275.00
Toy Soldier, marching with gun at side, saluting, crimson uniform, lace ascot, designed by Christian Ulbritch, Germany, #758, 18" h	240.00
Twist and screw type, nickel-plated cast iron	15.00

O

Occupied Japan

Collecting Hints: Buyers should be aware that a rubber stamp can be used to mark "Occupied Japan" on the base of objects. Fingernail polish remover can be used to test a mark. An original mark will remain intact since it is under the glaze; fake marks will disappear. This procedure should not be used on unglazed pieces. Visual examination is the best way to identify a fake mark on an unglazed item.

Damaged pieces have little value unless the item is extremely rare. Focus on pieces which are well-made and nicely decorated. There are many inferior examples.

From the beginning of the American occupation of Japan until April 28, 1952, objects made in that country were marked "Japan," "Made in Japan," "Occupied Japan," or "Made in Occupied Japan." Only pieces marked with the last two designations are of major interest to Occupied Japan collectors. The first two marks also were used during other time periods.

History: The Japanese economy was devastated when World War II ended. To secure necessary hard currency, the Japanese pottery industry produced thousands of figurines and other knickknacks for export. The variety of products is endless—ashtrays, dinnerware, lamps, planters, souvenir items, toys, vases, etc. Initially, the figurines attracted the largest number of collectors; today many collectors focus on other types of pieces.

References: Florence Archambault, *Occupied Japan for the Home,* Schiffer Publishing, 2000; Monica Lynn Clements and Patricia Rosser Clements, *Pocket Guide to Occupied Japan,* Schiffer Publishing, 1999; Gene Florence, *Price Guide to Collector's Encyclopedia of Occupied Japan,* Collector Books, 2001.

Collectors' Club: Occupied Japan Club, 29 Freeborn St., Newport, RI 02840; Occupied Japan Collectors Club, 18309 Faysmith Ave., Torrance, CA 90504.

Ashtray
Frog, ceramic, sitting on lily pad, 5" l, 3" w, 2-1/2" h 32.00
Pikes Peak, metal, emb scene, oval...3.00

Young boy smoking cigar, bobbing head, metal, 4-3/4" h...................55.00
Basket, china, miniature, floral dec 5.00
Bell, chef holding wine bottle and glass, 3" h..24.00
Bookends, pr, sailing ships, emb wood..75.00
Box, cov, inlaid, dog motif 15.00
Candleholder, 4" h, 4-1/2" w, two-lite, seated angel holding bouquet....24.00
Children's Play Dishes, Blue Willow, 18 pc set...375.00
Cigarette Box, cov, china, rect, blue floral dec, gold trim..............................15.00
Cigarette Lighter, silver colored metal, mkd..10.00
Cigarette Set, plated metal, cov box, Scottie dog dec, matching lighter..20.00
Clicker, beetle, silver colored 5.00
Clock, bisque, dancing couple in colonial garb, floral encrusted case, 10-1/2" h 250.00
Coaster Set, papier-mâché box, floral dec, price for six-pc set...............18.00
Coffee Set, 7-3/4" h coffee pot, creamer, sugar, six cups and saucers, white ground, pink flowers 165.00
Compass, pocket watch shape 20.00
Cornucopia, china, white, pink roses, gold trim 35.00
Creamer and Sugar, 3-3/4" h, hand-painted flowers, mkd "Hand Painted Prudence 1954" 18.50
Crumb Tray, metal, emb New York scenes...10.00
Cup and Saucer
Checkered borders, black and white...6.00
Floral dec, blue 12.50
Demitasse Cup and Saucer, white, yellow and red flowers 10.00
Dinnerware Set, eight 6-1/2" d bread plates, twelve 10" d dinner plates, six 7-3/4" d salad plates, eight 5-1/2" d fruit bowls, three cups, eleven saucers, 8" d covered bowl, gravy boat with underplate, two platters, open sugar, all mkd "Made in Japan Royal Embassy China, Wheeling, Made in Occupied Japan" 525.00
Doll, celluloid, baby wearing snowsuit, jointed...40.00
Doll House Furnishings, china
Couch, white, pink roses, 3" l 15.00
Lamp, white base, green shade, gold trim..10.00
Figure
1-1/4" x 5", farm girl with scarf, egg basket beside her, red mark........15.00
2-1/2" h, 3-1/4" w, three puppies in a basket, red mark.........................10.00
3" h, Colonial lady, red stamped mark...12.00
3" h, seated gentleman playing grand piano, two pcs..............................15.00
3-3/4" h, metal, cowboy on rearing horse...15.00
4-1/4" h, girl with milk pails 17.50
4-1/2" h, Hummel-type, Best Pal, American Children series, red mark.. 160.00

Figure, three puppies in basket, tan, gray, and brown, 2-7/8" w, 2-1/2" h, $12.

4-3/4" h, ballerina, bisque 35.00
5" h, jumping horses 12.00
5-1/2" h, lady seated in chair, reading sheet music 15.00
6" h, lady with netted skirt, mkd "Len-wille" and "Occupied Japan" 30.00
6" h, 2" w, man 25.00
6-1/2" h, French couple.............. 35.00
7" x 4-1/2", couple 35.00
8" h, woman, porcelain, lavender and yellow dress................................ 20.00
8" h, 3-1/2" w, man holding flower 40.00
8-1/2" h, lady, china, hp............. 145.00
9" h, lady sitting on bench, colonial garb 135.00
9-1/2" h, lady playing accordion, colonial garb.................................... 125.00
Flower Frog, bisque, girl with bird on shoulder, pastel highlights, gold trim 48.00
Harmonica, Butterfly, orig box 17.50
Head Vase, Oriental girl, china 18.00
Honey Jar, bee hive, bee finial......... 25.00
Incense Burner, woman 20.00
Lantern, 4-1/2" h, owl motif.............. 35.00
Match Holder, hanging type
2-3/4" h, Hummel-type Goose Girl... 15.00
4" h, Colonial lady, green and white background 12.00
Mat, hooked, 4-1/4" d, cream center, brown, teal, and green border with three daisy-like flowers, orig label 20.00
Miniature Tea Set, china, floral dec.. 25.00
Mug, china
Boy Handle................................ 14.00
Indian Chief 35.00
MacArthur.................................. 55.00
Napkins, damask, orig paper labels, price for set of six........................ 45.00
Necklace, pearls, double strand, orig paper label 12.00
Nodder, celluloid, figural, elephant, white body, green and gold trim, 3-1/2" l, 2-1/2" h...................................... 25.00
Noise Maker, horn, gold.................. 25.00
Perfume Bottle, glass, blue, 4" h...... 15.00
Piano Baby, hp 65.00

Pincushion, metal, grand piano shape, red velvet cushion 15.00

Planter, figural
  Baby booties, blue trim 9.00
  Cat, sitting up.............................. 10.00
  Dog, with basket........................... 20.00
  Donkey Pulling Cart...................... 10.00
  Facing boy and girl, each standing next to shell planter, bisque, sgd "Palauax," price for pair 125.00
  Rabbit.. 15.00
  Regal Carriage 12.50
  Wheelbarrow, floral dec, red mark, 2-1/2" h, 3-1/2" l.............................. 5.00

Plate
  Cabin Scene, chickens in yard ... 18.00
  Cherries, lacy edge 25.00
  Wooded scene by water's edge, 8-1/8" d 7.50

Platter, Courley pattern, heavy gold trim 30.00

Powder Jar, cov, Wedgwood style, blue and white, 3" d 15.00

Salt and Pepper Shakers, pr
  Arab Boys 17.50
  Coolies, orig box........................... 25.00
  Hat, one brown, one black 15.00
  Mammy and Chef 185.00
  Pigs, large ears............................ 15.00

Shelf Sitter, Little Boy Blue 15.00

Silent Butler, metal 15.00

Stein, man and woman with dog, 8-1/2" h 40.00

Tape Measure, pig, stamped "Occupied Japan"... 45.00

Teapot, 6-3/4" h, individual size, chocolate brown mirror glaze............... 12.00

Tea Set, Cottage, 6-3/4" w x 4-3/4" h cov teapot, 4-1/2" w x 2-1/2" h creamer, 5-1/4" w x 4" h cov sugar, each pc mkd "Made in Occupied Japan" 125.00

Toby, 3" h, 2" w, cobalt blue jacket, yellow knee britches, black tricorn hat, green handle, mkd "Hand Painted, Occupied Japan" 175.00

Toothpick holder, puppy in barrel 6.00

Toy
  Baby Pontiac, litho tin windup, car, orig box 65.00
  Boy on Sled, windup, litho tin, MIB.. 150.00
  Camel, walker, celluloid, MIB 120.00
  Cherry Cook, windup 90.00
  Dancing Couple, celluloid, MIB.. 95.00
  Hopping Dog, windup................. 22.50
  Minstrel Monkey, celluloid, MIB.. 175.00
  Monkey, windup, plays banjo, orig box 75.00
  Trick Seal, windup 880.00

Tray, rect, papier mâché, black ground, gold floral dec................................. 8.00

Vase
  3" h, white ground, painted flowers... 7.50
  5-1/4" h, Hummel type boy reading book 25.00

Wall Plaque, 5" w, 6-1/2" h, unglazed, pastel scene of man holding musical string instrument, woman dancing 135.00

Ocean Liner Collectibles

Collecting Hints: Don't concentrate only on ships of American registry, although many collectors try to gather material from only one liner or ship line. Objects associated with ships involved in disasters, such as the *Titanic*, often command higher prices.

History: Transoceanic travel falls into two distinct periods—the era of the great Clipper ships and the era of the diesel-powered ocean liners. The latter craft reached their golden age between 1900 and 1940.

An ocean liner is a city unto itself. Most have their own printing rooms to produce a wealth of daily memorabilia. Companies, such as Cunard and Holland-America, encourage passengers to acquire souvenirs with the company logo and ship's name. Word-of-mouth is a principal form of advertising.

Certain ships acquired a unique mystic. The *Queen Elizabeth, Queen Mary,* and *United States* became symbols of elegance and style. Today the cruise ship dominates the world of the ocean liner.

References: John Adams, *Ocean Steamers,* New Cavendish Books, 1992 Karl D. Spence, *How to Identify and Price Ocean Liner Collectibles,* published by author, 1991; James Steele, *Queen Mary,* Phaidon, 1995.

Collectors' Clubs: Oceanic Navigation Research Society, Inc., P.O. Box 8005, Studio City, CA 91608; Steamship Historical Society of America, Inc., 300 Ray Dr., Ste. 4, Providence, RI 02906; Titanic Historical Society, P.O. Box 51053, Indian Orchard, MA 01151.

Periodical: *Voyage,* P.O. Box 7007, Freehold, NJ 07728.

Museums: Mystic Seaport, Mystic, CT; South Street Seaport Museum, New York, NY; University of Baltimore, Steamship Historical Soc Collection, Baltimore, MD.

Ashtray, SS Argentina, Moore-McCormick Lines, brass, marked "Made in Switzerland," 5-1/2" d, $38.

Advertisement, framed
  Andrea Doria, 1952 adv for French market to sail on maiden voyage to USA, 8" x 11", acid free mat, 17" x 21" custom frame 175.00
  Normandie and *Ile de France*, Lafayette, Paris, and Champlain, NY Times May 31, 1936 color adv describing arrival of ships, 16" x 21" 250.00

Ashtray
  5" d, *Normandie*, porcelain, transatlantic map view, crackle finish 275.00
  6-1/2" d, 3" h, Le Chiminee Qui Fume, figural, smoke goes up funnel shape, French, 1950s..................... 265.00

Baggage Tag, French Line, first class, unused... 7.50

Belt Buckle, *RMS Queen Elizabeth II*, Cunard Line, chrome plated solid brass, black outline of ship, name in red... 15.00

Birthday Candle Holder Set, *SS Pleasure Cruise*, 5" l boat, three 2" l boats, hand carved, hand dec, each mkd "Japan," c1950... 5.00

Booklet
  Independence, American Export Lines, 1966 Gala Springtime Cruise, itinerary and deck plan inserts ... 24.00
  White Star Line, sailing list, 1933... 40.00

Bottle Opener, *RS Queen Mary*, ship floats in handle 30.00

Brochure
  Cunard and Anchor-Donaldson Line, Canadian Service. The Historic St Lawrence River Route to Europe, late 1920s 7.50
  Cunard Line, Getting There is Half the Fun, 16 pgs, 1952 .... 6.00
  Empress of Japan, Transatlantic sailings, 1930-31............................... 10.00
  Italian Line, Six Cruises to the Mediterranean and Egypt, 1934 .... 12.00

Change Tray, American Line Ship . 100.00

Cigarette Lighter, *RMS Queen Mary*... 32.00

Coffee Cup, *SS United States*.......... 32.00

Compact, *Empress of Canada*, Canadian Pacific Line, Stratton, line flag logo, ship's name in enameled front medallion... 40.00

Cruise Book, *Scythia*, 1929 ....40.00
Deck Card, Concordia Lines,
  Norway...18.00
Deck Plan
  MV Westerdamn 1950,
  multicolored 15.00
  RMSP Avon, The Royal Mail Steam
  Packet, December 1909 ....32.00
  RMS Samaria, Cunard Line, Plan of
  Tourist Accommodation 15.00
  SS Hamburg, 1930, fold out........35.00
Dish, *RMS Queen Mary*, Cunard Line,
  ceramic, 5" l, oval, color portrait, gold
  edge, Staffordshire 37.50
Display, Mediterranean *Americhe*, 1927,
  easel back, artwork by
  Riccobaldi...................................165.00
Excursion Announcement, SS
  Cuba 20.00
Goblet, *RMS Queen Elizabeth II*, Cunard
  Line, souvenir, etched image and
  name, manufactured by Stuart Crystal,
  #1305..225.00
Illustration, framed
  Le Paquebot Normandie Le Harve,
  engineering specs given in French,
  1936, 11-1/2" x 24" 250.00
  Nord-Lloyd Bremen, at sea, 1932,
  5-1/2" x 7-1/2" image, acid free mat,
  orig tourist class stateroom sticker on
  reverse, dated 12/9/32 ....125.00
  R.M.S. Queen Elizabeth, stern view,
  12" x 15-1/2" image with slight wrinkling to upper portion, 1940s vintage
  18-1/2" x 22-1/2" frame 150.00
  R.M.S. Queen Mary, under full steam
  at sea, 20" x 30" image size, acid free
  mat, slight wrinkling, slight foxing in
  margins 125.00
Key Chain, *Carnival*, Lucite, ship
  photo...4.00
Landing Arrangements Card, *RMS Caro-
  nia*, July 28, 1950...........................5.00
Letter Opener, *HMS Liverpool*, silver,
  enamel dec, 1921..........................75.00
Medal, *Normandie CGT*, bronze, given to
  passengers on maiden voyage, Le
  Harve to New York, June, 1935,
  designed by Jean Vernon,
  2-1/2" d...300.00
Menu
  Grace Line, *SS Santa Rose*, dinner,
  June 18, 1964.................................5.00
  Ile de France, July 12, 1938,
  dinner..5.00
  RMS Caronia, breakfast, Aug. 2, 1950,
  1 page card......................................6.00
  SS Leonardo Da Vinci, January,
  1973...6.00
  SS Lurline, Matson Lines, Commo-
  dore's Dinner, March 3, 1959, 12" x
  9"..20.50
  SS Manhattan, United States Lines, 6"
  x 10", 4 pgs, 1933, dinner, cream colored cover with Arch of Triumph, deck-
  led edges 7.50
Newspaper
  RMS Caronia, Ocean Times, Aug. 1,
  1950, 4 pgs...................................10.00
  RMS Queen Mary, May 10, 1950, 12
  pgs 15.00

Note Paper
  Cunard *White Star*, blue.................5.00
  M/S Osloofjord, two color views of
  ship...6.00
  RMS Queen Mary, beige 6.00
Passenger List
  RMS Aquitania, full color illus of
  ship...50.00
  SS Leviathan, 1924......................15.00
  SS Olympia, The Black Star Line,
  c1920, 5" x 8", 2 pgs 660.00
  St Louis, American Line, eastbound
  trip, Feb. 10, 1906.......................35.00
Passport Cover, Red Star Line, fabric,
  ship illus.......................................27.50
Pencil, mechanical, Cunard liner *Mauret-
  ania*, black and white, 5" l, "Right
  Point," gold metal accent tip, metal
  clip with black and white illus of pas-
  senger ship, name in black and red
  letters, c1930 ....24.00
Photograph, *Normandie*, sepia, engineer-
  ing specifications in French, 9-1/4" x
  18-1/2" custom frame................ 300.00
Pinback Button
  Carnival Cruises............................3.00
  Lusitana, 1-1/4" d, multicolored...50.00
  Mauertana, 1-1/4" d, multicolored,
  early 1900s....................................35.00
  RMS Queen Elizabeth I, Cunard Line,
  1-3/4", photo, "World's Largest Liner"
  at bottom 8.00
Playing Cards
  Alaska Steamship 15.00
  Eastern Steamship Corp.,
  c1950 ....15.00
  Holland American Line, double
  deck...25.00
  SS Badger, double deck 20.00
  SS Spartan, double deck 20.00
  Swedish American Lines, orig slip
  case...18.00
Pocket Mirror, *Queen Mary*, sepia photo,
  New York harbor scene, c1930...75.00
Post Card
  Andania, Cunard Line...................6.00
  Aurania, Cunard Line....................6.00
  RMS Olympia, unused.................75.00
Poster, Grace Line, Caribbean, 1949 C
  Evers, illus of tourists, ship, cars, and
  boats, 23" x 30" 200.00
Print
  Moor-McCormack Lines 85.00
  Titanic, 15 x 22-1/2", black and white,
  text of sinking, published by Tichnor
  Bro, Boston...................................60.00
Program of Events
  Cunard, *RMS Caronia*, Aug. 1,
  1950...6.00
  Cunard, *RMS Queen Mary*, May 12,
  1950...6.00
Race Card, Cunard White Star
  RMS Caronia..................................7.00
  RMS Queen Mary, some ink
  marks..7.00
Razor Towel, Cunard White Star,
  paper..5.00
Souvenir Spoon
  Cunard *White Star*, demitasse, silver
  plated 20.00
  Transylvania Anchor Line, silver
  plated, twisted handle, blue enameled
  ring, flag, and crest......................75.00

Stationery
  RMS Queen Mary, Cunard Line, note
  paper, matching envelope, color portrait, line, and ship name, 5" x
  7"..10.00
  Royal Mail Steamer, two sheets of
  paper, matching envelope..........20.00
  Sylvania, Cunard Line, beige, color
  portrait, line, and ship name, 5-1/4" x
  6-3/4"...8.00
Steamer Directory, Clyde-Mallory Lines,
  c1920...12.00
Steamship Card
  3-1/4" x 5-3/4", *City of Richmond*, published by Inman Line/Royal Mail
  Steamers, full-color engraving of stem
  and sail ship crossing choppy waters,
  back with list of other Inman steamers,
  also ink stamped by rubber stamp
  dealer from Machinery Hill, Centennial
  International Exposition, 1876 .... 35.00
  3-1/2" x 6", *SS Egypt*, published for
  National Line Steamships by Hatch
  Lithograhy Co., New York City, full
  color engraving of steam and sail ship
  crossing chopping waters under full
  color design of U.S. and British flags,
  extensive transportation description to
  European ports on back, c1884. 35.00
Tea Set, Cunard steamship, Art Deco
  cube shape, cov teapot, two salts, two
  sugars, creamer, sherbet, two teacups, cereal bowl, two salad plates,
  luncheon plate, three saucers, two
  demitasse saucers 800.00
Ticket Folio, Cunard Line, c1928..... 50.00
Tie Clasp, Cunard Line *RMS Queen Mary*,
  gold tone, red, white, and blue enam-
  eled ship 18.00
Timetable, Monticello Steamship Co., "On
  the Bay of San Francisco," 1907 65.00
Tin, *US Bremen* at sea on front panel,
  1930s 50.00

Olympics
Collectibles

Collecting Hints: Collectors of Olympic materials should remember that
the Olympic Games have been a
multi-language event. Collectors may
not wish to limit their collections to
English-only examples. The other
important fact to remember is that the
more recent the Olympiad, the
greater the number of items that have
survived. Items from the 1996 Olympics have not yet reached the secondary market, but things from 1988
are beginning to surface. More collectibles tend to enter the antiques
and collectibles marketplace during
the years the games are scheduled,
creating more interest in this fast-
growing field.

History: Organized amateur sports
games originated in ancient Greece.

The games were held every four years beginning about 776 B.C. At first, running events were the only type held, but many different events have been added over the years. The Olympics as we know them were revived in Athens about 1896. After that date, the games were held in a different city around the world every four years. The number of participants, competing nations, and events have increased steadily.

Women were first allowed to participate in the games in 1912. The winter games began in 1924 and were held on a four-year schedule until 1992 when they were rescheduled so that they would alternate at a two-year interval with the more traditional summer games.

References: Michael McKeever, *Collecting Sports Memorabilia*, Alliance Publishing, 1966.

Periodicals: *Olympic Collectors Newsletter*, P.O. Box 41630, Tucson, AZ 85717; *Sports Collectors Digest*, 700 E. State St., Iola, WI 54990.

Collectors' Clubs: Olympic Pin Collector's Club, 1386 Fifth St., Schenectady, NY 12303.

Badge
  1969 Soviet Olympic Trials Judge, silvered metal hanger bar, unmarked red fabric ribbon, suspending smaller silvered metal bar 20.00
  1980 Winter Olympics, 2-1/2" d, celluloid, color image of mascot raccoon as hockey player, white ground, black letters 20.00
  1988 Calgary Olympics, ABC-TV, gold luster finish metal, star shape, white porcelain enamel disk, five color accents 65.00
Bank, 1988, rounded 6-1/2" x 7" x 2" hard plastic replica of Olympic main stadium, Seoul, Korea 25.00
Barbie, Mattel
  Barbie as Olympic gymnast, 1995, NRFB 20.00
  Barbie and Ken as African-American Olympic skaters, #18727, released 1998 .... 25.00
Beer Can, 1996 Summer Olympic Set, Budweiser, sports include biking, baseball, soccer, boxing, and basketball, Olympic facts and history, cans carefully opened, price for five-can set 20.00
Beer Lighter, Scripto Vu Olympic 80.00
Book, *Sarajevo 1984 Winter Olympics* 12.00
Bowl, Campbell Kids, 1984 Sarajevo 12.00

Cabbage Patch Doll, 1996 Olympic set, tennis player with black hair and green eyes, four smaller female athletes, price for set of five in orig box 30.00
Calendar, 1992, Coca-Cola 5.00
Cigarette Lighter, 1976, Montreal 12.00
Cookie Jar, cov, Olympic Tunes, Warner Brothers, 14" h, MIB 100.00
Doll, 1980 Winter Olympics raccoon mascot, Chiquita, 14" h, stuffed cloth, gray, black, and white face, blue body, orange gloves, skating boots, separate white vinyl racing bib pullover vest, orig stitched tag with licensing authorization, Chase Bag Co. 40.00
Fan, Tenth Olympic Games/1932/Los Angeles, folding paper type, balsa sticks, chapel building illus, Olympic symbol, Japan 40.00
Gasoline Truck, Texaco, 1996 Olympics dec, MIB 30.00
Glass, 5-1/2" h, 1932 Olympics, clear, frosted white picture 50.00
Hand Puppet, 1980 Moscow, Misha, R. Dakin Co., card with scenes and Olympic rings, unopened 12.00
Keychain, 1984, Los Angeles 6.50
License Plate Holder, 1932, aluminum, two athletes holding the world, "Los Angeles" in raised letters 150.00
Magazine, Sports Illustrated, Sept. 5, 1960, Rome Olympics Ceremonies 7.50
Map, 1960, Rome Olympics, 6" x 10" folder opens to 10" x 35", eight color maps on both sides, Automobile Club of Italy sponsor 15.00
Pamphlet, 1936 Berlin 80.00
Paperweight, 1992, Coca-Cola McDonald's 12.00
Pennant, 1968 Mexico, felt 24.00
Pin
  1928, Olympic Fund, red, and white enameled brass, miniature shield, sold for 50¢ to help defray expenses of American team, orig card 25.00
  1964, Innsbruck Winter Olympics, Austrian made, black, white, and red accent enamels, gold finish 65.00
  1980, Moscow Olympics, figural mascot bear as soccer player, blue, white, and brown enamels, gold luster .. 20.00
  1980, Moscow Olympics, official symbol flanked by deep red porcelain enamel under Russian inscription, gold luster 15.00
  1984, Calgary Winter Olympics, official symbols in five colors, white ground, double needle post and clutch fasteners 8.00
  1984, Los Angeles Olympics, Fuji, domed acrylic on metal, symbolic cartoon U.S. eagle holding Olympic torch, needle post and clutch fastener . 10.00
  1988, Seoul Summer Olympics, domed acrylic, three enamel colors, gold luster, needle post and clutch fastener 5.00
  1992, Albertville Winter Olympics, CBS, domed acrylic, gold luster, white enamel, tiny Olympic rings in five colors 5.00

1996, Atlanta Olympics pre-event promotion pin, cartoon baseball player, four colors, gold above bar inscription "Atlanta 1996/1000 Days/October 23, 1993" 10.00
  1996, Balfour 21.00
Pinback Button
  1976, Edwin Moses, USA Gold Medalist, white celluloid, maroon lettering, photo, inscription lists alma mater and credits, bar pin fastner 20.00
  1980, VII Olympic Winter Games Messenger, red lettering, white ground 40.00
Pin Display, 1988 Olympics, 1-3/4" x 6" x 8" cover box, wooden display frame, high gloss finish, very dark mahogany enamel, frame holds recessed glass over gold luster metal title plate identifying Jeep as official sponsor of U.S. Olympic team, five different jeep pins comprising limited edition set 30.00
Plate, 7" d, 1968, gold leaf, Mexico and torch dec 60.00
Postcard
  1912 Stockholm Olympics, black and white photo 30.00
  1936, view of Berlin Olympics, Olympic cancel 15.50
  1988, Korea, Coca-Cola, set #1 ... 7.50
Program, 1996 Centennial Olympic Games, July 19-August 4, 1996, 10-1/2" l, 9" w 32.00
Smurf, Olympic outfit 40.00
Souvenir Dish, 7-1/4" d, Munich 72, porcelain, mkd "Made in Denmark, #8000/9472, First Issue" 40.00
Stadium Cushion, 11" x 13-1/2", 1956 Summer Olympics, red vinyl, yellow, white, and blue Olympics logo ... 48.00
Statue, 5" h, bronzed white metal with patina, 1900-20 athlete 75.00
Stick Pin
  1940, sterling-like silvered metal, Helsinki, Finland, torch flame under Olympics rings symbol, above 1940 date 80.00
  1964, silvered metal, Tokyo, rings above Olympic symbol 35.00
  1972, gold luster, Sapporo, winter, red, white, and blue enamels 30.00
  1978, gold luster, Innsbruck, winter, red and blue enamels, blue ground 25.00
  1980, Moscow Olympics, miniature Gold Olympics rings under miniature image of Soviet flag, dark red porcelain enamel accents 18.00
  1984, Swedish Team, blue enamel on brass, three crowns above Olympic rings 15.00
Token, 1984 Olympiad, Los Angeles, transit fare set, designed by N. Harris, orig 7" x 11" case 30.00
Toy, 1992 Olympic Bobsled Run, wooden replica, 1-1/2" h x 2" w x 8-1/2" l, wire handgrip rail and bumper bar, two front skis swivel left and right, driver unit inscribed "U.S.A.," thumb tack steering wheel, Olympic symbols on riding surface 200.00

Tray, 1976 Olympics, Montreal, litho
metal, Coca-Cola adv 40.00
Venue Guide, staff, 1996 .... 12.00

Owl Collectibles

Collecting Hints: If you collect the
"creature of the night" or the "wise old
owl," any page of this book might
conceivably contain a related object
since the owl theme can be found in
hundreds of collectible categories,
including advertising trade cards,
books, buttons, and postcards, to
name a few.

Don't confine yourself just to old or
antique owls. Owl figurines, owl
themes on limited edition collectors'
plates, and hand-crafted items from
modern artisans are plentiful. There
are many examples available in every
price range.

History: Owls have existed on earth
for more than 60 million years. They
have been used as a decorative motif
since before Christ. An owl and Ath-
ena appeared on an ancient Greek
coin.

Every culture has superstitions
surrounding the owl. Some believe
the owl represented good luck, others viewed it as an evil omen. The owl
has remained a popular symbol in
Halloween material.

Of course, the owl's wisdom is
often attached to scholarly pursuits.
Expanding this theme, the National
Park Service uses Woodsey to "Give
A Hoot, Don't Pollute."

Reproduction Alert: Reproduction
fruit crate labels with owl motifs are
common.

Westmoreland Glass molds have
been sold to several different manufacturers. The owl sitting on two
books is being reissued with the original "W" still on top of the books. The
three-owl plate mold also was sold.
Imperial Glass owl molds have also
found new owners.

Advertising Trade Card, Colburn's Phila-
delphia Mustard, diecut 10.00
Ashtray, ceramic, three cut owls,
figural 30.00
Bank, tin, owl illus on each side 50.00
Blotter, "Whoo? Oswald, I told you we
couldn't get away with that bone!," two
puppies under a tree, owl sitting on
branch, Harry N. Johnson, Real Estate
& Insurance, Highlands, NJ 10.00
Book
An Owl Came To Stay, Clair Rome,
Crown Pub., NY, 1980 .... 7.50
Owls in the Family, Farley Mowat, Lit-
tle, Brown & Co., 1961.................... 1.00

**Cheese dish, dome cover and tray,
Owl and Pussy Cat pattern, $500.
Photo courtesy of Joy Luke Fine Art
Brokers and Auctioneers.**

Bookends, pr
Brass, Frankart.......................... 135.00
Bronze, head, sgd "M Carr" 120.00
Book Rack, expanding 55.00
Box, cov, Limoges, France, owl on cover,
small rocks painted on inside... 175.00
Calendar Plate, 1912, owl on open book,
Berlin, NE 25.00
Calling Card Tray, 8-1/2" x 7", quadruple
plate, emb music staff and "Should
Owl's Acquaintance Be Forgot," two
owls sitting on back of tray 85.00
Candy Container, owl on branch 50.00
Clock, 6-1/2" h, wood, hand
carved 100.00
Coal Hod, brass, figural 300.00
Desk Set, metal, letter holder, book rack,
note spike, letter opener, envelope
holder, inkwell, blotter, four blotter corners, sgd "CV" 650.00
Figure
3" h, pottery, Winnie the Pooh owl,
Beswick Walt Disney series, 1968-
1990.. 125.00
4" h, porcelain, Karl Ens Factory .80.00
4-1/2" h, porcelain, Cybis 98.00
7-1/2" h, 6" w, porcelain, pair of naturalistic colored owls perched upon
books.. 75.00
Inkwell, figural, Noritake................. 125.00
Lamp, candle, 5-1/4", snow white china,
owl shaped shade, stump shaped
base, fitted candleholder, mkd "R S
Germany" 225.00
Letter Opener, brass 25.00
Limited Edition Plate, Goebel, Wildlife
Series, barn owl, 1976................... 35.00
Mask, papier-mâché, c1915............. 90.00
Match Holder
2-1/2" h, dark green, Wetzel Glass
Co. 8.00
8" h, 3" w, metal, hanging type 18.00
Medal
Leeds International Exhibition, 1890,
2-1/4", metal, white bust of Queen Vic-
toria on one side 25.00
Natural History Society of Montreal,
1-3/4", bronze, cast, owl with branch in
beak... 20.00
Mustard Jar, cov, 5" h, milk glass, screw
top, glass insert, Atterbury 165.00
Napkin Ring, standing owl, silver
plated 150.00
Owl Drug Co.
Bottle, 3-1/2" h, cork top, clear, Oil of
Sweet Almond label, 1 oz.............. 5.00

Shot Glass, one wing 17.50
Soda Bottle, 9-1/2" h, blob top, teal
green, two wings, San
Francisco 50.00
Paperweight, cast iron, owl family, two
babies, third baby in papa's
arms.. 45.00
Pin
2" w, 2" h, molded plastic, ivory color,
airbrushed and painted details .. 75.00
1-1/2" w, 2-1/2" h, cabochon belly and
eyes, green rhinestone wings, Alice
Caviness.................................... 95.00
Pitcher
8" h, 6" d top, pressed glass, owl
shape.. 110.00
9-1/2" h, cov, china, semi-vitreous,
Edwin M Knowles China Co. 37.50
Plate, milk glass
6" d, three owl heads, fluted open work
edge, gold paint......................... 65.00
7-1/2" d, owl lovers, 7-1/2" d 40.00
Salt and Pepper Shakers, pr, 3-1/4"h,
china, brown and white, mortarboard
hats, scholarly expression, horn rim
glasses 10.00
Sculpture, 4-3/4" x 3-3/4" x 12-1/4" h,
carved bark, mounted on enameled
wood base, artist sgd, Maiku Collection certificate of authenticity 75.00
Sheet Music
Beautiful Ohio, owl on cover 3.50
The Pansy and the Owl................. 4.50
Shot Glasses, head removes to show 4
shot glasses, stamped "Viking, Ger-
many," each shot glass stamped "Ger-
many," some use marks.............. 42.00
String Holder, 5-3/4" h, ceramic, mkd
"Made in England, Babbacombe Pot-
tery"... 75.00
Tape Measure, brass, glass eyes, mkd
"Germany".................................. 40.00
Thermometer, 6" h, plaster body...... 75.00
Tin, Owl Brand Shoe Polish 37.50
Toothbrush Holder, figural, Syroco .. 12.50
Valentine, 15" l, girl and boy riding bal-
loon, owl sitting on moon above,
"Nobody's looking but the owl and the
moon!" 8.00
Vase, 7" h, gold owls, white ground, Phoe-
nix Glass 175.00

**Tape measure, brass, glass eyes,
marked "Germany," 1-3/4" d, $40.**

P

Padlocks

Collecting Hints: There is a wide range of padlocks that can interest a collector, so many collectors specialize in just one category, such as railroad or logo. Collectors can also specialize in one manufacturer, or in miniatures. Just being old and scarce is not usually enough. They must have some special appeal, have an interesting design or have historical significance. The most competitive and expensive area is the embossed brass locks from the old defunct short line railroads and the very early locks from the larger railroads.

There is a new dimension in lock collecting—auctions on the Internet. You can see a great variety of locks, but watch out for pitfalls. The first is that you tend to bid more than you had intended. Many of the locks are sold at much more than they would sell for at a lock or railroad show. Another is the inadequate or misleading information on many of the locks offered. The sellers do not usually intend to mislead with their information; they just do not know enough about old locks to describe them properly. Sellers do not understand that a dent in an old lock is equivalent to a chip in a cut glass dish, and a lock that has been taken apart is equivalent to a Roseville teapot with a glued-on handle. Most collectors do not place much value on keys unless they are original. Do not let the Internet replace your presence at auctions, lock shows, antique shops, and flea markets. Just recently, a collector bought a lock, valued at $3,000, for $15 at a small-town auction. So locks are where you find them.

There are a number of words and phrases used in the Internet lock descriptions that must be completely disregarded. Some of them are "rare," "Civil War," "railroad," "old," "odd," "must have," "professional," "cool," "antique," "large," "huge," etc. Also, "Wells Fargo" and "Keenkutter" (see Reproduction and Fake Alert). Buyers must look at the photos to decide for themselves and not hesitate to e-mail sellers to eliminate any doubts about the condition, markings, size, etc.

A lock stamped with the name of a small company from the 1850s can be worth many times more than a similar lock made by a large manufacturer. There are always exceptions. For example, the Wrought Iron Lever locks, called "Smokies," do not have much value no matter how old or scarce. Locks in some categories can be several times more valuable than similar appearing locks in other categories. For example, locks in the Story category are worth several times more than similar locks in the Warded category.

Identifying many old padlocks is possible with either markings on the lock or illustrations from old catalogs, but for some padlocks, this is difficult or impossible. They are not marked, and the manufacturer evidently did not publish catalogs. Identical locks can be marked by different manufacturers as a result of one company acquiring another. Dating can also be a problem. Some of the manufacturers made the same locks for more than fifty years, and there are Yale models that were made for almost 100 years. A lock can be made the same year as the patent date, or the date can still be marked on the lock long after the patent expired. A definitive book on United States lock companies, their padlocks, and padlock construction has not been published.

Original keys can increase the value of locks, but other keys have little value to most collectors. Having a key made can cost more than the value of the lock, and locksmiths who are not familiar with the antique value of old locks can do irreparable damage. If you have repairs or a key made, make sure that the locksmith is an expert on old locks, and that you have complete agreement on the cost. Repairs, cracks, holes, internal damage, or appreciable dents drastically reduce the value of locks.

History: Padlocks of all shapes and sizes have been made in Europe and Asia since the 1600s; however, American collectors generally prefer American manufactured locks. In the 1830s, Elijah Rickard was making screw-key padlocks. He stamped some of them "B & O RR" for the Baltimore & Ohio Railroad. These were the first marked railroad locks. In the 1840s, safe lock manufacturers were adapting their lever tumbler designs to padlocks. Also in the 1840s, the first pin tumbler padlocks were made in the Yale Lock Shop. In the 1850s, a few companies were making lever tumbler padlocks simpler than the safe lock designs. Other companies started making low-quality padlocks based on cabinet and door lock designs. The United States Post Office was ordering locks with various postal markings, and Linus Yale, Junior, patented the pin tumbler lock. In 1860, Wilson Bohannan returned from the California gold fields, patented a simple, reliable brass lever padlock and started his manufacturing company. The brass lever and similar iron lever padlocks were subsequently manufactured in large quantities by many companies. Wilson Bohannan is still an independent company, and the pin-tumbler lock is the worldwide standard medium security lock.

Lock Companies: About 250 United States Lock manufacturers have been identified. Eight prolific companies were:

Adams & Westlake, 1857--, "Adlake" tradename started c1900, made railroad locks.

Eagle Lock Co., 1833-1976, a general line of padlocks from 1880, with padlock dates from 1867.

Mallory, Wheeler & Co., 1865-1910, partnership history started in 1834, predominant manufacturer of wrought iron lever (Smokies) padlocks.

Miller Lock Co. (D.K. Miller from 1870 to c1880) Miller Lock Co. to 1930, a general line of padlocks, and a pre-dominant manufacturer of railroad locks.

Slaymaker Lock Co. 1888-1985, dates include name changes, partnership changes, mergers. A general line of padlocks, and a predominate manufacturer of railroad switch locks.

Star Lock Works, 1836-1926, largest manufacturer of Scandinavian padlocks, also made many other types.

Yale & Towne Mfg. Co., 1884--, Yale Lock Mfg. Co. from 1868 to 1884, started c1840 by Linus Yale, SR as the "Yale Lock Shop," started producing padlocks c1875.

Wilson Bohannan, 1860--, made mostly brass lever padlocks to the early 1900s, then changed to the pin-tumbler type. Made many railroad and logo locks.

Padlock Types: Padlocks are categorized primarily according to tradition or use: Story, Railroad, etc. The secondary classification is according to the type of construction. For example, if a brass lever lock is marked with a railroad name, it is called a Railroad lock. Scandinavian locks have always been called "Scandinavians." Story locks became a common term in the 1970s; in the catalogs of the late 1800s, they were listed in various ways.

Railroad, Express and Logo locks are identified with the names of the companies that bought and used them. Story locks are a series of odd- and heart-shaped cast iron padlocks with decorative or figural embossments.

Governmental agencies and thousands of companies had locks custom made with their names to create Logo locks. Logo locks are not to be confused with locks that are embossed with the names of jobbers. This applies particularly to the six-lever push key locks. If "6-Lever" is included in the name, it is not a Logo lock. Since 1827, about 10,000 railroad companies have crisscrossed the United States. Most of these companies used at least two types of locks; some used dozens of types.

Reference: Franklin M. Arnall, *The Padlock Collector, Illustrations and Prices of 2,800 Padlocks of the Last 100 Years*, sixth edition, 1996, The Collector.

Collectors' Clubs: American Lock Collectors Assn., 8576 Barbara Dr., Mentor, OH, 44060; West Coast Lock Collectors, 1427 Lincoln Blvd., Santa Monica, CA 90401.

Museum: Lock Museum of America, P.O. Box 104, Terryville, CT 06786

Advisor: Franklin M. Arnall.

Reproduction and fake alert: A reproduction is new but made as a copy of an old item. A fake is not necessarily a copy of an old item. The "Wells Fargo" locks with the plaques fastened to the back, old locks with "Wells Fargo," "W F Co." or "W F Co. Ex" stamped on the lock, a newer one with W F CO EX embossed down the back, and the "KeenKutter" locks with the barrel-type keyholes are good examples of fakes.

The most common fakes now are the Asian locks with plaques fastened to the back saying that they are from various prisons, and one that claims to be a Winchester factory lock. The steel "Winchester" six-lever locks with the crude rivets and the small notches in the upper corners are reproductions. Beware of bargains, especially locks on the Internet when bids seem too low. Beware of

brass Story locks, locks from the Middle East and India, yellow brass switch locks, and switch lock keys. All Story locks are embossed cast iron, except the small "N H" and the small "Japanese Pattern" were made in both cast iron and brass; however, there are excellent cast-iron reproductions of the Skull & Crossbones lock. Some of the cast iron Story locks were brass plated and some were nickel plated.

Screw key, trick, iron lever, and brass lever padlocks are being imported from the Middle East. The crudely cast new switch lock keys are obvious. The high quality counterfeits are expertly stamped with various railroad initials on old blanks, tumbled to simulate wear, and aged with acid. They can be detected only by an expert.

Authentic Railroad, Express, and Logo locks will have only one user name. The size and shape will be like other locks that were in common use at the time, except for a few modified locks made for the U.S. government. All components of an old lock must have exactly the same color and finish. The front, back, or drop of an old lock can be expertly replaced with a reproduced part embossed with the name or initials of a railroad, express company, or other user.

Warning: The United States Forest Service and the United States Postal Service are repossessing their locks whenever they see them.

Lock Prices: The prices shown are for padlocks in original condition and without keys.

Favorite, six-lever, $25. Photo courtesy of Franklin Arnall.

Brass Lever

Brown's Patent, July 4, 1891,
  3 " h 30.00
Chubb Detector, 5" h 600.00
Dietz 373, 3" h 25.00

Dietz 213, fancy embossed,
  2-3/4" h 95.00
Good Luck, both sides, 2-3/4" h 40.00
Good Luck, one side, 2-3/4" h 35.00
Keenkutter, both sides, 3-3/4" h 75.00
New Champion 6 Lever 4.00
W. Bohannan, 3-1/8" h 15.00
Winchester, emb raised letters 175.00
Yale, Y & T, rect, keyhole in bottom, emb
  1-1/2 to 2" w 3.00
  3" w 65.00

Combination

4 brass lettered dials, 2 " w 60.00
J.B. Miller Keyless Lock Co. 5.00
Dean's Patent Combo 575.00
Miller Keyless Lock Co., Pat March 18,
  1902 .... 110.00
Steel case & brass dial, 2-1/2" h 4.00
W.A. Harrison, Inc. Insurance Lock,
  2-1/2" w 85.00

Commemorative

C Q D, Simmons Wireless, brass,
  2" h 125.00
P.P.I., 1915, steel 250.00
Sesquicentennial, 1776-1926, brass
  case 550.00

Express

Adams Express Co., Penna Div, Lever
  push key type, 2-1/4" dia 1,250.00
AM. EX. Co., emb in vertical panel down
  the back, brass lever type 600.00
AM RY EX, stamped on shackle and
  back, steel, iron lever type 50.00
U. S. Ex Co. Stamped on shackle, Brass
  lever type 250.00

Iron Lever (includes steel locks)

Dragons embossed, steel 15.00
Hatchet lock (shaped like a hatchet),
  steel with brass shackle 450.00
Pioneer, embossed ax, 3-1/4" h 35.00
Pyes Patent, Sept. 8, 1856, Oct. 16,
  1860 .... 30.00
Ten Star, 10 stars embossed,
  3-3/4" h 65.00
Trick lock – push square plate over to
  open keyhole, 4" h 190.00
Wilson Bohannan, 3-1/4" h 15.00
York, embossed, steel 10.00

Lever Push Key

Baffler 6 Lever, 2-3/4 " h 5.00
Champion 6-Lever, 2-1/4" dia 5.00
Crank, S B Co., emb, 2-7/8" h 35.00
Empire 6-Lever, emb, 2-1/4" dia 15.00
Harvard 6-Lever, emb, 2-1/4" dia..... 40.00
Miller, Six Secure Levers, iron case, brass
  panels, 3-7/8" h 15.00
TEN STAR 6 lever, emb,
  2-1/4" dia 170.00
Townley 6-Lever, emb, 2-1/4" dia... 205.00

Keen Kutter, E. C. Simmons, brass lever tumbler, $75. Photo courtesy of Franklin Arnall.

Logo

A-B, MHH Co, pin tumbler push key
type 55.00
Bechtel, American 20.00
Cudahy, Yale, embossed 80.00
Empire, Yale, emb............................55.00
F.W.W. Co., Best..............................40.00
Gulf, embossed, Corbin 75.00
I.D.B.R., Corbin................................40.00
Iroquois Gas, W B............................35.00
L.B.U.S.D., Best...............................25.00
Ordinance Dept., crossed rifles, emb,
Yale..10.00
Shell, Best 15.00
S O Co., Best 20.00
U.S. Internal Revenue, lever push
key 220.00
U S N, Several manufacturers..........10.00
Western Union Tel Co., brass lever
type 30.00
Western Union Telegraph, lever push key
type 500.00

Pin Tumbler

Corbin, brass case
1-1/4" to 2" w, keyhole in bottom ...2.00
3" w, keyhole in bottom................50.00
3" w, keyhole in front 15.00
Corbin, steel case..............................5.00
Hurd, brass case, 3-1/8" h.................5.00
O V B, Our Very Best, H.S.B. Co.,
brass 150.00
S & CO, emb, intertwined, brass,
3" h..20.00
Segal, brass case, 4-1/4" h 30.00
Segal, keyhole in front, brass,
3-5/8" h..45.00
Simmons, S H Co, emb, brass
case 35.00
Yale
Brass case, emb both sides 2.00
Iron case, round brass panels......5.00
Nickel plated, with dust cover.....30.00

Railroad

General Purpose and Signal
CCC&StL RR, steel, iron lever
type 15.00

D & H RR, emb, lever push key
type..190.00
D L W RR, emb, brass lever
type...45.00
I C RR, emb, lever push key
type...90.00
Illinois Central Signal, emb, brass lever
type 20.00
N Y C, emb, pin tumbler push key
type...50.00
New Jersey Central, Corbin, pin tum-
bler type 30.00
P. R.R., S D, Keystone logo, push key
type...35.00
Santa Fe, Keenkutter emb on opposite
side 400.00
SO Pacific Co. CS 24, Roadway &
Bridge 30.00
Union Pacific, CS 21, Roadway &
Bridge 30.00
Wabash RR, Yale, emb, pin tumbler
type...50.00
Switch, Brass
B & M RR, Williams Page, stamped on
back...130.00
C & A RR, stamped on shackle ..60.00
CCC & StL Ry, emb in panel down
back...135.00
C M & St P RR, emb in panel down
back...150.00
L & NW RR, stamped on
shackle..35.00
L S & M S RR, emb in panel down
back...250.00
P RR, emb across back, A & W or
Fraim, emb across back...........140.00
SO PAC Co., emb on panel & on
drop...80.00
U S Y of O, stamped on back 15.00
Union Pacific, emb in panel down
back...70.00
V RR , emb in panel down
back...300.00
W U RR, Loeffelholz, stamped on
back...120.00
Switch, Steel
AT & SF Ry, other common
railroads...5.00
FRISCO emb on brass drop........25.00
I C RR, Adlake...............................5.00

Scandinavian

Brass, 2-1/2" h.................................30.00
Corbin, emb, brass, 2-1/2" h..........125.00
Iron, 2-1/2" h....................................20.00
Iron, 5" h..150.00
J.H.W. Climax, iron, 3-1/2" h 40.00
R & E, No. 5, iron, 2-1/2" h 35.00
Star emb on bottom, iron
1-1/2" h 15.00
3-1/2" h 40.00
4-1/2" h 130.00

Six Lever & Eight Lever
Blue Chief Eight Lever, steel.............25.00
Eagle Six Lever, steel.........................5.00
John Pritzlaff Six Lever, steel 15.00
Quality Six Lever, Simmons, steel 5.00
Samson Eight Lever, brass...............20.00
Samson Eight Lever, steel 10.00
Super Lever, steel 5.00

Story, emb cast iron

Floral & Scroll, shield shape
2-3/8" h..80.00
3-3/8" h......................................175.00
4" h 250.00
Mail Pouch emb, shaped like a mail
pouch, Russell & Irwin Mfg.
Co. 200.00
Skull & Crossbones emb, 3-1/4" h . 200.00
"The Evil Eye," an eye and eyebrow emb,
with floral, 3-1/4" h 1,150.00

Warded

Floral & scroll, emb, rect. case, cast iron,
2-1/2" h..20.00
Hawk, a hawk emb, brass, 2-5/8" h. 40.00
Hibbard, emb, brass case, 2-5/8" h 15.00
Horsehead emb on front, floral on back,
brass, 2-1/8" h 45.00
Magic, emb, brass case, 2-3/4" h......5.00
1904, emb, brass case, 2-1/8" h........5.00
S. E. Co., Patd Mar 31, 1887, iron,
3-3/4" h..95.00
Shapleigh, brass case, 2" h 15.00
Simmons, iron case, brass panels .. 20.00
U.S., emb, brass, 2" h 15.00
Van Camp, emb, brass case,
2-3/4" h 20.00
W emb in diamond, brass case,
2-1/2" h 10.00
Winchester, both sides, brass case,
2-1/8" h 125.00

Wrought Iron Lever (Smokies, Shield),
with brass drops

D.M. & Co., 4-1/2" h.........................30.00
Floral emb on drop, 3-5/8" h 25.00
Head of dog emb on drop, 4-1/2" h 50.00
Improved tumbler lock, 5-3/4" h.......60.00
M, W & Co, 3-1/2" h 15.00
R & E Co, 3-1/8" h.............................20.00
S & Co, intertwined, 3-5/8" h............15.00

Paper Dolls

Collecting Hints: Most paper dolls that are collected are in uncut books, on intact sheets, or in boxed sets. Cut sets are priced at 50 percent of an uncut set, providing all dolls, clothing, and accessories are still present.

Many paper doll books have been reprinted. An identical reprint has just slightly less value than the original. If the dolls have been redrawn, the price is reduced significantly.

History: The origin of the paper doll can be traced back to the jumping jacks (pantins) of Europe. By the 19th century, boxed or die-cut sheets of paper dolls were available featuring famous dancers, opera stars, performers such as Jenny Lind, and many general subjects. Raphael Tuck began to produce ornate dolls in series form in the 1880s in England.

The advertising industry turned to paper dolls to sell products. Early magazines, such as *Ladies' Home Journal, Good Housekeeping,* and *McCall's,* used paper-doll inserts. Children's publications, like *Jack and Jill,* picked up the practice.

Cardboard-covered paper doll books first appeared and were mass-marketed in the 1920s. Lowe, Merrill, Saalfield, and Whitman were the leading publishers. The 1940s saw the advent of paper doll books featuring celebrities drawn from screen and radio, and later from television. A few comic characters, such as Brenda Starr, also made it to paper doll fame.

By the 1950s, paper-doll books were less popular and production decreased. Modern books are either politically or celebrity oriented.

References: Lagretta Metzger Bajorek, *America's Early Advertising Paper Dolls,* Schiffer Publishing, 1999; Lorraine Mieszala, *Collector's Guide to Barbie Doll Paper Dolls, Identification & Values,* Collector Books, 1997; Marci Van Audsdall, *Betsy McCall,* Hobby House Press, 2000; Mary Young, *Collector's Guide to Magazine Paper Dolls,* Collector Books, 1990; Mary Young, *Tomart's Price Guide to Lowe and Whitman Paper Dolls,* Tomart Publications, 1993.

Periodicals: *Celebrity Doll Journal,* 5 Court Pl, Puyallup, WA 98372; *Loretta's Place Paper Doll Newsletter,* 808 Lee Ave., Tifton, GA 31794; *Midwest Paper Dolls & Toys Quarterly,* P.O. Box 131, Galesburg, KS 66740; *Northern Lights Paperdoll News,* P.O. Box 871189, Wasilla, AK 99687; *Paper Doll Gazette,* Route #2, Box 52, Princeton, IN 47670; *Paper Doll News,* P.O. Box 807, Vivian, LA 71082; *Paperdoll Review,* P.O. Box 584, Princeton, IN 47670; *PD Pal,* 5341 Gawain #883, San Antonio, TX 78218.

Collectors' Clubs: Original Paper Doll Artist Guild, P.O. Box 176, Skandia, MI 49885; United Federation of Doll Clubs, 10920 N. Ambassador, Kansas City, MO 64153.

Museums: Children's Museum, Indianapolis, IN; Detroit Children's Museum, Detroit, MI; Kent State University Library, Kent, OH; Margaret Woodbury Strong Museum, Rochester, NY; Museum of the City of New York, New York, NY; Newark Museum, Newark, NJ.

American Family of Confederacy.....12.00
Ancient Egyptian Costumes.............12.00
Baby Sister and Baby Brother Dolls, Merrill, uncut book............................10.00
Baby Sparkle Plenty, Saalfield, 1948, uncut book............................60.00
Ballerina Barbie, Whitman, uncut.....12.00
Ballet, Nancie Swanberg...................8.00
Barbie, uncut book 15.00
Betsy McCall and Sandy McCall, 1958, uncut sheet 17.50

Ballet Dancers, Merrill Co., #3497, 1947, $22.

Children from Other Lands, Whitman, 1961, unused 20.00
Cinderella Steps Out, Lowe, 1948, uncut book............................20.00
Dionne Quintuplets, cut 75.00
Doris Day, Whitman, 1956, uncut book............................60.00
Drayton Paper Doll, uncut
    Alice, two outfits 12.00
    Anna, three outfits 10.00
    Baby and Baby Doll, three outfits 15.00
    Betty, two outfits 12.00
    Fido, five outfits 10.00
    Fred, two outfits 15.00
    Harriet, three outfits.....................15.00
    Jane, four outfits.........................15.00
    Kitty, six outfits 12.00
    Phyllis, four outfits 10.00
Dude Ranch, Saalfield, 11" x 14", unused 18.00
Family Affair, 1968, orig box 12.50
Girl Scouts, Brownies, c1950, MIB...40.00
Happy Bride, Whitman, 1967, uncut book............................20.00
Heidi and Peter, Saalfield, 1960s, 6 pgs, 8-1/4" x 11-3/4", uncut..................15.00
Indians, Artcraft series, Saalfield, 10-1/2" x 12-1/2", unused.............18.00
Janet Leigh, Lowe, album #2405, 1957, some pages neatly cut 20.00
Judy Holiday Paperdolls, Saalfield, #159110, 1954, 11" x 12", uncut..45.00
Laugh-In, unused.............................35.00
Lennon Sisters, Whitman, copyright 1958, 9" x 12", neatly cut....................28.00
Liberty Fair Dressing Doll, Miss Liberty cardboard doll, flags on wood stick, cut, c1900, 7" x 13" blue and white box...65.00

Little Lulu, boxed 25.00
Little Miss America, Saalfield, unused.......................................20.00
Little Women, 1981, uncut 12.00
Loretta Young Paper Dolls and Coloring Book..52.00
Majorette Paper Dolls, Saalfield, 1957, unused book 10.00
Malibu Francie, Whitman, uncut 12.00
Malibu Skipper, Whitman, 1973.......17.50
Mary Martin, Saalfield, #365, copyright 1944, 10-1/2" x 12-1/2", uncut.....48.00
Millie the Model..............................10.00
Nancy, Whitman, 1971, unused.......40.00
Nanny and the Professor, Saalfield, 1970, uncut book..................................15.00
Nursery Rhyme, Hallmark, uncut.....27.50
Nutcracker Ballet, Tom Tierney, full color, 1981, uncut..................................15.00
Pat and Pru, 1958..........................15.50
Patty Duke Paper Doll Book, punch-out type, 1964, partially used 20.00
Playhouse Dolls, Stephens Co., 1949, uncut book..................................20.00
Princess Diana 15.00
Raggedy Ann & Andy Paper Dolls Book, Saalfield, 1944, Johnny Gruelle Co., 4 pgs of clothes.............................50.00
Rosemary Clooney, Bonnie Book, 1958, uncut...70.00
Secret Garden 15.50
Shari Lewis, Saalfield, 1958, uncut book..20.00
Skipper, Whitman, boxed, uncut......12.00
Sonny and Sue, Lowe Co., copyright 1940, 10-1/4" x 13-1/2", uncut.....15.00
Southern Belles 14.50
Sports Time, Whitman, 1952, uncut book..20.00
Storybook Kiddle, Mattel, Whitman......................................15.75
Teen Time Dolls, Whitman, early 1950s, 7" x 10-1/2" box, neatly cut..............15.00
The Nutcracker Ballet, Cut and Assemble Toy Theater by Tom Tierney, 1981, Dover, unused 15.00
Tubsy, Whitman, 1968 ....35.00
Tuesday Weld, Saalfield, 1960, orig box, unused..60.00
Twins Around The World 7.50
Vivien Leigh, uncut..........................15.00
Walt Disney's Snow White, 1972......15.50
Wedding Party, Saalfield, 1951, unused book..20.00

Paperback Books

Collecting Hints: For collecting or investment purposes, buy only items in fine or better condition because books of lower-quality are too numerous to be of value. Unique items, such as paperbacks in dust jackets or in boxes, often are worth more.

Most collections are assembled around one or more unifying themes, such as author (Edgar Rice Burroughs, Dashiell Hammett, Louis L'Amour, Raymond Chandler, Zane Grey, William Irish, Cornell Woolrich, etc.), fictional genre (mysteries, science fiction, westerns, etc.), publisher (early Avon, Dell, and Popular Library are best known), cover artist (Frank Frazetta, R. C. M. Heade, Rudolph Belarski, Roy Krenkel, Vaughn Bode, etc.), or books with uniquely appealing graphic design (Dell map backs and Ace double novels).

Because paperbacks still turn up in large lots, collectors need to be cautious. Books that are in fine or excellent condition are uncommon. Currently, many dealers charge upper-level prices for books that are not in correspondingly good condition. Dealers' argument that top-condition examples are just too scarce is not valid, just self-serving.

History: Paperback volumes have existed since the 15th century. Mass-market paperback books, most popular with collectors, were printed after 1938. These exist in a variety of formats, from the standard-size paperback and its smaller predecessor to odd sizes like 64-page short novels (which sold for 10¢) and 5-1/4- by 7-1/2-inch volumes known as "digests." Some books came in a dust jacket; some were boxed.

Today there are not as many companies publishing mass-market paperbacks as there were between 1938 and 1950. Books of this period are characterized by lurid and colorful cover art and title lettering not unlike that of the pulp magazines. Many early paperback publishers were also involved in the production of pulps, and merely moved their graphic style and many of their authors to paperbacks.

References: *Collectible Vintage Paperbacks at Auction 1995*, available from Spoon River Press (2319C W. Rohmann, Peoria, IL 61604, 1995; Bob and Sharon Huxford, *Huxford's Paperback Value Guide*, Collector Books, 1994; Gary Lovisi, *Collecting Science Fiction and Fantasy*, Alliance Publishing, 1997; Kurt Peer, *TV Tie-Ins: A Bibliography of American TV Tie-In Paperbacks*, Neptune Publishing, 1997; Dawn E. Reno and Jacque Tiegs, *Collecting Romance Novels*, Alliance Publishers, 1995; Frank M. Robinson and Lawrence Davidson, *Pulp Culture: The Art of Fiction Magazines*, Collectors Press, Inc., 1998; Lee Server, *Over My Dead Body: The*

Sensational Age of the American Paperback, Chronicle Books, 1994.

Periodicals: *Books Are Everything*, 302 Martin Dr., Richmond, KY 40475; *Paperback Parade*, P.O. Box 209, Brooklyn, NY 11228; *Pulp and Paperback Market Newsletter*, 5813 York Ave., Edina, MN 55410.

Museum: University of Minnesota's Hess Collection of Popular Literature, Minneapolis, MN.

Notes: Prices are given for books in fine condition. Divide by three to get the price for books in good condition; increase price by 50 percent for books in near mint condition.

Adventures of Creighton Holmes, Ned Hubbell, Popular 10.00
Baa Baa Black Sheep, Gregory Boyington, Dell 3.00
Baby and Child Care, Dr. Benjamin Spock, 1956, 502 pgs 5.00
Baby Talk, Bruce Lansky illus, Meadowbrook, 1985 ....4.50
Battle Cry, Leon Uris, Bantam 3.00
Bedroom Tramp, Bill Adams, Playtime.......................................12.00
Beverly Hillbillies Book of Country Humor................................20.00
Bluebeard's Seventh Wife, William Irish, Popular Library 9.00
Bright Path to Adventure, Gordon Sinclair, Harlequin................................5.00
Conquest of the Planet of the Apes, John Jakes, 5th printing, 1974, ink mark...5.00
Crowded Ways, Murray H. Leiffer, Frederick A. Shippey, Mrs. E. Cranston, Mrs. Mabel G. Wagner, Earl D. C. Brewer, illus, Board of Missions of the Methodist Church, 1950s.........................5.00
Cry Slaughter, Avon 3.00
Dr. Prescott's Secret, Peggy Gaddin, Beacon......................................3.00
Fighting Coach, Jackson Scholz, Comet..3.00
Future Science Fiction, 1950s 20.00
Get Smart, complete set of 9............50.00
Girl from U.N.C.L.E., The Birds of a Feather Affair, #11 ....12.50
Grabhorn Bounty, Clifton Adams, Ace 7.50
Guide Book for the Edison Institute Museum and Greenfield Village, ©1937..20.00
He Who Laughs Lasts...And Lasts...And Lasts, Roy H. Hicks, DD, 1976, 63 pgs...5.00
I'll Be Glad When You're Dead, Dana Lynn, Quick Reader......................5.00
Jackie Robinson Story, Arthur Mann, J Low Co. 45.00
Judy Garland, James Juneau, Pyramid, 1974..18.00
Julia's Children, Margaret Chrislock Gilseth, Askeladd Press, 1987 ......5.00

Land of the Giants.............................15.00
Leave It To Beaver.............................15.00
Life and Loves of Lana Turner, W. Wright, Windom House..............................3.50
Living Letters, The Paraphrased Epistles, Kenneth N. Taylor, Tyndale House, 1962...5.00
Murder of the Circus Queen, Anthony Abbot, Popular 10.00
Open Heart Open Home, Karen Burton Mains, David C. Cook Publishing, 1976, 199 pgs 5.00
Return of a Fighter, Ernest Haycox, Corgi, 1956...15.00
Second Antiques Treasury, Edwin G. Warman, 1st edition, 1968................12.00
Sgt. Bilco...15.00
Songs Everyone Loves, Zondervan Publishing House, 9" x 6"....................5.00
Spider, 2/43, 6/43, 12/43, each........75.00
Super Eye Adventure Treasure Hunt, Jay Leibold, Ray Zone and Chuck Roblin illus, Bantham Skylar Books, 1995...5.00
Tarzan and The Lost Empire, Edgar Rice Burroughs, Ace 8.00
The Avengers, The Magnetic Man, #8, Berkley, 1968 ....8.00
The Book of Revelation, Harry R. Boer, ©African Christian Press, 1979, USA edition by William B. Erdmans Publishing, 157 pgs 5.00
The Democratic Book, 1936, 14" x 11", 394 pgs...55.00
The Flood, Alfred M. Rehwinkle, G C News Publishers, Illinois, some wear 5.00
The Go Gospel, Daily Devotions and Bible Studies in the Gospel of Mark, Manford George Gut, Rel Books, 1968...5.00
The Real Life Story of Fess Parker, Dell Magazine.......................................50.00
The Story, adapted by T. Miller, Tyndale House Publishers, Inc., 1986........5.00
The Story of Walt Disney, Martin and Miller, Dell 5.00
The Wedding Journey, Walter Edmonds, Dell 5.00
We Are The Public Enemy, Alan Hynd, Gold Medal.......................................5.00
Withering Heights, Emily Bronte, Quick Reader 7.50

Patriotic Collectibles

Collecting Hints: Concentrate on one symbol, e.g., the eagle, flag, Statue of Liberty, or Uncle Sam. Remember that the symbol is not always the principal attraction; don't miss items with the symbol in a secondary role.

Colored material is more desirable than black and white. Many items are two-dimensional, e.g., posters and signs. Seek three-dimensional objects to add balance and interest to a collection.

Much of the patriotic material focuses on our national holidays, especially the Fourth of July; but other holidays to consider are Flag Day, Labor Day, Memorial Day, and Veterans' Day.

Finally, look to the foreign market. Our symbols are used abroad, both positively and negatively. A novel collection would be one based on how Uncle Sam is portrayed on posters and other materials from Communist countries.

History: Patriotic symbols developed along with the American nation. The eagle, among the greatest of our nation's symbols, has appeared on countless objects since it was chosen to be part of the American seal.

Uncle Sam arrived on the American scene in the mid-19th century and was firmly established by the Civil War. Uncle Sam did have female counterparts—Columbia and the Goddess of Liberty. He often appeared together with one or both of them on advertising trade cards, buttons, posters, textiles, etc. His modern appearance came about largely as the result of drawings by Thomas Nast in *Harper's Weekly* and James Montgomery Flagg's famous World War I recruiting poster, "I Want You." Perhaps the leading promoter of the Uncle Sam image was the American toy industry, aided by the celebration of the American Centennial in 1876 and Bicentennial in 1976. A surge of Uncle Sam-related toys occurred in the 1930s led by American Flyer's inexpensive version of an earlier lithographed tin, flat-sided Uncle Sam bicycle string toy.

Reference: Gerald Czulewicz, *Foremost Guide to Uncle Sam Collectibles*, Collector Books, 1995; Nicholas Steward, *James Montgomery Flagg: Uncle Sam and Beyond*, Collector's Press, 1997.

Periodical: *Pyrofax Magazine*, P.O. Box 2010, Saratoga, CA 95070.

Collectors' Club: Statue of Liberty Collectors' Club, P.O. Box 535, Chautauqua, NY 14722.

Museum: 4th of July Americana & Fireworks Museum, New Castle, PA.

Additional Listings: Flag Collectibles.

Eagle

Badge, U.S.N.R., dark copper luster, eagle and patriotic symbols, inscription for Naval reserve 20.00
Bookends, 5-1/2" l, cast white metal, worn 50.00
Change Tray, 4" d, Hebbrun House Coal, eagle in center, holding banner, wood grain ground 50.00
Cookie Cutter, 6-1/2" l, tin 90.00
Fan, 8" x 9" diecut cardboard, 4" wood handle, full color eagle front, black and white illus text on back for Ontario Drill Co, Baltimore, © 1908 .... 85.00

Sheet music, "Father of the Land We Love," George Cohen, copyright 1931 by Sol Bloom, cover artist James Montgomery Flagg, $12.

Figure, 6" h, pot metal, gold paint 35.00
Pinback Button, 7/8" d
  Homecoming and Made in LaCross Celebration, red, white, and blue enamel, patriotic shield and eagle, war commemorative scene, c1920 .... 15.00
  Milwaukee July 4th, 1911, multicolored, eagle, shield, and flags, white rim, red lettering 35.00
  2nd Liberty Loan, Let The Eagle Scream Appeal, multicolored, blue letters 20.00
Postcard, 3-1/2" x 5", eagle on front with "E. Pluribus Unum," flags, slogan "In God We Trust To Save America," flags of other countries on right side, copyright 1941, Harry Reiter, NY, dated 1941, unused 60.00
Ring, Sam the Olympic Eagle, adjustable brass band, high relief colorful plastic eagle head, 1984 Olympics symbol 15.00
Watch Fob, 1" d, silvered brass, shield shape, attached silvered brass horseshoe, raised eagle on front, red, white, and blue enameled name "American Badge Co.," c1900 .... 45.00

Fans and Shields

Fan, diecut shield, red, white, and blue cardboard, "America First," sailor raising deck flag, warships in background, biplane flying overhead, back with sponsors names and song lyrics, 7" x 9" 45.00

Lapel Stud, Colonial Bicycles, red, white, and blue shield symbol 20.00
Medal, Victory Liberty Loan, U.S. Treasury Dept. 15.00
Note Pad Holder, kitten with red, white, and blue shield, wearing U.S. Navy cap, 7-1/4" x 9", some wear 25.00
Paperweight, 3" d, celluloid over weighted metal, mirror bottom, full color images of 12 Allied flags, local sponsor art center 35.00
Pocket Mirror, Beautifers of Homes, red, white, and gold patriotic shield shape, black lettering 40.00
Stickpin
  Advertising, diecut celluloid red, white, and blue American flag on front, black and white adv on back for Artistic Pianos, brass stickpin, early 1900s 30.00
  G. A. R. Encampment, stiff paper red, white, and blue flag, mounted to metal stickpin, "Welcome Comrades" .. 35.00
Watch Fob, silvered brass, shield shape, attached silvered brass horseshoe, raised eagle on front, red, white, and blue enameled name, American Badge Co., c1900 .... 48.00

Liberty Bell

Book, *The Centennial Liberty Bell*, Philadelphia, 1876, hard cover 18.00
Button, Liberty Bell, plastic shelf shank, 3/4" d 2.50
Paperweight 6" h, cast iron 60.00
Pinback Button, National Relief Assurance Co, Philadelphia, multicolored eagle and Liberty Bell, dark blue ground, c1900 .... 20.00
Pocket Mirror, Bell's Coffee, green Liberty bell trademark, mocha and java specialties, J H Bell & Co., Chicago. 60.00
Postcard
  Glorious 4th of July, minor wear.... 6.00
  Independence Hall, Philadelphia, sepia 8.50
  Liberty Bell Trolley, insignia on front 10.00
Sheet Music, "Liberty Bell Time To Ring Again," 1918 .... 10.00
Tape Measure, 1-3/4" d, celluloid case, blue and white design, logo and inscription for Missouri and Kansas telephone company, reverse "When You Telephone, Use The Bell," cloth tape, c1900 .... 40.00

Statue of Liberty

Bell, hand painted, Fenton 35.00
Bookends, pr, leather, carved design, 1930s 70.00
Brooch, silver-tone, red, white, and blue rhinestones, sgd "Wendy Gell," 4" h 65.00
Cigarette Case, painted metal, 1940s 30.00
Clock, Seth Thomas 400.00
Hat, heavy paper, "Liberty," red, white and blue, picture of Statue, c1918 .... 25.00

Lamp, 5-1/2" h, dark copper finished white metal, holds small electrical bulb, wooden base, sliding base opens to hold battery, c1920 ...... 40.00

Needle Book, World's Best, airplane, ship, world, six needle packets .. 20.00

Paperweight, glass and plaster, 1880 .... 150.00

Playing Cards, "606," U.S. Playing Card Co, Cincinnati, OH, picture of Statue of Liberty and flags of nations, gold edges, complete, orig box 20.00

Sheet Music, Liberty Enlightening The World, 1885 .... 100.00

Tin, Wiles Biscuit Company, Bakers of Sunshine Biscuits, NY, signing of Constitution, Gold Rush, Statue of Liberty, bail handle, some wear 25.00

Uncle Sam

Advertising Trade Card, 3-1/2" x 6-1/4", Hub Gore, Uncle Sam holding shoe, saying "Hub Gore Makers of Elastic For Shoes...It Was Honored At The World's Fair of 1803" 15.00

Candy Container, Fanny Farmer, some paper loss to label, 9-1/4" h 98.00

Cookie Jar, American Cookie Jar Co. 150.00

Doll, eagle, striped top hat, Japan, 1984, 18" h, MIB 200.00

Fruit Crate Label, 10-1/2" x 9", illus of sad Uncle Sam, hat in hand, red background 6.00

Magazine Tear Sheet, 5-1/2" x 8-1/2", Uncle Sam Holding a "Health Bill" under his arm, looking at Cream of Wheat advertising billboard, © 1915 .... 22.00

Pinback Button
America Always, red, white, blue, and fleshtone, 1-1/4" d 25.00
Spanish American War, multicolored image of Uncle Sam lowering Spanish flag and raising U.S. flag, witnessed by soldier and sailor, caption "We Have Remembered the Maine," Peitler Patriot Publishing CO., Denver . 110.00

Pocket Mirror, *Watertown Times Newspaper* 75.00

Salt and Pepper Shakers, pr, 1-1/2" x 2-1/2" x 2", painted plaster, glossy white, black, and red accents, red, white, and blue top hat 65.00

Stickpin, 1", diecut, white metal, tinted cherry red trousers and hat, blue coat, marching pose, c1898 .... 35.00

Tray, Cascade Beer, San Francisco, Uncle Sam and five ethnic people 675.00

Watch Fob, brass, detailed Uncle Sam kicking large bullet into stomach of Kaiser, red, white, and blue flags 75.00

George Washington

Fruit Crate Label, 10-1/2" sq, illus of George Washington on white horse, red, white, and blue ground 6.00

Lapel Stud, celluloid on metal, black and white portrait flanked by full color U.S. and Canadian flags, gold background, blue lettering "Division 268 Feb 1932" 15.00

Pinback Button
Bicentennial, black and white, 1932 .... 15.00
Cherry Smash, multicolored portrait of George, background shades from burgundy to olive green, inscription "Cherry Smash," early 1900s 20.00
Two flags on white background, orange and blue ribbon with token with emb Theme Building on one side, George Washington on other 45.00

Sheet Music, "Father of the Land We Love," lyrics and music by George M. Cohan, cover artist James Montgomery Flagg, illus of George Washington on cov, 1931 .... 12.00

Spoon, 4-1/2" l, George at top of handle, stars on handle, flags and staffs, shield with NY World's Fair in bowl, National Silver Co. 35.00

Teapot, white ironstone, portrait of George Washington, excerpts from Declaration of Independence, mkd "Ellgreave Adin of Woods and Sons, England, Genuine Ironstone," 5-3/4" h 40.00

Watch Fob, silvered brass, 7/8" d center multicolored portrait, c1932 .... 10.00

Pennsbury Pottery

Collecting Hints: Concentrate on one pattern or type. Since the wares were hand carved, aesthetic quality differs from piece to piece. Look for those with a strong design sense and a high quality of execution.

Buy only clearly marked pieces. Look for decorator and designer initials that can be easily identified.

Pennsbury collectors are concentrated in the Middle Atlantic states. Many of the company's commemorative and novelty pieces relate to businesses and events in that region, thus commanding the highest prices when sold within that area.

History: In 1950, Henry and Lee Below established Pennsbury Pottery, named for its close proximity to William Penn's estate "Pennsbury," three miles west of Morrisville, Pennsylvania. Henry, a ceramic engineer and mold maker, and Lee, a designer and modeler, had previously worked for Stangl Pottery in Trenton, New Jersey.

Many of Pennsbury's forms, motifs, and manufacturing techniques have Stangl roots. A line of birds similar to those produced by Stangl were among the earliest Pennsbury prod-

ucts. The carved-design technique is also of Stangl origin; high bas-relief molds are not.

Most Pennsbury products are easily identified by their brown-wash background. The company also made pieces featuring other background colors so do not make the mistake of assuming that a piece is not Pennsbury if it does not have a brown wash.

Pennsbury motifs are heavily nostalgic, often farm- or Pennsylvania German–related. Among the most popular lines were Amish, Black Rooster, Delft Toleware, Eagle, Family, Folkart, Gay Ninety, Harvest, Hex, Quartet, Red Barn, Red Rooster, Slick-Chick, and Christmas plates (1960-1970). The pottery made a large number of commemorative, novelty, and special-order pieces.

In the late 1950s, the company had 16 employees, mostly local housewives and young girls. By 1963, at the company's peak, there were 46 employees. Cheap foreign imports cut deeply into the pottery's profits, and by the late 1960s, just more than 20 employees remained.

Marks differ from piece to piece depending on the person who signed it or the artist who sculpted the mold. Some initials still have not been identified.

Henry Below died on December 21, 1959, leaving the pottery in trust for his wife and three children with instructions that it be sold upon the death of his wife. She died on December 12, 1968, and in October 1970, the Pennsbury Pottery filed for bankruptcy. The contents were auctioned off on December 18, 1970. On May 18, 1971, a fire destroyed the pottery and support buildings.

References: Susan and Al Bagdade, *Warman's American Pottery and Porcelain*, 2nd ed., Krause Publications, 2000; Lucile Henzke, *Pennsbury Pottery*, Schiffer Publishing, 1990; Mike Schneider, *Stangl and Pennsbury Birds*, Schiffer Publishing, 1994.

Look-Alike Alert: The Lewis Brothers Pottery, Trenton, New Jersey, purchased 50 of the Pennsbury molds. Although they were supposed to remove the Pennsbury name from the molds, this was not done in all instances. Further, two Pennsbury employees moved to Lewis Brothers when Pennsbury closed, helping to produce a number of pieces that are reminiscent of Pennsbury's products. Many of Pennsbury's major lines, including the Harvest and Rooster patterns, plaques, birds, and highly unusual molds, were not reproduced.

Glen View, Langhorne, Pennsylvania, continued marketing the 1970s Angel Christmas plate with Pennsbury markings. The company continued the Christmas plate line into the 1970s, utilizing the Pennsbury brownwash background. In 1975, Lenape Products, a division of Pennington, bought Glen View and continued making Pennsbury-like products.

Ashtray

Don't Be So Doppish, 5" l 20.00
Doylestown Trust 30.00
Hex Sign, earthtones 27.50
Outen the Light 20.00
Such Schmootzers 20.00
What Giffs, Amish pattern 20.00
Bank, jug, pig, "Stuff Me" 100.00
Beer Mug, Red Rooster 28.00

Bird

Bird on Nest 300.00
Goldfinch, #102 .... 200.00

Bowl

Fruit, shades of gray, 5-1/2" w, 2" h 12.00
Rooster, 6-1/2" d 24.00
Bread Tray, rect, wheat motif 45.00
Cake Stand, Amish 75.00
Candleholders, pr, Red Roosters 85.00
Canister set, cov, Black Rooster dec, 9" h flour and sugar, 8" tea and coffee 425.00
Coaster, Shultz 17.50
Coffeepot, cov, 8" h, Rooster 110.00
Creamer and Sugar, Rooster 40.00

Cream Pitcher

Large, Hex Sign 55.00
Medium, Distilfink 45.00
Small, Hex Sign 25.00
Cruet, stopper, Amish 40.00

Cup and Saucer

Black Rooster 20.00
Red Rooster 17.50
Desk Basket, Exchange Club 40.00
Dinner Plate, Hex pattern 17.50
Egg Cup, Red Rooster pattern 25.00

Milk Pitcher

6-1/2" h, Amish farm scene 175.00
7-1/4" h, Yellow Rooster 150.00

Mug

Eagle 25.00
Schiaraflia Filadelfia, owl and seal 30.00
Sweet Adeline 20.00

Pie Plate

Apple Tree pattern 37.50
Mother serving pie 75.00
Rooster, 8" d 65.00

Pitcher

Amish man, 2-1/2" h 12.00
Amish woman, 5" h 45.00
Eagle pattern 65.00
Hex Sign, 4" 20.00
Red Rooster, 3-3/4" 18.00

Plaque

Amish Family, 8" d 55.00

B & O Railroad, Lafayette engine and coal car, 5-3/4" x 7-3/4" 48.00
It is whole empty, 4" 20.00
Pennsylvania RR 1888, Tiger Locomotive, 5-5/8" x 8" 48.00
Pops half et already, 4" 20.00

Plate

Black Rooster, 10" d 15.00
Hex Sign, 8" d 20.00
Hex Sign, 10" d 20.00
Pretzel Bowl, large, Sweet Adeline ... 60.00
Salt and Pepper Shakers, pr, Amish heads 60.00
Snack Set, Red Rooster, set of four 5-1/2" x 9" kidney shaped plates, four 3" d x 3" h mugs 255.00
Snack Tray, matching cup, Red Rooster 25.00
Teapot, Red Rooster pattern 65.00
Tea Tile, 6" d, skunk, "Why Be Disagreeable" 60.00
Tray, 14-1/2" x 11-1/2", Amish Family 100.00
Vegetable Dish, divided, Red Rooster 30.00
Wall Pocket, 10" h, bellows-shape, eagle motif 60.00

Pens and Pencils

Collecting Hints: Price is lessened dramatically by any defects such as scratches, cracks, dents, warping, missing parts, bent levers, sprung clips, nib damage, or mechanical damage. Engraved initials or names do not seriously detract from the price.

History: The steel pen point, or "nib," was invented by Samuel Harrison in 1780. It was not commercially produced in quantity until the 1880s when Richard Esterbrook entered the field. The holders became increasingly elaborate. Mother-of-pearl, gold, sterling silver, and other fine materials were used to fashion holders of distinction. Many of these pens can be found along with their original velvet-lined presentation cases.

Lewis Waterman invented the fountain pen in the 1880s. Three other leading pioneers in the field were Parker, Sheaffer (first lever filling action, 1913), and Wahl-Eversharp.

The mechanical pencil was patented in 1822 by Sampson Mordan. The original slide-type action developed into the spiral mechanical pencil. Wahl-Eversharp was responsible for the automatic "clic," or repeater-type, mechanism which is used on ball-points today.

The flexible nib that enabled the writer to individualize his penmanship came to an end when Reynolds intro-

duced the ball-point pen in October 1945.

References: Deborah Crosby, *Victorian Pencils: Tools to Jewels*, Schiffer Publishing, 1998; Giorgio Dragoni and Giueseppe Fichera, *Fountain Pens, History and Design*, Antique Collectors' Club, 1999; Paul Erano, *Fountain Pens*, Collector Books, 1999; George Fischler and Stuart Schneider, *Fountain Pens and Pencils*, Schiffer Publishing, 1990; ——, *Illustrated Guide to Antique Writing Instruments*, 3rd ed., Schiffer, 2000; Henry Gostony and Stuard Schneider, *The Incredible Ball Point Pen*, Schiffer Publishing, 1998; Regina Martini, *Pens & Pencils: A Collector's Handbook*, 2nd ed., Schifer Publishing, 1998.

Periodicals: *Pen World Magazine*, P.O. Box, 6007, Kingwood, TX 77325; Pens, P.O. Box 64, Teaneck, NJ 07666.

Collectors' Clubs: American Pencil Collectors Society, 2222 S. Milwood, Wichita, KS 67213; Pen Collectors of American, P.O. Box 821449, Houston, TX 77282; Pen Fancier's Club, 1169 Overcash Dr., Dunedin, FL 34698.

Combination, pencil turns out, pen pulls out, gold plated, point marked "E. J. Johnson & Co., New York, No. 4," 2-3/8" l closed, $80.

Desk Set

Conklin, Endura Model, black marble base, two pens, side lever fill, double narrow gold color bands, mkd "Patent Nov. 17, 1925," on pen barrel, black-brown overlay color 125.00
Epenco, fountain pen and pencil, 5-1/2" l 30.00
Moore, gray and black marble base, black pen, 12 carat nib, side lever fill 75.00
Sheaffer, Triumph Lifetime, green marble base, two black snorkel design pens, c1940 .... 95.00

Display Case, "Rexall Pens Smooth Elastic Durable Steel Pens Warranted Highest Grade," wooden, open compartment trays on top side, sliding drawer pulls out at rear, gold lettering, c1920, some wear, 14" w, 13" d, 5" h 40.00

Pen

Advertising
Coca-Cola, 1996, polar bear, Coca-Cola bottle clip 8.00

Planters Snacks, Cheese Curls, Corn Chips, Pretzels written on barrel, Mr. Peanut top, 1970s, 5-1/4" l 20.00
Westinghouse, emblem in window, Garland, maroon and silver 8.00
Character
Mickey Mouse, mkd "Walt Disney Mickey Mouse," nib marked with Mickey's face, manufactured by Inkograph Co., New York, mkd "Ink-O-Gator" 470.00
Playboy, red ink 7.50
Roy Rogers, Stratford, unused .. 145.00
Taz, Looney Toons, Stylus Pen, Tax on clip 9.00
Columbia, Safety Fountain Pen, three engraved designs on cap top, professionally restored 300.00
Conklin
Model 20, 5-5/16" l, #2 Conklin pint-nib, black crescent filler #20, gold clip, narrow gold band on cap, patent date May 28, 1918 stamped on clip ... 75.00
Model 25P, ladies filigree cap ribbon, black, crescent filler, 1923 .... 70.00
Model 30, black hard rubber, 1903 .... 75.00
Symetrick, self filing, Pat 5-28-1918 and 11-17-1925, green and black, Conklin nib 150.00
Cross, gold colored, seashells engraved on clip 10.00
Dunn, black, red barrel, goldplated trim, c1920 .... 40.00
Epenco, black case, goldplated trim 25.00
Esterbrook, Dripless Inkwell, No. 444, clear glass base, black inset at bottom, black Bakelite top with penholder, matching Dipless pen with black section, clear taper 55.00
Eversharp
CA Model, ball point pen, black, gold filled cap, 1946 .... 42.00
Doric, gold seal, green marble cov, lever fill, large adjustable nib, c1935 .... 55.00
Fountain, gold bands, maroon body, 14K tip 90.00
Presentation, fountain pen, Dubonnet red, 14K nib 95.00
Hallmark, wood, dark colored 9.00
Marvel, black chased hand rubber, eyedropper, 1906 .... 75.00
Moore
Black, lady's ribbon pen, three narrow gold bands on cap, lever fill, patent nib #2 .... 70.00
Rose color, fancy band around cap, warranted nib, side lever filler 65.00
Onoto, 18K yg, fountain, 6" l, engraved "R. D. Charman" 190.00
Osmiroid, black, name on clip, tip mkd "Osmiroid, England," medium 20.00
Parker
Blue-Diamond-51, black, goldplated cap, button filled, 1942 .... 70.00
Duofold, Deluxe, pen and pencil set, black and pearl, three narrow gold color bands on cap, push button fill, 1929 .... 575.00

Duofold, Senior, Flashing Black, 1923 .... 185.00
Duofold, Streamline, burgundy and black, double narrow band on cap, 1932 .... 125.00
Lucky Curve, ring pen, black hard rubber, gold filled trim, 1921 .... 85.00
Model 48, ring top, gold filled barrel and cap, button filled, 1915 ..... 150.00
Parker 51, brown, jewel on cap, Vacumatic filler, mkd "Made in USA" .. 75.00
Vacumatic, gray-black, arrow clip, arrow design engraved on nib, silver color clip and band on cap, oversized model, 1932 .... 125.00
Political
Bush-Quayle '92, bluetone bald eagle, red, white, and blue stars and strips design 7.50
George Bush for President in '88, elephant emblem, red lettering, white ground 9.00
Mike Dukakis for President in '88, donkey emblem, blue lettering, white ground 8.00
Reynolds, Model 2, orig ball point, c1945 .... 75.00
Security, check protector, red hard rubber, gold filled trim, 1923 .... 85.00
Sheaffer
Strato Writer, ball point pen, gold filled metal mountings, 1948 .... 65.00
White Dot, green jade, goldplated trim, lever filled, 1923 .... 95.00
White Dot Lifetime, classic torpedo design cap and body, lever filler on side, 1930 .... 115.00
Wahl
Lady's, ribbon pen, double narrow band on cap, 14 carat #2 nib, lever fill, 1928 .... 75.00
Store display, oversized fountain pen, solid brass and wood, 24" l, 1-1/2" d, c1930 .... 500.00
Tempoint No. 305A, gold filled metal mounted, eyedropper, 1919 ..... 145.00
Wahl-Eversharp, gold seal, black, gold filled trim, lever filled, 1930 .... 125.00
Waterman
Model #12, mottled brow, 14 carat gold bands, 1886 .... 125.00
Model 42-1/2V, Safety, gold filigree, retractable screw action nib, 1906 .... 135.00
Model #71, ripple red, hard rubber case, goldplated trim, white clip, lever filled, 1925 .... 150.00
Taperite, black, gold filled metal mounted cap, gold filled trim, lever filled, c1949 .... 75.00
Webstar Four Star, 14K, green marbleized stripes, black bottom band .95.00

Pencil
Advertising
A. J. Spaulding Brothers, NY, silver lettering "Put Importance to the History and Tradition," Reimei 8.00
Broadman Supplies, red logo, 23rd Psalm printed in blue 8.50
Guy M. Grove Co. Plumbing & Heating. Funkstown, MD, 1968 monthly calendars, black on orange, Rite Graph brand 9.00

Planter's Peanuts, mechanical, blue and yellow, Mr. Peanut on top, 1950s 28.00
RCA, gold-colored Cross, "RCA" on clip 8.00
Tom's 24 Hour Service, Electric Motor, Pick Up and Delivery, phone number and Bakersfield, CA address, "USA" on clip, mechanical type 8.00
Eversharp, lady's, silverplated, c1920 .... 25.00
Souvenir
"1898-1948 - Golden Anniversary, New York City" emb on side, blue and orange stripes, brass sq eraser head, 12" l 8.50
"Souvenir of Saginaw" in silver writing on side, red, white, and blue, metal dome cap, thick, 1920s, 12-1/2" l. 8.50
Wahl-Eversharp, gold filled, metal mounted, 1919 .... 35.00
Zippo, black, gold trim 10.00

Pepsi-Cola Collectibles

Collecting Hints: Items advertising Pepsi, Hires, and a number of other soft drink companies became hot collectibles in the 1980s, fueled in part by the pricey nature of Coca-Cola items. The Pepsi market is still young, and, some price fluctuations occur.

Pepsi-Cola enjoys a much stronger market position in many foreign countries than it does in the United States.

Reproductions, copycats, and fantasy items are part of the Pepsi-collecting scene. Be on the alert for the Pepsi and Pete pillow issued in the 1970s, a 12-inch-high ceramic statue of a woman holding a glass of Pepsi, a Pepsi glass-front clock, a Pepsi double-bed quilt, and set of four Pepsi glasses. These are just a few of the suspect items, some of which were done under license from Pepsi-Cola.

History: Pepsi-Cola was developed by Caleb D. Bradham, a pharmacist and drugstore owner in New Bern, North Carolina. Like many drugstores of its time, Bradham provided "soda" mixes for his customers and friends. His favorite was "Brad's Drink," which he began to call "Pepsi-Cola" in 1898. Its popularity spread, and in 1902, Bradham turned the operation of his drugstore over to an assistant and devoted all his energy to perfecting and promoting Pepsi-Cola. He sold 2,008 gallons of Pepsi-Cola syrup his first three months and by

1904 was bottling Pepsi-Cola for mass consumption. He sold his first franchise within a short time.

By the end of the first decade of the 20th century, Bradham had organized a network of more than 250 bottlers in 24 states. The company's fortunes sank shortly after World War I, when it suffered large losses in the sugar market. Bankruptcy and reorganization followed. Roy Megargel, whose Wall Street firm advised Bradham, helped keep the name alive. A second bankruptcy occurred in 1931, but the company survived.

In 1933, Pepsi-Cola doubled the size of its bottle but held the price at 5¢. Sales soared. Under the direction of Walter Mack, 1938 to 1951, Pepsi challenged Coca-Cola for market dominance. In the 1950s, Pepsi advertising featured slogans such as "Pepsi Cola Hits the Spot, Twelve Full Ounces That's a Lot."

PepsiCo. is currently a division of Beatrice. It has a worldwide reputation and actually is the number-one soft drink in many foreign countries.

References: James C. Ayers, *Pepsi-Cola Bottles Collectors Guide*, published by author (P.O. Box 1377, Mt. Airy, NC 27030), 1995; Phillip Dillman and Larry Woestman, *Pepsi Memorabilia*, Schiffer Publishing, 2000; Don and Elizabeth Johnson, *Warman's Advertising*, Krause Publications, 2000; Everette and Mary Lloyd, *Pepsi-Cola Collectibles*, Schiffer Publishing, 1993; Bill Vehling and Michael Hunt, *Pepsi-Cola Collectibles*, Vol. 1 (1990, 1993 value update), Vol. 2 (1990, 1992 value update), Vol. 3 (1993, 1995 value update), L-W Book Sales.

Collectors' Clubs: Ozark Mountain Pepsi Collectors Club, P.O. Box 575631, Modesto, CA 95357; Pepsi-Cola Collectors Club, P.O. Box 1275, Covina, CA 91722.

Museum: Pepsi-Cola Company Archives, Purchase, NY.

Award Pin, bronze luster finish metal bar pin and pendant, domed image of figural softball, inscribed "Scholastic Softball Champs, 1942," bar pin with Pepsi-Cola sponsor name above inscription "Tournament Award" flanked by single leaf symbols....30.00

Bottle Cap, 1910, never crimped..50.00

Bottle Opener, slight rust..................20.00

Calendar, 1955, card stock, 12" x 20"..400.00

Carrier, aluminum, to hold six bottles, handle slides down for storage, some scratches.....................................60.00

Cigarette Lighter, 4" l, metal, bottle cap illus on side, 1950s 150.00

Clock, wall type................................40.00

Cooler, aluminum 200.00

Crate, wooden
   Four compartments, wear, 18" x 6" x 12"..48.00
   Six compartments, bright markings, 1940s..145.00
   Twenty-four compartments, mkd "Pittsburgh, Pa.," c1940 ....30.00

Door Push, wrought iron, 1960s.......65.00

Drinking Glass
   Boris and Natasha, 1970s...........30.00
   Daffy Duck and Pepe, mkd "part of a collector series, Warner Brothers Inc., 1976" with Pepsi logo, 6-1/4" h......8.00
   Uh-Huh Diet Pepsi 4.00

Fan, 10" sq, cardboard, wood handle, c1940 ....75.00

Figure, 5-1/2" h, 30 Anniversary, pewter, billboard center with bottle cap and "Cool" and cat figure leaning on it with one elbow, feet crossed, limited edition of 250..60.00

Fountain Glass, 5" h, syrup line, double dot...45.00

Key Chain, Pepsi Beach Club, 1960s...35.00

Letterhead, 8-1/2" x 11", Pepsi-Cola Bottling Works, Greensboro, NC, 1916..100.00

Napkin, 19" sq, cloth, c1940.............25.00

Notepad, 2-1/2" x 4-1/2", cardboard cov, red and black logo, 1914 calendar 35.00

Paper Cup and Cup Holder, Pepsi Double Dot, cone shape, made by Paper Container Mfg. Co., Chicago 75.00

Pinback Button, 2" d, red, white, and blue bottle cap design, slogan "More Bounce to the Ounce," 1950s.....25.00

Radio, transistor, 10" l......................55.00

Radio Premium, Certificate, 6" x 8-1/2", Counter-Spy Junior Agents Club, c1950 ....32.50

Record Set, set of six records, 1960s, orig cardboard jacket......................100.00

Salt and Pepper Shakers, pr, 4-1/2" h, bottle shape, glass, plastic lids 25.00

Sign
   3-1/2" x 10", emb tin, dark green, white, and red, mkd "Crown Cork & Seal Co., Baltimore, USA" c1910 ....650.00
   9" d, celluloid and tin, "Ice Cold Pepsi-Cola Sold Here," 1930s 300.00
   12" x 8", plastic, "Take Home Pepsi," light-up type, bottle cap illus, 1950s...160.00
   13" d, bottle cap, double-sided, Pepsi Double Dot, painted emb metal, late 1940s or early 1950s, some yellowing to white 250.00
   16" w, 15" h, double sided, Pepsi-Cola, masonite, red, white, and blue . 200.00
   22" x 7", paper, "Have A Pepsi," man, woman, and bottle cap illus, 1950s..35.00

24" x 28", tin, "Drink Pepsi-Cola," bottle cap illus, 1950s 55.00

Thermometer, 27-1/4" h, 7-1/8" w, double dot, some wear and stains 365.00

Thimble, plastic, red and blue on yellow, "America's Choice," Pepsi logo ... 7.50

Toy
   Car, diecast, #38, 1993, 1:64 scale, MOC 6.50
   Delivery Truck, 2-1/2" x 7-1/2" x 2", white plastic body, black wood wheels, red, white, and blue ...... Pepsi decal, three white plastic cases with 24 plastic bottles, Marx Toys, c1940..95.00
   Dispenser, 6" x 12" x 12", red, white, and blue plastic, 2" h scaled Pepsi plastic cups, some play wear, c1970..30.00

Tray
   Bottle cap shape, round, 1940. 325.00
   Coney Island, 1955.....................50.00

Uniform Patch, 7"............................. 15.00

Walkie-Talkie, bottle shape.............. 25.00

PEZ

Collecting Hints: PEZ became a hot collectible in the late 1980s. Its rise was due in part to the use of licensed cartoon characters as heads on PEZ dispensers. Initially, PEZ containers were an extremely affordable collectible. Generic subjects often sold for less than $5, character containers for less than $10.

Before investing large amounts of money in PEZ containers, it is important to recognize that: 1) they are produced in large quantities—millions, 2) PEZ containers are usually saved by their original buyers, not disposed of when emptied, and 3) no collecting category stays hot forever. PEZ prices fluctuate. Advertised price and field price for the same container can differ by as much as 50 percent, depending on who is selling.

Starting a PEZ collection is simple. Go to a local store that sells PEZ and purchase the current group of products. Your initial cost will be less than $3 a unit.

History: Vienna, Austria, is the birthplace of PEZ. In 1927, Eduard Haas, an Austrian food mogul, invented PEZ and marketed it as a cigarette substitute, i.e., an adult mint. He added peppermint oil to a candy formula, compressed the product into small rectangular bricks, and named it PEZ, an abbreviation for the German word *Pfefferminz*. Production of PEZ was halted by World War II. When the product appeared again after the war, it was packaged in a dispenser that resembled a BIC lighter. These early 1950s dispensers had no heads.

PEZ arrived in the United States in 1952. PEZ-HAAS received United States Patent #2,620,061 for its "table-dispensing receptacle," but the public response was less than overwhelming. Rather than withdraw from the market, Haas repositioned his product to appeal to children by adding fruit flavors. PEZ's success was assured when it became both a candy and a toy combined into one product. In some cases, the shape of the dispenser mimics an actual toy, e.g., a space gun. Most frequently, appealing heads were simply added to the tops of the standard rectangular containers.

PEZ carefully guards its design and production information. As a result, collectors differ on important questions such as dating and numbers of variations. Further complicating the issue is PEZ production outside the United States. A company in Linz, Austria, with PEZ rights to the rest of the world, including Canada, frequently issues PEZ containers with heads not issued by PEZ Candy, Inc., an independent privately owned company which by agreement manufactures and markets PEZ only in the United States. PEZ Candy, Inc., is located in Connecticut.

The American and Austrian PEZ companies use a common agent to manage the production of dispensers. The result is that occasionally the same container is issued by both companies. However, when this occurs, the packaging may be entirely different.

PEZ Candy, Inc., issues generic, seasonal, and licensed-character containers. Container design is continually evaluated and upgraded. The Mickey Mouse container has been changed more than a dozen times.

Today, PEZ candy is manufactured at plants in Austria, Hungary, Yugoslavia, and the United States. Previously, plants had been located in Czechoslovakia, Germany, and Mexico. Dispensers are produced at plants in Austria, China, Hong Kong, Hungary, and Slovenia.

References: Richard Geary, *PEZ Collectibles*, 4th ed., Schiffer Publishing, 2000; Shawn Peterson, *Collector's Guide To Pez, Identification & Price Guide*, Krause Publications, 2000.

Periodicals: *PEZ Collector's News*, P.O. Box 124, Sea Cliff, NY 11579;

Positively PEZ, 3851 Gable Lane #513, Indianapolis, IN 46208.

 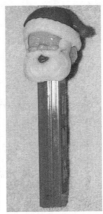

Mickey Mouse PEZ, $5.   **Santa PEZ, $8.**

Aardvark, orange stem, loose	10.00
Alpine Boy, purple hat and shoes, loose	6.50
Ant, green stem, loose	8.00
Aral, Gas, blue hat and shoes, loose	6.00
Barney, Flintstones	3.00
Boy with Hat, PEZ Pal, 1960	12.00
Captain Hook, 4-1/4" h	125.00
Charlie Brown, frown, MIP	8.00
Clown, Merry Melody Maker, MOC	5.00
Donald Duck, no teet, MIP	27.50
Fozzie Bear, 1991	3.00
Icee	5.50
Inspector Clouseu, yellow stem, loose	6.00
Kermit, mkd "Made in Hungary"	7.50
Lamb mkd "Made in Yugoslavia"	6.00
Mariner, blue hat, black shoes, loose	7.50
Mickey Mouse	5.00
Muselix, orange stem, loose	12.00
Parrot, Merry Melody Maker, MOC	8.50
Pebbles, Flintstones	3.00
Penguin, Melody Maker, MOC	12.00
Pilot, white hat, black shoes, loose	6.00
Pink Panther, pink stem, loose	12.00
Pluto	4.00
Rabbit	7.50
Santa, mkd "Made in Yugoslavia"	8.00
Sheep	3.00
Sheik, green stem, white burnoose, band missing, 4-1/4" h	18.00
Shell Gas, yellow hat, red shoes, loose	7.00
Smurf	
Boy, blue stem	3.00
Papa, red stem	3.00
Smurfette, yellow stem	14.00
Snowman	3.00
Tom	6.00
Tuffy	7.50
Tweety Bird	4.00
Whistle, 1960s	4.00
Yosemite Sam	5.00

Phoenix Bird China

Collecting Hints: Within this particular design of primarily blue and white Japanese chinaware, there are more than 500 different shapes and sizes, and more than 100 different factory marks that have been cataloged. The pieces vary greatly, not only in the quality of chinaware itself—from very thick to eggshell thin—but also in design execution, even the shades of blue vary from powder blue to deep cobalt. All of these factors, as well as condition, should be considered when determining prices. Especially important is the border width of the design—"superior" widths are preferred over the more common, narrower border. Another important consideration is that pieces with "Japan" appearing below the cherry blossom mark generally have a better-quality print and also were made in some of the more unique shapes.

Note that the Phoenix Bird's body is facing *forward* while its head is facing *back over its wings*; that is, the head looks opposite the direction the body is facing. Occasionally, on one side of a rounded piece, such as a creamer, sugar, or teapot, the phoenix's stance is reversed, but this is not the norm. Note, too, the phoenix always has at least four and no more than seven spots on its chest, and its wings are spread out and upward.

Green and white pieces are *very rare*. Do not confuse the Phoenix Bird pattern with the Flying Dragon design that does, in fact, come in either green and white or blue and white. Multicolored Phoenix Bird pieces are also rare and these oddities are generally carelessly painted, not the usual high-quality of the blue and white examples. Another pattern that can be confused with Phoenix Bird is Flying Turkey. The latter design was more often hand-painted, while Phoenix Bird was generally decorated by transfer printing. Furthermore, Flying Turkey has a heartlike border with a dot inside each heart. The few pieces of Phoenix Bird with this border, rather than the "cloud & mountain" (C/M) border are referred to as HO-O and rarely have a mark.

Because there are so many different shapes available, buying Phoenix Bird sight unseen can be risky. Insist on a sketch of the shape or a photocopy of the actual piece if at all possible—flat pieces copy well—but a photograph is best. Also ask for the dimensions as well as the mark on the bottom. The latter will sometimes give you a clue as to the quality of the piece.

History: The manufacture of the Phoenix Bird design began in the late 19th century, and pieces were marked "Nippon" from 1891 to 1921. Large quantities of this ware were imported into the United States from the 1920s through the 1940s. A smaller amount went into a few European countries and are so marked, each in their own way. The vast majority of Phoenix Bird was of the transfer-print variety; hand-painted pieces with Japanese characters underneath are rare.

The pattern was primarily sold, retail, through Woolworth's 5- and 10¢-stores. It could also be ordered, wholesale, from the catalogs of Butler Brothers and the Charles William Stores in New York. However, only the most basic shapes were offered through the catalogs. The pattern was also carried by A. A. Vantine Company, New York. The products, which were exported by Morimura Brothers, Japan, were known at that time as Blue Howo Bird China. Morimura used two different marks: "Japan" below a convex "M" under two crossed branches or "Made in Japan" beneath a concave "M" inside a wreath with an open bottom.

Phoenix Bird pieces could also be acquired as premiums. A simple breakfast set could be obtained by selling a particular number of subscriptions to *Needlecraft* magazine. During the early 1900s, two different brands of coffee and tea included a cup and saucer with purchase, and some pieces were available as premiums into the 1930s.

While no ads have yet been found, three-piece tea sets (teapot, creamer, and sugar) in children's play sets, were made at some point in time. To date, six different sets have been cataloged along with small cups, saucers, and plates.

There are several other patterns which are considered to be in the phoenix family: Flying Turkey (an all-over pattern that was hand-painted or transfer-printed), Twin Phoenix (a Noritake border-only pattern), Howo (a Noritake allover pattern), Flying Dragon (available in blue and white and green and white, and marked with six Japanese characters), and

Firebird (the bird's tail flows downward; usually hand-painted and character-marked). Most Japanese potteries were destroyed during World War II making it difficult to trace production of these related patterns.

Two different styles of coffeepots and after-dinner cups and saucers, as well as child-size and adult-size cups and saucers, have been found marked "Made in Occupied Japan" and/or "Maruta." Myott, Son & Company copied Phoenix Bird in England around 1936 and named the pattern Satsuma. These earthenware pieces do not have the same intense blue of the Japanese-made wares

References: Joan Collett Oates, *Phoenix Bird Chinaware*, Books I-IV, 1984-1989, published by author (685 S. Washington, Constantine, MI 49042).

Periodical: *Phoenix Bird Discoveries* (PBDs), 685 S. Washington, Constantine, MI 49042.

Museums: Alice Brayton House, Green Animals Topiary Gardens, Newport, RI; Charles A. Lindberg Home, Little Falls, MN; Historic Cherry Hill, Albany, NY; Huntingdon County Historical Society, Huntingdon, PA; Laura Ingalls-Wilder/Rose Lane Historic Home, Mansfield, MO; Majestic Castle (Casa Loma), Toronto, Canada; W. H. Stark House, Orange, TX; Val-Kill Cottage, Hyde Park, NY.

Reproduction Alert: Approximately 20 pieces of Phoenix Bird were produced in the late 1960s; these are now called Post-1970 Phoenix Bird. They are not reproductions, as such, because the pieces are not identical to nor of the same shape as earlier Phoenix Bird. Generally, these later pieces do not have a backstamp, although they did originally come with a "JAPAN" sticker that could be easily removed. Distinguishing characteristics of the newer wares are a milk-white rather than a grayish body, sparsity of design, especially near the bottom, and a more brilliant blue color in the designs.

Takahashia Imports, California, created a new style of "Phnx" (their term) that has been on the market since the late 1970s and was featured in gift catalogs in the 1980s. The phoenix itself is different on these blue and white porcelain pieces and the wares have no border design, making it easy to distinguish them from true Phoenix Bird. Phnx is a

unique pattern in its own right and has been purchased by many Phoenix Bird collectors as conversation pieces. Some Takahashi pieces come with a blue backstamp, but most were originally marked with a round, gold sticker naming the firm. Collectors call it "T-Bird," for short.

Advisor: Joan Collett Oates.

Note: Since there are several different shapes within some categories of Phoenix Bird, the various shapes are given a style number in the listings below. This numbering system corresponds to that used in the books by Joan Collett Oates.

Centerpiece bowl, 10" d, 4-1/2" h, mark #45, $250. Photo courtesy of Joan Oates.

Bread and Butter Plate, 6" d	8.00
Butter Dish, cov, drain	105.00
Castor Set, boat shape, 5 pcs, rare	500.00
Celery Tray, 13-1/2" l	145.00
Children's Creamer and Sugar, No. 3	45.00
Children's Tea Set, No. 2, partial set, 13 pcs	122.50
Chocolate Pot, #2, scalloped base, HO-O	375.00
Coaster	35.00
Coffee Pot, post 1970	55.00
Condensed Milk Holder	150.00
Cup and Saucer, common shape	5.00
Dessert Plate, common, 7-1/4" d	12.00
Dessert Plate, swirled, scalloped, 7-1/4" d, rare	24.00
Dinner Plate, 9-3/4" d	35.00
Fruit Bowl, 10" d, 4-1/2" h, rare	250.00
Egg Cup, double cup	20.00
Gravy Tureen, No. 2, attached underplate	145.00
Luncheon Plate, 8-1/2" d	16.00
Ramekin and Underplate	35.00
Relish Tray, No. 4	50.00
Salt Dip, scalloped, three footed	16.00
Soap Dish, cov, drain, rare	395.00
Teapot, cov, No. 25-D, (Book IV)	105.00
Tea Tile, 6" d	28.00
Toothpick, No. 6, rare	110.00
Vegetable Tureen, cov	150.00

Pig Collectibles

Collecting Hints: Bisque and porcelain pig items from late 19th-century European potters are most widely sought by collectors. Souvenir items should have decals which are in good condition; occasionally, the gilding wears off from rubbing or washing.

History: Historically, the pig has been important as a source of food and has also been an economic factor in rural areas of Europe and America. It was one of the first animals imported into the American colonies. A fatted sow was the standard gift to a rural preacher on his birthday or holiday.

As a decorative motif, the pig gained prominence with the figurines and planters made in the late 19th century by English, German, and Austrian potters. These "pink" porcelain pigs with green decoration were popular souvenir or prize items at fairs and carnivals or could be purchased at five-and-dime stores.

Many pig figurines were banks, and by the early 20th century, "Piggy Bank" became a synonym for coin bank. When tourist attractions became popular along America's coasts and in the mountain areas, many of the pig designs showed up as souvenir items with gilt decals identifying the area.

The pig motif appeared on the advertising items associated with farm products and life. Movie cartoons introduced Porky Pig and Walt Disney's "Three Little Pigs."

In the late 1970s, pig collectibles caught fire again. Specialty shops selling nothing but pig-related items were found in the New England area. In a 1981 issue, *Time* magazine devoted a page and a half to the pig phenomena.

Reproduction Alert: Reproductions of three German-style painted bisque figurines have been spotted in the market. They are pig by outhouse, pig playing piano, and pig poking out of large purse. The porcelain is much rougher and the green is a darker shade.

Additional Listings: Cartoon Characters, Disneyana.

Advisor: Mary Hamburg.

Water pitcher, opposite side as ham shank hung from red ribbon, unmarked pottery, 8-1/4" h, $90.

Advertising
  Cutting Board, Arnold Kent Feeds, wood, pig shape, 14" x 19-1/2" ...22.00
  Mirror, Newtown Collins Short Order Restaurant, St. Joe, MO, yellow and orange, 2-1/8" d 55.00
  Trade Card, Try Wright's Little Liver Pills, five pigs 10.00
Bank
  Front of pink pig sticking out of one end, back of pig sticking out of other end, 3-1/2" h.................................85.00
  Heart, green, two pigs on each side of sheet music, mkd "Germany" 85.00
  My System, money bag, pig along side, 3-3/4" h 125.00
Barometer, pig shape 125.00
Bottle, Benedictine Liqueur, pig popping out of bottle, orange seal, 5-3/4" h 120.00
Cork, Heidisieck Dry Champagne, two pigs, 3" h...................................85.00
Crock, orange pig along side, 3" h...85.00
Dice, with large pig 110.00
Figure
  A Fine Looking Couple, two fat pink pigs sitting................................200.00
  Black bisque pig jumping over fence, 4-1/2" l, 3-1/2" h.......................80.00
  Black cook holding frying pan, pink pig in basket, 4-1/4" h...............450.00
  Canoe, single gold pig in yellow canoe, 1930s 85.00
  Car, old-fashioned type, rumble seat, two pigs inside, 3" l, 2-1/4" h........90.00
  Good Old Annual, water pump with piglet inside, mkd "Made in Germany," 3-3/4" h 100.00
  Hearts are Trumps, two pigs playing cards, 3-1/2" h, 3/4" h 105.00
  Let Me Also Have Some Mother, Mother pig and piglet, 2" h, 3" w.....................................95.00
  Lobster, pulling leg of red pig .. 125.00
  Mammy, spoon and bandanna, pink pig in basket, 4-1/4" h...............450.00
  Mind How You Fall, swinging piglet, larger pig looking on, tree, 3-3/4" h 100.00
  Money Bag, large pig with binoculars, brown and green coat and hat, 5" h...125.00
  Pig beside large basket, 3" h ... 125.00
  Pink pig with devil, pulling on hose..200.00

Purse, green, black bisque pig sitting on top, 2-1/4" h 80.00
Shoe, green, one pink pig inside, 4-1/2" l...85.00
Shoe, two pigs inside looking out...85.00
Souvenir of Chicago, IL, gold pig, orange top, wishing well, mkd "Made in Germany," 1930s, 3" h.............65.00
The Heavenly Twins, mother pig wheeling two piglets, incised "Made in Germany," 3-3/4" l, 3" h 98.00
Typewriter gentlemen, pink pig...1255.00
Water Trough, bisque, surrounded by four pigs, 4" l, 3-3/4" h 110.00
Hummel, Farm Boy, Goebel...........150.00
Inkwell, pink pig sitting on top of green inkwell, 3" h 100.00
Match Holder
  Large bisque pink pig with "Scratch My Back," small pig with "Me Too," 5" l 125.00
  Pig holding flag, 2 black kids in boat, striker on match holder 450.00
Nodder, china, dressed as man and woman 90.00
Pin Dish
  Good Luck, horseshoe, large yellow and green horseshoe, pink pig, stamped "Made in Germany," 5" w 85.00
  Older couple pink pigs, top hat, green bow tie, umbrella, yellow bonnet and bow, "Grandma" on dish, 4-3/4" w, 3-1/2" h,.....................................135.00
Pitcher, figural, dressed in tie and tails, brown, 4" h.................................30.00
Salt Dish
  Casino Wash, fat pig, two dishes 100.00
  Chef pig with shamrocks, salt cellars on each side, 4-1/4" h 135.00
Toothpick Holder
  2-1/2" h, small and large pig in front of open mushroom 95.00
  2-3/4" h, two little pigs in front of egg..75.00
  3" h, pig with mug in hand, leaning on fence...75.00
  3-1/4" l, pink pig pushing wheel barrow, worn 65.00
  3-3/4" h, pig with racquet, "Lawn Tennis" 85.00
  4" h, three large pigs in front of water trough..80.00
Toy
  Squeak, painted papier-mâché, 5" h..350.00
  Stuffed, Steiff, velvet, 2-1/2" h ... 115.00
  Wind-Up, tin litho, Porky Pig, cowboy outfit, yellow hat, Marx, MIB......200.00
Vase, 7-1/4" l, red devil's arm around pink pig, sitting on log......................110.00
Weather Van, metal 130.00

Pinball Machines

Collecting Hints: Cosmetic condition is of paramount importance.

Graphics are unique to specific models, especially backglass and playfield plastics, making replacements scarce. Because they are complex, graphics are difficult, if not impossible, to repair. Prices in this listing are for games in working condition that are considered cosmetically good and have 95 percent or more of backglass decoration present.

Some wear is expected in pinballs as a sign that the game was a good one, but bare wood detracts from overall condition. Watch for signs of loose ink on the rear of the glass. Unrestorable games with good cosmetics are valuable because they can be used to help restore other games. A non-working game is worth 30 to 40 percent less than a working one.

Add 10 percent if the paper items, such as score card, instruction card, and schematic, are present and in good condition. It is fair to suggest that regardless of mechanical condition, a game in good cosmetic condition is worth roughly twice that of the same game in poor cosmetic condition.

Pinball collecting is a new hobby which is still developing. It can be started inexpensively, but requires space to maintain. The tremendous diversity of models made has prevented the market from becoming well developed. There are relatively few people who restore antique pinball machines and then sell them. Expect to buy games in non-working condition and learn to repair them yourself.

Prices for specialty games and newer high tech theme machines have aroused new interest and better prices in certain categories. Collecting has also been helped by newer homes having bigger sized gamerooms.

History: Pinball machines can be traced back to the mid-1700s. However, it was not until Gottlieb introduced Baffle Ball in 1931, during the Depression, that pinball machines caught on and became a popular and commercial success because people were hungry for something novel and for the opportunity to make money. Pinball machines offered both. The first games were entirely mechanical, cost about $20, and were produced in large numbers— 25,000 to 50,000 machines of the same model were not uncommon.

Pinball developments include:
- 1932—addition of legs
- 1933—electric, at first using batteries
- 1936—addition of bumpers
- 1947—advent of flippers
- 1950—kicking rubbers
- 1953—score totalers
- 1954—multiple players
- 1977—solid-state electronics

The size of the machines changed over the years. The early countertops were 16 by 32 inches. Later models were freestanding, with the base measuring 21 by 52 inches and the back box, 24 by 30 inches.

Most pinballs were made in Chicago. Major manufacturers were Gottlieb, Williams, and Bally.

The total number of pinball models that have been manufactured has not been precisely determined. Some suggest more than 10,000 different models from 200-plus makers. After 1940, most models were produced in quantities of 500 to 2,000; occasionally, games had production figures as high as 10,000. Pinball machines have always enjoyed a high attrition rate. New models made the most money and were introduced by several of the major manufacturers at the rate of one entirely new model every three weeks during the mid-1940s and 1950s. Today, new models are introduced at a slower rate, averaging four to six new games per year.

Most pinball owners used the older games for spare parts to repair newer models. Earning life was less than three years in most markets. Many games were warehoused or destroyed to keep them from competing with the newest games. At the very least, the coin mechanisms were removed before the game was sold.

Pinball art is part of the popular culture and the kinetic art movement. The strength of its pinball playfield design made D. Gottlieb & Co. the premier maker through the 1950s and into the 1970s. During the 1960s, its fame grew because of its animated backglasses, which both amused and attracted players. The combination of animation and availability make the 1960s' machines a target for collectors.

The advent of solid-state games in 1977, coupled with the video-game boom, dramatically changed the pinball-machine market. Solid-state game production increased as manufacturers attempted to replace all obsolete electromechanical games. Initially, Bally was the predominant maker, but Williams has since attained this position. Although solid-state games made electromechanical ones commercially obsolete, collectors who are rediscovering the silver ball are helping the pinball machine recover some of its popularity.

References: Richard Bueschel, *Collector's Guide to Vintage Coin Machines*, Schiffer Publishing, 1995; —, *Encyclopedia of Pinball: Contact to Bumper, 1934-1936, Vol. 2*, Silverball Amusements, 1997; Heribert Eiden and Jurgen Lukas, *Pinball Machines*, Schiffer Publishing, 1992, 1997 value update; Bill Kurtz, *Arcade Treasures*, Schiffer Publishing, 1994; —, *Slot Machines and Coin-Op Games*, Chartwell Books, 1991; Donald Mueting and Robert Hawkins, *Pinball Reference Guide*, Mead Co., 1979.

Periodicals: *C.O.C.A. Times*, 3712 W. Scenic Ave., Mequon, WI, 53092; *Gameroom*, P.O. Box 41, Keyport, NJ 00735; *PinGame Journal*, 31937 Olde Franklin Dr., Farmington Hills, MI 48334; *Pinhead Classified*, 1945 N. St., Suite 111, Newman, CA 95360; *Pinball Trader*, P.O. Box 1795, Campbell, CA 95009.

Notes: Pinballs are listed by machine name and fall into various classifications: novelty with no awards, replay which awards free games, add-a-ball which awards extra balls instead of games, and bingo where players add additional coins to increase the odds of winning. Some payout games made in the mid- to late 1930s paid out coins for achieving scoring objectives. After the first add-a-ball games in 1960, many game designs were issued as both replay and add-a-ball, with different game names and slight modifications to the game rules, but similar art work.

Advisor: Bob Levy.

Bally

1933, Airway, first mechanical scoring	350.00
1951, Coney Island, bingo	400.00
1963, Moon Shot, replay	400.00
1968	
Rock Makers, replay, unusual playfield	500.00
Safari, replay	400.00
1972, Fireball	1,500.00
1973, Nip-It, ball grabber	700.00
1975, Bon Voyage, replay	350.00
1978, Lost World, electronic	475.00

Chicago Coin, 1948, Spinball, spinner action 175.00

Exhibit, 1941, Big Parade, patriotic theme, classic art 450.00

Genco, 1936, Daily Races, 1-ball .375.00

Gottlieb

1936, Daily Races, 1-ball 375.00

1948, Buccaneer, replay, mirrored graphics 700.00
1950, Knockout, playfield animated 2,500.00
1951, Mermaid, backglass animated 3,000.00
1955, Duette, replay, first two-player 500.00
1956, Auto Race, replay 800.00
1960, Flipper, first add-a-ball 1,000.00
1965, Cow Poke, animation classic 1,750.00
1966, Subway, backglass animation 1,500.00
1967, King of Diamonds, replay, roto 1,100.00
1977, Target Alpha, multiplayer 500.00
1981, Black Hole, electronic, multi-level 800.00
Mills Novelty Co., 1932, Official, push-button ball lift 350.00
Pacific Amusement, 1934, Lite-A-Line, first light-up backboard 400.00
Rock-Ola
1932, Juggle Ball, countertop, road ball manipulator 300.00
1934, World Series, desirable sports theme 850.00
United, 1951, ABC, first bingo 400.00
Williams
1948, Yanks, baseball theme, animated 600.00
1951, Jalopy, mechanical car race 1,000.00
1953, Army-Navy, replay, reel scoring 750.00
1958, Gusher, disappearing bumper 900.00
1958, Turf Champ, playfield animation 1,500.00
1961, Metro, replay 400.00
1964, Palooka, add-a-ball 600.00
1973, Travel Time, timed play 300.00
1977, Grand Prix, replay 350.00
1980, Firepower, electronic 610.00

Pin-Up Art

Collecting Hints: Try to collect calendars that are intact. There is a growing practice among dealers to separate calendar pages, cut off the date information, and sell the individual sheets in hopes of making more money. Buyers are urged not to support this practice.

Concentrate on the work of one artist. Little research has been done on the pinup artists so it is a wide-open field. The original art on which calendar sheets and magazine covers are based has begun to appear on the market. High prices are being asked for both the oil paintings and pastel examples, but the market is not yet stabilized—beware!

Pinup material can be found in many other collectible categories. Usually the items are referred to as "girlies." Many secondary pinup items are not signed, but a collector can easily identify an artist's style.

History: Charles Dana Gibson introduced the first true pinup girl when he created the Gibson Girl in the early 1900s. Other artists who followed his example included Howard Chandler Christy, Coles Phillips, and Charles Sheldon. The film magazines of the 1920s, such as *Film Fun and Real Screen Fun*, developed the concept further. Their front covers featuring minimally clad beauties were designed to attract a male readership.

During the 1930s, popular cover artists included Charles Sheldon, Cardwell Higgins, and George Petty. Sheldon did calendar art, as well as covers for Brown & Bigelow. *Esquire* began in 1933; its first Petty gatefold appeared in 1939.

The golden age of pinup art was 1935 to 1955. The 1940s brought Alberto Vargas (the final "s" was dropped at *Esquire's* request), Gillete Elvgren, Billy DeVorss, Joyce Ballantyne, and Earl Moran into the picture. Pinup art appeared everywhere—magazine covers, blotters, souvenir items, posters, punchboards, etc. Many artists besides those mentioned here adopted the style.

Photographic advertising and changing American tastes ended the pinup reign by the early 1960s.

References: Max Allen Collins, *For The Boys: The Racy Pin-Ups of World War II*, Collectors Press, 2000; Max Allen Collins and Drake Elvgren, *Elvgren: His Life & Art*, Collectors Press, 1998.

Periodicals: *Glamour Girls: Then and Now*, P.O. Box 34501, Washington, DC 20043; *The Illustrator Collector's News*, P.O. Box 1958, Sequim, WA 98382.

Desk calendar, The Esquire Girl Calendar, 1947, Albert Varga, artist, $80.

Ashtray, metal, 4" sq, Elvgren picture, made for King Klub
  Titled "A Peek-A-Knees" 80.00

Titled "Catchy Number," 80.00
Titled "French Dressing," wear ... 60.00
Titled "Help Wanted" 80.00
Titled "Sport Model" 80.00
Blotter, 3-1/2" x 6", cardboard, full color sgd art by Rolf Armstrong, blond haired nude seated at edge of pond waters, 1935 Brown & Bigelow ©, unused 45.00
Box, 4-1/4" x 4-1/4" x 1-3/4", red and white, color graphics of high heeled smiling girl, bow and arrow, large red heart background, logo "Hit For His Heart," Pioneer Belts, c1940 ...... 28.00
Calendar
  1942, Esquire, Varga Girl, plastic spiral binding, 12 pgs, horizontal format, verses by Phil Stack, 8-1/2" x 12" 75.00
  1945, Starlight, Earl Moran, full color nude blond, dark green drape, black ground 40.00
  1948, Esquire Glamour Gallery, paper wall type, full color pin-up art for each month, contributing artists include Ben-Hur Baz, Fritz Willis, Joe DeMers, Al Moore, J Frederick Smith, Ron Wicks, 8-1/2" x 12" 65.00
  1948, Varga, adv Reliance Elevator Co., 9" w, 14" h 175.00
  1951, Esquire, desk type, Al Moore graphics, 12 pgs, 5-1/2" x 6" 38.00
  1952, Thompson Studio, sketches, orig envelope 50.00
Calendar Page
  Howard Chandler Christy, titled "When Sammy Comes Marching Home," July, August, September 1918, edge pcs missing top and bottom, 8-1/2" ... 80.00
  Varga, April, brunette in prone position, naval cap on her foot held high in air 25.00
  Varga, February, 1946, redhead dressed in translucent bathing suit, few stains 18.00
  Varga, Jaunary, 1944, seductively dressed redhead, verse by Phil Stack, minor stains 18.00
  Varga, March, redhead dressed in Hawaiian outfit 20.00
  Varga, September, 1946, blond in summer attire, some creases 18.00
Date Book, 5" x 7", Esquire, color cover, spiral binding, full color pin-up photos, 1943 © George Hurrell 35.00
Drawing, Munson
  Titled "Doc Said All I Needed Was Glasses," wood frame, 10" x 12" 95.00
  Titled "Shall I Turn Around," wood frame, 10" x 12" 95.00
Drinking Glass
  2-1/2" d, 5-1/2" h, titled "Regarde, Maman, Pas de mains!" artist sgd "McQuiddy," set of four 85.00
  3" d, 5" h, keyhole allows viewer to see pin-up girl on inside, two red and two black, set of four 95.00
Greeting Card
  Christmas, illus of Bettie Page, by Olivia 0.50
  Happy Birthday, illus of Bettie Page, by Olivia 7.50

Wedding, Varga bride, 5-1/2" x 8", blank int..................9.00

Hair Pin, orig 4" x 5-1/2" yellow, red, black, and white card, Petty, artist sgd, 1948, MOC..........................25.00

Hand Towel, printed pin-up gal, 1950s 22.00

Keychain, Elvgren insert, 1-1/2" x 2", slotted plastic case, full color insert, metal keychain, c1950
A Hitch In Time, girl adjusting stocking as dog looks on 35.00
Belle Ringer, girl doing laundry, skirt caught in ringer 25.00
Look What I've Got, leggy girl fishing.............................25.00
See-Worthy, leggy girl boating....25.00

Letter Opener, 8-1/2" l, 2" w, plastic, shaped like lady's leg, clear and blue rhinestone accents, sgd "Remembrance" on back..................70.00

Magazine
Esquire, June, 1942, Jane Russell centerfold by Petty, anti-Nazi theme 60.00
Pin-Up Photography, Vol. 1, No. 1, Betty Page cover, 1956..............65.00
Prevue, Jan 1953, Marilyn Monroe cov, article 35.00

Magazine Ad
Kentucky Club, 1956..................10.00
Perma-Lift Brassiers, black and white, woman wearing bra, girdle, and stockings, 1954, 10" x 13" 15.00
Spun Lo, pin-up lifeguard, 1950, 5" x 13"...................................12.00

Money Clip, 1-1/4" x 2", Betty Page .75.00

Mutoscope Card, minor edge wear, 3-1/4" x 5-1/4"
A Peek-A-Knees 14.00
Flaming Youth 14.00
Free As A Breeze..................14.00
Some Chicken, sgd "Earl Moran," copyright B&B 12.00
Sure Shot....................................14.00

Notepad, adv
Deltronix, sgd Gil Elvgren cov, titled "Stepping Out," unused, 4" x 6-1/2".....................................12.00
Geo. E. Failing Supply Co., 1945, captioned "This is just between us," 3-1/4" x 6"...................................22.00

Pencil, nude pin-up, plastic, 4-3/4" l, 1-1/2" d..........................70.00

Pendant, rect plaque
2" x 2-1/2", pin-up girl with bird that pulls on her skirt, turning pendant causes to show skirt falling off, mirror on back 75.00
2" x 2-1/2", pin-up girl watering plant, turning the pendant causes sunflower to bloom and her to jump back...85.00
2" x 2-3/4", pin-up girl covering herself up with feather fans, turning the pendant causes her to appear to be undressing, mirror on back 85.00

Pill Box, 1-1/4" x 1-1/4" 70.00

Playing Cards
Al Moore, copyright Esquire, Inc., two decks, one in orig plastic shrink wrap 125.00

Art Studios, nudes 65.00
Gil Elvgren, made by Brown & Bigelow, made for Henry Schaeffer Inc., Brooklyn, NY, wear to box............75.00
Gil Elvgren, made by Brown & Bigelow, made for Loring and Sykes Service Station, Elizabethtown, OH, Don Loring and Joe Sykes.................95.00

Pocket Knife, 4" l, silvered steel, single blade, black and white cello side panel insert photos, one with full figure nude, holding garment, similar photo on other side, knife blade mkd "U.S.A.," c1940s 35.00

Postcard, Curt Teich Co.
Sea Nymph, C-259, previously glued in album...............................8.00
Una-veil-able, 2B-21420, previously glued in album 8.00

Print
Moran, Dreamin,15-1/2" x 15-1/2", minor flaws, matted................... 125.00
Mozert, Zoe, calendar top, Sweet Dreams, framed, 16" x 20"....... 300.00
Munson , Doc Said All I Needed Was Glasses, sgd, wood frame, 10" x 12"...................................... 110.00
Munson, Don't You Just L-O-O-OVE These Cushions, sgd, wood frame, 10" x 12"................................95.00
Munson, Oh You Do Remember My Voice, sgd, wood frame, 10" x 12"..95.00
Withers of Hollywood, artist and models, 1952.....................................225.00

Punch Card, "Watch their dresses disappear when you pour a cold drink," pull flap at base of card to release dress..15.00

Sample Calendar, wall type
Armstrong, 11" x 23", full color art sgd by Rolf Armstrong, brunette model, red and white two-pc swimsuit, titled "Tip Top," text for Brown & Bigelow, St. Paul, Minn, calendar for March, 1951...75.00
Frahm Art, 16" x 33", art print titled "Spare?" 1958 copyright of A. Fox, credit line to artist Arthur E. Frahm, blond bowler, calendar for January 1960...85.00

Stand-Up Card, 4-3/4" x 10" diecut cardboard, perforations for folding to form model figure standing on triangular display, full color Moran art, titled "Not So Dusty," pretty brunette in sheer green cleaning outfit, high heels, c1950, unused 15.00

Tape Measure and Pin Cushion, 4-1/4" h, "Miss Pin-Up," figural pin cushion and tape measure, manufactured by Prestige, orig box, c1960 ....40.00

Planters

Collecting Hints: Planters are available in a wide array of shapes and colors. Seek out the best examples available. Because many planters were made inexpensively and meant to be used with dirt, water, and growing plants, it is not unusual to find wear and minor interior scratches and damage.

Collectors of modern planters should carefully save any packaging or brochures which illustrate the planter. The brochures issued as sales promotions by florists will become the advertising collectibles of tomorrow. Collectors of specialty planters should check to make sure all decorations are included, e.g., ladies' heads should be complete with original necklaces and earrings.

Collectors should be careful to determine that the object is a true planter and not a mismatched canister or vase that has been home to a plant.

History: As soon as houseplants became an important part of interior decoration, planters were created. Some planters are simply vessels given a new lease on life, such as crock or chamber pot. Other items, such as jardinieres, window boxes, and hanging baskets were designed specially to hold growing materials. Many manufacturers created these interesting shapes and colors to compliment not only the plant but also the interior design of the room where it was placed.

Like cookie jars, wonderful figural planters were created in the 1940s and have continued to present times. Many major companies, such as McCoy and Roseville, created an inexpensive line of planters for use by florists. Some of these same planters are now eagerly sought by collectors. Florists have learned this valuable lesson, and today planters issued by organizations like FTD are dated.

Some planters, such as the popular ladies' heads, were made by small firms and were distributed regionally. These charming figural planters give a wonderful perspective on the fashion and colors that were popular at the time of their manufacture.

References: Pat and Keith Armes, *The Collector's Guide to Lady Figure Planters*, Schiffer Publishing, 2000; Kathleen Cole, *Head Vases Identification & Values*, Collector Books, 1989, 2000 value update; Betty and Bill Newbound, *Collector's Encyclopedia of Figural Planters & Vases*, Collector Books, 1997; Mike Posgay and Ian Warner, *World of Head Vase Planters*, The Glass Press, 1992; Mary Zavada, *Lady Head Vases*, revised ed., Schiffer Publishing, 1994.

Periodocal: *Head Hunter Newsletter*, Box 83H, Scarsdale, NY 10583.

Collectors' Club: Wall Pocket Collectors Club, 1356 Tahiti, St. Louis, MO 63128.

Planter, lamb, white, pink bow at neck, American Art Potteries, 8-1/2" x 3", $25. Photo courtesy of Doris and Burdell Hall.

Figural

Auto, 9" x 4-1/2", ceramic, Birchwood line, McCoy, some wear to yellow trim 45.00

Bambi, mkd "Walt Disney Productions" 65.00

Bamboo, pale green, tan highlights, incised "0376 USA," 6-1/2" d, 5" h 12.00

Basket, yellow and brown, McCoy ..35.00

Birds on a Perch, four white, yellow, and black birds, brown tree branch, glossy glaze, mkd "Shawnee 502".........35.00

Blackamoor, heavy gold trim............35.00

Butterfly on Log, brown and white, glossy glaze, mkd "Shawnee USA 524" 10.00

Cactus and Cowboy, natural colors, Morton Pottery......................................15.00

Cart, blue exterior, yellow interior, glossy glaze, Shawnee, mkd "USA 775".......................................10.00

Cat, coral glaze, green box, McCoy, c1950 ....12.00

Cat, white, mkd "Haeger"...................7.50

Conch Shell, yellow and green, glossy glaze, Hull 35.00

Covered Wagons, one with boy walking beside donkey, other with girl, 6" x 4-1/4", price for pr.......................25.00

Cradle, pink, McCoy..........................10.00

Dachshund, brown, glossy glaze, Hull..75.00

Deer, pale brown and greens, glazed, unmarked......................................55.00

Dog, figure on pair of rockers, Morton Pottery 18.00

Donkey, standing, small Mexican figure sleeping in front of legs, baskets on back, high gloss, white, 6" h 9.00

Elephant, curved trunk, #94E, American Art Pottery 18.00

Elephant, figure on pair of rockers, Morton Pottery.....................................20.00

Elf, sitting on large shoe, multicolored, glossy glaze, mkd "Shawnee 765" 10.00

Fawns, standing pair, 5" x 3-1/2", McCoy, 1957...38.00

Flamingo, 10" l, 7-1/4" h, c1940, unmarked, price for pr............. 175.00

Ford, dark green, gold trim, detailed, Metlox, 8-1/2" l 75.00

Giraffe, 9" h, green, glossy glaze, Hull..35.00

Globe, blue and green, yellow stand, glossy glaze mkd "Shawnee USA"...15.00

Goat, gray, red harness, McCoy 15.00

Gondola, yellow, McCoy...................18.00

Goose, Hull, #80 ....30.00

Guitar, black, semi-gloss, mkd "Red Wing USA #M-1484" 15.00

Hen, figure on pair of rockers, Morton Pottery..16.00

Horse, figure on pair of rockers, Morton Pottery 16.00

Lady, two wolfhounds, Brayton Laguna, 11"h, 7-1/2" w 175.00

Lamb, white, blue bow, McCoy........15.00

Lamb, white, pink bow, #456D, American Art Pottery....................................25.00

Lion, white, McCoy, c1940 ....12.00

Log, 7" l, white, Niloak.....................18.00

Mallard, head down, Royal Copley ..20.00

Mouse, leaning on cheese wedge, multicolored, glossy glaze, Shawnee, mkd "USA 705" 15.00

Parrot, 5", white, orange accents 18.00

Pelican, turquoise, matte glaze, McCoy, mkd "NM USA" 12.00

Piano, upright, green, glossy glaze, Shawnee, mkd "USA 528"...........18.00

Pig, figure on pair of rockers, Morton Pottery..18.00

Policeman and Donkey, 5", blue, Niloak..35.00

Quail, 9-1/2" h, natural color spray glaze, American Art Potteries.................25.00

Raggedy Ann, holding baby bottle, 6" h, incised "Relpo 6565" 45.00

Ram, mkd "USA 6/3," 6" l, 4" h, price for pr 50.00

Rooster, figure on pair of rockers, Morton Pottery 16.00

Santa Claus, fleshtone, red, and white, Morton 25.00

Scottie Dog, Royal Copley................15.00

Shoe, bronzed-type, McCoy 8.00

Skunk, 6-1/2" h, black and white, pastel pink and blue basket, airbrushed, Brush-McCoy, #249 ....35.00

Snoopy, 7" h, ceramic, "Snoopy" on round planter container, paint wear on figure...40.00

Stork, McCoy 10.00

Surrey, metal fringe, dark green, wire wheel and top, Metlox, 15-1/2" l ..85.00

Swan, pink/mauve/gold decor, #319G, American Art Pottery....................27.00

Swan, turquoise, purple wing tips, unmarked 7.50

Turkey, brown, red wattle, Morton 12.00

Wally Walrus, ceramic, 1950............50.00

Whale, 10" l, black, Freeman McFarlin, ...50.00

Wishing Well, 7-1/4" h, dusty rose, Niloak..20.00

Head Types

Baby, 5-3/4" h, blond hair, open eyes, pink cheeks, open mouth, pink ruffled bonnet tied under chin, pink dress, unmkd 18.50

Betty Grable type, Morton Pottery Co. 35.00

Black Lady, 5" h, young, downcast eyes, yellow turban, red sarong, large gold hoop earrings, three-strand pearl necklace, Japan...........................45.00

Blond

5" h, green bonnet, mkd "Lew Woods Exclusive, Japan"..................... 150.00

7" h, black hat, white plume, blue bow tied under chin, mkd "#959," Philadelphia, 1950s............................... 295.00

7-1/2" h, Ardco...........................265.00

7-1/2" h, Relpo, Japan, #C1633 ....250.00

Bonnie, Ceramic Arts Studio..........160.00

Cowboy, 6" h, brown hair, blue eyes, yellow hat and neckerchief, white shirt, yellow star badge, unmkd 35.00

Girl, 5-1/4" h, long blond hair, straight bangs, blue flowers at ponytail on top of head, eyes looking right, raised hand, slender neck, blue press, Parma by AAI, Japan, A-222......12.50

Lady, 7" h, brown hair, downcast eyes, raised right hand, black hat with white and gold ribbon, black dress, white glove with gold accents, pearl drop earrings and necklace, Inarco, C-2322 ....35.00

Madonna, 4-1/2" h, blue head covering, slight crazing 12.75

Napco, Japan, all in mint condition, orig jewelry

6" h, #C3307 ....150.00

6" h, #C5428, orig paper sticker 165.00

6-1/2" h, #C5047.......................210.00

7-1/4" h, #C348B 175.00

7-1/2" h, #C6429.......................210.00

7-1/2" h, #C7495.......................295.00

8-1/2" h, #C7314, blond 250.00

8-1/2" h, #C7496.......................295.00

9-1/2" h, #C7487.......................525.00

10-1/2" h, #C6987.....................725.00

11" h, #C7487...........................725.00

Nurse, 5-3/4" h, short blond hair, downcast eyes, raised right hand, white cap with Red Cross insignia, white uniform with gold accents, painted fingernails, unmarked 45.00

Polynesian, Shawnee.......................60.00

1920s hairstyle, wide floppy brim hat, Morton Pottery Co. 60.00

1940s hairstyle, pillbox hat, Morton Pottery Co. 50.00

Wall pocket, cone shape, matte ivory/turquoise, Cliftwood Art Potteries, 5" w, 8" l, $40. Photo courtesy of Doris and Burdell Hall.

Wall Pocket

Acorn, light brown, mkd "Frankoma 190"..25.00
Apple on leaf, McCoy.......................50.00
Baby and Diaper, mkd "4921, Japan"...15.00
Bellows, McCoy...................................40.00
Broom, inverted, mkd "L & C Ceramics © Hollywood Hand Made"..............25.00
Cocker Spaniel, head, mkd "Royal Copley"...20.00
Cornucopia basket, green and white, McCoy..40.00
Cowboy Boot, figural, blue and white, speckled, mkd "Frankoma 133".30.00
Cup and Saucer, blue, B-24..........265.00
Fan, blue, McCoy...............................45.00
Fan, 24K overlay, McCoy.................40.00
Fan, white, pink floral, McCoy..........60.00
Fish, yellow stripes, mkd "Gilner Calif C"...25.00
Gardenia, brown, #666-8, Roseville..................................150.00
Geisha Girl..70.00
Grape Cluster, mkd "Royal Haeger R-745 USA"..25.00
Harlequin heads, boy and girl, Japan..65.00
Homemade Plaster, yellow iris dec, unmarked, 8" l.............................20.00
Horseshoe, horse head center........30.00
Iris, blue, 8-1/2" l, Weller...................50.00
Leaf, blue and pink, McCoy.............40.00
Lily, yellow, McCoy.............................25.00
Morning Glory, McCoy......................50.00
Peacock, mkd "West Coast Pottery, California, USA-441".........................45.00
Post Box, green, McCoy..................50.00
Sandy and Jean, head-type, boy and girl, blue plaid shirts, minor damage, price for pr...75.00
Snowberry, blue, #1WP-8, Roseberry..................................180.00
Straw Hat, mkd "Stewart G McCullock © Calif"..15.00
Sunflower, blue, McCoy....................30.00
Sunflower, yellow, with bird, McCoy.45.00
Teapot, pink apple dec, Shawnee...30.00
Tulips, emb flowers, white, Roseville....................................60.00

Tulips, white, green leaves, McCoy..40.00
Umbrella, black, white handle, mkd "McCoy USA"...............................40.00
Whisk Broom, blue, B-27..............265.00
Woman in bonnet and bow, white, red trim, McCoy..................................40.00
Woodrose, Weller.........................110.00

Planters Peanuts

Collecting Hints: Planters Peanuts memorabilia is easily identified by the famous Mr. Peanut trademark. Items made between 1906 and 1916 have the "Planters Nut And Chocolate Company" logo.

Papier-mâché, die-cut, and ceramic pieces must be in very good condition. Cast-iron and tin pieces should be free of rust and dents and have good graphics and color.

History: Amedeo Obici and Mario Peruzzi organized the Planters Nut And Chocolate Company in Wilkes-Barre, Pennsylvania, in 1906. Obici had conducted a small peanut business for several years and was known locally as the "Peanut Specialist."

At first, Spanish salted red skins were sold for 10¢ per pound. Soon after, Obici developed the whole, white, blanched peanut, and this product became consumers' favorite.

In 1916, a young Italian boy submitted a rough version of the now-famous monocled and distinguished Mr. Peanut as an entry in a contest held by Planters to develop a trademark. A wide variety of premium and promotional items were soon based on this character.

Planters eventually was purchased by Standard Brands, which itself later became a division of Nabisco.

Reference: Jan Lindenberger, *Planters Peanut Collectibles Since 1961*, Schiffer Publishing, 1995.

Collectors' Club: Peanut Pals, P.O. Box 4465, Huntsville, AL 35815.

Reproduction Alert.

Ashtray, 4-3/4" h, center figural Mr. Peanut, 1906-1956, mkd "Made in the USA by Diecasters Inc., Ridgefield, NJ"...30.00
Bar Wrapper, 6" x 7" waxed paper liner, red and blue adv inscription, c1929, unused..14.00
Book, 7-1/4" x 10-1/2", *Mr. Peanuts Presidents of the United States*, 1932, cover loose, worn.........................20.00
Bracelet, metal, 8" l, five plastic 1" charms, 1960s.........................30.00

Burlap Sack, 16" h, Mr. Peanut Roasted Peanuts, 1 lb, 8 oz, c1970..........18.00
Can, tin
  2-3/4" h, Mr. Peanut Cashew Nuts, Planters Nut and Chocolate Co., orig lid with wear, 1944......................32.00
  2-3/4" d, 2-3/4" h, Planters Nut & Chocolate Co., Suffolk, VA, Wilkes-Barre, PA, San Francisco, CA, Mr. Peanut standing on both sides of label, 4 oz, key wind lid, some fading, C-7...45.00
  2-3/4" d, 3" h, Planters the Name for Quality, Mr. Peanut, recipe on back for Pecan Coffee Cake and Pecan Meringue Frosting, 4 oz, key wind lid, mkd "Canco," C-9.....................45.00
Charm, 2-1/8" h, hard plastic, figural Mr. Peanut, emb "Mr. Peanut," 1950s..15.00
Coloring Book, *Mr. Peanut American Ecology Coloring Book*, 1970, unused...15.00
Cookbook, *Cooking The Modern Way*, Planters Peanut Oil, 1948, 40 pgs...12.00
Counter Jar
  7" d clear heavy glass, orig lid, 8" x 8" x 9-1/2", corrugated cardboard shipping carton, c1960s...........................90.00
  12" h hard plastic, 10-1/2" d blue hat, 1979...30.00
Dish Set Coupon, 6-3/4" x 8-1/2", shows single serving dish and four individual smaller dishes, mail-in premium offer on back, expiration date of Sept 30, 1939, folds...............................14.00
Figure, 6" h, flexible vinyl, black and white with yellow/orange body, cane in hand, Russ sticker on back, 1991 copyright...................................20.00
Jacket, Racing Team, dark blue, yellow lining, Mr. Peanut on front, larger one on back, unworn........................30.00
Lapel Pin, hard plastic, figural Mr. Peanut..15.00
Limited Edition Plate, 6" d, Wilton, pewter, 75th anniversary........................60.00
Mug, 4-1/4" d, 5" h, pewter, engraving of Mr. Peanut on side with date 1983...15.00
Olympic Coin, 2" d, 1980, incised with Mr. Peanut, Winter Games, Lake Placid mascot on other side.................15.00
Paint Book, Planters Seeing the USA, 1950, Mr. Peanut's trip through 48 states, Alaska, Hawaii, and Puerto Rico, unused.............................38.00
Pen, 5-1/4" l, "Planters Snacks, Cheese Curls, Corn Chips, Pretzels" written on barrel, Mr. Peanut top, 1970s.....20.00
Pencil, mechanical, blue and yellow, Mr. Peanut on top, 1950s.................28.00
Straw, 8" l, plastic, figural Mr. Peanut..15.00
Tray, 15-5/8" x 11-5/8", tin................18.00

Plastics

Collecting Hints: Thermoplastic collectibles can be ruined when exposed to heat, flame, or a hot-pin test.

History: The term "plastic" is derived from the Greek word "Plastikos," which means pliable. Therefore, any material which can be made pliable, and formed into a desired shape, technically falls into the category of plastic. For the collector, two categories of plastics should be recognized: natural and synthetic.

Natural plastics are organic materials which are found in nature. The most common natural plastics are tortoiseshell and cattle horn. They have been used for hundreds of years to make both utilitarian and luxury items. Natural plastics were harvested and cleaned, then softened in hot liquid. Once pliable, they were manipulated into shape by a variety of methods including carving, sawing, and press molding.

Semi-synthetic and synthetic plastics are those which are man-made from combinations of organic and/or chemical substances. The most commonly collected plastics in this category include the earliest examples: 1870—Celluloid (pyroxylin plastic), 1890—Casine (milk protein and formaldehyde), and 1907—Bakelite (phenol formaldehyde).

The years between World Wars I and II gave birth to the modern plastics age. Beetleware, a urea formaldehyde plastic with properties similar to Bakelite, was introduced in 1928. Lumarith, a trade name for cellulose acetate plastic, was introduced in 1929 and served as a nonflammable replacement for celluloid.

During the Great Depression, the plastics industry developed at an astounding rate with the introduction of acrylic and polymer plastics: Polystyrene and Poly-vinyl-chloride—PVC (1930), Methylmethacrylic (1934), Melamine (1935), and Polyethylene (1939). Today all of these plastics are collected in hundreds of forms.

All plastics fall into one of two categories: thermoplastic or thermoset. Thermoplastics are those which are molded by the application of heat and pressure, then cooled. Additional applications of heat will resoften or melt the material. Tortoiseshell, horn, celluloid, cellulose acetate, polystyrene, polyethylene, and acrylic fall into this category.

Thermoset plastics are those which are molded by the application of heat and pressure, then upon cooling, permanently hardened. While they are resistant to high temperatures, they are subject to cracking over time. Thermoset plastics include Bakelite, Beetleware, and Melmac.

Acrylic Plastic, introduced in 1927 by Rohm & Haas as "Prespex" or "Plexiglas," is used instead of curved glass in airplane cockpits In 1937 Dupont introduced Lucite, a thermoplastic acrylic resin that could be either crystal clear or opaque, tinted any color and cast, carved or molded.

Bakelite is the registered trade name for the first entirely synthetic plastic. It was developed by Leo H. Baekeland in 1907 using carbolic acid and formaldehyde. Commonly called phenolic resin, Bakelite is a tough, thermoset plastic that can be cast or molded by heat and pressure.

Celluloid was the first commercially successful semi-synthetic plastic. Introduced as a denture-base material in 1970, it reigned supreme as the most versatile man-made plastic for 40 years.

References: Shirley Dunn, *Celluloid Collectibles*, Collector Books, 2001; Bill Hanlon, *Plastic Toys*, Schiffer Publishing, 1993; Lyngerda Kelley and Nancy Schiffer, *Plastic Jewelry*, Schiffer Publishing, 1987, 1994 value update; Keith Lauer and Julie Robinson, *Celluloid, A Collector's Reference and Value Guide*, Collector Books, 1999, 2001 value update; Joan Van Patten and Elmer and Peggy Williams, *Celluloid Treasures of the Victorian Era*, Collector Books, 1999.

Museum: National Plastic Museum, Leominster, MA.

Advisor: Julie P. Robinson.

Purse, Lucite, white, $18.

Acrylic

Bedside Stand, three-pc twisted acrylic rod base, round glass top 250.00
Bracelet, 3/4" bangle, green, opaque, orig tag "Genuine Lucite" 10.00
Brush and Comb, translucent pink set, nylon bristles, mkd "Dupont Lucite," orig box 15.00

Business Card Holder, sea shells suspended in rect base, c1965 .... 6.00
Buttons, pearlescent pink squares, metal loop, set of eight on orig card 4.00
Clock, electric, chrome and lucite, cylinder shaped, rotating disc that changes color, pink, yellow, purple, and green reflect in fact, c1970s 65.00
Compact, 4" sq translucent case, applied sunburst medallion gold glitter acrylic, Roger & Gallet, mfg by Donmark Creations, Co, 1946 .... 150.00
Cufflinks, pr, Krementz, toggle findings, paperweight style, fishing fly suspended in lucite 35.00
Drafting Tools, Rhom & Haas Plexiglass, set of two rulers, two triangles, and semi-circle, c1940 .... 20.00
Dress Clips, green opaque lucite, triangular, chevron design, rim set with rhinestones 18.00
Etagere, 60" h, free standing triangular shape shelf, clear acrylic with four mirror shelves, pointed finial 550.00
Hand Mirror, beveled acrylic handle and frame, U-shaped mirror, sterling floral ornament, c1946 .... 55.00
Lamp, chrome cylinder base, 3" d solid lucite ball top, flickering red, white, and blue lights in base reflect through bubbles in acrylic globe, c1976 . 22.00
Napkin Ring, translucent lucite, square shape, rounded edges, circular center, c1960, price for four-pc set .. 10.00
Paperweight
    2" x 1", rect cube, suspended purple rose 5.00
    3" cube, translucent lucite, suspended JFK 50 cent piece, c1965 .... 8.00
Pin
    Apple, pink lucite, gold plated stem and leaf, Sarah Coventry, c1970 20.00
    Dragonfly, pearlescent green lucite wings, enamel paint over pot metal, c1960 .... 8.00
    Turtle, jelly belly, aqua lucite center, pot metal, red painted eyes, c1950 .... 12.00
Purse
    Basketweave chrome, 8" x 4", clear lucite bottom, black lucite hinged to and handle, c1955 .... 55.00
    Clutch, smoky gray lucite, camera case shape, hinge opening, c1950 .... 45.00
    Vanity, 4-1/2" x 4-1/2", envelope type front, white marbleized, Elgin American 100.00
Tumbler, clear 8 oz octagonal shape, chevron design, Art Deco revival, Norse Products, price for four-pc set 25.00

Bakelite

Ashtray, 8" d, black and white 45.00
Bar Pin, dangling heart, bright red catalin 150.00
Bracelet, bangle
    1/2" wide, carved leaf design, red catalin, ... 45.00
    3/4" wide, reverse carved floral design, translucent amber 150.00
Buckle, circular, interlocked red, yellow, green, and blue rings 25.00

Button, 1 large, four small, oval, two holes, translucent amber and brown swirl, price for five-pc set 12.00

Cake Server, green handle............... 12.00

Chess set, butterscotch and marbleized brown 400.00

Clock, 12" h, Western Electric, Gothic shape, dark brown 65.00

Crib Toy, amber, green, and orange opaque catalin, shape of girl doll, 17 separate pieces strung together...................................... 125.00

Dress Clip, triangular, chevron grooves, green, price for pr....................... 65.00

Manicure Box, Cleopatra, mfg by GE, black and red Art Deco............. 165.00

Napkin Ring, figural
   Animal shape, red, green, or butterscotch 45.00
   Trylon and Perisphere, orange, green, red, and yellow, price for pr 75.00

Pie Crimper, marbleized butterscotch handle 4.00

Pin, figural, cat, yellow catalin, chrome 95.00

Poker Chips, black, maroon, butterscotch, maroon holder 130.00

Rattle, barbell shape, five rings, red, green, and butterscotch.............. 90.00

Ring
   Dome top, floral carving, butterscotch........................... 75.00
   Square, starburst carving, brown 65.00

Ring Box
   Clam shell style, streamline modern grooves, orange and butterscotch swirl 85.00
   Semi-circular, hinged lift top, square base, mottled green and yellow,. 75.00

Salt and Pepper Shakers, pr
   Figural brown bird shaped holder, amber shakers........................... 120.00
   Gear shape, chrome lids, marbleized caramel, 2" h................................. 85.00
   Washington Monument souvenir, obelisk shape, cream colored.......... 65.00

Serving Tray, oval dark blue with inlaid strips of chrome, Art Deco style.. 350.00

Stationery Box, 7" x 8", molded brown, Art Deco winged horse design, American Stationery Co., 1937 .... 75.00

Toothpick Holder, dachshund, green....................................... 95.00

Utensil set, knife, fork, spoon, marbleized red and yellow handles 16.00

Yo-Yo, mottled green, mkd "Regal PDC" 30.00

Celluloid

Animal
   Cow, 6", purple, red rhinestone eyes, mkd "Made in Occupied Japan" 22.00
   Dog, 3", black Scottie, mkd "Made in USA".. 20.00
   Horse, 7" l, cream color, brown highlights, hp eyes, intertwined VCO mark 45.00

Bar Pin, 2-3/4" l, ivory grained, orange and brown layered pearlessence, hp rose motif 12.00

Bookmark, 4-1/2" l, cream colored diecut celluloid, poinsettia motif, Psalm 22, printed by Meek Co. 15.00

Bracelet, bangle, translucent amber celluloid, double row of green rhinestones 25.00

Collar Box, 6" x 6", olive colored, emb celluloid with floral motif, picture of beautiful woman on top.................... 45.00

Doll, 5" h, Kewpie-type, movable arms, molded clothing and cap, mkd "Made in Japan" 22.00

Dresser Set, comb, brush, mirror, tray, powder, box, and hair receiver, marked "Ivory Pyralin," price for six-pc set... 65.00

Dresser Tray, 8" oval, imitation tortoise shell rim, glass and lace center .. 35.00

Fan, 6" w, ivory colored, hp floral motif, blue satin ribbon 20.00

Haircomb, 6" l, pale amber, blue rhinestones, painted blue bird motif.... 55.00

Ink Blotter Booklet, 8-1/2" l, 1-1/2" w, wood grained celluloid, black lettering, "Jennison Co., Engineers & Contractors, Fitchburg, Mass," 1917 calendar, 8" ruler markings 30.00

Match Safe, 2-1/4" x 1-1/2", color photo scenes from Atlantic City, NJ....... 18.00

Necktie Box, 12-1/2" x 3-3/4", reverse painted Art Nouveau design, cream, brown, and coral 48.00

Picture Frame, 8" x 10", oval, ivory grained celluloid, easel back 20.00

Pinback Button, 1-1/4" d, dangling 1" celluloid camel, Shriner's logo.......... 55.00

Pocket Mirror, 2-1/2" oval, souvenir of Niagara Falls, printed colored drawing of Falls 18.00

Purse, 4-1/4" d, clam shell-type, amber colored celluloid, leather strap.... 45.00

Rattle
   4" l, blue and white egg shape, white handle 18.00
   4-3/4" l, figural, little girl playing lute, pink 45.00

Roly-Poly, 2-1/2" d, realistic chicken, weighted base 35.00

Playboy Collectibles

Collecting Hints: Antique shows typically do not offer a Playboy collector a vast selection of items to choice from and searching for them can become frustrating. Currently, Playboy collectibles are very popular and most easily obtained on the Internet. Literally thousands of listings can be found on a daily basis by searching on-line auctions.

When buying a *Playboy* magazine, who is on the cover or in a pictorial of an issue is many times more important than how old the magazine is. For the most part, there is no reason to buy a magazine if the centerfold has been removed. Having the subscription cards in tact, especially if there is a popular centerfold model on the front, will slightly add to the issue's value. Because *Playboy* has been printing more than a million copies since 1955, only purchase magazines that are in fine condition or preferably better.

History: The first *Playboy* magazine was released in December of 1953. Owner and publisher Hugh M. (Marston) Hefner did not put a date on the cover because he was not sure if there would be another copy. Fortunately for *Playboy*, and collectors, there was at least one more copy because that issue debuted the famous Rabbit Head logo. The popular Femlin was introduced into Party Jokes section of the August, 1955 magazine. She was drawn by LeRoy Neiman.

The first Playboy club opened in 1960. In just over a year, it had become the most visited night club in the world. After yielding a seemingly endless supply of ashtrays, mugs, swizzle sticks and other collectibles, the last state-side club closed in 1988. Currently, *Playboy* has more than 4 million subscribers and still offers its own line of merchandise.

Advisor: Patrick M. Leer.

Ashtray
   Clear glass, rabbit head in center, mint 12.00
   Orange, 3-3/4" x 3-3/4", Femlin logo in center, mint 10.00
   Smoked black glass, 3-3/4" x 3-3/4", Femlin logo in center, mint 12.00
   White, 5-5/8" x 5-5/8", black rabbit head in center, mint................... 15.00
   White and gold, 3-3/4" x 3-3/4", VIP in center.. 15.00
   Yellow, 3-3/4" x 3-3/4", Femlin logo in center, mint 18.00

Book, *Playboy's Host & Bar Book*, Thomas Mario, Playboy, 1971, hard cover, 339 pages 25.00

Cigarette Lighter
   Playboy Bunny, George Petty, Zippo, orig collector's case, mint 55.00
   Rabbit head logo on front, black case, Japan, mint................................. 18.00
   Rabbit head logo on front, cream/yellow case, Japan, mint 20.00
   White rabbit head logo on front, black case, 6-1/2" x 4-1/2", mint 85.00

Crock, 3" d, 3" h, stoneware, red insignia, chip on int. lip 28.00

Magazine, *Playboy*
   First Issue, Marilyn Monroe on cover, good condition 1,500.00
   First Issue, Marilyn Monroe on cover, near-mint condition................. 2,500.00
   1955, January, Bettie Page centerfold, good condition 300.00
   1955, January, Bettie Page centerfold, near-mint condition................. 475.00
   1965, February, Beatles interview, mint 18.00

1968, November, with centerfold, fine...9.00
1985, September, Madonna on cover, last stapled issue...........................15.00
1994, November, Pamela Anderson on cover, autographed, mint.......50.00
1995, January, Drew Barrymore cover, mint..20.00

Mug
Black, Playboy Club, gold Femlin logo, mint...15.00
Clear, black rabbit head logo, 9-3/4" h, mint...............................12.00
Green, black rabbit head logo, 9-3/4" h, mint...............................18.00
White, black rabbit head logo, 9-3/4" h, mint...............................15.00

Olive Pick, set of 28 black and 38 white plastic picks................................13.00
Pen, red...8.00
Pin, Playmate, circular, bunny logo, gold-tone, orig price tag, orig package..32.50
Plaque, 5-1/4" x 7-1/2", wood.........125.00
Playing Cards, 1971, nudes, orig plastic box, orig cardboard sleeve.........48.00
Poster, Miss January, 11" x 24".......65.00

Puzzle, centerfold, box
1967, Playmate Paige Young, opened, no centerfold picture, very good 25.00
1970s, Playmate Life Size Puzzle, MIB...200.00

Puzzle, centerfold, canister
1968, Playmate Jean Bell, opened, fair...12.00
1970, unopened, with centerfold picture, excellent..............................45.00
1973, Bonnie Large, unopened, excellent...50.00

Ring, man's, 14k yg, bunny logo...85.00
Shot Glass, 2" x 3", Femlin.................18.00

Stein
3-1/2" d, 6" h, glass, logo on two sides...8.00
4" d, 5" h, pewter, Playboy Bunny on front and back, glass bottom, mkd "Made in Hong Kong".................12.00

Swizzle Stick, 8-1/4" l
Black or white, Playboy on side, each...1.00
Blue, orange, red, or green, Playboy on side, each...................................4.00
Red plastic, Bunny on one end, "Playboy Club" down one side............10.00

Tankard, aluminum, rabbit head logo engraved on side, mint..............10.00
Tumbler, 3-1/4" h, Playboy Club.......14.00
Video, 1990-98 Video Playmate Review..17.50

Wall Calendar
1958, first, fine, no sleeve............70.00
1960-64, Playmate Calendar, orig envelope, mint, each...................55.00
1961, Stella Stevens as Miss March, 8" x 12"..70.00
1969, orig envelope.....................25.00
1976, orig envelope, mint...........18.00

Playing Cards

Collecting Hints: Always purchase complete decks in very good condition. Know the exact number of cards needed for a full deck—an American straight deck has 52 cards and usually a joker; pinochle requires 48 cards; tarot decks use 78. In addition to decks, collectors seek very early uncut sheets and single cards.

Many collectors focus on topics, for instance, politics, trains, World's Fairs, animals, airlines, or advertising. Most collectors of travel-souvenir cards prefer a photographic scene on the face.

The most valuable playing card decks are unusual either in respect to publisher, size, shape, or subject. Prices remain modest for decks of cards from the late 19th and 20th centuries.

History: Playing cards were first used in China in the 12th century. By 1400, playing cards were in use throughout Europe.

French cards are known specifically for their ornate designs. The first American cards were published by Jazaniah Ford, Milton, Massachusetts, in the late 1700s. United States innovations include upper-corner indexes, classic joker, standard size, and slick finish for shuffling ease. Bicycle Brand was introduced in 1885 by the U.S. Playing Card Company of Cincinnati.

Card designs have been drawn or printed in every conceivable size and on a variety of surfaces. Miniature playing cards appealed to children. Novelty decks came in round, crooked, and die-cut shapes. Numerous card games, beside those using the standard four-suit deck, were created for adults and children

References: Phil Bollhagen (comp.), *Great Book of Railroad Playing Cards*, published by author, 1991; Everett Grist, *Advertising Playing Cards*, Collector Books, 1992.

Collectors' Clubs: American Antique Deck Collectors Club, 204 Gorham Ave., Hamden, CT 06514; American Game Collectors Assoc., P.O. Box 44, Dresher, PA 19025; Chicago Playing Card Collectors, Inc., 1559 West Platt Blvd., Chicago, IL 60626; 52 Plus Joker, 204 Gorham Ave., Hamden, CT 06514; International Playing Card Society, 3570 Delaware Common, Indianapolis, IN 46220; Playing Card Collectors Assoc., 337 Avelon St. #4, Roundlake, IL 60073.

Museum: Playing Card Museum, Cincinnati Art Museum, Cincinnati, OH.

Notes: The following list is organized by both topic and country. Although concentrating heavily on cards by American manufacturers, some foreign-made examples are included.

Advertising, Reese's Peanut Butter Cups, 40th Anniversary, Brown & Bigelow, St. Paul, MN, $12.

Advertising
Blue Bonnet Margarine, Blue Bonnet Girl illus...17.50
Champion Spark Plugs, repeating logo...15.00
IGA Food Store, line drawing of store...10.00
Inclinator Company of America, Harrisburg, blue.................................12.00
Jefferson Motor Company, Jefferson, GA, Mercury outboard motors, two decks, slip case.............................75.00
Kool Cigarettes, cigarette pack image...15.00
Life Savers, multicolored.............12.00
Monarch Better Outdoor Garments, clothing tag with lion logo............15.00
Playboy Playmate, nudes, 1968, orig plastic box, orig cardboard sleeve...48.00
Robbins Potato Co., sailboat on ocean, rope and anchor border.12.00
Sinclair Oil, red oil well logo, white ground, gold and red borders....15.00
Superior Dairy, National Pro Football Hall of Fame building.................12.00
Tartan Coffee and Tea, 1/2" x 2-1/2" x 3-1/2" box, warrior in tartan plaid uniform, kilt and cloak, Lowry Coffee Co., c1930, 52 cards, no jokers, orig box...14.00

Aviation
Delta Air Lines, New York, traffic cop...15.00
Northwest Orient, Oriental phrases...10.00
WWII, airplane spotter, orig box.12.00

Brewery
Arrow Beer, gold arrows, lettering, and border, red ground.....................15.00
Old Tavern Lager Beer, black and white factory scene.....................18.00

Casino
Caesars Palace, Las Vegas, Nevada, gold logos, dark blue ground.......8.50
Golden Nugget Gambling Hall, mirror image of white lettering surrounded by gold scrollwork and nugget........12.00

Cause
Eisenhower College of Seneca Falls, NY, Dwight D. Eisenhower paintings of

George Washington and Abraham Lincoln, velour-topped box with label stating royalties go to Eisenhower College, late 1960s 60.00
Prince of Wales National Relief Fund, WWI, 1914, MIB 40.00

Railroad
Chicago, Milwaukee & St. Paul, 53 scenic views, 1919, orig box 50.00
New York, New Haven & Hartford RR, orig box and wrapper 75.00
Southern Pacific Railroad, 1930s 55.00

Souvenir
Boys Town, tax-stamped, 2 deck set by Brown & Bigelow, plain edges, scenes from Boys Town, Nebraska, orig box 60.00
Chicago, Sears Tower, skyline 15.00
Holland American Line, blue or red 9.00
Kennedy Space Center, FL, Space Shuttle, lift-off photo 12.00
Royal Caribbean, red, anchors, and ships 10.00

World Fairs and Expositions
Century of Progress, Belgian Village, plastic case 85.00
Golden Gate Exposition, two sets, one with distant view of Tower of the Sun during day, other night view, orig box 95.00
New York, 1965, tax-stamped deck, Stancraft, gold edges, orig two-part plastic box with promotional outer sleeve 55.00
Pan-American Exposition, Official Souvenir, different fair scenes 95.00

Pocket Knives

Collecting Hints: The pocket knife collector has to compete with those who collect in other categories.

The pocket knife with a celluloid handle and advertising underneath dates back to the 1880s. Celluloid-handled knives are considered much more desirable than the plastic-handled models. Collectors also tend to shy away from purely souvenir-related knives.

History: Pocket knife collectors fall into two main types: 1) those who concentrate on the utilitarian and functional knives from firms such as Alcas, Case, Colonial, Ka-Bar, Queen, Remington, Schrade, and Winchester; and 2) those interested in advertising, character, and other knives, which, while meant to be used, were sold with a secondary function in mind. These knives were made by companies such as Aerial Cutlery Co., Canton Cutlery Co., Golden Rule Cutlery Co., Imperial Knife Company, and Novelty Cutlery Co.

The larger manufacturing firms also made advertising, character, and figural knives. Some knives were giveaways or sold for a small pre-mium, but most were sold in general stores and souvenir shops.

References: Jerry and Elaine Heuring, *Keen Kutter Collectibles*, 2nd ed., Collector Books, 1990, 1993 value update; Jacob N. Jarrett, *Price Guide to Pocket Knives*, L-W Book Sales, 1993, 1995 value update; Bernard Levine, *Levine's Guide to Knives and Their Values*, 4th ed., Krause Publications, 1997; Jim Sargent, *Sargent's American Premium Guide to Knives and Razors*, 5th ed., Krause Publications, 1999; J. Bruce Voyles, *American Blade Collectors Association Price Guide to Antique Knives*, Krause Publications, 1995; Ken Warner, ed., *Knives 2000*, 20th ed., Krause Publications, 1999; Richard D. White, *Advertising Cutlery*, Schiffer Publishing, 1999.

Periodicals: *Blade*, 700 E. State St., Iola, WI 54990; *Edges*, P.O. Box 22007, Chattanooga, TN 37422; *Knife World*, P.O. Box 3395, Knoxville, TN 37927.

Collectors' Clubs: American Blade Collectors, P.O. Box 22007, Chattanooga, TN 37422; Canadian Knife Collectors Club, 3141 Jessuca Ct, Mississauga, ON L5C 1X7 Canada; Ka-Bar Knife Collectors Club, P.O. Box 406, Olean, NY 14760; National Knife Collectors Assoc., P.O. Box 21070, Chattanooga, TN 37421.

Museum: National Knife Museum, Chattanooga, TN.

Reproduction Alert: Advertising knives, especially those bearing Coca-Cola advertising, have been heavily reproduced.

Advertising
Canadian Club, The Best in the House, mkd "Stainless Steel, Japan," pocket knife and nail file, 2" x 1" .. 20.00

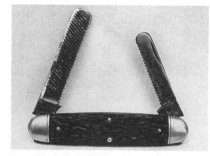

Remington, dog grooming, stag horn handle, 3-3/4" l, $125.

Champion Spark Plugs 35.00
Kaiers Beer 55.00
Phillips 66, knife and file, Zippo .. 20.00
Platts Bros., 4 blades, Congress type 55.00
Purina, checkerboard dec, 3-3/4" l 30.00

Snap-On, Captain DL-2, Dura-Lens diamond nail file, precision scissors, 1-1/2" blade, Schrade Cutlery 12.00
Swift's Canned Foods, 5" l, ivory celluloid 150.00

Barlow, one of two blades mkd "Colonial Prov. USA," 6-1/4" open, etched design on handle, used 95.00

Baseball
Babe Ruth, 2-1/2" l, facsimile signature, Camillus Cutlery Co. 125.00
Chicago Cubs, 3-3/8" l, two blades, plastic grips 18.00

Character
Dick Tracy, red and white, celluloid 45.00
Jimmie Allen, silver wings 70.00
Roy Rogers, 3-13/4" l, black and white 55.00
The Little Colonel, orig display with 12 knives on board, late 1950s 250.00

Figural
Dachshund, key chain and knife 12.00
Fish, 2-3/4" l, silver, Kero Co., Curby, Pat. 1885 .... 120.00
Shoe, 5-1/8" l, horn, steel blade, 19th C 350.00

Forestmaster, four blades, mkd "Colonial," used, some rust, 3-3/4" folded 25.00

Fraternal, Odd Fellows, porcelain handle, silver and enamel inlays of skull and crossbones, hand with red heart in the center, letters "FLT," orig box 185.00

Hunter, Puma, folding
Game Warden 45.00
Plainsman 40.00
Prince 60.00
Single blade 175.00

Political, Nixon Agnew, Re-elect President in 1972, blue lettering, white marble-ized surface, portrait sketches, two blades, 2-3/4" l 30.00

Souvenir, Ricordo Di Pompei, red plastic case, one blade, 2-3/4" l 12.50

Unmarked
Gold filled, two tone, 2-1/2" x 11/16", blade mkd "stainless steel," some wear 30.00
Stainless Steel, three different size blades, largest 2-1/4" l, stamped "Stainless Steel" 5.00
Sterling Silver, 3" l, two blades, engraved initials "CGHH," German 10.00

World's Fair and Expositions
1836-1936, Texas Centennial, cream colored handle with bull, hay, state flag and emblem, two blades 72.00
1935 .... 40.00
1939, Golden Gate Bridge, 5-1/2" l, two blades, cream colored pearl-type handle, name of fair and city 80.00

Political and Campaign Items

Collecting Hints: Items priced below $100 sell frequently enough to establish firm prices. Items above that price fluctuate according to supply and demand. Many individuals now recognize the value of acquiring political items and holding them for future sale. As a result, modern material has a relatively low market value, unless few examples were produced.

Knowledgeable collectors also keep in touch with Presidential libraries to find out what type of souvenir items they are offering for sale. This information is helpful in determining which items on the market originated at the time of actual campaigns, and these are the ones collectors should concentrate on acquiring.

The pioneering work on the identification of political buttons has been done by Theodore L. Hake, whose books are listed below. Two other books have greatly assisted in the identification and cataloging of pre-1896 campaign materials: Herbert R. Collins's *Threads of History* and Edmund B. Sullivan's *American Political Badges and Medalets 1789-1892*.

History: Since 1800, the American presidency always has been a contest between two or more candidates. Initially, souvenirs were issued to celebrate victories. Items issued during a campaign to show support for a candidate were widely distributed beginning with the William Henry Harrison campaign of 1840.

There is a wide variety of campaign items—buttons, bandannas, tokens, pins, etc. The only limiting factor has been the promoter's imagination. The advent of television campaigning has reduced the quantity of individual items, and modern campaigns do not seem to have the variety of materials that were issued earlier.

Modern collectors should be aware of Kennedy material. Much has been reproduced and many items were issued after his death.

References: Herbert Collins, *Threads of History*, Smithsonian Institution Press, 1979; Theodore L. Hake, *Encyclopedia of Political Buttons, United States, 1896-1972*, Americana & Collectibles Press, 1985, (P.O. Box 1444, York, PA 17405); ——, *Political Buttons, Book II, 1920-1976*, Americana & Collectibles Press, 1977; ——, *Political Buttons, Book III, 1789-1916*, Americana & Collectibles Press, 1978; Note: Theodore L. Hake issued a revised set of prices for his three books in 1998; ——, *Hake's Guide to Presidential Campaign Collectibles*, Wallace-Homestead, 1992; Margaret Brown Klapthor, *Official White House China: 1789 to the Present*, 2nd edition, Harry N. Abrams, Inc., 1999; Edward Krohn, *National Political Convention Tickets and Other Convention Ephemera*, David G. Phillips Publishing Co. Inc. (P.O. Box 611388, No. Miami, FL 33161), 1996; Keith Melder, *Hail to the Candidate*, Smithsonian Institution Press, 1992; James W. Milgram, *Presidential Campaign Illustrated Envelopes and Letter Paper 1840-1972*, David G. Phillips Publishing Co. Inc. (P.O. Box 611388, No. Miami, FL 33161), 1996; Edmund B. Sullivan, *American Political Badges and Medalets, 1789-1892*, Quarterman Publications, 1981; ——, *Collecting Political Americana*, Christopher Publishing House, 1991; Mark Warda, *Political Campaign Stamps*, Krause Publications, 1998.

Periodicals: *Autograph Times*, 2303 N. 44th St., #225, Phoenix, AZ 85008; *Political Bandwagon*, P.O. Box 348, Leola, PA 17540; *Political Collector Newspaper*, P.O. Box 5171, York, PA 17405.

Collectors' Clubs: American Political Items Collectors, P.O. Box 340339, San Antonio, TX 78234; Button Pusher, P.O. Box 4, Coopersburg, PA 18036; Ford Political Items Collectors, 18222 Flower Hill Way #299, Gaithersburg, MD 20879; Indiana Political Collectors Club, P.O. Box 11141, Indianapolis, IN 46201; NIXCO, Nixon Collectors Organization, 975 Maunawili Cr, Kailua, HI 96734; *Rail Splitter* (Abraham Lincoln), Box 275, New York, NY 10044; Third Party Hopefuls, 503 Kings Canyon Blvd., Galesburg, IL 61401.

Museums: Museum of American Political Life, Hartford, CT; Smithsonian Institution, Washington, DC; Western Reserve Historical Society, Cleveland, OH.

Advisor: Ted Hake.

Abraham Lincoln, 1860, 1864

Book, cartoon history, hard-bound set, Albert Shaw, volume 1 signed by author, gold imprinted spines, political cartoons and photographs, 1929...80.00

Campaign Envelope, 1860 jugate, 3-1/8" x 5-1/4", pale yellow, corner jugate in black, slight wear.....................125.00

Medalet, one side with spread wing eagle and slogan "Success To Republican Principles," other side emb "Millions for Freedom, Not One Cent For Slavery" 100.00

Benjamin Harrison, 1888, 1892

Pinback, 2" h, mechanical, Presidential Chair, silvered brass, real sepia photo of Harrison, seat is on a spring and can be closed, seat reads, "Who Shall Occupy It?" 1888.....................250.00

Print, sepia portraits of Pres. And Mrs. Harrison, 4-1/4" x 6-1/2", brown card mount, c1888..............................20.00

Silk, 2-1/2" x 4", Harrison and Morton, red, white, and blue flag design, names in dark blue, 1888 ....40.00

William McKinley, 1896

Jugate, black and white photos of McKinley and Teddy Roosevelt, red, white, and blue accent bow, backpaper reads "National Equipment Co.," Whitehead and Hoag, 1900 ....20.00

Lapel Stud, black and white photo in center, dark blue and bright red stars on cream rim....................................20.00

Paperweight, 2-1/2" x 3", solid brass bust, c1896...60.00

Paperweight, 2-1/2" x 4", glass, rect, center sepia portrait, c1896..............40.00

Pinback Button, 7/8" d, black and white photo, gold trim, diamond design flanked by red, white, and blue star and stripe motif, bright gold outer motif 30.00

Pinback Button, 1-1/4" d, rebus, black on cream, "Count Me For (picture of McKinley) And A Full" (picture of dinner pail)..225.00

Ribbon, 2-1/2" x 7", "Our Standard" platform, black and white, cream ground, brass eagle and flags bar pin hanger at top..90.00

Teddy Roosevelt

Figure, 6" h, Syroco, Great American series, 1941 copyright, old glue repair......................................125.00

Match Holder, 3" h, ceramic, Teddy Roosevelt on his knees, Rough Rider outfit, bear figure climbing tree stump, base inscribed, "Jamestown, NY," white, green and gold accents, c1904, slight wear 125.00

Paperweight, 2-1/2" x 4", sepia photo of Teddy Roosevelt in center 70.00

Pinback Button, rebus, "For President" large full-color design of red rose, green stem, center above lettering "Velt," no back paper...............200.00

Pinback Button, "Vote For Roosevelt Use Maple City Soap," dark red, cream lettering, 1904 ....210.00

Sheet Music, *Teddy You're A Bear*, credits to Ring H. Larder for worlds, music by Lee S. Robert, published by Jerome h. Remick & Co., 1916, 4 pgs.........25.00

Woodrow Wilson, 1912, 1916

Ashtray, 3" x 4", raised imp of young Wilson, inscription "Justice" on sword handle and "Humanity" on side of book, 1908-20 ....18.00

Campaign Ribbon, 3" x 6", red, white, and blue, "Democratic" ticket, above and below crossed flags, Wilson/ Marshall 35.00

Pinback Button, 1-7/8", red, white, and blue, blue name 20.00

Postcard, 3-1/4" x 5-1/2", "Our Next President," black on pale green, "Magic Moving Pictures Cared," push/pull black and white flicker of Teddy Roosevelt, Taft, or Wilson, 1912...40.00

Warren G. Harding, 1920

Pinback Button, "For President Warren G. Harding," photo center, white rim, blue lettering 15.00

Stereoscopic Card, set of five, showing Harding and wife at visits, speeches, and vacations, c1920 .... 20.00

Herbert Hoover, 1928, 1932

Campaign Ring, Hoover 1928, non-adjustable silvered brass, ornate enameled designs 30.00

Pinback Button, "Be Safe Be Hoover," emb brass, bright brass raised areas, dark blue painted background ... 15.00

Pinback Button, "Engineers For Hoover," 9/16" l diecut building, brass letter, dark blue enameled ground 35.00

Franklin D. Roosevelt, 1932, 1936, 1940, 1944

Button

1-3/4" d, black and white photo surrounded by bold rim design in red, white, and blue 35.00

2-1/8" d, portrait in blue and white, pale red accent under face, white background with narrow red circles surrounded by wide dark blue rim, "Franklin Delano Roosevelt" in white letters, 1936 .... 45.00

Inaugural Souvenir, 1-1/4" d black and white button with 1-3/4" x 3-1/4" attached gold type on red, white, and blue ribbon which reads, "Inauguration Franklin D. Roosevelt, Our First Third Term President/January 2, 1941/Washington, D.C." 50.00

Magazine Section, 11-1/2" x 15-3/4", 20 pgs, Sunday, Nov. 3, 1940, front cover collage of campaign materials ...20.00

Mug, 3" x 3-1/4" h, New Deal, brown and yellow, raised image of FDR on raised shield, c1933-35 .... 25.00

Newspaper, "F.D.R. Is Laid To Rest," Daily Mirror, 11-1/2" x 15", 20 pg section, April 18, 1945, large 10" x 10" black and white photo on cover, follow-up stories.. 25.00

Pillow Cover, 16" x 18", large black photo of FDR in wicker chair on front, navy border, blue piping, bright orange fabric back, c1932-36 .... 60.00

Poster, 11" x 14" red, white, and blue, bluetone photo of FDK and several Missouri Democrats, including Harry S. Truman for United States Senator... 70.00

Ribbon Badge, 1-3/4" x 5", "We Want Roosevelt," brass and fabric ribbon, red, white, and blue fabric, gold type, brass framed bar pin at top with blank cardboard insert for name, light general wear 50.00

Sheet Music, 9" x 12"

On With Roosevelt, red, white, and blue, four pgs, words and music by Louise Graeser, 1938 .... 10.00

The Road is Open Again, lyrics by Irving Kahal, music by Sammy Fain, red, white and blue glossy cover, four pcs 18.00

Sign, 14" x 22", thin cardboard, bluetone photos, red and blue type, white ground, titled, "Insure Wisconsin For Roosevelt/General Election/Tuesday Nov. 3, 1936"............................. 250.00

Transit Pass, 2" x 4-1/2", brown, red, and yellow, weekly pass for Inauguration Week, Jan. 19-25, 1941, 1-1/2" h oval black and white portrait of FDR on left side, punch-out for E. Washington Bus at top 25.00

Wall Hanging, 3-1/2" d, white molded plastic rim, eagle and star accents, 2" x 3-1/2" black and white raised dimensional center portrait, metal loop at top, 4" l faded red, white, and blue fabric 75.00

Alfred Landon, 1936

Campaign Card, 2-1/4" x 4" heavy paper card for election day, 1936 ....10.00

Napkin, 13-1/2" sq brown on white in paper, Landon's sunflower art in center as compass, folds to 7" sq, c1936 .... 18.00

Derby Pin, celluloid, "Al for our Next President," browntone, c1928 ....25.00

Pinback Button, brown and yellow sunflower, dark green rim 10.00

Wendell Willkie, 1940

Car Attachment, 3-1/2" h, black and white, 1940 ....50.00

Pinback Button, "Democrats for Willkie," blue and cream litho, red rim 12.00

Pinback Button, "Willkie Contributor," white lettering, red and blue segments 8.00

Harry S. Truman, 1948

Booklet, "The Democratic Digest, June-July 1950," 7-1/2" x 10-3/4", 32 pgs, black and white, photos, text of Democratic stand 20.00

Inauguration Button, 3-1/2" d, red, white, and blue, black and white center photo 90.00

Button

1-1/8" d, cream, reddish-brown litho, Harry S. Truman 40.00

3-1/2" d, red, white, and blue rim, large black and white center photo, For President, Harry S. Truman.........90.00

Hand-out Card, 2-1/2" x 3-1/2", glossy coated card, black and white picture and facsimile signature, 1948 Democratic National Committee Officially Authorized Votes by States on back..20.00

Mechanical Card, 4" x 7" stiff red, white, and blue card, center window shows browntone photo of Truman or Dewey, which changes as tab is pulled, reads, "Mystery of the Year, Who Will Be Our Next President," © 1948 by Alan Murray 75.00

Ribbon Badge, 1-1/4" x 5-1/2", Democratic National Convention, Philadelphia, brass and enamel, green fabric ribbon, raised image of "Birthplace of Old Glory" and furling flags on either

side, 1-1/4" dia bras medal with raised image of William Penn, Liberty Bell, and Independence Hall 48.00

White House Dinner Ticket, 2-1/2" x 4" stiff card, handwritten guest's name and date, May 27, 1946 .... 20.00

Dwight Eisenhower, 1952, 1956

Button

2-1/4" d, dark blue letters on cream ground, Fight with Dwight, made by The American Badge Co., Chicago, IL 50.00

2-1/2" d, red, white and blue, bluetone photo in center of shield, "Give Ike A Republican Congress"................ 20.00

Inauguration Invitation, 9" x 12-1/2" stiff paper, printed in script, presidential emblem emb in gold at top, 1957 .... 20.00

Jugate Button with Ribbon, 2" x 4-1/2" blue on gold and yellow ribbon, pin at top, "Montgomery County, Penna, Leading County For Ike," 3" lustrous gold rim edge 100.00

License Plate, 3" x 5", black on orange steel, Ike 35.00

Matchbook, "Citizens for Eisenhower," red, white and blue pack, Reading, PA, hotel sponsor, used 12.00

Pennant, 9" x 26" l, red felt pennant, white type "I Like Ike," yellow felt strip at left 20.00

Pinback Button, "I Like Ike," red, white, and blue rim, bluetone photo 7.50

Pinback Button, "Peace-Progress-Prosperity/I Like Ike," bluetone photo, white ground, blue and red slogan 10.00

Plate, 10-1/2" d, first birth in the White House, red, white, blue, and gold Pennsylvania Dutch sign surrounded by green type, red, white, and blue stars and gold facsimile signature, "Castleton China, New Castle, Pennsylvania" back-stamp................. 25.00

Stickpin Charm, brass pin holds clear plastic charm with back and white photo under plastic on the front, open back, paper insert reads I Like Ike 15.00

Token, 1-1/2" d, aluminum, profiles of Lincoln, Eisenhower, and Nixon, A Profile of Integrity, reverse with eagle and slogan Your Country, Your Dollar, Vote Republican 15.00

Richard M. Nixon, 1960, 1968, 1972

Autograph, dinner ticket, 3" x 6" stiff black and white card, $100 Per Person/Dinner Sponsored By Republican Finance Committee of Pennsylvania, Feb. 10, 1965, Bellevue Stratford Hotel, Philadelphia, sgd "Dick Nixon," minor wear 175.00

Bendee, 4" h, painted rubber figure of Nixon, jointed swivel arms, hands giving victory sign, 1" d suction cup attached to top of head, c1972 .. 20.00

Bubble Gum Cigars, 4-1/2" x 5", red, white, and blue box, 22 cigars, "Win with Dick" on labels, black and white photo of Nixon on box lid............ 35.00

Button, Member National Nixon Lodge Club, black and gold.................10.00

Campaign Hat, 11" d, 3" h, Styrofoam, red, white, and blue paper headband with bluetone photo of Nixon on either side of name and stars,.............20.00

Car Antenna Flag, 4" x 9-1/2", Pat for First Lady, plastic, 1960....................25.00

Game, Who Can Beat Nixon, 9" x 11-1/2" x 2", red, white, and blue box, light aging of box lid...........................15.00

Handout, Victorygram, 5-1/2" x 8-1/2", handout designed as replica of paper telegram sent to Texas supporter in 1968, stamped with date "1968 Nov 4 PM 2 29"....................................15.00

Hand Puppet, 15" h, painted stiff vinyl head of Nixon and Agnew, 9" h fabric smocks with sewn-in hands, price for pr..45.00

Inauguration Button, ribbon badge, 2" d blue on gold button, 2" x 7" blue fabric ribbon, gold type, "President Richard M. Nixon Inauguration, January 20, 1973, Lancaster County, Pennsylvania"..25.00

Inflatable Bag, 18" x 11", Keep Kicking Nixon, red, white, blue, and tan vinyl, Nixon image giving victory sign, sealed in orig plastic bag with header card, "Kick It Around, Always Makes a Comeback," sticker reads, "Who Says You Don't Have Nixon to Kick Around Anymore?" © 1982.....................40.00

Jugate, Nixon/Agnew, 1972, black and white photos, red, white, and blue eagle and shield design, white background..15.00

Key Fob, shield shaped clear plastic fob, red, white, and blue paper label, bluetone jugate photos........................10.00

Label Dispenser, 2-1/2" h sq cardboard box that held 5" d black and white paper "Vote for Nixon" stickers...10.00

Magazine, *Newsweek Election Preview '60*, illus of Nixon and Kennedy on cover, 126 pgs, Nov. 7, 1960......15.00

Mask, 13" h, rubber, 1983, well made..20.00

Pinback Button, Inauguration Day, black and white photo, black, red, and blue lettering, white background, red, white, and blue stylized flag........18.00

Ribbon, 2" x 6", "Pat & Dick Nixon in Philadelphia," brass frame, cardboard name tag bar pin attachment to white fabric ribbon with blue "Guest" type, c1960..20.00

Ticket, 3-1/2" x 6", Nixon/Lodge Campaign Breakfast, October 5, 1960, Hotel Commodore, New York City, 7/8" d red, white, and blue "Nixon/Lodge" button attached..........................30.00

John F. Kennedy, 1960

Ashtray, 4" x 4-1/2", smoked glass, black and white photos of JFK and RFK at center, gold trim, birth and death dates, gold stars, famous quotes, c1968..25.00

Bottle Stopper, 3-1/2" h, 1-1/4" deep cork, 3-D painted wood composition c1962...48.00

Button, Kennedy for President, blue and white flicker, slogan and portrait set in clear plastic case, red plastic rim, reverse with bar pin, black and white donkey, "Vote Democratic"..........35.00

Charm, 1-1/8" h, three dimensional bust, c1964..10.00

Coloring Book, 10" x 13", stiff paper, red, white, blue, and black cover, 24 pgs, satirical cartoons, 1962...............20.00

Gum Cards, 2-1/2" x 3-1/2" black and white cards, Rosan Printing Co., New York, 1964, complete set of 64....60.00

Jugate, 2-1/8" d, America Needs Kennedy-Johnson, black and white photos, red, white, and blue background...30.00

Magazine

Photoplay, March 1964, full color cover of Pres and First Lady, special section titled, "Jack & Jackie - Their Courtship," 7 page article on "JFK, the Assassin Was Not Alone," black and white and color photos................15.00

US News & World Report, Nov. 21, 1960, full-color photo of Kennedy on cover...25.00

Paper Dolls, Jackie and Caroline, Magic Wand Paperdoll Set, 10" x 14" set, c1982-83, unused....................60.00

Souvenir Plate, 6-1/2" d, President and Mrs. John F. Kennedy, painted full color illus, c1961.........................20.00

Johnson-Humphrey, Vote Democratic, $15.

Lyndon Johnson, 1964

Bumper Sticker, 4" x 11-1/2", New Hampshire, green, black, and white, issued by NH Democratic Committee, 1968...20.00

Delegate Badge, Indiana State, silvered brass bar, purple ribbon with "Delegate" in silver lettering, dark blue o silver luster aluminum diecut picturing LBJ with name below...................20.00

Glass, 5-1/2" h, clear glass, Kosygin Summit, Glassboro State College, NJ, June, 1967, black and white illus of meeting place.............................20.00

Hat, 4" x 11", plastic, campaign style, red, white, and blue stripes, black and white illus of Johnson on right, "LBJ for the USA".....................................10.00

Jugate, 4" d, bluetone photos of Johnson and Humbert Humphrey, white ground, red lettering "Great Day for USA"..24.00

License Plate, 6" x 12", inauguration souvenir, 1965......................................5.00

Pen, give-away, gold presidential logo, facsimile signature on black plastic, gold metal top and clip, felt tipped pen frayed..15.00

Viewmaster Reel Packet, 4-1/2" sq full color paper envelope, three reels, "LBJ Country," orig booklet.........12.00

Barry Goldwater, 1964

Antenna Attachment, 4" x 6-1/2", red and blue lettering, white background, spring tension.............................15.00

Pinback Button, "Goldwater In '64," light blue tone lettering and photo, white ground, red rim............................7.50

Stickpin, elephant, diecut plastic, wearing Goldwater-style eyeglasses..........5.00

Tie Tack, diecut letters, brass luster, needlepost and clutch back..............5.00

Gerald Ford, 1976

Button, full color photo, "For President Gerald Ford '76"...........................8.00

Poster, 19" x 25", President Ford '76, serious looking Ford, minor damage..12.00

Jimmy Carter, 1976

Bandanna, 28" sq, Carter-Mondale, white and green, 1980.........................25.00

Hand Puppet, 6" x 9", painted hollow rubber head, blue fabric coat, stuffed tan fabric hands, red, white, and blue header reads, "Puppet President/ Never Promised You A Rose Garden"......................................20.00

Inauguration Medal, 5" x 6" x 2" white cardboard box, blue presidential seal on top, solid bronze medal, antique finish, diecut repository lined in dark blue felt, parchment authenticity certificate, "Sculptured by Julian Harris/ Minted by the Franklin Mint".......30.00

Inauguration Pocket Mirror, black and white photo, bluetone photos of White House and Capitol in background, 1977...12.00

Jugate, Carter/Mondale

Light brown and white photos, bright yellow circles against off-white background, center eagle with red, white, and blue shield, bright green wreath, date in red above.......................10.00

Rectangular badge, black and white photo in diamond shape, red, white, and blue flag designs, browntone photos of Thomas Jefferson, White House, Statue of Liberty, and eagle, 1980...15.00

Playset, Amy At The White House, 9-1/2" x 18" x 1", sealed box, Toy Factory, c1978.................................25.00

Press Badge, ABC News, Democratic National Convention, black on pink...5.00

Watch, 1-1/4" d. dial with brown, rd, gray, and blue caricature figure, reads, "Official Jimmy Cater from Peanuts to President," Goober Time Company, 1976, stainless steel back, gold colored metal bezel 50.00

Ronald Reagan, 1980, 1984

Christmas Card, 1982, unused, 6" x 8", orig envelope 15.00

Inauguration Ticket , 2-3/4" x 7-1/4", Jan. 20, 1981, silver background, red, blue, and black type, red outlined eagle at center 20.00

License Plate, Presidential Inauguration, red, white, and blue aluminum, 1981 .... 17.50

Pinback Button, "Carry On For The Duke/ Reagan in 80," 3" d, bluetone photo, blue lettering, white ground, center illus of John Wayne 12.00

Pinback Button, "NJ/Reagan Youth Staff," dark blue on white 5.00

Poster, 2" x 24", Regan-Bush '84, full color, matte finish, titled, "Bringing America Back," D. Kilmer artist, "Paid for by Reagan-Bush '84" 18.00

Sheet Music, *Stand Up And Cheer for Ronald Reagan*, music and lyrics by E. F. Moss, black and white photo on cover, copyright 1980 by Apex Music 15.00

George Bush, 1980, 1984, 1988

Bumper Sticker, 3-1/2" x 9-1/2", "Bush/ Quayle '88," red, white, and blue .. 2.50

Inauguration Media Tag, 2-1/2" x 4", blue, yellow, brown, CBS, laminated in clear plastic, slot at top for wearing, 1989 .... 15.00

Pinback Button, "Bush Defeats Clinton," black and white photo of Truman holding copy of newspaper with Dewey headline, 1992 .... 3.00

Pinback Button, "I Was There, Bush/ Quayle Re-Nomination," bright red on white 5.00

Bill Clinton, 1992, 1996

Convention Delegate Button, 4" d, red, white, and blue, "Bill Clinton for President," 1992 .... 45.00

Inauguration Program, 8-1/2" x 11", 24 pgs, full color photos 15.00

Jugate, black and white photos, bright red rim, "Clinton for President, Carol Moseley Braun for U.S. Senate" ... 5.00

Pinback Button, "Blow Bill Blow," full-color photo of Clinton playing sax, red, white, and blue vertical striped background, 1992 .... 2.00

Pinback Button, "Just Say No," back and white photo of Clinton over printed by bright red, black lettering, 1992 .... 5.00

Police Badge, Inauguration Day, D. C. police, 2-3/4" h, heavy brass, Bastian 80.00

Postcards

Collecting Hints: Concentrate on one subject area, publisher, or illus-

trator. Collect cards in mint condition, when possible.

The more common the holiday, the larger the city, the more popular the tourist attraction, the easier it will be to find postcards on the subject because of the millions of cards that were originally available. The smaller runs of "real" photo postcards are the most desirable of the scenic cards. Photographic cards of families and individuals, unless they show occupations, unusual toys, dolls, or teddy bears have little value.

Stamps and cancellation marks may sometimes affect the value of cards. Consult a philatelic guide.

Postcards fall into two main categories: view cards and topics. View cards are easiest to sell in their local geographic region. European view cards, while very interesting, are difficult to sell in America.

It must be stressed that age alone does not determine price. A birthday postcard from 1918 may sell for only 10¢ while a political campaign card from the 1950s may bring $10. The price of every collectible is governed by supply and demand.

Although cards from 1898 to 1918 are the most popular with collectors, the increasing costs of postcards from this era have turned attention to postcards from the 1920s, 1930s, and 1940s. Art-Deco cards from the 1920-1930 period are the most desirable. The 1940s "linens," so called because of their textured linenlike paper surface, are the most popular cards of that time period.

Cards from the 1950 to 1970 period are called "Chromes" because of their shiny surface.

History: The golden age of post cards dates from 1898 to 1918. Cards printed earlier are collected for their postal history. Postcards prior to 1898 are called "pioneer" cards.

European publishers, especially in England and Germany, produced the vast majority of cards during the golden age. The major postcard publishers are Raphael Tuck (England), Paul Finkenrath of Berlin (PFB-German), and Whitney, Detroit Publishing Co., and John Winsch (United States). However, many American publishers had their stock produced in Europe, hence, "Made in Bavaria" imprints. While some Tuck cards are high priced, many are still available in the "10¢" boxes.

Styles changed rapidly, and manufacturers responded to every need.

The linen postcard which gained popularity in the 1940s was quickly replaced by the chrome cards of the post-1950 period.

References: Janet A. Banneck, *Antique Postcards of Rose O'Neill*, Greater Chicago Productions, 1992; Jody Blake and Jeannette Lasansky, *Rural Delivery: Real Photo Postcards from Central Pennsylvania*, Union County Historical Society (Union County Courthouse, Lewisburg, PA 17837), 1996; Michael Goldberg, *Bathing Beauties: French Photo Postcards of the 1920s*, Collectors Press, 1999; Juli Kernall, *Postcard Collector 1999 Annual & Price Guide*, 8th ed., Antique Trader Books, 1998; J. L. Mashburn, *Artist-Signed Postcard Price Guide*, Colonial House, 1993 (Note: all Mashburn books are available from Box 609, Enka, NC 28728); ——, *Black Americana Postcard Price Guide*, 2nd ed., Colonial House, 1996; ——, *Fantasy Postcards with Price Guide*, Colonial House, 1996; ——, *Postcard Price Guide*, 3rd ed., Colonial House, 1997; ——, *Super Rare Postcards of Harrison Fisher*, Colonial House, 1992; Frederic and Mary Megson, *American Advertising Postcards*, published by authors, 1985; ——, *American Exposition Postcards*, The Postcard Lovers, 1992; Ron Menchine, *Propaganda Postcards of World War II*, Krause Publications, 2000; Susan Brown Nicholson, *Antique Postcard Sets and Series Price Guide*, Greater Chicago Productions, 1993; ——, *Encyclopedia of Antique Postcards*, Wallace-Homestead, 1994; *Postcard Collector Annual*, 6th ed., Antique Trader Books, 1996; Cynthia Rubin and Morgan Williams, *Larger Than Life; The American Tall-Tale Postcard*, Abbeville Press, 1990; Nouhad A. Saleh, *Guide to Artist's Signatures and Monograms on Postcards*, Minerva Press, 1993; Robert Ward, *Investment Guide to North American Real Photo Postcards*, Antique Paper Guild, 1991; Naomi Welch, *American and European Postcards of Harrison Fisher Illustrator*, Images of the Past, 1999; Jane Wood, *Collector's Guide to Postcards*, L-W Book Sales, 1984, 2000 value update.

Periodicals: *Barr's Postcard News*, 70 S. 6th St., Lansing, IA 52151; *Gloria's Corner*, P.O. Box 507, Denison, TX 75021; *Postcard Collector*, 121 N. Main St., Iola, WI 54945.

Collectors' Clubs: *Barr's Postcard News* and the *Postcard Collector* publish lists of more than 50 regional clubs in the United States and Canada.

Notes: The following prices are for cards in excellent to mint condition—no sign of edge wear, no creases, untrimmed, no writing on the picture side of the card, no tears, and no dirt. Each defect reduces the price given by 10 percent.

An' You Know What Men Are? French subtitle, Mabel Lucie Attwell, $20.

Advertising

Adv on linens, large product image 10.00
Adv on chromes, large product
image 4.50
Automobile adv
  American prior to 1920 .... 24.00
  European prior to 1920 .... 14.50
  Oldsmobile 88 Super, four-door
  sedan, 1952 .... 8.50
  Pontiac Chieftan, two-door sedan,
  1949 .... 8.50
  Pontiac Streamliner, four-door sedan,
  1949 .... 9.00
Campbell Soup adv
  Horizontal format 32.00
  Vertical format............................ 100.00
Coca-Cola adv
  Duster girl in car 450.00
  Hamilton King 250.00
Diner Adv, linen era 12.50
DuPont Gun
  Birds.. 30.00
  Dogs.. 100.00
  Zeppelin...................................... 150.00
Elgin Watch Co 8.00
Formica, chrome era 3.50
Heinz, Ocean Pier, Atlantic City, NY,
  1910s 6.00
Hotel-Motel
  Chrome 3.50
  Early 5.50
  Linen era 8.50
Kellogg Co., Toasting Ovens, Battle
  Creek, Michigan, black and white,
  some color tinting, 1920s 7.50
McDonald's chrome era 4.00
Michelin Tire Company, featuring Michelin
  man 30.00
R. J. Reynolds, chrome era 10.00
Rockford Watch, calendar
  series... 18.50

Wells Fargo, colored sketch, Wells Fargo stage racing with Indians, history on back, postmarked 1915 ....12.00
Wood's Boston Coffees, black and white oval portraits of George and Martha Washington 8.50
Zeno Gum, mechanical 35.00

African-Americans

Bill Cosby, Las Vegas Hilton, "Now at the world famous Las Vegas Hilton," names of stars on back, 11" w, 4-1/2" l, fold-up type, unused 8.00
Cotton Pickers in the Field, #11277, Post Tint Card, Detroit Publishing Co..12.00
Greetings from Mann, S. C., cotton pickers at work, #90473, published by The Asheville Post Card Co., Asheville, N.C., linen, unused 12.00
Hope You'll Drop In Soon, published by The Asheville Post Card Co., Asheville, N.C., white borders, 1943 postmark, 1 cent stamp, addressed in pencil 12.00
King Cotton at Home on A.B. & A.R.R., #C5837, published by The A.B.& A. R.R. Line, Atlanta, Georgia, litho chrome, made in Germany, slight wear..15.00
Old Slave Market, St. Augustine, FL, Duy News Company, Jacksonville, FL, #5A-H, Curtech-Chicago, unused 15.00
Picking Cotton in the South, unused 14.00
Seven-Up in Dixieland, #E-5405, published by The Asheville Post Card Co., Asheville, N.C., linen, unused 12.00

Artist Signed

Atwell, Mabel Lucie
  Early by Tuck...............................20.00
  Regular, comic 15.00
Bertiglia, children 18.00
Boileau, Philip
  By Reinthal Neuman....................20.00
  By Raphael Tuck 100.00
  By other 35.00
Boulanger, Maurice, cats
  Large images...............................25.00
  Many, in action 15.00
Brisman, M., Greetings from Coney Island, yellow, black, white, and red, butcher slicing tail from dog as another dog with bandage over tail serves as waiter of frankfurters, copyright E. Zaitchick, artist sgd, unused, 1940s, 3-1/2" x 5-1/2", ...22.00
Browne, Tom
  American Baseball series, green
  background..................................15.00
  English comic series.....................8.00
Brundage, Frances
  Children..5.00
  Early Tuck Chromolithograph 35.00
Caldecott
  Early 12.00
  1974 reprints 1.00
Carmichael, comic............................5.00
Carr, Gene, comic............................17.50
Chiostri, Art Deco.............................20.00
Christy, Howard Chandler................24.50
Clapsaddle, Ellen Hattie
  Children..20.00
  Floral, sleds, crosses 10.00
  Unsigned, Wolf Publishing
  Co 12.00

Valentine, mechanical 45.00
Corbella, Art Deco...........................12.50
Corbett, Bertha, sunbonnets............15.00
Curtis, E., children 5.00
Daniell, Eva, Art Nouveau, Tuck 85.00
Drayton/Weiderseim, Grace (Campbell's Kids)..35.00
Dwig
  Comic 7.50
  Halloween.....................................15.00
Fidler, Alie Luella, women 8.00
Fisher, Harrison................................24.50
Gear, Mabel
  Cairn Terrier, Pekingese, Sealyham Terrier, and Cocker Spaniel, published by Valentine & Sons, Ltd., unused...30.00
  Cocker Spaniel and Scottish Terrier, published by Valentine & Sons, Ltd., unused...30.00
Gibson, Charles Dana, sepia...........12.00
Golay, Mary, flowers 7.50
Greenaway, Kate, sgd...................365.00
Greiner, M
  Blacks.. 22.50
  Children 9.00
  Molly and Her Teddy 15.50
Griggs, H. B. 10.00
Gutmann, Bessie Pease 17.50
Hays, Margaret.................................12.00
Humphrey, Maud, sgd......................75.00
Innes, John, western 6.00
Johnson, J., children 7.50
Kirchner, Raphael
  First period...................................125.00
  Second period...............................75.00
  Third period 50.00
  Santa...200.00
Klein, Catherine
  Floral 7.50
  Alphabet.......................................15.00
  Alphabet, letters X, Y, Z 25.00
Koehler, Mela, early 65.00
Mauzan, Art Deco.............................15.00
May, Phil, English comic series........15.00
McCay, Winsor, "Little Nemo" 25.00
Mucha, Alphonse
  Art Nouveau, months of the year..200.00
  Slavic period, murals 75.00
  Women, full card design...........600.00
O'Neill, Rose
  Gross Publishing Company....................................125.00
  Ice Cream adv...........................100.00
  Kewpies.......................................35.00
  Pickings from Puck-Blacks 100.00
  Suffrage, Babies........................200.00
  Suffrage, Kewpies 125.00
Opper, Frederick, comic 12.00
Outcault 15.00
Parkinson, Ethel, children..................9.00
Patella, women 15.00
Payne, Harry.....................................15.00
Phillips, Cole, fade-away style 25.00
Price, Mary Evans 9.00
Remington, Frederic..........................35.00
Robinson, Robert 15.00
Rockwell, Norman 35.00

Russell, Charles 15.00
Sager, Xavier 15.00
Schmucker, Samuel
   Halloween greetings 65.00
   New Years 25.00
   Silk, any greeting 55.00
   St. Patrick's Day greetings 18.00
   Valentine greetings 20.00
Shinn, Cobb 8.00
Smith, Jessie Wilcox, seven different
   images 15.00
Studdy, Bonzo Dog 12.50
Tam, Jean, women 20.00
Thiele, Arthur
   Blacks, large faces 25.00
   Blacks, on bikes 45.00
   Cats, in action 15.50
   Cats, large heads 20.00
   Pigs, large heads 25.00
Twelvetrees, Charles, comic,
   children 14.50
Underwood, Clarence 12.00
Upton, Florence, Golliwoggs,
   Tuck 35.00
Wain, Louis
   Cat 45.00
   Dog 30.00
   Frog 35.00
   Paper doll, cat 200.00
   Santa and cat 100.00
Wall, Bernhardt, sunbonnets 20.00
Wood, Lawson 12.00

Folder

Carlsbad Caverns, 10 cards, glossy
   black and white photos, 1930s 8.00
Corning Glass, 10 cards of glass pat-
   terns, 1950s 9.00
Hialeah Racing, 1940s 7.50
PA Turnpike, 18 view, Minsky Bros. ... 9.00

**William H. Taft for President, stars
and stripes, wear to corner, $12.**

Greetings

April Fools
   American comic 4.50
   French litho with fish 12.50
Birthday
   Floral 3.00
   Children 4.50
Christmas, no Santa 3.25
Christmas, Santa
   Artists signed 15.00
   Black face, Coontown series 100.00
   German, highly embossed 15.00
   Hold to light type 100.00
   Installment, unused 100.00
   Kirchner 200.00
   P.F.B. Publishing Company 20.00
   Red Suits 15.00
   Silk Applique 40.00

Suits other than red 17.50
Easter, printed in Germany
   Boy in sailor suit, holding chick, high
   top boots, hens and roosters, "Best
   Easter Wishes," postmarked Grand
   Rapids, MI, 1912 .... 8.00
   Boy on egg cart, wheels of forget-me-
   nots, pulled by two chicks, "Happy
   Easter-Tide," postmarked Kalamazoo,
   MI, 1913 .... 8.00
   Boy with arm full of pussy willows and
   forget-me-nots, three lambs, "Easter
   Greetings," postmarked Columbus,
   Ohio, 1910 .... 9.00
   Children playing in open egg, "Happy
   Easter" 6.00
   Victorian boy and girl gathering Easter
   eggs, "Easter Greeting," unused 12.00
   Victorian boy pushing egg entwined
   with roses, "Easter Greeting,"
   unused 15.00
   Victorian child pushing egg buggy
   filled with forget-me-nots and back
   chick, "A Very Happy Easter To You,"
   postmarked 1903 .... 10.00
Fourth of July
   Children 8.00
   Uncle Sam 12.00
   Others 4.50
Ground Hog Day, after 1930 .... 20.00
Halloween
   Children 7.00
   Children, extremely colorful or artists
   sgd 15.00
   Winsch Publishing 45.00
Labor Day
   Lounsbury Publishing 125.00
   Nash Publishing 95.00
Leap Year 7.00
Mother's Day, early 9.00
New Year
   Bells 4.25
   Children or Father Time 9.50
   Winsch Publishing, beautiful
   women 15.00
St. Patrick's Day
   Children 7.50
   No children 5.50
Thanksgiving
   Children 7.50
   No children 3.50
   Uncle Sam 9.50
Valentines
   Children, women 9.50
   Hearts, comic 5.00
   Winsch Publishing, beautiful
   women 18.00

Humor

It's the Same Old Moon - -But OH! How It
   Has Changed!, Curt Teich & Co., Chi-
   cago, unused 12.00
Me Worry?, Plastichrome, late 1950s,
   Neuman-like character set against
   blue/gray background, unused 8.00
Will You Be My Teddy Bear? Red Cliffe,
   CO, leather, postmarked 1909 ..... 7.50

**Hellertown Views, Saucon Furnace,
Calvin Burgstresser Photographer,
dated 1911, $15.**

Miscellaneous

Avalon Bay from Mt. Ada, Wrigley resi-
   dence, Casino on Santa Catalina, CA,
   postmarked 1949 .... 5.00
Boulder, Colorado, Turnpike, back reads,
   "Denver-Boulder Turnpike approach to
   Boulder, Colo., Long Peak and the
   Arapahoe Range in the background,"
   mkd "Color Photo by Robert Commercial Photo Dist., by Ray Surguine, Co.,
   Inc., P. O. Dr. J., Boulder, Colo.," 5-1/2"
   x 3-1/2", unused 4.00
Coney Island, Surf Avenue, hold to light,
   3-1/2" x 5-1/2" 35.00
Fantasia, sketch of Hyacinth Hip and Ben
   Ali Gator, Disney's Animation Gallery,
   7" x 4-1/2" 18.00
Jordan Boarding House, Greenfield Vil-
   lage, Dearborn, Michigan, mkd "Artcraft Photo Co., East Rutherford, NJ,"
   3-1/2" x 5-3/4", unused 3.00
Movie Star, Bob Hutton, black and white
   photo, printed signature, Warner
   Bros., Burbank, CA, 1946 postmark,
   some damage to corners 3.50
San Antonio Aviation Cadet Center, San
   Antonio, TX, San Antonio Card Co.,
   1940s, unused 4.00
Seals at Catalina Island, C. T. Photo-
   chrome, Los Angeles, tinted
   view 15.00
The Gen'l U. S. Grant Bridge, Portsmouth,
   Ohio, The Ohio Valley Famous in Song
   and Story, mkd "H. A. Lorberg, C. T.
   American Art Reg. U. S. Pat. C. T. Co.,
   Chicago," linen 4.00
The Inspector, C-14, giant grasshopper
   climbing up oil derrick, Multrakrom
   Postcard Co., Dodge City, Kansas,
   c1950 .... 10.00
University of Pennsylvania, Philadelphia,
   Victorian structure, numerous tiny win-
   dows that illuminate when held to light,
   unused, 3-1/2" x 5-1/2" 22.00
What We Saw at Catalina, Sam Hernan-
   dez, Deep Sea Diver, Glass Bottom
   Boat, early, unused 10.00
Wonderland Park, Revere Beach, MA,
   amusement park, 3-1/2" x 5-1/2", early
   1900s
   Administration Building, color 4.00
   Beautiful Orient exhibit building,
   color 4.75
   Hell Gate exhibition building, black
   and white 3.00
   Shooting the Chutes amusement ride,
   color 4.50

Patriotic

Declaration of Independence, Flag Series No. 14, Tichnor Bros., Inc., Boston MA, 5-1/2" x 4-1/2" 5.00
Decoration Day 9.00
Lincoln..12.50
Patriotic Songs....................................6.00
Uncle Sam 15.00
Washington 17.50
World War II, linen...............................7.50

Photographic

Atlantic City Boardwalk, postmarked 1919 ....9.00
Children under Christmas trees 14.50
Children with animals or toys 12.00
Christmas trees 9.50
Circus Performer, identified and close-up 15.00
Constitution Mall, government area, theme center, used 9.00
Diamond Green Ramblers, Silver City 7.00
Exaggerations
   Conrad Publishing, after 1935 ....10.00
   Martin Publishing 12.50
   Martin Publishing, US Coin 75.00
Indian chiefs, five chiefs in full regalia, emb, postmarked 1910 ....12.00
Lincoln Statue on Lincoln Memorial Bridge, Milwaukee, WI, used 6.50
Main Streets
   Large cities 12.50
   Unidentified towns 7.50
   With trains or trolleys 19.50
Men peeling potatoes, Co. B, 311th Inf. Kitchen Mechanics, Camp Dix, unused 10.00
People
   Military with flags 5.00
   Occupation, American 15.00
   Portraits, instant relatives 1.00
   Unusual studio backdrops............5.00
Railroad Depots 20.00
Railroad Depots, with trains 22.50
Shop Exteriors, identified 12.00
Shop Interiors, identified location.....25.00
The Belles of California, three elderly Indian women sitting in field, color, postmarked 1907 CA 12.00
The Old Indian Whale Hunter of Puget Sound, kneeling on the shore and leaning against dug-out 10.00
Visit Backstage at Radio City, NBC Studio Tour, black and white, postmarked 1937 ....7.50

Political and Social History

Blacks...15.00
Campaign
   1900 ....100.00
   1904 ....65.00
   1908 ....35.00
Col. Roosevelt's Home, Oyster Bay, Long Island, NY, postmarked 1922........7.50
McKinley Monument, Buffalo, NY, needle-work type emb, postmarked 1907 ....15.00
McKinley Monument, Canton, OH, emb, muted gray and pink 9.00

St. Patrick's Day, child riding pig, $32.

Muriel Humphrey, portrait and facsimile signature, reverse with Muriel Humphrey's Beef Soup recipe 8.50
President Franklin Roosevelt
   Posing with rangers in front of giant CA redwoods 9.50
   Speaking at dedication of Great Smoky Mountains National Park, linen finish 8.50
President and Mrs. Woodrow Wilson, tinted..10.00
Prohibition...8.00
Richard Nixon, Vote Republican, 1960, colored 7.50
School Delinquency, fill-in the blank 1932 post card, mailed in Baltimore, MD 7.50
Suffrage
   Cargill publisher............................18.00
   Clapsaddle...................................50.00
   General...12.50
   Kewpie 125.00
   Parades 17.50
Taft and Sherman, oval portraits with facsimile signatures, Capitol building in background.................................10.00
Washington DC, The New White House Sideboard designed by Mrs. Roosevelt, large marble top sideboard with two eagles 7.50
William H. Taft, dark sepia tone photo 7.50
William Jennings Bryan
   Addressing his Sunday School Class, Miami, Florida, huge crowd in amphitheater, palm trees, color tinted, used..7.00
   Home of F. R. Rogers, Dayton, Tenn. Where Wm. Jennings Bryan died July 26, 1925, unused 9.00
   Sepia tone photo.............................8.00
Willkie, "Think! Who Nominated Hitler? -- Hitler. Who Nominated Mussolini? - Mussolini. Who Nominated Stalin? -- Stalin. Who Nominated Roosevelt? -- Roosevelt. Who Nominated Willkie? -- The People. Vote for Willkie"........12.00

World Fairs and Expositions

Chicago, 1933-34
   Electrical Building at night, postmarked 1934 ....10.00
   Federal Building at night, postmarked 1934 ....10.00
   Havoline Thermometer, postmarked 1933...10.00
Golden Gate, 1939, black and white, unused
   Court of Reflections.....................12.00
   Court of the Moon 12.00
   Court of the Pacifica...................12.00
Tower of the Sun 8.00
New York, 1939, Aeroplane view, full color, linen, unused 8.50
New York, 1964-65, Coca-Cola Company Pavilion, unused 7.50
St. Louis 1764-1964 Bicentennial, city flag, unused...................................6.50
St. Louis, 1904, Compliments of Rice & Hutchins, Shoemakers, Boston, Manufactures Building, souvenir inscription at upper right corner, unused 70.00

World War II

Man of the Time, Adolf Hitler, #91, Hindenburg postage stamp, postmarked 1939..30.00
Mortars at Fort Wright, No. 19, published by American Colortype Co., Chicago, Photo International Film Service Inc., unused..6.00
U.S.S. Utah rescues torpedo, No. 13, published by American Colortype Co., Chicago, Photo International Film Service Inc., unused...........................6.00

Elvis Presley

Collecting Hints: Official Elvis Presley items are usually copyrighted and many are dated.

Learn to differentiate between items licensed during Elvis's lifetime and the wealth of "fantasy" items issued after his death. The latter are collectible, but have nowhere near the value of the pre-1977 material.

Also accept the fact that many of the modern limited edition items are purely speculative investments. It is best to buy them because you like them and plan to live with them for an extended period of time, not because you might realize a profit.

History: As a rock 'n' roll star, Elvis Presley was one of the first singers to target teen-agers in his promotional efforts. The first Elvis merchandise appeared in 1956. During the following years new merchandise was added both in America and foreign countries. After his death in 1977, a vast number of new Elvis collectibles appeared.

References: Pauline Bartel, *Everything Elvis*, Taylor Publishing, 1995; Jerry Osborne, *Official Price Guide to Elvis Presley Records and Memorabilia*, House of Collectibles, 1994.

Collectors' Clubs: Elvis Forever TCB Fan Club, P.O. Box 1066, Pinellas Park, FL 34665; Graceland News Fan Club, P.O. Box 452, Rutherford, NJ 07070.

Museums: Graceland, Memphis, TN; Jimmy Velvet's Elvis Presley Museum, Franklin, TN.

Barbie, Barbie Loves Elvis, 1996, MIB..........130.00

Beverage Tent Card, Sahara Tahoe concert, logo........15.00

Book
Meet Elvis Presley, Favius Friedman, © 1971, 1973, 1977, paperback, 128 pgs, includes epilogue written after Presley's death, 7-3/4" x 5-1/4"....10.00
Operation Elvis, Alan Levy, Henry Holt and Co., © 1960, hardcover.......12.00

Bubble Gum Card, series one, 1992, unopened pack, 12 cards..........85.00

First Day Cover, pink Cadillac, issued January 1993, Memphis, TN, canceled Tupelo, MS..........7.50

Calendar, 1977, Tribute to Elvis, Boxcar Enterprises, 12" x 13"..........50.00

Cookie Jar, riding, in car..........100.00

Decanter, McCormick Dist. Co., musical, plays Love Me Tender..........120.00

Flicker Button, 2-1/4" d, black and white photos of Elvis playing guitar, titled "Love Me Tender," © 1958 Elvis Presley Enterprises..........25.00

Game, Elvis Presley, King of Rock, Santa Clara, CA, copyright 1979..........80.00

Guitar, Emenee Toys, 1956, 31" l, color emblems, white ground, orig box, full color insert, mint..........1,175.00

Limited Edition Plate, '68 Comeback Special, In Performance Collection, Delphi, platinum edge, certificate of authenticity, MIB..........100.00

Limited Edition Stein, 9-1/4" h, Anheuser-Busch Co., Model CS375, 1968 Comeback..........75.00

Magazine, *Saturday Evening Post*, July/August, 1985, "Legends that Won't Die"..........10.00

Poster Book..........10.00

PEZ Container, stem gold outfit, hand-painted..........85.00

Photo Album, official Elvis Presley Collection, personal message from Elvis, Vernon Presley, and the Colonel, Boxcar Enterprises, 1977, certificate of authenticity..........85.00

Poster, movie, 22" x 28", Elvis Presley Kid Galahad, half-sheet, © 1962 United Artists..........40.00

Puzzle, The King, Springbok, 1992, 1000 pieces..........50.00

Radio, figural, MIB..........50.00

Record
Blue Suede Shoes/Tutti Fruiti, RCA Victor, 45 rpm, 1956..........60.00
Fun in Acapulco, RCA Victor, orig soundtrack, 1963..........50.00
Our Memories of Elvis, black label, DNT..........75.00
Personally Elvis, blue label, double pocket, silhouette..........50.00
Roustabout, RCA Victor, orig soundtrack, 1964..........50.00
Spinout, black label, DOT, RCA, white top..........35.00
Welcome to My World, black label, DNT, LP..........30.00

Sheet Music, *Love Me*, 1954..........35.00

Tab, 2" d, litho tin, blue, gold lettering, "I Love Elvis," metallic gold background, 1970s..........15.00

Toy, car, 1:24 scale funny car, limited edition John Force Castrol GTX, officially licensed NHRA on outside, 1998 Mustang, MIB..........90.00

Tumbler, early 1970s..........48.00

Waste Can, litho tin, c1977..........55.00

Punchboards

Collecting Hints: Punchboards which are unpunched are collectible. A board which has been punched has little value unless it is an extremely rare design. Like most advertising items, price is determined by graphics and subject matter.

The majority of punchboards sell in the $8 to $30 range. At the high end of the range are boards such as Golden Gate Bridge ($85) and Baseball Classic ($100).

History: Punchboards are self-contained games of chance made of pressed paper that has holes and coded tickets inside each hole. For an agreed amount, the player uses a "punch" to extract the ticket of his or her choice. Prizes are awarded to the winning ticket. Punch prices can be 1¢, 2¢, 3¢, 5¢, 10¢, 20¢, 50¢, $1, or more.

Not all tickets were numbered. Fruit symbols were used extensively as well as animals. Some punchboards had no printing at all, just colored tickets. Other ticket themes included dice, cards, dominoes, and words. One early board featured Mack Sennet bathing beauties.

Punchboards come in an endless variety of styles. Names reflect the themes of the boards: Barrel of Winners, Break the Bank, Baseball, More Smokes, Lucky Lulu and Take It Off are just a few.

At first punchboards winners were awarded cash. As a response to attempts to outlaw gambling, prizes were switched to candy, cigars, cigarettes, jewelry, radios, clocks, cameras, sporting goods, toys, beer, chocolate, etc.

The golden age of punchboards was from the 1920s to the 1950s. Attention was focused on the keyed punchboard in the film "The Flim Flam Man." This negative publicity hurt the punchboard industry.

Museum: Amusement Sales, Midvale, UT.

Advisor: Clark Phelps.

Ace High, 13" x 17", deck of cards for jackpot..........90.00

Barrel of Cigarettes, 10" x 10", Lucky Strike Green..........44.00

Bars & Bells, 13" x 8-1/2", deck of cards, fruit symbols..........135.00

Baseball Push Card, 7" x 10", 1¢ candy prize..........10.00

Basketball Push Card, 6" x 9", thin, 1¢ candy prize..........10.00

Beat the Seven, 10" x 10", card tickets determine winners..........35.00

Best Hand, poker hand tickets, 6-1/2" x 11", 1-1/4" thick, pays out in cigarettes..........40.00

Big Game, 8" x 10-1/2"..........30.00

Buck-A-Roo, silver dollars..........500.00

Candy Special, 4-1/2" x 7-1/2", penny candy board..........24.00

Cash In, 8-1/2" x 9", sack of money.18.00

Double of Nothing, 9" x 10", trade stimulator..........36.00

Extra Bonus, 13" x 12"..........40.00

Fin Baby, 19" x 6", folding pull tab...32.00

Five on One, 11" x 11"..........18.00

Five Tens, 10" x 13"..........18.00

Glades Chocolates, 7" x 9", set of three boards, factory wrapped..........75.00

Good Punching, 9-1/2" x 10", cowboy motif..........36.00

Hang It, factory paper..........95.00

Home Run Derby, 10" x 12", baseball theme, green baseball park.......75.00

Jackpot Bingo, 10" x 8", thick card jackpot..........10.00

Joe's Special, 11" x 14"..........20.00

Johnson's Chocolates, 9" x 11", Elvgren girl..........35.00

Lu Lu Board, 10" x 11", colored tickets..........28.00

McCoy, six cutouts, old lighters and sterling silver bolo tie..........100.00

More Smokes, 10-1/2" x 10-1/2", red, white, and blue tickets..........24.00

Nestle's Chocolate, 9" x 8-1/2", 2¢ board..........45.00

Nickel Fins, 12" x 15", cash board, colorful jackpot..........40.00

Odd Pennies, 6-3/4" x 11", small change, 2¢ and 3¢ board..........45.00

Palm Chart, 20" x 11-1/2", 1936, orig envelope..........8.00

Perry's Prizes, 9-1/2" x 13"..........60.00

Pocket Board, 2" x 2-3/4", great action cartoon graphic..........8.00

Positive Prizes, 12" x 17", diecut field for prizes of your choice..........25.00

Pots A Plenty, 11" x 17-1/2"..........26.00

Premium Prizes, 10" x 12"..........20.00

Professor Charley, 1946, Superior Mfg. Typical 25¢ cash board..........18.00

Race Track, Pimlico and Churchill Downs, minor shelf wear..........50.00

Section Play, 8-1/2" x 10"..........18.00

Select Your Smokes, 9-1/2" x 7-1/4".55.00

Ship Ahoy, factory wrapped, 9" x 15"..........95.00

So Sweet, 13-1/2" x 13"..........40.00

Speedy Tens, 10" x 13"..........18.00

Stars & Stripes, 9" x 14", red, white and blue, jackpot card..........26.00

Take It Off, minor shelf wear..........45.00

Tavern Maid, 9-1/2" x 13-1/2", cans of beer prize..........55.00

Three Sure Hits, 10" x 13"..........24.00

Tropics, diecut, hula dancer...........110.00
Tu Pots, 12" x 18"................................44.00
Win A Buck, 4-1/2" x 7-1/2"...............12.00
Win A Seal, 1920s, wooden puncher, 6 numbers on a ticket, colored foil.70.00
Win Twice, quarters and dimes, orig wrapper present but turn 175.00

Purinton Pottery

Collecting Hints: The most popular patterns among collectors are Apple, Intaglio (brown), Normandy Plaid (red), Maywood, and Pennsylvania Dutch. Variations, e.g., Intaglio with a green ground, are known for many of these patterns.

Purinton also made a number of kitchenware and specialty pieces. These should not be overlooked. Among the harder-to-find items are animal figurines, tea tiles, and the Tom and Jerry bowl and mug set.

History: Bernard Purinton founded Purinton Pottery in 1936 in Wellsville, Ohio. This pilot plant produced decorative dinnerware as well as some special-order pieces. In 1940, Roy Underwood, President of Knox Glass Company, approached Purinton about moving his operation to Knox's community, Shippenville.

In 1941, the pottery relocated to a newly built plant in Shippenville, Pennsylvania. The company's first product at the new plant, a two-cup premium teapot for McCormick Tea Company, rolled off the line on December 7, 1941.

Dorothy Purinton and William H. Blair, her brother, were the chief designers for the company. Maywood, Plaid, and several Pennsylvania German designs were among the patterns attributed to Dorothy Purinton. William Blair, a graduate of the Cleveland School of Art, designed the Apple and Intaglio patterns.

Initially, slipware was cast. Later it was pressed using a Ram Press process. Clays came from Florida, Kentucky, North Carolina, and Tennessee.

Purinton Pottery did not use decals as did many of its competitors. Greenware was hand painted by locally trained decorators who then dipped the decorated pieces into glaze. This demanded a specially formulated body and a more expensive manufacturing process. Hand painting also allowed for some of the variations in technique and colors found on Purinton ware today.

Purinton made a complete dinnerware line for each pattern, plus a host of accessory pieces ranging from candleholders to vases. Dinnerware patterns were open stock. Purinton's ware received national distribution, and select lines were exported.

The plant ceased operations in 1958, reopened briefly, and finally closed for good in 1959. Cheap foreign imports were cited as the cause of the company's decline.

References: Jamie Bero-Johnson, *Purinton Pottery*, Schiffer Publishing, 1997; Pat Dole, *Purinton Pottery*, Denton Publishing, 1990; Susan Morris, *Purinton Pottery*, Collector Books, 1994.

Periodical: *Purinton Pastimes*, 20401 Ivybridge Ct, Gaithersburg, MD 20879.

Collectors' Club: Purinton Pottery Convention, P.O. Box 9394, Arlington, VA 22219.

Baker
Apple, 6" x 4"................................30.00
Intaglio, ivory, hand dec with brown slip, 11-1/4" l.......................22.00
Bank, Raggedy Andy, 6-1/2" h.........80.00
Canister
Flour, Intaglio, square, wooden lid...................................95.00
Set, Apple, four-pc, wire rack......................................225.00
Set, Pennsylvania Dutch...........195.00
Sugar, Intaglio, square, wooden lid...................................95.00
Sugar, Fruit dec, cobalt blue trim...................................95.00
Casserole, cov
Apple, oval...............................25.00
Intaglio, 9" d..............................50.00
Cereal Bowl
Apple..18.00
Intaglio.......................................12.00
Pennsylvania Dutch.....................15.00
Chop Plate
Apple..20.00
Intaglio, 12" d.............................40.00
Coffee Mug, Plaid..........................1.00
Coffeepot, cov, Apple.....................60.00
Cornucopia....................................20.00
Cookie Jar, cov
Apple..40.00
Howdy Doody...........................250.00
Intaglio, ivory, hand dec with brown slip, 9" h..........................30.00
Pennsylvania Dutch.....................55.00
Creamer
Apple, double spout, 1-1/2" h......12.00
Fruits..10.00
Normandy Plaid..........................40.00
Cruet, Pennsylvania Dutch, jug-shape, price for pr.....................50.00
Cup and Saucer
Apple..24.00
Estate...12.00
Normandy Plaid..........................17.50
Dessert Bowl
Estate...6.00
Intaglio, brown...........................10.00
Dinner Plate
9" d, Normandy Plaid..................20.00

9-1/2" d, Fruits.............................15.00
9-3/4" d, Plaid..............................15.00
10" d, Intaglio, brown..................16.00
Drip Jar, cov
Apple..20.00
Daisy..80.00
Plaid...20.00
Dutch Jug, Apple, 6" h, 8" w...........35.00
Fruit Bowl, Estate.............................6.00
Grill Plate, Apple, 12" d...................25.00
Honey Jug
Red Intaglio...............................95.00
Red Ivy.......................................35.00
Jug
Dutch, Fruits, 2 pint...................12.00
Rebecca, Mountain Rose.............40.00
Juice Tumbler
Fruits, apple and pear................12.00
Maywood.....................................15.00
Lazy Susan, Fruits, apple finial, painted pear, plum, pineapple, and cherries......................................250.00
Luncheon Plate, Apple, 8-1/2" d......24.00
Marmalade, cov, Maywood.............32.00
Pitcher
Apple, 6" h.................................45.00
Fruits...32.00
Platter
Intaglio, ivory, hand dec with brown slip, 12-1/2" l......................24.00
Maywood, 12" l, oblong..............30.00
Normandy Plaid, 12" l..................55.00
Relish Dish
Fruits, divided, three parts, handle..18.50
Starflower, divided......................30.00
Roll Tray, Intaglio, brown, 11" l...35.00
Salad Plate, First Love......................6.00
Salt and Pepper Shakers, pr
Apple..18.00
Palm Trees................................100.00
Plaid...15.00
Shake and Pour, 4-1/4" h.............65.00
Snack Set, Intaglio, brown...............20.00
Soup and Sandwich Set, Rubel, bowl and plate...7.50
Sugar Bowl
Apple, open................................20.00
Intaglio, ivory, hand dec with brown slip...20.00
Normandy Plaid, cov..................40.00
Tea and Toast Set, Apple, plate and cup...30.00
Teapot, cov
Apple..35.00
Fruits, 2 cup.................................7.50
Maywood, 6 cup.........................35.00
Red Ivy, 5" h..............................35.00
Tea Tile Trivet..............................115.00
Tumbler, Apple................................20.00
Vase, 5-3/4" h, 5" w, hand painted..20.00
Vegetable
Apple, oval.................................20.00
Intaglio, brown, 8-1/2" d.............25.00
Normandy Plaid, 10-1/2" l, divided.......................................50.00

R

Racing Collectibles

Collecting Hints: This is a field of heroes and also fans. Collectors love the winners; a household name counts. Losers are important only when major races are involved. Pre-1945 material is especially desirable because few individuals were into collecting prior to that time.

The field does have problems with reproductions and copycats. Check every item carefully. Beware of paying premium prices for items made within the last 20 years.

Auto racing items are one of the hot collectible markets of the 1990s. Although interest in Indy 500 collectibles remains strong, the market is dominated by NASCAR collectibles. In fact, the market is so strong that racing collectibles have their own separate show circuit and supporting literature.

There are so many horse-racing collectibles that specialization is required from the beginning. Collector focuses include a particular horse racing type or a specific horse race, a breed or specific horse, or racing prints and images. Each year there are a number of specialized auctions devoted to horse racing. These range from sporting prints sales at the major New York auction houses to benefit auctions for the Thoroughbred Retirement Foundation.

History: Man's quest for speed is as old as time. Although this category focuses primarily on automobile and horse racing, other types of racing memorabilia are included. If it moves, it will and can be raced.

Automobile racing began before the turn of the century. Many of the earliest races took place in Europe. By the first decade of the 20th century, automobile racing was part of the American scene.

The Indianapolis 500 began in 1911 and was interrupted only by World War II. In addition to Formula 1 racing, the NASCAR circuit has achieved tremendous popularity with American racing fans. Cult heroes such as Richard Petty have become household names.

The history of horse racing dates back to the domestication of the horse itself. Prehistoric cave drawings illustrate horses racing. The Greeks engaged in chariot racing as early as 600 b.c. As civilization spread, so did the racing of horses. Each ethnic group and culture added its own unique slant.

The British developed the concept of the Thoroughbred, a group of horses that are descendants of three great Arabian stallions—Carley Arabian, Byerley Turk, and Goldolphin Arabian. Horse racing received royal sponsorship and became the Sport of Kings.

Horse racing reached America during the colonial period. By the 1800s, four-mile match races between regional champions were common. In 1863, Saratoga Race Track was built. The first Belmont Stakes was run at Jerome Park in 1867. As the 19th century ended, more than 300 race tracks operated seasonal cards. By 1908, the number of American race tracks had been reduced to 25 as a result of widespread opposition to gambling.

The premier American horse race is the Kentucky Derby. Programs date from 1924 and glasses, a favorite with collectors, from the late 1930s.

References: Mark Allen Baker, *Auto Racing Memorabilia*, Krause Publications, 1996; — *Collector's Guide to Celebrity Autographs*, 2nd ed., Krause Publications, 2000; Bill Coulter, *Stock Car Model Kit Encyclopedia and Price Guide*, Krause Publications, 1999; Jack Mackenzie, *Indy 500 Buyers Guide*, published by author (6940 Wildridge Rd, Indianapolis, IN 46256), 1996.

Periodicals: *Collector's World*, P.O. Box 562029, Charlotte, NC 28256; *Racing Collectibles Price Guide*, P.O. Box 608114, Orlando, FL 32860.

Collectors' Clubs: National Indy 500 Collectors Club, 10505 N Delaware St., Indianapolis, IN 46280; Sport of Kings Society, 1406 Annen Lane, Madison, WI 53711.

Museums: Aiken Thoroughbred Racing Hall of Fame & Museum, Aiken, SC; Harness Racing Hall of Fame, Goshen, NY; Indianapolis Motor Speedway Hall of Fame Museum, Speedway, IN; International Motor Sports Hall of Fame, Talladega, AL; Kentucky Derby Museum, Louisville, KY; National Museum of Racing & Hall of Fame, Saratoga Springs, NY.

Additional Listings: Horse Collectibles.

Auto

Bank, Robert Yates, diecast, 1994 .... 7.50

Banner, Coors Light, slight wear 10.00

Book

Barney Oldfield-The Life and Times of America's Legendary Speed King, William F. Nolan, Putnam, NY, 1961 .... 35.00

The Speed Merchants, The World of Road Racing, The Men, The Machines, The Tracks, Michael Keyser, Prentice Hall, 1973, 1st edition, dj 15.00

Bubble Gum Cards, Grid, Formula I, factory set, 200 cards 15.00

Calendar, 1995, Nascar, Winston Cup Series 10.00

Coca-Cola Bottle, commemorative, honoring Jeff Burton, Nascar series . 10.00

Display, Pepsi Racing, Jeff Gordon, life size 325.00

Drinking Cup, 6-1/4" h, plastic, racing car theme, Pepsi 89 Car, "Pepsi Official Soft Drink of the Daytona 500," red plastic cap, reverse side with racing flags and their meanings 1.00

Game, Daytona 500, Milton Bradley, 1990, officially licensed by NASCAR 35.00

Helmet, 1950s, used 17.50

Jacket, Racing Team, dark blue, yellow lining, Mr. Peanut on front, larger one on back, unworn 30.00

Lunch Box and Thermos, Speed Racer, King Seeley Thermos, 1987, C8 .... 125.00

Magazine, *National Speed Sport News*, 65 issues, 1970s 55.00

Magazine Tear Sheet, MGB, British Racing Green 12.00

Patch, Ford Racing, 1960s 7.50

Phone Card, Nascar, Assetts Racing 2.50

Photograph, 11" x 13", color, titled, "One Last Lap, A Final Tribute to Davey & Alan, November 14, 1993, Atlanta Motor Speedway" 15.00

Pepsi Bottle, long neck, painted label with Richard Petty 6.00

Pinback Button, Gilmore, celluloid, Souvenir of Gilmore Auto Races, some discoloration, 1930s 25.00

Pinball Game, Mickey & Donald Speed Way, Ideal, tin and plastic 80.00

Playing Cards, Dale Earnhardt 4.50

Postcard

Fairway Park, Casey, IL, postmarked 1908 .... 10.00

Miami Jockey Club, postmarked 1930 .... 7.50

Palm Beach, FL, early view, postmarked 1907 .... 9.00

Saratoga Race Track Grand Stand, postmarked 1911 .... 7.50

Press Kit

Kenny Schrader Kodiak, 1991 .... 15.00

Ricky Rudd Tide, 1994 .... 12.00

Rusty Wallace Miller, 1994 .... 12.00

Terry Labonte, Skoal, 1990 .... 18.00
Press Pass, Nascar 45.00
Stein, Avon 17.50
Stock Certificate, Western Racing, Inc.,
1958 .... 5.00
Toy
Diecast, Jeff Gordon Car, #24,
three-pack, MOC 25.00
Hot Wheel, Winner's Circle Nascar
#24, Jeff Gordon, collectible tin with
two decks of playing cards, diecast
replica race car, 1999 Motorsports,
Inc., unopened 25.00
Train Set, Dale Earnhardt, Revell Collection, 1996
.......#2234, Wrangler, curb tender, four
pcs 200.00
#3113, Olympic Games H.O., Good-
wrench Service, four pcs 150.00
#3114, Olympic Games H.O., Good-
wrench Service, six pcs 200.00
T-Shirt, Rusty Wallace, black, front, "Midnight Hour Approaches #2 Rusty Wallace," back reads "#2 Rusty Wallace
Miller Penske Racing," size XL ... 10.00

Horse

Badge, 3" d, Budweiser Million, Second
Running, Aug 29, 1982, full color
illus 10.00
Drinking Glass
Kentucky Derby, 1964, frosted, brown
illus, gold lettering....................... 35.00
Saratoga Travers Stakes, 1995 ... 12.00
Figure, 5" x 2-1/2", mkd "Occupied
Japan".. 85.00
Lobby Card, Pride of the Blue
Grass.. 15.00
Mug, 5-1/2" h, Hollywood Gold Cup, Hol-
lywood Park
Seabiscuit, 1938........................... 6.00
Slew of Damascus,1949 .... 6.00
Needle Book, 4-1/2" x 4-3/4", Steeple
Chase, cardboard, full color art,
1930s 30.00
Pinback Button
Churchill Downs Derby Day, blue let-
tering on white, c1930-40.............. 8.00
Female Jockey, wearing white and
black Duke of Portland colors racing
outfit, early 1900s 15.00
Male Jockey, wearing red and blue
Dwyer colors racing outfit, early
1900s 15.00
Pimlico Preakness, multicolored, horse
head illus, white ground, blue lettering,
1960s 20.00
Preakness Day, black lettering on
gold, 1960..................................... 8.00
Saratoga Race Horse, full color por-
trait of Four Star Dave, white ground,
blue and red lettering 12.00
Plate, "Compliments of Peterson & Wallin,
Orion, IL," 8-1/4" d, horse race
dec 65.00
Postcard
Going to the Post at Hialeah Park,
Miami, FL, unused 6.50
Man O' War, unused 6.00
Sunshine Park, Oldsmar, FL,
unused 8.50

Stickpin, brass, jockey cap over entwined
initials, green and white enamel
accents, 1906 ....30.00
Ticket, Kentucky Derby, May,
1936..12.00

Radio Characters and Personalities

Collecting Hints: Many items associated with radio characters and personalities were offered as premiums.
This category focuses mostly on the
non-premium items. Radio premiums
are listed separately in this book.

Don't overlook the vast amount of
material related to the radio shows
themselves. This includes scripts,
props, and a wealth of publicity material. Many autographed photographs
appear on the market. Books, especially Big Little Books and similar
types, featured many radio-related
characters and stories.

Radio characters and personalities found their way into movies and
television. Serious collectors exclude
the products which spun off from
these other two areas.

History: The radio show was a dominant force in American life from the
1920s to the early 1950s. "Amos 'n'
Andy" began in 1929, "The Shadow"
in 1930, and "Chandu the Magician"
in 1932. Although many of the characters were fictional, the individuals
who portrayed them became public
idols. A number of figures achieved
fame on their own—Eddie Cantor,
Don McNeill of "The Breakfast Club,"
George Burns and Gracie Allen,
Arthur Godfrey, and Jack Benny.

Sponsors and manufacturers were
quick to capitalize on the fame of the
radio characters and personalities.
Premiums were offered as part of the
shows' themes. However, merchandising did not stop with premiums.
Many non-premium items, such as
bubble gum cards, figurines, games,
publicity photographs, and dolls,
were issued. Magazine advertisements often featured radio personalities.

References: Mark Allen Baker, *Collector's Guide to Celebrity Autographs*, 2nd ed., Krause
Publications, 2000; Jim Harmon,
Radio & TV Premiums, Krause Publications, 1997; Rex Miller, *The Investor's Guide to Vintage Character
Collectibles*, Krause Publications,
1999; Jon D. Swartz and Robert C.
Reinehr, *Handbook of Old-Time
Radio*, Scarecrow Press, 1993.

Periodicals: *Friends of Old Time
Radio*, P.O. Box 4321, Hamden, CT
06514; *Hello Again*, P.O. Box 4321,
Hamden, CT 06514; *Nostalgia Digest
and Radio Guide*, Box 421, Morton
Grove, IL 60053; *Old Time Radio
Digest*, 4114 Montgomery Rd, Cin-
cinnati, OH 45212.

Collectors' Clubs: Friends of Vic
& Sade, 7232 N. Keystone Ave.,
Lincolnwood, IL 60646; Golden
Radio Buffs of Maryland, Inc., 301
Jeanwood Ct, Baltimore, MD
21222; Illinois Old Radio Shows
Society, 10 S. 540 County Line Rd,
Hinsdale, IL 60521; Manuscript
Society, 350 N. Niagara St., Bur-
bank, CA 91505; National Lum &
Abner Society, #81 Sharon Blvd.,
Dora, IL 35062; North America
Radio Archives, 134 Vincewood
Dr., Nicholasville, KY 40356; Old
Time Radio Club, 56 Christen Ct,
Lancaster, NY 14086; Old Time
Radio Collectors Traders Society,
725 Cardigan Ct, Naperville, IL
60565; Oldtime Radio Show Col-
lectors Assoc., 45 Barry St., Sud-
bury, Ontario P3B 3H6 Canada;
Pow-Wow, 301 E. Buena Vista
Ave., N. Augusta, SC 29841;
Radio Collectors of America, Ard-
sley Circle, Brockton, MA 02402;
Society to Preserve & Encourage
Radio Drama, Variety & Comedy,
P.O. Box 7177, Van Nuys, CA
91409.

Museum: Museum of Broadcasting,
New York, NY.

Additional Listings: Big Little Books,
Comic Books, Radio Premiums,
Super Heroes.

Amos 'n' Andy

Book, *Amos 'n' Andy*, Rand McNally &
Co., © 1929, hardcover,
autographed.............................. 265.00
Game, Card Party, M. Davis Co., two
score pads, eight tallies, orig box,
1938 .... 75.00
Get Well Card, 4-1/2" x 5-1/2", black and
white photo, Hall Brothers, 1931 32.00
Photo, 5" x 7", browntone, matte finish,
Pepsodent Co., 1929 .... 30.00
Record Set....................................... 50.00

Captain Midnight

Mug, Ovaltine, red plastic, colorful decal,
c1953.. 70.00
Patch, iron-on 30.00
Photo, Chuck Ramsey, 6" x 7-1/2", black
and white, white facsimile signature,
Skelly Oil, 1939........................... 70.00
Token Medallion, Skelly Oil 35.00

Don Winslow

Bank, 2-1/4" h, Uncle Don's Earnest Saver Club, oval, paper label, photo and cartoon illus, Greenwich Savings Bank, New York City, 1930s 40.00
Salt and Pepper Shakers, pr, full color, plaster 75.00

Edgar Bergen and Charlie McCarthy

Bubble Gum Wrapper, Bergen's Better Bubble Gum 10.00
Game, Charlie McCarthy Radio Party Game, orig envelope 65.00
Pencil Sharpener, figural, diecut plastic, color decal, 1930s 72.00
Soap, 4" h, figural, orig box, Kerk Guild, 1930-40 .... 75.00

Fibber McGee and Molly

Fan Card, 8" x 10", black and white glossy, 11 cast members, Kolynos Dental Cream, © 1933 .... 60.00
Menu, 9-1/2" x 12-1/4", Brown Derby, autographed 120.00
Record, 10-1/4" x 12", four 78 RPM records, live broadcasts, colorful cover, 1947 .... 55.00

Flying Family, Cocomalt, puzzle, 1932, orig envelope 60.00

Jack Armstrong

Bomb Sight Kit, MIB 525.00
Patch, Jack Armstrong, Future Champions of America, 1943 .... 22.00
Ped-o-Meter 30.00
Photo, Blackstar, 1933 .... 20.00
Reel, magnetic tape, The All American Boy Radio Shows, 15-minute episodes, 1940-41, 7 pcs 75.00
Ring, baseball 500.00
Sound Effects Kit, mint in orig mailer 300.00

Jack Benny

Booklet, Zenith Radios, Burns & Allen, Boswells, 1930s 45.00
Magazine, Jack Benny and Rochester, *Look* 22.00
Program, 9" x 12", black and white photos, Phil Harris signature, 12 pgs, late 1930s 27.50

Jimmie Allen

Model, 19" l airplane, Thunderbolt, orig box, 1930s 120.00
Photo, teenage aviator 40.00
Whistle, Jimmy Allen, brass, c1936 . 30.00

Joe Penner

Sheet Music, *Don't Never Do-o-o that*, black and yellow cover, © 1934 T. B. Harms Co. 25.00
Valentine, 4-1/2" x 7", mechanical, diecut, holding duck on shoulder, "I'll Gladly Buy A Duck," 1930-40 .... 24.00

Little Orphan Annie

Book
   Little Orphan Annie and the Circus, Cupples & Leon, 1927, 7" x 9", hardcover 60.00
   Secret Society Signs & Signals, Little Orphan Annie, 1937 .... 115.00
Coloring Book, *Little Orphan Annie*, McLaughlin, 10" x 13" 120.00
Decoder, Little Orphan Annie, 1936 .... 40.00
Game, Little Orphan Annie, Milton Bradley, 1927 .... 125.00
Manual, Secret Society, orig mailer 125.00
Puzzle, 9" x 12-1/2", Tucker County Horse Race, orig instruction sheet and mailing box, Ovaltine, c1933 .... 75.00
Ring, Secret Message 335.00
Shake-Up Mug, 1982 anniversary ... 50.00
Shake-Up Mug, vintage, brown 130.00
Sheet Music, *Little Orphan Annie's Song*, Harold Gray illus cov, Ovaltine, 1931, four pgs 27.50
Watch Box, 1938, white 250.00

Major Bowes, clock, 5-1/2" h, Ingersol, metal, brass luster, raised numerals, 1930s 145.00

Quiz Kids, game, Rapaport Bros, electric, orig box and instructions 25.00

The Shadow

Book, *The Living Shadow*, Maxwell Grant, c1931 .... 10.00
Figure, 7" h, china, glossy black cloak and hat, c1930 .... 265.00
Ring, Secret Agent, MIB 130.00
Rubber Stamp 40.00
Toy, super jet, plastic, orig package 45.00

Young Explorers Club, badge 50.00

Radio Premiums

Collecting Hints: Most collections are centered around one or two specific personalities or radio programs.

History: Radio premiums are nostalgic reminders of the radio shows of childhood. Sponsors of shows frequently used their products as a means of earning premiums, such as saving box tops to exchange for gifts related to a program or personality.

References: Ted Hake, *Hake's Price Guide to Character Toy Premiums*, Collector Books, 1996; Jim Harmon, *Radio & TV Premiums*, Krause Publications, 1997; Robert M. Overstreet, *Overstreet Premium Ring Price Guide*, Gemstone Publishing, 1995; ——, *Overstreet Toy Ring Price Guide*, 2nd ed., Collector Books, 1996; Tom Tumbusch, *Tomart's Price Guide to Radio Premium and Cereal Box Collectibles*, Wallace-Homestead, 1991.

Periodical: *Box Top Bonanza*, 3403 46th Ave., Moline, IL 61265.

Reproduction Alert.

Additional Listings: Radio Characters and Personalities.

Advertising Card, store window display-type, 8-1/2" x 11-1/2", Radio Stars, art by Early Christy, showing Harriet Hillard, c1937 .... 28.00
Autographed Book, *The Friskies Book of Dog Care*, Gracie Allen signature, 5-1/2" x 7-1/4" color cover, 1955 . 15.00
Autographed Photo
   Captain Tim Healy, 5" x 7" still paper black and white fan card, issued by Ivory Soap, c1938, dark blue inscription 28.00
   Lyman, Abe, 8" x 10" glossy black and white fan photo, printed text at bottom "The World's Biggest 15 Minute Show," sgd in black ink, 1934 .... 15.00
   Rubinoff, Dave, 8" x 10" matte black and white photo of pensive looking Rubinoff seated at table holding violin, white ink fountain pen autograph, 1934 .... 20.00
Autographed Postcard, Wallace Butterworth, 3-1/2" x 4-1/2", night scene of Chicago Merchandise Mart, imprint of Century of Progress, 1933, on reverse, pencil inscription 8.00
Bank, Treasure Adventures of Donald Ayer, Bond Flashlights, 2-1/4" h, battery shape, cardboard body, red, white, green, and yellow paper label, metal top and bottom, c1930 ..... 48.00
Beanie Cap, RCA, felt, child size, alternating red and white panels, blue inscription, "Victor RCA Steel Pier Day," c1940 .... 35.00
Book
   Bachelor's Children, 5" x 7-1/4" red hardcover book, silver accent, orig 6" x 8" white envelope with return address of Old Dutch Cleanser, 28 pgs, copyright 1939 .... 24.00
   Olsen & Johnson, Pocket Guide to What's Doing in San Francisco, 1954, 32 pgs, 3" x 8-1/8", age discoloration 5.00
   The Quiz Kids, Questions and Answers, Saalfield, copyright 1941, Louis G. Cowan, full-cover cover art, 6-3/4" x 7-3/4" 8.00
Booklet
   Lum and Abner's Adventures in Hollywood and 1938 Family Album, 6" x 9" booklet, 6-1/4" x 9-1/4" manila envelope, return address of Horlick's Malted Milk 18.00
   Ted Maone's Mansions of Imagination Album, Pilgrimage of Poetry, 5-3/4" x 9", 84 black and white text and photo pgs, NBC Blue Network, 1940, Columbia University Press 5.00
   Tom Breneman's Breakfast in Hollywood, 4" x 6", black and white, dark blue accents, eight pgs, two pgs of Tom promoting Ivory Flakes, c1945 .... 5.00
Bookmark, 2" x 5-3/4" stiff paper, Omar the Mystic, two sided, radio station call letters CKLW, Windsor, Ontario, show time, and text on both sides, issued by Taystee Bread, c1936 .... 40.00

Card
3" x 5" black and white, one side addressed "To Mother" promoting Dick Daring Radio Programs by Andrew "Coach" Rogers, Quaker Oats premium, c1933 .... 25.00
4-1/4" x 5-1/2", Gather Round Kids, Thanks for Listening, opens to red and green Christmas text message on left, call letters KYM, greentone photo image of smiling black-haired woman at piano, facsimile autograph "Love Mary Lou," Philadelphia, c1940 .... 8.00
4-1/4" x 7" black and white card, red accent text, cartoon of man kneeling on floor surrounded by hearts while woman on couch ignoring him, nose, mouth, and chin are comprised of thin link chain which moves to make strange and funny faces, text "please be our valentine from Maude and Bill" on A&P's radio program, orig 4-3/8" x 7-1/4" manila envelope 12.00

Certificate, "H.C.B. Club Grand Officer Award," (Hot Cereal Breakfast), 5-1/4" x 7-7/8" parchment-like certificate with black and white art, orange accents, 3/4" dia foil insignia, printed signature of Grand Commander, 1931, 5-1/2" x 8-1/4" orig mailing envelope with Cream of Wheat return address, crease in certificate 30.00

Child's Book, *Frank Bring 'Em Back Alive Buck Capturing Wild Elephants*, Merrill #M3840, copyright 1934 Frank Buck, 9" x 12" 20.00

Comic Book, Foldess, #36 .... 15.00

Decoder, Lil Orphan Annie, Secret Society, brass, silver outer rim, 1935 . 65.00

Fan Card, Tennessee Jed, Star of Tip-Top Bread Thrilling Radio Program, 3" x 4-3/4", black and white photo of Jed wearing buckskin jacket, name on back, age discoloration, 1945 .... 25.00

Flashlight, Sgt Preston, 3" l, plastic, black, red, and green color discs, facsimile signature, © 1949 .... 25.00

Folder
3-1/2" x 6-1/4" eight page black and white folder, Jack Benny, Helen Hayes, Conrad Thibault, Lanny Ross, General Foods list of products o back, late 1930s 12.00
9-1/4" x 9-1/4" folder, Eddie Cantor How to Make A Quack-Quack, black and white photo of Cantor, text on back for Dr. Cantor Examines Uncle Sam, orig 9-1/4" x 12-1/4" envelope with Standard Brands text, tear and slight wear 15.00

Game
Drew Pearson's Predict-A-Word, Deejay Products, copyright 1949, orig instructions, booklet adv Pearson's ABC radio show, slight oxidation to metal spinner, 10 sheets of 50 used, 6" x 8-1/2" x 3/4" black, white, red, and yellow box 10.00
Jack Armstrong's Adventure with the Dragon Talisman, map and game board with spinner, 7" x 10-1/2" manila envelope with return address of Jack Armstrong, General Mills............. 95.00

Identification Bracelet, Tom Mix, silvered brass chain, disc, two six guns, Ralston address and serial number, 1947..55.00

Ink Blotter
Bond Bread, 3-1/2" x 6-1/4", featuring "All-Plastic Radio-Purse of the Future," small ad for Bond Bread, late 1940s, unused 14.00
The Shadow, 4" x 9", white thin cardboard, blue and pink photo of smiling boy getting in bed, text "The Shadow Radio's Master Detective Is On The Air Every Sunday Afternoon," 1-1/8" h image of Shadow holding smoking gun, black text for New Jersey Blue Coal company, c1930.................40.00
The Shadow Knows, 3-3/8" x 5-3/4", black silhouette image of The Shadow, red, white, and black text for Canadian Blue Coal dealer, radio show listings, 1930s, scattered color rubs, visible moisture stains on front, back slightly discolored...............65.00

Jar, 2-1/2" d x 3-1/2" h clear glass jar, label with red, white, and blue tin litho lid with image of Gildersleeve looking at viewer, cigar in mouth, crown on head, text promoting, "The Great Gildersleeve Radio's Laugh King, NBC," c1948-51...........................8.00

Magic Answer Box, Jack Armstrong, 1" x 3-3/4" x 1", bright red litho, diecut viewing area, c1940, heat sensitive needle 48.00

Map, 11" x 25-1/2", Map of Countries Visited in Air Adventures of Jimmie Allen, full color, west coat and Far East on one side, black and white reverse with text letter from Allen, facsimile autograph and sketches, article by Capt. Ernie Smith, copyright 1934 Skelly Oil Co., folds 190.00

Member Certificate, David Harding Counter-Spy, 6" x 8" paper sheet, radio sponsor Pepsi-Cola, upper part is member certificate for Counter-Spy Junior Agents Club, members name sgd twice in ink, blue border, red, white, and blue Pepsi bottle camp, some age yellowing.....................15.00

Newsletter
49th State Safety Legion, orig membership certificate and mailer, issued by St. Louis Globe-Democrat, station KMOX, 1936................................12.00
Renfro Valley, four pgs, photos and articles of cast members, sponsored by Ballard's Obelisk Flour, Vol. 8, #10, Nov. 15, 1945, 12" x 16"...............15.00

Newspaper, *Jack Armstrong Tru-Flite News*, 10" x 11", four pgs, Vol. 1, #2, Oct., 1944, published by General Mills Inc., horizontal center fold 10.00

Pencil Box, Ripley Believe It Or Not, red box, black text, yellow accent lettering, Sgt. Maj. Jiggs Marine mascot dog on top, reverse with images and facts on Roger Bacon and Christopher Columbus, college pennant design inside, 1930s, 3-3/4" x 8-1/4" x 3/4", worn around edges 38.00

Pinback Button
Lone Ranger Safety Club, 1934..22.00

Olsen & Johnson's Winter Garden Farm Restaurant, black and white, red text on rim "I Had Chicken and I Like It At Olsen & Johnson's Winter Garden Farm Restaurant, Carmel, New York," center imge of Johnson dressed as chef, 3-1/2" d 20.00
Philips Audio/Video Appliances, litho, orange, red, and blue logo, early 1950s.. 12.00
Philco Week, red and white, sales promotion event for radio products, c1930s 8.00
RCA Micro Mike, 3" d, ivory white celluloid, red image and title, radio tube torso, arms and legs resembling other wiring elements, 1940s-50s........ 40.00

Portrait Sheets, RCA Victor, Red Seal Recording Artist, high-gloss paper, full-color portrait illus sheets with prominent performing artists, including Yehudi Menuhin, Vladimir Horowitz, Gladys Swarthout, Arthur Rubinstein, Alexander Kipnis, Jose Iturbi, Allan Jones, late 1930s-40s, set of seven 14.00

Postcard
3-1/4" x 5-1/2", Fred Allen's Town Hall Tonight Audition Notice, pre-printed, dated Aug. 25, 1935, booking agent name on bottom 12.00
3-1/4" x 5-1/2", Jimmie Allen Flying Club, pilot's wristlet award notification, postmarked Dec. 11, 1934, typed address of Oregon recipient, slight wear 24.00
3-1/2" x 5-1/2", WGN Studios, Chicago, full-color image of Gothic-style radio station, copyright Curt Teich & Co., Inc., J. G. Stoll Co., Chicago, unused 5.00
4" x 6", Uncle Don, black and white photo, personalized signature in blue ink, orig typed address and cancelled stamp, facsimile poem and signature on back, late 1930s.................... 24.00

Poster, The Rexall Theater, 10" x 32-1/2", blue, white, and orange, promoting NBC Friday night summer show, photos of Lynn Bari and Pat O'Brien, 1948, folds.................... 48.00

Premiums Catalog, 8-1/4" x 10-1/4", Tom Mix premiums, orig folder 35.00

Premium Club Kit Card, Mandrake the Magician, 3" x 5", black and white, both sides welcoming new member to club, promotes Taystee Bread, 1934... 30.00

Premium Dial
Radio Quiz Master, 9-1/4" x 9-1/2" stiff paper, diecut openings, copyright 1944 C. Cloud, Cloudcrest Creations, Chicago 30.00
Uncle Don, 40 Wonders/Great Inventions of the World, 10" d, stiff paper diecut wheel, Compliments of Uncle Don and Silver Wings, copyright 1931 Knapp, New York 24.00

Premium Letter
7-1/2" x 10-1/4" letter, The Cruise of the Blue Dart, vignettes of various pirate scenes, explains shark's tooth (missing), 3" x 4-1/2" gray mailer with Maltex Co., Inc. Vermont, return address, late 1930s, folded as issued.............. 15.00

7-1/2" x 10-1/2" letter, Jimmie Allen, typewritten, Allen letterhead with photo, sgd with facsimile signature, 6" x 8" sepia tone stiff cardboard fan photos of Speed Robertson and Jimmie Allen, Skelly Oil Co., 1934 .... 75.00

8-1/2" x 14", Jimmie Allen's Second Letter to Flying Cadets, brown and white, two sided printed letter, photo at top of Allen and Speed Robertson, Flash Lewis, and Ah Chow beside their amphibian plane, Hispeed Gas, copyright 1935 Hickok Oil Corp., 2" archival tape repair 38.00

8-3/8" x 10-3/4", Jimmie Allen Flying Club, Flight Lesson #3, Flight Chart, black and white, orange accent Jimmie Allen Flying Club letterhead, facsimile signature in blue ink, welcoming cadet and promoting Skelly Oil, 1933 .... 90.00

Premium Order Form, 4-1/2" x 6" pink sheet, black text for Dick Steel Detective Bureau badge, Educator Hammered Wheat Thinsies, 1934, unused 20.00

Premium Photo

Amos and Andy, 9" x 12", black and white photo, simulated frame border design, mkd "Supplement Detroit Sunday Times," c1930s 28.00

Keep Hardy Says Captain Ezra and Mary Diamond and Tommy, 5-5/8" x 8-1/2", black and white stiff paper real photo of cast members in costume, facsimile inscription and autographs, 1933 .... 15.00

Northwest Chronicle, 7-7/8" x 9-5/8", glossy black and white, pretty girl seated on piano, two guys standing next to her, old crone lectures older man, text notes members as Rhiny, Alice, Buck, Aunt Hessie, and Mr. Dudley, NBC show, Yeast Foam sponsor, mid 1930s 15.00

Peggy Joan and Maryanne Moylan, 7-1/8" x 10-1/4" black and white, serious pose, facsimile autographs, c1940 .... 7.50

Radio Explorers, 5" x 7" sepia photo of jungle hunter beside felled rhino, "To My Friends/The Radio Explorers/James R. Clark,"1930s, tear and several light creases 10.00

The Story of Mary Marlin, 8" x 14" semiglossy vertical paper formal with 8" x 10" real photo of three cast members, white facsimile autographs of Joe, Sally and Mary Marlin, headlines "Change in Time, Change in Stations" listing times, cities, and stations, sponsored by Kleenex, 1936 .... 15.00

Premium Prize List Folder, 3-1/2" x 6-1/4", Hey Members of the Joe E. Brown Club, 8-pg colorful folder, shows 32 prizes available through Grape-Nuts Flakes, expiration date of Dec. 31, 1936 .... 24.00

Print

8" x 10" full-color image of Capt. Tim Healy in uniform, NBC microphone, dark blue band along left side, name in white, reverse with biographical data, plus additional photos, c1939 .... 18.00

10" x 14", Check and Double Check, black and white, Scotty dogs, Grace G. Drayton, mkd "Courtesy of R. K. O. Radio Pictures," issued for 1930 Amos N' Andy movie 30.00

Puppet, hand, Charlie McCarthy... 200.00

Puzzle, 9" x 12", Just Plain Bill, Kolynos Dental Cream, 150 pcs, orig envelope 32.00

Radio Log

2-3/4" x 4", marbleized green celluloid front cover, high relief of owl's head in red celluloid, black celluloid back, two blue celluloid rings, 10 stiff page of "Index of Cities Alphabetically Listed," 1930s 10.00

5-1/2" x 10", New Dealers Official Radio Log, black, white, and red cover, 32 black and white pages of text, map of U.S., listings for radio stations in U.S., Canada, and Mexico, Cuba, and principal stations of the world, 1929, 3" splint on spine, scattered pencil notations 8.00

Record Set

Eddie Cantor, 10" x 12" cardboard cover, set of four 78 rpm records, distributed by Monitor, copyright 1947, minor damage to cover, one record broken 12.00

Fibber McGee and Molly with Teeny, 10-1/4" x 12" cardboard cover, set of three 78 rpm records, Capitol label, 1930s, some wear 30.00

Sea Chart, Captain Silver on Board the Sea Hound, 6-1/2" x 10" folded map, opens to 20" x 26-1/2", North and South America, image of sailing yacht, copyright 1942 Captain Silver Syndicate Inc., New York, Blue Network Inc., Radio City, NY, artist sgd "Neff"...20.00

Sheet Music

Lonely Heart, Today's Children theme song, 9" x 12", black and white photo of well dressed cast members, caption "Eilene's Wedding Party," 6 pgs, back cover photo showing Eilene's Wedding Cake, Pillsbury, Minneapolis, copyright 1936 .... 10.00

Smoke Your Troubles Away, Henry George theme song, 9-1/4" x 12-1/4", black and white cover with red accents, Henry and George smoking cigars, copyright 1930 .... 12.00

Sign, 11" x 14", Adam-Drew Pearson Radio Program, image of broadaster Pearson at microphone, large image promoting Knickerbocker hat by Adam, ABC radio show, 1949-51, white easel back 24.00

Spoon, Charlie McCarthy, orig mailer 50.00

Statuette, 11-1/4" h serviceman figure, holding RCA orbital symbol, RCA logo and "A Tribute To The Nation's Television Service Technicians for Their Tremendous Accomplishments in Installing and Serving the Million TV Sets Now in Active Use/National Television Servicemen's Week/March 7-12th, 1955," 3-1/4" sq black, pedestal base, orig box 70.00

Sticker, 2-1/4" x 3-1/2", Amos and Andy, black and white, red border, gummed back, "Check N Double Check That's Amos and Andy, We Don't Want Any Double Checks, Just a Single Check for $...Will Satisfy Us How About It?" Hartford Insurance Co., 1930s ... 30.00

Thank You Card, 3" x 5", orange and black illus, message to broadcasters, Art Deco style art of jazz band, copyright 1924 Exclusive Co., Philadelphia, orig envelope, unused 10.00

Tray, 13" x 17", litho metal tray, Lunch with Uncle Pete, Pete, cartoon-like squirrel, and loaf of Uncle Pete's Favorite Bread, red, white, blue, yellow, and green, litho map of U.S. for playing "Coast to Coast Road Trip Sleeper Hop" game, spinner missing, c1950, surface wear 8.00

Radios

Collecting Hints: Radio collectors divide into three groups: those who collect because of nostalgia, those interested in history and/or acquiring radios that represent specific periods, and collectors of personality and figural radios. Most collectors find broadcasting, and therefore broadcast receivers, of primary interest.

Broadcast receivers can be divided into these significant categories:

- Crystal sets and battery powered receivers of the early 1920s
- Rectangular electric table models of the late 1920s
- Cathedrals, tombstones, and consoles of the thirties
- Midget plastic portables and wood-cabinet table models built before and after World War II
- Shaped radios with cases made of Bakelite or other plastic.
- Personality and figural radios made between the 1930s and the 1960s.

Because the prime nostalgic period seems to be the decade of the thirties, the cathedral style, socket-powered radios (e.g., the Philco series) have become sought after items. Recently young collectors have exhibited interest in the plastic-cabinet radios built between 1945 and 1960.

Newer radio collectors are influenced by novelty, with the outside appearance the most important feature. The radio must play; but, shape, color, decoration, and condition of the case far outweigh the internal workings of the set in determining desirability and, consequently, price. Enclosures that resemble things or figures (e.g., Mickey Mouse) command premium prices. The square table models of the later thirties and the midget sets of the late 1930s and 1940s have recently attracted the attention of collectors.

The value of a radio is directly proportional to its appearance and its operating condition. Minor scratches are to be expected as is alligatoring of the surface finish, but gouges, cracks, and delaminated surfaces adversely affect prices, as will a crack, a broken place where plastic closures belong, or missing parts, tubes, or components. If major repairs are required to make the set work, the price must reflect this potential expense.

Many collectors specialize in radio-related memorabilia, brand names, or in a facet of radio paraphernalia such as loudspeakers, tubes, or microphones. As a result, auxiliary and radio-related items are becoming collectibles along with radios themselves.

Very rare radios usually go directly to major collectors, seldom appearing in the general market. Wireless equipment and radios used commercially before World War I are considered rare and are not listed here.

History: The radio was invented more than 100 years ago. Marconi was the first to assemble and employ the transmission and reception instruments that permitted electric messages to be sent without the use of direct connections. The early name for radio was "Wireless," and its first application was to control ships in 1898. Early wireless equipment is not generally considered collectible since its historic value makes it important for museum display.

Between 1905 and the end of World War I, many technical advances, including the invention of the vacuum tube by DeForest, increased communication technology and encouraged amateur interest. The receiving equipment from that period is desired by collectors and historians, but is rarely available.

By 1920, radio technology allowed broadcasts to large numbers of people simultaneously and music could be brought directly from concert halls into living rooms. The result was the development of a new art that changed the American way of life during the 1920s. The world became familiar through the radio in an average listener's home.

Radio receivers changed substantially in the decade of the twenties, going from black boxes—with many knobs and dials—powered by expensive and messy batteries, to stylish furniture, simple to use, and operated from the house current that had become the standard source of home energy. During the twenties, radios grew more complicated and powerful, as well as more ornate. Consoles appeared, loudspeakers were incorporated into them, and sound fidelity became an important consideration.

In the early 1930s, demand changed. The large expensive console gave way to small but effective table models. The era of the "cathedral" and the "tombstone" began. By the end of the thirties, the midget radio had become popular. Quality of sound was replaced by a price reduction, and most homes had more than one radio.

Shortly after World War II, the miniature tubes developed for the military were utilized in domestic radios. The result was further reduction in size and a substantial improvement in quality. The advent of FM also speeded improvements. Plastic technology made possible the production of attractive cases in many styles and colors.

The other development that drastically changed the radio receiver was the invention of the transistor in 1927. A whole new family of radio sets that could be carried in the shirt pocket became popular. Their popularity grew as they became less and less expensive, but their low cost meant that they were frequently thrown away when they stopped working. Today they are not easy to find in good condition and are, therefore, quite collectible.

References: John H. Bryant and Harold N. Cones, *Zenith Trans-Oceanic*, Schiffer Publishing, 1995; Marty and Sue Bunis, *Collector's Guide to Antique Radios*, 4th ed., Collector Books, 1997; ——, *Collector's Guide to Transistor Radios*, 2nd ed., Collector Books, 1996; Marty Bunis and Robert F. Breed, *Collector's Guide to Novelty Radios*, Books I and II, Collector Books, 1995, 1999 value update; *Evolution of the Radio*, Vol. I (1991, 1994 value update), Vol. II (1993), L-W Book Sales; Harold Cones and John Bryant, *Zenith Radio: The Early Years, 1919-1935*, Schiffer Publishing, 1997; Chuck

Dachis, *Radios by Halicrafters*, Schiffer Publishing, 1996; Roger Handy, Maureen Erbe, and Aileen Farnan Antonier, *Made in Japan: Transistor Radios of the 1950s and 1960s*, Chronicle Books, 1993; David Johnson, *Guide to Old Radios: Pointers, Pictures, and Prices*, 2nd ed., Wallace-Homestead, 1995; Ken Jupp and Leslie Piña, *Genuine Plastic Radios of the Mid-Century*, Schiffer Publishing, 1998; Harry Poster, *Poster's Radio & Television Price Guide*, 2nd ed., Wallace-Homestead, 1994; ——, *Illustrated Price Guide to Vintage Televisions and Deco Radios*, published by author, 1991; Ron Ramirez, *Philco Radio*, Schiffer Publishing, 1993; B. Eric Rhoads, *Blast from the Past*, available from author (800-226-7857), 1996; Norman Smith, *Transistor Radios: 1954-1968*, Schiffer Publishing, 1998; Mark Stein, *Machine Age to Jet Age, Radiomania's Guide to Tabletop Radios—1933-1959*, published by author (2109 Carterdale Rd., Baltimore, MD 21209.

Periodicals: *Antique Radio Classified*, P.O. Box 2, Carlisle, MA 01746; *Antique Radio Topics*, Box 28572, Dallas, TX 75228; *Horn Speaker*, P.O. Box 1193, Mabank, TX 75147; *Radio Age*, 636 Cambridge Rd, Augusta, GA 30909; *Transistor Network*, RR1, Box 36, Bradford, NH 03221.

Videotape: Roger Handy and Eric Wrobbel, *Favorite Transistor Radios*, available from producers (20802 Exhibit Ct., Woodland Hills, CA 91367).

Collectors' Clubs: Antique Radio Club of America, 300 Washington Trails, Washington, PA 15301; Antique Wireless Assoc, 59 Main St., Bloomfield, NY 14469; New England Antique Radio Club, RR1 Box 36, Bradford, NH 03221; Vintage Radio & Phonograph Society, Inc., P.O. Box 165345, Irving, TX 75016.

Museums: Antique Radio Museum, St. Louis, MO; Antique Wireless Association's Electronic Communication Museum, Bloomfield, NY; Caperton's Radio Museum, Louisville, KY; Muchow's Historical Radio Museum, Elgin, IL; Museum of Broadcast Communications, Chicago, IL; Museum of Wonderful Wireless, Minneapolis, MN; New England Museum of Wireless and Steam, East Greenwich, RI; Voice of the Twenties, Orient, NY.

Advisor: Lewis S. Walters.

Notes: The prices listed are for sets in average to good condition and are based upon an electrically complete receiver that operates when powered.

Admiral
Portable
  #33 ....30.00
  #35 ....30.00

Transistor, Coca-Cola Bottle, plastic, marked "Made in Hong Kong," 8" h, $40.

  #37 ....30.00
  #218, leatherette...........................40.00
  #909, All World 85.00
Y-2127 - Imperial 8, c1959 ....45.00

Air King- tombstone - Art Deco .3,000.00

Arvin
Mightymite #40 ....30.00
Rhythm Baby #417 ....275.00
Hoppy with lariatenna.....................575.00
Table
  #444 ....100.00
  #522A...65.00
Tombstone, #617 Rhythm Maid 215.00

Atwater Kent
Breadboard Style
  Model 9A.....................................550.00
  Model 10, with orig tags.........1,300.00
  Model 10................................1,100.00
Cathedral, 80, c1931 ....200.00
Table, 55 Keil.................................225.00
Tombstone, #854 ....155.00
#318 table radio, dome 115.00
Type R Horn 200.00

Bulova - clock radio
#100 ....30.00
#110 ....25.00
#120 ....30.00

Colonial "New World Radio" 1,000.00

Columbia - table radio – oak 125.00

Crosley
ACE V 170.00
Bandbox, #600, 1927 ....80.00
Gemchest, #609 ....425.00
Litfella -1N cathedral 175.00

Pup , with box................................500.00
Sheraton, cathedral 290.00
Showbox, #706 ....100.00
Super Buddy Boy............................125.00
#4-28 battery operated..................130.00
10-135 ....45.00
Dashboard 120.00
Sleigh 125.00

Dumont, RA346, table, scroll work,
1938...110.00

Emerson
AU-190 Catalin Tombstone......... 1,600.00
BT-245..1,200.00
Patriot 900.00
Snow White..................................1,200.00
274 Brown Bakelite 165.00
#400 Aristocrat...............................475.00
#409 Mickey Mouse.....................1,400.00
#411 Mickey Mouse.....................1,400.00
#570 Memento 110.00
#640 Portable 30.00
#888 Vanguard................................80.00
Porcelain Dealer Sign 150.00

Fada
#43...240.00
#53X...200.00
#60W..75.00
#115 bullet shape 1,000.00
#136..1,000.00
#252...575.00
#625 rounded end, slide rule dial . 700.00
#1000 red/orange bullet 1,100.00
#L 56 Maroon & White 2,600.00

Federal
#58DX...500.00
#110..550.00

General Electric
#400 .... 0.00
#410...30.00
#411...30.00
#414...30.00
#515, clock radio 25.00
#517, clock radio 25.00
K-126 ....150.00
Tombstone.....................................250.00
#81 c1934 ....200.00

Grebe
CR-8..500.00
CR-9..400.00
CR-12 ....600.00
MU-1 ....250.00
Service Manual 50.00

Halicrafters
TW-600 ....100.00
TW-200 ....125.00

Majestic
Charlie McCarthy 1,000.00
Treasure Chest 150.00
#92 ....125.00
59 Wooden Tombstone...............375.00
#381 ....225.00

Metrodyne Super 7 1925..............265.00

Motorola
#68X11Q Art Deco...........................75.00
Jet Plane...55.00
Jewel Box..80.00
M logo..25.00
Pixie 45.00

Ranger, Portable............................60.00
Ranger #700...................................30.00
Table, plastic 35.00

Olympic, radio w/phonograph........60.00

Paragon
DA-2 table......................................475.00
RD-5 table......................................600.00

Philco
T-7 126, transistor 65.00
T1000, clock radio...........................80.00
#551, 1928......................................175.00
#17, cathedral 250.00
#20, athedral..................................200.00
#37 – 62, table 2tone......................60.00
#37 – 84, cathedral 1937 ....175.00
#38, cathedral 250.00
#40 – 180, console wood 150.00
#46 – 132, table 20.00
#49 – 506, Transitone 35.00
#52 – 544, Transitone 40.00
#49 – 501, Boomerang 475.00
#60, Cathedral...............................125.00

Radiobar - w/glasses and
decanters................................. 1,500.00

Radio Corporation of America – RCA
LaSiesta 550.00
Radiola
  #17..120.00
  #18, with speaker 125.00
  #20..165.00
  #24..170.00
  #28 console 200.00
  #33..60.00
  #6X7 table - plastic 25.00
  8BT-7LE portable...........................35.00
  40X56 Worlds Fair 1,000.00

Silvertone - Sears
#1, table 75.00
#1582, cathedral - wood 225.00
#1955, tombstone 135.00
#9205, plastic transistor 45.00
Clock Radio – plastic 15.00

Sony - transistor
TFM-151, 1960 ....50.00
TR-63, 1958 ....145.00

Sparton
#506 Blue Bird -art deco.............3,30000
#5218..95.00
Blue Bird, reproduction 50.00

Stewart-Warner, table, slant 175.00

Stromberg Carlson # 636A
console 125.00

Westinghouse, Model WR-602 ...... 50.00

Zenith
#500 transistor - owl eye 75.00
#500D transistor 55.00
#750L transistor w/leather case.......40.00
Trans-Oceanic 90.00
#6D2615, table w/boomerang dial .. 95.00
Zephyr, multiband 95.00

Railroad Items

Collecting Hints: Most collectors concentrate on one railroad as opposed to one type of object. Railroad material always brings a higher price in the area in which it originated. Local collectors tend to concentrate on local railroads. The highest prices are paid for material from railroads which operated for only a short time. Nostalgia also influences collectors.

There are many local railroad clubs. Railroad buffs tend to have their own specialized swap meets and exhibitions. A large one is held in Gaithersburg, Maryland, in the fall each year.

History: It was a canal company, the Delaware and Hudson, which used the first steam locomotive in America. The Stourbridge Lion moved coal from the mines to the canal wharves. Just as America was entering its great canal era in 1825, the railroad was gaining a foothold. The Commonwealth of Pennsylvania did not heed William Strickland's advice to concentrate on building railroads instead of canals.

By the 1840s, railroad transportation was well-established. Numerous private companies were organized although many remained in business for only a short time.

During the Civil War, the effectiveness of the railroad was demonstrated. Immediately following the war, the transcontinental railroad was completed, and entrepreneurs such as Gould and Vanderbilt created financial empires. Mergers generated huge systems. The golden age of the railroad extended from the 1880s to the 1940s.

After 1950, the railroads suffered from poor management, a bloated labor force, lack of maintenance, and competition from other forms of transportation Thousands of miles of track were abandoned. Many railroads failed or merged together. The 1970s saw the federal government enter the picture with Conrail and Amtrak. Today railroads still are fighting for survival.

References: Stanley L. Baker, *Railroad Collectibles*, 4th ed., Collector Books, 1990, 1999 value update; Richard C. Barrett, *Illustrated Encyclopedia of Railroad Lighting*, Railroad Research Publications, Vol. 1 (1994), Vol. 2 (1999); *Collectible Lanterns*, L-W Book Sales, 1996; Tad Burness, *Classic Railroad Advertising, Riding the Rails Again*, Krause Publications, 2001; Barbara J. Conroy, *Restaurant China: Restaurant,*

Airline, Ship & Railroad Dinnerware, Collector Books, Volume I (1998), Volume 2 (1999); Bill and Sue Knous, *Railroadiana*, Krause Publications, 2001; Allan W. Miller, *Getting Started in Garden Railroading*, Krause Publications, 2001; Larry R. Paul, *Sparkling Crystal: A Collector's Guide to Railroad Glassware*, Railroadiana Collectors Association, Inc., 1990; Don Stewart, *Railroad Switch Keys & Padlocks*, 2nd ed., Key Collectors International, 1993; Joe Welsh, et. al., *The American Railroad*, MBI Publishing, 1999.

Periodicals: *Key, Lock and Lantern*, 3 Berkeley Heights Park, Bloomfield, NJ 07003; *Main Line Journal*, P.O. Box 121, Streamwood, IL 60107; *Railfan & Railroad*, P.O. Box 700, Newton, NJ 07860-0700; *Trains*, P.O. Box 1612, Waukesha, WI 53187; *US Rail News*, P.O. Box 7007, Huntingdon Woods, MI 48070.

Collectors' Clubs: Canadian Railroad Historical Association, 120 Rue St. Pierre, St. Constant, Quebec J5A 2G9 Canada; Chesapeake & Ohio Historical Society Inc., P.O. Box 79, Clifton Forge, VA 24422; Illinois Central Railroad Historical Society 14818 Clifton Park, Midlothian, IL 60445; New York Central System Historical Society, Inc., P.O. Box 58994, Philadelphia, PA 19102-8994; Railroad Enthusiasts, 102 Dean Rd, Brookline, MA 02146; Railroad Club of America, Inc., P.O. Box 8292, Chicago, IL 60680; Railroadiana Collectors Association, 795 Aspen Drive, Buffalo Grove, IL 60089; Railway and Locomotive Historical Society P.O. Box 1418, Westford, MA 01886; Twentieth Century Railroad Club, 329 West 18th St., Suite 902, Chicago, IL 60616.

Museums: Baltimore and Ohio Railroad, Baltimore, MD; California State Railroad Museum, Sacramento, CA; Museum of Transportation, Brookline, MA; New York Museum of Transportation, West Henrietta, NY.

Baggage Check, Texas Central RR, 1-5/8" x 2", brass, Poole Bros., Chicago 38.50
Blanket, Canadian Pacific 85.00
Blotter, Soo Line, 1920s, unused........5.00
Bond, New York Central, January 1948..4.00
Book
  Electric Railways of Northeastern Ohio, Central Electric Railfans Assoc., 1965...37.50
  Grand Central, David Marshall, 1945..20.00
  Highball, A Pageant of Trains, Lucius Beebe, Bonanza Books, 1945, 225 pgs 22.50

Guide Book, *Chicago Railroad Fair*, 1918-19, 16 pgs, $12.

  Northern Ohio's Interurban's & Rapid Transit Railways, Trolleys, & trains Too, Harry Christiansen, 1965, 176 pgs.. 37.50
  The Great Trains of North America, P. Whitehouse, Crescent Publishing, 1974... 11.00
Booklet
  By The Way Of The Canyons, Soo Line, 1907................................... 20.00
  Union Pacific RR, 1926 .... 15.00
Box, tin, black, paper attached to handle reads "Pittsburgh, Cincinnati, Chicago, St. Louis Railway Co., June 15, 1901" 40.00
Brochure
  Eastern Summer Trips, B & O..... 12.00
  Florida East Coast Railway & Steamship Co., January, 1900, 39 pgs...................................... 150.00
  Holiday Haunts, Adirondacks & 1,000 Islands, NYC, 1940, 63 pgs........ 20.00
Caboose Marker, Atlantic Coast Line RR Co., 1900, four-way lamp.......... 385.00
Calendar Card, 2-1/4" x 3-3/4", Gulf, Mobil & Northern, celluloid, red, white, and blue vest type, 1937, shows "The Rebel/The South's First Streamlined Air Conditioned Train," reverse with railway route from Illinois to Gulf of Mexico 35.00
Calendar
  1943, Burlington Zephyr 90.00
  1961, PA RR Transportation Center, Six Penn Center Plaza, Philadelphia, plastic, wallet size 5.00
Catalog, Hibbard Spencer Barlett & Co, Railway and Manufacturer's Supplies, 1907, 632 pgs 55.00
Car Inspector's Record, D & RGW, Ridway, filled in, 1928 .... 10.00
Cereal Premium, tin sign, set of ten. 35.00
China
  Bouillon Cup, WP, feather Friver, top logo, Shenango........................... 75.00
  Butter Pat, Santa Fe, California Poppy pattern, 3-1/2" d, price for pr 75.00

Celery Dish, Union Pacific, 10" l, oval, blue and gold pattern, backstamped "Scannel China" 40.00

Coffee Cup, Illinois Central, Coral pattern 20.00

Creamer, B & O, Centenary pattern, Scammell's Lamberton China, 3-1/2" d, 3-3/4" h 210.00

Cup and Saucer, B & O, Capital . 60.00

Cup and Saucer, NYC, Mercury, Syracuse, backstamped 65.00

Cup and Saucer, Southern Pacific 75.00

Demitasse Cup and Saucer, CMSTP & P, Traveler, Syracuse, backstamped 85.00

Dinner Plate, B & O, Scammell's Lamberton China, 10-1/2" d 120.00

Dinner Plate, B & O, Shenango, 10-1/2" d....................................120.00

Dinner Plate, Missouri Pacific, state flowers 275.00

Dinner Plate, NYC, Mohawk, salmon pink and black, top mkd 55.00

Dish, Santa Fe Super Chief.........65.00

Mustard Container, cov, small, white china, red PR RR keystone logo . 45.00

Platter, Southern, Peach Blossom, top mkd with logo and "Southern Serves The South," Buffalo China 125.00

Platter, Union Pacific, 8" l, oval, Challenger pattern, top mkd "The Challenger," backstamped Union Pacific RR...65.00

Sauce Dish, NYNH & H, Indian Tree pattern, Buffalo China backstamp.................................35.00

Sherbet, PRR, Keystone, Buffalo China.......................................65.00

Soup Plate, B & O, Capitol, Shenango China.......................................85.00

Soup Plate, PRR, Purple Laurel, 6-1/2" d, broad lip, Sterling China.......................................40.00

Coaster, Central RR, New Jersey, Statue of Liberty logo, set of 6 ....15.00

Coloring Book, *Union Pacific RR* giveaway, 29 pgs, 1954, 8" x 10" 20.00

Commemorative Plate, 10-1/2" d, B & O Railroad, blue transfer scene of Harper's Ferry, Lamberton China, 13-1/4" d turned wood frame 165.00

Conductor's Report, Wiscasset, Waterville & Farmington Railway, CO, filled in, 1920s 5.00

Creamer, Canadian Pacific, SP, mkd "England" 25.00

Drinking Glasses and Stemware
Bar Glass, Pere Marquette, 3-7/8" h, price for pr 20.00
Highball Glass, clear, gold and white dec, PR RR, set of four 150.00
Martini Glass, Pere Marquette, price for pr 25.00

Freight Receipt, NY, Lake Erie & Western RR, dated 1883 ....4.00

Hat Rack, overhead type, coach, wood and bras, six brass double-sided hooks.....................................200.00

Head Rest Cover, PRR, tan ground, brown logo, 15" x 18"....................15.00

Kerosene Can, tin
AT & SFRY, spout cap missing, 11" h...75.00

Texas & Pacific, spout cap missing, shallow dent, 13" h......................70.00

Lamp
Caboose, side, int., C & O Railroad, c1920, price for pr 350.00
Pullman, brass, early electric, white Bakelite shade, heavy wall brackets, 7-1/2" h, price for pr 145.00

Lantern
Adams & Westlake, conductor's, carbide, nickel over brass 195.00
Dietz, Acme Inspector, orig globe, hood and silvered reflector at rear of wick, 15" h, globe mkd "Dietz Fitzall, NY, USA, 4H Loc-Nob"................85.00
Dietz, Monarch style, orig red paint, orig red glass globe mkd "Dietz, Fitzall N.Y.U.S.A."...............................85.00
Dietz, Nightwatch, deep red globe, some wear..................................60.00
Dietz, #1, painted blue, red globe, mkd "Made in Hong Kong" 45.00
Dietz, #2, Blizzard, orig clear glass globe sgd "Dietz Fitzall" 95.00
Dietz, #100, painted blue, red globe, mkd "NY USA" 45.00
Meva 863, mkd "Made in Czechoslovakia," clear glass globe, 10" h...45.00
Missouri Pacific, hand, 4" clear globe 75.00
N.Y.C.S., New York Central System, mkd "Canada, 1821-1923" clear globe 95.00
Southern Railway, red globe 150.00

Magazine, Railway Age, 190, 64 pgs, 9" x 12"..9.00

Map, Atlantic Coast Line, large route, c1950 ....150.00

Mechanical Pencil, Northwestern Transit, Michigan City, Benton Harbor, Valparaiso, South Bend, La Porte, Chicago, Detroit, celluloid, made by Ritepoint, St. Louis...................10.00

Membership Card, American Association Railroad Ticket Agents, issued, 1931..10.00

Menu, Amtrak, Good Morning, single card, 7" x 11" 3.50

Napkin, linen
Burlington Route, 20" sq, white, woven logo..10.00
C & O, blue monogram 8.50
Rio Grande, white, woven logo ...12.00

Oil Can, Locomotive Oil................ 100.00

Padlock, Rock Island, orig key.........35.00

Pamphlet No. 10033, American Locomotive Co., New York, NY, 1908, 31 pgs, 6" x 9", Walschaert Valve Gear, Read Before the Brotherhood of Locomotive Engineers at Columbus, OH 35.00

Paperweight, 6" x 2" x 2-1/2", General American Car Co., Modern Milk Transportation, Refrigerated Glass lined Tank Car 120.00

Pass
Ft Wayne, Cincinnati & Louisville and White Water, 2-1/2" x 3-3/4" white card, green accents, purple ink stamp facsimile signature of president, 1889..12.00
Grand Trunk Railway Co. of Canada, 2-1/2" x 4", black and white, red year date, printed facsimile signature of general manager, 1889 ....15.00

Hartford & Connecticut Western railroad, 2-1/4" x 3-5/8", black and white, red accent, number sgd in black ink by president, 1889 .... 12.00
Ohio, Indiana, and Western, 2-1/4" x 3-3/4", black and white, ornately printed, signed in ink by general manager, 1889...................................... 12.00

Photograph, cabinet card, Baggage Master, Rochester, NH, double breasted uniform, holding gloves in left hand, photo by S. Swaine Photographer, Rochester, NH................ 45.00

Playing Cards
Chessie......................................20.00
Denver & Rio Grande Railways .. 35.00
EJ & ERR 20.00

Postcard
Fresh Air Pullman, C-4, giant grasshopper in open cargo car, Multrakrom Postcard Co., Dodge City, Kansas, c1950 .... 10.00
White River at Sharon, VT, New England States Limited, scenic, 5-3/4" x 3-3/4" 22.00

Print, The Hummingbird, Biloxi Bay Crossing, by Robert Weset, sgd and numbered 350/750, 19-1/4" x 24-3/4" silver frame 190.00

Record Book, Pennsylvania Railroad, C. T. 1930 Line for Train, Engine Number, etc., 194_, unused......................25.00

Ribbon, Brotherhood of Railroad Men, Grand Union Picnic, Harrisburg, PA, June 27, 1901, 1-7/8" x 5-1/2", dark red, gold accent lettering............ 12.00

Sign, Seaboard RR, "Explosives," 1948 .... 19.00

Steam Whistle, American Steam Gauge, Pat. Oct 14, June 16, 85, 100 lbs, brass 145.00

Step, Pullman RR Station, wood, hand cut out on top, 21" w, 10" h................ 25.00

Stock Certificate
Milwaukee Street Railway Co., 1897, vignette of two old wheel trolleys, motorman, conductor, passengers in derbys and top hats.................... 50.00
Penn Central Transportation Co., 100 Shares, blue on white, black vignette.................................... 50.00

Sugar Tongs, Canadian Pacific, SP, mkd "England" 20.00

Ticket, Pennsylvania Railroad Co, identification check, exchange ticket, and passenger's ticket 15.00

Timetable
Erie Railroad, 1907...................... 32.00
L&N Kansas City Southern, 1955... 8.50
Southern Pacific RR, 1915......... 22.00

Voucher, Union Pacific, Denver and Gulf Railway, 1890s............................. 5.00

Watchman's Station Box, iron 25.00

Reamers

Collecting Hints: Reamers are seldom found in mint condition. Cone and rim nicks are usually acceptable, but cracked pieces sell for considerably less. Ceramic figurals and American-made glass examples are collected more than any other types.

Reamer collecting, which can be an endless hobby, first became popular as a sideline to Depression glass collecting in the mid-1960s. It may be impossible to assemble a collection that includes one of every example made. One-of-a-kind items do exist, as some examples were never put into mass production.

History: Devices for getting the juice from citrus fruit have been around almost as long as the fruit itself. These devices were made from all types of material—from wood to glass and from nickel plate and sterling silver to fine china.

Many different kinds of mechanical reamers were devised before the first glass one was pressed around 1885. Very few new designs have appeared since 1940, when frozen juice first entered the market. Modern-day ceramists are making clown and teapot-shaped reamers.

References: Gene Florence, *Kitchen Glassware of the Depression Years*, 6th Edition, Collector Books, 2001; Mary Walker, *And Many More Reamers*, BNMC, 1998 (14542 Ventura Blvd., Suite 206, Sherman Oaks, CA 91403.)

Collectors Club: National Reamer Collectors Association, 47 Midline Court, Gaithersburg, MD 20878. -- , e-mail: reamesr@erols.com.

Reproduction Alert: Many glass reamers are being reproduced at this time. Some are American reissues from original molds, while others are made from old reamers in Asia. The Asian reamers are usually easy to spot since they are made from poor quality glass that feels greasy and is generally thicker than that used in the originals. Many reproductions are being made in colors which were never used originally, but some of the reamers being made from the original molds are the same colors as the originals, making them harder to detect. There are also several new ceramic reamers being made. One series looks like an old piece of flow blue or English china, and is mkd with a crested "Victoria Ironstone" on the bottom.

An old 5" Imperial Glass Co. reamer, originally made in clear glass, was reproduced for Edna Barnes in dark amethyst; 1,500 were made. The reproduction is mkd "IG" and "81."

Mrs. Barnes has also reproduced several old 4-1/2" Jenkins Glass Co. reamers in limited editions. The reproductions are also made in a 2-1/4" size. All Jenkins copies are mkd with a "B" in a circle. These limited editions have become collectible in their own right and should not be considered or valued the same as the reproduction reamers described above.

Collectors should consult Gene Florence's book for information about glass reproductions. Also, the National Reamer Collectors Association keeps its members up to date on the latest reproductions.

Notes: The first book on reamers, now out of print, was written by Ken and Linda Ricketts in 1974. Their numbering system was continued by Mary Walker in her first two books, *Reamers (200 Years)*, 1980 and *More Reamers (200 Years)* 1983, both published by Muski Publishers, Sherman Oaks, CA, and both now out of print, and in her newest book, *And Many More Reamers*. The Ricketts-Walker numbers will be found in the china and metal sections. The numbers in parentheses in the glass section are from Gene Florence's *Kitchen Glassware of the Depression Years*, and indicate the page number, row number and item number to be referenced.

Advisor: Judy Smith (e-mail: reamers@quiltart.com).

Elegant reamer, Austrian, white with pink flowers, royal blue and gold trim, E-36, 3-1/4" h, $125. Photo courtesy of Judy Smith.

China and Ceramic

Austria, 3-3/4" h, white, pink flowers, green trim (D-106) 90.00
Bavaria, 3-1/2" h, white, red, yellow and green flowers, gold trim, two-pc (E-119) 105.00
Czechoslovakia, 6" h, orange shape, white, green leaves, mkd "Erphila," two-pc (L-17)..............................60.00
England
3-1/2" h, white, orange and yellow flowers (D-107)..........................85.00
3-3/4" h, orange shape, orange body, green leaves, two-pc (L-20)........ 45.00
Germany
3-1/2" h, scrolling flow blue dec, white ground (E-60) 80.00
5" d, Goebel, yellow (E-108) 90.00
Japan
3" h, saucer-type on pedestal, loop handle fruit dec (D-59) 60.00
3-1/4" h, hand painted, white, floral dec, mkd "Nippon," two pc 175.00
3-3/4" h, strawberry shape, red, green leaves and handle, mkd "Occupied Japan," two pc (L-38) 90.00
4-3/4" h, lemon, yellow, white flowers, green leaves (L-40) 60.00
5" h, orange, textured orange-peel exterior, yellow, green leaves, white interior (L-39) 55.00
8-1/2" h, pitcher and tumbler, blue and white windmill dec (P-87)............ 75.00
United States
Jiffy Juicer, large bowl, cone center, elongated loop handle, 10 colors known, U.S. Pat. 2,130,755 Sept. 20, 1938, (A-5) 95.00
Red Wing (A-7)......................... 135.00
United States Ade-O-Matic Genuine, 8" h, green (A-11) 135.00
Universal Cambridge, 9" h, beige w/pink flowers (A-28) 195.00
Zippy, 3-1/4" h, 6-1/2" w, hand crank cone, Wolverine Products, Detroit, MI, several colors (A-4).................. 135.00

Figural reamer, house, Japanese, tan with brown and green trim, blue windows, pink door, 5-3/4" h, $110. Photo courtesy of Judy Smith.

Glass (measurements indicate width, not including spout and handle)

Anchor Hocking Glass Co., 6-1/4" d, lime green, pouring spout (155-4-3) 35.00
Federal, transparent green, pointed cone (151-3-4).......................... 30.00
Fluted ruffle, rose (149-5-3)........... 250.00
Fry, 6-5/16" d, opalescent, pouring spout (149-6-1)..................................... 55.00
Hazel Atlas
Criss-Cross, orange size, pink (153-2-2).................................... 325.00
Criss-Cross, crystal, tab handle, small (153-5-3).................................... 25.00
Indiana Glass Co., green, horizontal handle (151-5-3)........................ 35.00

Jeannette Glass Co.
Delphite Jennyware, small,
(159-3-1) 100.00
Light Jadite, two cup, two pc
(159-2-3) 45.00
Pink Jennyware, small
(159-4-4) 135.00
McKee
Chalaine blue, embossed Sunkist
(162-3-3) 235.00
U.S. Glass Co., light pink, 2-cup
pitcher set (167-2-1)....................55.00
Vaseline green embossed Sunkist
(162-5-4) 55.00
White, embossed Sunkist
(163-1-4) 15.00

Metal
Aluminum, Pat, 8" 1, 161609, Minneapolis, MN 5.00
Bernard Rice & Sons, Apollo EPNS, 3-3/4" h, two pc (PM-70) 130.00
Cocktail Shaker set, Kinsway Plate, German, one pint (PM-49).................85.00
Derby S.P. Co., International Co., 1923 EPNS W.M. Mounts (PM-74) 225.00
Dunlap's Improved, 9-1/2" l, iron hinge (M-17)...35.00
Gem Squeezer, aluminum crank handle, table model two pc (M-100)........12.00
Hong Kong, 2-1/2" h, stainless steel, flat, two pc, (M-205) 9.00
Kwicky Juicer, aluminum, pan style, Quam Nichols Co. (M-97) 9.00
Nasco-Royal, 6"1, scissors type, (M-265)...8.00
Presto Juicer, metal stand, porcelain juicer (M-112)...............................135.00
Wagner Ware, 6" d, cast aluminum, skillet shape, long rect. seed dams beneath cone, hole in handle, two spouts (M-96)..45.00
Williams, 9-3/4" l, iron , hinged, glass insert (M-60)...................................50.00
Yates, EPNS, 4-3/4" d, two pc (PM-73) 195.00

Records

Collecting Hints: Collectors tend to focus on one particular music field, e.g., jazz, the big bands, or rock 'n' roll, or on one artist. Purchase records with original dust jackets and covers whenever possible.

Also check the records carefully for scratches. If the sound quality has been affected, the record is worthless.

Proper storage of records is critical to maintaining their value. Keep stacks small. It is best to store them vertically. Place acid-free paper between the albums to prevent bleeding of ink from one cover to the next.

History: The first records, which were cylinders produced by Thomas Edison in 1877, were played on a phonograph of his design. Edison received a patent in 1878, but soon dropped the project in order to perfect the light bulb.

Alexander Graham Bell, Edison's friend, was excited about the phonograph and developed the graphaphone, which was marketed successfully by 1889. Early phonographs and graphaphones had hand cranks to wind the mechanism and keep the cylinders moving.

About 1900, Emile Berliner developed a phonograph which used a flat disc, similar to today's records. The United States Gramophone Company marketed his design in 1901. This company eventually became RCA Victor. By 1910, discs were more popular than cylinders.

The record industry continued to develop as new technology improved processes and sound quality. Initially 78-RPM records were made. These were replaced by 45 RPMs, then by 33-1/3 RPMs, and, finally, by compact discs.

References: John Clemente, *Girl Groups, Fabulous Females That Rocked The World*, Krause Publications, 2000; Les R. Docks, *American Premium Record Guide, 1900-1965*, 5th ed., Krause Publications, 1997; *Goldmine's Price Guide to Alternative Records*, Krause Publications, 1996; *Goldmine Roots of Rock Digest*, Krause Publications, 1999; Anthony J. Gribin and Matthew M. Schiff, *The Complete Book of Doo-Wop*, Krause Publications, 2000; Ron Lofman, *Goldmine's Celebrity Vocals*, Krause Publications, 1994; Tim Neely, *Goldmine's Price Guide to Alternative Records*, Krause Publications, 1996; *Goldmine Country & Western Record Price Guide*, Krause Publications, 2000; *Goldmine Record Album Price Guide*, Krause Publications, 1999; *Goldmine Standard Catalog of American Records*, 1950-1975, 2nd ed., Krause Publications, 2000; *Goldmine Christmas Record Price Guide*, Krause Publications, 1997; *Goldmine Jazz Album Price Guide*, Krause Publications, 2000; *Goldmine Price Guide to Alternative Records*, Krause Publications, 1996;

Goldmine Price Guide to 45 RPM Records, Krause Publications, 1996; Tim Neely and Dave Thompson, *Goldmine British Invasion Record Price Guide*, Krause Publications, 1997; Charles Szabla, *Goldmine 45 RPM Picture Sleeve Price Guide*, Krause Publications, 1998; Neal Umphred, *Goldmine's Price Guide to Collectible Jazz Albums*, 2nd ed., Krause Publications, 1994; Neal Umphred, *Goldmine's Price Guide to Collectible Record Albums*, 5th ed., Krause Publications, 1996; —, *Goldmine's Rock 'n' Roll 45 RPM Record Price Guide*, 3rd ed., Krause Publications, 1994.

Periodicals: *Cadence*, Cadence Building, Redwood, NY 13679; *DIScoveries Magazine*, P.O. Box 309, Fraser, MI 48026; *Goldmine*, 700 E. State St., Iola, WI 54990; *Joslin's Jazz Journal*, P.O. Box 213, Parsons, KS 67357; *New Amberola Graphic*, 37 Caledonia St., St. Johnsbury, VT 05819; *Record Collectors Monthly*, P.O. Box 75, Mendham, NJ 07945; *Record Finder*, P.O. Box 1047, Glen Allen, VA 23060.

Collectors' Clubs: Collectors Record Club, 1206 Decatur St., New Orleans, LA 70116; International Assoc. of Jazz Record Collectors, P.O. Box 75155, Tampa, FL 33605.

Note: Prices are for first pressings in original dust jackets or albums.

Additional Listings: Elvis Presley, Rock 'n' Roll.

Walt Disney Productions, "The Black Hole," child's read-along type, $24.

ABC Wide World of Sports, 33 rpm, 1970, narrated by Jim McCay, 7-1/4" sq......................................25.00
Annie Oakley, 45 rpm......................15.00
Bonic Woman 20.00
Bonzana
Chevrolet promo..........................25.00
High Chapparal............................35.00
Bourbon Street Beat........................25.00
Brady Bunch, membership application..................................38.00
Clint Eastwood, Rawhide, Cameo #C-1056, autographed 245.00
Dark Shadows, orig poster 30.00

Disneyland Davy Crocket Record Story Book, Walt Disney Productions, © 1971, 7-1/4" sq.............................35.00

Drag Boats, 33-1/3 rpm, factory sealed 25.00

Dragnet, 78 rpm, Jack Webb cover 30.00

Evel Knieval..65.00

Farrah Fawcett, 45 rpm 40.00

Godzilla, 1985, 45 rpm, I Was Afraid to Love You, Jill Elliott 30.00

Goober Sings, Andy Griffith 35.00

Green Acres 25.00

Groovy Goolies 50.00

Hair Bear Bunch, 45 rpm, 1970s, illus sleeve 10.00

Hot Rod Granny, Hanna-Barbera 50.00

Howdy Doody

   Christmas.....................................24.00

   Clowns with Jazz, Normal Paris Trio, Golden Crest, 1950s 50.00

Jackie Robinson/Pee Wee Reese, double set..185.00

James Bond, Hanna-Barbera..........40.00

Joe DiMaggio, Little Johnny Strikeout, double, 78 rpm 135.00

Johnny Quest, Hanna-Barbera, 45 rpm...28.00

Josie & the Pussycats, Capitol, soundtrack, 1970......................300.00

Kung Fu..25.00

Les Adventures of Tin Tin, French, Decca, 33 rpm...65.00

Little Black Jacobs and the Twins, double set..85.00

Lone Ranger, 3-1 ....25.00

Mad Magazine...................................35.00

Mannix 25.00

Mighty Hercules.................................95.00

Mr. Ed, TV series soundtrack, Colpix CP209 ....125.00

Ozzie and Harriet..............................25.00

Pepsi-Cola, six record set, orig cardboard jacket, 1960s 100.00

Petticoat Junction, 45 rpm 24.00

Return of The Pink Panther, United Artists, 1970s, 45 rpm...........................30.00

Ronald Reagan on GE Theatre........25.00

Secret Squirrel, Hanna-Barbera, 45 rpm...30.00

Shotgun Slade 25.00

Spike Jones, Kiddies Nutcracker Suite, RCA, three 78 RPM records in orig portfolio......................................35.00

Squiddly Diddly, Hanna-Barbera, 45 rpm...35.00

The Big Gun, 33-1/3 rpm, blue and white record jacket, from Revell model kit...4.00

Winnie the Pooh and Christopher Robin Songs, 1948, 78 rpm, Decca Record 40.00

Zorro, by The Chardettes, promo 40.00

Red Wing Pottery

Collecting Hints: Red Wing Pottery can be found with various marks and paper labels. Some of the marks include a stamped red wing, a raised "Red Wing U.S.A. #___," or an impressed "Red Wing U.S.A. #___."

Paper labels were used as early as 1930. Some pieces were identified only by a paper label that was easily lost.

Many manufacturers used the same mold patterns. Study the references to become familiar with the Red Wing forms.

History: The category of Red Wing Pottery covers several potteries which started in Red Wing, Minnesota. The first pottery, named Red Wing Stoneware Company, was started in 1868 by David Hallem. The primary product of this company was stoneware. The mark used by this company was a red wing stamped under the glaze. The Minnesota Stoneware Company was started in 1883. The North Star Stoneware Company opened a factory in the same area in 1892 and went out of business in 1896. The mark used by this company included a raised star and the words "Red Wing."

The Red Wing Stoneware Company and the Minnesota Stoneware Company merged in 1892. The new company was called the Red Wing Union Stoneware Company. The new company made stoneware until 1920 when it introduced a line of pottery.

In 1936, the name of the company was changed to Red Wing Potteries Incorporated. It continued to make pottery until the 1940s. During the 1930s, it introduced several lines of dinnerware. These patterns, which were all hand painted, were very popular and were sold through department stores, Sears Roebuck and Company, and gift stamp centers. The production of dinnerware declined in the 1950s. The company began producing hotel and restaurant china in the early 1960s. The plant was closed in 1967.

References: Dan and Gail DePasquale and Larry Peterson, *Red Wing Collectibles*, Collector Books, 1985, 1997 value update; ——, *Red Wing Stoneware*, Collector Books, 1983, 2000 value update; B. L. Dollen, *Red Wing Art Pottery*, Collector Books, 1997; B. L. and R. L. Dollen, *Collector's Encyclopedia of Red Wing Art Pottery, Identification and Values*, Collector Books, 2000; ——, *Red Wing Art Pottery Book II*, Collector Books, 1998; Ray Reiss, *Red Wing Art Pottery Including Pottery Made for Rum Rill*, published by author (2144 N. Leavitt, Chicago, IL 60647), 1996; ——, *Red Wing Dinnerware: Price and Identification* Guide, Property Pub-

lishing, 1997; Gary and Bonnie Tefft, *Red Wing Potters and Their Wares*, 2nd ed., Locust Enterprises, 1987, 1995 value update.

Collectors' Clubs: Red Wing Collectors Society, P.O. Box 50, Red Wing, MN 55066; RumRill Society, P.O. Box 2161, Hudson, OH 44236.

Vase, green-blue, marked "Red Wing, USA, 1563," 10" h, $30.

Ashtray, horse's head, ochre............ 75.00

Basket, white, semi-gloss 35.00

Bean Pot, cov, Tampico 40.00

Beverage Server, cov, Tampico 130.00

Bookends, pr, fan and scroll, green.. 25.00

Bowl, 9" d, 4-1/4" h, blue dec......... 195.00

Bread and Butter Plate, 6-1/2" d

   Bob White 8.50

   Pepe 5.00

   Pompeii... 6.00

   Random Harvest 6.50

Butter Dish, cov, Bob White 48.00

Candy Dish, three-part, hexagon, gray, semi-gloss 18.00

Casserole, cov, Tampico.................. 40.00

Casserole, open, Town & Country, Eva Zeisel, 14-1/2" x 10" x 3-1/4" h 65.00

Celery Tray, Random Harvest 15.00

Cereal Bowl, Damask........................ 9.00

Chip and Dip Set, Tampico, 12" d serving bowl and six 8" d plates, 1950s, minor usage wear................................ 90.00

Chop Plate, Capistrano, 12" d 22.00

Compote, orchid, cherub................... 65.00

Console Bowl, 12" d, Renaissance, brown dec... 45.00

Console Set, bowl and pr candleholders, Renaissance Deer..................... 125.00

Cookie Jar, cov

   Drummer Boy 600.00

   Friar Tuck, blue...................... 200.00

   Katrina, beige 145.00

   King of Tarts, blue speckled dec... 1,250.00

Cornucopia, white, pr 75.00
Creamer and Sugar, Smart Set 90.00
Crock, 9" h, #2, stoneware, Redwing
   stamp mark 175.00
Cup and Saucer
   Bob White 20.00
   Capistrano 18.00
   Lute Song 9.50
   Magnolia 9.50
   Tampico 12.00
Custard Cup, Fondos, green and
   pink 18.00
Dinner Plate, 10" d
   Bob White 12.00
   Lotus 9.50
   Town and Country, blue 9.50
Flower Frog, 10" h, Deer, white 25.00
Fruit Bowl, Lute Song 10.00
Gravy Boat, Driftwood, blue
Jardiniere, 10-1/2" d, 9-3/4" h, deep
   green, mkd "Redwing USA
   445-10" 65.00
Mug, blue bands 40.00
Mustard Jar, Town & Country, Eva Zeisel,
   sand, 4-1/4" d, 5-3/4" h 400.00
Nappy, Lotus 9.50
Pitcher
   Bob White, 12" h 65.00
   Stoneware, blue Dutch boy and girl
   kissing, windmill, rough molding,
   7" h 275.00
Planter
   #242, 5-1/2" x 4-1/2", light blue ... 18.00
   #789, 10-1/2" w, 3-1/4" h, eight sides
   with triangles, rose, white int., orig
   decal 30.00
   #1037, 7-1/2" sq, 2" h, white, green
   int. 15.00
Platter, Town & Country, Eva Zeisel, char-
   treuse 24.00
Relish, Town & Country, Eva Zeisel
   Bronze, 6" l 1-3/4" h 65.00
   White, 7" x 5" x 2-1/4" h 95.00
Salad Bowl, Pheasant, blue and
   green 48.00
Salt and Pepper Shakers, pr
   Bob White 30.00
   Brittany, Provincial 18.00
Sugar Bowl Bronze Lid, Town & Country,
   Eva Zeisel 65.00
Syrup, Town & Country, Eva Zeisel, forest
   green, 3-1/4" d, 5-3/4" h 325.00
Teapot
   Mediterranean 65.00
   Town & Country, Eva Zeisel, chartreuse, 11-1/2" l, 7" w, 4-3/4" h ... 625.00
Vase
   #144, Brushed Ware, crane
   motif 55.00
   #651, boot 70.00
   #892, fan shape, blue, pink int. 50.00
   #1155 .... 45.00
   #1182, ivory and brown wipe glaze,
   c1943 .... 60.00
   #1376, 11" h, green swirls, two long
   loop handles 95.00
Vegetable Bowl, divided, Lute Song 27.50
Wall Pocket, Gardenia, matte ivory .. 38.00

Robots

Collecting Hints: Robots are identified by the markings on the robot or box and from names assigned by the trade. Hence, some robots have more than one name. Research is required to learn exactly what robot you have.

Condition is critical. Damaged lithographed tin is almost impossible to repair and repaint. Toys in mint condition in the original box are the most desirable. The price difference between a mint robot and one in very good condition may be as high as 200 percent.

Working condition is important, but not critical. Many robots never worked well, and larger robots stripped their gearing quickly. The rarer the robot, the less important the working condition.

Finally, if you play with your robot, do not leave the batteries in the toy. If they leak or rust, the damage may destroy the value of the toy.

History: Atomic Robot Man, made in Japan between 1948 and 1949, is the grandfather of all robot toys. He is an all-metal windup toy, less than five inches high and rather crudely made. Japanese robots of the early 1950s tended to be the friction or windup variety, patterned in brightly lithographed tin and made from recycled materials.

By the late 1950s, robots had entered the battery-powered age. Limited quantities of early models were produced; parts from one model were used in later models with slight or no variations. The robot craze was enhanced by Hollywood's production of movies such as "Destination Moon" (1950) and "Forbidden Planet" (1956). Robby the Robot came from the latter movie.

Many Japanese manufacturers were small and remained in business only a few years. Leading firms include Horikawa Toys, Nomura Toys, and Yonezawa Toys. Cragstan was an American importer who sold Japanese-made toys under its own label. Marx and Ideal entered the picture in the 1970s. Modern robots are being imported from China and Taiwan.

The TV program "Lost in Space" (1965-1968) inspired copies of its robot character. However, the quality of the late 1960s toys began to suffer as more and more plastic was added; robots were redesigned to reduce sharp edges as required by the United States government.

Modern robots include R2D2 and C3PO from the "Star Wars" epics, Twiki from NBC's "Buck Rodgers," and V.I.N.CENT from Disney's "The Black Hole." Robots are firmly established in American science fiction and among collectors.

References: Jim Bunte, Dave Hallman and Heinz Mueller, *Vintage Toys: Robots and Space Toys*, Krause Publications, 2000; Stuart W. Wells, III, *Science Fiction Collectibles: Identification & Price Guide*, Krause Publications, 1999.

Periodical: *Robot World & Price Guide*, P.O. Box 184, Lenox Hill Station, New York, NY 10021.

Marvelous Mike, litho tin, plastic robot, rubber tract tires, yellow body, Saunders, Aurora, IL, 1954, $600.

Astronaut, Daiya, Japan, 1950s, blue, battery operated, complete, 14" h, C-8.5 .... 1,075.00
Attacking Martian, tin, green circles and squares dec, door opens and closes, double barrel tin guns shooting with blinking, walks and stops 175.00
Atomic Robot Man, Japan, litho tin, pressed tin arms, windup, orig box, 5" h 1,800.00
Big Loo, Your Friend From The Moon, Marx, 1950s, 38" h 785.00
Cone Head, Yonezawa, Japan, tin, plastic eyes, rubber antennae, windup, 8-1/4" h 2,750.00
Dingaling Boxer, Topper, MIB 35.00
Durham Industries, battery operated, plastic, silver colored, 9-1/2" h 35.00
Dux Astroman, Dux, Germany, tin and plastic, battery operated, orig box, 12" h 1,650.00
Earth Man, Kitahara #144, TN, Japan, litho tin, battery operated, remote control, 9-1/4" h 625.00
Fighting Robot, tin litho, battery operated, Japan, 1960s, C-8.5 .... 245.00
Gear Robot, 9" h, battery operated, tin, Japan 500.00
Great Garloo, Marx, 1960s, battery operated, 24" h, C-9 toy, C-8 box 745.00
Lost in Space, battery operated, Remco, C-9 .... 685.00
Machine Gun, battery operated, tin litho, dark brown, red feet, silver face accents, green transparent doors on chest which open to reveal machine

gun unit, mkd "Made in Japan," c1960, wear, lights and noise, but does not walk, 3" x 5-1/2" x 10-3/4" h....................................115.00

Marvelous Mike, tractor, USA, orig box 600.00

Moon Stroller, wind-up, arms swing, moving radar, mkd "Made in Hong Kong," 3-1/4" h, orig box with slight wear 35.00

Mr. Atom, Advance Toy, West Haven, CT, plastic, battery operated, orig box, 18" h 750.00

Mr. Machine, take-apart, MIB.........375.00

Mystery Action, battery operated, bump and go action, plastic, mkd "Made in Hong Kong," orig box, 8-1/2" h...25.00

Nando Robot, Italy, tin, air powered, gray unpainted finish, decal facial features, 1950s, orig box, 5" h..................550.00

NASA Robot, 1960s, tin litho, 6" h, mkd "Japan" 350.00

Planet Robot, KO, Japan, tin and plastic, windup, orig box, 9" h..................325.00

Radar Robot, Kitahara #8, Japan, tin, battery operated, primitive style, walking mechanism, orig box and insert, 9" h 750.00

Rascal, wind-up, mkd "1978, Tomy Corp., Made in Taiwan," MIP, 2" h 20.00

Robert Robot, Ideal, orig box.........275.00

Robot and Son, Marx, burgundy and silver, battery operated, 1950s, orig box, C.85 toy in C.8 box....................475.00

Robocon, 16" h, vinyl, MIB 100.00

Robot R-35, Modern Toys, Japan, 1950s, 8" h, remote control...................590.00

Robot 2500, silver, blinking lighted eye and chest, moving arms and legs....................................175.00

Robot Sentinel, battery operated, walks, arms move, lights, four shooting missiles, plastic, mkd "Made in China by Kamco," 1980s, 13" h, MIB 55.00

Rock'em Sock'em, full-color display box, 1960s 250.00

Saturn, battery operated, walks, lights up eyes, mkd "Made in Hong Kong by Kamco," missiles missing, 13" h .38.00

Silver colored, wind-up, mkd "Made in Hong Kong," 4" h, orig box 35.00

Silver Warrior, battery operated, Amico, storm trooper action, unused, orig box, 1970s 95.00

Smoking, lighted see-through piston action, emits smoke, walks 175.00

Space Conqueror X-70, Cragstan, Japan, 1950s, red, battery operated, 12" h, C-8.5 ....975.00

Space Man, 6-1/2" h, tin litho, litho face in astronaut space helmet, air tanks, regulator, large space rifle, 1950s, mkd "Japan" 1,800.00

Sparky Robot, wind-up, silver and red, flashes, 1950s, Japan, 8" h, C-9...355.00

SP-1, friction, blue and red space ship, Japan, 1950s, 6-1/2" l................330.00

Takra, Japanese, 190s, 8-1/4" h, litho tin wind-up 150.00

Television Spaceman, Alps, Japan, tin, battery operated, orig box, 11" h 750.00

Ultra 7, tin wind-up, Biliken, Japan, 8-1/2" h, MIB............................. 300.00

Video, all tin body, scene of moon and space on TV big screen, walks 175.00

Walk, wind-up, illustrated window box..25.00

Zeroid Zintar, Ideal 125.00

Zoomer, Japan, 1950s, 10" h, battery operated...................................485.00

2-XL Talking Robot, hard plastic, Mego, copyright 1978, wear and tears to orig box, 6" x 8" x 11"..........................30.00

Rock 'n' Roll

Collecting Hints: Many rock 'n' roll collections are centered around one artist. Flea markets and thrift shops are good places to look for rock 'n' roll items. Prices depend on the singer or group, and works by stars who are no longer living usually command a higher price.

Glossy, non-authographed 8 by 10-inch photographs of singers are generally worth $1.

History: Rock music can be traced back to early rhythm and blues. It progressed and reached its golden age in the 1950s. The current nostalgia craze for the 1950s has produced some modern rock 'n' roll which is well received. Rock 'n' roll memorabilia exists in large quantities, each singer or group having had many promotional pieces made.

References: Mark A. Baker, *Goldmine Price Guide to Rock 'N' Roll Memorabilia*, Krause Publications, 1997; John Clemente, *Girl Groups, Fabulous Females That Rocked The World*, Krause Publications, 2000; Dr. Anthony J. Gribin and Dr. Matthew M. Schiff, *The Complete Book of Doo-Wop*, Krause Publications, 2000; Joe Hilton and Greg Moore, *Rock-N-Roll Treasures*, Collector Books, 1999; David Loehr and Joe Bills, The *James Dean Collectors Guide*, L-W Book Sales, 1999; Editors of Goldmine Magazine, *The Beatles Digest*, Krause Publications, 2000.

Periodicals: *Kissaholics Magazine*, P.O. Box 22334, Nashville, TN 37202; *New England KISS Collector's Network*, 168 Oakland Ave., Providence, RI 02908; *Tune Talk*, P.O. Box 851, Marshalltown, IA 50158.

Collectors' Club: American Bandstand 1950's Fan Club, P.O. Box 131, Adamstown, PA 19501; Kissaholics, P.O. Box 22334, Nashville, TN 37202.

Additional Listings: Beatles, Elvis Presley, Records.

Action Figure
Dave Clark Five, Remco, Rick, Mike, Dennis...95.00
KISS, © 1978 Mego, 12" h, set of Ace, Gene, Peter, and Paul, MIB, price for set 500.00

Book
Kisstory, autographed by band members, coffee table size.. 175.00
Mike Jagger: Primitive Cool, Christopher Sanford, St. Martin's, 1994 . 12.00
Picture Life of Stevie Wonder, A. Edwards and G. Wohl, 1977......... 7.00
The Honeymoon Is Over, Shirley and Pat Boone, autographed, 1977, 185 pgs..................................... 22.50
Woodstock 69, Summer Pop Festivals, A Photo Review, Joseph J. Sia, Scholastic Book Services publisher, © 1970, 70 pgs,. 5-1/4" x 7-1/2"...... 30.00

Book Cover, orange and red title paper, three black and white book covers, one with Pat Boone, one with Sal Mineo, third generic signer, 1958 Cooga Mooga Products, Inc., NY, unused in clear plastic bag 18.00

Bracelet, gold chain link, burnished gold disc with raised Monkees guitar symbol, orig retail card, © 1967........ 27.50

Colorforms, KISS, MIB 27.50

Comic Book
Elton John, #62, 1993 .... 15.00
Frank Zappa, #32, 1991 .... 20.00
Janis Joplin #63, 1993 .... 15.00
Kiss, #9, March, 1990 .... 7.00
Metallic, 1990 .... 10.00
Queen, Night at the Opera, #9, 1992 .... 15.00
The Who, 1992 .... 8.00

Cuff Links, pr, Dick Clark, MIB 35.00

Doll
Boy George, LJN, 1984, 12" h, MIB.................................... 125.00
Andy Gibb, disco, Ideal, 1970s, MIB, C-10 .... 75.00
Donny Osmond, Mattel, © 1976, MIB..................................... 35.00
Michael Jackson, LIN, © 1984 MIJ Productions, Thriller outfit, MIB... 35.00

Finger Doll, Remco
Monkees, Davey 40.00
Monkees, Peter 40.00

Folder, 4-1/2" x 6", Swamp Notes, beige vinyl cover, emb image, note pad, reply cards................................. 50.00

Game, Duran Duran into the Arena, Milton Bradley, 1985 .... 18.00

Halloween Costume, child's, Donny, Marie, or Jimmy Osmond, orig costume, mask, box, each 35.00

Handkerchief, Buddy Holly, silk, red and gold paisley, authenticity card .. 450.00

Lunch Box
Monkees, plastic, Canadian, 1967.. 375.00
The Osmonds, metal, orig thermos, unused, 1973 .... 95.00

Magazine, *Frank Zappa Record Review*, Feb, 1980 .... 25.00

Microphone, toy, Michael Jackson .. 15.00

Nodder, 4-1/2" h, man, gold base, "Let's Twist" decal, Japan stick, c1960 75.00

Pinback Button
　　Frankie Avalon-Venus, black and white photo, bright pink ground 25.00
　　Bob-a-Loo, WABC, disc jockey, black and white photo 70.00
　　Dick Clark, black and white photo, dark green ground 15.00
　　James Dean, 2-1/2" d, color photo 60.00
　　Monkees, vending machine type, 1967, set of 6 .... 75.00
　　Pat Boone, 3-1/2" d, blue "Swoon with Pat Boone" inscription, white background, red rim 7.50
　　Rock-Ola, 3" d, red, white, and blue illus c1950 .... 17.50
Poster
　　Badfinger, April 1971, Fond du Lac, WI 495.00
　　Everly Brothers, August 1966, Colorado Springs 395.00
　　Fats Domino, Gerry & Pacemakers, March 1967, London 245.00
　　Fleetwood Mac, September 1972, Wilmington NC 225.00
　　Flying Burrito Brothers, Linda Ronstadt, Savoy Brown, March 1970, Los Angeles 400.00
　　Tom Jones, April 196, London Palladium 365.00
　　Kansas, January 1978, Seattle . 295.00
　　Amboy Dukes, 1968 .... 235.00
　　Conway Twitty, July 1973, Wellsville, OH 300.00
　　Tanya Tucker, June 1975, Portlane, OR 265.00
　　Dottie West, Homer & Jethro, Bill Anderson, blank for Grand Old Opry traveling show, 1965 .... 325.00
　　Beach Boys, Ike & Tina, Alice Cooper, Moby Grape, Chuck Berry, Wilson Pickett, and others, June 1972 . 200.00
　　Tony Bennett, Duke Ellington, March 1963, Philharmonic Hall, NY 395.00
　　Bobby "Blue" Band, March 1973, Fort Worth, TX 295.00
　　Johnny Cash, May 1965, Des Moines, IA 455.00
　　Ray Charles, May 1967, Santa Barbara, CA 225.00
　　Eric Clapton, Delaney & Bonnie, German tour, 1970 .... 295.00
　　John Prine, October 1976, Portland, OR 245.00
　　Joan Baez, April 1962, Santa Monica 400.00
　　Peter, Paul & Mary, May 1964, San Diego 350.00
　　Charlie Pride, April 1971, Waterloo, IA 200.00
　　Devo, November 1981, Paramount Theater 75.00
　　Bob Dylan, November 1978, Oakland 115.00
　　Eagles, Dan Fogelberg, Ozark Mountain Daredevils, July 1975, Iowa State Fair 145.00
　　Led Zeppelin, February 1970, Swedish tour 595.00
　　Led Zeppelin, Jethro Tull, August 1969, San Antonio, TX 995.00
　　King Crimson, May 1971, Plymouth, UK 295.00

Lovin' Spoonful, November 1966, Houston 395.00
Barry Manilow, December 1979 .... 185.00
Steve Miller Band, May 1973, Geneva, NY 125.00
Eric Clapton, Stevie Ray Vaughn, August 1990, Alpine Valley, WI. 250.00
Sly & The Family Stone, December 1972, San Francisco 345.00
War, November 1973, Memorial Coliseum 345.00
Dinah Washington, early 1950s 995.00
Who, November 1973, Cow Palace 295.00
Stevie Wonder, Beach Boys, Nov 1972, Greenville SC 365.00
Neil Sedaka, Adam Faith, April 1962, London Palladium 295.00
Grateful Dead, June 1966, Filmore West (Bill Graham) 375.00
Promotion Kit, 1993 "Riders in the Sky" concert, media releases, concert releases, postcard, bumper sticker, two 8" x 10" glossy photo, product catalog 10.00
Puzzle
　　Bee Gees, frame tray 20.00
　　George Simmons, Milton Bradley, 200 pcs, missing one piece, orig box 45.00
　　KISS, frame tray, 1964 .... 25.00
　　Shaun Cassidy, frame tray 20.00
Radio, KISS, 1977 .... 100.00
Record, KISS, "I Was Made For Loving You," 33 RPM, Casablanca, 1978, one-sided 35.00
Record Case, cardboard, full-color photo and signature of Dick Clark, blue, white plastic handle, brass closure, holds 45 RPM records 45.00
Salt and Pepper Shakers, pr, ceramic feet, mkd "Rock-N-Roll Indiana," mkd "Japan," 2-3/4" l 6.00
Scarf, AC/DC, EuroTour, 1980-81 ..... 60.00
Sheet Music
　　Green Tree Boogie, Bill Haley and the Comets, greentone photo, © 1955 Meyers Music 22.00
　　Substitute, The Who, bluetone photo, © 1966, Fabulous Music Ltd. 15.00
Ring, Monkees, club, flicker 50.00
Store Display, Jackson 5, Meagus, 27" x 22" 295.00
Thermos, Bee Gees, plastic, King Seeley, 1978 .... 27.50
Tie Clip, Dick Clark American Bandstand, gold-tone metal 15.00
Tour Book, Bob Dylan, 28 pgs, c1977 .... 30.00
Toy
　　Car, Monkees, tin 300.00
　　Guitar, Monkees, plastic, full-color diecut litho paper label, © 1966 .... 80.00
　　Saxophone, Spike Jones, hard plastic, mkd "A Trophy Product," c1950 .. 30.00
Trading Cards Box, unopened, Nu-Card, 1960, 36 unopened cello packs 360.00
Vending Machine Insert, showing Monkee pinback buttons, 1967 .... 75.00

Viewmaster Reel, Last Wheelbarrow to Pokeyville, Monkees, orig booklet 12.00
Window Card, 22" x 14", Rolling Stones, Gimme Shelter, blue, yellow, and white 165.00

Norman Rockwell

Collecting Hints: Learn all you can about Norman Rockwell if you plan to collect any of his art. His original artworks and illustrations have been transferred onto various types of objects by clubs and manufacturers.

History: Norman Rockwell, the famous American artist, was born on February 3, 1894. When he was 18, he did his first professional illustrations for a children's book, *Tell Me Why Stories* His next projects were done in association with *Boy's Life*, the Boy Scout magazine, and after that his work appeared in many other magazines. By his death in November 1978, he had completed more than 2,000 paintings, many of which were done in oil and reproduced as magazine covers, advertisements, illustrations, calendars, and book sketches. More than 320 of these paintings became covers for the *Saturday Evening Post*.

Norman Rockwell painted everyday people in everyday situations with a little humor mixed in with the sentimentality. His paintings and illustrations are well loved because of this sensitive nature. He painted people he knew and places with which he was familiar. New England landscapes are seen in many of his illustrations.

Because his works are so popular, they have been reproduced on many objects. These new collectibles, which should not be confused with the original artwork and illustrations, make Norman Rockwell illustrations affordable for the average consumer.

References: Denis C. Jackson, *Norman Rockwell Identification and Value Guide*, 2nd ed., published by author (P.O. Box 1958, Sequim, WA 98392), 1985; Mary Moline, *Norman Rockwell Collectibles Value Guide*, 6th ed., Green Valley World, 1988.

Collectors' Club: Rockwell Society of America, 597 Saw Mill River Rd, Ardsley, NY 10502.

Museums: Museum of Norman Rockwell Art, Reedsburg, WI; Norman Rockwell Museum, Northbrook, IL; Norman Rockwell Museum, Philadelphia, PA; The Norman Rockwell Museum at Stockbridge, Stockbridge, MA.

Bell, Love's Harmony, 1976, wooden handle, 9" h 45.00
Book, *Norman Rockwell's Growing Up in America*, Margaret Rockwell, Metro Books, 1998, 1st ed. 15.00
Child's Puzzle, 5" x 6-1/2" puzzle, Rockwell's "A Serious Case," Tuco Junior Picture Puzzle, 1930s 35.00
Dealer Sign, porcelain figure standing next to plaque, c1980, 5-1/4" h . 125.00
Doll, limited edition, Danbury Mint, MIB
    Girl and Her Doll 175.00
    Young Ladies 175.00
Ignot, Franklin Mint, Spirit of Scouting, 1972, 12 pc set 295.00
Limited Edition Figurine (also see Limited Editions)
    Bride and Groom, Rockwell Museum, 1979 .... 115.00
    Cradle of Love, Lynell Studios, 1980 .... 85.00
    First Haircut, Dave Grossman, 1995 .... 70.00
    Gramps at the Reins, Dave Grossman 35.00
    Marriage License, Dave Grossman 65.00
    Marriage License, Goebel 100.00
    Marriage License, Gorham 450.00
    No Swimming 65.00
    Saying Grace, Gorham, 1976 ... 165.00
    Taking Mother Over The Top, Hamilton, 1982 .... 225.00
    The Graduate, Dave Grossman, 1983 .... 35.00
    Triple Self Portrait, Gorham, bisque, 1978 .... 315.00
Limited Edition Plate (also see Limited Editions)
    A Mother's Love, Rockwell Society 1976 .... 38.00
    Angel with Black Eye, 1975 .... 40.00
    Boy Scout, Gorham, 1975 .... 65.00
    First Prom, Rockwell Museum, 1979 .... 35.00
    Four Seasons, 1975, set of four .. 85.00
    Huckleberry Finn, Dave Grossman, 1980 .... 45.00
    Jennie & Tina, River Shore, 1982 .... 45.00
    Mother's Day, Lynell Studios, 1980 .... 45.00
    One Present Too Many, Royal Devon, 1979 .... 30.00
    Ringing in Good Cheer, Rockwell Museum, 1981 .... 85.00
    Santa's Helpers, Gorham, 1979 .. 25.00
    Snow Queen, Lynell Studios, 1979 .... 30.00
    The Carolers, Franklin Mint, 1972 .... 175.00
Magazine Cover
    Boys' Life, June, 1947 .... 45.00
    Family Circle, December, 1967 ... 15.00
    Red Cross, April, 1918 .... 25.00
    Saturday Evening Post, Jan. 26, 1918 .... 95.00
    Saturday Evening Post, Feb. 18, 1922 .... 90.00

    Saturday Evening Post, April 19, 1950 .... 85.00
    Saturday Evening Post, Sept. 7, 1957 .... 35.00
    Saturday Evening Post, Jan. 13, 1962 .... 20.00
    Scouting, December, 1944 .... 15.00

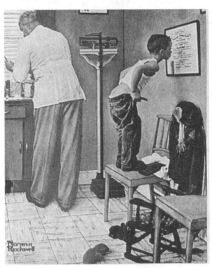

Print, Before the Shot, c1958, $25.

Print
    Bottom of the Sixth, brass plate "Norman Rockwell Centennial Edition," 9-1/2" x 11-1/2" framed 25.00
    Doctor and the Doll, brass plate "Norman Rockwell Centennial Edition," 9-1/2" x 11-1/2" framed 25.00
    Elderly couple sitting on bench with cat and dog, 14" x 11", metal frame 12.00
    Little girl reading to pairs of animals, 14" x 11", metal frame 12.00
    Santa, 12" x 13-1/4" 12.00
    The Gossips, brass plate "Norman Rockwell Centennial Edition," 9-1/2" x 11-1/2" framed 25.00
    The Self Portrait, brass plate "Norman Rockwell Centennial Edition," 9-1/2" x 11-1/2" framed 25.00

Roseville Pottery

Collecting Hints: The prices for Roseville's later commercial ware are stable and unlikely to rise rapidly because it is readily available. The prices are strong for the popular middle-period patterns, which were made during the Depression and produced in limited numbers. Among the most popular patterns from this middle period are Blackberry, Cherry Blossom, Falline, Ferella, Jonquil, Morning Glory, Sunflower, and Windsor.

The Art Deco craze has increased the popularity of Futura, especially the more angular-shaped pieces. Pine Cone pieces with a blue or

brown glaze continue to have a strong following as do the earlier lines of Juvenile and Donatello.

Desirable Roseville shapes include baskets, bookends, cookie jars, ewers, tea sets, and wall pockets.

Most pieces are marked. However, during the middle period paper stickers were used. These often were removed, leaving the piece unmarked.

Roseville made more than 150 different lines or patterns. Novice collectors would benefit from reading one of the several books about Roseville and should visit dealers who specialize in art pottery. Collections generally are organized around a specific pattern or shape.

History: In the late 1880s, a group of investors purchased the J. B. Owens Pottery in Roseville, Ohio, and made utilitarian stoneware items. In 1892, the firm was incorporated, and George F. Young became general manager. Four generations of Youngs controlled Roseville until the early 1950s.

A series of acquisitions began: Midland Pottery of Roseville in 1898, Clark Stoneware Plant in Zanesville (formerly used by Peters and Reed), and Muskingum Stoneware (Mosaic Tile Company) in Zanesville. In 1898 the offices also moved from Roseville to Zanesville.

In 1900 Roseville developed its art pottery line—Rozane. Ross Purdy designed a line to compete with Weller's Louwelsa. Rozane became a trade name to cover a large series of lines by designers such as Christian Neilson, John J. Herold, and Gazo Fudji. The art lines of hand-decorated underglaze pottery were made in limited quantities after 1919.

The success of Roseville depended on its commercial lines, first developed by John J. Herold and Frederick Rhead in the early decades of the 1900s. Decorating techniques included transfers, pouncing (a method which produced the outline of a pattern which could then be used as the basis for further decorating), and air brushing or sponging over embossed motifs. Dutch, Juvenile, Cameo, and Holland are some of the lines from this early period.

George Young retired in 1918. Frank Ferrell replaced Harry Rhead, who had replaced Frederick Rhead, as art director. Ferrell developed more than 80 lines, the first being Sylvan. The economic depression of the 1930s caused Roseville to look for new product lines. Pine Cone was introduced in 1935, made for 15 years, and issued in more than 75 shapes.

In the 1940s, a series of high-gloss glazes were used to try to revive certain lines. Other changes were made in response to the fluctuating contemporary market. Mayfair and Wincraft date from this period. In 1952, Raymor dinnerware was produced. None of these changes brought economic success back to Roseville. In November 1954, Roseville was bought by the Mosaic Tile Company.

References: Mark Bassett, *Bassetts Roseville Prices*, Schiffer Publishing, 2000; John and Nancy Bomm, *Roseville In All Its Splendor*, L-W Book Sales, 1998; Virginia Hillway Buxton, *Roseville Pottery for Love or Money*, updated ed., Tymbre Hill Publishing Co. (P.O. Box 615, Jonesborough, TN 37659), 1996; Sharon and Bob Huxford, *Collectors Encyclopedia of Roseville Pottery*, 1st Series (1976, 2001 value update), 2nd Series (1980, 2001 value update), Collector Books; Randall B. Monsen, *Collector's Compendium of Roseville Pottery*, Monsen and Baer (Box 529, Vienna, VA 22183), 1995; *Collector's Compendium of Roseville Pottery*, Volume II, Monsen and Baer, 1997.

Collectors' Clubs: American Art Pottery Association, 125 E. Rose Ave., St. Louis, MO 63119; Roseville's of the Past Pottery Club, P.O. Box 656, Clarcona, FL 32710.

Reproduction Alert: Reproductions of several Roseville patterns have plagued the marketplace in the late 1990s.

Candleholders, pair, Moderne, ivory, triple, #1112, incised mark, 5-1/4" d, 6-1/4" h, $325. Photo courtesy of David Rago Auctions.

Basket
    Bittersweet, 810-10 .... 185.00
    Bleeding Heart, 360-10, 1938, 9-1/2" h 395.00
    Monticello, brown, 632 .... 555.00
    Pine Cone, brown 365.00
    Poppy, pink, 347-10 .... 425.00
Basket with Frog, Pine Cone, 352-8, incised initial 450.00
Bookends, pr
    Gardenia, gray 300.00
    Silhouette 150.00
    Zephyr Lily, green 195.00
Bowl
    Blueberry, blue, 412-6 .... 130.00
    Florentine, 7"d 85.00
    Lombardy, dark teal 85.00
    Mauve, matte, 3-1/2" h, 5" w, orig paper label 75.00
    Moss Blue, high sides, #294-12 .... 275.00
    Nursery Rhyme 150.00
    Peony, yellow, 428-6 .... 95.00
    Pine Cone, green 115.00
    Water Lily, brown, 437-4 .... 95.00
Bowl and Flower Frog, Clematis, mkd "Roseville USA 458-10," c1944 .... 195.00
Bud Vase, double
    Dahl Rose 175.00
    Foxglove, green with peach blush 375.00
Candleholders, pr
    Carnelian II 70.00
    Gardenia, 652-4-1/2" 150.00
    Zephyr Lily, 1162-2 .... 115.00
Candlesticks, pr
    Carnelian I 140.00
    Pine Cone, 451-4 .... 325.00
Child's Feeding Plate, rolled edge
    Duck with Hat, c1916 .... 395.00
    Nursery Rhyme 150.00
    Tom Tom 90.00
Compote, Magnolia, 13" h 110.00
Conch Shell, Peony, blue 185.00
Console Bowl
    Bushberry, #414-10 .... 180.00
    Freesia, brown 115.00
    Snowberry, IBL-8, 17-1/2" w 375.00
Cookie Jar, cov, Clematis, blue, 10-1/2" h, 9" d, two small rim chips 350.00
Cornucopia, mkd "Roseville U.S.A. 321-6," rim chips, repairs 85.00
Creamer
    Juvenile, duck 100.00
    Wincraft, 271-C, glossy, 1940s 75.00
    Zephyr Lily, blue 80.00
Cup and Saucer, Zephyr Lily, blue 125.00
Ewer
    Clematis, 5" h 165.00
    Louwelsa, artist sgd "LM" for Lille Mitchell, 12-1/2" h 595.00
    Water Lily, 15" h, pink, #12 .... 500.00
Floor Vase, Gardenia, 689, green, matte finish, int. rim chip 550.00
Flower Frog, Clematis, 50 .... 90.00
Flower Pot
    Jonquil, attached frog, 6" h, 6-3/4" d top 600.00
    Thorn Apple, blue, matching underplate 215.00
Hanging Planter, Freesia, blue 450.00

Jardiniere
    Bushberry, brown, 657-3 .... 95.00
    Clematis, blue, 667-4 .... 90.00
    Pine Cone, 632-6, blue 550.00
    White Rose, 653-6 .... 375.00
Lamp, Rozane Royal, c1905, 17" h 600.00
Mug
    Duck with boots 150.00
    Dutch 110.00
    Rabbit 140.00
Pitcher
    Blended Landscape, 7-1/2" h 140.00
    Carnelian II, mottled green and cream, rough bottom 175.00
    Flute Player and Jester, c1915, small crack 400.00
    Freesia, 11", blue, yellow flowers, chip 385.00
Planter
    Magnolia, 388-6 .... 110.00
    Pine Cone, 12-1/2" x 4-1/2" 125.00
    Poppy, blue 85.00
Plate, Juvenile, rabbit, rolled edge, 7" d 155.00
Tea Set, Zephr Lily, teapot, creamer, sugar, small manuf defect on sugar lower rim 495.00

Vase, Wisteria, bulbous, foil label, 9" d, 6" h, restoration to chip at base, $1,100. Photo courtesy of David Rago Auctions.

Vase
    Baneda, pink 750.00
    Bushberry, green and brown, 8" h 300.00
    Dahl Rose, 4" x 10" 190.00
    Donatello, 10" h 230.00
    Freesia, 128-16, brown, rim defect 400.00
    Futura, 397-6, square cone, blue/gray 575.00
    Imperial II, 469-6 .... 425.00
    Iris, blue, 927-10, restored base chip 285.00
    Ivory II, 740-10, white, two repaired chips 90.00
    Laurel, 6" h, brown 185.00
    Magnolia, 14" h 550.00
    Moss, 6" x 9" 450.00
    Pine Cone, 839-6, blue 395.00
    Poppy, 872-9, base chips 120.00
    Primrose, blue 175.00
    Rozane, 8" h, honeycomb, pastel roses 375.00

Russco, 7" h	160.00
Silhouette, blue, nude, fan, 783-7,	
small base repair	400.00
Sunflower, 5" h	695.00
Wincraft, panther, 10-1/2" h,	
4-3/4" w	800.00

Wall Pocket

Apple Blossom, green	550.00
Carnelian	185.00
Clematis, green	180.00
Cosmos, blue	375.00
Foxglove, brown, 1296-8"	190.00
Gardenia, brown, 666-8"	150.00
Green, matte, 8" l	120.00
Maple Leaf, 8-1/2"	75.00
Snowberry, blue, 1WP-8	180.00
Three sided, green, 11" l	110.00
Tulips, emb flowers, white	60.00
White Rose, pink	325.00

Royal China

Collecting Hints: The dinnerware has become very collectible and increasingly popular. It can be found at flea markets and antiques malls across the country. Prices are steadily increasing, and it is becoming more difficult to find some of the serving pieces.

The backstamps usually contain the name of the pattern. In addition to many variations of company backstamps, Royal China also produced objects with private backstamps. All records of these markings were lost in a fire in 1970.

The following are some of the items that are considered scarce: clocks, grill plates, snack plates, and tab handled items, and some glasses and beverage sets. Items that are more sought after by collectors are items with decorated handles such as: cups, sugar bowls, creamers, teapots, and casseroles. Also items with backstamps such as the ashtray and the gravy underplate.

History: The Royal China Company manufactured dinnerware in Sebring, Ohio, from 1934 to 1986. The original officers were Beatrice L. Miller, William H. Hebenstreit, and John Briggs. Miss Miller became known as the "Queen of China" and sold Royal in 1969 upon retiring. She passed away in 1979. John Briggs passed away in 1980. Bill Habenstreit retired from Royal in 1946, moved to California, and passed away in 1964. They started the company with $500, six months free rent, and a handful of employees working without pay in the depths of the depression. Four months later, they had 125 people on their payroll. At the height of Royal's popularity in 1970, the company had

700 employees, seven acres under roof, and annual sales of around $16 million. It was the largest manufacturer of popular-priced dinnerware in the United States.

Royal produced a large variety of dinnerware patterns, the most popular being the blue and white Currier and Ives. Other patterns made by the company include Bucks County, Colonial Homestead, Fair Oaks, Memory Lane, Old Curiosity Shop, and Willow Ware. The blue Currier & Ives and blue Willow Ware were continued through the years, while most of the other patterns were discontinued when Royal sold to Jeannette in 1970 which as probably a mistake. Bucks County and Fair Oaks were reintroduced in 1985, but probably too late. These popular dinnerware patterns were made in four basic colors: blue, pink, green, and brown. Some were also made in black and multicolored.

Royal China was sold through retail department stores, catalog mail-order houses, and supermarket chains. They were also given as premiums. Numerous serving pieces as well as advertising and decorative items to compliment the dinnerware were available.

In the last few years that they were in business, Royal made many different cake plates, pie bakers, coasters, and holiday related items, including Christmas items. These items are becoming very collectible and sought after.

The company had various owners including the Jeanette Glass Corporation from 1969 to 1976. In 1970, the building and records were destroyed by fire and the operation was moved to the French Saxon China Company building. In 1978, the company was purchased by Coca-Cola and was operated by them until 1981, when it was sold to the J. Corporation. It was sold for the last time in 1984 to Nordic Capital, who filed for bankruptcy in 1986 and ceased production in March of that year.

References: Eldon R. Aupperle, *Collector's Guide for Currier & Ives Dinnerware by Royal China Co.*, published by author (27470 Saxon Rd, Toulon, IL 61483), 1996; Susan and Al Bagdade, *Warman's American Pottery and Porcelain*, 2nd ed., Krause Publications, 2000; Jo Cunningham, *Collector's Encyclopedia of American Dinnerware*, Collector Books, 1982, 1995 value update; Lois

Lehner, *Lehner's Encyclopedia of U.S. Marks on Pottery, Porcelain & Clay*, Collector Books, 1988.

Collectors' Club: Currier & Ives Dinnerware Collectors Club, RR 2, Box 394, Holidaysburg, PA 16648.

Advisor: David J. and Deborah G. Folckemer.

Bucks County, coffee mug, 2-3/4" x 3-3/4", $40. Photo courtesy of David Folckemer.

Bucks County

Introduced c1950; prices given are for yellow pieces with a dark brown printed farm scene. Also made in a green and white version.

Accessories

Beverage Tumbler, 5-1/2"	15.00
Hostess Table Tidbit, two tiers, 10" d and 13" d plates, wood legs	125.00
Juice Tumbler, 3-1/2"	15.00
Old Fashion Tumbler, 3-1/4"	15.00
Promotional Jug, 2" x 2-3/4"	100.00
Tidbit, 3 tiers, 6" d, 9" d, and 12" d plates	60.00

Dinnerware

Bread and Butter Plate, 6-3/8" d	3.00
Breakfast Plate, 9" d	12.00
Butter Dish, cov, 1/4 lb	45.00
Casserole, cov, angle handles	75.00
Cereal Bowl, 6-1/4" d	8.00
Coffee Mug, 2-3/4" x 3-3/4"	40.00
Creamer	4.00
Cup and Saucer, 6" d	4.00
Dinner Plate, 10-1/4" d	4.00
Fruit Bowl, 5-3/4" d	3.00
Gravy Boat	15.00
Gravy Ladle, white	40.00
Gravy Underplate, tab handles	12.00
Grill Plate, 3 sections	15.00
Lug Soup/Cereal Bowl	20.00

Platter

Lug, meat, 11-1/2" l	20.00
Oval, 10" x 13"	20.00
Round, 12" d	22.00
Round, 13" d	30.00
Rim Soup Bowl, 8-3/8" d	9.00
Salad Plate, 7-3/8" d	8.00
Salt and Pepper Shakers, pr	20.00

Sugar Bowl, cov

Angle handles	20.00
Tab handles	15.00

Teapot, cov 100.00
Vegetable Bowl
   9" d 15.00
   10" d 20.00

Colonial Homestead, tab handle gravy boat, $85. Photo courtesy of David Folckemer.

Colonial Homestead

Introduced c1950. Design consists of colonial home scenes of about 1750. Prices given are for white pieces with a green print. Also made with black and pink prints.

Accessories

Ashtray, 5-1/2" 12.00
Batter Set, large waffle pitcher and smaller syrup pitcher 150.00
Beverage Set, frosted pitcher and six tumblers 200.00
Beverage Tumbler, 5-1/2" 14.00
Canasta Tray, two tier, 7" d and 10" d plates, brass heart shaped handle 50.00
Clock, 10", electric, Charles Denning, spinning wheel........................... 400.00
Hostess Table Tidbit, two tier, 10" d and 13" d plates, wood legs 100.00
Juice Set, frosted pitcher and 6 tumblers 150.00
Juice Tumbler, 3-1/2" 14.00
Old Fashion Tumbler, 3-1/4" 14.00
Tile and Rack, 6" x 6", Wheeling . 75.00
Water Tumbler, 4-3/4"................... 14.00

Dinnerware

Bread and Butter Plate, 6-3/8" d ... 2.50
Breakfast plate, 9" d 12.00
Butter Dish, cov, 1/4 lb 25.00
Casserole, cov
   Angle handles 65.00
   Tab handles 200.00
Cereal Bowl, 6-1/4" d................... 10.00
Coffee Mug 20.00
Creamer 4.00
Cup and Saucer, 6" d 4.00
Dinner Plate, 10-1/4" d................... 4.00
Fruit Bowl, 5-3/4" d......................... 3.00
Gravy Boat, regular 15.00
Gravy Boat, tab handles 85.00
Gravy Ladle, white........................ 40.00
Gravy Underplate, tab handle 15.00
Grill Plate, 10-1/2" d, three sections.. 100.00
Lug Soup/Cereal Bowl 20.00
Pie Plate, 10" d............................. 25.00
Platter
   Lug, meat, 11-1/2" 20.00
   Oval, 10" x 13"......................... 25.00

Round, 12" d 20.00
Round, 13" d 30.00
Relish Dish 125.00
Rim Soup, 8-3/8" d...................8.00
Salad Plate, 7-3/8" d 10.00
Salt and Pepper Shakers, pr
   Angle handles......................... 20.00
   Round handles........................ 25.00
   White Hinge, decorated tops 30.00
Snack Plate with Cup, 9-1/4" d....65.00
Sugar Bowl, cov, angle handles..10.00
Teapot, cov................................ 90.00
Vegetable Bowl
   9" d 15.00
   10" d 20.00

Currier and Ives, tile and rack, Wheeling, Snowy Morning, 6" x 6", $150. Photo courtesy of David Folckemer.

Currier and Ives

Introduced late 1940s; prices given are for white pieces with a blue print. Also made in pink, green, black, brown, and multicolored.

Accessories

Ashtray, Central Park, 5-1/2"
   White and blue........................ 12.00
   White and pink........................ 50.00
Beverage Set, frosted pitcher and 6 tumblers 425.00
Beverage Tumbler, 5-1/2" 12.00
Calendar Plate, 1973 through 1986, white and blue, each 15.00
Calendar Plate, 1974, white and pink 60.00
Candle Lamp, with globe, Grist Mill, mid 1980s 300.00
Clock Plate, electric, Charles Denning
   10-1/4" d, Old School House................................... 500.00
   12" d, Grist Mill.................... 650.00
Hostess Table Tidbit, 2 tiers, 10" d and 13" d plates, wood legs 125.00
Juice Tumbler, 3-1/2".................... 12.00
Old Fashion Tumbler, 3-1/4" 12.00
Placemats, vinyl, foam back, Marcrest, set of four 100.00
Tidbit, three tiers, 6" d, 9" d, and 12" d plates, brass heart hardware 75.00
Tile and Rack, Snowy Morning, Wheeling, 6" x 6"
   White and blue.................... 150.00
   White and pink.................... 225.00
Tumbler, frosted, white and pink
   3-7/8" h 25.00

   5-1/8" h................................. 25.00
Wall Plaque, Rocky Mountains, 5-1/4" x 6-3/4" 500.00
Water Tumbler, 4-3/4" 12.00

Dinnerware

After Dinner Cup, Fashionable Turnouts 50.00
After Dinner Saucer, border only 20.00
Bread and Butter Plate, Harvest, 6-3/8" d 3.00
Breakfast plate, Grist Mill, 9" d.... 15.00
Butter Dish, cov, 1/4 lb
   Fashionable Turnouts............. 45.00
   Road Winter 30.00
Casserole, cov, Fashionable Turnouts, white and blue
   Angle handles 75.00
   Tab handles 200.00
Casserole, cov, Fashionable Turnouts, white and pink
   Angle handles 200.00
   Handleless 400.00
   Tab handles 500.00
Cereal Bowl, School House, 6-1/4" d 12.00
Creamer
   Angle handle, Express Train.... 5.00
   Round handle, Express Train 20.00
Cup, flared, round handle, Star of the Road 12.00
Cup and Saucer, 6" d, Star of the Road, Low Water on Mississippi .. 6.00
Dinner Plate, Grist Mill, 10-1/4" d .. 4.00
Gravy Boat, Road Winter
   Regular 20.00
   Tab handles 75.00
Gravy Ladle, white
   6-1/2" l, ftd, Royal/Harker 25.00
   7" l, hold in handle................. 40.00
Gravy Stand and Underplate
   Tab handles, Oaken Bucket .. 15.00
   White tab handles, Washington's Birthplace 75.00
Grill Plate, three sections, Partridge Shooting, Hens and Snipe........ 100.00
Lug Soup/Cereal Bowl, Suburban Retreat 35.00
Mug, coffee
   Express Train, 3-3/8" x 3-1/4"..................................... 30.00
   Fashionable Turnouts, 2-3/4" x 3-3/4"..................................... 25.00
   Woodcock Shooting.............. 60.00
Pie Plate, 10" d, nine different scenes American Homestead
   Winter..................................... 35.00
   Early Winter 25.00
   Getting Ice 25.00
   Grist Mill.................................. 35.00
   Home on Mississippi.............. 30.00
   Maple Sugaring...................... 50.00
   Old Inn Winter 30.00
   Return from Pasture 30.00
   Snowy Morning 25.00
Platter
   Lug, meat, 11-1/2"................. 20.00
   Oval, Central Park Winter, 10" x 13"... 100.00
   Oval, Old Inn Winter, 10" x 13"... 25.00
   Round, Getting Ice, 11" d 30.00
   Round, Rocky Mountains, 11" d... 75.00

Round, Getting Ice, 12" d.......25.00
Round, Snowy Morning,
13" d...75.00
Rim Soup, Early Winter, 8-3/8" d . 10.00
Salad Plate, Washington's Birthplace,
7-3/8" d.................................... 15.00
.Salt and Pepper Shakers, pr, Fashion-
able Turnouts, angle handles......25.00
Service Plate, Pic-nic Party,
11" d....................................... 100.00
Snack Plate with Cup, Grist Mill,
9-1/8".................................... 125.00
Sugar Bowl, cov, Loading Cotton on
Mississippi, white and blue
   Angle handles 18.00
   Flared, no handles.................. 45.00
   Round, no handles................. 30.00
Sugar Bowl, cov, Loading Cotton on
Mississippi, white and pink
   Angle handles 25.00
   Round, inside lid..................... 50.00
   Round, overlapping lid........... 75.00
Teapot, cov, Clipper Ship Dread-
nought, off Tuskar Light, white and
blue 135.00
Teapot, cov, Clipper Ship Dread-
nought, off Tuskar Light, white and
pink
   Angle handle 200.00
   Round handle, white lid 400.00
Vegetable Bowl
   9" d, Maple Sugaring, shallow25.00
   10" d, Home Sweet Home,
   deep.......................................30.00

Hostess Set, gadroon edge, mid 1980s
Cake Plate, Getting Ice, 10" d
   Flat 50.00
   Footed.................................. 150.00
Candy Bowl, Maple Sugaring,
7-3/4" d.. 40.00
Deviled Egg Plate, Grist Mill,
10-3/4" d..................................... 150.00
Dip Bowl, 4-3/8" d, all white..........40.00
Pie Baker, Getting Ice, 11" d 70.00
Serving Plate, American Homestead
Winter, 7-3/4" d............................ 15.00

Royal China Co., Fair Oaks, tab handle cereal bowl, $20. Photo courtesy of David Folckemer.

Fair Oaks

Introduced 1950s. Pattern based on Currier and Ives scenes. Prices given are
pieces with a multicolored print. There
were at least four different color variations.

Dinnerware

Bread and Butter Plate, 6-3/8" d ...4.00
Butter Dish, cov, 1/4 lb, Fashionable
Turnouts.......................................35.00
Casserole, cov, angle handles....75.00
Cereal Bowl, 6-1/4" d 12.00
Cereal Bowl, tab handle 20.00
Creamer 6.00
Cup and Saucer. 6" d, Frontier Settle-
ment..6.00
Dinner Plate, Return from Pasture,
10-1/4" d 6.00
Fruit Bowl, 5-3/4" d 5.00
Gravy Boat 20.00
Gravy Ladle, white 40.00
Gravy Underplate, My Cottage Home,
tab handle 15.00
Lug Soup/Cereal Bowl.................25.00
Platter
   Lug, meat, Puzzle Picture, Old
   Swiss Mill, 11-1/2" l 45.00
   Oval, 8-3/4" x 11-1/4" 35.00
   Oval, 10" x 13" 40.00
Rim Soup Bowl, 8-3/8" d 12.00
Salad Plate, My Cottage Home,
7-3/8" d...10.00
Salt and Pepper Shakers, pr 25.00
Sugar Bowl, cov, angle handles..18.00
Teapot, cov................................. 125.00
Tidbit, 3 tiers, fruit bowl, 7" d, and 10" d
plates..60.00
Vegetable Bowl
   9" d 18.00
   10" d 25.00
   Divided, Haying Time, First Load-
   Last Load, 8-1/4" x 12"............40.00

Memory Lane, ashtray, 5-1/2" d, $15. Photo courtesy of David Folckemer.

Memory Lane

Introduced 1965. Pattern based on Currier and Ives scenes. Prices given are
for white pieces with a pink print. Also
made in blue and green prints.

Accessories

Ashtray, 5-1/2" 15.00
Beverage Tumbler, 5-1/2" 12.00
Juice Tumbler, 3-1/2"....................12.00
Old Fashion Tumbler, 3-1/4" 12.00
Serving Tray, 19" d, metal 50.00
Water Tumbler, 4-3/4" 12.00

Dinnerware

Bread and Butter Plate, 6-3/8" d ...3.00
Breakfast Plate, Return from Pasture,
9" d...15.00
Butter Dish, cov, 1/4 lb, Fashionable
Turnouts.......................................35.00

Casserole, cov, angle handles ... 75.00
Cereal Bowl, 6-1/4" d.................. 10.00
Coffee Mug, 2-3/4" x 3-3/4" 25.00
Creamer 5.00
Cup and Saucer, 6" d, Frontier Settle-
ment 4.00
Dinner Plate, Return from Pasture,
10-1/4" d 4.00
Fruit Bowl, 5-3/4" d 3.00
Gravy Boat.................................... 15.00
Gravy Ladle, white 40.00
Gravy Underplate, My Cottage Home,
tab handle 15.00
Pie Plate, Puzzle Picture, Old Swiss
Mill, 10" d 30.00
Platter
   Lug, meat, Puzzle Picture, Old
   Swiss Mill, 11-1/2" l 25.00
   Oval, 10" x 13" 30.00
   Round, Snowy Morning,
   12" d...................................... 25.00
Rim Soup Bowl, 8-3/8" d 9.00
Salad Plate, My Cottage Home,
7-3/8" d 10.00
Salt and Pepper Shakers, pr 25.00
Sugar Bowl, cov
   Angle handles 15.00
   Tab handles........................... 50.00
Teapot, cov 125.00
Vegetable Bowl
   9" d....................................... 20.00
   10" d..................................... 25.00

The Old Curiosity Shop, tab handle sugar bowl, $40. Photo courtesy of David Folckemer.

Old Curiosity Shop

Introduced early 1950s. Pattern was
based on a Charles Dickens book,
The Old Curiosity Shop. Prices given
are for white pieces with a green print.
Also made in blue, brown, and pink
prints.

Accessories

Ashtray, 5-1/2" 12.00
Beverage Set, frosted pitcher and six
tumblers..................................... 350.00
Beverage Tumbler
   5-1/4", tapered...................... 18.00
   5-1/2"..................................... 16.00
Hostess Table Tidbit, two tiers, 10" d
and 13" d plates, wood legs 150.00
Juice Set, frosted pitcher and six juice
tumblers..................................... 175.00
Juice Tumbler, 3-1/2" 16.00
Old Fashion Tumbler, 3-1/4" 16.00
Tidbit, three tiers, 6" d, 9" d, and 12" d
plates 75.00

Tile and Rack, 6" x 6",
Wheeling 150.00
Water Tumbler, 4-3/4" 16.00

Dinnerware

Bread and Butter Plate,
6-3/8" d...3.00
Breakfast Plate, 9" d 15.00
Butter Dish, cov, 1/4 lb 35.00
Butter Pat, 3-1/4" d 75.00
Casserole, cov, angle handles....75.00
Cereal Bowl, 6-1/4" d 12.00
Coffee Mug, 2-3/4" x 3-3/4" 40.00
Creamer 4.50
Cup and Saucer, 6" d 4.00
Dinner Plate, 10-1/4" d...................5.00
Fruit Bowl, 5-3/4" d.........................4.00
Gravy Boat......................................20.00
Gravy Ladle, white..........................40.00
Gravy Underplate, tab handle 15.00
Lug Soup/Cereal Bowl 25.00
Pie Plate, 10" d 30.00
Platter
   Lug, meat, 11-1/2" l 25.00
   Oval, 8-3/4" x 11-1/4" 25.00
   Round, 12" d................................25.00
   Round, 13" d................................40.00
Rim Soup Bowl, 8-3/8" d.............10.00
Salad Plate, 7-3/8" d 12.00
Salt and Pepper Shakers,
pr...25.00
Sugar Bowl, cov
   Angle handles 20.00
   Tab handles 40.00
Teapot, cov 125.00
Vegetable Bowl
   9" d..20.00
   10" d..25.00

Willow Ware

Introduced 1940s. Pattern based on Oriental scenes. Prices given are for white pieces with a blue print. Also made in pink, green, and brown prints.

Ashtray 5-1/2" 20.00
Batter Set, large waffle pitcher, smaller
syrup pitcher...............................125.00
Beverage Set, frosted pitcher and six
tumblers 175.00

Beverage Tumbler, 5-1/2" 15.00
Candle Holders, pr, brass, weighted,
6" d plate 85.00
Clock, 10" d, electric, Charles
Denning....................................... 150.00

**Willow Ware, coaster, 4-1/2" d, $30.
Photo courtesy of David Folckemer.**

Coaster, 4-1/2" d 30.00
Hostess Table Tidbit, two tiers, 10" d
and 13" d plates, wood legs..... 125.00
Juice Set, frosted pitcher and six tumblers..125.00
Juice Tumbler, 3-1/2".....................15.00
Old Fashion Tumbler, 3-1/4" 15.00
Serving Tray, 19" d, metal 50.00
Tidbit, three tiers, 6" d, 9" d, and 12" d
plates..60.00
Water Tumbler, 4-3/4" d...............15.00

Dinnerware

After Dinner Cup and Saucer,
5" d...25.00
Bread and Butter Plate,
6-3/8" d 4.00
Breakfast Plate, 9" d....................15.00
Butter Dish, cov, 1/4 lb................30.00
Casserole, cov
   Angle handles.........................75.00
   Round handles 75.00

Tab handles.........................200.00
Cereal Bowl, 6-1/4" d...................12.00
Coffee Mug, 2-3/4" x 3-3/4" 20.00
Creamer
   Angle handle 4.00
   Round handle............................6.00
Cup and Saucer, 6" d...................5.00
Dinner Plate, 10-1/4" d 4.00
Fruit Bowl, 5-3/4" d 3.00
Gravy Boat
   4-1/2" x 6"................................12.00
   5" x 6-1/2" 15.00
   Tab handle................................50.00
Gravy Ladle, white 40.00
Gravy Underplate
   Rounded tab handles 15.00
   Squared tab handles 40.00
Grill Plate, three sections
   10-1/2" d 18.00
   11-1/2" d 15.00
Lug Soup/Cereal Bowl 25.00
Pie Plate, 10" d 25.00
Platter
   Lug, meat, 11-1/2" l 20.00
   Oval, 8-3/4" x 11-1/4".............30.00
   Oval, 10" x 13"........................25.00
   Round, 11" d............................30.00
   Round, 12" d............................25.00
   Round, 13" d............................50.00
Rim Soup Bowl, 8-3/8" d 10.00
Salad Plate, 7-3/8" d...................10.00
Salt and Pepper Shakers, pr
   Angle handles 20.00
   Round handles.........................25.00
   White, "S" and "P" tops..........35.00
Snack Plate, with cup,
9-1/8" d 50.00
Sugar Bowl, cov
   Angle handles 15.00
   Handleless 30.00
   Round handle..........................18.00
   Tab handles.............................25.00
Teapot, cov 95.00
Vegetable Bowl
   9" d..20.00
   10" d..25.00

S

Salt and Pepper Shakers

Collecting Hints: Collect only sets in very good condition. Make certain the set has the proper two pieces, and base if applicable. China shakers should show no signs of cracking. Original paint and decoration should be intact on all china and metal figurals. All parts should be present, including the closure.

Collectors compete with those in other areas, e.g., advertising, animal groups, Black memorabilia, and holiday collectors. Many shakers were stock items to which souvenir labels were later affixed. The form, not the label, is the important element.

History: The Victorian era saw the advent of elaborate glass and fine-china salt and pepper shakers. Collectors were attracted to these objects by the pioneering research work of Arthur Goodwin Peterson that was published in *Glass Salt Shakers*. Figural and souvenir shakers, most dating from the mid-20th century and later, were looked down upon by this group.

This attitude is slowly changing. More and more people are collecting the figural and souvenir shakers, especially since prices are lower. Many of these patterns were made by Japanese firms and imported heavily after World War II.

Some forms were produced for decades; hence, it is difficult to tell an early example from a modern one. This is one of the factors that keeps prices low.

References: Larry Carey and Sylvia Tompkins, *1006 Salt and Pepper Shakers*, Schiffer Publishing, 2000; Melva Davern, *Collector's Encyclopedia of Salt & Pepper Shakers*, 1st Series (1985, 2000 value update), 2nd Series (1990, 2000 value update), Collector Books; Helene Guarnaccia, *Salt & Pepper Shakers*, Vol. I (1985, 1999 value update), Vol. II (1989, 1998 value update), Vol. III (1991, 1998 value update), Vol. IV (1993, 2001 value update), Collector Books; Mildred and Ralph Lechner, *World of Salt Shakers*, Vol. 3, Collector Books, 1999 value update; Arthur G. Peterson, *Glass Salt Shakers*, Wallace-Homestead, out of print; Sylvia Tompkins and Irene Thornburg, *America's Salt and Pepper Shakers*, Schiffer, 2000.

Collectors' Clubs: Antique and Art Glass Salt Shaker Collector's Society, 2832 Rapidan Trail, Maitland, FL 32751; Novelty Salt and Pepper Shakers Club, P.O. Box 3617, Lantana, FL 33465.

Museum: Judith Basin Museum, Stanford, MT.

Birds, white, gold trim, marked "Made in Japan," 3" h, $7.50.

Advertising

Budweiser, miniature bottles	7.50
Coca-Cola, miniature bottles	15.00
Dairy Queen	32.00
GE Refrigerators, 1930 style refrigerator, milk glass	30.00
Hormel, hash and egg	18.00
Nipper, 3" h, white china, black ears, eyes, and noses, base inscribed, "His Master's Voice/RCA Victor," orig cork stoppers, c1930	30.00
Pillsbury Dough Boy	12.00
Planters Peanuts	30.00
Schlitz Beer, miniature bottles	7.50
Tappan Baker, glossy finished glass, black on pale yellow salt, pale blue pepper, inscribed "Tappan Kitchen Ranges" on one, black threaded plastic caps, c1940	20.00

Ceramic

Amish Couple	5.00
Barber shaving pig	70.00
Barn and Silo	10.00
Baseball and Glove	12.00
Birds on Nest	10.00
Birds, standing, white, gold trim, mkd "Made in Japan"	6.50
Black Children in Basket, minor paint wear	145.00
Bugs Bunny and Taz with football	15.00
Chicks emerging from egg-shaped cups, script mark "Japan," 4-1/2" h	60.00
Chicks, salt and pepper, mustard inside egg box, luster, Japanese	45.00
Cowboys, Vandor	10.00
Cows	15.00
Dachshund and Tire	18.00
Donald Duck and BBQ	15.00
Donkeys, nodders, c1940-50	145.00
Duck and Egg	7.50
Feet	5.00
Frogs	7.00
Hen and Rooster, c1940, mkd "Made in Japan"	165.00
Indian Chief and Squaw, 3-1/4" h, composition wood, both mkd "1947 copyright, Multi Products"	18.00
Indian Chief and Squaw, nodders, fit in ceramic base, c1940, mkd "Made in Japan"	175.00
Kangaroos, Mother and baby, nodders, c1940, mkd "Made in Japan"	140.00
Kissing Dutch Boy and Girl, nodders, c1940, mkd "Made in Japan"	225.00
Kitchen Prayer Ladies, pink	10.00
Lawn Mower, moving wheels and pistons, 1950s	30.00
Lemons	5.00
Matador and Bull, c1940, mkd "Made in Japan"	245.00
Monkeys, nodders, c1940, mkd "Made in Japan"	175.00
Mrs. Gamp and Sam Weller, 3" h lady with brown bonnet, yellow bow, red shawl, male with brown hat, blue jacket, gray trousers, Czechoslovakia marks, c1930	40.00
Penguins, black and white body, orange bill and webbed feet, mkd "Japan," c1930s, 3" h	10.00
Pluto and Doghouse	15.00
Poodles	40.00
Puss 'n' Boots	30.00
Rabbits, yellow, snuggle type, Van Telligen	42.00
Rooster and Hen	7.50
Sailor and Anchor, figural glass shakers, wrought iron tray holder that has anchor and ships wheel, 2" h, most orig paint missing	48.00
Skunks, Enesco	12.00
Telephone and Directory, 1-1/2" x 2" x 2" black cradle telephone, 1-1/2" h brown telephone directory, SC souvenir decal, stoppers missing	15.00
Thermos and Lunch Pail	35.00
Thread and Thimble	30.00
Toilets	10.00
Tomatoes	5.00
Transistor Radio, 1" x 2-1/2" x 4", glazed bisque, brass wire carrying handle swivels to serve as support easel, tan circular simulated speaker with "S" or "P," soft pink salt, pale blue pepper, orig plastic stoppers, foil sticker for Enesco, Japan, c1960	28.00
Willie and Millie	10.00

Santa Claus

Collecting Hints: The number of Santa Claus–related items is endless. Collectors are advised to concentrate on one form (postcards, toys, etc.) or a brief time period. New collectors will find the hard-plastic 1950s Santas easily accessible and generally available at a reasonable price.

History: The idea of Santa Claus developed from stories about St. Nicholas, who lived about 300 A.D.

By the 1500s, "Father Christmas" in England, "Pere Noel" in France, and "Weihnachtsmann" in Germany were well established.

Until the 1800s, Santa Claus was pictured as a tall, thin, stately man wearing bishop's robes and riding a white horse. Washington Irving, in *Knickerbocker's History of New York* (1809), made him a stout, jolly man who wore a broad-brimmed hat and huge breeches and smoked a long pipe. The traditional Santa Claus image came from Clement C. Moore's poem "An Account of a Visit from St. Nicholas" (*Troy Sentinel, NY,* 1823) and the cartoon characterizations by Thomas Nast which appeared in *Harper's Weekly* between 1863 and 1886. The current appearance of Santa Claus is directly attributable to the illustrations of Haddon Sundblom for the Coca-Cola Company.

References: Beth Dees, *Santa's Guide to Contemporary Christmas Collectibles,* Krause Publications, 1997; Lissa Bryan-Smith and Richard Smith, *Holiday Collectibles, Vintage Flea Market Treasures Price Guide,* Krause Publications, 1998.

Reproduction Alert.

Additional Listings: Christmas Items.

Advisors: Lissa Bryan-Smith and Richard Smith.

Punch set, punch bowl and 12 matching mugs, Morton Pottery, rare, $360. Photo courtesy of Doris & Burdell Hall.

Advertising Trade Card, 3" x 5", "Santa Claus Soap, Gifts for Wrappers," N. K. Fairbanks Co, Chicago, St. Louis, New York, 1899 .... 12.00
Bank
   3" h, red hard plastic, egg shaped, Santa mask, mkd "Firestone Bank, Lisbon, Ohio" 8.00
   4" h, cardboard, Santa and box-shaped sleigh, 1960s 8.00
   11" h, chalkware, Santa sitting on chimney, waving, 1960s 32.00
Book
   Night Before Christmas, Samuel Gabriel Sons & Co., NY, 1947, linenette, 12" h.. 20.00
   Santa Claus In Storyland, pop-up, Doechia Greeting Cards, Fitchburg, MA, 1950, 11" h............................ 25.00
Candy Box
   3" x 4-1/2" x 1-3/4", Santa face, cotton string handle, USA, 1970s............. 6.00
   3-1/2" x 5-1/2" x 2", Merry Christmas, picture of Santa and his workshop, cloth handle, USA, 1940s............ 10.00
Candy Container
   4-1/2" h, red hard plastic, green skis, lollipops in open back on back, USA 10.00
   5-1/2" h, glass, Father Christmas in chimney, metal base, Victory Candy Co. 100.00
   8-1/2" h, papier-mâché, Father Christmas, white mica coat, holding feather tree, early 1900s 500.00
Candy Mold, tin, #427, 4-1/2" h..... 125.00
Chromolithograph, 10" h, standing Santa, tinsel trim, Germany, 1920s........ 45.00
Clicker, 1-1/2" l, green, red, black, and white, Grant's Toy Department, 1930s... 40.00
Cookie Jar
   10-1/2" h, Mickey Mouse wearing Santa hat, c1994, incised "Copyright Disney, Licensed by Enesco Corp".. 95.00
   14" h, Santa Workbench, Lenox, 24K gold trim, hand painted, limited edition, MIB 85.00
Figure
   2-1/2" h, 4-1/2" l, Santa in cardboard sleigh.. 50.00
   3" h, composition face, red chenille body, Japan 15.00
   4" h, hard plastic, Santa on bike, USA, 1960s.. 10.00
   6-1/2" h, composition face, skier, red cloth coat, blue pants, wood skis and poles, Japan 70.00
   6-1/2" h, 7" w, hard plastic, riding reindeer, waving, pink halters, orig bell, fur trim.. 65.00
   10" h, papier-mâché 35.00
   13-1/2" h, hard plastic, small pack in hand, hole for light in back, Union Products, Leominster, MA 20.00
Game, 10" h, Santa Claus Ring Toss, cardboard, First National Bank of Berwick giveaway............................... 12.00
Greeting Card, Santa riding plane over world, Merry Christmas, 1940s 8.00
Lantern
   12" h, chromed metal, battery operated 75.00
   24" h, two piece hard plastic, Santa face fits over outdoor light, early 1960s.. 35.00
Ornament
   3-1/4" h, blown glass, holding tree, German, 1930s 35.00
   4" h, cotton batting, paper face, chenille hanger................................... 15.00
   6" h, blown glass, holding sack, metal clip base, Germany, 1920s......... 55.00
Paint Book, *Santa's Surprise Paint Book,* Merrill Co, 1949, flocked Santa with pack on cover 15.00
Paper Toy, 6-3/4" x 13" diecut stiff paper, figural red, white, and green Santa, wearing Sears belt buckle, diecut eyes and mouth, winking motion tab, reverse with 28 different children from other countries all saying "Merry Christmas" in their native language, Sears Happi-Time Toy Town, copyright 1948... 40.00

Postcard, International Art Publishing Co., Ellen H. Clapsaddle artist, red outfit, $20.

Postcard
   Christmas Greetings, Father Christmas with candlelit tree and toys, German, 1908................................... 12.00
   Merry Christmas, Santa wearing emb green outfit, red ground, carrying presents and tree.......................... 15.00
Push Puppet, Santa, holding bell, mkd "Made in Hong Kong for Kohner"...................................... 60.00
Ramp Walker, hard plastic
   German, cloth coat, orig paper label, 6-1/2" h...................................... 35.00
   Marx, orig package.................... 85.00
Stuffed Doll, Applause, 9" h, plush, 1993, MIB... 70.00
Tin, 4" d, Santa face surrounded by poinsettias, early 1900s 24.00
Toy, 12" h, battery operated, Happy Santa, five actions, Japan......... 235.00

Scouting

Collecting Hints: Nostalgia is one of the principal reasons for collecting Scouting memorabilia; individuals often focus on the period during which they themselves were involved in the Scouting movement. Other collectors select themes, e.g., handbooks, jamborees, writings by scout-movement leaders or Eagle Scout material. Jamboree ephemera is especially desirable. The greatest price fluctuation occurs in modern material and newly defined specialized collecting areas.

Scouting scholars have produced a wealth of well-researched material on the Scouting movement. Many of these pamphlets are privately printed and can be located by contacting dealers specializing in Scouting items.

Girl Scout material is about five to ten years behind Boy Scout material in respect to collecting interest. A Girl Scout collection can still be assembled for a modest investment. While Boy Scout uniforms have remained constant in design throughout time, the Girl Scout uniform changed almost every decade. This increases the number of collectibles.

History: The Boy Scout movement began in America under the direction of William D. Boyce, inspired by a helping hand he received from one of Baden-Powell's English scouts when he was lost in a London fog in 1910. Other American boys' organizations, such as the one organized by Dan Beard, were quickly brought into the Boy Scout movement. In 1916, the Boy Scouts received a charter from the United States Congress. Key leaders in the movement were Ernest Thompson-Seton, Dan Beard, William D. Boyce, and James West. One of Norman Rockwell's first jobs was editor of Boys' Life in 1913, and this began the famous American illustrator's lifelong association with the Boy Scouts.

The first international jamboree was held in England in 1920. America's first jamboree was held in 1937 in Washington, D.C. Manufacturers, quick to recognize the potential for profits, issued a wealth of Boy Scout material. Local councils and Order of the Arrow lodges have added significantly to this base, especially in the area of patches. Around the time of the 1950 National Jamboree, everything from patches to lizards were traded.

The Girl Scout movement began on March 12, 1912, under the direction of Juliette Gordon Low of Savannah, Georgia. The movement grew rapidly, and in 1928 the Girl Scout manual suggested cookies be sold to raise funds. The Girl Scout movement received wide recognition for its activities during World War II, selling more than $3 million worth of bonds in the fourth Liberty Loan drive.

References: George Cuhaj, *Standard Price Guide to U.S. Scouting Collectibles*, 2nd edition, Krause Publications, 2001; Fred Duersch, Jr., *Green Khaki Crimped-Edge Merit Badges*, Downs Printing, 1993; Franck, Hook, Ellis & Jones, *Aid to Collecting Selected Council Shoulder Patches*, privately printed, 2001.

Periodicals: *Fleur-de-Lis*, 5 Dawes Ct, Novato, CA 94947; *Scout Memorabilia Magazine*, c/o Lawrence L. Lee Scouting Museum, P.O. Box 1121, Manchester, NH 03105; *ISCA*, Executive VP Communications, 5410 Fenwood Ave., Woodland Hills, Ca. 91367.

Collectors' Clubs: International Scouting Collectors Association, Inc., Executive VP Communications, 5410 Fenwood Ave., Woodland Hills, Ca. 91367; International Badgers Club, 7760 NW 50th St., Lauder Hill, FL 33351; Scouts on Stamps Society International, 7406 Park Dr., Tampa, FL 33610.

Museums: Girl Scout National Headquarters, New York, NY; Juliette Gordon Low Girl Scout National Center, Savannah, GA; Lawrence L. Lee Scouting Museum and Max J. Silber Scouting Library, Manchester, NH; Lone Scout Memory Lodge, Camp John J. Barnhardt, New London, NC; National Museum of the Boy Scouts of America, Irving, TX; Western Scout Museum, Los Angeles, CA; World of Scouting Museum, Valley Forge, PA.

Advisor: Richard Shields.

Reproduction Alert: Boy Scout jamboree patches, rare Council Shoulder patches, and rare Order of the Arrow patches.

Boy Scouts

Backpack, canvas, New York City logo 15.00
Bear Cub Scout book, 1960-80 .... 1.00
Bolo Tie, 1977 National Jamboree 6.00
Booklet, Philadelphia Enquirer, National Jamboree, 1950 .... 8.00
Campaign Hat (Smokey Bear), felt, leather band, chin strap 50.00

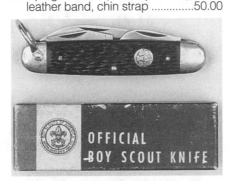

Official Boy Scout knife, Camillus, #1996, brown plastic handles, four blades, original box, $18.

Handbook
    Boys, 1950s 8.00
    Scoutmaster, 6th ed. 3.00
Key Chain, Cub Scout, "Be Square" in promise 3.00

Key Chain Medallion, National Jamboree, 1953 .... 8.00
Medal
    Ad Altare Dei 20.00
    Eagle, blue casket shaped box 100.00
    Eisenhower War Service 20.00
    God and Country, blue ribbon 20.00
Mug, ceramic, white 2.50
Neckerchief, National Jamboree, 1969, red 4.00
Neckerchief Slide
    New York World's Fair, 1964-65 .. 25.00
    Philmont brand, ceramic 3.00
Pamphlet, Merit Badge, full picture, 1950-60s 1.00
Paperback, *The Scout Law in Action*, MacPeek, 1966 .... 5.00
Patch
    Activity, 1960s 1.00
    Camporee, 1960s 1.00
    Historic Trails Award 1.00
    National Jamboree, 1950, canvas pocket 50.00
    National Office, Irving, TX 3.00
    New York World's Fair, 1939 .... 40.00
    Rank, Bear Cub, black on red felt 3.00
    Scout Show, 1960s 1.00
Pin
    First Class, thin metal, World War II era, 2" 50.00
    Fleur-de-lis, universal .... .50
Plate, Beyond the Easel, Rockwell .. 40.00
Pocket Coin, Scout Oath/Law 1.00
Postcard, World Jamboree, U.S., 1967 .... 1.00
Poster, Scout Week, cardboard, 1930s-40s 20.00
Shampoo Bottle, Snoopy Beagle Scout, plastic 20.00
Shirt, Explorer, dark green, circle V design emblem 8.00
Sundial, pocket, metal, orig box 50.00
Utensil Set, three pc, fits together, plastic case 5.00
Wash Basin, clear plastic, orig box . 15.00
Wolf Cub Scout book, 1960-80 .... 1.00

Girl Scouts

Belt, dark green web, trefoil emblem, metal buckle 15.00
Beret, dark green wool, with patch 8.00
Book, *Worlds to Explore*, 1980s 3.00
Camera, Herbert George Co., model 620 .... 50.00
Guide Book, leader's, nature, 1942 . 12.00
Handbook, Brownie, 1964 .... 3.00
Photo Album, dark green cover, small size 25.00
Pin, World Association, crude clasp .. 2.00

Dr. Seuss Collectibles

Collecting Hint: Collectors should learn which companies Seuss did advertising work for. People familiar with his drawings will almost always be able to spot his work, even if his name is not on the piece. It is often difficult to determine if one of his children's books is a first edition. Buyers should be aware of the order in which books were published as well as their original prices. Dr. Seuss also wrote under several pseudonyms including Theo, LeSieg (Geisel spelled backward) and Rosetta Stone. Prices for many Dr. Seuss items are still in a state of flux. The same Coleco plush character can vary in price by as much as $40 in for-sale ads in the same periodical.

History: The collector of Dr. Seuss memorabilia has far more to search for than children's books. Long before the Cat in the Hat first stepped onto the mat, Dr. Seuss had been busy producing cartoons, films, and advertising campaigns.

Dr. Seuss was born Theodor Seuss Geisel in 1904. In the 1920s, he started using his middle name and added the Dr. to the front. He began his career as a freelance illustrator and sent humorous pieces and cartoons to newspapers and magazines. Soon he began to get work in advertising. One of his first accounts was Flit insecticide, a product of Standard Oil of New Jersey. Other advertising work was done for Essolube Motor Oil, Essomarine Products, Ford Motor Co., National Broadcasting Co., Holly Sugar, Narragansett Lager and Ale, Brevo Shaving Cream, and Hankey Bannister Scotch Whiskey. Dr. Seuss won Academy Awards for the documentaries *Hitler Lives* in 1946 and *Design for Death* in 1947 and for the animated cartoon *Gerald McBoing-Boing* in 1951. In 1953, *The 5,000 Fingers of Dr. T* was released by Columbia. Seuss wrote the story, and those familiar with his work will recognize his characters in the movie.

Boners was the first book linked with the name Dr. Seuss. Published in 1931, it was a collection of humorous writings by children which Seuss illustrated. His first children's book was *And to Think I Saw It on Mulberry Street*, which was published in 1937 after it had been rejected by 28 publishing houses. *The Cat in the Hat* was published in 1957. Another famous Seuss work, *Green Eggs and Ham*, is the third-largest-selling book in the English language.

Many of the creatures which would later become famous in his children's works made their first appearance in the advertisements and cartoons that Seuss drew. The forerunner to Horton the kindly elephant first appeared in a 1929 *Judge* magazine.

Dr. Seuss died in 1991. Most of his children's books are still in print and his characters are still licensed to new products including toys and clothing items.

References: Richard Marschall (ed.), *The Tough Coughs as He Ploughs the Dough*, William Morrow and Co. Inc./Remco World Service Books, 1987; Neil and Judith Morgan, *Dr. Seuss and Mr. Geisel: A Biography*, Random House, 1995; *Dr. Seuss from Then to Now*, a catalog of the retrospective exhibition organized by the San Diego Museum of Art, 1986, Random House, 1986; *The Secret Art of Dr. Seuss,* with introduction by Maurice Sendak, Random House, 1995.

Web sites of interest: Random House has an interactive Dr. Seuss web site where children will find activities and can even write a letter to the Cat in the Hat. Events related to the famous cat and Dr. Seuss are often listed: http://www.randomhouse.com/seussville. Another good source is an online listing of the holdings of the University of California, San Diego, Geisel Library, Mandeville Special Collections. The URL is http://orpheus.ucsd.edu/speccoll/collects/seuss.html.

Advisor: Connie Swaim.

Mattel's See'n Say Talking Storybook.

Beer Tray, 12" d, Narragansett Beer, picturing Chief Gansett and Cat, slight rubbing on edges 95.00

Stuffed Grinch figure, from the 2000 movie, "The Grinch," Starring Jim Carrey.

Booklet, *The Log of the Good Ship*, Esso, 37 pgs, Seuss illustrations throughout, excellent condition 175.00
Coaster, 4-1/4" d, Chief Gansett on front, Narragansett Beer advertising on back 20.00
Drinking Glass, Esso Seuss Navy, "Official When Hen," 5-1/4" h 45.00
Figure, stuffed, Cat in the Hat,
Impulse Items Original, 24", slight stains 40.00
Macy's, 1995, excellent, no book 30.00
Lunch Box, 1970, metal, Aladdin Industries, Seuss characters on all sides, plastic handle, light wear consistent with use 85.00
Magazine
Judge, March 23, 1929, color illustration by Seuss on the cover 160.00
McCall's, October, 1970, four pages inside, Mr. Brown Can Moo Like a Cow, Can You? 20.00
Magazine Tear Sheet, talking Seuss toys adv, 1970 .... 5.00
Model, Revell, Gowdy, circa late 1950s, complete with box and instruction sheet 190.00
Plush figure, Coleco, 1983
Cat in the Hat, no box, with umbrella, 24", excellent condition 25.00
Cat in the Hat, with original box, all tags and excellent condition 100.00
Cat in the Hat, 48", excellent condition, body tag 80.00
Grinch, no box, excellent 75.00
The Lorax, no box, excellent 50.00
Thidwick, no box, no tags, excellent 25.00
Premium Booklet, 8" x 11", paper, McElligot's Pool, given away by Crest, Wonder or Prell, 1975 .... 10.00
Puzzle, "Foiled by Essolube," Esso advertising, paper mailing envelope, complete, 150 pieces, very good condition 90.00
Thermos, plastic, for lunch box, excellent condition 40.00

Sewing Items

Collecting Hints: Collectors tend to favor sterling silver items. However, don't overlook pieces made of metal, ivory, celluloid, plastic, or wood. Before buying anything which is metal-plated, be sure the plating is in very good condition.

Advertising and souvenir items are part of sewing history. Focus on one of these aspects to develop a fascinating collection. Other collectors may specialize in a particular instrument, i.e., tape measures. Figural items of any sort have a high value because of their popularity.

Most collectors concentrate on material from the Victorian era. A novice collector might look to the 20th century, especially the Art Deco and Art Nouveau periods, to build a collection.

History: Sewing was considered an essential skill of a young woman of the 19th century. The wealth of early American samplers attests to the talents of many of these young seamstresses.

During the Victorian era, a vast assortment of practical, as well as whimsical, sewing devices appeared on the market. Among these were tape measures, pincushions, stilettos for punchwork, and crochet hooks. The sewing birds attached to table tops were a standard fixture in the parlor.

Many early sewing tools, e.g., needle holders, emery holders and sewing boxes, were made of wood. However, the sterling silver tool was considered the height of elegance. Thimbles were the most popular of these, although sterling silver was used in other devices, particularly the handles of darning eggs, stilettos, and thread holders.

Needle cases and sewing kits were important advertising giveaways in the 20th century. Plastic sewing items are available, but they have not attracted much collector interest.

References: *Advertising & Figural Tape Measures*, L-W Book Sales, 1995; Helen Lester Thompson, *Sewing Tools & Trinkets*, Collector Books, 1997, 2000 value update; Estelle Zalkin, *Zalkin's Handbook of Thimbles & Sewing Implements*, Warman Publishing, 1988, distributed by Krause Publications.

Collectors' Clubs: International Sewing Machine Collectors Society, 1000 E. Charleston Blvd., Las Vegas, NV 89104; National Button Society, 2723 Juno Road, Apt. 4, Akron, OH 44313; Toy Stitchers, 623 Santa Florita Ave., Millbrae, CA 94030.

Museums: Fabric Hall, Historic Deerfield, Deerfield, MA; Sewing Machine Museum, Oakland, CA; Shelburne Museum, Shelburne, VT; Smithsonian Institution, Museum of American History, Washington, DC.

Additional Listings: Thimbles.

Advertising trade card, Singer No. 27-4, advertising on back, 5-1/2" l, 4-1/2" h, $12.

Basket, wicker, round, beaded lid 27.50
Bodkin, 2-1/2" to 3-3/8" l, sterling silver, mkd with intertwined B and U, "Sterling" and "925 fine," set of three..85.00
Book
    American Needlework, 1776-1976, Leslie Tillett, NY Graphic Society, 1975...15.00
    Crewel Embroidery in England, Joan Edwards, Wm Morrow, NY, 1974, 248 pgs, color and black and white drawings...34.75
    Designs in Patchwork, Dianne Logan, Oxmoor House, 1987, 143 pgs...15.00
    Gloria Vanderbuilt designs for your Home, 1077, 1st edition, dj 10.00
    Terrace Hill Needlepoint Designs, Orig Designs from Iowa Governor's Mansion, Billie Ray, 1980, sgd............10.00
    The Ornamental Branches Needlework and Arts from the Lititz Moravia Girls' School Between 1800 and 1865, Patricia T. Herr, Heritage Center Museum, Lancaster, PA, 1996, sgd by author, 87 pgs, color and black and white photos..............................36.75
Brooch, sewing machine shape, spool of thread, scissors and heart with Ladies Auxiliary VFW emblem, silvertone 30.00
Button
    Abalone, cut and polished, 3/4" d 12.00
    Bakelite, all colors, 12 on orig card 85.00
    Celluloid, figural, grape cluster, plastic shank, purple, blue, and green grapes, blue-green leaves 5.00
    Celluloid, figural, orange, plastic shank, brown leaf, orange body ...4.50
    Copper, man's head shape, 1/2" x 3/4", set of four 70.00
    Glass, cylinder shape, white, 1/2" l, 1/2" w 8.00

    Glass, honeycomb, black, early 1900s, set of six 5/8" d, one 1/2" d, two mkd "Costumaker" 30.00
    Glass, sweetheart shape, red, blue enameled zig-zag center, 1/4" 6.00
    Jade, green, floral, Qing Dynasty, 1-1/4" d 68.00
    Mother of Pearl, cut design, 1-3/8" d 8.00
    Plastic, figural, bowling pin, self shank, navy blue, 1/2" d, set of six 10.00
    Plastic, knot, metal stems, gray, 3/4" d, five buttons on orig card mkd "Costumakers Trade Mark, Made in U.S.A.," number stamped on back 10.00
    Rhinestone, black plastic backing, orig card with four buttons mkd "B. Blumenthal & Co., New York, NY" 8.00
    Silvertone, light blue rhinestones, 1-1/4" d 12.00
Button Display Card, The Ball & Socket Manufacturing Co., for Uniform Buttons, including buttons of Cardin, Paris; American Airlines; Western Union Pacific Railroad; Fire Department, etc., consisting of card and 25 buttons 70.00
Catalog
    Davis Sewing Machine Co., Watertown, NY, 1881, 64 pgs, 5-1/2" x 8-3/4", cover wear 24.00
    New Home Sewing Machine, New York, NY, c1900, 12 pgs, 3-3/4" x 6-1/4" 12.00
    Ormond Manufacturing Co., Baltimore, MD, 1878, 96 pgs, 4-1/2" x 5-3/4" 73.00
    United Thread Mills, New York, NY, c1930, 7 pgs, 6-3/4" x 10" 18.00
    White Sewing Machine, Cleveland, OH, c1923, 16 pgs, 3-1/2" x 6" ... 24.00
    Wilson Sewing Machine Co., Chicago, IL, pre-1900, 26 pgs, 6" x 9"........38.00
Clamp, wood, painted, pin cushion, cupid decal 115.00
Crochet Hook, metal, capped 15.00
Darning Egg, 4-1/4" l, 1-1/2" w egg, ebony, sterling silver handle, stamped "Sterling" on both sides 90.00
Dress Buckle
    3" x 2", sterling silver and turquoise, mkd "E. King Sterling"................. 40.00
    3" x 2-1/2", plastic, Art Deco, cream and black.................................... 28.00
Folder, full color, 4" x 5"
    Singer/Mother's Helper, The Handy Extension Leaf, copyright 1899, int. describes "The Light-Running Singer Sewing Machine No. 28," lightly browned...................................... 12.00
    The Refinement of Needlework, The Singer Automatic, c1900, describes "The Singer Automatic" and "The Singer Cabinet-Table," lightly browned...................................... 12.00
Hem Gauge, 4-3/4" l, poinsettias dec, mkd "Sterling," some corrosion on back... 95.00
Magazine
    McCalls, 1969, 8-1/4" x 11-1/4"..... 8.00
    Workbasket and Home Arts Magazine, 1976, 12 issues 10.00

Needle Book
Liberty National Life Insurance Company, Birmingham, Alabama, Statue of Liberty on front, 1 needle packet.. 7.50
Sears Roebuck and Co, A Gift to you from Kenmore - Fine Needlework, Japan 9.00
Sewing Circle, four ladies sewing, six needle packets and threader....... 10.00
Sewing Susan, Japan, four needle packets and threader, Japan...... 10.00
Sew Smart, Japan 9.00
The National Life and Accident Insurance Company Shields You, int. reads "A Stitch in Time Saves Nine -Presented by The Shield Man," 3" x 3" shield shape 9.00
Traveler, illus of two children and mother sewing, six needle packets and threader 9.00
Needle Case
Adv, Formamint, metal, adv "Wulfing's Formamint for Sore Throat" on side, mkd "Germany" on bottom, 2" h . 10.00
Barrel Shape, Piccadilly, wood, 3" h, 1-1/4" d 85.00
Needle Gripper, Nimble Thimble, orig package 20.00
Needle Sharpener
Cat 50.00
Strawberry 9.00
Photograph, cabinet photo of young man posed beside New York sewing machine, photographer's scenic backdrop, no photographer identified, 4-1/4" x 6-1/2" 15.00
Pin Cushion
Apple, satin, red and yellow, green leaves and stem, 2-1/2" h, 3" d ... 65.00
Calico Dog, holding flower pin cushion, mkd "Made in Japan," 3" l, 2-1/4" h 30.00

Pin cushion, white metal cat figure, pink cushion, 5-1/4" l, $135.

Calico Donkey, pulling club card sit pin cushion holder, mkd "Made in Japan," 3-3/4" l, 2-1/8" h 32.00
Doll face, bisque, blue glass eyes, blond hair, open mouth with teeth, mounted on purple orchid, orig box, German, 5" h, 5-1/2" w, ... 90.00
Round, pale orange satin, strawberry, mkd "Japan" 10.00
Strawberry, red velvet, green felt leaves, c1870, 5" h, 3" w 90.00
Pin Holder, adv, Prudential 10.00
Scissors, emb florals on handle, German 30.00
Sewing Bird, hand held, sgd "Turner" 80.00
Sewing Caddy
4" x 3-1/2", wood, red stain, three spools 28.00
8-1/2" h, figural chair, hand made, ply-

wood, drawer in front, scissors holder on back of chair, thimble holders on side, pin cushion seat 48.00
Sewing Machine, full size, working condition
Singer Featherweight 300.00
Wheeler & Wilson, treadle, c1871, flat belt, partial instruction manual, accessories 800.00
Sewing Machine, toy, working condition
Gateway Junior, Model NP-1, mkd "Gateway Engineering Company, Chicago, 51, Ill," stamped metal, some wear, needle missing, orig instruction sheet and box 85.00
Kay-an-EE, pink, mkd "Made in Germany, Berlin, U.S. Zone" 90.00
Singer, Little Touch & Sew, battery operated, plastic base cabinet, 26" h, 22-1/2" w, 12-1/2" d, some minor parts missing, wear 90.00
Spool Cabinet, JP Coats, metal, black, glass slant front 125.00
Tape Measure, figural
Apple, hard plastic, red, leaf pull 24.00
Clock, metal, hands turn, mkd "Germany" 125.00
Dress form 50.00
Fish, celluloid 30.00
Little Boy, clown hat, mkd "Germany" 45.00
Thimble Case
Brass, walnut 25.00
Crocheted 10.00
Sweet Grass 30.00
Thread Holder, 3-1/2" h, thimble top, red celluloid top, hand painted floral pattern 38.00
Tie Tac, men's, goldtone, zipper pull, mkd "Talon" 5.00
Tracing Paper, Singer, unopened back, c1960 .... 4.00
Travel Kit, 2" l, metal case, thimble as lid, wooden tube with needs and thread on outside, adv "J. B. Best & Co., Clothing & Shoes Since 1919, Woodville, Texas, Patent No. 2084780" 18.00
Zipper Pull
1-1/8" h, tassel, Bakelite, butterscotch, orig metal attachment 8.50
1-1/2" d, Mexican Hat, wood, hole at edge of brim, brightly colored 8.50

Shawnee Pottery

Collecting Hints: Many Shawnee pieces came in several color variations. Some pieces were both painted and decorated with decals. The available literature indicates some, but not all, of the variations.

Shawnee also produced artware and dinnerware lines. These include Cameo, Cheria (Petit Point), Diora, and Touche (Liana). New collectors might consider concentrating in one of these areas.

Shawnee pieces were marked "Shawnee," "Shawnee U.S.A.," "USA

#___," "Kenwood," or with character names, e.g., "Pat. Smiley" and "Pat. Winnie."

History: The Shawnee Pottery Co. was founded in 1937 in Zanesville, Ohio. The company acquired a 650,000-square-foot plant that had previously housed the American Encaustic Tiling Company. Shawnee produced as many as 100,000 pieces of pottery a day until 1961, when the plant closed.

Shawnee limited its production to kitchenware, decorative art pottery, and dinnerware. Distribution was primarily through jobbers and chain stores.

References: Jim and Bev Mangus, *Shawnee Pottery*, Collector Books, 1994, 2000 value update; Mark Supnick, *Collecting Shawnee Pottery*, L-W Book Sales, 2000; Duane and Janice Vanderbilt, *Collector's Guide to Shawnee Pottery*, Collector Books, 1992, 1998 value update.

Collectors' Club: Shawnee Pottery Collectors Club, P.O. Box 713, New Smyrna Beach, FL 32170.

Bank
Smiley, brown 550.00
Winnie, butterscotch 600.00
Bookends, pr, cattails and ducks 75.00
Bowl, 8-3/4" l, oval, Corn King, #95 . 45.00
Butter Dish, cov, 7" l, Corn King, mkd "#72, Oven Proof" 165.00
Casserole, cov
Corn King, large, mkd "Shawnee USA Oven Proof 74" 90.00
Lobster, 4-3/4" h, 11-1/4" l, 8" w, mkd "Oven Proof, USA Kenwood" 70.00
Cookie Jar
Dutch Boy, 11" h 200.00
Dutch Girl, tulip on skirt, mkd "USA" 250.00
Mugsy, 11-1/4" h, blue scarf, gold trim, mkd "Shawnee Mugsy, Patented, USA" 795.00
Puss & Boots 180.00
Smiley Pig, red bandana with chrysanthemums, mkd "USA" 475.00
Smiley Pig, shamrocks dec, gold trim, mkd "USA" 450.00
Corn Dish, Corn King, oval 25.00
Creamer
Cat, yellow and green 55.00
Corn King, #70 .... 25.00
Elephant 35.00
Puss N Boots 90.00
Smiley Pig, mkd "Shawnee USA 86" 165.00
Creamer and Sugar, Corn King 85.00
Cup, Corn King, #90 .... 20.00
Figure, deer 300.00
Fruit Dish, 6" d, Corn King, #92 .... 40.00
Incense Burner, 5" h, Chinaman, blue base, mkd "USA" 30.00

Jardiniere, 3-3/4" h, 4-1/4" w, muted orange, orig silver and red Shawnee sticker..15.00
Lamp, 12" h, pottery, orig shades, price for pr...175.00
Marmalade, cov, Fruits.....................40.00
Mixing Bowl, Corn King
  5" d, #5....................................40.00
  6-1/4" d...................................45.00
Mug, Corn King, 8 oz, #69..............45.00
Pie Bird, 5-1/2" h, yellow, made for Pillsbury..75.00
Pitcher
  Bo Peep, 1940s, mkd "Patented Bo Peep USA"..................................145.00
  Chanticleer.............................325.00
  Corn King, #71.........................70.00
  Fruits, juice..............................50.00
  Smiley Pig, 7-3/4" h, burgundy and blue flowers, mkd "Patented Smiley, USA"..170.00
Planter
  Dog and Jug.............................22.00
  Giraffe and baby, brown and rust...65.00
  Pixie Boot, green, gold trim.........15.00
  Polynesian Girl, 5-3/4" h, #896....35.00
  Pup, three button shoe, ivory......18.00
  Train, three pc, caboose, coal car, and engine..150.00
  Wishing Well, Dutch boy and girl...20.00
Plate
  8" d, Corn King..........................40.00
  9-1/2" d, Corn King, #68..............37.50
Platter, 12" l, Corn King, #96.............50.00
Range Shakers, pr
  Boy and Girl, 5" h.......................50.00
  Dutch Boy and Girl, large............95.00
  Mugsy.....................................245.00
  Pig, green bib............................125.00
  Rooster, 5-1/2" h........................50.00
Relish Tray, Corn King, #79..............40.00
Salad Plate, Corn King, #93.............40.00
Salt and Pepper Shakers, pr
  Bo Peep and Sailor.....................45.00
  Cats, orig paper labels...............85.00
  Corn King, tall............................35.00
  Dutch Boy and Girl......................95.00
  Mugsy
    Large....................................175.00
    Small....................................125.00
  Owls..75.00
  Puss n' Boots............................75.00
  Smiley and Winnie, 3-1/4" h, red heart on Winnie's hat and pocket.........95.00
  Swiss Children, 5" h, gold trim....75.00
  Watering Can, 2-1/4"...................45.00
Saucer, Corn King, #91....................20.00
Soup Bowl, Corn King, #94..............55.00
Spoon Holder
  Flower Pot, patent pending.........15.00
  Window Box, patent pending.....15.00
Sugar, Bowl, cov, Corn King...........42.00
Sugar Shaker, White Corn...............55.00
Teapot, cov
  Corn King, individual size.........325.00
  Granny Anne, peach apron......150.00
  Tom The Piper's Son..................115.00
Vase
  Bowknot, green...........................20.00

Dove, yellow, #829......................32.00
Wall Pocket, wheat...........................40.00
Water Pitcher, 7" h, 6-1/2" d, ball jug type, emb fruit design, yellow ground, mkd "Shawnee USA".........................135.00

Sheet Music

Collecting Hints: Pick a theme for your collection: show tunes, songs of World War I, Sousa marches, African-American material, songs of a certain lyricist or composer—the list is endless.

Be careful about stacking sheets on top of one another because the ink on the covers tends to bleed. The ideal solution is to place acid-free paper between each cover and sheet.

Unfortunately, tape was often used to repair tears in old sheet music, resulting in discoloration. This detracts from value. Seek professional help in removing tape from rarer sheets.

History: Sheet music, especially piano scores, dates to the early 19th century. The early music contains some of the finest examples of lithography. Much of this music was bound into volumes.

The covers of sheet music chronicle the social, political, and historical trends of all eras. The golden age of the hand-illustrated cover dates to around 1885. Leading artists such as James Montgomery Flagg used their talents to illustrate sheet music. Cover art work was critical to helping a song sell.

Once radio and talking pictures became popular, covers featured the stars. A song sheet might be issued in dozens of cover versions, each picturing a different personality. By the 1950s, piano playing no longer was popular and song sheets failed to maintain a high quality of design.

Reference: Anna Marie Guiheen and Marie-Reine A. Pafik, *Sheet Music Reference and Price Guide*, 2nd ed., Collector Books, 1995, values updated 2000.

Periodical: *The Rag Times*, 15522 Ricky Court, Grass Valley, CA 95949.

Collectors' Clubs: City of Roses Sheet Music Collectors Club, 13447 Bush St. SE, Portland, OR 97236; National Sheet Music Society, 1597 Fair Park Ave., Los Angeles, CA 90041; New York Sheet Music Society, P.O. Box 354, Hewlett, NY 11557;

Remember That Song, 5623 N. 64th St., Glendale, AZ 85301; Sonneck Society for American Music & Music in America, P.O. Box 476, Canton, MA 02021.

***Over the Rainbow*, Wizard of Oz, E. Y. Harbur, lyrics, Harold Arlen, music, cast photos and drawings, 1939, $25.**

Ain't You Coming Out Malinda? 1921, by Andrew Sterling, Edward Moran, and Harry Vontilizer, cover photo of Gus Van and Joe Schenck.................10.00

America I Love You, 1915, Tom Ward and Dolly McCue on cover with sketches of Statue of Liberty, Indian chief, covered wagon, Liberty Bell, pilgrims, farmer, New York City.................12.00

Archie's Little Love Song, Hoagy Carmichael and Ed "Archie" Gardner, © 1946...10.00

Battle of the Nations, "Companion Piece to the Celebrated Napoleon's Last Charge Descriptive March," E. T. Pauli, c1915, typical Pauli cover with chaotic battle scene with biplane, dirible, horses, cannons, flags and symbols for France, Belgium, Japan, Austria-Hungary, Germany, Turkey, and Russia...48.00

Carioca, 1933, movie "Flying Down to Rio," Fred Astaire and Dolores Del Rio cov.......................................9.00

Childhood Days Are Dear to Me, 1910, man looking into mirror with reflection as young boy, insert oval photo of Paulina Parks.............................10.00

Clicquot Fox Trot March, 1926, blue, white, and orange cover with Clicquot Club and trademark Eskimo boy, 6 pgs, 8" x 12"................................18.00

Comin' In On A Wing And A Prayer, 1943, Eddie Cantor and plane on cover...10.00

Country Style, Bing Crosby, Joan Caulfield, and Barry Fitzgerald on cover, 1947, Paramount, "Welcome Stranger" 10.00

Dawn of the Century, E. T. Pauli 48.00

Der Furherer's Face, Donald Duck ..35.00

Dope, Rag Novelties Two Step, 1908, blue, white, and orange cover, six pgs, 10" x 13" 12.00

Down in Jungle Town, African hut, 1908 .... 9.00

Enjoy Yourself (It's Later Than You Think), 1948, Guy Lombardo cover 9.50

Eatin' Time Rag, Irene Cozad, published c1913 by J. W. Jenkins Sons' Music Co., Kansas City 80.00

Everybody Two-Step Rag, by Wallie Herzer, published by Jerome H. Remick & Co; 1912, caricature of black man in checked suit, top hat, banjo 40.00

For Once in My Life, Stevie Wonder on cover, 1965 .... 9.00

Happy Go Lucky, Mary Martin, Dick Powell, Betty Hutton, Eddie Bracken, and Rudy Vallee 18.00

Harold Teen Songsheet, movie poster graphics cover, 1934 .... 45.00

Hop Scotch Polka, 1949, Gene Rayburn and Dee Finch in nightcaps, radio mike WNEW, caricature of two children in plaid playing hop scotch 10.00

Humpty Dumpty Heart, 1941, Kay Kyser, John Barrymore, Lupe Velez, Ginny Simms on cover dancing 9.25

If You Were But A Dream, Frank Sinatra on cover, 1941 .... 10.00

I Got The Sun In The Morning, Ethel Merman cover 9.00

I'm Drifting Back to Dreamland, 1922, Benson Orchestra, Chicago 8.50

I'm Sitting High On A Hill Top, Dick Powell, Fred Allen, Paul Whiteman, Ann Dvorak, Rubinoff, and Patsy Kelly, 1935, 20th Century Fox Production "Thanks A Million" 10.00

It Takes A Little Rain, boy and girl cover, 1913 .... 8.00

I Won't Dance, 1935, RKO Picture "Roberta," Fred Astaire, Ginger Rogers and Irene Dunn on cov 10.00

Just You, Just Me, 1929, soldiers and Marion Davies on cover, MGM "Marianne" 9.00

Lavender Blue (Dilly Dilly), Morey & Daniel, 1948 .... 10.00

Little Old Lady, 1936, Beatrice Lillie and Bert Lahr on cover 9.50

Lullaby Land, 1919, little girl, standing in surf 8.50

Ma Riza Love, The Warmest Yet-A Rag-Time Sensation, Frank S. Snyder, published 1899 by Norwood Publishing Co., Minneapolis 42.00

Muddy Waters, A Mississippi Moan, 1926, Nora Bayes on cover, lagoon background 10.00

Old Black Joe, Beaux Arts edition, 1906 .... 9.00

Old Folks at Home, composed by Stephen C. Foster, published by National Music Co., bluetone sketch on cover of old home, wear and soiling 8.50

Piccolino, 1935, RKO Picture "Top Hat," Fred Astaire and Ginger Rogers on cover 9.00

Pick Yourself Up, 1936, RKO "Swing Time," Fred Astaire and Ginger Rogers cov 10.00

Plantation Echoes, "Respectfully Dedicated to the Misses Drisiane," Otto M. Heinzman, c1899, cover with Southern river plantation, young dancing couple, banjo player, figures sitting around cotton bales, river boat 90.00

Plantation Melodies, arranged by Eugene Walter, 1905, several songs 8.50

Please, 1932, by Leo Robin and Ralph Ringer, Paramount "The Big Broadcast," cover montage with Bing Crosby, Burns & Allen, Cab Calloway, Boswell Sisters, Mills Brothers, Vincent Lopez, Kate Smith, Leila Hyams, Stuart Erwin, and Arthur Tracy 12.00

Rag-A-Tag Rag, Al W. Brown, published c1910 by Leo Feist, NY, five page instrumental 48.00

Ragging the Scale, Ed Claypoole 48.00

Ring Out Wild Bells, E. T. Pauli, c1912 .... 45.00

Rudolph the Red-Nosed Reindeer, 1949, sketch of Santa, sleigh, and reindeer 8.50

San Fernando Valley, I'm Packing My Grip, 1953, Bing Crosby cover 9.50

Seventh Heaven, 1937, Simone Simon and Jimmy Stewart 10.00

Something To Remember You By, 1930 .... 9.00

Sound Off, Duckworth Chant, Willie Lee Duckworth, 1950, sketch of army sergeant yelling on cover, Vaughn Monroe insert photo 10.00

Tam O'Shanter, 1909 .... 8.50

The Army Air Corps, Official Song of the United States Army Air Corps., 1939, logo, red, white and blue, "Buy War Bonds" stamp on cover 10.00

The Circus Parade, E. T. Pauli, c1904 .... 60.00

The Masquerade, March Two Step, E. T. Pauli, c1907 .... 55.00

There's A Girl in the Heart of Maryland, 1913 .... 9.00

There's a Mother Old and Gray Who Need Me Now, Harold Rossiter Music Co. 20.00

The Roaring Volcano, E. T. Pauli, c1912 .... 95.00

The Waltz In Swing Time, 1936, RKO "Swing Time," Fred Astaire and Ginger Rogers on cover 9.00

Topsy's In Town, Warner Crosby, published 1899 by Arthur W. Tams, five-page instrumental 45.00

Victory Polka, 1943, red, white, and blue cover with stars and "V" symbol ...8.00

Waiting For the Robert E. Lee, 1912 .... 10.00

We've Only Just Begun, 1970, full-color cover of the Carpenters 9.00

When the Daisies Bloom, 1909, field of daisies cover, insert photo of young girl 9.00

Will You Remember, 1944, Nelson Eddy & J. McDonald 10.00

Yip-i-addy-i-ay, 1908 .... 9.50

You Belong To My Heart, 1945, Disney movie "The Three Caballeros," by Augustin Lara and Ray Gilbert, Aurora Miranda, Carmen Molina, and Dora Luz on front cover, back cover with signed photo of Andy Russell 12.00

Shelley China

Collecting Hints: The familiar Shelley mark—a script signature in a shield—was used as early as 1910 even though the firm's name was still Wileman & Co. Dainty White was one of the company's most popular shapes, and pieces are, therefore, relatively easy to acquire.

History: While the Shelley family has been producing pottery since the mid-1880s, it wasn't until 1925 that the company bore the family name. Joseph Shelley and James Wileman became partners in 1872, operating their pottery under the name Wileman & Company. Joseph's son, Percy, joined the company in 1881 and assumed full control after his father's death in 1896. It was under Percy's direction that the company introduced its most popular shapes— Dainty White, Intarsio, Queen Anne, and Vogue.

Percy's three sons became involved in the business following World War I. During the 1920s and 1930s, the pottery produced miniatures, heraldic and souvenir china, Parian busts of military figures, tea wares, and nursery items, in addition to its fine dinnerware lines. Percy retired in 1932. After World War II, the company concentrated solely on its dinnerware lines. In 1965, the firm's name was changed to Shelley China Ltd. The Shelley family ties to the company were severed in 1966 when Allied English Potteries took control. Allied merged with the Doulton Group in 1971.

References: Chris Davenport, *Shelley Pottery, The Later Years*, Heather Publications, 1997; Robert Prescott Walker, *Collecting Shelley Pottery*, Francis Joseph Publications, 1997.

Collectors' Club: National Shelley China Club, 5585 NW. 164th Ave., Portland, OR 97229.

Children's dishes, Little Red Riding Hood bowl, Three Bears plate, bowl, and pitcher, The Babes in the Wood baby dish, sold together for $550. Photo courtesy of Joy Luke Fine Art Brokers and Auctioneers.

Bowl, 10" d, 3" h, satin glaze, abstract design 150.00
Bread and Butter Plate, Rock Garden .... I 15.00
Cake Plate
  Begonia, Dainty shape, #13427 ....215.00
  Blue Bubbles, slight wear 150.00
  Charm, #13752, Richmond shape, 10" x 9", tab handles trimmed in gold 90.00
Child's Plate, "Little Blue Bird, How He Sings, So Happy on My Plates and Things," Mabel Lucie Attwell illus, 7" d 150.00
Coffee Pot, Chintz, 7-1/2" h 300.00
Creamer and Sugar, Meisenette 95.00
Cream Soup, Sheraton, pattern #13291, double handles, 6-1/2" d saucer 85.00
Cream Soup and Saucer, Begonia, ribbed, #13427 ....170.00
Cup and Saucer
  Anemone, #12879, Henley shape 75.00
  Bananas, Queen Anne shape, black print, blue and yellow enamel, #11562 ....145.00
  Country Garden, #2500, Ludlow shape 85.00
  Crochet, Henley shape, mauve, reverse white dec 100.00
  Dainty Blue.....................................85.00
  Daffodil, #13677, Henley shape .85.00
  Footed Oleander, stocks transfer dec, green and pink ribbon border, c1940 ....225.00
  Lily of the Valley, Athol shape......95.00
  Maytime, #13452, Henley shape, beige trim 155.00
  Morning Glory, Dainty shape 85.00
  Orange 170.00
  Primrose, #13430, Richmond shape, oversized 80.00
  Red Daisy, Queen Anne shape, #11326 ....145.00
  Scilla, #2511 ....85.00
  Shamrock 85.00
  Sunrise and Tall Trees, Queen Anne shape, #11678..........................185.00

Syringa, Dainty shape 85.00
Demitasse Cup and Saucer
  Begonia, pattern #13427, Dainty shape, tall 85.00
  Dainty Blue, tall cup.....................95.00
  Duchess 80.00
  Red Rose and Daisy, #12425, tall 85.00
  Rosebud, #13291, Dainty shape, tall 85.00
  Sheraton, #13291........................90.00
Dinner Plate
  Dainty Blue............................... 175.00
  Harebell, 10-3/4" d 70.00
  Rose Spray, #13545.................. 190.00
Eggcup
  Charm, #13752, ftd.....................95.00
  Rose 18.00
Gravy Boat and Underplate, Dainty Blue 525.00
Luncheon Plate, Blue Rock, 8-1/4" d 75.00
Mocha Cup and Saucer, Primrose, #13430, 2-1/2" h cup 90.00
Pin Dish, 4 3/4" d, Primrose, pink edge trim...95.00
Platter
  Serenity, #13791, medium........ 210.00
  Serenity, #13791, small............. 210.00
  Sheraton, #13289 ....170.00
Salad Bowl, Drifting Leaves, R13848 .... 175.00
Salad Plate, Woodland, #13348, 8" d..80.00
Souvenir Plate, Bermuda, powder blue print and border "The Bermudas, Admiral Sir George Somers, Wrecked on the Island 1909," mkd "Fine Bone China, Shelley England, Made especially for H. A. & E. Smith, Ltd. Hamilton, Bermuda," 1959, 4-3/4" d.....45.00
Sugar Bowl, cov, Drifting Leaves, R13848 .... 140.00
Teapot, cov
  Begonia................................... 175.00
  Rosebud, Dainty shape, #13426 .... 395.00
Tea Set, Woodlands, cov teapot, plate, two cups and saucers, milk jug, sugar bowl 750.00
Toothpick Holder, Stocks, 2-1/8" h, 2-1/8" d 70.00
Trio, cup, saucer, and plate
  Art Deco, Vogue shape, white, green banding...................................200.00
  Begonia.................................... 125.00
  Bowl of Fruit, Queen Anne shape, #11566, 1927, black print, coral, yellow, pink, and purple enamel, orange edge 150.00
  Charm, #13752, Richmond shape, 6" plate...75.00
  Wileman, #3730, 6-1/2" d plate, c1898 .... 275.00
Vase
  3-1/2" h, 3-1/2" d base, Japanese Lake Scene, #4142............................ 150.00
  8-1/4" h, hand painted storks, c1930, backstamp "Shelley, Made in England"....................................125.00

Vegetable, open, oval, Sheraton, #13289...................................... 135.00

Slot Machines

Collecting Hints: Check the laws in your state. Some states permit the collecting of slot machines manufactured prior to 1941, while other states allow the collecting of all machines 25 years old or older, provided that they are not used for gambling. A few states prohibit ownership of any gambling machine.

A complete slot machine is one that is in working order, has no wood missing on the case and no cracked castings. Restoration work to improve appearance can cost from $100 to more than $1,000. The average restoration includes plating of all castings, refinishing the cabinet, repainting the castings to the original colors, rebuilding the mechanism, tuning up the operation of the mechanism, and adding new reel strips and award card. A quality restoration will increase the value of a machine by $400 to $800. A guarantee usually is given when a restored machine is purchased from a dealer.

Most collectors stay away from foreign machines, primarily because foreign coins are hard to find. Machines that have been converted to accept American coins frequently jam or do not pay out the correct amount.

Condition, rarity, and desirability are all very important in determining the value of a machine. Try to find one that is in as close to new condition as possible since "mint original" machines will resell for at least the same amount as restored machines.

The past few years have shown how the age of collectors and their interests can change a collecting field. The Baby Boomers surely desire the forties and fifties and not the earlier style slots.

History: The Liberty Bell, the first three-reel slot machine, was invented in 1905 by Charles Fey in San Francisco. Only three of these can be accounted for, and one of them is housed at the Liberty Bell Saloon, the inventor's grandson's restaurant in Reno, Nevada.

In 1910, the classic fruit symbols were copyrighted by Mills Novelty Company. They were immediately copied by other manufacturers. The first symbols still are popular on contemporary casino machines. The wood cabinet was replaced by cast iron in 1916. By 1922, aluminum fronts were the norm for most machines, and in 1928, the jackpot was added.

Innovations of the 1930s included more reliable and improved mechanisms with more sophisticated coin entry, and advanced slug detection systems. In the 1940s, drill-proof and cheat-resistant devices were added. Electronics, including electronic lighting, were introduced in the 1950s.

Although the goosenecks of the 1920s and 1930s often are more intricate and rarer than the models of the 1930s and 1940s, the gimmickry and beauty of machines of the latter period, such as Rolatop, Treasury, Kitty or Triplex, bring more money.

References: Jerry Ayliffe, *American Premium Guide to Jukeboxes and Slot Machines*, 3rd ed., Books Americana, 1991; Richard M. Bueschel, *Collector's Guide to Vintage Coin Machines*, Schiffer Publishing, 1995; ——, *Lemons, Cherries and Bell-Fruit-Gum,* Royal Bell Books (5815 W 52nd Ave., Denver, CO 80212), 1995; Marshal Fey, Slot Machines: *A Pictorial History of the First 100 Years*, 4th ed., published by author; David L. Saul and Daniel R. Mead, *Slot Machine Buyer's Handbook*, 2nd ed., Mead Publishing Co., 1998.

Periodicals: *Antique Amusements, Slot Machines & Jukebox,* 909 26th St. NW, Washington, DC 20037; *Coin-Op Newsletter,* 909 26th St., NW, Washington, DC 20037.

Museum: Liberty Belle Saloon and Slot Machine Collection, Reno, NV.

Notes: All machines listed are priced as if they are in good condition, meaning the machine is complete and working. An incomplete or non-working machine is worth only 30 to 70 percent of the listed price.

Machines listed are those which accept nickels or dimes. Quarter and 50¢-piece machines can run several hundred dollars more. A silver-dollar machine, if you are lucky enough to find one, can cost $400 to $800 more than those listed.

Advisor: Bob Levy.

Bally, Double Bell, 1936, only all mechanical unit produced 5,000.00
Bones, 1937, very desirable auto payout dice machine 5,500.00
Buckley, Criss-Cross, c1948, revamp of 1946 Mills "Golden Falls," Art Deco styling, guaranteed jackpot window 1,500.00
Caille
　Cadet, c1934, Art Deco style 700.00
　Centaur, c1904, single wheel upright floor model, superb cast iron feet and dec 15,000.00

Superior Jackpot, c1928, first counter-top machine during Depression to make a jackpot 1,500.00
Dewey, 1896, upright single wheel payout 10,000.00
Jennings
　Little Duke, c1932, most unusual in that reels spin concentrically, Art Deco style 2,000.00
　One Star Chief, c1936, large bronze Indian head on front, hunting Indian scene at bottom 1,800.00
　Standard Chief, c1946, chrome face, first basic slot after WW II 1,500.00
　Sun Chief, c1948, illuminated colored front panels, introduced for the glitz of Las Vegas 2,500.00
Mills
　Black Cherry, c1946, silver and black painted, raised red cherries .. 1,500.00
　Castle front, c1939, golden age machine 1,800.00
　Diamond front, c1938, ten raised diamonds on chrome front 1,600.00
　Golden Falls, c1946, gold and black painted, raised red cherries .. 1,600.00
　Jewel Hightop, c1948, colorful, bright, wringle-painted design in car-like style 1,70.00
　Operator Owl, c1925, classic gooseneck coin entry 1,400.00
　War Eagle, c1931, very colorful, often reproduced, price for vintage model 1,800.00
Pace
　Bantam, 1928, three-quarter size counter machine 1,300.00
　Comet, c1935, fancy front, Art Deco style 1,600.00
　Harrahs Club Special, c1962, all chrome plated 900.00
Watling
　Blue Seal, 1931 .... 1,200.00
　Rolatop Coin Front, c1937 ..... 4,000.00
　Treasury, c1936, extremely ornate, raised gold coins top and front castings 4,000.00

Snowdomes

Collecting Hints: There are two distinct types of snowdomes: 3- to 4-inch leaded-glass balls set on ceramic, plastic, wood, or "marble" bases; and plastic figurals averaging 2-1/2 inches in height, with plastic globes in shapes ranging from simple designs, such as drums, cubes, and bottles, to elaborate figurals. There are also two kinds of figurals. In one, the design incorporates the entire object, including the water ball. In the other, a plastic figurine sits on top of the dome.

Either type of snowdome can be collected by any number of subgroups or themes, e.g., Christmas (probably the most familiar), tourist souvenirs, Biblical scenes, Disney

and other cartoon characters, commercial advertisements, fairy tales, scenic railroads, famous buildings, sailing ships, geographic regions, or states (the goal being to collect one from each of the 50). There are also snowdomes with a variety of novelty features such as battery-powered flashing lights which illuminate the inner scene, salt and pepper snowdomes, those with perpetual calendars or banks included in the base, and pieces that contain water/ring toss games. Some snowdomes have parts that move: a seesaw, bobbing objects attached to strings, or small objects that move back and forth on a groove in the bottom of the dome. The objects themselves range from ferries to buses to Elvis Presley figures.

Value rests primarily on the physical condition of the paperweight itself and the condition of the water inside. Make sure there are no cracks in ceramic bases or in the globes themselves, check the condition of the label (if there is one) and the figurine, determine whether the paint has chipped or the colors seem faded, and be certain that the scene inside is not obscured by any streaking on the front of the dome.

The most common snowdomes do not have a specific label on the base, but do have a single figurine and a glass, ceramic, or Bakelite base. If the only difference between two snowdomes is the existence of a decal on the base identifying one as a "Souvenir of _____," the one with the decal is more valuable because a smaller number of that exact item would have been made. The same figurine was probably used for any number of places, and there is often no connection between the object and the place. An incongruous match-up may have value to a particular collector but would not necessarily affect the market price. Of greater value are those snowdomes which were obviously made for a specific place or event, where the object and the decal match, e.g., the ceramic-base snowdome containing a bisque Trylon and Perisphere and a "1939 Worlds Fair" decal.

While mismatched figurines and decals of the glass/ceramic style should not have a higher price than logical match-ups, there are many examples of obvious mistakes in the plastic snowdomes. These are worth more than a perfect one, e.g., a dome with "Milano" printed upside down or a souvenir of a religious shrine with a "Kings Island" plaque.

Generally, early snowdomes (1950s and 1960s) have greater detail and more sophisticated colors than the later snowdomes, which are simpler and have an unrefined, mass-produced appearance

Age can affect a dome's physical deterioration—fading, chipping paint, even bleaching of the words on the plaque must be constantly evaluated by the collector. The plastic snowdomes that were introduced in the 1950s, were fragile objects, easily broken, and often discarded. It is indeed a challenge to find unusual survivors.

History: A snowdome is a clear globe- or dome-shaped paperweight which is filled with water and loose particles which swirl when the paperweight is turned upside down. A visible figurine and/or decorated panel inside the globe is magnified by the water.

Snowdomes originated during the mid-19th century in Europe. In France, they evolved from round, solid-glass paperweights, and by 1878, there were seven French manufacturers of snowdomes. They also were produced in what is now Germany, Austria, Poland, and the Czech Republic, often as cottage industries.

During the Victorian era, snowdomes were very popular as paperweights, souvenirs, and toys. Early domes featured religious scenes, tourist sites, and children and animals associated with winter or water. A variety of materials were used to create the "snow," ranging from ground porcelain and bone to rice. The figurines inside were made of carved bone, wax, porcelain, china, metal, or stone. The bases were made in a variety of shapes and from many materials, including marble, wood, glass, and metal.

German companies exported their snowdomes to North America in the 1920s. The bases, which were cobalt blue glass, were occasionally etched with the name of a town or tourist attraction. The first American patent was granted in 1927 for a design of a fish floating on a string among seaweed The Novelty Pond Company of Pittsburgh was the original manufacturer of this snowdome, but the idea was soon copied by others. American manufacturers used a black plastic base, either smooth or tiered; Japanese companies used a glazed brown ceramic base.

Italian snowdomes from the late 1940s have a distinctive scallop-shaped base covered with seashells and pebbles, and a glass globe containing a flat, rubberized panel with the name of the tourist attraction or a Saint's name written inside a shell on the base.

Three West German companies used plastic to create small cubed or domed snowdomes in the 1950s. Koziol and Walter & Prediger, two of these companies, remain in business manufacturing hand-painted domes with blizzards of white snow. Herr Koziol claims it was the "domed" view of a winter snow scene as seen through the rear window of a Volkswagen that inspired the shape. As a result of court action, Walter & Prediger gained the right to the dome shape and Koziol was restricted to the round shape.

The Atlas Crystal Works was an American firm founded in the early 1940s to fill the void created when the popular glazed style which had been made in Japan became unavailable. Atlas became the giant in the snowdome field, creating hundreds of different designs. Other American firms that made a variety of snowdomes are the Driss Company of Chicago, Illinois (1950s) and Progressive Products of Union, New Jersey (1940s and 1950s)

In addition to an enormous number of figurine designs, either in painted or unpainted bisque, domes also feature Art Deco buildings, saints, and snow babies. Another design form consists of a flat, rubberized insert showing a photograph of a tourist attraction, such as Niagara Falls or the Skyline Drive.

The majority of plastic and glass snowdomes made in the 1990s come from the Orient. There are currently no American manufacturers, but rather dozens of large gift companies who design and import an array of styles, shapes, and themes. Enesco Corporation, Elk Grove Village, Illinois, is one of the largest.

Reference: Nancy McMichael, *Snowdomes*, Abbeville Press, 1990.

Collectors' Club: Snowdome Collectors Club, P.O. Box 53262, Washington, DC 20009.

Advisor: Nancy McMichael.

Advertising
　Jell-O, plastic dome, 1970s, 3-3/4", 2-1/2" w, 2-3/4" h 38.00
　Philco Radios, glass ball, oily liquid, brown Bakelite base, 3" w, 4" h, 1950s................................50.00
　Sears Kenmore, America's Largest Selling Washers and Dryers, rect, 1 pc

salt and pepper shaker, woman standing next to appliances, 1970s, 3-1/2" x 2-1/2" x 1"................................30.00

Amusement Park
　Coney Island, bathing beauty, scalloped base with sea shells, 1940s, 2" d glass ball 20.00
　Kings Dominion, plastic, two dolphins on seesaw, gold printed letters on plaque on waved base, 1970s ... 10.00

Ashtray, Radio City, black bakelite, bisque finish, early 1940s, 2-3/4" d, glass ball 70.00

Bank, Mackinac Bridge, plastic, printed on front, red base, 1960s, 2-3/4" d ball................................12.00

Bottle
　Flat Side, Rhode Island, four plaques, early 1970s, 5" l 30.00
　Upright, Mennonite male and female figures, silver, snow, red cap, 1970s, 4-1/2" x 1-1/2" price for pr 15.00

Boxed Set, winter snow scenes, assorted, Marx, set of six small plastic domes, c1960
　Sold individually 11.00
　Sold as set................................110.00

Calendar, plastic, red base with four openings where date shows, San Francisco, CA, bridge and city scene, cable car moves on slide, 1970s, 2-3/4" d ball................................7.50

Cartoon Character
　Pink Panther, plastic dome, Panther skating around Inspector Clouseau, 1980s 12.00
　Popeye, seated plastic figure, holds water ball between hands, Olive Oyl, Sweetpea and Wimpy in moving row boat, King Features Syndicate, 1950s 75.00
　Sleeping Beauty and Prince Charming, castle, rounded dome, green ground and base, "Made in West Germany," 1970s..............................10.00

Character
　Elvis, singing into microphone, figure moves back and forth in front of Graceland mansion panel, Graceland plaque, rect, 1970s 25.00
　General Eisenhower, glass ball, black ceramic base, bisque bust "General Dwight D. Eisenhower, Commander in Chief, Allied Invasion Forces" decal, mkd "Atlas Crystal Works, Covington, TN, U.S. Patents 231423/4/5," 1940s 65.00
　Lone Ranger, round glass ball, Bakelite base, green, yellow, and red, "Lone Ranger: The Last Round-Up" decal, 1950s..............................65.00
　Sailor, glass glove, saluting figure, black ceramic base, 1940s 25.00

Christmas
　Boot, clear, five pine trees, red house, waving snowman and children, holly trim, 1970s 10.00
　Elf, figural, red suit, green jester collar, ball in tummy, snowman, trees, and house scene, 1960s....................50.00
　Fireplace, child sleeping in pajamas on hearth, Santa in sled on seesaw in

dome, mkd "CSA Inc., Curt S. Adler, Inc., NY, NY 10010," 1970s, 3-1/2" x 3-1/4" x 2-1/4"..............................50.00
Nativity Scene, small plastic dome, 1980s 5.00
Rudolph the Red-Nosed Reindeer, green plastic base, "Rudolph the Red-Nosed Reindeer in the Snow, RLM" decal, 1950s..............................45.00
Santa, driving sleigh, two reindeer, rect dome with elf sitting under mushroom, 1960s, 5-1/4" x 3-1/2" x 1"............30.00

Figural, left: Old Salt, plastic, 5-1/2" h, 2-3/4" d water ball, 1970s, $20; right: Mickey Mouse, 5-1/2" h, Disneyland in 2-3/4" d water ball, 1970s, $35.

Figural
Church, steeple, plastic, altar, bride and groom, mkd "W. Germany" on bottom, 1980s, 2-1/4" x 2-3/4" x 2-1/2"...25.00
Mickey Mouse, plastic, castle scene, 1960s, holds 2" d ball in lap, 5" h..75.00
Treasure Chest, gold-colored plastic frame, clear sides, Nassau on plaque, red lobster, fish and seaweed, 1970s, 2-1/2" x 3-1/2" x 1-3/4" 8.00
Game, ring toss, plastic dome
Giraffe, hoops go over necks of two giraffes, "The Pacifier" decal, 1970s 12.00
Lobster, plastic hoops, mkd "Maine," early 1980s, 3" x 2" x 1" 10.00
Moving Parts
Champagne, shot and martini glass on strings, naked lady, "The Bar is Open" bar scene painted backdrop, "This one is on me" plaque, "Las Vegas" on outside, 1960s, 3-3/4" x 2-3/4" x 2-1/2".............................25.00
Trolley, Golden Gate Bridge, San Francisco, Chinatown background, small dome, 1970s...................................7.00
Souvenir
Detroit, MI, four tiers, painted figure of girl on angled sled, brown ceramic base, 1930s, 4" x 2-1/2" x 2-3/4" .45.00
Empire State Building, New York City, gold letters, inverted glass cone, black Bakelite base, 1950s, 4-3/4" h 15.00
Niagara Falls, salt and pepper shakers, TV shape, plastic blue "P," pink "S," tour boat on seesaw, side compartments, 1970s, 3" x 2-1/4" x 1"...20.00
Ocean City, MD, plastic dome, seagull and sea shells, 1960s, 2-3/4" x 2-1/4" x 2" 10.00

Ontario, Canada, gold decal, painted, bisque lighthouse, glass top, blue glass base, mkd "Germany," 1920s...40.00
Queen Mary, Long Beach, CA, plastic dome, cutout of ship on ocean, printed and town panels, 1970s 14.00
Roy Rogers and Dale Evans Museum, Victorville, CA, plastic dome, barn scene, Trigger moves on slide, 1960s...30.00
Terminal Tower Building, Cleveland, OH, plaque, 1970s 12.00
States
Florida, the Sunshine State, bottle, flat sides, plastic, two alligators on see-saw, tree, and mountain, 1960s, 5" l 12.00
New York, figural, black bear, plastic, two deer on seesaw, state name on chest, mkd "UVC-Inc. 1972" on bottom, 2-1/2" ball, 5" h 20.00
West Virginia, small dome, state outline and bird on branch, late 1970s..15.00
World's Fair
Expo 67, Montreal Canada, plaque, fireworks background..................16.00
New York, 1939, Trylon and Perisphere bisque figure, brown ceramic base... 100.00

Soda Fountain Collectibles

Collecting Hints: The collector of soda fountain memorabilia competes with collectors in many other categories—advertising, glassware, ice cream, postcards, food molds, tools, etc. Material still ranges in the 25¢ to $200 range.

When buying a tray, the scene is the most important element. Most trays were stock items with the store or firm's name added later. Always look for items in excellent condition.

History: From the late 1880s through the end of the 1960s, the local soda fountain was the social center of small-town America, especially for teenagers. The soda fountain provided a place for conversation and gossip, a haven to satisfy the mid-afternoon munchies, and a source for the most current popular magazines.

References: Douglas Congdon-Martin, *Drugstore and Soda Fountain Antiques*, Schiffer Publishing, 1991; Don and Elizabeth Johnson, *Warman's Advertising*, Krause Publications, 2000; Ray Klug, *Antique Advertising Encyclopedia*, Vol. I (1978, 1993 value update), Vol. II, (1985, 1990 value update), L-W Book Sales; Tom Morrison, *Root Beer*, Schiffer Publishing, 1992.

Collectors' Clubs: Ice Screamers, P.O. Box 5387, Lancaster, PA 17601; National Assoc. of Soda Jerks, P.O. Box 115, Omaha, NE 68101.

Museums: Greenfield Village, Dearborn, MI; Museum of Science and Industry, Finigan's Ice Cream Parlor, Chicago, IL; Smithsonian Institution, Washington, DC.

Reproduction Alert.

Additional Listing: Ice Cream Collectibles.

Advertising trade card, Hires Rootbeer, boy and dog, 3-1/8" w, 5" h, $9.

Advertising Trade Card, Rush's Soda Fountain 5.00
Ashtray, Breyers, 90th Anniversary, 1866-1956..22.00
Blackboard, Frostie Root Beer, tin, 1950s..75.00
Booklet, Moxie Menu Book, 4-3/4" x 7", 12 pgs, some wear, c1910 ....32.00
Bottle
7-Up Salutes 1973 Notre Dame, Fighting Irish, National Championship, pack of eight bottles in orig cardboard carrier...200.00
Welch's Grape Juice, Howdy Doody, paper label 65.00
Bottle Label
Dartmouth Ginger Ale, Dartmouth College pennant, red, blue, green, and gilt, unused stock from Newport Bottling Works, Newport, NH, 3-1/2" w 9.00
Wunder Pale Dry Ginger Ale, 2-3/4" l, set of five 2.00
Calendar, Squirt, 1947, 25" h 300.00
Can, Abbott's Ice Cream, half gallon, Amish girl, c1940 ....15.00
Catalog
Bastian-Blessing Co, Chicago, IL, Soda Fountain Parts & Carbonators, 1955, 65 pgs, 8-1/2" x 11" 30.00
Foot & Jenks, Jackson, MI, c1935, 8 pgs, 5-3/8" x 7", "Start the Season Right With These 3 Proven Winners,

Killarn Ginger-Ale, CXC Cherrystone & CXC Lemon & Limes Combined," picture of bottle, return post card 14.00
National Licorice Co, New York, NY, early 1900, 19 pgs, 3-1/4" x 6-1/4", licorice specialties, lozenges, penny sticks, cigars, pipes, etc. 65.00
Stanley Knight Corp, Chicago, IL, Soda Fountains, Instructions and Specifications, c1944, 52 pgs, 7" x 10" 32.00
Container, Lutted's S. P. Cough Drops, house shaped, name engraved on door, 7" x 7 3/4" 400.00
Counter Bin, 9" x 13-3/4" x 4-1/4", Quaker Brand Salted Peanuts 42.00
Counter Display, Moxie, Fred Archer diecut, cardboard, easel back, 10-3/8" w, 8" h 185.00
Coupon, 1-3/4" x 3", Hires Root Beer, illus of ugly boy, good for free fountain Hires, druggist stamp on front, one rounded corner 95.00
Display Card, 5" x 8-1/2", 7-Up, diecut cardboard, full color image of infant in red playsuit, copyright 1950 .... 15.00
Display Rack
  Beech-Nut Chewing Gum, c1920 .... 300.00
  Lance Candy, four shelves.......... 25.00
Dispenser, white ceramic body
  13-1/2" h, "Drink Dr. Swett's The Original Root Beer, On The Market Seventy Five Years," picture of boy holding glass of root beer, silhouette shows older profile, picture on front and back, replaced pump 3,200.00
  13-1/2" h, Hires Root Beer, hour glass shape, "Drink Hires It Is Pure" on front and back, orig pump mkd "Hires" 800.00
  14" h, Birchola, birch leaves around "Drink Birchola" on front and back, not orig pump 1,800.00
  14" h, Ward's Lemon Crush, lemon shape, porcelain ball pump, minor paint loss to base 2,200.00
  14" h, Ward's Lime-Crush, lime shape, porcelain ball pump, some staining.................... 2,800.00
  14-1/2" h, Cherry Smash, round, trio of cherries on stem on front and back, "Always Drink Fowler's Cherry Smash Our Nation's Beverage," orig pump.. 1,800.00
  14-1/2" h, Fowler's Root Beer, bulbous, "Drink Fowler's Root Beer The Best" on two sides, orig pump mkd "Fowler's Root Beer"................................. 700.00
  14-1/2" h, Ward's Orange-Crush, orange shape, porcelain ball pump, some paint loss, hairline cracks 950.00
Festoon, diecut cardboard, Hires
  11" h, 49-1/2" l, full bottles of Hires on each end, logo in center 800.00
  14" h, 52" l, lady in winter scene reaching for bottle, c1940 .... 400.00
Game Sheet, 13" x 17" mailer envelope, paper playing sheet, "Undo It" 7-Up game, c1970............................... 20.00
Hat, soda jerk style 5.00

Hot Plate, commercial, Nestle's Hot Chocolate, 8" x 12", standing metal sign, red and white snowman graphics, late 1940s.................................. 95.00
Ice Chipper, Gilchrist, 1930s 95.00
Ice Cream Scoop
  Dover, brass 70.00
  Erie, round, size 8, aluminum ... 180.00
  Gilchrist, #30, size 8, polished 70.00
Jar, Borden's Malted Milk, glass label 175.00
Magazine Cover, *Saturday Evening Post*, young soda jerk talking to girls at counter, Norman Rockwell, Aug. 22, 1953.. 15.00
Malt Machine
  Arnold #15............................... 145.00
  Dairy Bar, metal, white Bakelite canister, logo 115.00
Milkshake Machine
  Gilchrist, orig cup, c1926 .... 100.00
  Hamilton Beach, push-down type.. 150.00
Mug
  Belfast Root Beer, Tepco China, price for pr 65.00
  Rochester Root Beer, 6" h, 3-1/2" d, clear heavy glass, tankard style, c1940 .... 28.00
Paper Cone Dispenser, 11" l, glass tube, metal holder, "Soda Fountain Drinks & Ice Cream Served in Vortex," gold label, wall mount 40.00
Pinback Button
  1/2" d, Cherry Smash, diecut cherry, string stem, Whitehead & Hoag 115.00
  1" d, Cherry Smash, George Washington, Whitehead & Hoag 95.00
  1" d, Cleo Cola Knothole Gant, red and white litho, figural baseball, 1939 Red Birds 15.00
  1" d, Sanderson's Drug Store, blue and white, soda fountain glass illus, "Ice Cream, Soda/Choice Cigars/Fine Candies," 1901-12 .... 28.00
  2-1/4" d, Hi-Hat Ice Cream Soda, 10¢, McCory's, c1940 .... 15.00
Postcard
  Bodie's Ice Cream Store, diecut..12.00
  Gunther's Soda Fountain, Chicago....................................... 15.00
Poster, 24" h, 57-1/2" w, heavy paper, Hires R-J Root Beer, So Good With Food, lady with bottle in glass in hand, bottle and glass beside finger sandwiches, framed 225.00
Pretzel Jar, 10-1/2" h, Seyfert's Original Butter Pretzels, glass, orig lid......60.00
Seltzer Bottle, Sun Shine, 11" h 150.00
Set, black and chrome, Art Deco styling, price for 11 pcs 495.00
Sign
  Orange County Fountain, porcelain on steel, yellow oval center, blue and white lettering, dark blue ground...................................... 110.00
  Purity Brand Pretzels, diecut cardboard, easel-back, multicolor, smiling blond boy carrying giant pretzel, white lettering, black, red, and gold ground, Harrisburg, PA, early 1930s 75.00

Straw Jar, glass
  Frosted panel 225.00
  Green panel.............................. 410.00
  Pattern glass, Illinois pattern, orig lid 450.00
  Red, metal lid, 1950s 175.00
Syrup Jug, Cherry Smash, paper label with George Washington, glass, one gallon 45.00
Tin, Schraftt's Marshmallow Topping, 25 lbs 35.00
Toy, Kool-Ade Soft Drink Kooler, plastic dispenser holds inverted glass jar, 12 orig waxed paper cups, Trim Toys of Trim Molded Products Co., 1970s, 7-1/2" x 8-1/2" x 9" h orig box...... 20.00
Tray, 13" x 11", Schuller's Ice Cream, ice cream sodas and cones 200.00
Wafer Holder, Reliance.................. 175.00

Soft Drink Collectibles

Collecting Hints: Coca-Cola items have dominated the field. Only recently have collectors begun concentrating on other soft drink manufacturing companies. Soft drink collectors compete with collectors of advertising, bottles, and premiums for the same material.

National brands such as Canada Dry, Dr. Pepper, and Pepsi-Cola are best known. However, regional soft drink bottling plants do exist, and their products are fertile ground for the novice collector.

History: Sarsaparilla, a name associated with soft drinks, began as a medicinal product. When carbonated water was added, it became a soft drink and was consumed for pleasure rather than medical purposes. However, sarsaparilla was only one type of ingredient added to carbonated water to produce soft drinks.

Each company had its special formula. Although Coca-Cola has a large market share, other companies provided challenges in different historical periods. Moxie was followed by Hire's, which in turn gave way to Pepsi-Cola and 7-Up.

In the 1950s, large advertising campaigns and numerous promotional products increased the visibility of soft drinks. Regional bottling plants were numerous and produced local specialties such as Birch Beer in eastern Pennsylvania. By 1970, most of these local plants had closed.

Many large companies had operations outside of the United States, and there is a large quantity of international advertising and promotional material. The current popularity of diet soda is a response to the modern American lifestyle.

Reference: Allan Petretti, *Petretti's Soda Pop Collectibles Price Guide*, Antique Trader Books, 1996.

Collectors' Clubs: Club Soda, P.O. Box 489, Troy, ID 83871; Dr. Pepper 10-2-4 Collectors Club, P.O. Box 153221, Irving, TX 75015; Moxie Enthusiasts Collectors Club of America, Route 375, Box 164, Woodstock, NY 12498; National Pop Can Collectors, P.O. Box 7862, Rockford, IL 61126; New England Moxie Congress, 445 Wyoming Ave., Millburn, NJ 07041.

Museums: Clark's Trading Post, North Woodstock, NH; Matthews Museum of Maine Heritage, Union, ME.

Additional Listings: Coca-Cola, Pepsi, Soda Bottles, Soda Fountain Collectibles.

Advertising Trade Card
    Cherry Smash, 4-3/4" x 3-1/2" 60.00
    Hire's Root Beer, late 1800s 12.00
Badge, Dad's Root Beer, Finest Draw in the West 35.00
Baseball Counter, 3" h, 2-1/2" w, Hires Root Beer, celluloid, Josh Slinger face, changeable eyes and scoring numbers, 1915...................................450.00
Book, adv, *1940 Football Book*, Hire's Root Beer, schedules and rules, 40 pgs 30.00
Bottle
    3-1/2" h, Canada Dry, c1950.........7.50
    7" h, Ting, Wild Cherry...................2.00
    7-1/2" h, Hire's, Old Homemade Root Beer from Hires Extract, brown and white stoneware, half pint size, minor crazing and pitting 125.00
    10" h, Hire's Root Beer Concentrate, glass, paper label, orig seal and contents, slight damage to paper label..25.00
Bottle Carrier
    7-Up, aluminum, holds 12 bottles 10.00
    Spur Cola, unused, 1940s 10.00
Calendar, 1927, Nehi, woman leaning on boat at beach 125.00
Card, Drink Squirt, 5" x 6-1/2", diecut, scalloped border, full color art, © 1947 Squirt Co. 30.00
Charm, 1" h figural plastic soda bottle, multicolored paper label wrapper, 1940s-50s
    Canada Dry Ginger Ale, orange...12.00
    Royal Crown Cola, orange 10.00
    White Rock Crown Cream, yellow 12.00
Clock
    7-Up, oak frame, c1950 ....100.00

Sprite, wood frame, quartz, c1980 ....30.00
Doll, Sparky, 7-Up, vinyl head, cloth body 45.00
Door Push
    Canada Dry Ginger Ale, tin litho, 9" h.. 175.00
    Real Orange-Ade, Green Spot, emb tin, 10" x 3-1/2"..........................185.00
Drinking Glass
    Buddy-Ginger, 5" h, clear glass, red script and small boy with "B" and "G" initials on shirts, boy holds chain leash which extends around to radio microphone and monkey wearing fez, c1930 ....10.00
    Grapette 10.00
    Vernors Ginger Ale, Deliciously Different, 4" h.......................................40.00
Fan, Moxie
    8" x 7", copyright 1925, edge wear on corner 95.00
    8-3/8" x 5-1/4", Eileen Pery, stain on back...95.00
    9" x 8-1/4", Muriel Ostriche, edge chip..95.00
    13-1/2" x 8", cardboard fan, wood handle, Cherry Smash, black waiter serving George and Martha Washington on lawn of Mt. Vernon 300.00
Lamp, 7-Up, metal bottle..................45.00
Match Holder, Dr. Pepper 6.50
Mobile Store Display
    Cheer Up, green bottle, red label, double sided cardboard, unused 20.00
    Quiky Soda Pop 40.00
Mug, ceramic
    5" h, Hires Root Beer, older trademark boy holding identical mug with his likeness of it, Mettlach, very minor crazing.. 375.00
    5-1/2" h, Hires Root Beer, blue and gray, emb intertwined roots encircling mug at top and bottom, handle simulates a tree branch....................150.00
    6" h, Dr. Swett's Root Beer, highly emb, likeness of Dr. Swett against brown ground on front, back with emb cupids among fancy filigree 200.00
    6" h, Dr. Swett's Root Beer, highly emb, likeness of Dr. Swett against green ground on front, back with emb water greenery 225.00
Pin
    1" h, diecut tin, Moxie, boy's head 75.00
    1-3/4" h, diecut thin celluloid, flipper type, Gold Label Ginger Ale, youngster with brimmed hat 40.00
Pinback Button, Orange Crush, orange and black figure, white ground, c1930 ....25.00
Pocket Knife, Nehi, "Drink Nehi 5 cents Quality Beverages" on one side and "Take a good look at the bottle to be sure it's Nehi" on other side, boot shaped, blade mkd "Remington, Made in U.S.A.," 1920s, 3-3/16" l.................................... 165.00
Pocket Mirror
    3" d, Dr. Swett's Original Root Beer, celluloid, earthenware bottle, Ameri-

can Art Works litho, very light scratch to celluloid 200.00
    3" h, 1-3/4" w, Hires Root Beer, oval, celluloid, titled "Put Roses in Your Cheeks Drink Hires Root Beer," young girl with rosy cheeks, holding armful of roses 200.00
Postcard, Moxie.............................28.00
Puppet, hand, Bubbles, Booth Soda 250.00
Radio, Royal Crown, can shape, late 1970s 40.00
Salt and Pepper Shakers, pr
    Squirt, bottle shape, unused, MIB...30.00
    7-Up, bottle shape, unused, MIB...25.00

Tray, Cherry Sparkle, Graf's, Northwestern Extract Co., Milwaukee, WI, yellow lettering, red soda, green ground, 10-1/2" w, 13-1/4" h, $125.

Sign
    Dad's Old Fashioned Root Beer, emb tin, oversized bottle, 29" h, 13-1/2" l.......................................200.00
    Diamond Beverages, porcelain, 13-3/4" h, 41-3/4" l, some edge chipping..100.00
    Drink a Bunch of Grapes from Welch Juniors, 19-5/8" x 13-1/2" 535.00
    Drink Hires The Genuine Root Beer, emb tin, white letters, 5-1/2" h, 19-3/4" l, ...375.00
    Drink Sun Spot, tin, 9-3/4" x 12" 185.00
    Hires Root Beer, 6" x 15", tin, 1930s, later frame..................................335.00
    Moxie, tin on cardboard, 10" x 2-1/2", minor scuffs 325.00
    Pennsylvania Dutch Birch Root Beer, JUC Orange of America, from barrel dispenser, Amish man hoisting mug of birch beer, 1955, 9-1/2" x 13", some light scratches 150.00
    Sun Drop, bottle cap type, 33-1/2" d 485.00
    Sun-Rise Beverages, bottled by Coca-Cola Bottling Co., tin, 12" x 27" .325.00
Stickpin, Moxie, diecut litho tin man's face, very minor scratches 125.00
Thermometer
    Chicquot Club Pale Dry Ginger Ale, 6" w, 13-1/2" h, poor condition 6.00

Dr. Pepper, round 90.00
Frostie Root Beer, illus of
Frostie...85.00
Hire's, diecut bottle shape...........90.00
Moxie, 25-1/2" h, 9-1/2" w, "Drink
Moxie take home a case tonight,"
Moxie man points to viewer, green,
red, and black, unused, orig
box 1,100.00
Royal Crown RC, 9-3/4" w,
25-5/8" h 155.00
Tip Tray, Royal Crown Cola 40.00
Toy, truck, Canada Dry-Special Sparkle,
4" l..27.50
Tray, 13" x 10", Ace-Hy, blue, orange, and
white..40.00
Uniform Patch, 10" d, Dr. Pepper, Good
for Life 27.50
Watch Fob, Hire's Root Beer, octagonal,
emb image, early 1900s 75.00

Soldiers, Dimestore

Collecting Hints: Figures of soldiers are preferred over civilians. The most valuable figures are those which had short production runs, usually because they were less popular with the youthful collectors of the period.

O'Brien and Pielin use numbering systems in their books to identify figures. Newcomers to the field should study these books, taking note of the many style and color variations in which these soldiers were made.

Condition, desirability, and scarcity establish the price of a figure. Repainting or the presence of rust severely reduce the value.

Auction prices often mislead the beginning collector. While some rare figures have sold in the $150 to $300 range, most sell between $10 and $25.

History: Three-dimensional lead, iron, and rubber soldier and civilian figures were produced in the United States by the millions before and after World War II. These figures are called dimestore soldiers because they were sold in the "five and dime" stores of the era, and usually cost a nickel or dime. Although American toy soldiers can be traced back to the early 20th century, the golden age of the dimestore soldier lasted from 1935 until 1942.

Four companies—Barclay, Manoil, Grey Iron, and Auburn Rubber—mass produced the three-inch figures. Barclay and Manoil dominated the market, probably because their lead castings lent themselves to

more realistic and imaginative poses than iron and rubber.

Barclay's early pre-war figures are identifiable by their separate glued-on and later clipped-on tin hats. When these are lost, the hole in the top of the head identifies the piece as a Barclay.

The Manoil Company first produced soldiers, sailors, cowboys, and Indians. However, the younger buyers of the period preferred military figures, perhaps emulating the newspaper headlines as World War II approached. Manoil's civilian figures were made in response to pacifist pressure and boycotts mounted before the war began.

Figures also were produced by such companies as All-Nu, American Alloy, American Soldier Co., Beton, Ideal, Jones, Lincoln Log, Miller, Playwood Plastics, Soljertoys, Tommy Toy, Tootsietoy, and Warren. Because most of these companies were short-lived, numerous limited production figures command high prices, especially those of All-Nu, Jones, Tommy Toy, and Warren.

From 1942 through 1945, the wartime scrap drives devoured tons of dimestore figures and the molds that produced them.

In late 1945, Barclay and Manoil introduced modernized military figures, but they never enjoyed their pre-war popularity. Military operations generally were phased out by the early 1950s. Similarly, the civilian figures could not compete with escalating labor costs and the competition from plastic products.

References: Bertel Bruun, *Toy Soldiers*, Avon Books, 1994; Norman Joplin, *Great Book of Hollow-Cast Figures*, New Cavendish Books, 1992; Norman Joplin, *Toy Soldiers*, Running Press, 1994; Richard O'Brien, *Collecting Toy Soldiers*, No. 3, Krause Publications, 1996.

Periodicals: *Old Toy Soldier*, 209 N. Lombard, Oak Park, IL 60302; *Plastic Figure & Playset Collector*, P.O. Box 1355, LaCrosse, WI 54602; *Plastic Warrior*, 905 Harrison St., Allentown, PA 18103; *Toy Soldier Review*, 127 74th St., North Bergen, NJ 07047.

Reproduction Alert: Some manufacturers identify their newer products; many do not.

Notes: Prices listed are for figures in original condition with at least 95 percent of the paint remaining. Unless otherwise noted, uniforms are brown.

Advisor: Barry L. Carter.

Barkley, messenger boy, $10.

Civilian Figure

Auburn Rubber
Baseball...30.00
Football 30.00

Barclay
Cowboy
    Mounted, firing pistol (190).........22.00
    With lasso (752)............................18.00
Indian
    Standing, bow and arrow (757).....9.00
    Tomahawk and shield (754)..........9.00
Miscellaneous
    Girl Skater (636) 10.00
    Mailman (853) 10.00
    Newsboy (621)..............................10.00
    Pirate (714) 12.00
    Policeman, raised arms (850) 10.00
    Redcap with bag (614)...............15.00
    Santa Claus on skis (500)...........45.00
    Woman passenger with dog
    (610)..10.00

Grey Iron
American Family Series,
2-1/4" h.................................5.00-25.00
Western
    Bandit, hands up..........................55.00
    Cowboy, hold-up man..................25.00
    Cowboy, standing 9.00

Manoil
Happy Farm Series
    Blacksmith, horseshoes (41/7) ...20.00
    Blacksmith, wheel (41/22)...........21.00
    Farmer sowing grain (41/10) 18.00
    Man chopping wood (41/18) 18.00
    Man with barrel (41/36) 20.00
    Watchman with lantern (41/16)...25.00
    Woman with pie (41/35) 20.00
Western
    Cowboy, arms raised (18a)........17.00
    Cowboy, one gun raised (18) 14.00
    Cowgirl riding horse (two
    pieces)..25.00
    Indian with knife (22)...................10.00

Military Figure

Auburn Rubber

Charging with tommy gun	15.00
Grenade thrower	15.00
Machine gunner, kneeling	11.00
Marching with rifle	15.00
Motorcycle with sidecar	55.00
Motorcyclist	37.00
Kneeling with binocolars	11.00
Searchlight	25.00

Barclay

Podfoot Series, 2-1/4" h

Bugler (909)	7.00
Flag bearer (901)	10.00
Gunner, prone (928)	8.00
Machine gunner charging (937)	7.00
Nurse (962)	18.00
Officer standing (908)	8.00
Sailor, blue (920)	10.00
Soldier, charging (906)	6.00
Soldier, marching, with rifle (977)	7.00

Post War, pot helmet

Flag bearer (701)	18.00
Machine gunner, prone (728)	18.00
Officer with sword (708)	18.00
Rifleman, standing (747)	18.00

Pre-War

AA gunner (774)	18.00
At attention (707)	14.00
Aviator (741)	15.00
Bugler, tin helmet (709)	15.00
Cameraman, kneeling (758)	35.00
Cook holding roast (769)	25.00
Crawling, tin hat (750)	18.00
Dispatcher with dog (952)	38.00
Doctor, white, with bag (745)	16.00
Lying wounded (761)	12.00
Machine gunner, kneeling (702)	15.00
Marching, with rifle, tin hat (704)	12.00
Marine officer, marching (708)	35.00
Mortar, two-man (791)	20.00
Nurse, kneeling, cup (767)	18.00
Parachutist (784)	18.00
Peeling potatoes (771)	22.00
Prone with binoculars (729)	18.00
Releasing pigeons (737)	18.00
Running with rifle (748)	18.00
Sailor, marching (179)	12.00
Sailor with flag (756)	15.00
Sailor with signal flags (730)	22.00
Searchlight (776)	25.00
Stretcher bearer (759)	15.00
Telephone operator (732)	15.00
Wireless operator with antenna (951)	30.00
Wounded crutches (775)	18.00
Wounded, sitting, arm in sling (752)	15.00

Grey Iron

Cavalryman	25.00
Colonial Soldier	20.00
Doctor, white, with bag	20.00
Doughboy, crawling	15.00
Drum Major	17.00
Drummer	15.00
Ethiopian	
Charging	25.00
Marching	28.00

Flag bearer	15.00
Kneeling, with rifle	15.00
Machine gunner	
Kneeling	10.00
Prone	15.00
Marching	10.00
Nurse	18.00
Radio Operator	45.00
Sailor marching	14.00
Sentry	15.00

Manoil

Post-War

Bazooka (45/13)	25.00
Marching with rifle (45/8)	18.00
Mine detector (45/19)	30.00
Tommy-gunner, standing (45/12)	22.00

Post-War, 2-1/2" h, mkd "USA"

Aircraft spotter (527)	25.00
Aviator with bomb (525)	24.00
Bazooka (528)	18.00
Flag bearer (521)	20.00
Grenade thrower (535)	24.00
Machine gunner, seated (531)	20.00
Observer, with binoculars (526)	27.00

Pre-War

At searchlight (47)	20.00
Bicycle rider (50)	30.00
Bomb thrower, with 3 grenades (31)	14.00
Boxer (68)	70.00
Cameraman with overhead flash (61)	45.00
Cannon loader (24)	14.00
Charging with bayonet (36)	28.00
Cook's helper with ladle (60)	30.00
Deep-sea diver (65)	15.00
Doctor, white (20)	12.00
Firefighter, Hot Papa, gray (92)	75.00
Flag bearer (7)	18.00
Gas mask with flare gun (63)	20.00
Hostess, green (35)	45.00
Machine gunner, prone (12)	15.00
Marching (8)	16.00
Navy deck gunner (48)	30.00
Navy signalman with 2 flags (17)	24.00
Nurse, white, red dish (21)	16.00
Observer with periscope (45)	30.00
Radio operator, standing (88)	35.00
Rifleman, standing (26)	15.00
Running with cannon (94)	30.00
Sailor (14)	18.00
Sharpshooter, camouflage (57)	20.00
Sitting, eating (54)	26.00
Stretcher carrier, with medical kit (32)	17.00
Wounded (30)	15.00
Writing letter (59)	50.00

Soldiers, Toy

Collecting Hints: Consider three key factors: condition of the figures and the box, the age of the figures and the box, and the completeness of the set.

Toy soldiers were meant to be playthings. However, collectors consider them an art form and pay premium prices only for excellent to mint examples. They want figures with complete paint and intact parts, including the moving parts.

The box is very important, controlling 10 to 20 percent of the price of a set. The style of the box is a clue to the date of the set. The same set may have been made for several decades; the earlier the date of manufacture, the more valuable the set.

Sets have a specific number of pieces or parts. These must all be present for full value to be realized. The number of pieces in each set, when known, is indicated in the listings below.

Beware of repainted older examples and modern reproductions. Toy soldiers still are being manufactured, both by large companies and private individuals. A contemporary collection may prove a worthwhile long-term investment, at least for the next generation.

History: The manufacture of toy soldiers began in the late 18th century by individuals such as the Hilperts of Nuremberg, Germany. The early figures were tin, pewter, or composition. By the late 19th century, companies in Britain (Britain, Courtenay), France (Blondel, Gerbeau, and Mignot), and Switzerland (Gottschalk, Wehrli) were firmly established. Britain and Mignot dominated the market into the 20th century.

Mignot established its French stronghold by purchasing Cuperly, Blondel, and Gerbeau who had united to take over Lucotte. By 1950, Mignot had 20,000 models representing soldiers from around the world.

Britain developed the hollow cast soldiers in 1893. Movable arms also were another landmark. Eventually bases were made of plastic, followed finally by the entirely plastic figures. Production ceased in the 1980s.

Between 1930 and 1950, the English toy soldier was challenged in America by the dimestore soldiers made by Barclay, Manoil, and others. Nevertheless, the Britains retained a share of the market because of their high quality. The collecting of toy soldiers remains very popular in the United States.

References: Bertel Bruun, *Toy Soldiers*, Avon Books, 1994; *Elastolin, Miniature Figures and Groups from the Hausser Firm of Germany* (1990), Vol. 2 (1991), Theriault's; Norman

Joplin, *Great Book of Hollow-Cast Figures*, New Cavendish Books, 1993; Norman Joplin, *Toy Soldiers*, Running Press, 1994; Richard O'Brien, *Collecting Toy Soldiers*, No. 3, Krause Publications, 1996; James Opie, *Collecting Toy Soldiers*, Pincushion Press, 1992; Joe Wallis, *Armies of the World*, published by author, 1993.

Periodicals: *Old Toy Soldier*, 209 North Lombard, Oak Park, IL 60302; *Plastic Figure & Playset Collector*, P.O. Box 1355, LaCrosse, WI 54602; *Plastic Warrior*, 905 Harrison St., Allentown, PA 18103; *Toy Soldier Review*, 127 74th St., North Bergen, NJ 07047.

Collectors' Clubs: American Model Soldier Society, 1528 El Camino Real, San Carlos, CA 94070; Military Miniature Society of Illinois, P.O. Box 394, Skokie, IL 60077; Northeast Toy Soldier Society, 12 Beach Rd, Gloucester, MA 09130; Toy Soldier Collectors of America, 6924 Stone's Throw Circle, #8202, St. Petersburg, FL 33710.

Reproduction Alert.

Advisor: Barry L. Carter.

African Warriors, Zulus, W. Britain, No. 147, $200.

Authenticast, Russian Infantry, advancing with rifles at the ready, two officers, carrying pistols and swords, 8 pcs 75.00

Bienheim, sets only, mint, orig excellent box

B2, Coldstream Guards Colors, 1812, two color bearers, escort of four privates, six pcs 115.00

B17, Royal Marines, 1923, marching at the slope, officer, sword at carry, six pcs 75.00

B63, Royal Co of Archers Colors, two color bearers, escort of four privates, six pcs 100.00

C13, 17th Lancers, 1879, foreign service order, officer, bugler and trooper with lance, six pcs 130.00

US Naval Academy Color Guard, two standard bearers, escort of two midshipmen 100.00

Britains, sets only

28, Mountain Gun of the Royal Artillery, with gun, gunners, mules, and mounted officer, 14 pcs, mint, orig good box 250.00

33, 16th/5th Lancers, mounted at the half in review order, officer turned in the saddle, excellent orig illus box. 170.00

44, 2nd Dragoon Guards, The Queen's Bays, mounted at the gallop, lances and trumpeter, c1940, five pcs, excellent, good orig Whisstock box.. 135.00

117, Egyptian Infantry, at attention in review order, c1935, eight pcs, good, orig Whisstock box 150.00

122, The Black Watch, standing, firing, tropical service dress, officer holding binoculars, c1930, eight pcs, good orig Whisstock box 150.00

136, Russian Cossacks, mounted at the gallop with officer, five pcs, excellent, orig box 135.00

138, French Cuirassiers, mounted at the walk, review order with officer, five pcs, excellent, orig box 140.00

167, Turkish Infantry, standing on guard, review order, d1935, five pcs, good/ fine, orig Whisstock box 150.00

190, Belgian 2nd Regiment Chasseurs a Cheval, mounted in review order, officer, five pcs, good, orig box... 140.00

201, Officers of the General Staff, comprising Field Marshal, General officer and two Aides-de-Camp, four pcs, good 120.00

216, Argentine Infantry, marching at the slope, review order, c1940, eight pcs, excellent, good orig "Types of the Argentine Army" box 275.00

217, Argentine Cavalry, mounted in review order, lances and officer, eight pcs, excellent, orig box 225.00

1323, The Royal Fussilers, The Royal Sussex Regiment and the Seaforth Highlanders, marching at the slope, mounted and foot officers, 23 pcs, excellent, orig box 300.00

1339, The Royal Horse Artillery Khaki Service Order, six-horse team, lumber, gun, drivers with whips, four mounted outriders on trotting horses, officer on galloping horse, 13 pcs, excellent, good orig "Types of the British Army" box with gold and black label 1,700.00

1343, The Royal Horse Guards, mounted in winter cloaks, officer, c1940, five pcs, good orig "Armies of the World" box 130.00

1631, The Governor General's Horse Guards of Canada, mounted in review order, officer on prancing horse, five pcs, mint, orig excellent box 110.00

1632, The Royal Canadian Regiment, marching at the slope, officer, c1940, eight pcs, good, fine orig "Soldiers of the British Empire" box 400.00

1836, Argentine Military Cadets, marching at the slope, review order, officer, c1940, eight pcs, excellent, orig "Armies of the World" box...... 1,250.00

1935, Argentine Naval Cadets, marching at the slope, review order, officer, 1948-49, excellent, good orig box 1,800.00

2009, Belgian Grenadier Regiment, marching in review order, officer, eight pcs, excellent, orig box............. 180.00

2028, Red Army Cavalry, mounted at the halt in parade uniforms, officer, five pcs, excellent, orig box............. 120.00

2035, Swedish Life Guard, marching at the slope, officer, eight pcs, mint, tied in excellent, orig box 200.00

2059, Union Infantry, action poses, with officer holding sword and pistol, bugler and standard bearer, 87 pcs, excellent, orig box...................... 90.00

9217, 12th Royal Lancers, mounted in review order, officer, five pcs, mint, good orig window box 80.00

9265, Egyptian Camel Corps, mounted on camels, detachable riders, five pcs, mint, tied in excellent orig window box 180.00

9291, Arabs of the Desert on Horses, with jezalls and scimtars, excellent, good orig window box 80.00

9402, State Open road Landau, drawn by six Windsor Grays, with three detachable positions, attendants, Queen Elizabeth and Prince Philip as passengers, 13 pcs, mint, tied in excellent orig box...................... 375.00

9407, British Regiments on Parade, comprising General Officer, Royal Horse Artillery at the walk, 17th Lancers in review order on trotting and cantering horses with officer, Life Guard with trumpeter and officer, Royal Norfolk Regiment at the slope with officer, Scots Greys on trotting and walking horses with officer, The Black Watch marching at the slope with piper and officer, Band of the Line, 67 pcs, excellent, orig two-tray display box 2,500.00

Elastolin/Lineol

Flak Gunner, blue and gray uniform, kneeling with shell, very good 40.00

Medic, walking, helmet, back pack with red cross.................................... 35.00

Nurse, attending wounded, kneeling, olds foot of soldier sitting on keg, excellent 40.00

Staff Officer, pointing, field glasses, aristocratic pose................................. 35.00

Heyde

Chicago Police, 1890s, on foot, with billy clubs, policeman with dog, standard bearer, and mounted policeman, very good 225.00

French Ambulance Unit, horse-drawn ambulance, two-horse team, rider with whip, stretcher bearers, stretchers, casualties, mounted and foot medical officers, medical orderly, very good, fair orig box 275.00

German Infantry, World War I, attacking with fixed bayonets, officer with extended sword, very good 90.00

Heissan Infantry, 1777, marching at the slope, officers, standard bearer, four mounted dragoons, movable reins on horses, good 375.00

Mignot

15, French Muskeeters Period of King Louis XIII, marching with muskets at shoulder arms, officer and standard bearer, c1960, 12 pcs, excellent, orig box 275.00

17, Infantry of King Louis XIV, marching at the slope, officer, standard bearer, drummer, c1950, 12 pcs, excellent, orig box 400.00

28/C, Napoleon's Imperial guard Band, 1812, marching will full instrumentation, band director with baton, 12 pcs, excellent 350.00

36, French Napoleonic Skirmishers of the 17th Line Regiment, 1809, marching in blue and white uniforms, faced in red, tall plumed shakos, gloss paint, c1965, mint four-piece set in excellent orig window box and outer cardboard box 80.00

39, Italian Light Infantry, Regiment de Beauhamais, 1810, marching at the slope, green uniforms, pale blue facings, plumed shakos, drummer and officer, 12 pcs, excellent, orig box 225.00

43/H, Austrian Infantry, 1805, standing at attention, shoulder arms, officer, drummer, and standard bearer, 12 pcs, limited issue, mint, tied in excellent orig box 225.00

45/A, Bavarian Infantry, 1812, marching at the slope, blue and white uniforms, yellow facings, plumed light infantry caps, standard bearer and bugler, excellent eight-pc set in orig box 250.00

200, Ancient Gaul Cavalry, mounted with swords, spears, and shields, five pcs, excellent, orig box 275.00

200/8, Ancient Greek Cavalry, mounted with swords, spears and shields, five pcs, excellent, orig box 250.00

231/B, Austrian Cavalry, 1814, mounted in review order, officer, trumpeter and standard bearer, six pcs, mint, excellent orig box 250.00

255, Spanish Hussars, 1808, mounted in green uniforms, red facings, tall plumed shakos, officer, trumpeter, and standard bearer, mint, excellent orig box 375.00

1016, Drum Majors of the Empire, French Napoleonic regiments, including Orphans of the Guard, Marines of the Guard, St. Cyr Academy and various line infantry regiments, special limited edition, all mint, excellent orig boxes 475.00

Militia Models

Gatling Gun Team of 3rd London Rifles, Gatling gun and gunner, two ammunition carriers, officer holding binoculars, mint, excellent orig box 90.00

The Pipes and Drums of 1st Battalion Royal Irish Rangers, pipe major and four pipers, two snare and two tenor drummers, drum major, limited edition, mint, excellent orig box 125.00

Nostalgia, mint, excellent orig box

1st Gurkha Light Infantry, 1800, red and blue uniforms, marching with slung rifles, officer with sword at the carry 80.00

Kaffrarian Rifles, 1910, gray uniforms, plumed pith helmets, marching at the trail, officer with sword at the carry, mint 125.00

New South Wales Irish Rifles, 1900, marching at the trail, officer holding sword at the carry 95.00

New South Wales Lancers, 1900, marching, carrying lances on the shoulder, khaki uniforms, trimmed in red and plumed campaign hats, officer holding swagger stick 65.00

S.A.F., mint, excellent orig box

1358, Royal Horse Guards, 1945, mounted at the halt, officer 50.00

1761, French Cuirassiers, mounted at the walk, ... 85.00

3310, 1st Bengal Lancers, mounted at the half 115.00

Souvenir and Commemorative Items

Collecting Hints: Most collectors of souvenir and commemorative china and glass collect items from a region which is particularly interesting to them—their hometown or birthplace, or place of special interest such as a President's home. This results in regional variations in price because a piece is more likely to be in demand in the area it represents.

When collecting souvenir spoons be aware of several things: condition, material, subject, and any markings, dates, etc. Damaged spoons should be avoided unless they are very rare and are needed to complete a collection. Some spoons have enamel crests and other decoration. This enameling should be in mint condition.

History: Souvenir and commemorative china and glass date to the early fairs and carnivals when a small trinket was purchased to take back home as a gift or remembrance of the event. Other types of commemorative glass include pattern and milk glass made to celebrate a particular event. Many types of souvenir glass and china originated at the world's fairs and expositions.

The peak of souvenir spoon collecting was reached in the late 1800s. During that time, two important patents were issued. One was the December 4, 1884, patent for the first flatware design, and it was issued to Michael Gibney, a New York silversmith. The other important patent was the one for the first spoon design which commemorated a place. That patent was given to Myron H. Kinsley in 1881 for his spoon which showed the suspension bridge at Niagara Falls. This was the first of many scenic views of Niagara Falls which appeared on spoons over the years.

Spoons depicting famous people soon followed, such as the one of George Washington which was issued in May 1889. That was followed by the Martha Washington spoon in October 1889. These spoons, made by M. W. Galt of Washington, D.C., were not patented but were trademarked in 1890.

During the 1900s, it became popular to have souvenir plates made to memorialize churches and local events such as centennials and homecomings. These plates were well received in their respective communities. Collectors search for them today because they were made in a limited number. They are especially interesting as an indication of how an area changed architecturally and culturally over the years.

References: Wayne Bednersch, *Collectible Souvenir Spoons: Identification and Values, Book II*, Collector Books, 2000; Barbara J. Conroy, *Restaurant China*, Volume 2, Collector Books, 2000; Dorothy T. Rainwater and Donna H. Fegler, *American Spoons*, Schiffer Publishing, 1990; —-, *Spoons from around the World*, Schiffer Publishing, 1992.

Collectors' Club: American Spoon Collectors, 7408 Englewood Lane, Raytown, MO 64133; Antique Souvenir Collectors News, Box 562, Great Barrington, MA 01230; Northeastern Spoon Collectors Guild, 52 Hillcrest Ave., Morristown, NJ 07960; The Scoop Club, 84 Oak Ave., Shelton, CT 06484.

Busts, all frosted glass, James Garfield, M. J. Owens, U. Grant, Wm. McKinley, sold as group, $175. Photo courtesy of Joy Luke Fine Art Brokers and Auctioneers.

Booklet
 Souvenir of Coney Island, Brighton, and Manhattan Beaches, 1904, 40 pgs with black and white illus, 8" x 5"..65.00
 Views of Coney Island, 7-3/4" x 9-3/4", green softcover, gold accent title, 32 pgs, photos and text of Luna Park, Dreamland, and bathers, © 1906, LH Nelson Co. 35.00
 Steel Pier, Atlantic City, NJ, summer program, 32 pgs, pictures and ads 45.00
Bottle Opener, San Diego, 1912 ......25.00
Calling Card Receiver, Philadelphia, 1907, copper, moose, tree, lake, and mountains 40.00
Card Game, Excursion to Coney Island, Milton Bradley, c1885.................20.00
Condiment Set, Gettysburg, 1863, hp china, salt and pepper shakers, condiment jar with lid and spoon, 5-1/4" x 5-1/2" base, orange, yellow flowers, green leaves, gold, irid slate blue, and white accents, mkd "Nippon," 1930s 28.00
Cup, china, white
 St Charles Hotel, New Orleans ...15.00
 Souvenir of the Midget's Palace, Montreal, well-dressed male and female midgets illus, late 1800s...............65.00
Cup and Saucer, Niagara Falls, marked "Carlsbad, Austria".......................18.00
Demitasse Cup and Saucer, Hotel Roosevelt, New Orleans..............35.00
Doll, Icey the Ice Man, 9" h, Ice Capades 1950s tour, plastic, soft vinyl head, glued flannel felt Deutch boy cap, turquoise flannel jacket, blue flannel trousers, name and "Ice Capades" marks 45.00
Figure, 3-1/2" h, Chinatown, NY, Chinese couple 25.00
Guide Book, 7" x 10", New York, softcover, full color, airships and planes flying over city skyline and Statue of Liberty, 64 black and white pgs, © 1932 Manhattan Card Co Publishing Co. ...24.00
Hatchet, 6" l, Hazelton, PA, white milk glass, red letters 40.00
Medal
 Coney Island, steeplechase face, orig ribbon, 1924 ....90.00
 Souvenir of Wisconsin, green with gold 30.00
Mug
 Hardwick, VT, custard glass, gold trim 35.00

Lincoln Hotel, Reading, PA, white ceramic 10.00
New Rockford, ND, custard glass 35.00
Mustard, cov, Central School, Owosso, MI, mkd "Made in Germany," 3-1/2" h 35.00
Paperweight, glass, round
 Brainard, MN, lake scene, 3" d....40.00
 New Salem State Park, 2-3/4" d ..35.00
Pennant, felt
 Coney Island, maroon, white title, yellow, green, orange, and white scene of Steeplechase Pool, amusement rides, Luna Mill Sky Chaser building, c1930...30.00
 Hershey Park, brown ground, white letters, c1950 ....25.00
Photo Album, New Orleans, various scenes, 1885.............................45.00
Pinback Button, 1-1/4" d
 Asbury Park, black and white, bathing beach scene, c1900...................12.00
 Coney Island, multicolored, bathing beauty scene, rim reads "Citizens Committee of Coney Island," c1915 ....35.00
 Dreamland, NY, white lettering, red ground, 1900s...........................10.00
 Hershey Park, multicolored, child emerging from cocoa bean, c1905 ....35.00
 New Virginia Reel, Luna Park, two men and four ladies on ride, Bastian Brothers back label 125.00
 Wonderland Stamford, CT, multicolored, c1900................................90.00
Pinback Button Name Tag, attached ribbon
 Charter Day Celebration, July 5-6-7, MCMIX, 1884-1909, North Plainfield, Plainfield, Member of Citizen Committee, 1-3/4" d 42.00
 18th Annual Saengerfest, Philadelphia, Pa, June 21-24, 1897, Aurora Singing Society, New Brunswick, NJ, double sided, 1-1/2" d 45.00
Pin Cushion, 1-1/2" h, 5" l, Dutch shoe, thimble and thread holder, wood burned picture of Dutch windmill on one side and "Galveston, Texas" on other side 12.00
Pitcher, Bar Harbor, ME, custard glass, gold trim, beaded base 95.00
Plate
 Alabama, state capital in center, blue, Vernon Kilns 22.00
 Albany, Minnesota 40.00
 Along 101 The Redwood Highway, maroon, Vernon Kilns..................25.00
 Baltimore & Ohio Railroad, Harpers Ferry, blue and white, 10-1/2" d...95.00
 Birmingham, AL, The Industrial City, maroon, Vernon Kilns..................22.00
 Boston, MA, Filene's, brown, Vernon Kilns..22.00
 Carlsbad Caverns, White's City, New Mexico..25.00
 Chicago, clock in center, maroon 22.00
 Daytona Beach, FL, World's Most Famous Beach, maroon, Vernon Kilns..22.00
 Delaware Tercentenary Celebration, 1938, black and white, Spode 35.00

Denver, CO, state capital in center, blue, Vernon Kilns 22.00
Greenville, SC, blue, Vernon Kilns 22.00
Hollywood, CA, NBC Studios, Hollywood Bowl, Ciro's, Graumann's, Earl Carroll's, Brown Derby, blue, Vernon Kilns 35.00
Jacksonville, FL, Gateway to Florida, maroon..22.00
Laguna Beach, CA, Festival of Arts..25.00
Maine, state capital in center, multicolored, Vernon Kilns 30.00
Mississippi, blue, Vernon Kilns ...22.00
My Old Kentucky Home, 10" d, cobalt blue, Adams 75.00
Nevada, The Silver State, Hoover Dam in center, brown, Vernon Kilns 22.00
New Mexico, picture map...........22.00
Northwestern University, multicolored, Vernon Kilns 35.00
Our West, Vast Empire, maroon, Vernon Kilns 35.00
Portsmouth Virginia Bicentennial, 1752-1952, light brown, Vernon Kilns 22.00
Saint Augustine, FL, brown, Vernon Kilns 22.00
San Diego County Fair, Delmar, CA, Don Diego Welcomes You, blue 35.00
SE Missouri State College, Diamond Jubilee, brown, Vernon Kilns 25.00
Sonoma, CA, Cradle of California, maroon, Vernon Kilns 35.00
South Dakota, state capital in center, maroon, Vernon Kilns 22.00
Spokane, Washington, The Inland Empire, blue, Vernon Kilns..........25.00
SS Grand View Hotel, A Steamboat in the Allegheny Mountains, 10" d, cobalt blue, Adams 95.00
Statue of Liberty, mkd "Made expressly for James Hill, Bedloe's Island, NY, The New Colossus by Emma Lazarus" on back, blue, Vernon Kilns 35.00
Vermont, Green Mountain State, brown, Vernon Kilns 22.00
Washington, state capital in center, brown, Vernon Kilns 22.00
West Virginia, state capital in center, brown 22.00
Platter, 12" d, aluminum, 1665-1965 Halden, back mkd "Catherine Holm" 25.00
Program
 Ice Follies of 1953, Shipstads & Johnson 25.00
 Radio City Music Hall Pictorial, 1945 ....20.00
 Sonja Henie and Her Hollywood Ice Review, 1940 ....25.00
 The Eighth World Championship Rodeo, Boston, Garden Area Sports News, Vol. VII, No. 1, c1939 ....25.00
Salt and Pepper Shakers, pr
 Alscar de Segovia, emblem, Limoges 32.00
 Lafayette, TN, black maid and butler, white uniforms, c1940...............125.00
 Penn State, ceramic, blue logo 5.00
Spoon, sterling silver
 Athens, PA, engraved high school bowl 35.00

Battle Monument, Trenton, NJ.....35.00
Ben Franklin, Philadelphia...........55.00
Bethesda Springs, Waukesha,
WI 55.00
Bismarck, ND, post office bowl...45.00
Boston, emb sites and scenes on front
and back, mkd "Watson,"
5-7/8" l 35.00
Brooklyn, NY, 13th Regiment 35.00
Calumet, MI, mining, Helco Shaft
#2 ....35.00
Chicago, IL, US Government Building,
Fort Dearborn 40.00
Columbus, OH, Lancaster pattern
handle 35.00
Cuba, Morro castle......................50.00
Detroit Skyline............................70.00
Elgin Watch Factory 85.00
E.P.N.S. and crown, mkd "Made in
Holland" 18.00
Fishers Peak, CO, bowl with mule,
prospector, and state flower, CO
scenes on handle, 5-1/2" l...........70.00
Fredericton, New Brunswick, spiral
handle, gold wash bowl 60.00
Girard College, Irian pattern
handle 45.00
Golden Gate, San Francisco 45.00
Grant Monument, Chicago 45.00
Halifax, 3-1/2" l 18.00
Hope, Idaho................................30.00
Hot Springs, Arkansas, Indian head,
corn 45.00
Inclined Plane, Cincinnati, OH....35.00
Kansas City, Missouri, Convention
Hall 45.00
Lake Worth, Palm Beach, FL 65.00
Mammoth Cave, KY, ornately dec
bowl with view of Bridal Altar, c1910,
back mkd "Sterling," 5-3/4" l 24.00
Minneapolis, 4" l...........................6.00
Montreal, 3-1/2" l 18.00
Mt Vernon...................................20.00
Newtown, demitasse,
hallmarked 12.00
Niagara Falls, fleur-de-lis bowl with
engraved view of Falls, mkd "Sterling,"
4-1/2" l 20.00
Old Hickory, Jackson
monument......................................75.00
Paul Revere, Midnight Ride 95.00
Prairie de Chien, WI....................28.00
Providence, bowl engraved, mkd
".925 Sterling 1000," 4-1/2" l 20.00
Quebec, horse and buggy with three
passengers in bowl, "Quebec Citadel"
on handle, mkd "Sterling, G. Seifert,"
4-1/2" l 30.00
Reading, PA, Mt. Penn Tower, demi-
tasse..40.00
Salt Lake City, UT, Mormon Temple
handle, demitasse 45.00
San Francisco, Mission Dolores 1776,
bear on dec handle, gold bowl...45.00
Sioux City, IA, Corn Palace,
1891 ....80.00
Springfield, IL, Abraham
Lincoln...60.00
Statue of Liberty, Tiffany 75.00
Texas, enameled star,
demitasse 25.00
Union Station, Dayton, OH, picture
bowl..35.00
Vassar, MI, high school engraved in
bowl..35.00
Waseca, MN, grape pattern........55.00

Washington, lacy design handle, bowl
engraved "Washington," 4" l........20.00
Washington's Tomb......................30.00
Wilmington, NC, floral handle, gold
wash bowl, demitasse 35.00
Yellowstone Park, etched falls bowl,
bear, stag's head, and buffalo head on
handle 45.00
Tape Measure, New York City, celluoid,
pig..25.00
Teapot, Morrison Hotel, Chicago......35.00
Thermometer, Florida, figural flamingo, 6"
h, c1940-50 ....60.00
Tip Tray, Hotel Coronado, china.......15.00
Toothpick Holder
  Glen Ullen, ND, ruby stained glass,
  gold 35.00
  Lewistown, ME, Georgia Gem pat-
  tern, custard glass, gold trim 45.00
  Providence, Shamrock pattern, ruby
  stained glass..................................40.00
Trowel, Acme Portland Cement, engraved
eagle, 5-1/2" l 40.00
Vase
  Camp Lake View, Lake City,
  MN..20.00
  Catalina Island, two handles, blue,
  dragon dec, gold accents,
  2-1/2" h 5.00
  Opera House, What Cheer, IA, china,
  multicolored scene 45.00

Souvenir Buildings

Collecting Hints: Collectors look for rarity, architectural detail, and quality of material, casting, and finishing. As in real estate, location affects price: European and East Coast buildings are more expensive on the West Coast and vice versa.

Many souvenir buildings are now sold via internet auction sites. Common items sell at low prices, often under $15. Rare and unusual buildings can command prices in the $500 to $700 range.

History: Small metal replicas of famous buildings and monuments first became popular souvenirs among Victorian travelers returning from a Grand Tour of Europe. In the 1920s and 1930s, metal replicas of banks and insurance company headquarters were made as promotional give-aways to new depositors and clients. In the 1950s and 1960s, Japanese-manufactured metal souvenir buildings were the rage for motorists visiting attractions across America.

Souvenir buildings are still being manufactured and sold in cities and capitals around the world. They depict churches, cathedrals, skyscrapers, office buildings, capitols, TV and radio towers, castles, and museums. They can often be found in gift or souvenir shops located in or near the structure. Most souvenir

buildings are made of white (or pot) metal with a finish of brass, copper, gold, silver, or bronze. They have also been made in sterling silver, brass, silvered lead, plastic, resin composition, and ceramic. Today many are made of resin polymer, which can be "cold cast," a less expensive process than metal casting. Resin can be mixed with marble or metal dust to closely mimic the actual substance. Although many collectors may have frowned on resin souvenir buildings, they are becoming more common in the souvenir building shops Quality, detail, and workmanship continue to improve. Collectors with a long time horizon should consider them.

Where to look: Flea markets, antique malls, souvenir shops and antique shows are good sources for beginning collectors. The internet, especially eBay, is also well supplied with common items. Advanced collectors still scour the above sources, but also exchange trading lists with each other or try to outbid each other on eBay for unusual or rare pieces. Prices can escalate swiftly in cyberspace.

References: Margaret Majua and David Weingarten, *Monumental Miniatures/Souvenir Buildings from the Collection of Ace Architects*, Antique Trader Books, 1999; —, *Souvenir Buildings/Miniature Monuments*, Harry N. Abrams, 1996.

Collectors' Club: Souvenir Building Collectors Society, P.O. Box 70, Nellysford, VA 22958-0070. President: Art Ratner, 2871 San Pablo Ave., Berkeley, CA 94702. email: toyomanusa@netscape.net

Periodical: *The Souvenir Building Collector*, Journal of the Souvenir Building Collectors Society, P.O. Box 70, Nellysford, VA 22958-0070.

Advisor: Dixie Trainer.

Neuschwanstein Castle, 4" l, 2" w, 3-1/2" h, mid-1980s, $85. Photo courtesy of Dixie Trainer.

Arc de Triomphe, Paris, 1-3/4" x 1-1/2" x 1", copper finish 15.00

Brandenberg Gate, Berlin, 4" x 3-3/4" x 2", antique bronze, wood base 65.00

Bunker Hill Monument, Boston, MA, copper finish 14.00

Capitol, Washington DC
Jewelry Box, 4-1/4" x 5" x 3-1/2", gold, mkd "JB" on bottom 55.00
Souvenir, 2-1/4" x 3-1/2" x 2" 6.00
Coit Tower. San Francisco, 6-1/2" h, 2-1/4" sq base, antique bronze finish 98.00
Cologne Cathedral, Germany, 4-1/8" x 3-3/4" x 1-1/2", antique pewter or silver finish 18.00
Coliseum, Rome, 1-1/2" x 2-1/4" x 2", copper finish 15.00

Confederate Monument, Shiloh National Park, TN, 2-1/4" h x 2-3/4" l x 1" w, copper 100.00

Dollar Savings Bank, Pittsburgh, PA, 3-1/8" x 4" x 3", silvered lead bank 95.00

Eiffel Tower
3" x 1" x 1", copper, antique brass or silver finish 10.00
6" x 2-1/2" x 2-1/2", copper, antique brass or silver finish 18.00

Empire State Bldg
Prewar, no spire, 3-1/2" x 1-1/2" x 1", antique brass finish 30.00
Prewar, no spire, 5-3/4" x 2-1/2" x 2", silver finish 68.00
Postwar, with radio antenna spire, 3-1/2" x 1-1/4" x 3/4", gold plastic .5.00
Postwar, with radio antenna spire 5" x 1-3/4" x 1-1/4", antique brass finish 12.00
Postwar, with radio antenna spire 7-1/2" x 2-3/4" x 1-1/4", copper finish 18.00

Equator Monument, Ecuador, 5-1/2" h on 5" square wooden base, brass . 125.00

Field Museum of Natural History, Chicago, IL, 1" x 4-1/4" x 3", silver or copper finish 65.00

Franklin Trust Co., Patterson, NJ, 2-3/4" h x 3" x 2-1/4", coin bank, silver finish 400.00

Gateway Arch, St. Louis, MO., with cityscape, silver finish, 2-1/4" x 2-1/4" x 1-1/4" 45.00

General Motors Building, Detroit, MI, 3-3/4" x 6-1/4" x 4", antique bronze finish 250.00

Goodyear Zeppelin Hangar, Akron, OH, 2-1/4" h x 7" l x 2-3/4" w, aluminum 325.00

Johnson's Wax Tower, Racine, WI, 5-1/2" h on 2-1/2" diameter base, silver and red 185.00

La Giralda, Seville, Spain, 7-1/2" h, antique brass, 2-1/4" black marble base 65.00

Lincoln Memorial, Washington, DC, 1-1/2" x 3" x 2", copper finish 10.00

Loch Ness Castle, Scotland with swimming monster, bronze color, 3-1/2" h x 3" x 3" 50.00

Louisiana State Capitol, Baton Rouge, LA, 7" x 5-1/2" x 2-3/4", antique copper finish 68.00

Metropolitan Life Insurance Co., New York City, 5-1/4" x 3-3/4" x 2-1/4", silver or gold finish 125.00

Miami Beach Federal Savings, Miami, FL, 5-1/2" x 3-1/2" x 3-1/4", brass finish, Banthrico Bank 68.00

Mormon Temple, Salt Lake City, UT, 4" x 2-1/4" x 3-3/8", copper finish 45.00

Notre Dame, Paris, 2" x 3" x 1-1/2", bronze finish 16.00

Pan Am Building, New York City
Lighter, 4-1/2" h on 1-3/4" x 1-1/4" base, gold finish 350.00
Ruler, 2-3/4" h building on 6" ruler, gold finish 250.00

Petronas Towers, Kuala Lumpur, Malaysia, pewter
4-1/2" h x 3" x 1-1/4" 65.00
10-1/2" x 4-3/4" x 3-1/4" 110.00

Piaget Building, New York City, 6" h x 2-3/4" w x 2-1/4", gold finish 285.00

Prudential Building, Chicago, IL, 4-3/4", brass finish 125.00

Rockefeller Center, New York City
2-5/8" x 2" x 1", copper finish 75.00
4-1/4" x 3" x 1-3/8", silver finish . 125.00

Rose Bowl Stadium, Pasadena, CA, 1-1/4" x 6" x 5-1/2", bronze finish 145.00

Royal Observatory, Copenhagen, Denmark, 6" h x 2-1/4" diameter, silver plate 225.00

Sacre Coeur, Paris, 4-1/2" x 4-1/4" x 2-1/2", antique brass 32.00
Singing Tower, Bok Tower, Lake Wales, FL, 5" h, 1-3/4" d base 25.00
Space Needle, Seattle, WA, 6" h, revolving turret, silver or copper finish 30.00

Speyer Dom, Speyer, Germany 3-1/2" h x 4" l x 2" w, copper 110.00

Statue of Liberty, New York City
2" h 5.00
4-1/2" h 8.00
6" h 15.00

Stockholm City Hall, copper finish, 6-1/2" l, 4-1/4" w, 8" h, $195. Photo courtesy of Dixie Trainer.

St. Basil's Cathedral, Moscow, 4" x 3-1/2" x 3-1/2", solid brass, marble base 300.00

St. Peter's Cathedral, Rome, 3-1/2" h x 3-1/2" x 2-1/2", silver finish 35.00

Syracuse Savings Bank, Syracuse, NY, 5-1/2" x 4" x 3", copper finish 68.00

Tallinn, Estonia, City Hall, 3-1/4" h x 2" x 1", brass 55.00

United Nations Building, New York City, 3" x 4" x 2-1/2", antique brass 65.00

Washington, DC, cityscape, 5" h x 6" w x 3-1/2" d, brass finish 150.00

Washington Monument, Washington, DC
Salt and Pepper Shakers, 3-1/4" h, silver 27.00
Thermometer, 6" h, copper 9.00

Woolworth Building, New York City, 4" x 1-3/4" x 1-1/4", gold finish 55.00

Space Adventurers and Exploration

Collecting Hints: There are four distinct eras of fictional space adventurers: Buck Rogers, Flash Gordon, the radio and television characters of the late 1940s and 1950s, and the Star Trek and Star Wars phenomenon. Because Buck Rogers material is rare, condition is not as much of a factor as it is for the other three areas. Beware of dealers who break apart items, especially games, and sell parts separately.

In the early 1950s, a wealth of tin, battery-operated, friction, and windup toys not associated with a specific Space Adventurer were marketed. The popularity of these robots, space ships, and space guns is growing rapidly.

Trekkies began holding conventions in the early 1970s. They issued many fantasy items which must not be confused with items issued during the years the TV show was broadcast. The fantasy items are numerous and have little value beyond the initial selling price.

The American and Russian space programs produced a wealth of souvenir and related material. Beware of astronaut-signed material; it may have a printed or autopen signature.

History: In January 1929, "Buck Rogers 2429 A.D." began its comic strip run. Buck, Wilma Deering, Dr. Huer, and the villain Killer Kane were the creation of Phillip Francis Nowlan and John F. Dille. The heyday of Buck Rogers material was 1933 to 1937, when premiums were issued in conjunction with products such as Cream of Wheat and Cocomalt.

Flash Gordon followed in the mid-1930s. Buster Crabbe gave life to the character in movie serials. Books, comics, premiums, and other merchandise enhanced the image during the 1940s.

The use of rockets at the end of World War II and the beginning of the space research program gave reality to space travel. Television quickly capitalized on this in the early 1950s with programs such as "Captain Video" and "Space Patrol." Many other space heroes, such as Rocky Jones, had short-lived popularity.

In the 1950s, real-life space pioneers and explorers replaced the fictional characters as the center of the public's attention. The entire world watched on July 12, 1969, as man first walked on the moon. Although space exploration has suffered occasional setbacks, the public remains fascinated with its findings and potential.

"Star Trek" enjoyed a brief television run and developed a cult following in the early 1970s. "Star Trek: The Next Generation" has an established corps of watchers. "Star Wars" (Parts IV, V, and VI) and "ET" also initiated a wealth of merchandise which already is collectible.

References: Dana Cain, *UFO & Alien Collectibles Price Guide*, Krause Publications, 1998; Kelly Hoffman, *The Unauthorized Handbook and Price Guide to Star Trek Toys by Playmates*, Schiffer Publishing, 2000; James T. McCullum, *Irwin Toys: The Canadian Star Wars Connection*, Collector's Guide Publishing, Inc., 2000; Rex Miller, *The Investor's Guide to Vintage Character Collectibles*, Krause Publications, 1999; Frank M. Robinson, *Science Fiction of the Twentieth Century, An Illustrated History*, Collectors Press, 1999; Toy Shop, *Star War Collectibles*, Krause Publications, 1999; Stuart W. Wells, III, *Science Fiction Collectibles: Identification & Price Guide*, Krause Publications, 1999; —, *Star Wars Collector's Pocket Companion*, Krause Publications, 2000.

Periodicals: *Starlog Magazine*, 475 Park Ave. S., New York, NY 10016; *Strange New Worlds*, P.O. Box 223, Tallevast, FL 34270; *Star Wars Collection Trading Post*, 6030 Magnolia, P.O. Box 29396, St. Louis, MO 63139; *Trek Collector*, 1324 Palm Blvd., Dept. 17, Los Angeles, CA 90291.

Collectors' Clubs: Galaxy Patrol, 22 Colton St., Worcester, MA 01610; International Federation of Trekkers, P.O. Box 3123, Lorain, OH 44052;

Lost in Space Fan Club, 550 Trinity, Westfield, NJ 07090; Society for the Advancement of Space Activities, P.O. Box 192, Kent Hills, ME 04349; Star Trek: The Official Fan Club, P.O. Box 111000, Aurora, CO 80011; Starfleet, P.O. Box 430, Burnsville, NC 28714; Starfleet Command, P.O. Box 26076, Indianapolis, IN 46226.

Museums: Alabama Space & Rocket Center, Huntsville, AL; International Space Hall of Fame, The Space Center, Alamogordo, NM; Kennedy Space Center, Cape Canaveral, FL.

Additional Listings: Robots, Space Toys.

Battlestar Galactica

Comic Book, 1978, large size format 15.00
Electronic Game, working condition......................................50.00
Figure, Cylon Centurian, Mattel, MIB 150.00
Magazine, glossy periodical unfolds to 33" x 22"
   #1, Boxey & Muffey poster 25.00
   #2, Battlestar Spacecraft poster .25.00
   #3, Cyclon Warriors poster..........25.00
Model, Cylon Base Star, Revell Monogram, copyright 1997, MIB..........25.00

Magazine Cover, *Time*, July 25, 1969, $12.

Puzzle, Parker Brothes, Universal City Studios, 1978, No. 109, 140 pgs, 14" x 18"..5.00
Script, 1970s 20.00

Buck Rogers

Atomic Disintegrator, Hubley, 1930s, missing holding pin................... 290.00
Atomic Pistol, Daisy, silvered metal, C-8.5... 240.00
Badge, Solar Scouts 100.00
Battle Cruiser................................. 100.00
Big Little Book, CocoMalt 80.00
Book, *Buck Rogers Solar Scouts Handbook*, © 1936 .... 275.00
Comics, orig Sunday Funnies 100.00

Comics Page with Cut-Out, Omaha World Herald, 22-3/4" x 15", 1932 .... 45.00
Figure, lead...................................... 15.00
Helmet, lightning bolt design, 1935..800.00
Membership Kit
   1938, Rocket Rangers, card, letter, orig mailer...................................200.00
   1945, letter, card, and ship poster, envelope................................500.00
Paint Book, Whitman, 11" x 14", unused.......................................600.00
Photo, Buck Rogers, Buck and Wilma, 7-1/2" x 10", black and white, facsimile signatures, Cocomalt, c1934......85.00
Rocket Fighter, Wyandotte, 1936, 6" l 295.00
Space Ranger Kit, Sylvania TV premium, 1952, sealed..............................275.00
Thermos, plastic, Aladdin, 1979......35.00
Whistle Badge, Spaceship Commander 275.00

Captain Video

Decoder, 1-1/2" d, Capt Video Mysto-Coder, brass, plastic wheels, lightning bolt design.................................165.00
Gun, 2-1/2" x 3-1/2", Captain Video Secret Ray Gun, red plastic flashlight, secret message instructions, glow-in-the-dark card, Power House Candy premium..85.00
Magazine, *TV Star Parade*, two-pg photo article, Ideal Publishing Co., 1953.. 20.00
Pen Rocket 30.00
Press Book, 12" x 18", black, white, and blue cover, newspaper headline style..90.00
Rocket Sled, orig rockets............... 125.00
Space Figure, rubber 20.00
Spaceship, all parts 50.00

Flash Gordon

Bank, metal, rocket.......................... 35.00
Better Little Book, *Flash Gordon And The Perils of Mongo*, Whitman, 1940. 45.00
Big Little Book, *Flash Gordon and the Tournament of Mongo*.................. 55.00
Comics, Sunday Comics Page, 1935 .... 15.00
Book, pop-up, *Tournament Of Death*, Blue Ribbon Press and Pleasure Books, © 1935, 20 pgs............. 145.00
Eight-Pager, Flash Gordon, copyright 1950, 2-7/8" x 4-1/4" 38.00
Figure, Defender of the Earth
   Flash Gordon, MIP 15.00
   Ming, MIP 15.00
Gun, Radio Repeater, 1935, slight wear 800.00
Pencil Case, 1951 .... 160.00
Playset, Tootsietoy, figures, 1978, MIB... 100.00
Water Pistol, holster, King Features, 1975, MOC 45.00

Lost in Space

Blueprint Set 20.00

Comic Album, 7-3/4" x 10-1/4", Space Family Robinson/Lost In Space, stiff cover comic album, English reprints of Western Publishing Co full color comic book stories, © 1965 by World Distributors Ltd, 64 pgs 18.00
Game 180.00
Gum Wrapper, Lost in Space, US Gum, C-9.5 .... 100.00
Lunch Box, Lost in Space, dome..... 35.00
Model, Cyclops with Chariot, Aurora, MIB 2,350.00
Viewmaster, unopened 250.00

Outer Limits

Bubble Gum Cards, complete set, 1960s 250.00
Model, 6th Finger, vinyl, MIB 150.00
Television Poster 20.00

Space Cadet, Tom Corbett

Binoculars 125.00
Book
   Tom Corbett Space Cadet/Sabotage In Space, Grosset & Dunlap, hardcover, 212 pgs, dj 15.00
   Tom Corbett Push Out Book, unpunched, 1952, 14" x 10-1/2" 125.00
Decoder, 2-1/2" x 4", Tom Corbett Space Cadet Code, black, white, and red cardboard, membership card printed on back 45.00
Flashlight, 7" l, Space Cadet Signal Siren Flashlight, full color illus, orig box, c1952 .... 65.00
Lunch Box, red, C-8 .... 185.00
Membership Kit Fan Photo, 3-1/2" x 5-1/4", glossy black and white photo, Tom with Space Rangers, facsimile blue ink signature, c1952 .... 28.00
Patch, 2" x 4", cloth, Space Cadet, red, yellow, and blue, Kellogg's premium 35.00
Photo, 3-1/2" x 5-1/2", black and white glossy, blue signature "Spaceman's Luck/Tom Corbett/Space Cadet," early 1950s 45.00
Thermos, tin litho, Space Cadet, C-9 .... 95.00
Viewmaster Reel, set of three, orig story folder and envelope 45.00
Wrist Watch 250.00

Space Patrol

Belt and Buckle, 4" brass buckle, rocket, decoder mounted on back, glow-in-the-dark belt, Ralston premium, early 1950s 175.00
Coin Album, 3" x 7-3/4", thin cardboard black, white, and blue folder, spaceship landing and men rushing toward it, diecut slots for plastic Ralston premium or Schwinn Bicycle dealer coins, c1953 .... 175.00
Film Projector, pocket 185.00
Gun, Satellite 40.00
Handbook 165.00
Microscope, orig slides 195.00

Paper Cup, package of six, rocket ships, stars, and planets motif, orig cellophane and company label 70.00
Premium Card, 2-1/2" x 3-1/2", full color scene on front and back, text, ad for Wheat and Rice Chex Cereal, Rockets, Jets, and Weapons Series, seven cards from 40 card set, early 1950s 135.00
Space Helmet, diecut cardboard, six sided, yellow, green, red design, black top with printed red lightning flashes 1230.00
Watch, silvered chrome, stainless steel back, black leather straps, "Space Patrol" inscription on dial, black numerals, U.S. Time, early 1950s 165.00

Star Trek

Action Figure
   Borg Queen, loose 20.00
   Captain Kirk, Tholian Suit, loose.. 10.00
   Chekov, 9" h 15.00
   Cheron, 8" h, carded 250.00
   Data Transporter Figure, loose 12.00
   Gorn Captain, loose 10.00
   Guian, 9" h 50.00
   Jem Hadar, 9" h 25.00
   Keeper, loose 75.00
   Kira, 9" h 15.00
   Kirk, City on the Edge of Forever, loose 10.00
   Kirk and Spock, #1, Piece of the Action, Kaybee Set 200.00
   Klingon, 8" h, carded 60.00
   Lt. Commander La Froge Interstellar, loose 10.00
   McCoy, 8" h, carded 125.00
   Mugato, loose 300.00
   Neptuneman, loose 100.00
   O-Brien, 9" h 15.00
   Professor Data, All Good Things, loose 10.00
   Q, Judge's robe, flesh, 9" h 25.00
   Riker, 9" h 50.00
   Romulan, loose 700.00
   Scotty, 8" h, carded 125.00
   Sisko Dress, 9" 15.00
   Spock, City on the Edge of Forever, loose 10.00
   Talos, 8" h, carded 400.00
   Talos, 8" h, loose 200.00
   Ulhura, 8" h, carded 125.00
   Warrior Worf, 9" h 50.00
   Wolf Transporter Figure, loose..... 13.00
Bike Scout and Bike, Target Exclusive, MISB 60.00
Children's Book, *The Truth Machine*, hardcover, 1977 .... 10.00
Christmas Ornament, Hallmark
   1991, Enterprise 325.00
   1992, Shuttle 35.00
   1993, 1701-D, 1993 .... 30.00
   1994, Bird of Prey 30.00
   1995, Warbird 30.00
   1996, Voyager 30.00
   1997, Defiant 30.00
   1998, 1701-E 40.00
   Store display for 1992 ornament 100.00
Classic Communicator, lights and sounds
   Calculator 40.00
   Recorder 40.00
Universal Garage Door Opener 50.00

Cup, plastic, Deka, 1701 ship and crew, 1975 .... 30.00
Doll, Commander Sulu, 15" h, MIB 135.00
Drinking Glasses, set of four, orig Taco Bell display, Star Trek 3 .... 60.00
Halloween Costume, Mr. Spock, 1975 .... 85.00
Inflatable Enterprise, Star Trek 5, Kraft Foods promo, 24" l 15.00
Limited Edition Figure, Franklin Mint, pewter, orig stand, MIB
   Borg Ship 155.00
   Space Station 145.00
   U.S.S. Enterprise 160.00
Lunch Box, Borg, head, talking, 1992 .... 40.00
Manual, *Star Fleet Technical Manual*, hardcover, 1975 .... 60.00
Model
   AMT Enterprise, promo diecast TNG 100.00
   Galileo 7 Space Ship, AMT, 1974, orig contents sealed in box 150.00
   Klingon Battle Ship, AMT, 1968, orig contents sealed in box 150.00
   Mr. Spock, AMT, 1968, orig contents sealed in box 250.00
   USS Enterprise, AMT, 1968, orig contents seated in box 200.00
   USS Enterprise Command Bridge, AMT, 1975, orig contents sealed in box 150.00
Playset, Mego
   Bridge, 1975, sealed, MIB 300.00
   Combat Klingon Warrior, 9" 25.00
   Command Console 250.00
   Communicators, carded 200.00
   Galileo, shuttlecraft 35.00
   Gorn, 12" 30.00
   Insurrection Captian Picard, 12". 30.00
   Insurrection Enterprise 35.00
   Insurrection Phaser 20.00
   Mission to Gamma VI 400.00
   Mugato, 12" 30.00
   Seven of Nine, 9" 30.00
   Sulu, 12" 30.00
   Trekulator 250.00
   Tricarder 250.00
Playset, Playmates, Bridge, NRFB 100.00
Puzzle, boxed, Canadian 20.00
Ring, USS Enterprise
   Red plastic, raised image of spaceship, planets, and stars, bright gold luster accents, mkd "Hong Kong," 1970s 20.00
   White plastic, ship design, black accents, white stars, stamped "Canada," 1970s 20.00
Stamp Cachet, Trek Artwork, Shuttle, 1991, limited edition 50.00
Record, book and record, MIP 5.00
Towel, Voyager Promo, Fritts Candy, full color 50.00
Vehicle and Accessories
   Borg Cube 50.00
   Communicators, loose, pr........... 85.00
   DS9 Station 70.00
   Enterprise B 140.00
   Excelsior 140.00

Ferengi Fighter, Galoob, 1989, mint, C-8 box 35.00
Insurrection Phaser 15.00
Klingon Disruptor.........................25.00
Pikes Laser Pistol........................20.00
Romulan Warbird..........................50.00
Shuttlecraft, Goodard, battle sounds, MIB..75.00
Spacecraft Galileao, Galoob, 1989, mint, C-8 box 35.00
Voyager 140.00
Wall Clock, 1701-E Ship, Wesco......50.00
Watch, Timex, Cloaking Romulan, 1993, orig case 75.00

Space Exploration

Autograph, envelope, inked Jack Swigert signature on back, Man on Moon stamp, canceled Kennedy Space Center, April 11, 1970..................50.00
Bank, Apollo Astronaut in Space Suit, ceramic 40.00
Book
First American Into Space, Robert Silverberg, Monarch Books, 142 pgs, 1961 ....20.00
NASA Astronauts Biography Book, NASA, 1968, 8" x 10-1/4", softcover 40.00
The Space Eagle: Operation Doomsday, Jack Pearl, Whitman 1578, 1967 ....6.00
Candy Container, 2-3/4" h, hard plastic, moon module, red, blue, and green, Triumph Candy, 1970s, one black plastic wheel missing 12.00
Children's Book, *The Conquest of Space*, Willy Ley, illus by Chesley Bonestell, Viking, 1952, 7th printing...............9.00
Clock, 4" x 4-1/2" x 2", Apollo 11, animated wind-up, ivory case, red, white, and blue diecut, metallic blue dial, Apollo craft illus, gold colored numerals, brass hands, mkd "Lux Clock Mfg Co." 145.00
Dish, 8" d, Apollo II Commemorative, iridescent glass, raised design, inscription "One Small Step," 1970s......18.00
Glass
Astronaut Neil Armstrong, 5-1/2" h, clear glass, brown and white graphics of Armstrong wearing suit, gold lettering "Wapakoneta Astronaut Neil Armstrong," list of 1961-1966 manned space flights on reverse.............37.00
Columbia Space Shuttle, 4-1/2" h, clear, weighted bottom, black and white facsimile of NY times, April 15, 1981, Wendy's 15.00
Gyroscope, Gemini, plastic, 1960s, MOC..30.00
Letter Opener, 7" l, Apollo 11, gold colored metal, insignia on handle, grained black leather-like scabbard 30.00
Magazine, *Life*
1966, July 1, Moon Shot cover 5.00
1969, July 25, Leaving for Moon cover, article on Armstrong..................10.00
1969, Aug. 8, On the Moon with Flag cover, color photos 12.00

Magazine, *Look*, 1960, Feb. 2, The Lady Wants To Orbit, cov article, six pgs, Betty Skelton article and photos .17.50
Magazine, *Newsweek*
1969, Jan. 6, Apollo, Anders, Lovell, Borman cover 8.00
1969, July 28, Moonwalk cover, black and white..9.00
1969, Aug. 11, Moonwalk cover, color..9.00
Magazine, *Time*
1962, March 2, John Glenn cover..6.00
1962, Aug. 24, Russian Astronauts cover..5.00
1969, Jan. 3, US Astronauts cover..5.00
Medal, 1-1/2" d, commemorative, SS, astronaut descending from landing module onto moon, "One Small Step" inscription, plaque left on moon on reverse, acrylic case...................40.00
Model, Space 1999
MPC, Moonbase Alpa, MIB...... 300.00
MPC, Eagle, MIB...................... 100.00
Mug, 3" h, china, black St. Louis Globe-Democrat newspaper design of July 20, 1969, moon landing...............35.00
Patch, 9" x 9", cloth, Apollo 16, white background, full color, 3-1/2"d astronaut patch in center of red, white and blue shield, eagle at top against lunar background, blue and white star border, astronaut names Young, Matlingly, and Duke...................................24.00
Pennant, 29" l, felt, red and white, blue trim, First Man On Moon 20.00
Photograph, Space Program, 1965/66, set of five UPI and WW photos....20.00
Pinback Button
1-1/4" d, New Frontier, Man of the Year, Astronaut John Glenn, blue and white 35.00
3" d, Challenger 7, black and white photo, purple background 15.00
3-1/2" d, Gemini 4, black and white photos of McDivitt and White, red, white, and blue ground, June 3-7, 1965 walk in space mission 35.00
Plate
7-1/2" d, Apollo 13, glass, brown and tan lunar landscape, white silhouette of astronaut on moon surface, rim inscribed, "General Electric" and "United States Atomic Energy Commission," back and white NASA symbol..40.00
9-1/4" d, John Glenn, white china, black and white illus, stylized gold pattern, Feb. 20, 1962 flight.............30.00
Poster, Apollo Astronaut, set of three, large 35.00
Press Pass, 3" x 4-1/4", laminated, ABC News, June 18-24, 1983, Challenger Mission, black and white photos, blue, white, and orange design...........60.00
Puzzle, Apollo 11, 1969, MIB 25.00
Record, America's First Man In Orbit, John Glenn, 33-1/3 rpm, orig envelope.......................................35.00

Ring, Astronaut, adjustable aluminum ring, mkd inside band "Copyright Uncas Mfg Co.," top with atom symbols surrounding rocketships, large raised image of astronaut wearing helmet and oxygen mask, 1960s, slight wear 18.00
Rug, 19-1/2" x 37-1/2", woven, full color moon landing scene, red, white, and blue stars and stripes motif border, made in Italy, orig label 60.00
Ruler, 6", Space Shuttle 3-D Picture Ruler, blue, red, and white, illus 4-1/2" x 7" card, diecut opening, five images of space shuttle in flight, Vari-Vue, Mt Vernon, NY, unopened, orig display bag................................. 8.00
Salt and Pepper Shakers, pr, 3" h, china, blue symbol and Columbia shuttle design, inscription "Johnson Space Center, Houston, TX," early 1980s.. 20.00
Tie Clip, 1-1/2", Apollo 11, brass, black accents, raised moon landing design, landing date and astronaut names on rim, orig plastic display case...... 42.00

Space Related

Bank, Satellite, Duro, mold diecast rocket, 11" h................................. 100.00
Birthday Card, 1950s, 6" x 7" 20.00
Book
Rockets to Explore The Unknown, 1964.. 20.00
Science Fiction Films Pictorial History, Jeff Rovin, 1975..................... 25.00
Calendar, Alien, Heavy Metal, 1989.. 25.00
Cap
Beacon Beanie, signal cap, 1950s, orig box.................................... 100.00
Junior Astronaut, 1950s 45.00
Costume, child's
Alien, 1992, MIB 100.00
Micronauts, Baron Karza, Ben Cooper, 1978.. 125.00
Space Commander, uniform and hat 100.00
Space Man, 1950s 250.00
Flashlight
Alien head, green plastic 30.00
Johnny Astro Explorer, Topper, 1960s, MIB.. 95.00
Folder, Mead, colorful 20.00
Globe, moon, tin 45.00
Little Golden Book, *Exploring Space*, 1958.. 20.00
Nodder, Martian couple, plastic, 4" h.. 65.00
Pajamas, child's, Voltron 45.00
Pinback Button, Space Angel.......... 40.00
Planter, Space Shuttle and Astronaut, Inarco... 75.00
Poster, Space Age Brand Fireworks, 24" x 10", 1960s.................................. 15.00
Radio, Star Command, Calfax, 1970s, AM Robark, mascot robot, MIB........ 60.00
Space Ship, yellow, MIB 50.00
Record, child's, Space: 1999, book and record, MIP................................... 5.00

Ring, spaceship, white plastic, mkd "Canada," 1970s 15.00

Store Display
    Atomic Jet Flying Saucer, helicopter 50.00
    Spaceman Air Freshner, 1950s space outfit.................................... 150.00

Toy, Space Alien, pop-up, green plastic, 3" h 20.00

Writing Tablet, Frontiers of Space, 8-1/2" x 11", 1950s, unused 20.00

Space Toys

Collecting Hints: The original box is an important element in pricing, perhaps controlling 15 to 20 percent of the price. The artwork on the box may differ slightly from the toy inside; this is to be expected. The box also may provide the only clue to the correct name of the toy.

The early lithographed tin toys are more valuable than the later toys made of plastic. There is a great deal of speculation in modern toys, e.g., Star Wars material. Hence, the market shows great price fluctuation.

Collect toys in very good to mint condition. Damaged and rusted lithographed tin is hard to repair. Check the battery box for damage. Don't ever leave batteries in a toy when it is not in use.

History: The Hollywood movies of the early 1950s drew attention to space travel. The launching of Sputnik and American satellites in the late 1950s and early 1960s enhanced this fascination. The advent of manned space travel, culminating in the landing on the moon, further increased interest in anything space-related, and the toy industries of Japan and America. Lithographed tin and plastic models of astronauts, flying saucers, spacecraft, and space vehicles became quickly available. Some were copies of original counterparts; most were the figments of the toy designer's imagination.

During the 1970s, there was less emphasis on the space program and a corresponding decline in the production of space-related toys. The earlier Japanese- and American-made products gave way to less-expensive models from China and Taiwan.

References: Jim Bunte, Dave Hallman and Heinz Mueller, *Vintage Toys: Robots and Space Toys*, Krause Publications, 2000; Dana Cain, *UFO & Alien Collectibles Price Guide*, Krause Publications, 1998; Toy Shop, *Star War Collectibles*, Krause Publications, 1999; Stuart W. Wells, III, *Science Fiction Collectibles: Identification & Price Guide*, Krause Publications, 1999.

Periodical: *Robot World & Price Guide*, P.O. Box 184, Lenox Hill Station, New York, NY 10021.

Reproduction Alert.

Additional Listings: Robots, Space Adventurers and Explorers.

Buck Rogers Super Sonic Ray Gun, Norton-Homer Mfg. Co., plastic, copyright 1955, $65.

Aero Jet Range Rocket, red and blue plastic 11" h rocket, Ranger Steel Products Corp, Roslyn Heights, NY, c1950, 12" x 12" x 3" orig box 10.00

Astronaut
    Astro-Scout, 9-1/2" h, Yonezawa, Japan, litho tin, advances using crank friction lever, separate litho tin chest plate with #3, clear plastic helmet visor over litho tin face 2,500.00
    Man in Space, 8" l, Alps, Japan, battery operated, litho tin and plastic, orig box 950.00
    Mark Apollo Astronaut, 7-1/2" h, Marx, jointed plastic, orange space suit, white helmet, plastic accessories, orig instructions and box 175.00

Atomic Pistol, Bucks Rogers, Daisy, silvered metal, C-8.5 .... 240.00

Cap Gun
    Jet Jr Space, chrome, MIB 425.00
    Strato Gun, chrome, mint 465.00

Card Game, Space-O 30.00

Chalk, rocket ship illus, Creston 10.00

Colored Pencils, Dixon, space graphics 25.00

Colorforms, Battlestar Galactica 35.00

Coloring Book Set, Galacica 40.00

Doll, Mars Attack, Spygirl, talking, MIP 65.00

Drafting Set, Space Scientist, 1950s 80.00

Eagle Lunar Module, Daishin, Japan, battery operated, 1969, MIB 300.00

Figure
    A-Ok Astronaut, helmets, plastic, 1950s, MIP 10.00

Astronaut, 6" h, Marx, set of six different poses 100.00

Close Encounter of the Third Kind, Alien, bendee, MOC 45.00

Space Alien, 11" l, suction cup walker 40.00

Spaceman, plastic, Hong Kong, MIP 15.00

Firecrackers, Chinese, Rocket brand 20.00

Flying Saucer
    Air Commanders, sling powered glider, MIP 25.00
    Atomic Jet, Flying-O-Saucer, 1950s, orig instructions 20.00
    Blue, clear plastic and tin, 5" d ... 75.00
    Flying Saucer and Pilot, Cragston, Japan, 1950s, battery operated, 7-1/2" d 285.00
    Jupiter, litho tin, clear dome, sparks, mkd "K, Japan" 45.00
    King, tin, battery operated, MIB 140.00
    Z-101, litho tin, friction, 1950s, 6-1/2" l 225.00

Game
    Astro Launch, Ohio Art 110.00
    Blast Off, 1960s, MIP 35.00
    Countdown Arithmetic Space Game, Whitman, 1962 .... 30.00
    Moon Blastoff, Schaper, unused, sealed, MIB 48.00
    Planet Patrol, interplant space game, 1950s 75.00
    Space Faces, Pressman Toys, 1950s, Mr. Potato Head-type space kit, unplayed with condition, C-8 box 340.00
    War of the Daleks, 15" x 19" x 3", Strawberry Fayre, England, orig playing pieces, game board, and box, copyright 1975 B.B.C., wear 48.00

Gumball Machine, Rocket to the Stars, rocketship shape 225.00

Gun
    Astroray, tin friction, Japan, 10" l, MIB 100.00
    Cosmic Ray Space Gun, 1950s 100.00
    Cosmic Space Rifle, tin, Korea, 13" l 75.00
    Dan Dare Planet Gun, Eagle Toys, England, 1950s, unplayed with 165.00
    Jet Ray Gun, friction, graphic box 35.00
    Jet Space Gun, KO, Japan, tin litho, 1960s, 10" l 55.00
    Junior Jet Play Gun, open faced box with Space Girl graphics 45.00
    Rocket Jet Space Gun, silver plastic, 7" l 45.00
    Space Fazer, Kusan, 12" l 65.00
    Space Flash, battery operated, plastic, 6" l, MIB 65.00
    Space Gun, litho tin, friction window, yellow, Toy Hero, Japan 30.00
    Space Gun, Mickey Mouse, green plastic, Young Epoch Co., Japan, 1928 .... 90.00
    Space Gun, plastic, 6" l 60.00
    Space Gun, western style, red plastic, M&L Toys, 9" l 75.00

Space Jet, litho tin, Japan, 10" l..75.00
Space Pilot Jet Ray Gun, Hong Kong, friction, 1970s, 10" l 45.00
Space Pistol, Arco, © 1982, MOC.. 15.00
Space 1999, stun gun, MIB, some damage to box 100.00
Kite, Gayla Space Craft, unused, MIP..35.00
Lunar Bug Mooncraft, battery operated, 1960s, unused, MIB 150.00
Mask, 7" x 8" x 2", robot, tin gray plastic, dayglo orange and black, c1970 .5.00
Missile Launcher, 1950s, MIB 45.00
Model Kit
  Cyclops with Chariot, Lost in Space, Aurora, MIB...........................2,350.00
  Russian's First Spacecraft, Vostok, Revell, copyright 1969, 8" x 14-1/2" x 3" box, unassembled...................38.00
  Space Buggy, Monogram, copyright 1969, 7" x 14" x 2" box, some assembly.. 18.00
Moon Platoon, rubber robot figures, Japanese, Imperial, 1969, on card.....70.00
Motorized Astrobase, Ideal, 10" x 10" x 20" base, 12" x 12" x 20" h blue, white, and orange box, c1980, damage to orig box, play wear....................115.00
Pinball Game, bagatelle, space scene, 1950s, 14" l 45.00
Plane, NASA 905 Space Shuttle Challenger, 1/175 scale, Boeing 747 metal body, plastic wings, decals and flags, 12" l, 7" w.....................................75.00
Playset
  ID4 Los Angeles Invasion, buildings, tanks, men, MIB...........................35.00
  Space: 1999 Adventure Playset, unpunched, mint 145.00
  Space: 1999 Moonbase Alpha..125.00
  Star Station Seven, Marx #4115, 1978, MIB..75.00
Puzzle
  Moon map, Rand McNally, 1960s, unused, sealed..........................25.00
  Rip Foster, frame tray, 1953 ....35.00
Race Car
  Fire Wings, Marusan, Japan, Pontiac Experimental Car, 8" l, all tin, yellow, orange, and red, tin litho rider, C-8.5 ....285.00
  Rocket 7, Japan, 1950s, tin, 6-1/2" l, C-7 ....40.00
  Space Rocket Patrol Ship, Courtland Toys, 1950s, friction, 7" l 140.00
Ring, 2-1/4" x 4-1/2" neatly opened black and white envelope, instructions, hard plastic black base, 1-3/4" d red soft plastic Flying Jet saucer, black string attached to orig paper insert, 1960s cereal premium............................70.00
Rocket
  Interplanetary Rocket, Japan, early 1960s, 15" h, battery operated, tin, NASA emblems, orig insert, C-9 box 370.00
  Moon Rocket, Modern Toys, Japan, battery operated, late 1950s or early 1960s, 9-1/2" l, all tin, astronaut revolving on top, another beneath dome, C-9..455.00

Satellite, Orbiters, Frisbee type, 1950s, unused, MOC..............................55.00
Space Car, Pyro, plastic, 4" l, played with condition.................................30.00
Space Helmet, metal, bullet shaped, 1950s, 10" h 75.00
Space Rocket, Marx, 11" h 70.00
Space Ship
  Space 1999 Eagle 1 Spaceship, 30" l, MIB..225.00
  Space Ship X-5, battery operated, tin and plastic, 1970s, orig box........95.00
  Transcontinental Rocket Ship, Buck Rogers, 4" l, 1930s......................95.00
Space Tank, Robby, China, 1980s, MIB.. 145.00
Space Vehicle, plastic, red, yellow, and blue, Irwin, 1950s, 9" l 200.00
Spinner, Space Patrol 20.00
Squeeze Toy, Space Boy in rocket, figural, unused 40.00
Strato-Scout Space Phones, red and black hard plastic, attached soft plastic antenna, 1-1/2" x 2" x 5-1/2" h, orig mailing envelope, instruction sheet, mkd "J.V.Z. Co.," 1954 postmark 50.00
Target Game, tin
  Rocket and spaceship, 1950s, 15" x 23"... 100.00
  Rocket Patrol, magnetic, 14" x 16"... 100.00
Transformer, Space Mummy, Ultraman, diecast, 1980, MIB.................... 225.00
Viewmaster, Lost in Space, unopened 250.00
Whistle, Space Signal, rocket shape, red and yellow plastic, 5" l 25.00
Yo-Yo, Orbit, small white plastic satellite, green plastic ball used to represent Earth, string, copyright 1969 Tom Boy Inc., blue, white, and orange blister card 10.00

Sports Collectibles

Collecting Hints: The amount of material is unlimited. Pick a favorite sport and concentrate on it. Within the sport, narrow collecting emphasis to items associated with one league, team, individual, or era, or concentrate on one type of equipment. Include as much three-dimensional material as possible.

Each sport has a hall of fame. Make a point to visit it and get to know its staff, an excellent source of leads for material that the museum no longer wants in its collection. Induction ceremonies provide an excellent opportunity to make contact with heroes of the sport, as well as with other collectors.

History: Individuals have been saving sports-related equipment since

the inception of sports. Some material was passed down from generation to generation for reuse. The balance occupied dark spaces in closets, attics, and basements.

In the 1980s, two key trends brought collectors' attention to the sports arena. First, decorators began using old sports items, especially in restaurant decor. Second, card collectors began to discover the thrill of owing the "real" thing. Although the principal thrust was on baseball memorabilia, by the beginning of the 1990s all sport categories were collectible, with automobile racing, boxing, football, and horse racing especially strong.

References: Mark Allen Baker, *All Sport Autograph Guide*, Krause Publications, 1994; *Collector's Guide to Celebrity Autographs*, 2nd ed., Krause Publications, 2000; Jeanne Cherry, *Tennis Antiques & Collectibles*, Amaryllis Press (Box 3658, Santa Monica, CA 90408), 1996; Chuck Furjanic, *Antique Golf Collectibles, A Price and Reference Guide, 2nd Edition*, Krause Publications, 2000; Tom Mortenson, *2000 Standard Catalog of Sports Memorabilia*, Krause Publications, 1999, Tom Mortenson, *Warman's Sports Collectibles*, Krause Publications, 2001.

Periodical: *Sports Collectors Digest*, 700 E. State St., Iola, WI 54990.

Museum: National Bowling Hall of Fame & Museum, St. Louis, MO; New England Sports Museum, Boston, MA; University of New Haven National Art Museum of Sport, W Haven, CT.

Additional Listings: Baseball Collectibles, Basketball Collectibles, Boxing Collectibles, Fishing Collectibles, Golf Collectibles, Hunting Collectibles, Olympics Collectibles, Racing Collectibles, Wrestling Collectibles.

Autograph
  Agassi, Andre, photograph 40.00
  McEnroe, John 40.00
  Navratilova, Martina 40.00
  Perry, Fred, canceled check....... 50.00
  Sabatina, Gabriella...................... 40.00
  Witt, Katarina, photograph.......... 40.00
Bank
  4-1/2" d, composition, soccer ball, orig rubber stopper, c1950 .... 25.00
  4-1/2" d, metal, emb enameled fishing, golf, and travel scenes, changing date feature, 1950s, Cada Co., Chicago 60.00

5-1/4" h, Garfield bowling, mkd "Garfield Copyright 1981 United Features Syndicate, Licensee Eneseco," orig foil label 58.00

Book

American Sports Heroes of Today, Fred Katz, Random House, 1970, illus profiles of 40 champions 12.00

Bowditch For Yacktsmen: Piloting, Nathenial Bowditch, David McKay Co., 1976, 1st ed., 405 pgs 9.50

Hail to Pitt: Sports History of the University of Pittsburgh, Jim O'Brien, Wolfson Publ, 1982, 1st ed., 294 pgs, dj 25.00

How to Improve Your Tennis, Consultant Harry "Cap" Leighton, Tennis Coach, Senior High School, Chicago, and Forest Tennis Club, Athletic Institute Publishers 9.00

Modern Tennis, P. A. Valle, Funk and Wagnalls, Co., 1915, first edition 70.00

The Sportsman's Encyclopedia, A Practical, Detailed Guide to the World's Most Popular Team and Solo Sports, Bill Burton, ed., Grossett & Dunlap, 1971, 638 pgs 13.75

Youth Soccer Parent/Coach Primer, Basic Philosophy & Techniques for Coaching Young Players, U.S. Youth Soccer, 1993 .... 10.00

Bowling Shirt, woman's, white, red trim, name "Betty" stitched on pocket, numerous bowling related patches on back and shoulder, c1950 .... 48.00

Brooch

Goldtone, soccer angel, 2-1/4" l . 28.00

Platinum, tennis racquet, pearl as ball 125.00

Silvertone, lady bowling, peach enameled skirt, bright blue rhinestone on ball, 2" w, 2" h 32.00

Silvertone, tennis racquet, 1" l 2.00

Calendar Plate, 1967, bowling, football, water skiing, tennis, gold trim, 10" d 5.00

Cigarette Card, John Player and Sons, Imperial Tobacco Co., Great Britain, showing tennis stars, set of 50 cards 150.00

Cigarette Lighter, Scripto VU, bowling motif 30.00

Counter Display Sign, 17-1/2" h, Budweiser, scoring soccer player, MLS soccer logo 8.00

Decanter, tennis player, Ezra Brooks, Heritage China, 1973 .... 20.00

Dexterity Game, 2-1/4" d, soccer motif, sgd "D.R.G.M. in US Zone Germany" 25.00

Figure, 6-1/2" h, caricature, zealous lady bowler who rocks back and hits male bowler, © 1941 L. Ritgers, painted plaster 195.00

Game, Bowling-A Board Game, Parker Bros, orig box, 1896 .... 60.00

Hair Bow, 3" x 8" x 7-1/2" orig package, "Queen of the Roller Derby," 12 orig cellophane packages with rayon fabric hair bow and roller skating theme, each also includes black and white photo of female roller derby star, Gerry

Murray, Toughie Brasuhn, or Mary Gardner, by Burlington Mills, 1950s 60.00

Magazine

Life, Roy Campanella, June 8, 1953 .... 15.00

Life, November 1971 .... 7.50

Sport Revue, Quebec publication, February 1956, Bert Olmstead, Hall of Fame cov 15.00

Sports Illustrated, July 15, 1974, Jimmy Connors and Chris Evert . 10.00

Sports Illustrated, Sept. 6, 1954, sailing 17.50

Medal

1-1/8" d, tennis, back inscribed "1st Category Champion" 15.00

1-3/8" d, 1950 World Cup Soccer Cup Commemorative, issued 1983 by Uruguayan Association of Professional Footballers 24.00

Medallion, 10" x 12", wood frame, American Youth Soccer Organization .. 15.00

Mug, 5" h, gentleman playing with balls, two ladies shaking hands on reverse, Arthur Wood, Royal Bradwell, England, c1945 .... 45.00

Necklace, 16" l twisted rope cord, 1-3/4" l wood bowling pins, brass clasp, c1925 .... 125.00

Nodder, 6" h, "You're Right Down My Alley," composition, man holding bowling ball, mounted on wood block base 50.00

Pencil, Mechanical, 3-7/8" l, Odessa, TX, souvenir 20.00

Pencil Sharpener, 1-1/4" x 1-3/4" x 2", green and plastic, portable TV shape, full color flicker as screen, Kohner Products, c1950 .... 25.00

Pennant, 9" l, soccer ball and shoe, Sportvyroba Bardejov 20.00

Pinback Button

American Bowling Congress, 1932, 32nd Annual Tournament, Detroit, silver dollar size, red, blue, and blue, large luxury car in center 80.00

Congressional Country Club Caddie, red and white center, blue and gold trim, c1930 .... 20.00

Dallas Turnverein Bowling Club, "There's No Use Crying Baby Houston, You Can't Have This Cup," blue, white, and black, 1901-10 .... 42.00

Devil's Lake Regatta, blue and white, speedboat races, July 1934, 1-3/4" d 15.00

National Association of Amateur Oarsmen, black and white illus, competition roaring crews, late 1890s 30.00

Outboard Regatta, black lettering, tan ground, 1930s, 2-1/8" d 15.00

U.S. Open Tennis Championship, 1975, 2-1/8" d 15.00

Poster, Play Helps Study, colorful tennis motif, 1924 .... 30.00

Program, United States Lawn Tennis Championships, 9" x 12", official souvenir program, men's singles, women's singles, mixed doubles, September

1947, West Side Tennis Club, Forest Hills, NY, 56 pages, photos and player profiles, ads 40.00

Sculpture, 14-7/8" h, metal, tennis player holding racquet, sgd by Mexican artist 85.00

Snow Dome, 3" d pale transparent amber glass globe, 1-1/2" x 3" x 3" hard plastic black base, gold lettering on front "York County Lions/Team-High Average 1959," three miniature golden bowling pins and black ball in center with gold granules 40.00

Soccer Ball, Always Coca-Cola, 1997 .... 12.00

Telephone

Centra II, soccer motif, orig owner's manual, MIB 60.00

Sports Illustrated, speakerphone 25.00

Tennis Balls, Wilson Match-point, c1945, orig can never opened 30.00

Tennis Racket

Dayton, 1923 patent date, 26-1/2" l 70.00

Magnan, vintage 80.00

Maureen Connolly, full color portrait on handle, Wilson Sporting Goods, 1950s 20.00

Wright & Ditson Championship, 26" l 50.00

Tie Tac, 14kt yg, bowling ball and pin, patchwork Florentine texture, c1960 .... 135.00

Trophy, 3-1/4" h, crystal soccer ball on pedestal, sgd "Val St. Lambert" 125.00

Wire Service Photo, Chicago Bulls Scottie Pippen and Detroit Pistons Vinnie Johnson, 1989 .... 3.50

Stangl Pottery

Collecting Hints: Stangl Pottery produced several lines of highly collectible dinnerware and decorative accessories, including the famed Stangl birds. The red-bodied dinnerware was produced in distinctive shapes and patterns. Shapes were designated by numbers. Pattern names include Country Garden, Fruit, Tulip, Thistle, and Wild Rose. Special Christmas, advertising, and commemorative wares also were produced.

Bright colors and bold simplistic patterns make Stangl pottery a favorite with Country collectors. Stangl sold seconds from a factory store long before outlet malls became popular. Large sets of Stangl dinnerware currently command high prices at auctions, flea markets, and even antiques shops.

As many as ten different trademarks were used. Dinnerware was marked and often signed by the decorator. Most birds are numbered; many are artist signed. However, signatures are useful for dating purposes only and add little to value.

Several of the well-known Stangl birds were reissued between 1972 and 1977. These reissues are dated on the bottom and are worth approximately half as much as the older birds.

History: The origins of Fulper Pottery, the predecessor to Stangl, are clouded. The company claimed a date of 1805. Paul Evans, a major American art pottery researcher, suggests an 1814 date. Regardless of which date is correct, by the middle of the 19th century an active pottery was located in Flemington, New Jersey.

When Samuel Hill, the pottery's founder, died in 1858, the pottery was acquired by Abraham Fulper, a nephew. Abraham died in 1881, and the business continued under the direction of his sons, Edward, George W., and William.

In 1910, Johann Martin Stangl began working at Fulper as a chemist and plant superintendent. He left Fulper in 1914 to work briefly for Haeger Potteries. By 1920, Stangl was back at Fulper serving as general manager. In 1926, Fulper acquired the Anchor Pottery in Trenton, New Jersey, where a line of solid-color dinnerware in the California patio style was produced.

William Fulper died in 1928, at which time Stangl became president of the firm. In 1920, Johann Martin Stangl purchased Fulper, and Stangl Pottery was born. During the 1920s production emphasis shifted from art pottery to dinner and utilitarian wares.

A 1929 fire destroyed the Flemington pottery. Rather than rebuild, a former ice cream factory was converted to a showroom and production facility. By the end of the 1930s, production was concentrated in Trenton with the Flemington kiln used primarily for demonstration purposes.

Stangl's ceramic birds were produced from 1940 until 1972. The birds were made in Stangl's Trenton plant, then shipped to the Flemington plant for hand painting. During World War II the demand for these birds and Stangl pottery was so great that 40 to 60 decorators could not keep up with it. Orders were contracted out to private homes. These pieces were then returned for firing and finishing. Different artists used different colors to decorate these birds.

On August 25, 1965, fire struck the Trenton plant. The damaged portion

of the plant was rebuilt by May 1966. On February 13, 1972, Johann Martin Stangl died. Frank Wheaton, Jr., of Wheaton Industries, Millville, New Jersey, purchased the plant in June 1972 and continued Stangl production. In 1978, the Pfaltzgraff Company purchased the company's assets from Wheaton. Production ceased. The Flemington factory became a Pfaltzgraff factory outlet. One of the original kilns remains intact to commemorate the hard work and to demonstrate the high temperatures involved in the production of pottery.

References: Susan and Al Bagdade, *Warman's American Pottery and Porcelain*, 2nd ed., Krause Publications, 2000; Harvey Duke, *Stangl Pottery*, Wallace-Homestead, 1993; Robert Runge, Jr., *Collector's Encyclopedia of Stangl Dinnerware*, Collector Books, 2000; Mike Schneider, *Stangl and Pennsbury Pottery Birds,* Schiffer Publishing, 1994.

Collectors' Club: Stangl/Fulper Collectors Club, P.O. Box 64-A, Changewater, NJ 07831.

Additional Listings: See *Warman's Antiques and Collectibles Price Guide* for prices of bird figurines.

Plate, Colonial Rose, pink decoration, scalloped edge, 10-1/2" d, $15.

Dinnerware

Amber Glo, pitcher, pint 40.00
Arbor, dinner plate 22.50
Bittersweet
  Tidbit Tray, 10" d...........................45.00
Blueberry
  Coffeepot.................................. 100.00
  Creamer 15.00
  Platter, 14" d 75.00
  Salt and Pepper Shakers, pr........24.00
  Vegetable Bowl, 8" 50.00
Brittany, dinner plate,
  10-1/2" d 125.00
Colonial, #1388
  Candleholders, pr, blue 40.00
  Carafe, pottery stopper, wooden handle..65.00

Cigarette Box.................................60.00
Creamer and Sugar, green 20.00
Cup and Saucer............................12.00
Dinner Plate, 10" d, yellow 12.00
Salad Bowl, Round, 10" d 35.00
Salad Plate, 8" d, tangerine 8.00
Salt and Pepper Shakers, pr 20.00
Teapot..75.00
Teapot, individual 45.00
Dogwood
  Bowl, ruffled rim..........................55.00
  Cup and Saucer 11.50
Festival, vegetable bowl, open,
  round..45.00
Fruit
  Casserole, 8" d 85.00
  Chop Plate, 14" d 65.00
  Creamer, individual 25.00
  Cup and Saucer...........................18.00
  Dinner Plate, 10" d.......................25.00
  Eggcup..18.00
  Platter, round, 12-1/2" d, green ...35.00
  Salad Bowl, 11-1/2" d, green 40.00
  Salt and Pepper Shakers, pr 24.00
  Sherbet 20.00
  Teapot..100.00
  Teapot, individual 60.00
  Vegetable Bowl, divided 38.00
Garland, sugar bowl, light gray, maroon
  flowers and trim, 6-1/2" d,
  3-1/2" h 35.00
Golden Blossom, soup bowl,
  7-1/2" d 12.00
Golden Glo, bowl, pink and white, mkd
  "GG 3786" 20.00
Golden Grape, platter, palette
  shape...30.00
Golden Harvest
  Butter Dish, cov, 1/4 lb 35.00
  Cup and Saucer...........................11.50
  Dinner Plate, 10" d.......................12.00
  Gravy Boat...................................15.00
  Platter, 13-3/4" l, casual shape ...25.00
  Salt and Pepper Shakers, pr 12.50
  Vegetable Bowl, cov 50.00
  Vegetable Bowl, open, 8" d,
  round...28.00
Harvest, dinner plate, 10" d............18.00
Holly, pitcher, pint 38.00
Jeweled Christmas Tree
  Chop Plate, 14" d 175.00
  Cigarette Box..............................250.00
  Creamer.......................................40.00
  Cup and Saucer...........................50.00
  Dinner Plate, 10" d.......................65.00
  Pitcher, 2 qt.................................100.00
  Punch Bowl, 12" d 200.00
  Punch Cup...................................25.00
  Salad Plate, 8" d 40.00
  Sugar 40.00
Kiddieware
  Bowl, Goldilocks...........................150.00
  Child's Feeding Dish, 3 compartments
      Ducky Dinner 125.00
      Kitten Capers 100.00
      Playful Pups....................125.00
  Cup
      Goldilocks 150.00
      Kitten Capers 75.00
      Little Bo Peep..................150.00
      Little Boy Blue 50.00
      Ranger Boy 100.00
  Plate
      Little Quakers 110.00
      Mary Quite Contrary 200.00

Peter Rabbit...................175.00
Pony Trail 200.00
Set, Little Boy Blue, bowl, cup, and plate 550.00

Magnolia
Berry Bowl........................30.00
Bread and Butter Plate.................6.00
Cereal Bowl........................35.00
Coffeepot, individual size 100.00
Creamer and Sugar....................20.00
Cup and Saucer 12.50
Dinner Plate 15.00
Fruit Bowl 30.00
Platter, round, 14" d 40.00
Salad Plate..........................30.00
Salt and Pepper Shakers, pr.......25.00
Soup Bowl........................30.00
Vegetable Bowl, cov...................60.00
Vegetable Bowl, open, round, 8" d 24.00
Vegetable Bowl, open, round, 10" d 28.00
Maize, yellow, butter dish, 1/4 lb, corn 25.00

Orchard Song
Butter Dish, cov, 1/4 lb 35.00
Chop Platter, 14-1/2" d 45.00
Creamer and Sugar, cov 24.00
Gravy Boat and Underplate........28.00
Salad Bowl, 12" d, 4" h 50.00
Vegetable Bowl, divided 25.00
Vegetable Bowl, round, 8" d........17.50

Thistle
Coffeepot, cov 100.00
Cup and Saucer 13.50
Dinner Plate, 10" d 20.00
Eggcup 15.00
Fruit Dish 12.00
Gravy Boat...................................20.00
Pitcher, 1 qt.................................35.00
Platter, oval................................35.00

Town and Country
Bowl, blue, 10" d.........................60.00
Butter Dish, cov 60.00
Candlesticks, pr, 7-1/2" h 60.00
Coffeepot, yellow.......................100.00
Creamer 20.00
Cup and Saucer 20.00
Dinner Plate, 10-1/2" d, brown 20.00
Mug, blue......................................40.00
Salad Plate, 8-1/2" d, brown........15.00
Salt and Pepper Shakers, pr, handles 35.00
Soap Dish 75.00
Spoon Rest 35.00
Sugar, cov....................................30.00
Toothbrush Holder 75.00
Wash Pitcher and Basin, large, blue 175.00

Tropic, # 3338
Carafe, wood handle.....................5.00
Chop Plate, 14" d.........................75.00
Cup and Saucer 15.00
Dinner Plate, 10" d 25.00
Salad Plate, 7" d 12.00
Salt and Pepper Shakers, pr, figural 60.00
Vegetable Bowl, oval..................40.00

Miscellaneous and Artware
Ashtray, Pheasant, Sportsman Giftware, teardrop shape, hand painted, 10-1/2" l, 8" w..................65.00
Christmas Coasters
Carolers 125.00
Holly & Bells 125.00
Snowman................................ 125.00
Cigarette Boxes, cov
Daisy, #3666.........................50.00
Pagoda Lid, Marsh Rose, #3799 ....75.00
Granada Gold
Candle Holders, pr, Cosmos, 2-1/2" d............................45.00
Cornucopia, 22k gold, 8-1/2" l, 5" h...................................40.00
Pitcher, curving handle, 6" h........40.00
Sunburst Artware ("Rainbow")
Planter, swan, large.................. 400.00
Vase, Acanthus Leaf, #1540 .... 125.00
Vase, Deco, #1185, 9" h 150.00
Vase, Twist, #1124, three handles 125.00
Terra Rose Artware
Box, cov, hand painted, sgd, 5-1/2" l, 4-1/2" w 45.00
Bowl, Lily of the Valley, green, #3620 ....75.00
Bowl, Seahorse, handles, green, #3671 ....50.00
Candleholders, pr, Starfish, mauve, #3712 ....75.00
Candy Jar, cov, bird finial, #3676 ....60.00
Nautilus Shell, blue #3705...........75.00
Teapot, cov................................60.00
Vase, Butterfly, blue #3701 .... 300.00
Vase, Gazelle Head, blue #3708 .... 400.00
Watering Can, yellow tulip, #3511 .... 150.00
Watering Pitcher, blue tulip, #3211 ....50.00
Wigstand
Female.................................. 250.00
Male................................ 1,000.00

Star Wars

Collecting Hints: With the 1999 release of "Star Wars, Episode I, The Phantom Menace," many "Star Wars" collectibles are being offered for sale. Look for completeness when collecting vintage toys and figures.

When Kenner originally introduced "Star Wars" figures in 1977, the line contained only 12 figures. One way to identify those early figures when mint on the card is by the 12 photographs on the back. Collectors have nicknamed these "12 backs" to be able to tell the difference from "20 backs" and later issues.

If buying new release items, be aware their value is speculative and also be prepared to store them care-fully for several years. Remember that the anticipated revenue from the new release is estimated to be $4 billion in sales. That should give collectors many buying opportunities.

History: "Star Wars," 1977, "Empire Strikes Back," 1980, and "Return of the Jedi," 1983, have delighted movie-goers with special effects and stunning music as George Lucas has created a classic for all times. The new release, "Episode I, The Phantom Menace," successfully takes the story line back in time to reveal the origins of Anakin Skywalker who later becomes that dastardly villian, Darth Vader.

While most collectors know the details of each of the movies, hopefully they will not be disappointed with the wide range of collectibles being offered for this release. The first three movies have yielded many collectibles and rare items now going to auction are showing signs of high prices and keen collector interest.

Besides the toys and collectibles licensed by Hasbro and Kenner, the fast food companies have also created items which collectors eagerly seek. So strap yourself down in the old Land Speeder and enjoy the collecting ride of the millennium.

References: Sharon Korbeck and Elizabeth Stephan, *Toys & Prices 2000*, 7th ed., Krause Publications, 1999; *Toy Shop Presents Star Wars Collectibles*; Stuart W. Wells, III, *Science Fiction Collectibles Identification & Price Guide*, Krause Publications, 1998.

Periodical: *The Star Wars Collector,* 20982 Homcrest Court, Ashburn, VA 22011.

Collectors' Clubs: Alabama Star Wars Club, eformatt@traveller.com; Carolina Star Wars Collector Club, rlcox@uncg.edu; clubtokyo.simplenet.com/cswee/; Chicago Area Collectors Club, cesba@aol.com; members.aol.com/cesba/club.htm; Houston Star Wars Club, abrower@argohoustom.com; users.argolink.net/abrower/sw/index.html; Long Island's Network of Collectable Star Wars, RobotFan@aol.com; members.aol.com/robotfan/LINCS.html; Ohio Star Wars Collectors Club, webster@oswcc.com; www.osmcc.com; Official Star Wars Fan Club, PO Box 111000, Aurora, CO 80042-1000; Pennsylvania Star Wars Club, guzpro@ezonline.com; ajmay@postoffice.ptd.net; Seattle Area Lucasfilm Artifact Collectors Club, lopez@halcyon.com; www.tosrgus.com/seattle.html; The Wisconsin Collector Page, heybtbm@aol.com; members.aol.com/heybtbm/index.html.

Note: Loose, mint condition (LMC) means accompanied by all small accessory pieces, but not in orig package.

Kenner's Princess Lei Organa doll, 11 d, $450.

Kenner's R2-D2 and Chewbacca figures, $50 and $220, respectively.

Action Figure

ATAT Commander, Empire Strikes Back, MOC 85.00
Blue Snaggletooth, Kenner, 1977, only issued with playset 150.00
Bobba Fett, 3" h, 1978, MIP 920.00
C-3PO, Kenner, 1980, removable limbs
  LMC 8.00
  MIP 50.00
Chewbacca, Kenner, 1977, 3-3/4" h,
  MIP 220.00
Chief Chirpa, Return of the Jedi,
  MOC 35.00
Darth Vader, 12" h, Kaybees Exclusive,
  MISB 60.00

Patch, featuring Darth Vader, $5.

Darth Vader, 12" h, with cape 30.00
Death Squad Commander, Kenner, 1977,
  3-3/4" h, MIP 175.00
Death Star Droid, 3" h, 1978, MIP.. 155.00
Emperor's Royal Guard, loose 14.00
"Empire Strikes Back," six figures,
  MIP 1,000.00
FX-7, Kenner, 1980
  LMC 8.00
  MIP 55.00
Gammoran Guard, Return of the Jedi,
  MOC 75.00
Greedo, Kenner, 1977
  LMC 15.00
  MIP 135.00
Greedo, JC Penney 45.00
Hammerhead, Kenner, 1977
  LMC 15.00
  MIP 135.00
Han & Tauntaun, Kenner, 1997, Toys R' Us exclusive
  LMC 65.00
  MIP 185.00
Han Solo, Kenner, 1980, Hoth outfit
  LMC 10.00
  MIP 80.00
Hans Solo, 12 back, small head,
  MOC 700.00
Han Trench, "Return of the Jedi,"
  MOC 60.00
Hoth Snowtropper, "Empire Strikes Back,"
  MOC 150.00
Imperial Commander, loose 8.00
Jawa, Kenner, 1977, 3-3/4" h
  Cloth cape, MIP 220.00
  Vinyl cape, MIP 3,200.00
Lando Calrissian, Kenner, 1980
  LMC 10.00
  MIP 40.00
Leia Bespin, turtleneck, C-9.5 .... 295.00
Leia Combat, Return of the Jedi,
  MOC 65.00
Luke Skywalker, Kenner, 1977, 3-3/4" h,
  MIP 320.00

Obi-Wan, Kaybees Exclusive, 12" h,
  MISB 60.00
Obi-Wan Kenobi, Kenner, 1977
  LMC 30.00
  MIP 300.00
Power Droid, loose 10.00
Princess Leia, Kenner, 1977, Benspin outfit
  LMC 20.00
  MIP 100.00
Red Snaggletooth, Kenner, 1977
  LMC 24.00
  MIP 140.00
Ree Yees, "Return of the Jedi,"
  MOC 25.00
Romba, "Power of the Force," MOC 50.00
R2-D2, Kenner, 1980, retractable sensorscope
  LMC 10.00
  MIP 50.00
R5-D4, 3" h, 1978, MIP 130.00
Sand Person, 12 back, MOC 325.00
Sand Trooper, Diamond Exclusive,
  12" h 75.00
Snaggletooth, 3" h, 1978
  Blue body, Sears Exclusive,
    MIP 200.00
  Red body, MIP 160.00
Snow Trooper, loose 10.00
Stormtrooper, Kenner, 1977, 3-3/4" h,
  MIP 220.00
Tie Pilot, "Empire Strikes Back,"
  MOC 185.00
Tusken Raider, Kenner, 12" h
  With blaster rifle 50.00
  With gafi stick 50.00
Walrus Man, Kenner, 1977
  LMC 25.00
  MIP 135.00
Wequay, loose 7.50
Wicket, loose 25.00
Yak Face, Power of the Force,
  MIP 1,700.00
Yoda, loose 25.00
Zuckuss, loose 12.00
Activity Book, Darth Vader, Black Falcon, Ltd., 1970, some pages completed in pencil 5.00
Backpack, Yoda, Sigma 30.00
Bank
  Darth Vader, Leonard Silver, 1981, silver plated 95.00
  Yoda, litho tin, combination dials 25.00
Box, Star War Cookies, no contents 50.00
Candy Tin, Episode 3, England 20.00
Carrying Case
"Empire Strikes Back"
  Darth Vader, 1982 .... 35.00
  Mini figure, 1980 .... 30.00
  R2-D2, Droid 14.00
"Return of the Jedi"
  C-390, 1983 .... 40.00
  Darth Vader, 1983 .... 210.00
"Star Wars" 45.00
Child's Book, *Princess Leia* 25.00
Clock, Bradley, 1980-84 .... 45.00

Coat Rack, Jedi 400.00
Collector Drinking Glass, Jedi, set of four with matching tray, Burger King 35.00
Costume, Stormtrooper, Ben Cooper, 1973 .... 50.00
Doll, 12" h, sealed in orig box
Ben Kanobi 550.00
Chewbacca 150.00
Darth Vader 450.00
Han Solo 800.00
Jawa 350.00
Leia 450.00
Luke Skywalker 550.00
R2D2 .... 300.00
Gum Card Box, 1st issue 25.00
Halloween Costume, Darth Vader, 1977 .... 45.00
Light Saber, inflatable, 1977, MIB 250.00
Lithograph, limited edition, signed and numbered by Ralph McQuarrie
Cantina 175.00
Hoth Battle, AT-AT 175.00
Luke and Darth Vader Duel 195.00
Mailer
Han Solo, Fruit Loops 35.00
Spirit Obi 20.00
Mask, Lucasfilm Archive Collection
Jar Jar Binks 100.00
Naboo Starfighter Helmet 50.00
Nute Gunray 75.00
Pod Racing Helmet 50.00
Rune Haako 75.00
Sebulba 65.00
Pencil Tray, C-3PO, Sigma 50.00
Pez Dispenser, Naboo, MIB 8.00
Photograph, autographed, certificate of authenticity
Fisher, Carrie 35.00
Ford, Harrison 95.00
Guiness, Alex 95.00
Hamill, Mark 35.00
Jones, James Earl 35.00
Lloyd, Jake 35.00
McGregor, Ewan 50.00
Playset
Dagabah, Jedi offer 300.00
Endor Ambush, 1997 .... 20.00
Ewok Village, Kenner, 1983
LMC 30.00
MIP 90.00
Hoth Battle, 1997 .... 20.00
Ice Planet Hoth Action Fleet, Galoob, 1996
LMC 10.00
MIP 25.00
Land of the Jawas, Kenner, 1978
LMC 50.00
MIP 200.00
Snowspeeder, Action Fleet, Galoom, 1995
LMC 8.00
MIP 16.00
Postcard, Greetings from Another World, removed from *Cracked Magazine*, c1978, full color, Star Wars movie scene, 3-3/4" x 5-1/2" 8.00
Poster
Boba Fett, 10th anniversary 195.00
Burger King, 1978-80 .... 10.00

"Empire Strikes Back"
Advance 100.00
Re-release, 1981-82 .... 35.00
Nestea, 1980 .... 10.00
"Revenge of the Jedi"
With date 150.00
Without date 200.00
"Return of the Jedi"
1986 re-release 80.00
Special edtion 20.00
"Star Wars"
Advance, mylar 1,200.00
Second advance 175.00
Portfolio, art, Darth Vader, sealed with medallion and two prints, 1979 .... 250.00
Press Kit, first movie 90.00
Print, lithograph, Willitts, framed
Death Star Scene 150.00
Jabba's Throne Room 150.00
Rancor Creature 150.00
Speeder Bike Chase 150.00
Pulltoy, R2-D2, talking 400.00
Puppet, Chewbacca, 40" h, plush, Regal Limited 1,925.00
Radio, child's, Ewoks, MIB 35.00
Ring, "The Force," black plastic base, diecut letters finished in bright silver against black, late 1970s 12.00
Shampoo, Stormtrooper 3.00
String Dispenser, R2-D2, Sigma 45.00
Store Display, designed to hold orig 12 action figures 575.00
Tape Dispenser, C-3PO, Sigma 80.00
Vehicle
Cloud Car, MIB 95.00
Darth Vader's TIE Fighter, Kenner, 1978
LMC 60.00
MIP 150.00
Empire Rebel Transport, MIB ... 150.00
Jawa Sandcrawler, contents sealed, MIB 1,000.00
Jedi AT-AT Walker, MIB 325.00
Jedi Millennium Falcon 250.00
Jedi Speederbike, MIB 35.00
Landspeeder, Kenner, 1978, 5" l, diecast
LMC 30.00
MIP 70.00
Landspeeder, Kenner, 1978
LMC 20.00
MIP 75.00
Landspeeder, Kenner, 1996
LMC 6.00
MIP 15.00
Millennium Falcon, orig sealed box 350.00
Snowspeeder, MIB 85.00
Taun Taun 75.00
X-Wing Fighter, Kenner, white, 1978
LMC 50.00
MIP 320.00
Y-Wing, MIB 185.00
Weapon, Blaster, Kenner, 1977
LMC 25.00
MOC 85.00

Stereo Viewers

Collecting Hints: Condition is the key to determining price. Undamaged wooden-hood models are scarce and demand a premium price if made of bird's-eye maple. The presence of all-original parts increases the value. Plentiful engraving adds 20 to 30 percent.

Longer lenses are better than smaller ones. Lenses held in place by metal are better than those shimmed with wood.

Because aluminum was the same price as silver in the late 19th century, aluminum viewers often are the more collectible.

History: There are many different types of stereo viewers. The familiar table viewer with an aluminum or wooden hood was jointly invented in 1860 by Oliver Wendell Holmes and Joseph Bates, a Boston photographer. This type of viewer also was made in a much scarcer pedestal model.

Three companies—Keystone, Griffith & Griffith, and Underwood & Underwood—produced hundreds of thousands of hand viewers between 1899 and 1905.

In the mid-1850s, a combination stereo viewer and picture magnifier was developed in France and eventually was made in England and the United States. The instrument, which was called a Graphascope, usually consisted of three pieces and could be folded for storage. When set up, it had two round lenses for stereo viewing, a large round magnifying lens to view cabinet photographs, and a slide, often with opaque glass, for viewing stereo glass slides. The height was adjustable.

A rotary or cabinet viewer was made from the late 1850s to about 1870. Becker is the best-known maker. The standing floor models hold several hundred slides; the table models hold 50 to 100.

From the late 1860s to 1880s there were hundreds of different viewer designs. Models had folding wires, collapsible cases (Cortascope), pivoting lenses to view postcards (Sears' Graphascope), and telescoping card holders. The cases, which also became ornate, were made of silver, nickel, or pearl and were trimmed in velvets and rosewood.

Collectors' Clubs: National Stereoscopic Association, P.O. Box 14801,

Columbus, OH 43214; Stereo Club of Southern California, P.O. Box 2368, Culver City, CA 90231.

Corte-Scope, folding aluminum or metal, came in box with views, c1914...50.00
Hand, common maker
    Aluminum hood, folding handle...................................65.00
    Bird's eye maple hood, folding handle...................................85.00
    Walnut, screw on handle, velvet hood.....................................85.00
    Wide hood for people who wear glasses, dark brown or green metal....................................80.00
Hand, scissors device to focus, groove and wire device to hold card 120.00
Pedestal
    Foreign, French or English, nickel plated with velvet hood.............300.00
    Keystone, school and library type, black crinkle metal finish with light.......................................85.00
Sculptoscope, Whiting, counter top style, penny operated........................500.00
Stand, Bates-Holmes, paper or wood hood..150.00
Stereographascope, Sears Best, lens rotates to allow viewing of photos or postcards...................................90.00
Telebinocular, binocular style, black crinkle metal finish, excellent optics, came with book-style box.....................50.00

Stereographs

Collecting Hints: Value is determined by condition, subject, photographer (if famous), rarity, and age—prior to 1870 or after 1935. A revenue stamp on the back indicates the item dates between 1864 and 1866, the years a federal war tax was imposed. Lithograph printed cards have very little value.

Collect stereographs that are in good condition or better, unless the image is extremely rare. Very good condition means some wear on the mount and a little dirt on the photo. Folds, marks on the photo, or badly worn mounts reduce values by at least 50 percent. Faded or light photos are worth less than bright ones.

Don't try to clean cards or straighten them. Curved cards were made to heighten the stereo effect, an improvement made in 1880.

It pays to shop around to get the best price for common cards, but it is a good idea to buy rarer cards when you see them since they are harder to find and values are increasing annually. Dealers who are members of the National Stereoscopic Association are very protective of their reputation and their establishments are good places for the novice collector to visit.

Using the resources of the public library to thoroughly study the subject matter you are collecting will help you assemble a meaningful collection.

History: Glass and paper stereographs, also known as stereo views, stereo view cards, or stereoscope cards, were first issued in the United States in 1854. From the late 1850s through the 1930s, the stereograph was an important visual record of every major event, famous person, comic situation, and natural scene. It was the popular news and entertainment medium until replaced by movies, picture magazines, and radio.

The major early publishers were Anthony (1859-1873), Kilburn (1865-1907), Langeheim (1854-1861), and Weller (1861-1875). Between 1880 and 1910, the market was controlled by large firms, including Davis (Kilburn), Griffith & Griffith, International View Company, Keystone, Stereo Travel, Underwood & Underwood, Universal Photo Art, and H. C. White.

References: William C. Darrah, *Stereo Views*, published by author, out of print; ——, *World of Stereographs*, published by author, out of print; John S. Waldsmith, *Stereo Views*, Wallace-Homestead, 1991.

Collectors' Clubs: National Stereoscopic Association, Box 14801, Columbus, OH 43214; Stereo Club of Southern California, P.O. Box 2368, Culver City, CA 90231.

Notes: Prices given are for cards in very good condition, i.e., some wear and slight soiling. Pieces in excellent condition bring 25 percent more; those with a perfect image and mount are worth twice as much. Reverse the mathematical process for fair, i.e., moderate soiling, some damage to mount, minor glue marks, some foxing (brown spots) and poor folded mount, very dirty and damage to tone or both images. Where applicable, a price range is given

Animal

Birds, Hursts', 2nd series, #7, birds in tree....................................5.00
Cat
    Keystone #2314 ....6.50
    Keystone #9651, man and cat......5.00
    Soule, The Pickwickian Ride 20.00
Dog
    Kilburn #1644, "Home Protection," dog close up...............................6.50
    U & U, the puppies singing school...5.00
    Universal #3231............................5.00
Farm Yard, Kilburn #739, sheep and cows, 1870s.................................5.00
Horses, Schreiber & Sons, Jarvis and sulky, early..................................18.00
Walrus, Keystone #V21232, Bronx Zoo..4.50
Zoo, London Stereo Company, animals in London Zoo.................................10.00

Astronomy

Comet, Keystone #16645, Morehouse's...................................9.50
Mars, Keystone #16767T, the planet...6.50
Moon
    Beer Bros. 1866, photo by Rutherford..................................15.00
    Kilburn #2630, full moon...............6.50
    Soule #602, last quarter...............8.00
Planetarium, Keystone #32688, Adler's, Chicago......................................10.00

Aviation

Air Mail Plane
    Keystone #29446, at Cleveland . 30.00
    Keystone #32372, Inaugural, Ford Tri-motor, air-rail service NY to LA, 7/2/29......................................20.00
Aviators, Keystone #26408T, six men who first circled earth.......................25.00
Balloon, Anthony #4114, Prof. Lowe's flight from 6th Ave. in NYC........100.00
Dirigibles, and Zeppelins, Keystone
    #17397, *Los Angeles* at Lakehurst...........................45-50.00
    #17398, *The Los Angeles*..........45.00
    #18000, flying over German town...6.50
    #32277, *Gray Zeppelin* in hanger at Lakehurst, NJ 35.00
    #32740, framework of ZRS-4, Akron.......................................65.00
    #V19216, 1918, R-34 at Mineola, from WW I set.....................................15.00
Doolittle, Keystone #28031, Major Doolittle, 1931..................................65.00
General View, Keystone #32785, five biplanes fly over Chicago's field museum.....................................20.00
Lindbergh, Keystone
    #28029, in plane with wife 55.00
    #30262T, next to Spirit of St. Louis...30.00
Plan, Keystone
    #18920, Michelin bomber...........20.00
    #19049, Nieuport 10.00
    #V18921, twin seat fighter 9.00
Wright Bros., Keystone #V96103, in flight at Ft. Meyers...............................85.00

Black memorabilia

Keystone #9506, "We done all dis'a'morning," picking cotton 6.50
Kilburn #14317, boy and mule 3.00
Singley
    #10209, "one never came up," swimmers...12.00
    #10217, "one got an upper cut," fighting..10.00
U & U, "Cotton is King," picking 5.00

U & U, "Keystone, Kilburn," Whiting, etc., cheating at cards, stealing millions, infidelity, etc. 15.00

Whiting
#960, "there's a watermelon smiling on the vine" 10.00
#961, "Happiest Coon" 8.00

Cave

Keystone
#9586, man in front of Great Oregon Caves 6.50
#33516, int. of Crystal Springs Cave, Carlsbad 4.50
U & U, Luray Caverns 8.00
Waldack, 1866, Mammoth Cave, typical early magnesium light view 15.00

Christmas

Brownies & Santa, Universal #4679, Graves, sleigh in foreground....... 20.00
Children with Tree
Griffith #16833, children's Christmas dinner 18.00
Keystone, 1895, #987, Santa in front of fireplace 15.00
Santa coming down chimney, Keystone #11434, Santa with toys 25.00
Santa with Toys, Keystone 1898, #9445, Santa loaded with toys 15.00

Comics

Bicycle Bum, Graves #4551-58, "Weary Willie," four-card set..................... 20.00
Drinking
Kilburn 1892, #7348, "Brown just in from the club" 3.00
R.Y. Young 1901, woman drinking, two cards 16.50
U & U, 1897, man sneaks in after drinking, two-card set.................. 7.50
English, boy carves roast, "The Attack," ivory mount, hand tinted................ 5.00
Humor
Keystone #2346-7, before (cuddling) and after (reading) marriage....... 70.00
U & U, 1904, "Four queens and a jack," four girls and a jackass....... 6.50
Infidelity
"Foolin-around," 1910, husband fools around with his secretary, 12 cards 48.00
Keystone #12312-22, The French Cook- Communist version........... 50.00
U & U
Sneaking-in, 1897, caught by wife after night on the town.............. 8.00
The French Cook, 10 card set 50.00
Romance
U & U, "Going with Stream," hugging couple 6.50
Weller #353, "Unexpected," necking 5.00
Rumors, H. C. White, 5576-5578, quickest way to spread news: "Tell a graph, tell a phone, tell a woman," three-card set.. 20.00
Sentimental, American Stereo, #2001-2012, He goes to war; wounded; returns; reunited, etc., 12 card set.. 60.00

Wedding Set, White #5510-19, getting ready, wedding, reception, alone in bedroom......................................45.00

Disaster

Boston Fire, 1872, Soule, ruins...........8.00
Chicago Fire, 1871, Lovejoy & Foster, ruins....................................9.00
Galveston Flood, 1900, Graves, ruins....................................20.00
Johnstown Flood, ruins
Barker....................................9.00
U & U....................................7.00
Mill Creek Flood, 1874, popular series, house....................................5.00
Portland Fire, 1866, Soule #469, ruins....................................8.00
St. Pierre Eruption, Kilburn #14941, ruins....................................3.00
San Francisco Earthquake Scenes
Keystone #13264, Market St 9.00
U & U #8180, California St...........16.50
White #8713, wrecked houses 20.00
Train Wreck, Dole 50.00
Worcester, MA, Flood, 1876, Lawrence......................................5.00

Doll

Graves #4362, Sunday School Class......................................20.00
Kilburn
#15, tired of play 15.00
When will Santa come? 12.00
U & U
#6922, playing doctor...................15.00
#6952, girl asleep with cat and doll......................................9.00
Webster & Albee #160, doll's maypole......................................20.00

Entertainer

Actress, J. Gurney & Son, 1870s, Mrs. Scott or Mrs. Roland, etc. 10.00
Dancers, Keystone #33959, Bali, Dutch Indies......................................2.00
Natives, Keystone #16423, Java, good costumes......................................3.00
Singer
J. Gurney & Son, Annie Cary 15.00
James Cremer, opera, studio pose in costume......................................12.00

Exposition

NY Sanitary Fair, Anthony #1689-2864, fountain view 15.00
1872, World Peace Jubilee, Boston Pollock, interior view 8.00
1876, U.S. Close Up Centennial, Centennial Photo Co.
Common view of grounds and buildings 5.00-10.00
Corliss Engine 12.00
Monorail......................................65.00
Statue of Liberty Han 85.00
1894
California Mid-Winter, Kilburn #9474-2984..............................12.00
Columbian Chicago, Kilburn
Most views 7.00
Ferris Wheel 10.00
1901, Pan American Buffalo, Kilburn
Most views 6.50

President McKinley 9.00
1904, Louisiana Purchase Exposition, St. Louis
Graves for Universal Photo or U & U 8.00
White #8491, Education & Manufacturing buildings.................... 8.00
Whiting, #620, Missouri Fruit Exhibit 12.00
1905, Lewis & Clark Centennial, Portland, Watson Fine Art #34, building 9.00
1907, Jamestown Exposition, Keystone #14219, life saving demonstration 7.00
1908, West Michigan State Fair, Keystone #21507.................................. 12.00
1933, Century of Progress, Chicago, Keystone #32993, Lief Ericksen Dr... 20.00

Hunting and Fishing

Bass, Ingersoll #3159, string of bass 10.00
Deer, Keystone #26396, hunters and kill 5.00
Halibut, Keystone #22520, commercial fishing 5.00
Moose, Keystone #9452, 1899, big game kill 6.50
Trout, Kilburn, #115, a day's catch 5.00
Wildcat, Keystone 312264, man shoots sleeping wildcat 6.50

Indian

Burge, J.C., Apaches bathing 125.00
Continental Stereo Co., Pueblo eating bread 65.00
Griffith #11873, Esquimau at St. Louis Fair 8.00
Hayes, F. J.
#865, Crow burial ground 25.00
#1742, Sioux........................... 30.00
Jackson, Wm. H., #202, Otoe, with bow 100.00
Keystone
#23095, Chief Black Hawk 12.00
#23118, Indian girl 5.00
#V2181, Blackfeet 9.00
Montgomery Ward, squaw.................. 6.50
Soule #1312, Pieute squaw 60.00
U & U
Hopi 12.00
Wolpi 10.00
White #12279, pueblo 15.00

Mining

Alaska Gold Rush
Keystone
#9191, men with supplies getting ready to climb the "golden stairs" at Chilkoot Pass........................... 9.00
#9195, preparing to climb the golden stairs 9.00
#21100, panning for gold 12.00
U & U #10655, looking into glory hole 15.00
Universal, Graves, 1902, man working sluice, scarce card by scarce publisher 40.00
Easter, Anthony #474, working gold chute 45.00
Gold Hill, Houseworth #743, city overview..................... 75.00

Hydraulic, Houseworth #799, water spraying 70.00
Virginia City
    Houseworth #713, street view.....95.00
    Watkins
        Opera House.........................95.00
        Panorama, new series..........125.00

World's Peace Jubilee, coliseum, 1872, William G. Preston, $20.

Miscellaneous

Auto
    Keystone #22143, employees leaving Ford..8.00
    U & U, early auto in Los Angeles, 1903 ....20.00
Beach scenes, H. C. White, #476, bathers, Atlantic City............................5.00
Bicycles
    Kilburn #11924, women and bike...6.50
    Thorne, big two wheeler, early 1870s 45.00
Circus
    U & U, Chicago 20.00
    Windsor & Whipple, Olean, NY, people with elephant 40.00
Crystal Palace, yellow mount, outside general view 25.00
Firefighting
    Early 18702, unknown maker, close view of pumpers 40.00
    Keystone #11684, action view of pumpers....................................25.00
Glass Stereos
    Foreign Scenes...........................75.00
    United States Scenes..................80.00
Groups, various, Rogers statuaries 9.00
Gypsies, unknown maker, in front of tent 20.00
Hawaii, Keystone
    #10156, hula girls 9.00
    #10162, Waikiki Beach..................9.50
Lighthouses
    Keystone #29207..........................5.00
    Williams, Minot Ledge Light........20.00
New York City, Anthony #3938 ....20.00
Opium Dens
    X82, 1900...................................25.00
    Unknown Maker, two tier bed, pipe for smoking opium 60.00
Prisons, Pach, view of cabinets of rifles 15.00
Tinted Views
    Foreign...6.50
    United States 10.00
Toy Train, Keystone P-21329, boy playing with Lionel trains 25.00

Tunnel, Ward #808 Hoosac tunnel, just completed 15.00

National Park

Death Valley, Keystone #32666, pool..9.00
Garden of the Gods, Rodeo McKenney, Pike's Peak 5.00
Grand Teton, Wm. H. Jackson, #503, average for this prized photographer 20.00
Yellowstone
    Jackson, Wm. H., #422 ....15.00
    Universal, peak view.....................5.00
Yosemite
    Keystone #4401, Nevada Falls 5.00
    Kilburn #9284, Bridal Veil Falls......5.00
    Reilly, tourists at Yosemite Falls.....8.00
    U & U, Glacier Point 5.00

Niagara Falls

Anthony #3731, falls 5.00
Barker, ice bridge................................2.00
U & U
    Tourist..4.00
    Whirlpool rapids............................2.00
White #7, tourists, 1903 ....5.00

Occupational

Blacksmith, Keystone #18206, many tools in picture......................................5.00
Cowboys, Keystone
    #12465, Kansas............................7.00
    #13641, Yellowstone, Montana 7.50
Farming, Kilburn #1796, hay, 1870s ..7.00
Fireman
    G. K. Proctor, Mid-distance hook & ladder, horse drawn...................35.00
    1870s, good view of steam pumper......................................45.00
Milkman, Keystone #P-26392, horse-drawn wagon 10.00
Mill, U & U, linen factory, typical industrial view..3.00
Store, Keystone #18209, grocery store int...15.00

Oil

Pennsylvania
    Detlor & Waddell, #76, burning tanks...15.00
    Keystone #20352T, shooting a well..5.00
    Robbins #32, Triumph Hill 13.00
    Robbins, #88, gas well 8.00
    Wilt Brothers, Allegheny area........8.00
Texas, Keystone #34864, tanks near Kilgore 6.50

Person, Famous

Barton, Clara, Keystone #28002, founder of American Red Cross 60.00
Buffalo Bill, American Scenery #1399, on horseback in New York City 50.00
Buntline, Ned, J. Gurney, portrait .. 150.00
Burbank, Luther, Keystone #16746, with a cactus...8.00
Bryan, W. J., Keystone #15539, on way to hotel in NYC 30.00
Coolidge, President, Keystone
    #26303, President and Cabinet ..50.00
    #26303 ....30.00

#28004, at desk.........................12.00
Custar, General
Lovejoy & Foster, with bear he killed..350.00
Taylor #2438, with his dog in camp...500.00
Czar of Russia, U & U, with President of France...10.00
Edison, Thomas
    Keystone, #V28007, in lab 100.00
    U & U, in lab 150.00
Edison, Ford and Firestone, Keystone
    #18551................................75-125.00
    #45612................................75-125.00
Eisenhower, President, Keystone, at table with microphones, about 1954 ....250.00
Farqutt, Admiral, Anthony, from Prominent Portrait Series 40.00
Ford, Henry, Keystone #28023 ....60.00
Gandhi, Mahatma, Keystone #33852, portrait..35.00
Gehrig, Lou, Keystone #32597, baseball player...200.00
Grant, President, Bierstadt Bros., on Mount Washington 75.00
Hayes, B., President, party at Hastings......................................100.00
Harding, W., President, addressing boy scouts 20.00
Hoover, President, Keystone #28012, close portrait..................................35.00
Kettering, C. F., Keystone, inventor of auto self starter...................................60.00
Kingman, Seth, no maker, famous California Trapper 120.00
Lincoln, Abraham, Anthony
    Funeral, #4596 ....50-65.00
    President, #2969, scarce, highly prized view 900.00
Marconi, Keystone #V11969, radio inventor...45.00
McKinley, President, Keystone, Kilburn, U & U, most views.........................15.00
Morse, Samuel, J. Gurney 225.00
Queen Victoria, U & U 1897, having breakfast with Princesses 35.00
Rockefeller, J.D., Keystone #V11961, world's richest man 25.00
Rogers, Will, Keystone #32796, at 1932 Chicago Democratic Convention 75.00
Roosevelt, Theodore, President
    Keystone, Kilburn, U & U............30.00
    U & U, on horseback..................15.00
Ruth, Babe, Keystone #32590.......250.00
Sarazen, Gene, Keystone #32436, golfer..35.00
Schmeling, Max, Keystone #28028, boxer..75.00
Shaw, Dr. Anna, Keystone #V26151, suffrage leader 25.00
Shaw, George Bernard, Keystone #34505, on ship..........................60.00
Strauss, Johann, Gurney 90.00
Taft, President, U & U #10062, at desk...20.00
Thomas, Lowell, Keystone #32812, world travel expert and newsman 50.00

Twain, Mark
    Evans & Soule..........................350.00
    U & U #8010 or White #13055, in bed
    writing..250.00
Washington, Booker T., Keystone
    #V11960, with Andrew
    Carnegie 70.00
Wirewalkers, Barker
    Bellini on wire 10.00
    Blondin on rope 15.00
Young, Brigham, C. W. Carter, bust por-
    trait 20.00

Photographer, Famous

Brady, Anthony
    1863, Tom Thumb Wedding......125.00
    #428, Captain Custer with Confeder-
    ate prisoner...................................900.00
    #3376, Jeff Davis Mansion..........50.00
Houseworth, San Francisco, e.g.
    #150, show photo studio...........150.00
    #429, Golden Gate........................45.00
Langenheim, 1856, Trenton Falls, typical
    view, but scarce, on glass........135.00
Muybridge
    #318, The Golden Gate...............80.00
    #880, Geyer Springs 45.00
    #1623, Indian scouts.................250.00
O'Sullivan, T.H., Anthony #826, Men's
    Quarters..60.00
Pond, C.L., #786, Mirror Lake 30.00
Watkins, C.E.
    Panoramic, #1338, from Telegraph
    Hill..55.00
    San Francisco street scene, e.g.,
    #767, panorama from Russian
    Hill..55.00
    Trains..150.00
    Virginia City, NV, Panorama, new
    series..90.00
    Yosemite series, #1066, Yosemite
    Falls...25-30.00

Photographica

Camera, Houseworth #1107, wet plate
    camera in Yosemite......................75.00
Comic, Keystone #423, many viewers
    and cards in this comic "mouse" rou-
    tine...15.00
Gallery, American scenery, street with
    gallery sign visible.......................50.00
Photo Wagon, Weitfle's Photograph Van,
    close view with sign on
    wagon 125.00
Photography with stereo camera above
    street, Keystone #8283 ....65.00
Viewing, Keystone #11917, looking
    through viewer 10.00

Railroad

American stereo, view in Penn
    Station 15.00
Centennial, 1876 Monorail, World's Fair,
    scarce 65.00
Keystone
    #2367, loop at Georgetown 5.00
    #7090, interior of Baldwin Works ..8.00
    #37509, The Chief, 1930s...........75.00
Kilburn
    #135, pushing car up Jacob's
    Ladder...7.00
    #432, large side view of
    locomotive.......................................35.00

#779, train with engineer posed,
    1870...55.00
#2941, silver ore train 5.00
U & U
    #52, train going through Pillars of Her-
    cules..7.00
    #6218, Royal Gorge.......................5.00
Universal Photo Art #2876, Columbian
    Express 20.00
Unknown Maker, dramatic close-up of a
    1870 locomotive...........................75.00

Religious

Bates, open Bible, St. Luke 3.00
Keystone, Billy Sunday, evangelist...20.00
Keystone, Kilburn, U & U, Holy
    Land 2.00
Pope 7.50
Life of Christ, unmarked, usually set of
    photos of drawings or lithographed
    set, per set of 10-12....................10.00
Shakers, Irving, view of people 65.00

Risque

1820s, unmarked, typical
    "Peek-a-boo"..................................20.00
Griffith #2427, two girls, arms around
    each other, lightly clad.................20.00
Keystone, #9489, school girls retiring, in
    nightgowns.......................................7.00
Nude, early, bare breast 45.00
Nude, 1920s or 1930s 40.00

Sets

Boxer Rebellion, U & U 1901, 72
    cards 200.00
Bullfight, U & U, set of 15............... 100.00
China, Stereo Travel, set of 100, unusual
    subject... 400.00
Egypt, U & U set of 100 .... 310.00
France
    Stereo Travel, set of 30 ....70.00
    U & U, set of 100...................... 250.00
Glacier Park, Forsyth, set of 30 ..... 150.00
India, U & U, set of 100................. 250.00
Italy, U & U, set of 100 .... 200.00
Jerusalem, U & U, set of 30.............40.00
Switzerland, U & U, set of 100, guidebook
    and maps..................................... 200.00
United States, U & U, set of 100, good
    U.S. tour...................................... 350.00
Wild Flowers, Keystone, 100, hand
    tinted... 400.00
World Tour, Keystone
    Set of 200, trip from U.S. around world
    and back 350.00
    Set of 400 .... 700.00
    Set of 600, trip from U.S. around world
    and back, oak cabinet.............. 950.00
Yellowstone, U & U, set of 30 ....95.00
Yosemite, U & U, set of 30 .... 125.00

Ship

Battleships
    Griffith #2535, 1902, *USS
    Brooklyn* 8.00
    Universal Photo Art, *USS
    Raleigh* 9.00
Cruiser, White #7422, 1901, *USS New
    York*..10.00

Deck View, American Stereo, 1899, *USS
    Iowa* 8.00
Foreign, Keystone #16090, *HMS Albe-
    marie* 6.50
Riverboat, Anthony #7567, sternwheeler
    at Cincinnati...................................25.00
Sailboat, Anthony #22 ....20.00
Steamships
    Anthony #8691, *Bristol*, good average
    early view..15.00
    London Stereo, *Great Eastern*, early
    view...75.00
Submarine, Keystone #16667, at San
    Diego 8.00

Survey

Amundsen, Keystone, #13327, at Antore-
    tic Glacier, 1911 ....7.00
Gerlache, Keystone #13328, hunting
    seals at South Pole 6.50
Hayden, Jackson #796, people
    view...25.00
Lloyd, Grand Canyon, U & U, at work on
    mountain, 1903.............................25.00
Perry, Greenland, Keystone #13325,
    ships 6.50
Powell, #13, the wall.........................20.00
Wheeler, William Bell
    #14, Canon de Chelle, wall,
    1873...40.00
    #15, Canon de Chelle, wall,
    1872...25.00
Tissue, French
    Balloon, close view.......................70.00
    Diablo, 1870s, devils, skeletons, etc.,
    good shape with lots of "evil" 30.00
    Interior scene, 1870s, minor damage,
    viewable..7.50
    Interior scene, 1870s, nice stereo, pin-
    pricked, no tears 20.00
    Wedding, Young #7....................10.00

War

Boer, U & U, artillery firing 9.00
Boxer Rebellion, U & U, 1901 ....9.00
Civil War
    Anthony
        #3031, Dunlop Home.............20.00
        #3365, Brady, Libby Prison, yellow
        mount...25.00
        #3406, chair in which Lincoln was
        shot 60.00
    Gardner, #237, home of Rebel sharp-
    shooter...50.00
    Taylor & Huntington
        #458, Confederate
        fortifications 25.00
        #2557, pontoon boats............25.00
        #6705, powder magazine......35.00
Russo-Japanese, U & U #4380, general
    view of Port Arthur.........................5.00
Spanish American, U & U 12.00
World War I
    Set of 100...................................175.00
    Set of 200...................................300.00
    Set of 300...................................400.00

Whaling

Freeman, beached whales 50.00
Keystone
    #14768T, floating whale station ..10.00
    #V27198T, whalers cruising.........8.00

Nickerson, beached whales 70.00
Unknown maker, beached whale 30.00

Stock and Bond Certificates

Collecting Hints: Some of the factors that affect price are: 1) date (with pre-1900 more popular and pre-1850 most desirable), 2) autographs of important persons (Vanderbilt, Rockefeller, J. P. Morgan, Wells and Fargo, etc.), 3) number issued (most bonds have the number issued noted in text), and 4) attractiveness of the vignette.

Stocks and bonds are often collected for the appeal of their graphics or as a record of events or people which have impacted American history, such as gold and silver mining, railroad development, and early automobile pioneers.

History: The use of stock to raise capital and spread the risk in a business venture began in England. Several American colonies were founded as joint-venture stock companies. The New York Stock Exchange on Wall Street in New York City traces its roots to the late 18th century.

Stock certificates with attractive vignettes date to the beginning of the 19th century. As engraving and printing techniques developed, so did the elaborateness of the stock and bond certificates. Important engraving houses which emerged include the American Bank Note Company and Rawdon, Wright & Hatch.

Periodical: *Bank Note Reporter,* 700 E. State St., Iola, WI 54990.

Collectors' Club: Bond and Share Society, 26 Broadway, New York, NY 10004.

Museum: Museum of American Financial History, New York, NY.

Mt. Tamalpais Muir Woods Railway, H. S. Crocker Co., 1914, 7-3/8" x 10-1/2", $195.

Bonds

Cairo & Norfolk RR co., Kentucky, 1908, issued, not canceled, orange, speeding train vignette, coupons 45.00

Chicago & Wisconsin Valley Street Railways Co., 1912, $1,000, issued and canceled, first mortgage gold, black and white 25.00

Columbus & Southern Ohio electric co., issued and canceled, blue, engraved 7.50

Consolidated Edison Co., New York, $1,000, issued and canceled, engraved, blue or purple 8.00

Long Island Lighting Co., issued and canceled, orange, engraved, woman, child, generator, and light vignette 7.50

New Paltz, & Highland Electric RR, 1893, $500, issued and canceled, trolley car vignettes, gold seal, two pages of coupons 95.00

New York City, 1858, city seal, signed by Mor 45.00

New York, New Haven & Hartford, 1920, $10,000, issued and canceled, engraved, electric train vignette .. 48.00

Pennsylvania Canal Company, issued and canceled, 1870, canal and surrounding area vignette, two revenue stamps 125.00

Sacramento & Woodland RR, California, 1911, issued, not canceled, rust-brown, logo around capitol building vignette, coupons 165.00

Southern Indiana, 1908, $1,000, issued and canceled, green 28.00

Sovereign Gold Mining, issued and canceled, $5,000, Canadian, 1903, peach borders, coupon 10.00

Union Pacific RR, 1946, $1,000, issued and canceled, two engraved angels and company logo 15.00

West Shore Railroad, $10,000 First Mortgage Bond, 1948 .... 20.00

Stocks

American Express Co, issued and canceled, 1860s, bulldog vignette, sgd "Henry Wells" and "William Fargo" 750.00

American Locomotive Co., 50 shares, canceled, 1947 .... 20.00

American Tobacco Co., Indian Chief illus, 10 shares, 1968 .... 20.00

Anglo American Mining Corp., 1937, 1 share, blue and white 10.00

Associated Telephone Company, Ltd., 1945 .... 10.00

Broadway Joe's, issued and canceled, green or blue border, sports figure's restaurant 10.00

California Street Cable RR Co., San Francisco, CA, 1884, unissued, cable car vignette 35.00

Cambridge Railroad Co, MA, 1880s, unissued, black and white 8.00

Chico Gold & Silver Mining Co., 1867, sgd by company president John Bidwell 310.00

Colorado Milling & Elevator Co., issued and canceled, gold border, company buildings vignette, 1890s 25.00

Communications Satellite Corp., 1960s, issued and canceled, green or blue, space vignette 5.00

Edison Portland Cement Co, issued and canceled, engraved, rust or green, Thomas Edison vignette, 1900s . 35.00

Erie-Lackawanna Railroad Co., 100 shares, green on buff, black vignette with male and female allegorical figures standing along either side of laurel wreath, holding diamond box with name in script lettering, corporate seal at bottom center, issued 1967 .... 15.00

Falstaff Brewing Co., Falstaff logo surrounded by Greek gods and goddess, 100 shares, 1965 .... 16.00

F. W. Woolworth Co., eagle over two hemispheres vignette, brown 8.00

General Foods, issued and canceled, green, brown, or orange, engraved, vignette scene on right 2.50

Gulf, Mobile & Ohio, issued and canceled, engraved, blue or brown, two women and diesel train vignette .. 3.50

Heppner Railroad & Coal Co., Oregon, 1904 .... 165.00

Hornell Airways Inc., issued and canceled, NY, two women and sun rising over mountains vignette, 1920s . 65.00

Illinois, Central, issued and canceled, engraved, orange or brown, diesel train vignette 3.50

International Business Machines Corp, issued, brown 5.00

International Immigration & Colonization Assn., Hawaii, 1911, issued, not canceled, map vignette 100.00

International Telephone & Telegraph, 1930s, blue, engraved, goddess and globe vignette 8.00

Isabella, Gold Mining Co., Colorado, 1890s, issued and canceled, engraved, eagle vignette 8.00

Jantzen Knitting Mills, 1930s, issued and canceled, engraved, swimmer vignette, orange or green 20.00

Kelly-Springfield Motor Truck Co., issued and canceled, 1910-20 seated woman, anvil, and gears vignette, green or purple, American Bank Note Company 35.00

Maryland Telecommunications, issued and canceled, green, drawn 1957 TV and TV camera vignette 10.00

Nashville & Decatur, 1880s, issued and canceled, green border, train vignette 25.00

Nassau Electric Railroad, unissued, 1800s 40.00

Nickel Plate Road, 1957 .... 40.00

Norfolk and Western Railroad, 1887 .... 25.00

Omaha & Council Bluffs Street Railway, 1906, issued and canceled, blue, green, or pink 20.00

Packard Motor Car Company, one share, 1951 .... 30.00

Pennsylvania Railroad Company, dated Jan. 17, 1949 .... 8.00

Pennsylvania Salt Manufacturing Co., 100 shares, 1952 .... 18.00

Penn-Yan Mining Co., Montana Territory, 1888, colorful vignette of gold and silver coins 195.00

Philippine Long Distance Telephone Co., 1950s, issued and canceled, blue, engraved, woman on two globes vignette 5.00

Phillipsburg Mining Company, 1933, five shares 10.00

Pullman Company, vignette of George Pullman, 56 shares, 1922 .... 30.00

Raleigh & Gaston, 1870s, issued and canceled, two vignettes 65.00

Rochelle & Southern, Illinois, 1900, unissued, black and white 12.00

Rock Island & Eastern, Illinois, 1900, black and white, curved company name 15.00

Sentinel Radio Corp, issued and canceled, green or brown, goddess and two radio towers vignette 5.00

Sheba Gold & Silver Mining, Humboldt County, Nevada, issued, not canceled, three mining vignettes, gold seal 20.00

Solid Gold & Silver Mining Co., Colorado, 1884 .... 135.00

Texas Oil, 1901, sgd by A. M. Britton 140.00

Tuolumne County Water Co., 1850s, issued and canceled, mining methods vignette 75.00

Uncas National Bank of Norwich, 1900, green, gray and white, Indian, blacksmith, and sailing ship vignette .. 15.00

Wells Fargo Bank & Union Trust, 1940s, issued and canceled, green pony express ride vignette 25.00

Western Union Telegraph Co., 100 shares, 1960 .... 15.00

Stuffed Toys

Collecting Hints: Collectors tend to focus on one type of animal and to collect material spanning a long time period. The company with the strongest collector following is Steiff.

Collectors are mainly interested in items in very good to mint condition. Often stuffed toys had ribbons or clothing. All accessories must be intact for the toy to command full value.

History: The stuffed toy may have originated in Germany. Margarete Steiff GmbH of Germany began making stuffed toys for export beginning in 1880. By 1903, the teddy bear had joined Steiff's line and quickly worked its way to America. The first American teddy bears were made by the Ideal Toy Corporation. Not much is known about earlier manufacturers since

companies were short-lived and many toys have lost their labels.

The stuffed toy has always been an American favorite. Some have music boxes inserted to enhance their appeal. Carnivals used stuffed toys as prizes. Since the 1960s, an onslaught of stuffed toys have been imported to America from Japan, Taiwan, and China. These animals often are poorly made and are not popular among serious collectors.

Periodicals: *National Doll & Teddy Bear Collector*, P.O. Box 4032, Portland, OR 97208; *Soft Dolls & Animals*, 30595 Eight Mile, Livonia, MI 48152; *Teddy Bear and Friends*, 6405 Flank Dr, Harrisburg, PA 17112; *Teddy Bear Review*, 170 Fifth Ave., New York, NY 10010.

Collectors' Clubs: Collectors Club for Classic Winnie the Pooh, 468 W. Alpine #10, Upland, CA 91786; Good Bears of the World, P.O. Box 13097, Toledo, OH 43613; Steiff Collectors Club, P.O. Box 798, Holland, OH 43528; Teddy Bear Boosters Club, 19750 SW Peavine Mtn Rd, McMinnville, OR 97128.

Siamese Cat, R. Dakin Co., San Francisco, 14" l, $18.

Alligator, 9-1/2" l, vinyl, green and brown, glass eyes, c1950 .... 35.00

Bambi, Gund, c1953 .... 65.00

Beagle, plush, glass eyes, 9" h 28.00

Beaver, mohair, brown, Steiff 45.00

Boa Constrictor, plush, multicolored, felt eyes and tongue, c1958 .... 12.00

Buddy, 5-1/4" h, Clinton's dog 30.00

Camel
  4-1/2" h, leather, tan, single hump, straw saddle, c1955 .... 12.00
  8" h, plush, tan, single hump, glass eyes, c1950 .... 65.00

Cat
  4" h, Tabby, orig bell, Steiff........... 60.00
  5" l, sleeping, mohair, 5" l 100.00
  5-1/4" h, mohair, green plastic eyes, movable head and legs, Steiff, c1950 .... 45.00
  11" h, Diva, long white fur, sitting, orig Steiff tag and button 110.00

Cow, 5-1/2" h, felt, brown and white, glass eyes, wooden wheels 65.00

Deer, 15" h, Bambi, plush, Gund, c1953 .... 60.00

Dog
  4-1/2" h, Scottie, cotton, plaid, embroidered features and collar, hand made, c1950 .... 5.00
  6" h, Boxer, Steiff 75.00
  7" h, Dalmatian, sitting, mohair, swivel head, orig collar, Steiff 75.00
  8" h, plush, amber, swivel neck, oversized head, milk glass and amber bead eyes, embroidered nose and mouth, stitched tail and ears, early 20th C 75.00
  8-1/2" h, Poodle, pink, standing, glass eyes 18.00
  9" h, Beagle, plush, glass eyes .. 25.00
  10" h, Snoopy, black and white .. 15.00
  11" h, Terrier, white plush, black spots, swivel head, white muzzle, yellow glass eyes, embroidered features, red ribbon, c1925 .... 50.00
  12" h, Poodle, curly, gray, plaid coat, hat, and boots, c1960 .... 15.00
  16" h, Huckleberry Hound 14.00

Donkey, gray plush body, brown glass eyes, brown yarn mane, gray tail, wheeled base, c1950 .... 110.00

Duck, 8" h, plush, standing, yellow, straw hat, blue suspender pants 45.00

Elephant
  4" h, gray mohair , black glass eyes, red saddle, Steiff, c1953 .... 100.00
  6-1/2" h, standing, gray, red suspender pants 65.00

Elsie the Cow, 12" h, 1950s 300.00

Frog, green velvet back, white satin underside, c1960 .... 15.00

Giraffe, 42" h, plush, yellow, brown spots, brown button eyes, brown yarn tail, c1957 .... 20.00

Goat, 6-1/2" h, standing, white, brown felt horns, Steiff 50.00

Hedgehogs, 22" h, Micky & Mecky, vinyl swivel heads, pressed mask face, tan, squinting eyes, smiling mounts, bristly hair, felt bodies sewn on shoes, checkered costumes, c1950, price for pr 475.00

Hen, 7" h, gold and black spotted feathers, yellow plush head, felt tail, black button eyes, Steiff, c1949 .... 75.00

Hippo, plush, purple, plastic eyes and teeth, c1962 .... 18.00

Horse, 15" h, amber hopsacking, straw stuffing, reinforced stitching, pale yellow underbelly, amber glass eyes, stitched smiling mouth, applied ears, black fur mane, horsehair tail, velvet and leather saddle and harness, c1890 .... 85.00

Kangaroo, 11" h, plush, glass eyes, two plastic Joeys, Steiff button in ear marked "Linda" 65.00

Lamb, 9" h, white, fluffy, glass eyes, embroidered features, bell, flowers and ribbon at neck, paper label. 90.00

Leopard, 15" l, silver button, Steiff . 185.00

Llama, 11" h, standing, white, brown spots, Steiff 100.00

Misha, 10-1/2" h, Moscow
   Olympics.......................................25.00
Monkey
   11" h, mohair, jointed, felt paws and
   face, Steiff.....................................85.00
   36" h, Curious George, plush, knit yel-
   low sweater, red cap, c1975.......48.00
Mother Goose, 22" h, muslin, white, yellow felt feet, white cotton bonnet, blue
   floral apron, c1962.......................30.00
Owl, 10" h, Steiff.............................70.00
Owl, 8-1/2" h, Steiff Wittie Owl, Marguerite
   Steiff's nephew's signature on bottom
   of foot 70.00
Paddington Bear, Holiday, orig tags,
   16" h..20.00
Panda, 47" h, plush, black and white,
   jointed, humpback, pie shaped eyes,
   straw filled.................................225.00
Parrot
   9" h, Lora, glass eyes, Steiff........75.00
   15" h, Merrythought...................325.00
Penguin, 10" h, black and white, black
   plastic wings, c1960....................10.00
Pig, 6" h, plush, pink, pink felt cork screw
   tail, black and white felt eyes......20.00
Pinocchio, 8" h, orig Walt Disney tag.5.00
Polar Bear, 10" h, Coca-Cola............10.00
Rabbit
   6-1/2" h, mohair, jointed, Steiff...100.00
   12" h, plush, glass eyes, embroidered
   features, jointed body, paper
   label..70.00
   15" h, felt, eating carrot, Lenci 24.00
Raccoon, Gund.................................20.00
Seal, 10" h, fur, black, glass eyes 85.00
Socks, 11" h, Clinton's black and white
   cat..40.00
Squirrel, plush, Perri, Steiff...............42.00
Teddy Bear
   4" h, plush, dark brown, jointed ..40.00
   5" h, plush, standing, swivel head,
   "Character" label........................40.00
   6" h, plush, jointed, fully dressed orig
   clothes, "Berg" label....................65.00
   9" h, plush, blonde, black shoe button
   eyes, shoulder hump, small tail, straw
   filled, c1905 ....165.00
   9-1/2" h, 13-3/4" l, brown curly hair
   bear on all fours, mohair, early 20th C,
   unjointed, glass eyes..............1,380.00
   11" h, brown woven mohair, black
   shoe button eyes, embroidered features and claws 115.00
   11-1/2" h, Jeane Steele Original, straw
   hat, felt collar, big fabric bow, jointed,
   tag "Kent Collectibles/Jeane Steele
   Originals/©1985" 48.00
   12" h, mohair, blond, c1910, black
   shoe button eyes, fully jointed ..275.00
   12" h, plush, amber, swivel head,
   jointed arms and legs, stitched on
   ears, felt paws, functioning grower,
   straw filled, c1915.......................200.00
   14" h, Knickerbocker, 1950s 26.00
   14" h, Zotty, Hermann, platinum
   frosted mohair...........................155.00
   15" h, mohair, brown, black shoe button eyes, black embroidered nose,
   mouth, and claws, fully jointed, label
   "Bruin Mfg Co," c1907 ....250.00

16" h, Anker, German, mohair, hang
   tag mkd "Pluschtiere Aus
   Munchen".....................................215.00
16" h, Steiff, Molly Koala bear, gray
   and tan 135.00
17" h, mohair, blond, 1910, black steel
   eyes...517.50
17" h, plush, brown, tan paws, molded
   muzzle, Ideal Toy 50.00
18" h, gold mohair, unmarked, brown
   glass eyes, applied ears, felt pads on
   paws...375.00
18" h, Shug, Laveen Bear Country,
   long gray fur, long leather nose,
   leather pads on feet, blue corduroy
   vest, large blue marble eyes, orig
   hang tag......................................165.00
20" h, mohair, brown, jointed, flat face,
   Knickerbocker.............................100.00
24" h, mohair, brown, glass eyes,
   black cloth nose, fully jointed,
   c1925 ....600.00
25" h, Ideal, light yellow mohair, c1905,
   black shoe button eyes 13,800.00
Tiger
   6" h, plush, Steiff...........................60.00
   8" h, Tony, Esso Tiger, orange and
   black, felt trim...............................45.00
   13" h, plush, Shere Khan, black-green
   eyes, 8" l tail, button in ear,
   Steiff..175.00
Turtle, 5-1/2" l, plush and felt, Steiff ..40.00
Walrus, pink, Gund 25.00
Weasel, 7-5/8" h, Steiff, 1970's, "Wiggy,"
   synthetic white winter fur, black plastic
   eyes, ear button and chest tag 258.75
Zebra, 7" h, belt and white, button in ear,
   Steiff..75.00

Super Heroes

Collecting Hints: Concentrate your collection on a single super hero. Because Superman, Batman, and Wonder Woman are the most popular, new collectors are advised to focus on other characters or on one of the modern super heroes. Nostalgia is the principal motivation for many collectors; hence, they sometimes pay prices based on sentiment rather than true market value.

Comics are a fine collectible but require careful handling and storage. An attractive display requires inclusion of a three-dimensional object. Novice collectors are advised to concentrate on these first before acquiring too much of the flat paper material.

History: The super hero and comic books go hand in hand. Superman made his debut in 1939 in the first issue of Action Comics, six years after Jerry Siegel and Joe Shuster conceived the idea of a man who flew. A newspaper strip, radio show, and movies followed. The popularity of Superman spawned many other

super heroes, among them Batman, Captain Marvel, Captain Midnight, The Green Hornet, The Green Lantern, The Shadow, and Wonder Woman.

These early heroes had extraordinary strength and/or cunning and lived normal lives as private citizens. A wealth of merchandising products surround these early super heroes. Their careers were enhanced further when television chose them as heroes for Saturday morning shows as well as for prime time broadcasts.

The Fantastic Four—Mr. Fantastic, The Human Torch, The Invisible Girl, and The Thing—introduced a new type of super hero, the mutant. Other famous personalities of this genre are Captain America, Spider-Man, and The Hulk. Although these characters appear in comic form, the number of secondary items generated is small. Television has helped to promote a few of the characters, but the list of mutant super heroes is close to a hundred.

References: Les Daniels, *Superman: the Complete History*, Chronicle Books, 1998; Tom Heaton, *The Encyclopedia of Marx Action Figures*, Krause Publications, 1999; Rex Miller, *The Investor's Guide to Vintage Character Collectibles*, Krause Publications, 1999; Jeff Rovin, *Encyclopedia of Super Heroes*, Facts on File Publications, 1985.

Collectors' Clubs: Air Heroes Fan Club, 19205 Seneca Ridge, Gaithersburg, MD 20879; Batman TV Series Fan Club, P.O. Box 107, Venice, CA 90291.

Additional Listings: Action Figures, Comic Books, Radio Characters and Personalities.

Plastic cup, Captain Midnight touting Ovaltine, $65.

Mattel's Marvel Super Heroes Secret Wars Doom Roller, 1984, $25.

Aquaman

Action Figure, MOC 35.00
Bathtub Toy, Burger King Kids Meal premium 12.00
Comic Book, DC, #4, August, 1962 ....40.00
Costume, Ben Cooper, 1967..........200.00
Glass, 1973 ....15.00
Puzzle, Whitman, action scene, 1967 ....40.00
Tattoo, 1967, unused, orig wrapper..50.00

Batman & Robin

Action Figure, diecast, fully jointed, Mego, 5-1/2" h, C-9, orig box 115.00
Batcopter, Batman the Dark Knight, Kenner, 1990, MIB.............................65.00
Bank, plastic, full color, arms crossed 75.00
Batmobile
  Animated....................................90.00
  Radio controlled, Richman's Toys, 1989, some damage to remote 350.00
  Tin, red, Taiwan, some damage to orig box 300.00
Batmobile Gift Pack, batmobile and boat, Corgi, 1979, MOC 395.00
Coloring Book, 1963, used..............20.00
Cosmetics, Robin goes to a Weekend, Travel Time Cosmetics, Hasbro, 1960s, unused, MIB 65.00
Costume, Switch & Go, orig box....150.00
Desk Set, calendar, stapler, and pencil sharpener, MIB 150.00
Doll, Batman, 15" h, 1992, DC Comics..85.00
Figure, McDonald's Happy Meal, never removed from plastic bag Batman, press and go car, © 1991 ....6.00
  Ridler, © 1993................................5.00
Halloween Mask
  Batgirl, 1977, Ben Cooper, unworn, orig elastic....................................25.00
  Batman, 1960s, tears on lower chin section..36.00
Joker Cycle, Batman the Dark Knight, Kenner, 1990, MIB.....................25.00
License Plate, Batmobile, 1966 ....45.00
Lunch Box, Batman & Robin, C-8.75 ....225.00
Model, MPC Super Powers, Aurora 75.00

Movie Viewer, cassette, Galoob, 1984, MIB 20.00
Pez Dispenser, European, Dark Knight, TAS, MOC 20.00
Plane, friction, plastic, MIB 65.00
Playset, Ideal, Sears Mail Order, 1966, orig box opened from bottom, mint condition box and all accessories, one figure neatly trimmed, rest unplayed with 4,000.00
Puppet
  Hand, Robin, vinyl, Ideal, 1966... 185.00
  Marionette, hard plastic, Hazelle, c1966
    Batman.................................... 195.00
    Robin....................................... 195.00
Puzzle, Batman Returns, 1992, MIB 10.00
Ring, sterling silver, batwing logo, DC Comics, MIB..................................90.00
Statue, WB Resin, Batgirl.............. 100.00
Watch, Fossil, MIB 60.00

Bionic Woman

Bank, figural, wearing running suit, pile of rocks base....................................42.00
Card Set, 44 color cards, colorful wrapper with Jamie 40.00
Doll, Kenner, 1977 ....45.00
Game, The Bionic Woman Board Game, Parker Bros..................................35.00
Model, Repair Kit, Jamie on operating table, computerized medical equipment, Oscar Goldman, snap together, 1976..30.00

Buck Rogers

Action Figure, 12" h, Mego, NRFB 30.00
Rubber Stamp Kit, MIB....................35.00
View-Master Set, Battle of the Mon, cartoon version, 1978, MISP.............24.00

Captain Action

Doll, red shirt, fully dressed, complete accessories, orig box 225.00
Outfit, cap, chains............................95.00

Captain America

Action Figure, 12" h, Mego, MIB.... 125.00
Badge, Sentinels of Liberty, very good condition.................................... 750.00
Comic Book, Marvel
  #27... 195.00
  #217..3.00
  #264..3.00
Doll, 8" h, Super Baby, vinyl head, white hair, stuffed body, uniform, shield, gloves, Amsco, 1970s, orig box .85.00
Game, Captain America game, Milton Bradley, 1977 ....30.00
License Plate, 2-1/4 x 4" , metal, full color graphics, green background, © 1967 Marvel Comics Group, Louis Marx & Co, Japan....................................28.00
Pop-On Ring, pale green plastic base, top with diecut brown plastic head, charm loop on to, copyright symbol and "MC," c1966 ....30.00

Premium Ring, white, expansion bands, metallic blue raised image, 1960s 20.00
Puzzle, Whitman, 1976 .... 28.00
Transfer Sheet, 11" x 12-1/4" , white sheet, colorful day-glow image, © 1971 Marvel Comics Group 18.00
Tricycle, worn................................. 95.00
Wrist Watch, figural, digital, MIP 30.00

Captain Marvel

Christmas Card 150.00
Code Wheel.................................... 350.00
Figure, lead, British, set of Captain Marvel, Captain Marvel Jr., and Mary Marvel.. 275.00
Magic Blotter 225.00
Magic Flute, MOC 125.00
Magic Pictures, Fawcett Publications, 1945, unused 25.00
Membership Kit, card, pin, letter, code sheet 300.00
Pencil Clip...................................... 75.00
Pennant, blue felt, name and drawing in red and white, 1940s 125.00
Pinback Button, club 100.00
Power Siren.................................... 250.00
Punch-Out Book, Captain Marvel's Rocket Raider, Fawcett Publications, 1940s, unused............................ 75.00
Shoulder Patch, multicolored......... 150.00
Slurpee Cup, 7-11 .... 15.00
Toy, Captain Marvel Buzz Bomber, Fawcett Publications, 1945.................. 22.00
Wrist Watch, Mary Marvel, Shazam, wear 140.00

Captain Midnight

Book, Joyce of the Secret Squadron..................................... 35.00
Decoder, 1946................................. 95.00
Leaflet, 6" x 9" , Herald, radio introduction, Skelly Oil, 4 pgs, listing radio stations, October 1939, black, white, and blue printing.. 275.00
Manual
  Captain Midnight Manual, 5" x 6-1/2" mailer, 1957 Ovaltine premium, 12 pgs, code book, cover letter 145.00
  Captain Midnight's Secret Squadron Manual, 6" x 8-3/4" , 1942 Ovaltine premium, 12 pgs 145.00
Mug, Ovaltine, very good decal 65.00
Patch, 3" w fabric shoulder insignia, blue and gold, red border, 1943 Ovaltine premium.. 135.00
Premium Photo, 6" x 7-1/2" matte finish black and white, Chuck Ramsey, smiling close-up, facsimile signature, Skelly Oil premium, 1939 .... 80.00
Ring
  Flight Commander, signet......... 900.00
  Secret Compartment................. 150.00
Salt and Pepper Shakers, pr, full color, plaster 75.00
Service Ribbon, letter, orig mailer .. 395.00
Shake-Up Mug, orig box, 1957 ..... 250.00
Whistle Decoder, 1947.................... 75.00

Fantastic Four

Action Figure, Mego, set of four figures, MOC 200.00
Comic Book, Marvel, #375 .... 4.00
Figure, 5" h
   Human Torch 5.00
   Thing 5.00
Lunch Box 50.00
Puzzle, Marvel, 1970s 120.00

Green Hornet

Annual, British, hardbound, 1966, some ink marks 75.00
Big Little Book 75.00
Cutlery Set, MOC 85.00
Halloween Costume, Ben Cooper, c1966, MIB 275.00
Magic Rub-Off Slate, Whitman, 1966 .... 200.00
Membership Card 15.00
Pennant, orange and green, felt, 28" l 185.00
Puzzle, frame tray, 1966, set of four . 95.00
Ring, seal/secret compartment 850.00
Spoon 20.00
Trading Card 8.00
Walkie Talkies, Remco, © 1966, MIB 800.00

Incredible Hulk

Figure, jointed, flat, litho, 1978, MIP . 27.50
Lunch Box, C-8 .... 85.00
Playing Cards, MIB 15.00
Premium Ring, white, expansion bands, metallic green raised image, 1960s 20.00
Utility Belt, Remco, 1978, MIB 45.00

Legion of Super Heroes, figure, gold tone, MIB 55.00

Mr. Fantastic, Marvel, flashlight, 1978, unused 55.00

Shadow

Photo, 8" x 10" black and white, masked, facsimile autograph 285.00
Toy, Crime Fighter Helicopter, battery operated, MIB 200.00

Spider-Man

Action Figure, 9-1/2 x 14-3/4", diecut card, Spider-Man on rope, red, blue, and black costume, Fly Away Action version sticker, Mego, © 1979 Marvel Comics, MOC 90.00
Doll, Energized Spider-Man, Mego, copter, trap, accessories 165.00
Game, Spider-Man Web Spinning Action Game, Ideal, 1979, factory sealed 130.00
Halloween Candy Container, plastic, black and white eyes, AJ Renzy Corp., Leominster, MA, 1979 Marvel Comic copyright 20.00
Model Kit, MPC, 1978 .... 50.00
Motorcycle, Super Moto, MIP 40.00
Patch, iron-on, set of six different poses, Marvel 5.00

Premium Ring, red plastic, black and white face on to, mkd "Hong Kong," 1970s 18.00
Race- Car, Ricochet, 1974 .... 85.00
Sign, adv Spider-Man comic strip in Bee Comics, autographed by Stan Lee, 1977 .... 150.00
Toy, Helicopter, NRMIB 95.00
Wrist Watch, figural, digital, MIP 35.00

Spiderwoman

Premium Ring, white, expansion bands, black raised image, 1960s 20.00

Super Heroes, DC Comics

Activity Set, Prestofix, Tarco, 1977, MIB 50.00
Plaster Set 25.00

Superman

Animation Art, cel, Superman with three lava monsters, flying to left, matted and framed 300.00
Catalog, Superman at the Gilbert Hall of Science, toy catalog, Superman cover, illus, 8-1/2" x 5-1/2", 1948 .... 175.00
Cake Topper, Wilton, set in orig box, 1979 .... 20.00
Coloring Book, Saalfield, 11" x 15", 1940, 52 pages, some colored 120.00
Comic Book, *Amazing World of Superman*, Official Metropolis Edition, 14" x 12", 1973, NPP 30.00
Cookie Jar, ceramic, brown telephone booth 595.00
Figure, rubber, flexible, Ben Cooper, 1978 .... 65.00
Game, Superman Match Game, Ideal, 1978, MIB 85.00
Hair Brush, 2-1/4" x 4" x 1-1/2" tan wooden brush, curved top surface, black and brown bristles, 1-1/4" x 2" red and dark blue image of flying Superman carrying red, white, and blue stars and stripes banner reading "Superman America" gold background, c1942 .... 90.00
Lunch Box, thermos, C8 .... 65.00
Membership Card, 1940 .... 24.00
Movie Viewer, cassette, Galoob, 1984, MIB 20.00
Record Player, child's, 1970s 40.00
Ring
   Logo, DC Comics, sterling silver 100.00
   Superman of America, silver, diamond, metal tin container, membership kit 375.00
Squirt Gun 65.00
Toy, roll-over tank, C9 .... 650.00
Wallet, vinyl, 1966, unused 45.00

X-Men, premium ring, thin plastic diecut, bright yellow accent on Wolverine mask, 1980s 12.00

Wonder Woman

Action Figure, MOC 25.00
Animation Art, cel, Wonder Woman and Firestore, 3/4 poses, matted and framed 50.00

Bath Sponge, unopened package 70.00
Book and Record Set, 33-1/3 rpm, Peter Pan, 16 pg comic story, 1977, orig cardboard sleeve 20.00
Cake Pan Set, Wilton, 16" h figural aluminum pan, orig plastic Wonder Woman face, MIB 40.00
Card Game, Superhero Color-A-Deck, 1977, MIP with colored pencils, unused 90.00
Collector Drinking Glass, Pepsi 30.00
Coloring and Fun Activity Book, mask 12.00
Comic Book, #134 .... 14.00
Doll, Mego, Nubia, 1981, 8-1/2", MIB 200.00
Drinking Cup, Burger King Kid's Meal premium 12.00
Greeting Card, orig envelope, unused, risqué verse 16.50
Light Switch Cover 15.00
Lunch Box, vinyl, C8-8.5 .... 95.00
Pencil Case, vinyl, C-9.5 .... 72.00
Playing Cards, MIB 15.00
Pocket Superhero, Mego, 1980, MOC 105.00
Puzzle, 130 pcs, 10-3/4" x 5-1/2" 15.00
Set, mask, cloak, wrist band, lasso, MIB 15.00
Skates 20.00
Squeeze Toy, rubber 24.00
Sticker, 3-D, unused sheet 3.00
Sunglasses 4.00

Swarovski Crystal

Collecting Hints: Sophisticated design and custom fabricated components of the clearest crystal are some of the criteria that distinguish Swarovski crystal from other collectible crystal figurines. The most popular array of Swarovski items falls within the Silver Crystal line, which has included animals, candlesticks, paperweights, and decorative accessories since 1977. Most items are marked, and this is helpful to collectors. The first mark for Silver Crystal items was a block style "SC," sometimes accompanied by the word "Swarovski." Since 1989 an impressionistic swan has been used as the Swarovski symbol. The logo accompanied by a small copyright symbol indicates that the piece was manufactured for the American market.

Other items produced by the Swarovski company are also of interest to collectors, and these include Trimlite, Savvy, Swarovski Selections, Daniel Swarovski Collection, Ebeling & Reuss, and Giftware Suite assortments.

Swarovski crystal collecting has attracted a worldwide following, with a vigorous secondary market. New collectors will find the Swarovski company's Product Listing leaflet very helpful as a beginning checklist of retired and current items. Condition is critical when contemplating an item for resale, and presence of original packaging with enclosures, where applicable, is important. Also desirable is an artist's autograph, occasionally found on the underside of a figurine. Some figurines were produced in more than one version, and the pursuit of various configurations of a design is one type of collection pursued by some Swarovski enthusiasts.

Some crystal figurines have metal trim, usually in one of two colors: shiny silvertone is called "Rhodium" and usually predates the goldtone version of the same item. Examples include the In Flight series of Bee, Butterfly, and Hummingbird, which were produced with both types of trim.

In addition to stunningly clear crystal, color appears in some Swarovski items. For a number of years paperweights were produced in assorted colors, few of which were sold at retail in the United States. These paperweights, which were colored by applying a vaporized chemical coating to the bottom, have sparked interest among collectors. Recently, the company has introduced several figurines with integrally colored glass.

Few Swarovski pieces are serially numbered, and the items that are numbered have attracted considerable interest. In 1995, the Eagle was produced in an edition of 10,000 pieces. In 1995 and 1996, the company collaborated with perfume makers to create serially numbered perfume flacons in limited quantities.

History: The Swarovski family has been perfecting the glassmaker's art in Wattens, Austria, since 1895, and is responsible for many technical advances in the glass industry. For decades, this company has been a leading producer of colored and faceted stones for the costume jewelry and fashion industry, and also is widely respected for its industrial abrasives and quality optics.

Silver Crystal collectible figurines and desk accessories were introduced in 1977, with the creation of a sparkling crystal mouse, followed soon after with a spiny crystal hedgehog. Formed of crystal with lead content of at least 30 percent, these crystal critters have unmistakable

sparkle, and were immediately popular.

The Swarovski Collectors Society, which was formed in 1987, extends exclusive offers to members to purchase annual limited editions. The first SCS series, called Caring and Sharing, features three different pairs of birds. The second series, entitled Mother and Child, focuses on three sets of sea mammals with their young. The third SCS series, with the Inspiration Africa theme, offers three different African wildlife figurines. A fourth series, called Fabulous Creatures, was launched in 1997, and offered mystical creatures. The new series, Masquerade, debuted in 1999 with the introduction of "Pierrot." All SCS figurines are limited to one per member during the year it is offered, and each piece comes with special packaging and a certificate of authenticity.

References: *Swarovski, The Magic of Crystal,* Harry N. Abrams, 1995; Jane and Tom Warner, *Warner's Blue Ribbon Book on Swarovski Silver Crystal,* 3rd ed. (separate pocket guide included), published by authors (7163 W Frederick-Garland Rd, Union, OH 45322), 1996.

Periodical: *Swarovski Collector,* General Wille Strasse 88, SH-8706, Feldmeilien, Switzerland.

Collectors' Clubs: Swan Seekers, 9740 Campo Rd, #134, Spring Valley, CA; Swarovski Collectors Society, 2 Slater Rd, Cranston, RI 02920.

Reproduction Alert: Nefarious reproductions haven't been a problem, but copycats are widespread. Collectors who are alert to correct proportions and quality material rarely are mistaken about a piece of Swarovski crystal, and the presence of the maker's mark and correct packaging make acquisition almost foolproof. Replica mouse, replica hedgehog, and replica cat were issued by the company in 1995. Although similar to early figurines, these reissues are clearly marked with the swan logo and also have design distinctions that will keep collectors from becoming confused.

Advisor: Jimer De Vries.

Notes: All prices shown are approximate retail replacement cost for items in perfect condition with correct original packaging and enclosures. Deduct 15 percent for missing boxes or certificates

Accessories

Apple, photo, apple hinged at side, when top is tilted back, it reveals a photograph
#7504NR030R, 30 mm d, rhodium, SC logo.................................300.00
#7504N050, 50 mm d, gold, SC or swan logo.................................325.00
#7504NR060, 60mm d, SC logo, gold.................................690.00
Ashtray, #7641NR100, sculpted crystal, 3-3/8" d, SC or swan logo.........350.00
Bell, #7467NR071000, 5-3/4" h, SC or swan logo.................................210.00
Candleholder
#7600NR116, for five candles, found with sockets or pickets, SC logo.................................3,850.00
#7600NR123, waterlily, medium.................................235.00
#7600NR131, pickets, set of six, 15/16" h, SC logo.................................300.00
#7600NR136001, gold metal foliage, pineapple, SC logo.................600.00
Christmas Ornament
1981, not dated, crystal snowflake, hexagonal metal trim ring and neck chain, hexagonal ring is stamped "SC" at top on back side, orig blue velour pouch, silver logo box, called the "First Annual Edition," only ornament produced in the Silver Crystal Line.................................525.00
1987, dated, Giftware Suite, etched baroque teardrop shape, first in "Holiday Etching" series, no mark....375.00
1991, dated, Giftware Suite, star/snowflake series.................................350.00
Cigarette Holder, #7463NR062, sculpted crystal, 2-3/8" h, SC or swan logo.................................175.00
Cigarette Lighter, #7462NR062, 3-1/2" h, chrome lighter in crystal base, SC or swan logo..............410.00
Eagle, 1998, edition of 10,000....6,000.00
Grapes, #7550NR30015, cluster of fifteen 1-1/8" d clear grapes, gold stem, SC logo, USA only.......................2,700.00
Paperweight
#7450NR40, pyramid, helio, retired 1990.................................600.00
#7451NR60095, Carousel, 2-3/4" h, flared sides, vertical facets, clear, SC logo, often found without logo, sometimes paper label on felted bottom.................................1,200.00
#7452NR600, Cone, 3-1/8" h, facets that spiral around cone, Bermuda Blue, shades from dark to light blue, SC or swan logo.......................575.00
#7452NR600, Cone, 3-1/8" h, facets that spiral around cone, Volcano color, SC or swan logo.......................700.00
#7452NR600878, Cone, 3-1/8" h, facets that spiral around cone, clear, SC or swan logo.............................300.00
#7453NR60088, Barrel, 2-5/8" h, rect facets that line up vertically, Bermuda Blue, shades from dark to light blue, SC logo, often found without logo, sometimes paper label on felted bottom.................................800.00

#7453NR60095, Barrel, 2-5/8" h, rect facets that line up vertically, clear, SC logo, often found without logo, sometimes paper label on felted bottom 450.00

#7454NR600, Atomic, 2-3/4" h, hexagonal facets, Bermuda Blue, shades from dark to light blue, SC logo, often found without logo, sometimes paper label on felted bottom..............2,875.00

#7454NR600, Atomic, 2-3/4" h, hexagonal facets, clear, SC logo, often found without logo, sometimes paper label on felted bottom.....................1,500.00

#7454NR600, Atomic, 2-3/4" h, hexagonal facets, Vitrail, medium color, SC logo, often found without logo, sometimes paper label on felted bottom..2,100.00

Perfume Bottle, Lancome Tresor, 1994 edition of 5,000 serially numbered, full, with box 450.00

Picture Frame
#7505NR75G, oval, 3" h, gold trim, SC or swan logo 500.00
#7506NR60, square, gold or rhodium trim, SC or swan logo 400.00

Pineapple, rhodium metal foliage
#7507NR060002, 2-1/2" h.........200.00
#7507NR105002, 4-1/8" h, SC logo 600.00

Salt and Pepper Shakers, pr, #7508NR068034, 2-3/8" h, rhodium screw on tops, SC logo 500.00

Schnapps Glass, #7468NR039000, approx. 2" h, SC or swan logo
Europe, set of three 200.00
USA, set of six 625.00

Treasure Box, removable lid
#7464NR50, round shape, flowers on lid, SC or swan logo 300.00
#7464NR50/100, round shape, butterfly on lid, SC logo 300.00
#7465NR52, heart shape, flowers on lid, SC logo 600.00
.#7465NR52/100, heart shape, butterfly on lid, SC or swan logo.........350.00
#7466NR063000, oval shape, flowers on lid, SC or swan logo 350.00
#7466NR063100, oval shape, butterfly on lid, SC logo 425.00

Vase, #7511NR70, 2-7/8" h, sculpted crystal, three frosted crystal flowers, SC or swan logo 220.00

Figurine

Baby Beaver, #7616NR000002, sitting, retired December 1999 ....215.00

Baby Lovebirds, #7621NR005.......115.00

Bear
#7636NR112, 4-1/2" h, SC mark only, USA only, SC logo 3,500.00
#7637NR92, 3-3/4" h, USA only, SC logo 2,650.00
#7670NR32, 1-1/8" h, SC logo ..375.00

Bee, crystal and metal bee feeding on crystal lotus flower, 4" w, SC logo
#7553NR100, gold metal bee 2,250.00
#7553NR200, silver metal bee 5,225.00

Butterfly
#7551NR100, 4" w, crystal and metal butterfly feeding on crystal lotus flower, gold metal butterfly, SC logo 1,400.00
#7551NR200, 4" w, crystal and metal butterfly feeding on crystal lotus flower, silver metal butterfly, SC logo 5,150.00

#7671NR30, 1" h, crystal, metal antennae, no base, USA only SC logo 225.00

Cat
#7634NR52, 2" h, flexible metal tale, SC logo 700.00
#7634NR70, 2-7/8" h, SC or swan logo 150.00
#7659NR31, 1-1/4" h, flexible metal tail, SC or swan logo 75.00

Cathedral, #7474NR000021, Silver Crystal series, designed by Gabriele Stamey, retired December 1994... 215.00

Chaton, #SW-7433NR080000 .... 260.00
Chaton, #SW-7433NR050000 ....65.00
Cheetah, #7610NR000001 .... 500.00

Christmas Angel
1996.. 300.00
1997, #9443NR9700001 .... 215.00

City Gates, #7474NR000023, Silver Crystal series, designed by Gabriele Stamey, retired December 1994... 215.00

City Hall, #7474NR020027, Silver Crystal series, designed by Gabriele Stamey, retired December 1994 .... 215.00

Dachshund, metal tail
#7641NR75, 3" l, rigid, limp, or gently arched, SC or swan logo 150.00
#7642NR42, 1-1/4" l, SC logo... 200.00

Dog (Pluto on European list), SC or swan logo 150.00

Dolphin, #7644NR000001 .... 210.00

Dragon, #D01X971, 1997.............. 600.00

Duck
#7653NR45, 1-7/8" l, silver beak, SC logo 100.00
#7653NR55, 2-1/8" l, silver beak, USA only, SC logo 225.00
#7653NR75, 3" l, crystal beak, USA only, SC logo 600.00

Eagle, #7607NR000001, 1995, edition of 10,000 serially numbered, gray train case type box, wood display pedestal 8,100.00

Elephant
#7640NR60, 2" h, frosted tail, swan logo 150.00
#7640NR55, 2-1/2" h, flexible metal tail, SC logo 275.00
#7640NR100, Dumbo, 1990, black eyes, clear hat, only 3,000 made, most have swan logo, few unmarked 1,150.00
#7640NR1000001, Dumbo, 1993, blue eyes, frosted hat, swan logo and Disney copyright symbol 1,500.00

Falcon Head, SC or swan logo
#7645NR45, 1-3/4" h................. 230.00
#7645NR100, 4" h.................. 3,500.00

Frog
#7642NR48, black eyes, clear crown, SC or swan logo...................... 150.00
#7642NR48, clear eyes, clear crown, usually found with SC logo 350.00

Grand Piano, with stool, #7477NR000006 ....260.00

Hedgehog, silver whiskers
#7360NR30, 1-1/4" h including spines, 30mm body, SC logo, USA only 565.00
#7360NR40, 1-3/4" h including spines, 40mm body, found only with SC mark, worldwide distribution 180.00
#7360NR50, 2" h including spines, 50mm body, SC logo, worldwide distribution 200.00
#7630NR60, 2-3/8" h including spines, 60mm body, SC logo, USA only 1,150.00

Hummingbird, crystal and metal hummingbird feeding in crystal lotus flower, 4" w, SC logo #7552NR100, gold metal hummingbird, green stones on wings 1,500.00
#7552NR200, silver metal hummingbird, red stones on wings 6,500.00

Lion, #D01X951, Inspiration Africa series, 1995 ....750.00

Mallard, #7647NR80, 3-1/2" l, frosted beak, SC or swan logo..............225.00

Mouse, silver whiskers, metal coil tail
#7631NR23, 13/16" h, SC logo 100.00
#7631NR30, 1-3/4" h to top of ears, 30mm body, octagonal base, SC or swan logo 130.00
#7631NR50, 2-7/8" h to top of ears, 50mm body, sq base, USA only, SC mark 1,500.00
#7631NR60, 3-3/4" h to top of ears, 60mm body, sq base, USA only, SC logo 2,200.00

Mushrooms, #SW-7472NR030000 .... 45.00

Peacock, #7607NR000002, 1998, edition of 10,000 ....6,000.00

Pig, #7638n65, 1-3/4" l, crystal "J" shaped tail, SC logo..................500.00

Poodle, #7619NR000003, retired 1997 ....225.00

Rabbit, ears lay flat on top of head, SC logo
#7652NR20, 1" h 110.00
#7652NR45, 1-1/2" h 550.00

Roe Deer Fawn, #SW-7608NR000001 .... 75.00

Rose, #7478NR000001 .... 155.00

Santa Maria, #7473NR000003 ......375.00

Shell with Pearl, #7624NR055000 ....175.00

Sparrow, silver metal open beak
#7650NR20, 3-/4" h, SC or swan logo 75.00
#7650NR32, 1-1/4" h, SC logo....80.00

Squirrel, 10-Year Anniversary 210.00

Swan, Centenary, 100th Anniversary, 2" h 195.00

Swan, #7658NR27, 1" h, delicate crystal neck connected to body, two wings, tail, SC logo 190.00

The Harp, #SW-7477RR000003 ....210.00

Three South Sea Fish, #SW-7644NR0570000 ....140.00

Turtle, #SW-7632NR045000.............75.00

Whale, mother and child, #D01X921, 1992..475.00

T

Taylor, Smith and Taylor

Collecting Hints: Collector interest focuses primarily on the Lu-Ray line, introduced in 1938 and named after Virginia's Luray Caverns. The line actually utilized forms from the Empire and Laurel lines. Lu-Ray was made from the 1930s through the early 1950s in coordinating colors, which has encouraged collectors to mix and match sets.

Pieces from the Coral-Craft line are very similar in appearance to pink Lu-Ray. Do not confuse the two.

Vistosa, introduced in 1938, is another example of the California patio dinnerware movement that featured bright, solid-color pieces. Unfortunately, the number of forms was restricted. As a result, many collectors shy away from it.

Pebbleford, a plain colored ware with sandlike specks, can be found in gray, dark blue-green, light blue-green, light tan, and yellow. When in production, it was the company's third most popular line, but it is only moderately popular among today's collectors.

Taylor, Smith, and Taylor used several different backstamps and marks. Many contain the company name as well as the pattern and shape names. A dating system was used on some dinnerware lines until the 1950s. The three-number code identifies month, year, and crew number.

History: W. L. Smith, John N. Taylor, W. L. Taylor, Homer J. Taylor, and Joseph G. Lee founded Taylor, Smith, and Taylor in Chester, West Virginia, in 1899. In 1903, the firm reorganized and the Taylors bought Lee's interest. In 1906, Smith bought out the Taylors. The firm remained in the family's control until it was purchased by Anchor Hocking in 1973. The tableware division closed in 1981.

Taylor, Smith, and Taylor started production with a nine-kiln pottery. Local clays were used initially; later only southern clays were used. Both earthenware and fine-china bodies were produced. Several underglaze print patterns, e.g., Dogwood and Spring Bouquet, were made. These prints, made from the copper engravings of ceramic artist J. Palin Thorley, were designed exclusively for the company.

During the 1930s and through the 1950s, competition in the dinnerware market was intense. Lu-Ray was designed to compete with Russel Wright's American Modern. Vistosa was Taylor, Smith, and Taylor's answer to Homer Laughlin's Fiesta.

References: Susan and Al Bagdade, *Warman's American Pottery and Porcelain*, 2nd ed., Krause Publications, 2000; Lois Lehner, *Lehner's Encyclopedia of U.S. Marks on Pottery, Porcelain & Clay*, Collector Books, 1988; Kathy and Bill Meehan, *Collector's Guide to Taylor, Smith & Taylor Lu-Ray Pastels* U.S.A., Collector Books, 1995.

Magazine tear sheet, China and Glass Tablewares, February 1962, $3.

Autumn Harvest, Ever Yours
Butter Dish, cov 30.00
Casserole, cov, 10-3/8" x 7" 38.00
Coffee Pot, cov 30.00
Vegetable Bowl, cov 40.00
Vegetable Bowl, open, round,
7-1/2" d 38.00
Beverly, platter 12.00
Bonnie, sugar, cov 30.00
Boutonniere, Ever Yours
Gravy Boat, with underplate 35.00
Platter, 13-1/2" l, medium 35.00
Break O' Day
Sugar, cov 30.00
Vegetable Bowl, round 30.00
Chateau Buffet, skillet, cov, 10" d, aqua
int. 45.00
Classic Heritage, sugar, cov 35.00
Delphian, cup and saucer 7.50
Empire
Butter Dish, cov 20.00
Dinner Plate, 10" d 12.00
Fairway
Casserole 20.00
Dinner Plate, 9-1/2" d 8.50
Indian Summer
Gravy Boat, underplate, orig
ladle 45.00

Platter, large 35.00
Vegetable Bowl, round, open 30.00
Laurel, cake plate, 10-1/4" d 12.00
Lazy Daisy, platter, 13-5/8" x 11" 30.00
Lu-Ray
Berry Bowl, Chatham Grey 14.00
Bowl, c1936
Persian Cream 60.00
Surf Green 60.00
Windsor Blue 60.00
Bread and Butter Plate, 6" d, Windsor
Blue 6.00
Breakfast Plate, 9" d, Persian
Cream 7.50
Bud Vase, Windsor Blue 135.00
Butter Dish, Persian Cream 35.00
Cake Plate
Persian Cream 110.00
Sharon Pink 110.00
Casserole, cov
Sharon Pink 150.00
Surf Green 140.00
Windsor Blue 140.00
Chop Plate, 14" d
Sharon Pink 30.00
Surf Green 25.00
Creamer, Persian Cream 6.00
Cream Soup and Underplate
Persian Cream 125.00
Sharon Pink 125.00
Windsor Blue 125.00
Demitasse Creamer, Sharon
Pink 50.00
Demitasse Cup and Saucer
Persian Cream 20.00
Surf Green 45.00
Dinner Plate, 10" d
Sharon Pink 20.00
Surf Green 20.00
Egg Cup
Persian Cream 20.00
Surf Green 20.00
Windsor Blue 20.00
Epergne
Sharon Pink 145.00
Windsor Blue 145.00
Fruit Bowl, Persian Cream 8.00
Gravy Boat, attached underplate,
Windsor Blue 50.00
Grill Plate
Persian Cream 30.00
Surf Green 30.00
Juice Pitcher, Windsor Blue 225.00
Juice Tumbler
Persian Cream 70.00
Sharon Pink 70.00
Luncheon Plate, 8" d, Sharon
Pink 20.00
Nappy, Sharon Pink 15.00
Nut Dish
Persian Cream 125.00
Surf Green 125.00
Pickle Dish, Persian Cream 45.00
Pitcher
Persian Cream 135.00
Sharon Pink 65.00
Platter, 12" l, Surf Green 20.00
Relish, four sections, Surf
Green 220.00
Salad Bowl, Sharon Pink 45.00
Salt and Pepper Shakers, pr
Persian Cream 18.00
Windsor Blue 15.00

Sauceboat, underplate, Persian
Cream 18.00
Soup, flat, Windsor Blue..............15.00
Teapot, Sharon Pink....................50.00
Tidbit Tray, Chatham Grey...........80.00
Tumbler, Windsor Blue 98.00
Vase, bud, Surf Green...............150.00
Vegetable Bowl, 8" d
Sharon Pink.............................20.00
Windsor Blue 17.50

Marvel
Cup and Saucer............................6.00
Salad Bowl.................................17.50

#1377, Empire Shape
Casserole, cov, 8-1/2" l, red, blue,
green, and yellow floral border, gold
trim, 1941......................................45.00
Platter, 15" l, 1941, some usage
scratches 35.00

Paramount, gravy boat 12.50
Pebbleford, dinner plate, 10" d 10.00
Plymouth, chop plate.......................20.00
Ranchero, platter, large...................32.00
Scroll Border, sauceboat, attached
underplate, Laurel shape, ivory bor-
der, 1942.....................................30.00

Sea Shell
Casserole, cov, 8" d....................50.00
Platter, 13-1/2" l 30.00

Silhouette, vegetable bowl, cov 95.00

Summer Rose
Casserole, cov, 10" d, 3 quart.....45.00
Place Setting, 8 pcs 42.00

Versatile, Salt and Pepper Shakers,
pr 6.00

Vistosa
Bowl
8" d, Cobalt Blue.....................65.00
12" d, ftd, Mango Red 115.00
Chop Plate, 12" d, Light
Green 85.00
Creamer
Cobalt Blue.............................20.00
Light Green..............................20.00
Cup and Saucer
Deep Yellow............................15.00
Light Green..............................17.50
Demitasse Cup and Saucer, Deep Yel-
low..45.00
Dinner Plate, Cobalt Blue............20.00
Eggcup, Cobalt Blue...................25.00
Luncheon Plate, 9" d, Light
Green 17.50
Salad Bowl, 12" d, ftd, Light
Green 195.00
Salt and Pepper Shakers, pr
Deep Yellow............................22.00
Mango Red..............................20.00
Sauce Boat, Light Green...........145.00
Soup, coupe, Mango Red...........25.00
Soup, flat, Deep Yellow 24.00
Sugar, cov
Light Green..............................25.00
Mango Red..............................25.00
Teapot
Deep Yellow............................85.00
Light Green..............................95.00
Mango Red..............................85.00
Vegetable Bowl, Cobalt Blue 45.00
Water Jug, Deep Yellow 75.00
Water Pitcher, Mango Red 85.00

Vogue, cup and saucer....................6.50

Teapots

Collecting Hints: Most collectors
focus on pottery, porcelain or china
examples. Much attention has been
given recently to the unglazed pottery teapots referred to as Yixing.
These teapots are small in size and
feature earthy designs such as lotus
flowers, handles of twig, and insects
shaped on the body or lid finial. Yixing (traditionally Vis-Hsing or I Hsing)
is a Chinese province that has been
known for these artistic wares since
the 16th century. Since they are still
being produced, collectors need to
learn to differentiate the antique from
the modern.

History: The origin of the teapot has
been traced back to the Chinese
province of Yixing in the late 16th
century. The teapots, similar to ones
still being produced today, were no
bigger than the tiny teacups used at
that time.

By the 17th century, tea drinking
had spread throughout the world.
Every pottery or porcelain manufacturer from the Asia, Europe and
America has at one time produced
teapots. Forms range from the purely
functional, such as the English Brown
Betty, to the ornately decorative and
whimsical, such as individual artist
renditions or popular figurals depicting shapes of people, animals, or
things. The majority of teapots available in today's market date from 1870
to the present.

References: Edward Bramah, *Nov-
elty Teapots*, Quiller Press (available
from John Ives, 5 Normanhurst Dr.,
Twickenham, Middlesex, TW1 1NA,
London, England), 1992; Tina M.
Carter, *Teapots*, Running Press (avail-
able from author, 882 S. Mollison
Ave., El Cajon, CA 92020), 1995; —,
*Collectible Teapots, Reference and
Price Guide*, Krause Publications,
2000; Robin Emmerson, *British Tea-
pots and Tea Drinking*, distributed by
Seven Hills, 1996.

Periodicals: *Tea, A Magazine*, P.O.
Box 348, Scotland, CT 06264; *Tea
Talk*, P.O. Box 860, Sausalito, CA
94966; *Tea Time Gazette*, P.O. Box
40276, St. Paul, MN 55104.

Reproduction Alert: New and modern Yixing teapots mimicking the vintage pots. This category requires
extra study. Watch for teapots and
other porcelain with a celadon color
and cobalt design similar to flow

blue. These reproduction teapots
often have a blurred mark, including
a lion, unicorn and shield, which is
similar to many pottery marks from
England.

Advisor: Tina M. Carter.

**Variations of Rebekah at the
Well, brown glaze, left, 9-1/2" h,
$100; center, 7-1/2" h, $20; right,
7-1/2" h, $90. All with roughness
at spout. Photo courtesy of Joy
Luke Fine Art Brokers and Auctioneers.**

Brass, 8" d, 9" h, green handle, four small
feet 290.00

Ceramic, pottery or porcelain
Belleek, Shamrock dec, 2nd black
mark 295.00
Fraunfleter, ribbed body, marked "Ohio"
in diamond...................................32.00
Harker, Royal Gadroon pattern,
floral 25.00
Mammy, 4-1/4" h, mkd "Made in Japan,"
c1940 .... 195.00
Mulberry China, Washington's Vase, mis-
matched lid................................ 195.00
Rockingham Glaze, sterling silver appli-
qué design 145.00
Royal Winton, Chintz 195.00
Staffordshire, coralene raised decoration,
black ground, lion and Staffordshire
knot mark, made as fund raiser for
wartime efforts, c1948............... 40.00
Torquay, motto ware, small, Watcombe,
England 38.00
Vernon Kilns
Gale Turnball, 6-1/2" h, mkd "Vernon
Kilns 707".................................. 115.00
Linda, mkd on bottom............... 125.00
Wade, Scottie, 51/2" h, 8" w handle to
spout..300.00
Wedgwood, deep green, 4-3/4" h, 8" w
handle to spout 400.00

Chinese
Brass, hammered design, matching
warming stand, mkd "China"......85.00
China, white, large 8-cup teapot, rattan
handle, no mark 18.00
Floral, tiny spout, unmarked.............25.00
Set, teapot and 2 cups, in padded bas-
ket, mkd "China" 125.00

Figural
Colonial man and woman, Tony Wood,
England 40.00

Dickens characters, Beswick,
England...75.00
House, Cottage Ware, Price, Kensington,
England...32.00
Jim Bean Club, collector's edition, Wade,
1995..50.00
Santa, white glaze, Price Bros, England,
1960s...30.00
Sherlock Holmes, Hall China, 1988,
12" h...125.00
Snow White, dwarves around base, holds
1-1/2 cups, music box base plays "Hi
Ho, Hi Ho," c1940, 6" h..............130.00
Iron, 8" h, 7-1/2" d, Tetsubin, Japan,
c1920...250.00

Miniature

Aluminum, Swans Brand, 2 cup, England,
4" h...15.00
China
    Hand painted, dragonflies, Chinese
    mark, 2-1/2" h...............................12.00
    Peking Duck, teapot on stand,
    2" h...18.00
Copper, mkd "Italy," 1-3/4" h.............,10.00
Porcelain
    Children playing dec, no mark, attrib-
    uted to Germany, 4" h...................25.00
    Floral, lid screws on, Germany,
    3" h...25.00
    Relief flowers, white porcelain,
    England, 2" h...............................15.00
Precious Moments, Taiwan, 1992,
2" h...12.00
Thimble, pewter mouse peaks out of tea-
pot, 1" h...10.00

Pewter

5-3/4" h, 10" w handle to spout, mkd
"M209" with diamond shape.....145.00
6" h, 10" w handle to spout, Richard Franklin & Sons, Sheffield.................175.00

Television Personalities and Memorabilia

Collecting Hints: Collectors of television memorabilia fall into two categories. One includes those who
specialize in acquiring items from a
single television series. "Star Trek,"
"Hopalong Cassidy," "Howdy
Doody," "Roy Rogers," or "Leave It To
Beaver" are the most popular series.
The other category of collector spe-
cializes in TV memorabilia of one type
such as *TV Guides*, model kits, films,
or cards.

There have been more than 3,750
series on television since 1948.
Therefore, an enormous number of
artifacts and memorabilia relating to
television are available. Premiums
from the early space shows and cowboy adventure series are eagerly
sought by pop-culture collectors. As

a result, these items are beginning to
command high prices at auction.

Systematic scheduling of television programs developed a new type
of publication called *TV Guide*. The
early guides are avidly sought. The
first schedules were regional and
include titles such as *TV Today in
Philadelphia*, *TV Press in Louisville*,
and *Radio-Television Life in Los
Angeles*. The first national *TV Guide*
was published on April 3, 1953. Collectors enjoy these older magazines
because they are good sources for
early stories about the stars of the
time.

History: The late 1940s and early
1950s was the golden age of television. The first TV programming
began in 1948. Experimentation with
programming, vast expansion, and
rapid growth marked the period.
Prime-time live drama series were
very successful, and provided the
start for many popular stars, such as
Paul Newman, Steve McQueen, Rod
Steiger, Jack Lemmon, and Grace
Kelly. The stars signed autographs
and photographs to promote the dra-
mas. These items, plus scripts and
other types of articles, have become
very collectible.

When the period of live drama
ended, the Western assault began. In
1959 there were 26 Western series,
many of which were based on movie
or radio heroes. The Western era
continued until the early 1960s when
it was replaced by the space adventure series and science fiction.

The 1970s are remembered for
their situation comedies, including
"All In The Family" and "M*A*S*H*."
The collectibles resulting from these
series are numerous.

References: Jim Bunte, Dave Hall-
man and Heinz Mueller, *Vintage Toys:
Robots and Space Toys*, Krause Pub-
lications, 2000; Dana Cain, *Film & TV
Animal Star Collectibles*, Antique
Trader Books, 1998; Greg Davis and
Bill Morgan, *Collector's Guide to TV
Toys and Memorabilia*, 2nd ed., Col-
lector Books, 1999; Ted Hake, *Hake's
Guide to Character Toys*, 3rd ed.,
Gemstone Publishing; Rex Miller, *The
Investor's Guide to Vintage Character
Collectibles*, Krause Publications,
1999; Elizabeth Stephans, ed.,
O'Brien's Collecting Toys, Tenth ed.,
Krause Publications, 2001; Stuart W.
Wells, III, *Science Fiction Collecti-
bles: Identification & Price Guide*,
Krause Publications, 1999.

Periodicals: *Autograph Times*, 2303
N. 44th St., #225, Phoenix, AZ 85008;

Big Reel, P.O. Box 83, Madison, NC
27025; *Celebrity Collector*, P.O. Box
1115, Boston, MA, 02117; *Collecting
Hollywood*, 2401 Broad St., Chattanooga, TN 37408; *Norm's Serial
News*, 1726 Maux Dr., Houston, TX
70043; *Television History Magazine*,
700 E. Macoupia St., Staunton, IL
62088; *TV Collector*, P.O. Box 1088,
Easton, MA 02334.

Collectors' Club: TV Western Collectors Fan Club, P.O. Box 1361, Boyes
Hot Springs, CA 95416.

Museum: Smithsonian Institution,
Washington, DC.

Additional Listings: Cowboy
Heroes, Space Adventurers & Explorers, Super Heroes, Western Americana.

**Archie Bunker's Grandson Joey
Stivic, made by Ideal. The doll,
22" h, "drinks, wets, and is a physi-
cally correct male," $48.**

Action Figure, Dukes of Hazzard,
3-1/2" h
    Bo, MOC....................................25.00
    Luke, MOC.................................25.00
Alarm Clock, Mr. T., A-Team, metal, blue,
silvered metal bells, Zeon, © 1973
Ruby-Spears Enterprises............27.50
Autograph, color photo, Lost in Space,
Jonathan Harris...........................50.00
Bag, child's, Beany & Cecil, early 1960s,
C-9..55.00
Book
    *Mission Impossible: The Money Explo-
    sion*, Talmage Powell, Whitman 1512,
    1970...12.00
    *National Radio-Television News Direc-
    tory, Official Press Guide of the Work-
    ing Press Association*, 9th edition,
    1964, 11-1/4" x 8-1/2", 255 pgs ..55.00
Car
    Dick Dastardly, Corgi.................75.00
    Magmum PI, Burnin' Key Car Action
    Set, Kidco, 1981, MIB................40.00
    Muppet Show, die-cast, Corgi, com-
    plete set of four, 1979, MOC.....135.00
Colorforms
    Flipper, 1966...............................55.00
    Tammy..40.00
    Welcome Back Kotter, © 1976 ...30.00

Howdy Doody, bank, riding on pig, 7" h, $60.

Coloring Book
    Addams Family, © 1965, Saalfield, used 25.00
    Bewitched, Treasure Books, 1965, unused 75.00
    I Love Lucy, © 1954, Whitman, unused 75.00
    Jackie Gleason, © 1956, Abbott, unused 75.00
    Ozzie & Harriet, © 1973 Filmways Television Corp., Saalfield, unused 45.00
    Wagon Train, © 1959, Whitman, unused 35.00
Comic Book
    Captain Kangaroo, #1, 1956.......25.00
    Gidget, Dell, Dec, 1966...............15.00
    I Love Lucy, 1956 ....5.00
Cookbook, *Granny's*, Beverly Hillbillies, orig dust jacket 100.00
Cookie Jar, Howdy Doody, Purinton Pottery, 9-3/4" h 900.00
Display Box, Welcome Back Kotter, for pinback buttons, Canadian, 1976, slight wear 60.00
Doctor Kit, Dr. Kildare, C-9 ....20.00
Doll
    Bart Simpson 35.00
    Davy Crockett, orig coon skin cap and pouch, some soiling and wear....65.00
    Happy Days, Fonzie, Mego, 8" h, 1976, MOC 150.00
    Happy Days, Potsy, Mego, 8" h, 1976, MOC 75.00
    Happy Days, Ralph, Mego, 8" h, 1976, MOC 75.00
    Happy Days, Ritchie, Mego, 8" h, 1976, MOC 100.00
    Howdy Doody, composition face and hands, pull string to operate mouth 80.00
    I Dream of Jeannie, Remco, poseable, 1977, MIB...............................125.00
    John Wayne, 1981, MIB 185.00
    Redd Foxx, stuffed, double sided, pull string talker doesn't work 58.00
    Ricky Jr., 1950s...........................275.00
    Tabatha, Bewitched, MIB.......2,420.00
Drawing Set, Laugh-In, 1969 ....70.00
Fan Club Kit, Banana Splits 295.00
Figure
    Daisy, Dukes of Hazzard, Mego, 8" h, MOC...60.00

Howdy Doody Puppet Show, five plastic figures, MOC 285.00
Magilla Gorilla, Playtime Toys, 7" h, 1979...20.00
Sluggo, Bendy, 1950s, some paint loss 40.00
Fire Helmet, child's, Emergency, color photo on front with show stars.....50.00

The 3 Stooges Fun House Game and Colorforms, $45.

Game
    Columbo.......................................27.50
    Dick Van Dyke, Standard Toykraft, 1964...500.00
    Gilligan's Island, Game Gems, 1965...570.00
    Knight Rider, 1983 ....65.00
    Kukla, Fran & Ollie 27.50
    Leverne and Shirley....................27.00
    Merv Griffin's Word for Word Game, Mattel, © 1963 NBC, orig box.....37.50
    Perry Mason, Missing Suspect, 1959...42.00
    The Gomer Pyle Game, Transogram 120.00
Gum Card Wrapper
    Man from UNCLE, United Kingdom.......................................60.00
    Outer Limits 350.00
Halloween Costume
    Alf..10.00
    Banana Splits 85.00
    Beany, 1960s, some wear 175.00
    Big Bird..5.00
    Captain Kangaroo.......................85.00
    Dr. Kildare....................................45.00
    Dr. Kildare's Nurse 65.00
    Dukes of Hazzard, Bo, 1982 ......40.00
    Howdy Doody 125.00
    I Dream of Jeannie, 1960s 125.00
    I Love Lucy................................300.00
    Little House on the Prairie, Laura 10.00
    Miss Piggy..................................12.00
    Mr. Ed 110.00
    Six Million Dollar Man, Ben Cooper, 1974, C-9...................................40.00
    Thunderbirds.............................325.00
    Zorro, Ben Cooper, 1981, MIB 75.00
Handbook, *Operation Backstage*, NBC TV, 1951, 10-1/4" x 8-1/4" 65.00
Hat, My Favorite Martian, 1963 ....45.00
Hat Box, Buffy, Family Affair, 10" d, pink plastic, 1969...............................48.00
Kite, Knight Rider, 1982 ....28.50
Lunch Box
    Bonzana, brown, C-8................ 180.00

Fall Guy, box and thermos, C7 ... 40.00
Family Affair, King-Seeley, © 1969, no thermos.......................................95.00
Happy Days, orig thermos..........85.00
Land of the Giants, C-8.5..........250.00
Super Friends, box and thermos, C-7 ....80.00
Thundercats, box and thermos, C-9 ....90.00
Wagon Train, King Seeley, © 1964, no thermos.......................................160.00
Welcome Back Kotter, C-8..........90.00
Magazine
    Foto-Craft, Charlie McCarthy cover, 1940 ....20.00
    Philadelphia News, Our Miss Brooks...30.00
    Post, Laugh-In 15.00
    Star, Charlie's Angels, 1977 ....20.00
    TV Guide, Little House on the Praire, 1976...20.00
    TV Spotlight, Jackie Gleason, 1953...38.00
Magic Slate, Sea Hunt, 1960 ....60.00
Magic Transfers, Fall Guy, Rub-A-Doos, Imperil, 1982...................................5.00
Membership Card, 3" x 5" eight page black and white folder, red accents, Sky King Fan Club, membership card, Good Conduct Rules, photos with facsimile autographs of Penny and Sky King, dot-to-dot puzzle, Nabisco, 1959, wear to cover, orig owner's name written in 65.00
Mittens, pr, Howdy Doody and Clarabell, wool, red 40.00
Model Kit, Welcome Back Kotter, Sweathogs Dream Machine, MPC, 1986, sealed 55.00
Newspaper Advertisement, Sky King, Name-A-Plane Contest, 1950s ... 25.00
Night Light
    Church Lady, Saturday Night Live, 1991 ....30.00
    Howdy Doody, figural, Leadworks, Inc., 1988, 8" h...........................150.00
Oogie Boogie, Hasbro, NBC, 8" h, C-8.5 card...150.00
Ornament, Lost in Space, robot, MIB...50.00
Paint by Number, Dukes of Hazzard, acrylic, MIB...................................50.00
Paint Set, Winky Dink, 1950s, 12" x 18" x 2" box, slight use 70.00
Paperback, *Man from UNCLE*, #2, Ace...6.50
Paper Dolls
    Hee-Haw, punch-out type, 1972, unused...25.00
    Welcome Back Kotter, © 1976 Wolper Organization, Toy Factory, diecut figure, orig box 50.00
Paramedic Kit, Emergency, MOC ... 40.00
Party Hat, A-Team, mint in orig bag... 5.00
Pencil By Number Set, Buccaneers 40.00
Pinback Button, 3-1/2" d, America's Foist Family/The Bunkers, red, white, and blue, black and white photo, © 1972 Tandem Productions, Inc............17.50
Placemat, Howdy Doody, set of 8 ...50.00

Playset, Detective, tommy gun, leather holster, pistol, badge, handcuffs, orig box, 1958 .... 375.00

Portfolio, cardboard, Dukes of Hazzard......................... 15.00

Poster, Partridge Family, unopened pack 30.00

Post Card, The Rebel, Johnny Yuma, fan club 40.00

Premium Card, 4" x 6" glossy black and white photo card, Chuck Wagon Pete, holding carton of Sylvan Seal milk, viewers told to watch him on TV station WPTZ, North Pole, NY, c1950, minor wear 5.00

Press Kit, Polly, Walt Disney, three 8" x 10" black and white glossy photos, biographies, etc., 1989....................... 42.00

Produce Bag, clear plastic, Howdy Doody, 1950s, red, white, and blue graphics of 6 characters, 7" x 12".. 22.00

Punch Out Book, unused
  Beverly Hillbillies, Whitman 85.00
  Dr. Kildare, 1962...................... 22.00
  Heckle & Jeckle, 1978 .... 18.00

Puppet
  Flintstone's, Bam Bam................. 45.00
  Flintstone's, Pebbles.................... 45.00
  Pokey 35.00

Puzzle
  Beany & Cecil, frame tray, c1960 .... 95.00
  Charlie's Angels, Farrah, sealed, orig box 25.00
  Chicken Charlie, Jaymar, boxed. 90.00
  Dukes of Hazzard, boxed, Canadian 25.00
  Emergency, canned, sealed 32.00
  Flipper, frame tray, 1965.............. 20.00
  Gene Autry, Whitman, No. 261029, 1957, frame tray........................... 54.00
  Gumby, frame tray...................... 20.00
  Happy Days, The Fonz, #465-01, HG Toys, 1976, boxed 25.00
  Highway Patrol, Broderick Crawford, boxed... 75.00
  Lassie, Bilt Rite, 1950s, 6" x 9", real photo of Lassie and friend on dock fishing, frame tray...................... 24.00
  Rootie Kazootie, 10" x 14", 1950s, frame tray, set of two 85.00
  Six Million Dollar Man, British 50.00
  Super Six, Whitman, 1959, boxed.. 27.00
  Zorro, Whitman No, 4417, 1957, frame tray 40.00

Radio
  A-Team, MIB 40.00
  Knight Rider, car 55.00
  Six Million Dollar Man, Kenner, 1973, unused 45.00

Record, Laugh-In, 1969, 33 rpm.. 50.00

Ring
  Howdy Doody, raised face.......... 75.00
  Sky King, teleblinker.................. 225.00

Scrapbook, Dr. Kildare, 11" x 14", photo type, 1962, unused........................ 65.00

Sheet Music, theme song
  Jackie Gleason........................... 35.00

S.W.A.T. 20.00

Slide Puzzle, Knight Rider, Michael with K.I.T.T., 1982............................... 18.50

Stethoscope, Thumpy the Heart Beat Stethoscope, picture of Richard Chamberlain on package, MIP ... 40.00

Sticker Book, Flipper.......................... 25.00

Store Display, Beverly Hillbillies, Buddy Ebsen, adv flyswatters, 30" x 24".. 225.00

Stuffed Animal, Scooby Do, 13" h, orig tab, 1980 .... 35.00

Sweatshirt, child's, Pee Wee Herman, Penny 75.00

Tablecloth, paper, I Dream of Jeannie, MIB 30.00

Tee-Shirt, Lost in Space.................... 20.00

Thermos
  Partridge Family, metal 38.00
  The Banana Splits, tin litho, King Seeley, C-9.5 .... 185.00
  Wild Wild West 75.00

Toy
  A-Team Great Escape Stunt Set, motorized van, Lin, 1983, played with condition................................ 30.00
  Howdy Doody Power Tools, MIB. 20.00
  Knight Rider, K.I.T.T. dashboard, MIB 175.00
  Yogi, squeeze toy....................... 35.00

Trapeze, Atom Ant, Kohner, 1960s 100.00

Viewmaster Reel
  Fantastic Voyage 75.00
  Six Million Dollar Man, talking, 1970s, MISB.. 10.00

Walkie Talkie, Six Million Dollar Man Porta Communicator Set, Kenner, 1975, unused.. 48.00

Wallpaper, Howdy Doody, 36" section 30.00

Waste Can, litho tin, 13" h
  Grizzly Adams, 1977 .... 45.00
  Laugh-In.................................... 55.00
  Welcome Back Kotter, 1976........ 48.00

Wrist Watch, Dukes of Hazzard, Unisonic, 1981, orig case, unused.............. 25.00

Writing Tablet, Hogan's Heroes 35.00

Shirley Temple

Collecting Hints: Dolls are made out of many materials—composition, cloth, chalk, papier-mâché, rubber, and vinyl. Composition dolls are the earliest. When Shirley Temple's popularity was boosted by television in the 1950s, a new series of products was issued.

History: Shirley Jane Temple was born April 23, 1928, in Santa Monica, California. A movie scout discovered her at a dancing school. The 1932 film "Pie Covered Wagon" was her screen test, and during that decade she made 20 movies, earning as much as $75,000 per film.

Her mother supervised the licensing of more than 15 firms to make Shirley Temple products, including dolls, glassware, china, jewelry, and soap. The Ideal Toy Company made the first Shirley Temple dolls in 1934. These composition (pressed wood) dolls varied in height from 11 to 27 inches. Ideal made the first vinyl dolls in 1957.

Reproduction Alert.

Doll, 12" h, original wardrobe and carrying case, 1957, $1,800. Photo courtesy of McMasters Doll Auctions.

Doll, 20" h, Ideal, original dress, box, and pinback button, $2,000. Photo courtesy of McMasters Doll Auctions.

Advertisement, 4-1/4" x 6", for Shirley Temple Sewing Kit.......................... 8.00

Arcade Card, Educational Pictures, black and white 2.50

Book
  Heidi, orig production storybook, authorized edition, No. 337, 20th Century Fox Productions, copyright 1937, few waterstains, wear at top edge 100.00
  Shirley Temple and the Spirit of Dragonwood, Kathryn Heisenfelt, Whitman Publishing, 1945, cracked hinge, spine taped, fair 9.00
  Shirley Temple, My Life & Times,

1936 ....50.00
The Little Colonel, Annie Fellows Johnson, A. L. Burt, 1935, 20th Century Fox photos, cover worn 20.00
Candy Mold 35.00
Cereal Bowl, cobalt blue glass, white portrait image 50.00
Cereal Box, Quaker Puffed Wheat, c1930 ....110.00
Clothing
    Coat, cashmere, label, Bambury orig, c1937 ....285.00
    Dress, child's, satin, pink, ruffled, blue and white tag 50.00
Cereal Box, Quaker Puffed Wheat, c1930 ....110.00
Doll, Ideal, composition
    16" h, Ideal, Glad Rags to Riches, 1984, orig box............................195.00
    19" h, Ideal, vinyl head, hazel flirty sleep eyes, real lashes, feathered brows, open-closed mouth, six upper teeth, dimples, rooted hair in orig set, five-pc vinyl body, tagged pink and blue nylon dress, orig underclothes, socks and black shoes, orig wrist tag, mkd "Ideal Doll, ST-19" on back of head and on back, box label "Shirley Temple Doll, Made in U.S.A. by Ideal Toy Corporation, Hollis 23, N.Y.," worn orig box, unplayed with condition 650.00
Doll Carriage, 27" h at handle, brown wicker carriage on metal frame, excellent condition 900.00
Embroidery Set, tablecloth, four napkins, hoop, needle, threads, plastic thimble, unused, Gabriel, 1960s...............50.00
Fan, teen-age Shirley, with RC Cola, "I'll Be Seeing You" movie.................24.00
Figure, 8-1/2" h, rubber, black Scottie dog under one arm, marked "Made in Czechoslovakia," mid-1930s 90.00
Game, The Little Colonel, board, diecut figure pieces, box with Shirley's picture, Selchow & Righter, 1935.....70.00
Jewelry
    Charm, 5/8", brass rim, cut out center, 1930s 75.00
    Necklace, 14", brass, 5/8" cut out head disk, 1930s.................................100.00
    Ring, celluloid, red, black and white diecut head of Shirley, marked "Made in Japan" 25.00
Movie Still, 8" x 10", Little Miss Marker, Shirley on horse with Adolphe Menjou, Paramount Film, 1934 ....20.00
Mug 55.00
Paper Dolls, uncut 18.50
Pinback Button, 1" d, enamel on brass, "Sunday Referee/Shirley Temple League," English newspaper issue..110.00
Pitcher, 4-1/2" h, cobalt blue glass, white portrait image, Wheaties offer, c1938 ....65.00
Pocket Mirror, Quaker Puffed Wheat adv, 1937 ....18.00
Post Card, 3-1/2" x 5-1/2", glossy sepia picture, "Captain January" scene, unused, 1936..............................15.00

Print, 8" x 10" color photo, facsimile signature...10.00
Scrapbook, 11" x 15", Saalfield, 1937 copyright 25.00
Sewing Cards, six black and white cards, yarn, 5" x 7" box, marked "Made by Saalfield 1936" 45.00
Sheet Music
    "Good Night My Love," 1936 ......18.50
    "Pigskin Parade," Shirley on back..10.00
Slipper Box, child's, 6" x 10-1/2" x 3-1/4", gray and blue design, marked "Restful," mid-1930s 75.00
Song Album, 9" x 12", 36 pgs, words and music, pink tinted films scenes ...35.00
Souvenir Book, 9" x 12", 32 pgs, Tournament of Roses Parade, Shirley as Grand Marshal, 1939..................22.00
String Holder, 7" h, chalkware, orig scissors.. 375.00

Thimbles

Collecting Hints: There are many ways to approach thimble collecting. You can collect by material (metal or porcelain), by design (cupids or commemorative), by types (advertising or political), or limited editions (modern collectibles). However, in reality, there is only one philosophy that applies: collect what you like.

There are thousands of thimbles. The wise collector uses a narrow approach, thereby saving money and enabling a meaningful collection to be assembled.

The wonderful thing about thimble collecting is that there is something for every budget. The person with a limited budget might look at advertising or modern collectible thimbles, while the more prosperous could focus on gold examples.

History: Silver thimbles were imported from England during the colonial period, and only the wealthy could afford to buy them. By the late 18th century, advertisements appeared in the *New York Weekly Post, New York Gazette*, and *Philadelphia Directory* offering American-made thimbles. These were gold, silver, or pinchbeck thimbles, some with steel caps.

The 19th-century Industrial Revolution brought about the golden age of thimble production because of the availability of machinery which could produce fine thimbles. By the end of the 19th century, world production of thimbles was about 80 million per year.

Before the sewing machine became a permanent household fixture, all sewing and mending was done by hand. The frontier home-

maker guarded her thimble. Replacing it meant a visit to the general store, which was often miles away, or waiting until a traveling peddler came along. City ladies had no problem replacing a lost thimble. A selection was always available at the local dry good stores. The name "dry goods" assured a lady that no "wet goods," or alcoholic beverages, were sold in that store, and it was perfectly proper for her to shop there.

Needlework can be divided into two kinds: plain and fancy. Plain sewing required a utilitarian thimble made of steel, brass, or celluloid. A process for making celluloid thimbles was patented by William Halsey in 1880. Eugene Villiers patented a thimble-molding process in the same year. Because aluminum was a costly metal during the 19th century, it was not used to make thimbles until the 20th century, when it became less expensive and more practical to use the metal in such applications.

Fancy sewing was considered a parlor or social activity. Ornate thimbles made of precious metals were saved for this purpose. Many gold and silver thimbles were received as gifts. In years past, proper etiquette did not permit a young man to give his lady any gift that was personal, such as jewelry or clothing. Flowers, books, or sweets were considered proper gifts. The thimble somehow bridged this rule of etiquette. A fancy gold or silver thimble was a welcomed gift. Many of these do not show signs of wear, probably because either they did not fit the recipient or were considered too elegant to use for mundane work.

An extensive array of goods and services are advertised on thimbles, and many collections are built around these advertising thimbles because they are easy to find and inexpensive to buy advertising thimbles made of celluloid or metal are older than the modern plastic examples. These little advertising ploys helped salesmen open the door. Tradesmen knew that these tokens would constantly remind the customer of their product. There was no standard method of distributing advertising thimbles, although most were handed to a potential customer by a salesman. Others were packaged with a product, such as flour or bread.

The history of thimbles advertising political campaigns began with the amendment giving the vote to women, ratified on August 20, 1920, just in time for the political campaign that year. The first presidential candi-

Captain America...................5.00
Captain Kangaroo............10.00
Care Bears......................5.00
Casper, 1961, GAF.............25.00
Charlie Brown, Bon Voyage...............5.00
Charlotte's Web....................5.00
CHiPs.........................15.00
Christmas Story, 3 parts, Sawyer, 1948..........................22.00
Cisco Kid, single reel.........................2.50
Cowboy Stars......................25.00
Daktan, 1968, GAF..................35.00
Dale Evans.........................27.50
Daniel Boone......................15.00
Dark Shadows.......................32.00
Dennis the Menace.........................4.00
Deputy Dawg.........................30.00
Detroit, A583, 3 reels......................18.00
Dick Tracy........................7.50
Disneyland, 1962, Sawyers
    Adventureland......................20.00
    Fantasyland.......................25.00
    Frontierland........................25.00
    Main Street USA......................20.00
    Tomorrowland........................25.00
Donald Duck, 1960s, Sawyers.........25.00
Dr. Who........................35.00
Dracula.........................15.00
Duck Tales.........................5.00
Dukes of Hazzard, MOC.................15.00
Dumbo.........................7.50
Eight is Enough, 1980......................15.00
Emergency......................10.00
E. T..........................15.00
Expo, 1967, 3 reels
    A071..........................24.00
    A073..........................24.00
    A074..........................27.00
Family Affair......................24.00
Fantastic Four......................10.00
Fantastic Voyage......................75.00
Fat Albert & Cosby Kids......................10.00
Flintstones, View Master International, 1980 copyright, MOC..............15.00
Fraggle Rock......................3.50
France, Sawyers, sealed pack.........15.00
Frankenstein, 1976, GAF..................15.00
Full House......................3.00
Gene Autry......................40.00
Germany, GAF, sealed pack............15.00
Ghostbusters......................5.00
G.I. Joe Adventures, GAF.................20.00
Godzilla.........................14.00
Goonies.........................7.50
Great Muppet Caper......................4.50
Grizzly Adams......................10.00
Grotto of Redemption West Bend, IA, GAF......................10.00
Gunsmoke, 1972, GAF..................30.00
Happy days......................9.00
Hawaii Five-O.........................20.00
Hopalong Cassidy
    No. 955, Hopalong Cassidy and Topper, 1950........................12.00
    No. 956, The Cattle Rustler, 1950........................12.00
Howard the Duck......................8.00
Huckleberry Hound & Yogi Bear........5.00
Incredible Hulk, 3 reels, booklet, envelope, GAF Viewmaster Cartoon Favorites, J26, 1981......................12.00
Inspector Gadget......................6.00

International Swimming and Diving, ABC Sports......................60.00
Iowa, Sawyers......................15.00
Ironman......................3.50
Isis, MIP......................25.00
Italy, Sawyers, sealed pack............15.00
James Bond, Live & Let Die.............12.00
Jaws......................3.50
Jetson's, 1981, sealed pack.............24.00
John Travolta, 1979, MIP.................35.00
Julia, three reels, story booklet, no envelope, 1969......................40.00
King Kong......................9.00
Kiss Me Kate......................125.00
Knight Rider......................5.00
Korg, sealed......................10.00
Kotter, sealed......................18.00
Kung Fu......................9.00
Lake Tahoo, A161, 3 reels............14.00
Land of the Giants, Sawyer, B484, 3 reels, 1968......................45.00
Land of the Lost, #2, The Abominable Snowman, 1971, orig booklet, damage to envelope......................15.00
Lassie and Timmy, 1958, GAF........20.00
Lassie Look Homeward, 1965, GAF 20.00
Last Starfighter......................7.50
Laugh-In, three reels, orig envelope, 1968......................45.00
Legend of the Lone Ranger.............7.50
Little Black Sambo......................90.00
Little Mermaid......................2.50
Lost in Space, sealed......................250.00
Lost Treasures of the Amazon.......120.00
Love Bug......................10.00
Mannix, sealed......................15.00
Mary Poppins......................8.00
M*A*S*H......................10.00
Mexico, 1973, GAF, sealed pack.....15.00
Michael......................25.00
Mickey Mouse Club......................25.00
Mighty Mouse......................20.00
Mission Impossile......................15.00
Mod Squad, B478, 3 reels.................38.00
Monkees, talking, illus box.............80.00
Mount Rushmore, 1966, GAF..........15.00
Movie Stars, 1 reel......................15.00
Munsters, orig box......................200.00
Muppets Go Hawaiian......................5.00
Naval Aviation Training, World War II, test reel #13, hand lettered, plane identification......................25.00
NCAA Track & Field Championships, ABC Sports......................55.00
New Mickey Mouse Club......................4.50
New Zoo Revue......................12.00
Old Mexico, B206, 3 reels, sealed...15.00
One of Our Dinosaurs is Missing.....12.00
Partridge Family, talking, illus box, MIB......................50.00
Pee Wee's Playhouse, Tyco, 1987, MOC......................15.00
Pete's Dragon......................8.00
Pinocchio, B311, 3 reels, sealed,......16.00
Planet of the Apes, master set, orig envelope......................30.00
Pluto......................5.00
Polly in Venice......................18.00
Popeye, 1962, Sawyers......................20.00
Poseidon Adventure......................24.00
Quick-Draw McGraw, 1961, Sawyers......................25.00

Red Riding Hood, 1 reel......................3.00
Return to Witch Mountain.................7.50
Ringling Bros and Barnum & Bailey Circus, 1952, 3 reels......................35.00
Rin-Tin-Tin......................15.00
Road Runner, 1967, GAF,......................20.00
Robin Hood......................24.00
Romper Room......................8.00
Roy Rogers......................25.00
San Diego Zoo, A173, 3 reels..........15.00
Santa Catalina Island, CA, Sawyers, #201, single reel in sleeve..........3.00
Scenic USA, GAF, sealed pack.......15.00
Scooby Doo......................5.00
Sebastian......................28.00
Secret Squirrel & Adam Ant...........10.00
Sesame Street, Follow That Bird.......4.50
Silver Dollar City, 1971......................15.00
Silverhawks......................5.00
Silver Springs, FL, Sawyers, #A962, 1958......................20.00
Smurf, Flying......................3.50
Snoopy and the Red Baron.............8.00
Snow White and the Seven Dwarfs . 10.00
Sxnowman......................6.50
Space Mouse, 1964, Sawyer...........25.00
Space: 1999, 1975, GAF......................28.00
Spider-Man......................10.00
Star Trek, Mr. Spock's Time Trek, 1974, GAF......................20.00
Strange Animals of the World, 1958, GAF......................18.00
Superman Movie, sealed......................18.00
S.W.A.T., sealed......................15.00
Tailspin......................5.00
Tarzan, B444, 3 reels......................48.00
Teenage Mutant Ninja Turtles...........2.50
Thomas the Tank Engine......................7.50
Thor......................2.00
Thunderbirds......................45.00
Time Tunnel, Sawyer, 1966...........165.00
Toby Tyler......................30.00
Tom & Jerry......................10.00
Tom Sawyer......................9.00
Top Cat, 1962, MIP......................40.00
Tournament of Thrills, ABC Sports...35.00
TV Stars, 1 reel......................20.00
Tweety & Sylvester......................9.00
20,000 Leagues Under The Sea, 1962, Sawyers......................30.00
U.N.C.L.E., three reels, story booklet, no envelope, 1965......................36.00
U.F.O.......................40.00
US Spaceport, GAF......................15.00
Universal Studios Scenic Tour, 1974, GAF, sealed pack......................25.00
Virgin Islands, B036, 3 reels............16.00
Voyage to the Bottom of the Sea, 1966, Sawyers......................30.00
Walt Disney
    Mickey Mouse in Clock Cleaners, 1971, GAF......................20.00
    The Love Bug, 1968, GAF..........25.00
    World Adventureland, GAF.........20.00
Waltons......................10.00
Washington DC, Sawyers, sealed pack......................15.00
Water Ski Show, Cypress Gardens.. 15.00
Welcome Back Kotter, three reels, story booklet, color photo cover, 1977 24.00
Wild Animals of Africa, 1958, GAF .. 15.00

W

Watch Fobs

Collecting Hints: The most popular fobs are those related to old machinery, either farm, construction, or industrial. Advertising fobs are the next most popular group.

The back of a fob is helpful in identifying a genuine fob from a reproduction or restrike. Genuine fobs frequently have advertising or a union trademark on the back. Some genuine fobs do have blank backs; but a blank back should be a warning to be cautious.

History: A watch fob is a useful and decorative item which attaches to a man's pocket watch by a strap and assists him in removing the watch from his pocket. Fobs became popular during the last quarter of the 19th century. Companies such as The Greenduck Co. in Chicago, Schwabb in Milwaukee, and Metal Arts in Rochester produced fobs for companies that wished to advertise their products or to commemorate an event, individual, or group.

Most fobs are made of metal and are struck from a steel die. Enamel fobs are scarce and sought after by collectors. If a fob was popular, a company would order restrikes. As a result, some fobs were issued for a period of 25 years or more. Watch fobs still are used today in promoting heavy industrial equipment.

Reference: John M. Kaduck, *Collecting Watch Fobs*, Wallace-Homestead, 1973, 1995 value update.

Collectors' Clubs: Canadian Assoc. of Watch Fob Collectors, P.O. Box 787, Caledonia, Ontario, N0A IAO Canada; International Watch Fob Association, Inc., RR5, P.O. Box 210, Burlington, IA 52601; Midwest Watch Fob Collectors, Inc., 6401 W Girard Ave., Milwaukee, WI 53210.

Reproduction Alert.

Advertising
   Anheuser-Busch, 1-1/2" d, diecut silvered brass, enameled red, white, and blue trademark 60.00
   Brown Gin and Liquors, 1-1/2" d, brass, raised moose head, reverse "Sold by H Obernauer & Co, Pittsburgh, PA" 60.00
   Buster Brown Blue Ribbon Shoes, silvered white metal oval, attached 3-3/4" long black leather strap with detailed image of Mary Jane looking at her new shoes, Buster and Tige smiling and waving 150.00

Laddie Athletic, white metal, $28.

Caterpillar, MacAllister Machinery Co., Ft. Wayne-Indianapolis, Plymouth, IN, 1-1/2" 45.00
Engeman-Matthew Range, diecut range 85.00
Evening Gazette, baseball shape, scorecard back, 1912 .... 95.00
Gardner-Denver Co, jackhammer, silvered brass, tool replica, symbol and name on back, c1950 .... 25.00
General Motors Diesel Engine, bronze luster metal, detailed engine image, block inscription "GM/General Motors Diesel Power," block logo on back, engraved dealer name 15.00
Green River Whiskey 45.00
Huntingdon Pianos, dark white metal, 7/8" black, white, blue, and gold celluloid with Paderewski, inscription "Paderewski Bought One," early 1900s 65.00
Johnston's the Appreciated Chocolates, pretty woman offering platter full of candy, 2-1/8" 40.00
Kellogg Switchboard & Supply Co/ The Service Of The Telephone Proves The Worth Of The Line, dark copper luster brass, raised image of candlestick phone with receiver off the hook, "K" circular logo, 1920s 60.00
Kelly Sprfingfield Tires, 2" d, white metal, raised illus of female motorist, "Kelly Springfield Hand Made Tires" on back 75.00
Lima Construction Equipment, copper luster, large excavation tractor, world continents background, inscribed "Lima/Move The Earth With a Lima," back text for shovels, draglines, clamshells, and cranes .. 25.00
Lorain Construction Equipment, silvered brass, truck crane used to fill bed of pickup truck, inscribed "Loraine Cranes-Shovels/Draglines/ Moto-Cranes," back inscribed "Freeland Equipment Co," Baltimore, orig strap 30.00
Martin-Senour Paints, 1-1/2" d, silvered brass, 1" d multicolored celluloid insert, hand holding dripping paint brush, text on back 65.00
Moose Club Whiskey, silvered brass, center celluloid insert, inscribed

"Moose Club Whiskey, The Best in The Land, The Adler Co., Cincinnati, O," early 1900s 125.00
Old Dutch Cleanser, porcelain center with Dutch lady 75.00
Red Bird Coffee, silver luster finish, brass, black, white, and red celluloid disk, blank reverse 50.00
Red Goose Shoes, enameled red goose 95.00
Rosenthal Bros, NY, Adamant Suit, boy holding knickers, sitting on box holding extra pants 40.00
Schramm Tractors 60.00
Studebaker, enameled tire design 50.00
Ward's Fine Cakes, white porcelain, bluebird, silvered beaded rim... 45.00
Zeno Means Good Chewing Gum, brass 95.00
Brass, mechanical cigar cutter, mkd "D B Patent" 275.00
Bronze, emb United States Great Seal, back mkd "Genuine Bronze," 1-5/8" d 36.00
Carnelian, carved mask, gold filled frame, 1-3/8" x 1" 95.00
Citrine, gold filled, engraved floral design, 1-1/2" x 1" 275.00
Elk's Tooth, bone engraved "1888 Deer" on one side "Feb 10" on other, replaced leather strap 60.00
Gold Filled/Plated/Tone
   Coin, one cent, gold filled frame, 1-1/4" x 1-1/2" 75.00
   Elk, mkd "St. Louis Button Co.," very worn, 1-1/2" 20.00
   Horn, Victorian, c1870, 1-1/8" x 5" 75.00
   Jitney, stamped, 1-5/8" h 55.00
   Oval bezel set amethyst, 3-3/4" x 1-1/2" 100.00
Political
   Bryan, Our Next President 40.00
   Democratic National Convention, Baltimore, 1912, silvered brass, center shield with eagle standing atop 20.00
   Hughes, Charles E, 1908, silvered brass, head and shoulder portrait, from governor's campaign 60.00
   Republican National Convention, brass, 1920, bust of Lincoln 40.00
   Taft, brass, figural, padlock, "White House Lock, Taft 1908/Holds The Key" 50.00
Souvenir
   Cleveland State Convention, American Legion, 1946, diecut brass 30.00
   Mormon Temple, Salt Lake City 50.00
   Municipal Pier, Chicago, emb scene, initials "MWA" and cross hatchet and mallet, back mkd "Souvenir Chicago Camp, June 19-23, 1917," 1-7/8" l 30.00
   Princeton University, brass, 1908 .... 45.00
   World Championship Rodeo Contest, Chicago 45.00
Sterling Silver, Victorian, center shield, anchor, lion passant, "O" and "WHH" marks, English, c1850, 1" x 1-3/4" 145.00

Vegetable Ivory, carved face, mkd "Un Recuerdo," 7/8" x 1" 28.00

Watt Pottery

Collecting Hints: Since Watt pottery was hand painted, there is a great deal of variation in patterns. Look for pieces with aesthetically pleasing designs which have remained bright and cheerful.

Watt had a strong regional presence in New England and New York, where over 50 percent of its production was sold. Little of the output made its way west. Beware of placing too much emphasis on availability as a price consideration when buying outside the New England and New York areas.

Watt made experimental and specialty advertising pieces. These are eagerly sought by collectors. In addition, Watt made pieces to be sold exclusively by other distributors, e.g., Ravarino & Freschi Company's "R-F Spaghetti" mark.

History: Watt Pottery traces its roots back to W. J. Watt who founded the Brilliant Stoneware Company in 1886 in Rose Farm, Ohio. Watt sold his stoneware company in 1897. Between 1903 and 1921 W. J. Watt worked at the Ransbottom Brothers Pottery owned by his brothers-in-law.

In 1921, W. J. Watt purchased the Crooksville, Ohio, Globe Stoneware Company, known briefly as the Zane W. Burley Pottery between 1919 and 1921, and renamed it Watt Pottery Company. Watt was assisted by Harry and Thomas, his sons, C. L. Dawson, his son-in-law, Marion Watt, his daughter, and numerous other relatives.

Between 1922 and 1935, the company produced a line of stoneware products manufactured from clay found in the Crooksville area. The company prospered, exporting some of its wares to Canada.

In the mid-1930s, Watt introduced a kitchenware line with a background of off-white and tan earth tones. This new ware was similar in appearance to dinnerware patterns made by Pennsbury, Pfaltzgraff, and Purinton. It also can be compared to English Torquay.

Most Watt dinnerware featured an underglaze decoration. On pieces made prior to 1950, decoration was relatively simple, e.g., blue and white banding. Patterns were introduced in 1950; the first was a pansy motif. Red Apple began in 1952 and

Rooster in 1955. Floral series, such as Starflower and Tulip variations, were made. New patterns were introduced yearly.

Watt sold its wares through large chain stores such as Kroger's, Safeway, and Woolworth, and grocery, hardware, and other retail merchants. Most of their output was sold in New England and New York. The balance was sold in the Midwest, Northwest, and South.

In the early 1960s, Watt was grossing over three-quarters of a million dollars. Future prospects were promising, but on October 4, 1965, fire destroyed the factory and warehouse. The pottery was not rebuilt.

References: Susan and Al Bagdade, *Warman's American Pottery and Porcelain*, 2nd ed., Krause Publications, 2000; Sue and Dave Morris, *Watt Pottery*, Collector Books, 1993, 1998 value update; Dennis Thompson and W. Bryce Watt, *Watt Pottery, Revised*, Schiffer Publishing, 2000.

Periodical: *Watt's News*, P.O. Box 708, Mason City, IA 50401.

Collectors' Club: Watt Pottery Collectors USA, Box 26067, Fairview Park, OH 44126.

Reproduction Alert: A Japanese copy of a large spaghetti bowl marked simply "U.S.A." is known. The Watt example bears "Peedeeco" and "U.S.A."" marks.

Apple

Bean Pot...200.00
Bowl
  #4, ribbed, mkd "Watt Oven Ware 04 USA"....................................95.00
  #5, ribbed, mkd "Watt Oven Ware 05 USA"....................................90.00
  #6, ribbed, adv...........................70.00
  #8 ....50.00
  #8, adv for Hillsboro Farmers Co-Op Warehouse, mkd "Watt 8, USA," slight manuf flaw................................75.00
  #9 ....75.00
  #63 ....60.00
  #66 ....95.00
  #73, adv for W. C. Keinas Markesan, Wisconsin, mkd "Oven Ware 73 USA," some crazing................125.00
  #96, mkd "Watt 96 USA Oven Ware," 8-1/2" d.....................................75.00
  #601, cov, ribbed three leaves 125.00
Canister, cov, #72.........................265.00
Casserole, cov, individual size, two leaves, hairline.........................100.00
Cereal Bowl....................................24.00
Coffee Server, cov, #115............2,400.00
Cookie Jar, #503 ....375.00
Creamer, #62.................................175.00
Dinner Plate, #29, 10" d 250.00

Ice Bucket.....................................295.00
Mug...65.00
Nappy, #64.....................................65.00
Pie Plate..150.00
Pitcher
  #15..115.00
  #16..110.00
  #17..175.00
Salad Bowl, #73 ....65.00
Salt and Pepper Shakers, pr........175.00
Spaghetti Bowl, #39 ....150.00
Sugar, #98 ....400.00
Vegetable Bowl, cov 50.00

Autumn Foliage

Baker, cov 90.00
Bean Pot, #76.................................50.00
Cookie Jar, #76..............................95.00
Creamer, #62................................200.00
Pepper Shaker, hour glass shape . 90.00
Sugar, cov, #98.............................150.00
Teapot, #505................................995.00

Bleeding Heart

Bean Pot 125.00
Bowl, #7 ....30.00
Creamer 75.00
Pitcher, #15 ....55.00

Cherry

Baker, #53 ....100.00
Berry Bowl, #4 ....25.00
Bowl, #89 ....50.00
Pitcher, #15 ....60.00
Platter 150.00
Salt Shaker 50.00
Spaghetti Bowl, #39 ....50.00

Kolor Kraft, mixing bowl, green, mkd "Oven Ware USA 9," 9" d, some glaze skips 42.00

Pansy

Casserole, cov, individual, stick handle, mkd "Watt Oven Ware USA" ... 145.00
Creamer, 3-1/2" h.........................100.00
Pie Plate, #33, adv 60.00
Pizza Plate 275.00
Spaghetti Bowl, #39 ....95.00

Rooster

Baker, cov, #67 ....165.00
Bowl, adv 55.00
Casserole, cov, #18......................425.00
Cheese Crock, #80 ....1,500.00
Creamer, #62................................275.00
Ice Bucket 125.00
Mixing Bowl, #5 ....85.00
Pitcher, #15 ....165.00
Salt and Pepper Shakers, pr........300.00
Vegetable Bowl, adv 55.00

Starflower

Baker, #67 ....165.00
Bowl, #15, four petal flower............95.00
Casserole, cov, #67......................110.00
Cookie Jar, #21............................165.00
Creamer, #62................................185.00
Dinner Plate, 10" d.........................15.00
Grease Jug, #1.............................350.00
Mixing Bowls, nesting, set of four, #4, #5, #6, #7................................185.00

Mug, #501 ....95.00
Pitcher, #15 ....50.00
Platter, #31 ....50.00
Salt and Pepper Shakers, pr,
  barrel 160.00
Tumbler 300.00

Tulip
Baker, #600 ....350.00
Bean Pot, #76 ....100.00
Bowl
  #62, mkd "Oven Ware 62
  USA" 150.00
  #64, 5" h, 7-1/2" d, mkd "Oven Ware
  64 USA" 180.00
  #65, 5-3/4" h, mkd "Oven Ware 65
  USA" 190.00
  #73 ....115.00
Casserole, cov, #600 ....125.00
Cookie Jar, #503 ....375.00
Creamer, #62 ....225.00
Pitcher, #17 ....295.00
Salad Bowl, #73 ....145.00
Spaghetti Bowl, #39 ....100.00

Westwood
Baker, #96, yellow, brown glaze drip, imp
  "Watt 96 Oven Ware USA" 45.00
Mixing Bowl, 7-1/2" d 45.00

Weller Pottery

Collecting Hints: Because pieces of Weller's commercial ware are readily available, prices are stable and unlikely to rise rapidly. Forest, Glendale, and Woodcraft are the popular patterns in the middle price range. The Novelty Line is most popular among the lower-priced items.

Novice collectors are advised to consider figurals. There are more than 50 variations of frogs, and many other animal shapes also are available.

Pieces made during the middle production period are usually marked with an impressed "Weller" in block letters or a half-circle ink stamp with the words "Weller Pottery." Late pieces are marked with a script "Weller" or "Weller Pottery." Many new collectors see a dated mark and incorrectly think the piece is old.

There are well over 100 Weller patterns. New collectors should visit other collectors, talk with dealers, and look at a large range of pieces to determine which patterns they like and want to collect. Most collections are organized by pattern, not by shape or type.

History: In 1872, Samuel A. Weller opened a small factory in Fultonham, near Zanesville, Ohio. There he produced utilitarian stoneware, such as milk pans and sewer tile. In 1882, he moved his facilities to Zanesville. Then in 1890, Weller built a new plant in the Putnam section of Zanesville along the tracks of the Cincinnati and Muskingum Railway. Additions to this plant followed in 1892 and 1894.

In 1894, Weller entered into an agreement with William A. Long to purchase the Lonhuda Faience Company, which had developed an art pottery line under the guidance of Laura A. Fry, formerly of Rookwood. Long left in 1895, but Weller continued to produce Lonhuda under the new name "Louwelsa." Replacing Long as art director was Charles Babcock Upjohn who, along with Jacques Sicard, Frederick Hurten Rhead, and Gazo Fudji, developed Weller's art pottery lines.

At the end of World War I, many prestige lines were discontinued and Weller concentrated on commercial wares. Rudolph Lorber joined the staff and designed lines such as Roma, Forest, and Knifewood. In 1920, Weller purchased the plant of the Zanesville Art Pottery and claimed to produce more pottery than anyone else in the country.

Art pottery enjoyed a revival when the Hudson Line was introduced in the early 1920s. The 1930s saw Coppertone and Graystone Garden wares added. However, the Depression forced the closing of the Putnam plant and one on Marietta Street in Zanesville. After World War II inexpensive Japanese imports took over Weller's market. In 1947, Essex Wire Company of Detroit took control through stock purchases, but early in 1948 operations ceased.

References: Susan and Al Bagdade, *Warman's American Pottery and Porcelain*, 2nd ed., Krause Publications, 2000; Sharon and Bob Huxford, *Collectors Encyclopedia of Weller Pottery*, Collector Books, 1979, 1999 value update.

Collectors' Club: American Art Pottery Association, 125 E. Rose Ave., St. Louis, MO 63119.

Note: For pieces in the middle and upper price ranges see *Warman's Antiques and Collectibles Price Guide.*

Ashtray
  Coppertone, frog seated at
  end 115.00
  Roma, 2-1/2" d 35.00
  Woodcraft, 3" d 75.00
Basket
  Melrose, 10" 155.00
  Sabrinian 165.00
  Silvertone, 8" 350.00
  Wild Rose, 6" h, 5" d 65.00
Bowl
  Bonito, brown, green, and blue, int.
  crazing, 9" d 150.00

Cameo, 6" d 95.00
Claremont 325.00
Claywood, 4" d 40.00
Knifewood, swans, dark
  ground 255.00
Marbleized, 5-3/4" d, 1-5/8" d, shades
  of rose, pink and mauve 55.00
Sabrinian, 6-1/2" x 3" h 240.00
Scandia, 6-1/2" d 75.00
Woodcraft, squirrel, 5-1/4" d,
  3" h 195.00
Bud Vase, Muskota, double, 5-1/4" h,
  small rim chip 175.00
Candlesticks, pr
  Euclid, 12-1/2" h, orange
  luster 85.00
  Floraia, 11" h 235.00
  Lorbeek, 2-1/2" h, shape #1 ....125.00
  Pumila 65.00
  Silvertone 175.00
Children's Ware
  Feeding Dish, Strutting Duck .. 125.00
  Milk Pitcher, 4" h, Zona 75.00
  Plate, Zona, 7" d 70.00
Cigarette Holder, figural, frog, Coppertone 200.00
Compote, Bonito, 4" h 75.00
Console Set
  Ardsley, c1928, 12" d bowl, pr 4-3/8" h
  candlesticks 345.00
  Warwick, 10-1/2" d bowl, pr candlesticks 175.00
Cornucopia
  Softone, light blue 45.00
  Wild Rose 75.00
Ewer
  Cameo, 10" h, white rose, blue
  ground 65.00
  Etna, 9" h 150.00
  Forest, 8" h 175.00
  Greenbrier, 11-1/2" h 200.00
  Louwelsa, red and orange clover
  dec, 5-1/2" h, artist sgd 190.00
  Panella 55.00
Figure
  Brighton Kingfisher 350.00
  Elephant, bug-eyed, Cactus line, yellow 145.00
  Turtle, Coppertone, 5-1/2" l 95.00
Flask, Take a Plunge 135.00
Flower Frog
  Kingfisher, 6" 475.00
  Silvertone, 1928 ....100.00
  Woodcraft, figural lobster,
  c1917 ....120.00
Hanging Basket
  Ivory Ware, marked with half kiln ink
  stamp 110.00
  Marvo, 7" 145.00
  Woodcraft, 9" 225.00
Jardiniere
  Claywood, 8", cherries and
  trees 95.00
  Fairfield, 6-3/4" h 175.00
  Ivory, 5" 45.00
  Marvo, rust, 7-1/2" d 85.00
  Roma, cat chasing canary 175.00
Jug, Louwelsa, small 140.00
Lamp Base, Louwelsa, artist sgd,
  9" h 350.00
Mug
  Aurelian, 4-1/2" h 375.00
  Claywood, star shaped
  flowers 75.00

Pitcher, Eocean, cherries decorated on shaded gray ground, stamped "Weller," hand incised "Eocean," crude repairs, 11" h, $60. Photo courtesy of David Rago Auctions.

Dickensware, 5-3/4" h 375.00
Ivory, brown accents, cream
ground..55.00
Soucvo, #30 ....150.00

Pitcher
Bouquet, 6" h, ruffled top, lavender
flower, white ground, artist sgd
"M" 60.00
Pansy, 6-1/2" h 110.00
Pierre, 5" h 50.00
Zona, 8" h, kingfisher dec, green
glaze, c1920 ....140.00

Planter
Blue Drapery 60.00
Duck..75.00
Klyro, small.................................45.00
Sabrinian, 5" x 5" 170.00
Woodrose, 9" h...........................60.00

Spittoon, Louwelsa, 7" d,
5-1/2" h......................................225.00

Tub, Flemish, 4-1/2" d 75.00

Tumbler, Bonito, multicolored flowers,
4-1/4" h...70.00

Umbrella Stand, Ivory, 20" h 225.00

Urn, sculpted handles, matte blue,
unmarked, 5-1/2" h......................50.00

Vase
Art Nouveau, 9-3/4" h...............225.00
Atlas, yellow, white trim , mkd "C-3,
Weller," 6-1/2" d, 4" h...............165.00
Bonito, 9" h..............................350.00
Burntwood, pin-oak dec,
11" h 150.00
Chase, 9" h...............................350.00
Claremont, 5" h, 2 handles 60.00
Coppertone, 8-1/2" h 265.00
Dogwood, 13" h, 7-1/2" w handle to
handle, small rim nick 175.00
Eocean, 10-1/2" h.....................250.00
Floretta, 7-1/2" h, grapes dec, high-
gloss glaze...............................175.00
Forest, 6" h 165.00
Genova.......................................95.00
Glendale Thrush 250.00
Hudson, floral dec, sgd "D England,"
7" h 200.00
Ivory, peacocks, 11" h................85.00
Knifewood, 5-1/2" h, canaries, high
glaze, nick on inside rim 125.00

Louella, gray, hp, nasturtiums..220.00
Louwelsa, #595, 6-5/8" h..........180.00
Muskota, boy fishing, c1915,
7-1/2" h 200.00
Oak Leaf, 8-1/2" h 185.00
Paragon, gold, base chip,
6-3/4" h 145.00
Roma, grape, dec, 6" hScenic...65.00
Souevo, 7" h 115.00
Turkis, deep red, yellow and green
drip, script "Weller Pottery,"
5" h 195.00
Tutone, 4" h, 3-legged ball
shape 75.00
Viola, fan shape 65.00
Woodcraft, 1917, smooth tree-trunk
shape, molded leafy branch around
rim, purple plums, 12" h 195.00

Wall Pocket
Ardsley, double, 12" l 190.00
Blue, emb leaf, 7" l 60.00
Glendale, 9-1/2" l......................450.00
Iris, blue, 8-1/2" l.........................50.00
Klyro, 8" h 110.00
Roma, 7" l 130.00
Squirrel 375.00
Souevo 195.00
Sydonia, blue 225.00
Tutone, 11" l...............................170.00
Woodcraft, 10" h 300.00
Woodland 120.00
Woodrose 110.00

Vase, Coppertone, beaker shaped, incised "Weller Hand Made," 5-3/4" h, $400. Photo courtesy of David Rago Auctions.

Western Americana

Collecting Hints: The collecting category of Western Americana is as vast and as wide ranging as the West itself. Western art and books are collected, along with well-used cowboy gear like saddles and spurs. Western-theme furniture, decorative items, and dinnerware have become very collectible and are often priced as high as their antiques that are one hundred years older.

Western memorabilia has a strong regional following. For example, memorabilia from the early years of the Grand Canyon National Park has a stronger following in Arizona while "Let 'er Buck" souvenirs of the Pendleton Rodeo are more eagerly sought out by Oregon collectors.

Look for a hot spot in the market to be ethnic collectibles. Memorabilia from the black "Buffalo Soldiers" calvary units is sought after by Western and military collectors for its rarity as well as for the contribution to black Western history. Hispanic cultural influence in the settlement of the West cannot be overlooked. After all, it has been over four hundred years since the first Spanish settlers arrived in modern day New Mexico. Souvenirs from Mexico continue to be popular today, as more collectors come to recognize the fine craftsmanship involved in their manufacture of sterling silver jewelry, weavings and pottery.

Cowgirl memorabilia has long been a "sleeper" in this category and is now becoming a vibrant, exciting part of the Western Americana market. This is due, in part, to a growing number of books and short stories chronicling the role of women in settling the West. Just check out the auction prices for a signed Annie Oakley cabinet card! Posters, sheet music, or postcards featuring a cowgirl in vintage clothing is a hot item. Cowboy and cowgirl toys remain a good buy. Western-themed toys, especially Japanese tin lithographed toys from the 1950s and 1960s, are relatively inexpensive and sure to appreciate.

With popularity comes imitation, and Western memorabilia is no exception. Beware of the many "new" items of Western memorabilia that are in reality cheaply made imports. Be especially wary of spurs marked "Korea" or those that have scratch marks where the country of origin has been ground off. Most contemporary Western artists, whether their medium is leather, metal or oils, market their products honestly—as a new work of art.

History: Western American was sought out and preserved even before the turn of the century when astute historians saw their way of life disappearing before their eyes and made an effort to save all that they could through oral histories and artifacts. Much regional Western memorabilia is available in tiny local museums and historical societies. Early collectors were often ranchers, cowboys, and the descendants of early residents trying to keep their own family history intact. Today, collectors are more varied and you can find Western memorabilia on display in barns, high-class restaurants and attorney's offices. As the American West has become more popular, prices have risen and the fine line between the "real" old West and that of story, song and movie has blurred. Today, you can find a fine pair of wooly chaps displayed beside a vintage Gene Autry movie poster or a Red Ryder BB gun mounted on a gun rack right next to a Winchester.

References: Warren R. Anderson, *Owning Western History*, Mountain Press Publishing, 1993; Judy Crandall, *Cowgirls*, Schiffer, 1994; Ned & Jody Martin, *Bit and Spur Makers in the Vaquero Tradition*, 1998; William Manns with Elizabeth Flood, *Cowboys and the Trappings of the Old West*, Zon Publishing, 1998; Jim and Nancy Schaut, *Collecting the Old West*, Krause Publications, 1999.

Periodicals: *American Cowboy*, P.O. Box 54555, Boulder CO 80322; *Cowboy Magazine,* Box 126, La Veta, CO 81055; *Cowboys*, P.O. Box 6459, Santa Fe, NM 87502; *Lone Prairie Roundup*, 2931 South St., Lincoln NE 68502; *Persimmon Hill*, 1700 NE. 63rd St., Oklahoma City OK; *Wild West*, 6405 Flank Dr., Harrisburg, PA 17112.

Collectors' Club: American Barbed Wire Collectors Society, 1023 Baldwin Rd, Bakersfield, CA 93304; National Bit, Spur, and Saddle Collectors Association, P.O. Box 3035, Colorado Springs, CO 80904.

Museums: Autry Museum of Western Heritage, Los Angeles, CA; Buffalo Bill Historical Center, Cody, WY; Cowgirl Hall of Fame, Hereford, TX; Cowboy Museum of the West, Sheridan, WY; National Cowboy Hall of Fame, Oklahoma City, OK; Wells Fargo History Museum, Los Angeles, CA; Rockwell Museum, Corning, NY.

Advisors: Jim and Nancy Schaut.

Advertising
   Banner, 19-1/2" by 29", Winchester horse and rider in center, "Headquarters for Winchester Rifles and Shotguns," fringed hem 250.00
   Figure, cowboy with saddle, rope, Stetson cologne, composition ... 35.00
   Sign, Moccasin Agency, fierce Indian with headdress, emb tin 95.00
Artwork
   Buffalo Bill, pyrography, drawn and burnt of Albert J.Seigfried, NY, 1907 .... 150.00
   Wells Fargo Depot and Office Building, Moron Taft, CA, 1910, original ink drawing, 20" by 30" framed 750.00

Autograph, photo card, "Louise from W. F. Cody, 1906," (Buffalo Bill) .1,500.00
Belt Buckle, Heston, Rodeo, 1985..25.00
Bit
   Iron, rusted, marked "CSA," often used by former Confederate soldiers in the West................................ 500.00
   Silver inlay spade bit, full engraving of kissing birds, J. F. Echaverria, minor restoration 2,000
   G. S. Garcia, silver inlay, curved snake cheeks, large 2" domed conchos.. 1,500.00
Bolo, 3" diameter figural turtle, crushed turquoise inlay, marked ".925" (sterling silver) and "Taxco" 55.00
Book
   Children of the Covered Wagon, A Story f the Old Oregon Trail, Mary Jane Carr, illus Bob Kuhn, Thos Corwell, 1943 .... 6.25
   Cowboys North and South, Will James, 1924.............................. 45.00
   Doctor at Timberline, Charles Fox Gardiner, Caxton Printers, Caldwell, Idaho, 1939, 3rd printing, 315 pgs 10.00
   Famous Sheriffs and Western Outlaws, William MacLeod Raine, Doubleday, 1929, 1st ed., 294 pgs ..12.00
   The Border Outlaws, The Younger Brothers, Jesse & Frank James, J. W. Buel, 1994, reprint of 1882 edition, 488 pgs................................ 11.00
   The Earp Brothers of Tombstone, Frank Waters, Clarkson N. Potter, Inc., 1960, 1st ed, ... 48.00
   The Overland Trail, The Epic Path of the Pioneers to Oregon, Agnes C. Lad, Stokes, 1929, 1st edition, photos, maps, dwgs........................ 10.00
   The Story of the Outlaw, A Study of the Western Desperado, Emerson Hough, Grossett & Dunlap, 1915 .... 10.00
   The Trampling Herd, The Story of the Cattle Range in America, Paul I. Wellman, Doubleday, NY, 1951, 433 pgs, maps, illus 12.00
   Two on the Trail, A Story of the Far Northwest, Hubert Footner, Gross & Dunlap, 1912............................ 6.00
Bookends, pr, "End of the Trail," tired Indian on pony, cast metal......... 75.00
Buckskin Jacket, beaded, w/fringe, 1920s.................................... 250.00
Cabinet Card, Butch Cassidy & Sundance Kid............................ 2,200.00
Chaps
   Black woolies 500.00
   Edward Bohlin, batwing style, black, engraved sterling silver buckle mounted with eight 1878 silver dollars.................................... 2,800.00
   Shotgun (narrow leg) style, well-worn leather, initials "JS".................. 450.00
Cuffs, pr
   Plain leather, brass studs form star design, unmarked..................... 250.00
   Tooled leather, fancy floral engraving, no maker's mark...................... 150.00
Dinnerware, Wallace China
   Boots & Saddles, cup & saucer set.. 45.00
   Rodeo, salad plate, 7" d 75.00

Westward Ho, ashtray 55.00
Glass, frosted, painted cowboy on bucking bronco, 1950s era 25.00
Holster and belt, tooled leather, floral design, marked Mexico 95.00
Holster w/running iron (portable branding iron), crudely handmade..... 75.00
Magic Lantern Slides, set of 60, "Colorado by a Tenderfoot," shows mining towns, Pike's Peak, waterfalls, 1907 Denver.............................. 300.00
Neckerchief, bucking bronco motif, "Let 'er Buck" rodeo souvenir, 1920s.................................... 125.00
Parade Outfit, Bohlin, silver mounted, made 1937 for Eleanor Montana.............................. 22,000.00
Party Set, Covered wagon bean pot, ceramic coffeepot, beverage barrel, chip and dip bow with cowboy hat lid, ranch scenes, McCoy pottery, set.. 1,200.00
Pennant, Grand National Livestock Show and Rodeo, San Francisco, 1960s.................................... 35.00
Pinback Button, "Let 'er buck," celluloid, cowboy on bucking horse, 1" d 25.00
Pitcher, plastic, figural cowboy with gun, 1950s.................................... 45.00
Postcard, cowboys & cowgirls on picnic, by "Dude" Larsen..................... 15.00
Poster
   Yosemite National Park, 1931, Jo Mora 200.00
   101 Ranch Wild West Show, 28" by 42", 1915............................. 2,700.00
Program, Texas Prison Rodeo, 1970s.................................... 15.00
Rope
   Braided horsehair.................... 225.00
   Braided rawhide, "riata" 150.00
Rope box, tooled leather with initials "FS".. 450.00
Saddle
   Calvary, McClellan military issue 800.00
   Charo style, mother of pearl inlay, marked "La Moderna" 2,500.00
   Child's, Roy Rogers imprint.. 1,250.00
   Hamley, Pendleton, OR, exc condition...................................... 2,800.00
   Pack saddle, wood frame for burro 75.00
Saddle Bags
   Embossed floral leather, black, marked "Garcia, Mexico"........ 125.00
   R. T. Frazier marked, wooly angora trim...................................... 2,000.00
   "US" military saddle bags, fair condition...................................... 250.00
Saddle Blanket
   Navajo, densely woven, few stains, 1960s.................................... 475.00
   Pendleton, Indian style print, 1970s tag 125.00
Spittoon
   Brass and iron turtle................ 650.00
   Copper, 13" d, saloon-type, 1870s.................................... 275.00
Spurs
   Buerman, marked "Hercules Bronze," gal leg, old leathers............... 650.00
   Child's, marked "Made in USA," good leather.................................... 40.00

Mexican style, silver inlay, large rowels..450.00
Crockett, large conchos on leathers...................................1,500.00
Prison made, Thunderbird design.......................................950.00
Tie Holder, 3/4" x 1-1/2" x 4", Lone Wolf, steer head shape, brown, brown, red, and white beads, c1930.............35.00
Tobacco Felt, Indian rug design, "rolling logs" (swastikas) good luck motif.....................................25.00
Toy, Cortland, Rocking R Ranch, litho tin wind-up......................................295.00
Toy Chest, cowboy and Indian motif, burnt-wood designs, 1950s.....250.00
Trunk, Miller Bros. Rawhide cov., "101" and "MB" in brass nailheads, from the 101 Ranch show...................1,200.00
Vase, Wagon Wheel shape, stamped "Frankoma"..............................35.00
Watch Fob, sterling, 101 Ranch, shows the Miller Bros..........................650.00

Westmoreland Glass Company

Collecting Hints: The collector should become familiar with the many lines of tableware produced. English Hobnail, made from the 1920s to the 1960s, is popular. Colonial designs were used frequently, and accessories with dolphin pedestals are distinctive.

The trademark, an intertwined "W" and "G," was imprinted on glass beginning in 1949. After January 1983, the full name, "Westmoreland," was marked on all glass products. Early molds were reintroduced. Numbered, signed, dated "Limited Editions"" were offered.

History: The Westmoreland Glass Company was founded in October 1899 at Grapeville, Pennsylvania. From the beginning, Westmoreland made handcrafted high-quality glassware. During the early years, the company processed mustard, baking powder, and condiments to fill its containers. During World War I, candy-filled glass novelties were popular.

Although Westmoreland is famous for its milk glass, other types of glass products were also produced. During the 1920s, Westmoreland made reproductions and decorated wares. Color and tableware appeared in the 1930s; but, as with other companies, 1935 saw production return primarily to crystal. From the 1940s to the 1960s, black, ruby, and amber objects were made.

In May 1982, the factory closed. Reorganization brought a reopening in July 1982, but the Grapeville plant closed again in 1984.

References: Tom and Neila Bredehoft, *Fifty Years of Collectible Glass, 1920-1970, Volume 1, Volume II*, Antique Trader Books, 2000; Lorraine Kovar, *Westmoreland Glass*, Vols. I and II, The Glass Press, 1991; Hazel Marie Weatherman, *Colored Glassware of the Depression Era, Book 2*, Glassbooks, Inc., 1982; Chas West Wilson, *Westmoreland Glass*, Collector Books, 1996, 1998 value update.

Collectors' Clubs: National Westmoreland Glass Collectors Club, P.O. Box 372, Westmoreland City, PA 15692; Westmoreland Glass Collectors Club, 2712 Glenwood, Independence, 64052; Westmoreland Glass Society, 4809 420th St. SE, Iowa City, IA 52240.

Museum: Westmoreland Glass Museum, Port Vue, PA.

Magazine cover from China, Glass & Tablewares, showing assortment of animal dishes, $5.

Animal, covered dish type, white milk glass
Camel, kneeling.........................75.00
Cat, blue eyes...........................75.00
Chick on eggs, iridized..............85.00
Fox, brown eyes, lacy base.......75.00
Hen on Nest, white milk glass, blue head, diamond basket weaved nest, 5-1/2" l, 4-1/4" w.........................65.00
Hen on Nest, white milk glass, red painted top and eyes, 5-1/2" l, 4-1/2" h, WG mark................................60.00
Swan, raised wing....................115.00
Turkey, crystal, some Goofus glass dec remaining, 6-1/4" w, 5-1/4" d, 7" h...125.00
Appetizer Canape Set, Paneled Grape, milk glass....................................80.00
Ashtray, 5" d, Beaded Grape..........15.00
Basket, Pansy, milk glass...............20.00

Bon Bon, Waterford, #1932, ruby stained, 6" d, heart shaped, handle..70.00
Bowl, cov, 5" d, flared, Beaded Grape...55.00
Bowl, open
7" d, 2-3/4" h, English Hobnail, 3 legs..75.00
7-1/2" d, vaseline, crimped, round foil label...55.00
9" w, sq, ftd, Beaded Grape, milk glass..55.00
9" d, 6" h, ftd, Paneled Grape, milk glass..60.00
10-1/2" d, ftd, Paneled Grape, milk glass..100.00
Bud Vase, 10" h, Paneled Grape, milk glass, orig label..........................30.00
Butter Dish, cov, 1/4 lb
Old Quilt, milk glass..................28.00
Paneled Grape, milk glass........24.00
Cake Stand, Paneled Grape, milk glass...95.00
Candlesticks, pr
Dolphins, white opaque glass, 9" h..75.00
English Hobnail, green, 3-3/4" h..78.00
Old Quilt, milk glass..................30.00
Paneled Grape, milk glass, 4" h..25.00
Ring & Petal..............................22.00
Sleighs, cobalt blue, 4-1/4" h....75.00
Waterford, #1932, ruby stained, 6" h, 1-lite...130.00
Candy Dish, cov
Beaded Bouquet, blue milk glass..35.00
Beaded Grape, 9" d, ftd............40.00
Paneled Grape, milk glass, 3 legs, crimped.......................................35.00
Wakefield, crystal, low...............45.00
Waterford, ruby stained, 9" d....35.00
Cheese, cov, Old Quilt, milk glass. 52.00
Children's Dishes
Creamer, File & Fan, ruby carnival......................................20.00
Mug, chick, milk glass, #603, dec, orig label.....................................30.00
Pitcher, Flute, cobalt blue, white floral dec...40.00
Sugar, cov, File & Fan, ruby carnival......................................30.00
Table Set, cov butter, creamer, cov sugar, File & Fan, milk glass.....45.00
Tumbler, Flute, green, white floral dec...15.00
Compote
Vaseline, WG mark, 9" d, 7" h.. 145.00
Waterford, #1932, ruby stained, ruffled, ftd......................................120.00
Console Set, Dolphin, milk glass, three pcs..85.00
Cordial, Waterford, #1932, ruby stained...50.00
Creamer, 6-1/2 oz, Paneled Grape, milk glass, orig label..........................16.00
Cruet, stopper
Old Quilt, milk glass..................30.00
Paneled Grape, milk glass........30.00
Cup and Saucer, Paneled Grape, milk glass...22.00

Dinner Plate, Daisy Decal, #1800, 10-1/4" d, dark blue mist, scalloped edge..45.00
Dish, heart shape, handle, Della Robia, stained 70.00
Epergne, 8-1/2" h, Paneled Grape, milk glass...70.00
Flower Pot, Paneled Grape, milk glass...48.00
Fruit Cocktail, Paneled Grape, milk glass...25.00
Fruit Cocktail Underplate, Paneled Grape, milk glass..........................9.00
Goblet, 8 oz
  Della Robia, stained..................40.00
  Paneled Grape, milk glass 18.00
Gravy Boat and Underplate, Paneled Grape, milk glass......................58.00
Honey, cov, 5" d, Beaded Grape, milk glass, roses and garland dec....45.00
Ice Tea Tumbler, Paneled Grape, milk glass, 12 oz...........................25.00
Jardiniere, Paneled Grape, milk glass, 6-1/2" h, ftd...............................42.00
Jelly, cov, Paneled Grape, milk glass...30.00
Mayonnaise Set, Paneled Grape, milk glass, 3 pcs 65.00
Mint Compote, Waterford, #1932, ruby stained, crimped.........................60.00
Oil and Vinegar Cruets, English Hobnail, crystal..65.00
Pickle Jar, Deco pattern, frosted, flower dec, 4-1/4" d, 12" h 85.00
Pitcher
  Old Quilt, milk glass...................40.00
  Paneled Grape, milk glass
    16 oz 45.00
    32 oz 35.00
Planter, 5" x 9", Paneled Grape, milk glass...48.00
Plate, 7" d, Beaded Edge
  Goldfinch center 13.00
  Red edge 10.00
Puff Box, cov, Paneled Grape, milk glass...30.00
Punch Bowl Base, Paneled Grape, milk glass......................................115.00
Punch Cup, Fruits, milk glass...........6.00
Punch Set
  Fruits, milk glass, 12 pc set 150.00
  Paneled Grape, milk glass, red hooks and ladle, 13" d, 15 pc set.......595.00
Rose Bowl, 4" d, Paneled Grape, milk glass, ftd 30.00
Salad Plate, Della Robia, dark stain...22.00
Salt and Pepper Shakers, pr
  Della Robia, stained...................70.00
  Old Quilt, milk glass...................25.00
  Paneled Grape, milk glass 25.00
Sauceboat and Underplate, Paneled Grape, milk glass......................70.00
Saucer, Paneled Grape, milk glass...8.50
Sherbet, 10-3/4" h, Della Robia, light stain...26.00
Sleigh, cobalt blue, 9" l, 5" h 175.00
Slipper, figural, almond milk glass..20.00
Spooner, Old Quilt, milk glass, 6-1/2" h 28.00
Sugar
  Beaded Grape, milk glass, individual size...10.00

English Hobnail, ice blue, octagonal foot, 4-1/4" h 55.00
Old Quilt, milk glass, large, open 15.00
Sweet Meat, Waterford, #1932, ruby stained, ftd, crimped..................40.00
Toilet Bottle Stopper, English Hobnail, green 55.00
Torte Plate, 14" d, Della Robia, light stain...125.00
Tumbler, flat
  Della Robia, dark stain, 8 oz......28.00
  Paneled Grape, milk glass.........12.50
Vase
  6" h, ftd, bell-shape, Paneled Grape, milk glass 15.00
  7" h, horn-shape, Lotus, #9........35.00
  9" h, Paneled Grape, milk glass, bell shape, ftd 30.00
  15" h, swung-type, Paneled Grape, milk glass 20.00
Water Set, 1776 Colonial, amber, flat water pitcher, six goblets, price for seven-pc set 70.00
Wedding Bowl, Roses & Bows, milk glass, 10" d..............................130.00

Whiskey Bottles, Collectors' Special Editions

Collecting Hints: Beginning collectors are advised to focus on bottles of a single manufacturer or to collect around a central theme, e.g., birds, trains, or Western. Only buy bottles that have a very good finish (almost no sign of wear), no chips, and intact original labels.

A major collection still can be built for a modest investment, although some bottles, such as the Beam Red Coat Fox, now command over $1,000. Don't overlook miniatures if you are on a limited budget.

In many states, it is against the law to sell liquor without a license; hence, collectors tend to focus on empty bottles.

History: The Jim Beam Distillery began the practice of issuing novelty (collectors' special edition) bottles for the 1953 Christmas trade. By the late 1960s, more than 100 other distillers and wine manufacturers followed suit.

The Jim Beam Distillery remains the most prolific issuer of the bottle. Lionstone, McCormick, and Ski Country are the other principal suppliers today. One dealer, Jon-Sol, Inc., has distributed his own line of collector bottles.

The golden age of the special edition bottle was the early 1970s. Interest waned in the late 1970s and early 1980s as the market became

saturated with companies trying to join the craze. Prices fell from record highs, and many manufacturers dropped special edition bottle production altogether.

A number of serious collectors, clubs, and dealers have brought stability to the market. Realizing that instant antiques cannot be created by demand alone, they have begun to study and classify their bottles. Most importantly, collectors have focused on those special edition bottles which show quality workmanship and design and which are true limited editions.

References: Hugh Cleveland, *Bottle Pricing Guide*, 3rd ed., 1988, 1993 value update; Molly Higgins, *Jim Beam Figural Bottles*, Schiffer Publishing, 2000; Molly Higgins, *Jim Beam Figural Bottles*, Schiffer Publishing, 2000; Michael Polak, *Bottles*, 3rd ed., Avon Books, 2000.

Collectors' Clubs: Cape Codders Jim Beam Bottle & Specialty Club, 80 Lincoln Rd, Rockland, MA 02370; Hoffman National Collectors Club, P.O. Box 37341, Cincinnati, OH 45222; International Association of Jim Beam Bottle & Specialties Clubs, 5013 Chase Ave., Downers Grove, IL 60515; National Ski Country Bottle Club, 1224 Washington Ave., Golden, CO 80401; Space Coast Jim Beam Bottle & Specialties Club, 2280 Cox Rd, Cocoa, FL 32926.

Museum: American Outpost, James B. Beam Distillery, Clermont, KY.

Jim Beam, The Broadmoor, Royal China, 1968, $10.

Anniversary, Lincoln, 1973 .... 15.50

Ballantine

Golf Bag, 1969 .... 9.50
Mallard, 1969 .... 18.00
Zebra, 1970 .... 14.00

Jim Beam

Ahepa, 1972 ....5.00
Akron, Rubber Capital, 1973 ....24.00
Barney's Slot Machine, 1978 ....20.00
Bing Crosby, 1970s 15.00
BPO Does, 1971 ....5.00
Buffalo Bill, 1970s 10.00
Cable Car, 1983..............................66.00
Churchill Downs, Kentucky Derby.. 15.00
Civil War, 1961, South.....................50.00
Cowboy, 1981..................................15.50
Ducks Unlimited...............................50.00
Ernie's Flower Car, 1976 ....35.00
Evergreen State Club, 1974 ....15.50
Harolds Club, Covered Wagon, green,
    1969 ....6.00
Hawaiian Open 10.00
Horse, brown, 1967-68 ....21.50
Kansas City Convention Elephant,
    1976 ....15.00
Katz Cat, black, 1968 ....13.00
Key West, FL.....................................6.00
John Henry, 1972.............................72.00
London Bridge, Regal China, 1971.. 7.50
Louisiana Superdome, 1975 ....9.00
Marine Corps 35.00
New Jersey 40.00
New York World's Fair, 1964 ....12.00
Ohio, 1966 ....18.00
Opera Series
    Don Giovanni 170.00
    Figaro 185.00
    Madame Butterfly, 1977...........200.00
Pennsylvania Dutch Club, 1974 ..... 12.00
Pony Express 10.00
Rabbit, 1971 ....15.00
San Diego, 1968 ....7.00
Saturday Evening Post, 1970s 15.00
Stutz Bearcat 50.00
Thomas Flyer, cream, brown roof,
    empty 135.00
Train Caboose..................................50.00
Travelodge Bear 25.00
Twin Bridges Club, 1971 ....50.00
Volkswagen......................................55.00
Yellowstone 8.00
Yosemite...8.00
Zimmerman Liquors..........................10.00

Beneagle

Alpine Pitcher, 1969........................25.00
Amphora, 2 handles, 1950 ....20.00
Barrel, thistle 4.50
Bell House, 1960..............................12.00
Chess Pawn, John Knox, black, minia-
    ture 12.00
Fruit, canteen, 1969 ....18.00

Bischoff

Chinese Boy, 1962...........................36.00
Grecian Vase, 1969 ....15.50
Pirate..20.00

Ezra Brooks

Basketball Players, 1974 ....10.00
Card, Jack of Diamonds, 1969........10.00
Casey at Bat, 1973 ....16.00
Clown with balloons, 1973...............22.00
Club Bottle #1, Distillery, 1970........12.50
Clydesdale, 1974 ....10.00

Dummy Gallon, 1969 ....90.00
Elephant, Big Bertha, 1970................8.00
FOE Eagle, 179 ....15.00
Fresno Grape, 1970 ....12.00
Go Big Red #3, 1972 ....12.00
Greensboro Open, cup, 1975 ....50.00
Hereford, 1971.................................14.00
Iowa Farmers Elevator, 1978 ....36.00
Lion on Rock, 1971 ....10.00
Masonic, fez, 1976...........................10.00
Max "The Hat" Zimmerman, 1976 ..32.00
Mr. Merchant, 1970 ....10.00
Motorcycle, 1971 ....13.50
Oliver Hardy, 1976 ....17.50
Ontario Racer, #10, 1970.................21.00
Panda, 1972.....................................18.00
Penguin, 1973 ....15.00
Phoenix Bird, 1975...........................18.00
Spirit of St. Louis, 1977 ....12.00
Stonewall Jackson, 1974 ....32.00
Tank, 1972..30.00
Train, Iron Horse, 1969....................12.00
Vermont Skier, 1973 ....12.00
Whitetail Deer, 1974 ....20.00
Wichita Centennial, 1970..................7.50

Collector's Art

Basset Hound, miniature 25.50
Cardinal, miniature...........................30.00
Poodle, white, miniature...................21.00
Texas Longhorn, 1974 ....35.00

Cyrus Noble

Buffalo Cow & Calf, Nevada ed,
    1977 ....85.00
Burro, 1973......................................50.00
Carousel Series, pipe organ,
    1980 ....45.00
Harp Seal, 1979...............................50.00
Moose & Calf, 2nd ed, 1977...........80.00
Sea Turtle, 1979 ....50.00
Snowshoe Thompson, 1972 ....150.00
Whitetail Deer, 1979.........................35.00

Cabin Steel, 1969, matte finish, $12.

J.W. Dant

American Legion, 1968.....................10.00
Boeing 747.......................................14.00
Boston Tea Party 12.00

Field Bird
    #2, 1969, Chukar partridge....... 12.00
    #4, 1969, mountain quail............. 9.00
Mt Rushmore, 1968 .... 12.00
Patrick Henry, 1969 .... 5.00

Early Times, 1976

Cannon Fire
    Delaware 22.00
    Nevada..................................... 22.00
    New Mexico.............................. 28.00
Drum and Fife
    Florida...................................... 17.00
    Kansas..................................... 20.00
Minuteman
    Alaska...................................... 35.50
    Oklahoma 24.00
Paul Revere, Arizona....................... 21.00
Washington Crossing the Delaware,
    South Dakota........................... 17.00

Famous Firsts

Balloon, 1971 .... 65.00
Bears, miniature, 1981 .... 36.00
Bucky Badger Mascot 10.00
China Clipper, 1989 .... 120.00
Circus Lion, 1979 .... 20.00
Corvette, 1963 Stingray, white, miniature,
    1979.. 13.50
Fireman, 1980 .... 50.00
Golfer, 1973 .... 30.00
Hippo, baby, 1980.......................... 50.00
Hurdy Gurdy, miniature, 1979 .... 15.50
Minnie Meow, 1973 .... 17.50
National Racer, No. 8, 1972 .... 70.00
Panda, baby, 1980 .... 50.00
Pepper Mill, 1978 .... 20.00
Phonograph, 1969 .... 36.00
Porsche Targa, 1979 .... 44.00
Sewing Machine, 1979.................... 35.00
Swiss Chalet, 1974 .... 20.00
Winnie Mae, large, 1972 .... 85.00
Yacht America, 1978 .... 25.00

Garnier (France)

Baby Foot, 1963............................. 15.00
Bullfighter 18.00
Cat.. 70.00
Christmas Tree, 1956 .... 65.00
Diamond Bottle, 1969 .... 15.00
Inca, 1969 .... 15.00
Locomotive, 1969........................... 14.00
Meadowlark, 1969.......................... 12.00
Parrot 30.00
Soccer Shoe, 1962......................... 30.00
Trout 24.00
Young Deer..................................... 28.00

Grenadier

American Revolution Series
    Second Maryland, 1969............ 37.50
    Third New York, 1970 .... 22.00
British Army Series, Kings African Rifle
    Crops, 5th, 1970...................... 20.00
Civil War Series, General Robert E. Lee,
    1/2 gal, 1977 .... 150.00
George Washington, on
    horseback 20.00
Jester Mirth King, 1977 .... 56.00
San Fernando Electric Mfg Co.,
    1976.. 66.00
Santa Claus, blue sack 30.00

Hoffman

Aesop's Fables Series, music, six types,
1978 ....30.00
Canada Goose Decoy...................15.00
Cheerleaders, Rams, miniature,
1980 ....20.00
Doe and Fawn................................40.00

Hoffman, wildlife series, deer, musical, $30.

Fox and Eagle, 1978.......................45.00
Kentucky Wildcats, football, 1979..38.00
Mr. Lucky Series, music
Barber, 1980 ....38.00
Cobbler, 1973 ....25.00
Fiddler, 1974 ....25.00
Mailman, miniature, 1976 ....12.50
Pistol, Dodge City Frontier,
framed,.......................................25.00
Stage Coach Driver 30.00
Tennessee Volunteers....................28.00
Wood Duck, decoy 15.00

Japanese Firms

House of Koshu
Geisha, chrysanthemum, 1969.23.50
Sake God, white, 1969 ....14.00
Kamotsuru, treasure tower, 1966....18.00
Kikukawa
Eisenhower, 1970......................17.00
Royal couple, pr.........................32.00

Lewis and Clark

Clark, miniature, 1971....................15.50
General Custer, 1974.....................70.00
Grandfather, 1978..........................10.00
Indian, 1978 ....65.00
Lewis, 1971 ....85.00
Major Reno....................................25.00
Sheepherder 40.00
Trader..50.00

Lionstone

Annie Oakley, 1969........................60.00
Barber, 1976 ....40.00
Bartender, 1969 ....30.00
Baseball Player, 1974 ....27.50
Cherry Valley..................................20.00
Dance Hall Girl, 1973 ....60.00
Dove of Peace, 1977 ....40.00
Eastern Bluebird, 1972 ....20.00
Fireman, #8, fire alarm box, 1983...50.00
Hockey Player, 1974......................20.00
Indian, squaw, 1973 ....25.00
Riverboat Captain, 1969.................14.00
Stutz Bearcat, miniature, 1978 ....15.00

Telegrapher, 1969 ....20.00
Tennis Player, male, 1980 ....45.00
Turbo Car STP, red, 1972...............27.50

Luxardo

Apple, figural.................................14.00
Apothecary Jar 20.00
Bizantina.......................................26.00
Babylon, 1960................................
Calypso Girl, 1962 ....15.50
Coffeepot.......................................12.00
Mayan, 1960..................................50.00
Tower of Flowers, 1968 ....18.00
Venus, 1969 ....20.00
Zodiac, 1970..................................30.00

McCormick

Betsy Ross, miniature, 1976 ....48.00
Bluebird...20.00
Centurion, 1969.............................20.00
Chair, 1979 ....40.00
Eleanor Roosevelt 20.00
FOE, 1985 ....50.00
Henry Ford 30.00
Kit Carson, 1975 ....15.00
Mark Twain, 1977 ....32.00
Merlin..30.00
Nebraska Football Player, 1972......24.00
Oregon Duck..................................20.00
Robert E. Lee, 1976 ....40.00
Sir Lancelot 40.00
Texas Longhorn, 1974 ....36.50
Train Series, wood tender, 1969 .....22.00
Ulysses S. Grant, 1976 ....25.00
Victorian, 1964 ....20.00
Wood Duck, 1983 ....28.00

OBR

Caboose, 1973...............................21.00
River Queen, 1967 ....10.00
W.C. Fields, top hat, 1976..............16.00

Old Commonwealth

Apothecary Series, North Carolina Uni-
versity, 1979 ....30.00
Coal Miners, #5, coal shooter,
1983 ....40.00
Fireman, #5, Lifesaver, 1983..........72.50
Indian Chief Illini, University of Illinois,
1979 ....60.00
Irish at the Sea, 1989 ....24.00
Lumberjack, old time, 1979 ....20.00
Kentucky Peach Bowl.....................30.00
Kentucky Thoroughbreds, 1977 .....40.00
Sons of Erin 25.00
Symbols of Ireland, 1985 ....12.00

Old Crow

Chess Set, 32 pcs..........................450.00
Crow, 1974 ....14.00

Old Fitzgerald

America's Cup, 1970 ....27.00
Blarney, Irish toast, 1970................16.00
Candlelite, 1963.............................10.00
Classic, 1972 ....10.00
Davidson, NC, 1972.......................40.00
Hospitality, 1958............................9.00
Old Ironsides..................................9.00
Rip Van Winkle, 1971 ....34.50
West Virginia Forest Festival,
1973 ....22.00

Old Mr. Boston

Black Hills Motor Club, 1976.......... 12.00
Concord Coach, 1976.................... 17.00
Dan Patch 25.00
Deadwood, SD, 1975..................... 16.00
Eagle Convention, 1973................. 10.00
Hawk, 1975 .... 18.00
Lion, sitting 12.00
Nebraska, #1, gold, 1970 .... 20.00
Paul Revere, 1974......................... 15.50
Town Crier, 1976........................... 10.00
Wisconsin Football 25.00

Pacesetter

Camaro, Z28, yellow, 1982 .... 42.00
Coca-Cola Truck 135.00
Corvette, red, 1975 .... 40.00
Mack Pumper 140.00
Pontiac Firebird 35.00
Tractor Series, No. 2, Big Green
Machine, International Harvester,
1983.. 66.00
Vokovich, #2, 1974....................... 30.00

Ski Country

Antelope, pronghorn...................... 70.00
Bassett, miniature, 1978 .... 20.00
Blackbird 40.00
Bull Rider...................................... 15.00
Ceremonial Indian, Falcon 110.00
Chickadee 50.00
Cigar Store Indian, 1974 .... 40.00
Clown, bust, 1974, miniature 18.00
Eagle, paperweight........................ 190.00
Ebenezer Scrooge, 1979,
miniature.................................... 24.00
Jaguar, miniature........................... 30.00
Koala, 1973 .... 42.00
Labrador with mallard, 1977,
miniature.................................... 40.00
Mallard Drake................................ 40.00
Mill River Country Club, 1977 .... 44.00
Mountain Lion, 1973, miniature...... 30.00
Ringmaster, 1975, miniature 26.50
Salmon.. 40.00
Submarine, 1976, miniature........... 29.00
Tom Thumb.................................... 30.00
Woodpecker, ivory bill, 1974.......... 66.00

Wild Turkey

Crystal Anniversary, 1955 .... 2,000.00
Mack Truck 20.00
Series #1
No. 2, female, 1972.................... 150.00
No. 3, on wing, miniature,
1983... 65.00
No. 5, with flags, 1975 .... 40.00
No. 8, strutting, 1978................. 45.00
Series #2, No. 2, lore, 1980........... 30.00
Series #3
No. 5, with raccoon, 1984......... 40.00
No. 7, with fox, 1984, miniature. 30.00
No. 12, with skunk, 1986........... 90.00
Series #4, No. 2, habitat, 1989 ...... 90.00

World War I Collectibles

Collecting Hints: Be careful. Uniforms and equipment from World

War I were stockpiled at the end of the war and reissued in the early years of World War II. Know the source of the items before you buy, and scrutinize all materials. Some research and investigation might be necessary to correctly identify an item as an actual war artifact.

Collectors' clubs and re-enactment groups are among the best sources of information. These groups also are very knowledgeable about reproductions, copycats, and fantasy items.

History: Power struggles between European countries raged for hundreds of years. As the 20th century dawned, leading European countries became entangled in a series of complex alliances, many sealed by royal marriages, and a massive arms race. All that was needed to set off the powder keg was a fire. The assassination of Austrian Archduke Franz Ferdinand by a Serbian national ignited the fuse on June 28, 1914. Germany invaded Belgium and moved into France. Russia, England, and Turkey joined the war. Italy and the United States became involved by mid-1917.

In 1918, Germany sued for peace. A settlement was achieved at the Versailles Conference, January–June 1919, during which time the United Sates remained in the background. President Wilson's concept for a League of Nations failed to gain acceptance in his own country, opening the door to the events which culminated in World War II.

References: W. K. Cross, *Charlton Price Guide to First World War Canadian Infantry Badges,* The Charlton Press, 1995.

Periodicals: *Men at Arms,* 222 W. Exchange St., Providence, RI 02903; *Military Collector Magazine,* P.O. Box 245, Lyon Station, PA, 19536; *Military Collectors' News,* P.O. Box 702073, Tulsa, OK 74170; Military History, 6405 Flank Dr., Harrisburg, PA 17112; *Military Trader,* P.O. Box 1050, Dubuque, IA 52004; Wildcat Collectors Journal, 15158 NE. 6 Ave., Miami FL 33162.

Collectors' Clubs: American Society of Military Insignia Collectors, 526 Lafayette Ave., Palmerton, PA 18701; Association of American Military Uniform Collectors, P.O. Box 1876, Elyria, OH 44036; Company of Military Historians, North Main St., Westbrook, CT 06498; Orders and Medals Society of America, P.O. Box 484, Glassboro, NJ 08028.

Museums: Liberty Memorial Museum, Kansas City, MO; National Infantry Museum, Fort Benning, GA; The Parris Island Museum, Parris Island, SC; Seven Acres Antique Village & Museum, Union, IL; US Air Force Museum, Wright-Patterson AFB, Dayton, OH; US Army Transportation Museum, Fort Eustis, VA; US Navy Museum, Washington, DC.

Advertising, drawing book, Old Reliable Coffee, patriotic edition 8.00

Badge
    American Red Cross-Military Welfare, cap, enamel 20.00
    Rural Mail Carrier Award, brass, 1st place bar, profile bust of Benjamin Franklin 15.00

Bayonet, orig case 20.00

Beanie, ribbon and charms, 7" d, 3" h, dark brown corduroy, yellow felt trim, red, white, and blue stars and stripes V-ribbon shown in place on top, three charms sewn in place around sides, silver accent double flag, clear plastic star, silver accent Police Commissioner, ribbon slightly frayed 20.00

Belt, web 254.00

Book
    Building the Kaiser's Navy, Gary Weir, 289 pgs 27.00
    Granville: Tales and Tail Spins from A Flyer's Diary, Abingdon Press, 1919 .... 75.00

Candleholder, Germany, sword handle fits into candleholder, silver inlay reads "To Mom & Dad from Gordon" just above handle, no blade 85.00

Canteen, Army 15.00

Census Badge, diecut brass shield, state seal of NY in center, 1917 . 18.00

Easel Plaque, 6" d, convex celluloid over metal, wire easel, colorful Allied flags 35.00

Flip Book, 2" x 2-1/2" x 1/4", soldier, sailor, and Uncle Sam presenting the colors, pledge of Allegiance, Liberty Bone promotion, © 1917 .... 30.00

Gas Mask, carrying can, shoulder strap, canister attached to bottom, German 50.00

Handkerchief, 11" sq, "Remember Me," soldier and girl in center, red, white, and blue edge 20.00

Helmet, US, 3rd Army insignia 65.00

Key Chain Fob, Kaiser Bill's Bones, 1-1/4" l replica of shell casing holding miniature celluloid die set, inscription on firing cap end of brass cartridge, removable silver bullet head, loop for key chain 72.00

Medal, Iron Cross 45.00

Paperweight, weighted celluloid, full color image of 12 "Flags of the Allies-United For The Cause Of Liberty," white center, black letters, mirror base 40.00

Pinback Button
    Australia Day, 1916, light sepia portrait of English naval officer Lord Kitchener, white ground, blue letters, 1916 Unley event 20.00
    Australia Day, 1918, red, white, blue, and black, aborigine young lady puffing pipe, wearing red bandanna, blue and black rim depiction of tiny boomerangs 40.00
    French Orphans Fund, red, white, and blue, illus of woman holding two youngsters, inscribed "France Always Our Friend, Help the Orphaneliant Des Armees" 12.00
    Jewish Relief, red, white, and blue, silver accents, Hebrew man holding youngster in one arm, upper rim inscription in Hebrew, lower "The Jews Look to America For Help," back paper inscription "Remember Relief Ball Wed March 15, 1916 at Symphony Hall-Boston" 15.00
    Liberty Loan Committee, blue lettering on white ground, gold rim, red, white, and blue patriotic shield, c1918 .... 12.00
    Lloyd George, black and gray portrait of British Prime Minister, Welsh rim inscription 30.00
    On Active Service, multicolored image of English bulldog staunchly positioned on nationality flag, blue lettering 30.00
    Our Heroes Welcome Home, blue letters, white bordered by red victory wreath 20.00
    Port Pirie Repatriation, black cat on lower yellow ground, shaded blue top, black lettering, Australian, c1916 .... 35.00
    78th Division, red, white and blue, Welcome Home, issued for "The Fighting Demons" 35.00
    We Mourn Our Loss, black and gray photo celluloid of unidentified officer, spiked military helmet 20.00
    World Peace, multicolored, Allied flags around white dove carrying olive branch 60.00

Pin Holder, 2-1/4" d, celluloid, full color image of 12 Allies flags around white center, blue letters, perimeter ring holds glass mirror 35.00

Portrait, 5-3/4" x 8", full-color celluloid, sepia portrait, surrounding flags and patriotic symbols, inscription "Army and Navy Forever," single star service banner, black velveteen over metal back, wire easel stand 65.00

Ribbon, 2" x 5", Welcome Home 26th Division 25.00

Sheet Music
    If We Had A Million Like Him Over There, George Cohan songwriter, 10-1/2" x 13-1/2", 1918 copyright
    Spirit of France, "Respectfully inscribed to Ferdinand Foch Marshall of France and Generalissimo of Allied Armies," cover shows French WWI troops, inset portrait of General Foch, some wear 45.00

Tobacco Jar, cov, 6-1/2" h, ceramic, brown glaze, General Pershing 145.00

Uniform, US Army, Engineer, coat, belt, pants, cap, canvas leggings, wool puttees, and leather gaiters, canteen 400.00

Watch Fob, flag on pole, USA, beaded, blue 45.00

World War II Collectibles

Collecting Hints: To the victors go the spoils, or so World War II collectors would like to think. Now that the Soviet Block has fallen, a large number of dealers are making efforts to import Soviet Block World War II collectibles into the United States. Be careful when buying anything that has a new or unused appearance. Many Soviet countries continued to use stockpiled World War II equipment and still manufacture new goods based on World War II designs.

The Korean Conflict occurred shortly after World War II. The United States and other armed forces involved in this conflict used equipment and uniforms similar to those manufactured during World War II. Familiarize yourself with model styles, dates of manufacture, and your buying sources.

If you locate a World War II item, make certain to record all personal history associated with the item. This is extremely important. Collectors demand this documentation. If possible, secure additional information on the history of the unit and the battles in which it was engaged. Also make certain to obtain any extras that are available, such as insignia or a second set of buttons.

History: With the rise of the German Third Reich, European nations once again engaged in a massive arms race. The 1930s Depression compounded the situation.

After numerous compromises to German expansionism, war was declared in 1939 following Germany's Blitzkrieg invasion of Poland. Allied and Axis alliances were formed.

Although neutral, Americans were very supportive of the Allied cause. The December 7, 1941, Japanese attack on the U.S. Naval Station at Pearl Harbor, Hawaii, forced America into the war. It immediately adopted a two-front strategy.

From 1942 to 1945, the entire world was directly or indirectly involved in the war. Virtually all industrial activity was war related. The resulting technological advances guaranteed that life after the war would be far different from prior years.

Germany surrendered May 7, 1945. Japan surrendered on August 14, 1945, after the atomic bombing of Hiroshima on August 6, 1945, and Nagasaki on August 9, 1945.

References: Martin Jacobs, *World War II Homefront Collectibles*, Krause Publications, 2000; Jack Matthews, *Toys Go to War: World War II Military Toys, Games, Puzzles & Books*, Pictorial Histories Publishing, 1994; Ron Menchine, *Propaganda Postcards of World War II*, Krause Publications, 2000.

Periodicals: *Men at Arms*, 222 W. Exchange St., Providence, RI 02903; *Military Collector Magazine*, P.O. Box 245, Lyon Station, PA, 19536; Military Collectors' News, P.O. Box 702073, Tulsa, OK 74170; Military History, 6405 Flank Dr., Harrisburg, PA 17112; *Military Trader*, P.O. Box 1050, Dubuque, IA 52004; *Wildcat Collectors Journal*, 15158 NE 6 Ave., Miami FL 33162.

Collectors' Clubs: American Society of Military Insignia Collectors, 526 Lafayette Ave., Palmerton, PA 18701; Association of American Military Uniform Collectors, P.O. Box 1876, Elyria, OH 44036; Company of Military Historians, North Main St., Westbrook, CT 06498; Imperial German Military Collectors Association, 82 Atlantic St., Keyport, NJ 07735; Orders and Medals Society of America, P.O. Box 484, Glassboro, NJ 08028.

Museums: Liberty Memorial Museum, Kansas City, MO; National Infantry Museum, Fort Benning, GA; The Parris Island Museum, Parris Island, SC; Seven Acres Antique Village & Museum, Union, IL; US Air Force Museum, Wright-Patterson AFB, Dayton, OH; US Army Transportation Museum, Fort Eustis, VA; US Navy Museum, Washington, DC.

Bomber's Vest, $40.

Album Picture, Hi-Speed Victory Club, 6-1/4" x 8-1/2", bluetone photo and text, Hi-Speed Gas, c1943.......... 2.00

Arm Band, Civilian Defense Air Raid Warden, 4" w, white, 3-1/2" blue circle, red and white diagonal stripes within triangle.. 10.00

Bank, 3" d, 7-1/2" h, hollow plaster, gray paint, white letter "V," raised lettering "Bomb the Axis/Bonds Buy Bombs," red, white, and blue paper sticker...................................... 125.00

Better Little Book, *Fighting Heroes Battle For Freedom*, #1401, © 1942, 1943... 18.00

Binoculars, Army, M-17, field type, 7-1/2" l, olive drab, 7 x 50 power, clear, fixed optics 95.00

Book

Aerial Warfare, The Story of the Aeroplane as a Weapon, by Hal Goodwin, New Home Library, 1943, 273 pgs, hard cover.................. 10.00

Baa Baa Black Sheep, War Memoirs of Pappy Boyington, Marine Corps Pilot Ace with Flying Tigers, Boyington, 1958.................................... 38.00

Blood and Banquets, A Berlin Social Diary by a Jewish Reporter and Witness to Nazi Rise, Fromm, 1942... 30.00

Bunker's War-The World War II Diary of Colonel Paul D. Bunker, Barlow ed., 32- pgs 38.00

Day of Infamy, Dec 7, 1941, Walter Lord, 1957, Henry Holt, 243 pgs, illus, slightly worn dj 12.00

Europe & the Mediterranean, Dept. of History, West Point Military Academy, 1978, 366 pgs 35.00

From Hell to Heaven Memoirs from Patton's Third Army in WWII, McHugh, 1980........................... 30.00

Handbook of Hospital Corps, United States Navy, Government Printing Office, 1939.............................. 17.00

History of World War II, Armed Services Memorial Edition, Francis Trevelyan Miller, Reader's Service Bureau, war photos, official records, maps.. 18.00

Pearl Harbor Story, Capt. Wm. T. Rice, 1973, 9th printing 7.00

Semper Fi, Mac, Living Memories of the US Marines in WWII, Berry, 1982... 38.00

Song & Service Book for Ship & Field, Army & Navy, Ivan L. Bennett, 1942, A. S. Barnes Pub. 15.00

Ten Thousand Eyes-Spy Network That Cracked Hitlers Atlantic Wall Abefor D-Day, 1958, 300 pgs, plates, photos, maps........................... 38.00

The General Was A Spy-The Truth About German General Gehlen, Who Served Hitler, The CIA & West Germany, Heinzel-Hohne, H. Zolling, c1972, photos, dj 30.00

World War II Operations in North African Waters, Oct 1942-June 1943, Samuel Eliot Morison, Atlantic, Little Brown, 1955, 297 pgs, dj.......... 25.00

Calendar, 6-3/4" x 10", Co-Operative Elevator Co, Gen Douglas MacArthur, 1943, cream colored diecut sheet, red, and blue sword design at center, browntone portrait of general 45.00

Cap, AAF Officer's, 50-Mission, crash cap, small gilded eagle, front and back straps, soft bill, gabardine, mkd "Fighter by Bancroft, O.D." 95.00

Card Game, Navy Aircraft Squadron Insignia, 1" x 4" x 5", 17 pairs of cards 35.00

Figure, 3-3/4" h, Kilroy Was Here, plastic, wistful pregnant girl 35.00

Flight Suit, Army Air Force, Type A-4, olive drab gabardine, matching belt, zipper front 95.00

Glass
4-1/2" h, flying white eagle, blue and red "V" symbol 24.00
4-3/4" h, 2-1/4" d, clear glass, applied red, white, and blue, "Remember-Pearl Harbor, Dec. 7, 1941," image of US aircraft 20.00

Gunpowder Can, 18" h, 10" d, copper and brass, U.S. Navy, hinged brass port hole opening with tie dogs (wing nuts) 225.00

Helmet, MI, olive drab sand finish, olive drab chin strap, orig liner, thin mesh helmet net 145.00

Jacket, A-2 Army Air Force, leather, cowhide, light brown, name tag 495.00

Knife, Camillus USN Mark 5 Sheath, black finish blade, light scabbard wear, USN and name marked on guard, gray web belt loop, gray fiber scabbard 65.00

Lamp, 5" h base of painted figural plaster, 3-1/2" h figural soldier, fleshtone face, brown uniform, garrison cap, 3" h tan cardboard shade with printed red, and blue aviation scenes, parachuting Air Force figure 75.00

Magazine
Liberty, Aug. 24, 1940, 8-1/2" x 11-1/2", full color cover art for Lighting in the Night, A Story of the Invasion of America 18.00
Life, Occupation of Germany, Feb 10, 1947 .... 9.00
Pin-Up Parade, 8-1/2" x 11", black and white photo cov, purple and yellow accents, 48 pgs, full page black and white pin-up photos of Hollywood stars such as Lucille Ball, Barbara Stanwyck, Lana Turner, Ginger Rogers centerfold, © 1944 Bond Publishers 40.00
War Planes, Dell, 8-1/4" x 11", full-color cov, 28 black and white pgs, © 1942 .... 35.00

Manual
The Bluejackets Manual, 1946, 13th ed., US Naval Institute, Annapolis, 622 pgs 9.00
War Department Technical Manual Air Navigation, 1940, 296 pgs, U.S. Govt. Printing Office, maps, charts, illus 7.00

Matchbox, 5/8" x 1-1/2" x 2-1/4", cardboard slipcase cover, wooden safety matches, red, white, and blue war bonds and slogans, "Keep Em Rolling" and "Keep Em Flying" 15.00

Mirror and Thermometer Premium Picture, 4-1/2" x 9-3/4", cream colored cardboard mat, diecut opening, blue accent mirror, full color 3" oval art of Gen MacArthur, 2-1/4" diecut opening with thermometer, c1943 .... 48.00

Notebook, spiral-bound, pocket-type, bald eagle perched on sword on cover, "The Pen and the Sword for Victory," red, white, and blue 4.00

Patch
AAF, cloth, bombardier wings, embroidered silver and gray, tan cotton, unused 15.00
War Production Soldier, 3-1/4" x 7-1/2", red, white, and blue stitched fabric 70.00

Pencil Box, 1-1/4" x 5" x 8-1/2", "V for Victory," sturdy cardboard, snap fastener, early 1940s 70.00

Pin
Axe the Axis, hatchet shape, inscription on blade, marked "Sterling Silver" 85.00
Boston Paper Trooper, diecut white plastic, red and blue lettering "Salvage for Victory" 15.00
Marine Civilian Corps, diecut circular plastic, red spoked wheel design, inscribed "Depot of Supplies-San Francisco" 15.00
Remember Pearl Harbor, diecut white metal eagle, gold luster finish, inset pearl disk and slogan 65.00
Stage Door Canteen, red, white, and blue enamel, silver lettering "American Theatre Wing-Stage Door Canteen," mkd "Sterling" on bar pin 12.00
U.S. for Victory, bright luster brass frame, clear plastic insert cover over paper insert with red, white, and blue flag 20.00
USO Camp Shows, diecut brass, white enamel eagle, red ground, "Camp Shows," 15.00
Women's Service, diecut brass eagle and shield symbol, rim inscribed "National League for Woman's Service" 20.00

Pinback Button
Avenge Manila, red, white, and blue, on pale gray ground 40.00
Battleship USS Washington, green on gold, June 1, 1940 launch from Philadelphia Navy Yard 45.00
Beat the Schedule, red, white, and blue celluloid, Congress of Industrial Organizations 25.00
Eat To Beat The Devil, red, white, and blue litho, image of clenched fist belting head of devil 55.00
Gen MacArthur Welcome Home, red, white and blue, bluetone portrait 60.00
Gopher Ordinance Works, full color war production cartoon of determined gopher 35.00
Mothers of World War II, blue and white image 40.00
Pabst Breweries Bond Buyer, red, white, and blue, 10 percent salary contributor 30.00

Postcard, 3-1/2" x 5-1/2", Just A Little Something To Remember Pearl Harbor, full color cartoon showing Navy ship firing on and sinking Japanese ship, 1942 cancellation 18.00

Poster
Bunds-Bonds, 16-1/2" x 22", Hitler confusing German word "Bunds" for Bonds, discrepancy whispered by character representing Goebbels to Nazi cohort Herman Goering, government printing date 1942, #473829 .... 125.00
Buy War Bonds, 22" x 28", vivid color beachhead assault scene, artist Ferdinand Warren, facsimile signature, government printing date 1942, #497775 .... 75.00
Enemy Propaganda, 18" x 23" frame, art by Jack Betts, caricature images of Tojo and Hitler, sponsored by Veterans of Foreign Wars, early 1940s 110.00
Fatso-Ratso-Japso, 15-1/4" x 18" rigid cardboard, caricature art of Mussolini, Hitler and Tojo as the blame for "Higher Prices and Shortages!," cardboard easel back, paper stick for sponsor Schnaley, "Three Feathers Whiskey, and Coronet Brandy" 275.00

Premium, Navy Code Signal Flags, 5" x 12-1/2" brown paper mailer from Tootsie Rolls, pair of folded paper sheets, each opening to 12" sq 60.00

Record, "Remember Pearl Harbor," 10" d black wax, 78 rpm, RCA Victor Bluebird label 65.00

Sheet Music, Rosie the Riveter, 9" x 12", 1942 .... 25.00

Shovel, fox hole type 15.00

Sign, 18" h, 12" w, Kool Cigarettes, full color, graphics showing Kool penguin as Army sentry on duty, text at top "Keep Alert-Smoke Kools" 135.00

Stud, V symbol, white metal, gold luster finish, red, white and blue paint accents 15.00

War Stamp Card, 1-1/2" x 2-3/4" red, white, and blue card slotted to hold 1945 Liberty head dime, text promises one dime buys four bullets 40.00

World's Fairs And Expositions

Collecting Hints: Familiarize yourself with the main buildings and features of the early World's Fairs and Expositions. Much of the choicest china and textiles pictured an identifiable building. Many exposition buildings remained standing long after the fairs were over, and souvenirs proliferated. Prices almost always are higher in the city or area where an exposition was held.

There have been hundreds of local fairs, state fairs, etc., in the last 100 years. These events generally produced items of value mostly to local collectors.

History: The Great Exhibition of 1851 in London marked the beginning of the World's Fair and Exposition movement. The fairs generally featured exhibitions from nations around the world displaying the best of their industrial and scientific achievements.

Many important technological advances have been introduced at world's fairs, including the airplane, telephone, and electric lights. Ice cream cones, hot dogs, and iced tea were first sold by vendors at fairs. Art movements were often closely associated with fairs and exhibitions. The best works of the Art Nouveau artists were assembled at the Paris Exhibition in 1900.

References: Joyce Grant, *NY World's Fair Collectibles, 1964-1965*, Schiffer Publishing, 1999; Robert L. Hendershott, *1904 St Louis World's Fair Mementos and Memorabilia*, Kurt R. Krueger Publishing (5438 N. 90th St., Ste. 309, Omaha, NE 68134), 1994; Frederick and Mary Megson, *American Exposition Postcards*, The Postcard Lovers, 1992; *New York World's Fair Licensed Merchandise*, World of Tomorrow Co. (P.O. Box 229, Millwood, NY 10546), 1996; Howard M. Rossen, *World's Fair Collectibles: Chicago 1933 and New York 1939*, Schiffer Publishing, 1998.

Periodical: *World's Fair*, P.O. Box 339, Corte Madera, CA 94976.

Collectors' Clubs: 1904 World's Fair Society, 529 Barcia Dr., St. Louis, MO 63119; World's Fair Collectors' Society, Inc, P.O. Box 20806, Sarasota, FL 34276.

Museums: Atwater Kent Museum, History Museum of Philadelphia, Philadelphia, PA; Buffalo & Erie County Historical Society, Buffalo, NY; California State University, Madden Library, Fresno, CA; 1893 Chicago World's Columbian Exposition Museum, Columbus, WI; Museum of Science & Industry, Chicago, IL; Presidio Art Museum, San Francisco, CA; The Queens Museum, Flushing, NY.

1893, Chicago, The Columbian Exposition

Belt Buckle, brass, "Landing of Columbus," wheat husk tied with bow, 1492-1892, mkd "Made by Tiffany Studio, NY," 3-3/8" x 2-3/8" 100.00

Book, *Harper's Chicago and the World's Fair*, Julian Ralph, NY, Harper and Brothers, 1893, clothbound, 244 pgs, 70 illus 45.00

Brochure
Lundborg Perfuem, 8-1/2" x 6-1/2" 18.00
Mammoth Redwood Plank, Owned By The Berry Bros, Ltd, 4 pgs, 4" x 5" 25.00

Comb and Case, 4-1/2" l, gold colored, top of case mkd "1934 Chicago World's Fair," Golden Temple of Jehol, US Building, and Dairy Building, other side shows General Exhibits Building, Travel & Transportation Building and Electrical Building, yellow comb 60.00

Crumb Tray and Scraper, silverplated 30.00

Drinking Glass, 2-1/2" d, 3-1/2" h, clear, frosted white "World's Fair, Electrical Building" 35.00

Scarf, 17" x 15", silk, Chicago 1893, Expo, panorama of Expos overlaying American flag 45.00

Souvenir Book, *Official Guide To The World's Columbian Exposition*, 5" x 7", 192 pgs 50.00

Souvenir Spoon, profile of Columbus on handle, 1492 above, 1893 below sketch of ship, "Columbian Exposition" emb down handle, different scene and map on back 27.50

Table Cloth, 11" sq, Machinery Hall, fringed border, small stain and damage 70.00

1894, California Mid-Winter Exposition, souvenir spoon, bowl with drawing of ornate pavilion, SP, mkd "AMN Sterling Co" 25.00

1901, Pan Am Exposition, Buffalo

Bandanna, 20" sq, silk, Electrical Tower illus 195.00

Book, *The Pan American Exposition, Buffalo, N.Y., 1901*, softbound, green cover, gold lettering 25.00

Fan, flowers on front, back "Japan Welcome, Beautiful, Battleship Game, Fishing Game, Lucky Co., On the Zone, Pan. Pac. Int. Expo, San Francisco, 1915" 70.00

Match Holder, hanging type 25.00

Memo Pad, 1-1/2" x 2-1/4", Mother's Oats, diecut celluloid covered tablet, grommet fastner, "A Souvenir of the Pan-American Exposition and Mother's Oats" 75.00

Pinback Button, Lion Brewery, multicolored cartoon of man falling upside down from hot air balloon over city, "Drop In Buffalo 1901" 35.00

Souvenir Spoon, silver plated
4-1/2" l, Machinery & Transportation Building on bowl 13.00
6" l, buffalo sitting on earth on top of handle, waterfalls on bowl 15.00

Stud, diecut thin brass figural charging buffalo, silver luster finish, blue porcelain disk with North and South America continents 20.00

Tip Tray, King's Puremalt, woman holding tray with bottle, fair emblem at bottom, reads "Panama-Pacific International Exposition-Medal of Award," 6" l, 4-1/4" w, oval 165.00

1904, St. Louis, Louisiana Purchase Exposition

Bowl, Grant log cabin 165.00

Brooch, figural, diecut celluloid, apple applied on silvered tin backing, diecut opening at center for pin, Arkansas Exhibit Building, railroad train, floral motif 45.00

Coffee Tin, Hanley & Kinsella 30.00

Letter Opener, emb buildings on handle 45.00

Napkin Ring, aluminum, engraved "World's Fair, St. Louis, 1904," engraved US flag 50.00

Pinback Button, red, white, blue, and gold emblem on gray ground, white lettering "Louisiana Purchase Exposition-St. Louis 1904," back paper with design copyright by Louisana Purchase Exposition Co. 15.00

Postcards, set of three, sponsored by Regal Shoe Co., Boston, color view of Palace of Machinery, Palace of Varied Industries, U.S. Government Building, brief text, unused 15.00

Souvenir Book, *Souvenir Book of the Louisiana Purchase Exposition*, day and night scenes, published by the Official Photographic Company, 11" x 8-1/2" 45.00

1915, San Francisco, Panama-Pacific International Exposition

Badge w/ribbon, top pin "Guest-Los Angeles Produce Exchange," orange ribbon mkd "San Francisco Dairy Produce Exchange, Santa Barbara, May 6-8, 1910," attached hen charm reads "Laying For Panama-Pacific International Exposition" 95.00

Booklet, Panama-Pacific International Exposition, compliments of Remington Typewriter, 30 pgs, 7-1/4" x 11" 40.00

Handbook, *The Sculpture & Murals of the Panama-Pacific International Exposition*, Stella S G Perry, 1915, 104 pgs, 5 x 6-3/4", ex-library copy 45.00

Print, 6" x 26-1/2", Panoramic View of Panama-Pacific International Exposition, San Francisco, 1915, Tower of Jewels in center, some aging, traces of moisture 20.00

Tray, 3-1/2" x 5-1/2", hammered metal, bear figural, emb "Tower of Jewels, Panama Pacific International/San Francisco, Cal 1915," dark finish 45.00

Watch Fob, brass, orig black leather strap 95.00

1934, Chicago, Century of Progress

Ashtray, 5-1/2", Firestone, black rubber tire, transparent amber glass insert inscribed "Firestone/Century of Progress/Chicago 1934" 30.00

Automobile Accessory, rear view mirror, no glare, orig box 90.00

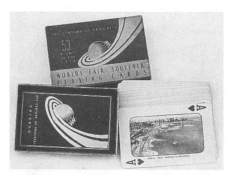

Chicago, 1933, Century of Progress, playing cards, Playing Card Co., Racine, WI, $30.

Bracelet, copper, scenic................35.00
Brochure
    Baltimore and Ohio Railroad World's Fair Exhibit 1934, 20 pgs, 4-1/2" x 9-3/4"...................................25.00
    57 At The Fair, Heinz 57 Exhibit, Agricultural Building, 16 pgs............22.00
    How! And Where! At Chicago and The World's Fair, Chicago and Northwestern (Railroad) Line, 16 pg guide to Chicago 20.00
    Official Pictures, Rueben H Donnelly, black and white, 7" x 10"...........35.00
    Sky-Ride, See The Fair From The Air, 4 pg, 3-1/2" x 5-3/4" 12.00
    The Why-What-and When of A Century of Progress, 10 pgs 10.00
Certificate of Attendance, Closing Day, Oct. 31, 1934, 3" x 5-1/4" 15.00
Coffee Mug, Stewart's.....................50.00
Coin, flattened
    1-3/8" l, Fort Dearborn 15.00
    1-1/2" x 3/4", General Motors Exhibit 15.00
Good Luck Key, 2" l, Master Lock, pavilions on shank..............................20.00
Handkerchief, 11" sq, painted silk, small stains..40.00
Magazine
    Liberty, 8-1/2" x 11-1/2", June 9, 1934, full color cover art by Carl Pfeufer of honeymooners arriving at fair, article about technical achievements and exhibits at fair............................15.00
    Marshall Field & Co, 9-1/2" x 13", 44 pgs, photos and articles............20.00
Map, City of Chicago and Century of Progress fairgrounds, Shell Oil..16.00
Needlecase, 6-3/4" x 4-1/2", A Century of Progress...................................27.00
Pin, Sharpshooter, vertical format, silvered brass, official 1933 symbol between inscription "Safety Glass" and "Sharpshooter/Chicago" 20.00
Pinback Button
    Black and white litho image of symbol, reverse "Cardinelli Century/Official Photographers for Century of Progress 1933" 15.00
    Blue lettering on white "Century of Progress Tour-New York Farm Bureau-Chicago, 1933"..............12.00
Playing Cards, gold leaf edges, orig red leather case 30.00
Pocket Mirror.................................25.00

Press Pass, 2-1/2" x 4-1/4", Short Term Press Pass, typewritten name of user and "Postal Telegraph Co.," 1934 ....20.00
Puzzle, 16-1/2", aerial view of fair opening, 300 pcs 50.00
Ring, silvered adjustable brass ring, image of Hall of Science, 1934 date in vertical letters on band 20.00
Snowglobe 50.00
Souvenir Book
    1933 Century of Progress Souvenir Book, 8-1/2" x 11-1/2"...............20.00
    Official Guide Book of the Fair, foldout map and Firestone colored adv insert..25.00
Souvenir Bottle, 3-1/2" x 6" x 6" h, clear glass, threaded red enameled tin cap, emb image of skyscraper flanked by frontier log cabin and Indian teepee, inscribed, "A Century of Progress, 1833-1933"............35.00
Souvenir Spoon, silverplate
    Electrical Group on bowl, Fort Dearborn on handle, dated 1934......10.00
    Travel & Transport on bowl, Hall of Science on handle, dated 1933 ..8.00
Tray, Hall of Science, emb buildings, bridge...30.00
View Book, 9" x 12", A Century of Progress Exhibition Official Book of Views, watercolor views and painting reproductions, published by Donnelly 30.00
Wings 25.00

1939, New York, New York World's Fair

Album, 5" x 6-3/4", Snapshots, cardboard covers, 15 pages of black paper...30.00
Ashtray, 3" x 3-1/2", Trylon and Perisphere, Manuf by Almar, Point Marian, PA 60.00
Banner, 10" x 8", multicolored paint on blue felt..45.00
Belt Buckle, goldtone, enameled Trylon, and Perisphere..........................20.00
Bookends, pr, alabaster, figural, Trylon and Perisphere.........................110.00
Booklet
    Around the Grounds, Greyhound, 2-1/2" x 5" opens to 9" x 12" sheet, orange and blue printing, white ground...18.00
    General Motors Highway & Horizons, 20 pgs 24.00
    The Foods of Tomorrow, Birdseye..8.00
Bowl, 10" d, 2-1/5" h, pottery, color design of fair motifs, musical notes, mkd "Paden City Pottery, Paden City, W Va," and Union Made logo 95.00
Brochure, 12 pgs, fold-out, Trylon and Perisphere...............................16.00
Cake Server, 10" l, National Silver Co., view of man with five stars on handle "New York World's Fair 1939" with symbols and flags surrounding words..60.00
Cane, 34" l, wood, blue, round wooden knob, Trylon and Perisphere decal 85.00

Charm Bracelet, brass link bracelet, five 3/4" brass disk charms, each with major exhibit building...............40.00
Clock, travel, chrome silver case, Trylon, Perisphere, and fair buildings on cover, blue and orange enamel accents...................................125.00
Coin, flattened, World of Tomorrow, Trylon and Perisphere...................13.00
Commemorative Plate..................150.00
Compact, 2-3/4" d, metal, full color celluloid insert, ivory white enameling................................40.00
Cuff Links, pr, Trylon, and Perisphere 45.00
Cup...25.00
Flashlight, 2-7/8" l, metal barrel, white plastic cap, blue finish, two orange and silver accent bands, fair emblem..................................55.00
Fountain Pen, 5" l, ivory white celluloid, matching cap, semi-iridescent, orange and blue Trylon and Perisphere symbols, mkd "Stratford".................................85.00
Glass, 4-1/4" h
    Business Administration Building, dark blue top and center, orange base, NYWF 39 and row of stars at base......................................20.00
    Textile Building, yellow top and center, green base, center shows building...20.00
Guide Book, *Official Guide to World of Tomorrow*, first edition, 1939.....25.00
Handkerchief, 10-1/2" x 11", sheer white silk-like fabric, printed images of 13 couples, each in different ethnic costume, red trim, mkd "Made in Hungary".....................................20.00
Hat, employee, wool, navy, orange Trylon and Perisphere, and "1940" on front......................................42.00
Hot Plate, silver, engraved fair scenes.....................................15.00
Identification Check, Greyhound Bus, Sightseeing Bus Trip Through Grounds..................................7.50
Kerchief, 20" sq, deep blue, cluttered yellow, green, and red artwork of Fair buildings, Trylon, and Perisphere 65.00
Key Ring..20.00
Magazine
    Band World, Summer, 1939......18.00
    Life, Trylon, and Perisphere on cover......................................30.00
Map, Transit Map of Greater New York, Compliments of Franklin Fire Insurance Co....................................25.00
Match Case, 1-1/2" x 2", leather, Trylon and Perisphere.........................35.00
Motion Pictures Reel, 1" x 3-3/4" x 3-3/4" boxed metal reel, black and white 16mm silent film for home projection use, black, white, and orange box dec, 1940 ....70.00
Music Box.......................................65.00
Night Light, ceramic, oval base with Trylon and Perisphere, ivory white finish, gold accents 100.00
Photo, 25" x 20", American Jubilee, dry-mounted 55.00

Pin

I Have Seen The Future 25.00
Little Miss Junket, black and white litho of serving girl, Junket Food Products Exhibit.................................15.00
Shield shaped logo, 5/8" h, 3/8" w, 1-1/2" chain to "39" on smaller shield, blue enamel on brass.................25.00
Trylon and Perisphere, brass, figural, inscribed, "New York World's Fair 1939"...60.00

Plate

7-1/4" d, Joint Exhibit of Capital & Labor, The American Potter, New York World's Fair, 1940, National Brotherhood Cooperative Potteries.......45.00
9" d, Homer Laughlin Pottery, potter, turquoise 38.00
10" d, Cronin, crazed 85.00

Playing Cards, two decks, orig box, U.S. Playing Card Co.........................50.00

Postcard

Jungland Jiggs, high gloss, sepia photo of costumed chimp riding tricycle, "Frank Buck's Jungleland At N. Y. World's Fair, Jiggs, The Mayor of Jungeland," unused 15.00
Set of 10 double faced cards, orig folder, unused 18.00

Postage Stamps, 54 licensed stamps in orig envelope, unused...............25.00

Pot Holder, 7-1/2" x 8-1/2", woven terry cloth, blue and white design, inscribed, "Macy's Pot Holder"..50.00

Program, Opening Day, April 30, 1939 ....150.00

Ring

Brass, adjustable, oval disk with raised relief of Trylon and Perisphere.................................30.00
Sterling silver, 5/8" d, 3/8 x 5/8" top with Trylon and Perisphere........45.00

Rug, 9" x 13", woven Oriental-type, image of Trylon and Perisphere surrounded by flowers, shades of green, yellow, red, and orange highlights, Italian.......................................95.00

Salt and Pepper Shakers, pr, Trylon and Perisphere, 3" h, gold trim 60.00

Scarf, 18" x 17", white, orange, yellow, and maroon, blue ground, trees and buildings, Trylon and Perisphere around edge, clouds center 45.00

Spoon

4-1/2" l, flags, Sphere and Trylon, date "1939" and two stars on handle, bowl with "New York World's Fair," tarnished silver...............................24.00
6" l, three stars, flags, Theme Bldg, date "1939" and two more stars on handle, bowl with "New York World's Fair," rim of stars, silverplated ...30.00

Table Lighter, 2-1/2" d, 2-5/8" h, metal globe, gloss black baked enamel finish, chromed mechanism, applied 3/4" brass disk symbol emblems, orange and blue enamel accents 150.00

Table Mat, 11" x 21", red felt, yellow, green, and white graphics, Statue of Liberty, Fair Administration Bldg., Empire State Bldg, Trylon, and Perisphere 95.00

Tape Measure, 2-1/2" w, egg shape, metal, blue finish, bee figure on both sides, orange Trylon and Perisphere on one side, mkd "New York World's Fair 1939"..................................60.00

Teapot, white glazed china, blue Trylon, and Perisphere...........................50.00

Thermometer, 8-1/4" l, key shape, aerial view 32.00

Thermos, 10" h, steel, threaded aluminum cap, orange Trylon and Perisphere, Universal Thermos......100.00

Ticket, 3" x 4", black and white photo, starched black fabric holder......45.00

Tie Clip, 2-3/4" w, brass, raised center emblem of Trylon and Perisphere..................................25.00

Valet Holder, clothes brush holder and tie rack, syrocco wood, raised Trylon and Perisphere, orig brush........50.00

View-Master, set of three reels, orig booklet and envelope 40.00

1939, San Francisco, Golden Gate International Exposition

Ashtray, 1939 Golden Gate Expo, Homer Laughlin Pottery 125.00

Belt Buckle, silver colored metal, badge emblem in center, aerial view of Treasure Island, name at top, 1-1/2" l 1" w..60.00

Handkerchief, 12-1/2" sq, Treasure Island, minor stains....................40.00

Labels, set of five, 1-1/2" d, "1939 Golden Gate International Exposition 1939 - a Pageant of the Pacific" around edge, center with woman arms up, flags at her feet, sunset, Treasure Island in background ..30.00

Matchbook Cover, Golden Gate Bridge scenes, pr 25.00

Pinback Button, 1-1/4" d, yellow, blue, and white....................................25.00

Plate, 10" d, Homer Laughlin 125.00

Stamps, set of six, San Francisco, Oakland and Bay Cities Invite the World in 1939, "1939 Golden Gate International Exposition 1939, A Pageant of the Pacific," one stamp stuck to another, orig packaging.............45.00

Ticket, 3-1/2" x 2-1/4", general admission, slight glue and paper on back 15.00

1962, Seattle, Century 21 Exposition

Glass, set of eight 80.00

Lobby Card, 11" x 14", Elvis Presley, It Happened at the World's Fair, MBM copyright, 1963, #3, small tack holes...20.00

Pinback Button, 1-1/4" d, red, white, and blue, Space Needle scene 17.50

Postal Cover, 2-3/4" x 10", glossy cardboard self mailer, full color night photo of Space Needle................8.00

Souvenir Plate, 10-3/4" d, gray outer rim band, silver bands, white center with multicolor view of grounds, inscribed, "Century 21-Seattle World's Fair, 1962," back mkd "Made Expressly for Frederick & Nelson-Seattle".......18.00

Token, gold....................................10.00

Tray, metal, Space Needle scene...12.00

New York, 1964-65, plate, Unisphere center, six medallions, 10-1/4" d, $37.50.

1964, New York, New York World's Fair

Ashtray, 4" x 5", glass, white, orange, and blue graphics, two Fair Kids, Unisphere, 1964 ....25.00

Bank, dime register, orig card........40.00

Bookmark, orig cello package.......35.00

Change Tray..................................12.00

Coaster, 4" d, plastic, white, emb gold Unisphere, title and date, price for 4 pc set...32.00

Comic Book, Flintstones at the World's Fair...22.00

Doll, 8-1/2" h, © 1963 Sun Rubber, New York World's Fair, 1964-1965.....85.00

Envelope, Unisphere as Christmas tree ornament, unused.....................10.00

Flash Card Set, New York World's Fair Attractions
Full Size, 3-1/2" x 6", 28 cards... 25.00
Miniature Size, 24 cards............ 20.00

Fork and Spoon Display, 11" l, mounted on wooden plaque, Unisphere decals on handles...............................45.00

Hat, black felt, Unisphere emblem, white cord trim, feather, name "Richard" embroidered on front 25.00

Lodge Medallion, bronze luster finish, image of Unisphere and two exhibit buildings, brass hanger loop, inscribed "The Grand Lodge I.O.O.F. of the State of New York"...........15.00

Mug, 3-1/4" h, milk glass, red inscription 17.50

Paperweight, panoramic scenes... 40.00

Placemat, 11" x 17-1/2", plastic, full color illus, Swiss Sky Ride and Lunar Fountain, price for pr 25.00

Postcard, ten miniature pictures, twenty natural color reproductions, unused...20.00

Puzzle, jigsaw, 2" x 10" x 11", Milton Bradley, 750 pcs, unopened 20.00

Ring, silvered plastic, small clear plastic dome over blue and orange image of Unisphere, inscription "NY World's Fair 1964-1965".......................10.00

Salt and Pepper Shakers, pr, Unisphere, figural, ceramic 50.00

Souvenir Book, *Official Souvenir Book of the New York World's Fair,* 1965...25.00

Stein, 6" h, ceramic, blue, German-style, emb Unisphere, German village scene, beer drinke.....................25.00

Thermometer, 6" x 6", diamond shape, metal and plastic, full color fair buildings and attractions 25.00

Ticket
    Belgian Village 7.50
    General Admission, adult, unused 20.00
    Pavilion of American Interiors, unused prepaid ticket, courtesy of International Silver Co.................15.00
    Travelers Pavilion, The Travelers Insurance Companies stockholders courtesy card............................12.00

Tray, 10-1/2" x 11-1/2", oval, plastic, raised fair attractions 42.00

Tumbler, Science Hall, 6-1/2" h.......17.50

Videotape, Lowell Thomas, shows construction through models and pictures 20.00

1967, Montreal, Montreal Expo

Bookmark, multicolored picture of sphere...8.00

Lapel Pin, brass, repeated motif around edge, threaded post fastener on back 12.00

Tab, 1-1/2" l, litho tin, blue and white, U.S. Pavilion, Compliments of Avis Car Rental 6.00

1982, Knoxville, World's Fair

Glass, 5-1/2" h, clear, tapered, Energy Turns The World theme, trademark for McDonald's and Coca-Cola 8.00

Sailor Cap, black and red inscription on brim...5.00

Wright, Russel

Collecting Hints: Russel Wright worked for many different companies in addition to creating material under his own label, American Way. Wright's contracts with firms often called for the redesign of pieces which did not produce or sell well. As a result, several lines have the same item in more than one shape.

Wright was totally involved in design. Most collectors focus on his dinnerware; however, he also designed glassware, plastic items, textiles, furniture, and metal objects. He helped popularize bleached and blonde furniture. His early work in spun aluminum often is overlooked as is his later work in plastic for the Northern Industrial Chemical Company.

History: Russel Wright was an American industrial engineer with a passion for the streamlined look. His influence is found in all aspects of domestic life. Wright and his wife, Mary Small Einstein, wrote *A Guide To Easier Living* to explain their concepts.

Russel Wright was born in 1904 in Lebanon, Ohio. His first jobs included set designer and stage manager under the direction of Norman Bel Geddes. He later used this theatrical flair for his industrial designs, stressing simple clean lines. Some of his earliest designs were executed in polished spun aluminum. These pieces, designed in the mid-1930s, include trays, vases, and teapots. Wright garnered many awards, among which were those he received from the Museum of Modern Art in 1950 and 1953.

Chase Brass and Copper, General Electric, Imperial Glass, National Silver Co., Shenango, and Steubenville Pottery Company are some of the companies that used Russel Wright designs. In 1983, a major exhibition of his work was held at the Hudson River Museum in Yonkers, New York, and at the Smithsonian's Renwick Gallery in Washington, DC

References: Susan and Al Bagdade, *Warman's American Pottery and Porcelain*, 2nd ed., Krause Publications, 2000; Joe Keller and David Ross, *Russel Wright Dinnerware, Pottery & More*, Schiffer Publishing, 2000; Ann Kerr, *Collector's Encyclopedia of Russel Wright Designs*, 2nd ed., Collector Books, 1998; Leslie Piña, *Pottery, Modern Wares 1920-1960*, Schiffer Publishing, 1994.

American Modern

Made by the Steubenville Pottery Company, 1939-1959. Originally issued in Bean Brown, Chartreuse Curry, Coral, Granite Grey, Seafoam Blue, and White. Later color additions were Black Chutney, Cedar Green, Cantaloupe, Glacier Blue, and Steubenville Blue.

Baker, small, Chartreuse Curry.......25.00
Bread and Butter Plate, 6" d
    Coral...4.00
    Granite Gray...................................5.00
Butter, cov
    Black Chutney...........................285.00
    Chartreuse Curry 285.00
    Coral..285.00
    White 625.00
Carafe, Granite Grey....................175.00
Casserole, cov, stick handle, Seafoam Blue 40.00
Celery
    Bean Brown..................................24.00
    Black Chutney...............................30.00
    Granite Grey..................................20.00
Children's Dish Set, 7" d cov bowl, six sets of chartreuse cups and saucers, 8" rect tray, three 6" d coral plates, three 6" d blue plates, blue, creamer, cov sugar, teapot and lid, made by Ideal 110.00
Chop Plate
    Black Chutney.............................50.00

Chartreuse Curry......................20.00
Coral..20.00
Granite Grey..............................25.00
Seafoam Blue............................25.00
Coaster, White 24.00
Cocktail, 2-3/4" h, 2-1/2 oz, Seafoam Blue, glass............................. 17.00
Creamer
    Chartreuse..................................18.00
    Coral..20.00
    Granite Gray...............................18.00
Creamer and Sugar, Chartreuse Curry...20.00
Cup, Seafoam Blue........................12.00
Cup and Saucer
    Chartreuse Curry......................24.00
    Coral..24.00
    Glacier Blue................................28.00
    Granite Grey..............................28.00
Demitasse Cup
    Chartreuse Curry........................8.50
    Granite Grey..............................17.00
Demitasse Cup and Saucer, coral...20.00
Demitasse Pot, cov
    Coral..120.00
    Granite Grey............................150.00
    Seafoam Blue...........................150.00
Dinner Plate, 10" d
    Bean Brown................................20.00
    Black Chutney............................18.00
    Cedar Green 15.00
    Granite Gray...............................16.00
    Seafoam Blue............................18.00
Dinner Service, Seafoam Blue, 74 pcs.................................... 600.00
Fruit Bowl, lug handle
    Bean Brown................................20.00
    Chartreuse Curry......................12.00
    Coral..15.00
Hostess Plate
    Chartreuse Curry......................75.00
    Granite Grey..............................85.00
Iced Tea Tumbler, 5" h, Coral, glass, slight use 24.00
Pickle
    Chartreuse Curry......................15.00
    Granite Grey..............................18.00
Pitcher
    Chartreuse Curry......................65.00
    Coral..120.00
    Seafoam Blue...........................185.00
Refrigerator Dish, cov
    Coral..225.00
    Granite Grey............................175.00
Relish
    Chartreuse Curry, rosette........145.00
    Seafoam Blue............................28.00
Salad Bowl
    Coral..75.00
    Granite Grey..............................85.00
    Seafoam Blue............................85.00
Salad Fork and Spoon, Chartreuse Curry and Granite Gray, 10" l 175.00
Salad Plate, 8" d
    Coral..18.00
    Granite Grey..............................15.00
Salt and Pepper Shakers, pr
    Black Chutney............................40.00
    Cedar Green 45.00
    Chartreuse..................................20.00
    Coral..30.00
    Granite Grey..............................20.00
    Seafoam Blue............................25.00
Sauceboat
    Black Chutney............................80.00

Coral..45.00
Sherbet, 5 oz, Seafoam Blue,
   glass...20.00
Soup Bowl
   Bean Brown, lug handle 24.00
   Coral..18.00
   Granite Grey, lug handle............18.00
   Stack Server, Cedar Green......250.00
Sugar, cov
   Cedar Green 15.00
   Chartreuse Curry 20.00
   Coral..30.00
   Seafoam Blue..............................15.00
Teapot, cov
   Coral..95.00
   Granite Grey................................75.00
Tumbler
   Black Chutney..............................65.00
   Cedar Green 72.00
   Coral..60.00
   Granite Grey................................95.00
Vegetable Bowl
   Chartreuse Curry 15.00
   Coral..20.00
   Granite Grey................................22.00
   Seafoam Blue..............................20.00
Vegetable Bowl, divided, Chartreuse
   Curry 80.00

Iroquois Casual

Made by the Iroquois China Company
and distributed by Garrison Products,
1946-1960s. Initially issued in Ice Blue,
Lemon Yellow, and Sugar White. Later
colors produced were Aqua, Avocado
Yellow, Brick Red, Cantaloupe, Char-
coal, Lettuce Green, Oyster, Nutmeg
Brown, Parsley Green (later called Forest
Green), Pink Sherbet, and Ripe Apricot
Yellow.
Bread and Butter Plate, 6-1/2" d
   Avocado Yellow..............................4.00
   Ice Blue 4.00
   Ripe Apricot 4.50
   Sugar White 7.50
Butter, cov
   Avocado Yellow............................75.00
   Ice Blue 150.00
   Lemon Yellow...............................65.00
   Pink Sherbet................................85.00

Ripe Apricot 95.00
Sugar White................................85.00
Carafe
   Avocado Yellow............................90.00
   Ripe Apricot 175.00
Casserole, cov, 2 qt
   Avocado Yellow............................35.00
   Oyster..20.00
Cereal Bowl, 5-1/4" d
   Cantaloupe...................................18.00
   Ice Blue 12.00
   Oyster..15.00
Chop Plate, 13" d
   Ripe Apricot 24.00
   Sugar White................................30.00
Coffeepot, cov
   Ice Blue 135.00
   Nutmeg Brown 125.00
Coffee Service, Nutmeg Brown, 10 pc
   set..135.00
Creamer and Sugar, cov, stacking
   Avocado Yellow............................25.00
   Ice Blue 22.50
   Oyster..95.00
   Sugar White................................37.50
Cup and Saucer
   Charcoal 15.00
   Ice Blue, ear handle....................12.00
   Lemon Yellow...............................12.00
   Pink Sherbet................................12.00
   Sugar White................................15.00
Demitasse Pot, cov
   Avocado Yellow............................65.00
   Nutmeg Brown 75.00
Demitasse Cup and Saucer
   Avocado Yellow..........................150.00
   Ice Blue 150.00
Dinner Plate, 10" d
   Avocado Yellow............................12.00
   Charcoal 12.00
   Lemon Yellow...............................12.50
   Lettuce Green 15.00
   Oyster..18.00
Fruit Bowl
   Avocado Yellow..............................6.00
   Oyster..7.50
Gumbo
   Ice Blue 35.00
   Pink Sherbet................................30.00
   Hostess Plate, Ice Blue..............85.00

Luncheon Plate, 9" d
   Avocado Yellow............................. 9.00
   Ice Blue 9.50
   Oyster... 12.00
Mug, Ripe Apricot 75.00
Pitcher, cov, Parsley, 6-1/2" h 475.00
Pitcher, Coral, 6" h 95.00
Platter, 12-1/2" l, Ice Blue 40.00
Platter, 12-3/4" l, Charcoal............. 60.00
Platter, 14-1/4" l, Pink Sherbet........ 55.00
Salad Plate, 7-3/8" d
   Ice Blue 8.00
   Lemon Yellow 9.00
   Oyster 10.00
   Sugar White 12.00
Salt and Pepper Shakers, pr, stacking
   Oyster 18.00
   Sugar White 19.50
   Soup Bowl, Cantaloupe 95.00
Vegetable, 8" d, open
   Avocado Yellow 15.00
   Ice Blue 15.00
   Nutmeg Brown 15.00
   Pink Sherbet 17.50
Vegetable, 10" d, cov
   Chartreuse, pinch lid, 2 pt 30.00
   Nutmeg Brown 55.00
   Pink Sherbet 50.00

Iroquois Casual, Redesigned

In 1959 Iroquois Casual dinnerware was
produced in patterns and offered in 45
piece sets. Cookware was another later
addition in the redesigned style.

Butter Dish, cov, ice blue 160.00
Cup, Charcoal 8.00
Cup and Saucer, Ice Blue.............. 10.00
Gravy, Ice Blue 220.00
Mug
   Apricot Yellow 80.00
   Ice Blue 75.00
   Lemon Yellow 75.00
   Pink Sherbet 70.00
   Ripe Apricot 70.00
   Sugar White, Christmas dec 85.00
Platter, Pink Sherbet, 14-1/4" l 55.00
Set, Pink Sherbet, 24 pcs............. 125.00
Teapot, Lemon Yellow 185.00
Vegetable, divided, Sugar White, some
   mottling on interior................. 200.00

Z

Zeppelins

Collecting Hints: All types of zeppelin material remain stable. Specialize in one specific topic, e.g., material about one airship, models and toys, or postcards. The field is very broad, and a collector might exhaust his funds trying to be comprehensive. The most common collecting trend focuses on material relating to specific flights.

History: The terms "airship," "dirigible" and "zeppelin" are synonymous. Dirigible (from Latin) means steerable and the term originally applied to bicycles although it evolved into a synonym for airship. Zeppelin honors the name of Count Frederick Von Zeppelin, the German inventor whose first airship flew on July 2, 1900, it's maiden flight lasting only eighteen minutes.

There are three types of dirigibles: 1) Rigid—a zeppelin, e.g., *Hindenburg, Graf, Shenandoah*; 2) Non-Rigid—a blimp, e.g., those flown by the Navy or bearing Goodyear advertising; and 3) Semi-Rigid—non-rigid with a keel, e.g., *Norge and Italia*. Only non-rigid and semi-rigid dirigibles were made prior to 1900. Hot-air balloons, barrage balloons, hydrogen balloons, and similar types are not dirigibles because they are not directable. They go where the wind takes them.

Zeppelins were made from 1900 to 1940, the last being the *LZ130*, sister ship to the *Hindenburg*. The *Graf* zeppelin was the most successful one, flying between 1928 and 1940. The *Hindenburg*, which flew in 1936 and 1937, was the most famous due to the spectacular fire that destroyed it in 1937.

America never used its four zeppelins for passenger travel; they were strictly for military use. The Naval Air Station at Lakehurst, New Jersey, where the well-known zeppelins docked, is still open, although its name has been changed to the Naval Air Engineering Center. The last Navy blimp flew from Lakehurst in 1962.

References: Walter Curley, *Graf Zeppelin's Flights to South America*, Spellman Museum, 1970; Arthur Falk, *Hindenburg Crash Mail*, Clear Color Litho, 1976; Sieger, *Zeppelin Post Katalog* (in German), Wurttemberg, 1981.

Collectors' Club: Zeppelin Collectors Club, c/o Aerophilatelic Federation, P.O. Box 1239, Elgin, IL 60121.

Museum: Navy Lakehurst Historical Society, Cinnaminson, NJ.

Reproduction Alert.

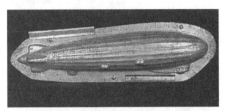

Candy Mold, #25647, Anton Reiche, Dresden, tin, two-piece clamp style, $145.

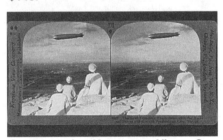

Stereograph, Keystone View Co., #7758632, The Great Zeppelin's Rendezvous with the Eternal Desert and Ancient Pyramids of Giza, historical information and facts on reverse, $35.

Badge, *Graf Zeppelin*, German, silver, mkd "800".............................. 2,500.00
Book
  Aircraft Carrier: Graf Zeppelin, Breyer, 48 pgs 10.00
  Nations of Europe in Great War, Charles Morris, 1914, zeppelin on colorful cover 30.00
  The Story of the Airship, Hugh Allen, Goodyear Tire & Rubber Co. 84 pages, 1937 .... 40.00
  The Zeppelin in Combat, A History of the German Naval Airship Division, Douglas H. Robinson, 400 pgs, black and white photos, charges, drawings.. 50.00
Candy Mold, two part type 95.00
Cocktail Shaker, silver plated, figural... 50.00

First Day Cover, "San Francisco Greets U.S.A.S. Macon Upon Arrival at Home Base," 8 cent airmail stamp, postmarked "Moffett Field, Oct. 15, 1933".. 30.00
Flight Schedule, from Germany to America, c1936 .... 60.00
Magazine Cover
  New Yorker Magazine, German *Graf Zeppelin* flying over NY skyscrapers, illus by Haupt, 1930, 8" x 11" image, acid-free mat 125.00
  Saturday Evening Post, black and white adv for Packard, showing US Navy Dirigible *Shenandoah*.......... 8.00
Needle Book, *Silver Flyer* Needles, one fold cardboard, showing Silver Flyer over New York skyline, harbor with Statue of Liberty on back, 6-3/4" x 3-3/4", wear.................................... 2.00
Newspaper, Pierce, SD, *Daily Capital Journal*, Nov, 1928, "Jones Holds Milwaukee Railroad Pass," *Graf* Zeppelin in Home Port, Seventy-One Hours to Port... 35.00
Pennant, 8-1/2" l, *Hindenburg,* airship and swastika symbols, black and gold, 1936 .... 150.00
Photograph, half tone, by Collier
  3" x 7", zeppelin sinking in English Channel, March 31, 1916 .... 20.00
  5" sq, French officers examining zeppelin bombs, 1917 .... 20.00
Pinback Button, Lakehurst Naval Air Station, red, white, and blue, attached ribbon and aluminum airship, 1930s 95.00
Postcard
  Advertising for Veedol Oil, showing *Graf Zeppelin*, descriptive text on back, 1929.................................... 35.00
  Dr. Hugo Eckener, *Luftscheiff Graf Zeppelin* am Ankermast................ 7.00
  Graf L2127, real photo of zeppelin about to enter hanger.................. 20.00
  Mooring scene, real photo, details about Dr. Z. Reederei, Frankfurt, unused 45.00
  Zeppelin flying over Montevideo, Uruguay, black and white 28.00
Pull Toy, *Graf Zeppelin*, Steelcraft, C-8 .... 490.00
Stamp, *Graf Zeppelin*, on postcard, postmarked Los Angeles, first European Pan-American round flight
  C14 .... 325.00
  C15 .... 310.00
Toy, cast iron, unknown maker
  Los Angeles, worn old repaint, one cabin damaged, 11-1/4" l 275.00
  Pony Blimp, old worn repaint, nickel finish wheels, light rust, 5-1/2" l. 180.00
  Zep, old repaint, 5" l 100.00

A

Abingdon Pottery, 18, 109
Action figures, 18-20
    Star Wars, 336
    Super heroes, 345
Advertising, 20-26
    Ashtray, 21
    Bank, 40
    Beanie Babies, 52
    Bill clip, 21
    Bill hook, 21
    Book, 21
    Bookcover, 21
    Bookmark, 21
    Bookmarks, 64
    Bottle openers, figural, 65-66
    Box, 21
    Bridge tallies, 21
    Brochure, 21
    Brush, 21
    Calculator, 21
    Calendar, 21
    Candy tin, 21
    Canister, 21
    Charm, 21
    Clickers, 100
    Clip, 21
    Clock, 22, 100
    Coffee tin, 22
    Collapsible cup, 22
    Comic book, 22
    Compass, 22
    Cookie jars, 109
    Counter sign, 22
    Creamer and sugar, 22
    Display cabinet, 22
    Display rack, 22
    Display, 22
    Doll, 22
    Fan, 22
    Figure, 22
    Flip pin, 22
    Flow Blue china,
            American, 153
    Folder, 22
    Handwriting analysis guide, 23
    Ink blotter, 23
    Key holder, 23
    Letter opener, 23
    Lunch box, 23
    Magazine ad, 23

Match safe, 23
Matchcovers, 230-231
Memo book, 23
Mirror pocket, 23
Movie memorabilia, 240
Ocean liner collectibles, 251
Paperweight, 23
Pencil clip, 23
Pendant, 24
Pens and pencils, 262, 263
Pig collectibles, 267
Pin holder, 24
Pinback button, 24
Plate, 24
Playing cards, 275
Pocket knives, 276
Post card, 24
Post cards, 281
Record, 24
Salesman's sample, 24
Salt and pepper shakers, 307
Sharpening stone, 24
Shoe horn, 24
Sign, 24-25
Snowdomes, 317
Spinner top, 25
Spoon rest, 25
Stud, 25
Thimble holders, 355
Tile, 25
Tip tray, 25, 26
Tobacco jar, 25
Tobacco tin, 25
Toys, 25
Trade cards, 25, 26
Tray, 26
Tumbler, 26
Watch fobs, 374
Western Americana, 378
Whistle, 26
Advertising characters, 26
    AC Spark Plug, 27
    Alka Seltzer, 27
    Aunt Jemima, 27
    Buster Brown, 27
    California Raisins, 27
    Campbell Kids, 27
    Charlie the Tuna, 27
    Dutch Boy, 27
    Elsie the Cow, 27
    Entenmann's, 28
    Esquire, 28

Exxon Tiger, 28
Florida Orange Bird, 28
Green Giant, 28
Hawaiian Punch, 28
Heinz, 57, 28
Hush Puppies, 28
Keebler, 28
Kellogg's, 28
Kool Cigarettes, 28
Mennon, 28
Mr. Bubble, 28
Nestle's Quick, 28
Philip Morris, 28
Pillsbury Co., 28
RCA Victor, 28
Red Goose Shoes, 28
Reddy Killowatt, 28
Sinclair Oil, 29
Tony the Tiger, 29
Willie Wiredhand, 29
Advertising-logo watches, 29-31
Akro Agate Glass, 31-33
    Children's dishes, 31
    Household items, 32
Aluminum, hand wrought, 32, 33
American Bisque, 33, 34
    Cookie jars, 110
Animation art, 34
Autographs, 34-36
    Autograph letters signed, 35
    Book signed, 35
    Cards signed, 36
    Document signed, 36
    Equipment, 36
    First day covers, 36
    Photograph signed, 36
Aviation collectibles, 36-38
    Commercial, 37
    General, 37
    Personalities, 38
Avon collectibles, 38-39
    Beauty products, 38
    Glassware, 39
    Jewelry, 39
    Miscellaneous collectibles, 39
    Sales awards and
            ephemera, 39

B

Banks, still, 40-41
    Advertising, 40
    Ceramic, 40

Metal, 40
Plastic and vinyl, 40
Porcelain, 40-41
Barbershop and beauty collectibles, 41
Barbie, 42-44
    Accessories, 42
    Clothing, 42
    Doll, 43
    Doll, Barbie's friends and family, 44
    Olympic collectibles, 253
    Ornament, 44
    Presley, Elvis, 284
    Trading card, 44
Baseball cards, 44-47
    Bowman era, 45
    Topps era, 45-47
    Upper Deck, 47
Baseball collectibles, 47-49
Basketball collectibles, 49, 50
Battery-operated automata, 50-51
Bauer pottery, 51
Beanie Babies, 51-52
    Advertising, 52
    Retired, 52
Beatles, 52, 53
Beer bottles, 53, 54
    Embossed, 54
    Painted label, 54
    Stoneware, 54
Beer cans, 54, 55
Beswick, 55, 56
Bicycle collectibles, 56-58
Big Little Books, 58-59
    Better Little Books, 58
Black memorabilia, 59-61
    Postcards, 281
    Stereographs, 338
Blue Ridge Pottery, 61, 62
Bookends, 62, 63
Bookmarks, 63, 64
    Advertising, 64
Books, 64, 65
Bottle openers, figural, 65, 66
    Advertising, 65
    Figural, 66
Boxing collectibles, 66, 67
Boyd Crystal Art Glass, 67, 68
Brastoff, Sascha, 68
Brayton Laguna Pottery, 68, 69
Breweriana, 69, 70

C

Calculators, 71, 72
Calendars, 72, 73
Cameras and accessories, 73, 74
Candlewick pattern, 74-78
Candy containers, 78
    Cardboard, 78
    Glass, 78
    Metal, 78
    Papier-mâché, 78
    Plastic, 78
Candy molds, 78, 79
    Chocolate mold, 79
    Hard candy, 79
Cap guns, 79, 80
Cartoon Characters Peanuts, 213
Cartoon characters, 80-83
    Andy Panda, 80, 81
    Archie, 81
    Barney Google, 81
    Betty Boop, 81
    Bringing Up Father, 81
    Bugs Bunny, 81
    Casper and Friends, 81
    Daffy Duck, 81
    Deputy Dawg, 81
    Dick Tracy, 81
    Felix the Cat, 81
    Flintstones, 81
    Heckle and Jeckle, 81
    Huckleberry Hound, 81
    Jetsons, 81
    Lil Abner, 81
    Mickey Mouse, 220
    Moon Mullins, 82
    Mutt and Jeff, 82
    Peanuts, 82, 216, 220
    Pogo, 82
    Popeye, 82
    Porky Pig, 82
    Rocky and Bullwinkle, 82
    Sylvester, 82
    Tom and Jerry, 82
    Underdog, 82
    Woody Woodpecker, 82, 83
    Yellow Kid, 83
    Yogi Bear, 83
    Yosemite Sam, 83
Catalina Pottery, 83
Catalogs, 83-85

Cat collectibles, 85, 86
Ceramic Arts Studio, 86
Cereal boxes, 86, 87
    Cereal box back, 87
    Cereal box cutout, 87
Cereal premiums, 87-89
Character and promotional glasses, 89-91
Children's books, 91-93
Children's dishes, 93, 94
    Aluminum, 94
    Cast iron, 94
    China, 94
Christmas collectibles, 94, 95
    Christmas village/garden, 95
    Non-tree related items, 95
    Tree-related items, 95
Cigar collectibles, 96
Cigarette items, 97, 98
Circus items, 98, 99
Cleminson Clay, 99
Clickers, 99, 100
Clocks, 100, 101
Clothing and clothing accessories, 101-103
Coca-Cola collectibles, 103, 104
Cocktail collectibles, 104, 105
Comic books, 105-108
Cookbooks, 108, 109
Cookie jars, 109, 110
    Abingdon Pottery, 109
    Advertising, 109, 110
    American Bisque, 110
    Avon, 110
    Brush, 110
    California Originals, 110
    Cardinals, 110
    Certified Internationl, 110
    Clay Art, 110
    Cleminsons, 110
    Doranne, 110
    Enesco, 110
    Fitz and Floyd, 110
    Goebel, 110
    Hall, 110
    McCoy, 110
    Metlox, 110
    Pearl China, 110
    Pottery Guild, 110
    Redwing Pottery, 110
    Regal, 110
    Shawnee, 110

Treasure Craft, 110
Twin Winton, 110
Warner Brothers, 110
Cow collectibles, 110-111
Cowboy heroes, 111-114
Annie Oakley, 112, 214
Bobby Benson, 112
Bonanza, 112
Buck Jones, 112
Buffalo Bill, 112
Cisco Kid, 112
Davy Crockett, 112
Gabby Hayes, 112
Gene Autry, 112
Gunsmoke, 113
Hopalong Cassidy, 113
John Wayne, 113
Ken Maynard, 113
Kit Carson, 113
Lone Ranger, 113
Maverick, 113
Rawhide, 114
Red Ryder, 114
Restless Gun, 114
Rin Tin Tin, 114
Roy Rogers, 114
Straight Arrow, 114
The Rifleman, 114
Tim McCoy, 114
Tom Mix, 114
Wagon Train, 114
Wild Bill Hickok, 114
Wyatt Earp, 114
Cracker Jack, 114, 115

D

Degenhart glass, 116, 117
Depression glass, 117-122
Aunt Polly, 118
Cherryberry, 118
Christmas Candy, 118
Cracked Ice, 118
Daisy, No. 620, 118, 119
Doric, 119
Early American Prescut, 119
Floral, Poinsettia, 120
Fortune, 120
Manhattan, 120, 121
National, 121
Old Colony, Lace Edge, Open
Lace, 121
Ring, Banded Rings, 121, 122

Round Robin, 122
Sierra, Pinwheel, 122
Star, 122
Disneyana, 122-125
Bambi, 123, 220, 221
Cinderella, 123
Disneyland, 123
Donald Duck, 123, 124
Dumbo, 124
Lady and the Tramp, 124
Lion King, 124
Mickey Mouse Club, 124, 220
Mickey Mouse, 124, 213, 220
Minnie Mouse, 124
Pinocchio, 125
Pluto, 125, 220
Snow White, 125, 220
Winnie the Pooh, 125
Zorro, 125
Dog collectibles, 125, 126
Dollhouse furnishings, 127
Dolls, 127-133
American Character, 129
Annalee 214
Arranbee, 129
Barbie, 43
Character and personality, 129
Cosmopolitan Doll
Company, 129, 130
Deluxe Reading, Deluxe Top-
per, Topper Corpora-
tion, Topper Toys, 130
Eegee Doll Mfg.
Company, 130
Effanbee Doll Corp., 130
Hasbro, 130
Horsman Dolls Company,
Inc., 130, 131
Ideal Toy Corp., 131
Madame Alexander, 131, 132
Mary Hoyer, 132
Mattel, 132
Stereographs, 339
Sun Rubber Co., 133
Terri Lee Dolls, 133
Vogue, 133
Dr. Seuss Collectibles, 309, 310
Drugstore collectibles, 133, 134
Beauty products, 134
Cold and cough, 134
Dental, 134
First aid, 134

Infants and children, 134
Miscellaneous, 134

E

Electrical appliances, 135-138
Blenders, 135, 136
Chafing dishes, 136
Coffee makers and sets, 136
Egg cookers, 136
Food cookers, 136
Hot plates, 136, 137
Miscellaneous, 137
Mixers, 137
Popcorn poppers, 137
Toasters, 137, 138
Waffle irons and sandwich
grills, 138
Elephant collectibles, 138, 139

F

Farm collectibles, 140-142
Fast food memorabilia, 142-144
A & W, 142
Archie's Lobster House, 142
Big Boy, 142
Burger Chef, 142
Burger King, 142
Colonel Sanders, 143
Dairy Queen, 143
Denny's, 143
Howard Johnson, 143
Kentucky Fried Chicken, 143
Little Caesar's, 143
McDonald's 143
Pizza Hut, 144
Taco Bell, 144
Wendy's, 144
Fiesta ware, 144, 145
Fire King, 146-148
Dinnerware, 147
Kitchenware, 147
Firehouse collectibles, 145, 146
Fishing collectibles, 148, 149
Flag collectibles, 149-151
Flashlights, 151, 152
Florence Ceramics, 152
Flow Blue china, American,
152-154
Football Cards, 154-155
Bowman Card
Company, 154, 155
Fleer, 155

Leaf, 155
Philadelphia, 155
Pro Set, 155
Score, 155
Stadium Club, 155
Topps, 155
Upper Deck, 155
Football collectibles, 155-157
Franciscan dinnerware, 157, 158
Apple, 157
Arcadia, 157
Carmel, 157
Coronado, 157
Daisy, 158
Del Monte, 158
Denmark, 158
Desert Rose, 158
Fremont, 158
Fresh Fruit, 158
Granville, 158
Hacienda, 158
Indian Summer, 158
Ivy, 158
Larkspur, 158
Magnolia, 158
Mariposa, 158
Meadow Rose, 158
Mesa, 158
Olympic, 158
Palomar, 158
Poppy, 158
Rosemore, 158
Starburst, 158
Sundance, 158
Westwood, 158
Wildflower, 158
Willow, 158
Woodside, 158
Fruit jars, 158, 159
Furniture, Modernism
Era, 159-165

G

Gambling collectibles, 166
Games, 167, 168
Card, 168
Gardening, 168-170
Gasoline Collectibles, 170, 171
G.I. Joe collectibles, 171-173
Accessories pack, 172
Action figures and dolls, 172
Coloring book, 173

Foot locker, 173
Gear, 173
Kite, 173
Outfit, 173
Playset, 173
Ring, 173
Set, 173
Thermos, 173
Vehicle, 173
Weapon, 173
Golf collectibles, 173, 174
Graniteware, 174, 175
Griswold, 175, 176
Muffin Pan, 176
Other, 176
Skillet, 175

H

Haeger Potteries, 177
Hall China, 177-180
Autumn Leaf, 178
Blue Garden/Blue
Blossom, 179
Chinese Red, 179
Crocus, 178
Dinnerware patterns, 178
Golden Glo, 178
Kitchenware patterns, 179
Orange Poppy, 178
Pastel Morning Glory, 178
Red Dot, 178
Red Poppy, 179
Refrigerator ware and
commercial ware, 179
Rose Parade, 179
Rose White, 179
Shaggy Tulip, 179
Taverne, 179
Teapots, 179, 180
Wild Poppy, 179
Handkerchiefs, 180, 181
Children's, 180
Designer printed, 180, 181
Lace, 181
Monogram, 181
Movie and cartoon, 181
Souvenir printed, 181
Harker Pottery, 181, 182
Amy, 181
Cameo, 182
Colonial Lady, 182
Deco Dahlia, 182

Ivy, 182
Kelvinator, 182
Mallow, 182
Monterey, 182
Petit Point Rose, 182
Red Apple, 182
Tulip, 182
Holiday collectibles, 182-184
Christmas 216, 217, 218,
219, 220
Easter, 182, 183, 218
Fourth of July 218
Halloween, 183
St. Patrick's Day, 183, 184
Thanksgiving, 184, 218
Valentine's Day 218, 220
Holt-Howard Collectibles, 184, 185
Christmas, 184
Cozy Kittens, 184
Jeeves, 185
Merry Mouse, 185
Miscellaneous, 185
Red Rooster, 185
Homer Laughlin, 185-187
American Provincial, 185
Amsterdam, 185
Best China, 185
Brittany Majestic, 186
Calendar Plate, 186
Cavalier, 186
Georgian, 186
Harlequin, 186
Kitchen Kraft, 186
Magnolia, 186
Marigold, 186
Mexicana, 186
Nautilus, 186
Oven Serve, 186
Priscilla, 186
Rhythm Rose, 186
Rhythm, 186
Riviera, 186
Silver Patrician, 187
Skytone Stardust, 187
Song of Spring, 187
Virginia Rose, 187
Horse collectibles, 187-189
Horse equipment and related
items, 188
Horse theme items, 188
Racing collectibles, 287
Hull Pottery, 189, 190

Post-1950 patterns, 189
Pre-1950 patterns, 189, 190
Hummel items, 190, 191
Hunting collectibles, 191, 192
    Stereographs, 339

I

Ice cream collectibles, 193, 194
Insulators, 194-196
Irons, 196, 197
    Charcoal, 196
    Children's, 196
    Flat irons, 196
    Fluters, 196, 197
    Gasoline, 197
    Goffering, 197
    Liquid fuel, 197
    Slug, 197
    Special purpose, 197

J

Jewelry, costume, 198-201
    Bracelet, 198
    Brooch/pin, 198, 199
    Chatelaine, 199
    Choker, 199
    Clip, 199, 200
    Cuff links, pair, 200
    Earrings, pair, 200
    Necklace, 200
    Pearls, 200
    Pendant, 200
    Ring, 200
    Sash ornament, 200
    Stickpin, 200
    Suite, 200, 201
Jukeboxes, 201, 202

K

Kewpies, 203
Kitchen collectibles, 203-206
Kitchen glassware, 206, 207

L

Labels, 208-211
    Apple, 208
    Baking powder, 208
    Blueberry can, 208
    Grape, 208, 209
    Lemon, 209
    Orange, 209, 210

Pear, 210
Tin can, 210
Vegetables, 210, 211
Yam and sweet potato, 211
Lamps, 211, 212
Limited edition collectibles, 212-220
    Ashton Drake, 214
    Bareuther, 216
    Bells, 213
    Berlin, 216
    Bing and Grondahl, 213, 216
    Christmas ornaments, 213
    Cybis, 215
    Danbury Mint, 213
    Davis, Lowell, 215, 217
    Dolls, 214
    Enesco Corp., 213, 214, 215
    Ferrandiz, Anri J., 213, 216
    Figurines, 215
    Franklin Mint, 213, 214, 215, 217
    Gorham, 213, 214, 216
    Grossman, Dave, 213, 215
    Hallmark, 213
    Hamilton Collection, 214
    Haviland & Parlon, 214, 217
    Hummel, 213, 215
    International Silver, 214
    Knowles, Edwin M., 218
    Lawton, 214
    Lenox, 213, 214, 218
    Lladro, 213, 214, 215, 218
    Lunt, 214
    Mann, Seymour, 214
    Music boxes, 216
    Pickard, 213
    Plates, 216
    Reco, 218
    Reed and Barton, 213, 214, 218
    River Shore, 213, 215
    Rosenthal, 218, 219
    Royal Copenhagen, 215, 219
    Royal Doulton, 214, 215, 219
    Royal Orleans Porcelain, 215
    Schmid, 214, 215, 216, 220
    Towle, 213, 214
    Wallace Silversmiths, 214
    Walt Disney, 213, 214, 216
    Wedgwood, 213, 216, 220
Little Golden Books, 220-222

Little Red Riding Hood, 222, 223
Lottery tickets, 223, 224
Lunch kits, 224, 225

M

Magazine covers and tear sheets, 226
Magazines, 226-229
Marbles, 229
    Akro Agate, 229
    Christensen Agate Co., 229
    End of Day, 229
    Handmade, 229
    Lutz, 229
    M.F. Christensen & Son, 230
    Machine-made, 229
    Marble King Co., 229
    Master Marble Co., 230
    Mica, 229
    Other, 229
    Peltier Glass Co., 230
    Swirl, 229
    Transitional, 230
    Vitro Agate/Gladding Vitro Co., 230
Matchcovers, 230, 231
    Special covers, 230
    Topics, 231
McCoy Pottery, 231, 232
    Coockie jars, 110
McKee Glass, 232
Metlox pottery, 232-234
    Antique Grape, 233
    Blue Provincial, 233
    Brown Eyed Susan, 233
    California Ivy, 233
    California Provincial, 233
    California Strawberry, 234
    Camelia California, 234
    Colonial Homestead, 234
    Contempora, 234
    Cookie jars, 110, 233
    Della Robia, 234
    Dinnerware, 233
    Homestead Provincial, 234
    Provincial Rose, 234
    Red Rooster, 234
    Sculptured Daisy, 234
    Sculptured Grape, 234
    Sculptured Zinnia, 234
    Vernon, Antiqua, 234
Model kits, 234-236

Monsters, 236, 237
 Dracula, 236
 Elvira, 236
 Frankenstein, 236
 Godzilla, 236
 Hammer, 237
 Miscellaneous, 237
 Munsters, The, 237
 The Creature from the Black
    Lagoon, 237
 The Exorcist, 237
 The Nightmare Before
    Christmas, 237
 The Nightmare on Elm Street/
    Freddy Krueger, 237
 Wolfman, 237
Morton Potteries, 237-239
 American Art Potteries,
    1947-1963, 239
 Cliftwood Art Potteries Inc.,
    1920-1940, 238
 Midwest Potteries Inc.,
    1940-1944, 239
 Morton Pottery Company,
    1922-1976, 239
 Morton Pottery Works, Morton
    Earthenware
    Co., 1877-1917, 238
Movie memorabilia, 239-241
Movie personalities, 241-243

N

Napkin rings, 244
New Martinsville-Viking
Glass, 244, 245
Newspapers, headline
editions, 245, 246
Niloak pottery, 247
Nippon china, 1891-1921,
247, 248
Noritake Azalea China, 248, 249
Nutcrackers, 249

O

Occupied Japan, 250, 251
Ocean liner collectibles, 251, 252
Olympic collectibles, 252-254
Owl collectibles, 254

P

Padlocks, 255-257

Brass lever, 256
Combination, 256
Commemorative, 256
Express, 256
Iron lever, 256
Lever key push, 256
Logo, 257
Pin tumbler, 257
Railroad, 257
Scandinavian, 257
Story, 257
Warded, 257
Wrought iron lever, 257
Paper dolls, 257, 258
Paperback books, 258, 259
Patriotic collectibles, 259-261
 Eagle, 260
 Fans and shields, 260
 Liberty Bell, 260
 Statue of Liberty, 260
 Uncle Sam, 261
 George Washington, 261
Pennsbury Pottery, 261, 262
Pens and pencils, 262, 263
 Desk set, 262
 Display case, 262
Pepsi-Cola collectibles, 263, 264
PEZ, 264, 265
Phoenix Bird China, 265, 266
Pig collectibles, 267
Pinball machines, 267-269
 Bally, 268
 Chicago Coin, 268
 Exhibit, 268
 Genco, 268
 Gottlieb, 268
 Mills Novelty Co., 269
 Pacific Amusement, 269
 Rock-Ola, 269
 United, 269
 Williams, 269
Pin-up art, 269, 270
Planters, 270-272
 Figural, 271
 Head types, 271
 Wall pocket, 272
 Weller pottery, 377
Planters Peanuts, 272
Plastics, 272-274
 Acrylic, 273
 Bakelite, 273, 274
 Celluloid, 274

Playboy collectibles, 274, 275
Playing cards, 275, 276
Pocket knives, 276
Political and campaign items,
276-280
 Abraham Lincoln, 277
 Alfred Landon, 278
 Barry Goldwater, 279
 Benjamin Harrison, 277
 Bill Clinton, 280
 Dwight Eisenhower, 278
 Franklin D. Roosevelt, 278
 George Bush, 280
 Gerald Ford, 279
 Harry S. Truman, 278
 Herbert Hoover, 278
 Jimmy Carter, 279
 John F. Kennedy, 279
 Lyndon Johnson, 279
 Postcards, 283
 Richard M. Nixon, 278
 Ronald Reagan, 280
 Teddy Roosevelt, 277
 Warren G. Harding, 278
 Wendell Willkie, 278
 William McKinley, 277
 Woodrow Wilson, 277
Postcards, 280-283
 Advertising, 281
 African-Americans, 281
 Artist signed, 281
 Folder, 282
 Greetings, 282
 Humor, 282
 Miscellaneous, 282
 Patriotic, 283
 Photographic, 283
 Political and social history, 283
 World fair and expositions, 283
 World War II, 283
Presley, Elvis, 283, 284
Punchboards, 284, 285
Purinton Pottery, 285

R

Racing collectibles, 286
 Auto, 286
 Horse, 287

Radio characters and personalities, 287
    Amos 'n' Andy, 287
    Captain Midnight, 287
    Don Winslow, 288
    Edgar Bergen and Charlie McCarthy, 288
    Fibber McGee and Molly, 288
    Flying Family, 288
    Jack Armstrong, 288
    Jack Benny, 288
    Jimmie Allen, 288
    Joe Penner, 288
    Little Orphan Annie, 288
    Major Bowes, 288
    Quiz Kids, 288
    Young Explorers Club, 288
Radio premiums, 288
Radios, 290-292
    Admiral, 292
    Air King, 292
    Arvin, 292
    Atwater Kent, 292
    Bulova, 292
    Colonial, 292
    Columbia, 292
    Crosley, 292
    Dumont, 292
    Emerson, 292
    Fada, 292
    Federal, 292
    General Electric, 292
    Grebe, 292
    Halicrafters, 292
    Majestic, 292
    Metrodyne, 292
    Motorola, 292
    Olympic, 292
    Paragon, 292
    Philco, 292
    Radiobar, 292
    RCA, 292
    Silvertone, 292
    Sony, 292
    Sparton, 292
    Stewart-Warner, 292
    Stomberg Carlson, 292
    Westinghouse, 292
    Zenith, 292
Railroad items, 292
    Stereographs, 341
Reamers, 294-296

China and ceramic, 295
Glass, 295
Metal, 296
Records, 296
Red Wing Pottery, 297
    Cookie jars, 110
Robots, 298
Rock 'n' roll, 299
Rockwell, Norman, 213, 215, 217, 300
Roseville Pottery, 301
Royal China, 303-306
    Bucks County, 303
    Colonial Homestead, 304
    Currier and Ives, 304
    Fair Oaks, 305
    Memory Lane, 305
    Old Curiosity Shop, 305
    Willow Ware, 306

S

Salt and pepper shakers, 307
    Advertising, 307
    Ceramic, 307
Santa Claus, 213, 217, 218, 220, 307, 308
Scouting, 308, 309
Sewing items, 311, 312
Shawnee pottery, 312, 313
    Cookie jars, 110
Sheet music, 313, 314
Shelley China, 314, 315
Slot machines, 315, 316
Snowdomes, 316-318
Soda fountain collectibles, 318, 319
Soft drink collectibles, 319-321
Soldiers, dimestore, 321, 322
    Auburn Rubber, 321
    Barclay, 321
    Civilian figures, 321
    Grey Iron, 321
    Manoil, 321
    Military figures, 322
Soldiers, toy, 322-324
    Authenticast, 323
    Bienheim, 323
    Britains, 323
    Elastolin/Lineol, 323
    Heyde, 323
    Mignot, 324
    Militia models, 324

Nostalgia, 324
S.A.F., 324
Souvenir and commemorative items, 324-326
Souvenir buildings, 326, 327
Space adventurers and exploration, 327-331
    Battlestar Galactica, 328
    Buck Rogers, 328
    Captain Video, 328
    Flash Gordon, 328
    Lost in Space, 328, 329
    Outer Limits, 329
    Space Cadet, Tom Corbett, 329
    Space exploration, 330
    Space Patrol, 329
    Star Trek, 329
Space toys, 331, 332
Sports collectibles, 332, 333
Stangl Pottery, 333-335
    Amber Glo, 334
    Arbor, 334
    Bittersweet, 334
    Blueberry, 334
    Brittany, 334
    Colonial, 334
    Dinnerware, 334
    Dogwood, 334
    Festival, 334
    Fruit, 334
    Garland, 334
    Golden Blossom, 334
    Golden Glo, 334
    Golden Grape, 334
    Golden Harvest, 334
    Harvest, 334
    Holly, 334
    Jeweled Christmas Tree, 334
    Kiddieware, 334
    Magnolia, 335
    Maize, 335
    Miscellaneous and artware, 335
    Orchard Song, 335
    Thistle, 335
    Tropic, 335
Star Wars, 335-337
Stereo-Viewers, 337, 338
Stereographs, 338-342
    Animal, 338
    Astronomy, 338

Aviation, 338
Black memorabilia, 338
Cave, 339
Christmas, 339
Comics, 339
Disaster, 339
Dolls, 339
Entertainers, 339
Expositions, 339
Famous people, 340
Famous photographers, 341
Hunting and fishing, 339
Indian, 339
Mining, 339
Miscellaneous, 340
National parks, 340
Niagra Falls, 340
Occupational, 340
Oil, 340
Photographica, 341
Railroad, 341
Religious, 341
Risque, 341
Sets, 341
Ships, 341
Survey, 341
War, 341
Whaling, 341
Stock and bond
certificates, 342, 343
    Bonds, 342
    Stocks, 342
Stuffed toys, 343, 344
Super heroes, 344-346
    Aquaman, 345
    Batman & Robin, 345
    Bionic Woman, 345
    Buck Rogers, 345
    Captain Action, 345
    Captain America, 345
    Captain Marvel, 345
    Captain Midnight, 345
    Fantastic Four, 346
    Green Hornet, 346
    Incredible Hulk, 346
    Legion of Super Heroes, 346
    Mr. Fantastic, 346
    Shadow, 346
    Spider-Man, 346
    Spiderwoman, 346
    Super Heroes,
        DC Comics, 346

Superman, 346
Wonder Woman, 346
X-Men, 346
Swarovski crystal, 346-348
    Accessories, 347
    Figurine, 348

T

Taylor, Smith and Taylor, 349, 350
    #1377, 350
    Autumn Harvest, 349
    Beverly, 349
    Bonnie, 349
    Boutonniere, 349
    Break O' Day, 349
    Chateau Buffet, 349
    Classic Heritage, 349
    Delphian, 349
    Empire, 349
    Fairway, 349
    Indian Summer, 349
    Laurel, 349
    Lazy Daisy, 349
    Lu-Ray, 349
    Marvel, 350
    Paramount, 350
    Pebbleford, 350
    Plymouth, 350
    Ranchero, 350
    Scroll Border, 350
    Sea Shell, 350
    Silhouette, 350
    Summer Rose, 350
    Versatile, 350
    Vistosa, 350
    Vogue, 350
Teapots, 350, 351
    Brass, 350
    Ceramic, pottery or
        porcelain, 350
    Chinese, 350
    Figural, 350
    Iron, 351
    Miniature, 351
    Pewter, 351
Television personalities and
memorabilia, 351-353
Temple, Shirley, 353, 354
Thimbles, 354, 355
Toys, 355-364
    Acme Toys, 357
    Advertising, 25

Alps, 357
Arcade, 357
Auburn Toys, 357
Bachman, 357
Bandai Co., 357
Buddy L, 357
Chein, 357
Chilton Toys, 358
Circus, 99
Coca-Cola, 104
Con-Cor, 358
Corgi, 358
Cragston, 358
Dinky, 358
Distler, 358
Doepke, 358
Ertl, 359
Fisher-Price, 359
Gabriel, 359
Gama/Schuco, 359
Gay Products, 359
Gilbert, 359
Gong Bell, 359
Hasbro, 359
Hot Wheels, 359
Hubley, 359
Ideal, 360
Japanese, post war, 360
Kenner, 360
Knickerbocker, 360
Lesney Products & Co., 360
Lido Toys, 360
Lincoln Toys, 360
Line Mar (Linemar), 360
Marusan, 360
Marusyo Toys, 361
Marx, 361
Matchbox, 361
Mattel, 362
Mego, 362
Modern Toys, 362
MTU, 362
Nylint, 362
Occupied Japan, 362
Playsets, 362
Promo car, 362
Radio Flyer, 362
Remco, 362
Schuco, 363
Slinky, 363
Structo, 363
Sun Rubber, 363

SY Toys, 363
Taiyo, 363
TN, 363
Tonka, 363
Tootsietoy, 363
TPS, 363
TT, 363
Unidentified makers, 363
Williams, A.C., 363
Wolverine, 364
Wyandotte, 364
Yone, 364
Trains, toy, 364-366
    American Flyer O Gauge, 364
    American Flyer S Gauge, 364
    Ives, 365
    Lionel O Gauge, 365
    Lionel S Gauge, 365
    N Gauge, 366

U

Uhl Pottery, 367
Universal pottery, 367, 368
    Ballerina, 368
    Bittersweet, 368
    Calico Fruit, 368
    Cattails, 368
    Circus, 368
    Rambler Rose, 368
    Woodvine, 368

V

Valentines, 218, 369, 370
    Animated, 369
    Comic, 369
    Diecut, 369
    Flat, 369
    Folder, 369
    Hanger and string, 369
    Honeycomb tissue, 369
    Paper lace, 369
    Parchment, 369
    Pull-down, 370
    Pullout, 370
    Silk fringed, 370

    Standup with easel back, 370
    Victorian novelty, 370
    Wood, 370
Vending machines, 370, 371
Vernon Kilns, 371, 372
View-Master products, 372, 373

W

Watch fobs, 374
Watt pottery, 375, 376
    Apple, 375
    Autumn Foilage, 375
    Bleeding Heart, 375
    Cherry, 375
    Kolor Kraft, 375
    Pansy, 375
    Rooster, 375
    Starflower, 375
Weller Pottery, 376, 377
Western Americana, 377-379
Westmoreland Glass
Company, 379, 380
Whiskey bottles, collectors' special
editions, 380-382
    Anniversary, 380
    Ballantine, 380
    Beneagle, 381
    Bischoff, 381
    Collector's Art, 381
    Cyrus Noble, 381
    Early Times, 381
    Ezra Brooks, 381
    Famous Firsts, 381
    Garnier, 381
    Grenadier, 381
    Hoffman, 382
    J.W. Dant, 381
    Japanese Firms, 382
    Jim Beam, 381
    Lewis and Clark, 382
    Lionstone, 382
    Luxardo, 382
    McCormick, 382
    OBR, 382
    Old Commonwealth, 382

    Old Crow, 382
    Old Fitzgerald, 382
    Old Mr. Boston, 382
    Pacesetter, 382
    Ski Country, 382
    Wild Turkey, 382
World War I collectibles, 382-384
World War II collectibles, 384, 385
    Postcards, 283
World's fairs and
expositions, 385-389
    1893, Chicago, the Columbian
        Exposition, 386
    1894, California Mid-Winter
        Exposition, 386
    1901, Pan Am Expisition,
        Buffalo, 386
    1904, St. Louis, Louisiana Pur-
        chase Exposition, 386
    1915, San Francisco, Pana-
        ma-Pacific Internation-
        al Exposition, 386
    1934, Chicago, Century of
        Progress, 386
    1939, New York, New York
        World's Fair, 387
    1939, San Francisco, Golden
        Gate International Ex-
        position, 388
    1962, Seattle, Century 21
        Exposition, 388
    1964, New York, New York
        World's Fair, 388
    1967, Montreal, Montreal
        Expo, 389
    1982, Knoxville, World's
        Fair, 389
Wright, Russel, 389, 390
    American Modern, 389
    Iroquois Casual, 390
    Iroquois Casual,
        Redesigned, 390

Z

Zeppelins, 391